THE ENCYCLOPEDIA OF
WARFARE

THE ENCYCLOPEDIA OF
WARFARE

amber
BOOKS

Published by
Amber Books Ltd
74–77 White Lion Street
London
N1 9PF
United Kingdom
www.amberbooks.co.uk
Appstore: appstore.com/amberbooksltd
Facebook: www.facebook.com/amberbooks
Twitter: @amberbooks

ISBN: 978-1-78274-023-0

Publishing Manager: Charles Catton
Project Editors: Sarah Uttridge and Michael Spilling
Design Manager: Mark Batley
Design: Colin Hawes, Andrew Easton and Rick Fawcett
Cartographer: Alexander Swanston at Red Lion Media
Consulting Editors: Marcus Cowper and Chris McNab
Proofreader: Alison Worthington and David Worthington
Indexers: Malcolm Henley, Michael Forder and Penny Brown
With thanks to Patrick Mulrey, Ben Way and Martin Dougherty for their assistance

Printed in China

Endpaper Credits:
The first of a set of three paintings by Paolo Uccello
depicting The Battle of San Romano shows
Niccolò da Tolentino leading the Florentine cavalry.
This painting is currently on display at the
National Gallery, London. (AKG-Images/Erich Lessing)

CONTENTS

WARS AND CAMPAIGNS

MAPS

AUTHORS AND CONTRIBUTORS

Ralph W. Ashby

Dr Ralph W. Ashby is a member of the History Department at Eastern Illinois University and has a PhD from the University of Illinois at Chicago. His military experience includes completing a training programme with the United States Marine Corps, and more than three years of active service in the United States Army, during which he participated in the First Gulf War. He is the author of *Napoleon Against Great Odds: The Emperor and the Defenders of France, 1814.*

Nell Aubrey

Nell Aubrey has a BA in History, an MA in Medieval Studies and is completing a PhD in the History of Medicine, all at University College London. She has also taught early medieval history and the history of torture at University College London.

Tim Benbow

Dr Tim Benbow is a Senior Lecturer in the Defence Studies Department at the Joint Services Command Staff College, Oxfordshire. He previously taught at Britannia Royal Naval College, the University of Exeter and Oxford University. He has a BA in Philosophy, Politics and Economics from Brasenose College, Oxford and an MPhil and DPhil in International Relations from St Antony's College, Oxford. He is the author of *British Naval Aviation: The First 100 Years* and *The History of World War I: Naval Warfare 1914-1918* and *The Magic Bullet? Understanding the Revolution in Military Affairs.*

James Bosbotinis

James Bosbotinis is a UK-based analyst specialising in military and strategic developments. He is an Associate Member of and Editorial Assistant to the Corbett Centre for Maritime Policy Studies, King's College, London. He holds memberships of the Royal United Services Institute for Defence and Security Studies, the Royal Institute of International Affairs, the International Institute for Strategic Studies and *The Naval Review.* He also holds an MA in Diplomatic Studies from the University of Westminster and a BA in Economics and International Relations from London Guildhall University.

Thomas D. Conlan

Thomas D. Conlan is Associate Professor of Asian Studies at Bowdoin College, Maine. He studied Japanese history at the University of Michigan and Kyoto University before earning his Ph.D from Stanford University in 1998. His scholarship focuses on medieval Japanese history. He is the author of *Weapons & Fighting Techniques of the Samurai Warrior 1200–1877 AD* and has also published two monographs: *In Little Need of Divine Intervention: Takezaki Suenaga's Scrolls of the Mongol Invasions of Japan* and *State of War: The Violent Order of Fourteenth Century Japan.*

Alejandro de Quesada

Alejandro de Quesada has more than 30 years of experience as an armourer, collector, museum curator, weapons wrangler and as a participant in living history presentations and reenactments. He is the founder of AdeQ Historical, which provides consulting for film and TV, museums and researchers. He is the author of more than 30 books, including *The Hunt for Pancho Villa: The Columbus Raid and Pershing's Punitive Expedition 1916–17, The Mexican Revolution 1910–20, The Spanish–American War and Philippine Insurrection: 1898–1902* and *Uniforms of the German Soldier: An Illustrated History from 1870 to the Present Day.*

Kelly DeVries

Dr Kelly DeVries is Professor of History at Loyola College in Maryland. He is the author of several books, including *Medieval Military Technology, Infantry Warfare in the Early Fourteenth Century, Joan of Arc: A Military Leader* and *Guns and Men in Medieval Europe.*

John Dorney

John Dorney studied history and politics in University College Dublin, completing an MA on the sixteenth century Irish chieftain Florence McCarthy. He is the author of *The Story Of The Easter Rising, 1916*, *The Story of The Irish War Of Independence*, *The Story Of The Irish Civil War* and *The Story of the Tudor Conquest of Ireland.*

Kevin J. Dougherty

Kevin J. Dougherty is an adjunct professor at The Citadel, The Military College of South Carolina in Charleston. He is a retired US Army officer who previously taught history at the University of Southern Mississippi. Dougherty is the author of *The Peninsula Campaign of 1862: A Military Analysis*, *Civil War Leadership and Mexican War Experience*, *Encyclopedia of the Confederacy* and *Campaigns for Vicksburg, 1862–63: Leadership Lessons.* He lives in Charleston, South Carolina.

Martin J. Dougherty

Martin J. Dougherty is a freelance writer and editor specializing in weapons technology, military history and combat techniques. He is the author of *Vikings: A History of the Norse People* and has previously contributed to *Battles of the Ancient World*, *Battles of the Medieval World* and *Battles of the Crusades.*

Lee W. Eysturlid

Dr. Lee W. Eysturlid is a history/social science instructor at the Illinois Mathematics and Science Academy. He has a PhD in history from Purdue University, Indiana, and is a member of the Citadel Historical Association. He has published on numerous military history topics and is author of *The Formative Influences, Theories and Campaigns of the Archduke Carl of Austria* and co-editor of *Philosophers of War: The Evolution of History's Greatest Military Thinkers.*

Westley Follett

Dr. Westley (Lee) Follett is Associate Professor in the College of Arts and Letters at the University of Southern Mississippi Gulf Coast, where he teaches courses in classical, medieval and world history. He received his doctorate from the Centre for Medieval Studies at the University of Toronto and held a post-doctoral scholarship in the School of Celtic Studies at the Dublin Institute for Advanced Studies. He is the author of *Céli Dé in Ireland: Monastic Writing and Identity in the Early Middle Ages* and has published or has forthcoming articles in Eolas: The Journal of the American Society of Irish Medieval Studies, Journal of Celtic Studies and Insignis Sophiae Arcator, an edited festschrift on medieval Latin studies.

Paul Gelpi

Dr Paul Gelpi is a Professor of Military History at the US Marine Corps Command and Staff College, Quantico, Virginia, where he is a faculty advisor teaching Operational Art and the Communications Program Director. He holds a PhD in History from the University of Alabama, as well as a BA and MA from the University of New Orleans. He is a contributor to several compendiums of military (US and world) history, twentieth century US history, an encyclopedia of Sino-American relations and academic journals.

Stephen Hart

Dr Stephen Hart is a Senior Lecturer with special responsibilities at the Department of War Studies, the Royal Military Academy Sandhurst. He has been published widely on military history topics, including *The Atlas of Tank Warfare* and *Colossal Cracks: Montgomery's 21st Army Group in Northwest Europe 1944–45.*

Phyllis G. Jestice

Dr Phyllis G. Jestice is Associate Professor of Medieval History and Chair of the History Department at the University of Southern Mississippi. A specialist in German history during the central Middle Ages, she is the author of *Wayward Monks and the Religions Revolution of the Eleventh Century* and has contributed to several works on the history of warfare, including *Battles of the Ancient World*, *Battles of the Bible*, *Fighting Techniques of the Early Modern World* and *The Timeline of Medieval Warfare.*

David Jordan

Dr David Jordan is a Senior Lecturer in Defence Studies, King's College London. A graduate of the Universities of Oxford and Birmingham, he previously held lecturing posts at Birmingham, Worcester and Keele. He is the author of *Wolfpack*, *Aircraft Carriers*, *The Fall of Hitler's*

Reich and *Atlas of World War II*. He has also contributed to the Dictionary of National Biography and has written a number of academic articles on subjects as diverse as the British involvement in Indonesia in 1945 and the prospects for Britain's future aircraft carriers.

Hunter Keeter

Hunter Keeter is a consultant in naval and military technology and operations. From 1998 to 2004 he worked as journalist and editor on several publications, including *Sea Power Magazine* and the trade newsletter *Defense Daily*. In addition, he has written articles for *Naval Forces International* magazine, and the US Navy publications *Undersea Warfare* and *Surface Warfare*, and is the author of *American Air Forces in Vietnam* and *American Ground Forces in Vietnam*, as well as a contributing author to books on US homeland security.

Savvas Kyriakidis

Dr Savvas Kyriakidis is a Post Doctoral Fellow at the University of Johannesburg. He studied classics at the University of Thrace, Greece, and obtained his PhD in Byzantine Studies from the University of Birmingham. He is the author of *Warfare in Late Byzantium, 1204–1453*.

Michael Neiberg

Dr. Michael Neiberg is Co-Director of the Center for the Study of War and Society at the University of Southern Mississippi. He specializes in the comparative history of War and Society since 1789 and is a founding member of the Société Internationale d'Étude de la Grande Guerre. He is the author of, among other books, *Dance of the Furies: Europe and the Outbreak of World War I*, *The Second Battle of the Marne*, *Fighting the Great War: A Global History*, *Warfare in World History*, *Foch: Supreme Allied Commander in the Great War*, *World War I: The Western Front 1914–1916*, as well as numerous articles, book chapters, encyclopedia entries and reviews. He is also the editor of *The Great War Reader*.

Peter Polack

Born in Jamaica in 1958, Peter Polack is a graduate of the University of the West Indies and Norman Manley Law School. A lawyer in the Cayman Islands since 1983, his first book, *Black Stalingrad*, is about the Battle of Cuito Cuanavale 1987–88 during the Angolan Civil War.

David Porter

David Porter has had a life-long interest in military history, particularly armoured warfare and armoured fighting vehicle technology. Since leaving the British Ministry of Defence in 2006 after 29 years' service, he has worked on a number of research projects. As well as writing four volumes in the World War II *Visual Battle Guide* series, he is the author of *The Essential Vehicle Identification Guide: Soviet Tank Units, 1939–45*, *The Essential Vehicle Identification Guide: Western Allied Tanks, 1939–45* and *World War II Data Book: Hitler's Secret Weapons*.

Rob S. Rice

Rob S. Rice is a Professor at the American Military University, teaching courses on ancient and modern naval warfare. He has published articles in the *Oxford Companion to American Military History* and contributed to B*attles of the Ancient World*, *Fighting Techniques of the Ancient World* and *Battles of the Bible*.

Scott M. Rusch

Dr Scott M Rusch has a PhD from the University of Pennsylvania. He has written on ancient military history for many publications. He is the author of *Sparta At War: Strategy, Tactics and Campaigns, 950–362 BC*.

Frederick C. Schneid

Dr. Frederick C. Schneid is a Professor of History at High Point University in North Carolina. He is the author of several books on European warfare, including *The Second War of Italian Unification 1859–61*, *Napoleon's Conquest of Europe: The War of the Third Coalition* and *Napoleonic Wars*. He has also contributed to *Fighting Techniques of the Early Modern World* and *Fighting Techniques of the Napoleonic Age*.

Gary Sheffield

Professor Gary Sheffield is Chair of War Studies at the University of Birmingham. He has written widely on twentieth century military history and defence issues. He is the author of *The Chief: Douglas Haig and the Transformation of the British Army*, *The War Studies Reader*, *The Somme: A New History* and *Forgotten Victory: The First World War – Myths and Realities*. With John Bourne he edited *Douglas Haig: War Diaries and Letters 1914–1918*. In 2003, he shared the Templer Medal for Military Literature for his contribution to *The British General Staff: Innovation and Reform c.1890–1939*.

Robert J. Thompson III

Robert J. Thompson III is a PhD student at the University of Southern Mississippi. Originally from Alexandria, Virginia, he received a BA in History from Virginia Wesleyan College in 2006 and an MA in History from Wilfrid Laurier University in 2007. His dissertation will examine how the US Army's pacification program in South Vietnam functioned after the 1968 Tet Offensive.

Stephen Turnbull

Dr Stephen Turnbull is Lecturer in Far Eastern Religions at the University of Leeds. Following an undergraduate degree from University of Cambridge, he has an MA and a PhD from the University of Leeds. He has published more than 60 books, including *Samurai: The World of the Warrior*, *Ninja AD 1460–1650*, *The Samurai Capture a King: Okinawa 1609*, *The Art of Renaissance Warfare: From the Fall of Constantinople to the Thirty Years War*, as well as *Samurai: The Japanese Warrior's (Unofficial) Manual*. He was a consultant for the PC games Shogun: Total War and Shogun 2: Total War, as well as the feature film *47 Ronin*.

Andrew Wiest

Dr Andrew Wiest is Professor and Director of International Studies in the Department of History at the University of Southern Mississippi. Specializing in the study of World War I and Vietnam, Dr. Wiest has served as a Visiting Senior Lecturer at the Royal Military Academy, Sandhurst and as a Visiting Professor in the Department of Warfighting Strategy in the United States Air Force Air War College. He is the author of *The Boys of '67: Charlie Company's War in Vietnam*, *Vietnam's Forgotten Army: Heroism and Betrayal*

in the ARVN, *Haig: The Evolution of a Commander* (Great Commander Series) and *The Illustrated History of World War I*, among other titles.

L.B. Wilson III

L.B. Wilson III holds a Masters Degree in War and Society from the University of Southern Mississippi and is currently a PhD student at Mississippi State University. A former US Army Sergeant, in 2003 he served in Iraq. He has written on irregular warfare, insurgency and terrorism in Afghanistan, Iraq, Lebanon, Ireland and Libya. He is a contributing author to *Culture, Power, and Security: New Directions in the History of National and International Security*.

CONSULTANT EDITORS

Marcus Cowper

Marcus Cowper studied history at the universities of Manchester and Birmingham and has worked in the field of military history as a writer and editor for the past 15 years. He is the author of a range of titles including *Cathar Castles* (2006), *The Words of War* (2009), *Henry V* (2010) and the National Geographic History Book: *An Interactive Journey* (2011). He lives and works in Oxford.

Chris McNab

Chris McNab is a writer, editor and historian, specializing in military history and military technology. He has written more than 80 books covering a broad range of periods and interests, his titles including *Native American Warrior* (2010), *Hitler's Armies: A History of the German War Machine 1939–45* (2012), *Third Reich Databook, 1933–45* (2009), *The Roman Army: The Greatest War Machine of the Ancient World* (2010), *Armies of the Napoleonic Wars* (2009) and *Campaigns of World War II: Day by Day* (2003). Chris has appeared on both TV and radio as an expert commentator in military affairs, and works internationally delivering training programmes in writing and editorial skills, particularly in the fields of history and education. Chris lives in Swansea, UK, where his other passions include hill running and percussion.

PUBLISHER'S NOTE

The Encyclopedia of Warfare – over four years in the making – relates the complete history of warfare in 1024 pages, using approximately 350,000 words and 600 maps. Almost five millennia of wars have been referenced: the entirety of military history in its strictest sense. It has been a vast undertaking in an age when reference publishing has fallen somewhat out of fashion.

History is constantly mutating. As new generations of historians emerge, new events occur and fashions change, certain wars and battles rise and fall in prominence. Subjective decisions have had to be made during the compilation of the encyclopedia, not least in determining the length of each entry. Key battles are given greater coverage than most; minor battles have but a brief mention. In a similar manner, naming conventions provided many an opportunity for debate and argument, while some ancient battles have disputed dating that can vary by centuries. Maps have been created for this volume where original sources either do not exist, or else wildly contradict each other. In each case we have striven to use whichever is the most widely accepted and/or correct variant.

The decision was made early in the creation of this book not to follow a strict chronology overall, but group related events together, so that the reader could get a sense of how a war or campaign developed without constant interruptions from other theatres or conflicts 'off stage'. This has led to some unfortunate quirks – Constantinople's fall in 1453 precedes its sack in 1204, for example, and Nelson is victorious at Trafalgar (1805) before the Nile (1801) – but a keen effort has been made for the contents to remain in an order as close to chronological as possible. (A strict chronological list of wars is provided in the front matter for those who would prefer the former. With the advent of digital publishing, reordering of entries according to the reader's preference will soon be available at the touch of a button.)

The decision was also taken to omit a bibliography, as to do justice to such a vast scope of history would require a volume beyond the capacity of current print binding machines, and space was required for the two exhaustive indexes. Inevitably the choices made in compiling this encyclopedia will be seen by some as indefensible or puzzling. However we trust that this volume will prove to be an invaluable reference tool and vehicle of discovery for many interested in military history.

FOREWORD
by Dennis Showalter

The fundamental purpose of a foreword is to persuade – in this case, to persuade committing time, money and not least shelf space, not merely to acquire but to retain a thousand-page encyclopedia: a print artifact some might consider obsolescent in an electronic age. *The Encyclopedia of Warfare* offers five characteristics justifying its possession. First, it is chronological. Its entries reflect a fundamental characteristic of history. History is linear. It starts somewhere in time. It goes somewhere in time. Its events interact in a temporal context. And the encyclopedia's chronological perspective enables making connections that otherwise might remain obscure. It contextualizes, for example, the 1147 siege of Lisbon with the Crusader-Turkish wars of the same period – and in the process demonstrating the comprehensive aspect of Christian–Muslim rivalry. Lisbon was far from Jerusalem only in terms of miles.

The encyclopedia is also comprehensive. It eschews a Western-centric perspective that too often sacrifices understanding for familiarity. The chronological chapters are subdivided by time and place. Thus they integrate the ancient wars of China and of South and South-East Asia, the battles of early Rome and those of Ireland in the twenty-fifth century BCE (a single entry, to be sure, but meriting consideration!) Cross-referencing cannot be easier. And that cross referencing enables not merely juxtaposition, but comparison on a global scale of war's methods and war's consequences.

The encyclopedia is concise. Its entries honour a time-tested formula. They address 'who', 'what', 'when', 'where', 'why', and thereby offer frameworks for further investigation of taproots and ramifications. But that does not mean a 'one size fits all' template. Events recognized as important – Hattin, Gettysburg, the Somme – are more fully developed without distorting the essentially economical format. Nor are the entries mere narratives. They incorporate analytical dimensions relative to their length and insightful whether phrases, sentences or paragraphs – like the comment that Crusader Jerusalem's 1187 surrender to Saladin involved ransoming most of the population 'at reasonable rates'!

The encyclopedia is user-friendly and clearly written. Not only are its more than five thousand entries individually intelligible. The graphics synergise with the text, enhancing rather than challenging or submerging it. The maps in particular are models of their kind, both accurate and informative.

Finally the encyclopedia is concentrated on warmaking. It eschews military history's framing concepts, whether economic, cultural or gender, in favour of presenting war at its sharp end. That enables covering the full spectrum: wars and revolutions, campaigns and counter-insurgencies, battle and sieges. And in turn the encyclopedia's format facilitates integrating, rather than compartmentalising, war's levels and war's aspects. In these pages Marathon and Hastings, the rise of the Roman Empire and the British Empire, become subjects for comparison and contrast.

The Encyclopedia of Warfare, in short, admirably fulfills the definition of a work that provides information on many elements of one subject. Its value, however, is also in context. This work makes broader contributions to military history's reference apparatus, and to its reference mentality, on two levels. The encyclopedia complements the electronic era's meme of 'six degrees of separation'. The idea that everything is no more than six steps away from everything else is a natural byproduct of websurfing, where a half-dozen mouse clicks can lead far away indeed from the original reference point. It also encourages diffusion: engagement on peripheries at the expense of the centre.

The Encyclopedia of Warfare encourages and facilitates refocusing on war's essential elements: the planning, conduct and result of using armed force. Diffusion is a natural aspect of the currently dominant approach to military history as an academic discipline. The concept of pivotal events has been overshadowed by an emphasis on underlying structures: reaching out from the operational towards the institutional, the political and the social dimensions. War's sharp end at best jostles for place. It can lose out to an intellectual disdain that is also aesthetic and moral. Warfare, in the sense of making war, is arguably to the twenty-first century what sex allegedly was to the Victorians. It involves emotions nice people do not feel and actions nice people do not perform. Writing about it becomes the new pornography, pandering to appetites best left neither nurtured nor acknowledged.

The encyclopedia contributes balance and perspective to this discourse. Its contents reinforce the specific, unique nature and function of armed forces compared to any other institutions. Its entries demonstrate that warmaking has had a direct, significant impact on human affairs; that combat has fundamentally altered history's course in both short and long terms. To understand this is to understand the world in which we live. And *The Encyclopedia of Warfare* enables that understanding in an impressive fashion.

Dennis Showalter
June 2013

TIMELINE OF NOTABLE CIVILIZATIONS

3500–3000 BCE

EGYPTIAN 3100 BCE

3500 BCE	3400 BCE	3300 BCE	3200 BCE	3100 BCE	3000 BCE

3000–2500 BCE

EGYPTIAN

SUMERIAN 2800 BCE

MINOAN 2700 BCE

3000 BCE	2900 BCE	2800 BCE	2700 BCE	2600 BCE	2500 BCE

2500–2000 BCE

EGYPTIAN

SUMERIAN

BABYLONIAN 2100 BCE

MINOAN

AKKAD 2500 BCE

ASSYRIAN 2100 BCE

INDUS 2500 BCE

CHINA 2500 BCE

2500 BCE	2400 BCE	2300 BCE	2200 BCE	2100 BCE	2000 BCE

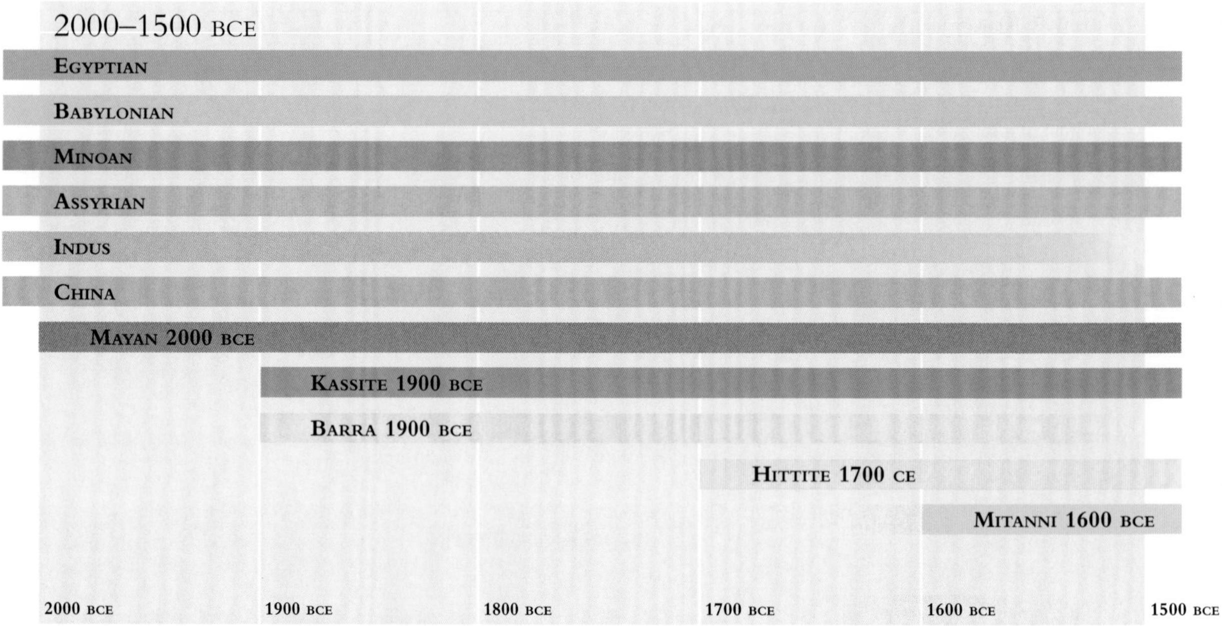

2000–1500 BCE

EGYPTIAN

BABYLONIAN

MINOAN

ASSYRIAN

INDUS

CHINA

MAYAN 2000 BCE

KASSITE 1900 BCE

BARRA 1900 BCE

HITTITE 1700 CE

MITANNI 1600 BCE

| 2000 BCE | 1900 BCE | 1800 BCE | 1700 BCE | 1600 BCE | 1500 BCE |

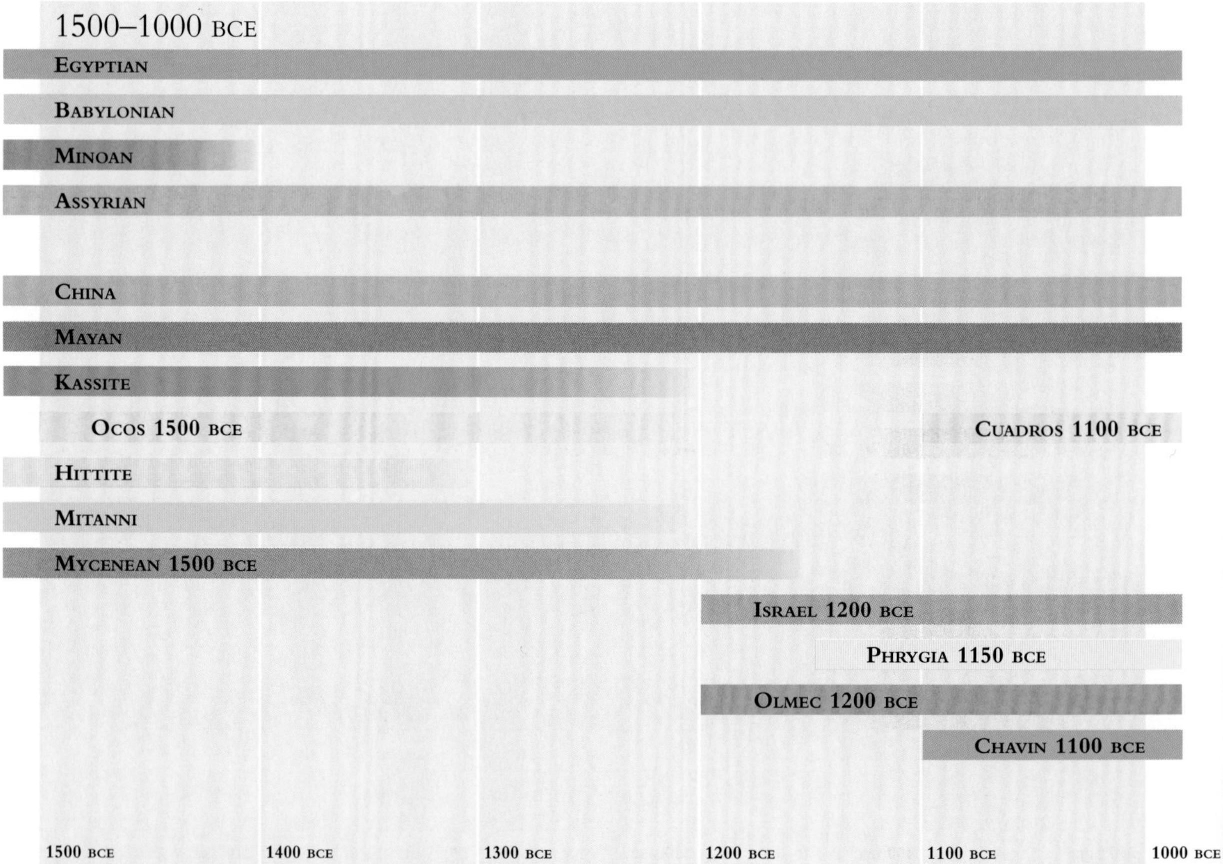

1500–1000 BCE

EGYPTIAN

BABYLONIAN

MINOAN

ASSYRIAN

CHINA

MAYAN

KASSITE

OCOS 1500 BCE

CUADROS 1100 BCE

HITTITE

MITANNI

MYCENEAN 1500 BCE

ISRAEL 1200 BCE

PHRYGIA 1150 BCE

OLMEC 1200 BCE

CHAVIN 1100 BCE

| 1500 BCE | 1400 BCE | 1300 BCE | 1200 BCE | 1100 BCE | 1000 BCE |

1000–500 BCE

EGYPTIAN					
BABYLONIAN					
PHOENICIA 1000 BCE					
ASSYRIAN					
		ROMAN KINGDOM 800 BCE			
CHINA					
MAYAN					
		CARTHAGE 800 BCE			
CUADROS					
				PERSIA 650 BCE	
ISRAEL					
PHRYGIA			**GREECE 700 BCE**		
OLMEC					
CHAVIN					

1000 BCE	900 BCE	800 BCE	700 BCE	600 BCE	500 BCE

500–0

EGYPTIAN					
					ROMAN EMPIRE 27 BCE
ROMAN REPUBLIC 509 BCE					
CHINA					
MAYAN					
CARTHAGE					
	MOCHE 400 BCE				
PERSIA 650 BCE					
ISRAEL					
GREECE 700 BCE	**MACEDONIA 400 BCE**	**SELEUCID EMPIRE 312 BCE**			
OLMEC					
			NAZCA 200 BCE		

500 BCE	400 BCE	300 BCE	200 BCE	100 BCE	0 BCE

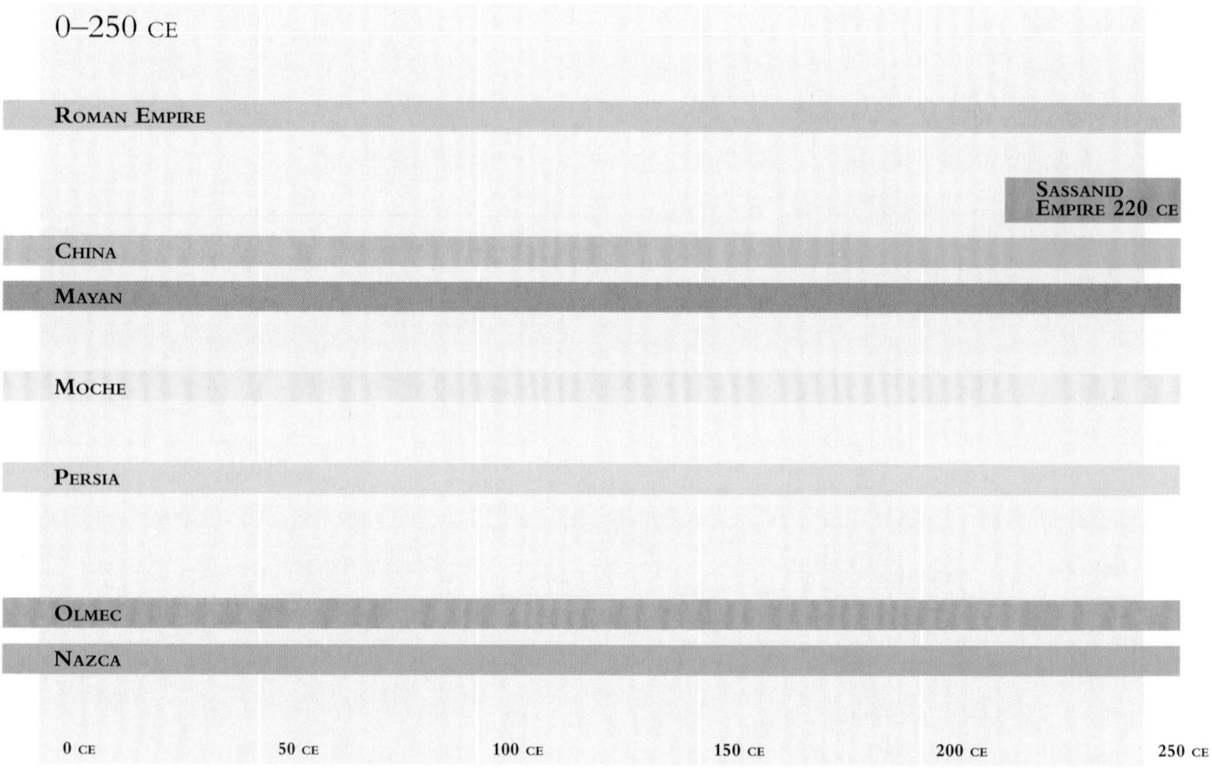

0–250 CE

ROMAN EMPIRE

SASSANID EMPIRE 220 CE

CHINA

MAYAN

MOCHE

PERSIA

OLMEC

NAZCA

0 CE	50 CE	100 CE	150 CE	200 CE	250 CE

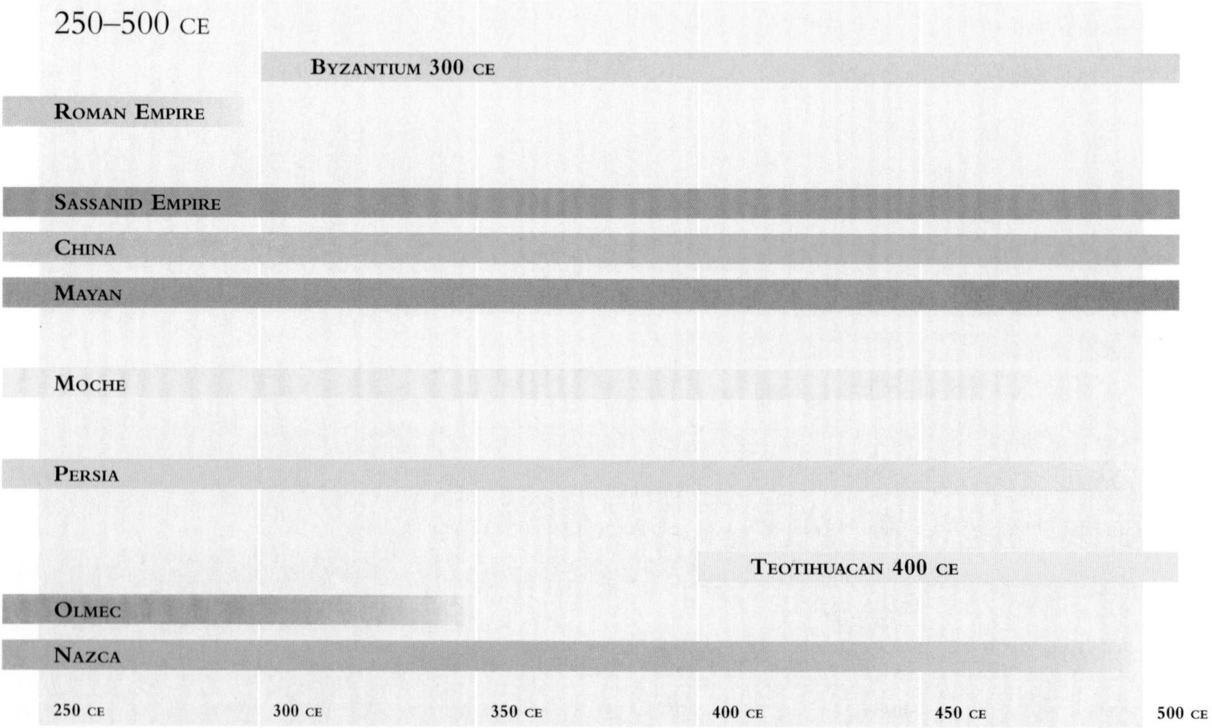

250–500 CE

BYZANTIUM 300 CE

ROMAN EMPIRE

SASSANID EMPIRE

CHINA

MAYAN

MOCHE

PERSIA

TEOTIHUACAN 400 CE

OLMEC

NAZCA

250 CE	300 CE	350 CE	400 CE	450 CE	500 CE

500–750 CE

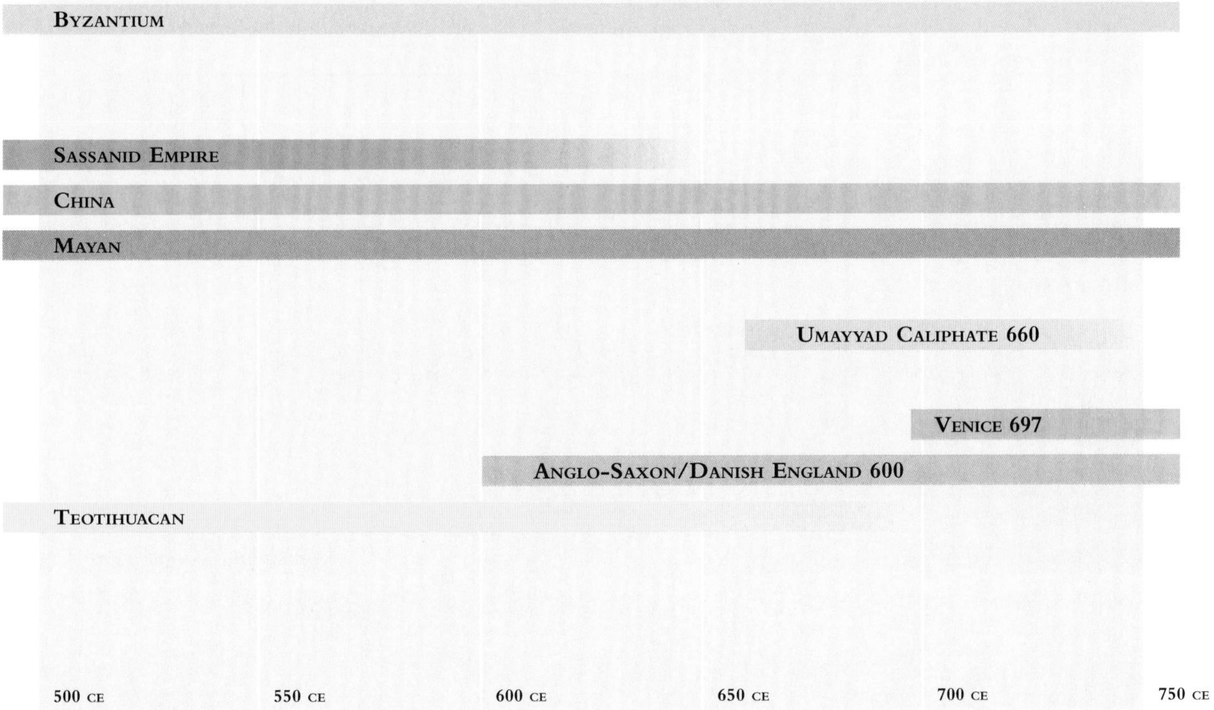

BYZANTIUM

SASSANID EMPIRE

CHINA

MAYAN

UMAYYAD CALIPHATE 660

VENICE 697

ANGLO-SAXON/DANISH ENGLAND 600

TEOTIHUACAN

500 CE	550 CE	600 CE	650 CE	700 CE	750 CE

750–1000 CE

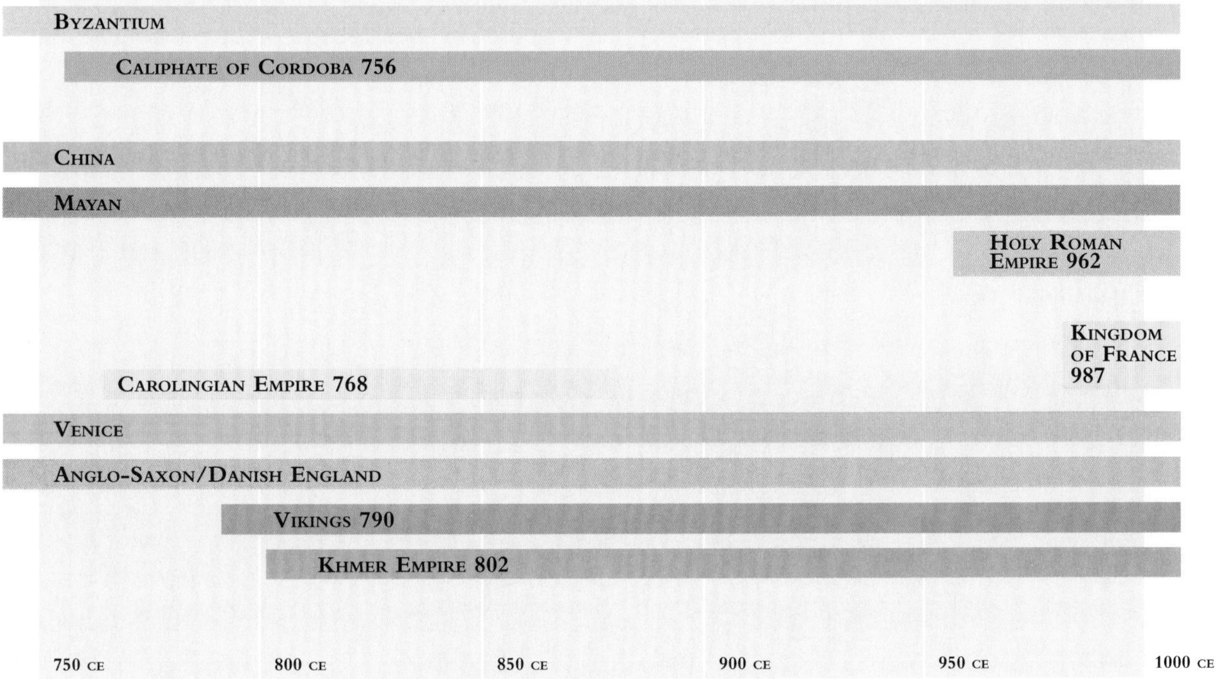

BYZANTIUM

CALIPHATE OF CORDOBA 756

CHINA

MAYAN

HOLY ROMAN EMPIRE 962

KINGDOM OF FRANCE 987

CAROLINGIAN EMPIRE 768

VENICE

ANGLO-SAXON/DANISH ENGLAND

VIKINGS 790

KHMER EMPIRE 802

750 CE	800 CE	850 CE	900 CE	950 CE	1000 CE

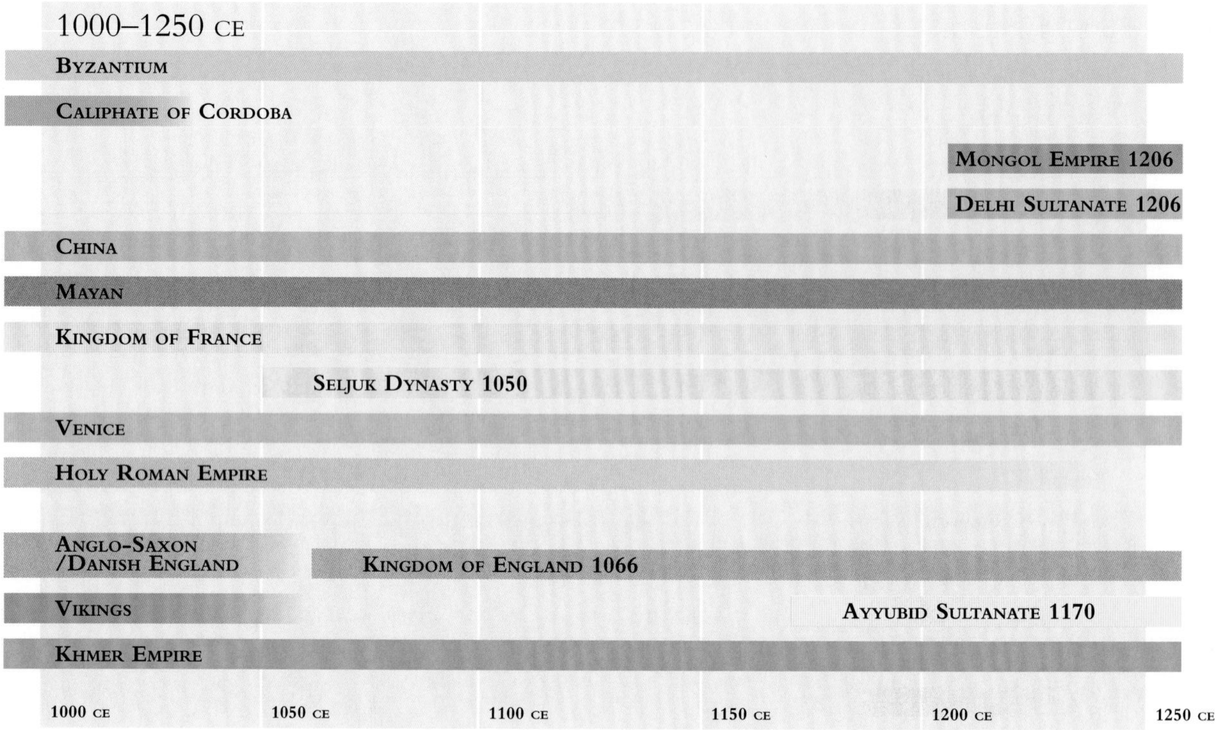

1000–1250 CE

BYZANTIUM

CALIPHATE OF CORDOBA

MONGOL EMPIRE 1206

DELHI SULTANATE 1206

CHINA

MAYAN

KINGDOM OF FRANCE

SELJUK DYNASTY 1050

VENICE

HOLY ROMAN EMPIRE

ANGLO-SAXON /DANISH ENGLAND

KINGDOM OF ENGLAND 1066

VIKINGS

AYYUBID SULTANATE 1170

KHMER EMPIRE

1000 CE	1050 CE	1100 CE	1150 CE	1200 CE	1250 CE

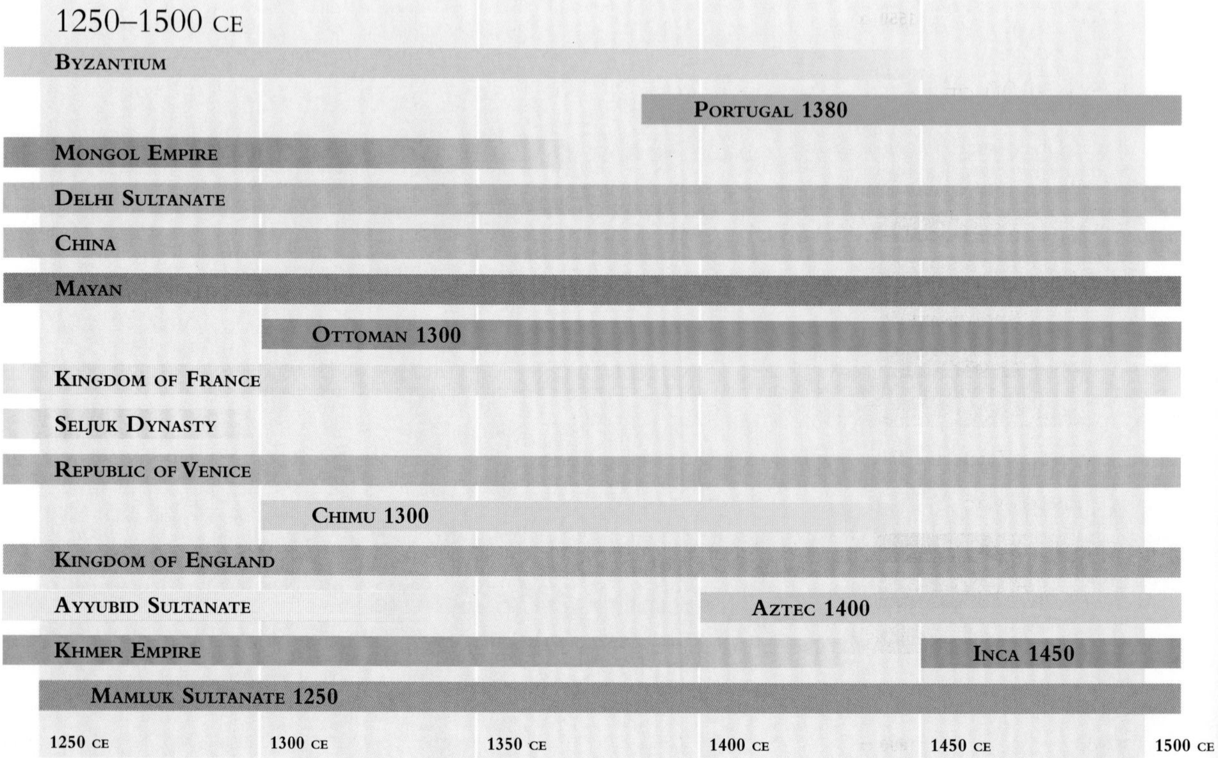

1250–1500 CE

BYZANTIUM

PORTUGAL 1380

MONGOL EMPIRE

DELHI SULTANATE

CHINA

MAYAN

OTTOMAN 1300

KINGDOM OF FRANCE

SELJUK DYNASTY

REPUBLIC OF VENICE

CHIMU 1300

KINGDOM OF ENGLAND

AYYUBID SULTANATE

AZTEC 1400

KHMER EMPIRE

INCA 1450

MAMLUK SULTANATE 1250

1250 CE	1300 CE	1350 CE	1400 CE	1450 CE	1500 CE

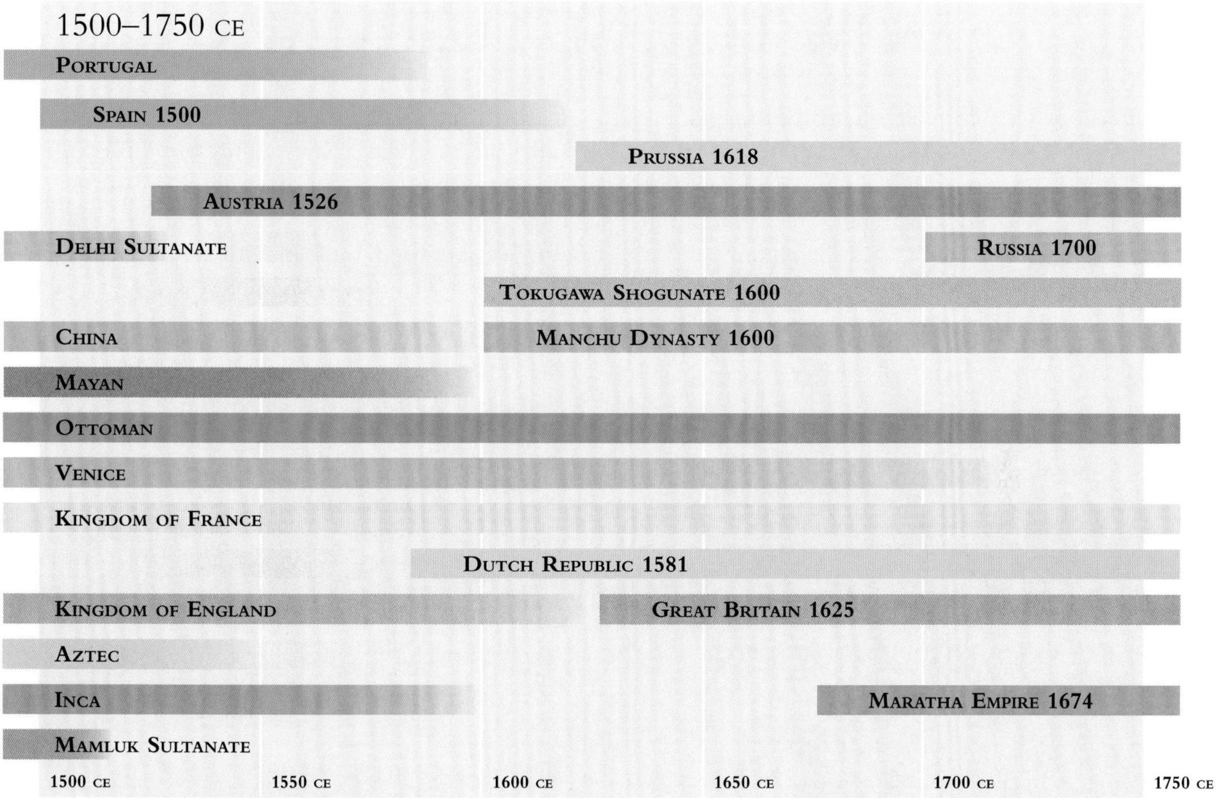

1500–1750 CE

PORTUGAL

SPAIN 1500

PRUSSIA 1618

AUSTRIA 1526

DELHI SULTANATE

RUSSIA 1700

TOKUGAWA SHOGUNATE 1600

CHINA   MANCHU DYNASTY 1600

MAYAN

OTTOMAN

VENICE

KINGDOM OF FRANCE

DUTCH REPUBLIC 1581

KINGDOM OF ENGLAND   GREAT BRITAIN 1625

AZTEC

INCA   MARATHA EMPIRE 1674

MAMLUK SULTANATE

| 1500 CE | 1550 CE | 1600 CE | 1650 CE | 1700 CE | 1750 CE |

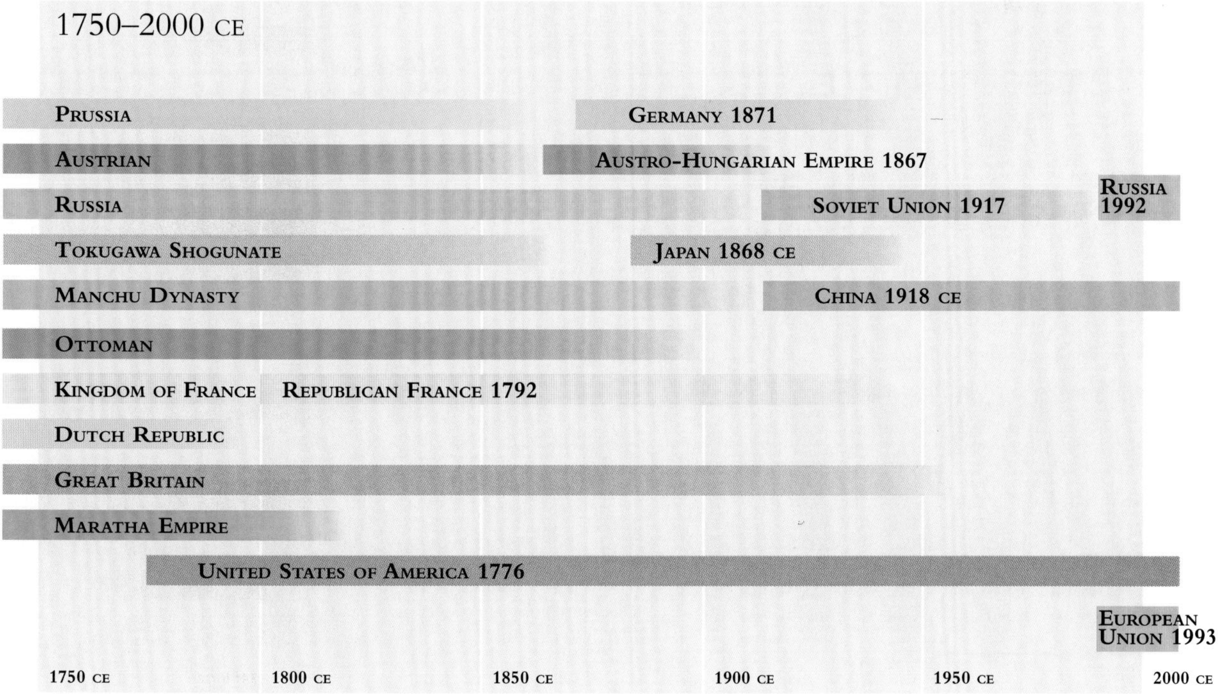

1750–2000 CE

PRUSSIA   GERMANY 1871

AUSTRIAN   AUSTRO-HUNGARIAN EMPIRE 1867

RUSSIA   SOVIET UNION 1917   RUSSIA 1992

TOKUGAWA SHOGUNATE   JAPAN 1868 CE

MANCHU DYNASTY   CHINA 1918 CE

OTTOMAN

KINGDOM OF FRANCE   REPUBLICAN FRANCE 1792

DUTCH REPUBLIC

GREAT BRITAIN

MARATHA EMPIRE

UNITED STATES OF AMERICA 1776

EUROPEAN UNION 1993

| 1750 CE | 1800 CE | 1850 CE | 1900 CE | 1950 CE | 2000 CE |

HOW TO USE THE MAPS

Each map in this book is designed to provide a concise picture of the battle as it unfolded. The dispositions of both sides are shown with red and blue blocks, the red forces indicating the recognized victors and the blue the defeated forces. Movement is shown with coloured arrows. Significant geographical features are also marked, such as towns, hills, ridges, roads, railway lines and rivers. A distance scale is also included. For battles after 1914, the standard NATO military unit symbols are used, indicating the type of force, its size, commander and number or other identifying mark.

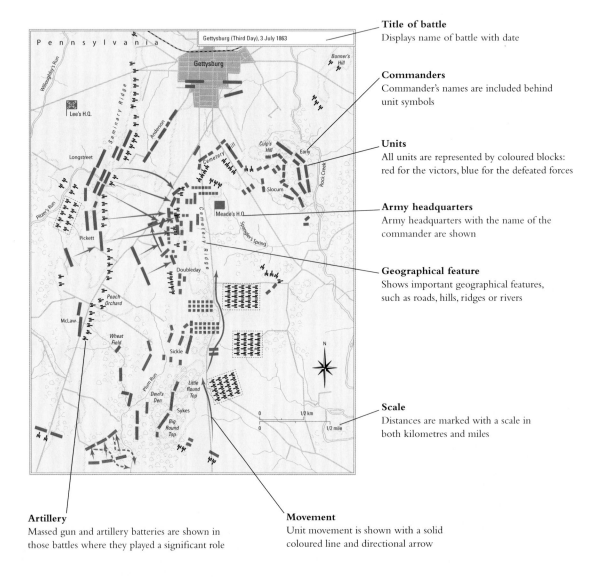

Title of battle
Displays name of battle with date

Commanders
Commander's names are included behind unit symbols

Units
All units are represented by coloured blocks: red for the victors, blue for the defeated forces

Army headquarters
Army headquarters with the name of the commander are shown

Geographical feature
Shows important geographical features, such as roads, hills, ridges or rivers

Scale
Distances are marked with a scale in both kilometres and miles

Artillery
Massed gun and artillery batteries are shown in those battles where they played a significant role

Movement
Unit movement is shown with a solid coloured line and directional arrow

KEY TO THE MAP SYMBOLS

Direction of movement
of victors

Direction of movement
of defeated forces

Secondary movement

Castle or fort

Camp

Cavalry

Infantry

Guns/artillery batteries

Ancient galleys

Ships

Ship sunk

Aircraft movement/attack

Airfield

U-boat

Conflict/flashpoint

Battle

Types of unit symbols (post 1914 maps)

Infantry

Cavalry

Armoured

Airborne

Combined (Corps level and above)

Unit sizes

XXXXX	Army Group/Front
XXXX	Army
XXX	Corps
XX	Division
X	Brigade
III	Regiment
II	Battalion
I	Company

How to understand a unit symbol

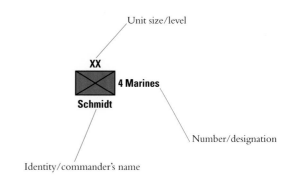

Unit size/level

Number/designation

Identity/commander's name

'I must study Politics and War that my sons may have liberty to study Mathematics and Philosophy.'

John Adams, 1780

Ancient Wars
c.2500 BCE—500 CE

It is a reasonable assumption to make that hundreds — if not thousands — of ancient battles took place for which no record survives today. Yet even those that history has chosen to preserve come to us with the scantest detail, frustrating students from a later era.

Mediterranean & Middle Eastern Wars
c.2500–500 BCE

■ HAIK VS NIMROD, C.2492 BCE

Nimrod came to rule Mesopotamia through military conquest, and founded several cities. According to Armenian legends, he was defeated near Lake Van by the Armenian patriarch Haik, who killed him with a bow shot from a great distance.

■ LAGASH VS UMMA, C.2450 BCE

The earliest battle currently known to history arose from a border dispute between the city-states of Lagash and Umma. Carvings of the battle suggest that the main fighting force involved was a dense phalanx of spearmen.

■ CONQUESTS OF SARGON, C.2234–2284 BCE

King Sargon of Akkad is credited with forming the world's first true army. Leading a force of 5000 professional soldiers armed with bows and bronze hand weapons, he subdued and conquered Mesopotamia.

■ URUK, C.2340 BCE

During the conquest of Sumer, Sargon the Great's army attacked and destroyed the city of Uruk. Surviving forces from the city formed

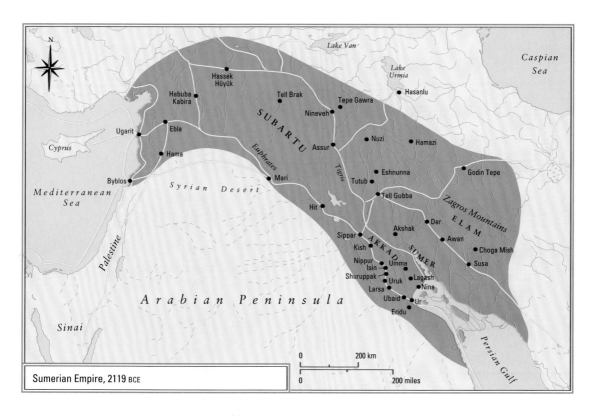

Sumerian Empire, 2119 BCE

part of a great Sumerian alliance, which was in turn defeated.

■ VICTORY OVER KASHTUBILA, C.2300 BCE

Among the foes faced by Sargon the Great was Kashtubila, king of Kazalla, a city to the west of Mesopotamia. Kashtubila opposed Sargon but was comprehensively defeated. His city was razed to the ground, so thoroughly destroyed that it was said that birds could not find anywhere to perch in the ruins.

■ MARI, C.2300 BCE

Sargon's early campaigns were directed against city-states in the fertile crescent, cementing his power over the whole region. The city of Mari on the Euphrates river was one of his targets. Once conquered, it became an Akkadian administrative centre.

■ YARMUTI (JARMUT), C.2300 BCE

The location of Yarmuti is unclear, but it may have been a trading port on the Phoenician coast. Many of Sargon's campaigns were directed at securing trade routes and valuable resources, which would make such a port a logical target.

■ EBLA, C.2250 BCE

Ebla was an important trade centre in northern Syria. It is claimed that Sargon of Akkad captured and destroyed the city, though the date and circumstances remain unclear. Ebla eventually regained some of its power, but was attacked again by Sargon's grandson, Naram-Sin.

■ CEDAR FOREST & TAURUS, C.2250 BCE

Sargon's campaigns took him northward into what is today known as Turkey, to the Amanus and Taurus mountains. It is unclear exactly what foes he faced here, possibly tribal peoples and small independent city-states.

■ FALL OF SUMER, C.2006 BCE

Changing agricultural conditions weakened the Sumerian city-states as pressure from Amorite tribes increased. Unable to feed its population, Sumeria was incapable of resistance and was gradually overrun by the invaders.

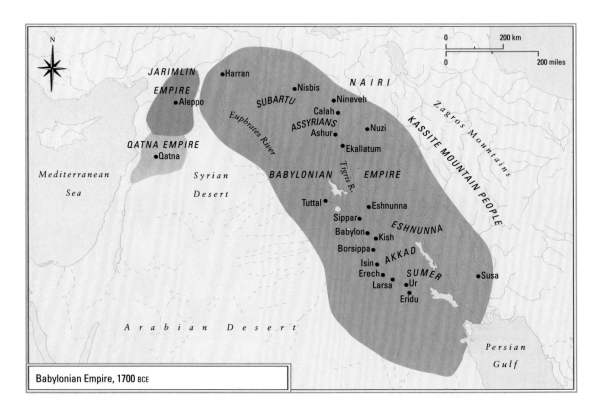

Babylonian Empire, 1700 BCE

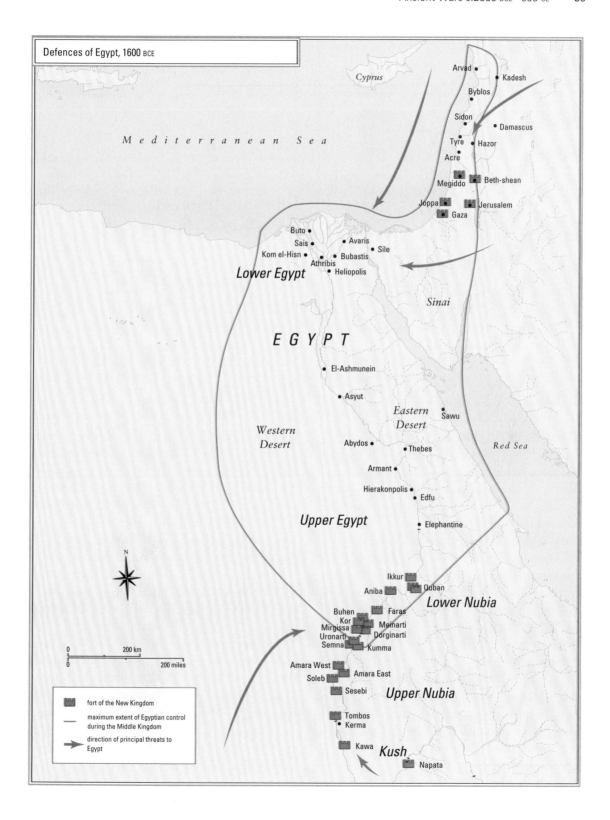

Defences of Egypt, 1600 BCE

Cyprus

Arvad •
• Kadesh
Byblos •
Sidon •
• Damascus
Tyre • Hazor
Acre •
Megiddo • Beth-shean
Joppa • Jerusalem
Gaza •

M e d i t e r r a n e a n   S e a

Buto •
Sais •   • Avaris
Kom el-Hisn •   • Sile
Athribis • • Bubastis
Lower Egypt   • Heliopolis

Sinai

E G Y P T

• El-Ashmunein

• Asyut

Eastern Desert   • Sawu

Western Desert   Abydos •   • Thebes   *Red Sea*

Armant •

Hierakonpolis • • Edfu

Upper Egypt   • Elephantine

Ikkur
Aniba   Quban
Lower Nubia

Buhen   Faras
Kor   Meinarti
Mirgissa   Dorginarti
Uronarti
Semna   Kumma

Amara West
Soleb   Amara East
Sesebi   *Upper Nubia*

N

Tombos
Kerma

Kawa   *Kush*   • Napata

0   200 km
0   200 miles

fort of the New Kingdom

maximum extent of Egyptian control during the Middle Kingdom

direction of principal threats to Egypt

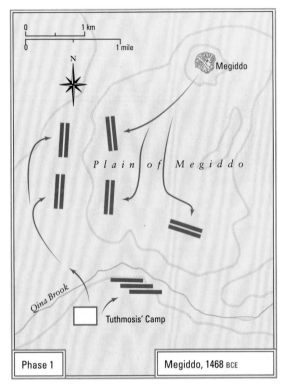

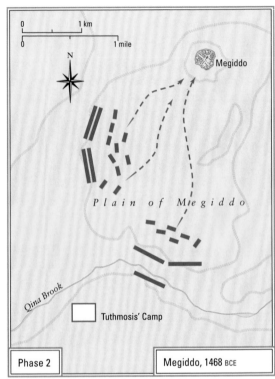

■ **FALL OF UR, C.1940 BCE**

The city-state of Ur was sacked by invading Elamite tribes from the east, after which Sumeria came under Amorite rule. The Amorites gradually became absorbed into the culture of the region, forming the basis for the Babylonian Empire.

■ **BATTLES OF HAMMURABI, C.1763–1758 BCE**

Predecessors of Hammurabi, the Amorite king of Babylon, had conquered some of the surrounding city-states. Hammurabi built on their success by making alliances then turning on his former allies, establishing Babylon as the dominant power in southern Mesopotamia.

■ **ALEPPO, 1590 BCE**

As Babylon declined in power, the Hittites were able to advance down the Euphrates river, sacking Aleppo. Internal troubles prevented the Hittites from consolidating their gains, and they ceased to be a major power for several decades.

■ **MEGIDDO, C.1468 BCE**

Pharoah Tuthmosis III was co-regent with his aunt, Hapshepsut, for the first 22 years of his reign. During this time he served as head of the army, gaining a reputation as an excellent commander. An alliance of Canaanite princes attempted to take advantage of the inevitable disruption caused by Hapshepsut's death in order to secede from Egyptian rule. However, they had miscalculated; Tuthmosis moved rapidly against them at the head of a well-organized army. The subsequent battle at Megiddo was extensively recorded at the behest of the victorious Tuthmosis, becoming the first fully documented battle in history.

The Egyptian army benefited from unified and cohesive command, while the opposing forces were led by allied princes who argued among themselves over matters of strategy and precedence. Their army was deployed near Megiddo, with a formidable ridge blocking the Egyptian approach. Had Tuthmosis taken either of the conventional routes, north or south around the ridge, the Canaanites would have been able to deploy against him in good time. Instead, he attempted a risky march through a narrow pass. Even a small blocking force could have successfully held the pass, but it had been left unguarded, perhaps due to problems within the Canaanite command structure. It was to be a fatal mistake on the part of the Caananites

The Canaanite forces became disorganized as they redeployed, while the Egyptians formed up in a far more disciplined manner. The initial Egyptian attack took the form of a mass chariot charge that threw back the disordered Canaanites. Organized resistance was impossible and the Cannanite army rapidly collapsed. Many of the survivors took refuge in Megiddo itself, where they were besieged until the city fell several months later.

■ **TUTHMOSIS' SYRIAN CAMPAIGNS, C.1460 BCE**
Tuthmosis III of Egypt undertook several campaigns into Syria, conquering numerous towns. These campaigns may have been supported by naval transport for supplies or even troops. The economies of Syria were left in ruins as a result, reducing the chances of a successful rebellion.

■ **TUTHMOSIS' CAMPAIGN AGAINST THE MITANNI, C.1458 BCE**
The Egyptian army gained the advantage of surprise by carrying out what appeared to be merely another campaign in Syria, then suddenly marching to the Euphrates and crossing in boats they had carried with them. The Mitanni were totally unprepared and easily defeated.

■ **FALL OF CRETE, C.1400 BCE**
The Minoan civilization arose on the island of Crete around 2700 BCE. Around 1400 BCE, a series of natural disasters weakened the Minoans, whose culture was displaced by the more warlike Mycenean Greek civilization.

■ **SUGAGI, C.1308 BCE**
In the late Bronze Age, Babylonia was ruled by the Kassites, who conquered Assyria. Assyria rebelled and began to rebuild its power, leading to the battle of Sugagi, which established the border between the two states.

■ **KADESH, 1294 BCE**
Egyptian dominance over Canaan waxed and waned several times as Egypt both lost territory to rebellions and invasions, then retook it. The region was somewhat too remote to maintain permanent strong control, but too close to permit a foreign power to dominate. The increasing power of the Hittites, who originated north of Canaan, resulted in several clashes and, consequently, improvements in military technology. Among these developments was an improved axe with better performance against armour. Egyptian chariots were also made lighter and faster, permitting the chariot force to become an elite striking arm.

There was nothing new about conflict between the Egyptians and the Hittities. Indeed, among the opponents of Tuthmosis III at Megiddo were the Mitanni people, forerunners of the Hittites. Like the Egyptians, the Hittites had a centralized empire and a well-organized military. They also wanted dominance over Canaan and were willing to fight for it. Pharoah Ramses II marched through Sinai into Canaan with an army of some 20,000 men. This army was divided into four divisions, each with its own identity and command structure. The Pharoah's bodyguard formed a separate body from the four main divisions and was held under his close command. The force also included significant numbers of mercenaries who were recruited partly to add fighting power and partly to deprive the enemy of using them.

The Egyptians at the time had a sophisticated system of intelligence gathering, using spies and agents who reported to officers trained to handle them. Information was obtained as the army advanced, though in this case it turned out to be faulty. Mutwallis, the Hittite king, had taken up position near Kadesh but sent men posing as deserters towards the advacing Egyptians. These men told Ramses that the main Hittite force was still distant. Seeing an opportunity for decisive victory, Ramses dispensed with reconnaissance and instead rushed forward to meet the enemy before they could be reinforced. He took with

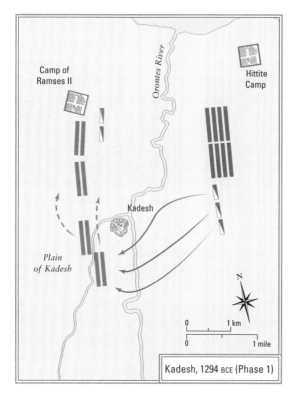

Kadesh, 1294 BCE (Phase 1)

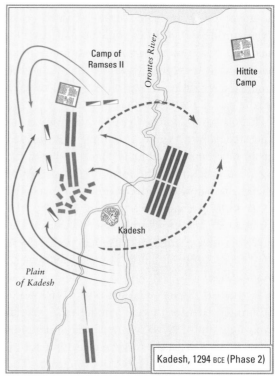

Kadesh, 1294 BCE (Phase 2)

him only his bodyguard force and one 5000-man division, which reached Kadesh unopposed. The Hittites had concealed their force using the city as cover and launched a chariot strike against a second Egyptian division, which was moving up in support. This was routed, the survivors seeking safety with the Pharoah's force. The Egyptian army came under severe pressure, with the Hittites blocking their line of retreat, but gained some respite when the Hittites paused to plunder their camp.

As the fighting became more confused, the Hittites failed to notice the approach of the other two 5000-strong Egyptian divisions and a force of mercenaries marching up from the coast. These divisions hit the Hittite flank and rear, taking the pressure off the Pharoah. Ramses took advantage of this opportunity to launch a disorganized counter-attack with his personal bodyguard in the lead. This decisive action rallied the wavering Egyptians, and it was the Hittite army that broke

under the pressure. They fell back into Kadesh and took up defensive positions that Ramses judged his army was too weak to take by force. A peace treaty – the earliest known to history – was negotiated and both kings returned home to claim victory. The Egyptians could perhaps claim a narrow victory, but they had not achieved enough to change the strategic situation. The treaty did, however, secure the northern frontier against greater Hittite incursions and it prevented further conflict for a time.

■ DAPUR, 1269 BCE

Dapur was one of several rebel Canaanite cities recaptured by Pharoah Ramses II. He chose to use assault rather than siege tactics. Ladders were used to scale the walls while axe-armed troops broke through the gates.

■ SIEGE OF TROY, C.1184 BCE

It is thought that legends of the 10-year siege of Troy are based on historical events, though proof is sketchy. Traditionally, Troy was besieged

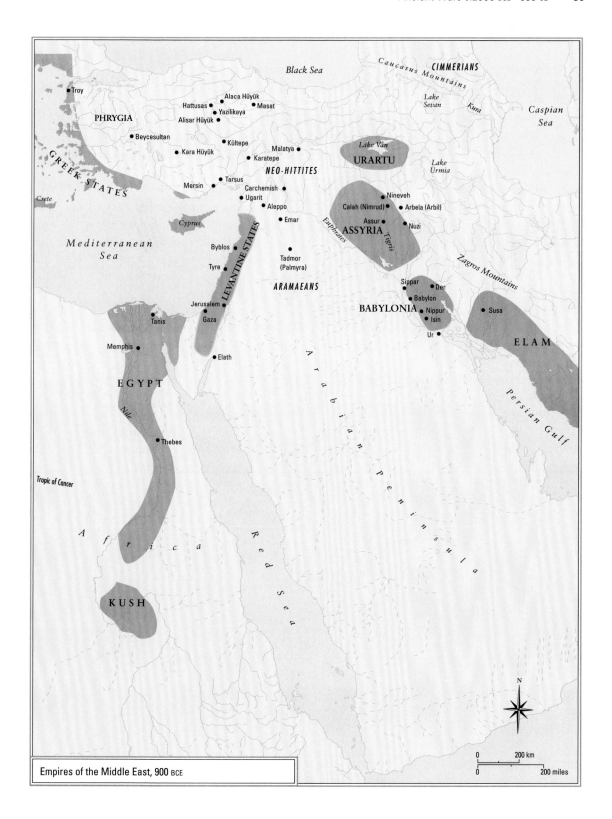

Empires of the Middle East, 900 BCE

by an alliance of Achaean Greeks who finally destroyed the city.

■ INVASION OF THE SEA PEOPLES, 1179 BCE

After sacking many cities around the eastern end of the Mediterranean, the Sea Peoples advanced on Egypt by sea and overland. The Pharoah constructed the world's first purpose-built war fleet to counter the seaward invasions.

■ MOUNT GILBOA, c.1000 BCE

Although traditionally opposed to the concept of kings, the early Hebrews appointed Saul as their first monarch. Saul's forces were mostly poorly equipped tribesmen, who faced much better equipped and organized troops fielded by the Philistines of the coastal region. With no real chance of success in a set-piece battle, the Hebrews conducted a guerrilla war, striking down into the coastal plain then retreating into the mountains. This was successful for a time, but eventually the Philistines forced a direct confrontation at Mount Gilboa. Saul was said to

have consulted a witch or oracle who told him he would lose the battle, and he had become dispirited as a result. Whether for this reason or simply the superior fighting power of the Philistines, Saul's army was gradually pushed back and, despite stubborn resistance, overwhelmed. Saul committed suicide to avoid capture and the Philistine army advanced to occupy Hebrew lands.

■ QARQAR, 853 BCE

The Assyrian King Salmaneser III led his army against a hostile alliance in what was at the time the largest battle ever fought. The battle was inconclusive, and it was not for several years that Assyrian dominance was established.

■ GEZER, 733 BCE

The city of Gezer occupied a strategic site above the coastal plain of what is today known as Israel. It was besieged and captured by the Assyrian Empire, which later used it as an administrative centre for the surrounding region.

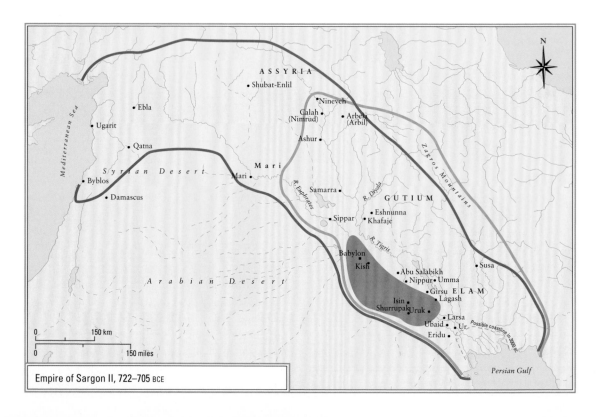

Empire of Sargon II, 722–705 BCE

■ ETHIOPIAN CONQUEST OF EGYPT, 730 BCE

Responding to a request for assistance from the city of Thebes, the Ethiopian King Piye marched his army into Egypt and was able to reunify the fragmented country under his rule. Ethiopian (Nubian) kings ruled Egypt for the next several decades.

■ SIEGE OF SAMARIA, 724–722 BCE

The expanding Assyrian Empire advanced into Jewish lands, which were divided into the kingdoms of Judah and Israel. Samaria, capital of Israel, was besieged for three years before finally falling. Its population was deported, a common Assyrian practice.

■ SIEGE OF LACHISH, 701 BCE

The Jewish kingdom of Israel fell to the Assyrians in 722-705 BCE. The capital was destroyed and its population deported, leaving only Judah as an independent Jewish state. Judah was small and insignificant, wholly unable to resist the powerful Assyrian army without outside help. Aware that an alliance of Egyptian, Phoenician and Philistine forces was forming against Assyria, King Hezekiah of Judah decided to stop paying his ruinous tribute to Assyria and rose in rebellion. The Egyptians were quickly defeated by Assyrian troops and the alliance fell apart. Judah escaped retribution on this occasion, despite the fact that the Assyrians normally followed a policy of harsh reprisals for rebellion. However, the tribute was reinstated and it seemed that it was only a matter of time before Judah was annexed. The death in 705 BCE of Assyrian King Sargon II at the hands of his own troops offered a second chance at independence. Judah sought allies and began a military campaign, but Sargon's successor, Sennacherib, broke Babylonian and Egyptian armies with ease. Judah surrendered and was again spared, until four years later when Sennacherib announced that he intended to settle the Judah problem by force. The Assyrian army was at that time virtually unbeatable in the field, and the greatly inferior forces of Judah did not even try. Instead they retreated to their fortresses, which were taken one by one. As the

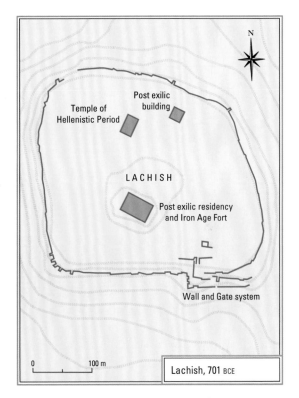

Lachish, 701 BCE

Assyrians advanced, the fortifications of Jerusalem, the capital, and other towns such as Lachish were strengthened against the inevitable siege.

When the Assyrian army reached Lachish, the town was offered a chance to surrender as per the usual Assyrian practice. This was accompanied by parades and a display of force by the Assyrians, underlining the threat to the town. The offer was refused, forcing Sennacherib to choose between a lengthy siege and a costly assault. He chose the latter. After first encircling the town to prevent aid and supplies from reaching it, the Assyrian army began preparations for the assault. A huge earthern ramp was constructed, giving access to the walls. This was built mainly by forced labour, using prisoners captured elsewhere. Assyrian archers, armed with powerful composite bows and protected by armour, shot at anyone trying to interfere with the work. Once the ramp was completed, it was faced with stone slabs, allowing a siege tower to be pushed up to the

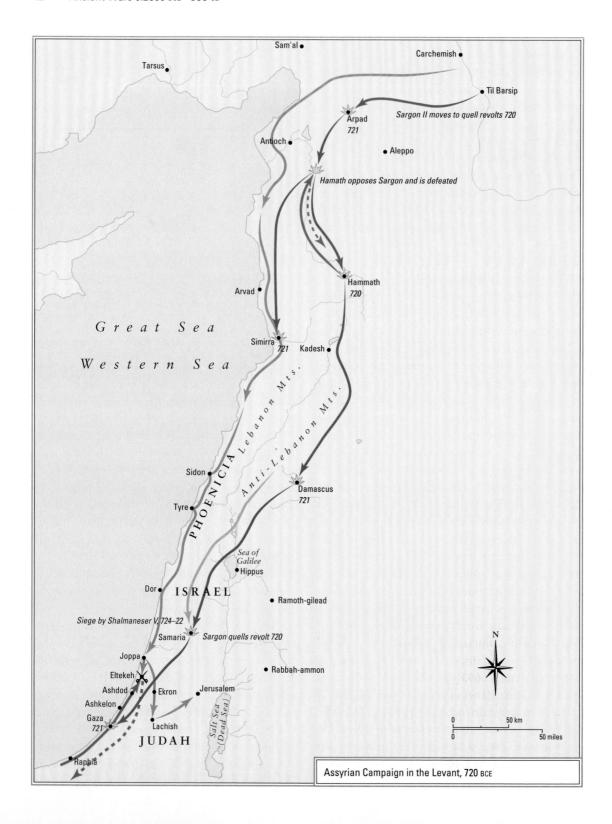

Sam'al

Carchemish

Tarsus

Til Barsip

Arpad
721

Sargon II moves to quell revolts 720

Antioch

Aleppo

Hamath opposes Sargon and is defeated

Hammath
720

Arvad

Great Sea

Western Sea

Simirra
721

Kadesh

Lebanon Mts.

Anti-Lebanon Mts.

PHOENICIA

Sidon

Damascus
721

Tyre

Sea of
Galilee

Hippus

Dor   ISRAEL

Ramoth-gilead

Siege by Shalmaneser V, 724—22

Samaria   Sargon quells revolt 720

Joppa

Rabbah-ammon

Eltekeh

Ashdod   Ekron   Jerusalem

Ashkelon

Gaza
721   Lachish

Salt Sea
(Dead Sea)

JUDAH

N

0   50 km
0   50 miles

Raphia

Assyrian Campaign in the Levant, 720 BCE

top. Diversionary assaults were made elsewhere, using iron-tipped rams against the walls. A breach was made, though the defenders were able to reinforce the threatened section of wall with a ramp of their own.

The final assault was made at several points, using ladders to gain access to the wall while the siege tower was advanced into position. Covered by archery, the Assyrian infantry assaulted the walls and drove the defenders from them. They then entered the town and ran riot. The Assyrians commited many atrocities in Lachish, impaling leaders and putting much of the population to the sword. These actions may have been deliberately encouraged as a means of spreading fear among potential enemies; the Assyrians typically used tactics like blinding captured soldiers and executing their leaders for this purpose, so they were unlikely to be squeamish during the aftermath of an assault.

■ JERUSALEM, 701 BCE

With disease in their camp and dwindling water supplies, the Assyrian army besieging the Jewish capital at Jerusalem finally broke off their siege. This decision ensured the survival of the Jewish state and religion.

■ LELANTINE WAR, c.710–650 BCE

The Lelantine War was fought over control of the Lelantine Plain on the island of Euboea. The principle combatants were Chalkis and Eretria but the conflict drew in many other cities due to their alliances and influence. It is likely that the forces involved included some hoplites, cavalry and chariots, but were primarily composed of lightly equipped swordsmen. The drawn-out conflict greatly diminished the importance of Euboea in Greek affairs.

■ DIYALA RIVER, c.693 BCE

After subjugating Babylonia, the Assyrian Empire launched a campaign against the kingdom of Elam. The decisive clash came at the Diyala river. Assyrian sources hail the battle as a great victory, but more likely it was both costly and inconclusive.

■ HALULE, 691 BCE

Rising in rebellion against the Assyrian Empire, Babylon was joined by allies including the Chaldeans and Elamites as well as several tribal peoples. The Elamite contingent contained cavalry and charioteers as well as infantry. After an indecisive clash in which the Assyrians probably suffered the most casualties, both sides claimed victory but the political situation remained unchanged. Babylon was besieged later in the year, falling after a siege that lasted nine months.

■ ASSYRIAN CAMPAIGNS INTO EGYPT, 668 & 661 BCE

During the reign of King Ashurbanipal, Assyrian armies launched two campaigns into Egypt. The second, in 661 BCE, succeeded in sacking Thebes, and Nubian influence was expelled from Egypt. However, Assyrian control was short-lived.

■ HYSIAE, 669 BCE

A clash between the Greek city-states of Argos and Sparta resulted in defeat for the Spartan army. The rise of Sparta to military pre-eminence in Greece is generally considered to have begun a few years later.

■ ULAI, 652 BCE

Elam, lying to the east of Mesopotamia, was an ally of Babylon and a threat to the trade routes upon which much of Assyria's power was based. Assyria launched a pre-emptive campaign to eliminate the threat, inflicting a decisive defeat at the River Ulai.

■ SUSA, 647 BCE

Ongoing conflict between the Assyrians and Elamites led to a major clash at Susa. The victorious Assyrians levelled the city and looted its treasures, depicting this act in their records as one of vengeance.

■ ASHDOD, 635 BCE

The city of Ashdod in Palestine was besieged by Egyptian forces for 29 years before finally being taken. Egypt had formerly been dominated by the Assyrian Empire, but had begun to reassert its power.

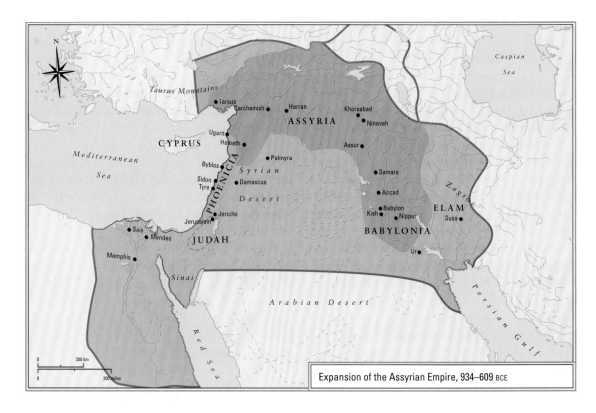

Expansion of the Assyrian Empire, 934–609 BCE

■ **ARRAPHA, 616 BCE**

Babylonia revolted against Assyrian rule in 627 BCE and campaigned against the collapsing Assyrian Empire right up until its final destruction. The Babylonians won a significant victory at Arrapha, capturing large numbers of horses and chariots.

■ **FALL OF ASSYRIA, 616–605 BCE**

After years of war with Babylon and Elam, Assyria was exhausted and unable to respond effectively to pressure from Scythia and Medea. Babylon, once more independent, led the final conquest of the Assyrian Empire.

■ **FALL OF ASSUR, 614 BCE**

After a failed attack on Nineveh, Babylonian forces marched on the old Assyrian capital of Assur. Joined by their Median allies, they laid siege. Even with the Assyrian army still at Nineveh, the city was able to hold out until 612 BCE.

■ **NINEVEH, 612 BCE**

The capital of the Assyrian Empire came under siege by combined forces from Babylon, Medea,

Elam and Scythia. After a period of vigorous resistance, Nineveh was taken and sacked. The Assyrian King Sin-shar-Ishkur was killed in the fighting.

■ **SECOND MEGIDDO, 609 BCE**

Marching to the assistance of their Assyrian allies, Egyptian troops entered the kingdom of Judah without permission and were attacked. After defeating the forces of Judah at Megiddo and slaying their king, the Egyptians continued their march.

■ **HARRAN, 608 BCE**

After the loss of the king at Nineveh, the Assyrian Empire proclaimed one of its generals as King Ashur-Urballit II. He ruled what was left of the Assyrian Empire from Harran, until the city's fall in 608 BCE.

■ **CARCHEMISH, 605 BCE**

The last remnant of the Assyrian Empire was centred on Carchemish. An Egyptian army, marching to assist its Assyrian allies, was delayed by a battle at

Megiddo, but arrived in time to confront the main Babylonian force. The joint army was defeated, bringing the Assyrian Empire to an end. Egypt's power and prestige were also greatly reduced, and Egypt ceased to be a major factor in Mesopotamian affairs while Babylon assumed prominence.

▪ Hama, 605 BCE

Egyptian forces, retreating from their defeat at Carchemish, were caught and attacked by a Babylonian army. The Egyptian army, exhausted from its march, was almost totally annihilated.

▪ Siege of Kirrha, c.590 BCE

The Amphictyonic League was formed to protect the Greek oracle at Delphi. Its forces besieged Kirrha as a result of Kirrhan interference with pilgrims bound for Dephi. Hellebore was used to poison the city's water supply.

▪ Jerusalem, 586 BCE

After displacing Assyria as the major power in the region, the Neo-Babylonian (or Chaldean) Empire expanded its territory at the expense of neighbouring states. Among those overrun was the Jewish kingdom of Judah, whose Egyptian allies abandoned her. Jerusalem withstood the siege for 18 months, but with the population starving, the Jews were forced to attempt a field battle to decide the campaign. They were defeated and Jerusalem fell, with much of the city's population taken as slaves.

▪ Halys, 585 BCE

Fighting between forces from Media and Lydia ended due to an eclipse, which was taken as a bad omen. Since the eclipse can be precisely dated, the battle of Halys can too, making it the earliest battle whose date can be exactly determined.

▪ Siege of Tyre, 585–573 BCE

The city of Tyre occupied a very strong position on an island just off the coast. It resisted siege by Babylonian forces for 13 years, but eventually agreed to pay tribute as part of a settlement.

▪ Egyptian Invasion of Palestine, 567 BCE

Deposed by General Amasis (Ahmose II), King Apries of Egypt sought refuge at the Babylonian court. He was given a Babylonian army to regain his throne but was defeated by an Egyptian expedition into Palestine.

▪ Hyrba, 552 BCE

A force of Persian cavalry and infantry under the command of Cyrus the Great defeated a smaller Median cavalry force. This was the first defeat Media had suffered in some time, and marked the beginning of the Median–Persian war.

▪ Battle of the Persian Border, 551 BCE

A Persian army under the command of Cyrus the Great and his father Cambyses I, consisting mainly of cavalry with some chariots, was engaged by a much larger Median force. The Medians were intent on invading the province of Persis and returning it to Median rule, while the Persians hoped to hold them at the border. The Persians offered battle before an unknown city on the Persian–Median border. Despite the disparity in numbers, the Persians inflicted heavy casualties on their opponents and ended the first day of battle undefeated. They then retired southwards, leaving the city lightly held. The Medians captured the city, killing Cambyses in the process, but the Persian army under Cyrus remained a potent force. Cyrus retreated to the capital, where his army prepared to make a final stand against the Medians.

▪ Battle of the Fetters, 550 BCE

An overconfident Spartan army, carrying fetters with which to bind the captives they intended to take, was heavily defeated by their Arcadian opponents. Many Spartans became prisoners and were bound in their own fetters and shackles.

▪ Pasargadae, 550 BCE

The revolt of Persis against its Median overlords resulted in a lengthy and bloody struggle. Defeated in the field, the Persians under Cyrus the Great retreated to Pasargadae, where they were attacked by a Median army. Cyrus won a decisive victory which established him as overlord of Media, thus creating the Persian Empire. It is thought that the Medians were able to recruit as many as one million infantry and 200,000 cavalry for this campaign, though

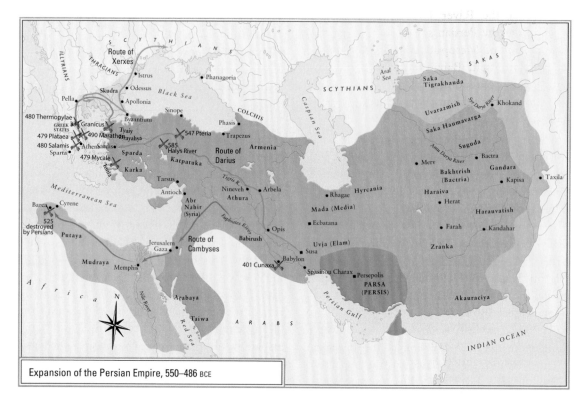

Expansion of the Persian Empire, 550–486 BCE

smaller numbers took part in the actual fighting. Median casualties were much higher than those suffered by the Persian opponents.

■ **PTERIA, 547 BCE**

Taking advantage of the defeat of Media by Persia, the Lydians invaded what had been Median territory. The first clash at Pteria was indecisive, but the Lydians chose to retreat, giving strategic victory to the Persians.

■ **THYMBRA, 547 BCE**

Cyrus the Great deployed his outnumbered Persian forces in a square formation, using camels to disrupt the opposing Lydian cavalry. As the Lydians became disordered, the Persians counter-attacked to win a decisive victory.

■ **SIEGE OF SARDIS, 547 BCE**

After defeating the Lydians at Thymbra, Cyrus the Great advanced on Sardis. The city fell after a 14-day siege. Lydia was then annexed into the Persian Empire, though it took several more years to put down revolts and pacify the region.

■ **300 CHAMPIONS, 545 BCE**

In an effort to minimize casualties, the Greek city-states of Argos and Sparta each agreed to field a force of 300 of their finest warriors against one another. At the end of the battle, only one Spartan champion remained alive against two warriors of Argos. The latter claimed victory and marched home. However, the lone Spartan was left in possession of the battlefield and announced that Sparta had won the battle. This disputed outcome resulted in a full-scale clash between hoplite armies, which was a decisive victory for Sparta.

■ **OPIS, 539 BCE**

Cyrus the Great of Persia launched a campaign against the Neo-Babylonian Empire, which required that he penetrate or bypass the Median Wall. This was a fortification constructed to prevent an invasion of Babylonian territory by the Medes from the north. The city of Opis lay at one end of the wall, and offered a good crossing point over the River Tigris. Capturing Opis would offer the Persian army an easy route into the interior of Mesopotamia, allowing a strike at Babylon itself. Babylonia was at that time in decline, contending with severe economic and political problems, but still remained a formidable power. However, the death in battle of the Babylonian commander and heavy casualties inflicted in the ensuing rout broke Babylonian resistance. Once past Opis, Cyrus was able to overrun the rest of Babylonia against minimal resistance.

■ BABYLON, 539–538 BCE

Cyrus the Great of Persia sent an army under one of his subordinate generals to besiege Babylon. This permitted him to take possession of the surrendered city under the guise of a liberator rather than a conqueror.

■ PERSIAN CONQUEST OF EGYPT, 525 BCE

After the death of Cyrus the Great, his empire was further expanded by his son Cambyses II. Brushing aside Egyptian resistance at Pelusium, the Persian army advanced almost unopposed to Memphis, making Egypt a Persian province.

■ PELUSIUM, 525 BCE

The fortified city of Pelusium controlled access to Egypt via the Sinai and Nile Delta. Here, an invading Persian army under Cambyses II was met by Egyptian forces, which were decisively defeated. The city surrendered after the field battle.

China
c.2500–200 BCE

■ BANQUAN, C.2500 BCE

The earliest recorded battle in Chinese history occurred at Banquan. Events are unclear, but it seems that the Yellow Emperor's forces defeated those of the Yan Emperor, bringing both groups under a single ruler as the Huaxia.

■ ZOULOU, C.2500 BCE

Soon after the battle of Banquan, the newly formed Huaxia tribes fought the Jiuli tribes over control of the Yellow River valley. The resulting Huaxia victory formed the basis for the Han dynasty, which ruled China after the fall of the Qin Dynasty.

■ MING CHIAO, C.1523 BCE

The Shang Dynasty was the first literate Chinese dynasty and was also notable for the development of bronze metallurgy. Their ascension began with the decisive defeat of the rival Shao Dynasty near Shang Chu in Honan province. The Shang deployed 70 chariots for this battle.

■ MUYE, C.1057 BCE

The Shang Dynasty, which ruled China at this time, became increasingly suspicious and fearful of the Zhou, a people whose king, Wen, had previously been a trusted vassal. As tensions increased, the Zhou began to overrun the territory of Shang allies, although they took care not to provoke the Shang. By 1046 BCE, the Shang had become heavy-handed and unpopular rulers and a revolt by the Zhou was viewed favourably by much of the populace. Although a sizable force was available to defend the capital, Yin, the Shang ruler, distributed weapons to thousands of slaves. Not only did most of the slaves immediately swap sides, so too did many Shang troops. Of the remainder, some stood aside and refused to fight for their unpopular ruler, and the rest were overrun in a bloody battle. Victory established the Zhou Dynasty as rulers of China.

■ RUGE, 707 BCE

A dispute between the Zhou kingdom and Count Zheng over a land deal concluded without Zhou's approval, resulted in a failed Zhou campaign into Zheng. The decisive battle became known as the battle of Ruge and served to underscore the declining prestige of the Zhou Dynasty.

■ CHENGPU, 632 BCE

The ruling Zhou Dynasty held direct control over only a fairly small area, with the remainder of China divided up between feudal lords and princes. Zhou dominance over these nobles was at times tenuous and gradually grew weaker. Some states, notably in the south, proclaimed independence while others fragmented into civil wars. The states of Jin and Chu became engaged in a series of increasingly direct conflicts, each attempting to draw allies away from the other state. This situation culminated in an invasion of Song, an ally of Jin, and a counterstroke against Wei and Cao, allies of Chu. The Jin army then encamped on the Wei–Cao border and awaited Chu's next move. The Jin army is said to have protected its chariot horses with tiger skins. Their tactics were sophisticated, using chariots for a rapid advance and switching the main axis of attack as necessary. Thus, when the Chu arrived, the Jin advanced on both flanks, making the main effort against the Chu right. This extremely aggressive attack was successful, breaking the forces opposite it. The Jin exploited this advantage by using their victorious left-flank force to make holding attacks against the Chu centre, preventing it from interfering as the Chu left was drawn into

Feuding States, 350 BCE

a trap. Here, the Jin had advanced to skirmish, then pulled back to draw the Chu forward. Chariots dragging branches were used to throw up dust and conceal the fact that the Jin were re-forming their lines. As the Chu left wing advanced, it was taken in the flank by chariots and frontally attacked by the reformed Jin. The centre, pinned in place by attacks from the front and threats from the flank, could not assist and the Chu left was smashed. With both flanks in tatters, facing an intact Jin force, the Chu centre retired from the field.

■ **BI, 595 BCE**

Skirmishing between Jin and Chu forces went badly for the Jin, who sent out a chariot force to assist. This brought about a more general engagement in which the Jin were flanked by Chu chariots and forced to withdraw by their more nimble opponents.

■ **YANLING, 575 BCE**

Continued conflict between Chu and Jin resulted in a clash at Yanling. Correctly predicting that the Chu would place their best troops in the centre of the line, the Jin attacked on the flanks and broke the weaker forces there.

■ **BAI JU (BOJU) C.506 BCE**

The state of Wu, sponsored by Jin as an ally against Chu, grew in power until it was able to challenge Chu directly. Forces led by the great military thinker Sun Tzu were temporarily able to occupy the Chu capital at Ying.

■ **LIZE, 478 BCE**

The state of Yue, to the south of Wu, was less significant than its northern neighbour until its forces inflicted a defeat at Lize and captured considerable territory. Yue became a major power in the region for several decades as a result of this campaign.

■ **JINYANG, 453 BCE**

The army of Zhao was besieged in Jinyang by the forces of Zhi, Wei and Han for three years until, desperate, the Zhao sent emissaries to the Wei and Han. Mistrusting their Zhi allies, these forces consented to change sides. The result was a crushing defeat for Zhi.

■ **GUILING, 353 BCE**

Forces from Qi and Zhao attacked the Wei capital, pulling Wei troops away from their own siege of the Zhao capital. Tired from the march and from crossing the Yellow River, the Wei army was ambushed at Guiling.

■ **MALING, 342 BCE**

The army of Qi retired in the face of an advance by Wei forces, engaging in a stratagem to draw the Wei into an ambush. The Qi commander ordered his troops to light fewer cooking fires each day, giving the impression that a portion of his army was deserting. Some artillery was also abandoned. Convinced that the Qi army was disintegrating, the Wei pursued recklessly and were ambushed in a narrow pass.

■ **YIQUE, 293 BCE**

Exploiting divisions within the Wei–Han alliance, Qin forces drew off Han troops with raids, then attacked the main Wei army. The subsequent defeat broke the alliance, allowing the Qin to defeat the Wei and Han separately.

■ **CHANPING, 260 BCE**

A Zhou force numbering about 400,000 men was drawn out by the retreating Qin, then cut off and besieged in its field fortifications. Unable to escape, the Zhou surrendered after 46 days. A large-scale massacre of prisoners followed, fatally weakening the Zhou.

■ **CONQUEST OF ZHOU BY QIN, 229–222 BCE**

Zhou was one of the 'Seven Great Powers' of the Warring States Period, but gradually declined as the years went by. Neighbouring Qin conquered the state of Han in 230 BCE, then turned on Zhou. Zhou's ablest generals were relieved or dismissed due to internal politics and Qin infiltration, and the Zhou army was badly outmatched. As a result the state fell to the Qin, bringing the Zhou dynasty to an end.

■ **CONQUEST OF YAN BY QIN, 227–222 BCE**

Qin forces serving King Zheng overran the province of Yan after destroying Zhou. Although the Yan were assisted by the last remnants of the Zhou army, they were unable to prevent

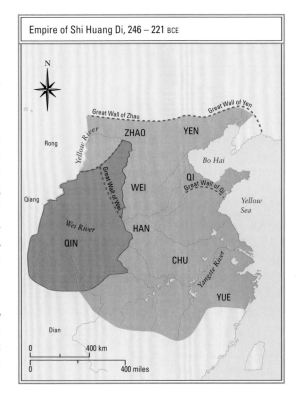

Empire of Shi Huang Di, 246 – 221 BCE

total defeat. After mopping up the remaining resistance, King Zheng proclaimed himself first emperor of a unified China and set about a programme of construction and improvements that included a standardized system of weights and measures.

■ **QIN CONQUEST OF CHU, 226–223 BCE**

After a year-long standoff, the massive Chu army became disaffected while the Qin secretly continued to make preparations for an assault. The weakened Chu force was defeated in a lengthy campaign, bringing the region under Qin control.

■ **UNIFICATION OF CHINA, 222–221 BCE**

The Qin overran Zhou in 222 BCE and advanced into Yan territory. Despite desperate measures, including an attempt to murder the Qin king, Yan was also briskly conquered. In 221 BCE the state of Qi surrendered, having taken no part in resisting Qin expansion. Qin was the last of the Warring States to be subjugated, ending the period and beginning Qin Dynasty rule over a unified China.

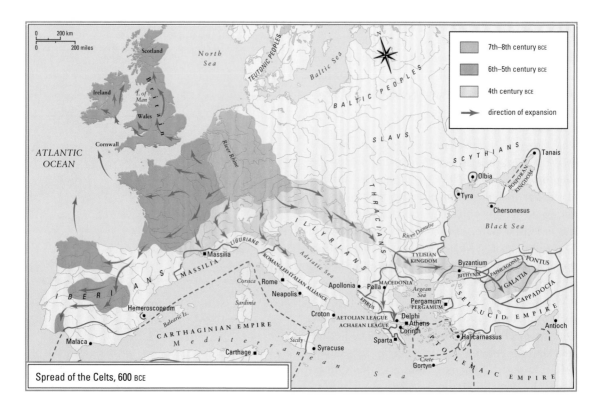

	7th–8th century BCE
	6th–5th century BCE
	4th century BCE
→	direction of expansion

Spread of the Celts, 600 BCE

Ireland 2530 BCE

■ MAGH ITHE, 2530 BCE
The earliest known battle in Ireland was fought between 800 Formorian invaders and an unknown number of local warriors. The *Annals of the Four Masters* record that all of the invaders were killed.

South & South-East Asia 1500–1 BCE

■ KURUSHETRA WAR, ESTIMATED DATE VARIES 5561–800 BCE
According to the Hindu epic *Mahabharata*, the Kurushetra War was an 18-day clash of huge armies, fighting over the throne of Hastinapur. Forces from all over India fought on both sides of the conflict, with almost all of the thousands of participants killed in the battle. Although very detailed in some places, the epic does not give clear and verifiable dates for the conflict, and cannot be taken as an accurate and detailed account of the fighting and the tactics actually used. It does, however, give a general picture of how wars were fought in India in antiquity.

■ DARIUS ON THE INDUS, 517–509 BCE
Darius I of Persia mounted a successful campaign eastwards into the Indus valley, overrunning the valley and the region now known as the Punjab. The campaign resulted in greater awareness of the incredible riches of India, causing an upsurge in trade and an increasingly cultural interchange between South-East Asia and the Middle East.

■ HYDASPES, 326 BCE
Alexander the Great's campaign eastwards brought him into conflict with King Porus of Paurava. Alexander's army won a costly victory over King Porus, but refused to go any further east than the Hydaspes river, forcing Alexander to curtail his ambitions.

Messenian Wars 743–668 BCE

■ **AMPHEIA, 743 BCE**

War between Sparta and Messenia arose out of increasing tensions and an incident at the temple of Artemis Limnatis, over which both sides accused one another of treachery. The first serious clash was a surprise Spartan attack on Ampheia, whose population was massacred.

■ **ITHOME, C.740 BCE**

Messenia managed to avoid losing any more cities to the Spartans for several years, but after failing to defeat their Spartan opponents in the field, the Messenians retired to the natural fortress of Mount Ithome.

■ **ITHOME, 724 BCE**

Hearing that the Messenians had obtained divine assistance from the Oracle at Delphi, the Spartans were hesitant to attack until they obtained advice of their own from the Oracle. The Messenian king was killed in the ensuing indecisive battle.

■ **DERES, 685 BCE**

The Greek city-state of Sparta conquered and enslaved the Messenians in a war lasting from 743 to 724 BCE. The Messenians revolted, bringing about the Second Messenian War as they sought independence. The first action of this war was the battle of Deres, fought in response to a Messenian invasion of Laconia, the region around Sparta. The outcome of the battle remains unclear, though subsequently the Messenians continued their advance into Spartan territory.

■ **GREAT FOSS, 682 BCE**

The Messenians suffered an overwhelming defeat. Reputedly, this occurred because the Spartans bribed the Messenians' allies to withdraw at a critical moment. It is not clear what role the great foss (trench) played in the battle.

■ **MOUNT EIRA, C.668 BCE**

The Messenians retired to a fortified city at Mount Eira, from which they launched raids against Spartan territory. Eventually the Spartans stormed the city and enslaved those who were not killed. Some Messenians fled to Italy.

Battles of Early Rome/Italy 509–275 BCE

■ **LAKE REGILLUS, 509–493 BCE**

The Roman forces, like their Latin League opponents, fought in the manner of Greek hoplites. The battle was decided by the intervention of dismounted Roman cavalry, who restored a deteriorating situation and eventually forced a Latin retreat.

■ **ROME, 509 BCE**

The Roman Republic came about as a result of the violent overthrow of King Tarquin the Proud, who attempted to regain his throne with Etruscan assistance. It is thought that Rome was besieged by Tarquin's forces, though few details are known.

■ **TIBER RIVER, 508 BCE**

Some accounts claim that the Etruscans did not besiege Rome, but were halted at the River Tiber. After breaking the Roman army in a field battle, the Etruscans tried to pursue them across the Pons Sublicius, but were single-handedly prevented from crossing by Publius Horatius Cocles.

■ **CREMERA, 477 BCE**

Roman forces established a fortress on the River Cremera, from which they were able to curtail raids from the city of Veii. They were eventually enticed out of their fortifications by a ruse, and ambushed by Veii troops.

■ **MONS ALGIDUS, 458 BCE**

A Roman army facing forces of the Aequi tribe became trapped, with the enemy building fortifications surrounding it. In turn, a relief force commanded by Cincinnatus encircled the Aequi, who succumbed to assault from two sides.

■ **CORBIONE, 446 BCE**

Rome gradually increased its dominance over the local tribes. Having defeated the Aequi at Mons Algidus, this second victory consolidated Roman control over the region. Few details of the action itself have survived.

■ **SECOND VEIENTINE WAR, 438–425 BCE**

The city of Veii was a frequent opponent of early Rome. Conflict arose over control of the Tiber

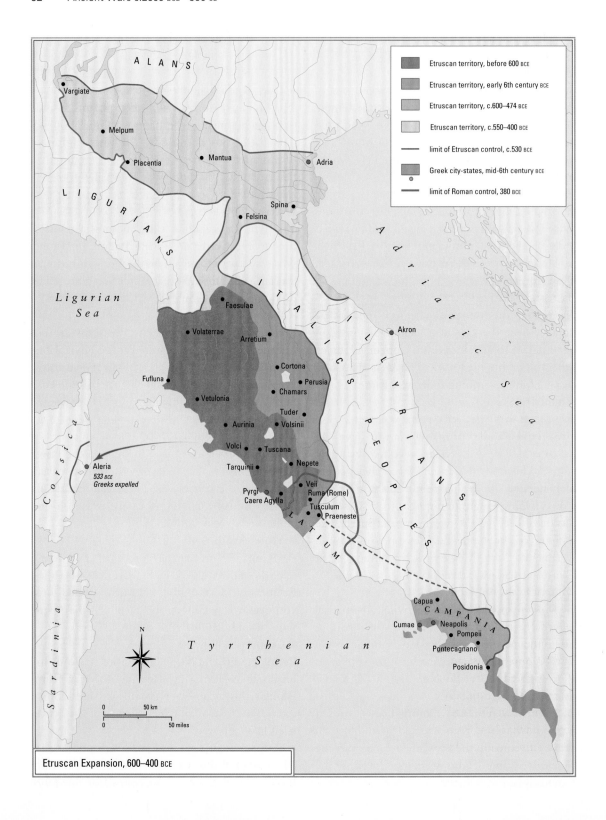

A L A N S

Vargiate

Melpum

Placentia

Mantua

Adria

L I G U R I A N S

Spina

Felsina

Ligurian Sea

A d r i a t i c   S e a

I T A L I C S

Faesulae

Volaterrae

Arretium

Akron

I L L Y R I A N S

Cortona

Fufluna

Perusia

Chamars

Vetulonia

Tuder

Aurinia

Volsinii

P E O P L E S

Volci

Tuscana

Tarquinii

Nepete

Aleria
533 BCE
Greeks expelled

Corsica

Veii

Pyrgi

Ruma (Rome)

Caere Agylla

Tusculum

Praeneste

L A T I U M

Sardinia

Capua

C A M P A N I A

Cumae

Neapolis

Pompeii

Pontecagnano

T y r r h e n i a n   S e a

Posidonia

N

	Etruscan territory, before 600 BCE
	Etruscan territory, early 6th century BCE
	Etruscan territory, c.600–474 BCE
	Etruscan territory, c.550–400 BCE
	limit of Etruscan control, c.530 BCE
	Greek city-states, mid-6th century BCE
	limit of Roman control, 380 BCE

0   50 km
0   50 miles

Etruscan Expansion, 600–400 BCE

crossing at Fidenae, resulting in a series of battles. After Rome captured and secured Fidenae, the war went against Veii and a truce was agreed.

FIDENAE, 435 BCE

The originally Etruscan city of Fidenae changed hands several times in the war between Rome and Veii. In 435 BCE it was conquered by the Romans and, with the defeat of Veii, permanently thereafter remained a Roman possession.

VEII, 396 BCE

The expiry of the long truce between Rome and Veii did not immediately result in hostilities, but a deteriorating diplomatic situation caused a declaration of war in 405 BCE. Veii was besieged, unsuccessfully at first, for a decade, while Roman forces fought campaigns elsewhere. Final victory was achieved by means of a tunnel with a concealed entrance. This enabled a Roman assault force to enter the city while other forces simultaneously rushed the walls.

ALLIA, 390 BCE

Responding to a Gallic invasion of Italy, a Roman army of six legions met the Gauls at the River Allia. The Romans were overrun by the more numerous Gauls, who marched on Rome and sacked it. These events prompted major changes in the Roman military system.

MOUNT GAURUS, 352 BCE

A request for Roman aid against the Samnite tribe by the people of Campania sparked off the First Samnite War. The first clash, near the base of Mount Gaurus, was a clear victory for Rome but did not end the war.

SUESSULA, 341 BCE

A second battle with the Samnites also resulted in a Roman victory, but little advantage could be derived from it. Instead, a peace settlement was quickly agreed to free Roman forces to deal with a revolt by their Latin allies.

VESUVIUS (OR VESERIS), 339 BCE

Displeased that Rome had entered into a war with the Samnites without consulting them, Rome's Latin allies revolted. The two forces met at Mount Vesuvius, where the Latins were heavily defeated.

TRIFANUM, 338 BCE

Rome's Latin foes retreated north after their defeat at Vesuvius, receiving reinforcements as they went. The Roman army advanced after them, bringing about a disorganized encounter battle at Trifanum. The Latins suffered worse from the surprise attack and were defeated.

NEAPOLIS, 327 BCE

The seizure of Neapolis by the Samnites resulted in the outbreak of the Second Samnite War. Initial Roman successes caused the Samnites to ask for terms, but those offered were so harsh that they were rejected, resulting in an intermittent 20-year war.

CAUDINE FORKS, 321 BCE

The Roman army fell victim to disinformation planted by Samnite agents and was lured into advancing through a narrow mountain defile. Finding the road ahead barricaded against them, the Romans turned back only to find they were now trapped. The Samnites debated whether to slaughter the trapped Romans or release them as a gesture of reconciliation. Instead, they compelled the Roman army to surrender under humiliating terms that virtually guaranteed further hostilities.

LAUTULAE, 316 BCE

Forced to accept a five-year truce after the surrender at the Caudine Forks, Rome expanded its military forces and resumed hostilities as soon as it could. The first clash of the renewed war was at Lautulae, where the Samnites inflicted a decisive defeat.

VADIMO, 310 BCE

War between Rome and the Etruscans began with an Etruscan attack on the city of Sutrium. The decisive clash of the war came at Lake Vadimo, on a narrow and restricted battlefield. Dismounted Roman cavalry turned the battle around after both sides ran out of infantry reserves.

BOVANIUM, 305 BCE

Although hard-pressed and having to fight the Etruscans as well as the Samnites, Rome gradually gained the upper hand in the Second Samnite

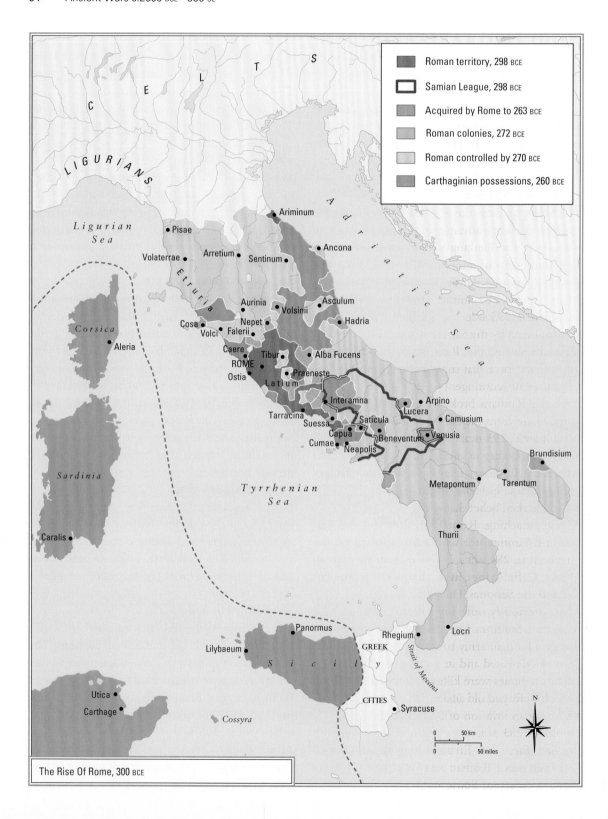

Legend:
- Roman territory, 298 BCE
- Samian League, 298 BCE
- Acquired by Rome to 263 BCE
- Roman colonies, 272 BCE
- Roman controlled by 270 BCE
- Carthaginian possessions, 260 BCE

CELTS

LIGURIANS

Ligurian Sea

Corsica

Aleria

Sardinia

Caralis

Tyrrhenian Sea

Utica
Carthage

Cossyra

Lilybaeum

Panormus

Sicily

Strait of Messina

GREEK

CITIES

Syracuse

Rhegium

Locri

Pisae
Volaterrae
Arretium   Sentinum
Etruria
Aurinia   Volsinii   Asculum
Cosa   Nepet   Hadria
Volci   Falerii
Caere
Tibur   Alba Fucens
ROME   Praeneste
Ostia   *Latium*
Interamna
Tarracina   Saticula   Lucera   Camusium
Suessa   Capua   Arpino
Cumae   Beneventum   Venusia
Neapolis

Ariminum
Ancona

Adriatic Sea

Brundisium

Metapontum   Tarentum

Thurii

0   50 km
0   50 miles

N

The Rise Of Rome, 300 BCE

War and inflicted a decisive defeat at Bovanium. It is possible that the concept of the manipular legion came from the Samnites' military system.

■ **CAMERINUM, 298 BCE**

The Third Samnite War began with the Samnites invading Roman territory. Their allies, including Etruscans and Gauls, also made war on Rome at the same time. Despite this, the first clash at Camerinum was a Roman victory.

■ **TIFERNIUM, 297 BCE**

After failing to draw the Romans into an ambush, the Samnite army advanced for a set-piece field battle. A Roman flanking force was mistaken for a large contingent of reinforcements by both sides, causing a Samnite defeat that the Romans were too exhausted to exploit.

■ **SENTINUM, 295 BCE**

Outnumbered by the Samnites and their Etruscan and Gallic allies, the Romans sent off a small diversionary force that succeeded in pulling away the Etruscan contingent. After a hard-fought battle, the Romans broke the Samnites then fell on the Gauls from the flank.

■ **AQUILONIA, 293 BCE**

Scraping together a new army, the Samnites mustered at Aquilonia. They were able to withstand Roman attack for some time, but began to waver in the mistaken belief that Roman reinforcements were approaching. Rout soon followed, ending the Third Samnite war with a Roman victory.

■ **ARRETIUM, 284 BCE**

Various Celtic tribes lived in Italy, notably the Boii and the Senones. The latter had clashed with Rome previously, suffering a defeat alongside the Samnites at Sentium. The Celts attacked Arretium, causing a Roman army to march to its relief. The army was defeated and its commander and seven military tribunes were killed. Encouraged by this, the Celts reforged old alliances with the Etruscans and began an invasion of Roman territory.

■ **VADIMO, 283 BCE**

A joint force of Etruscan troops and Boii tribesmen met a Roman army near Lake Vadimo and was defeated. Some of the Boii may have

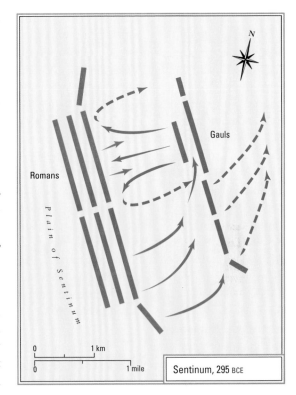

Sentinum, 295 BCE

been driven eastwards into the Danube region; others settled in northern Italy and accepted Roman rule.

■ **POPULONIA, 282 BCE**

Despite earlier defeats, the Etruscans continued their campaign against Rome. The battle of Populonia was a decisive Roman victory, finally ending the Etruscan threat to Rome.

Carthaginian & Sicilian Wars 650–300 BCE

■ **CARTHAGINIAN CONQUESTS, 650–500 BCE**

Carthage was a Phoenician colony which became independent in 650 BCE. Its location on the North African coast close to Sicily was ideal for sea trade, allowing a rapid increase in power. Many small campaigns were fought to protect the trade routes or against potential rivals, until in 509 BCE a treaty was agreed with Rome that divided the Mediterranean into Roman and Carthaginian spheres of interest. In the intervening time, Carthage fought off Greek forays into the western Mediterranean and conquered territories in Iberia, Sicily and Sardinia. Wars were also fought with the neighbouring Libyans and Numidians, but did not result in conquest.

■ ALALIA, 540 BCE

Dominance of the western Mediterranean by the Etruscans and Carthaginians was challenged by the arrival of Greek traders and colonists starting around 750 BCE. As a result, by 540 BCE an alliance between Etruscan cities and Carthage existed, aimed at curbing Greek expansion. A major clash between the Greek and Allied fleets occurred at Alalia. Although the allies did not win an outright victory, they caused sufficient damage that the Greeks withdrew and evacuated their holdings on Corsica.

■ HIMERA, 480 BCE

Fearing that Sicily would soon be completely dominated by Greek interests, Carthage sent troops to assist the deposed tyrant of Himera. The Carthaginians were attacked in their camp by a Greek force and defeated, beginning a period of truce.

■ CUMAE, 474 BCE

The cities of Cumae and Syracuse, originally founded by Greek settlers, were extremely powerful in the western Mediterranean. Their economies were largely based on sea trade and both maintained powerful fleets to protect their interests. The rising power of the Etruscan civilization led to conflict, and in 474 BCE a joint Cumae–Syracuse fleet defeated an Etruscan force. The Etruscans lost prestige as well as the economic benefits of sea trade, contributing to a decline that eventually led to absorption by Rome.

■ HIMERA, 409 BCE

A Greek relief army surprised and routed Carthaginians besieging the city. This force was in turn defeated by a Carthaginian counter-attack. False information caused the defenders to pull troops out of the city, which was then successfully assaulted.

■ AKRAGAS, 406 BCE

The Carthaginian army laid siege to Akragas, which was well provisioned and prepared. During the siege, a relief army from Syracuse arrived and drove off the Carthaginian force sent to prevent its approach. A standoff then ensued, with the Carthaginians suffering constant harassment by light Greek forces. The capture of a Greek convoy by Carthaginian naval forces solved the Carthaginians' increasing supply problems and deprived Akragas of badly needed grain. Many of the Greek troops were sent away due to lack of supplies, and the city was all but abandoned. The remnant was easily overcome by a Carthaginian assault.

■ GELA, 405 BCE

Syracusan forces attempted a complex three-pronged land and sea attack on a Carthaginian army besieging Gela. Coordination was poor, resulting in a defeat that forced the Greeks to abandon Gela and retire towards Camarina.

■ CAMARINA, 405 BCE

Retreating from defeat at Gela, the Syracusan leader Dionysius decided not to risk becoming besieged at Camarina and ordered the city abandoned. Morale in the Greek army plunged as a result, forcing Dionysius to seek a peace settlement with Carthage.

■ MOTYA, 398 BCE

The city of Motya lay on an island in a lagoon, forcing the Greek besiegers to build a mole towards the city. A Carthaginian fleet attempted to intervene, but was driven off. The city was then taken after savage urban combat lasting several days.

■ CATANA, 398 BCE

The Carthaginian fleet was attacked by a Greek force that was lesser in numbers but possessed better and heavier ships. The Greek admiral launched a reckless attack with part of his fleet, causing considerable damage at first. However, these vessels became surrounded and were defeated, with the survivors driven off. The Carthaginians reordered their formation and attacked the now leaderless and confused Greek fleet, inflicting a major defeat.

■ MESSENE, 397 BCE

The army of Messene marched out to confront the Carthaginians short of the city, but was outflanked by an amphibious movement. By the time the army returned, the city was in Carthaginian hands.

■ SYRACUSE, 397–396 BCE

The Carthaginian army encircled Syracuse and began ravaging the surrounding countryside to deny the city provisions. It was hoped that this might draw out a Syracusan force for battle. When this did not occur, the Carthaginians began preparations for a long siege. Although repeated raids made some progress against outlying parts of the city, plague weakened the Carthaginians and Syracusan counter-attacks forced a negotiated withdrawal.

■ SOLUS (SOLUNTUM), 396 BCE

The city of Soluntum resisted Greek influences early in its history and remained loyal to Carthage during the Sicilian Wars. In 396 BCE it was taken by Syracuse through treachery, but reverted to Carthaginian allegiance soon after.

■ ELLEPORUS, 389 BCE

The Italiote League, dominated by Tarentum, was formed of Greek settlements in southern Italy. An expedition led by Dionysius I of Syracuse defeated the League at the River Elleporus (modern Stilaro), bringing it under the control of Syracuse.

■ RHEGIUM, 386 BCE

Having defeated the Italiote League in battle at the Elleporus, Syracusan forces laid siege to the city of Rhegium, just across the Strait of Messina opposite Sicily. The city was captured and sacked, with the population sold into slavery.

■ CABALA, 378–375 BCE

Little is known about the battle of Cabala, not even the exact location. Allegedly the Syracusans won a victory over Carthage, in which some 15,000 Carthaginians including Mago II were killed or captured.

■ LILYBAEUM, 368 BCE

After the Greek sack of Motya, the Carthaginians built the city of Lilybaeum as their principal base on Sicily. The city was strongly defended, coming under siege by Greek forces in 368 BCE.

■ CRISSIMUS, 341 BCE

The vastly outnumbered Greeks attacked a Carthaginian army as it crossed the River Crissimus, first disordering them with a cavalry charge then following up with infantry. The Carthaginians were heavily defeated despite their numerical advantage.

■ AKRAGAS, 315 BCE

After capturing Messene, Syracusan forces advanced on Akragas and besieged it, hoping to remove the last Carthaginian holdings from Sicily. The Carthaginian response was direct and highly successful, pushing the Syracusans all the way back to their capital.

■ CARTHAGE, c.309–307 BCE

With Syracuse under siege, its tyrant Agathocles launched a campaign against Carthage itself. Although this was ultimately defeated, it did cause most of the Carthaginian army to be recalled, saving Syracuse from defeat.

■ HIMERA, 311 BCE

Syracuse caused the Third Sicilian War by violating the treaty that ended the second war and invading Carthaginian-controlled territory on Sicily. The Carthaginian response was to move an army into Sicily for a campaign against Syracuse. Carthage won a decisive victory at the battle of Himera in 311 BCE and, by the following year, had pushed the Syracusans all the way back to their capital, which was brought under siege. The war ended with a settlement that preserved Syracuse, though with greatly diminished power, and enabled Carthage to enjoy almost complete domination of Sicily and the surrounding sea lanes for several decades. The war had never been a clash of cultures, but was motivated primarily by the protection of commercial interests. Thus Carthage emerged as the clear victor despite not destroying her opponent.

Greek & Greco-Persian Wars
499–450 BCE

■ **NAXOS, 499 BCE**

The city of Miletus was one of many Greek colonies founded in Ionia and later conquered by the Persian Empire. Its ruler in 499 BCE was the Persian satrap Aristagoras. Feeling that his position was threatened by local politics, Aristagoras decided to intervene in a revolt on the island of Naxos. This action would obtain a forward base for the Persian invasion of Greece, greatly enhancing Aristagoras' status and securing his position. Aristagoras' ally Artaphernes supplied a fleet and a general in return for a share of the spoils. Disputes over command precedence caused the Persian general to betray the mission's intentions, allowing the people of Naxos to prepare a defence. As a result, what was envisaged as a short war of conquest turned into a four-month struggle of attrition before the Persians retreated. Aristagoras' prestige was further diminished.

■ **EPHESUS, 499 BCE**

Disgraced and in debt to his former ally Artaphernes, Aristagoras of Miletus risked being deposed as a result of his bungled invasion of Naxos. In desperation he turned against Persia and incited the whole of Ionia to revolt. The campaign initially went well, with Ionian troops capturing and burning Sardis. However, as the Ionian force retired, it was caught at Ephesus by a large force of Persian cavalry and routed.

■ **SARDIS, 498 BCE**

Forces from the states of Athens and Eretria and the Ionian rebels assembled at Ephesus and launched an attack on Sardis, which turned out to be weakly defended. Although the city was taken, the Greeks fell back rather than face a Persian relief army.

■ **LADE, 494 BCE**

After several years of revolt, Persian fortunes had waxed and waned, with a heavy defeat at Pedasus offsetting successes elsewhere. Reorganizing their forces, the Persians launched a major offensive directly at Miletus in the hope of striking a knockout blow to the rebellion. The rebels assembled a fleet of over 350 triremes off the island of Lade to try to counter the strong Persian force.

A standoff ensued, during which the Persians made secret agreements with some of the rebel contingents. As the battle commenced, the Samian force deserted the rebel lines, causing other contingents also to flee. What remained of the rebel army, notably the Chians, put up a stiff fight despite the chaos their line had fallen into. The rebels managed to capture several Persian ships but were eventually forced to break off, opening the way for an attack on Miletus.

■ **SIEGE OF MILETUS, 494 BCE**

With the rebel fleet cleared out of the way, the Persian army laid siege to Miletus. The walls were breached by undermining and the use of an extensive siege train. Much of the populace was enslaved or put to the sword.

■ **SEPIEA, 494 BCE**

A Spartan army under Kleomenes I inflicted a decisive defeat on Argos, causing 6000 casualties and cementing Sparta's position as the dominant power in the Peloponnese. Kleomenes then attempted to become a tyrant in Sparta, leading to civil war.

■ **NAXOS, 490 BCE**

Although the final goal of the operation was an invasion of mainland Greece, Persian forces first landed on Naxos, whose inhabitants had resisted a previous Persian expedition. The large Persian army quickly overwhelmed all resistance.

■ **ERETRIA, 490 BCE**

Unable to face the large Persian army in the field, the Eretrians retired behind their walls. Persian forces prosecuted the siege aggressively and after heavy fighting the gates were opened to them.

■ **MARATHON, 490 BCE**

The Ionian Revolt was something of a prelude to major war between the Persian Empire and the cities of Greece. Starting in 492 BCE, Persian forces captured several Aegean islands. They then landed on the island of Euboea and captured the city of Eretria, which had sided with the Ionian rebels. Euboea was an excellent forward base for operations against the Greek mainland, and from there the Persian force landed at Marathon. A Greek army from Athens was sent to oppose them and took up a blocking position between Marathon and Athens, about 40km distant. Sparta agreed to send a force to help the Athenians, but this was delayed by religious observances. While the Greeks waited, they were joined by allies from Plataea. Although this improved the numerical odds, the main problem facing the Greeks was tactical. Their heavy infantry was suited to a slow, deliberate advance that would make them an easy target for the Persian cavalry, who were armed with missile weapons.

The Greeks learned that the Persian cavalry would not be available for a time, though accounts differ regarding why this was so. Some historians have suggested that the Persians had begun re-embarking their forces for a move up the coast to attack the Athenian port at Phaleron. Others state that Persian deserters told the Greeks that the Persian cavalry was away on some mission. Within the Greek camp some leaders favoured a withdrawal to the defences of Athens, while others wanted to attack. According to Herodotus, the Greek general Miltiades argued that a withdrawal would shake the morale of the army and the citizens of Athens, possibly leading to surrender. There are also suggestions that the Greeks were swayed by favourable omens. Whatever the reason, they decided to attack without waiting for the Spartan contingent.

In order to match the length of the Persian line, the Greeks drew up in a dangerously thin formation that was stronger on the wings than in the centre. They then began to advance at a run. This almost suicidally reckless charge covered about 1.6km to strike the Persian line.

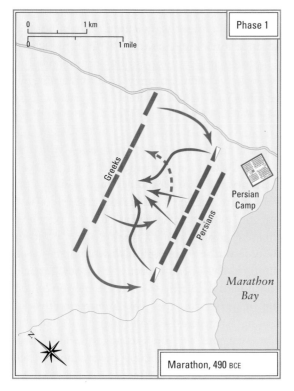

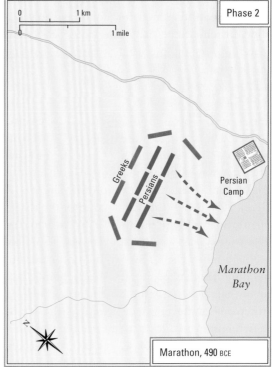

It may be that the rapid Greek advance caught the Persians by surprise and denied them time to form a solid battle line. The thin centre made little progress and was soon engaged in a losing battle against the Persians. However, the more powerful wings were more successful and broke their opponents. As the Persian flanking forces fled, the Greek wings then enveloped the Persian centre, forcing the rest of the Persian line to flee towards the beach. There, some of the Persians fought a rearguard action to allow the rest of their army to hurriedly embark. Most of the Persian ships escaped, although casualties were heavy among the troops. Sailing along the coast, the Persians considered an attack on Phaleron but were deterred by the obvious readiness of the Greek army to meet any new landing. The fleet withdrew to Persia, bringing the attempted invasion to an end.

The legend of Philippides, who ran to Athens with news of the victory, arose from this conflict but is untrue. Its origins probably lie in the story of Pheidippides, the messenger to Sparta who carried the request for aid, or possibly the rapid march of the Athenian army back from Marathon to oppose the threatened landing at Phaleron.

■ THERMOPYLAE, 480 BCE

For ten years after the defeat at Marathon, Persia made no serious attempts to invade Greece. This situation was largely due to revolts in other areas, notably Egypt. Once the internal situation was stabilized, extensive preparations began for a renewed invasion of Greece. A Greek alliance was formed to counter the threat of invasion, which could come by two routes. The narrow pass at Thermopylae was a suitable point to block the Greek advance on land, but it could be flanked by sea. Both points had to be held for either to be effective. Thus an Athenian-led fleet was deployed to the straits at Artemisium while an army marched to hold Thermopylae. This force was led by Sparta, which could not send its full army for religious

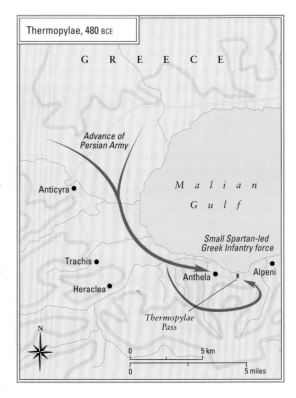

reasons. The intent was to hold the pass with an advance force until the main army could arrive. The force at Thermopylae was far too small to meet the vast Persian army on equal terms, but possibly sufficient to defend the narrow pass. The Persians first tried bribery, then waited for four days in the hope that the Greeks would become disheartened or fall out with one another. When neither happened, they attacked.

After two days of repeated attacks in which the Persian army failed to make any real impression on the defenders, a Greek traitor informed them of a route around the defensive position. A force was sent to exploit this opportunity on the third day of the battle, while frontal attacks continued. Realizing that they were outflanked, the majority of the Greek force retreated, leaving a rearguard in the form of the Spartan, Thespian and Theban contingents. This force fought on to buy time for the remainder and was annihilated.

▪ ARTEMISIUM, 480 BCE

Even after losing large numbers of ships to storms, the Persian fleet greatly outnumbered its opponents when they met. After two days of skirmishing a major clash took place. Although hard-fought, it was indecisive, with heavy losses on both sides. The Persian fleet could better afford such losses than could the Greeks, but more importantly, word had arrived that the pass at Thermopylae had been forced. This made holding the straits at Artemisium meaningless, so the Greeks retreated.

▪ ATHENS, 480 BCE

After forcing the pass at Thermopylae, the Persian army advanced on Athens, capturing and burning the city. The Athenian population and remaining military forces took refuge on the island of Salamis, protected by the Greek fleet.

▪ SALAMIS, 480 BCE

Having overrun Boeotia and Attica, further Persian progress in the invasion of Greece required sea power. Greek forces had heavily fortified the Isthmus of Corinth, making any advance in that direction a costly option unless the position could be flanked by sea. Meanwhile the Athenians had taken refuge on the island of Salamis and continued their defiance.

The Greek allied fleet was assembled at Salamis to oppose any further Persian advance. Its ships carried extra marines, mainly Athenian soldiers, but were outnumbered by their Persian opponents even though additional vessels had arrived from other Greek cities. Some of these fled in the face of the Persian fleet, leaving the Greeks confronting more than 700 Persian vessels with perhaps 300 of their own. The Persian fleet carried more marines aboard its vessels than was common Greek practice, and its ships were in better repair as they had been beached and overhauled in the early stages of the invasion. Their superior numbers were somewhat offset by the narrow waterway between Salamis and the mainland, which was just over 1.6km wide.

The Persians first tried to defeat the Greek fleet on land by building a causeway to the island that would allow an attack by the Persian army. This was prevented by archers who shot the workers as soon as the causeway came within range. A feint was made towards other Greek cities in the hope that elements of the allied fleet would rush to defend their homes. At first, this gambit appeared to have succeeded. Believing that some of the Greek forces intended to return to their homes, the Persian fleet positioned vessels to ambush them as they left the straits. However, this turned out to be a Greek ruse intended to draw out part of the Persian fleet and defeat it in detail. In due course Greek squadrons began sailing up the straits as if to depart homewards and the Persians advanced to attack them. The Greek ships fled, drawing their pursuers into a counter-ambush. As the pursued vessels turned to fight, others emerged from hidden side channels to attack the Persians. Caught in narrow waters

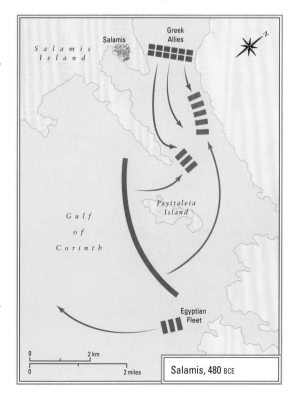

Salamis, 480 BCE

and disorganized from the pursuit, the Persian fleet was struck in the flanks and rear. Conditions in the straits favoured the heavier and more stable Greek vessels, which were comparatively unaffected by the swell. Conversely, the lighter Persian ships found their oar strokes badly disrupted. Whilst their opponents struggled to manoeuvre effectively, the Greeks found them easy targets for ramming attacks.

Part of the Persian fleet fled, allowing the Greeks to concentrate on those who remained. With their admiral dead and their fleet in disarray, the Persians were overwhelmed. Many ships ran aground in their haste to escape or in the chaos of the battle, while others managed to flee out of the straits. The Persian force lost more than 200 ships as opposed to about 40 Greek vessels lost. Many of the crews of defeated Greek vessels were able to swim the short distance to Salamis and were thus available to fight aboard other ships, whilst losses among Persians who went into the water

were much higher. Nevertheless, the Persian fleet remained a powerful force. The Greeks prepared for renewed battle, but the morale of the Persian fleet was broken. After a short time the Persian ships withdrew, leaving the army unsupported.

■ PLATAEA, 479 BCE

Defeated at Salamis, the Persian fleet withdrew, leaving the army to carry on the invasion of Greece without adequate support. Part of the army was also withdrawn, and with the Greek allies mustering large forces, the Persians were forced to retreat. Falling back into Boeotia, the Persians tried to exploit their main advantage over the hoplite-based forces of the Greeks. The slow-moving Greek infantry would be an easy target for Persian cavalry if they could be drawn into open country. The Persians thus built a fortified camp near Plataea and tried to induce the Greeks to attack them by raiding their supply lines.

Recognizing the danger they faced, the Greeks

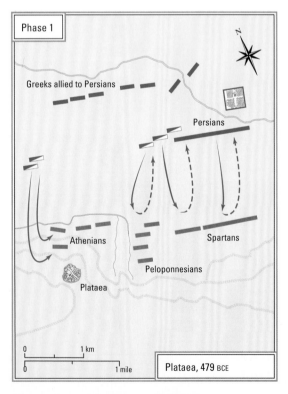

Plataea, 479 BCE

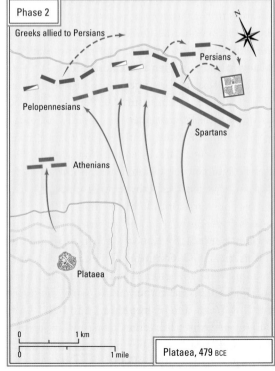

Plataea, 479 BCE

chose not to attack. The resulting standoff ended when the Greeks, perceiving the threat to their supply lines to be too great, began to withdraw. The Persian force seized this opportunity and launched an attack. What was intended to be a pursuit became a major battle. The Greek rearguard, composed of Spartans, came under attack by Persian cavalry, who pulled back once infantry came up to make their own attack. Meanwhile, the Athenian contingent became engaged with a phalanx of Thebans fighting on the Persian side. The heavily armed Greek hoplites gradually overcame the lighter-equipped Persian infantry. The Thebans put up determined resistance against their countrymen, but were eventually driven from the field. They retired homewards, away from the Persian army.

A significant Persian contingent was able to retreat towards the Hellespont, but many of the Persians took refuge in their camp, which was then surrounded by the Greeks. Once other elements of the allied army arrived, the camp was eventually stormed and the defenders slaughtered.

■ MYCALE, 479 BCE

Seeking to avoid a naval battle, the Persian fleet beached its ships and built a fortified camp. After the Ionian contingent of the Persian army defected, the Greeks stormed the camp and destroyed the Persian fleet.

■ CYPRUS, 479 BCE

With the Persian fleet defeated, an allied Greek force launched a raid in force against Cyprus. The Persian garrisons there were overcome and the island was looted, but did not become a Greek possession.

■ BYZANTIUM, 479 BCE

After looting Cyprus, the Greek fleet sailed to Byzantium and began a siege that was eventually successful. This gave them control of the straits between Asia and Europe, making a renewed Persian offensive unlikely.

■ EION, 475 BCE

Having formed the Delian League under Athenian leadership, the Greeks launched a campaign against Eion with the intent of removing the Persian garrison there. After a lengthy siege, the city was captured and became an Athenian possession.

■ SKYROS, 475 BCE

Skyros was not a Persian stronghold, but had become a haven for pirates. The Delian League conquered the island and set up an Athenian colony to secure their control of the surrounding seas.

■ EURYMEDON RIVER, 466 BCE

Recovering from earlier defeats, the Persian Empire began to build a large fleet with the obvious intention of renewing hostilities with the city-states of Greece. The Greeks had been harassing Persian territory for some years, and had captured several important coastal cities. It is likely that the initial Persian goal was to retake these cities before proceeding with an invasion of the islands and, eventually, mainland Greece. As the Persian fleet and its associated army assembled at Aspendos on the River Eurymedon, the Delian League launched a pre-emptive strike. First sailing to Phaselis, the Greeks harassed the city until its population agreed to join the League and contribute to the expedition. From there, the Greeks launched their attack.

The Persian fleet was at anchor at the mouth of the River Eurymedon, awaiting reinforcements before commencing operations. Upon sighting the approaching Greeks, the Persians first retreated into the river before accepting battle. Although outnumbered, the Greek fleet was quickly victorious. Most of the Persian fleet was able to escape by running aground. The crews took shelter in the Persian army nearby. The Greeks then landed troops and engaged the Persian force. As in previous engagements, the heavy equipment and long spears of the Greek hoplites proved superior to the lighter gear of the Persian infantry, and the Persian line was broken. Many Persians fled into their camp, but this was overrun soon afterwards. The Greeks were able to capture or destroy large numbers of beached Persian warships after the land battle, and according to some sources, went on to intercept and defeat the Persian reinforcements coming up the coast. Whether or not this is the case, the Greek victory at the Eurymedon prevented any major new Persian offensives for some time.

■ **THASOS, 465 BCE**

After the conquest of Eion, Athens founded the colony of Amphipolis, expanding its power base. Feeling that this colony threatened its interests, Thasos rebelled against the Delian League. After a three-year siege, Thasos was subdued and reincorporated into the League.

■ **PAMPRENIS, 460–459 BCE**

Rebelling against Persian rule, Egypt asked for aid from the Delian League. A joint Delian-Egyptian force engaged the Persian army near Pamprenis. After a hard-fought battle, the heavier-equipped Greeks broke the Persian line.

■ **MEMPHIS, 460–454 BCE**

Defeated in the field, elements of the Persian army took refuge in the citadel of Memphis where they were besieged by Athenian and Egyptian forces. The siege was finally raised by the arrival of another Persian army.

■ **PROSOPTIS, 454 BCE**

After being driven from Memphis, the Athenians retired to a fortified camp on the island of Prosoptis at the mouth of the Nile, where they were besieged for over a year. The Persians dug canals to drain the river, lowering its level sufficiently to gain access to the island. They then launched an attack that defeated the Athenian force. Accounts of the battle differ, but it is likely that the Athenians were virtually annihilated.

■ **MENDESIUM, 454 BCE**

Attempting to relieve Prosoptis, a Greek fleet entered the mouth of the Nile and was ambushed from the landward and seaward flanks. Only a small portion of the fleet was able to return to the open sea.

■ **SALAMIS, 450 BCE**

After a failed siege of Kition in Cyprus, the Athenian fleet sailed to Salamis where they were engaged by a Persian fleet. Defeating the Persians at sea, the Athenians landed troops at Salamis to complete the victory on land.

Peloponnesian War & Greek Wars 458–403 BCE

Athens vs Sparta

■ **AEGINA, 458–457 BCE**

Although Aegina lay very close to Athens, its people were allied with Sparta and Sparta's Peloponnesian allies. Athenians defeated the powerful Aeginetian fleet before landing to begin a siege. Aegina fell a year and a half later.

■ **TANAGRA–OENPHYTA, 457 BCE**

Drawn into conflicts in Boeotia by their allies, a Spartan army became cut off by an Athenian force positioned to block its line of retreat. After a standoff, the Athenians attacked near Tanagra. Despite heavy casualties on both sides, the Spartans were able to force a passage and return home. The Athenian force then advanced into Boeotia, capturing Locrida, Phocis and Tanagra. This success also paved the way for final victory at Aegina.

■ **CORONEA, 447 BCE**

An Athenian army advanced into Boeotia to restore control over regions that had been lost to rebellion. Although initially successful, the Athenians were defeated by a Boeotian force at Coronea and forced out of Boeotia.

■ **SYBOTA, 433 BCE**

Seeking independence, the Corinthian colony of Corcyra allied itself with Athens, which was hostile to Corinth's ally, Sparta. A Corinthian fleet sent to restore control was opposed by the powerful Corcyran fleet, with additional ships from Athens. The battle was characterized by boarding actions rather than ramming attacks. Despite the defeat of one wing of its fleet, Corinth emerged victorious. Reinforcements from Athens arrived in time to prevent a landing, and Corcyran independence was preserved.

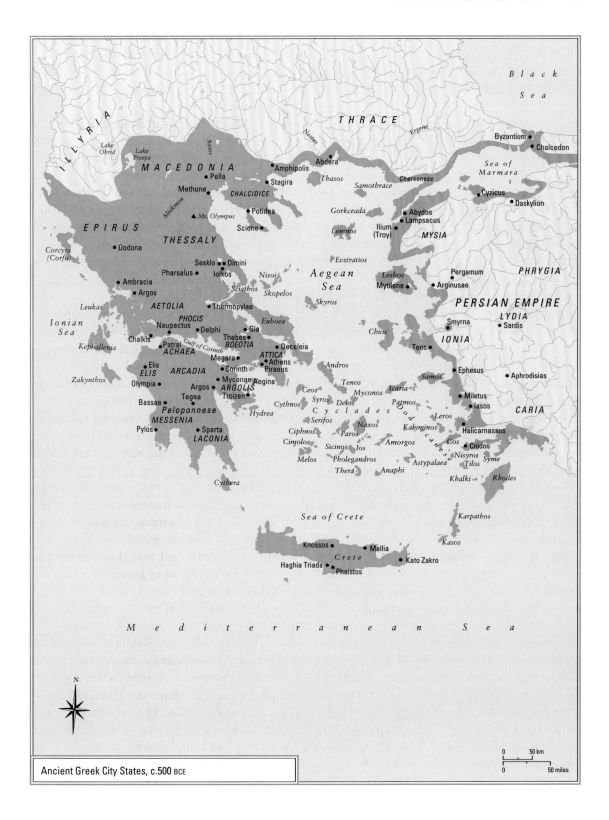

Ancient Greek City States, c.500 BCE

■ **POTIDAEA, 432 BCE**

The Delian League was founded as an alliance against Persia under Athenian leadership, but eventually grew into more of an Athenian Empire than an alliance of equals. Among the League members was the city of Potidaea, a Corinthian colony. Corinth was allied to Sparta and therefore hostile to Athens.

Having successfully supported Corcyra's bid for independence from Corinth, Athens attempted to cement its influence over Potidaea. Among the Athenian demands were the expulsion of Corinthian officials and the provision of hostages to Athens. These demands were underscored by an Athenian fleet sent to Potidaea.

With assurances of assistance from Sparta, Potidaea allied itself with King Perdiccas II of Macedon, who had been encouraging anti-Athenian revolts for some time. Corinthian troops also arrived in Potidaea, and together these forces attempted to prevent the Athenians, who had also been reinforced, from advancing on the city.

The Macedonian contingent did not engage, but the Corinthians put up stiff resistance and an additional force of Potidaeans also attacked the Athenian army. However, the Athenians were ultimately victorious and were able to continue towards the city. There they implemented a naval blockade and began siege operations.

Further reinforcements joined the Athenians during the siege, which nevertheless went on until 429 BCE. Potidaea was finally subdued and its population sent into exile. Athenian colonists were sent to establish a loyal population in the city. Despite its eventual success, the siege was extremely expensive and caused significant unrest in Athens. More importantly, tensions with Sparta came to a head during the period of the siege, resulting in the declaration of what would come to be known as the Peloponnesian War.

■ **CHALCIS, 429 BCE**

An Athenian army marched to Spartolos to compel the city's surrender, but was met by a force from Chalcidice, Olynthus and Spartolos. The initial clash was inconclusive, but reinforcements from Olynthos helped defeat the Athenians in a second battle.

■ **RHIUM, 429 BCE**

A Peloponnesian fleet, including many transports filled with troops for a land campaign, was attacked by Athenian triremes while crossing the Gulf of Patras. In order to protect the transport vessels from ramming attacks, the Peloponnesian force formed a circular defensive formation with the ships' bows pointing outwards. The Athenians sailed around the formation in a tightening circle, forcing the Peloponnesian vessels closely together. Once their opponents were too close to be able to manoeuvre effectively the Athenians attacked.

■ **PLATAEA, 429–427 BCE**

Spartan attempts to breach the high walls of Plataea resulted in a frenzy of engineering and counter-engineering works and a siege that dragged on for months. Part of the Plataean garrison escaped in the winter of 429–428 BCE, with the remainder finally starved into submission in 427 BCE.

■ **NAUPACTUS, 429 BCE**

The Peloponnesian fleet made a feint at the Athenian naval base at Naupactus, drawing Athens' fleet into a vulnerable position. A sudden attack routed the Athenians, with several ships driven ashore. The remaining Athenian ships were pursued into the harbour at Naupactus. There, reinforcements awaited and a vigorous counter-attack routed the Peloponnesian fleet. The Athenians retook the previously lost vessels, and naval dominance in the region was assured by the arrival of additional ships.

■ **MYTILENE, 427 BCE**

With Athens embroiled in the Peloponnesian War, the city of Mytilene led most of the cities of Lesbos in open revolt, attacking an Athenian force sent to restore the situation. Although initially defeated, the Athenians received reinforcements and implemented a close blockade of Mytilene. The Peloponnesian League agreed to assist Mytilene, but help failed to materialize in time to make any difference. Mytilene was starved into submission and surrendered after the population rebelled against their own leaders.

■ TANAGRA, 426 BCE

After pillaging Melos in the hope of forcing the island to join the Delian League, an Athenian fleet landed troops close to Tanagra where they encountered a joint Tanagran–Theban force. The Athenians were victorious but withdrew after the battle.

■ OLPAE, 426 BCE

The occupation of Olpae by a force from Ambracia caused its Acarnanian owners to request Athenian assistance. This was countered by a Spartan force which joined the Ambracians. The Spartan-led troops succeeded in enveloping the Athenian flank, but were driven off by the attack of a small ambush force previously concealed on that flank. After a day of hard fighting the Athenians emerged victorious.

■ IDOMENE, 426 BCE

Having defeated a Spartan–Ambracian force, the Athenian army was well positioned to ambush Ambracian reinforcements who were marching to join their countrymen, unaware of the presence of hostile forces in the area.

■ PYLOS, 425 BCE

Attempting to remove a small Athenian garrison established at Pylos, Spartan forces made several fruitless assaults before beginning siege preparations. They were then attacked by an Athenian fleet, destroying their ships and trapping a force of hoplites on the island of Sphacteria.

■ SPHACTERIA, 425 BCE

After peace negotiations failed, the Athenians attacked a force of Spartan hoplites who were cut off on Sphacteria. The Athenians drove their enemies into a fortified position where they held out until flanked and forced to surrender.

■ INVASION OF THRACE, 424 BCE

The Spartan general Brasidas marched into Thrace and began operating against Athenian allies there. He convinced or compelled several cities to rebel against Athens, forcing the Athenians to begin negotiations for a truce.

■ MEGARA, 424 BCE

As Peloponnesian pressure on Athens eased, the Athenians had gone over to the offensive, operating against Megara from 431 BCE onwards. The Megaran port of Minoa was captured in 427 BCE, and Megara came under siege by Athenian forces. A plot to open the gates to the Athenians was discovered, derailing a plan to storm the city. Instead the Athenians attacked a Peloponnesian army stationed nearby, inflicting a minor and inconclusive defeat.

■ DELIUM, 424 BCE

The Boeotian army attacked Athenian troops at Delium, while the Athenian commander was still in the middle of an oration. The Athenian right encircled the Boeotian left and defeated it, though Athenian troops ended up fighting one another in the confusion and were then set upon by cavalry. Meanwhile, the Theban phalanx, drawn up unusually deep on the Boeotian right, broke its opponents. The Athenians were driven back to their fort at Delium where they became besieged for a time.

■ AMPHIPOLIS, 422 BCE

An Athenian army arrived at Amphipolis to take back the city, which had surrendered two years earlier. The Spartan garrison retired into the city, then suddenly attacked and routed the unprepared Athenians.

■ MANTINEA, 418 BCE

Internal politics caused the Spartans to seek a battle with the forces of Argos and Athens by marching on Mantinea. The Argives initially retired rather than fight, but then advanced to attack the Spartans before the latter's allies could arrive. As was typical in hoplite warfare, the right flank of each army lapped around the enemy left, and the Mantineans were able to exploit the advantage this gave them. However, their allies from Athens and Argos were defeated, forcing a retreat.

■ SYRACUSE, 415–413 BCE

In the hope of weakening Sparta and its Peloponnesian allies, and gaining sufficient strength to win the ongoing war against them, Athens

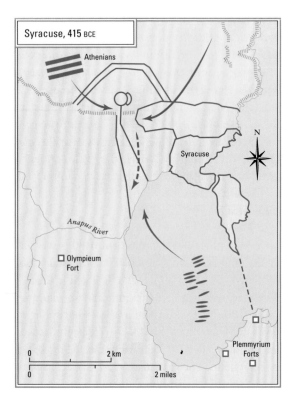

Syracuse, 415 BCE

Athenians

Syracuse

N

Anapus River

Olympieum
Fort

Plemmyrium
Forts

0   2 km

0   2 miles

themselves ashore and defeated the returning Syracusan army, but then entered winter quarters in Catana and Naxos.

The Syracusans made preparations for siege during the winter, and in the spring of 414 BCE the conflict began in earnest. Athenian forces eliminated Syracusan outposts, destroyed farmlands and built fortifications around the city. Syracusan sallies to try to disrupt the siegeworks were beaten off, and the Athenians began to surround the city with a wall.

If the siege lines were completed, the city would be entirely cut off from outside assistance and could be starved into submission. The Syracusans attempted to prevent this by building one of their own to intercept it. This construction was stormed and destroyed, so the Syracusans began another one which suffered the same fate.

A small force from Sparta then arrived on Sicily and began operating against the Athenians, while Syracusan forces made sorties from their city. The latter usually failed due to inexperience among the Syracusan troops, but the siege works were disrupted. Eventually, Spartan leadership enabled the Syracusans, making effective use of their cavalry, to defeat an Athenian force and build a third wall blocking the Athenian encirclement.

The arrival of Corinthian ships enabled the Syracusans and their allies to mount a credible challenge to Athenian sea power, while both sides received additional troops. A Spartan offensive against Athenian territory in Greece distracted attention, while efforts to recruit more troops on Sicily itself bore fruit. The Syracusans and their allies grew in strength relative to their opponents, and began attacking more boldly both on land and at sea.

Although unable to defeat the Athenian fleet, the Syracusans managed to force it into the harbour where it became trapped. This effectively placed the Athenians under siege, as their supplies had to come in by sea. Some of the forts surrounding the city were also captured, and supply depots established in Italy were raided by Syracusan and

decided to embark upon an ambitious expedition against Sicily. The main city on the island was the Corinthian colony of Syracuse, whose subjugation would considerably further Athenian aims.

The fleet that set out for Sicily represented what was at the time the largest military expedition in history. The journey was long and slow, especially since navigation on the open sea was not possible. As the fleet coast-hopped its way towards Sicily, there was plenty of time for the Syracusans to begin defensive preparations.

The fleet landed at the small city of Catana to the north of Syracuse, without opposition as the city lacked sufficient resources to resist such a large force. From there, the Athenians set up a camp and began operations on the island, drawing out an army from Syracuse to attack them.

As this force marched towards the Athenian camp, the Athenians boarded their ships and sailed to Syracuse itself, arriving well before the Syracusans could return. The Athenians established allied naval forces which could now operate freely. Reinforcements arrived to assist the Athenians, enabling an offensive that succeeded in destroying part of the Syracusans' defensive works. The operation dissolved into chaos soon after, and was soundly defeated. The arrival of yet more enemy reinforcements prompted the Athenians to begin preparing for a retreat, though Syracusan attacks on the fleet and their blockade of the harbour made this a difficult prospect.

The Athenian breakout attempt resulted in a huge close-quarters naval battle, which the Athenians eventually lost. Unable to escape by sea, they tried to break out on land and retire to another part of Sicily, but were harassed en route and finally forced to surrender.

■ MELOS, 415 BCE

Athens demanded that the Spartan colony of Melos join the Athenian side. Melos preferred to remain neutral and declined, so Athens conquered the city, executing all males and enslaving the women and children.

■ ERETRIA, 411 BCE

Athens sent a naval squadron to Eretria, whose loyalty was suspect. While the squadron was resupplying in harbour it was attacked by a Spartan fleet and defeated. Eretria then joined the Spartan side.

■ CYNOSSEMA, 411 BCE

The defeat of the Sicilian Expedition greatly diminished Athenian prestige and encouraged other cities to consider switching sides. Spartan diplomacy was successful in provoking several revolts, and the Athenian fleet was forced to act as a response force, putting down rebellions among the coastal cities. This enabled the Spartan fleet to operate more freely.

In response to Spartan naval forces operating in the Hellespont, Athens sent a fleet to remove the threat. This fleet was attacked as it rounded the point of Cynossema, becoming scattered. The divisions of the fleet were driven apart, with the central group largely driven aground. As the battle became increasingly disorganized, the Athenian right flank rallied and went on to the offensive, breaking the Spartan left flank force and then attacking the central group. The surviving Spartan vessels were able to break off and retire to Abydos.

■ SYME, 411 BCE

Attempting to prevent the junction of Spartan fleets, an Athenian force intercepted one contingent off the island of Syme. In a disorganized action fought during a storm, the Athenians were initially successful but were then defeated by the arrival of additional Spartan ships.

■ CYZICUS, 410 BCE

Using a small force as bait, the Athenians drew the Spartan fleet out of port, then cut off its retreat with larger groups of ships. The entire Spartan fleet was captured or destroyed.

■ ABYDOS, 410 BCE

After a closely contested battle between equal forces, the Spartan fleet was put to flight by Athenian reinforcements. Many ships were lost during the subsequent pursuit, until the Spartans found refuge in their base at Abydos.

■ NOTIUM, 406 BCE

Attempting to repeat the strategy used at Cyzicus by drawing the Spartan fleet out of port in Ephesus, the Athenians sent a small force to tempt the Spartans into an ambush. The decoy force was caught and savaged by the Spartans, who then pursued the survivors towards their base at Notium. The remainder of the Athenian fleet was caught unprepared and suffered heavy losses from a vigorous Spartan attack.

■ SELINUS, 409 BCE

The Sicilian city of Segesta requested Carthaginian assistance against aggression from Selinus, prompting a major expedition. The Carthaginians made extensive use of rams and siege towers, enabling them to take the city by storm after a 10-day siege.

■ BYZANTIUM, 408 BCE

Athenian forces besieging Byzantium gained entry when a demoralized segment of the population agreed to desert their posts at an appointed time. During the ensuing fighting, the

Athenians offered generous surrender terms, which were eventually accepted.

■ MYTILENE, 406 BCE

A badly outnumbered Athenian fleet was defeated by Spartan forces just outside the harbour at Mytilene, where it was forced to accept siege. This prompted the dispatch of another fleet from Athens.

■ ARGINUSAE, 406 BCE

Obtaining contributions from several allies, the Spartans managed to assemble a powerful fleet, which quickly captured Methymna. Using the city as a base enabled the Spartan fleet to threaten the rest of the island of Lesbos, which in turn would allow a move against the Hellespont.

To counter this threat, the Athenians had only a relatively small fleet. With no alternative but to move against the Spartans, this force moved close to Lesbos where it was attacked and quickly defeated. Finding refuge in Mytilene, the fleet became besieged, though a vessel did manage to escape to Athens with a request for aid.

Desperate measures allowed the Athenians to put together another fleet, which was jointly commanded by eight generals. Gathering allied vessels along the way, the fleet advanced to Lesbos. To offset the inexperience of the Athenian crews, their vessels operated as eight small independent combat groups and deployed in a double line to counter standard ramming tactics.

The numerically superior Athenian fleet was able to outflank its opponents, and after a period of intense fighting the Spartan right flank broke. The Athenians turned their full force on the remaining Spartan ships, which were forced to retreat with heavy losses. Leaving a small force to rescue survivors from sunken Athenian ships, the remainder of the fleet pushed on to relieve the fleet besieged in Mytilene. A storm drove the Athenians into port before either of these objectives could be achieved. Despite their victory the eight generals were recalled to Athens. The six who did return were condemned to death for their failure to complete the mission or rescue the survivors.

■ AEGOSPOTAMI, 405 BCE

After the losses at Arginusae, Sparta was able to build a large number of replacement vessels with the assistance of Persian funds. This new fleet operated in the Aegean, capturing a number of Athenian ports. The ultimate goal was control of the Hellespont, through which supplies of grain essential to Athens passed.

By raiding close to Athens, the Spartan fleet drew the main Athenian fleet away from its base at Samos. The Spartans then slipped past the Athenian fleet and entered the Hellespont, capturing the town of Lampsacus and threatening the Athenian grain and trade routes.

The Athenian fleet took station outside Lampsacus, but could not tempt the Spartans to come out and fight. A base was established on a nearby beach. This was not very secure and made supplying the fleet troublesome, but it did allow a close watch to be kept on the Spartans. All day the Athenian fleet waited outside the harbour, returning to its temporary base each evening.

Accounts of the battle that ensued vary. In one version, the Spartans declined to come out and fight, waiting until the Athenians had retired for the night. They then attacked the beached fleet and overran it. The other version is a repeat of the battle of Notium; a portion of the Athenian fleet attempted to draw out the Spartans and was also successful. After scattering the decoy force, the Spartans then fell on the main fleet, which was unprepared, and inflicted a crushing defeat.

Whichever version is correct, the Athenian fleet was all but annihilated. The Spartans then advanced westward, capturing cities as they went, and cut off grain supplies to Athens. This forced an Athenian surrender which brought to an end the Peloponnesian War.

■ PHYLAE, 405 BCE

After the end of the Peloponnesian War, a group of Athenian exiles entered Attica and tried to overthrow the Spartan-imposed government of Athens. A Spartan-led force sent against them was ambushed and decisively defeated.

■ MUNICHIYA, 403 BCE

Victorious at Phylae, Athenian exiles marched to Piraeus and captured the hill of Munichiya. The exiles charged down the hill and scattered the force assembled against them, killing some of the Spartan-imposed Athenian leaders.

■ PIRAEUS, 403 BCE

A Spartan army was sent to remove Athenian exiles who had occupied Piraeus. After initial successes against the Spartans' light troops and cavalry the exiles were defeated. Rather than crush the exiles, the Spartan commander then negotiated a settlement that ended the exiles' campaign.

The Anabasis
401–6 BCE

■ MARCH OF THE 10,000, 401–400 BCE

The Persian prince Cyrus the Younger recruited large numbers of Greek mercenaries to fight against his brother, who had inherited the Persian throne. At the battle of Cunaxa in 401 BCE, Cyrus was killed, leaving the mercenaries without a patron. Their services were refused by other Persian leaders, and they were unwilling to surrender to the local satrap.

The mercenaries were mostly hoplites, recruited from various regions of Greece. Their overall commander at the battle of Cunaxa was a Spartan named Clearchus, but along with many of the other Greek leaders he was betrayed by the local satrap and executed. With no alternatives remaining, replacement commanders were selected and the force set out to march home. The tale of the march is related by Xenophon, who became leader of the Ten Thousand, in the *Anabasis*.

The troops of the Ten Thousand, as they became known, were sufficiently disciplined to be able to remain a coherent fighting force despite the difficulties they faced. This permitted them to negotiate for supplies, with the threat of force to back up their requests. Where diplomacy failed, the Ten Thousand were able to forage or raid for what they needed.

Despite harassment and sometimes sterner resistance from local leaders or tribal peoples whose territory they passed through, the Ten Thousand were finally able to cross Mesopotamia and reach the shores of the Black Sea. Although this area contained many Greek cities, the march was not over.

Crossing into Thrace, the Ten Thousand took service there, fighting for a general who became King Seuthes II of Thrace. They then marched onward into Greece itself, where they were recruited into the Spartan forces. Under the command of General Thibron, the Ten Thousand fought against the Persians and took part in a siege of Larissa.

Wars of the Greek City-States
395–356 BCE

■ HALIARTUS, 395 BCE

The Spartans sent two armies against the Boeotians, one from the Peloponnese under King Pausanias, the other from Phocis under Lysander. Lysander won over Orchomenus in Boeotia and advanced faster than planned. Unknown to him, the Athenians allied with the Boeotians and deployed against Pausanias. Freed to act, the Boeotians attacked Lysander unexpectedly at Haliartus in Boeotia, killing him and dispersing his army. Pausanias had to retreat.

■ CORONEA, 394 BCE

Invading Boeotia, Sparta's King Agesilaus and some 15,000 Spartans, allies and mercenaries defeated the Boeotians and their allies near Coronea. However, the contingent from Thebes in Boeotia overcame its opponents and reached Agesilaus' baggage train. The king rallied Spartan infantry and attacked the Thebans head-on, seeking to block their escape. After hard fighting the Thebans broke through to their allies' defensive position. Wounded in battle, Agesilaus withdrew.

■ CNIDUS, 394 BCE

Years of naval stalemate between Sparta and Persia ended when the Spartan admiral Peisander engaged the fleet of the Persian satrap Pharnabazus and his admiral, Conon of Athens, near Cnidus in Asia Minor. Initially successful, Peisander's 85 triremes were defeated by over 90 Greek ships under Conon, supported by Pharnabazus and a Phoenician fleet. Peisander lost 50 triremes and his life, Sparta its dominance of the Aegean.

■ NEMEA, 394 BCE

A Spartan and allied army invaded Corinthian territory, forestalling an invasion of Laconia by a coalition force of over 24,000 Corinthian, Athenian, Argive and Boeotian hoplites. Near the Nemea river the coalition attacked, routing most Spartan-allied units. However, 6000 Spartans routed their Athenian opponents, turned and defeated in sequence several major coalition units as each returned in disorder from pursuit. The coalition never attempted to invade Laconia thereafter.

■ RAVAGING THE CORINTHIA, 394 BCE

Following Nemea and Coronea, the Spartans attacked Corinth's countryside, using raids and invasions. As a result, a pro-peace faction formed in Corinth, producing, ironically, civil strife and efforts to betray its defences.

■ LECHAEUM, 390 BCE

Trained and led by the Athenian Iphicrates, mercenary peltasts using javelins and pelta shields harassed to destruction a regiment of Spartan hoplites caught in the open west of Lechaeum, Corinth's port, killing 250.

■ THEBAN REVOLT, 379 BCE

Democratic conspirators rose against the pro-Spartan faction ruling Thebes, killing its leaders. Aided by Athenian forces, they then assaulted the Cadmea, the city's citadel. The small Spartan garrison evacuated on terms.

■ TEGYRA, 375 BCE

His retreat blocked by 1000 Spartans, Pelopidas attacked with 300 hoplites of the Theban Sacred Band and 200 Boeotian cavalry, killing the Spartan commanders, forcing the enemy formation to divide, and routing it.

■ LEUCTRA, 371 BCE

After isolating the Boeotians diplomatically, the Spartans sent against them King Cleombrotus,

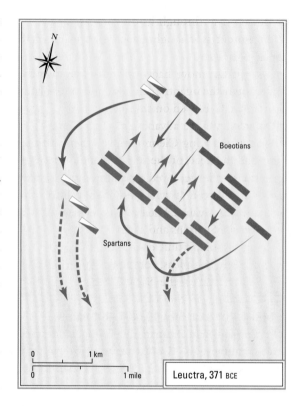

Leuctra, 371 BCE

then in Phocis with an army of 10,000 infantry and 1000 cavalry. The Boeotians tried to block his invasion, but he successfully crossed Mount Helicon and bypassed their defences, encamping at Leuctra, south of Thespiae. The Boeotians deployed 6000 infantry and cavalry against him. Their leaders were divided about seeking battle, but finally Epaminondas and others favouring action prevailed. Cleombrotus also felt he had to fight, for political reasons.

Cleombrotus formed his hoplites 12 deep, the Spartans on the right, the allies on the left, and deployed his cavalry in front of his formation. At Tegyra the Boeotian cavalry probably harassed the Spartan infantry there and stopped them from encircling the outnumbered Boeotian hoplites, helping to cause the Spartan defeat. Cleombrotus probably aimed to prevent another such effort. However, the Spartans had neglected their cavalry arm, while the Boeotian cavalry was battle-hardened. Its charge routed the Spartan cavalry, which burst in through its own infantry, catching it in disorder as it sought to extend its formation to the right.

This Spartan move had been meant to outflank and encircle the infantry of Thebes, the leading city in Boeotia. Deployed on the left wing and formed 50 deep, they were advancing against the Spartan unit in which King Cleombrotus stood, intending 'to crush the head of the serpent'. The rest of the Boeotians were deployed on the right wing, but had been ordered to stand fast. The Spartan allies also failed to advance. The battle would be decided between the Spartans and Thebans.

Seeing the king's unit disordered by the process of extension, Pelopidas, commander of the picked hoplite unit called the Sacred Band, led it in a charge ahead of the other Thebans. Although attacked unexpectedly, the Spartans held off the Sacred Band, retrieving their mortally wounded king from the fight. But then the massed Thebans arrived and attacked, probably on the Spartans' flank. The king's unit was crushed. Disordered, attacked by cavalry and facing the oncoming mass, the other Spartan units gave way as well. The survivors fell back onto the hill where they were encamped and stood on the defensive. Almost 1000 Spartans perished, including over 400 full citizens. Theban losses were minor in comparison.

Once word of the defeat reached Sparta, a relief army under Prince Archidamus was levied and sent north. Before it reached the scene, however, Jason of Pherae in Thessaly had arrived with his army, ostensibly to aid the Boeotians. He persuaded them to let the Spartans withdraw under truce, and persuaded the Spartans there to agree. Prevented by the sworn truce from attempting any further operations, Archidamus dismissed his army.

The Boeotian battleplan at Leuctra, Epaminondas' conception, combined a rapid attack in oblique order weighted on the left, concentration on the enemy command structure and use of a massed infantry attack column in coordination with cavalry. No one element was truly new in Greek warfare, but their use together in so bold an action

was remarkable. Leuctra ended the era of Spartan victories in major land battles, unbroken for 17 decades. Already weakened by population decline, loss of legitimacy and the increasing military skill of its foes, Sparta's power in Greece had been sustained chiefly by her reputation. This was dispelled by Leuctra.

■ CYNOSCEPHALAE, 364 BCE

In a meeting engagement, Pelopidas' Thessalian cavalry routed Alexander of Pherae's horsemen. Pelopidas then drove Alexander's infantry off Cynoscephalae ridge with hoplite frontal attacks and cavalry flank attacks. He died attacking Alexander's guards.

■ MANTINEA, 362 BCE

Seeking decisive battle, Epaminondas went against the Arcadian, Spartan and Athenian army deployed south of Mantinea between Mounts Mytika and Kapnistra. He led his army across the enemy front and made as if to encamp, only to mass his leading units and charge suddenly. His horsemen routed the enemy's right flank cavalry, and his Boeotian hoplites crushed their Spartan opponents. However, Epaminondas was slain, throwing all into confusion.

Athenian Social War
357–355 BCE

■ CHIOS, 357 BCE

During the Social War, Athenian troops under Chares attacked Chios but were driven off by the rebel coalition, while Chabrias perished in a simultaneous attempt to force the harbour with 60 Athenian ships.

■ LEMNOS, 356 BCE

During the Social War, the rebellious cities of Chios, Rhodes and Byzantium, together with their allies, manned 100 ships. This fleet ravaged the islands of Lemnos and Imbros, both Athenian possessions.

■ IMBROS, 356 BCE

During the Social War, the rebellious cities of Chios, Rhodes and Byzantium, together with their allies, manned 100 ships. This fleet ravaged the islands of Imbros and Lemnos, both Athenian possessions.

■ SAMOS, 356 BCE

After Lemnos and Imbros, the 100 ships from Chios, Rhodes, and Byzantium ravaged the island of Samos, an Athenian possession, and besieged its city, only to withdraw when Athens moved against Byzantium.

■ EMBATA, 356 BCE

During the Social War, two 60-ship Athenian fleets sought to intercept 100 rebel ships at Embata near Erythrae. Storms caused one Athenian fleet to abort action, and sunk several ships of the other.

Macedonian Wars 355–303 BCE

■ VICTORY OVER THESSALY, 355–353 BCE

Twice defeated by Onomarchus, the Phocian Philip II of Macedonia retreated, re-armed and re-invaded Thessaly in 353 BCE. In a pitched battle near the Pagasean Gulf, Philip and his cavalry killed Onomarchus and therefore become masters of Thessaly.

■ BATTLE OF THE CROCUS FIELD, 353 BCE

As Onomarchus moved north to join forces with his allies at Pherae, Philip II and the Macedonian cavalry won a large-scale battle at this uncertain location near the Thessalian coast. 6000 Phocians and Onomarchus perished.

■ THERMOPYLAE, 352 BCE

This celebrated strategic pass from Thessaly to Greece was held by an Athenian expeditionary force to protect the Phocians from Philip II after the Crocus Field. The Athenians' defences discouraged Philip from trying to move further southward.

■ VOLO, 352 BCE

This modern Greek town on the Thessalian coast was near the plain where the full Phocian army fought and lost the huge battle of the Crocus Field. That Macedonian victory gave Philip II Thessaly and ruined Phocis.

■ THRACE AND CHALCIDICE, 352–346 BCE

Athenian northern interests and support of Phocis prompted Philip to move against their allies in these regions. Philip picked off the Thracian tribes, culminating in his siege of a fort called Heraeon Teichos. Despite Demosthenes' urging, the Athenians were too preoccupied by a revolt Philip staged on Euboea to save their last ally, Olynthus, which Philip destroyed in 348 BCE. The 346 Peace of Philocrates, which spared some Athenian possessions, recognized Philip's dominance in the north.

■ BYZANTIUM, 340 BCE

Demosthenes' oratory undid Philip's efforts to sever Athens' Ukrainian grain route by making an alliance with the city on the Bosporus. Byzantium's alliance with Athens against Philip was a major blow to his northern objectives.

■ CHAERONEA, 338 BCE

Philip's sudden march southward prompted a rare alliance between Athens and Thebes, which met Philip north of Thebes in battle on 7 August. Alexander commanded the cavalry in a devastating rout that gave Greece to Philip.

■ THEBES, 335 BCE

After Philip II's assassination and a false report of Alexander's death, Thebes rose in revolt against a Macedonian garrison. Following a lightning march, Alexander destroyed the ancient city utterly as an example to the Greeks.

■ GRANICUS RIVER, 334 BCE

This was a major battle in May between the army of Alexander the Great and the Persian forces in Asia Minor. The effort of the Persian satraps to stifle the war at its beginning collapsed in a disastrous failure.

Ignoring the advice of Memnon to withdraw and devastate the Persian countryside before Alexander and his army's advance, the local satraps instead chose to protect their revenue base and launch a 'decapitation strike' against Alexander upon his actual entry into their territory, thus forfeiting the initiative and allowing Alexander to fight a cavalry battle upon his own terms with 1500 Macedonian elite *hetairoi* and 3500 allied horse. The Persians

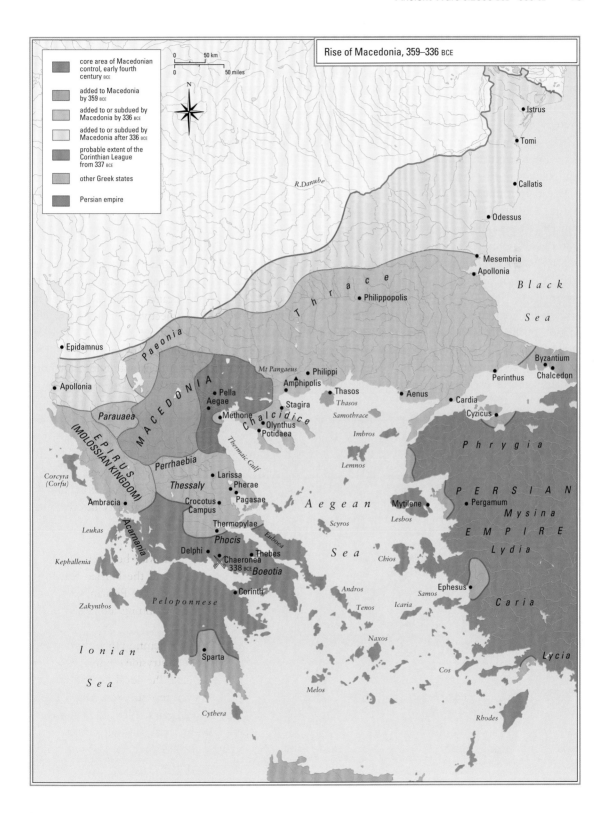

Rise of Macedonia, 359–336 BCE

core area of Macedonian control, early fourth century BCE

added to Macedonia by 359 BCE

added to or subdued by Macedonia by 336 BCE

added to or subdued by Macedonia after 336 BCE

probable extent of the Corinthian League from 337 BCE

other Greek states

Persian empire

0   50 km
0   50 miles

N

R.Danube

Istrus

Tomi

Callatis

Odessus

Mesembria
Apollonia

Black

Sea

T h r a c e

Philippopolis

P a e o n i a

Epidamnus

Byzantium
Perinthus   Chalcedon

Mt Pangaeus   Philippi
Amphipolis

Apollonia

MACEDONIA   Pella
Aegae

Methone
Olynthus
Potidaea

Chalcidice

Thasos
Thasos

Stagira

Samothrace

Aenus

Cardia
Cyzicus

P h r y g i a

Parauaea

E
P
I
R
U
S
(MOLOSSIAN KINGDOM)

Perrhaebia

Corcyra
(Corfu)

Ambracia

Imbros

Lemnos

Larissa
Pherae
Thessaly   Pagasae

Thermaic Gulf

Crocotus
Campus

Thermopylae

Leukas

Kephallenia

Acarnania

Phocis
Delphi   Thebes
Chaeronea
338 BCE *Boeotia*

Aegean

Sea

Scyros

Mytilene

Pergamum
Lesbos

P E R S I A N

M y s i n a

E M P I R E

L y d i a

Zakynthos

Peloponnese

Corinth

Ionian

Sea

Sparta

Chios

Andros

Tenos   *Icaria*

Samos

Ephesus

Caria

Naxos

Lycia

Cythera

Melos

Cos

Rhodes

awaited him on the far side of the stream with 20,000 elite cavalry and a reserve force of 18,000 Greek mercenary infantry, which they kept fatally far behind their frontline. Alexander, for the first time, unveiled what would become his usual strategy against the Persians in the early stage of the war – an oblique attack upon the enemy left while the phalanx of Macedonian pikeman, equipped with the long and counter-weighted sarissa, approached towards the enemy's left centre. Anticipating such tactics, Memnon had himself put the bulk of the Persian horse on the extreme left, which Alexander avoided, holding it in place with light troops and skirmishing cavalry while the main onslaught was further down the enemy line.

Parmenio commanded the more defensive portion of the army, the phalanx of some 30,000 infantry, the pike formation connected to the cavalry by elite troops called *hypaspists*. As the phalanx ground on towards the Persian centre-

left, Persian commanders including Rhoesaces, Spithridates and Darius's son-in-law Mithridates, took their own cavalry commands directly against Alexander. In the onset, the Macedonian cavalry version of the sarissa proved superior to the shorter Persian lance/javelin. Alexander's life, campaigns and empire were saved when one Cleitus 'The Black' severed Spithridates' arm and saved the king from a blow from behind. Under the fierceness of Alexander's onslaught, the Persian cavalry collapsed and fled, leaving the Greek mercenaries to buy time for the Persians' retreat with their destruction between Alexander's cavalry and arriving phalanx. Alexander set a pattern early on for exploiting each Persian collapse as vigorously as possible; Persians slain on the battlefield were enemies he would never have to fight or subdue again. The official report of Alexander's losses listed 95 dead from the cavalry, another 30 in the infantry. The wounded numbered as much as 1200, all of whom Alexander visited personally.

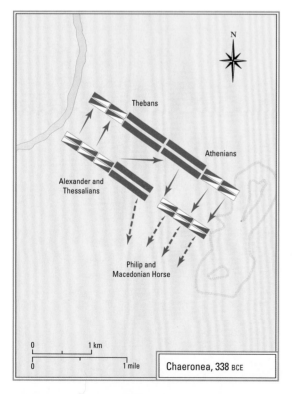

Chaeronea, 338 BCE

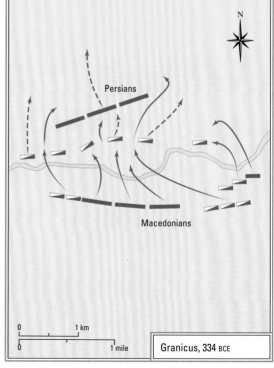

Granicus, 334 BCE

Alexander made significant practical use of his first major victory over the Persians, sending spoils of the battle to Athens. There they adorned the Acropolis and made reference to the refusal of the Spartans to join the League of Corinth, which Alexander had formed before the war to launch what he termed a Greek 'war of revenge' against the Persians for the Persian Wars of a century earlier. Extermination of the surrendering Greek mercenaries found convenient justification in the nature of this 'Holy War,' while removing those and potential future recruits from the battlefield. Statues of the 35 slain Macedonian *hetairoi* were placed on the Athenian acropolis and reminded visitors of the first major Greek success against the Persians since the Peloponnesian Wars. Alexander provided honourable burial for the Persian dead, and kept the existing offices and revenue streams of the Persian Empire in place by creating Calas satrap of the conquered Hellespontine Phrygia.

■ ISSUS, 333 BCE

The first battle fought in November by Alexander the Great directly against Darius, the 'Great King' of the Persian Empire, was a disastrous defeat for the Persian army at its full strength.

The speed of Alexander's southward advance after several checks combined to let Darius take the field personally with the largest force Alexander had yet faced: as many as 400,000 Persian infantry, including the Persian *kardakes*, armed as Greek hoplites, 100,000 Persian cavalry from throughout the empire, and a back-up force of actual Greek hoplite mercenaries numbering a total of 20,000–30,000 men. Alexander reversed his march with the objective of engaging Darius's army, Darius having taken his own force southward down the line of Alexander's advance, slaughtering Macedonian wounded at Issus itself. Alexander picked a battlefield at the far side of Bailan Pass, alerted to the Persian advance by scouts.

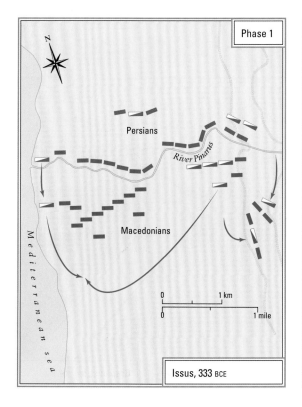

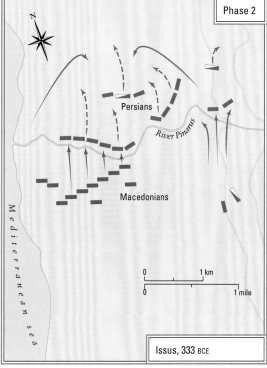

The Persian line consisted of their cavalry on the right, the Greek hoplites in the centre with the *kardakes* on their either flank in support and a flanking force of infantry and cavalry on the Persian extreme right. Alexander's archers repelled these while his cavalry once again crossed a river, the Pinarus, and surged upward into the Persians. As the phalanx climbed the river bank, a crisis occurred when the Greek hoplites struck its disordered ranks at the moment of greatest vulnerability. Alexander's victory in the cavalry skirmish allowed his horse and supporting infantry to take the Greeks in flank, some 8000 of them escaping over the mountains by holding formation.

Darius's flight from the battlefield allowed the war to go on, but left the Persians in disorder to be annihilated by the vengeful Macedonians. Darius's wives and treasury became Alexander's booty.

■ GORDIUM, 333 BCE

Gordum was the ancient capital of Phrygia at which Alexander reunited the halves of his army after separate winter quartering. When Alexander's sword cut the 'Gordian Knot' there, it fulfilled a prophecy that he would conquer Asia.

■ TYRE, 332 BCE

In the culminating battle of Alexander's campaign to reduce the Persian fleet by capturing its Phoenician bases, Alexander laid siege to the island city of Tyre for eight months, only capturing it when his own fleet arrived from Greece.

■ GAZA, 332 BCE

Alexander took two months to overcome a fierce defence by the Persian garrison of this port city in a very strategic position on the route from Syria to Eqypt. A Persian eunuch, Batis, commanded a force levied from the native Nabataean population, the city itself protected by a high wall, mud and the shifting sand dunes allowed to pile up against it. In the course of Alexander's seven-month siege of neighboring Tyre, there had been ample time to provision and fortify the bastion. Alexander unleashed his siege train on the city, the work of his engineer Aristobulus eventually managing to

breach the city's defences. Alexander was badly wounded during the siege and sold the population as slaves after Homerically dragging Batis's body around the walls behind his chariot. Gaza's fall severed Egypt from the rest of the Persian Empire.

■ ARBELA (GAUGAMELA), 331 BCE

Gaugamela was a decisive battle in which Alexander's war-seasoned army utterly crushed the full force of the Persian Empire under the command of the Great King. In a tactical masterpiece, Alexander destroyed organized Persian resistance to his conquest. Persian forces numbered some 200,000 infantry and 45,000 horse, while Macedonian forces totalled 40,000 infantry and some 7000 cavalry.

The Persian ruler Darius exploited Alexander's diversion south into Egypt to accumulate the full resources of his empire, which included a number of war elephants, transported at great expense from the easternmost frontiers. Untrained horses shied at the sight and scent of the strange monsters, which carried archers and javelin throwers.

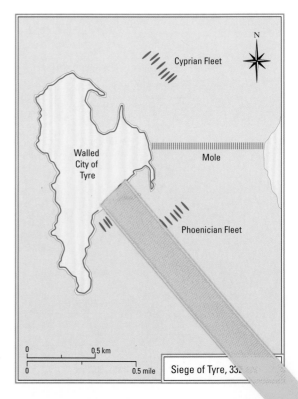

Siege of Tyre, 33.

Those and 200 scythe-equipped chariots buoyed Darius's hopes of finally cracking the deadly Macedonian phalanx.

Alexander's plan to capture and supplant him allowed Darius to control Alexander's movements, by being the primary objective of Alexander's campaign. He chose a wide and level battlefield near the city of Arbela, going so far as to have the terrain levelled to assist the action of his chariots. For his own part, Alexander had taken the precaution of scouting the battlefield thoroughly. Darius's preparations provided his enemy with an excellent preview of his plans.

Alexander camped 6.4km from Darius's army, just far enough to prevent a surprise attack. Such was Alexander's confidence in victory that he left his troops comfortably encamped, while the Persians passed a long, cold desert night in formation under arms. Alexander himself, having rejected Parmenio's suggestion for a night attack, had to be roused at daybreak.

Alexander's army stuck to his proven battle plan against the Persians: an oblique thrust with his elite cavalry supported by the grinding advance of the phalanx, the latter being set directly for Darius's visible position in the centre of his line. The movement of Alexander's thrust would create a gap in the ranks of the enemy as each man sought to cover himself with his neighbour's shield. Special forces of Thessalians and elite infantry called *hypaspists* protected Alexander's own flanks.

Behind his frontline, under the worried Parmenio, Alexander placed a reserve phalanx, another rectangle of bristling pikes as difficult to attack as the frontline. The Thessalians and *hypaspists* would fall back into contact with the second line. In effect, as his smaller army waded into the massed Persian forces, Alexander's forces were capable of forming a square in the event that Persian numbers engulfed them.

Alexander's archers and javelin throwers killed the charioteers of the scythed chariots,

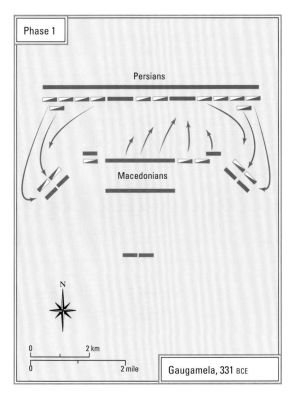

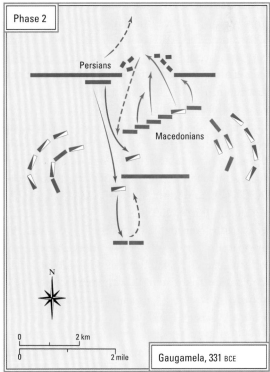

traditionally used to slaughter a disorganized and retreating enemy, the scythes taking a fearful toll on frightened and defenceless men. In the face of Alexander's veterans, they failed miserably. The elephants also failed; having no stake in the battle sufficient to wade into the bristling spears and arrows of the enemy army, they proved useless and uncontrollable.

Darius had nothing to stop the slow advance of the Macedonian infantry and cavalry towards where Darius and his court watched in terror. Onrushing Persian cavalry bypassed the Thessalians and *hypaspists* on a flank and drove for the Macedonian rear. Parmenio had not been able to keep the reserve in good order, which allowed those Persians to move kilometres to the rear to plunder the Macedonian camp. The only result was to prevent Alexander's pursuit of Darius when he instead had to respond to Parmenio's request for what proved to be unneeded support. An infuriated satrap, Bessus, however, executed Darius some time later.

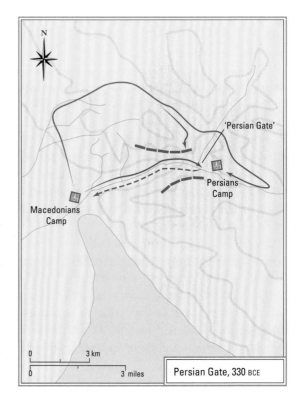

■ MEGALOPOLIS, 331 BCE

This was an unsuccessful siege of the capital city of Arcadia. With Alexander in Asia, Agis rallied the remnants of Sparta's army and allies and, with mercenaries, assaulted the city. Antipater and the Macedonians easily scattered them.

■ PANDOSIA, 331 BCE

This battle in southern Italy was between the Epirotes, allied Thurii and the rebel and powerful city of Taras. An assassin killed Alexander of Epirus during the battle, ending Epirus's efforts to create an Italian empire in Italy.

■ PERSIAN GATE, 330 BCE

This battle consisted of an effort at the pass by Ariobarzanes, satrap of Persis, to delay Alexander's eastern march from Persepolis. After a costly repulse, Alexander found a shepherd who showed him a trail by which he turned the pass.

■ SOGDIAN ROCK, 327 BCE

This Afghan mountain fortress held the remnants of Persian resistance, was considered impregnable and was the location of the hold-outs' families. The defenders taunted that Alexander would need flying soldiers to take it. Alexander found 300 mountaineers amongst his army who, with casualties and pitons, ascended a peak above the fortress during the night and occupied it. The Afghanis surrendered, Alexander finding and marrying Princess Roxane, becoming Afghan himself and pacifying the region.

■ AORNOS, 327 BCE

Fortress on the Indus, held by Pathans against Alexander. Alexander bridged the ravine to the fortress's spire with a combination bridge and dam under cover of his catapults, eventually taking the fortress after severe reverses.

■ HYDASPES RIVER, 326 BCE

This was a major battle fought near the summer solstice in which Alexander, with great difficulty, defeated the armies of the Rajahs Porus and Abisares as they sought to oppose Alexander and his army's entrance into India. The battle was Alexander's last decisive major victory.

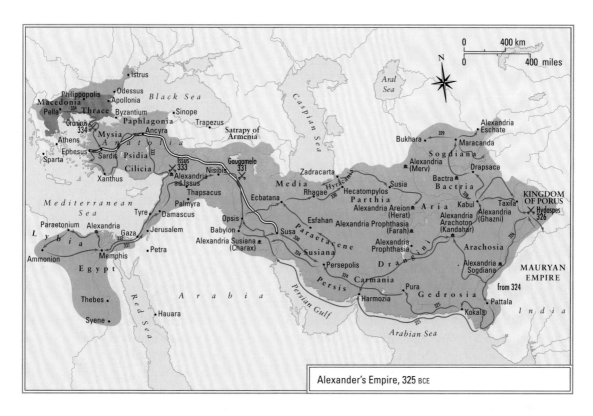

Alexander's Empire, 325 BCE

Porus and Abisares had mustered a very substantial force of 200 well-trained elephants and 300 war chariots, supported by 20,000 infantry. Some 4000 cavalry supported the Indians' flanks. The war chariots and elephants both carried javelin throwers and archers, the ancient sources remarking upon how the size of the Indian formation had the appearance of a fortified city. Alexander's army, reduced by forces left behind to occupy conquered territory, numbered roughly 6000 heavy infantry, 4000 lighter troops, 4000 conventional cavalry and 1000 mounted archers.

Alexander had to force the crossing of the Hydaspes river at the height of flood. With the Indian forces so ready to receive him, for several days Alexander made demonstrations and countermarches back and forth on his side of the river in order to fatigue the Indians and lower their wariness. Finally Alexander himself, after a night march, crossed upstream unopposed with

his most mobile 6000 infantry and 5000 cavalry, leaving the main body under Craterus at the original river crossing.

Porus shifted his formation and moved to engage, with Alexander refusing the left flank of his cavalry vanguard and engaging personally himself with his right. As the Indians rode into the attack, the refused left of the Macedonian cavalry under Coenus fell upon their flank, collapsing the Indian horse. The Indian cavalry retreated back into the elephants, throwing them into confusion and damaging Porus's formation. Alexander's forces now began a holding attack to keep the Indians' attention.

Craterus, meanwhile, had forced the river while Alexander and Coenus held Porus's attention and took the Rajah's army in flank. Drawing upon their experience at Gaugamela, the Macedonians targeted the drivers of the Indian chariots and the elephants' mahouts, neutralizing Porus's remaining mobile assets. As previously, the elephants would not attempt to penetrate the bristling pikes of the Macedonian phalanx, and became unmanageable, sowing further confusion within the collapsing Indian ranks.

Porus held his ground and fought to the last, but the rest of the Indian army fell into rout, which the Macedonian cavalry exploited, ruthlessly inflicting further casualties while daylight lasted. Porus was wounded and brought to Alexander after his capture, the two commanders beginning a firm friendship that made Porus Alexander's loyal vassal to the end of Alexander's life. Abisares, who had not been present at the battle, offered his submission later.

Alexander took advantage of the resulting stability of his new eastern frontier to found two Greek cities, one, Nicaea, on the site of his own crossing, and the other on the riverbank at Craterus's suggestion named after his deceased horse, Bucephala. By so doing, he both established Greek civilization at its furthest east and permanently secured his river crossing into India. Soon after the Hydaspes, however, Alexander's army exercised its technical sovereignty within the unwritten Macedonian constitution and refused to follow the king further eastward, thus forcing his return back to the Persia, where Alexander died of a fever at Babylon in 321 BCE.

■ CRANNON (ATHENS REVOLT), 322 BCE

This was a battle in Thessaly in which the converging Macedonian armies of Antipater and Craterus sundered a coalition army of Greeks in revolt after Alexander's death. The battle was nearly even, but the Greek allies surrendered individually.

■ CAMPAIGNS OF CHANDRAGUPTA, 310–303 BCE

Having seized power from the Nanda dynasty in 322 BCE, Chandragupta Maurya consolidated his control and then rapidly took control of North-west India. This required the conquest of several satrapies created by Alexander the Great, and caused a conflict with the successor state of Seleucid Persia. A Seleucid expedition was defeated in 305

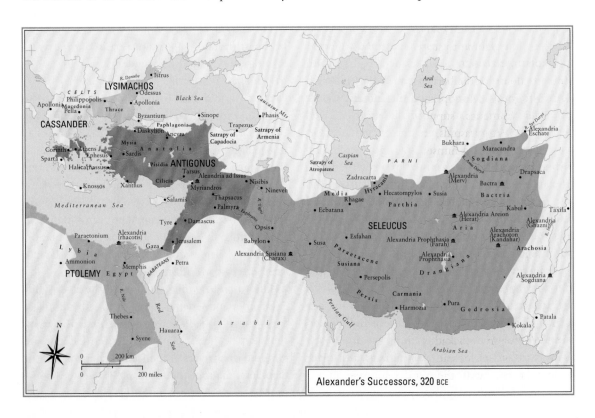

Alexander's Successors, 320 BCE

BCE opening the way for a campaign of conquest westwards. The war was concluded by a treaty that granted Chandragupta territory in return for military assistance.

Mauryan Wars
322–185 BCE

■ KALINGA, 262 BCE
The independent state of Kalinga had aligned itself with enemies of the Maurya Empire, prompting an invasion in overwhelming force. The resulting carnage prompted Emperor Ashoka to embrace Buddhism and to renounce violence.

Hellenistic/Diadochi/Greek Wars
322–146 BCE

■ PARAETAKENA (PARAECENE), 317 BCE
A battle in Media during the War of the Successors between the Macedonian forces of Eumenes of Cardia and Antigonus Monopthlamus. Eumenes anticipated Antigonus's river crossing, inflicting casualties, but failing to stop his rival's advance.

■ GABIENE, 316 BCE
Final battle in Media between Eumenes of Cardia and Antigonus Monopthalmus. After Antigonus captured Eumenes' supplies, Macedonian elite forces, the Argyraspids, betrayed Eumenes to Antigonus, who rid himself of a formidable rival by executing him.

■ GAZA, 312 BCE
Decisive strategic defeat for Antigonus Monopthalmus by the combined armies of Ptolemy and Seleucus. Antigonus's son, Demetrius, lost a large-scale battle near the city, costing his father control of Syria and hope of conquering Egypt.

■ SALAMIS (CYPRUS), 308 BCE
Demetrius Poliorcetes with 118 warships held 60 ships of Ptolemy blockaded at their Cyprian base with just 10 vessels, defeating 140 relieving Egyptian galleys at sea with the remainder. Demetrius's victorious left rolled up the Egyptian centre.

■ SALAMIS (CYPRUS), 306 BCE
Successful Antigonid storming of Ptolemy's Cyprian naval base by Demetrius Poliorcetes. Demetrius employed sea-borne catapults and a moving multi-storey siege tower against the Egyptian defenders. The capture of Salamis much improved the Antigonid position in the Mediterranean.

■ SIEGE OF RHODES, 305–304 BCE
An epic siege in which Demetrius Poliorcetes and his siege train failed to reduce the island democracy's capital. Demetrius's monster terrestrial and naval siege engines met equivalent responses from the defenders, supplied by the Antigonids' rivals.

■ IPSOS, 304 BCE
Catastrophic defeat of the Antigonid Empire in Asia, leading to the death of Antigonus Monophthalmus and Demetrius Poliorcetes' retreat to the islands and port cities of the eastern Mediterranean. The battle took place in eastern Central Asia Minor near where Lysimachus, ruler of Thrace, successfully eluded Antigonus's army in a southward march. Lysimachus rendezvoused with Seleucus, who had ceded Alexander's conquest in India to obtain 480 elephants, which he had transported at tremendous expense across Persia. The two allies combined 64,000 foot, 10,500 cavalry and 120 chariots to move against Antigonus's 70,000 infantry, 10,000 cavalry and 75 elephants. Demetrius's initial charge with the cavalry succeeded, but Demetrius was unable to prevent the allied infantry and elephants from crushing his father's infantry and body in the resulting disaster. Their success in this battle prompted the popularity of elephants in Hellenistic warfare.

■ THERMOPYLAE, 279 BCE
A Greek confederation failed to hold the pass against the Gauls under Brennus seeking to move into and plunder the cities of Greece. After a repulse, the Gauls bypassed the defenders, who evacuated by sea.

■ CORUPEDION, 281 BCE
Decisive defeat in late summer of Lysimachus, 80, by Seleucus, 77, invading Thrace from Asia Minor.

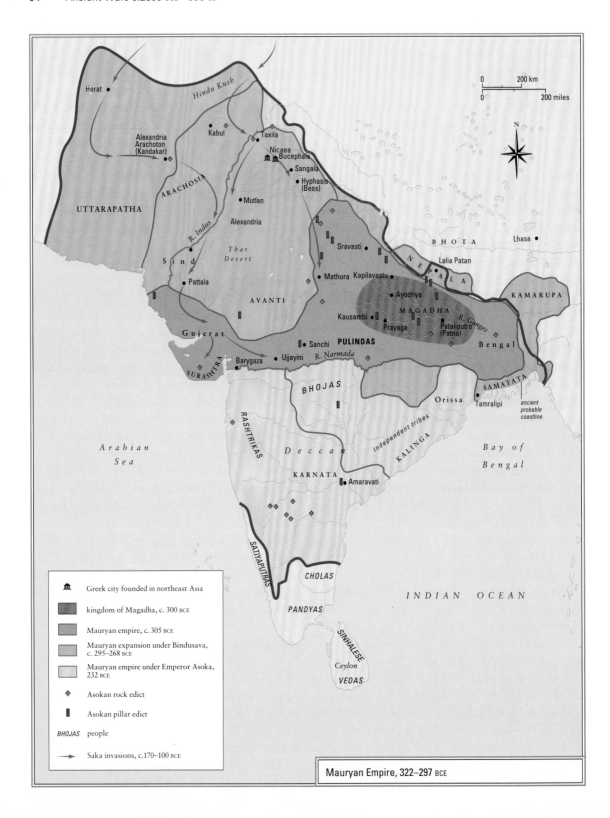

Herat

Hindu Kush

Kabul   Taxila
Alexandria   Nicaea
Arachoton   Bucephala
(Kandakar)   Sangala
ARACHOSIA   Hyphasis
(Beas)
UTTARAPATHA   Mutlan
R. Indus   Alexandria   Sravasti
Thar   BHOTA   Lhasa
Sind   Desert   Lalia Patan   NEPALA
Pattala   Mathura Kapilavastu   KAMARUPA
AVANTI   Ayodhya
Kausambi   MAGADHA   R. Ganges
Gujerat   Prayaga   Pataliputra
Sanchi   PULINDAS   (Patna)   Bengal
Barygaza   Ujjayini   R. Narmada
SURASHTRA   SAMATATA
BHOJAS   Tamralipi   ancient
Orissa   probable
Arabian   coastline
Sea   Deccan   Independent tribes   Bay of
RASHTRIKAS   KALINGA   Bengal
KARNATA
Amaravati
SATIYAPUTRAS
CHOLAS   INDIAN   OCEAN
PANDYAS
SINHALESE
Ceylon
VEDAS

🏛 Greek city founded in northeast Asia

⬛ kingdom of Magadha, c. 300 BCE

⬛ Mauryan empire, c. 305 BCE

⬛ Mauryan expansion under Bindusava,
     c. 295–268 BCE

⬜ Mauryan empire under Emperor Asoka,
     232 BCE

◆ Asokan rock edict

▮ Asokan pillar edict

BHOJAS people

→ Saka invasions, c.170–100 BCE

Mauryan Empire, 322–297 BCE

In this final battle between Alexander's former generals, the armies fought in western Asia Minor. Lysimachus perished in the fighting.

■ **ANDROS, 246 BCE**

Naval victory off the Greek coast by the Macedonian fleet of Antigonus Gonatus over the Egyptian squadron of Ptolemy II. Antigonus, 73, employed some of the largest vessels ever in combat in the ancient world.

■ **LAMIA, 1ST AND 2ND BATTLES, 209 BCE**

Two battles lost by the Aetolians under Pyrrhias attempting to defend their capital against Philip V of Macedon's advance southwards. Support from Attalus of Pergamon and a thousand Roman marines did not prevent the defeats.

■ **MANTINEA, 207 BCE**

The battle of Mantinea was caused by an attack by Machanidas, the tyrant of Sparta, against Philopoemen and the Achaean League, mustering in the nearby city. Machinadas's catapults scattered the Achaean mercenaries, but Philopoemen, rallying his forces on better ground, defeated and killed Machanidas.

■ **CHIOS, 201 BCE**

Large fleet action between the navies of Philip V of Macedon and the Rhodians and Attalus of Pergamon. The Macedonians recovered from initial reverses, but Philip had to abandon his effort to capture neighbouring Samos.

■ **LADE, 201 BCE**

Naval defeat by Philip V of Macedon of the Rhodian fleet as it sought to prevent his conquest of Rhodian possessions on the mainland opposite the island. The Rhodians afterwards appealed to Rome for aid.

■ **CORINTH, 198 BCE**

Unsuccessful siege of Philip V's southernmost fortress in Greece by the younger Flamininus and the fleets of Attalus of Pergamon and Rhodes. A naval bombardment breached the Macedonian defences, but a phalanx in the breach held.

■ **AOUS, 198 BCE**

Philip V's fortified position preventing a juncture of Flamininus's army with Rome's Aetolian allies to the south. Flamininus found a local guide to take the Romans behind and above Philip's lines, successfully routing the Macedonians.

■ **CYNOSCEPHALAE, 197 BCE**

Cynescephalae was the decisive battle of the Second Macedonian War, the set-piece clash of the Macedonian phalanx with the Roman manipular legion. Reinforced by veterans returning from Carthage, Flamininus took two legions in pursuit of Philip V's full strength, consolidated in Thessaly for battle. Roman skirmishers and allied cavalry moving up one side of a ridge encountered their Macedonian counterparts, prompting Flamininus to launch an all-out assault before the Macedonian formations were fully ready for battle. Philip's consolidated forces on the right formed a deep phalanx. This formation crested the ridge and drove down upon the legionaries, the long pikes of the Macedonians still proving effective in pushing the legionaries back. Flamininus took his elephants and unengaged right, rolling up the disorganized Macedonians opposite while the last line of the retreating legion took the Macedonians in flank, completing the rout with heavy casualties.

■ **GYTHEUM, 194 BCE**

City of the Achaean League besieged by Nabis, tyrant of Sparta. Philopoemen and the League moved before the Romans could effectively intervene, striking against Nabis by land and sea. The Achaeans lost at sea to Nabis's blockading squadron when a recommissioned war memorial foundered, and Gytheum fell. The Achaeans then destroyed Nabis's disorganized forces in a night attack and besieged Sparta, while Roman marines captured Gytheum and imposed a peace.

■ **THERMOPYLAE II, 191 BCE**

Antiochus III, with 14,000 infantry and 500 cavalry, held the historic pass against Roman forces seeking to evict the Seleucids from Greece. Cato the Censor led a detachment around an unguarded trail, causing a disastrous rout.

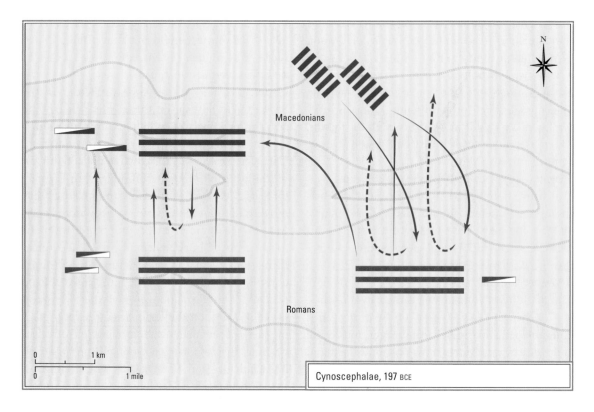

Cynoscephalae, 197 BCE

■ PYDNA (THIRD MACEDONIAN WAR), 172–167 BCE

Philip V's heir Perseus's efforts to restore Macedonian prestige in Greece led to friction and conflict with the Achaean League and Eumenes of Pergamon, both of whom were successful in drawing Rome's attention back to the tense situation in the Balkans. Upon Rome's declaration of hostilities, Perseus retreated behind the safety of his borders and prolonged the war with defensive campaigning. The strategy was a sensible one, which strained Rome's alliances and supply streams. Perseus moved his forces into a strong position near his capital at Pydna and awaited Aemelius Paulus's attack.

Two rivers protected the Macedonian flanks on the ridge where the phalanx awaited; Paulus accordingly was reluctant to engage. For unknown reasons Perseus's phalanx charged down the hill into the Roman line, unsupported by their cavalry. A sacrificial stand by the Achaeans apparently created enough disorder for the Roman legionaries to cut their way in and utterly destroy the Macedonian army and empire.

■ CALLICINUS, 171 BCE

Opening engagement of the Third Macedonian War. Perseus had 39,000 infantry and 4000 cavalry, while the Roman army of Licinius consisted of two legions containing 12,000 largely inexperienced Italian troops. Perseus forced the Romans to retreat.

■ PYDNA, 148 BCE

One Andriscus, claiming Perseus as his father, seized control of Macedonia in 149. After defeating a legion under Juventius Thalna, two legions under Caecilius Metellus crushed Andriscus near the capital of Pydna. Rome then annexed Macedonia.

■ CORINTH, 146 BCE

Site of the Achaean League's last effort against Roman domination of Greece; the army of Consul L. Mummius obliterated the League's final levy and levelled the ancient and prosperous city, selling its inhabitants into slavery.

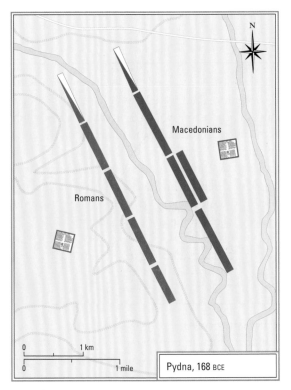

Pydna, 168 BCE

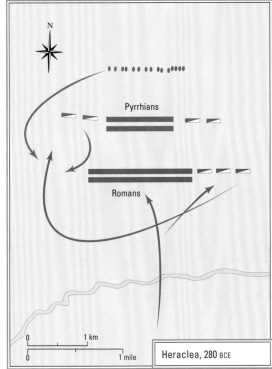

Heraclea, 280 BCE

Pyrrhic War
281–275 BCE

■ THURII, 281 BCE

The city of Thurii, an ally of Rome, was attacked and plundered by forces from Tarentum. This led to a clash between Rome and Tarentum, and ultimately to the intervention of Pyrrhus of Epirus.

■ HERACLEA, 280 BCE

Shortly after Pyrrhus of Epirus landed in Italy, Roman forces were sent to dislodge him. Pyrrhus preferred to avoid battle for the time being, as the Tarentines had not managed to raise a suitable army to fight alongside the newly arrived Greeks.

Pyrrhus needed time to train up a Tarentine force and to receive reinforcements from other cities that might be willing to fight against Rome. He thus positioned his army behind the River Siris and made camp. Determined to force a battle before the enemy was reinforced, the Roman commander detached his cavalry on a long flank march into the enemy rear. This attack was used to cover the Roman infantry's river crossing, forcing Pyrrhus to accept battle. Pyrrhus led from the front and came close to being killed. When it became obvious that the Romans were singling him out, the king switched clothing with a subordinate. This action may have saved his life, but it did cause the Greek army to lose heart when they apparently saw their king fall. Pyrrhus rallied his troops by showing them that he was still alive.

With morale restored, Pyrrhus deployed his war elephants, which the Romans had never before encountered. The Roman cavalry was routed and the infantry severely disordered by this assault. The Roman force was saved from complete disaster by the tendency of wounded elephants to run amok, disrupting their own side's formations.

The Roman force disengaged and the Greeks were able to advance almost as far as Rome itself. However, both sides had taken very heavy losses and Pyrrhus was not confident of victory if he assaulted the city. His force pulled back and wintered in Tarentum.

■ **ASCULUM, 279 BCE**

After first encountering Greek war elephants at Heraclea, the Romans had developed anti-elephant tactics. On the first day of the battle of Asculum, the wooded and hilly terrain impeded the elephants and cavalry, resulting in a bloody but inconclusive clash between infantry forces. An aggressive redeployment by the Greeks forced the Romans to fight in terrain better suited to the use of elephants and the dense phalanx of the Greeks. A flank attack by the Greek elephants broke the Roman cavalry and caused a hurried withdrawal, giving the Greeks possession of the battlefield. Heavy losses on the winning side led to the concept of the 'Pyrrhic Victory'.

■ **SYRACUSE, c.279 BCE**

To prevent King Pyrrhus from using Syracuse as a base for operations on Sicily, Carthaginian forces allied to Rome besieged the city. Pyrrhus

landed Eryx and Panormus, then marched to break the siege of Syracuse.

■ **BENEVENTUM, 275 BCE**

Taking advantage of defections among the Roman allies camped at Malaventum, King Pyrrhus launched a night assault on the Roman camp. This was thrown back in disorder. An initial Roman counter-attack was a failure, but a second attempt succeeded when their own war elephants stampeded though the Greek phalanx. King Pyrrhus called off his Italian campaign as a result of this defeat, and the Romans celebrated their victory by renaming the town Beneventum.

Syrian, Ptolemaic, Seleucid and Antignonid Wars 274–100 BCE

■ **INVASION OF MACEDONIA 274 BCE**

Returning home from Italy with what remained of his armies, Pyrrhus found that conditions in

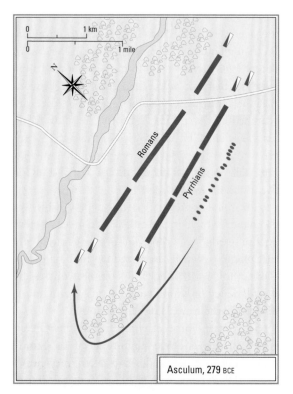

Asculum, 279 BCE

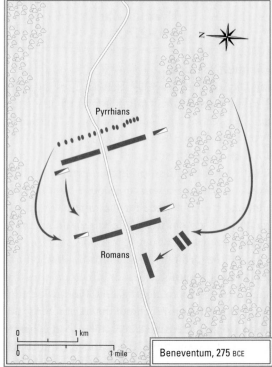

Beneventum, 275 BCE

neighbouring territories were ripe for a campaign of conquest. Hiring mercenaries, he launched a campaign to topple Antigonus of Macedonia.

■ CORINTH, 265 BCE

After two years of indecisive campaigning, the Greek coalition against Macedon had made some minor progress. The coalition suffered a severe defeat at Corinth, after which the war went very much against them.

■ MACEDONIA, 263 BCE

The Greek coalition against Macedonia collapsed with the fall of Athens to Macedonian troops and a peace treaty with Sparta. This cemented Macedonian control over Greece, though Egypt continued to interfere in Greek affairs.

■ INVASION OF SYRIA, 263 BCE

Entering into alliance with Seleucid Persia, Macedonian troops campaigned into Syria with the intention of driving Egyptian forces out of the Aegean region. Macedonian interest in the region waned as troubles grew on the northern borders.

■ COS, 258 BCE

The Egyptian and Macedonian fleets met off Cos in a clash that decisively weakened Egyptian naval power. Details are sketchy, and the date has been disputed by several historians. An alternate date of 255 BCE has been suggested.

■ ANDROS, 245 BCE

Continued naval clashes between Egypt and Macedon led to a battle off Andros in 245 or 246 BCE. Egyptian power in the Cyclades island group was broken as a result of this defeat.

■ ANCYRA, 236 BCE

Having been installed as regent in Asia Minor, Antiochus Hierax rebelled against his brother Seleucus II of Persia. Seleucus was decisively defeated in a clash at Ancyra, making a hasty retreat across the River Taurus.

■ RAPHIA, 217 BCE

After a period of skirmishing, the Egyptian and Seleucid armies clashed, with the Egyptian flanks soon broken. The phalangites of both armies fought on for some time, with the Egyptians finally emerging victorious.

■ INVASION OF PARTHIA, 209 BCE

After the failure of a first expedition by Seleucus II to retake Parthia from the Parni, a second campaign under Antiochus III brought the region under Seleucid control as a vassal state.

■ ARIUS, 209 BCE

A force of Parthian cavalry attempted to halt the Seleucid advance at the river Arius. The Seleucid advance guard, composed mainly of elite troops, crossed the river at night and surprised the Parthians in their camp.

■ WAR OF ANTIOCHUS, III 208–06 BCE

After securing his northern frontier by reducing Parthia to a vassal state, Antiochus III marched eastward, forcing a peace settlement upon the rebellious province of Bactria. He then forayed into India where he was gifted with war elephants.

■ PANIUM, 198 BCE

Having seized Syria and Palestine, the Seleucids held it for a short time before they were driven out by additional forces from Egypt. Antiochus

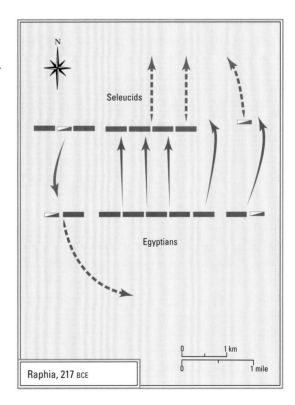

Raphia, 217 BCE

launched a new campaign to regain control of the province, culminating in the battle of Panium. The Seleucids' chief advantage was their use of cataphract cavalry, which defeated and drove off the Egyptian cavalry on the flanks, then attacked the rear of the enemy's main infantry body.

▪ EURYMEDON, 190 BCE

With the Seleucid intervention in Greece defeated by a Roman army at Thermopylae, Antiochus III was forced to abandon the campaign. Roman forces then went on the offensive, making control of the Aegean vital to both sides. The Seleucid fleet was commanded by the Carthaginian Hannibal, who was in exile at the Seleucid court. Hannibal's fleet suffered a heavy defeat at the hands of a combined Roman–Rhodian force.

▪ MYONESSUS, 190 BCE

Soon after the battle at Eurymedon, the Seleucid fleet was again defeated by a roughly equal-sized force of Roman and Rhodian ships. The superior experience of the Rhodians, and their use of fire-ships, were critical factors.

▪ MAGNESIA, 190 BCE

With the Roman army on the offensive and keen to seek a decisive battle before winter set in, Antiochus set up a fortified camp and awaited their arrival. The Roman formation was conventional, in three lines with the Roman legions in the centre and allied forces holding the flanks. The Roman force had some war elephants but these were African beasts, outmatched by the Indian elephants of the Seleucid force in both numbers and physical power.

The Seleucid cavalry broke its opposite numbers on the Roman left flank, but pursued them rather than turning on the Roman centre. The Seleucid left flank was broken soon afterwards. In the centre, the two infantry forces were evenly matched until a force of elephants mixed into the Seleucid formation were routed and the pike-armed infantry became disordered. The Seleucid force was then driven from the field.

▪ WADI HARAMIA, 167 BCE

Rising in revolt against Seleucid rule, Jewish forces under Judas Maccabeus established themselves in the mountains near Samaria, from where a force was sent against them. This was ambushed and overwhelmingly defeated.

▪ BETH HORON, 166 BCE

A Seleucid force under the command of the general Seron was sent to locate and destroy the Maccabean rebels. This force was surprised at the Pass of Beth Horon and resoundingly defeated.

▪ EMMAUS, 166 BCE

While Seleucid troops were in the field searching for his camp, Judas Maccabeus led an audacious attack against the Seleucids' base at Emmaus. His force then harassed the Seleucids during their subsequent retreat.

▪ BETH ZUR, 164 BCE

Facing a Seleucid army under Lysias, governor of Syria, the Maccabean forces resorted to guerrilla tactics to wear down the enemy. Once the Seleucids were weakened, they were attacked and defeated at Beth Zur.

▪ BETH ZACHARIAH, 162 BCE

After capturing and ritually cleansing the temple at Jerusalem, the Maccabees were faced with a new army under Lysias. The Jews attempted to fight a set-piece field battle and were defeated by the better-equipped Seleucids.

▪ ADASA, 161 BCE

The newly appointed governor of Judah, Nicanor, led a renewed attempt to crush the Maccabean revolt. Encountering the Jews at Adasa, near Beth-Horon, the Seleucids attacked but were defeated. This bought the revolt a brief respite.

▪ ELASA, 160 BCE

Facing a vastly larger Seleucid force, Judas Maccabeus launched an attack against the bodyguard of their commander, routing it. His force was then overwhelmed by the remainder of the Seleucid army, and Judas was killed.

▪ ANTIOCH, 145 BCE

The diminished Seleucid kingdom in Syria was attacked by forces backed by the Ptolemaic dynasty in Egypt. The Seleucids were defeated, though Pharaoh Ptolemy VI was killed in the fighting.

■ **ECBATANA, 129 BCE**

Antiochus VII led a campaign into Parthia to revive the fortunes of the declining Seleucid Empire. His force was overwhelmingly defeated at Ecbatana, bringing Seleucid ambitions in Parthia to an end.

Punic Wars 264–146 BCE

First Punic War 264–241 BCE

■ **MESSINA, 264 BCE**

In the hope of avoiding conquest by Syracuse, the city of Messina asked for aid from both Carthage and Rome. The result was a siege by Carthage, which was broken by the arrival of a Roman army.

■ **AGRIGENTUM, 261 BCE**

In order to prevent Carthage from using Agrigentum as a base of operations on Sicily, a Roman army was sent to capture it. This required a lengthy siege, allowing the Carthaginians to launch a relief expedition. This force established

itself across the Roman supply line, effectively besieging the besiegers. After a long period of skirmishing the Romans were able to inflict a decisive defeat on their opponents, before finally forcing Agrigentum to surrender.

■ **LIPARAEAN ISLANDS, 257 BCE**

Attempting to take advantage of an offer by the city of Lipara to join their side, the Romans sent a small fleet there. It was ambushed by a far more experienced force and utterly defeated.

■ **MYLAE, 260 BCE**

War with Carthage forced Rome to confront its enemy at sea, and early encounters with the more experienced Carthaginian fleet did not go well. As a partial counter, Roman ships were fitted with a boarding ramp known as a *corvus*. This was intended to play to Roman strengths by allowing their legionaries to act as marine infantry.

The Roman and Carthaginian fleets met in the Tyrrhenian sea off the north coast of Sicily, near Mylae. The Carthaginians were eager to fight and

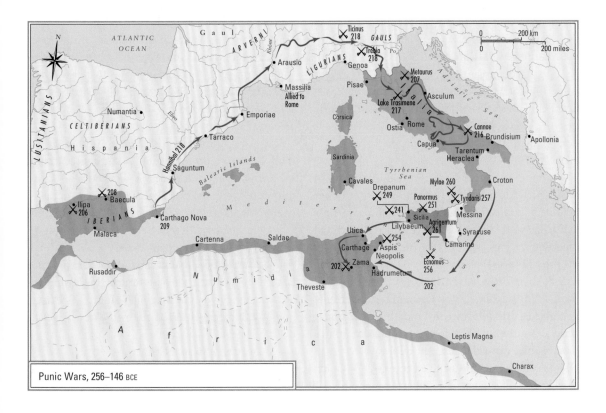

Punic Wars, 256–146 BCE

expectant of victory, but the Roman tactic of using the *corvus* to force boarding actions came as a surprise and many ships were captured.

Although the Carthaginians tried quickly to adapt their tactics, the Romans had gained a decisive advantage, forcing their opponents to retreat with heavy losses. Rather than seek a further naval action the Roman force then landed troops in Sicily.

■ SULCI, 258 BCE

Sea power was essential to the control of Sicily, and naval skirmishing was common throughout the First Punic War. The Romans gained naval experience in these clashes and won a small victory off Sardinia in 258 BCE.

■ TYNDARIS, 257 BCE

Roman naval forces, observing the Carthaginian naval base at Tyndaris, became aware of a hostile fleet which appeared to be in a vulnerable disordered state. The Roman fleet attacked, but itself became disordered with the leading ships too far ahead of the main body. These ships were roughly handled by the Carthaginians, who were then driven off with heavy losses by the arrival of the main Roman fleet.

■ CAPE ECNOMUS, 256 BCE

A large Carthaginian fleet, attempting to prevent an invasion of Africa, attacked the Roman transport fleet. Roman naval tactics had improved sufficiently that the attack was driven off with heavy losses, despite initial Carthaginian successes.

■ ADYS, 255 BCE

Attempting to oppose the Roman invasion of North Africa, a somewhat disorganized force under Hamilcar was resoundingly defeated near Adys. Carthage sued for peace, but ultimately rejected the offered terms as they were exceedingly harsh.

■ TUNIS (TUNES), 255 BCE

The Roman army, advancing on Carthage, made camp at Tunis where it was attacked by a hurriedly assembled Carthaginian army under the mercenary general Xanthippus. This force was a mix of militia, mercenaries, war elephants and elite cavalry.

The Roman legions struggled to resist the attack of the war elephants. Those that were able to

Cape Ecnomus, 256 BCE

engage the Carthaginian infantry at all did so in a piecemeal fashion and were driven off, although some Roman troops did manage to defeat their opposite numbers. These were able to fight their way clear of the disaster that followed and were able to reach the coast.

The Carthaginian cavalry hugely outnumbered their Roman opponents and soon routed them, after which they fell on the flanks and rear of the disordered legions. The Roman force was quickly overwhelmed, ending any chance of defeating Carthage in Africa.

■ LILYBAEUM, 251 BCE

After a series of setbacks, including the loss of a large fleet to storms, Rome returned to a strategy of wearing down Carthaginian strength. A naval raid on Lilybaeum, carried out by the newly rebuilt fleet, was beaten off.

■ PANORMUS, 251 BCE

After a long period of skirmishing on Sicily, a Carthaginian army under Hasdrubal launched an attack on a Roman force in the vicinity of Panormus. The Romans initially responded by retiring into the city, which permitted Hasdrubal to operate freely. His force foraged and ravaged the surrounding region before finally marching on the city itself.

The advance was led by war elephants, which came under attack from javelin men concealed outside the city and on top of the walls. Many wounded beasts ran amok, disordering the main Carthaginian body. This facilitated an assault by the main Roman force, which sallied out of the city to rout the enemy infantry.

Carthage abandoned any hope of gaining control of Sicily after this defeat, though skirmishing continued for some time. Hasdrubal was recalled to Carthage and executed, while the elephants captured by the Romans met the same fate at a public spectacle in Rome.

■ **DREPANUM (TRAPANI), 249 BCE**
The Roman siege of Lilybaeum was repeatedly broken by naval forces based in Drepanum, which outmanoeuvred the Roman fleet to carry supplies into the besieged city. This was not only a setback in the siege operations, but also an affront to the prestige of Rome. As a result, it was decided to remove the Carthaginians from Drepanum.

The plan was for a surprise attack, but the Roman fleet became disordered, giving the Carthaginians a chance to launch their ships. While the Romans were forming up their vessels, omens were sought. They were not good; the sacred chickens, whose feeding provided the omens, would not eat anything. The Roman commander, Publius Claudius Pulcher, threw them overboard and launched his attack anyway.

Outmanoeuvred by the Carthaginians, the Roman fleet was caught between the coast of Sicily and the Carthaginian ships. The two forces were roughly equal in size but the advantages of position and superior seamanship were with the Carthaginians. The Roman force was quickly driven onto the defensive and, unable to manoeuvre freely, was largely destroyed.

Some ships did manage to fight their way clear of the melee and flee, including the flagship. Publius Claudius Pulcher was recalled to Rome where he was charged with sacrilege for his actions towards the sacred chickens. The battle was followed by a further disaster, in which the remainder of the Roman fleet suffered huge losses in a storm.

Rome did not challenge Carthage at sea for some years thereafter, though the land campaign continued. Supplies and reinforcements were run across the Straits of Messina, preventing Carthage from using this opportunity to rebuild their strength on the island.

■ **AEGATES ISLANDS, 241 BCE**
A Carthaginian fleet sent to relieve the blockaded city of Lilybaeum was intercepted off the Aegates Islands. The inexperienced Carthaginian fleet was outmanoeuvred by the Romans and driven off, ultimately resulting in the fall of Lilybaeum.

Mercenary War c.240 BCE
■ **BAGRADAS RIVER, 239 BCE**
Marching to retake Utica from rebellious mercenaries, the Carthaginian army encountered a large but disorganized hostile force. Carthaginian commander Hannibal was able to outmanoeuvre his opponents and break through to the city.

■ **THE SAW, 239 BCE**
Hannibal was able to drive the main mercenary army into a canyon known as 'The Saw' where he laid siege. Eventually the starving mercenaries were forced to launch a hopeless attack on the Carthaginian positions.

■ **UTICA, 238 BCE**
Most cities that had rebelled during the Mercenary War surrendered, but Utica remained defiant and was besieged. Despite counter-attacks, the siege was eventually successful and the fall of the city brought the Mercenary War to a close.

Second Punic War 219–202 BC
■ **SAGUNTUM, 219–218 BCE**
Carthaginian ambitions in Iberia required that the heavily fortified city of Saguntum be captured. This

required a lengthy siege, giving time for assistance to arrive from Rome, with whom Saguntum had a treaty. However, the Romans were occupied with dealing with a revolt in Illyria and did not send assistance in time.

Over the course of several months, Carthaginian forces under the command of Hannibal Barca gradually reduced the defences and finally broke into the city. This gave Hannibal a secure port through which he could supply his army for a campaign to expand Carthaginian power in Iberia.

By taking Saguntum, Hannibal brought Carthage into direct conflict with Rome. Previous treaties limited Carthaginian expansion in the region, and attacking a Roman ally was a provocation that could not be ignored. Despite attempts at a diplomatic resolution, the Second Punic War was thus begun.

■ CISSA, 218 BCE

Roman forces arrived in Iberia after Hannibal had left, and were engaged in a set-piece battle by an outnumbered Carthaginian army. The Romans emerged victorious, in this, their first battle in Iberia, and succeeded in capturing the enemy camp.

■ RHONE CROSSING, 218 BCE

With hostile Gauls holding the Rhone crossings against him, Hannibal sent a force on a wide flank march across the river. With the Gauls' attention fixed on Hannibal's main force, they were struck in the rear and routed.

■ TICINUS RIVER, 218 BCE

Since a maritime strategy had failed in the First Punic War, Hannibal's strategy was to march overland against Rome, through southern Gaul and northern Italy. He hoped to recruit the tribes of that region, many of whom had no love for Rome, to his cause.

Rome used the time that Hannibal spent on the march to raise and train an expanded army and navy. Some of these forces were sent to Sicily to guard against renewed Carthaginian attempts to control the island. Attempts to rally the Gallic tribes against Hannibal failed, largely due to the fact that

Rome had recently allowed Saguntum to be taken without sending the aid required by treaty.

Some tribes did oppose the Carthaginian march, but by and large the Roman response was ineffective in preventing Hannibal's army from entering Italy. Once on Italian soil, he forced an alliance on the tribes of the region, many of whom were in a state of revolt against Rome.

The sudden appearance of Hannibal's army in Italy caused the Romans hurriedly to send an army against him, resulting in an encounter between the reconnaissance forces of both sides. The Roman force included some light foot troops; the Carthaginian detachment was entirely of cavalry.

The Carthaginian cavalry scattered the Roman light infantry, causing them to flee and disorder the cavalry behind. The ensuing melee was won by the Carthaginians, who came close to capturing the consul Publius Cornelius Scipio the Elder. He was rescued by a force of cavalry commanded by his son, the future Scipio Africanus.

The Roman reconnaissance was in some ways a success despite this defeat; having learned of the disposition of Hannibal's army the Roman force retired to await reinforcements.

■ TREBIA RIVER, 218 BCE

Hannibal's defeat of a Roman army at the Ticinus river drew additional forces to his banner, from tribes who wished to be free of the control of Rome. The Romans, for their part, were reinforced by the arrival of an army under Tiberius Sempronius Longus. As Scipio was wounded, Sempronius took command of the overall force.

A detachment from Sempronius' army was able to drive a Carthaginian foraging expedition back to their camp, which convinced Sempronius that he had the measure of this opponent. Hannibal, however, realized that Sempronius was predisposed to be rash and laid a trap. To draw his enemies into it, he sent Numidian cavalry to make a dawn attack on the Roman camp. Sempronius took the bait and pursued the Numidans across the River Trebia, where Hannibal's main force awaited him.

The Roman troops were forced to wade through cold water up to their chests. They emerged tired and chilled, and in no condition to fight.

Rather than engage the Romans when they were in the river, Hannibal chose to allow them to gain the bank, slightly reducing the odds of victory in return for greater results if the Romans were broken with their backs to the water. The Roman light infantry were first to engage but were ineffective because of the cold. They were soon driven off.

The heavily outnumbered Roman cavalry were defeated on the flanks, but despite being chilled and disordered by their river crossing the infantry were able to advance some distance from the riverbank. At this point, Carthaginian forces concealed by the river launched an attack from ambush. They were joined by cavalry from the flanks.

The rear elements of the Roman formation were first to break, with many men trying to cross the river to safety while under attack. The lead elements, composed of better-trained troops, remained effective and formed a square formation to defend themselves, as supporting units scattered around them. This force was able to continue to advance, while Hannibal's troops concentrated on the rout by the river.

The broken Roman and allied units were massacred as they tried to reform or escape across the river, and allied Gallic infantry who had not been able to join the square formation also suffered very heavy casualties. Among the troops by the river, the battle had become a massacre, and Sempronius wisely chose not to try to fight his way back to help comrades who were already comprehensively defeated. Instead, Sempronius' force beat off all attacks on it and was able to retire to Placentia.

Losses on the Roman side were enormous – about half the force committed, or around 15,000-20,000 men. This left Rome without an effective field army to oppose Hannibal's advance. However, the cold weather made further Carthaginian operations difficult for a time, other than some skirmishing.

Hannibal's losses at the Trebia were small, and fell mainly on allied Gallic tribesmen rather than native Carthaginians. The majority of the remaining elephants were killed in the battle, or died during the cold weather that followed, but Hannibal's strategic position was strong and he had reason to hope that he might be able to trigger a revolt among Rome's allies and subjects. To that end he released many of the prisoners he had taken, allowing them to return home in the hope of building goodwill in their cities.

◼ LILYBAEUM, 218 BCE

Mischance and bad weather caused a group of Carthaginian ships to be captured by the navy of Syracuse, whose ruler passed on information gained from their crews. Thus forewarned of a raid against the Sicilian coast, the Roman fleet was able to position itself to intercept.

Although numerically inferior, the Roman force was operating closer to its home ports.

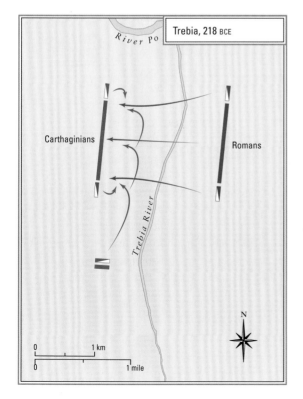

Trebia, 218 BCE

River Po

Carthaginians

Romans

Trebia River

N

0   1 km

0   1 mile

This permitted the ships to be fully manned with legionaries acting as marines, whereas the Carthaginians were forced to carry supplies in the place of additional fighting men.

Both sides played to their strengths, with the Carthaginians attempting to ram and the Romans preferring to grapple and board. Roman seamanship had improved since the First Punic War, and they were able to bring their superior manpower to bear in a series of boarding actions. Several Carthaginian ships were taken and the rest driven off.

■ LAKE TRASIMENE, 217 BCE

Faced with a successful Carthaginian invasion now firmly established on Italian soil, the Roman position was perilous. Hannibal's army began marching south, bypassing the Roman force under Gaius Flaminius. Flaminius was forced to hurry south, trying to get between Hannibal and Rome. This gave Hannibal the chance to defeat his force before it could be reinforced by a consular army under Servilius.

Hannibal decided to draw the Romans into an ambush by ravaging the countryside and offering provocations. At the same time, he tried to lure Flaminius into complacency by deception. A detachment of troops lit fires in the distance, making Flaminius think he was safe. The Romans thus took to the road without proper scouts, hoping to catch up with Hannibal's army by a rapid march.

Hannibal positioned part of his force in a blocking position on the Malpasso road where it ran close to Lake Trasimene. The remainder of the troops were concealed on the hills that loomed above the road. With no scouts out, the lead elements of the Roman army had no warning of the enemy to their front.

As the head of their column came under attack and struggled to deploy into battle formation, the Romans were also assailed from the flank positions, initially by light missile troops stationed on the high ground. Another force of Hannibal's infantry attacked the rear of the Roman column, cutting off the line of retreat. Essentially, the Romans were now trapped. The main Carthaginian force then charged down the slope to take the disorganized Romans in the flank.

The Roman force was broken into sections. The vanguard managed to fight its way out of the trap, but the rear segment was driven into the lake. The central part of the column defended itself for a time with complete desperation, but was eventually overwhelmed.

■ EBRO RIVER, 217 BCE

A Carthaginian fleet arrived at the mouth of the Ebro and sent personnel ashore to forage. It was surprised there by a Roman force. Many Carthaginian ships were beached when it became apparent that the battle was lost.

■ AGER FALERNUS, 217 BCE

Hannibal's army became trapped in the valley of Ager Falernus, with Roman garrisons on the exit passes. Drawing one out by deception, Hannibal inflicted a sharp defeat and broke out of the trap.

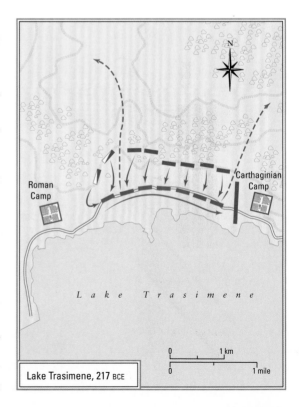

Lake Trasimene, 217 BCE

■ GERONIUM, 217 BCE

Wearying of the cautious strategy of the dictator Fabius Maximus, the Roman senate gave his second in command, Marcus Minucius Rufus, half the army. Hannibal was able to draw Minucius into a trap. Fabius, known for his cautious strategy of avoiding decisive battle, intervened to restore the situation. As Minucius' troops rallied and the whole Roman army prepared for a continued battle, Hannibal chose to break off and withdraw.

■ CANNAE, 216 BCE

Fabius Maximus' strategy of avoiding defeat became increasingly unpopular as Hannibal's Carthaginian army ravaged the countryside. Many Roman politicians had holdings in the affected regions. They were suffering financial losses and were not willing to wait for Hannibal's army to be worn down by campaigning in the field.

In 216, under pressure to achieve a decisive result, consuls Paullus and Varro were elected to command the Roman army. The arrangement was that each consul would be in overall command on alternate days. At the head of a body of reinforcements, they joined the army in close proximity to that of Hannibal.

Skirmishing had been ongoing for some time when Paullus and Varro arrived, and the cautious Paullus was content with small victories that would slowly bleed the Carthaginian army's strength. Not so Varro, who believed that he could defeat Hannibal in a decisive battle where others had failed so completely.

Aware of Varro's hot-headedness, Hannibal laid a trap for the Romans near the village of Cannae, offering battle on a somewhat restricted frontage. Woods and a river limited the Romans' freedom to manoeuvre, and the Carthaginians were deployed on higher ground than their Roman opponents. This positioning somewhat offset the numerical advantage of the Roman army.

The two Roman consuls held differing opinions about whether or not to attack. Paullus chose caution, but on Varro's day in command he resolved to fight. The Roman army advanced in its customary formation, with the heavy infantry in the centre and the flanks held by cavalry. The force was screened by skirmishers.

Hannibal's force also deployed behind a screen of skirmishers, with a line of mercenary infantry behind them to absorb the initial Roman assault. On the ends of this line were the Carthaginian infantry. Gallic and Spanish cavalry were deployed on the left flank, with Numidian horsemen on the right.

Hannibal's deployment of his infantry was designed to spare his own Carthaginian troops from the initial Roman charge. It also made economic sense, as dead mercenaries need not be paid. The line was bowed out towards the Roman force.

The battle began with a general clash between the skirmishers on both sides. Ideally, their role was to harass the main body of the enemy, inflicting casualties and disrupting its formation, but as usual the result was that the skirmishers fought their own inconclusive battle among themselves and

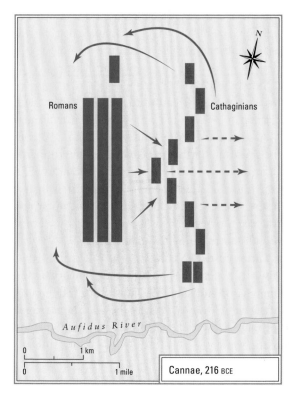

Cannae, 216 BCE

then fell back. Hannibal's left-flank cavalry was more successful, however, driving off its opposite numbers. The Roman cavalry were outmatched in terms of numbers, equipment and training, and were soon driven from the field. The Gallic and Spanish cavalry, some of whom had fought dismounted, remained under the control of their commanders and rallied, ready to launch another attack. Meanwhile, the Roman infantry drove forward confidently. The mercenary troops facing it were driven back, with the line now bowing back instead of forward. However, this forced the Roman infantry ever closer together as they penetrated the enemy formation, and Hannibal's Carthaginian infantry began to lap around the flanks.

As the Roman infantry advance ground to a halt, the Roman left-flank cavalry were attacked from the right by the Numidians. The Gallic/Spanish cavalry force fell on their rear and broke them, with the Numidians pursuing them from the field. The Roman infantry, now tightly packed together and surrounded on three sides, were attacked by cavalry in the rear and massacred. Those that escaped were vigorously pursued, with Paullus killed in a rearguard action, one of more than 50,000 Romans who died that day.

■ **NOLA, 216–214 BCE**

After the disaster at Cannae, Rome recalled the veteran commander Marcus Claudius Marcellus to its defence. He was given the remnant of the army shattered at Cannae to augment his own troops. Sending a detachment to protect Rome itself, Marcellus took his force into Campania where he was able to prevent an attempt by Hannibal to capture the city. This action did much to dispel the atmosphere of despondency in Rome; it established that Hannibal could in fact be defeated.

Hannibal attempted to capture the city again in 215 and a third time in 214 BCE, but was prevented from doing so each time. Whereas Rome could replace its losses, Hannibal's army was on foreign soil and supporting itself by foraging. Each failure to win a decisive battle was a step closer to defeat.

■ **DERTOSA, 215 BCE**

The Carthaginian commander in Iberia, Hasdrubal, hoped to draw in the Roman army and perform a double envelopment of the sort that was so successful at Cannae. However, the Roman cavalry wings were not broken and the legionaries in the centre were able to break the Carthaginian line. As a result of this defeat, forces intended to assist Hannibal in Italia had to be redirected to Iberia in order to shore up a worsening position there.

■ **CORNUS, 215 BCE**

A revolt against Roman rule in Sardinia prompted Carthage to send assistance, which was delayed by storms. After arriving, the Carthaginian forces became involved in a lengthy standoff with Roman troops, who had been reinforced. Both sides sought a decisive battle, which was won by the Romans. Some surviving Carthaginian troops were taken off by their fleet, which was then intercepted and defeated by a Roman naval force.

■ **BENEVENTUM, 214 BCE**

A Roman army, comprised mainly of slaves who had been offered their freedom in return for fighting, intercepted a Carthaginian detachment near Beneventum. The battle was notable for its ferocity rather than any tactical brilliance.

■ **SYRACUSE, 214–212 BCE**

Syracuse, long friendly to Rome, sided with Carthage in 214 BCE. A Roman army under Marcus Claudius Marcellus was sent to deal with the situation. Unable to take the city by storm, the Romans were forced to resort to a long siege in which the defenders benefited from the assistance of the Greek scientist Archimedes. The outer city was taken by a surprise assault, but it was several months more before the citadel fell.

■ **TARENTUM, 212 BCE**

A surprise night attack caught the Roman garrison unprepared and allowed Hannibal to take control of the city. However, some of the garrison managed to reach the citadel, which they held until the end of the war.

■ **CAPUA, 212 BCE**

Hannibal's successes, notably at Cannae, caused

Carthaginian Campaigns Against Rome, c.200 BCE

N

207 BCE: Hasdrubal invades Italy, intending to join Hannibal but is defeated at Metaurus

Aquileia

Trebia
December 218 BCE

Patavia

Ticinus
November 218 BCE

Placentia

204 BCE: Mago lands in Liguria but is defeated and returns to Carthage in 203

Hannibal's winter quarters 218–217

L i g u r i a n   S e a

Pisae

Florence

Metaurus
207 BCE

Ariminum

A d r i a t i c

Volaterrae

Arretium

Ancona

C o r s i c a

Aleria

E t r u r i a

Trasimene
April 217 BCE

Perusia

Sentinum

Cosa

Aurinia

Volsinii

Asculum

Hadria

Gerunium 217 BCE and Hannibal's winter quarters 217–216 BCE

Falerii

Volci

Caere

Ostia

Rome

Alba Fucens

S

L a t i u m

Praeneste

Beneventum
214–212 BCE

203 BCE: Mago and 5000 troops return to Carthage but Mago dies of his wounds en route

Tarracina

Capua
212 BCE

Nola
216 BCE
215 BCE
214 BCE

Asculum
208 BCE

Cannae
Aug. 216 BCE

Barium

Awaiting news from Hasdrubal in N. Italy

Brundisium

S a r d i n i a

Olbia

Sulcis

Grumentum
207 BCE

Tarentum
212–209 BCE

S i n u s   T a r e n t i n u s

T y r r h e n i a n

S e a

Thurii

209 BCE

Croton

204 BCE: Scipio launches invasion of Africa

215, 210 BCE

Rhegium

Panormus

Locri

203 BCE: Hannibal and 1800 troops sail for Africa to defend Carthage

Lilybaeum

212, 210 BCE

S i c i l i a

Syracuse
214–212 BCE

Great Plains
203 BCE

Utica

Carthage

0   50 km

0   50 miles

A f r i c a

Zama
202 BCE

Hadrentum

M e d i t e r r a n e a n   S e a

a number of cities to defect to his cause. Among them was Capua, and in 212 BCE a Roman army laid siege to the city. Hannibal sent a force to break the siege, which at first conducted raids against the Romans. When these raids failed to achieve a result, Hannibal offered battle. The ensuing action was bloody but inconclusive, leaving the strategic situation more or less unchanged.

BENEVENTUM, 212 BCE

Although forced to retire from Capua, Roman forces under Quintus Fulvius Flaccus were able to defeat a Carthaginian army near Beneventum and capture their camp before returning to besiege Capua once more.

SILARUS, 212 BCE

A Roman force under the command of the inexperienced Marcus Centenius Penula was ambushed by Hannibal's army, which for once enjoyed superiority of numbers. The Roman force was all but annihilated.

HERDONEA, 212 BCE

Hannibal lured the complacent Roman commander Gnaeus Fulvius Flaccus into a trap. With the Roman line of retreat blocked and attacked by ambush from the flanks as well as the front, Roman resistance collapsed.

UPPER BAETIS, 211 BCE

Reinforced with additional troops, Hasdrubal Barca went on the offensive in Iberia. In a series of connected actions he defeated the Roman army under the Scipio brothers, killing both. The surviving Roman force was pushed northwards.

HERDONEA, 210 BCE

Hannibal marched against a Roman force besieging the city of Herdonia, which had rebelled in his favour. The Roman force was surrounded and was all but annihilated in what would be Hannibal's last great victory.

NUMISTRO, 210 BCE

Although he had broken the siege of Herdonea, Hannibal did not attempt to hold it but retired in the face of a second Roman army under Marcus Claudius Marcellus. This resulted in an inconclusive clash at Numistro.

CARTAGENA, 209 BCE

Roman forces first implemented a sea and land blockade of the city, which was accessible by land only over a narrow isthmus. After containing a counter-attack by the Carthaginian defenders an initial, and unsuccessful, assault was launched. A second attempt was then made using much the same tactics. The Roman fleet attacked the south side of the city while a land assault was made from the north, dividing the defenders.

NEW CARTHAGE, 209 BCE

First isolating the city by establishing himself on the isthmus connecting it to the mainland, Scipio Africanus assaulted overland from the north while his fleet attacked from the south. New Carthage was taken after repeated assaults.

TARENTUM, 209 BCE

A Roman army under Quintus Fabius Maximus defeated a similarly sized Carthaginian force to retake Tarentum, which had previously thrown in its lot with Carthage. Hannibal gradually began to lose his hold on southern Italia.

ASCULUM, 208 BCE

Although now heavily outnumbered, and with his Italian allies turning against him, Hannibal continued to present a severe threat to Rome. Consul Marcus Claudius Marcellus, the 'Sword of Rome', was killed in a skirmish with the Carthaginian forces.

BAECULA, 208 BCE

Scipio Africanus deviated from standard Roman doctrine to outmanoeuvre a Carthaginian army deployed in a strong position. The Carthaginians were forced to sacrifice their light troops in order to preserve the core of their army.

GRUMENTUM, 207 BCE

Apparently offering a traditional set-piece battle, the Romans were able to conceal a detachment to the enemy rear. As the fighting intensified, this force assaulted the Carthaginian rear and provoked a disordered retreat.

METAURUS, 207 BCE

Attempting to reinforce Hannibal's army in Italy, his brother Hasdrubal marched from Iberia through

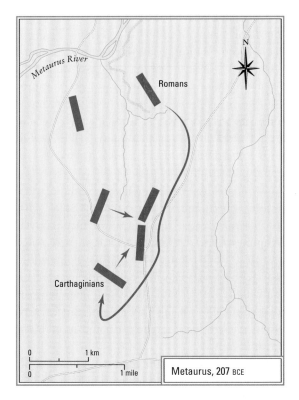

Metaurus, 207 BCE

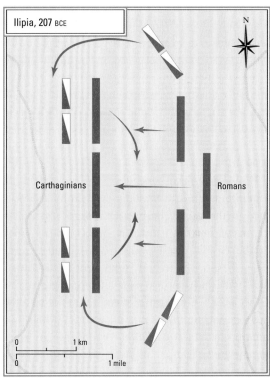

Ilipia, 207 BCE

southern Gaul. He was intercepted in northern Italy near the River Metaurus by a Roman army under Livius and Nero. The forces engaged were roughly equal, at around 50,000 on each side.

Roman generals had begun emulating Hannibal's tactics rather than simply launching the traditional frontal assault, and their fortunes improved correspondingly. At the Metaurus, the Roman commanders used dead ground to cover a flank march. This flanking attack caused the Carthaginian right wing to collapse. In the centre, the line was badly disordered by their own panicked war elephants running amok, and began to dissolve into rout upon seeing the Romans overrunning the right. Hasdrubal decided that all was lost and sought an honourable death by charging into the Roman line.

■ ILIPA (SILIPA), 207 BCE

Using a refused centre and reinforced wings, Scipio Africanus caught the Carthaginian army in a double envelopment, breaking the flanks

and then falling on the centre. Only a sudden rainstorm prevented the total destruction of the Carthaginian army.

■ CROTONE, 204 BCE

In 204 BCE a Roman force approaching the port of Crotone was defeated in an unplanned encounter battle, escaping disaster only by taking refuge in its camp. Inconclusive fighting in the area continued into the next year.

■ UTICA, 203 BCE

Scipio Africanus' army, forced to lift its siege of Utica, took refuge in a fortified camp. The two armies facing Scipio did likewise, creating a standoff. This was broken by a surprise Roman attack combined with the burning of the Carthaginian camps.

■ BAGBRADES, 203 BCE

A vigorous Roman charge quickly broke most of the Carthaginian army, leaving only its Spanish mercenary contingent on the field. This force was flanked by the second and third Roman lines, with few mercenaries escaping.

■ CIRTA, 203 BCE

The Numidian king Syphax, ally of Carthage, assembled a new force to oppose Scipio after the defeat at Bagbrades. He attempted to copy Roman tactics, but his newly raised force was not up to the task before it. After a hard fight, Syphax' army began to collapse and he was captured while trying to rally his troops. Carthage responded to the defeat at Cirta by recalling Hannibal from Italy.

■ PO VALLEY RAID, 203 BCE

Operating in north-western Italy from 205 BCE, the Carthaginian commander Mago succeeded in triggering insurrections among the tribes of the region. These added to his strength and alarmed Roman leaders, who sent an army to deal with him in 203 BCE. The battle did not go well for Rome at first, but the intervention of the second-line troops, as well as a serious wound suffered by Mago, caused the Carthaginian force to collapse in rout.

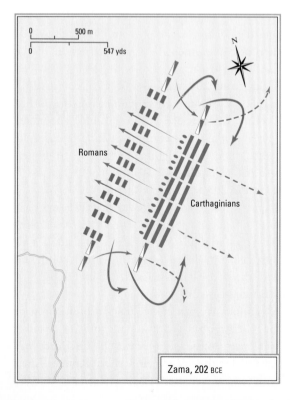

Zama, 202 BCE

■ ZAMA, 202 BCE

Recalled from Italy to defend Carthage itself from Rome, Hannibal Barca brought with him around 18,000 veteran troops. To augment these forces, Carthage raised around 30,000 more. However, most were little more than militia or were foreign mercenaries. The Carthaginian cavalry, once a formidable elite force, had suffered severe losses and was greatly diminished.

The opposing armies deployed with infantry in the centre and cavalry on the flanks, with the Carthaginians deploying war elephants in advance of their infantry. The Roman cavalry saw off its opponents after a brisk fight, while the elephant attack was dealt with by herding the beasts into gaps between the Roman formations. These gaps contained light infantry who killed those elephants that did not simply pass through.

The Roman cavalry pursued its opponents off the field, rather than rallying to attack the enemy infantry in the rear. This left the course of the battle down to the respective infantry forces, both of which were deployed in three lines.

The Carthaginian front line, composed largely of mercenaries, initially held the Roman advance. Superior training and discipline eventually allowed the Romans to push the mercenaries back, and the Carthaginian second line was easily overcome. The third line was composed of Hannibal's veterans, and these were a match for the Romans.

Both commanders ordered reserves onto the flanks, extending their lines in the hope of outflanking their opponents. The infantry fight went on for some time before the returning Roman cavalry launched an attack into the Carthaginian rear. Hannibal and what remained of his army retired into Carthage, which surrendered soon afterward. This brought about the end of the Second Punic War with a treaty sufficiently harsh as to ensure that the power of Carthage was broken forever.

Third Punic War 149–146 BCE

■ **CARTHAGE, 149–146 BCE**

Although Carthage was no longer a threat to Rome, many Roman leaders argued for its total destruction. Carthage attempted to appease Rome, but was forced into refusing when Roman demands became unacceptable. Roman attempts to storm the city failed, and a formal siege was implemented. The Carthaginians made a spirited active defence, raiding the Roman camps and even their fleet, but after a long siege the city was finally assaulted.

Rome vs Gauls/Celts 250–133 BCE

■ **FAESULAE, 225 BCE**

Faesulae was an Etrurian city in northern Italy, along Hannibal's invasion route, near which his allied Gauls invading across the Alps separately ambushed a smaller Roman army, inflicting 6000 casualties before the Romans withdrew.

■ **TELAMON, 225 BCE**

The consul Gaius Atilius Regulus, landing from Sardinia, intercepted the further advance of the Gauls in Telamon as they moved southward into Italy, while the army of the other consul, Lucius Aemilius Papus, pursued them from the north. Atilius' cavalry fought a sharp action with the Gauls' horse, in which Atilius fell. Papus noted the position of the action and hastened his own advance, his cavalry joining the earlier melee and prevailing. By the end of the cavalry action the infantry on both sides were engaged, the Gauls in a double formation. The heavy javelins, armour, and shields of the legionaries proved superior to the shock caused by the terrifying onset of the traditionally naked Gallic infantry, the result being the collapse of the invasion with 40,000 Gauls slain and their king Concolitanus captured.

■ **CLASTIDIUM, 222 BCE**

This Roman outpost in Cisalpine Gaul was relieved when the consul Marcus Claudius Marcellus led a cavalry charge against the besieging Insubrian Gauls. By slaying the chieftain Viridomarus, Marcellus won Rome's highest military honour, the Spolia Opima.

■ **MUTINA, 218 BCE**

The fortified Roman outpost in Cisalpine Gaul was attacked by the Boian Gauls, who were in revolt in anticipation of Hannibal's invasion of Italy. A relieving Roman army retreated after an ambush to nearby Tanetum. Mutina apparently survived the siege.

■ **CREMONA, 200 BCE**

The Gauls launched a dawn attack around the Roman fort at Cremona upon a relieving Roman army under Lucius Furius. Furius shifted reserves behind his outnumbered army to win decisively.

■ **MOUNT OLYMPUS, 189 BCE**

A Gallic mountain tribe, the Tolostobogii, moved into Roman-occupied Greece along the range that included this peak. The Gauls camped above collapsed under sustained missile attacks by Roman and allied forces under the consul Manlius.

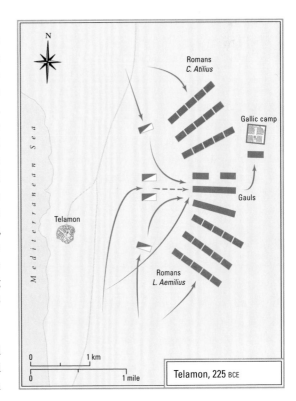

Telamon, 225 BCE

■ SIEGE OF NUMANTIA, 134–133 BCE

This powerful Celtic city had resisted six Roman efforts to reduce it before the final epic siege by Scipio Aemilianus and his Mauritanian allies. Aemilianus pragmatically resorted to circumvallation, surrounding the town and its 4000 inhabitants with a wall extending 9km supported by 13 legionary camps. After resisting for eight months, the bulk of the Numantians chose to fire their city and commit suicide rather than surrender to the Romans.

Cleomenean War
227–222 BCE

■ ELIS, 227 BCE

This strategic city in the northern Peloponnese was besieged by Aratus, commanding the Achaean League's forces. Cleomenes, one of the Spartan kings, surprised and drove off the Achaeans with a force of 5000 Spartans and loyal mercenaries.

■ LADOCEIA, 227 BCE

Cleomenes, withdrawing before an Achaean League force relieving Megalopolis, won an unexpected victory in pitched battle. Aratus had countermanded an engagement, but a subordinate crossing a ravine after a skirmish suffered defeat in detail.

■ DYME, 226 BCE

City of the Achaean League, before which Hyperbatos, having replaced Aratus as the Achean League's commander, engaged Cleomenes and the Spartans. Cleomenes' challenge drew out the Achaean phalanx, which the Spartans destroyed, inflicting severe losses.

■ LECHAEUM, 226 BCE

Outlaying port-suburb of Corinth, beyond which Cleomenes had driven the Achaean League, having taken or received in alliance nearly all the cities of the Peloponnese. The Macedonians' intervention under Antigonus Dosun forced Cleomenes' retreat southward.

■ TEGEA, 223 BCE

Town in Arcadia on the Spartan frontier, garrisoned and defended by Cleomenes against the advancing Macedonian army under Antigonus Dosun. Cleomenes returned suddenly to Sparta, and the Macedonians quickly took the town in his absence.

■ SELLASIA, 222 BCE

Valley battle in which Cleomenes fought the combined forces of Antigonus Dosun of Macedon and Philopoemen and the Achaean League. The Acheans dislodged the Spartan centre; Cleomenes expended his own troops against the Macedonian phalanx.

Chinese Chu-Han War
207–202 BCE

■ JULU, 207 BCE

The Qin Dynasty succeeded in unifying China but did not outlast its first emperor for long. Within months of his death in 210 BCE, unrest had become open revolt. Qin forces attempted to suppress the insurrection, with mixed success.

In 207 BCE, a Qin army laid siege to the city of Julu, which belonged to the state of Zhao. This prompted the state of Chu to send a relief force to the city. The Chu strategy was at first a cautious one, waiting for the Zhao defenders of Julu to wear down the Qin forces.

With the defenders of Julu beginning to starve, the Chu were forced to attack. After crossing the Yellow River, the army was ordered to destroy its boats and most of the available supplies in a deliberate ploy to make the Chu soldiers desperate. With no means to retreat and short of food, the Chu had to attack and win in order to feed themselves.

The Chu won several victories and succeeded in breaking the supply line between the force besieging Julu and the larger Qin army. The Chu commanders had hoped that success would inspire other rebel states to send assistance, but none was sent. With no alternative, the Chu army was forced to fight on alone and eventually succeeded in pushing the Qin away from Julu. The Qin army took up a new position at Jiyuan, but its retreat from Julu finally prompted the other rebel states to send assistance to the Chu. The enlarged Chu army then advanced against the Qin force, hoping for a decisive battle. Instead, the Qin army surrendered; its commander had become aware of an internal plot against him and sought sanctuary with his former enemies.

■ JINGXING, 205 BCE

Han forces drew their Zhao opponents onto a prepared position and fought a defensive battle while a diversionary force attacked the Zhao camp. Thinking they were under attack from the rear, the Zhao forces collapsed.

■ WEI RIVER, 203 BCE

The outnumbered Han army provoked its opponents into charging across the Wei river, which had been dammed with sandbags. They then smashed the dam, drowning many of their enemies and trapping a segment of the enemy army.

■ GAIXIA, 202 BCE

After the collapse of the Qin dynasty, Chu and Han fought over rulership of all China. Internal politics hamstrung the efforts of the Han, with rival generals and political leaders vying for position and precedence once victory was achieved. Thus, although the Han were successful in some engagements, they were not able to achieve lasting dominance and the Chu retained control of large parts of the country.

The Chu benefited from the strong leadership of Xiang Yu, who was a great fighting general but a poor logistician. The Han strategy of harassing Chu supply lines exacerbated this problem, preventing Xiang Yu from achieving decisive results. Having finally settled some of their internal differences, the Han decided upon a new strategy in 202 BCE.

Offering the Chu a peace settlement, the Han feigned a retreat, prompting the Chu army to retire also. The Chu had been under-supplied for some time, so their troops were tired and hungry as they began their march. They were also jubilant at returning home after a long war, and were unprepared for the sudden attack launched by the

Han. The Chu counter-attack was defeated by a Han retreat, leading the disorganized Chu into a series of ambushes. Xiang Yu then decided to continue with the retirement. His intent was to reach a friendly stronghold where his army could resupply and reorganize in safety. The Han set about channelling the Chu retreat by setting up blocking positions and ambushes on their route, herding the Chu into the region of Gaixia.

Correctly deducing that his force was being directed into a trap, Xiang Yu attempted to avoid the canyons around Gaixia. Learning that his wife had been captured and was being held there, he sent the bulk of his force by a different route and led a rescue mission with part of his army. Although they knew they would be ambushed, the Chu had no choice but to follow their general into the canyons. There, they were attacked in a series of hit-and-run raids designed to lead any pursuit into further ambushes. The rescue force remained a dangerous opponent, however.

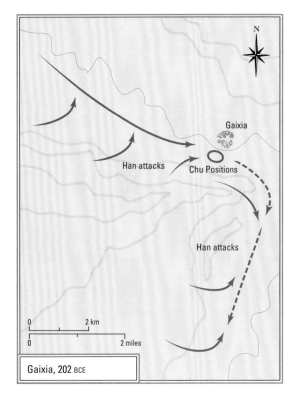

Gaixia, 202 BCE

Instead it was penned in the canyons for some months, while the Han used psychological gambits to reduce Chu morale. Among these was the tactic of forcing captured Chu soldiers to sing songs about their homes within earshot of the trapped army, making the Chu think that their nation had been conquered. This resulted in mass desertion.

Eventually, less than a thousand Chu remained with their general. The force was far more mobile than the host that had entered the canyons, making a breakout possible. Despite heavy losses, a small force did succeed in getting out of the trap. They were chased down by Han cavalry.

Xiang Yu committed suicide. His loss, as much as that of his army, crippled the Chu war effort. No other leaders of his calibre were available, and the war thereafter became a string of defeats for the Chu. The Han were able to achieve dominance over the regions originally unified by the Qin, and became the ruling dynasty of China.

Han Dynasty Wars
200 BCE–220 CE

■ BAIDENG, 200 BCE

Han forces operating against the Xiongnu (Hsiung-nu), a confederation of nomadic tribal peoples to the north, became surrounded at Baideng. It is unclear exactly what circumstances led to this event; the Han may have been responding to a raid or launching a campaign of conquest. In either case, the Han were defeated and implemented a diplomatic rather than military strategy to ensure stable relations with their tribal neighbours.

■ MAYI, 133 BCE

After many years of border raids, the Han attempted to draw Xiongnu forces into an ambush at the city of Mayi. The Xiongnu detected the trap in time and withdrew before the infantry-based forces of the Han could catch them.

■ KANSU/HE SI, 121 BCE

Han forces under General Huo Qubing launched a series of raids that forced the Xiongnu to seek a peace settlement with the Han. This gave the Han control over the Hexi Corridor, an important trade route.

■ MOBEI, 119 BCE

Initially the armies of the Han, based as they were on infantry and chariots, could only achieve success against the Xiongnu by luring them into an ambush. Increased use of cavalry gave the Han the option of launching offensive operations against the Xiongnu. A series of attacks drove the Xiongnu northwards, and in 119 BCE the Han followed up with a renewed offensive.

The eastern part of the operation was a complete success, pursuing the Xiongnu as far as Lake Baikal. The western segment was more difficult, running into a counter-attack by Xiongnu cavalry. The Han took up a defensive stance, using their chariots to create field fortifications. After several hours of indecisive fighting, the Han took advantage of a sandstorm to launch a flanking cavalry attack which broke the Xiongnu. This defeat forced the Xiongnu further north and secured the Han frontier.

■ LOULAN, 108 BCE

After securing their northern flank, the Han turned their attention to Central Asia. A small expeditionary force was able to overrun the kingdom of Loulan without difficulty, bringing it under Han rule.

■ TIEN SHAN, 99 BCE

Li Ling, a Han general, led a small force on a deep raid into Xiongnu territory, but was driven back by greatly superior numbers. The Han made a fighting retreat but eventually became surrounded, after which Li Ling surrendered.

■ JUSHI, 67 BCE

Although their power was greatly diminished, the Xiongnu intervened in a Han attempt to control Jushi. Their attempt to relieve the siege of Jiaohe, capital of Jushi, was driven off by the Han army.

■ KANG-CHU, 36 BCE

Fearing an invasion by the Xiongnu leader Zhizhi Chanyu, Han governor Gan Yanshou launched a pre-emptive campaign without the emperor's

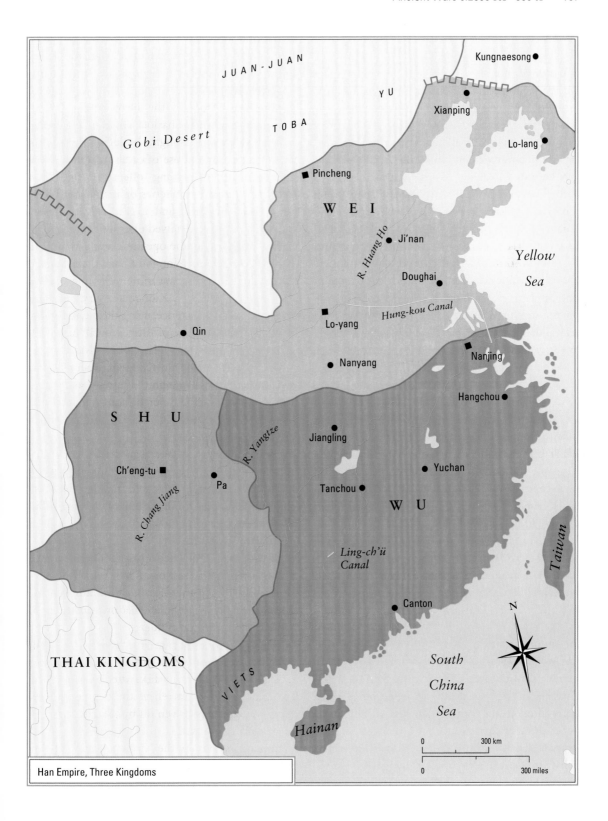

Han Empire, Three Kingdoms

permission. The Han force beat off an attack by Kangju cavalry en route.

■ TALAS, 36 BCE

The Xiongnu prince Zhizhi Chanyu fortified himself near Talas. Despite cavalry attacks by Kangju allies, he was unable to defeat the attack of a large Han army. Zhizhi's force may have included some Romans captured at Carrhae.

■ KUNYANG 23 CE

Rebellions against the Xin Dynasty permitted the Han Dynasty to be re-established under Liu Xuan. He provided a figurehead for the rebels and, conversely, a chance to suppress the revolts by killing him. Han forces were disjointed, operating under a number of leaders who did not always agree on what was to be done. A portion of the Han army, forced to retreat by the arrival of a greatly superior Xin army, took refuge in Kunyang.

As the Xin advanced on Kunyang, some rebel leaders wanted to disperse their forces and avoid a battle, but Liu Xuan persuaded them to fortify the city and hold it while other Han troops assembled to attack the Xin. While the rebels gathered their army, the defenders of the city were forced to endure repeated assaults with siege towers as well as attempts to undermine the walls. The city was still under Han control when the relief force arrived.

Despite setbacks against the city's defenders, the Xin were overconfident. When Liu Xuan led a small force against them, the Xin responded with only part of their army. The remainder was ordered to hold its siege positions unless directly ordered to intervene. The Xin commander was killed in the fighting with Liu Xuan's force, ensuring that the order to join the battle was never given.

Even when a diversionary force assaulted the Xin camp, there was little response from the main army, though the distraction was sufficient to allow the city garrison to sally out. This sudden attack caused a panic in the Xin army, which collapsed in rout. This defeat triggered further uprisings in support of the Han.

■ SOGDIANA, 36 CE

Continued Han intervention in Central Asia led to an expedition across the Jaxartes river and a battle with the people of the region, who were known as Sogdians. Among the Sogdian forces were, reportedly, a number of Roman soldiers. According to what records remain, the crossbows of the Han infantry were highly effective in penetrating the armour of the Romans, contributing to their defeat. If Roman troops were present, it is likely that they were military slaves, probably captured during Crassus' disastrous campaign into Parthia. These troops, perhaps captured at the battle of Carrhae, might have been offered their lives in return for military service in a remote region, a system often used by the Romans themselves. Accounts exist of Han encounters elsewhere with troops equipped in the Roman manner.

■ CHENGDU, 36 CE

Han forces advanced on Chengdu despite delays caused by the assassination of two generals. An assault failed but the Han used a ruse to trick the defenders into launching a counter-attack, which was decisively defeated.

■ YIWULU, 73 CE

A Han expedition against the Xiongnu proved largely inconclusive, but part of the Han force was able to drive the Xiongnu out of Yiwulu. This allowed the creation of a supply base in the region.

■ IKH BAYAN, 89 CE

A further expedition against the Xiongnu forced them to negotiate for peace, after which internal conflicts rendered them all but powerless. Within a few years the Xiongnu ceased to be a threat to the Han state.

■ YELLOW TURBAN REBELLION, 189 CE

A combination of weak central government and several crises prompted a widespread uprising. After taking steps to secure the capital, the imperial army gradually wore down the rebel forces, though the conflict flared up again for several years.

■ XINGYANG, 190 CE

Alleging that the chancellor, Dong Zhuo, was intending to seize power by controlling the child emperor, a coalition of regional leaders launched a campaign to remove him from his position. Dong Zhuo ordered the capital, Luoyang, to be abandoned and destroyed, moving the seat of government to the more defensible Chang'an. The capital was first thoroughly looted.

A coalition army advancing on Luoyang encountered Dong Zhuo's forces at Xingyang, where an intense but inconclusive battle resulted. The coalition force retreated to Suanzao towards nightfall, where it took up a defensive stance. Dong Zhuo's field commander declined to launch an attack and withdrew from the battlefield. After this setback, the coalition moved from a strategy of direct confrontation to one of blockade and harassment in the hope of wearing down their opponents.

■ YANGCHENG, 191 CE

The ruined remains of the imperial capital at Luoyang were abandoned by Dong Zhuo's forces and afterwards were captured by the coalition in a largely symbolic act. The coalition then began to break up; what had begun as a campaign against Dong Zhuo became a struggle between warlords for domination of China. This began with an attack on Yangchen by Yuan Shao and gradually expanded into a wider conflict.

■ JIEQIAO, 191 CE

What was primarily an infantry army under the warlord Yuan Shao encountered the more balanced force of Gongsun Zan. Zan's opening cavalry charge was routed by heavy crossbow fire and steady infantry, causing the rest of his army to collapse.

■ XIANGYANG, 191 CE

After defeating the forces of the warlord Liu Biao in the field, Yuan Shu's general, Sun Jian, besieged them in Xiangyang. A sortie under General Huang Zu was launched to break the siege, but was defeated and pursued away from the city. During the pursuit Sun Jian was killed and Liu Biao was able to claim victory. Yuan Shu's forces retired from the region, leaving it under Liu Biao's control.

■ FENGQIU, 193 CE

Forces of the warlord Yuan Shu occupied Fengqiu, causing Cao Cao to attempt to dislodge them. Defeating Yuan Shu's field army, Cao Cao advanced on Fengqiu and laid siege, driving off what remained of Yuan Shu's force.

■ YAN PROVINCE, 194 CE

While the warlord Cao Cao was on campaign elsewhere, his home province of Yan rebelled against him. Cao Cao was forced to fight a long campaign, including a very lengthy siege of Yongqui, to recapture it.

■ WANCHENG, 197 CE

The city of Wangcheng surrendered to Cao Cao, but its forces then launched a surprise attack on the fortified camp of Cao Cao's army. This assault was held at one entrance to the camp by Cao Cao's general, Dian Wei, and a handful of men, but Wangcheng troops were able to breach the other gates. Cao Cao himself fled the battle, in which his son was killed.

■ XIAPI, 198 CE

The warlord Cao Cao besieged the city of Xiapi amid complex and at times treacherous political manoeuvrings. A relief army and a sortie from the city were both beaten off. Eventually, hamstrung by internal politics, the defenders surrendered.

■ YIJING, 199 CE

After lengthy fighting, the warlord Yuan Shao gradually gained a dominant position in the northern provinces of China. His rival, Gongsun Zan, built a fortified city at Yijing for use as a supply base. While Gongsun Zan remained secure in his new fortress, his field armies were gradually defeated or surrendered as central command weakened.

This freed Yuan Shao to march on Yijing. His forces were unable to storm the city, but placed it under siege. A relief force was finally assembled, and a plan was developed to surprise the attackers. However, Yuan Shao's commanders became aware of the plan and laid an ambush. With the relief force defeated, Yuan Shao's army undermined part of the walls and gained entry to the city. Gongsun Zan committed suicide when defeat became inevitable.

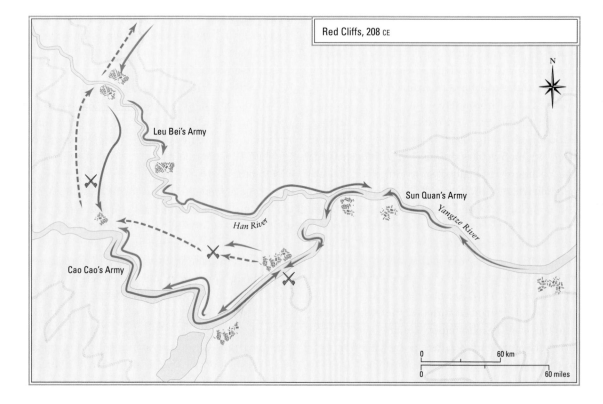

Red Cliffs, 208 CE

Leu Bei's Army

Sun Quan's Army

Han River

Cao Cao's Army

Yangtze River

0   60 km

0   60 miles

■ **GUANDU, 200 CE**

After several months of stalemate, both the forces of Yuan Shao and Cao Cao were short of food. Cao Cao's forces were able to destroy the main enemy supply bases, forcing Yuan Shao to withdraw across the Yellow River.

■ **BOWANG, 202 CE**

A detached force of Cao Cao's army engaged troops loyal to Liu Bei, who retreated southwards. The pursuit ran into an ambush, but was saved from utter defeat by the timely arrival of reinforcements.

■ **XIAKOU (JIANGXIA), 208 CE**

Hoping to capture the city as a base of operations, the warlord Sun Quan advanced on Jiangxia. His progress was blocked by large warships at the mouth of the Miankou river, with land forces nearby. Sun Quan's warships were unable to break through, but an assault force overran the blocking ships despite stiff resistance. With the collapse of Jiangxia's naval defences, Sun Quan's forces were able to reach and assault the city.

■ **CHANGBAN, 208 CE**

Cao Cao's forces, pursuing those of Liu Bei, caught up with them at Changban. Liu Bei was able to escape due to a determined rearguard action, though a large portion of his army was captured.

■ **RED CLIFFS, 208 CE**

As the Han Dynasty came to an end, the warlords of various regions grew beyond the control of the Emperor and eventually began to openly fight over rulership of all China. The most powerful of them was Cao Cao, who controlled the North China Plain.

Cao Cao was sufficiently successful in pacifying his home region, so much so that he was named imperial chancellor, possibly in an attempt to obtain his loyalty to the emperor or perhaps at his own demand. This position gave him control of the imperial government and legitimized his campaigns of conquest as an attempt to re-unify a divided China. Cao Cao then launched a campaign to gain control of the Yangtze river, which in turn would give him easy access to the southern regions. This would enable him to suppress the southern warlords and impose his dominance over a re-unified China, either in his own right or in the name of a figurehead emperor.

Cao Cao's forces were easily able to capture the city of Jiangxia and the nearby naval base of Jiangling. This gave Cao Cao control of that part of the Yangtze, as well as the naval forces necessary to exploit it. After the fall of Jiangxia, the warlord Liu Bei was forced to retreat and was heavily defeated at Changban, though he was able to escape with part of his army.

Unable to counter the greater strength of Cao Cao, Liu Bei made an alliance with his fellow warlord Sun Quan. The two set out to meet Cao Cao with a hastily assembled force of ships and marines which, although large, was still seriously outnumbered. Their main advantage was that Cao Cao was operating at the end of a long supply line. Furthermore, his troops were tired and possibly suffering from disease.

The allies sailed upriver to intercept Cao Cao at Red Cliffs where an indecisive skirmish took place. Cao Cao's advantage in numbers was offset by the weariness of his troops, resulting in a stalemate. The allies pulled back to reorganize and Cao Cao retreated to Wulin where he moored his fleet in a defensive position.

Cao Cao's forces were landsmen, unskilled at fighting aboard ships and, to take advantage of this, a squadron of large fireships was sent against Cao Cao's fleet. The northerners were unable to manoeuvre out of the way in time, and many of their vessels were set alight. The ensuing confusion and panic was exploited by the allies, who launched a successful assault on Cao Cao's fleet.

Cao Cao decided to fight on land rather than risk total defeat on the river, so his force disembarked and burned some of its remaining ships to prevent capture. A difficult retreat was then carried out towards Huarong. This took Cao Cao's army through swampy ground where it lost more of its strength to drowning, straggling, and

to skirmishes with the pursuing allies. Disease also claimed many lives, and by the time the army had reached a suitable position to reorganize itself, it was exhausted and fatally weakened. Cao Cao had no choice but to retreat northward with his main force, leaving garrisons to hold strategic points.

■ YILING, 208 CE

As Cao Cao retreated, Sun Quan's general Zhou Yu advanced towards Jiangling with the intention of recapturing it. To cover his flank he detached a force to Yiling, which was also garrisoned by Cao Cao. The governor of the city, who had been forced to serve Cao Cao, surrendered and offered his allegiance to Sun Quan.

Cao Cao's forces immediately launched an attack to capture Yiling. The heavily outnumbered defenders requested assistance from the main army, which was sent, despite the fact that this dangerously weakened the main force before Jiangling. In the meantime, Zhou Yu's forces engaged in deceptive operations and skirmishing to disguise their weakness. The unexpected arrival of reinforcements at Yiling enabled Sun Quan's army to inflict a serious defeat on Cao Cao's expedition and capture large numbers of horses.

■ JIANGLING, 209 CE

Cao Cao's army in Jiangling was extremely strong but was consequently difficult to supply. After months of skirmishing it became too costly for Cao Cao to maintain his garrison at Jiangling, so it was withdrawn.

■ TONG PASS, 211 CE

Cao Cao's army met a large force from Guanxi at Tong Pass. After a lengthy period of stalemate, Cao Cao launched an outflanking manoeuvre and, capitalizing on internal disputes among his enemies, finally routed them in open battle.

■ JICHENG, 213 CE

Under siege by the forces of Ma Chao, the governor of Jicheng sent an official out to make contact with any relief force. He was captured and executed after which the governor surrendered.

■ LICHENG, 213 CE

Rebelling against the rule of Ma Chao, forces

under Yang Fu made a fighting retreat until reinforcements from other rebellious factions and from the warlord Cao Cao arrived. Ma Chao was forced to withdraw.

■ Yi province, 214 CE

After the defeat of Cao Cao at Red Cliffs, Liu Bei decided to take control of Yi province by capturing Chengdu. This required a lengthy siege at Luo. Chengdu itself surrendered as Liu Bei's army approached.

■ Baxi, 215 CE

Cao Cao's forces, advancing on Baxi, were ambushed by troops loyal to Liu Bei in mountainous terrain. With their column under attack from different directions, Cao Cao's forces were defeated with only a small proportion escaping.

■ Yangping, 215 CE

Zhang Lu's forces fortified Yangping Pass against Cao Cao, and held out for some time. Feigning retreat, Cao Cao launched a surprise attack that overcame the defenders and opened the way for a continued advance.

■ Hefei, c. 217 CE

Hefei was a fortress city built to defend the state of Wei and was attacked repeatedly. Sun Quan launched a campaign to take it while its owner, Cao Cao, was elsewhere on campaign. The outnumbered defenders launched a pre-emptive attack on Sun Quan's army, which severely disrupted their plans. After a short siege Sun Quan was forced to withdraw. Pursuit by troops from Hefei resulted in a costly rearguard action.

■ Ruxukou, 218 CE

Cao Cao led a counter-offensive against Sun Quan in 217 CE, leading to a naval campaign against Ruxukou which was severely disrupted by a storm. After failing to break through Sun Quan's defences, Cao Cao retired.

■ Mount Dingjun, 219 CE

Liu Bei led an offensive against Cao Cao's forces in Hanzhong province, which was stalled for months at Yingpin Pass. A night attack eventually broke through Cao Cao's defences and pushed his army out of the pass.

■ Han River, 219 CE

Liu Bei launched a raid to destroy grain supplies held by Cao Cao's field army. The raiding force became cut off, prompting a rescue mission. After a confused series of engagements Liu Bei's forces regained their camp with Cao Cao in pursuit. Liu Bei tried to lure Cao Cao into an ambush at the camp, which partially succeeded. Cao Cao was forced to retire, and his supplies of grain were destroyed.

■ Fancheng, 219 CE

Taking advantage of setbacks suffered by Cao Cao, Guan Yu, a general serving Liu Bei, launched a campaign against his territory. After a series of engagements, Cao Cao's forces were caught in a flood and suffered massive casualties, forcing the remnant to stand on the defensive behind the walls of Fangcheng. Exploiting a dispute between Liu Bei and his ally Sun Quan, Cao Cao launched a counter-offensive that forced Guan Yu to retreat.

■ Jing Province, 219 CE

Sun Quan attacked Liu Bei's holdings in Jing province and overran them while Guan Yu was still fighting at Fangcheng. Guan Yu's attempt to retake the province failed, leaving Jing in the hands of Sun Quan.

Cimbrian War
113–101 BCE

■ Noreia, 112 BCE

The migrating Cimbri and Teutones threatened Roman allies near Noreia. A Roman army responded by attempting an ambush. Their plan was discovered and the Roman force was heavily defeated. The tribes then resumed their march.

■ Arausio, 105 BCE

Attempts to intercept the migratory Cimbri and Teutones highlighted deficiencies in the Roman military system that had been apparent for some time. The commanders of the two armies sent against them failed to cooperate, reducing their effectiveness considerably. In addition, the Roman army was in a period of transition from a militia force to one staffed by professionals.

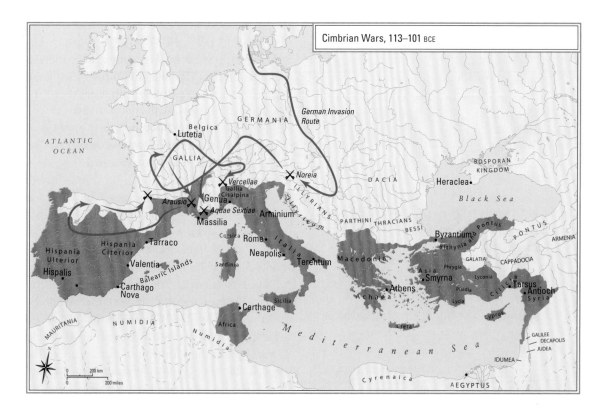

The burden of military service traditionally fell on the landed classes, whose absence from their businesses and estates had a serious impact on their finances and upon the Roman economy. Poorer citizens were recruited only in times of dire need. However, the system was evolving, with legions becoming permanently established and gaining regimental traditions.

The old system of recruits being assigned according to their age and experience to the *Hastati*, *Principes* and *Triarii* within a legion was also gradually supplanted. The *Triarii* were now equipped equivalently to the *Hastati* and *Principes*, with pila and swords instead of their traditional spears.

Although change had been ongoing for some time, the year of 107 BCE was highly significant. In this year Caius Marius implemented significant reforms, largely in order to circumvent laws that made it difficult to raise troops for a campaign in North Africa. However, the armies sent to

Gaul had probably not benefited much, if at all, from these reforms.

The two Roman forces made separate camps and failed to coordinate their operations, even after a screening force was overrun by the Cimbri and Teutones. One of the Roman forces launched an unsupported attack and was easily defeated, allowing the other to be overwhelmed by vastly superior numbers. Caught with their backs to a river, few of the Romans were able to escape.

■ AQUAE SEXTIAE, 102 BCE

After the loss of possibly as many as 80,000 troops in the disaster at Arausio, Rome turned to Caius Marius to defend against the Cimbri and Teutones. Marius assumed command of what forces then existed and implemented a training programme that had proven very effective during his North African campaign.

Marius' regime became the standard training system from Roman troops thereafter. He emphasized physical fitness and stamina, which

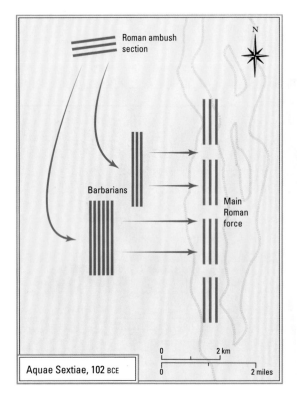

Roman ambush section

N

Barbarians

Main Roman force

0   2 km
0   2 miles

Aquae Sextiae, 102 BCE

army to rival even the catastrophe at Cannae. Thus Marius would not at first engage them, remaining fortified in his camp. He ridiculed challenges to single combat, holding his troops back until they had a chance to accustom themselves to the appearance of their enemies.

The tribesmen launched an attack on Marius' camp, which was defeated. This suited Marius' purposes; he had showed his men that the enemy was not unbeatable. But even after this, he would not come out to fight as the tribes passed by and headed for Roman territory. Once they were past, the Romans broke camp and followed.

Caius Marius announced to his troops that he would fight when the correct moment arrived. At Aquae Sextiae, he decided that the time had come. However, combat broke out before he was ready, as a result of a skirmish that developed while both sides were obtaining water. The fight escalated, with the Romans defeating part of the tribal force. This further improved morale, and after a period of standoff, with both forces in close proximity, Marius detached a flanking force to conceal itself behind the enemy, and made preparations for battle.

Marius drew up his infantry at the top of a slope and sent his cavalry to make an attack on the enemy. As he had hoped, this provoked the tribal warriors into charging up the slope, arriving within *pila* range of the Romans in a breathless and disorganized state. The Romans' volley of javelins compounded the situation and was followed by a charge, which Marius led from the front rank.

The tribesmen were pushed back to the flat ground at the base of this slope, where they formed a defensive shieldwall and were able to stabilize the situation. The sudden attack of Marius' detached force in their rear caused the line to collapse, giving the Roman force a decisive victory.

■ **VERCELLAE, 101 BCE**

Although Marius' victory at Aquae Sextiae removed the worst threat to Roman territory, a significant force composed mainly of Cimbri tribesmen was able to force its way past a smaller

were built by training with double-weight weapons and long marches. He required his troops to carry their own gear, earning them the nickname of 'Marius' Mules' and did away with many of the servants and other encumbrances that landed men were wont to bring with them to the army.

Thus Marius' army was well disciplined and in good fighting condition, but it was essential to remain between the migrating tribes and Italy rather than seeking a battle and possibly pulling his force out of position. Marius was thus required to maintain a defensive position on the banks of the Rhone and watch for an attack, while the tribes wandered as far away as the Pyrenees. Eventually, they advanced to the Rhone with the intention of crossing.

Well aware of the intimidating appearance of the tribesmen, Marius was careful to protect the morale of his troops. These tribesmen had defeated no less than five consular armies during their march and, at Arausio, had inflicted losses upon the Roman

Roman force under Catulus and enter Italy. Marius joined forces with Catulus to oppose the invasion. Accepting a formal challenge from the Cimbri, the Roman force met them at Vercellae and defeated them in a hard-fought and confused action.

Jugurthine War
111–104 BCE

■ **SUTHUL, 110 BCE**
King Jugurtha of Numidia understood both the Roman methods of war and their politics, and used both to his advantage. A combination of bribery and manoeuvring enabled him to defeat a Roman army near Suthul.

■ **MUTHUL, 108 BCE**
A divided Roman army was attacked by Jugurtha's forces whilst trying to obtain water. Caius Marius salvaged the situation with a display of initiative, but the Numidians were able to retreat in good order.

Rome's Social War
91–88 BCE

■ **AESERNIA, 90 BCE**
Remaining loyal to Rome, Aesernia was besieged by the Samnites but was able to resist for a long period. The city was eventually compelled to surrender by starvation and became an important administrative centre for the rebels.

■ **RAIDS INTO LUCANIA/APULIA, 90 BCE**
Roman control over Lucania and Apulia was greatly weakened by attacks launched by the rebels. The defeat of Roman field forces caused several cities to join the rebel cause, including Canusium and Venusia.

■ **ASCULUM, 89 BCE**
Disaffection among Rome's allies grew over time, and eventually resulted in open hostilities. Roman forces under the consul Gnaeus Pompeius Strabo besieged Asculum, blockading the city, despite Italian attempts to break the siege.

■ **FUCINE LAKE, 89 BCE**
The rebels had broken away from their alliance with Rome and declared their own nation, 'Italia'. However, support for their cause was reduced when Rome declared that cities that remained loyal (and some that had defected but returned to Roman allegiance) would receive citizenship and greater control over foreign policy. This was one of the main causes of the war, so the move weakened the Italians. Lucius Porcius Cato commanded Roman forces in the central region, and was mainly opposed by the Marsi tribe. Struggling with poor training levels and indiscipline among troops, as well as insubordination among the officers, Cato advanced to the Fucine Lake where he was killed in a failed attempt to storm a fortified Marsic camp.

■ **ASCULUM, 89 BCE**
A large Italian force attempted to break the siege of Asculum and was decisively defeated by Roman forces. This effectively decided the course of the war in the northern regions, breaking the rebels' strength.

First Mithridatic War
89–84 BCE

■ **RIVER AMNIAS, 88 BCE**
This battle was the opening engagement of the First Mithridatic War between Rome, its allies, and Mithridates VI of Pontus. A sudden devastating attack of Mithridates' Pontic scythed chariots scattered the Romans' Bithynian allies and forced a Roman retreat.

■ **MOUNT SCOROBAS, 88 BCE**
Following up on the Amnias victory, Mithridates captured and released more Roman allies here, afterwards falling upon the Roman general Manius's camp, capturing that with heavy casualties and evicting the Romans from Asia Minor.

■ **ATHENS, 86 BCE**
Athens joined with Mithridates in his war and slaughter of all Romans in the East. Mithridates' general Archelaus was not enough to stop L. Cornelius Sulla's conquest, devastation and partial sack of the historic city.

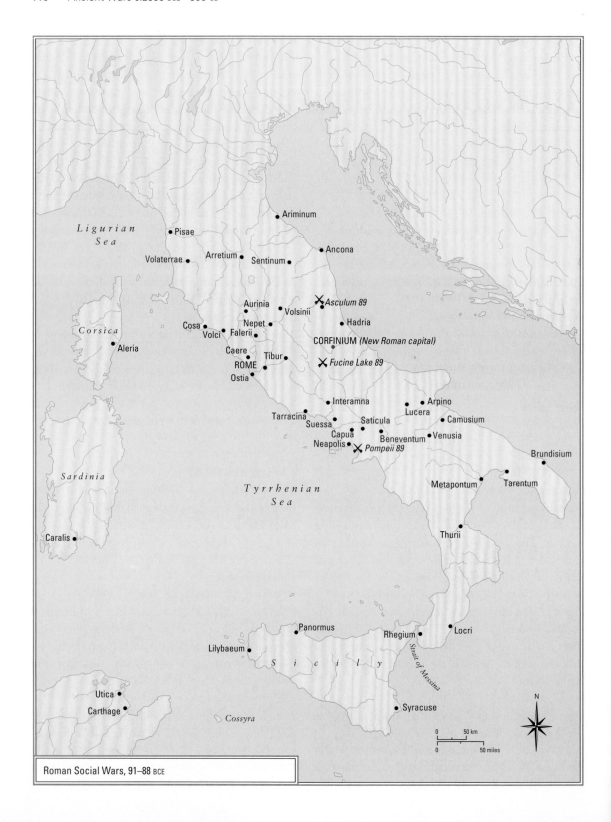

*Ligurian
Sea*

• Pisae

Volaterrae •

Arretium •   Sentinum •

• Ariminum

• Ancona

Corsica

• Aleria

Aurinia •
• Volsinii

Cosa •
Volci • Nepet
Falerii •

X *Asculum 89*

• Hadria

CORFINIUM *(New Roman capital)*

Caere •
• Tibur
ROME •
Ostia •

X *Fucine Lake 89*

Sardinia

Tarracina •
Suessa •
Capua •
Neapolis •

• Interamna

Saticula •

Beneventum •

• Arpino
Lucera •
• Camusium
• Venusia

X *Pompeii 89*

• Caralis

*Tyrrhenian
Sea*

Metapontum •

• Brundisium

• Tarentum

• Thurii

• Panormus

Rhegium •
• Locri

Lilybaeum •

S   i   c   i   l   y

Strait of Messina

Utica •
Carthage •

Cossyra

• Syracuse

N

| 0 | 50 km |
| 0 | 50 miles |

Roman Social Wars, 91–88 BCE

■ TENEDOS, 86 BCE

This battle was a naval defeat of the forces of Mithridates' admiral Neoptolemus by the Rhodian and allied fleet under Damagoras. Superb Rhodian ship-handling off the island's coast overcame superior Pontic numbers and larger ships in neutralizing Mithridates' navy.

■ CHAERONEA, 86 BCE

Mithridates' general Archelaus retreated north and eastward before Sulla's advance up from Athens, where he found reinforcement from a second Pontic army that had been consolidating Mithridates' gains in Macedonia and the north. Both sides had time to consolidate their forces and prepare for a decisive battle, Sulla having manoeuvered Archelaus into this small plain between mountain spurs that prevented escape or retreat. Archelaus had sought to delay battle pending the arrival of additional troops from a third Pontic army en route by sea.

Mithridatic forces numbered some 140,000 Pontic and allied infantry, scythed chariots and

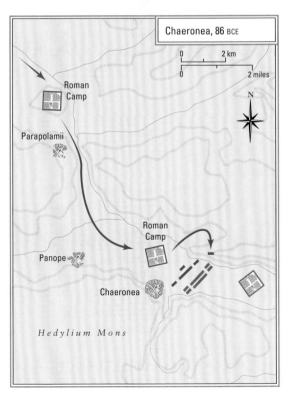

Chaeronea, 86 BCE

0   2 km

0   2 miles

N

Roman Camp

Parapolamii

Roman Camp

Panope

Chaeronea

Hedylium Mons

conventional cavalry. Sulla commanded 30,000 Romans in five legions with an additional 10,000 or so Greeks and Macedonians returned to their allegiance.

Archelaus invited the Roman's advance into a trap reminiscent of Hannibal's at Cannae by arranging his superior numbers in a crescent with infantry and scythed chariots in the centre. On the ends of his crescent he stationed his cavalry, with orders to envelop Sulla's forces as they advanced. Sulla, too, had read his history and the Roman formations opened as Alexander's had at Gaugamela, the scythed chariots charging harmlessly through the Romans' ranks. Sulla then attacked the Pontic left, with a Gaugamela-style rear reserve separately defeating the Pontic cavalry while Archelaus's centre collapsed. Mithridatic numbers surrounded both Sulla's main force and reserve, but superior Roman command and training allowed the separated forces to rejoin as the Pontic army collapsed in utter rout, unable to escape because of the surrounding mountains.

Pontic casualties in the ensuing slaughter may have been as many as 110,000, Roman losses orders of magnitude less.

■ ORCHOMENUS, 85 BCE

Having escaped in the confusion after Chaeronea with his surviving 10,000, Archelaus withdrew by sea until the final allotment of his reinforcements reached him, swelling the total numbers under his command to some 90,000 men. When these landed, Sulla moved his own command to this small Boetian village where he entrenched in the face of Archelaus's considerable numbers of cavalry. The Roman infantry in fact quailed in the trenches in the face of the Pontic horse, forcing Sulla to take personal command in the vanguard as he challenged his soldiers to save their general or live with the disgrace of his death. When their officers followed their commander's example, the infantry rallied and finally defeated the Pontic army, inflicting some 15,000 casualties. Sulla pursued the remnants of Archelaus's command into their camp, inflicting there still further casualties.

Roman Slave and Civil Wars
88–50 BCE

■ **MOUNT TIFATA, 83 BCE**

Returning from Asia Minor to take advantage of the power vacuum in Rome, Sulla was confronted by an army under Gaius Norbanus which had marched to intercept him. Defeated, Norbanus retreated to Capua.

■ **COLLINE GATE, 82 BCE**

Advancing on Rome, Lucius Cornelius Sulla was met at the Colline Gate by a large Samnite army. Largely through the efforts of Marcus Licinius Crassus, Sulla was victorious and drove off the Samnites. This spelled the end of Samnite power and ensured that the Social War did not flare up again. Sulla then entered the city and took control, declaring himself dictator.

■ **BAETIS RIVER, 80 BCE**

Forces loyal to Quintus Sertorius and opposed to Sulla were based largely in Hispania. A Roman army sent against them while they marched towards Lusitania was defeated at the Baetis river.

■ **PICENUM, 72 BCE**

The slave revolt led by Spartacus rapidly grew until he had around 70,000 followers, but their fighting ability may have been underestimated by the Roman authorities. At Picenum the rebels defeated a consular army before marching north towards Mutina.

■ **MUTINA, 72 BCE**

Marching north from Picenum, Spartacus' army continued to grow. A single legion based at Mutina was easily overrun, but internal conflicts among the rebels caused them to turn back southwards instead of crossing the Alps as originally intended.

■ **CAMPANIA, 71 BCE**

Marcus Licinius Crassus was given command of a large army with which to crush Spartacus' rebels. A part of his force attacked prematurely and was easily defeated, requiring a pause to regroup.

■ **CAMPANIA II, 71 BCE**

Renewing the offensive against Spartacus, Crassus inflicted a serious defeat and forced Spartacus to fall back to Rhegium. His attempt to cross into Sicily failed when the local pirates declined to provide transportation.

■ **SILARUS RIVER, 71 BCE**

Despite an attempt to break out of the toe of Italy, Spartacus' forces were crushed by Crassus' army near the headwaters of the Silarus river. This brought the rebellion to an end.

■ **KORAKESION, 67 BCE**

Charged with defeating the Cilician Pirates, Pompey the Great inflicted a sharp defeat at sea and then besieged his enemies in Korakesion. The siege was subsequently brought to a successful conclusion.

■ **PISTORIA, 62 BCE**

An attempt by the Senator Catiline to overthrow the Roman republic resulted in his army becoming caught between two republican forces. Launching an attack against one force, Catiline was defeated and killed in the fighting.

■ **BOVILLAE, 52 BCE**

An encounter between the supporters of rival Roman politicians Clodius and Milo near Bovillae led to a bloody clash in which Clodius was killed. This in turn caused further violence in Rome itself.

Gallic Wars
58–52 BCE

■ **ARAR, 58 BCE**

The Helvetii tribe asked Rome for permission to migrate westwards. Taking advantage of this situation, Julius Caesar stalled their emissaries for weeks while his troops built fortifications at the River Rhone. The Helvetii then attempted to march around the defended line, taking them into the territory of the Aedui tribe, who were friendly to Rome. The Aedui requested assistance, giving Caesar the excuse to attack the Helvetii that he had wanted all along.

Caesar's forces caught up with the Helvetii as they crossed the River Arar (the modern Saône).

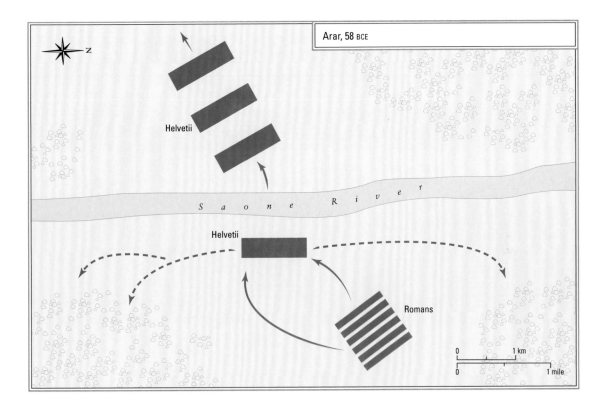

They were moving as four cantons, and three were already across the river. The fourth was attacked whilst thus isolated and suffered severe casualties, though many tribespeople were able to escape into nearby woods. Caesar's army then bridged the Arar and pursued the Helvetii.

■ **BIBRACTE (MOUNT BEAUVAY), 58 BCE**

In need of supplies, Caesar's army turned aside from pursuing the migrating Helvetii tribe and marched towards Bibracte. The Helvetii began to harass the rear of the Roman army, which drew up in battle order on Mount Beauvay. The initial Gallic attack was repulsed, but the legions were then flanked. The third line of the Roman force was tasked with holding off this attack while the first lines eventually outfought their opponents in battle.

■ **VESONTIO, 58 BCE**

After a period of manoeuvring and standoff near Vesontio, Caesar forced a battle by attacking the camp of the Suebi. As he had planned, Caesar's right-flank legions broke the enemy opposite them, driving the Suebi back across the Rhine.

■ **VOSGES, 58 BCE**

King Ariovistus of the Suebi avoided battle with the Romans for as long as possible, awaiting reinforcements from across the Rhine, but was eventually brought to action. Caesar's forces made a frontal attack, concentrating on the weaker German left. Their own left flank came close to defeat but was reinforced by reserves brought up from the third line. Ariovistus' troops were gradually outfought and eventually broke, after which they were pursued back across the Rhine.

■ **AXONA, 57 BCE**

An attack by the Belgae on a Roman-allied Gallic tribe caused Caesar to launch a campaign against them. An initial, inconclusive, skirmish led to an attempt by the Belgae to outflank the strong Roman position by attacking across the river Axona. Caesar launched an immediate counter-attack with cavalry and light troops, repelling the attack. The Belgae then began to retreat and, once he was sure this was not a trick, Caesar pursued and inflicted severe casualties.

■ Sambre River (Sabis), 57 BCE

Advancing into the lands of the Belgae, Caesar's force began making camp near the Sambre river, sending detachments to attack the Belgae as they attempted to flee across the river. A vigorous counter-attack by the Belgae caught Caesar's main body unprepared and, in the ensuing chaotic melee, the Romans came close to total defeat. Eventually, superior discipline and the arrival of reinforcements turned the battle in Caesar's favour.

■ Octoduros, 57 BCE

Detached from the main Roman army, a legion under the command of Servius Sulpicius Galba was sent on a foray into the lands of the Nantuates. The legion occupied the tribal stronghold at Octoduros, but was ultimately defeated.

■ Moribhan Gulf, 56 BCE

Caesar's fleet offset the superior ships of their Veneti opponents by using boarding tactics, augmenting the crews with legionaries. The Veneti were defeated piecemeal when their ships were left strung out by a changing wind.

■ Coblenz, 55 BCE

Facing an invasion of Gaul by Germanic tribes, Julius Caesar's forces inflicted a sharp defeat at Coblenz. The legions then built a bridge over the Rhine as a demonstration of Roman superiority, which helped subdue the tribes.

■ Tongres (Aduatuca), 57 BCE

After the defeat of the Belgic tribes by Caesar's forces, the Atuatuci retreated to their capital where they were besieged. After an attempt to break out of the town failed, it was stormed and the population sold into slavery.

■ Caesar's Invasion of Britain, 55–54 BCE

Caesar's initial invasion of Britain, in 55 BCE, was little more than reconnaissance in force, though lessons were learned from the expedition. These included the need for ships better suited to a beach landing and the expectation of significant resistance by the Britons.

In 54 BCE Roman forces probed inland, beating off attacks by the Britons, but were required to halt operations to repair their ships after a storm. A second foray inland was met by a large force of Britons, who quickly discovered that their odds in a pitched battle were poor. The Britons used their chariots to skirmish and wear down the Romans, who nevertheless reached the Thames and forced a crossing.

Some tribes surrendered to Caesar and offered tribute, while others launched an attack on the beachhead where the Roman ships remained under guard. The defeat of this assault marked the end of British resistance, after which Caesar returned to Gaul.

■ Agendicum, 52 BCE

Gallic troops positioned themselves across the rear of a detachment of Caesar's force under the command of Quintus Labeinus, then headed for Lutetia. The legions defeated this force to clear their line of communications.

■ Avaricum (Bourges), 52 BCE

Unable to defeat Caesar in open battle, the Gauls decided on a scorched-earth strategy, but left Avaricum intact as the city was strongly fortified. Caesar laid siege to the city, but was suffering from an acute shortage of supplies. Despite raids by Gallic troops, the legions were able to build siege towers and ramps to allow them to be moved up to the walls. The city was then successfully stormed and the defenders massacred.

■ Gergovia, 52 BCE

Caesar's campaigns in Gaul caused a degree of polarization among the Gallic tribes. Some remained friendly to Rome and supplied Caesar's army while others, overtly or otherwise, supported the leader of the Gauls, Vercingetorix. Support for Caesar depended greatly on his ability to demonstrate the effectiveness of his army; allies who felt that Caesar could not protect them were likely to defect. Thus, when Vercingetorix attacked Gergovia, Caesar needed to dislodge him quickly. This was made problematical by a poor supply situation, but while it may have been more

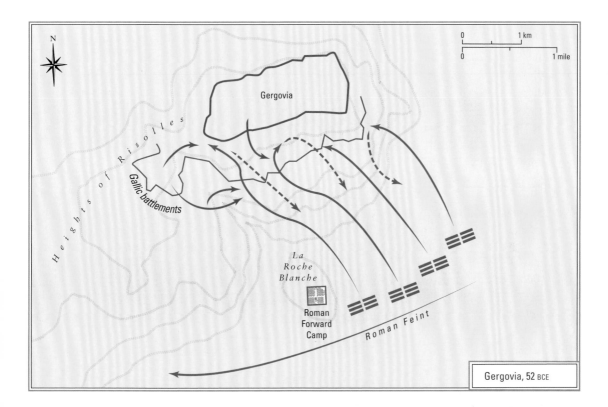

Gergovia, 52 BCE

prudent to remain in winter quarters, this was not an option as it would expose Roman weakness to their allies and possibly result in desertion.

Caesar detached four of his ten legions to campaign against the Senones and the Parisii. With the remainder he marched on Gergovia. Vercingetorix' army attempted to block his crossing of the River Allier, but was decoyed out of position by part of Caesar's army, while the rest of the force rebuilt a bridge and reached the far bank. Vercingetorix retreated to Gergovia, followed by Caesar who found the city strongly fortified and barricaded against him.

The Romans began siege preparations, capturing a hill and fortifying it against counter-attack. However, a rebellion among the previously allied Aedui tribe interrupted the siege. Caesar needed to reunite his forces without being seen to retreat, so ordered a limited attack on part of the Gallic defences. This developed into a large-scale assault which was defeated.

Despite this setback, Caesar drew up his army in battle order. When Vercingetorix did not accept the challenge to come out and fight, Caesar was able to portray this as weakness on his part and broke contact, marching north to concentrate his forces.

■ VINGEANNE, 52 BCE

As Caesar's army marched through the Vingeanne valley, it was attacked by a large Gallic force with a sizable cavalry contingent. The battle opened with a Gallic cavalry attack that fell mainly on the Roman flanks. Although hard pressed, the Roman cavalry, supported by infantry, were eventually able to defeat their Gallic counterparts. The Gallic army was vigorously pursued and sought refuge in Alesia, which was then besieged.

■ ALESIA, 52 BCE

The loss of Avaricum to Roman forces did not unduly concern Vercingetorix, leader of the Gallic opposition to Caesar. Vercingetorix had argued that the city should not be held against the

N

Oldbury   Bigberry

Cissbury   Mount Caburn

55 BCE
54 BCE

Oceanus Britannicus (English Channel)

MENAPII

MORINI

NERVI   EBURONES

55 BCE   ATUATUCI
56 BCE

ATREBATES

Sabis River

BELGAE   REMI

CALETI   Samarobriva (Amiens)
53 BCE   TREVERI

BELLOVACI   Durocortorum (Reims)

VENELLI   LEXOVII   SUESSIONES   *57 BCE*

57 BCE   AULERCI   *Sequana (Seine)*   *52 BCE*   LINGONES

CORIOSOLITES   PARISII

VENETI   SENONES   Alesia   *58 BCE*
Cenabum (Orléans)

56 BCE   CARNUTES   Approximate site of
the defeat of Arovistus

PICTONES   Avaricum (Bourges)   SEQUANI

51 BCE   BITURIGES   Bibracte (Mont Beuvray)
52 BCE

Lemonum (Poitiers)   AEDU   HELVETII

LEMOVICES   Matisco (Macon)   *58 BCE*
52 BCE   *52 BCE*   Lake Geneva

51 BCE   Gergovia   *52 BCE*

Mare Cantabricum (Bay of Biscay)

ARVERNI   *52 BCE*

AQUITANI   Uxellodunum   *Rhodanus (Rhone)*   **Gallia Transalpina**

Liger (Loire)

Garumna (Garonne)

52 BCE

Caesar's route (with date)

site of battle

major Gallic settlement

Roman Empire c.50 BCE

major British hill fort

major Roman city

Roman road

Tolosa (Toulouse)

Via Domitia   Aquae Sextiae (Aix-en-Provence)

Narbo (Narbonne)   Massilia (Marseille)   Antipolis (Antibes)

Mare Internum

Rhenus (Rhine)

0   50 km
0   50 miles

Caesar's Campaigns in Gaul, 58–51 BCE

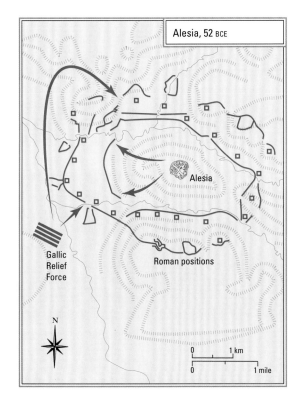

In front of this was a double ditch to impede attackers. Vercingetorix launched numerous raids as the siege lines were built, but was unable to prevent their completion. This meant that he was cut off, but not before Vercingetorix' cavalry fought its way out of the city to join a relief force.

As supplies began to run out in Alesia, Vercingetorix sent all non-combatants out of the town. They could not pass the Roman lines and were left to starve between the fortifications of the town and those of the besiegers. Hope for the defenders rested on the arrival of a relief force, which in due course appeared before the city.

The Gallic relief attempt opened with a cavalry attack, which resulted in a widespread running fight between the horsemen of both sides and some supporting light infantry. The battle was eventually won by the Romans, who inflicted severe casualties. Meanwhile, the Gauls within the siege line attempted to take advantage of this diversion to fill in parts of the Roman ditch, facilitating an assault.

Vercingetorix then launched a breakout attempt at night, while the relief army attacked the Roman positions from the outside. The fighting was intense and confused, but was eventually stabilized by the effective use of Roman reinforcements. The besieged and the relief force fell back, but attacked again the next day.

Under cover of diversionary assaults at various points on the Roman defences, the relief army attacked one of the main Roman forts. Vercingetorix became aware of the attack and once more led his forces out to attempt a breakout. Once again the Romans were hard-pressed, but the legionaries were well led and highly disciplined. Just as importantly, they were confident that reinforcements would be sent to them. Although some areas came under very heavy attack, most were able to hold out as Caesar transferred reinforcements along the line, and back again, to deal with the next crisis point.

Romans in the first place, so its fall simply proved him right. He thus retained the confidence of the many tribes involved in the conflict, and was able to field a large force that grew as more tribes joined the war.

After failing to storm Gergovia, Caesar decided to concentrate his forces, and called in reinforcements in the form of auxiliary troops and Germanic mercenaries. Vercingetorix followed Caesar's march to re-unite his forces, resulting in several skirmishes that developed into a more decisive action. This was lost by the Gauls, who retreated with the Romans in pursuit.

The Gauls made a stand at the city of Alesia, where Caesar besieged them. This required the construction of two parallel siege lines – one facing inward and one outward – as Alesia lay in hostile territory and the Roman force might well be attacked by a relief force or raiding parties. The lines consisted of earth-and-timber forts connected by a wall of the same construction.

At the height of the fighting, Vercingetorix' men managed to penetrate the Roman lines and destroy part of the defences. This final attempt was contained by a counter-attack that required virtually all of the available Roman troops, but decided the battle. The relief force fell back and Vercingetorix was unable to break out. The next day he agreed to surrender to Caesar.

Wars of the First Triumvirate/Rome 53–44 BCE

■ CARRHAE, 53 BCE

In choosing Parthia as the target for an invasion Marcus Licinius Crassus, political ally of Caesar and Pompey, made a serious mistake. Most of the eastern regions conquered by Rome were heavily influenced by the Greek or Macedonian methods of fighting, and were heavily dependent upon dense bodies of pike-armed infantry. Repeated clashes had shown that Roman armies were superior in fighting power, discipline and tactics to these forces, and Crassus therefore assumed that his army would be able to defeat whatever he encountered.

Crassus sailed from Italy with seven legions plus some Gallic cavalry, and hired Arab mercenaries to augment this force. He followed the River Tigris, using it to transport supplies, and thus brought his large army across the Euphrates into Parthian territory. Several cities surrendered and a successful assault on Zendotia brought in significant booty. Garrisoning these conquests reduced the Roman force, which waited out the winter in Syria and then advanced once again.

Crassus had failed to appreciate two important factors when he planned his campaign. One was the terrain in which he would have to fight. Lacking many clear objectives, it required long marches through dry and inhospitable terrain. Slow-moving infantry-based forces were confined to certain routes where water could be obtained or brought up, while a cavalry army could move more freely. This was the other

significant factor. Roman armies were ideally suited to breaking infantry-based forces but could not manoeuvre fast enough to catch an all-cavalry force such as that of the Parthians. The latter used armoured cavalry as their shock arm, but could afford to wait until their horse archers had worn down the enemy before committing to a charge.

As Crassus advanced on Seleucia, the Parthian army confronted him. Crassus' first response was to form a very long and thin line, suggesting that he had not considered how to deal with such a threat. He then ordered the line folded back to form a hollow square which had no flanks to be turned by more mobile cavalry.

Crassus' army then advanced, slowly, in this formation until they were close to the waiting Parthians. The Romans' mercenary Arab cavalry made off before the fighting started, leaving Crassus with little in the way of mobile forces.

The Parthians feigned a charge but instead

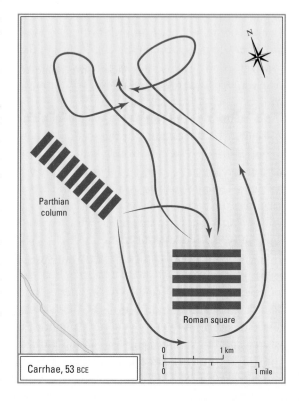

Parthian column

Roman square

Carrhae, 53 BCE

0   1 km

0   1 mile

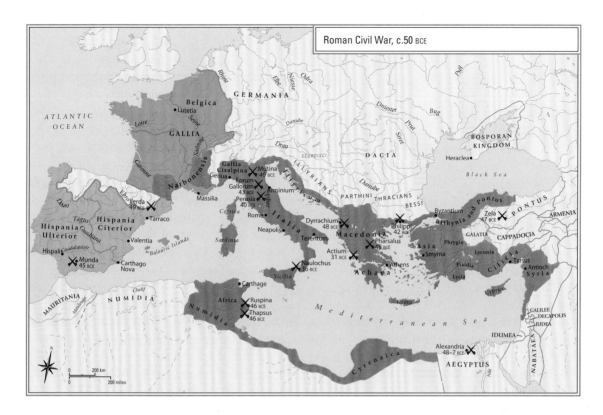

surrounded the Roman square with a cloud of horse archers who kept up a ceaseless barrage of arrows. The legionaries' pila lacked the range to return fire, though some of the light troops were able to shoot back with bows.

Crassus launched a counter-attack with cavalry and some legionaries, but the Parthians fell back before it and drew this force away from the main body before forcing it into a defensive formation with the threat of a charge. The detachment was then showered with arrows until the survivors surrendered. As the main square was worn down by archery, the Parthian heavy cavalry began making a series of charges, pulling back after each to avoid a counter-attack.

Nightfall saved the Romans from total destruction, allowing the survivors to reach the town of Carrhae. From there an attempt was made to escape by marching at night, but this ended in disaster as the retreating force was caught and attacked again. The majority of the remaining

Roman troops surrendered, though some were able to reach friendly territory.

■ ANTIGONEA, 51 BCE

After defeating Crassus' invasion, Parthian forces advanced into Roman-held Syria. Near Antigonea, the main Parthian army was drawn into an ambush by Roman cavalry, allowing the legionaries to achieve a decisive victory which ended the campaign.

■ RUBICON RIVER, 49 BCE

Rather than return to Rome without his army, which would make him vulnerable to his enemies, Caesar entered Italy with one legion. Crossing the Rubicon river was an act of war against Rome, and began a long civil war.

■ MASSILIA, 49 BCE

Caesar took control of Rome without undue difficulty, and from there marched towards Hispania, where some of his enemies were raising forces against him. The city of Massilia was held by his opponents, forcing Caesar's army to launch a siege to capture the city. Naval forces fought to prevent the city from being resupplied until the siege was brought to a successful conclusion. Massilia became a Roman possession after its conquest.

■ ILERDA, 49 BCE

While detached forces reduced Massilia, Caesar marched on into Hispania to confront forces loyal to Pompey the Great. A confrontation developed near Ilerda, with a Pompeiian army under Afranius. Caesar at first drew up in battle order to cover the construction of a fortified camp. Once the camp was established, Caesar attempted to gain control of high ground that dominated the battlefield. Pompey's force also sent troops to seize the rise.

As Caesar's detachment was pushed back towards the camp, Caesar counter-attacked with one of the Ninth Legion and drove them back in turn. As the defeated Pompeiian troops sought the safety of Ilerda's fortifications, Caesar's legionaries were drawn too close to the city and forced to retreat hurriedly.

The Ninth Legion made a fighting retreat as additional enemy reinforcements joined the action. Caesar sent detachments to support his legion, resulting in a larger-scale battle that lasted several hours. This was finally won by a charge launched by Caesar's forces, which again drove the enemy back to the town. Taking advantage of the situation, Caesar's forces broke off the action and fell back, supported by cavalry.

After a period of standoff, Afranius' forces began to retire and were pursued. They had hoped to join up with other forces from their faction, but were blocked by Caesar and forced to retire back to Ilerda. After a siege this force surrendered, allowing Caesar to confront the other Pompey-aligned army in Hispania.

This force surrendered without a battle, many troops coming over to Caesar's side, and with Hispania secured Caesar marched back to Massilia.

■ UTICA, 49 BCE

Caesar's opponents included Publius Attius Varus, who went to North Africa and began to raise troops. He was offered support by King Juba of Numidia, but Juba's army was defeated at Utica by Caesarean forces.

■ BAGRADAS RIVER, 49 BCE

After an initial success against Juba's army, Caesarean forces were drawn into an ambush and suffered massive casualties. Part of the Caesarean force gained the safety of a hilltop and held out for a time, but were eventually overwhelmed by the opposing forces.

■ ILLYRIA, 49 BCE

While Caesar was campaigning in Hispania, Pompey's forces attempted to clear pro-Caesar garrisons from Illyria. Caesar's governor in Illyria, Gaius Antonius, was besieged on the island of Curicta by Pompey's fleet, and was eventually starved into surrender.

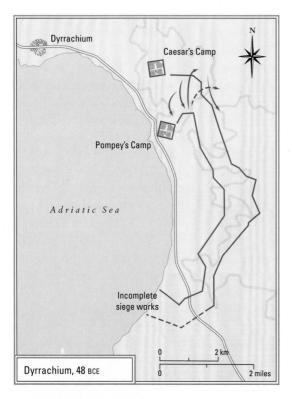

Dyrrachium, 48 BCE

■ **DYRRACHIUM, 48 BCE**

Besieged in his camp by Caesar's army, Pompey attempted a breakout. Despite a counterattack by the outnumbered Caesarean forces, Pompey was able to push through the siege lines and turn Caesar's flank, forcing a withdrawal.

■ **PHARSALUS, 48 BCE**

Having defeated Julius Caesar at Dyrrachium, Pompey pursued a cautious strategy but, in response to political pressure, engaged Caesar's forces in battle on the banks of the river Enipeus near Pharsalus. Caesar's army was outnumbered two to one and was desperately short of supplies.

Pompey deployed his forces in the conventional three lines, with the river covering his right flank. He massed his cavalry on the left. Caesar deployed his main force in a similar manner but less depth, reinforcing his outnumbered cavalry with a force of light infantry to cover his exposed flank. Caesar needed a decisive outcome whereas Pompey could afford to simply avoid defeat;

his army was well supplied whereas Caesar's force would starve if it did not win this battle. Expecting Caesar's troops to be weakened by lack of food, Pompey ordered his own men to receive their charge rather than counter-charging, forcing the Caesarean legions to further tire themselves by covering more ground. Caesar's experienced troops instead halted and reformed their lines, resting before moving up to the attack and depriving Pompey of his expected advantage. Pompey's cavalry charged but ran into unexpectedly heavy resistance, and were then attacked by Caesar's flank infantry force. They were driven off, allowing Caesar's troops to fall on the flank of the thus far indecisive infantry melee. Fearing all was lost, Pompey fled to his camp and from thence to Egypt where he was assassinated. Leaderless, his army collapsed, granting Caesar the decisive victory he needed at relatively low cost. Defeat at Pharsalus broke the power of the Senatorial faction and ensured

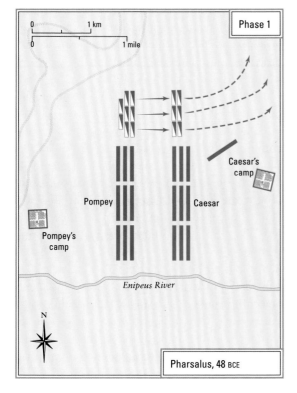

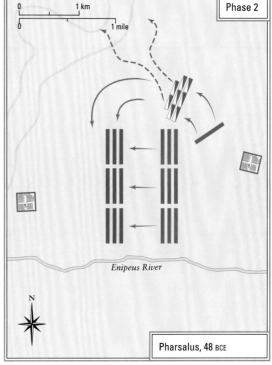

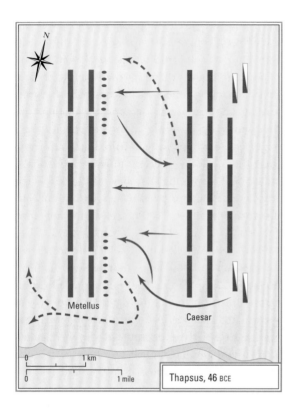

Thapsus, 46 BCE

Caesar's ultimate victory in the civil war, though resistance continued for some time.

■ **NICOPOLIS, 48 BCE**

As the focus of Caesar's campaign moved to Egypt, King Pharnaces II of Pontus invaded Roman territory. Roman forces intercepted the invaders but were forced to make a fighting withdrawal when their local auxiliaries fled the field.

■ **ALEXANDRIA, 47 BCE**

After defeat at Pharsalus, Pompey the Great fled to Egypt, where he was assassinated on the orders of Pharaoh Ptolemy XIII. Caesar had intended to be lenient upon his old friend Pompey, and was greatly displeased. He placed Cleopatra on the throne, causing Ptolemy to besiege Alexandria where Caesar was based. Caesar's forces were able to hold out until relief arrived from Judea and Asia Minor.

■ **NILE, 47 BCE**

Marching to break the siege of Alexandria, Mithridates of Pergamum was intercepted

by an Egyptian force which he was able to defeat. Upon hearing that his ally was within marching distance, Caesar left Alexandria lightly garrisoned and joined forces with his ally. Caesar's army defeated that of Ptolemy XIII on the banks of the Nile, breaking up the Egyptian spear phalanx with pila before closing to attack.

■ **ZELA, 47 BCE**

Caesar left Egypt to deal with Pharnaces II's invasion, and was attacked as his army made its usual fortified camp. Although initially hard-pressed the Romans were able to launch a counter-attack that drove Pharnaces' army from the field.

■ **RUSPINA, 46 BCE**

Defeat in Hispania and Greece left Caesar's enemies with significant holdings only in North Africa; Caesar's victory here would therefore bring the civil war to a close. Caesar faced forces under his former subordinate Titus Labienus, who managed to catch Caesar by surprise. Caesar's cavalry and some of his legionaries were driven off by a cavalry attack. The remainder managed to adopt a defensive position and held out until enemy reinforcements drove them back to their camp.

■ **THAPSUS, 46 BCE**

Caesar's army laid siege to Thapsus, forcing his opponents to offer battle. Their army included a large number of war elephants, which were countered by archers as far as possible. The arrows caused some of the elephants to stampede through their own lines; the remainder were fought off by the legionaries. As his infantry gradually gained the upper hand, Caesar's cavalry was able to outflank the enemy and capture their camp.

■ **MUNDA, 45 BCE**

After defeat in Africa, the last of Caesar's opponents fled to Hispania. Caesar followed, and after some skirmishing, Caesar defeated his enemies in an extremely hard-fought set-piece battle, bringing the civil war to a close. Ceasar lost more than 1000 killed and at least 5000 wounded.

Wars of the Second Triumvirate/ Rome
43–31 BCE

■ FORUM GALLORUM, 43 BCE

Intercepting an inexperienced Republican force sent to assist Brutus, who was cornered near Mutina, Mark Antony inflicted a defeat on the forces of Pansa, who was killed. But while Antony's men were celebrating their victory further Republican forces under Hirtius unexpectedly turned up and forced Antony to make a retreat. Antony in turn rallied his army and retreated to Mutina.

■ PHILIPPI, 42 BCE

War between the assassins of Julius Caesar and the Second Triumvirate of Octavian, Mark Antony and Marcus Aemilius Lepidus, came to a close near Phillippi in Macedonia. Having secured Italy, the Triumvirs left Lepidus in control there and took 28 legions to Macedonia where the assassins Brutus and Cassius were gathering strength.

Brutus and Cassius established themselves in strong positions within supporting distance of one another, though the reliability of some of their troops was questionable. These men had served Caesar and might now baulk at making war on his heir, Octavian, in the name of Caesar's assassins. Propaganda and bribery were used to improve loyalty.

Unable to entice the assassins out of their positions, Mark Antony attempted to outflank them by throwing a causeway across the marshes protecting their southern flank. Cassius's attempt to block this move resulted in an engagement in which Antony attacked Cassius's positions while the forces of Brutus finally left their strong positions to attack Octavian.

The overall outcome was inconclusive, with Cassius defeated on one side and Octavian on the other. However, whilst Octavian survived the battle, Cassius, the most able Republican commander, committed suicide in despair at what he thought was a complete disaster.

On the same day as the first battle of Philippi, the Republican fleet was able to intercept and destroy the triumvirs' reinforcements. The interception of reinforcements offset any gains that Antony and Octavian had made, and their supply situation was poor. However, they were able to push a line of fortifications towards Brutus' positions and to occupy what had been Cassius's camp.

Brutus wanted to avoid battle, but was forced to engage by, among other things, concerns about defection among his troops. His frontal assault was defeated after intense fighting and, cut off from his camp, Brutus committed suicide rather than be captured. His suicide brought the campaign to a close. The total casualties were not reported, but the close quarters fighting likely resulted in heavy losses for both sides, including many leading aristocrats. The battle marked the highest point of Antony's career: at that time he was the most famous Roman general and the senior partner of the Second Triumvirate.

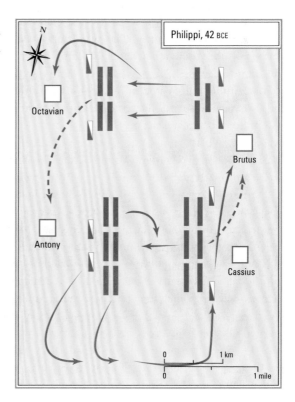

■ **PERUGIA, 41–40 BCE**

A political dispute between Mark Antony and Octavian led Antony's wife and brother to raise an army and occupy Rome. They were then forced to retreat to Perugia, which was successfully besieged by Octavian's forces.

■ **GINDARUS, 38 BCE**

Parthian cavalry invading Syria was met by Roman forces positioned on high ground. Making good use of supporting slingers, the Romans were able to defeat the Parthian cavalry attack and inflict a decisive defeat.

■ **PHRAASPA, 36 BCE**

Mark Antony invaded Parthia and besieged the capital, Phraaspa, without success. Depleted by disease and Parthian harassing attacks, the Roman army withdrew. Mark Antony ultimately established himself in Egypt, in alliance with Cleopatra.

■ **NAULOCHUS, 36 BCE**

Sextus Pompey, son of Pompey the Great, wielded significant influence over the affairs of Rome, through his control of Sicily and its grain supply. To secure his support, Mark Antony and Octavian offered Sextus an alliance. This was short-lived, and again the grain was cut off. Building a fleet of improved vessels. Octavian ordered a naval campaign that culminated in a hard-fought battle off Naulochus. Sextus' fleet was defeated, giving control of Sicily to Octavian.

■ **ACTIUM, 31 BCE**

The alliance between Mark Antony and Octavian collapsed largely due to Antony's association with Cleopatra of Egypt. This alliance not only snubbed Octavian, to whose sister Antony was married, but created suspicions that Antony intended to use Cleopatra's son Caesarion (allegedly the child of Julius Caesar) as a political tool to gain control of Rome. Rifts between Antony and Octavian had existed for some time, but now the conflict became open.

Both factions built up large fleets, and Antony attempted to strike the first blow. This was thwarted by Octavian's naval forces, so Antony set up a base at Actium. A period of skirmishing ensued, while

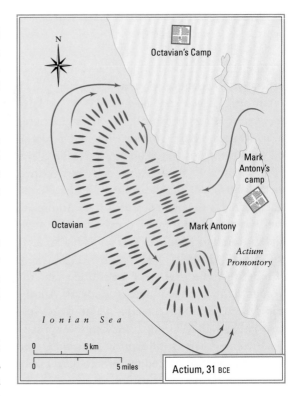

Actium, 31 BCE

Antony waited for additional forces to arrive. During this time Octavian's land forces closed in on Antony. He was advised by Cleopatra, who had supplied a large part of his fleet, to withdraw his fleet to Egypt, and eventually he conceded.

Learning that Antony intended to withdraw, Octavian resolved to force a battle. As Antony's fleet exited the straits, Octavian's ships launched their attack. Octavian also knew of Antony's battle plan and where he intended to strike his heaviest blow. Octavian's more manoeuvrable ships were able to concentrate against their chosen targets and avoid ramming attacks by the heaviest of Antony's vessels. The battle was hard-fought even though Antony's sailors were weakened by disease and some ships were undermanned. The issue was still in some doubt when Cleopatra's squadron broke off and fled. This caused Antony's fleet to dissolve into chaos and many of his ships followed suit. Both Antony and Cleopatra were able to break off and escape with a few ships, but most of the fleet was trapped against the shore and defeated.

■ **ALEXANDRIA, 30 BCE**
Although losing men to desertion, Mark Antony's army was able to defeat Octavian's first attempt at an invasion of Egypt. A second attempt overwhelmed the weakened Antonian forces, after which Egypt was annexed as a Roman province.

Second Mithridatic War
83–81 BCE

■ **HALYS, 82 BCE**
Quarrelling Roman generals Murena and Gordius provoked Mithridates by their looting and were routed in detail on either bank of the river, which bordered Pontus. The Pontic success re-inflamed resentment of the Romans in Asia.

Third Mithridatic War
75–65 BCE

■ **CYZICUS, 74 BCE**
Mithridates personally laid siege with 300,000 men to this vital city at the entrance to the Black Sea as he sought to follow up on Roman reverses in Asia. Defectors produced by Rome's ongoing civil wars aided him considerably in both strategy and tactics. Cyzicus's fortifications and defenders endured long months of continued assaults with Mithridates' engineers employing some of the more advanced siege equipment against their walls and harbour. Consul L. Licinius Lucullus and 30,000 legionaries moved to the city's relief and blocked Mithridates' supply lines in a fortified camp in a vital pass, from which they launched harassing attacks. With his own army starving faster than the inhabitants of Cyzicus, Mithridates abruptly retreated. Lucullus at once left his camp and attacked, inflicting still more casualties and driving Mithridates back into his own kingdom.

■ **CABIRA, 72 BCE**
Invading Pontus, Lucullus suffered reverses advancing to this fortress in the heart of Pontus,

even as residual Mithridatic forces cut his supply line to the coast. Alerted by beacons, Mithridates dispatched considerable cavalry against the Romans, trapping them on a neighbouring mountain. Mutual probing favoured the Romans until a sudden assault drove green Pontic troops in a disordered retreat, leading to the collapse and rout of the Pontic army.

■ **TIGRANOCERTA, 69 BCE**
Mithridates having fled to Armenia, Lucullus and 16,000 weary soldiers gave battle here to the Armenian king, Tigranes. Tigranes' contempt for the outnumbered Romans allowed Lucullus to defeat his arrayed forces in detail, capturing Tigranocerta.

■ **ARTAXATA, 68 BCE**
Facing two kingdoms with no support from Rome, Lucullus advanced to the Armenian capital in the face of Mithridates' and Tigranes' withdrawing armies. Having forced a fight and concentrated his foes, Lucullus defeated each separately.

■ **LYCUS, 66 BCE**
Pompey renewed Lucullus's advance into central Pontus with 50,000 men. Mithridates found his movements restricted by Roman field fortifications. With his 33,000 men at a loss for supplies, Mithridates attempted a retreat. His force disintegrated.

Roman Imperial Wars
27 BCE–200 CE

■ **LUPIA RIVER, 11 BCE**
Nero Claudius Drusus invaded the territory of the German Sugambri in the face of mounting unrest. Pressured in skirmishes, Drusus retreated. The Sugambris' head-on attack resulted in a repulse and the establishment of Roman bastions.

■ **TEUTOBERG FOREST, 9 CE**
(ALL DATES HENCE CE UNLESS OTHERWISE STATED)
The battle of Teutoberg Forest was Rome's worst military debacle of the 1st century CE, involving the annihilation of P. Quinctilius Varus and his three legions (some 20,000 men) by Arminius and

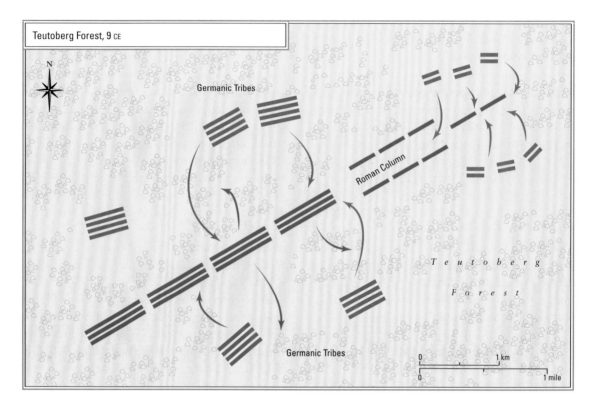

Teutoberg Forest, 9 CE

N

Germanic Tribes

Roman Column

Germanic Tribes

T e u t o b e r g

F o r e s t

0   1 km

0   1 mile

the German Cherusci. Despite considerable earlier successes, the 'Varian Disaster' drove Augustus to abandon all thoughts of extending Rome's influence across the Rhine.

Earlier expeditions by Augustus's stepsons Tiberius and Drusus had penetrated deep into German territory and defeated such federations and concentrations of German resistance as had risen in their path. In the course of such activity Arminius himself had enlisted as a Roman ally and was awarded equestrian rank for his service in Augustus's nascent 'province' of Germany. Varus as imperial governor provoked rebellion upon his arrival with premature efforts to impose taxation and Roman jurisprudence upon the trans-Rhenish population. Arminius took advantage of the resulting surge of quiet anger to employ his knowledge of Roman strategy and tactics against his instructors. Arminius and Segimerus, another German, were regular guests at Varus's table while the governor parceled out his forces throughout

his assigned territory. Having camped that summer on the Weser river, Varus moved back towards the Rhine in early Autumn with the XVII, XVIII and XIX Legions.

Varus had his troops in column when the blow fell, under cover of a series of violent rainstorms that would hit the area over the next four days. The onslaught began with superior concentrations of Germans slaughtering the Romans on more distant stations, then concentrating against Varus and his main army on ground where their numbers could be concealed from the Romans, who had a hard time communicating with their commanders and each other. German attacks began all along the line of march, with individual Roman units surrounded and destroyed without reinforcement from the rest of the column. The Romans had burdened themselves with families and a large supply train, such booty drawing still more Germans to the ongoing slaughter. At the evening of the first day of battle, Varus constructed a fortified camp and burned his wagon train, leaving the Romans surrounded by both the forest and ever-increasing numbers of Germans. On the second day, Varus and his forces struck out back through the woods towards Roman territory, that day and the next, the Romans enjoying some success against the Germans in open patches, but suffering still further casualties and hampered movement each time they re-entered the denser groves as the driving rain continued to obstruct communications and movement.

By the fourth day, Roman archery and equipment were too sodden to be of any use in the fighting, and the rain and Germans continued to pour in. At the news that Varus and his officers had committed suicide for fear of capture, resistance by the ranks collapsed, leaving Arminius and his allies to complete the slaughter and the plunder of the remaining Romans.

At the news, the Emperor Augustus suffered a nervous breakdown while surviving Roman outposts on the eastern side of the Rhine found themselves under still further attack. Panic spread as far as Italy, but German unity fractured under the lure of plundering the emptied Roman positions and over tribal antagonisms. Tiberius shifted the Roman army in Gaul into a position to prevent German crossings, while subsequent Roman expeditions would reach the battlefield, bury the remains of the dead, and with great difficulty retrieve the captured legionary standards, their loss a very great disgrace to Roman arms. Some survivors of Rome's efforts to extend the empire across the Rhine were ransomed from the Germans years later.

■ WESER RIVER, 16

At Idistaviso near the banks of the Weser river, Germanicus, 28,000 legionaries, 30,000 allies and 6000 cavalry brought Arminius and 40–50,000 Cherusci and other Germans to battle. Arminius coordinated a charge directly into the Roman centre, which resulted in the collapse of his own

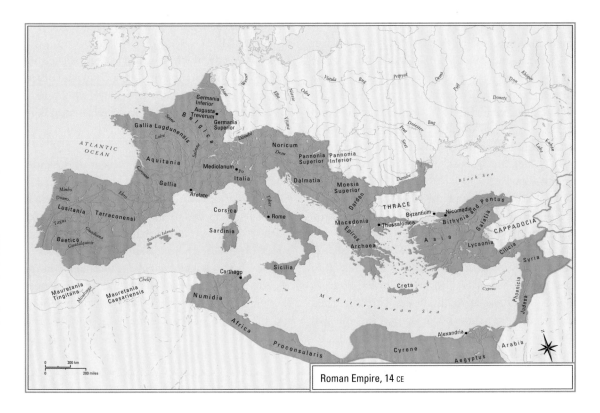

Roman Empire, 14 CE

middle and his flight during the slaughter of many of his countrymen by Roman cavalry moving around the German flanks. Germanicus withdrew in good order to the Rhine.

■ RHANDEIA, 62
L. Caesennius Paetus and his force marched boldly into Armenia where the Parthian king Vologeses promptly surrounded them and forced the unit's surrender. Rome secured their release by recognizing Armenia as a Parthian client state.

■ BETH HORON, 66
This saw the defeat of Cestius Gallus and 30,000 legionaries by the Zealots. Cestius abandoned his effort to take Jerusalem, and while retreating lost his baggage train, suffering heavy casualties when the Zealots broke his line and rear.

■ LOCUS CASTORUM, 69
Emperor Otho moved north to resist the Rhenish armies, who had proclaimed their commander Vitellius emperor. Caecina's detachment coming down from the Swiss passes fell back from Otho's army's unexpected effort to hold the Po here.

■ FIRST BEDRIACUM, 69
Lightning marches by the Rhenish armies over the French and Swiss Alps caught Otho's army unprepared to engage them in northern Italy before the commanders Valens and Caecina successfully united their forces after an abortive attack upon Placentia. Otho made his headquarters here, his staff urging him to await the arrival of loyal forces from Dalmatia, Moesia and Pannonia. Instead, having allowed his foes to consolidate, Otho sent most of his army against the Vitellians, waiting on the other side of Po among scattered vineyards. Casualties were heavy, with Otho's outnumbered troops doing well until Vitellian Batavian auxiliaries attacked the loyalist army's flank, forcing a retreat to their camp. Trapped on the far side of the Po from the rest of Otho's army, the beaten force defected to Vitellius. Hearing the news, Otho ended the civil war by committing suicide.

■ SECOND BEDRIACUM, 69
Vitellius's forces tried to hold the Po River against the arrival of the Eastern armies, who had proclaimed their commander Vespasian emperor. Antonius Primus brought 50,000 men against Vitellius's larger forces, prevailing by superior generalship.

■ JERUSALEM, 70
Jerusalem was stormed by the future emperor Titus during the Jewish Revolt after 66. Some 24,000 quarreling Zealots under Simon Bar Giora resisted 35,000 Romans and auxiliaries. As the Roman army approached, the feuding rebels drew together and did what they could to augment the city's already strong defences, consisting of two outer rings of walls on the city's plateau, and the citadels of the Antonia and the Temple. Jewish raiders almost killed Titus as he reconnoitred before his attack. Resistance to the Romans' ramps, walls and towers was heavy, employing artillery captured from the garrison. The repulse of the Romans at the final 'First Wall' prompted Titus to surround the entire city with a stockade. The final Roman assault crushed the defenders of the Temple, and the surviving zealots were scattering. Bar Giora was captured and subsequently executed.

■ TREVES, 71
This uprising by the Batavi was initially successful, with two Roman legions massacred. The end of the Romano-Jewish war allowed an overwhelmingly large Roman army to be deployed, forcing the Batavi to sue for peace.

■ MASADA, 73
This battle was the culminating event of the most famous of the Jewish revolts, in which Flavius Silva and 7000 troops from the X Legion surrounded and besieged Herod's palace-fortress on the banks of the Dead Sea, forcing the suicide of Jewish leader Eleazar Ben Y'ir and some 1000 followers.

Jewish forces rebelling against Roman control of their homeland had found considerable encouragement from the victory at Beth Horon and the failure of the Roman Empire, paralyzed by the fall of the Julio-Claudian dynasty, to chastise their insurrection. The end of the civil war brought a crushing Roman response and the nearly complete pacification of Judea.

Eleazar and his faction, called 'Assassins' by other sects, had continued destructive raids against the Romans even after the fall of Jerusalem and of Herodium and Machaerus, their two other fortresses. Masada had been built by Herod the Great as his own final refuge on a peak 450m above the surrounding territory. The fortress contained an elaborate water system and considerable stores of supplies, those features and its difficulty of access making the position impregnable, in most estimations. Flavius's command, however, had become a specialized siege unit, demonstrating its skills in three previous successful sieges.

A wall completely surrounded the edge of the plateau, with towers guarding the gate and other important sections of the defences. Silva began the siege with the classic Roman tactic of circumvallation. Large numbers of recently enslaved Jews joined the Romans in the construction of eight fortified camps linked by a stockade, preventing the Zealots from slipping

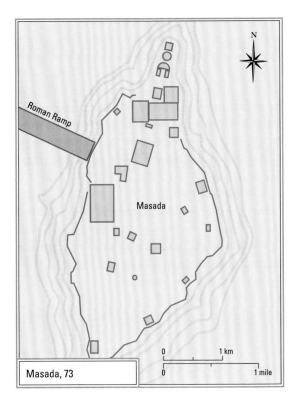

Masada, 73

away and provisions from being smuggled in. Silva secured his own supply line with long caravans of still more enslaved Jews bringing in provisions and potable water.

The Romans next began construction of a siege ramp by which they could move artillery and a battering ram up against the fortress. The engineers augmented a neighbouring height with earth and crushed stone to create an enormous siege ramp, upon which they laid a course of masoned stone to achieve strength and the required height of 100m to allow them to take the walls and gates under artillery fire. The ramp's construction began that autumn and finished in spring.

There was not much the Zealots could do in response, except for delivering harassing archery and preparing a section of wood-beam wall in front of the burgeoning ramp, covered with earth in an effort at fire-proofing the construction. Upon the completion of the ramp, the Romans sent a siege tower some 30m high up the ramp, with iron plates and smaller artillery protecting the machine from the Zealots' fire and incendiary missiles.

When the tower reached Herod's entrance, the Romans employed the massive bronze-tipped ram inside the device against the gate and beams behind it. The impacts of the ram served to shake the surrounding earth down inside the bulwark, making it more solid, but also rendering it vulnerable to fire, which the Romans soon employed. Shifting wind drove the flames back against the iron plates of the tower, but a second shift engulfed the beams in a roaring inferno.

The Romans withdrew that night to let the flames burn, manning their wall in anticipation of a break-out. What they found in the morning were the bodies of the defenders, who had slain each other and themselves along with their families.

■ TAPAE, 87

Responding to a Dacian incursion into Moesia, Roman forces invaded Dacia but were heavily defeated at Tapae. A renewed offensive the following year resulted in another battle at Tapae, this time a Roman victory.

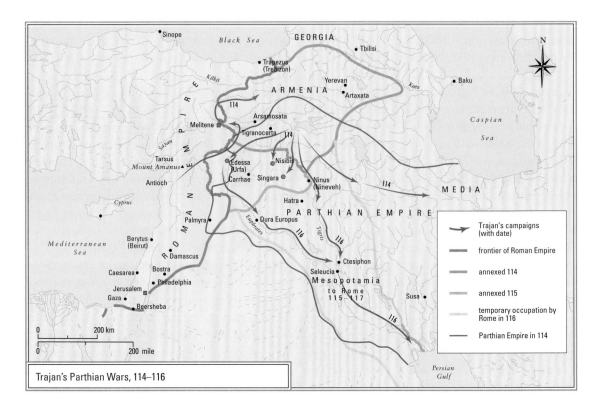

Trajan's Parthian Wars, 114–116

■ TAPAE, 101

A Roman invasion of Dacia was met at Tapae. After inconclusive fighting, the Dacians interpreted a storm as a divine omen and broke off the action. The Roman army then went into winter quarters.

■ ADAMCLISI, 102

Before the Romans could resume their offensive into Dacia, the Dacians attacked Moesia. After a major battle at Adamclisi, the Dacians withdrew to counter Roman advances into their home territory, but were defeated at Sarmisegetusa.

■ SARMISEGETUSA, 106

Having defeated the Dacians in 102, the Roman army enforced the partial dismantling of Sarmisegetusa's walls before retiring. By 106 the walls had been rebuilt and the Dacian king, Decebalus, did not observe the peace terms imposed upon him. A renewed Roman offensive, led by Emperor Trajan, was launched, using parallel routes which were already garrisoned by Roman forces as part of the 102 settlement. Brushing aside what resistance developed, Trajan's main force laid siege to Sarmisegetusa while detachments attacked other Dacian settlements to prevent a relief from being mounted. After the initial Roman assault failed, deliberate siege operations commenced, the Romans surrounding the city with fortified positions. The defenders of Sarmisegetusa were gradually worn down until Roman forces were able to enter the city. Decebalus escaped from the city with some troops but was chased down.

■ POROLISSUM, 106

After their defeat at Sarmisegetusa, the remaining Dacian forces were pursued and brought to action at Porolissum. A legion camp was set up at this location, which then became the capital of the province when it was annexed.

■ CTESIPHON, 165

After beating off Parthian attempts to take control of Armenia, Roman forces entered Parthia itself and besieged the capital, Ctesiphon. The city was taken but was returned to Parthia as part of the subsequent peace settlement.

■ **CYZICUS, 193**

The Praetorian Guard, formed to protect the Roman Emperor, had become such a power in Roman politics that in 193 its members were able to murder Emperor Pertinax and offer the throne to the highest bidder. Several claimants emerged, of whom Didius Julianus was placed on the throne. Septimus Severus first deposed and beheaded Didius Julianus, then marched east to Asia Minor, defeating rival claimant Pescennius Niger at Czyicus.

■ **NICAEA, 193**

Defeated at Czyicus, Pescennius Niger retreated to Nicea where a second encounter took place. Niger's outnumbered forces were defeated, but managed to conduct a retreat into the Taurus Mountains where Severus could not immediately follow.

■ **ISSUS, 194**

The final encounter between the forces of Septimus Severus and Pescennius Niger took place at Issus in 194. Although the issue remained in doubt for some time during the battle, Severus's legions outfought their opponents; Pescennius Niger was killed whilst fleeing.

■ **LUGDUNUM, 197**

Rival claimant Clodius Albinius initially allied himself with Severus, but later came into conflict with the Roman. Albinius's army, claimed to include 150,000 troops, was decisively defeated at Lugdunum. Severus thus emerged as undisputed Roman emperor.

■ **CTESIPHON, 198**

Roman forces succeeded in reaching Ctesiphon despite resistance from the declining Parthians. Once again the city was taken and Parthia was forced to make further concessions to Rome, hastening the end of Parthian power.

Romano-British Wars
55 BCE–410 CE

■ **FIRST INVASION, 55 BCE**

Julius Caesar undertook a number of endeavours during his wars in Gaul which were far beyond the remit of his mission, such as the bridging of the Rhine and two expeditions against Britain. The first of these, in 55 BCE, was probably an opportunistic foray rather than a full-scale invasion and was driven off, though it further increased Caesar's reputation in Roman politics.

After a personal reconnaissance of the shore, Caesar crossed the English Channel with two legions, with a force of cavalry to be brought across soon afterwards. Caesar's legions made an opposed landing against a force of Briton chariots and infantry, which was eventually pushed back enough to create a beachhead. In the face of repeated attacks, and unable to get the cavalry ashore due to bad weather in the Channel, Caesar decided to retire to Gaul.

■ **SECOND INVASION, 54 BCE**

Caesar's second invasion of Britain was carefully planned and involved around 27,000 troops; five legions plus cavalry support. This time the Britons felt unable to oppose the landing directly and mustered their forces inland. Caesar went on the offensive immediately, clearing the area around his beachhead, but was then forced to delay further action in order to repair damage to his fleet.

Defeated in open battle, the Britons attempted to wear down Caesar's force with skirmishing and guerrilla tactics, and made a stand at the Thames. Caesar's legions forced a crossing and soon afterwards an alliance was made with some of the Briton tribes. After further fighting the Britons agreed to pay tribute to Rome, and Caesar returned to his campaign in Gaul. It is highly unlikely that the tribute was paid, as Caesar could not spare any troops as garrisons or to enforce the treaty.

■ **THIRD INVASION, 43**

Taking advantage of conflict among the Britons, about 40,000 Roman troops were landed on the south coast in 43 CE. Within the year, 11 south-eastern tribes had surrendered and a capital was set up at Camlodunum.

■ **MEDWAY, 43**

The primary leader of Briton resistance to the Roman invasion was Caratacus, who chose to contest a crossing of the River Medway. An

Roman Conquest, 43 CE

VERULAMIUM (ST ALBANS), 60/61

After overrunning Camulodunum, Boudicca's forces overwhelmed a single legion sent to stop them and advanced on Londinium, sacking it, and thence to Verulamium. Unable to defend the town, Roman forces withdrew and Verulamium was sacked unopposed.

WATLING STREET, 60/61

Preserving what little remained of his force after the destruction of Legio IX Hispana, Roman governor Gaius Suetonius Paulinus did not oppose the Iceni in their destruction of Londinium and Verulamium, but once reinforced he sought a decisive battle. Although heavily outnumbered, the Roman legions were far more disciplined than their Iceni opponents and were more efficiently equipped.

The actual location of the battle is open to some speculation. It probably occurred on the route that became known as Watling Street, somewhere between Londinium and Viroconium. The Romans prepared a defensive position and awaited attack, trusting to difficult terrain on the flanks to somewhat offset Iceni numbers.

The Iceni made a straightforward frontal charge, which was met by the usual Roman tactic of hurling pila spears to disrupt the advance. This was followed up by a counter-charge against the disorganized Britons. Although more numerous, the Briton force did not have the sustained fighting power of the Romans. Tired legionaries were constantly replaced in the front lines by fresh men in a well-drilled cycle. Meanwhile the Briton warriors were unable to obtain respite due to the press of men at their backs.

The Iceni force was gradually outfought by the legions in a protracted action that resulted in massive Briton casualties. As the line advanced, space was created for the Roman cavalry to attack the Iceni flanks, contributing to an eventual collapse. Many Iceni warriors were unable to escape due to their own baggage train encamped at the rear of the army and were slaughtered. Boudicca herself is said to have committed suicide rather than face

aggressive Roman crossing caught the Britons unawares, but after a day of heavy fighting the situation was still in doubt. A renewed offensive on the second day inflicted a heavy defeat and the Britons fell back to the Thames. The exact location of this battle is open to much debate.

CAER CARADOC, 51

Defeated in the south-east, Caratacus retired to Wales and continued to resist Roman expansion in Britain. As the Romans pushed west Caratacus fought a final defensive battle at Caer Caradoc, but was outfought by the better-armed legions.

Revolt of Boudicca 60/61

CAMULODUNUM (COLCHESTER), 60/61

Mistreated by Roman officials, Queen Boudicca of the Iceni tribe took advantage of the absence of Roman legions, which were campaigning in the west of Britain. Her first target was Camulodunum, which was virtually undefended.

First Roman landing 43

Roman advance 43–47

Roman advance 47–59

Roman advance 61–74

Roman advance 78–84

Major Roman fort

Marching camps for Agricola's campaigns 78–83

Major battles with dates

ICENI Tribe names

Orkney Islands

CORNOVII

CAERENII

SMERTAE

Outer Hebrides

CARNONACAE Cawdor Bellie *TAEXALI* Ythan Wells
Thornshill Auchinhove Dumo
DECANTAE Mons Graupius? 84 BCE

CREONES *VACOMAGI*

CALEDONES Strathcathro
VERTURIONES Finavon
Cardean
Inchtuthil
Dalginross Carpow Bonnytown
Menteith Ardoch
Camelon Dunblane

DAMNONI *VOTADINI*

EPIDII Castledykes Newstead

Beattock *SELGOVAE*

NOVANTAE Dalswinton
Carlisle Corbridge
Nether Denton

CARVETII

BRIGANTES

North Sea

Irish Sea *PARISI* York

Ribchester

SETANTII

IRELAND

Anglesey Newton-on-Trent Lincoln
60 CE *DECEANGLI* Chester *CORITANI*

GANGANI *ICENI*

Wroxeter Longthorpe
ORDOVICES Wall Leicester
CORNOVII *TRINOVANTES*

Clyro *DOBUNNI*
Gloucester *CATUVELLAUNI* Colchester
DEMETAE St Albans
SILURES Usk London 43 BCE
Caerleon Richborough

BELGAE *ATREBATES* *CANTIACI*

South Cadbury *REGNI*
AD 44? Hod Hill Fishbourne Boulogne
AD 44?

North Tawton *DUROTRIGES*
DUMNONII Exeter
Maiden Castle
Nanstallon AD 44?

ATLANTIC OCEAN

English Channel

0   100 km
0   100 miles

ROMAN EMPIRE

Roman Conquest of Britain, 43–84

Boudican Revolt, 60

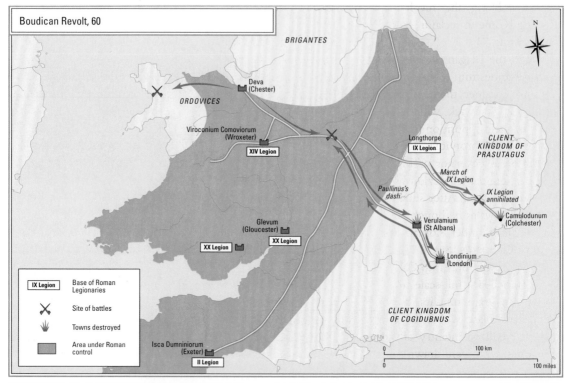

BRIGANTES

Deva (Chester)

ORDOVICES

Viroconium Comoviorum (Wroxeter)
XIV Legion

Longthorpe
IX Legion

CLIENT KINGDOM OF PRASUTAGUS

March of IX Legion

Paullinus's dash

IX Legion annihilated

Verulamium (St Albans)

Camulodunum (Colchester)

Glevum (Gloucester)
XX Legion   **XX Legion**

Londinium (London)

CLIENT KINGDOM OF COGIDUBNUS

Isca Dumniniorum (Exeter)
II Legion

IX Legion   Base of Roman Legionaries

✕   Site of battles

    Towns destroyed

    Area under Roman control

0 ——— 100 km
0 ——— 100 miles

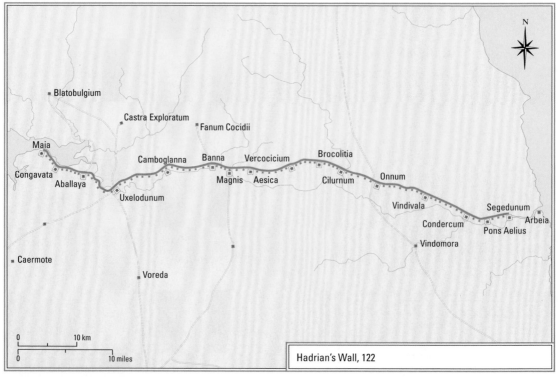

Blatobulgium

Castra Exploratum

Fanum Cocidii

Maia

Camboglanna   Banna   Vercocicium   Brocolitia

Congavata   Magnis   Aesica   Cilurnum   Onnum
Aballaya

Uxelodunum   Vindivala   Segedunum
    Condercum   Arbeia
    Pons Aelius

Vindomora

Caermote

Voreda

0 ——— 10 km
0 ——— 10 miles

Hadrian's Wall, 122

capture, robbing the revolt of leadership and allowing Rome to reclaim south-east Britain.

■ STANWICK, 71

Although the Brigantes tribe had formerly been allies of Rome, from 69 CE onwards attempts were made to conquer them. A Brigantes force was defeated at Stanwick, which may have been the centre of their opposition to Rome.

■ DEFEAT OF ORDIVICES, 78

Appointed as governor of Britain, Gnaeus Julius Agricola found the previously subdued tribes of Wales in rebellion. After subduing the Ordivices of northern Wales he bought all territory as far as Anglesey back under Roman control.

■ MONS GRAUPIUS, 84

Agricola made a foray into Caledonia in 79, and in 84 he launched a full-scale invasion. Threatening Caledonian grain supplies, he was able to force a battle at a place whose location remains vague. Tacitus' auxiliary infantry advanced against the Caledones, who were drawn up on high ground.

After driving in the front enemy ranks the auxiliaries were outflanked by Caledonian reserves, who where then flanked by Roman cavalry.

■ PICTISH RAIDS, c.105

Although much of Caledonia remained beyond Roman control, the lowlands were garrisoned and increasingly Romanized. Around 105, Pictish raids into the region coincided with a draw-off of troops to deal with crises elsewhere.

■ BRIGANTES REVOLT, 155–57

The Brigantes revolted against Roman rule and destroyed the fort at Olicana, but were subdued and placed under direct military rule for a period. Some tribes broke away at this time and became Roman allies.

■ BREACH OF HADRIAN'S WALL, 180

After retreating from the Antonine Wall in 163, Roman forces rebuilt the fortifications of Hadrian's Wall. This did not prevent a large-scale penetration of the wall by northern tribes, which was met by Roman punitive raids.

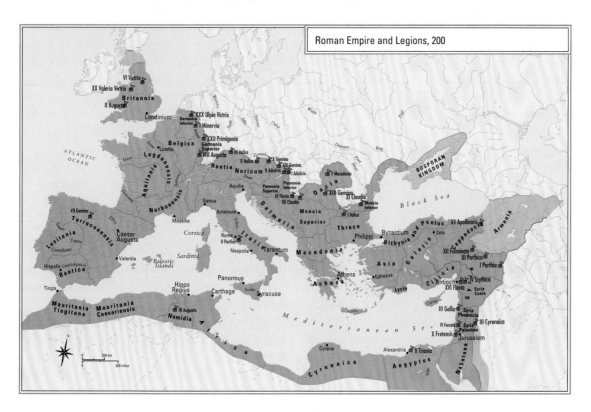

Roman Empire and Legions, 200

■ SOUTHAMPTON, 293

After retaking Gaul for the Western Empire, a Roman force landed near Southampton. There they engaged and defeated forces of Allectus, who had taken control of the country after assassinating the self-proclaimed Western Emperor Mausaeus Carausius.

■ BARBARIAN RAIDS, 4TH CENTURY

After the withdrawal of Roman troops to face the Goths, Romano-Britons elected their own emperors to lead the defence against raids from Ireland and the Continent. By 410 Britain had explicitly been abandoned by Rome.

Chinese Three Kingdom Wars 220–80

■ XIAOTING, 222

The warlord Liu Bei declared himself emperor of Shu Han and invaded Eastern Wu, using the Yangtze river for transport. A piecemeal response by Eastern Wu was easily defeated, until the forces of Eastern Wu abandoned attempts to intercept the invasion and retreated to concentrate for a decisive battle.

Bypassing the few places strongly held by Eastern Wu, Liu Bei's forces reached the city of Xiaoting but were unable to capture it, despite some local successes. Liu Bei's forces were operating at the end of a long supply line and were gradually worn down by the defenders, who remained in their fortified positions and refused to be drawn into open battle. Eastern Wu finally launched a counter-attack in the height of summer, driving Liu Bei's army from its camps by setting fire to them. Liu Bei was killed in the retreat.

■ WUZHANG PLAINS, 224

The last Northern Expedition led by the Shu Han chancellor Zhuge Liang became a lengthy stalemate, during which Zhuge Liang fell ill and died. His army then retreated to Shu Han territory.

■ XINGSHI, 224

A large Cao Wei force invaded Shu Han territory, which required passing through difficult terrain.

The route chosen was short but rugged and lacked water sources, imposing a severe logistical problem. The outnumbered Shu Han forces took advantage of the terrain to block the advance at Mount Xingshi. Deception operations were undertaken, convincing the Wei commanders that they faced a much greater force.

Large numbers of pack animals and human bearers died of thirst, along with some of the troops, before the Wei force began to withdraw. It was then attacked by Shu Han reinforcements which attempted to cut off the line of retreat. Although the Wei army was able to extricate itself from the trap, it suffered huge casualties from thirst as well as enemy action. This defeat had far-reaching consequences for internal and external politics within Cao Wei.

■ XINCHENG, 227–228

Meng Da, administrator of Xincheng, offered to betray his allegiance to Wei and join the forces of Shu Han if they moved against Wei. His intentions were discovered, causing him to assemble an army hurriedly. However, Wei's general deceived Meng Da into thinking that the information had been disregarded as part of an external plot. Meng Da became complacent and was easily defeated by the army of Wei, pre-empting his rebellion.

■ TIANSHUI, 228

Shu Han forces advanced against the city of Chang'an, triggering a series of revolts against Cao Wei. Tianshui opened its gates to the Shu Han forces, but these were forced to retreat by defeats elsewhere.

■ JIETING, 228

The First Northern Expedition launched by Shu Han forces achieved considerable success before it was halted at Jieting. Unable to use the region as a supply base, the expedition was forced to retreat.

■ SHITING, 228

Duped by a false promise that an Eastern Wu general would defect to their side, forces of Cao Wei were drawn into an ambush. Retreating into a fortified camp at Shiting, they were then attacked at night and part of the force was dispersed. Nevertheless,

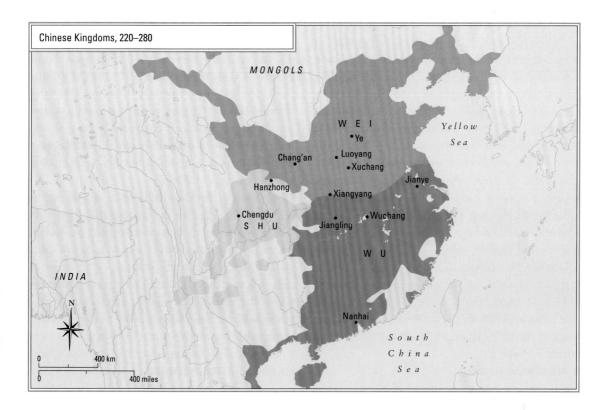

Chinese Kingdoms, 220–280

the Wei commander decided to launch an attack and was decisively defeated. Wu forces then pursued those of Wei and inflicted further casualties.

■ CHENCANG, 229

The Second Northern Expedition of Shu Han reached Chencang and found it heavily defended. Despite having a large siege train the siege was unsuccessful and the Shu Han were forced to withdraw as supplies ran out.

■ QUCHENG, 249

Cao Wei forces attempted to eliminate Shu Han fortifications in the Qu mountains, resulting in a counter-offensive and an inconclusive series of actions. A deteriorating supply situation caused the Shu Han to retreat.

■ DIDAO, 255

Rashly attempting to intercept invading Shu Han forces, the Cao Wei army was defeated and then besieged in Didao. The Shu Han failed to take the city and were forced to retreat by enemy reinforcements.

■ DUANGU, 256

Shu Han forces advanced against the city of Qishan but found it heavily defended. The Han army was decisively defeated at Duangu by a Cao Wei force, after reinforcements failed to reach the Han in time.

Rome's Germanic and Barbarian Wars 250–500

■ PHILIPPOPOLIS, 250

A Goth force under King Cniva was driven away from Nicopolis by a Roman army commanded by Emperor Decius, which then followed the Goths. Cniva turned on his pursuers and routed them before successfully besieging Philippopolis.

■ ABRITTUS, 251

As the Goths marched home from sacking Philippopolis, they were caught by Emperor Decius' army, which had been reinforced after its recent defeat. The Goths' king, Cniva, gave battle on ground of his own choosing, concealing part of his force from the Romans. According to some accounts of the battle, Emperor Decius' son was killed in the early stages. The initial fighting nevertheless went in favour of the Romans at first.

As the Goth line collapsed, the Romans attempted to pursue them from the battlefield but instead were led into a swamp. Here, the concealed Goth force launched a counter-attack that inflicted great slaughter on the Romans. Emperor Decius (and possibly his son) were killed in the fighting. Rome was forced to accept an unfavourable treaty which may have included tribute paid to the Goths.

■ **GOTHIC SEA RAIDS, 253–268**

Despite the terms of a treaty requiring them to respect Roman territory, the Goths raided the Black Sea and Balkan coasts. Weakened by a long plague, the Roman Empire was unable find an effective counter.

■ **MEDIOLANUM, 259**

Facing an incursion into Italy by the Alemanni, the Roman senate threw together a militia force which caused the tribesmen to retire. They were intercepted at Mediolanum by a Roman army and defeated with heavy casualties.

■ **LAKE BENACUS, 268**

A very large Alemanni force remained at large in Italy despite the victory at Mediolanum, posing a severe threat to Rome itself. Relatively few troops were available to Emperor Claudius II due to the needs of campaigns in the east against the Goths. Thus the emperor attempted to negotiate an Alemanni withdrawal. When the talks broke down, the much smaller Roman force attacked and inflicted a decisive defeat.

■ **NAISSUS, 269**

As Rome recovered its strength after plague had deprived its legions of manpower, the Goths continued their raids and incursions into Roman territory. They were met by a Roman army under Emperor Gallienus, who managed to inflict defeats upon the invaders. Further casualties were caused by the Roman fleet, which attempted to prevent the Goths from raiding along the coast.

Gallienus was assassinated, probably in 268, and was succeeded by Claudius II. There is some doubt as to which emperor was reigning at the time of the battle at Naissus, though it seems likely that it was Claudius. The emperor was also distracted for a time by an incursion of the Alemanni into Italy. After defeating this invasion, he marched east in time to meet a huge Gothic force which was moving into the Balkans.

The Roman fleet did what it could to oppose the invasion, defeating or driving off part of the Gothic fleet, but it was not possible to prevent several cities from being besieged. Some were sacked, others successfully resisted.

Hearing that the Roman emperor was approaching with a large army, the Goths concentrated their forces and met their opponents as the Romans came down from the north. A bloody set-piece battle ensued for a time before the Romans gained an advantage by means of a ruse. Some units feigned a retreat and drew part of the Gothic force into an ambush, causing a general collapse.

Forced to discard their baggage train and many pack animals, the Goths suffered additional causalities from starvation and disease as they retired. The Roman pursuit was so vigorous and inflicted such losses on the Goths that they ceased to be a major threat for some time.

■ **PLACENTIA, 271**

Defeat at Lake Benacus did not end the Alemanni threat to Rome. Taking advantage of the army's absence on the frontiers, the Alemanni invaded Italy and marched on Placentia. Emperor Aurelian brought his army rapidly from Pannonia to meet the invasion but was ambushed and defeated. With Aurelian's army in retreat the Alemanni then resumed their advance towards Rome, which was virtually undefended and possessed inadequate fortifications.

■ **FANO, 271**

Recovering from his defeat at Placentia, Emperor Aurelian pursued the Alemanni and defeated them near Fano. The Alemanni were caught with their backs to the River Metaurus; many drowned as they tried to escape.

■ **PAVIA, 271**

Pursuing the Alemanni from Fano, Emperor Aurelian caught them again at Pavia and was able to block their retreat through the Alpine passes. The Alemanni force was virtually annihilated, ending the threat to Rome for the time being.

■ **CHALONS, 274**

From 260 onwards, former Roman possessions in Gaul and the surrounding areas had been part of the Gallic Empire. Already diminished, the Gallic Empire was reintegrated after Emperor Aurelian defeated its forces at Chalons.

■ **LINGONES, 298**

The city of Lingones, an important economic and administrative centre, was sacked by the Alemanni. They were then defeated and driven off by a Roman army under the command of Emperor Constantius Chlorus.

■ **VINDONISSA, 298**

Emperor Constantius Chlorus campaigned against the Alemanni along the Rhine frontier, defeating them at Vindonissa and other locations. These victories restored stability to the region at a time when Rome was severely threatened by barbarian incursions.

■ **AUTUN, 356**

Autun was blockaded by the Alemanni, who were prevented from breaching its inadequate walls by a force of retired veterans who resided in the town. At the approach of a Roman army, the Alemanni retreated.

■ **REIMS, 356**

After relieving Autun, Julian the Apostate's Roman army advanced directly towards Reims despite a series of ambushes on the road. His force was outflanked by the Alemanni and narrowly avoided a serious defeat.

■ **BRUMATH, 356**

Most Alemanni war bands fell back before Julian's force, but at Brumath one offered battle. Julian's force enveloped the Alemanni flanks, inflicting a defeat that discouraged other Alemanni bands for a time.

■ **SENOE, 356**

Julian's army went into winter quarters and was attacked at Senoe. The Alemanni assault was repulsed but Julian lacked the forces to counter-attack, so had to remain besieged until the Alemanni ran out of supplies and dispersed.

■ **ARGENTORATUM, 357 (STRASBOURG)**

Julian the Apostate was appointed Caesar of the West by the Roman Emperor, Constantius II, and was sent to Gaul where he campaigned against the Alemanni, who had overrun several Roman towns. After a somewhat successful first campaign year Julian was reinforced but was also beset with political problems within his command.

Nevertheless, Julian conducted a successful campaign against the Alemanni who were marauding west of the Rhine, then moved to intercept a large force which was crossing the river. Although outnumbered, Julian gave battle with his cavalry massed on the right flank.

The battle opened with a cavalry clash which was indecisive for a time, before the Roman cavalry suddenly collapsed and began to rout. The infantry maintained their discipline, allowing some of the cavalry to rally, but they played little part in the remainder of the action, other than to keep the Germanic cavalry from attacking the Roman flank.

After a long period of hand-to-hand fighting the Alemanni were able to penetrate the first Roman line and attacked the second, which repelled the assault after hard fighting. This setback, coupled with exhaustion and heavy casualties, caused morale among the Alemanni to fall, and soon their whole force dissolved into rout.

With the river at their backs, many Germanic warriors were unable to escape or were killed with arrows and javelins as they tried to cross. Julian restrained his force from chasing their opponents into the water, instead pulling back to a defensive camp for the night. Julian's force crossed the Rhine thereafter and launched a punitive raid into Alemanni territory. The Romans pulled back once serious resistance materialized, and the Alemanni were granted a temporary peace agreement.

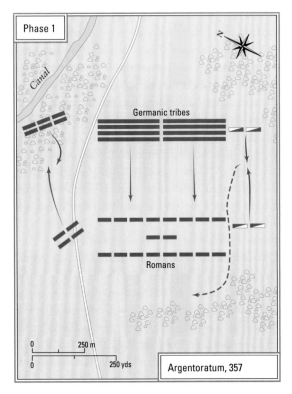

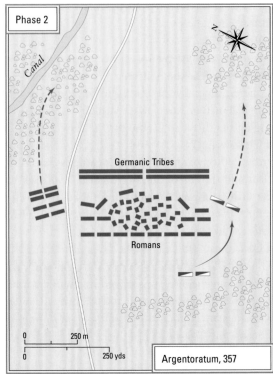

CHALONS, 366

After the defeat of Roman forces by the Alemanni, Emperor Valentian I led a campaign agasint them. Following victory over the Alemanni at Chalons, Valentian advanced across the Rhine; he was the last Roman emperor to campaign there.

SOLICINIUM, 367

Facing an alliance of Germanic tribes, Roman forces under Emperor Valentian I launched a vigorous attack which forced the barbarians back to a defensive position on a hill. Heavy losses were suffered by both sides.

TANAIS RIVER, 373

As the Huns moved westwards they pushed into the territory of the Alans, resulting in a clash at the Tanais river (the modern Don). Details are sketchy, but the Huns apparently defeated the Alans in the battle.

BATTLE OF THE WILLOWS, 377

Rebellious Goths began plundering Roman provinces in search of food. A joint force from the Eastern and Western Empires fought the Goths to a bloody draw in what was the first battle of the Gothic War.

ARGENTOVARIA, 378

The Lentienses, part of the Alemanni tribal group, crossed the frozen Rhine to enter Roman territory in search of plunder. They were defeated by Roman forces, and their king killed, at Argentovaria.

ADRIANOPLE, 378

Driven by the Hun invasion, large numbers of Goths asked permission to settle in Roman territory; in return they would help defend the frontiers of the Empire. A famine, and Roman indifference to their starvation, forced the Goths into revolt. After initial attempts to put down the rebellion failed, the Goths advanced on Adrianople and launched an unsuccessful assault. Help was promised by the Western Emperor, Gratian, but he was forced to deal with an incursion by Alemanni tribesmen. The Eastern

Emperor, Valens, was thus forced to choose between taking on the Goths with only his own forces or waiting for assistance from the west.

Marching from Constantinople, Valens made contact with the Goth army and used his cavalry to track it while his main force moved up. He reached Adrianople and made camp, expecting Western Roman forces to join him before offensive operations began. However, an opportunity arose to attack the Goth army, and Valens decided to make the most of it.

Valens' army somewhat outnumbered the Goths, and was composed of a good mix of legions, auxiliaries and cavalry. Many of the Roman troops were veterans, giving Valens further reasons to be confident. The Goths, for their part, seemed to have a force composed entirely of infantry and archers. They camped in a defensive wagon laager and awaited the Roman approach.

Valens deployed for battle in conventional manner, with infantry in the centre and cavalry forming the flanks. These included heavily armoured cataphracts as well as lighter cavalry. Faced with this threat the Goths adopted a very defensive deployment, using their wagon laager to protect their infantry from cavalry attack.

Valens was not aware that the Goths had a large body of cavalry in the area, which had been out foraging. Hoping to buy time for this force to return, the Goths offered a parlay. Valens had already rejected an earlier suggestion of peace negotiations, but now agreed to talk. Fussing over minutae of protocol regarding who was of sufficient rank to meet with whom bought more time for the Goths, who started brushfires in order to increase the discomfort of Valens' hungry, hot and tired troops.

Before the parlay could finally get underway, cavalry skirmishing escalated into an attack on the Goths' main positions. The Roman cavalry were easily repelled, and at the same time the Gothic cavalry reached the field. It launched an immediate charge at the disorganized Roman left flank cavalry.

The Roman left flank rapidly gave way, permitting the Gothic cavalry to charge into the infantry in the centere They were rapidly joined by the Gothic infantry, who came out of their laager to engage the Romans from the front. Despite a collapsed flank, the Roman infantry proved extremely resilient and held out against repeated assaults.

Hot, hungry and tired from their long march, the Roman infantry had started the battle at a disadvantage, and as the fighting went on exhaustion took its toll. Units began to falter and then melt away, although some fought a stubborn rearguard action that allowed at least part of the army to escape. When Roman resistance finally collapsed, the Gothic pursuit was extremely vigorous. As much as two-thirds of the Roman army may have been annihilated. Emperor Valens himself was killed in the fighting, although his exact fate is not known for certain.

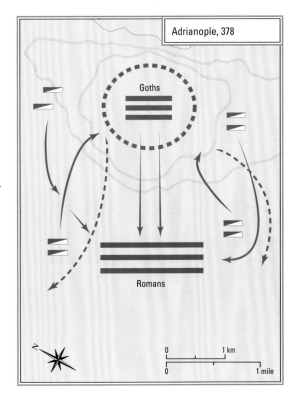

Adrianople, 378

Goths

Romans

0   1 km

0   1 mile

■ AQUIELA/FRIGIDUS, 394

Attempting to re-unify the Eastern and Western Empires, Eastern Emperor Theodosius marched towards Italy. His army was intercepted near Aquileia by a Western army under the Western Emperor Eugenius. Theodosius sent his barbarian allies into a headlong attack, which was repulsed with heavy losses on both sides. The next day, reinforced by deserters from the Western army, Theodosius attacked again. His victory permitted a temporary re-unification of the Roman Empire.

■ MILAN, 402

The Visigoths under Alaric I advanced into Italy, forcing Emperor Honorius to take refuge behind the fortifications of his capital at Milan. Meanwhile, Roman forces were hurriedly gathered from the frontiers to oppose the invasion.

■ ASTA, 402

As the Visigoths closed in on Milan, Emperor Honorius tried to move to Arles but was driven into Asta where they were besieged. Roman reinforcements fought their way into the city to assist the defenders.

■ POLLENTIA, 402

The arrival of a Roman army caused the Visigoths besieging Emperor Honorius in Asta to withdraw to Pollentia. There, they were attacked by surprise during their Easter Day ceremonies. The attack was led by Alans, allied to Rome, who were eventually driven off. In the ensuing bloody hand-to-hand struggle, Roman troops gradually outfought the Visigoths, who managed to withdraw at the price of leaving their baggage and loot behind.

■ VERONA, 403

Defeated at Pollentia, the Visigoths agreed to withdraw from Italy but instead besieged Verona. They were attacked there by a Roman army and forced to withdraw eastwards, out of Italy and towards Illyricum.

■ SIEGE OF FLORENCE, 406

Florence was besieged by Gothic tribesmen under Radagaisus, and brought to the point of surrender.

A Roman army under Stilicho then surrounded the Goths and besieged them in turn, starving them into surrender.

■ ROME, 410

Suspicion that their able commander Stilicho, who had defeated King Alaric of the Visigoths, was now in league with his former enemy prompted the Roman authorities to execute the general. This caused disaffected elements of the Roman army to go over to Alaric's side.

In 408 the Visigothic army reached Rome and placed the city under siege. With no relief force available in time, the city was starved into surrender and forced to pay a large ransom. Alaric made demands of Emperor Honorius, including a homeland for his people and recognition for himself as a Roman official.

Honorius would not grant these concessions, so Alaric returned to Rome in 409. He took control of Rome's port, Ostia, and destroyed its granaries. Again the city was forced to surrender, and Alaric demanded that the Senate depose Emperor Honorius and replace him with Priscus Attalus. Alaric's army then marched on Ravenna to enforce this decision upon Honorius. This was thwarted by the arrival of troops from the Eastern Empire to reinforce Ravenna.

A dispute between Alaric and Attalus, and failure to reach a settlement with Honorius, caused Alaric to depose Attalus and march back to Rome, laying siege a third time. The gates were opened to Alaric's army by sympathizers within the city, which was then sacked for the first time in 800 years. Rome was not at this time the capital of the empire; government had previously been relocated to Milan and then Ravenna. Alaric died soon after the fall of Rome, and after a plan to relocate to Africa came to naught the Visigoths instead moved to Gaul in search of a new home.

■ VIENNE, 411

Having originally supported Constantine III's revolt against Emperor Honorius, Gerontius turned against him. He besieged Constantine's forces in Vienne. After capturing the city along

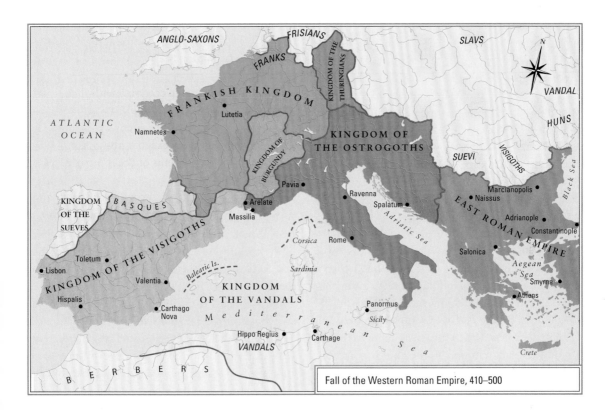

Fall of the Western Roman Empire, 410–500

with Constantine's son Constans, Gerontius then marched against Constantine himself.

ARELATE, 411

While Gerontius was besieging Constantine III in Arelate, a Roman army loyal to Emperor Honorius arrived, causing Gerontius to retreat into Spain. The siege was continued by the loyalists, who captured and executed Constantine III.

ARELATE, 427–430

A Visigoth force besieging Arelate (Arles) was driven off by a Roman army under the command of Flavius Aëtius. A renewed attack in 430 was again defeated, leading to a peace treaty between Rome and the Goths.

HIPPO, 430–431

Bonifacius, the Roman governor in Africa, hired Vandal mercenaries to his side, but then dismissed them. They revolted in response, and besieged him in Hippo Regius for over a year. A Roman army rescued the defenders but was driven to Carthage by the Vandals.

ARELATE AND NARBO, 436–437

Theodoric I of the Visigoths took advantage of Rome's internal troubles, attacking Narbo and Arelate. This move was countered by Roman forces and Hun mercenaries, though the siege of Narbo was not broken until 437.

ATTILA INVADES EASTERN EMPIRE, 441

After an unsuccessful campaign into Persia, the Huns returned to the Danube region. Roman garrison strengths had been reduced to provide troops for service elsewhere, leaving Illyricum and the Balkans open to attack.

UTUS, 447

A Roman army including imperial troops and local forces met the Huns at the River Utus. The Huns were eventually victorious, but their heavy losses may have caused an abandonment of plans to attack Constantinople; instead the Huns pillaged much of the Balkans. A peace treaty was agreed a year later, creating a demilitarized buffer zone around the Danube.

■ ATTILA CROSSES THE RHINE, 451

In the spring of 451 the Huns crossed the Rhine and pushed into Gaul. Aided by local allies they pillaged Divodurum (Metz) and besieged Orleans. Roman commander Flavius Aëtius began assembling an alliance to counter the invasion.

■ SIEGE OF ORLEANS, 451

Unwilling to be pinned down against the defences of Orleans, Attila broke off his siege at the approach of an allied Roman and Visigoth army under the command of Flavius Aëtius and Theodoric.

■ CHALONS/CATALAUNIAN FIELDS, 451

Interrupted in their siege of Orleans by the approach of a Roman and allied army, the Huns under Attila moved off. However, they were burdened by large quantities of loot gathered during their campaign in Gaul, and were caught by the Romans. On the Catalaunian Fields, probably somewhere between Chalons and Troyes, the Huns formed up for battle. The Huns had traditionally been horse archers, and many still fought in this way. However, the

majority of Attila's force were infantry. This may have been due to a shortage of mounts, perhaps because of poor grazing conditions, or it could have been a tactical decision. The Huns had been fighting infantry-based forces for some years and may have decided to adopt their tactics.

The army facing the Huns was commanded by Flavius Aëtius, who had been expecting an invasion for some years. He was familiar with his enemies, having commanded Hun mercenaries in the past. He had also been for a time a hostage of the Huns when they were led by Rua, Attila's uncle. Flavius Aëtius had spent some time preparing for the Huns' arrival and had forged alliances with other leaders in Gaul, notably among the Visigoths and the Alans.

The 'Roman' portion of Flavius Aëtius' force was different from the legions of previous centuries. His troops were largely recruited from barbarians who had settled along the frontiers of the empire and were less well disciplined than the former legions. The Visigoths sent a contingent of heavy cavalry and infantry while the Alans, who had recently been attacked at Orleans, provided cavalry. Contingents also came from other allies, such as Burgundy.

Although the two forces were of equivalent size, the Huns had the advantage of a more unified command structure, and Attila did not need to worry about the political reliability of his allies. Flavius Aëtius was suspicious of the Alans in particular, and there was always the chance that King Theodoric of the Visigoths might decide it was in his best interests to throw in his lot with the Huns.

Flavius Aëtius was forced to work with what he had, so deployed his Roman troops on the left flank and the Visigoths, who had provided the strongest and most numerous 'barbarian' contingent, on the right. Between them were the Alans. Facing them was the main Hun force, with allied Ostrogoths opposite the Visigoths and a force of Gepids facing the Roman contingent. Both sides advanced rapidly, seeking to gain control of high ground

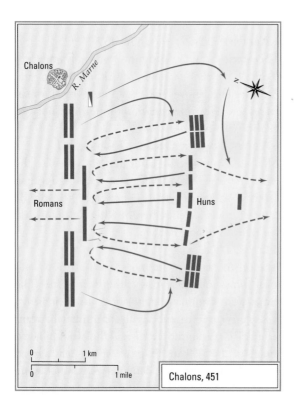

Chalons, 451

in the centre of the battlefield. The Romans won this fight, driving back the Huns who were then personally rallied by Attila.

Renewed hand-to-hand fighting ensued, in which the Visigothic king Theodoric and his son Thorismund were killed. The enraged Visigoths then drove the Huns back and forced them to seek refuge in their camp, but night fell before anything more could be made of the advantage thus gained.

The following morning, both armies formed up for battle again, with the Romans and their allies deployed defensively on the high ground they had captured. No attack materialized and the standoff continued for several days before the Visigoth contingent began to withdraw. This left the Roman force too weak to interfere as the Huns and their allies also began a withdrawal. They took with them their booty, but Flavius Aëtius was still able to claim a victory over the invaders.

■ ROME, 455
A dispute between the Vandal kingdom of North Africa and Roman Emperor Petronius Maximus resulted in an invasion of Italy. Little opposition materialized. Petronius Maximus was killed, and Rome was sacked for 14 days.

■ CAMPI, 456
Assisted by Frankish and Burgundian forces, a Visigoth army invaded Spain. At Campus Paramus a Seuevic army under King Rechiar attempted to drive them back but was defeated. Rechiar was captured and executed.

■ CARTAGENA, 460/461
Roman Emperor Majorian planned to invade North Africa and take it back from the Vandal Kingdom. This move was forestalled by the Vandals, who surprised the Romans at Cartagena. Some ships defected; the remainder were destroyed.

■ TRIPOLI, 468
Despite successes, including the destruction of a Vandal fleet and the capture of Tripoli, a Roman expedition against the Vandal kingdom failed. The loss of its supporting fleets, and strong resistance on land, made victory impossible.

Wars of the Eastern and European Tribes 250–500

■ THERMOPYLAE, 267
The Heruli, a Germanic tribe, invaded the Balkans and Black Sea coastal regions in the 260s. Local forces, unsupported by the Legions, attempted to hold the pass of Thermopylae against them but were overrun.

■ MAINZ, 406
Attempting to prevent an invasion of Gaul by the Alans, Suevi and Vandals, the Franks attacked them as they crossed the Rhine. Although initially successful the Franks were counter-attacked by Alan forces and driven off.

■ AQUILEIA, 452
Defeated at the Catalaunian Fields, the Huns crossed into northern Italy and laid siege to Aquileia. The city held out for a time but was eventually taken, opening the way for attacks on other cities in the region.

■ NEDAO, 454
After the death of Attila, internal conflict over leadership weakened the Huns sufficiently that many of their subject peoples rose up against them. A Hunnic force led by the sons of Attila clashed with an alliance of Germanic peoples under the leadership of King Ardaric of the Gepidae at Nedao. Heavy casualties were taken on both sides, including Attila's favourite son Ellac, with the result that the power of the Huns in Europe was broken.

■ AYLESFORD, 455
Aylesford was the site of a clash between Britons and Saxons, who had settled in Kent. Historical accounts vary, and it is not clear which side won, though the Saxon leader Horsa was killed.

■ URBICAS, 456
Hoping to reclaim Hispania for the Roman Empire, the Western Emperor requested aid from the Visigothic kingdom in Gaul. The Visigoths defeated the Suevi and Vandals, eventually adding Hispania to their territory.

WIPPEDESFLEOT, 466

The battle of Wippedesfleot was a minor but fiercely fought skirmish between Saxon forces under the command of Hengist, and a force of Britons. The outcome of the battle is not recorded.

SOISSONS, 486

The Domain of Soissons survived the collapse of the Roman Empire and retained its stability during the chaotic period that followed. Its wealth made it a target for outside aggression, which was kept at bay until the Franks united under Clovis I. Clovis made war on Soissons and finally issued a challenge to Syagrius, its ruler. The ensuring Frankish victory in the battle of Soissons greatly increased Frankish power.

SIRMIUM, 489

A huge Gothic army, marching west towards Italy, was opposed by forces of the Gepidae at Sirmium in Pannonia. Victory over the Gepidae allowed the Goths access to the Julian Alps and opened the route into Italy.

ISONZO/SONTIUS, 489

The Ostrogoths had been allies of the Eastern Roman Empire for some time, but tensions were increasing. Thus the Eastern Emperor suggested that King Theodoric take his forces west against Flavius Odoacer, King of Italy, who had deposed the last Western Emperor. Theodoric defeated Odoacer's forces at the River Isonzo and was able to gain entry into Italy, after which he marched on Verona and won another victory.

FAENZA, 490

Having failed to halt Theodoric the Great's campaign at the Isonzo, Odoacer, King of Italy, was besieged at Ravenna. A sortie from the city inflicted a sharp defeat on the Ostrogoths, forcing a retreat.

ADDA, 490

Retreating from his defeat at Faenza, Theodoric the Great fought a defensive battle on the River Adda, forcing Odoacer to fall back to Ravenna where he was once again placed under siege.

SIEGE OF RAVENNA, 490–493

Ravenna, capital of King Odoacer of Italy, was besieged by the forces of Ostrogothic King Theodoric the Great for three years. Although unable to gain entry to the city, Theodoric convinced Odoacer to accept a treaty whereby they would jointly rule Italy. Theodoric murdered Odoacer at a banquet held to celebrate the peace treaty. He ruled Italy ostensibly as a viceroy of the Eastern Empire, but in practice was independent of imperial authority.

TOLBIAC, 496

Having united the Franks under his rule, Clovis I was seriously challenged by the Alemanni. At the battle of Tolbiac he vowed that if he won, he would become a Christian, with profound implications for religion in Europe.

Roman Empire's Eastern Mediterranean Wars 200–400

NISIBIS, 217

In 216, Emperor Caracalla treacherously initiated a new conflict with Parthia in the hope of exploiting internal differences. He was assassinated the following year, and in the meantime a large Parthian force was assembled to recapture territories taken by Rome. The decisive clash, fought between the primarily infantry army of Rome and the cavalry forces of Parthia, came at Nisibis.

Roman forces adopted a defensive deployment, using caltrops to break up the Parthians' charge. Light infantry were sent forward to skirmish with the Parthians, retiring between the heavier cohorts when hard pressed. In this manner the Romans withstood three days of attacks.

By the end of the third day both sides had suffered such heavy losses that morale threatened to collapse. The Parthians agreed to accept reparations in return for a peace treaty with the new Roman Emperor, Mancrinus.

ANTIOCH, 218

Emperor Mancrinus' rule was challenged by Elagbalus, a juvenile cousin of the assassinated Emperor Caracalla. Some of Mancrinus' legions defected, weakening his position. Mancrinus was decisively defeated at Antioch, and was captured whilst trying to flee.

■ CARTHAGE, 238

The province of Africa revolted against Emperor Maximinus Thrax. Although supported by the Senate, the rebels could muster only a force of militia, which was crushed by a single legion from neighbouring Numidia.

■ RESAENA, 243

Emperor Gordian III initiated a campaign against Sassanid Persia, hoping to recapture territory lost while Rome was distracted by internal conflicts. Roman victory at Resaena returned the cities of Carrhae and Nisibis to Roman control.

■ MISICHE, 244

A continued Roman advance into Sassanid territory resulted in a major clash at Misiche. Accounts of the battle vary. Some claim that Rome won, some the Sassanids. Emperor Gordian III may have been killed in the battle; other accounts suggest that he was assassinated by unpaid legionaries afterwards.

He was replaced by Philippus Arabs, Prefect of the Praetorian Guard, who made peace with the Sassanids by paying a vast sum in tribute.

■ BARBALISSOS, 253

Conflict over Armenia led to renewed Roman–Sassanid hostilities, this time initiated by the Sassanids. The Roman force was defeated in a major battle at Barbalissos, opening the way for a Sassanid advance on Antioch.

■ EDESSA, 259

Responding to repeated Sassanid incursions into Syria, a large force under Roman emperor Valerian returned the region to Roman control before marching on Edessa. There, the army was decisively defeated and Emperor Valerian captured.

■ EUPHRATES RIVER, 261

Hoping to prevent Sassanid supremacy in the region, Palmyra rescinded its neutrality and sent forces to intercept a Sassanid army as it retired after sacking Antioch. The Palmyrans attacked before the Sassanids could cross the Euphrates to safety.

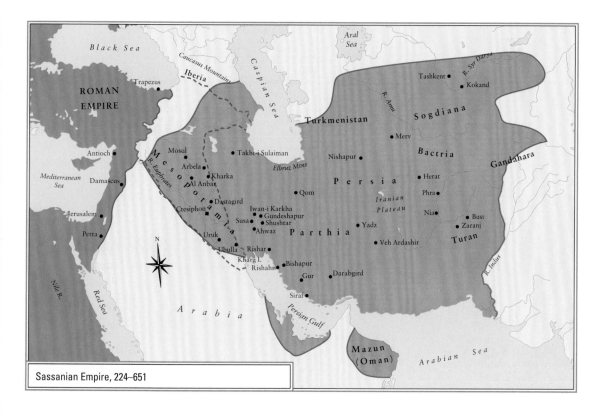

Sassanian Empire, 224–651

■ NISIBIS AND CARRHAE, 262

Continuing his campaign against the Sassanids, Odaenathus of Palmyra was able to return Nisibis and Carrhae to Roman rule. He was subsequently assassinated. His wife and successor, Zenobia, then came into conflict with Rome.

■ IMMAE, 271

Facing a superior force of Palmyrian cataphracts, the Roman cavalry feigned a retreat and drew the Palmyrians into an ambush. The remainder of the Palmyrene army collapsed in the face of superior Roman infantry.

■ EMESA, 272

Defeated at Immae, the Palmyrians attempted to defend Emesa. After defeating their Roman opposite numbers, the Palmyrian heavy cavalry became disorganized and was overwhelmed by Roman infantry. Palmyrian Queen Zenobia was captured while fleeing.

■ NILE VALLEY, 273

With Roman forces tied down besieging Palmyra, Firmus led a revolt in Egypt, threatening the Roman corn supply. The revolt was put down by Emperor Auralian, who then marched back to Palmyra to deal with a renewed uprising.

■ CALLINICUM, 296

The Sassanid king Narseh launched a campaign in 294 to retake Roman gains in Armenia. Then turning south, he inflicted a serious defeat on Roman forces at a point somewhere between Callinicum and Carrhae. The disaster was blamed on the Roman commander, Galerius, rather than his troops, with Emperor Diocletian taking steps to distance himself from the stigma of defeat. Diocletian did, however, arrange for reinforcements to be sent to Galerius.

■ TIGRIS RIVER, 297

Although defeated at Callinicum, Galerius was twice victorious over the Sassanids in Armenia, all but annihilating their army. This permitted an advance down the Tigris river and the capture of the Sassanid capital at Ctesiphon.

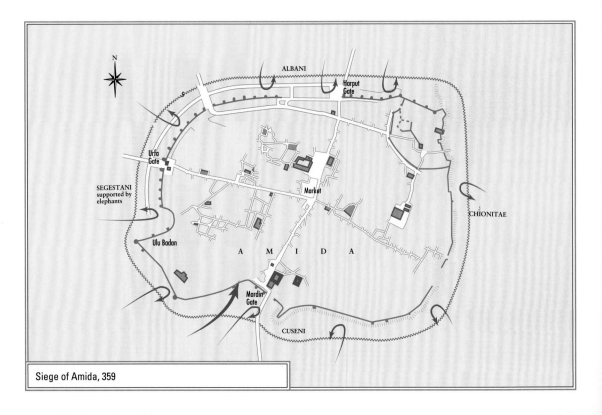

Siege of Amida, 359

■ SINGARA, 344/48

Attempting to retake previously lost territories, Sassanid forces besieged Singara. Raids against other parts of Sassanid territory caused the campaign to be broken off. A mutual non-aggression treaty was subsequently agreed with Rome.

■ SIEGE OF AMIDA, 359

The non-aggression treaty with Rome permitted other threats to be eliminated, opening the way for renewed hostilities in 359. The city of Amida withstood siege and repeated assaults by a Sassanid army for several weeks before eventually falling.

■ JULIAN INVASION OF PERSIA, 363

Seeking to cement his position as emperor, Julian undertook a new campaign against Sassanid Persia. He personally commanded the main force, with additional troops marching via Armenia, whose king was instructed to lend his assistance.

■ CTESIPHON, 363

Emperor Julian's campaign against Sassanid Persia was waged, ostensibly, to secure the eastern frontier of the empire. It was, in reality, just as much about gaining the support of the Eastern legions. Thus when the Sassanids attempted to negotiate a treaty, Julian refused to consider their overtures. Instead he assembled his army at Antioch and advanced towards the Euphrates.

The Armenian contingent and some Roman troops were detached to ravage the countryside of Media, and he made a feint towards Carrhae. Rather than take the same route as his predecessors, down the Tigris, Julian instead marched along the Euphrates supported by a purpose-built fleet which carried supplies for his army.

Some garrisons along the route of Julian's march were neutralized by diplomacy, essentially being left unmolested if they agreed not to act against his force. Others were reduced by a series of quick sieges. There was little serious opposition on the march, though the Sassanids did flood areas to slow down the Romans' progress. Only at Ctesiphon itself did opposition materialize.

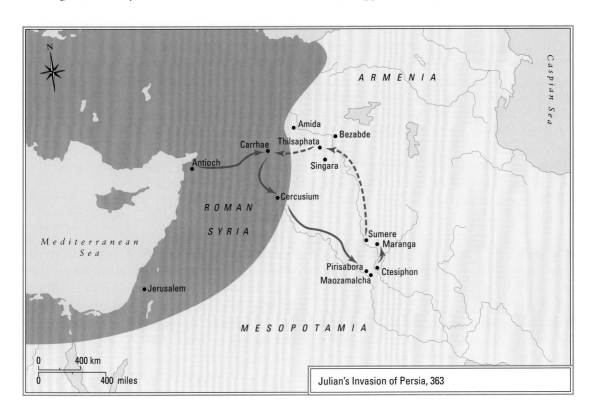

Julian's Invasion of Persia, 363

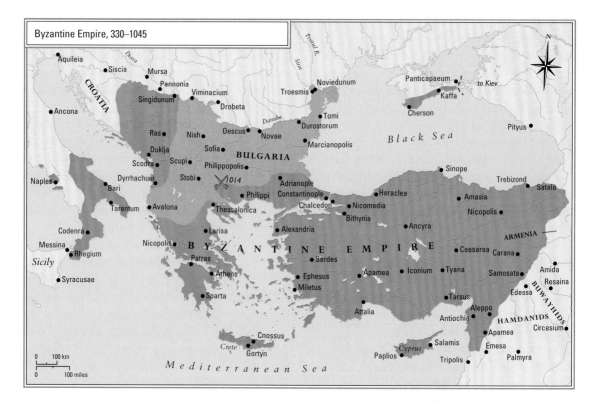

The Roman army launched a double-envelopment attack, crushing the wings of the Sassanid force and driving the centre back into the city. Although the Sassanids had fielded cataphract cavalry and war elephants, their army collapsed before these could make much impression on the battlefield.

Julian rejected a peace offer from the Sassanids and laid siege to the capital, but could not gain entry. With a larger Sassanid army approaching, and the failure of his detached forces to rejoin, Julian was forced to retreat from Ctesiphon. He was killed during the retreat and thereafter all Roman emperors followed a defensive strategy, bringing to an end the age of Roman conquests.

■ SAMARRA, 363

During Emperor Julian's retreat from Ctesiphon, his army was attacked at Samarra. Although the attack was beaten off, the emperor received a fatal wound. His successor, Jovian, agreed to a very unfavourable peace with Sassanid Persia.

■ MARITZA RIVER, 378

While Emperor Valens awaited reinforcements, he sent out a detachment under Count Sebastian, his Master Peditum, to harass the Goths. Sebastian's force made a successful attack against a Goth camp on the River Maritza.

Rome's Internal Wars 285–500

■ MARGUS, 285

Diocletian, commanding the Eastern armies, fought Carinus, the son of the murdered emperor Carus. Carinus's Western troops at first prevailed over Diocletian's troops, veterans of a difficult Persian campaign. Carinus's sudden assassination left Diocletian sole emperor.

■ INVASION OF ITALY, 307

Galerius moved west into Italy after Maxentius proclaimed himself Emperor at Rome. Finding Italy mobilized and fortified against him, Galerius withdrew, shadowed by Maxentius's army, devastating the heart of the empire and ruining his reputation.

■ SUSA, 312

Constantine's bid for sole rule of the empire began with storming this northern Italian city after his army descended from the Rhine. Bombardment with incendiaries and an escalade reduced the city to ruins and surrender.

■ TURIN, 312

Maxentius's forces, with a contingent of protected cavalry equipped like those the Romans had fought in the East, awaited Constantine's advance before the walls of this city. Maxentius's commanders arranged these armoured men and horses in a crescent formation with a central wedge designed to pierce Constantine's line. Constantine's troops, drawing on previous experience, successfully eluded their charges, and the retreating survivors found the gates of the city closed against them.

■ MILAN, 312

When Constantine captured it, the official capital of the Western Roman Empire contained an imperial palace. The news of the city's fall contributed to Maxentius's decision to advance northwards out of Rome to engage Constantine.

■ VERONA, 312

At the news of Constantine's advance, Maxentius's general Pompeianus mustered a large concentration of troops near Verona. Constantine suddenly doubled the length of his formation, prevailing and killing Pompeianus, leaving Constantine master of northern Italy.

■ MILVIAN BRIDGE, 312

Although Maxentius had fortified and provisioned Rome for a long siege, Constantine's uninterrupted series of victories in the north of Italy contributed to Maxentius's unease about his hold on the Western Empire. His subordinates beaten or dead, Maxentius himself advanced up the Appian Way with his personal core of Praetorian Guards and the balance of his heavy cavalry and infantry. The speed of Constantine's ongoing advance southward found the two armies colliding just on the far

side of the Tiber bridge, the stone bows of which Maxentius had previously ordered demolished, his forces crossing over a pontoon structure. Maxentius put his heavy cavalry and lighter horse in the front, hoping to shatter and scatter Constantine's line.

Inspired by a vision or hope of victory, Constantine proclaimed an alliance with the Christian deity and blazoned a Christian symbol on his army's shields. His own seasoned cavalry attacked Maxentius's horse pell-mell, which, morale undoubtedly suffering from previous defeats, collapsed in disorder back upon Maxentius's advancing column, leaving it disordered and its flanks exposed. Notwithstanding the reverse, the Praetorian Guard stood firm, but their resistance to the last was insufficient to overcome the onset of Constantine's victorious veterans. Maxentius's untried Italian levies broke and fled immediately.

Maxentius himself seems to have wavered at the last moment and decided to return to Rome and there try to withstand Constantine's siege, a tactic

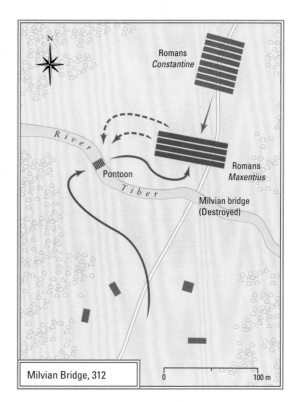

Milvian Bridge, 312

which had previously succeeded against Galerius, although Maxentius had lost heavily in this battle. The stress of the resulting panicked retreat collapsed the wooden structure of the pontoon bridge and drowned Maxentius and many of his soldiers, leaving Constantine to enter Rome in triumph the following day with Maxentius's head on a pike.

■ TZIRALLUM, 313

Battle between Licinius and Maximin for control of the Eastern Empire, ceded to Licinius by Constantine. Some 70,000 Legionaries faced Licinius's 30,000 levies from Illyria, but Licinius's superior ability as commander steadied his men to victory.

■ CIBALAE, 314

Constantine took 20,000 men across the border of his territories and faced Licinius with 35,000 in upper Pannonia. Terrain protected Constantine's flanks as his forces launched a charge that routed Licinius's forces with heavy losses.

■ MARDIA, 314

Constantine advanced into Thrace and again faced Licinius on favourable ground. A reserve of 5000 men in Licinius's rear attacked during the day-long struggle, forcing Licinius's forces to retreat and Licinius to ask for terms.

■ ADRIANOPLE, 323

Adrianople was the final show-down between Licinius and Constantine for control of the empire. Constantine had sent forces into Licinius's territory to repel invading Goths, which remained in position after evicting the barbarians. Licinius mustered a considerable army in the plains near the city and moved a fleet into the Hellespont behind it. Constantine moved 120,000 seasoned infantry and cavalry against Licinius's 150,000 infantry and 15,000 cavalry. Licinius waited on the far bank of the Hebrus river as Constantine's army moved towards him.

Initial skirmishing and the river's current led Constantine to lead the crossing personally, in which he was wounded while his engineers began constructing a wooden bridge. With Licinius and

his soldiers' attentions drawn to the bridgehead, Constantine's force of 5000 sent around to Licinius's rear drove the larger army down to level ground. Constantine prevailed with 34,000 slain and Licinius dislodged.

■ CHRYSOPOLIS, 323

Licinius raised a new levy of 50–60,000 men and engaged Constantine's army on these heights once Constantine's fleet had ferried it over the Bosphorus. Licinius's green troops fought surprisingly well before dispersing after 25,000 casualties.

■ HELLESPONT, 324

Licinius's collected naval forces before Constantine's attack numbered some 350 fleet units drawn up in the Hellespont. Licinius retreated into Byzantium's fortifications. Constantine entrusted his own force of some 200 smaller vessels to his son Crispus and his admirals, with orders to force the Hellespont. In the strait's close quarters, the smaller vessels proved less hampered, destroying 130 vessels and 5000 men. Licinius surrendered after the assault on Byzantium began.

■ REVOLT OF MAGNENTIUS, 350

In a palace coup, the Illyrian Magnentius, a trusted senior officer, sent loyal cavalry who murdered the Emperor Constans while he was hunting in central Gaul. His own troops proclaimed him emperor in the west.

■ MURSA, 351

Constantius separated or cowed Magnentius's allies, whose forces augmented his as he moved west. Magnentius moved east and attacked the city of Mursa with a strong force, defeated by Constantius's heavy cavalry with 54,000 casualties.

■ PAVIA, 351

An over-extended pursuit of Magnentius allowed his remaining loyal forces to drive off the vanguard of Constantius's cavalry here. Magnentius was able to raise an army in the furthest west and resume the civil war.

■ MONS SELEUCUS, 353

Constantius's troops crossed the French Alps and bore down on the last of Magnentius's levies.

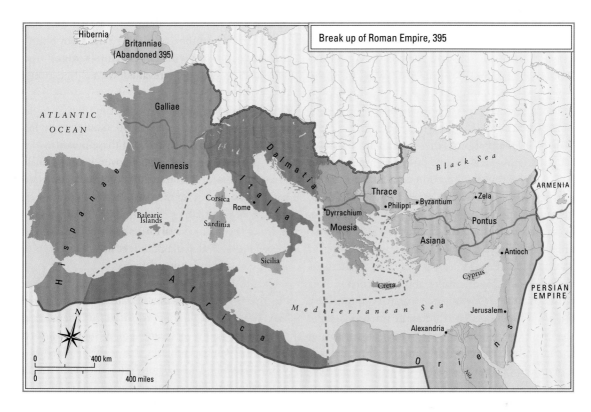

Magnentius's forces collapsed. Unable to enlist more soldiers and with the cities of Gaul supporting Constantius, Magnentius fell on his sword.

■ THYATIRA, 366

Valens, the Eastern Emperor, found Procopius, a friend of Julian, proclaimed emperor in Constantinople. Senior commanders in the field remained loyal to Valens, defeating Procopius's forces in this battle. Procopius himself was afterwards captured and executed.

■ SAVE, 388

Theodosius I and Maximus, who had made himself Western Emperor, fought here in 388, Theodosius moving to restore Valentinian II to single authority. Theodosius's allies rushed Maximus's army across this river, with Maximus's army surrendering at dawn.

■ RAVENNA, 432

Western generals Boniface and Aëtius fought for control of the West. Boniface prevailed but fell, mortally wounded. Aëtius fled to the Huns, with whom he would later return as a conqueror.

Sassanid Persia and South-west/Central Asia 200–500

■ HORMOZGAN, 226

Adarvan, the last Parthian shah, lost his battle and dynasty to the first Sassanian emperor, Ardashir I, in this valley in southern Persia. The Sassanians moved to consolidate and centralize power in a soon-resurgent Persia.

■ CONQUEST OF ARMENIA, 295–298

Under the shah Nersi, the Persian army had undergone reorganization and become a more formidable force, invading and occupying the Roman client kingdom. An initial Roman counter-attack had met with disaster at Haran in 296. Galerius, later emperor, invaded with the intention of restoring King Tiridates. The Romans moved through the mountains and scattered the Persians with a surprise attack, securing Armenia for Tiridates. Persia agreed to the Tigris boundary.

◼ MEROE, C. 350

The Kushite kingdom to the south of Egypt had its capital here for centuries, despite Egyptian and Roman incursions. Invasions northward from the Christianized Aksumite kingdom of Ethiopia led to the kingdom and city's destruction.

◼ AVARAYR, 451

Shah Yazdegerd II of the occupying Persians sought to impose Zoroastrianism on his Christian Armenian subjects. Instrumental in this effort was an Armenian-born Persian viceroy, Vasak of Siuniq, fiercely loathed by his countrymen. With invasions along the frontier by the powerful Heptalian tribe and a revolt in Georgia tying down considerable Persian resources, the Armenians under Vardan Mamikonian rose to protect their faith. Promised Byzantine support evaporated, but the Armenians enjoyed some success against smaller Persian detachments while accumulating an army by late May of some 60,000 peasant infantry and traditional heavy cavalry. The Persian Empire mustered 300,000 under Mushkan against them, including 10,000 elite cavalry, war elephants and 40,000 Armenians under Vasak. The Armenian elites fought well against their former comrades in the Persian army, but Vardan's death resulted in defeat but religious toleration for the Armenians.

Britain 450–500

◼ AEGELSTHREP, 455

Crushing of the last British resistance under Vortigern by the Saxons under Hengist and Horsa. Having been invited in as mercenaries against invading Picts, the Saxons turned upon the British and occupied Sussex and Essex.

Chinese Jin Dynasty Wars 265–420

◼ FEI RIVER, 383

The Former Qin state, having succeeded in unifying northern China, began pushing southwards. The Eastern Jin Dynasty launched an offensive to forestall an invasion, but was defeated. The Former Qin then assembled a large but poorly trained army from its many subject states, and advanced southwards. After capturing Shouyang, the Former Qin vanguard was ambushed and defeated by the Jin. The Former Qin then brought up their main force, which set up camp at the Fei river. A relocation order caused confusion in the disorganized Former Qin ranks, resulting in panic as the Jin attacked in force. The Jin then launched a vigorous pursuit, driving the Former Qin before them and annihilating some units. This triggered a series of revolts in Former Qin territory, leading to the eventual collapse of the Former Qin Empire and the rise of the Later Qin.

◼ CAHNE SLOPE, 395

Northern Wei had been a vassal state to the Later Yan, but had begun to assert its independence. This prompted a military expedition to return Northern Wei to vassalage. The army of Northern Wei sheltered behind the Yellow River, but a sudden freeze allowed the Later Yan forces to cross over the ice and launch an attack.

Pursuing the army of Northern Wei to Cahne Slope, the Later Yan became distracted by the need to forage for supplies, enabling the Northern Wei army to move into position undetected. A surprise attack routed the Later Yan, driving many troops into the river; others were captured and later executed. The losses taken at Cahne Slope sufficiently weakened the Later Yan that Northern Wei was subsequently able to launch an invasion of its own, overrunning much of what had been Later Yan territory.

◼ YEH, 528

Advancing on the rebel army of Ge Rong, which was encamped on the plains of Hebei north of Ye, a force of 7000 elite cavalry under Erzhu Rong caught the more numerous enemy by surprise and routed them.

◼ SHAYUAN, 537

An invasion of Western Wei by a large Eastern Wei force was decisively defeated at Shayuan. This enabled Western Wei to occupy large areas of territory and capture Chang'an before pushing further east.

Medieval Wars 500–1500

The wars of the medieval period were brutal affairs, conducted primarily at close range with edged and impact weapons, supported by the bow and arrow and the crossbow. Yet by the end of the era, gunpowder weapons were starting to reshape the nature of the battlefield, from infantry battles to siege warfare against fortresses.

Post-Roman Britain 500–1100

■ Camlann, 537

The *Annales Cambriae* record the deaths of King Arthur and Mordred, often interpreted as belligerents. Gildas' contemporary descriptions of internal discord suggest civil war, but neither this nor the location are certain.

■ Arfderydd, 573

Gwendoleu of Arfderydd, the area encompassing Hadrian's Wall and Carlisle, fought against Peredur and Gywri of Strathclyde. The *Annales Cambriae* record that Gwendoleu fell and Merlin went mad.

■ Deorham, 577

The forces of Gloucester, Cirencester and Bath united to dislodge Ceawlin's 'Wessex' forces from Hinton Hill, overlooking the Avon valley. The towns were defeated and their kings Connmail, Condida and Farinmail were slain. The victory extended Ceawlin's power from the Solent to the Thames and the Severn Estuary, isolating the West Country Britons from those of the Welsh Marches and Wales.

■ Degsastan, c. 603

Aidan, king of the Scotti, attempted to halt the expansionist warfare of Ethelfrid of Northumbria. Ethelfrid defeated the numerically superior army at Degsas' Stone. His brother, Theobald, was killed with all his men.

■ Chester, 616

Ethelfrid of Northumbria vanquished an army from the British kingdoms of Powys and Rhos, possibly allied with the Anglo-Saxon Cearl of Mercia. Despite heavy losses, Ethelfrid was victorious and King Selyf Sarffagadan of Powys

and Cadwal Crysban of Rhos fell. Notably, 1200 British monks from Bangor-on-Dee were slaughtered. The victory isolated the British kingdoms in Wales from those of Strathclyde and Rheged in the north.

■ Hatfield Chase, 12 October 633

Edwin of Northumbria was defeated by an alliance of Cadwalla of Gwynedd and Penda of Mercia. Edwin was killed, his army destroyed and Northumbria fragmented as Cadwalla pursued a year of rapine in the north.

■ Heavenfield, 634

Oswald of Northumbria, possibly with allies from Dal Riata, defeated Cadwalla's numerically superior forces. Oswald took a defensive position alongside Hadrian's Wall and hemmed in Cadwalla's advancing army.

■ Maserfelth, 642

Penda of Mercia defeated Oswald of Northumbria. The location is uncertain; contenders include Oswestry, 'Oswald's Tree'. Tradition states Penda had Oswald's body ritually dismembered and displayed in a tree as a sacrifice to Woden.

■ Winwaed, 655

Oswy of Bernicia defeated the superior forces of Penda of Mercia and his Deiran and East Anglian allies. Mercians and their allies were killed, including the East Angle Ethelhere. Oswy beheaded Penda.

■ Invasion of North Wales, 1063

Harold Godwinson led a land and sea campaign from Gloucester to curb the power of Gruffudd ap Llewellyn, 'King over all of the Welsh'. Harold attacked Rhyddlan, razed Gruffudd's fleet and put his men to flight. Harold secured the submissions of Welsh sub-kings as Tostig led a campaign of plunder. Gruffudd was murdered by his own men and Harold sent his head to Edward the Confessor.

■ NORTHUMBRIAN REVOLT, 1065

Following a series of murders, the northern aristocracy rebelled against Tostig Godwinson, Earl of Northumbria, slew his men and declared him an outlaw. The lords of Northumbria and Mercia marched south to confirm Morcar of Mercia as their new Earl and plundered the area around Northampton. Harold Godwinson allied himself with Morcar against his brother. Tostig fled into exile in Flanders and sent emissaries to Harald Hardrada of Norway.

Early Medieval Scotland 500–1100

■ DUNNICHEN, 20 MAY 685

Ecgfrith of Northumbria attempted to reinforce his power in northern Britain in an attack against the Pictish Kingdom of Fortiu, to the north of the Mounth. The southern Pictish zone above the Forth acknowledged Northumbrian suzerainty, but Bridei of Fortiu challenged Northumbrian power and harassed its allies.

The Northumbrians marched into north Angus near the Lake Lunn Garan, an area marked by deep hills, a narrow pathway and boggy terrain. Feigning retreat, the Picts led Ecgfrith's men into a narrow mountain pass where they were ambushed. Ecgfrith was killed and the greater part of his army slaughtered. The defeat marked the independence of the Pictish kingdoms from Northumbria and the end of their tributary status. The recovery of lands from Northumbrian control coincided with the rejection of the newly established See at Abercorn, which was symbolic of Northumbrian-sponsored 'Roman' Christianity.

■ CARHAM, 1018

Huctred, Earl of Northumbria, marched against Malcolm II of the Scots Kingdom (south of the Forth and Clyde) and Owain of Strathclyde. Huctred was defeated and killed and the Scots gained control of Lothian.

■ DUNSINANE (BATTLE OF THE SEVEN SLEEPERS), 1054

Siward of Northumbria led land and sea forces against Macbeth of Scotland, following Scottish attacks on Northumbria. Battle was met north of the Firth of Forth on the feast of the Seven Sleepers of Ephesus. Siward was victorious; 3000 Scots and 1500 English fell and Macbeth put to flight. The English regained control of Cumbria, installing Malcolm III as King of Strathclyde.

■ LUMPHANAN, 15 AUGUST 1057

Malcolm III of Scotland mortally wounded his rival Macbeth at an engagement north of the Mounth. Retreating over the Cairnamounth pass, Macbeth staged a last stand and was defeated. He died at Lumphanan.

■ ALNWICK, 13 NOVEMBER 1093

Malcolm of Scotland led his fifth and last invasion of northern England, besieging the castle at Alnwick. Robert de Mowbray, Earl of Northumbria, set out to relieve the castle. Although lacking the manpower to engage the Scots in open battle, Robert succeeded in taking them unawares and attacked Malcolm's besieging forces before the ramparts. Malcolm and his son were both killed, resulting in ongoing dynastic struggles in Scotland.

Wars of the Franks 500–1000

■ VOILLE, 507

Clovis' victories over the Alemanni east of the Rhine and the Burgundian Kingdom on the Rhone valley brought the Franks into the orbit of the Gothic kingdoms and the scene of Mediterranean politics. Despite the mediation of Theodoric, Clovis moved against the Visigothic kingdom of Aquitaine. The superior army of Alaric II of Toulouse met Clovis' forces in the northern marches of Visigothic territory. Fighting took place with javelins and hand-to-hand combat, the Goths deserted the field and the Senatorial leaders of the Auvergnats under

Frankish Empire, *c.* 730–900

N

0   200 km

0   200 miles

Kaupang   Birka

North Sea

DENMARK

BALTIC PEOPLES

Baltic Sea

SCOTTISH KINGDOMS

KINGDOM OF PICTS

STRATHCLYDE

NORTHUMBRIA

Lindisfarne

Ripen

York

Hamburg

Vistula

IRISH KINGDOM

WELSH STATES

MERCIA

London

WEST WALES   WESSEX

Friesland

Saxony

S   L   A   V   S

Aachen   *Rhine*   Hessen

France   Mainz   Frankfurt

Bohemia

Paris   Metz

Nordgau   Moravia

Britanny

F R A N K I S H   E M P I R E

Strasbourg   Bavaria

ATLANTIC OCEAN

Alamannia

Carinthia   Pannonia   *Danube*

AVAR EMPIRE

Geneva   Lyon   Italian Kingdom

Aquitaine   Milan   Venice   Dalmatia

Bordeaux   Burgundy   Turin   Genoa   Ravenna

Nish

ASTURIAS

Toulouse   Septimania   Florence

Marseille   Papal States   Rome

Adriatic Sea   Ragusa

V   L   A   C   H   S

Spanish March

Barcelona

Corsica

PRINCIPALITY OF BENEVENTO

Salonica

EMIRATE OF CORDOVA

Balearic Is.

Sardinia

Naples   Otranto

Cordova

Cartagena

B Y Z A N T I N E   E M P I R E

Panormus   Calabria

Mediterranean   *Sicily*   Catania

Sea

IDRISIDS   RUSTAMIDS   ABBASIDS

the command of Appollinarius were all killed. Clovis killed Alaric and plundered his treasury at Toulouse. He drove the Goths from Angoulême and his son, Theuderic, subdued the Visigothic kingdom south to the Pyrenees. Clovis was made consul by the Emperor Anastasius.

■ VEZERONCE, 25 JUNE 524

Following the death of Clovis, his four sons continued the Frankish Wars against Burgundy. Clotair and Childebert finally defeated Gundomar and his Ostrogothic allies and the Burgundian Kingdom was annexed into the Merovingian lands.

■ WOGASTISBURG, 631

Dagobert I sent three armies recruited from the Austrasians, Alemanni and Lombards to stem the growing cohesion of Slavic power united under Samo, once a Frankish merchant. Dagobert's armies were heavily defeated, probably in Bohemia.

■ COMPIÈGNE, 26 SEPTEMBER 715

The first in a series of battles in the Frankish civil wars following the death of Pepin of Heristal. Pepin's grandson Theudoald succeeded him briefly as Mayor of the Palace to Dagobert III. Theudoald was ousted in favour of Ragenfrid of Neustria and Pepin's illegitimate son, Charles Martel, was declared mayor by the nobles of Austrasia. Ragenfrid defeated Theudoald with the support of Eudo, Duke of Aquitaine.

■ COLOGNE, 716

Chilperic II and Ragenfrid, Mayor of the Palace of Neustria, led a force against Austrasia. A simultaneous invasion was led by their ally Radbod of Frisia. Charles Martel, recently escaped from imprisonment by Plectrude and Theudoald in their power base at Cologne, retreated rather than face insuperable odds. Cologne fell after a short siege and Chilperic II and Ragenfrid were declared king and mayor respectively by the Austrasians.

■ AMBIEVE, 716

Charles Martel defeated the army of Chilperic II and Ragenfrid of Neustria. Attacking as they rested at midday, Charles Martel employed a feigned retreat to draw them from their defensive position into open ground.

■ VINCY, 717

Charles Martel routed the troops of Chilperic II and Ragenfrid of Neustria. Having pursued them to Paris, Charles Martel moved against Plectrude in Cologne and secured the remains of Pepin's treasury.

■ SOISSONS, 718

Chilperic II, Ragenfrid and Eudo, Duke of Aquitaine were defeated by Charles Martel's army of veterans. Ragenfrid fled to Angers, Eudo and Chilperic II to lands south of the Loire. Eudo handed Chilperic II over to Charles Martel in return for recognition of his Dukedom. On the death of Chlothar IV, Charles Martel recognized Chilperic II as king in return for royal legitimization of his mayoralty.

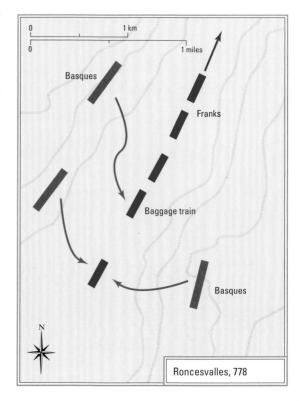

Roncesvalles, 778

THE BOARN, 734

Charles Martel's army was ferried over the Aelmere to the Boarn, where he defeated and killed Poppo, king of the Frisians. Looting and destruction of heathen temples followed. Charles Martel annexed the Frisian kingdom.

RONCESVALLES, 778

The rearguard of the Frankish Army was ambushed and defeated in the Pass of Roncesvalles by an alliance of Christian Basques of Pamplona and the forces of the Emir of Cordova.

BALLON, 22 NOVEMBER 845

Charles the Bald of West Francia was defeated by the numerically inferior troops of Nominoe, Duke of Brittany. The Bretons lured the Frankish troops into the treacherous marshlands between the Oust and the Aff.

SOISSONS, 923

The climax of the rebellion by West Frankish nobles against Charles III (the Simple), led by his brother, Robert, Count of Paris. Charles III was defeated and deposed and Robert was killed.

Wars of the Germanic Migrations 500–750

THE ICE OF LAKE VANERN, C. 530

Onela of Sweden was defeated by the exiled Swedish princes Eanmund and Eadgils and the Geatish King Heardred. The battle, fought on the frozen lake, is recorded in *Beowulf* and Norse sagas.

ASFELD, 552

Audoin, leader of the Lombards and allied to the Emperor Justinian, defeated the Gepid army of Thorisind. Jordanes records the battle as one of the bloodiest of his time, with the loss of 60,000 lives.

CORONATE, 689

Cunipert, King of the Lombards, returned from exile with an army of Piedmontese and defeated the rebellion of Alahis, Duke of Trent and Brescia, along with his Venetian forces. Alahis was killed in the battle.

BRAVALLA, 750

Legend recorded by Saxo Grammaticus and Norse saga. Harald Wartooth of Denmark is defeated by Sigurd, King of Sweden, in a battle replete with heroes, berserkers, fighting bears and Valkyries.

Wars of the Byzantine Empire 500–1000

AMIDA, 502–03

A Sassanian Persian siege of Byzantine-held Amida is noted for a spirited defence in which Byzantine soldiers undermined the Persian siege ramp from inside the walls until it collapsed. Nonetheless, the city fell.

DARA, 530

One of Byzantine Gen Belisarius' earliest victories. The Byzantine field army of the east, about 25,000 men, was camped near Dara when a 40,000-strong Sassanian force under Firuz approached. Belisarius assumed defensive positions outside the town, digging a series of ditches with narrow passages left for his troops to cross. The Persians began with a cavalry charge that temporarily drove the Byzantine left flank back, but the Byzantines regrouped and the first day concluded with two fights between champions of each army. On the second day, 10,000 more Persians arrived. After arrow exchanges at midday, the Persians launched a general assault. The Byzantines threw them into confusion with a flank attack by cavalry that had been concealed. In the final phase, the Byzantines divided the Persian army into two parts and defeated each in turn.

CALLINICUM, 19 APRIL 531

A Sassanian cavalry force of 15,000 under Azarethes invaded Byzantine territory; Belisarius brought a mixed Byzantine force of 25,000 to challenge him, pursuing the withdrawing Persians. In an Easter Day battle, both sides began with arrow exchanges. Under their cover, Azarethes reinforced his left-wing cavalry. Their charge then crumbled the Byzantine right wing.

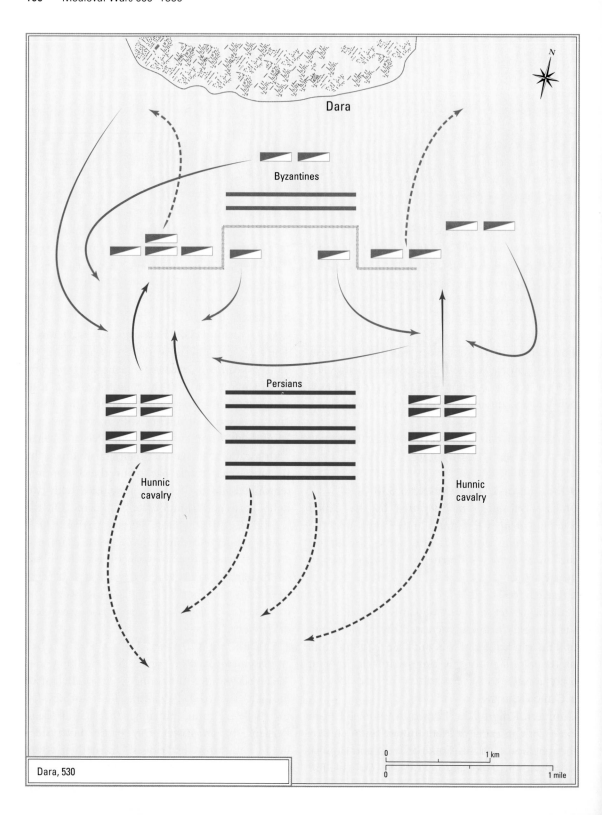

Dara

Byzantines

Hunnic
cavalry

Persians

Hunnic
cavalry

Dara, 530

0   1 km

0   1 mile

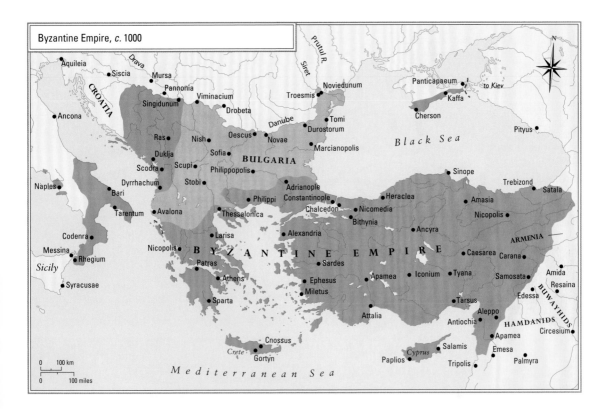

Byzantine Empire, *c.* 1000

The Byzantine cavalry fled. Belisarius' infantry, in close formation, survived the attack until dark, then escaped.

■ CONSTANTINOPLE I, 532

In the Nika revolt, massive rioting and property destruction in Constantinople threatened Emperor Justinian. Eastern veterans under Belisarius and Herul mercenaries under Mundus charged the mob in the Hippodrome, slaughtering an estimated 30,000.

■ AD DECIMUM, 13 SEPTEMBER 533

In 533, a Byzantine army under the command of Belisarius invaded the former Roman province of Africa, currently ruled by Vandals under King Gelimer. After his unopposed landing, Belisarius marched rapidly toward Carthage. The Vandal army ambushed the Byzantine force on 13 September at Ad Decimum, the 10-mile marker on the road south of Carthage, at a point where the road passed through a narrow defile. Gelimer's plan was apparently to bottle the Byzantine force

in and attack it from both sides, but the Vandal attack was badly coordinated. The first Vandal contingent, commanded by Gelimer's brother, Ammatas, was not yet organized for battle when it ran into the Byzantine advance guard. This force was almost completely destroyed, the dead including the Vandal prince. A second Vandal force soon engaged with Belisarius' Hun mercenaries, but proved to be so terrified of the Hunnic force that they hardly fought back. The Byzantines pursued them nearly to the walls of Carthage.

Gelimer then appeared on the scene with the largest of the three Vandal forces. He drove the Byzantines back from the field, the Vandal cavalry routing Belisarius' mercenary cavalry. Gelimer then discovered his brother's body and stopped to bury it. Belisarius was able to regroup his forces and his counter-attack found the Vandal force completely unprepared. The Vandals were routed, Gelimer fleeing away from Carthage,

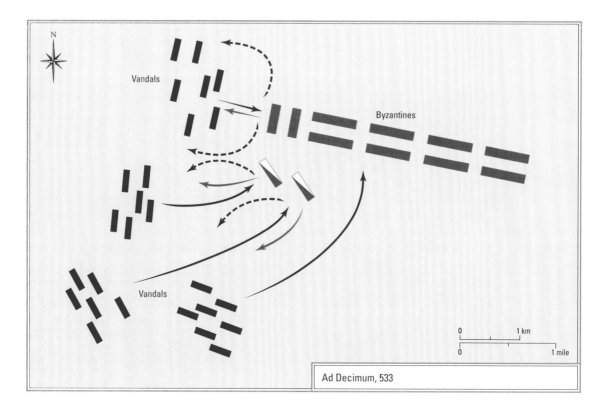

Ad Decimum, 533

apparently in the mistaken belief that Byzantine forces already blocked the way to his capital city. Belisarius lost at most 1800 men, while Vandal casualties numbered 10–12,000. Although most of the Vandal army still remained intact, Belisarius was able to march on to Carthage, which opened its gates to him.

▪ TRICAMARUM, 15 DECEMBER 533

The Byzantine invasion army under Belisarius had taken Carthage, but the Vandal king Gelimer's army was still largely intact. Belisarius marched out to meet Gelimer 27km from Carthage; the Byzantine force numbered about 8000 infantry and 5000 cavalry and the Vandal army was slightly larger.

Belisarius first tried to lure the Vandals into a disordered charge, but Gelimer held his ground. The Byzantines then attacked the Vandal centre. In a hard fight, the Vandals were driven back, but their wings did not come to support them. The Vandal centre eventually collapsed into a rout,

whereupon the wings of the Vandal force also fled back to their camp. Belisarius began to organize an assault on the Vandals' fortified camp. Before he could attack, Gelimer fled, precipitating a mass flight before the Byzantines stormed the by-then empty camp.

▪ ROME III, 537–538

Byzantine general Belisarius defended Rome with 5000 soldiers. Vitigis, the Gothic king, established a partial siege, his seven fortified camps blocking supplies and breaking the aqueducts. An attempted assault in March 537 failed, but Vitigis' seizure of Portus increased pressure on Rome. Belisarius offered battle, but was driven back into the city. Stalemate ended when Roman reinforcements arrived and the Goths were defeated as they withdrew.

▪ ROME IV, 546–47

Gothic king Totila besieged Byzantine-held Rome. Gen Belisarius tried to break the siege, but his small army was driven off. Much of

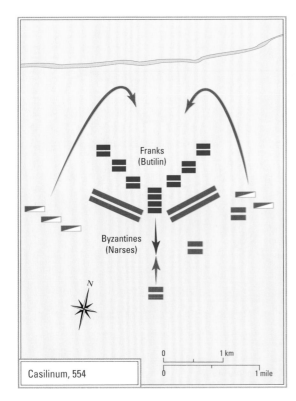

Casilinum, 554

held. The Byzantine advance then drove the Goths through their own infantry in a bloody rout.

■ MONS LACTARIUS, 552
A Byzantine army under the eunuch Narses trapped a Gothic force under King Teïas as it marched to relieve Cumae. In a two-day fight, Teïas and much of his army was killed.

■ CASILINUS, 554
Frankish raiders with some Goths invaded Byzantine-held Italy. Narses met them with 18,000 men near Capua; the Franks under Butilin had a similar force. When the Byzantines struck a Frankish foraging party, the Franks left their fortified camp to fight. The Franks, formed into a wedge (*cuneus*), broke through the Roman centre, only to be hit by Byzantine cavalry on their flanks and rear, suffering a massive defeat.

■ CONSTANTINOPLE II, 559
A Kotrigur Hun force of 7000 advanced on undefended Constantinople. Belisarius assembled a scratch force of guardsmen, veterans and volunteers and defeated the Huns in an ambush. Justinian then paid them to withdraw.

■ MELITENE I, 576
In a cavalry battle, Byzantine Gen Justinian defeated the Sassanian Persian king Khusrau near Melitene and sacked the Persian camp. Fleeing Persians looted Melitene, but many drowned in the Euphrates as they fled.

■ SOLACHON, 586
A Byzantine army under Philippicus halted a Persian invasion in northern Mesopotamia. Both armies were apparently all cavalry; the Byzantine right flank broke the Persian left; the Persians fled when threatened with double envelopment.

■ VIMINACIUM, 601
Part of a long campaign against the Avars, the Byzantine Balkan army heavily defeated the Avars at Viminacium by dismounting their cavalry and withstanding repeated Avar cavalry charges. Avar losses were heavy.

■ ANTIOCH, 613
Emperor Heraclius, personally commanding the Byzantine army, tried to stop invading Persians in

the population starved; others attempted flight, although most were killed. Finally, part of the garrison betrayed the city to Totila. Early in 547, Totila abandoned Rome and Belisarius reoccupied it, restoring the walls Totila had slighted. Totila tried and failed to force Belisarius out again.

■ SENA GALLICA, 551
A total of 50 Byzantine warships attacked 47 Gothic ships blockading Ancona. The Goths came out to meet the Byzantines; in missile exchange and then boarding, the Goths, inexperienced at sea, were completely defeated.

■ TADINAE, 552
Byzantine Gen Narses with 20,000–25,000 men met a somewhat smaller Gothic army under Totila. Battle commenced with the Goths' unsuccessful attempt to take a gully and outflank the Byzantines, followed by single combats between champions. Totilo then launched an attack of cavalry with lances along the entire battle front, but the Byzantines

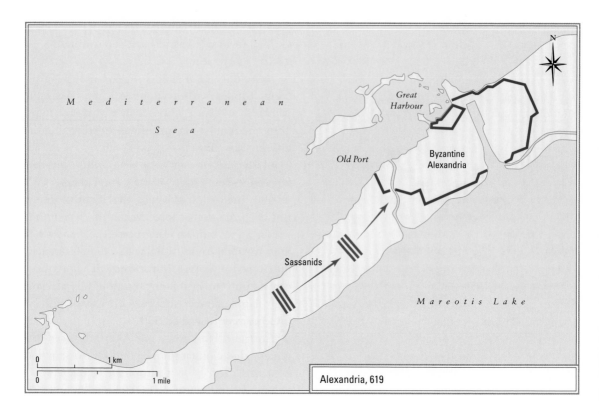

Alexandria, 619

a bloody battle that was at first indecisive, but the Persians regrouped and routed the Byzantines, consolidating their hold on Cilicia.

■ JERUSALEM V, 614

A Sassanian Persian army under Shahrbaraz invaded Byzantine Palestine. Jerusalem surrendered peacefully, but when Shahrbaraz marched on, the inhabitants expelled the Persian garrison. Shahrbaraz turned back and placed the city under siege. Strongly fortified, but with a mostly civilian and clerical populace, Jerusalem withstood the siege for 21 days, its garrison vastly outnumbered by the Persians and a large number of Jewish rebels under the command of Benjamin of Tiberias. When the wall was finally breached, Shahrbaraz took the city by storm. Many relics and churches were destroyed and priests killed in revenge for the Christians' duplicity. The Persian conquerors deported much of the Christian population to Persia and also carried off the relic of the True Cross. They left the city under the control of their Jewish allies.

■ ALEXANDRIA, 619

The Sassanian Persian invasion of Byzantine Egypt began in 617 or 618. In 619, they reached Alexandria, which was highly defensible, but had a large civilian population that could not be fed since the Persians held the surrounding countryside. Byzantine governor Nicetas and Orthodox patriarch John the Almsgiver both soon fled to Cyprus. The city surrendered in June 619, although one source reports that it was betrayed to the Persians.

■ ISSUS, 622

Byzantium's Emperor Heraclius defeated a large Persian army under Shahrbaraz in eastern Anatolia, discovering an ambush and responding with a feigned retreat that drew the Persians out. Although not decisive, Issus restored Byzantine morale.

■ SARUS, 625

The Byzantine vanguard crossed the Sarus, but was lured into an ambush and nearly destroyed by their Persian opponents. Emperor Heraclius then led the rearguard over the unguarded bridge, driving the Persians off.

■ CONSTANTINOPLE, 626

A Sassanian Persian army under Shahrbaraz and the Avars jointly besieged Constantinople. Emperor Heraclius sent part of his field army to reinforce the garrison. The Avars, unskilled in siegecraft, tried to bring Persians to the European side of the city in canoes, but they were destroyed by the Byzantine fleet, leaving the Avars to attempt primitive siege towers. When another Byzantine army arrived, the Avars and Persians both withdrew.

■ NINEVEH, 12 DECEMBER 627

All available Persian forces gathered under Gen Rahzad to meet a Byzantine invasion of Assyria. Emperor Heraclius feigned retreat, then turned and attacked the disorganized Persian force, winning a decisive victory. The Persians retreated after eight hours of fighting. About 6000 Persians died in the battle, including Rahzad, who may have been killed in single combat with Heraclius. A force of Persian reinforcements numbering 3000 then arrived, but were too late to fight in the battle.

■ RAVENNA, 729

Byzantine troops sent to restore order in Italy after a tax revolt met an Italian army near Ravenna. The Byzantines were defeated and thousands were killed, helping loosen Byzantine control of northern Italy.

■ PLISKA, 26 JULY 811

In 811, Byzantine emperor Nicephorus I launched a great campaign against the Bulgars, personally leading a very large army that included many courtiers and court officials. The Bulgar khan Krum tried to make peace, but Nicephorus rejected his offers.

On crossing the frontier, the emperor took Pliska, the Bulgar capital, slaughtering the garrison and a relief force that arrived too late, then proceeded to lay waste to the countryside. He then marched on, believing that Krum's army had been destroyed, allowing discipline to slacken despite pleas for greater caution. The Byzantine army soon found itself caught in a trap: the Bulgars had blocked the end of the river valley they were traversing with a log palisade and ditch. When Nicephorus' scouts brought word, he fell into depression and took no immediate action. The Bulgars, reinforced by Avar and Slav allies, attacked before dawn on 26 July, targeting the imperial encampment. Nicephorus was among the first to fall in the surprise attack and uncontrollable panic rapidly spread among the Byzantine troops. Many fleeing Byzantine soldiers drowned in the nearby marshes; in fact, so many were trampled to death in their haste that the Bulgars were able to cross the marshes on their bodies. Some Byzantines reached the palisade to the south and tried to climb, only to fall to their deaths in the ditch on the far side. The desperate soldiers burned a section of the palisade and it fell outward over the ditch, but when they tried to cross on it, it gave way and many were burned to death in the ditch. It was perhaps the worst Roman defeat since Adrianople in 378. Khan Krum made Nicephorus' skull into a drinking bowl.

■ VERSINIKIA, 22 JUNE 813

Bulgars defeated a much larger Byzantine army because an impatient Byzantine general led his wing forwards without orders. He did not receive support; the wing was slaughtered and the rest of the army fled in panic.

■ LALAKAON, 3 SEPTEMBER 863

Emir Omar of Melitene raided to the Black Sea with about 8000 men. His force was surrounded by 13 Byzantine corps under Petronas and almost completely destroyed, outnumbered at least three to one.

■ BATHYS RYAX, 878

Two Byzantine divisions (4,000–5000 men) shadowed retreating Paulician rebels. They got in an argument over which was bravest and disobeyed orders in a dawn attack that created panic and broke the rebel army.

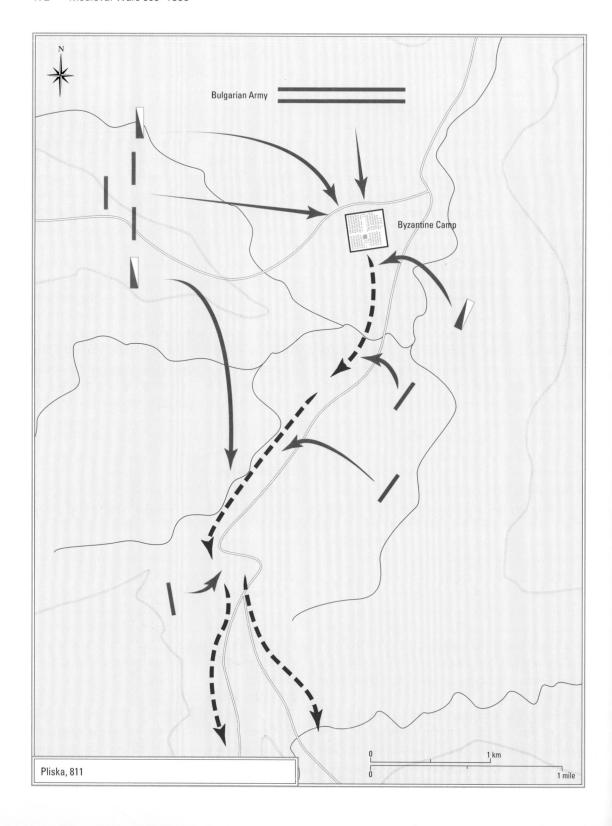

Bulgarian Army

Byzantine Camp

N

0 ___ 1 km

0 ___ 1 mile

Pliska, 811

■ **ACHELOOS, 20 AUGUST 917**

Byzantines under Leo Phocas attacked the Bulgars under Tsar Symeon. The Byzantines were winning, but a rumour spread that their commander was dead, causing panic. Symeon turned his troops and routed the Byzantines.

■ **DOROSTOLON, 971**

Byzantine emperor John I Tzimiskes led an army of about 30,000 to drive the Rus' under Svyatoslav out of Bulgaria. They met outside the fortress of Dorostolon. The Russians began the action with a charge, only to be stopped; a second charge was similarly contained. Finally, John sent in heavy cavalry on both wings, breaking through the Rus' shieldwall and causing a complete route.

■ **ADRIANOPLE, 972**

A Byzantine army under John I Tzimiskes defeated the larger, but inferior Rus' army of Svyatoslav. Russian advance was halted with archery, then a cavalry charge; the Rus' withdrew to Kiev.

■ **PANKALIA, 24 MARCH 979**

In a surprise attack, Byzantium's Gen Bardas Phocas crushingly defeated a rebel army under Bardas Sclerus, Phocas wounding Sclerus in single combat. The battle ended the rebellion and Sclerus escaped to Muslim territory.

■ **GATES OF TRAJAN, 17 AUGUST 986**

Byzantine emperor Basil II retreated after unsuccessfully besieging Sofia. Bulgarians under Tsar Samuel surrounded his army in the mountains and nearly annihilated it as the Byzantines fled; Basil himself barely escaped.

■ **SPERCHEIOS, 996**

Byzantines under Nicephorus Uranus surprised a Bulgarian army under Tsar Samuel as they returned from raiding Greece. The Byzantines daringly crossed the flooded Spercheios River, completely routing the Bulgarians in a dawn attack.

Chinese Sui/Tang Dynasty 581–950

■ **BOHAI SEA, 598**

A Chinese army and supporting fleet invaded the Korean kingdom of Goguryeo (Koguryo). The fleet was badly damaged in storms and repulsed by a Korean fleet. The army, depleted by disease, withdrew.

■ **YODONG REGION, 612**

A large Sui Dynasty/Chinese army invaded the Korean kingdom of Goguryeo (Koguryo). While medieval accounts suggest that the Chinese invasion included over a million troops, this is doubtlessly an exaggeration. A system of fortresses in northern Goguryeo tied down the Chinese invasion. In the Yodong region (present-day north-east North Korea) a Korean fortress withstood a lengthy siege by Chinese forces purportedly numbering over 300,000, another exaggeration. The garrison of the fortress finally began negotiating surrender terms, but Korean reinforcements arrived and the fortress continued to hold. Chinese forces were meanwhile depleted, unable to obtain sufficient supplies in the region. The siege was lifted when Goguryeo Gen Ŭlji Mundŏk (Eulji Mundeok) led forces that cleared the Chinese from the region. It is thought that the Chinese lost all but 2700 out of their force of over 300,000 during the campaign.

■ **PYONGYANG, 612**

During the Chinese invasion of the Korean kingdom of Goguryeo (Koguryo), a Chinese amphibious force attempted to seize the city of Pyongyang. The amphibious force entered Pyongyang, but was ambushed and retreated to the coast.

■ **SALSU RIVER, 612**

During a Chinese invasion of the Korean kingdom of Goguryeo (Koguryo), a large Chinese army began the process of crossing the Salsu River (present-day Chongchon river in north-eastern North Korea). In response the Koreans broke a dam upstream, flooding the river and isolating part of the Chinese army. The Gorguryeo gen Ŭlji Mundŏk (Eulji Mundeok) attacked the isolated Chinese and badly defeated them. Exaggerated accounts give Chinese losses of more than 300,000 troops.

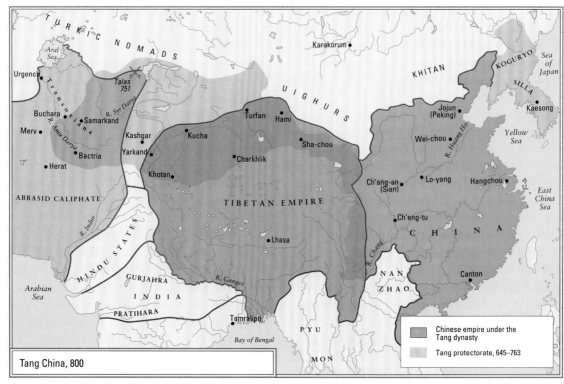

Tang China, 800

Chinese empire under the Tang dynasty

Tang protectorate, 645–763

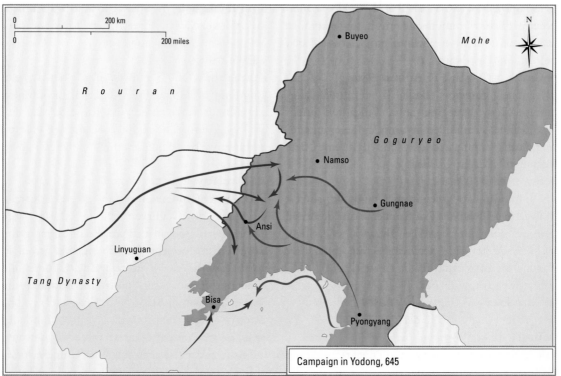

Campaign in Yodong, 645

■ **HUOYI, 8 SEPTEMBER 617**
As the Chinese Sui Dynasty began to collapse, the Sui Gen Li Yuan joined a rebellion against the dynasty. Li Yuan's 70,000 troops defeated Sui loyalists at Huoyi, near the Yellow River.

■ **HULAO, 28 MAY 621**
Li Shimin, the second emperor of the new Chinese Tang Dynasty, led an army against two rebellious warlords, Dou Jiande and Wang Sichong. The warlords were defeated at Hulao, in central China.

■ **ANSI FORTRESS, 645**
The Chinese Tang Dynasty, like the previous Sui Dynasty, invaded the Korean kingdom of Goguryeo (Koguryo), which, at the time, included parts of present-day China, including the Liaodong peninsula. The Ansi Fortress guarded part of this area, being located just southeast of the Liao river. A Chinese army reportedly as large as 60,000 led by Emperor Taizong defeated Goguryeo forces outside of the fortress and then began a siege. The fortress proved impregnable to assault, so the Chinese laboriously built an earthen ramp designed to overlook the fortress walls. The Koreans foiled this effort by building higher wooden ramparts atop their walls in the path of the Chinese ramp. The fortress continued to hold while winter approached and the Chinese forces withdrew, being unable to obtain adequate supplies in a hostile area with worsening weather.

■ **BAEKGANG, 27 AUGUST 663**
Forces of the Korean kingdom of Baekje, with their Japanese allies, were badly defeated by forces of the Korean kingdom of Silla and their Chinese allies at Baekgang, in present-day South Korea.

■ **TA-FEI, 670**
A Tibetan army attacked an invading Chinese army near Mount Ta-Fei in the Tarim Basin. The Chinese forces had separated into an advance force and rearguard; both were decisively defeated.

■ **KAO YU, 685**
A Chinese Tang Dynasty army crushed a rebel force in the province of Jiangsu, near the central-west coast of China. Tang forces inflicted at least 7000 casualties on the rebels.

■ **TIANMENLING, 698**
Chinese Tang Dynasty forces had defeated rebel Mohe peoples and pursued them into the former Korean kingdom of Goguryeo. There, the Mohe and Belhae Koreans joined forces and defeated the invading Chinese army.

■ **SHIBAO, 745–59**
Chinese forces invaded the Tarim Basin in present-day western China, which was held by Tibetans. Shibao was a strong Tibetan position in the Red Hills, continually resupplied by Tibetan cavalry, while besieging Chinese forces lacked adequate supplies. The Chinese appointed a Turkish general, Qosu Khan, who ordered a massive assault with 63,000 men. The assaulting force suffered huge losses in the attack, but finally captured Shibao, finding only 400 dead Tibetans inside.

■ **YONGQIU, 756**
During the An Shi Rebellion against the Chinese Tang Dynasty, loyal forces under Zhang Xun successfully defended the walled city of Yongqiu in Henan Province, inflicting heavy losses on much larger rebel forces.

■ **SUIYANG, 757**
During the An Shi Rebellion against the Chinese Tang Dynasty, 130,000 rebels under Yin Ziqi besieged the city of Suiyang in Henan Province. Zhang Xun, having successfully defended Yongqiu the previous year, was chosen to command 10,000 loyalists defending Suiyang. Suiyang repelled all assaults for several months. Food supplies in Suiyang were exhausted and the defenders eventually resorted to cannibalism. The city finally fell, but the costly siege crippled rebel strength.

■ **HENSHU, 781**
Chinese Tang Dynasty emperor Dezong, intending to establish firmer control within the Tang Empire, dispatched Imperial troops who defeated warlord forces under Tian Yue in modern-day Hubei Province in central China.

■ **HUANG CHAO REBELLION, 874–84**

As the power of the Tang Dynasty in China declined, rebellions were numerous. Huang Chao, a charismatic merchant, led a particularly destructive rebellion. Huang's territorial successes throughout China were temporary, resulting in the sacking of major cities and the devastation of rural regions, while Tang generals unenthusiastically pursued the mobile rebels. Huang escaped capture, but died during a clash with rival rebels.

■ **TING HSIEN, 945**

Khitan forces led by Liao emperor Taizong clashed with Jin Chinese forces in present-day northern China. Taizong was defeated and barely escaped capture in this attempt to expand the Khitan Liao Empire.

Wars of the Turkish Empires 600–1299

■ **DERBENT, 627**

During the Third Perso-Turkic War, the western Turkic Khaganate fought against the Sassanid Empire in alliance with the Byzantine emperor Heraclius. The Khagan Tong Yabghu led a Göktürk and Khazar force that stormed the newly fortified Sassanid city of Derbent in the southern Caucasus. In the aftermath of this victory, Heraclius led a Byzantine offensive, which defeated the main Sassanid army at Nineveh in December 627, while the Khagan's forces took Tbilisi.

■ **DANDANAQAN, 23 MAY 1040**

A Seljuq force of 20,000 that had been raiding the western provinces of the Ghaznavid Empire defeated a 50,000-strong Ghaznavid army at Dandanaqan in Khorasan. The disputed territory was incorporated into the Great Seljuq Empire.

■ **DIDGORI, 12 AUGUST 1121**

A 56,000-strong Georgian army under King David IV intercepted and defeated a Seljuq invasion force totalling at least 150,000 men at Didgori, near Tbilisi. David followed up his victory with the capture of Tbilisi in the year 1122.

■ **YASSI CHEMEN, 10–12 AUGUST 1230**

The last Khwarezmian ruler, Jalal ad-Din, captured the Ayyubid city of Ahlat, provoking an Ayyubid alliance with the Seljuq Sultanate of Rûm. Jalal ad-Din was defeated in a three-day battle by the Seljuq sultan Kayqubad I.

Korea 600–1100

■ **HWANGSANBEOL, 660**

A 50,000 strong Silla army commanded by Gen Kim Yushin attacked a force of no more than 5000 Baekje troops under Gen Gyebaek, which was defending Sabi, the Baekje capital. Despite being heavily outnumbered, the Baekje army inflicted heavy casualties, beating off at least four Silla attacks before being overwhelmed and annihilated. Sabi was then captured by the Silla army, leading to the surrender of King Uija of Baekje.

■ **HEUNGHWAJIN, 1018**

Khitan troops numbering 100,000 under the command of Gen Xiao Baiya invaded the Korean kingdom of Goryeo. Their line of advance crossed a stream near Heunghwajin, where Goryeo's army under Gen Gang Gam-chan had set a trap. Gen Gang had the stream blocked and broke the dam as the Khitan force crossed the stream bed. Many Khitans were drowned. These losses increased the already considerable numerical superiority of the 208,000 strong Goryeo army.

■ **KWIJU, 1019**

Despite his defeat at Heunghwajin, Gen Xiao Baiya advanced on the Goryeo capital, Kaesong, but his army suffered badly in the harsh Korean winter. The Khitan army was virtually annihilated by Gen Gang Gam-chan at Kwiju.

Chinese Nanchao War 650–774

■ **CHANG'AN, 763**

A 100,000-strong Tibetan army surrounding the Chinese capital, Chang'an, was panicked into retreat by the renowned Chinese Gen Guo Ziyi

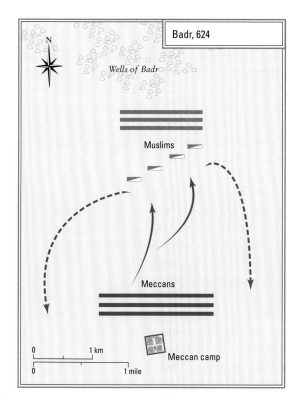

Badr, 624

N

Wells of Badr

Muslims

Meccans

Meccan camp

0   1 km

0   1 mile

who had spread rumours of his advance at the head of a huge army.

Muslim Expansion 624–1100

■ BADR, 13 MARCH 624

In the earliest days of Islam, Muhammad and his followers had to flee their hometown of Mecca in Arabia and set up a Muslim community in Medina, roughly 320km to the north of Mecca. Mecca was controlled by the Quraish tribe, who were polytheistic and hostile to Islam. A clash between the Muslims of Medina and the Quraish of Mecca initially took place along the important caravan route that ran north and south along the western edge of the Arabian peninsula. The wells at Badr, 130km south-west of Medina, were a key point along that route, which became the scene of the first significant battle between the Muslims and the Quraish. Muhammad commanded 313 men, two horses and 70 camels, taking up defensive

positions near Badr as the Quraish approached with over 900 men, 100 horses and 170 camels. Both sides included archers and swordsmen. By tradition, the battle opened with personal combat between champions from each side. Both sides sent out three champions, including Ali, Hamza and Ubayda for the Muslims. All three Muslim champions slew their opponents, although Ubayda was mortally wounded. After the combat of champions, the Quraish mounted a general attack. The Quraish attack faltered and the Muslims counter-attacked. The Quraish fled in disorder, pursued by the Muslims, who gathered over 40 prisoners.

The Muslims had lost 14 killed, while the Quraish lost more than 70 killed. The Muslims executed some Quraish captives immediately after the battle, but Muhammad then ordered the lives of prisoners spared. Some of the prisoners became converts to Islam. Although small, the battle was decisive in terms of the survival of the seminal Muslim community.

■ OHOD, 625

The battle of Ohod (often rendered Uhud) was the second battle between the Quraish tribe of Mecca and the Muslims of Medina in Arabia. The Quraish with 3000 men advanced on Medina. Muhammad led 1000 Muslims around the rear of the Quraish force, which then turned to attack the Muslims. The Muslims repulsed the initial attack, but ultimately lost the battle and retreated to Medina.

■ MEDINA, 627

The polytheistic Quraish tribe of Mecca in Arabia had been engaged in war with the Muslims of Medina, led by Muhammad since 624. The Quraish allied with other Arab tribes and gathered an army of 10,000 to march on Medina in early 627. Muhammad, with only 3000 combatants and alerted to the approach of the Quraish, ordered ditches dug around Medina. The Quraish army consisted largely of mounted warriors on horses and camels, which could not cross the Muslim ditches nor assault the walls of

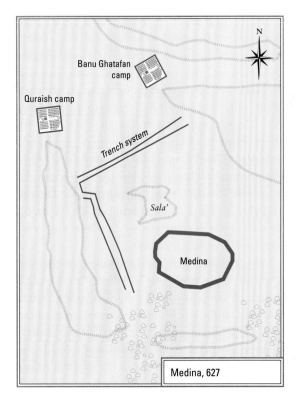

Banu Ghatafan
camp

Quraish camp

Trench system

N

Sala'

Medina

Medina, 627

Medina. Unprepared for siege warfare, probing attacks by the Quraish failed. In personal combat between champions, the Muslim Ali slew the Quraish champion Amr. Total casualties are unknown, but the Muslims suffered few losses, while the Quraish army became badly depleted and was compelled to withdraw.

■ MUTA, 629

Zaid Ibn Harithah was defeated while leading a small force into modern-day Jordan to avenge the murder of Muslim emissaries by local Arab tribes in the first confrontation between Muslims and the Christian Byzantine Empire.

■ MECCA, 630

Muhammad's followers from Yethrib-Medina and allied Arab tribes numbering 10,000 forced the eventual submission of Mecca and the ruling Quraish tribe in an almost bloodless assault. The idols in the Ka'ba were subsequently destroyed.

■ YAMAMA, 632

After two failed attacks under the commanders Ikrimah and Shurahbil, Khalid ibn al-Walid led a force of 13,000 to defeat Musailama and the Banu Hanifa tribe and subjugated central Arabia.

■ HIRA, 633

Khalid ibn al-Walid besieged the fortified city of Hira, capital of the Lakhmid Kingdom until it was annexed by Persia in 602. The Lakhmids surrendered, allied with Khalid and acted as spies against the Sassanids.

■ ULLAIS, 633

Khalid pursued Persian and Christian Arab forces from Walaja to the plain between the Euphrates and Khaseef. Light cavalry massacred the Sassanians in retreat in the Khaseef. Ullais was also known as the battle of Blood River.

■ ZUMAIL, 633

Khalid's spies identified the location of imperial camp at Zumail. The Islamic forces conducted a co-ordinated three-sided attack at night, nearly destroying the Christian Arab corps.

■ WALAJA, 633

Khalid ibn al-Walid led an army of the Rashidun Caliphate numbering around 15,000 against the numerically superior Sassanid forces of Yazdegerd III. The Sassanids sent two armies to intercept the Islamic forces at Walaja near the Euphrates, recruiting Arab allies en route. Khalid moved his forces to meet the armies separately before they coalesced. The battlefield consisted of a plain between two high ridges, bordered by the Euphrates and the desert. Khalid deployed the terrain and his superior numbers of cavalry, positioning them behind the western ridge until he was able to entrap the entire Persian army. After assuming an initial defensive position, the Persian commander Andarzaghar launched a counter-attack. Following a period of retreat, the light cavalry charged the more unwieldy Persian heavy cavalry. Khalid's forces then gradually surrounded and decimated the Persian army.

■ SALASIL, 633

Khalid ibn al-Walid tricked the heavily armed Persian army into a series of marches until they

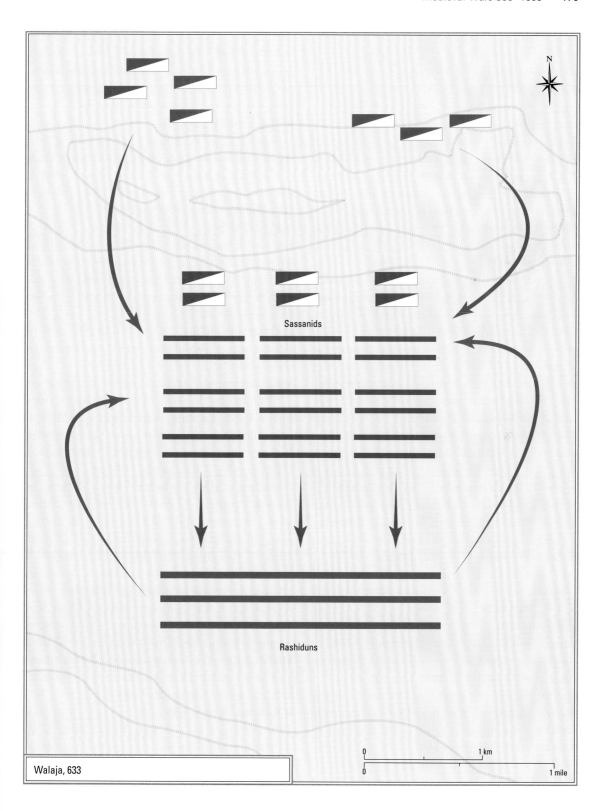

Sassanids

Rashiduns

Walaja, 633

0   1 km

0   1 mile

were exhausted. The Islamic cavalry broke through the infantry lines of the Persian army, who were massacred in retreat.

■ FIRAZ, 633

Khalid defeated an alliance of the Byzantine and Sassanian forces both garrisoned in the border region of Firaz. Khalid led a force of around 18,000 against a force of up to 180,000. After giving the enemy the option to cross the Euphrates, Khalid caught them in a pincer movement with the river at their back. Some 50,000 Byzantine and Sassanids fell and Firaz surrendered.

■ AJNADAIN, 634

The combined Islamic forces of several armies, numbering 20,000, were summoned to Ajnadain by Khalid ibn al-Walid to meet a local Byzantine force of around 9000. Islamic archers were ordered to fire in controlled barrages against the initial forays of lightly armed Roman infantry and archers, but these remained out of range. Al-Waqidi records that after suffering initial losses, Khalid sent individual warriors to challenge their Roman counterparts. Numerous Roman commanders were killed by Dharar Ibn al-Azwar, then, as the duelling became widespread, Khalid ordered a general advance. On the second day of the battle, the Roman lines collapsed after the loss of their commander Theodore, following a failed ambush against Khalid. The Byzantine forces were routed by the Islamic cavalry as they fled towards Jerusalem, Jaffa and Gaza. Despite a decisive victory, many Islamic commanders fell.

■ BOSRA, 634

Islamic forces attack the Byzantine Army at Bosra, the capital of the Ghassanid kingdom. After several days of battle, the Islamic forces besiege the city. As reserve forces were moving towards Ajnadain, the Byzantine commander surrendered.

■ SANIYYAT-UL-UQAB, 634

Khalid laid siege to Damascus and formed an isolating cordon around the city; the largest detachments covered the southern road to Palestine and the northern road to Emesa. Heraclius sent 12,000 Byzantines reinforcements to break the siege; these were intercepted and routed in a pass 32km north of the city.

■ MARJ-UD DEEBAJ, 634

Following the surrender at Damascus, the Byzantine Army were given a three-day truce to disperse. Leading the cavalry, Khalid pursued and attacked the Byzantine army on the plain of Jabal Ansariya, close to Antioch.

■ PELLA, 635

Khalid defeated the Byzantine army under Theodore the Sacellarius, the military commander in Syria. As imperial treasurer, Theodore's role was to provide reassurance to unpaid soldiers and mercenaries.

■ DAMASCUS, 635

Khalid ibn al-Walid laid siege to Damascus, the stronghold of Byzantine Syria. The fortifications of Damascus were intimidating, surrounded by an 11m high wall and guarded by six gates. Lacking siege equipment, Khalid surrounded the city, with each gate guarded by a general commanding over 4000 troops. One cavalry detachment reconnoitred for Byzantine relief columns from Emesa as another protected lines of communication with Medinah and engaged the Byzantine garrison at Fahal. Following the defeat of a relief column, the Byzantine defenders attempted a series of counter-attacks. Infantry covered by archers rushed first from one and then from several gates, but suffered serious losses and could not break the siege lines. On receipt of insider information, Khalid launched a surprise attack against the lightly guarded Eastern Gate and, after initial resistance, the city surrendered and was spared further bloodshed.

■ YARMUK RIVER, 636

Vahan's ethnically mixed force of 50,000 pursued Khalid's army of 25,000 in retreat from Damascus. After six days of single combat, cavalry charges and negotiations, Khalid's

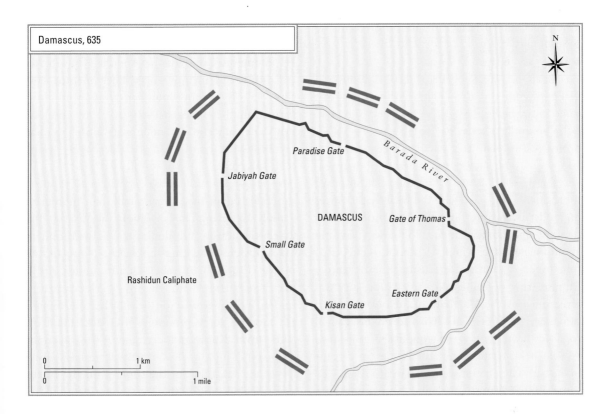

Damascus, 635

N

Paradise Gate

Jabiyah Gate

Barada River

DAMASCUS   Gate of Thomas

Small Gate

Rashidun Caliphate

Eastern Gate

Kisan Gate

0   1 km

0   1 mile

forces routed the Byzantines. The survivors fled towards Egypt.

■ Qadisiya, 637

Sa'd ibn abi-Waqqas led an Islamic force of 30,000 against a numerically superior, but inexperienced Persian army of infantry, heavy cavalry and elephant corps. The decisive Islamic victory effectively ended the Persian control of Iraq.

■ Hazir, 637

Meenas commanded a garrison force of around 70,000 against Khalid's mobile guard in an offensive aimed at preventing a full-scale siege of Qinnasrin. Meenas was killed, the garrison slaughtered and the city surrendered.

■ Iron Bridge, 637

Following the Rashidun victory at Yarmuk, the Islamic army marched into Anatolia. Approaching Antioch from the east, they encountered the Byzantine army outside modern-day Mahruba, near an Iron Bridge over the Orontes. Few

details remain beyond the prominent role played by Khalid and the Islamic mobile guard. The Byzantine Army suffered catastrophic losses and fled to Antioch, which was then besieged.

■ Jalula, 637

Following the capture of Ctesiphon, 12,000 Islamic troops engaged the Sassanian armies regrouping at Jalula. The Sassanian commander Mihran dug entrenchments in an attempt to slow the opposing cavalry, but his forces were defeated.

■ Jerusalem, 637

With the defeat of the Byzantine field army, Jerusalem was gradually besieged by Islamic armies marching from the east. Heraclius could not offer any assistance and the surrender of Jerusalem solidified Islamic control over Palestine.

■ Aleppo, 638

The Roman general Joachim unsuccessfully defended the fort of Aleppo with 4000 garrison troops against the Islamic forces of Khalid. After a siege, Aleppo surrendered and the garrison was permitted to depart.

■ BABYLON, 639

In one of the initial engagements of the conquest of Egypt, Amr ibn al-Asl defeated the Byzantine force near Heliopolis, then besieged Egyptian Babylon until its surrender in 641.

■ NIHAWAND, 641

Known as 'The Victory of Victories'. Nihawand saw the decisive defeat of the Sassanian imperial forces marshalled to defend the wealthy provinces of modern-day Iraq. The desert frontier was in disarray and undermanned following Sassanid abolition of the client Lakhmid state that functioned as a buffer zone against the Byzantine Empire. After defeat at Jalula in 637, the city was abandoned by the Marzbans of the north-eastern provinces. Yazdegerd III had moved his capital to Merv from which he conducted raids into Islamic-held territory and raised levies for a major offensive. The commander Mardan Shah led some 60,000 against an Islamic army numbering 30,000, led by numerous commanders including Caliph Omar. The Persian cavalry may have been tricked into an ill-prepared attack on a Bedouin force that feigned flight, only to surround the Persians in pursuit.

■ ALEXANDRIA, 642

The Islamic forces of Amr were bombarded from within the heavily fortified walls for months, but the death of Heraclius prevented Byzantine reinforcements being sent and the city fell after a siege of over a year.

■ TRIPOLI, 643

Abdullah ibn Zubayr captured the last of the Byzantine coastal enclaves in North Africa after a siege lasting one month.

■ BALANJAR, 650

Abd ar-Rahman ibn Rabiah invaded the northern Caucasus intent on conquering the Khazar Khagagnate, but was defeated. A ninth-century source describes catapults used by both sides.

■ BATTLE OF THE MASTS, 655

Fought off the coast of Mount Phoenix in Lycia, this naval battle was a crucial victory for Islam over a naval force of some 500 ships led by Emperor Constans II. Abdullah bin S'aad led a relatively inexperienced fleet of some 200 ships. The Byzantine ships were moored in close formation; the Islamic victory may have resulted from the superior boarding and close combat techniques of their forces.

■ BASRA, 656

Also known as the 'battle of the Camel'. A rebel group in Egypt first imprisoned, then murdered Caliph Uthman. The accession of Ali ibn Abi Taleb (the cousin and adopted son of the Prophet) led to dissension within the Sahaba (companions of the Prophet). A rebel faction under Aisha marched to Basra with an army of 3000 warriors to demand vengeance for the murder of Uthman. Ali raised a force of several thousand aided by allies from Kufra and defeated Aisha's faction. The spiral into civil war and eventual schism leaves the reliability of the sources for the battle questionable, but both factions are reputed to have suffered great losses.

■ SIFFIN, 657

Ali led an army against Mu'awiya, Governor of Syria, who was in revolt against him. After three days of battle with many casualties, the belligerents withdrew to Kufa and Damascus respectively.

■ CONSTANTINOPLE, 673–78

Mu'awiya's forces failed to defeat the Byzantine fleet at sea, but remained in possession of the Asiatic shore of the sea of Marmora in 672. The army returned the next year and formed a land and sea blockage along the Bosphoros river, keeping the city in an intermittent state of siege. The fifth-century Theodosian Walls remained unbreached and the city defences under Emperor Constantine IV Pogonatus were unbroken. The defeat of the Islamic navy at the battle of Syllaeum in 677 owed much to the use of Greek fire and ensured that the city was re-supplied by sea. The harsh winter of 677–78 and the starvation suffered by the Islamic forces resulted in the siege being lifted. Mu'awiya sued for peace in 678.

■ **KERBALA, 680**

Husain ibn Ali led a revolt of the Banu Hashim, the clan of the Prophet, against the Umayyad Yazid I in defence of the hereditary principle of the Caliphate. Accounts of the battle have uncertain veracity in view of their doctrinally partisan nature. Shi'a traditions describe the massacre of Husain's companions by onslaughts of lances and arrows and the decapitation of the remaining members of the Prophet's family.

■ **SEBASTOPOLIS, 690–92**

The Umayyad Gen Marwan defeated an army led by the Byzantine emperor Leontios who had successfully subjected Islamic forces to a series of humiliating defeats in Georgia, Armenia, Azerbaijan and Albania. The Byzantine Army included a force of 30,000 Slavs (forcibly resettled within the empire by Justinian II) under the Bulgar-Slav commander Neboulos. Marwan secured victory by persuading Neboulos and some 20,000 of the Slavic contingent to defect.

■ **CARTHAGE, 698**

Following the Byzantine reconquest of Carthage under John the Patrician and Tiberius Aspimarus. Hasan ibn al-Nu'man led a counter-attack with the Islamic forces who had fled to Kairouan. Hasan's force of 40,000 outnumbered the Carthaginian defenders, although the Byzantines had called on their traditional Amazigh allies, plus Franks and Visigoths. Hasan launched a successful land and sea offensive and the Byzantine forces withdrew to Corsica, Sicily and Crete.

■ **KABUL (MASKIN), 701**

Abd ul Malik dispatched Syrian reinforcements to his general Al-Hajjaj ibn Yusuf, governor of the eastern Muslim provinces. Al-Hajjaj successfully defeated the revolt of Ibn Al Ashath, who then retreated to Kabul.

■ **RIO BARBATE, 711**

Internal dissensions in the Visigothic kingdom in Spain resulted in an alliance between the remaining Byzantine governor in North Africa, Count Julian of Ceuta, and Musa ibn Nusair. Tariq ibn Zayid, governor of Tangiers, led an initial raid

on Gibraltar with 1700 men, possibly aided by a fleet of Count Julian's ships. Subsequently he led a force of 7000 Syrians, Berbers and Yemenis on to Cartagena. The Visigothic king Roderick had been campaigning against Basques and Franks in the northern town of Pamplona. His force of 25,000 marched south and encountered Tariq's army at Rio Barbate near Cadiz. Roderick's commanders Sisbert and Osbert either deserted or defected during the battle. Roderick was killed with the majority of his court and the defeated Visigoths fled to Seville.

■ **CONSTANTINOPLE, 717–18**

Leo the Isaurian defeated the fleet of Maslama and Suleiman and drove their remaining ships into the Sea of Marmara. Leo repulsed several more attacks before the arrival of Bulgar allies saw the besiegers withdraw.

■ **COVADONGA, 718**

The Visigoth Pelayo successfully repulsed a Moorish advance in the first major Christian victory against the Islamic invasion of the Iberian peninsula.

■ **TOULOUSE, 9 JUNE 721**

Al-Samh ibn Malik al Khawlani besieged the city of Toulouse. Eudo, the Duke of Aquitaine, retreated at the start of the siege to gather allies and defeated the Moors in a surprise attack.

■ **BALANJAR, 723**

According to the ninth-century historian al-Tabari, al-Djarrah ibn Abdullah captured the town of Balanjar and massacred much of the population who had tried to defend the city with a cordon of 3000 wagons.

■ **TOURS, 732**

Abd er-Rahman led a force of Arab and Berber cavalry from the Kingdom of Al-Andalus across the mountains by the valley of Roncesvalles and into Gascony. At Bordeaux, the Islamic force of some 50,000 defeated the alliance of Eudo of Aquitaine and Munuza, once a Berber commander in Spain. From here, the army overran southern Gaul for several months, reaching as far as the Loire. The anonymous Arabic source describes

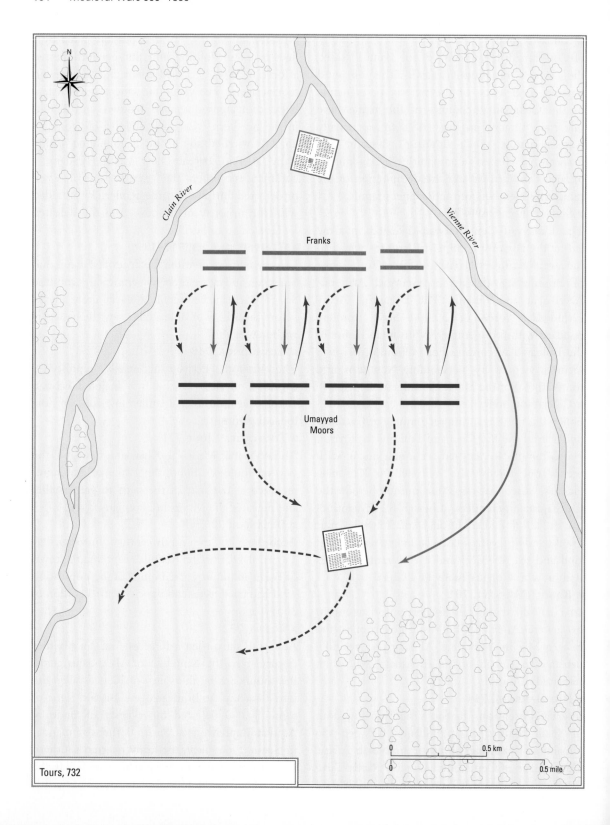

Tours, 732

the army reputedly laying waste to the country and ladening themselves with captives and spoils. Both the Mozarabic Chronicle and Isidore Pacensis attest to the destruction of churches and of the general population and suggest that the aim of the expedition was raid and pillage, not conquest.

Eudo of Aquitaine fled to Austrasia with the remnants of his army and sought the assistance of Charles Martel, with whom he had previously contested the status of Major of the Palace. Charles Martel reordered his forces and marched south from the upper Danube. Abd's forces had looted the extra-mural church of St Hilary at Poitiers, but made no serious attempt to besiege the city itself. The forces then separated into several raiding parties and pillaged the area between Tours and Poitiers. Upon hearing the advance of the armies of Charles Martel and Eudo from the east, Abd withdrew towards Poitiers, covering the slow dispatch of the train of booty with a series

of skirmishes to delay the approaching Frankish forces. An anonymous Arabic source makes pointed reference to the disorder caused by the baggage train and Abd's reluctance to order his troops to abandon their spoils.

The discipline and mobility of the lightly armed Islamic cavalry made it difficult to counter in mounted combat and they could easily outmanoeuvre the Frankish heavy cavalry. Although probably possessing superior numbers and both cavalry and infantry forces, Charles dismounted his cavalry to present a strong defensive line. Isidore Pacensis describes the solid phalanx of the Frankish forces as 'a belt of ice frozen together, and not to be dissolved, as they slew the Arabs with the sword'. This defensive position resisted the repeated charges of the Islamic cavalry until nightfall. An Arabic anonymous Aramic source describes the Islamic assault breaking the Frankish lines, but deterred by the enemy looting the baggage train and then

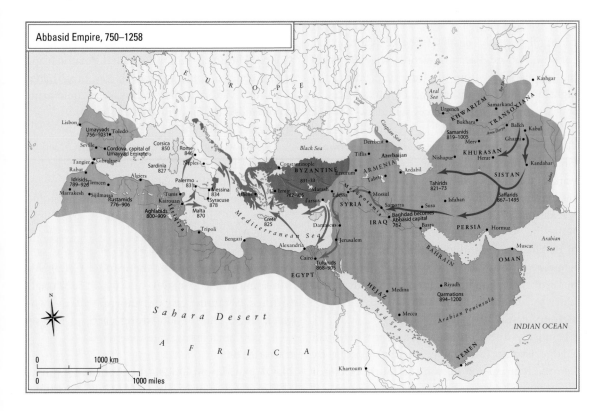

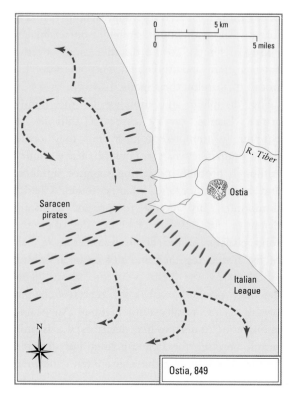

Ostia, 849

taking flight at the death of Abd er-Rahman. By contrast, Isidore Pacensis records the retreat of the Islamic forces from the battlefield during the night. Despite the divergence of the sources, it appears that the Islamic forces withdrew, perhaps lacking the weight to deal an effective blow and desirous of protecting their remaining booty. Charles refused to send the cavalry in pursuit, wary of the risk posed by a feigned retreat to men and reclaimed spoils alike.

■ KASHGAR, 736
Nassr ibn Sayyar, Governor of the garrison city of Balkh, unsuccessfully defended the city against Khurasani troops led by al-Harith ibn Surayj, in revolt over conditions for native converts in Umayyad-controlled Khurasan.

■ ACRONIUM, 739
Theophanes the Confessor records the defeat of a large Islamic force raiding across Anatolia by Leo the Isaurian and his son the future Emperor Constantine V.

■ RUPAR THUTHA, 746
The last Umayyad caliph, Marwan II, occupied Kufa and Mosul in a series of campaigns to reunite the Umayyad Empire and put down Syrian and Kharijite rebellions.

■ ZAB, 25 JANUARY 750
The final defeat of the Umayyad Dynasty by the first Abbasid caliph Abu al-'Abbas al-Saffah. Around 300 members of the Umayyad family were killed. Marwan fled to Egypt and was later executed.

■ TALAS, 751
Islamic and Tibetan allies defeated the Tang Gen Kao Hsien-chih. The number of combatants is uncertain. The Abbasid army of Ziyad ibn Salih may have numbered 20,000, including their Tibetan and Uyghur allies. The Tang forces including their Ferghana allies may have numbered 10,000, plus 20,000 Karluk mercenaries. The retreat of their allies and the desertion of the Karluks left the Tang army outnumbered and outmanoeuvred.

■ HERACLEA PONTICA, 806
An Arab army of up to 135,000 men under Caliph Harun al-Rashid invaded Anatolia and took Heraclea Pontica (modern-day Eregli) after a decisive victory against a Byzantine field army commanded by Emperor Nikephoros I.

■ ANZEN, 22 JULY 838
A 25,000-strong Byzantine army commanded by Emperor Theophilos was decisively defeated at Anzen in Anatolia by Gen Afshin's Arab army of 20,000 men. Theophilos fled to Constantinople, allowing Caliph al-Mu'tasim's army to besiege Amorium.

■ AMORIUM, AUGUST 838
An Arab army of 80,000 men under Caliph Al-Mu'tasim invaded Anatolia and took the strongly fortified Byzantine city of Amorium after a two-week siege. The 30,000-strong garrison and up to 40,000 inhabitants were massacred.

■ OSTIA, 849
Naval expeditions under the Aghlabid Emirate of Tunisia systematically raided the coastlines

of Provence and Italy. A fleet for the common defence of the coastline, formed by Naples, Amalfi and Gaeta, gathered at Ostia. The engagement opened with an attack from Neapolitan galleys, but midway through the battle, a storm scattered the Islamic ships, allowing survivors to be easily defeated. Islamic booty and prison labour helped build the Leonine Walls.

■ SAMOSATA (SAMSAT), 873

The Byzantine emperor Basil I advanced from Anatolia, penetrating deep into Arab territory and reaching the valley of the Euphrates, which was temporarily incorporated into the empire, together with the city of Samosata.

■ APULIA, 875–80

Islamic attacks conquered Bari, Taranto and Brindisi and saw the formation of numerous Emirates claiming independence from the Aghlabid Emirate of Tunisia. Islamic and Lombard control of Apulia was gradually eradicated in the 870s, first by a series of campaigns under Louis the Pious and, in 880, by the navy of Byzantine emperor Basil I.

■ TAORMINA, 1 AUGUST 902

Byzantine control of Sicily was steadily eroded by a series of Arab offensives that began in 827. The coastal fortress of Taormina was the last Byzantine stronghold on the island and was captured in August 902.

■ GARIGLIANO, JUNE 915

The Fatimid Caliphate conquest of Minturno on the Garigliano river in 883 posed a serious threat to Rome. Pope John X led a combined Italian and Byzantine force in an offensive which destroyed the Fatimid army.

■ MELITENE, 934

The city of Melitene (Malatya) in eastern Anatolia had been a major Byzantine stronghold until its conquest by the Arabs in 638. A Byzantine counter-offensive by a 50,000-strong army under John Kourkouas recaptured the city in 934.

■ SIMANCAS, 934

Abd al-Rahman III led a large army with the assistance of the Moorish governor of Zaragoza, Abu Yahya. Ramiro II of Leon headed a combined force from Navarre, Galicia and Asturias. The forces gathered near the walls of the city of Simancas, but a total eclipse caused such terror that battle was not joined for two days. After several days of combat, the Christians emerged victorious and held control of the Douro.

■ CANDIA, 960–61

In 960, a 50,000-strong Byzantine army under the future emperor Nicephoros II Phokas invaded Muslim-held Crete. Although the island was quickly overrun, the capital of Candia was only taken in 961 after a long siege.

■ ADANA, 964

After defeating Sayf al-Dawla, Emir of Aleppo, and sacking the city in 962, the Byzantine emperor Nicephoros II Phokas launched an offensive into southern Anatolia. He captured Adana, despite fierce resistance by Sayf al-Dawla's garrison.

■ ALEPPO-ANTIOCH, 969

After the recapture of Anatolia the armies of Byzantine emperor Nicephoros II Phokas invaded Syria and stormed Antioch, before retaking Aleppo from the chamberlain Karguyah, who had overthrown the emir Sayf ad-Dawla. Both cities became Byzantine protectorates.

■ CROTONE, 982

Emperor Otto II and his Italo-Lombard allies fought the numerically inferior forces of the Kalbid emir of Sicily, Abu al-Qasim. German heavy cavalry killed al-Qasim, but, following his death, the Islamic troops surrounded the German forces. The resulting slaughter included the deaths of Landulf IV of Benevento; Henry I, Bishop of Augsburg; Günther, Margrave of Merseburg; numerous German counts and Otto II, who subsequently died on his journey north.

■ CIVITATE, 18 JUNE 1053

Robert Guiscard, Humphrey de Hauteville and Richard of Aversa faced Leo IX with an army of Lombard, Italian and Swabian troops. The forces met on the banks of the Fortore river. Richard led a cavalry charge, which put the ramshackle Lombards to flight. Humphrey attacked the formidable Swabian mercenaries, at the centre,

Viking Campaigns, 900

N

400 km

0

0   400 miles

ICELAND

Norwegian Sea

FINNIC PEOPLES

Hladir

NORWAY

Kaupang

SWEDEN

Uppsala

Birka

Staraya Ladoga
(Aldeigjuborg)

Novgorod
(Holmgard)

KIEVAN
RUS

North Sea

Baltic Sea

DENMARK

Roskilde   • Lund

BALTIC PEOPLES

KINGDOM OF ORKNEY

NORTHUMBRIA

IRISH
KINGDOMS

York

Dublin

Danelaw

Hedeby

Bremen

S   L   A   V   S

Kiev

Cork

WELSH
STATES

WESSEX

London

Rhine

Cologne

Aachen

Frankfurt

Cracow

ATLANTIC
OCEAN

Normandy

Paris

EAST FRANKISH
KINGDOM

Lorch

Nitrava

HUNGARY

Mosapurc

PECHENEGS

Orléans

WEST FRANKISH
KINGDOM

Besançon

UPPER
BURGUNDY

Lyon

LOWER
BURGUNDY

Milan

Venice

Danube

Presov

Bordeaux

Genoa

KINGDOM OF ITALY

CROATIA

Serbia

Nish

BULGARIA

Corunna

Bayonne

Avignon

Nice

Adriatic Sea

LEÓN

Oporto

NAVARRE
ARAGON

Fraxinetum

Barcelona

MUSLIM
STATES

Tarragona

PAPAL ITALY

Rome

Corsica

Sardinia

Pr. of Benevento

Barium

BYZANTINE EMPIRE

Phillippopolis

Adrianople

Thessalonica

Aegean Sea

Smyrna

Toledo

Balansiyah

Balearic Is.

EMIRATE OF CORDOBA

Ishbiliyah

Ibn
Hafsun
(autonomous)

Cartagena

M   e   d   i   t   e   r   r   a   n   e   a   n

Panormus

Sicily

Naples

Chandax

Crete

IDRISIDS

RUSTAMIDS

ABBASIDS
(AGHLABIDS)

Sétif

Tunis

Malta

S   e   a

Kairawan

Tripoli

eventually decimating them with the assistance of Robert's reserve and Richard's cavalry.

■ SAGRAJAS (AZ-ZALLAQAH), 1086

King Alfonso VI's Castilian and Leónese force of 2500 men was defeated by a 7000-stong Andalusian army under Yusuf ibn Tashfin at Sagrajas, near Badajoz. Alfonso barely managed to escape and his army was effectively destroyed.

Norse Expansion 800–1066

■ ELLANDUN, 825

Egbert of Wessex defeated Beornwulf of Mercia, overturning the balance of power and resulting in the submission of the Mercian subject kingdoms (Kent, Surrey, Sussex, Essex, East Anglia) to the overlordship of Wessex.

■ HINGSTON DOWN, 837

A great Viking 'Ship-Army' joined with Cornish Britons resisting submission to Wessex to raid across the south-west. Egbert of Wessex defeated the combined forces on the Cornish side of the Tamar.

■ ACLEA, 851

Aethelwulf of Wessex defeated a large force of Viking ships raiding along the Thames, described by *The Anglo-Saxon Chronicle* as the 'greatest slaughter of a heathen raiding-army that we have ever heard tell of'.

■ YORK, 867

The Viking army of Ivar and Halfdene wintered in York and repaired the Roman fortifications. Osberht and Aella, rival claimants to the Northumbrian throne, combined their forces and succeeded in breaching the walls behind which the Vikings had fled. Once inside the fortifications, the Northumbrians were slaughtered and both kings killed; Aella subjected to the Blood-Eagle. The submission of the survivors effectively ended the Anglo-Saxon kingdom of Northumbria.

■ ENGLEFIELD, 31 DECEMBER 870

Earldorman Aethelwulf of Berkshire led the shire levies to victory against a contingent of Vikings on a plundering expedition from their base at Reading, killing one of their earls.

■ HOXNE, 870

The Viking army annihilated the army of Edmund of East Anglia at Hoxne. Edmund died fighting fiercely with a great many of his men and East Anglia became subject to Viking control.

■ READING, 4 JANUARY 871

Aethelred and Alfred of Wessex attacked the Vikings at their stronghold in Reading. The Wessex forces succeeded in taking the gate, but were seriously defeated once confronted with the main Viking army.

■ ASHDOWN, 8 JANUARY 871

Aethelred and Alfred of Wessex defeated a large Viking army, killing five earls and two kings, Bagsecg and Haldan. Both sides divided their forces into two divisions and employed shieldwalls.

■ WILTON, 871

In his first engagement as king of Wessex, Alfred's depleted forces suffered a serious defeat by the reinforced Viking army. Following a long battle, the Vikings feigned a retreat, killing those who broke ranks in pursuit.

■ HAFRSFJORD, 872

In one of the most decisive sea battles of medieval Scandinavia, Harald Fairhair defeated a loose confederation of kings and jarls opposed to his conquests and consolidation of power throughout Norway.

■ CHIPPENHAM, 6 JANUARY 878

The Viking Guthrum attacked the Royal Vill of Chippenham on the feast of Epiphany and overrode much of Wessex. Alfred and his remaining thegns fled to Athelney, many others fled overseas or submitted to Guthrum.

■ EDINGTON, 878

Alfred of Wessex with the Shire levies of Somerset, Wiltshire and Hampshire routed the entire Viking army, put them to flight, then besieged them for a fortnight at Chippenham until they sued for peace.

■ CYNWIT, 878

The men of Devon routed a force of 23 Viking ships

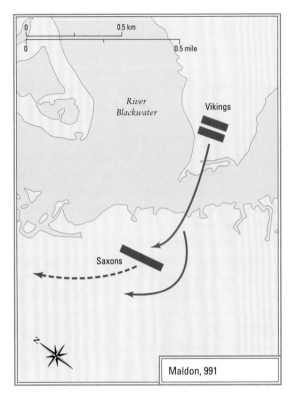

River
Blackwater

Vikings

Saxons

Maldon, 991

and Ealdred, son of Eadwulf, of Northumbria at Corbridge. In 918, Ragnall established himself as king at York.

■ TEMPSFORD, 918

Edward the Elder stormed the Burh, fortified by Vikings from Huntingdon and East Anglia, killing the East Anglian leader Guthrum II and the earls Toglos and Manna.

■ BRUNABURH, 937

Aethelstan of Wessex, his brother Edmund and forces of Wessex and Mercia defeated a confederacy of Irish Norse led by Olaf, Constantine of Scotland and the Strathclyde Welsh of Eugenius.

■ BAUDS, 962

Vikings colonized the Orkneys and Hebrides and systematically attacked the Scottish mainland. Indulf, King of Scotland, defeated a party of Norse 'pirates', but then fell in battle.

■ MALDON, 10 AUGUST 991

The Earldorman of Essex, Brythnoth, his housecarls and the local fyrd faced a large Danish raiding party, possibly led by Olaf Tryggvason, across the causeway at Northey Island on the Blackwater Estuary. The poem *The Battle of Maldon* depicts Brythnoth refusing to pay ransom and inducing the Vikings to cross the causeway. Following Brythnoth's death, the shield wall eventually disintegrated and his men fled or were overwhelmed.

■ GLEN MAMMA, 30 DECEMBER 999

Brian Boru of Munster and his ally, Mael Sechanaill II, routed the combined armies of Mael Morda of Leinster and Sygstrygg Silkbeard of Dublin in a narrow valley of the Wicklow Mountains.

■ SWOLD, 1000

Olaf Tryggvason, and his fleet, headed by the 'Long Serpent,' was defeated and killed by a coalition of Olaf of Sweden, Swein Forkbeard of Denmark and Eric Hakonson.

■ NAIRN, 1009

Swein Forkbeard of Denmark besieged the town of Nairn and defeated Malcolm of Scotland in his attempt to raise siege. Malcolm was wounded, but the Danes withdrew.

surrounding their stronghold on the earthwork at Countisbury. Around 1200 were killed, including their kings, and the 'Raven' banner was captured.

■ LEUVEN, 891

Arnulf, king of East Francia, defeated a force of mounted Vikings riding in advance of their fleet towards Louvain, blocking the run of the river Dyle with the bodies of dead Norsemen.

■ TETTENHALL, 5 AUGUST 910

The Vikings of Northumbria mounted an attack on Mercia, believing Edward of Wessex to be with his forces in Kent. Edward commanded the combined levies of Wessex and Mercia, surrounding the Viking forces between Wednesfield and Tettenhall in Staffordshire. The decisive Anglo-Saxon victory and the death of the Viking kings Eowils and Healfdan signalled the end of Viking raids in Britain south of the Humber.

■ CORBRIDGE, 915/918

Vikings from Waterford, led by Ragnall, fought an indecisive battle with Constantine of Scotland

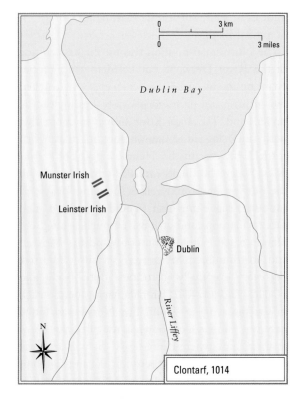

Clontarf, 1014

■ MORTLACK, 1010

Swein of Denmark's forces were routed after a desperate struggle. Three Scottish thains were lost but Malcolm of Scotland is reputed to have strangled the Danish leader Enetus.

■ CLONTARF, 23 APRIL 1014

Brian Boru and his Ui Neill and Manx allies defeated an alliance of Vikings from Orkney, Man and Dublin and Leinstermen. Thousands fell on both sides including Brian Boru, his son and grandson.

■ NESJAR, 1016

At Nesjar in 1016 Olav Haraldsson fought off an attack from the Swedish Sveinn Hakonarson and the Norwegian chieftain Erling Skjalggson, in the first of several sea battles for control of the waters around Norway.

■ PEN, 1016

Edward Ironside repulsed the invading army led by his Danish rival Cnut, from Kenwalh's Castle, an Iron Age hillfort in Castle Wood, defended

by a single rampart and ditch.

■ ASHINGDON OR ASSANDUN, 18 OCTOBER 1016

Edmund Ironside and his entire English forces tracked Cnut's forces heading inland. Following the desertion of his Mercian ally Eadric Streona, Edmund was defeated and Ulfkell Snilling of East Anglia killed.

■ SHERSTON, 1016

The raiding army of Cnut, aided by Eadric Streona of Mercia, faced Edmund Ironside in an indecisive encounter with great slaughter on either side.

■ HELGEAA, 1026

Olaf II Haraldsson of Norway and Anund Jakob of Sweden attacked the coast of Skane. Cnut met them with a combined English and Danish fleet, and the battle was indecisive.

■ STRANGEBJERG, 1028

Cnut arrived on the coast of Norway with a powerful fleet, having suborned the chieftains of Norway. Olaf II Haraldsson fled to Russia

■ STIKLESTAD, 29 JULY 1030

Olaf II Haraldsson, aided by Harald Hardrade and a muster of 4000 from Sweden and south-eastern Norway, was defeated and killed by rebel Norwegian chieftains leading a force of some 14,000.

■ NORWEGIAN INVASION OF BRITAIN, 1066

In 1038, Harthacnut of Denmark and Magnus of Norway named each other their successor, should they die without a male heir. Harthacnut died in 1042, as king of Denmark and England. Harald Hardrada succeeded Magnus in 1047, but preoccupation with extending his power in Denmark and Sweden delayed pursuit of his claim until the death of Edward the Confessor. Harald received emissaries offering support from Scandinavian Orkneyers and Tostig Godwinson. Tostig sought to reclaim the earldom of Northumbria from which he had been deposed by his brother and was already harrying the English coast with Norse pirates. Hardrada sailed to Northumbria with 200 ships the combined forces with his allies numbered 300 ships and 9000 men.

Nowegian Invasion, 1066

Hardrada raided the coast of Yorkshire to the Humber, then pursuing a few retreating English ships, followed the Ouse to disembark at Riccall.

■ FULFORD, 20 SEPTEMBER 1066

Edwin of Mercia and Morcar of Northumbria blocked Hardrada's route to York at Gate Fulford. The English broke from the battle after suffering a rout, but there were severe losses on both sides.

■ STAMFORD BRIDGE, 25 SEPTEMBER 1066

Following the defeat of the Mercian and Northumbrian levies at Gate Fulford, Hardrada accepted surrender from the citizens of York and demanded hostages from throughout the shire. To receive these hostages, he marched the main body of his army away from his ships to Stamford Bridge. Harold Godwinson headed north, having demobilized the Essex levies at Sandwich. Taking only his housecarls, reinforced with what levies could be mustered en route, Harold met with the English ships and remnants of the army at

Tadcaster and surprised Hardrada's forces at Stamford Bridge.

The Norwegian position was on the eastern side of the River Derwent, but failed to set a proper guard on the bridge. The forces were well-matched but surprise and preparedness gave the English the upper hand. *The Anglo-Saxon Chronicle* reports that both sides slogged it out on foot in 'a stubborn battle'. However in the 'Heinskringla' (*Lives of the Norse Kings*) the English are depicted riding in on the Norwegians from all sides, throwing spears and shooting, suggesting that Harold may have used mounted troops and archers. Through a long and bloody battle Harold's housecarls and the Mercian and Northumbrian levies were seriously depleted, but were eventually victorious. Both Tostig and Harald Hardrada fell, Hardrada having been struck in the throat by an arrow. The Norwegian forces gave way and were cut down as they fled the 19km to their ships, where Harold gave them quarter. Of the 300 invading ships, between 20 and 24 ships sailed home.

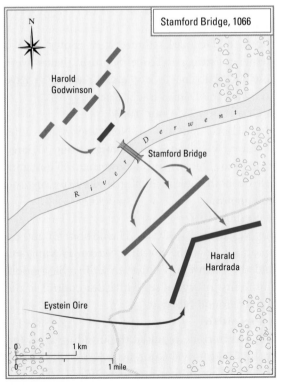

Stamford Bridge, 1066

Wars of Norman England 1066–1200

■ HASTINGS, 14 OCTOBER 1066

Harold marched south with his housecarls from York to London in five days and waited five days to muster all the available militia, gathering forces in the region of 9000 men, including some 3000 housecarls. Had he waited longer in London, he might have gathered musters from the southern counties and the remnants of the Northern Levies. William of Normandy had landed at Pevensey on 28 September. His forces included feudal contingents and mercenaries from Normandy, Brittany and Flanders and have been estimated to number between 7000 and 50,000, including cavalry of 12,000 and infantry of 20,000. William moved his forces to Hastings and began construction of a castle, raiding for supplies across the Sussex countryside, much of it Harold's ancestral land.

Harold arrived at Senlac Hll on 13 October and organized his forces in a defensive position on a ridge 13km northwest of Hastings, overlooking a marshy valley and brook. The housecarls stood at the highest point and at the centre of the line with the mass of infantry positioned on either side. The next morning, he formed a solid shield wall, 400m broad and 800m deep, behind which his forces were armed with javelins, swords, pikes and axes.

William led the Normans from the centre with the French and Flemish on his right and the Bretons on his left. The Norman archers and crossbow-men advanced shortly after dawn, but as they were firing uphill, they made little initial impact on the housecarls' shields. William ordered the infantry advance, which was hampered by the slope and marshy terrain. A contingent of Breton infantry retreated down the hill under a barrage of javelins and collided with the archers and cavalry who became mired in the marsh. The Bretons were pursued down the hill and the rest of the Norman infantry retreated. William, his brother Odo of Bayeux and Count Eustace of Boulogne

rallied the centre and right. The Anglo-Saxon charge was cut off by a contingent of the cavalry, rallied to protect the Bretons. William led a cavalry charge up the slope, which eventually broke, but, as it was pursued downhill, manoeuvred a devastating counter-attack. The use of feints and counter-attacks was a regular Breton tactic assimilated and deployed by Norman cavalry at Arques (1053) and Messina (1060). William led another charge against the centre, which was repulsed, followed by another feigned flight. The shieldwall wavered despite Harold's orders to hold fast. This reflects a definite contrast with the level of discipline apparent from the concerted actions of the Normans and the device of feigned flight and counter-attack. The dwindling Anglo-Saxon line held as the Normans wrought ongoing mounted attacks. These alternated with coordinated high-angle fire volleys and repeated infantry assaults, gradually demolishing the shieldwall. Harold's two brothers, Gyrth

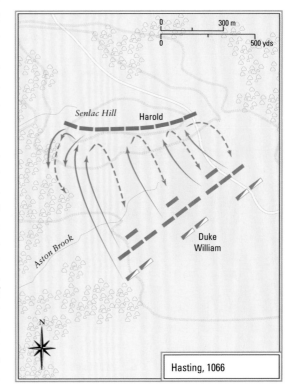

Hasting, 1066

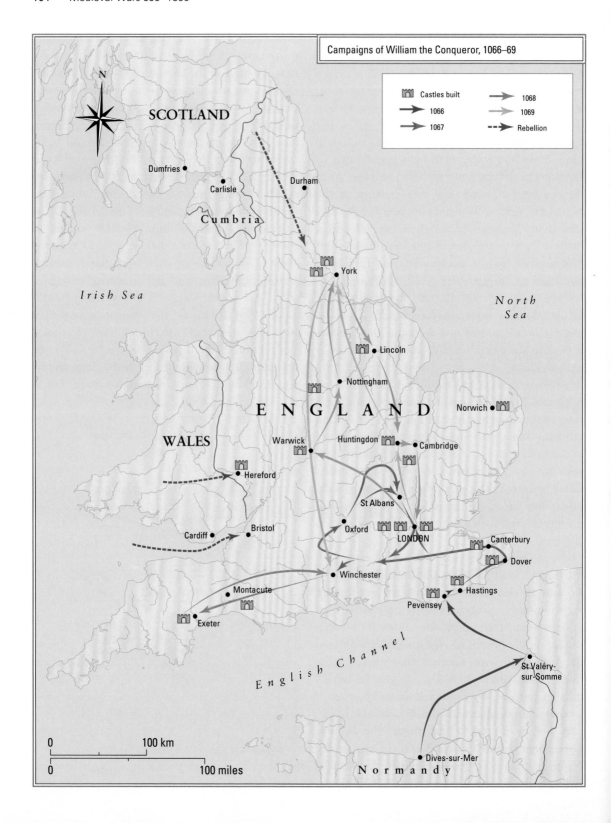

Campaigns of William the Conqueror, 1066–69

Castles built

1066

1067

1068

1069

Rebellion

and Leofwine, plus a number of his bodyguard fell before Harold was struck in the eye with an arrow and mortally wounded. The Fyrd levies gave way, leaving only the housecarls surrounded on the crest of the ridge. William imperilled his victory and barely escaped when the contingent of housecarls he pursued rallied themselves in retreat to slaughter a large number of Normans in a deep ditch called Malfosse.

■ ELY, 1071

Ely was a refuge for rebels, including Hereward 'the Wake' and Morcar. William surrounded the island with ships and soldiers, constructed a bridge and broke in after several bloody assaults. Morcar was captured, but Hereward escaped.

■ TINCHEBRAY, 28 SEPTEMBER 1106

Robert of Normandy attacked the army of Henry I as it besieged the castle of his ally, Mortain, but was defeated and captured together with the Count of Mortain, Robert Belleme and Edgar the Aetheling.

■ CRUG MAWR, 1136

An alliance of Deheubarth and Gwynedd, with armoured horsemen, defeated the Norman lords of south Wales, pursuing them to the River Teifi, where many drowned and to Cardigan, which the Welsh burned.

■ NORTHALLERTON, 22 AUGUST 1138

The marauding army of David of Scotland, supported by northern nobles, was defeated by the forces of Archbishop Thurstan of York, under the standards of the Northern Saints.

■ COED EULO, 1157

The army of Henry II and his Welsh allies, including Madog of Powys, was routed in a deep wooded valley by the sons of Owain Gwynedd. Henry himself narrowly avoided capture.

■ ALNWICK, 1174

William the Lion of Scotland besieged castles and raided across northern England in support of Henry the Young King's rebellion against Henry II. As William headed to Alnwick with Norman knights and Frankish mercenaries, the English army under Richard de Lucy approached from Newcastle under the cover of mist and took them unawares. William was captured as his horse fell, bringing the rebellion to a halt.

■ TAILLEBORG, 1179

Richard I, then Duke of Aquitaine, attacked the cliff-top fortress, first looting surrounding lands. Left with no reinforcements or lines of retreat, the defenders attacked Richard outside the walls and were easily subdued.

■ GISORS, 27 SEPTEMBER 1198

Richard I and Brabancon mercenaries routed Philip Augustus and 300 knights. Pursued to the Gisors, the bridge collapsed with 20 knights drowned and 100 captured. Lacking siege machinery, Richard then retreated to Dangu.

Wars of the Holy Roman Empire 900–1259

■ MERSEBERG (RIADE), 15 MARCH 933

A large Magyar army commanded by the warlords Bulcsú, Lél and Súr invaded central Germany, but was decisively defeated by the German heavy cavalry of King Henry I the Fowler near the Unstrut river.

■ LECHFELD, 10 AUGUST 955

A Magyar army of 25,000 light cavalry commanded by the warlords Bulcsú, Lél and Súr invaded central Germany in an attempt to repeat the large-scale raid of the previous year. However, on this occasion, Otto I the Great, King of the Germans, was prepared to meet the threat. He ordered his troops, which were drawn from across Germany, to concentrate on the Danube, around Neuburg and Ingolstadt. This placed his army across the Magyar line of communications in a good position to attack their rear while they were raiding north-east of Augsburg. Otto also anticipated the probable Magyar route for their return journey; he believed that, as in the past, they would head back towards Hungary via Lotharingia (Lorraine), the West Frankish Kingdom (France) and finally Italy. He therefore ordered his brother Bruno, Archbishop of

Cologne and Duke of Lotharingia, to keep his forces concentrated in Lorraine to block their line of retreat.

The German army probably totalled 8000 cavalry in eight 1000-strong *legiones* (divisions) – three from Bavaria, two from Swabia, one from Franconia and one from Bohemia under Prince Boleslav I. The eighth division, which was commanded by Otto and slightly larger than the others, included Saxons, Thuringians and the king's personal guard. Otto's forces caught the Magyar army as it attacked Augsburg, which was fiercely defended by a garrison led by Bishop Ulrich.

The arrival of the German army forced the Magyars to abandon their attacks on Augsburg and to deploy on the Lechfeld, the flood plain to the south of the city. The Magyar cavalry launched a frontal attack on the Bavarians, while a detachment made a wide outflanking move, routed the baggage guards and charged into the

rear of the Swabians. This dangerous threat was finally contained when the attackers were driven off by the Franconian division.

The Magyars' frontal attack was beaten off by Otto's more heavily armoured cavalry, which inflicted severe casualties on their opponents. In such close combat, the Magyar horse archers were at a marked disadvantage, lacking the space to effectively use their deadly shoot-and-run tactics. Bulcsú feigned a retreat with part of his force in an attempt to lure Otto's men into breaking formation and pursuing, but the German line held and routed the Magyars.

In an exceptional move for an army of this period, the German forces maintained their discipline and methodically pursued the Magyars for the next couple of days, rather than dispersing to loot the enemy camp. Many fugitives were killed, or drowned attempting to cross the Lech river. Bulcsú and several other Magyar leaders were captured and executed. It seems likely that

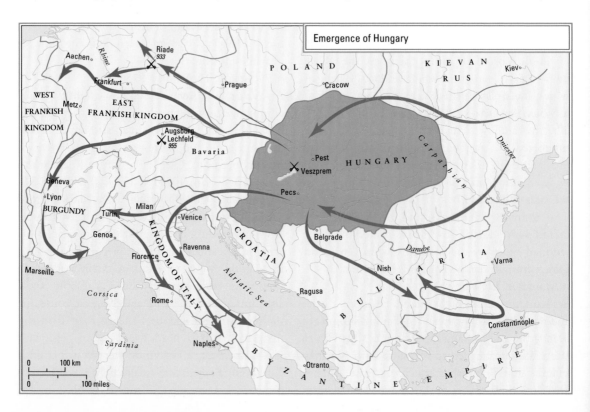

German casualties totalled approximately 3000. Although the Magyars may well have lost no more than 1000 men in the battle itself, a further 2000 were probably killed afterwards by the pursuing German cavalry, while another 1500 or so were slaughtered by German peasants as they made their way back to Hungary.

The victory effectively ended the Magyar threat to Germany and boosted Otto's prestige as a warrior and commander. He was hailed as emperor by his troops on the Lechfeld battlefield and, in 962, was formally crowned as Holy Roman Emperor by Pope John XII. Militarily, the battle at Lechfeld is often regarded as marking the beginning of the dominance of heavy cavalry in battle, which was soon to evolve into the armoured knight on the battlefields of northern Europe.

■ Cedynia, 24 June 972

Odo I, Margrave of the Saxon Ostmark, invaded Poland with an army of about 4000 men, but was defeated near Cedynia, West Pomerania, by a Polish force commanded by Duke Mieszko I.

■ Vlaardingen, 29 July 1018

Godfrey II, Duke of Lower Lorraine, led an imperial force of possibly 1000 men against the rebellious Count Dirk III of Friesland. The imperialists sailed west, along the rivers Waal and Merwede, to Dirk's stronghold in Vlaardingen. On landing, Godfrey's men found that the numerous ditches made it impossible to deploy near the castle and attempted to move to more open ground, but were ambushed and routed with heavy losses.

■ Nakło, 10 August 1109

Prince Bolesław III Wrymouth of Poland invaded Pomerania to secure his northern borders against the pagan Pomeranian tribes. The Poles captured the stronghold of Nakło nad Notecią after defeating a Pomeranian relief force near the town.

■ Głogów, 14 August 1109

King Henry V of Germany's invasion of Poland in support of the exiled Zbigniew, Duke of Poland, was halted by the defenders of Głogów in Silesia. Harassment by Polish guerillas forced Henry to abandon the siege.

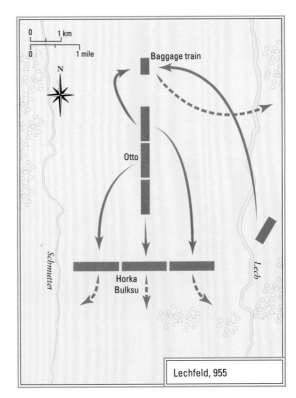

Lechfeld, 955

■ Hundsfeld (Psie Pole), 24 August 1109

An imperialist army under King Henry V of Germany invaded Polish territory in support of the exiled Zbigniew, Duke of Poland, but was defeated by Prince Bolesław III Wrymouth's Polish army near Wrocław in Silesia. The battle was dubbed 'Dogs' Field' (*Hundsfeld* in German; *Psie Pole* in Polish) after Bishop Wincenty Kadłubek of Kraków wrote of 'dogs which, devouring so many corpses, fell into a mad ferocity, so that no one dared venture there'.

■ Welfesholz, 11 February 1115

Saxon and Thuringian nobles led by Duke Lothar of Saxony rose against the Holy Roman Emperor Henry V. They defeated imperial forces at Welfesholz, near Mansfeld in Saxony, forcing Henry to relinquish effective control of the province.

■ Nocera, 1132

A rebel army under Prince Robert II of Capua and Ranulf II, Count of Alife, destroyed King Roger

II of Sicily's royalist forces at Nocera Inferiore in southern Italy. Roger escaped, accompanied by only four knights.

■ RIGNANO, 30 OCTOBER 1137

King Roger II of Sicily's army was defeated at Rignano in Apulia by Ranulf II, Duke of Apulia and Count of Alife, supported by 800 German knights sent by the Holy Roman Emperor Lothair III.

■ WEINSBERG, DECEMBER 1140

King Conrad III of Germany seized the lands of Henry the Proud, Duke of Saxony and Bavaria. On Henry's death, his brother Welf, reclaimed Bavaria, but was defeated by Conrad at Weinsberg, near Heilbronn.

■ MONTE PORZIO, 29 MAY 1167

An imperialist army of 1600 men commanded by Christian I, Archbishop of Mainz, defeated Oddone Frangipane's 10,000-strong army of the Commune of Rome. The poorly equipped Roman militia were routed by Christian's knights, losing over 4000 men.

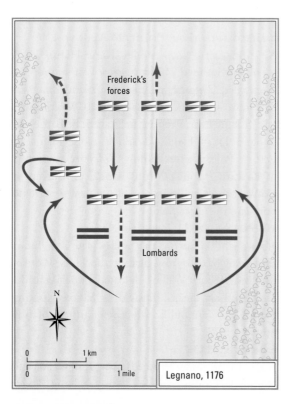

Legnano, 1176

■ LEGNANO, 29 MAY 1176

Attempts by the Holy Roman Emperor, Frederick I Barbarossa, to assert control of northern Italy led to the formation of the Lombard League in 1167, an anti-Imperialist alliance of northern Italian city-states, backed by Pope Alexander III.

In 1174, Frederick attempted to finally crush the League and invaded northern Italy. He took the towns of Susa and Asti in Piedmont, but was forced to abandon the long siege of Alessandria in 1175. By 1176, he had received reinforcements, but his forces were no more than 3000 strong (mainly German knights). The League was able to raise an army of 4000 men and the two forces clashed at Legnano near Milan. Frederick's knights broke much of the League's cavalry, but were repulsed by the elite Lombard infantry protecting their standard. A final counter-attack by the League's Brescian cavalry routed the Imperialists.

■ CORTENUOVA, 27 NOVEMBER 1237

The Second Lombard League was formed by the northern Italian city-states in 1226 to counter attempts by the Holy Roman Emperor, Frederick II, to impose his authority on the region. In August 1237, Frederick led a 10,000-strong army into northern Italy in an attempt to crush the League. After prolonged manoeuvring, he surprised and defeated the League's army of 15,000 men under Pietro Tiepolo near Cortenuova in Lombardy, inflicting 10,000 casualties.

■ BRESCIA, AUGUST–OCTOBER 1238

Following his victory at Cortenuova, Frederick II besieged Brescia, one of the few cities of the Lombard League that had continued to resist him. The city held during a three-month siege and Frederick was forced to withdraw.

■ VITERBO, 1243

The Holy Roman Emperor, Frederick II, installed an imperial garrison in Viterbo in 1240, which was expelled by a popular uprising in 1243. Frederick besieged the city, but was persuaded to withdraw by Pope Innocent IV.

■ PARMA, 18 FEBRUARY 1248

The Holy Roman Emperor Frederick II's siege

of Parma ended abruptly when his fortified camp was surprised and captured by a sortie on 18 February 1248. The 5600-strong Imperialist army lost at least 3000 men.

■ FOSSALTA, 26 MAY 1249

The Lombard League's army of 8800 men under Filippo Ugoni was marching to attack Modena when it was intercepted near the city by a 15,000-strong imperialist army commanded by King Enzio of Sardinia, the illegitimate son of the Emperor Frederick II. Despite being heavily outnumbered, the League's forces made repeated attacks, finally routing the Imperialists. Casualties were heavy on both sides and Enzio and 400 of his knights were captured.

■ CASSANO, 16 SEPTEMBER 1259

The Ghibellines under Ezzelino da Romano were defeated at the Ada river by Guelphs under Azzo VII d'Este. Azzo won a significant victory for the Guelphs; Ezzelino was wounded and captured.

Wars of the Balkan and Slavic Peoples 900–1250

■ BOSNIAN HIGHLANDS, 927

A Bulgarian force of 30,000–70,000 men under Duke Alogobotur invaded Croatia, but was heavily defeated as it crossed the Bosian Highlands in May 927 by a far larger Croatian army commanded by King Tomislav.

■ PRESLAV, 971

The Byzantine emperor, John I Tzimiskes invaded Bulgaria with an army of 40,000 men and stormed the capital, Plevna. The Bulgarian tsar, Boris II, was captured and deposed and his country became a Byzantine province.

■ STUGNA RIVER, 1093

An army led by three princes of Kievan Rus', Sviatopolk II of Kiev, Vladimir Monomakh of Chernigov and Rostislav of Pereyaslav, was attacked and defeated by 8000 Cuman tribesmen near the Stugna river.

■ GVOZD MOUNTAIN, 1097

An Hungarian army led by King Coloman I crossed the River Drava and invaded Croatia. King Petar Svačić of Croatia attempted to intercept the invaders before they reached the Adriatic coast and the two armies clashed at Gvozd Mountain. Petar was defeated and killed, marking the end of the Svačić dynasty. Croatia was then linked to Hungary in a personal union between the two crowns, which continued until 1918.

■ LIPITSA, 22 APRIL 1216

This was the decisive battle in the wars of succession for the Grand Princely throne of Vladimir-Suzdal, following the death of Vsevolod the Big Nest. In the battle, fought on 22 April 1216, the forces of Mstislav the Daring and Konstantin Vsevolodovich defeated the army of Konstantin's younger brothers, Yuri Vsevolodovich and Yaroslav. Konstantin seized the throne of Vladimir-Suzdal and ruled as Grand Prince until his death two years later.

■ KLOKOTNITSA, 9 MARCH 1230

An 85,000-strong Epirote army led by Theodore Komnenos Doukas invaded the Bulgarian Empire, but was defeated by a Bulgarian force of 25,000 men commanded by Tsar Ivan Asen II.

Chinese Song, Jin, Yuan and Ming Dynasty Wars 960–1644

■ TANGDAO, 16 NOVEMBER 1161

A Southern Song fleet of 120 warships equipped with trebuchets hurling gunpowder bombs surprised and defeated a Jurchen Jin force of 600 naval vessels off the island of Tangdao in the East China Sea.

■ BACH DANG, 1288

The attempted Mongol invasion of Champa in 1288 was frustrated at Bach Dang. The defenders placed sharpened stakes in the sea near the shore. When the tide retreated, the ships caught on the stakes.

■ LAKE POYANG, 30 AUG 1363–4 OCT 4 1363

The largest naval battle in history, 300,000 Han crews and marines in 'tower ships' faced 200,000 Ming in smaller, similar vessels. In long weeks of

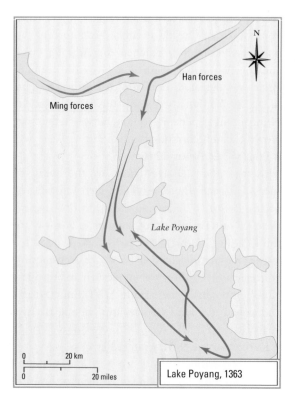

Lake Poyang, 1363

fighting on the huge, shrinking lake, the Ming eventually prevailed.

■ TUMU, 1449

In July 1449, Oirat Mongol forces totalling 20,000 men led by Khagan Esen Tayisi carried out large scale raids into Chinese territory. The Ming Zhengtong emperor was persuaded by the influential eunuch, Wang Zhen. to lead his 500,000-strong army in person against the raiders. However, Wang Zhen held effective command and conducted an incompetent campaign, which culminated in the defeat of the Ming forces and the capture of the Zhengtong emperor.

■ PYONGYANG, 8 JANUARY 1593

The Chinese attack on Pyongyang in 1593 was the turning point in the Japanese invasion of Korea. They drove the Japanese out of the city to begin a retreat that ended with them leaving Korea.

■ ULSAN, 1597

Ulsan, a small castle guarding a harbour on the eastern coast of Korea, was one of the Japanese fortresses established to provide control of the country and to ensure communications with Japan. In 1597, while still incomplete, Ulsan came under attack from a huge Chinese and Korean army in one of the last battles of the invasion. Repeated attacks using waves of troops were beaten back from the walls so that even further assaults could be mounted across piles of corpses. Starvation and very cold weather took their toll on the defenders, who froze to death at their posts. Desperate foraging parties searched the pockets of dead soldiers in the moat to find scraps of food. The castle was defended by Kato Kiyomasa, who held out until a Japanese relieving army arrived and attacked the rear of the Chinese lines.

■ SARHU, 1619

During the winter of 1618–19, a 160,000-strong Ming army advanced in four detachments on the Manchu city of Hetu Ala. Although he had only 60,000 men, the Manchu khan Nurhaci beat each of the first three Ming detachments in turn. The final 40,000-strong Ming force was badly demoralized as it retreated through the mountains and was routed when a shadowing 20-man Manchu scouting force sounded horns, giving the signal to attack.

■ NINGYUAN, 1626

The Manchu khan Nurhaci led an army of at least 60,000 men in assaults on the city of Ningyuan. Nurhaci was mortally wounded by artillery fire and the attacks were beaten off by the city's 10,000-strong Ming garrison.

■ NANYANG, 1642

Li Zicheng took the Ming city of Nanyang with a 20,000-strong peasant rebel army, following up his victory with the capture of Beijing, after which he proclaimed himself as the first emperor of the Shun Dynasty.

■ SHANHAI PASS, 28 MAY 1644

After taking Beijing, Li Zicheng attacked a 100,000-strong Ming and Manchu army in the Shanhai Pass. Li's 60,000 men had almost defeated the Ming contingent when his army was broken by a Manchu cavalry charge.

■ Fort Zeelandia, 1661

Fort Zeelandia was the most important Dutch colonial outpost on the island of Taiwan. In 1661, it was captured by Zheng Chenggong (Koxinga) in an action that marked the beginning of Chinese rule over Taiwan.

Scandinavian Kingdoms 1157–1471

■ Grathe Heath, 1157

Three claimants to the Danish throne, Sweyn III, Cnut V and Valdemar I the Great, had agreed to partition the country between them. Sweyn broke the pact, killing Cnut and wounding Valdemar, who managed to escape to Jutland. Sweyn then invaded Jutland, but his army was broken by Valdemar's forces in a surprise attack at Grathe Heath. Sweyn managed to escape, but was hunted down and killed by local peasants.

■ Visby, 27 July 1361

The battle of Visby in 1361 was fought on the island of Gotland between King Valdemar IV of Denmark and the local yeomanry. After overcoming the defenders, the Danish king laid siege to the town of Visby, which soon surrendered. According to legend, its inhabitants then paid money to persuade the Danes not to carry out looting. Mass graves found at Visby have yielded important archaeological finds concerning medieval warfare.

■ Helsingborg, 1362

A Danish fleet commanded by King Valdemar IV defeated a Hanseatic squadron under Johann Wittenborg, the mayor of Lübeck, at Øresund, off Helsingborg. Twelve Hanseatic ships were lost and Wittenborg was executed on his return to Lübeck.

■ Brunkeberg, 10 October 1471

A Swedish force of at least 8000 peasant levies and 1000 knights led by Sten Sture the Elder attacked and defeated a 6000-strong Danish army under King Christian I of Denmark at Brunkebergsåsen near Stockholm.

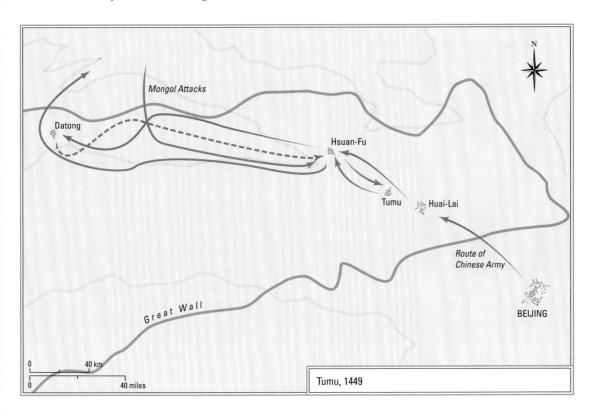

Tumu, 1449

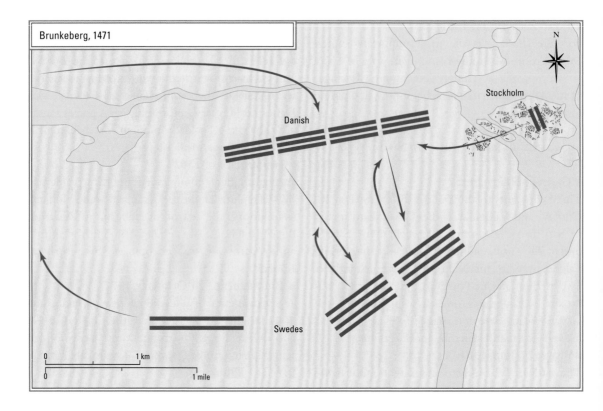

Brunkeberg, 1471

Stockholm

Danish

Swedes

0   1 km

0   1 mile

N

The Iberian Peninsula and the *Reconquista* 1000–1250

■ GRAUS, 1063

King Ramiro I of Aragon attacked Graus, a town on the border of the Moorish Emirate of Zaragosa. Ramiro was defeated and killed by the Emir's army, which was supported by a force of 300 Castilian knights.

■ CABRA, 1079

Emir Abd Allah of Granada invaded the Emirate of Seville with the tacit support of Alfonso VI of León and Castile, but was defeated at Cabra by a Granadine army under Rodrigo Díaz de Vivar (El Cid).

■ UCLÉS, 29 MAY 1108

A 2300-strong Castilian and Leónese force under Alfonso VI was defeated here by an Almoravid army commanded by Tamim ibn-Yusuf. The *infante*, Sancho Alfónsez, was murdered by villagers while trying to escape from the battlefield.

■ ALARCOS, 18 JULY 1195

A large Almohads army, commanded by Emir Abu Yusuf Ya'qub al-Mansur, defeated a smaller Castilian force under Alfonso VIII. The emir deployed the veteran Almohades and Andalusian cavalry in the first line, supported by a second line of African archers and javelin-armed infantry and a third line to act as a reserve. After three charges, Alfonso's 8000 cavalry broke through the centre of the emir's frontline, but the gap was closed behind them and they were surrounded by the archers and infantry of the second line. The Castilian infantry, supported by Alfonso's bodyguards and the knights of the Military Orders, attempted to follow up the initial breakthrough, but were defeated by the emir's first line, which had reformed. Alfonso's army then broke in rout with the loss of 20,000–25,000 men, including three bishops and much of the Castilian nobility.

■ LAS NAVAS DE TOLOSA, 16 JULY 1212

Las Navas de Tolosa was a turning point in the

Christian *Reconquista* of Moorish Spain. The allied Christian army was led by a local shepherd along a path to take the Muslim army by surprise.

■ MURET, 12 SEPTEMBER 1213

Simon IV de Montfort led the Albigensian Crusade to destroy the Cathar heresy and bring Languedoc under the crown of France. He invaded Toulouse and exiled its count, Raymond VI, who sought aid from his brother-in-law, King Peter II of Aragon. De Montfort's conquests in Languedoc threatened Aragon's borders and Peter agreed to cross the Pyrenees and deal with Montfort's crusaders who had just taken Muret.

On 10 September, Peter's army of 3000 cavalry arrived at Muret, where it was joined by 30,000 militia infantry from Toulouse. The crusader infantry drove off the first of three allied cavalry divisions under the Comte de Foix, which attacked an open gate in the city walls. As this action was being fought, three divisions of crusader cavalry sortied via another gate. The first

charged the Comte de Foix's disordered men in flank, breaking them after a short melee. It was then joined by the second division commanded by William d'Encontre and both formations charged the allies' main battle led by King Peter. At this stage, the crusaders' third division under de Montfort charged the allied left flank. King Peter was killed and the surviving allied cavalry broke, with many fugitives killed in the ruthless pursuit.

So far, the allied infantry had not been seriously engaged; they misinterpreted the confused cavalry actions as a crusader defeat and surged forward to attack the town walls. They broke as de Montfort's cavalry rallied and reformed to attack their rear. Thousands were killed in the crusader pursuit and many drowned trying to ford the Garonne river. Allied losses totalled 15,000–20,000 dead, while crusader casualties were very light, although almost certainly greater than their claims of only one knight and eight sergeants.

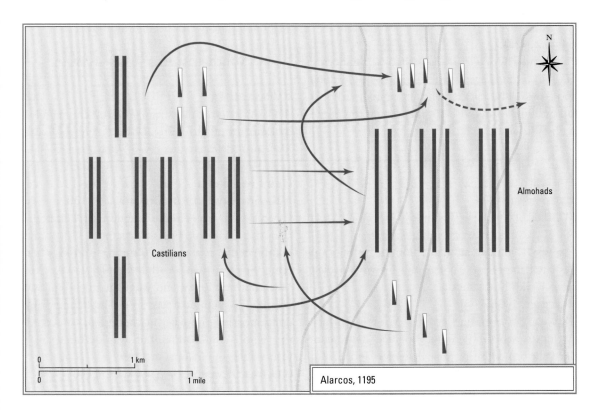

Alarcos, 1195

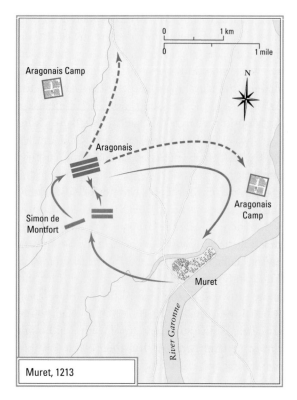

Muret, 1213

■ Jerez, 1231

Ferdinand III of Castile launched a plundering raid or *cavalgada* against the Emirates of Cordoba and Seville. The raiders defeated a Moorish force led by Emir Ibn Hud before returning to Castile with their loot.

Indian Wars 1000–1200

■ Peshawar, 1009

Mahmud of Ghazni led his Turkic-Afghan warriors out of present-day western Afghanistan to victory against a confederation of Hindu princes at Peshawar, in present-day Pakistan. Victory enabled further raids by Mahmud.

■ Gujrat, 1025

Mahmud of Ghazni led his Muslim Turkic-Afghan warriors into Gujrat Province (in present-day Pakistan) defeating local defenders and seizing the Hindu temple of Somnath. The temple was looted of its riches and destroyed.

■ Koppan, 1052

Rajadhiraja, the ruler of the Chola Empire in present-day southern India and Sri Lanka, was killed fighting the rebellious Chalukya kingdom. His younger brother, Rajendra, defeated the Chalukyas and maintained the Chola Empire.

■ Gujrat, 1178

Muhammad of Ghur led a Muslim Turkic-Afghan army into the province of Gujrat, in present-day Pakistan. His army was weak after crossing a desert and local forces under Raja Bhimdev II repulsed the invaders.

■ Tarain, 1191

Muhammad of Ghur led his Muslim Turkic-Afghan army into north-central India. A confederation of Hindu princes formed a large army and stopped the invasion at Tarain, north of Delhi. The Hindus used superior numbers to defeat the left and right wings of Muhammad's army. Muhammad himself was badly wounded in personal combat with Govindraj, the brother of the Hindu commander, Prithviraj. Muhammad withdrew northwards beyond the Indus river.

South-east Asia 1000–1200

■ Vijaya, 1044

A Dai Viêt (North Vietnamese) army commanded by Emperor Lý Thái Tông invaded Champa (South Vietnam), defeated the Cham king Sa Dau and sacked his capital of Vijaya. An estimated 30,000 Cham were killed.

■ Khmer Invasion of Champa, c. 1130

Operations by the Khmer kingdom of Cambodia against Champa began around 1130 and culminated in an attack on Champa in 1145, when King Suryavarman II, the founder of Angkor Wat, captured Vijaya and went on to pillage and destroy the temples at My So'n. The Khmer king continued his campaign in an attempt to control the whole of Champa, but was defeated by a future ruler of Champa in 1149.

■ Khmer Invasion of Annam, c. 1150

Having subdued Champa during his initial

campaigns, the Khmer king Suryavarman II sought to control the whole of Vietnam by conquering Annam in the north. However, instead of marching against Annam with allies from Champa, he discovered that a Champa–Annam alliance had been created against him. In a series of actions, the alliance managed to drive the Khmers out, to be followed by an invasion of Cambodia on their own behalf.

Byzantine Wars 1000–1453

■ KLEIDION, 29 JULY 1014

Confronted by the high palisade erected by the Bulgarians under their ruler Samuel, the Byzantines, led by Emperor Basil II, initially tried to storm the obstacle. They suffered high losses in the attempt and the emperor was ready to call off the campaign. The Byzantine general Nikephoros Xiphias volunteered to lead a small force over the mountains in an attempt to find a way behind the enemy position. Basil's troops maintained their position and launched small-scale assaults to keep the defenders busy. Xiphias followed a difficult track to the west of the pass, which led across Mount Belasica and fell on the rear lines of the Bulgarians. The Bulgarian army was crushed. According to later traditions, Basil II captured and blinded 15,000 prisoners and ordered every hundred to be led back to Samuel by a one-eyed man.

■ CANNAE, 1018

A Byzantine force under the governor of Italy, Basil Boioannes, defeated an army of rebels led by Melo from Bari. The Varangians sent by the emperor Basil II played a decisive role to the Byzantine victory.

■ SHIRIMNI, 11 SEPTEMBER 1021

The Byzantine army under Emperor Basil II defeated the forces of King George I of Georgia. The Georgians were reinforced by Armenian auxiliaries. The Georgians began the battle and put to flight a part of the Byzantine army. However,

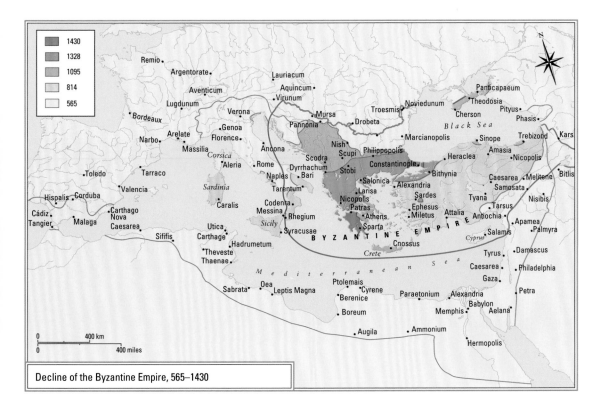

Decline of the Byzantine Empire, 565–1430

the Byzantines, led by Basil, counter-attacked and won the battle. The most effective part of the Byzantine army was the Varangians, who led a ferocious attack on the enemy.

■ SVINDAX, 1022

The Byzantine army under Emperor Basil II defeated the forces of King George I of Georgia. As a result, the Georgian king abandoned his claims to Tao and surrendered many possessions to Basil II.

■ SYRIA, 1030

A campaigning force of 20,000 men under the emperor Romanos III was crushed by an Arab force near Aazaz. The Byzantine army broke and fled because many soldiers were exhausted by thirst and dysentery.

■ ADRIATIC, 1032

After capturing Cassano, the Sicilian Arabs carried out a naval raid across the Adriatic to Corfu, where they burnt the city. However, they were defeated at the hands of the Byzantine and Ragusan fleets.

■ INVASION OF SICILY, 1038

George Maniakes led a Byzantine invasion of eastern Sicily. His aim was to exploit the civil conflicts among the local Arabs and bring the entire island under Byzantine control. Maniakes' army included Varangian and Norman mercenaries.

■ MESSINA, 1038

A Byzantine army of up to 15,000 under George Maniakes stormed Messina and defeated the Sicilian Arabs. The Byzantine force relied on Varangian soldiers under Harald Hardrada and on Norman and Lombard mercenaries under Arduin.

■ RAMETTA, 1038

The Arabs of Sicily and a force of 5000 Arabs from Africa attacked the Byzantines under George Maniakes. A fierce battle was fought and eventually Maniakes put the Arabs to flight.

■ DRAGINA, 1040

The Byzantines under George Maniakes defeated an army of Arabs under Umer. The charge of the Byzantine and Norman heavy cavalry demolished

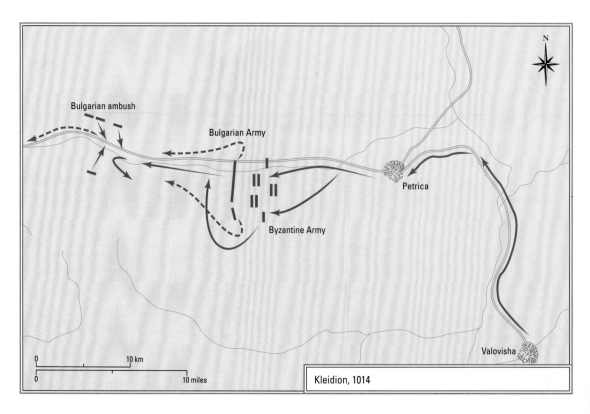

Kleidion, 1014

the Arab battle line at the first attack. Umer barely escaped with his life.

■ BULGARIAN REVOLT, 1040–41

Emperor Romanos III's decision to force the Bulgarians to pay their taxes in coin and not in kind triggered a revolt. A certain Peter Deljan raised an army and marched southwards. The army that was sent to fight Deljan and their leader, Tihomir, joined the rebels. However, Deljan had Tihomir killed. The rebels defeated the Imperial army close to Thessalonica. However, another Bulgarian leader, Alusjan, seized control over the revolt and replaced Deljan as its head. Leading 20,000 men, Alusjan marched to besiege Thessalonica. After six days, the besieged carried out a sortie and caught the rebels by surprise. Around 15,000 Bulgarians were captured. In the aftermath of this defeat, Alusjan had Deljan blinded and withdrew to the interior. The Imperial army invaded Bulgaria and Emperor Michael IV defeated the Bulgarians in Prilep. The revolt was crushed.

■ MONOPOLI, 1042

A Byzantine force of 3500 men under George Maniakes defeated the forces of the rebel Argyros from Apulia and the Normans. The rebels numbered around 7000. Maniakes made a terrible example and had many civilians executed.

■ SASIRETI, 1042

Feudal lords under Liparit IV, Duke of Kledkari, revolted against the king of Georgia Bagrat IV. The rebels attempted to place the king's half-brother Demetrius on the throne and requested Byzantine military aid. The forces of the rebels under Liparit and their Byzantine allies defeated the royal army. The royal army commanded by Bagrat was reinforced by 700 Scandinavians, who were campaigning under the Viking Ingvar.

■ KORSUN, 1044

After leading an unsuccessful naval campaign against the Byzantines, the Russian prince, Vladimir of Novgorod advanced on Korsun and captured it from the Byzantines. He retained it until he signed a treaty with the Byzantines.

■ KARS, 1048

A force of Seljuq Turks under Ibrahim, the brother of Togrul, launched the first large-scale Seljuq raid on Byzantine Armenia. The Byzantines and the Armenians were defeated and a large number of Armenians were enslaved.

■ KAPITRON, 1048

Following their defeat in Erzerum, the Byzantines, under the command of Katakalon Kekaumenos and Liparit regrouped and fought against the advancing Seljuqs. The Byzantines won the battle, but Liparit was captured by the enemy.

■ PECHENEG RAIDS, 1048–54

The Pechenegs raided the Balkans, crushing a Byzantine army under Constantine. A second battle near Adrianople had the same outcome, despite the bravery of the Byzantine commanders Dokeianos and Arianites. The Byzantines reorganized their defence. They stopped seeking pitched battles and the field army was dispersed through fortified camps. From these, the Byzantines launched surprise attacks on the Pechenegs, seizing booty and prisoners. These tactics proved successful and pushed the enemy back to Bidin. However, a large-scale Byzantine attack failed because of the lack of co-ordination between the Byzantine generals. A large Byzantine force suffered heavy casualties. The emperor Constantine IX Monomachos was forced to recognize the settlement of the Pechenegs between the Haemus and lower Danube. In 1054, the emperor signed a 30-year peace treaty and, through titles and gifts, appeased the Pechenegs.

■ STRAGNA, 1049

The Byzantine troops under Aaron Vladishtlav abandoned their camp and established themselves in hiding places. The Seljuqs under Hasan started plundering the camp. The Byzantines emerged from their hiding places and routed the Seljuqs.

■ MANZIKERT, 1049

The Seljuqs under Togrul besieged the city for 30 days. They tried to mine the walls. The Byzantines, under Basil Apokapes, destroyed the siege engines of the Seljuqs and forced them to lift the siege.

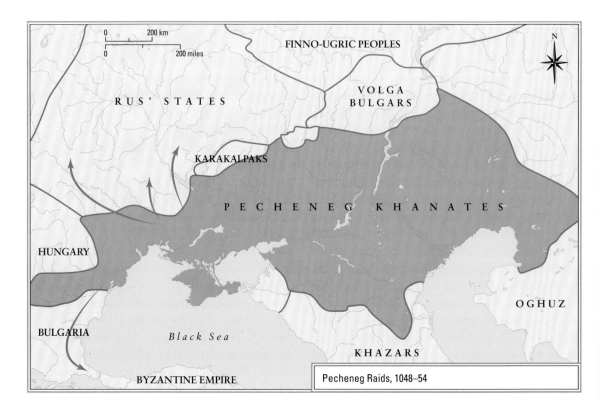

FINNO-UGRIC PEOPLES

VOLGA
BULGARS

RUS' STATES

KARAKALPAKS

P E C H E N E G   K H A N A T E S

HUNGARY

OGHUZ

BULGARIA

Black Sea

KHAZARS

BYZANTINE EMPIRE

Pecheneg Raids, 1048–54

0   200 km
0   200 miles

N

■ ANATOLIA, 1064

A Seljuq army under Sultan Alp Arslan besieged Ani, which fell after 25 days. The city was pillaged and much of its population was slaughtered. Around 50,000 people were captured.

■ SEBASTIA, 1068

When Emperor Romanos IV was stationed in Lykandos, he was informed that the Seljuqs had sacked Neokaisareia. Leading a mobile cavalry force, the emperor forced the Turks to abandon the booty and prisoners they had captured.

■ HERAKLEIA, 1068

While Romanos IV was in Herakleia, the Seljuqs defeated the Byzantines under Philaretos Bacharamios, destroyed Ikonium and retreated. Romanos ordered the army of Chatatourios to attack the retreating Turks. He failed to carry out the attack.

■ OTRANTO, 1068

The Normans captured the city from the Byzantines. The besiegers bribed a niece of the city's governor whose house was attached to the wall. They entered the city with ropes through her house.

■ SEBASTIA, 1070

The Byzantines under Manuel Komnenos were defeated by a Seljuq force under Arisghi. By feigning retreat, the Seljuqs enticed the Byzantines into an undisciplined charge. Many Byzantines were killed and their general was captured.

■ BARI, 1071

Leading a large army, the Norman leader Robert Guiscard laid siege to the city in 1068. The Byzantines pushed back the numerous Norman assaults. Guiscard blockaded the city's port by building a fortified bridge, which prevented Byzantine reinforcements from entering Bari. Although the defenders destroyed the bridge, the Byzantine navy failed to provide effective support to the besieged. The city was starved into submission and surrendered after negotiations in 1071.

■ Manzikert, 26 August 1071

A Byzantine force of 40,000 under Emperor Romanos IV marched against the Seljuqs in Anatolia. On the march, Romanos was forced to dismiss his German mercenaries. He also sent a large part of the army, including Varangians and Frankish mercenaries, to Chliat. These forces played no further role in the campaign. Romanos reached Manzikert on 24 August and sent Nikephoros Bryennios to chase off Seljuq raiders. Bryennios' army was ambushed and withdrew. Similarly, by feigning retreat, the Seljuqs ambushed and annihilated a cavalry force under Nikephoros Basilakes. Realizing that the Turks were present in greater strength than he had previously assumed, Romanos ordered the left wing of the army under Bryennios to attack. However, the Seljuqs forced Bryennios to withdraw. On 26 August, the Imperial army launched a full-scale attack. The Byzantines advanced, with the rearguard protecting the main line and flanks. The Seljuqs harried the Byzantine line with arrows while constantly moving back. The Seljuq wings attacked the Byzantine wings at close range before withdrawing again. Consequently, the Byzantine wings marched at slower pace than the centre. By mid-afternoon, the Byzantines had reached the empty Seljuq camp. However, they failed to come to grips with the enemy and the emperor's forces were no longer in close contact with the wings. It was dusk and the emperor gave the order to withdraw. However, the signal was misunderstood by some officers and soldiers who believed that the emperor had fallen. Andronikos Doukas, the head of the rearguard, deliberately failed to cover the withdrawal of the army. He reversed his own lines and marched towards the camp. Romanos' division was isolated and the emperor was captured by the Seljuqs.

■ Kalavryai, 1078

A force of 6000 mercenaries under Alexios Komnenos defeated a force of 12,000 under the rebel Nikephoros Bryennios. Komnenos won the battle because he exploited the plundering of the enemy camp by Bryennios' own Pecheneg allies.

■ Nicaea, 1080

Nikephoros Melissenos revolted and became the self-proclaimed emperor. He captured Nicaea, where he established a garrison of Turkish mercenaries. When he moved to Thessalonica, these mercenaries seized the city, which became the capital of a Seljuq state.

■ Durrachium, 18 October 1081

The Normans under Robert Guiscard defeated the Byzantines under the emperor Alexios I Komnenos. Robert detached some cavalry to entice the Byzantines into an undisciplined charge. They were pushed back by Byzantine archers. The Norman right under Count Ani charged the left flank of the Varangians. The Byzantines under Pakourianos attacked and broke Ani's troops. Consequently, the Norman knights who were engaged in skirmishes with the Byzantine right were outflanked. The Varangians joined the pursuit of the enemy and became separated from Alexios' main line. Tired by the chase and the weight of their equipment, they were unable to resist the assault of Norman spearmen sent by Guiscard. The whole Varangian detachment perished. The main battle line of the Byzantines, which was situated behind the Varangians, was crushed by the charges of Guiscard's heavy cavalry that had been held in reserve.

■ Antioch, 1084

The Seljuq leader, Suleyman, took advantage of the absence of Philaretos Bachramios, who had established his own independent principality and captured the city. With the assistance of accomplices, the Seljuqs entered the city without resistance.

■ Dorostorum, 1086

The Pechenegs defeated the Byzantines under Alexios I Komenos. The Pechenegs used their wagons as a fortified camp. It was an equal fight until Pecheneg reinforcements arrived late in afternoon. This relief force routed the Byzantines.

■ Leburnion, 1091

The Byzantines under Alexios I Komnenos and their Cuman allies inflicted a severe defeat on the

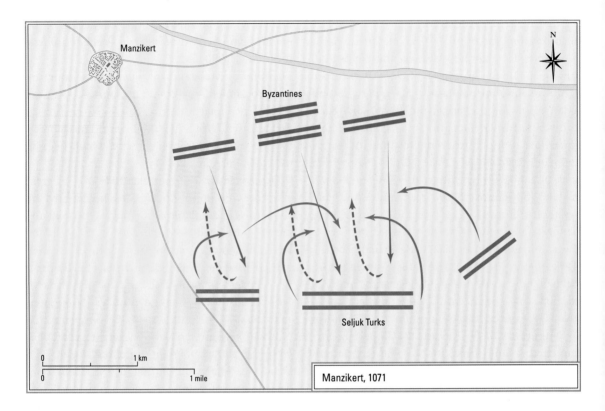

Manzikert

Byzantines

N

Seljuk Turks

0   1 km

0   1 mile

Manzikert, 1071

Pechenegs. Many prisoners were captured. The Byzantine victory was followed by the slaughter of a large number of Pechenegs.

■ NORTHERN SYRIA, 1099–1104

Bohemond, the Prince of Antioch, with the support of several Pisan ships, led an unsuccessful attack on Laodikeia. In 1101, Tancred captured Kilikia and Maras and blockaded Laodikeia, which capitulated in 1103. In 1104, the Byzantine generals Boutoumites and Monastras seized Kilikia and Maras, while Kantakouzenos, leading a surprise attack from the sea, recaptured Laodikeia. However, he failed to capture the fortress from the Normans. Jocelin of Courtenay recaptured Laodikeia in the name of the crusaders.

■ DURRACHIUM, 1107–08

The king of Sicily, Bohemond, besieged the city. The Byzantines, together with the Venetian fleet, blockaded the Normans from land and sea. Many Normans died and Bohemomd was forced to sign a peace treaty with Alexios I.

■ PHILOMELION, 1116

The Seljuq ruler Malik-Shah led a major assault on the rearguard of the army of Alexios I while it was marching towards Nikomedia. The attack was driven off by Nikephoros Bryennios. The Byzantine cavalry pursued the Seljuqs.

■ ANATOLIA, 1120–21

The emperor John II Komnenos led a campaign against the Seljuqs. After successive victories on the battlefield, the Byzantines captured the fortified city of Laodikeia. The following year, the Byzantines captured Sozopolis through trickery. Paktarios, a cavalry commander, was instructed to fire arrows at the enemy troops who occupied the gates. When the Turks sallied out in frustration, Paktarios' troops feigned retreat and the emperor's main force ambushed the Seljuqs.

■ BEROE, 1122

The Byzantines under John II Komnenos fought a large-scale battle with the Pechenegs. The

Pecheneg cavalry charged and fired missiles constantly to the Byzantines. The Byzantines forced the enemy back to their wagon circle, but they failed to penetrate it. This fortified enclosure withstood many attacks. Eventually, the emperor's intervention took charge of the Varangians, who broke the wagons with their axes, causing the defeat of the Pechenegs.

■ CORFU I, 1147

A Norman fleet of 70 galleys under George of Antioch captured Corfu. The island surrendered thanks to bribes and the dissatisfaction of the population over the tax burden.

■ CORFU II, 1149

Byzantine and Venetian galleys under Stephen Kontostephanos captured the island from the Normans. The allies attacked from towers and ladders attached to ships and occupied the city. The defenders of the citadel were starved into submission.

■ SERBIAN REBELLION, 1150–51

The revolt under Uroš II was incited by the Normans of Sicily and backed by the Hungarians. Manuel I Komnenos defeated the Hungarians before they could join the Serbs. The battle took place at Tara. Manuel I and his generals performed individual acts of valour and the emperor's duel with the Hungarian commander Bagin sealed the Byzantine victory. Afterwards, the Serbian leader swore to remain loyal to Manuel I.

■ SIRMIUM, 8 JULY 1167

The Byzantines under Andronikos Kontostephanos defeated the Hungarians under Dionysios. The Byzantines won the battle because of intelligent tactical dispositions, mainly the weakening of the Hungarian line by the feigned withdrawal of the Byzantine left.

■ EGYPTIAN EXPEDITION, 1169

A Byzantine army and a naval force of 200 ships under the command of Andronikos Kontostephanos joined forces with the king of Jerusalem, Amalaric, at Ascalon and laid siege to Damietta. The siege failed, according to the Byzantine sources, because Amalaric, not wanting to share the profits of victory, dragged out the operation until the Imperial army ran short of provisions and suffered from famine. Meanwhile, the besieged received reinforcements and supplies from Cairo, whereas the Byzantines began to run out of material for the construction of siege engines. Eventually, the Byzantines assaulted the walls using ladders and archers. Their attack was aborted when they were informed that Amalaric had negotiated a truce with the defenders. Being demoralized and pressed by the lack of supplies, the Byzantines lifted the siege and departed. The siege had lasted for three months.

■ AEGEAN, 1170

The emperor Manuel I ordered the arrest of all Venetians throughout the empire and confiscated their properties. Venice forbade its subjects to trade with the Byzantines and sent a fleet to attack the Aegean islands.

■ RAGUSA, 1171

The Venetian fleet of 120 ships attacked the city, which was under Byzantine control. After some fighting, the city surrendered, was forced to pay tribute to Venice and to demolish part of its walls.

■ CHIOS, 1171

The Venetian fleet captured the island from the Byzantines. In April 1172, the Venetians were forced to abandon Chios. Famine and disease claimed the life of 6000 men and depleted the Venetian army.

■ MYRIOCEPHALON, 17 SEPTEMBER 1176

A Byzantine army of about 25,000 soldiers under Manuel I Komnenos was defeated by the Seljuqs under Sultan Kilij Arslan II. The Byzantines were marching towards Iconium when they were ambushed by the Seljuqs.

■ INVASION OF GREECE, 1185

A large Norman fleet sailed from Messina and captured Durrachium. Following the Via Egnatia, the Normans under Baldwin sacked Thessalonica and captured much booty. The Normans were stopped in Mosynoupolis, where they were defeated by Alexios Branas.

■ **CONSTANTINOPLE UPRISING, 1185**

When an agent of Andronikos I went to arrest Isaak II Angelos, the latter killed the agent and sought asylum in Hagia Sophia. Isaak appealed to the people of Constantinople and was declared emperor. Andronikos I was executed.

■ **STRYMON, 1185**

Following their victory in Mosynoupolis, the Byzantines under Alexios Branas continued to pursue the Normans until the banks of Strymon. In Dimitriza, the Byzantines plundered the enemy camp and captured generals Richard and Baldwin.

■ **CONSTANTINOPLE, 1186**

General Alexios Branas revolted against the emperor Isaak II Angelos. He was defeated and killed by Conrad of Montferrat, who was the emperor's brother-in-law, in a battle at the walls of Constantinople.

■ **BERRHOE, 1189**

The Vlachs and the Cumans, who led unremitting attacks on Byzantine territories from fortified strongholds, ambushed and scattered the Byzantine army in a narrow defile. The emperor Isaak II Angelos barely escaped with his life.

■ **ANTALYA, 1207**

The Seljuqs, under Sultan Kay-Khusraw I, exploited the fragmentation of the Byzantine Empire by the armies of the Fourth Crusade and captured this port from the Italian adventurer Aldobrandini. The siege lasted for two months.

■ **ADRIANOPLE, 1254**

A small army under Emperor Theodore II Laskaris defeated a Bulgarian force under Michael I Asan. Laskaris led a surprise attack on the enemy camp. Most of the Bulgarian soldiers managed to flee unscathed.

■ **PELAGONIA, 1259**

The Nicaeans under John Palaiologos defeated the forces of Michael Angelos of Epiros, Guillaume II of Villehardouin and 400 German knights. The Cuman and Turkish cavalry archers ambushed the Franks and many knights were taken prisoner.

■ **CONSTANTINOPLE, 1261**

An army of 800 men under Alexios Strategopoulos captured Constantinople. Strategopoulos took advantage of the absence of the Latin fleet and, with the help of the city's inhabitants, his army entered Constantinople using ladders.

■ **BURSA, 1317–26**

The Ottomans blockaded the city, destroyed its countryside and built forts to prevent it from receiving reinforcements. Being pressed by starvation, the local authorities surrendered the city to Orhan, who made it his capital.

■ **CONSTANTINOPLE, 1422**

The Ottomans had taken almost all of the Byzantine Empire and penetrated deep into the Balkans, but Constantinople remained Byzantine. Sultan Murad II besieged the city for several months, but could not breach the walls and finally withdrew.

■ **CONSTANTINOPLE, 6 APRIL–29 MAY 1453**

On 2 April, the advanced units of the Ottoman army pitched camp in the landward side of the city. The emperor Constantine XI Palaiologos ordered the great chain of iron and wood on wooden floats be placed across the Golden Horn to prevent the Ottoman fleet from entering it. On 5 April, Sultan Mehmed II arrived and set up camp along the land walls close to the Gate of Romanos. The size of the Ottoman army is unknown, with eyewitnesses providing estimates ranging from 60,000 to 300,000. The defenders were around 5000 and many of them were western European reinforcements. The Ottomans had large cannons, bombards and arquebuses. The largest of their cannons was some 8.8m long and hurled stones weighing 544kg. Because of the heat and pressure generated, it could be fired only seven times a day. It was designed by the Hungarian engineer Urban. Lacking men, the defenders decided to man only the outer section of the city's land walls. They had crossbows, small arms, small canons and arquebuses. However, their canons proved ineffective and damaged the walls, because the fortifications of Constantinople were unable to support them. The core of the Ottoman fleet was 16 to 18 galleys, 60 to

80 galliots and around 20 vessels for carrying horses. The defenders had between 10 and 39 ships. On 20 April, the defenders received minor reinforcements and supplies commissioned by the Pope and the king of Aragon. This indicates that the Ottomans were unable to control the sea fully. To deal with this, on 22 April, the Ottomans wheeled their ships overland from the Bosporus to the Golden Horn. They bypassed the iron chain and were able to harass the defender's ships in the harbour. The defenders' plan to attack the Ottoman fleet was delayed due to dissension among the Venetian and Genoese. When the attack was launched on 29 April, it failed. Meanwhile, the defenders were able to deal with the Ottoman bombardment and to rebuild damaged sections of the walls with wood, stones, earth and hides. On 18 May, the Ottomans filled in part of the moat and attempted to wheel a wooden turret up to the walls. The defenders burnt it down. Consequently, from 16 May to 25

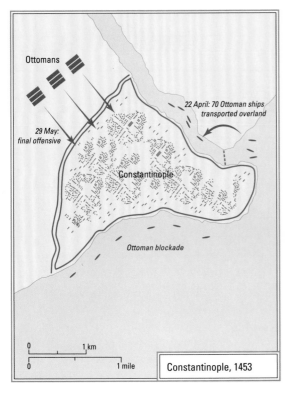

Constantinople, 1453

May, the Ottomans carried out extensive mining operations. All of them were successfully foiled by the defenders who were led by John Grand. On 28 May, when the land walls were sufficiently weakened, Mehmed II ordered a general assault. This assault was concentrated around the gates of Romanos and Charision, where Giustiniani, the leader of the Genoese reinforcements, and the emperor were positioned. After an artillery barrage, the Ottomans led a disorganized assault that was repelled. However, it managed to weary the defenders. A second attack was carried out by the Anatolian Turks, but this was repelled. Then the Janissaries attacked the defenders and, after an hour of fierce fighting, they succeeded in advancing to the inner walls. About 50 Ottomans entered the city through a small gate called Kerkoporta. They climbed the tower above the gate. At the same time, Giustiniani was wounded and withdrew. The defenders panicked and the Janissaries poured into the city through this position. Constantine XI, who was at Charision Gate, perished, although his body was never found. It is calculated that about 4000 people were killed and at least 50,000 were taken prisoner.

The Crusades 1096–1291

First Crusade 1096–99

■ **NICAEA, 14 MAY–19 JUNE 1097**
United crusader and Byzantine forces (perhaps 60,000) besieged Seljuq-held Nicaea, suffering heavy losses in an attempted escalade. After crusaders repelled a relief force under Kilij Arslan, the Turkish garrison surrendered to the Byzantines.

■ **DORYLAEUM, 1 JULY 1097**
The First Crusade army became divided while marching in Anatolia. Turkish sultan Kilij Arslan attacked the vanguard of 20,000 with 6000–7000 cavalry. Bohemond rallied the crusaders and the noncombatants and infantry made a strong camp while he, with about 3000 knights, shielded them, then fell back on the camp. Fighting

continued until the main crusader force of *c.* 30,000 arrived and attacked the Turkish flank.

■ TARSUS, 1097

Tancred and Baldwin of Boulogne cleared the south flank of the First Crusade's advance, taking Tarsus and liberating the Armenian Christians from Turkish rule. Baldwin garrisoned Tarsus after fighting Tancred for possession.

■ ANTIOCH, 1097–98

The First Crusade army besieged the very strong city of Antioch, erecting camps outside the major gates. They defeated a relief effort from Damascus in December, but a sally from Antioch killed many and made morale plummet. Crusaders crushed another relief force from Aleppo in February. A traitor let crusaders into the city on the night of 2–3 June, as a third relief force under Kerbogah of Mosul approached.

The crusader army, now numbering under 30,000, was vastly outnumbered and suffering from starvation and lack of horses. Heartened

by discovery of the Holy Lance, they broke out of the city and attacked Kerbogah on 28 June. Exiting the city in five divisions, the crusaders counted on speed. The overconfident Kerbogah threw forces into the fight piecemeal, where they were defeated in turn. The main Mosul force fled without engaging.

■ SIEGE OF JERUSALEM, 1099

The First Crusade army, numbering around 12,000–14,000 combatants, reached Fatimid-held Jerusalem on 7 June. Jerusalem was strongly fortified and garrisoned and the crusaders had to bring water in from a distance since the Fatimid governor had poisoned the local wells. The crusaders decided on an immediate assault (13 June), despite having only one siege ladder, but were driven off with heavy losses. The crusaders then established a siege, with the troops of Godfrey of Bouillon, Robert of Flanders and Robert of Normandy to the north and Raymond of Toulouse on the west. Two Genoese ships then

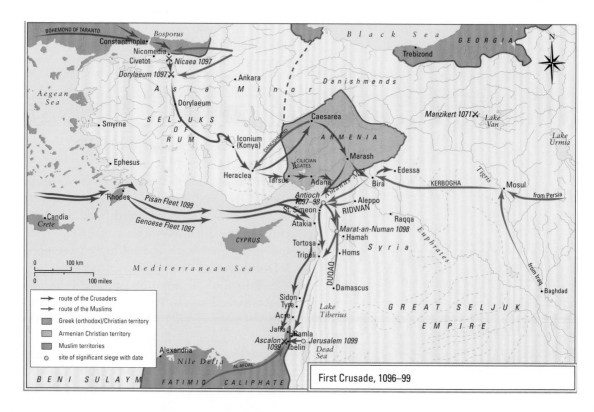

First Crusade, 1096–99

Siege of Jerusalem, 1099

Muslim Quarter

Crusaders

Christian Quarter

Har Ha-Moriyya
(Har Ha-Bayit)
(Temple MT)

J E R U S A L E M

Jewish Quarter

Armenian Quarter

Crusaders

0   400 m

0   400 yds

arrived, which were dismantled, their timber used to build a ram and catapults. The crusaders also constructed two great siege towers, one in Raymond's camp and the other under Godfrey's command. Under heavy missile attack from the walls, the crusaders filled in the ditch surrounding the city so the siege towers could approach. The assault began on 13 July, impelled by news that a Fatimid relief army was approaching. Raymond's men were unable to manoeuvre his siege tower to the wall, but on the north side of the city, a ram brought down part of the outer wall early on 14 July. The crusaders then burned the ram, clearing the way to the inner wall. The siege tower was dragged up to the wall in the course of the day. Normally, siege towers were used to fire at the defenders, but, on 15 July, two Flemish knights used spare timber to bridge the gap and established themselves on the wall, opening the gate to their comrades. The crusaders flooded into the city, massacring most of the populace.

■ **ASHKELON, 1099**

A Fatimid army of 15,000–20,000 under Vizier al-Afdal gathered at Ashkelon and the First Crusade army of about 9000 marched against them from the recently conquered Jerusalem. On 12 August, the crusaders caught the Fatimids by surprise in their camp north of the city, the crusaders attacking in three divisions. The Fatimid Ethiopian infantry charged valiantly, but the bulk of their army never deployed properly and was overwhelmed.

■ **MERSIVAN, 1101**

The Danishmend Turkish army surrounded a Lombard and French crusader force in Anatolia. After days of fighting and several efforts to break out, the Christians panicked. Most of the crusaders were massacred or captured.

■ **EREGLI I, 1101**

The crusader army of William of Aquitaine and Welf of Bavaria suffered a surprise attack by Kilij Arslan's Seljuqs in early September and was routed. Many leaders escaped, but most crusaders died.

■ **EREGLI II, 1101**

A 15,000-man crusader army under Count William II of Nevers was ambushed near Eregli, Anatolia, by Kilij Arslan and almost entirely destroyed. Only William and a few knights made it to Antioch.

■ **RAMLEH, 1102**

A Fatimid army several thousand strong invaded the Kingdom of Jerusalem from Ascalon. Baldwin I underestimated their numbers and attacked with a disorganized cavalry force of only 500 knights, without waiting for his infantry to catch up with his vanguard. Most of Baldwin's army was lost, including Count Stephen of Blois. Baldwin escaped with only a few men, who barricaded themselves in a tower and escaped at night.

■ **HARRAN, 1104**

Seljuq emirs Soqman ibn Ortuq and Jikirmish attacked a combined Christian force led by Bohemund of Antioch and Baldwin of Edessa, which had been besieging Harran. Details of the battle are unknown, except that the Christians were heavily defeated and Count Baldwin was captured, ending Frankish expansion toward the Euphrates. Consequences of the battle were slight, as the Turkish leaders fought each other over division of the spoils.

■ **ARTAH, 1105**

Tancred, regent of Antioch, was besieging Artah when a Muslim relief force under Ridwan of Aleppo attacked. Tancred defeated the Muslim force, perhaps employing a feigned retreat, then completed his siege of the city.

■ **SARMIN, 1115**

Bursuq bin Bursuq's Seljuq army invaded Antiochene territory in 1115. Prince Roger of Antioch, aided by Baldwin of Edessa, gathered an army of Franks and Muslim allies several thousand strong that caught the Turks by surprise on 14 September. The crusader left wing rapidly broke the Turks facing them. The Turcopoles on the Frankish right were thrown back, but the Christians soon rallied, winning an easy victory.

Crusader-Turkish Wars 1119–49

■ Ager Sanguinis, 28 June 1119

The 'Field of Blood' was a catastrophic defeat of the Franks of Antioch. When Il-Ghazi of Mardin invaded the Principality of Antioch, Roger of Antioch mobilized immediately instead of awaiting reinforcements from the south. His force of 700 knights and about 3000 infantry marched against the enemy only to be caught by surprise in a steep-sided valley; Il-Ghazi's force, travelling on little-used paths, appeared suddenly on all sides. The fight began with archery on both sides and heavy casualties. When the forces engaged, the Frankish right enjoyed considerable success. However, the Turcopoles on the Frankish left were driven back, which threw the men behind them into confusion, leaving the Frankish force unable to recover as a strong wind blew sand in their faces. Roger and most of his army died in the encounter.

■ Azaz, 11 June 1125

The Seljuq Il-Bursuqi of Mosul invaded Edessa and besieged Azaz. King Baldwin II of Jerusalem, Joscelin I of Edessa and Pons of Tripoli assembled a relieving army about 3000 strong. They attacked Il-Bursuqi on 13 June, Baldwin feigning a retreat and thus drawing the larger Turkish army into a close engagement in which Frankish superior armour had a decisive advantage. The Turks were defeated in a bloody battle.

■ Marj es-Suffar, 1126

In King Baldwin II of Jerusalem's second major battle against the Turks, the Franks, although badly hurt by Turkish archery, rallied with a strong attack late in the day, winning the victory.

■ Edessa, 28 November–24 December 1144

Edessa, weakest of the crusader states, was the first to fall to a resurgent Islam. Count Joscelin II of Edessa had made an alliance with his Turkish neighbour, Kara Arslan, against Imad ad-Din Zengi, ruler of Mosul and Aleppo. Joscelin left with most of his army to support Kara Arslan, leaving Edessa almost undefended. Zengi seized

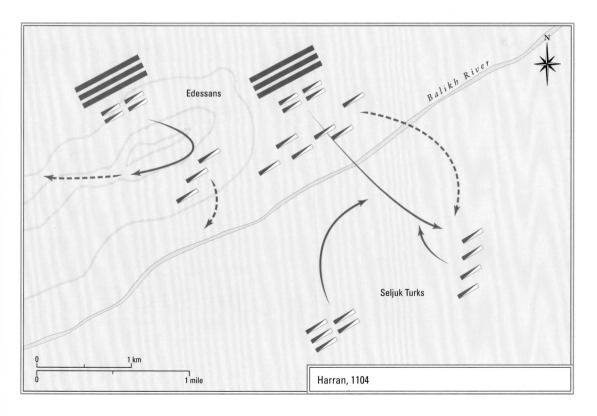

Harran, 1104

the opportunity, rushing his army to attack the city in its lord's absence. He arrived on 28 November and laid the city under siege. The few trained soldiers and civilians, under the command of Archbishop Hugh II and the Armenian and Jacobite bishops of the city, attempted a defense, but did not have sufficient force to man the entire circuit of walls or the knowledge to combat Zengi's efforts to undermine them. The Edessans held out for nearly a month, as Count Joscelin frantically tried to muster a force from the other crusader states to raise the siege. But Zengi's siege engines and mines worked too quickly. The Muslim army took Edessa on 24 December, sacking and slaughtering the panicked defenders, many of whom were trampled to death while trying to reach the citadel. The citadel fell on 26 December. Zengi had all the Frankish survivors killed, but spared the native Christians. He was able to go on to take Saruj, but returned to Mosul as a Jerusalemite army approached. The fall of Edessa led to the calling of the Second Crusade.

■ **LISBON, 1147**

Northern crusade armies numbering about 10,000 with a fleet of 150–200 ships stopped in Portugal, where Afonso Henriques convinced them to help attack Muslim-held Lisbon. They invested the city in late June, finding vast food stores in the suburbs. A massive attack in early August failed, but a mine brought down part of the wall in mid-October. The governor surrendered, but the city was still sacked.

Second Crusade 1145–49

■ **DORYLAEUM II, 1147**

Emperor Conrad III's large crusading army fell into a Turkish trap. Their cavalry was drawn away, leaving the crusader infantry unprotected. The German retreat became a rout after their rearguard was destroyed.

■ **DAMASCUS, 23–28 JULY 1148**

The forces of the Second Crusade led by Louis

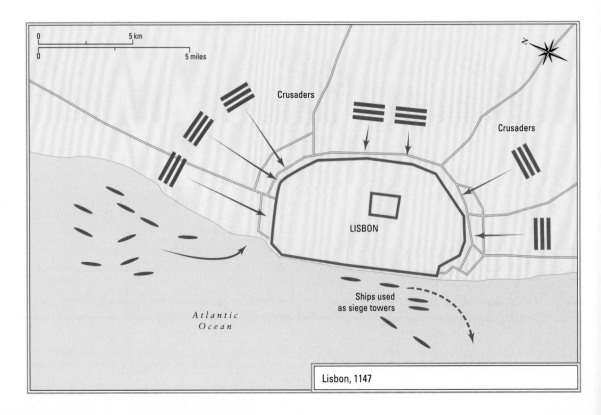

Lisbon, 1147

VII of France and Conrad III of Germany decided with Baldwin III of Jerusalem to attack Damascus. Their army, perhaps 50,000 strong, approached Damascus from the west, driving back outlying Muslim forces. Word came that Nur ad-Din's army was marching to relieve the city, so the crusaders knew they had to take the city quickly. The crusaders shifted operations to the east, believing the wall to be weaker, but found themselves trapped with no water, little food and no easy way into the city. They could not return to the western wall because the area had been reoccupied by Muslim forces. After a siege of only four days, the Crusader army had to withdraw, effectively ending the Second Crusade. They suffered heavy casualties on their march back to Christian territory

■ INAB, 29 JUNE 1149

Nur ad-Din of Aleppo besieged Inab with about 6000 men; Raymond of Antioch came with a relieving force of 1400. The Muslims withdrew, but attacked Raymond's camp, killing most of the Antiochenes, including Raymond.

Crusader-Turkish Wars 1153–87

■ ASCALON, 1153

Ascalon was the last port to fall to the Kingdom of Jerusalem. In a seven-month siege by Baldwin III, the large Fatimid garrison waged a strong defense behind Ascalon's strong walls, conducting a series of skirmishes and resupplied by sea in May. In August, the defenders' destruction of a siege tower backfired when the tower collapsed and brought down part of the wall, allowing the successful Christian assault.

■ HARIM, 12 AUGUST 1164

A large Christian force came to raise Nur ad-Din's siege of Harim. The Muslims retreated and the Christians pursued, losing all cohesion. The Muslims turned and defeated the Christians piecemeal, then took Harim.

■ AL-BABEIN, 18 MARCH 1167

Amalric of Jerusalem invaded Egypt, pursuing Shirkuh's Egyptian force up the Nile with his cavalry. The Muslims turned at the edge of the desert, where sand limited the Frankish cavalry's effectiveness. Amalric, with his 374 Frankish knights, attacked the centre, which retreated to draw Amalric away. The main battle broke down into small fights. When Amalric returned, he rallied some of his Turcopole troops. There was no clear victor.

■ MONTGISARD, 25 NOVEMBER 1177

This was Saladin's worst defeat. The Ayyubid sultan launched a raid from Egypt against Jerusalem. He bypassed Templar-held Gaza and Ascalon, held by King Baldwin IV with 500 men. Baldwin managed to get word to the Templars at Gaza, who helped his men break out of Ascalon. The combined force caught Saladin's larger army by surprise. Those who stood were annihilated; those who fled were harried back to Egypt.

■ JACOB'S FORD, 1179

Baldwin IV of Jerusalem began constructing a strong castle, Chastellet, to defend the vulnerable Jacob's Ford on the Jordan river. Saladin tried to bribe Baldwin to cease construction, then attacked. A large Muslim force reached the incomplete Chastellet on 23 August. They immediately undermined a wall and, after several attempts, broke in on 30 August, killing 700 soldiers and builders, taking 800 captives and destroying the fortress.

■ KERAK, 1183

Saladin invested Kerak castle with a vastly superior force of about 20,000. Baldwin IV led a relieving army of perhaps 8000. Saladin feared being caught between the castle and Christian field army and withdrew.

■ CRESSON, 1 MAY 1187

Saladin's son al-Afdal raided Galilee with about 7000 men. A Templar and Hospitaller force of 130 knights and 300 mounted sergeants attacked them. In fierce fighting, the Christians were destroyed, only four knights managing to escape.

■ TIBERIAS, 2 JULY 1187

Saladin invaded the Kingdom of Jerusalem with a force of about 30,000. To lure the Christian army out, Saladin sent a detachment against Tiberias on 2 July; the town fell on the same day, although Eschiva of Galilee withdrew with her garrison to the citadel. The decision to rescue Eschiva, the wife of Raymond of Toulouse, led to the crusader defeat at Hattin. Eschiva was forced to surrender the day after the battle.

■ HATTIN, 4 JULY 1187

Saladin invaded the Kingdom of Jerusalem with a force probably numbering 30,000, the culmination of years of mounting pressure on the crusader settlements. The controversial King Guy rallied all available forces to counter the threat, raising perhaps 20,000 men (including 1200 knights); the largest army ever assembled by the kingdom. To bring together this force, Guy assembled most of the manpower of the military religious orders, as well as stripping garrisons from fortresses throughout the kingdom.

To lure the Christians into battle, Saladin sent a detachment to take the fortress of Tiberias; the main city fell on 2 July, although Raymond of Tripoli's wife Eschiva was able to withdraw to the citadel with the garrison. When word reached the Christian army, Guy decided after long and acrimonious debate to march to the relief of Tiberias' garrison.

The Christian army's march on 3 July proved to be very slow, with the men suffering constant Muslim attacks on their right flank and to their rear. Instead of reaching Tiberias, they camped for the night at Markana, on a waterless plateau, the men and their horses already suffering grievously from thirst in the summer heat. By the morning of 4 July, Saladin's army had completely surrounded the demoralized and disunified Christian force. Guy desperately needed to push forward to the Sea of Galilee for water.

Action opened when Raymond of Tripoli launched a charge to break through the Muslim line, which just opened ranks and let him through. Instead of turning back to attack the Muslim rear, Raymond continued toward Tiberias, adding to suspicions that he was a traitor. The rest of the Christian army suffered a barrage of arrows and smoke from the grass fires the Muslims had set that aggravated their thirst even more. Some of the rearguard broke free, but the main Frankish cavalry was left unsupported by the infantry, which retreated against orders to the Horns of Hattin, an extinct volcano whose lip was littered with Bronze- and Iron-Age walls that gave them some protection. This 'mutiny' rendered it impossible for the Christians to break out, since the cavalry could not advance without infantry support. Through the day, the Frankish predicament grew ever more desperate, fatigue and thirst taking their toll as they fought off constant Muslim harassment. Late in the day, Guy led two desperate charges, both aimed directly at Saladin in the hope of killing the Muslim sultan and disheartening his troops, but the Christians were thrown back both times. Later in the fight, the Christian relic of the True Cross was captured and its bearer, the bishop of Acre,

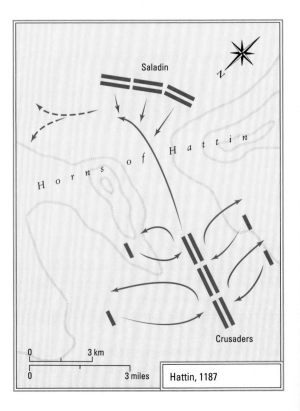

Hattin, 1187

was killed, further disheartening the surviving crusaders. When the Muslims broke through the Frankish defences, they found Guy and his knights slumped on the ground, so weakened by exhaustion and thirst that they could fight no longer. The battle of Hattin destroyed the fighting force of the Kingdom of Jerusalem. Most of the leaders received courteous treatment and were soon ransomed, although Saladin personally executed his enemy, Reynald of Châtillon. The 200 Templar and Hospitaller prisoners were butchered, while the surviving foot soldiers were enslaved. The destruction of the Christian army made it possible for Saladin to take control of most of the Kingdom of Jerusalem over the next few months, including Jerusalem itself. The desperate plight of the crusading cause led to the calling of the Third Crusade.

■ Jerusalem, 1187

After delivering his crushing victory at Hattin, Saladin easily took most of the kingdom of Jerusalem. The most important point symbolically was Jerusalem. Although Jerusalem was denuded of its garrison, Patriarch Heraclius and Lord Balian of Ibelin decided to resist. Only two other knights and few professional soldiers were within the walls, although Balian knighted all noble boys over the age of 16 and 30 burgers to stiffen the defence. Saladin's army numbered at least 20,000.

Saladin invested the city with his army on 20 September, but attempted no escalade, as the Christians put up a show of resistance by manning the walls. It became a battle of negotiation, Saladin threatening to put all Christians to the sword and Balian threatening to destroy the Dome of the Rock. Jerusalem opened its gates on 2 October, ransoming most of the populace at reasonable rates.

Third Crusade 1189–92

■ Acre, 1189–91

When Saladin released King Guy of Jerusalem in July 1188, almost all his kingdom was in Muslim hands and Guy's own leadership was under threat.

His response was to take a small force to besiege the Muslim-held town of Acre, which started on 28 August 1189. At first, Guy's force was far too small even to invest the large and strongly-fortified city, but gradually more and more men joined him, including his political rivals and gradually crusaders from Europe.

Saladin soon arrived and camped close to the strong Christian field camp, but failed to overrun Guy's force on 15 September. Soon a first wave of crusaders arrived – Germans, Dutch, English, Danish and northern French – bringing the number of besiegers to 30,000. On 4 October, Saladin failed again to dislodge the Christians in a major battle during which the crusaders broke into Saladin's camp, but were soon driven out again.

On 5 May 1190, the crusaders launched a major assault against Acre, employing three great siege towers in an attempt to break their way in, but they were driven off, with the flammable towers destroyed by Greek fire. Saladin's response was an eight-day assault on the crusader camp, which began on 19 May. A large French crusader army arrived in July 1190 and, on 25 July, the army launched a massive assault on Saladin's camp. The assault failed, resulting in 4000–5000 Christians being killed.

Acre's plight became more desperate as crusader fleets blocked off its harbour, but the deadlock was only broken after Kings Philip II of France and Richard I of England arrived in mid-1191. The city surrendered on 12 July 1191, after Saladin's final effort to drive off the crusader army failed. The crusaders took 3000 Muslim prisoners, but massacred them when negotiations for their ransom broke down.

■ Arsuf, 7 September 1191

After taking Acre, the army of the Third Crusade, under Richard the Lionheart, set out to march the 129km to Jaffa. Saladin's army shadowed the Christian march, harrowing the flank and especially the Hospitaller rearguard. Skirmishes were so frequent that the crusaders made barely 8km progress a day. An attempt to negotiate with

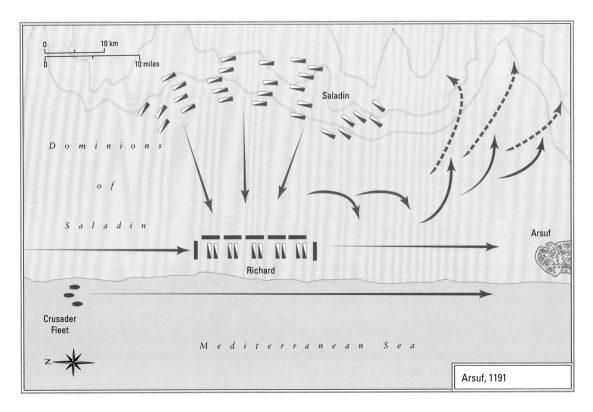

Arsuf, 1191

Saladin rapidly broke down. On 7 September, the crusader army north of Arsuf suffered such heavy attacks that Richard stopped to face the enemy. Each army numbered about 20,000, although the Muslim force was mostly cavalry, compared to about 4000 knights, 2000 Turcopoles and 14,000 infantry on the Christian side. The battle started at about 900 hours, Saladin launching his Turkish light cavalry against the Christian line in the hope of provoking a disorganized charge.

The Christians were harried for hours, but managed to hold their positions, the more vulnerable cavalry sheltering behind a shield of infantry that responded to the Muslims with their own crossbows and bows. King Richard prepared the cavalry for a decisive envelopment of the Turks, but, before he could do so, the Christian line finally broke when the Hospitallers on the left flank, goaded beyond bearing, charged the enemy, sweeping the neighbouring northern French contingent along with them. Richard the

Lionheart ordered a general attack to keep his force from disintegrating. His forceful action managed to keep the Christian army from breaking up in pursuit, while Richard's Anglo-Norman reserve force repulsed Turkish counter-attacks. A series of crusader charges finally drove Saladin's army from the field and looted his camp. Although a Christian victory, Arsuf was not decisive; Saladin lost perhaps 7000 men (to Christian losses of 700), but retained a sufficient force to dog the crusaders' footsteps.

■ JAFFA, 1192

In the last engagement of the Third Crusade, Muslims attacked King Richard's camp of 2000 men outside Jaffa. Richard had time to organize a solid defence of lances and crossbows; the Muslims never closed.

Fourth Crusade 1202–04

■ CONSTANTINOPLE, 8–13 APRIL 1204

The Fourth Crusade, a mostly French army of about 10,000 accompanied by a large Venetian fleet of over 200 vessels, including 60 galleys, reached Constantinople in June 1203. Their goal was to support the claim of Byzantine prince Alexius against a usurper. In an initial assault in 1203, the crusaders took a section of Constantinople's walls and forced the usurper to flee. Relations between the crusaders and the Constantinopolitans soon broke down and the emperor friendly to them was killed in a coup early in 1204. The crusaders decided on revenge and conquest.

In 1203, the crusaders had found the great land walls of the city impenetrable, so in 1204 they focused their assault on the sea walls that overlooked the Golden Horn. The Venetians under Doge Enrico Dandolo prepared for the assault by lashing cargo ships together for stability and creating flying bridges that could be connected to Constantinople's towers with grappling hooks. They also protected the ships from enemy missiles with meshes of vines. The first assault on 9 April failed as adverse winds blew the ships away from the towers. A second assault on 12 April was more successful. Some crusaders crossed onto Constantinopolitan towers by means of the flying bridges, while others landed on the narrow shore and scaled the wall at other points. As the crusaders broke into the city, they purposely set a fire to discourage resistance. That night, the usurper fled and resistance had ended by the morning of the 13th. The Westerners systematically pillaged the Christian city of everything they could find, their loot including a great wealth of holy relics and important historical artefacts. They then proceeded to choose one of their own, Baldwin of Flanders, as emperor.

Crusader-Bulgar Wars 1205–08

■ ADRIANOPLE, 14 APRIL 1205

Western Emperor Baldwin I of Constantinople besieged Adrianople with a relatively small force early in 1205. Kaloyan, the Bulgar tsar, brought a relieving force to the city's aid. An attack on the heavily fortified crusader camp was impractical

and the force of 300 knights was formidable, so Kaloyan turned to guile. The Bulgar sent his Cuman allies against the crusaders, who had formed before their camp. These lightly armed cavalrymen feigned flight, drawing the crusaders into a disordered pursuit; the Cumans then turned and wounded many with arrows. The same stratagem was accomplished with even more success the following day. Despite warnings, a force under Count Louis of Blois pursued the seemingly fleeing Cumans, who led them into an ambush. Baldwin came to support Louis and most of the crusader force was killed; Baldwin was captured and soon died. The Bulgars overran Thrace and Macedonia.

■ PHILIPPOPOLIS, 30 JUNE 1208

Henry of Constantinople with a strong army including 2000 knights defeated a Bulgar army of 30,000 with a direct assault against Tsar Boril that forced his flight. The crusaders then harried the Bulgar retreat.

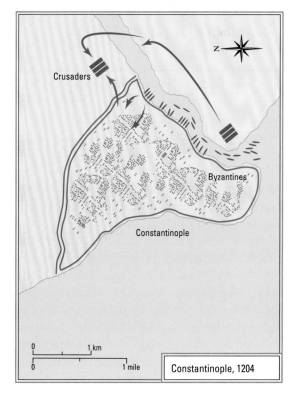

Constantinople, 1204

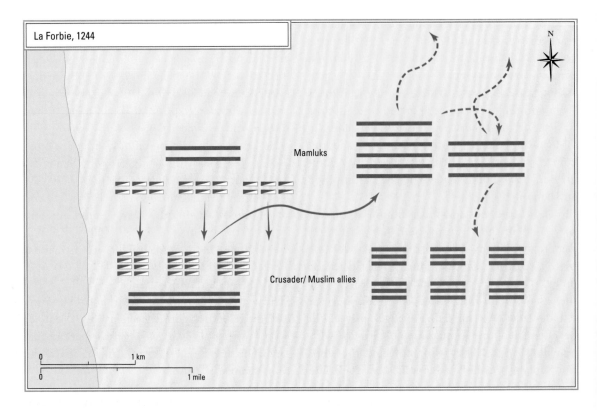

La Forbie, 1244

Mamluks

Crusader/ Muslim allies

0   1 km

0   1 mile

Fifth Crusade 1213–21

■ **DAMIETTA, 1218–19**

A crusading army decided in April 1218 to attack the strongly fortified city of Damietta on the Nile delta. The 18-month siege was marked by constantly departing and arriving groups of crusaders.

The first stage of the siege was a series of attempts to take Chain Tower on an island in the Nile. The crusader force succeeded in this objective after constructing a floating miniature castle with a revolving scaling ladder. The Muslims then blocked the Nile to the crusaders by sinking ships.

October 1219 saw two major attacks on the crusader camp, but, in February 1219, the crusaders were finally able to cross to the Damietta bank. Direct assaults on the city started on 8 July but failed, as did a 29 August attack on the Muslim camp. On the night of 4 November, however, crusader sentries discovered an unguarded tower and scaled the wall.

Crusader Battles 1244

■ **LA FORBIE, 17–18 OCTOBER 1244**

After Khwarazmian mercenaries sacked Jerusalem, the Christian settlers in Outremer and their Ayyubid allies from Damascus and Homs marched south to confront a combined Khwarazmian–Mumluk force. Each side's army numbered about 11,000. The Christian knights on the right wing were at first successful against the Egyptians, but the Khwarazmians overran the Damascenes in the centre, then fell on the crusaders' rear. The Christian-Ayyubid force was annihilated.

Seventh Crusade 1248–54

■ **EL MANSURA, 1250**

King Louis IX's crusader cavalry crossed the Nile to attack the Ayyubid Muslim camp, but without infantry support, the cavalry was pinned in a day-long battle. Louis held the field, but without decisive victory.

Crusader–Turkish Wars 1268

■ ANTIOCH, 1268

Mamluk sultan Baibars attacked Antioch, which was strongly fortified, but defended only by a small force. The city surrendered after a short siege, after which Baibars massacred or enslaved the population despite a promise of mercy.

Eighth Crusade 1270

■ TUNIS, 1270

On his second crusade, King Louis IX attacked Tunis. Dysentery soon ravaged the crusader camp and, on 25 August, the king himself died. The crusaders withdrew under Charles of Anjou, having accomplished nothing.

Crusader–Turkish Wars 1289–91

■ TRIPOLI (LEBANON), 1289

Mamluk sultan Kalavun brought a large force against Christian Tripoli. Venetian and Genoese defenders deserted and the city offered little organized resistance to a general assault. Most of the defenders were massacred.

■ ACRE, 4 APRIL–18 MAY 1291

Mamluk sultan al-Ashraf Khalil attacked Acre with a huge Muslim army, determined to take the last major outpost of the Kingdom of Jerusalem. The Muslim force probably outnumbered the 30,000–40,000 people in Acre, about 15,000 of whom were fighting men.

The city's double walls were in good repair, but the Mamluks undermined them and launched missiles against them, including jars of explosive material. The Christians responded with repeated sorties, until defenders feared that not enough men survived to defend the walls. The outer walls had to be abandoned on 8 May and, on 18 May, Acre fell to a general assault. As Muslim troops entered, much of the populace fled to the port, fighting and capsizing ships in their frenzied effort to escape. The Templar convent held until the 28th, when it collapsed, killing both attackers and defenders.

Russian/Russo-Swedish Wars 1142–1500

■ NOVGOROD, 1164

Seeking to control the Gulf of Finland, the Kingdom of Sweden attempted to send a fleet up the Neva river onto Lake Ladoga. The fleet was driven off, with many of its ships captured.

■ NEVA, 15 JULY 1240

The declaration of a crusade against the pagans of north-east Europe suited the interests of the Kingdom of Sweden. The nominally Swedish component of the crusade, including Finns, Norwegians and some Teutonic Knights, advanced up the Neva river. A hurriedly raised army under the command of Prince Alexander of Novgorod caught the Swedes by surprise and routed them, probably close to the point where the River Izhora flowed into the Neva.

■ LAKE PEIPUS, 1242

As part of the crusade to bring Christianity to the largely pagan lands of north-eastern Europe, the Teutonic Knights sent an expedition towards Pskov, on Lake Peipus. Other allied forces also invaded the region, creating a crisis for Novgorod, to whom Pskov owed allegiance.

The loss of Pskov caused Novgorod to raise an army under Prince Alexander, which retook the town and launched raids designed to draw out the Crusader army. As the Crusader army advanced over the ice of Lake Peipus, it was outnumbered by Alexander's army and many allied troops fled the field.

The core of the crusader force, the Teutonic Knights, led a charge at the Russian centre, becoming embroiled in a melee. Russian cavalry crushed the crusader flanks and surrounded the knights, inflicting a severe defeat. Prince Alexander was afterward known as 'Nevski' for his leadership in the battle.

■ TURKU, 1318

Novgorodian forces made several forays into Finland, often causing great destruction. In 1318, the town of Turku was attacked and heavily damaged, probably as part of a campaign

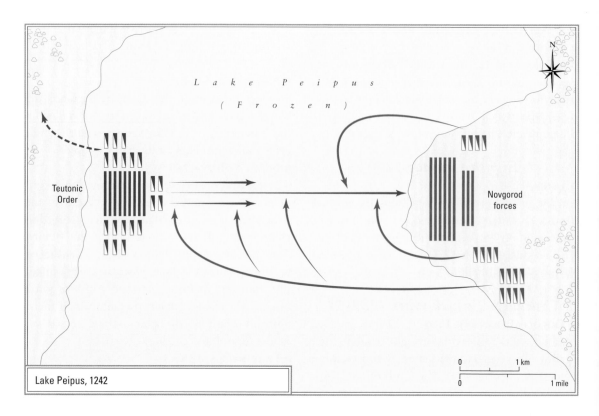

Lake Peipus, 1242

to consolidate Novgorodian control over the Baltic coastal region.

■ **VYBORG, 1495**

In the early months of the Russo-Swedish War of 1495-97, Russian forces besieged Vyborg castle. During the final assault a mine was detonated by the defenders, causing the Russians to retreat in disorder and break off the siege.

■ **IVANGOROD, 1495**

In response to the Russian offensive, Swedish forces attacked and captured the newly built Russian fortress at Ivangorod. Once it became apparent that the fortress could not be held, it was demolished and the Swedes retreated.

The Celtic West – Ireland and Wales 1150–1500

■ **MÓIN MHÓR, 1151**

An invading army of Connachtmen and Lenistermen ambushed a Munster force led by Toirdhelbach Ó Briain, King of Thomond, as he emerged from a mountain pass. Ó Briain lost two of his three battalions, some 3000 men.

■ **BATTLE OF ABERCONWY, 1194**

A hard-fought battle near the estuary of the Conwy river between Llywelyn ap Iorwerth, a prince of Gwynedd, and his uncle, Dafydd ab Owain Gwynedd. Llywelyn's victory allowed him to seize control of northern Wales.

■ **DÚN BEAL GALLIMHE, 1230**

Richard Mór de Burgh led an inconclusive Norman assault on Galway fort, held by Áed Ó Flaithbertaig for the king of Connacht. After several days of fighting, reinforcements from Connacht arrived and the Normans withdrew.

■ **BRYN DERWIN, 1255**

Llywelyn ap Gruffudd, co-heir of the Welsh principality of Gwynedd, fought and defeated his brothers, Owain and Dafydd, at Bryn Derwin, south-west of Snowdonia. Llywelyn's army outnumbered the combined forces of Owain and Dafydd who were captured after not much more than an hour of fighting, thereby ending the battle. Llywelyn's victory gained him the sole rulership of Gwynedd and positioned him as the effective leader of the rest of Wales.

■ CADFAN, 1257

Welsh forces led by Maredudd ap Rhys Gryg and Maredudd ap Owain, lords of Deheubarth, defeated an English royal army in the Tywi Valley in Carmarthenshire, southern Wales. As the English army, under the command of Stephen Bauzan and Nicholas FitzMartin, lay encamped in the valley, the Welsh, hidden in the woods, harassed them through the night. In the morning, the English began to withdraw to Carmarthern, but experienced continued harassment until about midday, when the Welsh outflanked them and captured the English supply train at Coed Llathen. The following day, the English moved to the west, toward Cymerau, but ran into a marsh where their mounted troops were bogged down. The Welsh promptly attacked and, in the ensuing battle, many English knights were pulled from their horses and trampled to death. English casualties included Bauzan and as many as 3000 of his men.

■ CREADRAN CILLE, 1257

Cenél Conaill forces led by Goffraid Ó Domnaill halted the northward advance of Maurice FitzGerald, Lord Justiciar, near Sligo. The battle turned into a rout of the Anglo-Normans who were then driven from lower Connacht.

■ CALLAN, 1261

Munstermen led by Fíngen Mac Carthaig, King of Desmond, engaged a royal army commanded by John FitzThomas, 1st Baron of Desmond, at Callan near Kenmare in south-west Munster. The mountainous terrain was not suited to the Anglo-Norman force, many of whom were mounted, and an immense slaughter occurred. According to the Annals of Ireland, their losses included FitzThomas, his son Maurice, eight barons, 15 knights and countless soldiers.

■ ÁTH AN CHIP, 1270

Connachtmen attacked an Anglo-Norman force fording the Shannon river near Carrick-on-Shannon. After breaking up the vanguard, the Connachtmen then dislodged the enemy rear, forcing the Normans to leave nine dead knights and 100 horses on the field.

■ OREWIN BRIDGE, 11 DECEMBER 1282

A mounted English force supported by archers surprised the army of Llwelyn ap Gruffudd, Prince of Gwynedd, near Orewin Bridge on the Yfron river. Attacked from the rear, the Welsh broke and fled. Llwelyn himself was killed.

■ DENBIGH, 1294

During a general Welsh revolt led by Madog ap Llywelyn, the tenants of Denbigh rose up against the earl of Lincoln and drove him out with heavy losses. Edward I responded with overwhelming force and quickly retook Denbigh.

■ MAES MOYDOG, 5 MARCH 1295

The Welsh revolt led by Madog ap Llywelyn against Edward I effectively ended at Maes Moydog in Caereinion when the earl of Warwick defeated Madog with a combined force of cavalry, crossbowmen and archers.

■ ATHENRY, 10 AUGUST 1316

A force of Anglo-Norman colonists and allied Munster Irish defeated an army of Connachtmen led by Feidlim Ó Conchabair, the king of Connacht, who was killed. Over 1500 heads were collected from the battlefield and sent to Dublin.

■ DYSERT O'DEA, 10 MAY 1318

Conor O'Dea of Thomond and a small contingent of Munstermen held the ford of the Fergus river against an advancing Anglo-Irish force under Richard de Clare. De Clare heedlessly rushed across the river with some of his knights, only to be surrounded and killed. De Clare's main force then crossed over and surrounded the O'Deas in turn, but were thrown into disarray by the arrival of Irish reinforcements and routed.

■ ARDNOCHER, 10 AUGUST 1329

Thomas Butler, brother to Edmund, Earl of Carrick, led an unsuccessful Anglo-Norman

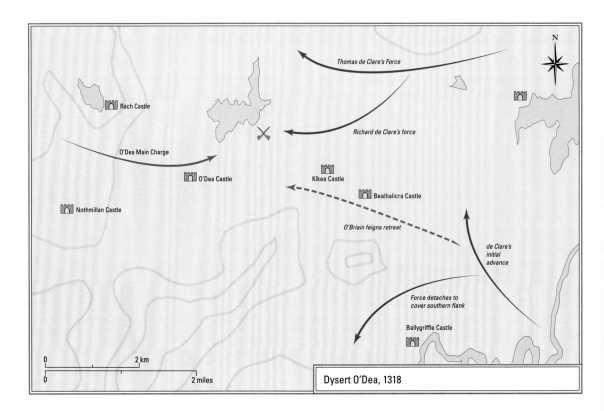

Dysert O'Dea, 1318

attack on the MacGeoghegan fort of Ardnocher in Westmeath. Butler and several other Norman leaders were killed, along with some 140 soldiers.

■ FIODH-AN-ÁTHA, 1330

Ualgarg Ó Ruairc, King of Breifne, led an Irish force against Fiodh-an-Átha (Finnea, Co. Westmeath), but was repulsed by the town's Anglo-Norman population. Among the slain was Art Ó Ruairc, in line to the kingship of Breifne.

■ LOUGH NEAGH, 1345

Aodh Reamhair Ó Néill, King of Tyrone, invaded Clandeboye (Co. Down) across Lough Neagh, but was repulsed in a naval encounter with Clandeboye ruler Éinri Ó Néill. Aodh escaped with difficulty back across Lough Neagh.

■ CALRY-LOUGH-GILL, 1346

An engagement between Ualgarg Ó Ruairc, King of Breifne, and Ruaidrí Ó Conchobair of the Clann-Donough near Lough Gill (Co. Sligo). Ó Ruairc was routed and subsequently slain with all his foreign (probably Scottish) mercenaries.

■ BAILE LOCH DEACAIR, 1356

Aided by Clann an Baird's men, Donnchadh Ó Ceallaigh of Uí Maine slew Aodh Ó Conchobair, King of Connacht, at Baile Loch Deacair (Balloughdacker) in a personal act of revenge.

■ TRIAN CONGAIL, 1383

Niall Mór Ó Néill, King of Tyrone, led a large Irish force into Clandeboye (Counties Down and Antrim) and attacked and burned several English settlements there. An opposing English force formed up near Carrickfergus where, in a mutual cavalry charge, Aodh Óg Ó Néill, presumably the son of Niall Mór, and Roland Savage, son of English baron Henry Savage, wounded each other with spears. Aodh Óg died three days later.

■ TOCHAR CRUACHAIN-BRI-ELE, 1385

Near Croghan (Co. Offaly), Murchad Ó Conchobhair and the men of Uí Failghe (Co. Offaly), joined by the Cenél Fiachach, defeated the English of Meath. Among the English dead were Nugent of Meath and his son Chambers.

■ Ros-mhic-Thrúin, 1394

In October 1394, King Richard II of England landed with a large army at Waterford. In defiance, Leinster king Art Mac Murchadha Caomhánach attacked, plundered and burned the English port of New Ross (Ros-mhic-Thrúin, Co. Wexford).

■ Tragh-Bhaile, 1399

The Clann Enrí Ó Néill, led by Domhnall mac Enrí of Tyrone, mounted an excursion against the English of Tragh-Bhaile (Dundalk, Co. Louth). The English repulsed them, killing many, and Domhnall was taken prisoner to England.

■ Mynydd Hyddgen, June 1401

A few hundred Welsh bowmen led by Owain Glyn Dŵr, Prince of Wales, defeated a larger and better-armed, but undisciplined English force in the Cambrian mountains of Wales. English losses were around 200 men.

■ Tuthill, 2 November 1401

This was a skirmish between a Welsh army commanded by Owain Glyn Dŵr and the English defenders of the town and castle of Caernarfon, in northern Wales. The battle was inconclusive, with some 300 Welsh casualties reported.

■ Bryn Glas, 22 June 1402

The county levy of Herefordshire under Edmund Mortimer pursued the smaller force of Owain Glyn Dŵr, Prince of Wales, to a hill near Pilleth. There the Welsh turned and overwhelmed the English, taking Mortimer prisoner.

■ Shrewsbury, 21 July 1403

In 1403, the earls of Northumberland and Worcester in northern England rose up in rebellion against King Henry IV. Henry Percy ('Hotspur'), son of the earl of Northumberland, joined by his uncle Thomas Percy, raised an army of some 14,000, including a significant force of Cheshire longbowmen, and then marched on Shrewsbury, in Shropshire. A royal army near the same size, led by King Henry himself, met them three miles north of Shrewsbury. After an unsuccessful effort to negotiate a settlement, battle began around midday with a massive, mutual exchange of arrows. However, the Cheshire longbowmen

proved superior to the royal archers and collapsed the king's right wing, commanded by the earl of Stafford. According to a contemporary monastic source, the king's men 'fell like autumn leaves, every arrow striking a mortal man'. Stafford himself was killed and his men fled the field. The king's left wing, under the command of his son Henry, Prince of Wales (the future Henry V), held fast, although the 16-year old prince himself withdrew with a grievous arrow wound to the face. Hotspur then led a charge of knights directly against the king, hoping to kill him, and managed to take the royal standard. Unfortunately, upon lifting the visor of his helmet Hotspur himself took an arrow to the face and was instantly killed. However, confusion on the battlefield led some of the Northumbrian forces to believe that Hotspur lived and the king was dead, prompting Henry IV to show himself and shout out 'Henry Percy is dead'. When realization of this sunk in, the battle came to a halt. The royalist army had taken

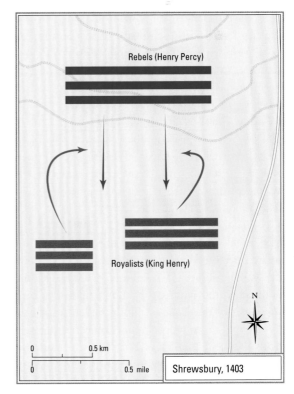

Shrewsbury, 1403

the heavier losses, but Hotspur's death ended the Percy rebellion.

■ **PWLL MELYN, 1405**

A Welsh force, led by Gruffudd ap Owain Glyn Dŵr, attacked Usk castle in south-east Wales, but were repulsed by the English defenders. The castle garrison pursued the retreating Welsh into nearby Monkswood where Gruffudd was captured.

■ **CLUAIN IMMORRAIS, 1406**

At Cluain Immorrais (near Geashill, Co. Offaly), Murchadh Ó Conchobair, Lord of Uí Failghe (Offaly), led a small mounted troop to victory against a combined force of English and Connacht mercenaries, who took some 300 casualties.

Japanese Genpei War 1180–85

■ **UJI, 23 JUNE 1180**

The Minamoto clan once again resumed their efforts to unseat the powerful Taira family from their control of the Shogunate and the Emperor. With a decree of Prince Mochihito supporting their uprising, the small Minamoto army moved south from Kyoto commanded by Minamoto Yorimasa, seeking promised support from warrior-monks at Nara. At the ruined bridge over the Uji, superior Taira forces destroyed the Minamoto and rebellion in a sharp combat.

■ **NARA, 1180**

Taira forces in great number attacked the Nara monastery, which had allied to the Minamoto clan. Around 3500 monks and their followers fell when the Taira burned the monastery and two temples after a spirited defence.

■ **ISHIBASHIYAMA, 14 SEPTEMBER 1180**

Minamoto Yoritomo took advantage of the sudden death of Taira Kiyomori in a raid to move the Minamoto up out of Izu towards Edo with his supporters, the Miura. Oba Kagechika, a strong supporter of the Taira, promptly rallied his forces for a rapid movement in pursuit, amassing ten times Yoritomo's numbers. The Taira overtook the Minamoto in the narrow isthmus near the ravine of Ishibashiyama. Under cover of darkness and a

torrential rainstorm, the Taira launched an all-out attack up the valley into the surprised Minamoto samurai. In the murk and muck, the Minamoto were entirely annihilated, but Yoritomo escaped the Taira's vengeance into the surrounding foothills in the confusion. Kagechika continued the pursuit in vain for three days, finally abandoning it and leaving Yoritomo alive, then fleeing to the coast to Awa Province by sea to resume the fighting.

■ **FUJIGAWA, 9 NOVEMBER 1180**

Invading Minamoto territory, the Taira army paused at the Fujigawa river to find the Minamoto and their Takeda allies mustered on the far bank. An attack or disturbance during the night provoked a Taira retreat.

■ **SUNOMATAGAWA, 6 AUGUST 1181**

Minamoto Yukiie's attack upon a Taira force invading Owari Province disintegrated when the Taira on the far side of this river allowed his approach and then smothered the attack in showers of arrows and samurai.

■ **YAHAGIGAWA, 1181**

Retreating defeated before the Taira advance, Minamoto Yukiie attempted to hold the river with a stockade made of timbers from a dismantled bridge. Only the illness of Taira Tomomori saved the Minamoto after another rout.

■ **HIUCHI, APRIL–MAY 1183**

Taira Koremori and his main army succeeded in capturing this palisaded hilltop bastion, garrisoned by a detachment of Minamoto Yoshinaka's troops. A traitor suggested breaching the moat's dam; the Taira stormed and took the position.

■ **KURIKAWA, 1183**

The main Taira army moved southward out of Kyoto, overcoming isolated Minamoto detachments placed along the line of Kiso Yoshinaka, the Minamoto commander's, advance. Alerted to the quality and quantity of the Taira force, Yoshinaka discovered that the Taira had split their army in two, with the larger portion under Taira Koremori and Michimori camped just before this pass, which Yoshinaka convinced them was already defended. A deep, blind valley opened

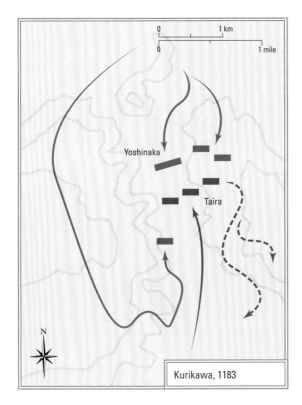

Kurikawa, 1183

out of the pass. The Minamoto drew the Taira army into a protracted fight, while special units circled around to the enemy's rear. As night fell, Yoshinaka's infiltrators attacked and stampeded a herd of cattle into the Taira, their onset made all the more startling by torches tied to the animals' horns. The panicked Taira fled into the blind valley where the Minamoto butchered them. This marked the first Taira defeat.

■ SHINOHARA, 1183

Minamoto Yukiie joined his force with Kiso Yoshinaka's, the combined Minamoto armies rapidly pursuing the Taira forces retreating after the disaster at Kurikawa. The Taira made a fierce stand here, but lost and resumed their retreat.

■ MIZUSHIMA, 17 NOVEMBER 1183

The defeated Taira evacuated Kyoto and moved south back to their own territory, rallying and readying their forces in expectation of Kiso Yoshinaka's pursuit. The Minamoto army had looted the Imperial capital, with Yoshinaka and

Minamoto Yukiie forfeiting imperial and popular support with that action and other rude conduct. Yoshinaka divided his forces and engaged the Taira here, losing badly and retreating back to Kyoto with weakened numbers in still further disgrace.

■ MUROYAMA, 1183

Minamoto Yukiie took the smaller portion of the Minamoto army and moved into Taira territory, finding the enemy's morale and numbers rallied sufficiently to thrash his army soundly and send them limping back to Kyoto.

■ FUKURYŪJI, 1183

Seno Kaneyasu, one of the more clever Taira allies, held this palisaded keep for a while against Kiso Yoshinaka's army under Imai Kanehira, slowing the Minamoto advance with archery directed into the surrounding rice paddies.

■ HOJUJIDONO, 1184

Kiso Yoshinaka sought sole control of his Minamoto clan and declared himself Japan's first shogun. He began by attacking the Hojujidono palace where the Minamoto had installed their puppet-emperor, Go-Shirakawa, after the clan's triumphant entry into Kyoto. The emperor's retinue and allied warrior-monks resisted the attack, but with the defenders slaughtered and the palace in flames, Yoshinaka took the emperor and fled while the rest of the clan moved against him.

■ UJI, 19 FEBRUARY 1184

Miyamoto Yoshitsune moved to drive Kiso Yoshinaka from Kyoto after his attempted coup. Having demolished the bridge into the city, Yoshinaka's forces found themselves flanked and beaten by Yoshitsune's Kamakura army, which forded the Uji river.

■ AWAZU, 21 FEBRUARY 1184

Kiso Yoshinaka was in flight to the city of Awazu when his horse became enmired in a frozen rice paddy. His retainers and warrior-wife failed to hold off Minamoto Yoshitsune's pursuing forces long enough for his suicide.

■ ICHI-NO-TANI, 18 MARCH 1184

This Taira fortress on advantageous ground obstructed the Minamoto advance under Yoshitsune near Kobe. Two loosed riderless horses proved its impassable cliffs passable and Yoshitsune, with 200 samurai, entered the bastion's rear and seized it.

■ **Kojima, 1184**

The Taira navy on the Inland Sea supported this bastion on the coast against Minamoto Noriyori's advance into their territory. The Minamoto cavalry managed to swim an intervening strip of ocean and overrun the position.

■ **Yashima, 22 March 1185**

Minamoto Yoshitsune's nascent fleet, during a fierce storm, launched a seaborne assault upon this Taira stronghold near the Taira fleet's anchorage. The Minamoto advancing under a cloud of smoke drove the Taira to their ships.

■ **Dan-no-ura, 25 April 1185**

Strengthened by allies and ships, Minamoto Yoshitsune led his clan in superior force against the Taira at sea. After a bloody defeat, the Taira and their puppet-emperor plunged into the sea.

Mongol Wars 1190–1402

Conquests of Genghis Khan 1211–27
■ **Beijing, 1215**

Following a series of Mongol victories under Genghis Khan, the Jin's northern capital of Zhongdu (Beijing) came under threat. The Juyong Pass to the north of the capital was well defended, so the Mongols were forced to make a detour and began a long siege of Zhongdu. The city surrendered when the garrison were reduced to cannibalism and the Jin emperor fled to his other capital at Kaifeng in the south.

■ **Otrar, 1219**

Genghis Khan conducted a fierce five-month siege against Otrar, a well-defended outpost of the Khwarazm Empire. According to legend, when it fell, the governor was executed by having molten silver poured into his eyes.

■ **Bukhara, 1220**

While the siege of Otrar was in progress, Genghis Khan led his main army to assault

Bukhara. The 20,000-strong garrison fled, leaving only a handful of troops to be defeated by the Mongol besiegers.

■ **Samarkand, 1220**

The fall of Samarkand was the decisive action of the Khwarazm War. A brave sortie was made using elephants, but the Mongol horsemen broke the attack and a surrender was negotiated after the citadel fell.

■ **Herat, 1220**

The Mongol conquest of Central Asia was accompanied by much slaughter. The armies divided in pursuit of the Khwarazm Shah Jalal-al-Din. After Genghis Khan captured Nishapur, his son Tolui captured Herat after fierce fighting.

■ **Merv, 1221**

The Khwarazm outpost of Merv fell to the Mongols after much fierce fighting. The Mongol general Tolui is said to have sat on a golden chair to watch the execution of the numerous prisoners taken.

■ **Nishapur, 1221**

During the preliminary attack on Nishapur, Toghachar, Genghis Khan's son-in-law, was killed by an arrow. The subsequent sack of the well-defended city was far more terrible than normal and the area was laid to waste.

■ **Indus River, 1221**

Jalal al-Din of Khwarazm evaded the Mongols as far as the Indus river. Here, his army were encircled, so Jalal al-Din swam his horse across the river. Admiring his bravery, the Mongols let him escape.

■ **Kalka River, 31 May 1223**

The battle of the Kalka river was one of the greatest victories achieved under the Mongol general Subadai. By 1223, the Mongols had regrouped in the southern Russian steppes. The Russian princes would appear to have had no intelligence about the campaigns and conquests of Genghis Khan. The first information that a new enemy had appeared in the southern steppes was brought to Mstislav Mstislavitch in Galich by his father-in-law, Khan Kotyan, whose nomadic

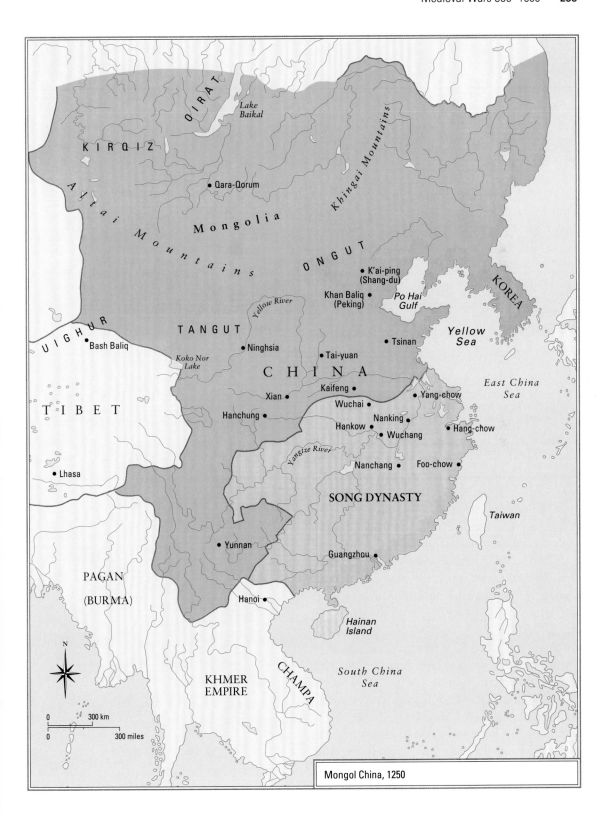

Mongol China, 1250

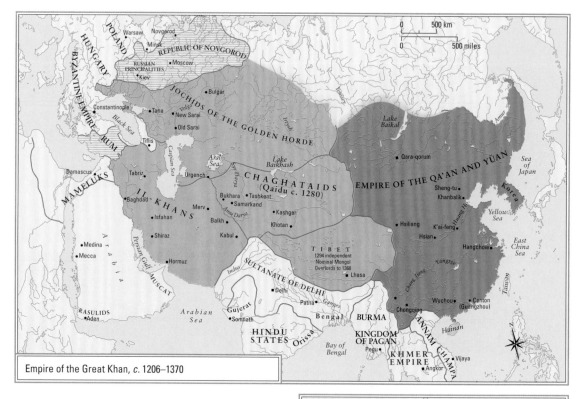

Empire of the Great Khan, *c.* 1206–1370

territory lay close to the easternmost bend of the Dnieper. Mstislav of Galich immediately summoned a council of war in Kiev. They made the decision that the Russians and Polovtsians should move east to seek out and destroy the Mongols wherever they might be found. When the expeditionary force was on its way, the Mongol envoys met the main body at Pereyaslavl and tried to dissuade them from fighting. However, when a second attempt at parley failed, the army crossed the Dnieper and marched eastwards across the steppes for nine days, little knowing that they had in fact been misled by a Mongol false retreat, a favourite tactic conducted on a grand scale. They soon encountered a Mongol army at the Kalka river. The Kumans retreated in such haste that they galloped over the Russian camp and trampled it underfoot. There was complete confusion and a terrible slaughter. Mstislav of Kiev defended himself inside a hastily erected stockade until he was persuaded to give himself up. The princes

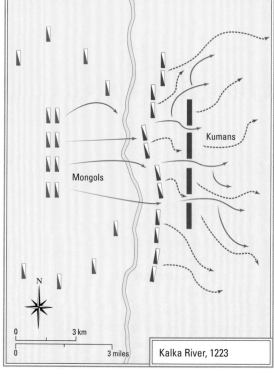

Kalka River, 1223

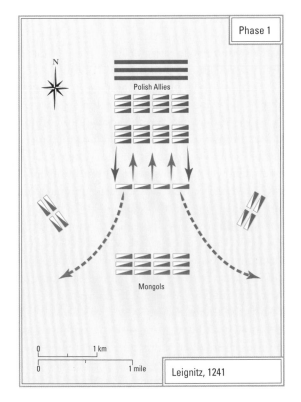

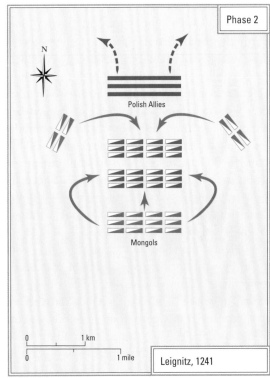

were taken by the Mongols and crushed beneath platforms placed over their bodies. Subadai led the Mongol army home, having covered 6430km in less than three years.

■ SIT RIVER, 1226

While the main body of the Mongol army was besieging Vladimir, their vanguard, went to reconnoitre the position of Prince Yuri located on the Sit river. Vladimir was demoralized when the Mongols presented the head of one of Yuri's sons at the gate and thousands of Russian prisoners began erecting palisades. After a fierce bombardment, the city surrendered and the army moved against, and defeated, Prince Yuri at Sit.

Mongol Campaigns 1232–1336

■ KAIFENG, 1232

Kaifeng was the southern capital of the Jin, who defended it against the Mongols in a long siege celebrated for using iron bombs and fire lances. The city only fell when the Jin emperor fled.

■ KIEV, 1240

The city of Kiev fell to the Mongols after a short, but brave resistance. Many of the civilians took refuge on a certain church roof, which collapsed under their weight. The city was then almost completely destroyed.

■ CRACOW, 1241

The Mongols had not intended to capture Cracow as they were already satisfied with the booty they had collected during their raid, but, on hearing that its prince had fled, they entered Cracow virtually unopposed.

■ LEIGNITZ, 9 APRIL 1241

The Mongol army in Poland continued westwards towards Breslau (Wroclaw), the capital of Silesia. Crossing the Oder river at Ratibor, some on rafts and some swimming, the Mongols approached Breslau ready for a siege, but found that its inhabitants had done their work for them, burning the town themselves and taking refuge in the citadel.

Here the Mongol main body was rejoined by a detachment under Kaidu that had taken a more northerly route. Scouts informed them that a hostile army had taken up a position against them not far to the west of Breslau at Wahlstatt, near Leignitz (Legnica). A decision now had to be made over whether to attack the castle of Breslau first or to take on the Polish army, which was under the command of Henry the Pious, Duke of Silesia. Czech and German knights were also present and a persistent tradition claims that a contingent of Teutonic Knights was also there, possibly under their Grand Master Poppo of Osterna, although this has been called into question.

As Henry marched out from Liegnitz with his army, a stone fell from a church and nearly struck him. This was taken as a bad omen and it was therefore with some trepidation that he arranged his forces into four divisions on the fateful battlefield. The Mongols left Breslau and advanced to fight him and appear to have adopted their favourite tactic of a false withdrawal to lure their enemies on. The allied army seems to have been initially thrown into confusion by volleys of Mongol arrows, but rallied sufficiently to mount a charge against the Mongols, at which the Mongols carefully withdrew.

At this point great alarm was caused in the allied ranks by a man who appeared out of the Mongol ranks on horseback and galloped around crying out in Polish: 'Fly, fly!' This apparition no doubt accompanied the Mongol counter-attack. Some of the army retreated, but Henry the Pious charged the Mongols once again. The chronicler Dluglosz includes a vivid description of the Mongol tuk (standard) made from crossed bones and yak tails, which he describes as being 'a Greek cross, on top of which was a grey head with a beard'. He also mentions the strange phenomenon of clouds of burning, foul-smelling smoke that the Mongols used at Leignitz. It was probably produced by burning reeds, fanned by a favourable wind. With this smoke acting as both an irritant and a smoke screen, the Mongols pressed home their advantage. Henry the Pious escaped with four of his followers. Three were killed and then the duke's own horse gave way. After a brave combat, Henry was slain and his head was cut off.

The body of Henry the Pious was identified later by his wife only because of the six toes he had on one foot. He was the most distinguished out of thousands of casualties at Leignitz on 9 April, because we are told that the Mongols filled nine sacks with the ears cut off from the slain as trophies. Henry's head was impaled upon a spear and paraded outside the walls of his castle. The defenders were suitably terrified, but Leignitz was not a major Mongol target, so the Mongols abandoned Poland and marched on into Bohemia and Moravia, heading in the general direction of their main military objective of Hungary.

■ MOHI, 11 APRIL 1241

The newly reunited Mongol army withdrew to the Sajo river, where they inflicted a tremendous defeat on King Bela IV at the battle of Mohi. The king had summoned a council of war at Gran (Esztergom). As Batu was advancing on Hungary from the north-east, it was decided to concentrate at Pest and then head north-east to confront the Mongol army. When news of the Hungarians' apparent intentions reached the Mongol commanders, they slowly withdrew, drawing their enemies on. The Mongols took a stand near Eger to the east of the River Sajo. It was a strong position. Woodland prevented their ranks from being reconnoitred, while across the river on the plain of Mohi, the Hungarian army appeared to be very exposed. Subadai launched his attack during the night of 10–11 April 1241, only one day after his compatriots won the great battle of Leignitz. One division crossed the river in secret to advance on the Hungarian camp from the south-east. The main body began to cross the Sajo by the bridge at Mohi. This met with some resistance, so catapults were used to clear the opposite bank. When the crossing was completed, the other contingent attacked at the same time. The result was panic and, to ensure that

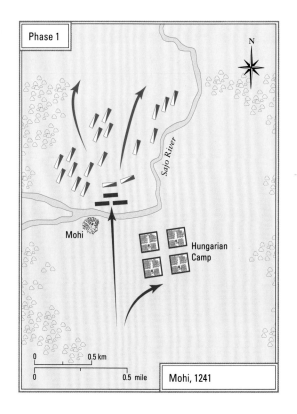

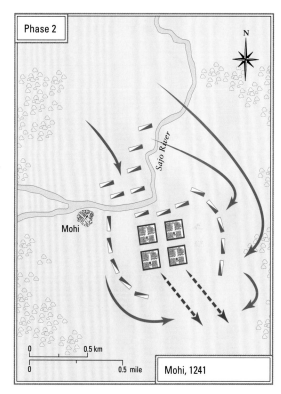

the Hungarians did not fight desperately to the last man, the Mongols left an obvious gap in their encirclement. As they had planned, the fleeing Hungarians poured through this trap that led to a swampy area. When the Hungarian knights split up, the light Mongol archers picked them off at will. It was later noted that corpses littered the countryside for the space of a two days' journey.

■ Köse Dağ, 26 June 1243

The Mongols attacked the Seljuq Sultanate of Anatolia late in 1242. The sultan was joined by the Empire of Trebizond and their combined army was larger than the Mongol one. The Mongols stated that they welcomed the odds because it promised more loot. The result was a decisive Mongol victory at Köse Dağ early in 1243 that led to the decline of the Seljuqs and the absorption of Trebizond into the Mongol Empire.

■ Baghdad, 29 January–10 February 1258

The Mongol siege of Baghdad began with arrow letters threatening to spare only non combatants.

A bombardment led to the capture of the eastern wall. Those who tried to escape were killed before the city fell.

■ Ain Jalut, 3 September 1260

Qutuz's Mamluks followed the Mongols up the coast to Acre, which was then held by a crusader army. The crusaders were enthralled by the prospect of a battle between Mongols and a Muslim army and chose to remain neutral, although they sent supplies to Qutuz in acknowledgement of the recent sacking of Sidon by the Mongols.

Ketbugha was in the Biqa valley when he received the news that the Mamluks had entered Syria, so he gathered his troops who were then widely scattered on garrison duties or grazing and headed south. He took up a position at Ain Jalut ('Goliath's spring') north-west of Mount Gilboa. It was an excellent place for a cavalry battle, and the adjacent valley offered good pasture. Baybar's Mamluk vanguard made contact with the Mongol through some extensive skirmishing, and on

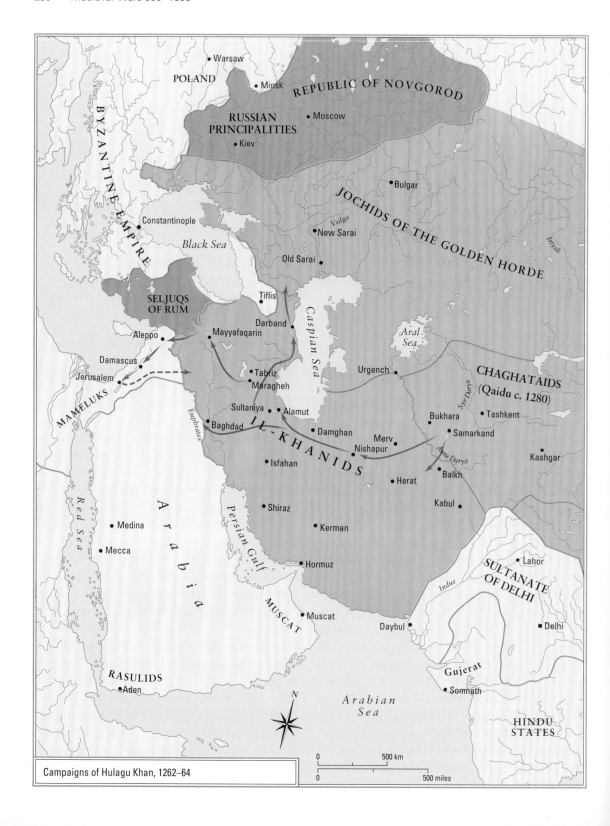

POLAND

• Warsaw

• Minsk

REPUBLIC OF NOVGOROD

RUSSIAN
PRINCIPALITIES

• Moscow

• Kiev

BYZANTINE EMPIRE

• Bulgar

JOCHIDS OF THE GOLDEN HORDE

Volga

Constantinople

Black Sea

• New Sarai

• Old Sarai

Irtysh

SELJUQS
OF RUM

• Tiflis

• Darband

Caspian Sea

Aral Sea

Aleppo •

Mayyafaqarin

Damascus •

• Tabriz
• Maragheh

Urgench

CHAGHATAIDS
(Qaidu c. 1280)

Jerusalem •

MAMELUKS

Sultaniya
• Alamut

Baghdad •

Euphrates

IL-KHANIDS

• Damghan

Merv
Nishapur

• Isfahan

Syr Darya

Bukhara •

• Tashkent

• Samarkand

Amu Darya

• Kashgar

• Herat

• Balkh

Kabul •

Red Sea

A
r
a
b
i
a

Persian Gulf

• Shiraz

• Kerman

• Medina

• Mecca

• Hormuz

Indus

SULTANATE
OF DELHI

• Lahor

MUSCAT

• Muscat

Daybul •

■ Delhi

RASULIDS
• Aden

*Arabian
Sea*

Gujerat

• Somnath

HINDU
STATES

N

0 ———— 500 km

0 ———— 500 miles

Campaigns of Hulagu Khan, 1262–64

ascending a hill observed the Mongol positions. The Mongols had also noted him, so he beat a hasty retreat to join Qutuz and the main body. The battle of Ain Jalut took place on Friday 3 September 1260. The Mamluks approached from the north-west, and the Mongols charged into them, destroying the Mamluk left flank. But Qutuz rallied his troops and launched a counter-attack that shook the Mongols. They again attacked, but Qutuz again rallied his men to the cry of 'Allah – help your servant Qutuz against the Mongols!'. He then launched a frontal attack that led to a complete Mamluk victory. Ketbugha was killed and the Mongol army disintegrated. There followed a pursuit of the Mongol stragglers. Ain Jalut had therefore provided that rarest of events, a Mongol defeat, so that it is often regarded as being the turning point in their conquests.

■ TEREK RIVER, 1262

The Golden Horde was a Mongol state brought about by the submission of the Khanate of Kipchak. At its height, it enjoyed great wealth (hence the name). In 1262, the Golden Horde became embroiled in the civil war arising from the disputed succession to the position of Great Khan of the Mongols after the death of Ogedei Khan. The battle of the Terek river was a victory won by Mongol general Nogai, nephew of Berke Khan of the Golden Horde, during the civil war between his uncle and Hulagu. Taking the initiative, Hulagu marched north and defeated Berke in a surprise attack beside the Terek River. However, victory was rapidly turned into defeat when many of Hulagu's troops were drowned as the ice of the frozen river gave way under them. Nogai's army then successfully counter-attacked and the survivors fled.

■ XIANGYANG, 1268–73

The long siege of Xiangyang displayed great ingenuity on the part of the Song defenders and the Mongol besiegers. Xiangyang was supplied by paddle boats driven by men working treadmills. Two Song officers led a relief convoy of a hundred paddle boats laden with supplies, but were intercepted by the Mongols during the night, with bales of burning straw providing artificial illumination from the banks. In 1272, the Song built a pontoon bridge to link the two cities, but the Mongols constructed mechanical saws that cut the bridge into sections, after which it was burned. Both sides also had exploding bombs with fragmenting iron cases. These were used largely as anti-personnel weapons. A provisioning operation of Xiangyang was carried out later on in the siege, helped by Southern Song ships that were equipped with fire lances, siege crossbows and trebuchets shooting fire bombs. Yet, even when a river blockade was finally put in place and firmly maintained, the Mongol siege weapons of traction trebuchets, bombs and siege crossbows proved incapable of causing any real damage to the walls, so Muslim counter weight trebuchets and their operators were summoned to China from the lands of the west. The weapons were constructed at the Mongol capital, where Khubilai Khan attended some of the trials in person, before being transported to Xiangyang. This may have been done by dismantling the machines, although they could have been mounted on wheeled carriages. Projectiles could now be launched weighing ten times greater than any stone thrown beforehand. One particular shot launched on target brought down a tower of Xiangyang with a noise like thunder. The destruction of the walls in this way eventually led to Xiangyang's surrender.

■ BUN'EI, 1274

The first Mongol invasion of Japan takes its name from the year period of Bun'ei during which it occurred. A fleet carrying defeated Chinese and Korean troops sailed from the coast of Korea and first ravaged the island of Tsushima, where great heroism was displayed by the samurai warriors. They were the first to encounter this strange and terrible enemy who used exploding bombs flung by catapult. Their tactics were also unfamiliar because the Mongol troops were organized in huge phalanxes, unlike the samurai who were used to a more individual style of combat. Arrows (some poisoned) were loosed in dense volleys. From Tsushima, the Mongols sailed to Iki, where the local governor put up a fierce resistance before being killed. Captives were taken from Iki as the Mongols prepared for their landfall on Japan's southern main island of Kyushu.

■ HAKATA BAY, 1274

When the Mongols landed at Hakata Bay, they were subjected to attacks by groups of samurai, who were driven back inland. The Mongols soon withdrew, satisfied with the intelligence they had gathered about Japanese defences.

■ NGASAUNGYYAN, 1277

In Burma, the Mongol horses were startled by war elephants, but the Mongols refused to be panicked and calmly took their mounts to the rear, then returned to loose arrows against the elephants, stampeding them.

■ YAMEN, 19 MARCH 1279

The Mongol conquest of the Song was initially hampered by their lack of ships and naval expertise for use both at sea and on rivers. In 1265, many ships were captured as the nucleus of a fleet. The advance against the Song was stepped up and it was a sea battle at Yamen that brought about the final eclipse of the Southern Song. Bayan crossed the Yangtze in 1275 and, from 1277, the war against the Song developed into a seaborne chase from one port to another. The pursuit reached its climax at Yamen, situated off Guangdong Province. The Mongols blockaded the Song fleet, which attempted to break out. In the ensuing battle, the Song imperial ship was one of the casualties, so, before the Mongols reached them, an official took the child emperor in his arms and jumped into the sea, drowning them both.

■ KYUSHU, 1281

During the second Mongol invasion of Japan the Mongols were forced to wait on their ships before landing. There, the fleet was caught by a typhoon (the *kamikaze* or divine wind) that sunk their ships.

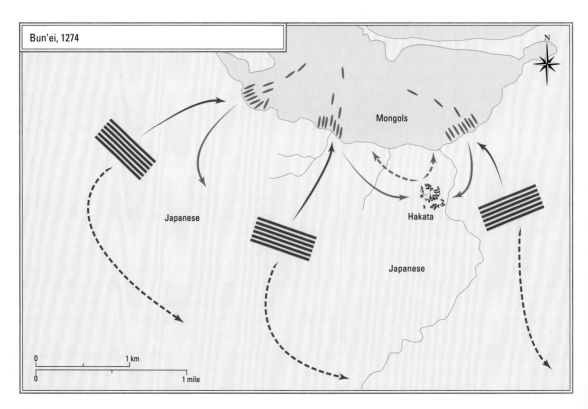

Bun'ei, 1274

Mongols

Japanese

Hakata

Japanese

0   1 km

0   1 mile

■ **Homs, 29 October 1281**

The second battle of Homs was an indecisive encounter between the Mamluks of Egypt and the Mongol Ilkhanate, including Armenian and Georgian auxiliaries. The Mamluk left flank and the Ilkhanate centre were broken in succession.

■ **Kaungsin, 1283**

Following their victory at Ngasaungyyan in 1277, the Mongols advanced to Kaungsin in northern Burma, but were driven back by the heat. They took Kaungsin in 1283, an operation resulting in the fall of Pagan.

■ **Kulikovo, 8 September 1380**

Grand Duke Dimitri of Moscow (Dimitri of the Don) fought an important battle against the Golden Horde of the Mongols at the field of Kulikovo, at the confluence of the Don and the Nepryadva rivers.

Conquests of Tamerlane 1370–1405

■ **Kandurcha, 1391**

The battle of Kandurcha (the Battle of the Steppes) was won by Tamerlane against his protégé Toktamish, who first defeated Tamerlane's left wing, only for reserve troops to circle round and attack Toktamish's rear.

■ **Panipat, 1398**

The battle of Panipat in 1398 was a defeat inflicted upon Sultan Nasir-u Din Mehmud of the Tughlaq Dynasty in the north Indian city of Delhi by Tamerlane, as part of his campaign to control India.

■ **Baghdad, 1401**

Tamerlane besieged Baghdad, but the defenders held out for 40 days before Tamerlane decided to storm the city. This was followed by a brutal sack of the city, in which almost every inhabitant was killed.

■ **Angora/Ankara, 20 July 1402**

Tamerlane approached Ankara knowing that it had been left lightly defended by Bayezid the Thunderbolt and gave orders for immediate siege operations against Ankara's mighty Byzantine walls. The city's water supply was diverted and the mining of the ramparts began. Mongol troops were already scaling the walls when the news came that Bayezid had abandoned his march to Sivas and was two days away from Ankara, but when the Ottoman army arrived, they were in a very poor state. The only source of water available for Bayezid's troops was a spring that Tamerlane had arranged to be fouled. Therefore, they were in no position to fall upon the rear of a besieging army, so Tamerlane was given ample opportunity to organize his battle lines. They looked magnificent, being crowned at the front by the presence of war elephants from India. Bayezid's army included Serbian troops under his brother-in-law Stephen Lazarevic and, in fact, the Serbs scored the first gain of the day by driving back Tamerlane's left wing. However, there were problems among the Ottoman ranks. Certain contingents from Anatolia were from a similar ethnic background to Tamerlane's own troops and his agents had been active among them, so some came over to Tamerlane's side. Faced by rear attacks along with the frontal assault, the Ottoman army began to give way. On the right wing, Lazarevic's Serbs hung on until forced to retreat to cover other contingents' withdrawal. Soon, only Bayezid and his janissaries were left. He held on until nightfall, then retreated with only 300 warriors left to accompany him. The enemy followed in hot pursuit and killed Bayezid's horse as he was being ridden. Bayezid the Thunderbolt was taken prisoner.

Teutonic and Livonian Wars 1198–1500

■ **Umera, 1210**

The crusading Brothers of the Sword, consisting of Livonians, Germans and Latgalians, pursued Baltic pagans into present-day Estonia. The Brothers were ambushed and repulsed. Several captured Brothers were executed by the Pagans.

■ **Viljandi, 1211**

The crusading Livonian Order attacked the fortified pagan town of Viljandi in present-day Estonia. The town held, but negotiations allowed

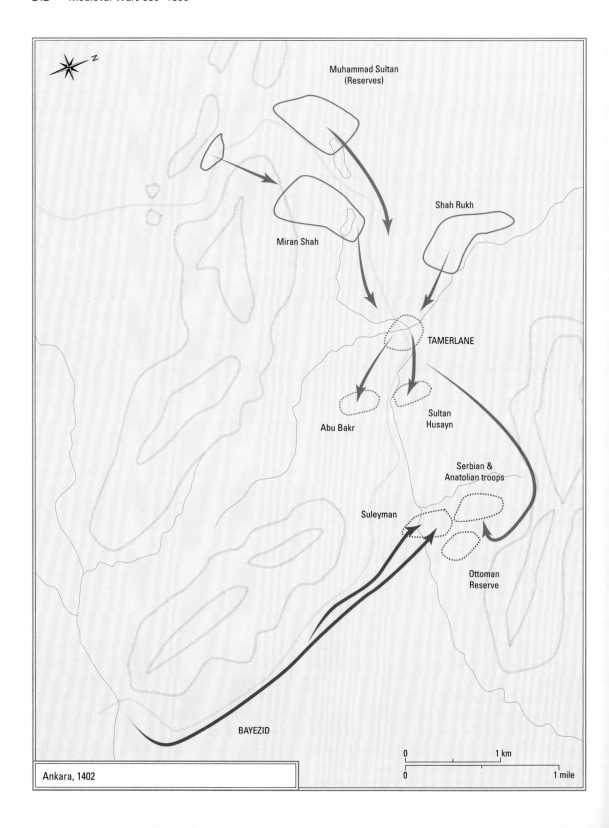

Ankara, 1402

priests with holy water to enter the town before the Livonian Order withdrew.

ST MATTHEW'S DAY, 21 SEPTEMBER 1217
The crusading Sword Brothers, including Germans and converted Baltic Christians, attacked and defeated the pagans in present-day Estonia. Killed in battle was convert leader Caupo, but the pagan commander, Lembitu, also died.

OTEPÄÄ, FEBRUARY 1217
Estonians allied with Russians, totalling 20,000 men, besieged the crusader Sword Brothers' outpost at Otepää. The town was strongly fortified and could not be taken by assault, but provisions were scanty, even for the small garrison. A relief column of 3000 Germans and Baltic Christians arrived, but could not break the siege. Negotiations allowed the garrison to evacuate the town and the Sword Brothers withdrew from Estonia.

LYNDANISSE, 15 JUNE 1219
The king of Denmark, Valdemar II, invaded Estonia and defeated an army of Baltic pagans. The battle is linked to the origins of the Danish flag; a white cross on a red field.

LIHULA, 8 AUGUST 1220
A large army of combined pagan tribes in Estonia attacked the Swedish fortified outpost of Lihula. The Swedes had only 500 men in the garrison, which attempted to fight its way out of Lihula once the town had caught fire. Only about 50 Swedes escaped to the Danish outpost of Tallinn. The defeat discouraged further Swedish crusades in Estonia, leaving such efforts to Denmark and the Livonian Order.

SAAREMAA, 1227
The Livonian Sword Brothers invaded the Baltic island of Saaremaa, the last major stronghold of pagans in Estonia. The island was captured, converted to Christianity and held by the Sword Brothers until 1236.

SAULE, 22 SEPTEMBER 1236
Estonia had been mostly conquered and converted by the crusading Livonian Sword Brothers. An expedition built around the Sword Brothers, reinforced by Baltic Christians and German knights from Holstein, was organized to invade present-day Lithuania. The army of 3000 was commanded by Master Volkwin and advanced into the lands of the Lithuanian Samogitian tribe. Local defenders under Vykintas organized behind the invaders and Volkwin turned his army back towards Estonia. The path was blocked by thousands of Samogitians at a swampy area near a stream.

The Holstein knights and Sword Brothers attempted to break through, but their heavy horses and armour bogged them down in the swampy terrain, where they were showered with javelins and swarmed by the more mobile Samogitians. Volkwin and at least 48 knights were killed, and the invading army was routed with heavy losses.

SKUODAS, 1259
Lithuanian Samogitians raided Courland near the border of present-day Lithuania and Latvia. A party of Livonian knights sent to pursue the raiders was ambushed by the Samogitians, who killed 33 of the knights.

DURBE, 13 JULY 1260
A crusading army of Teutonic Knights, Danes and Baltic Christians, led by Hornhausen, was organized to invade Lithuania. Instead, Samogitian Lithuanians raided Courland (Latvia) and Hornhausen turned his army against them. The swampy terrain hampered the heavy knights and allied Baltic tribes switched sides during the battle. Hornhausen and 150 knights were killed in the defeat, which was followed by pagan rebellions in Prussia and Livonia.

RAKOVAR, 18 FEBRUARY 1268
A large Russian army advanced into present-day Estonia and fought the Livonian branch of the Teutonic Knights. Both sides claimed victory after the fierce battle, called the battle of Wesenberg by the knights.

KARUSE, 16 FEBRUARY 1270
An army of the Grand Duchy of Lithuania under Traidenis defeated an army of the Livonian Order of the Teutonic Knights. Lutterberg, commanding the knights, was killed in the battle.

■ **AIZKRAUKLE, 5 MARCH 1279**
Grand Duchy of Lithuania forces under Traidenis defeated a force of the Livonian Order of the Teutonic Knights in present-day Latvia. Ernst von Rassburg, the knights' commander, was killed in battle.

■ **GAROZA, 1287**
The Semigallian tribe had been in revolt against the Livonian Order of the Teutonic Knights in present-day Latvia and won a battle at Garoza. Despite the victory, the Semigallians were pacified by 1290.

■ **PLOWCE, 27 SEPTEMBER 1331**
The Teutonic Knights with 7000 troops advanced into central Poland, where they fought 5000 Poles. The seesaw battle was claimed as a victory by both sides, each losing a third of their force.

■ **PÖIDE, 4 MAY 1343**
During the Estonian Uprising against the Teutonic Knights, the knights invited four rebel Estonian kings to Pöide castle for negotiations. The kings and their retinues were attacked and killed in the courtyard.

■ **GRUNWALD (TANNENBERG), 15 JULY 1410**
War began between the Teutonic Knights, based in Prussia, and Poland and their ally the Grand Duchy of Lithuania in 1409. After an advance by the Teutonic Knights into Polish territory, both sides called a truce and mobilized larger armies. Once the truce expired in 1410, the Poles and Lithuanians began a counter-offensive. The armies clashed between the towns of Grunwald and Tannenberg, in present-day northern Poland.

The Teutonic army, commanded by Grand Master Jungingen, consisted of German knights and foot soldiers from Prussia, Pomerania and Stettin, plus volunteers and mercenaries from different parts of Europe. The Polish king, Jagiello and Lithuanian Grand Duke Vytautas commanded the Polish-Lithuanian forces, which also included volunteers and mercenaries from Bohemia, Russia and elsewhere.

The Polish-Lithuanian army totalled between 30,000 and 39,000 men, significantly outnumbering the Teutonic army of 20,000–27,000 men. However, the Teutonic army included more heavy knights, more trained troops, better armour and weapons, plus some bombards. The Polish-Lithuanian army had a lower proportion of heavy knights, consisting largely of light cavalry and raw infantry levies.

The Teutonic army was drawn up facing east by south-east. The Polish-Lithuanians were opposite, drawn up on a few low hills and partly in woods, with the Poles on the left and the Lithuanians further north on the right. Grand Master Jungingen expected the larger Polish-Lithuanian force to attack his position. When they failed to do so, he sent envoys across the battlefield to provoke King Jagiello. Legends suggest that Jagiello was delaying battle in order to force the Teutonic army to stand for hours in their heavy armour in the hot July sun, while his forces were in partial shade. The Teutonic envoys reportedly threw down two swords in front of Jagiello as part of the provocation, suggesting that if the king of Poland was afraid, here were more weapons and that the Teutonic army would fall back to weaker positions.

Shortly afterwards, Vytautas and the Lithuanians on the right did launch an attack against Jungingen's position. The Teutonic bombards managed two shots against the rapidly advancing Lithuanian light cavalry. A counter-attack by heavy Teutonic Knights drove back the Lithuanians in disorder. As the Lithuanians retreated beyond their original line, the right flank of the Polish line was exposed. Jungingen wheeled his knights towards the Poles, hoping to complete the victory.

The Teutonic army drove back the Poles and captured the royal banner of Cracow. Polish reserve heavy cavalry counter-attacked, recapturing the banner in fierce fighting. Spotting King Jagiello on a hill, some Teutonic Knights attacked that position. One knight identified as von Kökeritz nearly reached the king, but was stopped at the last moment by the royal secretary, Oleśniscki. Teutonic victory seemed imminent, but their

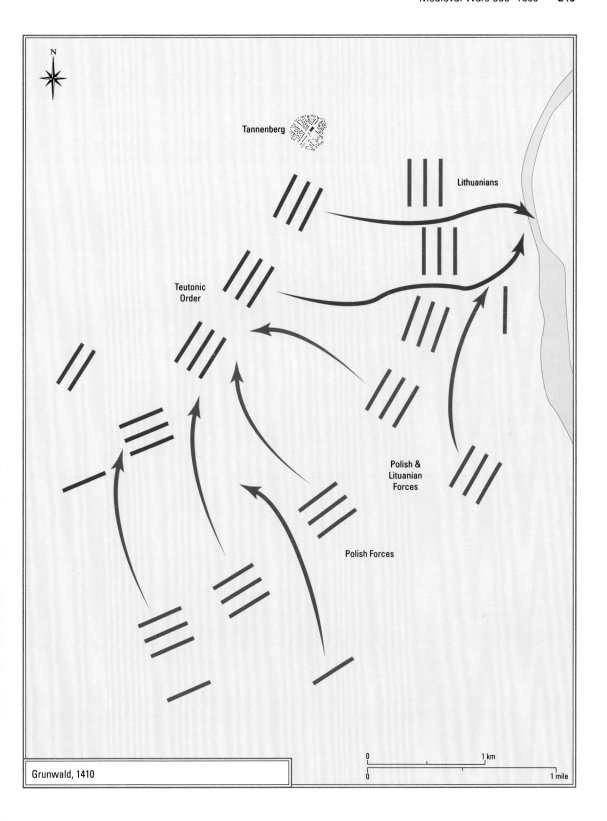

Tannenberg

Lithuanians

Teutonic
Order

Polish &
Lituanian
Forces

Polish Forces

0   1 km

0   1 mile

Grunwald, 1410

main force was fully engaged facing south-east against the Poles, when Grand Duke Vytautas, having rallied his Lithuanians, attacked Jungingen's rear and left flank. Nearly surrounded by superior numbers, the Teutonic Knights attempted to cut their way through their converging enemies. Jungingen was killed, as were several other high-ranking Teutonic Knights. The Teutonic force was shattered and routed. A futile last stand at their camp using wagons as barricades was overrun.

The Teutonic army was annihilated, with nearly 8000 killed and 14,000 captured. Polish-Lithuanian losses in victory had been heavy, with those killed and wounded totaling 12,000. The Peace of Thorn followed, in which the Teutonic Order ceded some territory and agreed to pay an indemnity.

■ CHOJNICE, 18 SEPTEMBER 1454

A Polish and Prussian confederation army besieged a small Teutonic Order garrison in the fortified town of Chojnice in present-day northern Poland. A Teutonic army of 9000 cavalry and 6000 infantry under Bernard Szumborski advanced to relieve Chojnice. Near the town, they were attacked by almost 20,000 Poles, Prussians and foreign mercenaries under the Polish king, Casimir IV.

The Teutonic force was driven back and Bernard Szumborski was captured. The Polish-Prussian advance was halted by a solid line of Teutonic infantry behind barricades and supported by bombards. The garrison of Chojnice then sallied out and attacked the Polish-Prussian rear, causing panic and confusion. The Teutonic army counter-attacked and Bernard Szumborski escaped. The Polish-Prussian force routed, losing 3300 killed or captured. The Teutonic force lost 100 knights and an unknown number of infantry in their victory.

■ SWIECINO, 17 SEPTEMBER 1462

A Polish force consisting largely of mercenaries, defeated a Teutonic force, also consisting largely of mercenaries, near Swiecino in northern Poland. Killed in action was the Teutonic leader Raveneck.

■ ZAKOTA SWIEZA, 15 SEPTEMBER 1463

Also known as the battle of Vistula Lagoon, a Teutonic Order fleet was destroyed by a Prussian Confederation fleet allied with Poland, near modern-day Kaliningrad, Russia.

India and South-East Asia 1200–1400

■ CONQUEST OF THE DECCAN, 1296–1323

The first stage of the conquest of the Deccan by the Delhi Sultanate began in 1296, when Alauddin Khilji, the son-in-law and commander of Sultan Jalaluddin's armies, raided and plundered Devagiri (Maharashtra). Khilji subsequently murdered the sultan and took control of the sultanate. The wealth of the Kakatiya Kingdom also attracted the attention of Khilji, who launched an attack against its Telugu Province in 1303. His armies were led by Malik Fakruddin, but were heavily defeated by the Kakatiya army in a battle at Upparapalli (Karimnagar District). A second attempt was made in 1309 by Malik Kafur, who managed to capture Siripur and Hanumakonda forts, although the fortress of Warangal was only taken after a prolonged siege. Malik Kafur's forces' atrocities at Warangal intimidated King Prataparudra sufficiently to induce him to offer an enormous amount of tribute, and sue for peace. According to contemporary accounts a total of 241 tonnes of gold, 20,000 horses and 612 elephants laden with the looted treasure (including the Koh-i-Noor diamond, at the time the world's largest diamond) were paraded through Delhi. However, Prataparudra re-asserted his independence in 1320 following the fall of the Khilji Dynasty and the accession of Ghiyasuddin Tughlaq as sultan of Delhi. Tughlaq sent his son Ulugh Khan in 1323 to defeat the defiant Kakatiya king. Ulugh Khan's (Muhammad bin Tughluq's) first attack was repulsed but he returned a month later with a larger and reorganized army. The unprepared and battle-weary forces of Warangal were finally defeated, and King Prataparudra was taken prisoner. He committed suicide by drowning

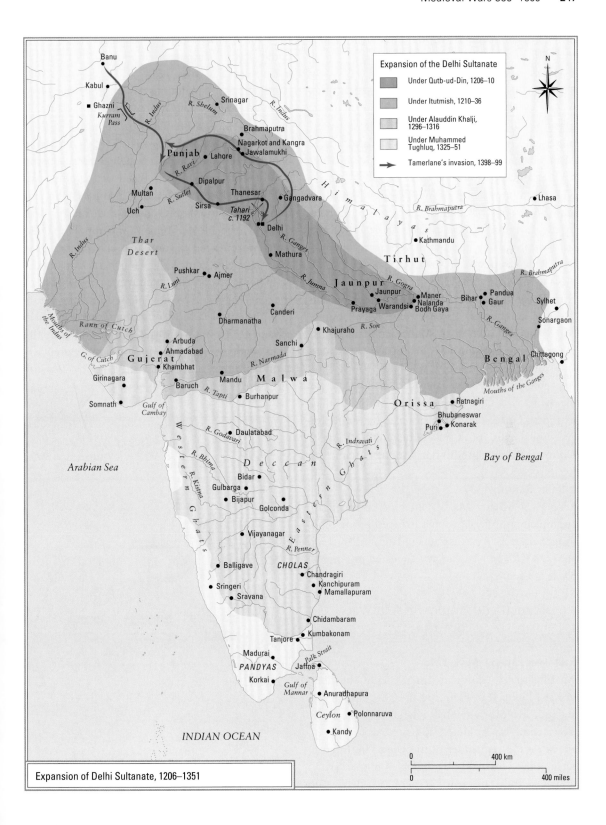

Expansion of the Delhi Sultanate

- Under Qutb-ud-Din, 1206–10
- Under Itutmish, 1210–36
- Under Alauddin Khalji, 1296–1316
- Under Muhammed Tughluq, 1325–51
- → Tamerlane's invasion, 1398–99

Expansion of Delhi Sultanate, 1206–1351

himself in the River Narmada while being taken to Delhi.

■ MYINSAING, 1299

The Burmese Pagan Empire fragmented into several small rival states following the Mongol capture of its capital in 1287. Antipathy between these states flared up in 1299, provoking a further Mongol attack, which was defeated at Myinsaing.

■ CHAKANGRAO, 1376

King Borommaracha I of Ayutthaya attempted to take the city of Chakangrao, which was reinforced by the governor of Nan and his army. This force set an ambush for the Ayutthayan army, but was heavily defeated.

■ KAMPHAENG PHAT, 1378

King Borommaracha I launched a further offensive to seize Sukhothai's frontier city, Chakangrao. The king of Sukhothai, Mahathammaracha II, realized the hopelessness of further resistance and surrendered the city. He was allowed to rule part of his former lands as a tributary state of Ayutthaya. The western part of Sukhothai, including Chakangrao, was annexed by Ayutthaya and the cities of Chakangrao and Nakhon Chum were merged under the new name of Khampaeng Phet.

■ SAEN SANUK, 1387

King Saen Müang Ma of Chiang Mai foiled an attempted coup by his uncle Prince Phrom, who sought aid from Ayutthaya. King Borommaracha I attacked Chiang Mai, but was defeated in a fierce battle at Saen Sanuk.

French and Anglo-French Wars 1200–1337

■ DAMME, 30–31 MAY 1213

An English expeditionary force caught the fleet of King Philip II of France in the port of Damme and quickly overwhelmed a large portion of it. The action was resumed the next day with an attack on the remainder of the fleet. The English were then repulsed by King Philip's army, which left its siege of Ghent to drive off the numerically inferior English before they could capture Damme itself.

■ BOUVINES, 27 JULY 1214

An allied force including troops from the Holy Roman Empire, England and rebellious French provinces met a French army commanded by King Philip II at Bouvines. The French chose the battleground and fought a largely defensive battle against superior numbers. Each of the allies had a different reason for fighting against Phillip, but found a common cause under the command of Otto IV, the Holy Roman Emperor. The allied vanguard engaged as soon as it arrived, bringing about a melée, which the French cavalry on the right wing eventually won. As the remainder of the allied army arrived, it hurried into the attack in a piecemeal fashion, offsetting their numerical advantage. Troops were still arriving to join the right wing of the allied army even after the centre and left had been defeated, but by then the outcome was no longer in doubt.

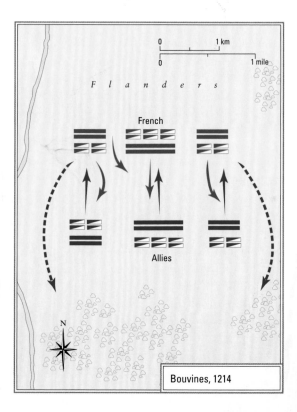

Bouvines, 1214

■ **TAILLEBOURG, 21 JULY 1242**

Large English and French armies under the command of Henry III and Louis IX respectively clashed at Taillebourg, both seeking to control the strategic river crossing there. A French cavalry charge decided the issue.

First Barons' War and England 1215–24

■ **ROCHESTER, 1215**

Rochester castle blocked King John's route from Dover to London and was besieged. Even after part of the keep was undermined, the defenders made a long and determined resistance until they were eventually starved into submission.

■ **DOVER, 1216–17**

Dover castle was key to communications with France and thus vital to the operations of the French force under Prince Louis, which was assisting the rebel barons against King John. Louis laid siege to the castle in 1216 using land and naval forces. Despite gaining entry by undermining a tower, the French were repulsed and the siege broken off. Operations against Dover Castle were renewed the following year, but Louis was again unsuccessful.

■ **LINCOLN, 20 MAY 1217**

With part of Louis' army involved in siege operations at Dover, the remainder was besieging Lincoln. An English relief army broke the siege and drove the remainder of the French army towards London.

■ **SANDWICH, 24 AUGUST 1217**

After a serious defeat off Dover, the remainder of the French fleet was again brought to action off Sandwich. The loss of his fleet deprived Prince Louis of reinforcements and made his position in England untenable.

■ **BYTHAM, 1220**

Having changed sides several times in the barons' wars, William de Forz rose in rebellion against Henry III. The fall of his castle at Bytham brought his rebellion to a temporary end; he revolted again in 1223.

■ **BEDFORD, 1224**

Bedford castle was besieged for eight weeks by the young king Henry III and eventually fell after four assaults. This brought the surrender of the rebellious Fawkes de Breauté and helped cement Henry's position as king of England.

Iceland 1246

■ **HAUGSNES, 19 APRIL 1246**

Although small by European standards, the clash between two rival chieftains at Haugsnes in 1246 saw the highest casualties (about 100) of any battle in Icelandic history. It established Þórður kakali Sighvatsson as the dominant Icelandic leader.

Eastern European and Ottoman Wars 1250–1500

■ **KRESSENBRUNN, JULY 1260**

Fighting for control of the duchies of Austria and Styria, the army of King Ottokar II of Bohemia routed that of King Béla IV of Hungary. Both forces were very large and were supplemented by mercenaries.

■ **BAPHEUS, 27 JULY 1302**

What seemed to be an inconsequential rebellious clan, the Ottoman Turks, led by founder, Osman I, stunned a Byzantine army sent to relieve their siege of Nicaea. The Turkish light cavalry drove the heavier Byzantine forces from the field.

■ **PELEKANON, 10–11 JUNE 1329**

The Ottoman Turks, led by Sultan Orhan I, defeated another Byzantine army, under Andronicus III, attempting to stop their expansion throughout Asia Minor. The smaller, but better-armoured Byzantine forces proved to be no match against the experienced Turks.

■ **POSADA, 9–12 NOVEMBER 1330**

Wishing to form an independent political entity, the Wallachians put together a military confederacy that raised an army led by Besarab I. It was a small force, estimated at around 10,000, which was not very experienced in warfare. Facing them was

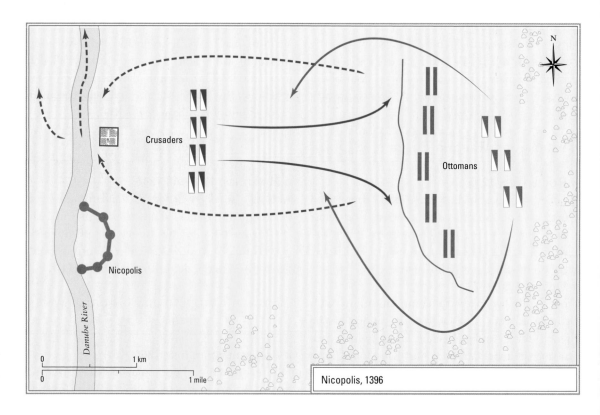

Nicopolis, 1396

the Angevin king of Hungary, Charles I Robert, whose army was much larger (estimated at 30,000) and far more experienced. Charles Robert took the offensive, attacking Wallachian sites, even if not sympathetic to his opponents. As he pushed further, fewer assisted him. Eventually, his own guides led him into an ambush in the Carpathian Mountains. There, the Wallachians quickly overwhelmed the Hungarians. In order to save himself, Charles Robert was forced to exchange his clothes with one of his soldiers, who was slain shortly thereafter. The Wallachians still had many conflicts to fight, but were effectively on their way to sovereignty.

■ ADRIANOPLE, 1365
A decade after Adrianople was captured by the Serbs from a weakened Byzantine Empire (1355) – however, it was regained shortly afterwards – the Ottoman Turks defeated the Byzantines outside it, although the city would not fall until 1369.

■ MARITSA, 26 SEPTEMBER 1371
As the Ottoman Turks moved further into the Balkan peninsula, the declining Serbian Empire determined to stop them. Assembling a large army, with exaggerated estimates of nearly 70,000, the Serbian king Vukašin Mrnjavčević tried to surprise the Ottomans, but was unable to do so. The smaller Ottoman force, under the able leadership of Lala Şâhin Pascha, defeated the Serbs and killed Vukašin, thus facilitating the conquest of south-eastern Europe.

■ SAVRA, 1385
Following Maritsa, the Ottoman Turks lost several engagements against small local armies, but nevertheless moved further into the Balkan peninsula. At Savra, the Turks faced and destroyed another of those forces, led by Balsa Balsich.

■ KOSOVO, 15 JUNE 1389
Perhaps the first major defence against Ottoman Turkish forces invading the Balkan peninsula was that made by Serbian forces under Prince Lazar Hrebeljanović at Kosovo in 1389. The Turks were led by their Sultan, Murad I. Both armies were

large, with (likely exaggerated) numbers always placing the Turks at a two-to-one advantage, athough the Serbians did have some heavy cavalry, which the Turks lacked. The two forces met in an open field, with their soldiers arrayed in a similar formation. The Serbs began the conflict with a heavy cavalry charge which, however, did not force the Turks to flee as was hoped. When the Turks counter-attacked, the Serbs fled and the battle ended. Both sides suffered extremely heavy casualties, including both commanders. Murad's son, Bayezid I, who had proven himself particularly valiant in the battle, succeeded to the Ottoman throne.

■ ROVINE, 17 MAY 1394

After several victories, the large Turkish army, led by Sultan Bayezid I, was defeated by a smaller, but very determined Wallachian force, although there is some dispute as to what caused the Ottoman rout.

■ NICOPOLIS, 25 SEPTEMBER 1396

The battle of Nicopolis was the first combined military effort of western European forces in a crusade against the Ottoman Turks. English, French and Burgundian crusaders marched without difficulty through central Europe – where they were joined by Hungarians, Wallachians, Transylvanians, Germans and Knights Hospitallers – and into Ottoman territory south of the Danube river. The initial campaign, including early attacks against fortified Turkish locations, was quite successful, with Vidin and Rahova surrendering after strong Crusader attacks. Eventually, they moved on to besiege Nicopolis. Bayezid I, the Ottoman Turkish Sultan, was attacking the remnants of Byzantium, but he quickly marched to Serbia to counter them.

John the Fearless seemed not to have known Bayezid's plans or progress. In fact, it was not until the day prior to the battle of Nicopolis, when the Ottomans were less than 7km away, that the crusader leaders learned that a large enemy army led by the Sultan approached their force and wanted to fight a battle. The crusaders broke off their siege of Nicopolis and prepared for a battle outside its walls. Both sides are said to have numbered more than 100,000, but are likely to have been between 12,000 and 15,000. The crusaders were led by a number of different generals: John the Fearless, Count of Charolais and heir to the Duchy of Burgundy; Philip of Artois, the Constable of France; Jean II le Meingre dit Boucicault, the Marshal of France; Jean de Vienne, the Admiral of France; Guillaume de la Trémoille, the Marshal of Burgundy; Sir Enguerrand de Coucy VII and the Hungarian king, Sigismund I.

Sigismund, the most experienced against the Ottomans, recommended that the Hungarians and other central European troops, almost entirely infantry, should be in the front of the crusader forces. He suggested that they meet the irregular infantry of the Turks who were always in front of their army. He would take a defensive stance to provoke the Ottomans into a charge that might be defeated at the contact of the two infantry forces or reinforced by the strong Franco-Burgundian cavalry in the second rank. However, Sigismund was overruled by the Franco-Burgundians. They believed that a heavy cavalry charge would defeat the Turks.

They charged headlong into the Turks, standing behind a line of stakes. Initially, the shock of this charge brought success, breaking through the stakes and pushing the Turkish irregular infantry back. However, these troops did not break, quickly reforming before a second attack could be made. That charge also pushed the Ottoman vanguard back, but did not break it and, when a counter-attack came from Bayezid's regular troops, the crusaders were finished. Although some German and Hungarian infantry tried to reinforce their cavalry, all were quickly defeated.

The battle of Nicopolis lasted only a very short time, no more than an hour. King Sigismund and his army, which had not participated in the battle because it had been so short, retreated to the Danube, boarded boats and sailed back to Buda.

The many captives were executed, until John the Fearless's nobility was recognized and some of the European nobles became held for ranson. No more than 300, from a total of up to 6000, were spared. The Turks had also suffered numerous losses, but far fewer than the crusaders.

■ **VORSKLA RIVER, 12 AUGUST 1399**

Wishing to halt the Golden Horde's expansion into north-eastern Europe, Grand Duke Vytautas of Lithuania formed an alliance of forces, including Teutonic Knights. led from their *Wagenburg* ('wagon fort') by a Mongol feigned retreat, the Europeans were defeated with heavy casualties.

■ **SUDOMER, 25 MARCH 1420**

Allied central European Catholic forces attacked the Hussities almost immediately after Pope Martin V called a crusade against them. In their second battle, the battle of Sudomer, the Hussites prevailed, using a wagenburg field fortification. Jan Žižka emerged here as an effective general.

■ **PRAGUE, 12 JUNE 1420**

The citizens of Prague joined the Hussite rebellion in 1419. Answering the call to crusade, a large German army arrived outside Prague on 12 June, but their siege was raised by the arrival of Žižka's soldiers.

■ **VITKOV HILL, 12–14 JULY 1420**

Following their relief of Prague, a Hussite force of 9000 retreated to nearby earthen fortifications. Armed mainly with agricultural implements and some rudimentary gunpowder weapons, the Hussite heretics on Vitkov Hill were attacked by Holy Roman Emperor Sigismund's army. However, Jan Žižka's peasant army's surprise flanking attack routed the crusaders.

■ **VYŠEHRAD, 1420**

A Catholic force from Plzeň was intercepted on their way to relieve Emperor Sigismund by soldiers under Jan Žižka. The Hussites, using their artillery-filled wagons, fired gunpowder artillery at the crusaders, chasing them from the field with heavy casualties.

■ **KUTNÁ HORA, 21 DECEMBER 1421**

Jan Žižka's Hussites once more defeated the crusaders in December 1421. Emperor Sigismund's superior forces surrounded the Hussites, but, after forming a column of cavalry and wagens, Žižka pushed his way through their lines and routed them.

■ **NEBOVIDY, 6 JANUARY 1422**

Having chased Sigismund from Bohemia, Jan Žižka went on the offensive by attacking the fortification at Nebovidy. The Hungarian garrison was small and easily defeated. The Hussite victory forced Sigismund from his winter quarters.

■ **NĚMECKÝ BROD (DEUTSCHBROD), 1422**

Two days after his victory at Nebovidy, Jan Žižka attacked Sigismund's relief army, defeating it and causing heavy casualties. Some crusaders escaped to nearby Německý Brod, which the Hussites quickly captured, massacring the inhabitants.

■ **HOŘICE, 27 APRIL 1423**

Having defeated the crusaders, the Hussites fell into two militant factions, the Taborites and the Ultraquists. Equal in numbers, the Taborites, led by Jan Žižka, defeated the Ultraquists of Čeněk of Wartenberg, ending the civil war.

■ **AUSSIG (ÚSTI NAD LABEM), 16 JUNE 1426**

Trying to take advantage of Žižka's death in 1424, another crusade was called against the Hussites. The response resulted in a huge army entering Bohemia. Learning from previous experience, the crusaders had built their own artillery-laden wagons. However, the Hussites held the higher ground, negating the effect of the crusaders' artillery. The crusaders' charge was initially successful, but their impetus failed and, fatigued, they were quickly defeated, with heavy losses.

■ **KHIROKITIA, 7 JULY 1426**

Attempting to halt the piracy of his ships, Barsbay, Mamluk sultan of Egypt, invaded Cyprus. His 5000-man army defeated the 4600 soldiers of King Janus of Cyprus. Janus, taken prisoner, agreed to become the vassal of Egypt.

■ **DOMAŽLICE, 14 AUGUST 1431**

A crusading army besieging Domažlice was surprised by a Hussite army, led by Prokop the

Bald, thought to be many kilometres north. The sight of the approaching and singing Hussite relief army led to mass panicking among the crusaders, who fled, with the Hussite army killing many.

■ Lipany (Český-Brod), 30 May 1434

Once again, the crusade having been quelled, Taborite Hussites faced Ultraquist Hussites (with Catholic allies) in a religious war. Lured from their *Wagenburg* by a feigned retreat, the Taborites were defeated by cavalry attack and artillery fire.

■ Grotniki, 4 May 1439

The end of the Hussites came when Polish crusaders, led by Hińcza of Rogów, defeated a small force, led by Spytko of Melsztyn, in a quick and ruthless battle of which few details are known.

■ Zlatica, 1443

After several defeats in the Balkans against the forces of János Hunyadi, the Ottoman Turks, led by Sultan Murad II, defeated the Hungarians and their allies, the Poles and Serbs, in a mountain pass.

■ Varna, 10 November 1444

Following on his victory the previous year, Sultan Murad II's large army of Ottoman Turks soundly defeated a smaller crusading force primarily drawn from central Europe. It was the last serious attempt by Christian Europe to save Constantinople from Ottoman rule. Folowing pleas from the Byzantines, Pope Eugenius IV agreed to organize a crusade. Largely composed of Hungarians, Germans and Poles, the 25,000-strong Crusader army was led by Hungarian king Uláiszló I. With a force of 40–50,000 troops, Murad II's army met the Christians near Lake Varna, close to the Black Sea coast. During the battle Uláiszló and many of his knights were killed after an unsuccessful charge against the elite Janissary infantry in the Ottoman centre. At the end of the day both sides disengaged, with no clear victor. The Christian losses were so heavy, however, that their army soon disintegrated and retreated from Ottoman territory.

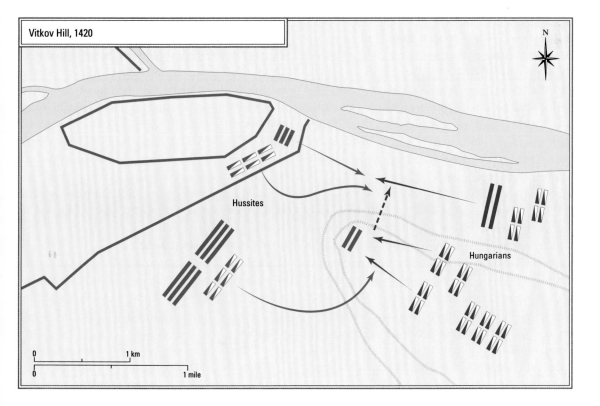

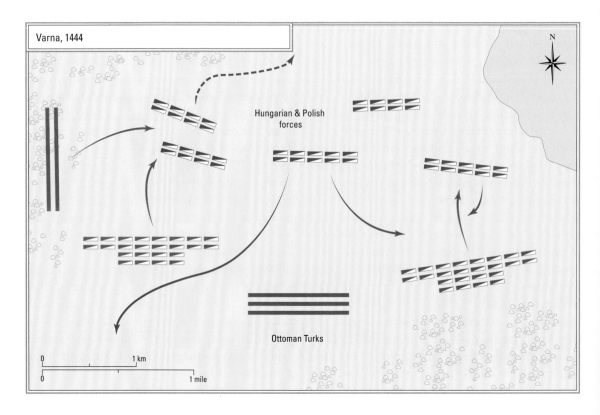

Varna, 1444

Hungarian & Polish
forces

Ottoman Turks

0   1 km

0   1 mile

■ KOSOVO, 17–20 OCTOBER 1448

A second battle at Kosovo was fought between
the Ottoman Turks, led by their sultan, Murad II
and the Hungarians, led by János Hunyadi. The
Serbs, who controlled the area where the battle
was fought, tried to remain neutral, although
their territory suffered from the destruction of
both forces. Both armies were large, although the
numbers reported – which place the Turks at a
significant advantage (24,000 against 40,000–
60,000) – are certainly exaggerated. Both also
had fairly large numbers of gunpowder weapons,
which opened the battle with a strong, but
ineffective barrage. The Hungarians then charged
their cavalry, which was initially successful, but
soon became fatigued and impotent. The Turkish
janissaries held and other troops rallied around
them. After a long and costly battle, the Hungarians
fled, followed by their remaining forces. The Serbs
captured Hunyadi, who was only released when a
ransom of 100,000 florins was paid.

■ BELGRADE, 4–22 JULY 1456

The Serbian capital Belgrade had remained an
island of defiance against the Ottomans in the
Balkans. Sultan Mehmed II (the Conqueror) tried
to follow up his victory at Constantinople by
besieging Belgrade. But, despite having the same
gunpowder artillery arsenal, he could not bring
down these walls. A counter-attack launched
by the townspeople, inspired by septuagenarian
Franciscan friar Giovanni da Capistrano, forced
the Turks into flight, with Mehmed only barely
escaping capture.

■ DIREPTATEA, APRIL 1457

In a battle for the right to rule Moldavia, the army
of Ştefan cel Mare, in alliance with Vlad III Dracul
(the Impaler), defeated that of Petru Aron and he
was crowned Stephen III of Moldavia.

■ TRABZON, 1461

The last remnant of the Byzantine Empire,
Trebizond, on the south-eastern coast of the Black
Sea, was attacked by Ottoman sultan Mehmed

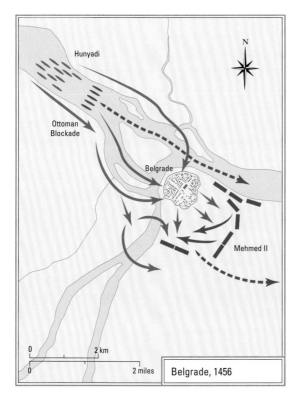

Belgrade, 1456

attacked Poland, Moldavia and Lithuania. These invasions ended when the Moldavian king Stephen III defeated a large force retreating to Horde lands with booty and slaves.

■ NEGROPONT, 1470

The Ottoman army, led by Sultan Mehmed II, was besieging Negropont when a Venetian fleet arrived to relieve the city. However, the admiral, Nicolò Canale, retreated rather than face the Turkish fleet and the city surrendered.

■ OTLUKBELI, 11 AUGUST 1473

After defeating the Byzantines, Sultan Mehmed II turned to the remnants of Mongol-controlled Asia Minor. One of these areas, the Ak Koyunlu (White Sheep), which had few soldiers and no gunpowder weapons, were easily defeated.

■ VASLUI, 10 JANUARY 1475

The only question about the Ottoman Turkish invasions by the mid-fifteenth century was how far north or west in Europe they would go. The Turks had already conquered the Byzantine Empire and

II. Besieging the capital city, Trabzon, Mehmed quickly forced the city into submission.

■ THE NIGHT ATTACK, 17 JUNE 1462

Vlad III's invasion of Bulgaria led to an attested 23,000 impalements of Bulgarians and Turks. Ottoman sultan Mehmed II responded by invading Bulgaria and Transylvania. Wanting to stop this invasion, but thinking that he lacked sufficient soldiers to fight a battle against Mehmed's troops, Vlad launched a night attack the Turkish camp. He hoped to cause confusion among the Ottomans and (possibly) assassinate the sultan. He did cause confusion, but neither killed Mehmed nor discouraged the Turks to end their invasion. Mehmed pursued the retreating Wallachians, reaching the capital, Târgoviste, but retreated on finding that Vlad had impaled a further 20,000 of his men.

■ LIPNIC, 20 AUGUST 1470

Testing the weakness of eastern Europe, Golden Horde leader Ahmed Khan simultaneously

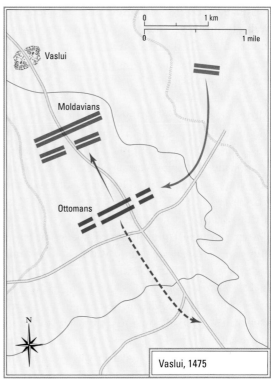

Vaslui, 1475

much of the Balkans; they showed no stopping. No kingdom was more active against the Turks than Moldavia. A large army of Moldavians, led by their king, Stephen III, faced an even larger army of Turks under Hadân Suleiman Pasha, the Beylerbey of Rumelia outside of Visuli. The Moldavians attacked with gunpowder artillery, handguns and bows, then launched their cavalry at the Turks, who were having difficulty seeing what was happening through the cold January fog. The Ottomans remained confused, until they fled or surrendered. The latter were impaled, with only the commanders being preserved. However, the defeat was far from decisive as the Turks would return the next year.

■ VALEA ALBA, 26 JULY 1476

Allied with the Crimean Khanate, Mehmed II again tried invading Moldavia. Arrayed in a forest, the Moldavians initially withstood Ottoman attacks using intensive handgun fire and forcing the attackers to suspend their assaults. Mehmed, using his own guards, rallied his janissaries, who eventually charged the forest and defeated the Wallachians. Both sides took heavy casualties. However, the Turks could not capitalize on their victory, being decimated by ensuing months of starvation and plague.

■ SHKODËR, 1478–1479

Albania had resisted Ottoman control, although Mehmed II determined to change that. Shkodër was besieged and, despite being bombarded continually by gunpowder artillery, hung on for nine months until the Ottomans allowed the citizens to leave.

■ BREADFIELD, 13 OCTOBER 1479

Wanting to repeat the success of his father, János Hunyadi, Hungarian king Matthias Corvinus determined to halt Turkish progress in the Balkans. Mustering a force of Hungarians and other Christian soldiers, he fought a larger Ottoman army. Early on, the Ottomans held sway, but eventually the Hungarians wore them down, causing them to flee. No quarter was given to the Turks, who were pursued and killed.

■ RHODES, 1480

The Knights Hospitaller had held the island of Rhodes, 26km off the coast of Asia Minor, since 1306. Their navy constantly harassed ships coming to or from the Ottoman Turkish ports. Sultan Mehmed II decided finally to put an end to this piracy. On his deathbed, he sent a large expeditionary force to the island in May 1480. They would besiege the fortifications for the next four months, using a large number of gunpowder weapons to bring the Hospitallers to surrender. But, assisted by the townspeople, they did not surrender, resisting attacks on Fort St Nicholas in the harbour and the Jewish quarter on the eastern side. Having suffered heavy casualties, the Turks retreated to the mainland and gave up their siege. It would be another 42 years before Rhodes would be attacked again.

■ OTRANTO 1480–81

A sizeable Ottoman army attacked Otranto, quickly defeating the city and castle. From the city, the Turks made several raids on southern Italy. However, their occupation was brief as Ferrante, King of Sicily, retook Otranto in September 1481.

■ YENIŞEHIR, 1481

Bayezid and Cem, Mehmed II's sons, fought a brief war to succeed him. This first battle was won by Bayezid, but Cem was able to escape and return with Mamluk supporters. He lost again and was sent into exile.

■ KRBAVA FIELD, 9 SEPTEMBER 1493

Pushing into Croatia, Ottoman armies faced little united resistance. Finally, several local lords combined in one army, led by Mirko Derenčin. However, these were inexperienced men fighting very experienced soldiers. Their enthusiasm quickly gave way to defeat.

■ ZONCHIO, 25 AUGUST 1499

For four days, Ottoman and Venetian ships fought in the Ionian Sea. The conflict went back and forth, with Venetian and Ottoman ships changing hands and at least one sunk by gunpowder artillery. Eventually, the Ottomans prevailed.

Wars of Sicily, Sardinia and Italy 1250–1500

■ CINGOLI, 1250

A Sicilian-Guelph invasion of southern Italy by Cardinal Pietro Capoccio was so resoundingly defeated by Imperial-Ghibelline troops that the baggage train – a large stock of papal arms – was captured. Capoccio escaped disguised as a mendicant friar.

■ MONTEBRUNO, 25 FEBRUARY 1255

At Montebruno, the army of one of the Guelph claimants – Thomas II of Savoy, Count of Flanders – was defeated by an army of Ghibelline citizens from Asti and the surrounding regions. Thomas was captured in the battle.

■ MONTAPERTI, 4 SEPTEMBER 1260

One of the largest of the Guelph-Ghibelline battles was fought between Florence and Siena at Montperti, outside the walls of Siena. The Sienese (Ghibellines), even with German heavy cavalry mercenaries, were outnumbered by more experienced Florentines (Guelphs). Both sides launched charges at each other, but the battle was likely decided by an act of treachery, when Florentine Bocca degli Abati, switching sides, caused a rout by the Guelph troops.

■ BENEVENTO, 26 FEBRUARY 1266

The forces of Charles of Anjou and Manfred of Sicily fought the most decisive battle of the Guelph-Ghibelline Wars. Manfred's army was better experienced and armed, although not more numerous, but Charles placed his soldiers in a defensive formation and forced Manfred's troops to cross a bridge before they attacked. Several charges could not break Charles' formation and he eventually gained victory, although with heavy casualties on both sides (including Manfred).

■ TRAPANI, 1266

Venetian-Genoese competition in the eastern Mediterranean resulted in this naval battle. Venetian galleys, numbering 24, led by Jacopo Dandolo, fought with 27 Genoese galleys, led by Lanfranco Borbonino. The Genoese were quickly defeated.

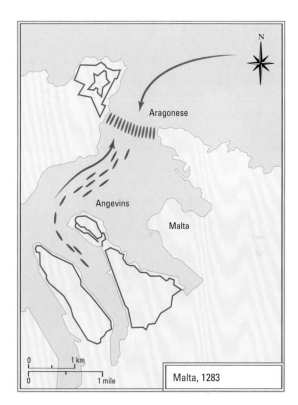

Malta, 1283

DESIO, 21 JANUARY 1277

In 1277 at Desio, control of the very important northern Italian city of Milan was decided between forces of the Visconti and Della Torre families. Interestingly, both families were led by ecclesiastical leaders, Ottone Visconti, Archbishop of Milan, and Raimondo della Torre, Bishop of Como. Visconti soldiers, taking refuge in the walled town of Desio, were attacked by the Della Torres, who eventually forced the gates open, but fell to defeat in fighting among the streets with both sides taking heavy casualties. As a consequence, the Viscontis assumed rule in Milan.

■ MALTA, 8 JULY 1283

During the War of the Sicilian Vespers, an Aragonese fleet, commanded by Roger of Lauria, soundly defeated an Angevin-Napolese fleet, commanded by William Cornut (who was killed), in the harbour mouth of Malta.

■ GULF OF NAPLES, 5 JUNE 1284

Roger of Lauria proved his naval expertise by

attacking the Neapolitan fleet, commanded by Charles II, in their home port. Lauria feigned a retreat, allowing his own galleys to surround and attack the less experienced Neapolitan galleys.

■ Meloria, 6 August 1284

Genoa, competing economically with Pisa, chose to settle matters in a large naval battle, with estimations of Genoese 88 galleys vs 72 Pisan ones. The more experienced Genoese made quick work of the Pisans.

■ Les Formigues (Las Hormigas), 4 September 1285

Fighting at night, Roger of Lauria's expertise and experience led to yet another victory in the War of the Sicilian Vespers. His Aragonese galleys destroyed more than half of the opposing Franco-Genoese galleys.

■ The Counts, 23 June 1287

Roger of Lauria's next victory was near Naples when his 40–45 Aragonese galleys defeated a superior Angevin fleet of 70 galleys. His less experienced opponents were forced to manoeuvre until confused and easily defeated.

■ Campaldino, 11 June 1289

In northern Italy, the larger towns – Florence, Pistoia, Lucca, Siena and Prato in this case – often favoured the pro-papal Guelphs – as they were likely to gain more economic and political sovereignty, while smaller towns – Arezzo – and principalities favoured the pro-imperial Ghibellines. The Guelph army adopted a defensive formation and, although Ghibelline charges pushed their centre formation back, Guelph counter-attacks eventually defeated them, causing huge Ghibelline casualties.

■ Curzota, 1296

In one of the numerous naval battles between Venice and Genoa for control of the Mediterranean Sea, Genoese galleys defeated Venetian ones. Marco Polo, recently returned from China, fought among the Venetians.

■ Curzola, 8 September 1298

A Genoese fleet of 66–75 galleys, led by Lamba Doria, defeated a larger Venetian fleet of 95 galleys, commanded by Andrea Doria, off the coast of Dalmatia. Marco Polo was among those captured by Genoa.

■ Ponza, 14 June 1300

Roger of Lauria continued to win naval battles during the War of the Sicilian Vespers with his – by then – very experienced Aragonese-Angevin galley crews. His fleet, outnumbering an opposing fleet of Sicilian galleys, captured 26 galleys.

■ Montecatini, 29 August 1315

The combined Florentine and Napolese army significantly outnumbered the Pisans. However, the Pisans, commanded by the condottere (mercenary) Uguccione della Faggiuola, outmanoeuvred their opponents, defeating them and causing huge casualties (including members of all Florentine noble families).

■ Zappolino, 15 November 1325

The Ghibellines of Modena faced the Guelphs of Bologna with equal numbers of cavalry, but a significantly smaller number of infantry. Yet the Modenese fought with greater unity and intelligence, more than making up for their numerical inferiority.

■ Parabiago, 20–21 February 1339

Mercenaries (condottieri) were used by everyone in northern Italy during the fourteenth century. When not employed, they often operated as private armies, raiding at will to keep occupied and supplied. At Parabiago, the Milanese decided to put an end to one of these armies. Interestingly, both sides were commanded by Visconti brothers. On the point of collapse, the Milanese rallied and eventually defeated the condottieri, with heavy casualties on both sides.

■ Gamenario, 22 April 1345

A Guelph queen of Naples, Joan I, seemingly pursuing peace, had her armies besieged at the Piedmontese castle of Gamenario. However, Ghibelline forces, under John II, Marquess of Montferrat, soundly defeated them in a battle fought nearby.

■ Porto San Lorenzo, 20 November 1347

Several Roman nobles and their retainers, including Stefano Colonna the Younger, tried to put down

Cola di Rienzo's rebellion by force. Rienzo discovered and defeated this 'army' at the gate of San Lorenzo, with Colonna dying in the melée.

■ **Bosporus, 13 February 1352**

To combat a Byzantine trade monopoly with the Venetians, a Genoese fleet fought a similarly sized Venetian fleet in the Bosporus strait. After a long and bloody battle lasting well into the night, the Venetians withdrew.

■ **Alghero, 25 August 1353**

Using their support of Aragonese claims to Sardinia as provocation for further conflict, a Venetian fleet fought and defeated a Genoese fleet off Alghero, although it had little overall effect on the continual warfare between these Italian states.

■ **Modon, 1354**

Wintering on the island of Sapienza and with two-thirds of their vessels beached, a Venetian fleet, led by Niccolò Pisani, was surprised by a Genoese fleet, led by Paganino Doria, who took most of the ships as prizes.

■ **Cascina, 28 July 1364**

Pisans and Florentines had fought against each other for several centuries, with little territory exchanged over that time. In the most recent engagements, both towns employed large numbers of mercenary forces, with those of Pisa led by the famous *condottieri*, John Hawkwood and Hanneken von Baumgarten.

Recently, they had led Pisan troops to several victories. In response, Florence replaced the ineffective Pandolfo II Malatesta with his cousin, Galeotto, insisting on positive results. The two armies met near Pisa, just outside Cascina, on the hot evening of 28 July 1364. The Florentines had camped and were resting, when Hawkwood and Baumgarten decided to attack their camp. The Florentines were surprised, but fought diligently and regrouped, counter-attacking the Pisans and driving them from the field. Both sides took huge casualties, especially among the Pisan mercenaries. However, Malatesta did not advance on Pisa and thus the city remained outside Florentine control for another 38 years.

■ **Cesena, 1377**

During the War of the Eight Saints, the rebellion of the small town of Cesena against the papacy provoked its recapture by *condottieri* leader John Hawkwood and Robert, Cardinal of Geneva. In retaliation, the cardinal, serving as papal legate for the expedition, supervised a massacre of between 2500 and 5000 citizens as punishment, gaining for himself the name 'The Butcher of Cesena'.

■ **Chioggia, August 1379–June 1380**

The Genoese captured Chiogga in the Venetian lagoon in summer 1379. Outmanoeuvring the Genoese fleet, that of Venice, led by Carlo Zeno, blockaded Chioggia. With no relief, after holding out for several months, the Genoese surrendered.

■ **Castagnaro, 11 March 1387**

John Hawkwood, employed as captain of the Paduan army, lured the Veronese to a field outside Castagnaro. Foolishly, the Veronese attempted to attack the Paduans, appearing to be haphazardly arrayed next to a canal, by crossing a make-shift bridge of fascines. However, when Hawkwood's cavalry charged from the nearby woods, the Veronese were quickly routed, in what must have been one of the shortest battles in medieval history.

■ **Alessandria, 1391**

After losing several battles to the Florentines, mostly against John Hawkwood, a Milanese force under Jacopo dal Verme surprised a French army outside Alessandria. The French, led by Count Jean III of Armagnac, were crushed, with Armagnac himself killed.

■ **Portomaggiore, 16 April 1395**

Azzo X d'Este's dispute with his family over control of Ferrara led to an attempt to capture the city. However, his army of 8000 *condottieri* were soundly defeated by Venetian allies of the Ferrarese and imprisoned.

■ **Casalecchio, 26 June 1402**

In 1402, armies of Bologna and Florence, led by Giovanni I Bentivoglio, were allied against those of Milan, Rimini and Mantua, led by Gian Galeazzo Visconti, Duke of Milan. The war was short-

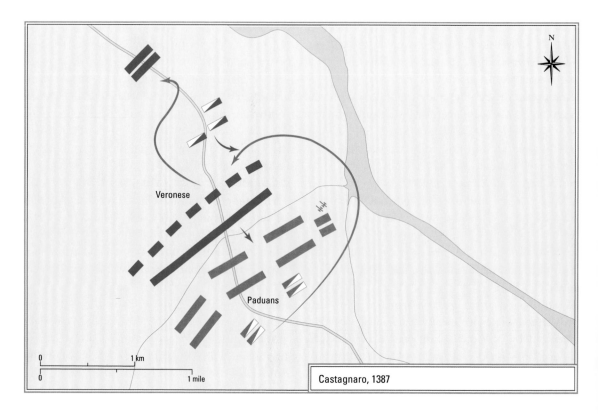

Veronese

Paduans

0   1 km

0   1 mile

Castagnaro, 1387

lived, however, as the Bolognese-Florentines were soundly defeated at Casalecchio.

■ SANLURI, 30 JUNE 1409

Fighting for the island of Sardinia, a smaller Spanish-Sicilian army of King Martin I of Sicily defeated an army largely of Franco-Italian mercenaries. However, Martin was unable to profit from this victory as he died shortly afterwards.

■ ARBEDO, 30 JUNE 1422

Milan's defence relied on the control of fortifications along the alpine passes. The Swiss cantons of Uri and Unterwalden bought the well-fortified town of Bellinzona, but then refused to resell it to the Milanese, who tried taking it by force. The Swiss chose to fight, initially stopping the Milanese cavalry, but could not sustain their efforts and were virtually annihilated.

■ L'AQUILA, 1424

Braccio da Montone, leading a Neapolitan army, had laid siege to l'Aquila for 13 years when a

force of Angevins, under Muzio Attendolo and Francesco Sforza, came to relieve the city, defeating the Napolese and killing Braccio.

■ ZAGONARA, 28 JULY 1424

Florence and Milan hired numerous *condottieri* to fight several wars in Lombardy. Attempting to raise the Milanese siege of Zagonara, laid by Angelo della Pergola, a Florentine force, led by Carlo I Malatesta, fought a lengthy battle and were ultimately defeated.

■ SONCINO, MARCH 1431

The first of two battles between the Milanese and Venetians in 1431, this one on land. Francesco I Sforza led the Milanese in a surprise attack of the Venetians, capturing more than 2000 men.

■ PAVIA (BATTLE OF THE PO), 6 JUNE 1431

A riverine battle between galley fleets from Venice, trying to aid their recently defeated army and Milan. After a lengthy conflict, the larger Milanese fleet defeated the Venetians, who suffered heavy losses in men and galleys.

■ SAN ROMANO, 1 JUNE 1432

The Chianti region had been fought over by Florence and Siena for centuries. However, the battle near Florence is most famous because it was memorialized in Paolo Uccelo's famous painting. The Florentines, led by Niccolò da Tolentino, met the invading Sienese, led by Francesco Piccinino. The battle, by similarly sized forces, lasted more than six hours and ended with no definitive result, although the Sienese returned to Siena.

■ DELEBIO, 18–19 NOVEMBER 1432

Late in 1431 Venice invaded the Valtelina. In November 1432, the duke of Milan, Filippo Maria Visconti, took a small army into the region, fighting two battles near Delebio, both of which losses by Venice.

■ PONZA, 5 AUGUST 1435

Fighting for control of the western Mediterranean, a Genoese fleet defeated an Aragonese one, capturing the future king of Aragon, Alfonso V and his brother Juan II. It was later memorialized by the poet Iñigo López de Mendoza.

■ ANGHIARI, 29 JUNE 1440

Filippo Maria Visconti, Duke of Milan, had so infuriated other Italian states that an Italian League of the Republics of Venice and Florence and the Papal States joined against him. The League attacked Anghiari and won, despite the Milanese outnumbering them.

■ CARAVAGGIO, 15 SEPTEMBER 1448

Although the Italian League fell apart, Venice remained at war with Milan. Both fielded armies of *condottieri*. The Milanese, a republic for only a brief time, were led by Francesco Sforza, later Duke of Milan, who defeated the Venetians.

■ SARNO, 1460

The fight to claim Naples between the Angevins and Aragonese took an Angevin turn when they ambushed an army led by King Ferdinand I. He escaped utter defeat and capture only when relieved by a nearby garrison.

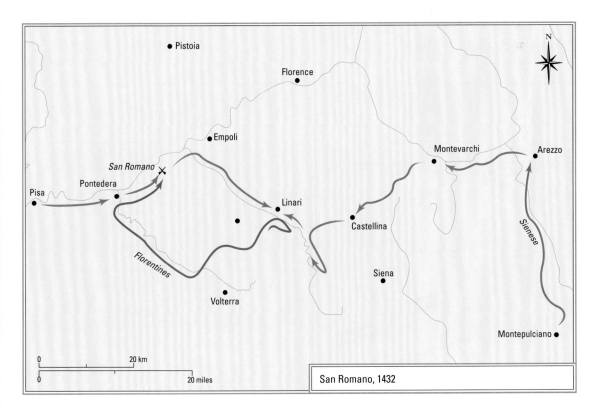

San Romano, 1432

■ **MOLINELLA, 25 JULY 1467**

Venice and Florence fought again in 1467. The battle was fought along the Idice river, near the village of Molinella. The armies were equal in numbers and technology, including artillery, but ended essentially without a clear victor. The Venetian general, *condottiere* Bartolomeo Colleoni, decided not to advance on Milan.

■ **MACOMER, 14 MAY 1478**

The Aragonese finally conquered Sardinia when they faced Leonardo Alagon, Marquis of Oristano. The local militias, a large part of the Sardinian force, could not compete against the more professional Aragonese and were soundly defeated.

■ **CAMPOMORTO, 21 AUGUST 1482**

In an early battle of the War of Ferrara, fought between the Papal States and Ferrara (with many allies on both sides), the papal army, led by Roberto Malatesta, defeated a Neapolitan force, led by Alfonso, Duke of Calabria.

Monarchic, Imperial and Noble Wars of Western Europe 1250–1500

■ **TAGLIACOZZO, 23 AUGUST 1268**

The Ghibelline Conrad V (Conradin) challenged the Guelph Charles of Anjou for the Sicilian crown. The Ghibellines had seemingly won the battle, before the Guelphs lured them into a trap and chased them from the field.

■ **ROCCAVIONE, 12 DECEMBER 1275**

Charles of Anjou's Guelph army was defeated by northern Italian Ghibellines. Numbers, experience and technology being equal, it is likely that the Ghibellines choosing the field and using defensive tactics was what won the battle in their favour.

■ **MARCHFELD, 26 AUGUST 1278**

Trying to exert his claim to the Holy Roman Empire, Ottokar II, King of Bohemia, campaigned in the Austrian lands of Emperor Rudolph I, with the two eventually meeting at the battle of Marchfeld. After a gruelling summer battle

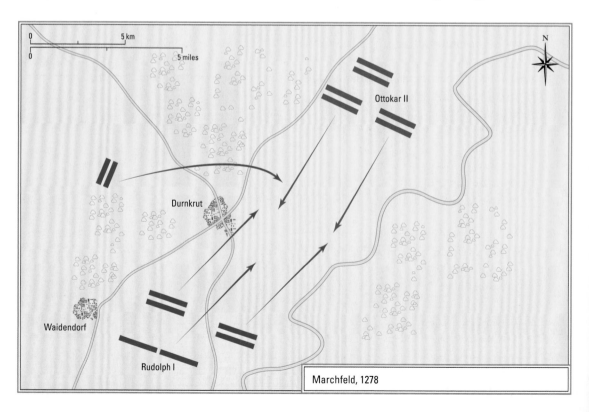

Marchfeld, 1278

between heavy knights, which essentially ended in a draw, Rudolph's concealed reinforcements attacked Ottokar's flank and drove the Bohemians from the field, although without Ottokar, who had been slain.

■ WORRINGEN, 5 JUNE 1288
A German army of Heinrich VI, count of Luxembourg and Siegfried II, Archbishop of Cologne, attacked the Brabantese besiegers of Worringen, led by Duke Jan I. The Brabantese won after killing Heinrich and capturing Siegfried.

■ FURNES, 20 AUGUST 1297
Guy de Dampierre, Count of Flanders, fought a French force led by Robert II of Artois. The French trounced the Flemings, although both armies were similar in size, type and technology. Guy was captured and imprisoned.

■ GOLDEN SPURS (COURTRAI), 11 JULY 1302
Flemish townspeople rose against French political and economic rule by massacring a garrison of soldiers in Bruges. Following this, the Flemings besieged Courtrai castle, while the French army marched north. The Flemings dug ditches on the battlefield – some filling them with water from the Lys river – and ordered their forces in solid lines behind them. Several French cavalry charges were repulsed, with many knights killed, before the French fled, giving the Flemings victory.

■ MONS-EN-PÉVÈLE, 18 AUGUST 1304
The Flemish army faced a large French army, fighting an unusually long battle that ended with neither side controlling the battlefield. However, with their leader, Willem von Jülich, slain, the Flemings withdrew.

■ GAMMELSDORF, 9 NOVEMBER 1313
Gammelsdorf was fought between two cousins claiming the German throne: Frederick I, Duke of Austria and Louis, Duke of Bavaria. Louis' soldiers, mostly Bavarian militia, defeated the Austrians more numerous and largely cavalry force.

■ MORGARTEN, 15 NOVEMBER 1315
In Morgarten Pass, Austrian Duke Leopold I, with a largely cavalry army of 2000–3000, was ambushed by 3000–4000 Swiss peasants, who shot

arrows at and rolled stones and logs onto them. The Austrians fled, taking huge casualties.

■ CASSEL, 23 AUGUST 1328
The county of Flanders rebelled against France in 1323, although the French did not respond until 1328. At that time, a large army, led by recently crowned Philip VI, surrounded an equally large Flemish force positioned in Cassel, on a hill 176m high. After several days, the Flemish soldiers attacked the French camp, nearly capturing the king. However, a French response routed the rebels, who suffered huge losses.

■ CHAMPTOCEAUX, 14–16 OCTOBER 1341
In the first large conflict of the Breton Civil War, Charles of Blois, allied to the French, besieged Champtoceaux from 10 October to 26 October. John of Montfort, allied to the English, attempted to relieve the siege but, despite coming close to capturing Charles at one point, he failed to do so and retreated, leading to the fall of the town and a shift in the war to Charles.

■ STAVEREN, 26 SEPTEMBER 1345
To subdue Frisian rebels, armies of William IV, Count of Holland, Hainaut and Zeeland, landed on the beach near Staveren, where the local forces, fighting tenaciously from trenches with pikes, spears and swords, defeated them.

■ BAESWEILER, 22 AUGUST 1371
Wenceslas, Duke of Brabant, led an army into Jülich to punish Duke William VI for not protecting travelling merchants. The Jülich army outnumbered the Brabantese, who were in disarray from the outset and defeated them fairly quickly.

■ SEMPACH, 9 JULY 1386
In an effort to regain some of the lands and control lost by the Austrians over the previous 75 years, as well as to counter recent raids into their lands, Duke Leopold III invaded Switzerland in 1386. Their opponents were an alliance of cantons, the Old Swiss Confederacy, principally Lucerne, Uri, Schwyz and Unterwalden. Leopold's army outnumbered the Swiss, and included a large number of heavy cavalry. Initially, the Austrians were successful, but, during a battle fought on

9 July 1386 outside the town of Sempach, the Swiss duplicated the results of their ancestors. Learning from past mistakes of fighting against the unconventional Swiss, the Austrians dismounted their cavalry, but they were unaccustomed to fighting in this way and were hindered by their heavier and hotter armour. The Swiss simply outlasted them. Among the dead was Leopold and a number of his greater nobles.

■ BILEĆA, 27 AUGUST 1388
The Ottoman Turks seemed unstoppable as they invaded south-eastern Europe. Only rarely did they face setbacks. One was when a Bosnian army defeated an Ottoman force outside of the town of Bileća.

■ OTHÉE, 23 SEPTEMBER 1408
Following an ineffectual artillery duel, the Burgundians, led by Count John the Fearless, quickly defeated the rebelling Liégeois by charging into their lines and, with a small force, circling around and attacking from the rear.

■ LA ROCHELLE, 1419
A Castilian fleet allied to the French was intercepted by an English fleet off the coast of La Rochelle. The Castilians won, but could not keep the English from controlling the Channel.

■ BRUSTEM, 28 OCTOBER 1467
The Liégeois, inexperienced in fighting battles, gathered an army and met the Burgundians, led by Charles the Bold, at Brustem, where they were soundly defeated. Charles then besieged and sacked Liège, ending their rebellion.

■ NEUSS, 29 JULY 1474–27 JUNE 1475
Assisting the Archbishop of Cologne, Charles the Bold laid siege to Neuss. The Burgundians possessed a large gunpowder artillery train and the walls held for nearly a year until a German army defeated the fatigued Burgundians.

■ NANCY, 5 JANUARY 1477
Following defeats against the Swiss at Grandson and Murten the previous year, Charles the Bold, Duke of Burgundy, gathered what forces and artillery he had left to meet the rebellion of Lorraine at Nancy on 5 January 1477. Heavily outnumbered by their opponents, the Burgundians were defeated by infantry forces; Charles was among those killed.

■ COSMIN FOREST (CODRII), 26 OCTOBER 1497
John I, King of Poland, and Ştefan cel Mare, Prince of Moldavia, decided a border dispute in the Cosmin Forest. Surprising the Poles, the Moldavians fought for three days until forcing them out of Moldavia.

The Iberian Peninsular and Balearic Islands 1250–1500

■ HALMYROS, 15 MARCH 1311
Walter V of Brienne, the Frankish duke of Athens, dismissed the mercenary Catalan Company without settling its arrears of pay. The Catalan's 2000 cavalry and 4000 infantry deployed on the plain of Orchomenus, near the Cephissus river, flooding the fields in front of their position. Walter launched a frontal attack with his 6000 cavalry and 8000 infantry, which bogged down in the swampy ground and was decisively defeated by the lightly equipped mercenaries.

■ MANOLADA, 5 JULY 1316
This action was fought by armies led by Louis of Burgundy and the Infante Ferdinand of Majorca, both of whom claimed the Principality of Achaea on behalf of their wives. Ferdinand's defeat ensured continued Angevin supremacy in Achaea.

■ RIO SALADA, 30 OCTOBER 1340
The sultans of Morocco and Granada besieged Tarifa with an 80,000-strong army. Alfonso XI of Castile and Alfonso IV of Portugal led a relief force of 12,000 infantry and 9000 cavalry, which decisively defeated the besiegers.

■ LLUCMAJOR, 25 OCTOBER 1349
In 1344, James III of Majorca was driven into exile by his cousin Peter IV of Aragon and was killed in the battle of Llucmajor on 25 October 1349, while trying to retake Majorca.

■ NÁJERA, 3 APRIL 1367
An Anglo-Gascon army of 24,000 men commanded by Edward, the Black Prince, intervened in the Castilian civil war in support

of Pedro the Cruel against his half-brother Henry II of Castile. The Black Prince's force (including 12,000 archers) was reinforced by 4000 Castilians led by Pedro and attacked Henry's 60,000-strong army near Nájera. English archery inflicted heavy casualties before Henry's force was routed with the loss of at least 5000 men.

■ MONTIEL, 14 MARCH 1369
Pedro the Cruel's 40,000-strong army was routed by a force of 6000 men under Henry II of Castile. Pedro's forces suffered at least 14,000 casualties and he was killed by Henry while trying to escape.

■ ATOLEIROS, 6 APRIL 1384
A Portuguese force of 1400 men under Dom Nuno Álvares Pereira intercepted a 5000-strong Castilian army besieging Fronteira. The Portuguese formed a defensive square that repelled several attacks before the demoralized Castilian army was routed.

■ TRANCOSO, 29 MAY 1385
A 600-strong Castilian raiding party was caught by

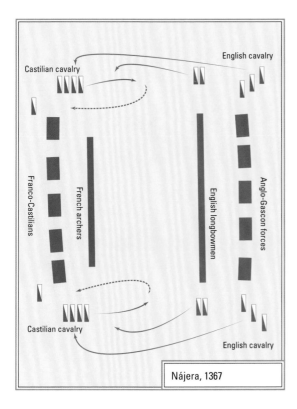

Nájera, 1367

a Portuguese force of 300 men, which dismounted and deployed in ploughed fields. The Castilians fled after making several charges that were beaten off with heavy losses.

■ ALJUBARROTA, 29 MAY 1385
Juan I of Castile invaded Portugal with an army of 8000 cavalry and 10,000 infantry. João I commanded the Portuguese field army of 2500 cavalry and 12,000 infantry (including 700 English archers), which intercepted the Castilians near the abbey of Aljubarrota.

The Portuguese took up a strong defensive position among orchards, cutting brushwood barricades to cover their flanks and digging a trench in front of their main line. Their crossbowmen and the English archers deployed on each flank with the dismounted knights and men-at-arms in the centre.

The Castilian nobles pressured a reluctant Juan into ordering a frontal attack, despite the fact that his army was exhausted after several hours march. Juan advanced in three lines, the first comprising French mercenaries, the second formed by his Castilian cavalry and the third containing crossbowmen and other infantry. The French cavalry dismounted and attacked before the rest of the Castilian army could come up to support their assault. They took heavy losses from archery and crossbow fire as the attack was funneled into the gap in the barricades in the centre of the Portuguese line. This attack was repelled with French losses of several hundred dead and 1000 captured, but Juan failed to realize the extent of the defeat and committed his cavalry to a charge, which lost impetus in crossing the trench and was also badly shot up by archery and crossbow fire. Unsurprisingly, the cavalry were defeated by the Portuguese knights and men-at-arms, suffering at least 500 casualties before breaking in rout. Juan escaped, but his army was shattered, losing 6000 dead and 2000 prisoners. Apart from Juan, virtually all the Castilian commanders were captured.

■ CEUTA, 1415
In August 1415, a 45,000-strong Portuguese army commanded by King João I surprised and stormed

the Moroccan city of Ceuta. João's son, Prince Henry the Navigator, distinguished himself in the assault on the city.

■ **ALFARROBEIRA, 20 MAY 1449**

Rivalries within the Portuguese royal family briefly flared up into civil war in 1449, when an army of 30,000 men commanded by King Alfonso V defeated a 6000-strong rebel force under Pedro, Duke of Coimbra.

Wars of Scotland 1263–1500

■ **LARGS, 2 OCTOBER 1263**

Hakon IV of Norway with a fleet of more than 100 ships invaded Scotland to claim the Hebrides; they also raided the Scottish mainland coast. To counter the threat, Alexander III of Scotland called up local militias as well as knights and their retainers. A Scottish force numbering perhaps 500 met a large Norse raiding force (800–900) at Largs in early October and drove them off in confused fighting.

■ **DUNBAR, 27 APRIL 1296**

The English under Earl Warenne attacked Dunbar castle. Relieving Scots arrived on 27 April, but mistook Warenne's manoeuvring for retreat and advanced in disorder. An English cavalry charge routed the Scots with heavy slaughter.

■ **LANARK, MAY 1297**

In a minor incident, the Scot William Wallace and his supporters attacked the English sheriff of Lanark in May 1297, killing him and burning several buildings. Lanark ignited the Scottish revolt against England.

■ **STIRLING BRIDGE, 11 SEPTEMBER 1297**

In early September, an English army under Earl Warenne entered Scotland to suppress a growing rebellion. William Wallace and Andrew Murray joined forces to oppose him with numbers of perhaps 3000–4000 men. They took position around Abbey Craig to protect strategically vital Stirling Bridge. Warenne, with an army perhaps twice as large, attacked northward across the bridge on 11 September, after losing the element

of surprise by oversleeping. The English vanguard crossed the narrow bridge two abreast. As they formed on the north side, the Scots attacked. The ground was waterlogged, so English cavalry could not manoeuvre and infantry became mired. Warenne tried to send reinforcements, but the bridge collapsed, either by sabotage or the sheer weight of men. Most of the English caught on the north bank were slaughtered, perhaps totalling 500, with a few dozen Scots casualties.

■ **FALKIRK, 22 JULY 1298**

Edward I responded to William Wallace's great raid of northern England with a massive invasion of Scotland to suppress the rebellion. The English army initially mustered 3000 cavalry and 25,000 English and Welsh foot, although numbers were smaller at the battle, as Edward suffered supply problems and a Welsh mutiny. Indeed, Edward considered retreat, but the Scots under William Wallace offered battle. Wallace's force was smaller than Edward's, perhaps 6000 pikemen,

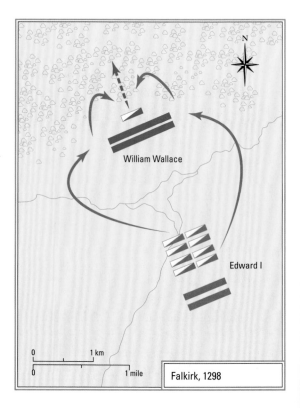

Falkirk, 1298

1000 archers and 500 cavalry, but he prepared a strongly defensive position on the road to Stirling. Four divisions of Scottish infantry formed into schiltrons, tightly packed ranks of pikemen brandishing 3.6m spears, protected by a line of stakes roped or chained together. Archers were placed between the schiltrons to protect the lightly armoured pikemen from English bowmen, while the Scots cavalry in turn protected the archers. The Scots were further defended by woods and marshes on the flanks and by a stream in front.

The battle on 22 July was bloody. The first English attack by heavy cavalry became mired in the wet ground and failed to penetrate the schiltrons, but the Scots horse fled as the English advanced on the right flank. The English cavalry was then able to ride down the unprotected Scots archers, leaving the schiltrons exposed to Edward's archers and Gascon crossbowmen. The men of the schiltrons – untried militia – held their ground, but they were unable to advance over the wet ground to meet the enemy, and fell in their hundreds. Finally, Edward sent his cavalry back in to break the schiltrons. Thousands of Scots were killed, with relatively light English casualties and the Scottish rebel army was effectively destroyed.

■ Stirling Castle I, 1299
Stirlingshire rebels led by Thomas Morham and Gilbert Malherbe besieged strategically vital Stirling castle, held by an English garrison. The Scots lacked siege equipment, but eventually starved the garrison into submission.

■ Stirling Castle II, 20 July 1304
Edward I of England besieged strategically vital Stirling. Heavy English trebuchets killed many and damaged the walls. The Scots 'rebels' finally surrendered on 24 July for fear of the massive trebuchet 'Warwolf'.

■ Methven, 19 June 1306
King Robert the Bruce advanced against English-held Perth. On 19 June, a force of 300 cavalry and 1300 infantry under the Englishman Aymer de Valence surprised and totally defeated the Scots; Robert fled.

■ Loudon Hill, 10 May 1307
Robert the Bruce of Scotland's first victory. Robert, with 600 Scots spearmen, chose his ground carefully, protecting his force with a bog and series of ditches. Aymer de Valence's English force numbered about 3000, but they had to advance with a tightly restricted front along the highway. Scottish spearmen pushed downhill into the disordered English ranks. A panic ensued and at least one hundred Englishmen were killed.

■ Bannockburn, 24 June 1314
Edward II of England invaded Scotland to suppress Robert the Bruce's rebellion. The English force numbered perhaps 10,000 infantry and 2000 cavalry; the Scots force was 5000–6000, mostly highly experienced light infantry. Robert deployed his Scots to keep the English from relieving Stirling castle. On 23 June, the English cavalry vanguard tried to slip between the Scots and Stirling castle, but a Scottish division under Thomas Randolph, Earl of Moray, drove them back in heavy fighting.

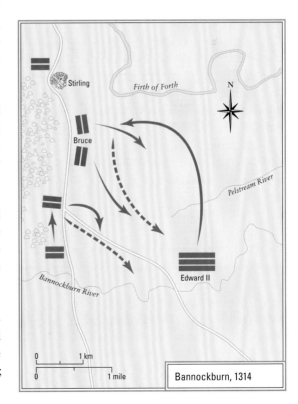

Bannockburn, 1314

The engagement disheartened the English, whose supplies had also failed and led them to expect a night attack.

King Robert had intended a defensive battle. The Scots had dug in on high ground, protected by pits, traps and caltrops. However, seeing the English in disorder, he ordered his schiltrons to advance onto the marshy plain on 24 June. Four Scottish schiltrons advanced in turn, striking a series of hammer blows against the English, who could not deploy along a front that was highly restricted, being trapped between a river, a number of streams and the Scots. The English and Welsh archers could not be placed properly to cut down the lightly armoured Scots; one group worked around a stream and began firing against the Scots, only to be ridden down by Scots cavalry. The English tried to stop the Scottish advance with isolated attacks, but failed.

King Edward's household finally forced him to withdraw. As the English force wavered, the Scottish 'small folk' charged from the high ground and precipitated an English rout. The bulk of the English army was killed or captured, hundreds drowning in the Forth or in the many streams like the Bannockburn that surrounded the battlefield.

■ FAUGHART, 14 OCTOBER 1318
Edward Bruce, Robert the Bruce's brother, invaded Ireland. On 14 October, Bruce's Scots-Irish army attacked a stronger Hiberno-Norman force and the three Scottish divisions were each defeated separately. Bruce himself was killed.

■ MYTON, 20 SEPTEMBER 1319
Archbishop Melton of York raised local levies to stop Scottish raiders. On 12 September, they attacked the Scottish camp. Scottish spearmen advanced and the English were disastrously defeated; many clerics fell in the rout.

■ BOROUGHBRIDGE, 16 MARCH 1322
English troops under Andrew Harclay held the bridge against rebellious Earl Thomas of Lancaster with archers supported by dismounted men-at-arms, preventing Lancaster from joining a Scottish force on 16 March. Lancaster was captured and executed.

■ INVASION OF SCOTLAND, 1332
Robert Bruce's death inspired Scottish exiles in England and France to return. The Disinherited, under Edward Balliol, landed at Kinghorn with an 88-ship fleet on 6 August, driving off local forces. Their army of about 1500 defeated young King David II at Dupplin Moor, then took Perth and won a naval battle on the Tay. Balliol was crowned king, but was forced to flee by a surprise attack in December.

■ DUPPLIN MOOR, 10–11 AUGUST 1332
Edward Balliol's 1500-man force defeated a superior Scottish royal army under the earl of Mar, storming Mar's camp and occupying the high ground. Many suffocated in the melee. About 2000 royalists fell.

■ DORNOCK, 25 MARCH 1333
In a small border incident, William Douglas with 50 men set on an English force of 800. Two Englishmen were killed as well as 24 Scots and William Douglas was captured and imprisoned.

■ HALIDON HILL, 19 JULY 1333
In the second Anglo-Scottish War, Edward III of England with his ally Edward Balliol besieged Berwick. Archibald Douglas, guardian of the young David II, marched with a large army to relieve the siege. The English chose their ground on Halidon Hill, Edward dismounting his men-at-arms and placing them in three divisions, each flanked by archers; his army numbered perhaps 8000. On 19 July, Douglas attacked uphill with about 1200 men-at-arms and 13,500 spearmen arrayed in four schiltrons. Slowed by the bogs at the base of the hill, the Scots were cut down by the English archers, then as the attack wavered, the English cavalry mounted and charged. They pursued the broken Scots for five miles. Douglas, five earls and thousands more Scots fell. Berwick surrendered to Edward and Balliol was restored as king of Scotland.

■ BOROUGHMUIR, 30 JULY 1335
Guy of Namur with 300 men marched to join

Edward III on 30 July, but was ambushed by Scots under John Randolph. Namur retreated into derelict Edinburgh Castle, but surrendered the next day.

■ CULBLEAN, 30 NOVEMBER 1335

In the Second Anglo-Scottish War, David Strathbogie besieged Andrew Murrey's wife in Kildrummy castle. On 30 November, Murrey, with 1000 men, defeated and killed Strathbogie in a surprise attack, scattering his larger force.

■ NEVILLE'S CROSS, 17 OCTOBER 1346

David II of Scotland invaded England with about 10,000 men. On 17 October, he stumbled on a northern English army of about 5000. The Scots advanced in schiltrons over rough ground, suffering heavy losses to archers. The Scottish right pushed the English back, but were thrown into disorder by a cavalry attack. The Scottish rearguard then withdrew, sealing David's defeat. Several thousand Scots, as well as hundreds of Englishmen, died in the battle.

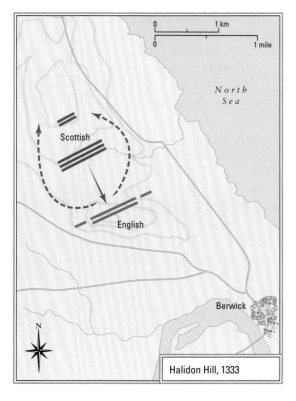

Halidon Hill, 1333

■ OTTERBURN, 5 AUGUST 1388

Hotspur (Henry Percy) raised an English force to pursue Scots raiders. Reaching them at twilight, he attacked the Scottish camp immediately. After heavy and confused fighting, Hotspur was captured and about 2000 English died.

■ NORTH INCH, SEPTEMBER 1396

This 'Battle of the Clans' was a staged battle between two Scottish highland clans. Thirty men from each side fought. Clan Chattan won with 11 survivors; 29 of the Camerons were killed.

■ NESBIT MOOR, 1402

A party of 400 Scottish raiders in Northumberland was ambushed by 200 Englishmen from the Berwick garrison under the earl of March. The Scots were badly cut up; several leaders were captured.

■ HOMILDON HILL, 14 SEPTEMBER 1402

A Scottish raiding force of perhaps 10,000 found their route blocked by an English army. The Scots took a defensive position, but were mowed down by archery. At least 1200 Scots died.

■ TUITEAM TARBHACH, 1406

A Scottish clan battle, in which Clan Mackay caught up with MacLeods of Lewis who had just raided their lands as the latter crossed Tuiteam Burn. The raiding party was completely destroyed

■ HARLAW, 24 JULY 1411

A bloody battle between Donald, Lord of the Isles and the Earl of Mar, whose force was smaller, but better armed. In the day-long struggle, Donald lost 900 men and Mar 500, with no clear victor.

■ INVERLOCHY, SEPTEMBER 1431

James I tried to assert his authority over the Highland clans, imprisoning Alexander, Lord of the Isles. In September, a force of Highlanders under Donald Balloch ambushed the army James I sent against them under the earl of Mar, with bowmen firing down on their camp while the Highlanders charged from the south. More than 1000 royalists are believed to have been killed in the encounter, with only 30 Highland losses.

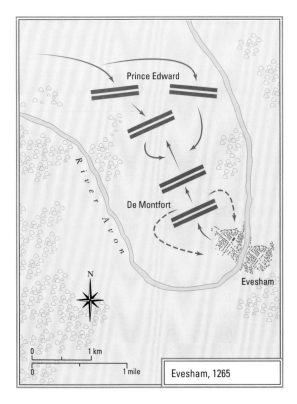

Prince Edward

River Avon

De Montfort

N

Evesham

0   1 km

0   1 mile

Evesham, 1265

■ **PIPERDEAN, 10 SEPTEMBER 1436**
About 4000 English soldiers under Henry Percy and the Earl of Mar moved against Dunbar castle, but Scots under William Douglas attacked them. The English were routed; perhaps 400 were killed and 300 captured.

■ **SARK, 23 OCTOBER 1448**
The Earl of Northumberland invaded Scotland with 6000 men. A total of 4000 Scots under the Earl of Ormond attacked the English camp, driving them into the rising tide at their back. Approximately 1500 English were killed, with another 500 drowned.

■ **ARKINHOLM, 1 MAY 1455**
This small engagement, fought on 1 May, ended the Scottish Civil War between James II and the Black Douglases. Royalist forces, perhaps under the earl of Angus, decisively defeated the rebels.

■ **LOCHMABEN FAIR, 22 JULY 1484**
Scots rebels Albany and Douglas came to Lochmaben Fair on 22 July with 500 English

cavalry to incite rebellion against James III. Townsmen took arms against the rebels, routing them and capturing Douglas.

■ **SAUCHIEBURN, 11 JUNE 1488**
On 11 June, as many as 30,000 troops under James III met a Scottish rebel army of 18,000 under Prince James at Sauchieburn. Details of the battle are confused. The rebels won and James III was killed.

■ **DRUMCHATT, 1497**
After James IV of Scotland revoked the MacDonald title 'Lord of the Isles' in 1495, Alexander MacDonald rebelled, claiming his traditional family lands. Clans Mackenzie and Munro, although normally rivals, joined forces against MacDonald as he invaded Ross. After a short battle at Drumchatt ('the Cat's Back') near Strathpeffer, MacDonald fled. He was hunted down and soon killed.

Second Barons' War, England 1264–67

■ **NORTHAMPTON, APRIL 1264**
A royalist army commanded by Henry III besieged Northampton, which was held by two of Simon de Montfort's sons. A royalist detachment led by Prince Edward broke into the town and forced the surrender of the castle.

■ **ROCHESTER, 1264**
Rebel forces commanded by Simon de Montfort and Gilbert de Clare took Rochester, but the castle held out for a week until the siege was raised by a relief force led by Henry III.

■ **LEWES, 14 MAY 1264**
A 5000-strong rebel army led by Simon de Montfort surprised a royalist army of 10,000 men commanded by Henry III and Prince Edward. De Monfort deployed his forces in three divisions, the right under his sons Henry and Guy, the centre led by Gilbert de Clare and the left of Londoners. Prince Edward's cavalry broke the Londoners, but then pursued them for several hours, during which time the rebels had defeated the main royalist army.

■ **EVESHAM, 4 AUGUST 1265**

A royalist army of at least 7000 infantry and 1000 cavalry commanded by Prince Edward trapped Simon de Montfort's 5000-strong rebel force in a loop of the River Avon near Evesham. De Montfort attempted to break the centre of the royalist line, but his Welsh troops deserted and the remainder of his force was quickly surrounded. The rebel army was shattered, losing 3000 men, including de Montfort who was killed in action.

■ **SIEGE OF AXHOLME, 1265**

After their defeat at Evesham, many rebels fled to the Isle of Axholme in the Lincolnshire Fens where they were besieged by royalist forces. Some eventually surrendered, but de Montfort's son, Simon the Younger, escaped.

■ **CHESTERFIELD, 1266**

Despite the royalist victory at Evesham, the Earl of Derby and other barons continued their resistance to Henry III, but were again defeated at Chesterfield. Some of the survivors then took refuge at Ely in the Fens.

■ **KENILWORTH, JUNE–DECEMBER 1266**

Undismayed by repeated royalist victories, a rebel garrison of 1200 men held Kenilworth castle against a six-month siege. Attempts to storm the castle failed, but the garrison was finally starved into surrender on 13 December 1266.

■ **ELY, 1267**

Prince Edward defeated rebel forces under John d' Eyvill, which were holding out on the Isle of Ely in the fens of Cambridgeshire. This royalist victory marked the end of the Second Barons' War.

Japanese Genko War 1331–33 and Fourteenth-Century Battles

■ **KASAGI, 1331**

Emperor Go-Daigo sought to wrest power back from a weak shogunate, taking refuge here while he sought alliances with warrior-monasteries. Bakufu troops stormed the temple and dragged the emperor into exile.

■ **AKASAKA, C. 31 OCT–20 NOV 1331**

Kusunoki Masashige, Go-Daigo's samurai, brilliantly held this flimsy fortress against Bakufu troops. With supplies and defenders exhausted, a fake funeral pyre convinced the besieging troops that the escaping clan had committed suicide in defeat.

■ **CHIHAYA, 1333**

With Go-Daigo returning from exile, Kusunoki Masashige successfully defended this impregnable hill-top fortress, inflicting by ruses extremely heavy casualties upon Bakufu attackers and resisting all assaults. Loyalist forces flocked to the emperor's cause as a result.

■ **BUBAIGAWARA, 1333**

Nitta Yoshisada proclaimed Go-Daigo's cause and marched against the Bakufu. Here Yoshisada had to retreat after attacking recently reinforced Bakufu troops, who – on the next day – found the Imperialist forces reinforced and, retreating, attacked from the rear.

■ **KAMAKURA, 1333**

Taking severe losses through defended narrows, Nitta Yoshisada ground toward this, the Hojo shogun's last bastion. Forces depleted by battle and the Chihaya siege, the shogun committed suicide after Yoshisada attacked across neighbouring tide flats.

■ **MINATOGAWA, 1336**

Ashikaga Takauji made his family's bid for the Shogunate, attacking here after an initial repulse. Having urged Emperor Go-Daigo's retreat in vain, Kusonoki Masushige and Nitta Yoshisda fought Takuji's landing. Masushige committed suicide in defeat.

■ **KANEGASAKI, 1337**

Nitta Yoshisda was left as Emperor Go-Daigo's last loyal general and concentrated his family's resources at this strategic fortress on Tsuruga Bay, in which he sheltered Prince Takayoshi. The army of Ashikaga Takauji closely besieged the castle, which fell after the defenders had been reduced to eating their horses and the dead. Nitta himself escaped, but his son, the prince and most of his family committed suicide upon the surrender.

Hundred Years War 1337–1457

■ CADSAND, NOVEMBER 1337

As a show of strength against France, Edward III of England sent a small fleet against the Flemish island of Cadsand. The troops, led by Walter Manny, raped and slaughtered the villagers.

■ ARNEMUIDEN, 23 SEPTEMBER 1338

In the first naval battle using artillery, a French fleet of 48 galleys overwhelmed five English carracks transporting a cargo of wool. The Englishmen who survived the battle were massacred, numbering about 1000 in total.

■ SLUYS, 24 JUNE 1340

Edward III invaded Flanders with a fleet of 120–160 ships. A French fleet opposed his landing, taking station at the opening of the Zwin estuary, then about 5km wide. The French admirals arrayed their 213 vessels in three lines, the ships of each line chained to their neighbours. As the English approached, the French fleet drifted eastward,

Sluys, 1340

as wind blew into the mouth of the river. They cast off their chains, but failed to re-form before the English hit their first line. It was a battle of archery, then grappling and boarding. The English ships were full of longbowmen intended for the invasion of France; they vastly outshot the Genoese crossbowmen in French employ. As evening fell, Flemings attacked the French third line from the rear. In an overwhelming victory, Edward captured 190 French ships and 16,000–18,000 Frenchmen died.

■ SAINT-OMER, 26 JULY 1340

Robert of Artois led 1000 English archers and 10,000–15,000 Flemings to attack Saint-Omer, which the Duke of Burgundy held with several thousand men. Robert offered battle and eventually some of the duke's men burst out and attacked. Robert's men were driven off and their camp breached, where many thousands were slaughtered. Meanwhile, the Duke of Burgundy emerged and Robert overwhelmed him, with the battle ending in stalemate.

■ BREST, 18 AUGUST 1342

The Earl of Northampton reached France with a fleet of 260 ships, but only a small land army. They caught by surprise 14 Genoese galleys anchored at Brest. Three of the galleys made it up the estuary of the Elorn river; the other 11 grounded in mud and were burned by the English. The French raised the siege of Brest and withdrew, thinking that a large army had come.

■ MORLAIX, 30 SEPTEMBER 1342

The Earl of Northampton with about 2400 Englishmen and an unknown number of Bretons attacked the French port town of Morlaix; after an initial assault on 3 September failed with heavy casualties, the earl settled down to a siege. Charles of Blois came to relieve the siege with perhaps 3000 cavalry, 1500 Genoese crossbowmen and some Breton infantry. Northampton received word of Charles' approach and made a night march with most of his men, digging in to block the French line of advance. The English protected themselves with pit-traps and trenches. The first French

Hundred Years War, 1337–1457

North Sea

ATLANTIC OCEAN

English Channel

ENGLAND

London

BRABANT

Sluys ✕ *1340*
Bruges
Antwerp
Ghent
Brussels
FLANDERS
Calais
Lille
Liège
Tournai
ARTOIS
Agincourt ✕ *1415*
Namur
1346 ✕ Crécy
Arras
HAINAULT
Abbeville
Cambrai
Amiens
Péronne
LUXEMBOURG
PICARDY
RETHEL
Barfleur
Harfleur
Soissons
1450 ✕ Formigny
Honfleur
Rouen
Reims
Caen
Chalons
NORMANDY
CHAMPAGNE
Morlaix
Avranches
Paris
Brest
St Malo
1424 ✕ Verneuil
BRITTANY
Chartres
Domremy
Brétigny
Rouvray
Rennes
MAINE
Patay
Le Mans
Troyes
1428–29 ✕ Orléans
Vannes
Blois
Angers
Tours
NEVERS
ANJOU
Chinon
Dijon
TOURAINE
BERRY
Besançon
Bourges
Bay of Biscay
POITOU
Châteauroux
BURGUNDY
1356 ✕ Poitiers
Lusignan
BOURBON
La Rochelle
SAVOY
Taillebourg
LE MARCHE
Saintes
ANGOULEME
Limoges
Lyons
SAINTONGE
LIMOUSIN
Périgueux
AUVERNE
Grenoble
PERIGORD
Bordeaux
Castillon
DAUPHINÉ
✕ *1453* Bergerac
English holdings, 1360
AGENAIS
Cahors
Rodez
Albret
GASCONY
Avignon
ARMAGNAC
PROVENCE
Bayonne
Toulouse
Montpellier
Aigues Mortes
Aix
BÉARN
LANGUEDOC
Carcassonne
Narbonne
NAVARRE
Foix

0   50 km
0   50 miles

cavalry charge was repulsed. When the second line charged in turn, they rode straight for the English traps, where 50 French men-at-arms were killed and another 150 captured. Northampton then withdrew into the forest, where the French besieged him inconclusively for several days.

■ **Auberoche, 21 October 1345**
The earl of Darby launched a surprise attack on French forces besieging the castle of Auberoche. Despite superior numbers, the French fell back, whereupon the garrison sortied, trapping the French and slaughtering them.

■ **St-Pol-de-Leon, 9 June 1346**
Charles of Blois' overwhelmingly superior army trapped an English commander with 80 men-at-arms and 100 archers. The English dug in on a hill and repelled attacks until dark, when the French withdrew.

■ **Caen, 26 July 1346**
The English seized Caen, which was garrisoned by 1000–1500 French troops. The French commanders decided to defend the suburb on Île Saint-Jean rather than the old town, although the island's defences were weak. A sudden, disorderly English assault proved effective. French defences failed at several points on the river and French troops at the bridge held, only to be outflanked. About 2500 French fighters and townspeople were slaughtered; others were ransomed.

■ **Blanchetaque, 24 August 1346**
The French Godemar du Fay held the Blanchetaque ford against Edward III's army. An English advance of 100 men-at-arms and 100 archers established a bridgehead and gradually pushed the French back until they broke.

■ **Crécy, 26 August 1346**
Preparatory to this first great land battle of the Hundred Years War, Edward III had raided deep into France with an army of about 4000 men-at-arms, 7000 archers and 5000 other infantry. They began to withdraw upon news that Philip VI had gathered a large French army (12,000 men-at-arms and 20,000–25,000 infantry) to meet them. Philip, determined not to suffer another

embarrassment, decided to cut the English army off and force battle.

On 26 August, Philip with his advance troops blocked the English retreat. English scouts had discovered the French presence and Edward responded by digging in his much smaller army on the gently rising ground near the village of Crécy. The English position was strong. The 16-year-old Prince of Wales commanded the first line of dismounted men-at-arms, while King Edward commanded the reserves. Edward posted his longbowmen on the wings, forward of the main lines, protecting them with circles of baggage carts and shallow pits, with the five English cannon also positioned on the wings. The men-at-arms' horses were also protected at the rear in a laager of baggage carts.

Although it was already late afternoon and most of the French army was still spread out along the road, Philip decided on an immediate attack. Inexplicably, the first troops he sent into action

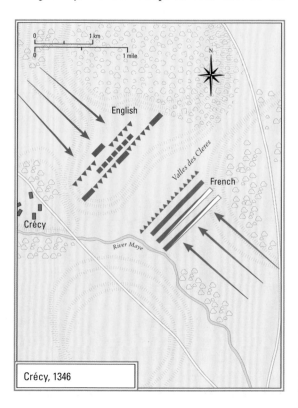
Crécy, 1346

were his 6000 Genoese mercenary crossbowmen. The Genoese were made to advance, shooting as they went, a tactic to which crossbows are ill suited. Increasing their difficulties, the large shields that normally protected crossbowmen as they reloaded were still in the baggage, as was most of their ammunition. Worst of all, it began to rain, which affected the crossbows' mechanisms and slowed their advance still further. The Genoese soon broke and fled under a storm of English arrows.

To the French leaders, the Genoese withdrawal appeared to be cowardice and treason. Without orders, the count of Alençon charged them with the elite French cavalry. While massacring their own mercenaries, the French inadvertently got within range of the English archers and soon suffered heavy losses. Some of the French men-at-arms reached the first English line, where a vicious fight developed around the Prince of Wales.

The French attack continued into the night, with repeated charges against the English positions as reinforcements reached the battlefield and threw themselves into the engagement. They failed, however, to break through to the English archers, who continued to inflict great damage on men and horses. As dark fell, the English men-at-arms mounted and charged the surviving groups of French horse and French infantry in turn. The bulk of the French infantry broke and ran, suffering heavy losses. King Philip himself was nearly killed; he escaped with his life, but left his personal standard and the Oriflamme on the battlefield. The battle was effectively over by the end of the day, although 2000 French infantry turned up the next morning. They mistook the English for their own army and were quickly scattered and slaughtered.

This great English victory displayed beyond doubt the power of well-positioned and well-defended longbowmen. Few Englishmen died at Crécy, but the French toll was enormous. About 2000 French men-at-arms perished, including eight princes of the blood and the blind King John of Bohemia. Nobody knows how many common

French soldiers also fell, but King Philip made the carnage even worse by ordering the massacre of the surviving 'traitor' Genoese mercenaries.

■ **Calais, 4 September 1346–3 August 1347**
The English siege of the strongly held seaport of Calais dragged on for 11 months. In November, an effort to storm the town from boats in the moat failed. Supplies and reinforcements reached Calais by sea as late as April, but famine finally took its toll. King Philip finally came to relieve Calais in late July, but withdrew in face of the stronger English army. Calais surrendered on 3 August.

■ **La Roche-Derrien, 1347**
An English force of 700 under Thomas Dagworth came to relieve this Breton town, under siege by Charles of Blois with about 1500 men. The French force was divided into four sectors. Dagworth attacked the largest before dawn, although his attempt at surprise failed. Fighting was heavy and confused until the garrison came to Dagworth's assistance. The English defeated the other French units in turn, inflicting heavy casualties.

■ **Lunalonge, 1349**
A stalemate between French and Anglo-Gascon armies. The English in an entrenched position typical of the early Hundred Years War beat off French cavalry attacks and the English were able to withdraw that night.

■ **Les Españols sur Mer, 29 August 1350**
Also known as the battle of Winchelsea, this battle developed when Edward III organized a fleet to stop raiders and intercepted 24 Castilian ships sailing southward. The English had twice the number of ships, but their vessels were smaller and lower, so they suffered heavy casualties while closing with the enemy. However, they quickly gained the advantage in hand-to-hand fighting, winning a complete victory.

■ **Thirty French Knights, 26 March 1351**
The French and English each provided 30 champions to fight this battle in Brittany. Fighting several hours in accordance with strict rules the French won the day. The battle accomplished nothing.

■ **SAINTES, 1351**

The French Guy de Nesle tried to halt an English advance, drawing his men up on foot before them on rising ground. The French were completely defeated, because another English force attacked their rear.

■ **ARDRES, 1351**

An English raiding party in France was cornered by French troops. Forced to defend themselves on open ground and with archers almost out of arrows, the English force was killed or captured.

■ **MAURON, 14 AUGUST 1352**

A superior French force attacked about 750 English troops. The English commander, Walter Bentley, dismounted his men-at-arms, placing archers on the wings. A French cavalry charge scattered the unprotected archers on one wing. Dismounted men-at-arms then attacked the English centre. After hard fighting, the French were driven back. Both English and French suffered heavy casualties, including 89 Knights of the Star, who had previously sworn never to retreat.

■ **POITIERS, 19 SEPTEMBER 1356**

Civil war in France led Edward III of England to renew his efforts at conquest. He planned an ambitious pincer strategy to trap Jean II's French army, his own large army attacking from the west while the Prince of Wales came up from Gascony to threaten the French rear. In the event, King Edward's army was delayed, while Edward the Black Prince began a pillaging thrust into France. His English-Gascon force consisted of about 2000 archers, 1000 Gascon infantry and 3000 men-at-arms, all mounted.

Jean II took the field with 8000 men-at-arms and 3000 infantry, his goal to force the Black Prince into a decisive battle. As they approached, the prince marched over fields to avoid detection, finding and routing part of the French rearguard. The prince then took up a defensive position on a hill north of Nouaillé, a forest to the rear, with a hawthorn hedge and vines in front. Marshes protected the left flank, while on the right, the English dug deep trenches. As usual, archers were

posted on the wings, with dismounted men-at-arms in the centre under the Prince's command. The thirsty, hungry English stood to arms, expecting immediate attack. Battle was delayed for a day as a cardinal tried to negotiate peace. The Prince of Wales proved willing to negotiate, but Jean II refused proposals out of hand.

By the morning of Monday 19 September, the English army was in bad straits, but the French delayed attacking such a strong position. Finally, the French planned a massed cavalry charge – 500 men-at-arms on armoured horses – to break up the English archers, the rest of the army following on foot. Meanwhile, the Black Prince planned a desperate retreat and started moving the Earl of Warwick's men. The French advance guard saw the enemy movement and launched a charge against the English wings, but not against the all-important archer positions. On one wing, archers were able to move behind the charging Frenchmen and fire at the horses' unarmoured rumps; on the other, the impetuous French charge brought them into close range of archers concealed in trenches.

The main French force was already advancing on foot, led by the dauphin. They suffered a barrage of arrows, which had less effect on footmen than they would on cavalry. Some Frenchmen were able to close with the English, where they fought hand-to-hand for about two hours before retreating, still in good order.

At this point, in a horrible miscalculation, King Jean ordered his son to withdraw to safety. The Duke of Orléans, seeing the dauphin and his entourage depart, misunderstood and pulled back with the entire French second line. In exasperation, the king himself advanced with the third line. By then, the English were running out of arrows, so Jean was able to close with the English men-at-arms. The English were tired and wounded, but still outnumbered the remaining French, especially as archers joined in with swords and knives. The decisive blow came when the Captal de Buch took 160 of the English reserve and charged the

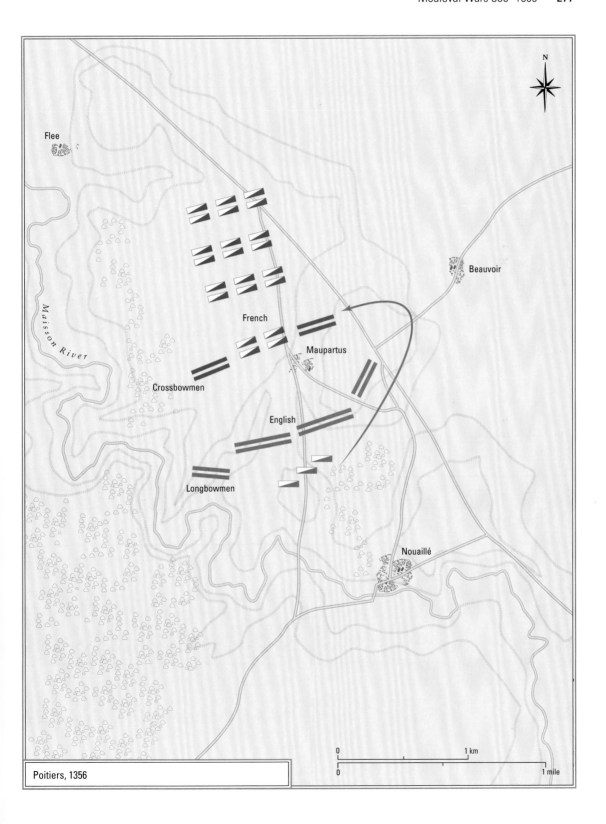

Flee

Beauvoir

French

Maupartus

Crossbowmen

English

Longbowmen

Nouaillé

Maison River

N

0   1 km
0   1 mile

Poitiers, 1356

French rear. The prince then mounted many of his men-at-arms and charged the unmounted French on open ground. Caught between two forces, the French were slaughtered and those who fled were cut down; Jean himself was captured, along with about 3000 of his army. About 2500 French men-at-arms died.

■ **MELLO, 10 JUNE 1358**

French peasant rebels, the 'Jacques', camped in a strong position on the plateau of Mello; a French army under King Charles of Navarre opposed them. Charles invited the peasant leader for a parley, but took him captive. Charles' army then charged the leaderless peasants. Despite their strong position in two lines with archers in front and carts and trenches protecting the flanks, the peasant army was overrun and destroyed.

■ **BRIGNAIS, 6 APRIL 1362**

The mercenary Great Company, about 5000 strong, attacked a French force of 4000 that had been sent against them. Accomplishing complete surprise, the Company captured 1000 French fighters, killing and scattering the rest.

■ **COCHEREL, 16 MAY 1364**

An Anglo-Gascon force of 1500–2000 under the Captal de Buch met 1200 Franco-Gascons under Bertrand du Guesclin. After a bloody engagement, du Guesclin committed his reserve against the Captal's flank, causing a rout.

■ **AURAY, 16 MAY 1364**

Charles of Blois with 3000–4000 men came to relieve the siege of Auray. The Anglo-British defenders, about 2000 men under Sir John Chandos, took a strong position on rising ground. Chandos drove off the first Franco-Breton attack, whereupon the Bretons of Charles' second division deserted, leaving Charles isolated. The English then charged, completing the French route with their reserves. Some 800 Franco-Bretons died, including Charles.

■ **PONTVALLAIN, 4 DECEMBER 1370**

In December, English bands were spread out in disorganized camps, preparing to enter winter quarters. With a series of forced marches, a French force under Bertrand du Guesclin completely surprised the largest group, under Grandeson. Another French force under Sancerre, hearing of the battle, attacked the English band under Fitzwalter and massacred them. The English suffered very heavy casualties and the rest of the English force was scattered.

■ **LA ROCHELLE, 22–23 JUNE 1372**

A Castilian-French fleet of 20–40 ships trapped an English convoy of about 20 merchant ships and three warships in La Rochelle's harbour. In a two-day battle the English suffered complete defeat.

■ **CHIZÉ, 1373**

Sir John Devereux brought an English force c. 800 strong to relieve Chizé castle. Initially successful, the English fled when French troops rallied. Almost the entire English force was killed or captured.

■ **CHATEAUNEUF-DE-RANDON, 1380**

Bertrand du Guesclin brought a French force to attack an independent mercenary band occupying this small town. The town surrendered after a short siege, but France's great General du Guesclin died of dysentery.

■ **ROOSEBEKE, 27 NOVEMBER 1382**

Charles VI's large French army completely defeated about 40,000 rebel Flemings under Philip van Artevelde. The untrained townsmen took a defensive position, but were outflanked and massacred until nightfall; about 27,500 died.

■ **MARGATE, 24 MARCH 1387**

About 200 armed merchant ships under Jan Buuc dared an English Channel blockade, but the Earl of Arundel with 47 great ships ambushed them, defeating Buuc in two engagements and capturing 68 vessels.

■ **BRAMHAM MOOR, 19 FEBRUARY 1408**

The rebellious Henry Percy, earl of Northumberland marched against York with a Northumbrian-Scottish army. Sir Thomas Rokeby met Percy with local levies, defeating and killing the earl.

■ **HARFLEUR, 18–22 SEPTEMBER 1415**

When Henry V invaded France in 1415, his first target was the town of Harfleur. King Henry invested the town with his force of about 2000 men-at-arms and 6000 archers; Harfleur had a garrison of 400. The 12 great guns of Henry's siege train inflicted serious damage on the town's walls. He then planned a general assault, but Harfleur's leaders surrendered on terms on 22 September.

■ AGINCOURT, 25 OCTOBER 1415

Henry V of England invaded France in 1415 to reignite the Hundred Years War, taking advantage of a French civil war. After taking Harfleur, the English force of perhaps 1500 men-at-arms and 7000 archers marched northward. The French mustered a much larger army, perhaps as many as 10,000 men-at-arms and a total force of 25,000, under Constable of France Charles d'Albret, to confront the invaders. At first, d'Albret shadowed the English route as he raised more men. However, the English force was rapidly weakening. The campaigning season was over, they were short on food and dysentery was running rampant. Finally, the French forced battle on 25 October.

King Henry chose his ground carefully, placing his men in a narrow defile between two forests. As usual, dismounted English men-at-arms were placed in the centre in three lines, with archers protected by stakes on the wings. Some archers may also have been positioned in the centre interspersed with the men-at-arms. Although their numbers were far superior, the French hesitated to attack, wary of the English archers and the narrow front, especially as they would have to advance through the thick mud of freshly ploughed fields. Henry finally started the fight in mid-morning by moving his army forward to within archery range; inexplicably, the French did not attack until after the English archers had driven in stakes to protect themselves against cavalry charges.

After English arrows began stinging the French, d'Albret sent his cavalry against the archers in a catastrophic charge. Unable to gain much speed on the muddy ground, the French men-at-arms and, more importantly, their horses were struck by a hale of arrows. Wounded horses threw their

riders into the mud or rampaged, maddened by pain. Even before the cavalry charge failed, the constable began leading a second charge consisting of dismounted men-at-arms. Their plate armour was largely proof against English arrows; the plan must have been that they would close with the English centre and overwhelm it with their superior numbers. They advanced in horrible conditions through knee-deep mud, trying to push forward despite the weight of 23–27kg of armour, trying to breathe through the slits in their helmets. Arrows were unlikely to pierce them, but many were knocked off their feet by the force of blows and they were advancing in such close order that those who fell were trodden into the mud.

Nonetheless, some of the French men-at-arms reached the English centre, certainly exhausted by their arduous crossing of the fields. The front was too narrow for the French to deploy their superior numbers and they were also harried by

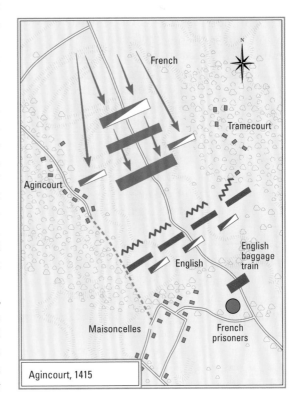

Agincourt, 1415

the English archers, who attacked them on the flank with hatchets and swords. In a three-hour fight, the English killed, captured, or drove off their attackers.

Much of the French never engaged with the English. In the afternoon, fearing an attack by the French rearguard, Henry ordered the execution of all but his highest-ranking prisoners. The attack never materialized, though, with the demoralized Frenchmen fleeing the battlefield.

While all sources agree that Agincourt was a great English victory, they vary widely in their accounts of the slain. The English suffered heavy casualties, about 1600, suggesting how desperate the fighting had been. Anywhere between 4000 and 10,000 fell on the French side, including their commander and a large number of other nobles.

■ ROUEN, 31 JULY 1418–19 JANUARY 1419

King Henry V besieged Rouen between July 1418 and January 1419. Soon running low on food, the town expelled 12,000 poor people who were left to starve outside the walls. The commander, Guy le Bouteiller, finally surrendered.

■ BAUGÉ, 21 MARCH 1421

A 6000-man Franco-Scottish army confronted a larger English army besieging Baugé. Their surprise attack failing, the English were defeated in a long, bloody fight in which their commander, the Duke of Clarence, was killed.

■ MEAUX, 6 OCTOBER 1421–10 MAY 1422

Henry V besieged Meaux in October 1421 until the garrison surrendered on 10 May 1422. Henry's artillery and miners brought down sections of wall, but no general assault was attempted as the besiegers fell prey to dysentery.

■ CRAVANT, 31 JULY 1423

A French royalist army 8000 strong marched into Burgundy, encountering the earl of Salisbury's Anglo-Burgundian army on the banks of the Yonne river. The English crossed under their archers' protective fire, both fording and crossing the narrow bridge. The French retreated, but their Scottish allies under the earl of Buchan stood their

ground. In the major English victory, 6000 French and Scots were killed and 2000 captured.

■ LA BROSSINIÈRE, 26 SEPTEMBER 1423

About 2800 French supporters of the dauphin caught an English raiding force of about 1500 under William de la Pole. The English were broken in a flank attack and nearly all were massacred.

■ VERNEUIL, 17 AUGUST 1424

A French royalist force of 14,000–16,000 (including about 6000 Scots) took Verneuil with a ruse, drawing the English army of 8000–10,000 under John, Duke of Bedford, out against them.

The French army was far from unified. Scots and French divisions were drawn up side by side, with Lombard mercenary cavalry on both wings. The English formed with dismounted men-at-arms in the centre and archers on the wings, then advanced to within arrow range. As the archers drove in protective stakes, the Milanese cavalry attacked and broke through the English right

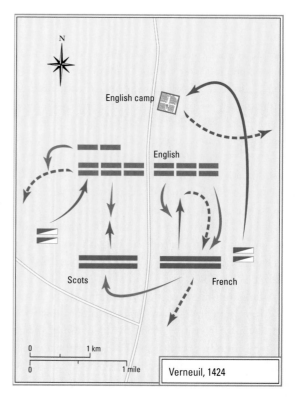

Verneuil, 1424

wing, but went on to attack the baggage train; the Lombard cavalry on the other wing soon joined them. Bedford pushed back the French, but broke off pursuit to attack the Scots, now fighting alone, on the right flank. More than 7000 Frenchmen and Scots died, with light English casualties.

■ BROUWERSHAVEN, 13 JANUARY 1426

Philip the Good of Burgundy invaded Zeeland, held by a mixed Zeelander-English force. The English attacked as Philip disembarked, but the Burgundian knights drove their enemies onto a dike and killed 3000.

■ ST JAMES, 1426

An English army raiding into Brittany took refuge at St-James-de-Beuvron, where a French force under Arthur de Richemont attacked them. The French were caught off guard by a sortie and withdrew.

■ ORLÉANS, 12 OCTOBER 1428–8 MAY 1429

After a series of triumphs, an English army under the earl of Shrewsbury reached the strategically placed city of Orléans, which still held out for Charles VII of France. Orléans was connected to the Duke of Orléans, England's inveterate enemy, so the Orléanais could expect brutal treatment from the enemy. As a result, they refused to surrender, after which Shrewsbury mounted a siege on 12 October 1428.

Orléans was a strongly fortified town with suburbs extending to the south bank of the Loire. The English effort to take the city opened in the south-bank suburb with an attack on the Augustins, a walled monastery. They soon took the Augustins, then went on to seize Les Tourelles, a heavily fortified gate that protected the southern end of the long bridge over the Loire that led into Orléans. The French defenders were forced back behind the city walls, destroying a section of the bridge as they went.

The walls of Orléans were invulnerable to the cannon of the day, so the English had no choice but to try to starve the defenders out. The death of their commander and a number of temporary

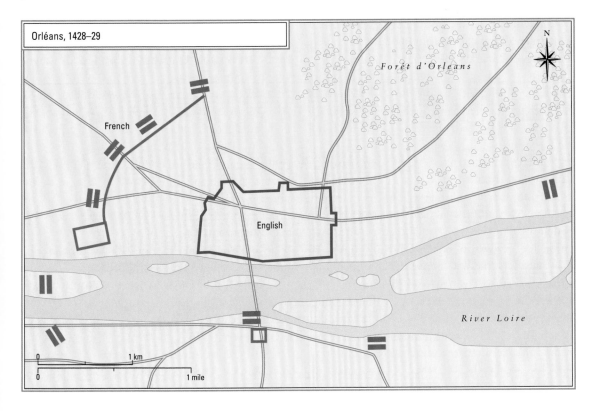

Orléans, 1428–29

commanders probably also added to English inactivity during the winter months. Eventually the Earl of Suffolk took charge. The English force was insufficient to invest the large town completely, but they created a series of fortified camps to control the surrounding countryside. Some food and reinforcements continued to find their way into the town, despite English patrols. Nonetheless, by spring 1429, the defenders were growing desperate.

Then came one of history's great surprises: a French peasant woman presented herself to the demoralized dauphin of France, proclaiming that God had sent her to raise the siege of Orléans and to see Charles crowned as true king. Joan of Arc quickly won credence. She was equipped with arms and armour, as well as a banner proclaiming her cause and was sent to Orléans with a hastily assembled relief force. She entered the city on 29 April. Jean de Dunois (the 'Bastard of Orléans') soon accepted Joan at least as a talisman, but his caution continued to clash with her fiery demands for immediate attack. Joan quickly gave heart to the dispirited French, inspiring the men to confess their sins and sing hymns.

At Joan's urging, the French made a direct assault on 4 May against the English fortress of St-Loup, taking the position after heavy fighting. Joan then wrote to the English demanding their withdrawal in God's name (the letter is still extant). The defenders joined with Joan in clamouring for a further assault until Dunois had to agree to attack Les Tourelles on 7 May. Again, the French abandoned subtlety in favour of a full frontal assault. The first escalade failed and Joan suffered an arrow wound, leading the English to chant gleefully 'the witch is dead'! However, Joan soon returned to the fight and the French force successfully overran Les Tourelles in the evening, killing or capturing all defenders.

On 8 May, Suffolk gathered the English garrisons from the fortresses surrounding Orléans and drew them up for battle. The French responded by taking up battle formations outside the city walls.

The two forced faced each other for an hour, neither side willing to start the conflict (it was a Sunday, so Joan was unwilling to attack). Finally, the English withdrew, ending the siege.

■ **ROUVRAY, 12 FEBRUARY 1429**
The 'Battle of the Herrings' developed when the French attacked an English supply convoy under Sir John Fastolf. The English fortified themselves with their wagons; the French failed to break through. About 400 Frenchmen were killed.

■ **JARGEAU, 11–12 JUNE 1429**
A French force of 3000 attacked the town of Jargeau, held by an English garrison of 700. French artillery brought down a tower and the French, rallied by Joan of Arc, scaled the walls.

■ **MEUNG-SUR-LOIRE, 15 JUNE 1429**
A French army led by Jean, Duke of Alençon and Joan of Arc attacked English-held Meung-sur-Loire. They took the fortified bridge in a single day, ignoring the English-held town and castle.

■ **BEAUGENCY, 16–17 JUNE 1429**
A French force under Jean, Duke of Alençon and Joan of Arc thrust into the Loire Valley. They attacked English-held Beaugency on 16 June, soon forcing the English to abandon the town and take refuge in the castle. The second day saw an artillery barrage against the castle. That night, Alençon received word of an English relief force, so he offered generous terms for the castle's surrender.

■ **PATAY, 18 JUNE 1429**
A 5000-man English army was caught unprepared by the 1500-man vanguard of the French army under La Hire. The English, mostly archers, had no time to fortify themselves and were scattered.

■ **COMPIÈGNE, 18 JUNE 1430**
Joan of Arc gathered 300–400 volunteers to protect Compiègne. After a failed surprise attack against the Burgundians at Margny, Joan fell back to Compiègne, but was captured because the gate was already closed.

■ **GERBEVOY, 1435**
English troops under the Earl of Arundel encountered a large French force near Gerbevoy. Many of Arundel's soldiers ran most who

remained were killed. Arundel himself suffered a culverin wound and later died.

■ ROUEN, 1449

A large French army under Dunois, the 'Bastard of Orléans', took Rouen, the English capital of France, after a three-week siege. Their victory was due to Dunois' modern and large artillery train.

■ FORMIGNY, 15 APRIL 1450

The increasingly desperate English gathered a force of 4000–7000 soldiers, two-thirds of them bowmen, to halt the French advance into Normandy. They encountered a 5000-man French army under the Comte de Clermont at Formigny on 15 April 1450.

The English under Thomas Kyrielle took up a defensive position, in line behind stakes and low earthworks. Action began with a series of ineffective French charges against the English flanks. Clermont then had two cannon brought forward, whose shot had little effect; the English soon charged and seized them. The battle turned when the Duke of Brittany with 1200 men arrived on the English flank. Forced out of their prepared position, the English (mostly lightly armoured archers) could be overwhelmed in a series of charges. Kyriell and 900 of his men were captured; about 2500 English were killed. French losses, however, were under 1000.

CASTILLON, 17 JULY 1453

A 9000-man English army led by Shrewsbury encountered a French force invading Gascony in July 1453. The French soldiers took refuge in a heavily fortified camp, their 300 cannon, archers and crossbowmen mowing down English charges. A Breton flank attack eventually completed the English rout.

Ethiopian War 1445

■ GOMIT, 1445

Ethiopia, led by Zara Yaqob, overcame the forces of the Adal Sultanate, led by Badlay ibn Sa'ad ad-Din who was killed. His body was then distributed around Ethiopia.

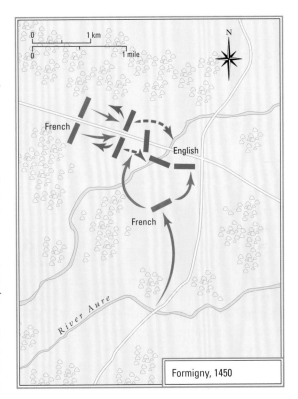

Formigny, 1450

Wars of the Roses 1455–85

■ ST ALBANS I, 22 MAY 1455

The first battle of St Albans is regarded as the first battle of the Wars of the Roses. It was fought between Richard, Duke of York, assisted by Richard Neville, Earl of Warwick, whose 3000 men overcame 2000 Lancastrians under Edmund, Duke of Somerset, who was killed in the fighting in the city streets of St Albans. An important outcome of the battle was the temporary seizure of Henry VI.

■ BLORE HEATH, 23 SEPTEMBER 1459

At Blore Heath, a Lancastrian army under Lord Audley attempted to intercept a Yorkist army marching to join up with the Yorkist main body at Ludlow. The ambush was foiled and Lord Audley was killed.

■ LUDFORD BRIDGE, 12 OCTOBER 1459

Richard, Duke of York made a stand at Ludford Bridge across the River Teme below Ludlow

Castle, but when some of his troops defected, he was forced to take refuge in Ludlow and then fled.

■ SANDWICH, JANUARY 1460

The battle of Sandwich was a minor naval engagement fought at sea off Sandwich between the Earl of Warwick, Captain of Calais and a Lancastrian fleet. It secured the English Channel for the Yorkist cause.

■ NORTHAMPTON, 10 JULY 1460

Landing at Sandwich, the Yorkists under Richard Neville, Earl of Warwick, advanced to London and headed north towards Coventry where King Henry VI was based. The King's Lancastrian army advanced to meet them and took up a position at Northampton behind some field defences. The Yorkista attacked in rain against a barrage of arrows. The Lancastrian Lord Grey of Ruthin changed sides as the battle began and their defence collapsed.

■ WAKEFIELD, 30 DECEMBER 1460

The battle of Wakefield was a major defeat for the Yorkists. Richard, Duke of York, was inside his castle of Sandal to the south of Wakefield and was expecting reinforcements, but before any supporters arrived, he made the strange decision to march out and give battle to the Lancastrians. He was heavily defeated and died in battle. His son, Edmund Earl of Rutland, was killed as he tried to escape.

■ MORTIMER'S CROSS, 2 FEBRUARY 1461

Mortimer's Cross was a victory gained by Edward, Earl of March (later Edward IV) as he successfully prevented a Lancastrian army under Owen Tudor from joining forces with the main Lancastrian body in England. Owen Tudor attempted an encirclement of the Yorkist left wing but his troops were defeated. During the flight from the battlefield, some of the Lancastrians were followed as far as Hereford, where Owen himself was captured and beheaded.

■ ST ALBANS II, 17 FEBRUARY 1461

The Earl of Warwick attempted to halt the progress to London of the Lancastrian army at St Albans, 38 km (24 miles) north of London. The Lancastrians outmanoeuvred him by making a wide sweep, but were unable to follow up their victory.

■ FERRYBRIDGE, 28 MARCH 1461

The minor conflict at Ferrybridge was a preliminary to the battle of Towton. The Earl of Warwick, leading the Yorkist vanguard of the newly proclaimed King Edward IV, forced their way under arrow fire across the broken bridge of the Aire river. The following day, the successful Yorkists were ambushed by Lancastrians, although their main body soon arrived. Crossing upstream at Castleford, they began a pursuit of the Lancastrian army.

■ TOWTON, 29 MARCH 1461

The battle of Towton was the largest battle of the Wars of the Roses and one of the bloodiest in English history. The Yorkists were led by King Edward IV, the Lancastrians by Henry Beaufort, Duke of Somerset. The battle began with a discharge of arrows by the Yorkists as snow began to fall. The wind carried the arrows far into the ranks of the Lancastrian army, who replied with a barrage of arrows that fell short. Both armies then advanced and began a long and bloody hand-to-hand struggle, constantly replenished from the rear. As the Lancastrians fell back, a panicked retreat began. A wooden bridge across the Cock beck broke under the weight of the retreat and as many as 30,000 soldiers died in all.

■ HEDGELEY MOOR, 25 APRIL 1464

This battle, a footnote to the Wars of the Roses, was an encounter between the families of Neville and Percy, during which the Percies attempted an ambush against the Yorkists. Sir Ralph Percy was killed in the battle.

■ HEXHAM, 15 MAY 1464

In another encounter in the north of England, John Neville, Lord Montague, attacked the camp of a Lancastrian raiding party located beside a river near Hexham. Three important Lancastrian leaders were captured and later beheaded.

■ EDGECOTE MOOR, 26 JULY 1469

The battle of Edgecote Moor arose from the defection to the Lancastrian side of the Earl of

Warwick, who reinforced the rebels. The rivals met almost unexpectedly near Banbury. The Earl of Pembroke was captured.

■ LOSECOAT FIELD, 12 MARCH 1470

Also known as the battle of Empingham, this was the main engagement of the Lincolnshire Rebellion. Although a victory for Edward IV, it was one of the factors that caused him to flee from England.

■ RAVENSPUR, 1471

King Edward IV returned to England to regain his throne. He landed at Ravenspur and avoided fighting Lancastrian armies by claiming that he acknowledged Henry VI and merely wished to reclaim his dukedom of York.

■ BARNET, 14 APRIL 1471

The battle of Barnet was fought between Edward IV and the Earl of Warwick. The fighting began early in the morning when fog obscured the battlefield and the flank attacks were dissipated while a fierce melee went on in the centre. An impetuous attack by the Earl of Oxford left the battlefield and, when they returned, they were attacked by their allies in mistake leading to a defeat for Warwick. While retreating, Warwick was killed by Yorkist soldiers.

■ TEWKESBURY, 4 MAY 1471

The battle of Tewkesbury came about when the Lancastrians, retreating into Wales, were caught while crossing the Severn river after being denied the safety of the city of Gloucester. The battle was evenly balanced until the Lancastrian Duke of Somerset accused an ally of treason and killed him, causing a split in the ranks. The Yorkists took advantage of the confusion and attacked in force, driving the Lancastrians towards the river where many drowned.

■ BOSWORTH FIELD, 22 AUGUST 1485

Bosworth Field, the battle that ended the Yorkist line, was one of the most decisive battles in English history. Henry Tudor, exiled in France, provided a nucleus of resistance for

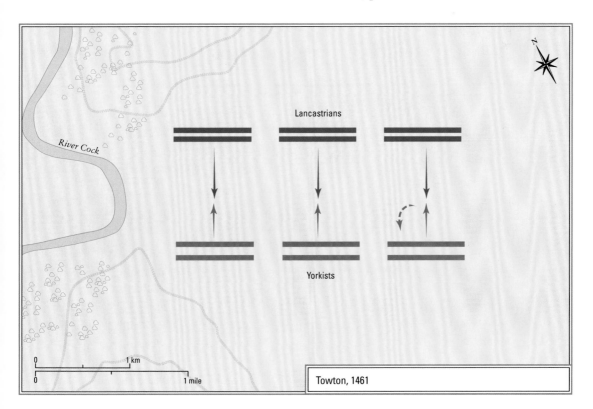

Towton, 1461

Wars of the Roses, 1455–85

Area supporting the House of Lancaster

Area supporting the House of York

Battle sites

SCOTLAND

Hedgeley Moor

Hexham

Durham

North Sea

Richmond

Scarborough

Isle of Man

Lancaster

Ripon

York

Hull

Ravenspur

Irish Sea

Towton

Wakefield

Isle of Anglesey

Chester

Lincoln

Derwent

Don

Trent

The Wash

Blore Heath

Stoke on Trent

Shrewsbury

Stamford

Lynn

Norwich

Bosworth

Ludlow

Lutterworth

Ely

Bury St Edmunds

Gloucester

Warwick

Mortimer's Cross

Edgecote Moor

Northampton

Tewkesbury

E N G L A N D

Milford Haven

Pembroke

Gloucester

Oxford

St Albans

Barnet

LONDON

Canterbury

Dover

Bristol

Bath

Thames

Salisbury

Winchester

Southampton

Hastings

Launceston

Exeter

Dorchester

Isle of Wight

Plymouth

Dartmouth

English Channel

0   50 km

0   50 miles

the Lancastrian lords who had been dispossessed following the triumph of Edward IV and his successor, Richard III. Henry and his army landed at Milford Haven in August 1485 and began to raise additional troops. King Richard III did the same and, owing to the locations of their allies and the directions of movement, the armies met at Bosworth Field near Leicester. The forces of Lord Stanley and the Earl of Northumberland were of questionable loyalty, so Richard treated the former as hostile and placed the latter, who had pledged loyalty to him, safely to his rear.

The battle of Bosworth Field began precipitately when Richard attacked first to prevent Henry from bringing into action his Burgundian gunners. The move was led by the Duke of Norfolk. Henry was still arranging his army and there was some confusion, but the line held and the Duke of Norfolk was killed. There followed something of a stalemate and, seeing Henry Tudor riding towards Lord Stanley to ask for his allegiance, Richard III unleashed a fierce cavalry charge.

The impact was considerable and Richard's own lance pierced the body of Henry Tudor's standard bearer. Although seemingly successful, at that point Lord Stanley declared for Henry and attacked Richard III's left flank. The Earl of Northumberland withdrew his forces and Richard III was killed on the field of battle. The coronet he wore on his helmet was hacked off, and presented as a crown to Henry Tudor.

■ EAST STOKE, 16 JUNE 1487

Regarded as being the final battle of the Wars of the Roses, at Stoke King Henry VII crushed the Yorkist rebellion under the pretender Lambert Simnel and the Earl of Lincoln, who led an army containing German and Irish mercenaries. The Yorkists immediately went on the attack, but after three hours the lightly armoured Irish troops suffered heavy losses and Lincoln's army was defeated. It was one of the deadliest fights of the war, with perhaps 7000 of the 20,000 combatants dying, as there was a mutual agreement that there

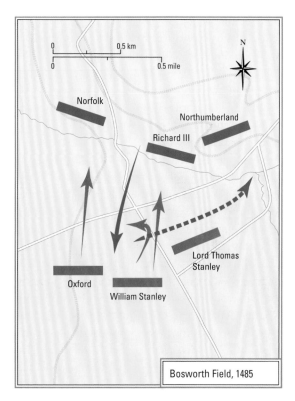

Bosworth Field, 1485

would be no quarter for those left standing. All of the main Yorkists commanders died at the battle apart from Simnel, who was captured and eventually pardoned.

Swiss-Burgundian War 1474–77

■ HÉRICOURT, NOVEMBER 1474

This was the first encounter of the Swiss-Burgundian War. An allied army of Austrians, Alsatians and Swiss besieged Héricourt and defeated Charles the Bold's relieving army, thus delaying his plans to annex Alsace and Lorraine.

■ PLANTA, NOVEMBER 1475

In November 1475, the army of the Duchy of Savoy engaged the Swiss Confederates who were initially driven back, but reinforcements forced the Savoyards to withdraw their left flank. During the attack, 1000 Savoyards died.

■ GRANDSON, 2 MARCH 1476

Grandson was a major defeat for Charles the

Bold at the hands of the Swiss Confederacy. It followed his capture of the castle of Grandson on Lake Neuchâtel. Charles assumed that the approaching Swiss vanguard was their entire army and withdrew his cavalry so that his artillery could deploy, but the rapid advance of the Swiss main body did not allow for the artillery to be used.

■ MORAT, 22 JUNE 1476

Also known as the battle of Murten, Morat was a castle besieged by Charles the Bold. The Swiss relieving army advanced steadily in a dense pike formation and overcame the Burgundian army, capturing much booty.

■ NANCY, 5 JANUARY 1477

During a severe winter, Charles the Bold laid siege to the city of Nancy, previously captured by the Duke of Lorraine, who sent a relieving army. Charles deployed his army of 3000 besiegers in a defensive position, which had a small stream, as well as 30 small cannon, in front of it. The position was sufficiently strong to dissuade the Duke of Lorraine's much larger army of 10,000 from a frontal attack. Instead, the largely Swiss vanguard was sent off in an encircling movement against Charles' left flank. Meanwhile, the centre took up a position on Charles' right. When they attacked, Charles tried to reorganize his forces, but was caught up in the overwhelming advance. Charles was hit on the head and knocked off his horse. His body was found three days later. Nancy was relieved and when Charles' death became known, the Swiss-Burgundian Wars ended.

Spanish-Muslim Wars 1481–92

■ ALHAMA DE GRANADA, 1482

Situated between Malaga and Granada, Alhama was strategically important to the Sultanate of Granada. In 1482, it fell to a Christian army as part of the reconquest of Moorish Spain.

■ LOJA, 1486

The attack on Loja in 1486 was led personally by King Ferdinand and proved to be a disaster for

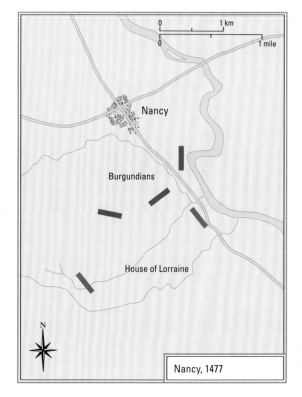

Nancy, 1477

the Christian army, who were driven off and pursued. A planned withdrawal then turned in to a panic retreat.

■ MALAGA, 18 AUGUST 1487

The siege of Malaga in 1487 began with a fiercely contested attempt by the Christian besiegers to find suitable places where they could locate their artillery. pieces A bombardment followed and Malaga was also the last occasion on which a trebuchet was used during a siege. When it was discovered that the garrison were beginning to suffer from the effects of starvation, a gunpowder mine was exploded under them and the city surrendered.

BAZA, 4 DECEMBER 1489

The Amir Muhammad the Valiant surrendered Baza to the Catholic monarchs rather than submit to his hated nephew Boabdil, whom he regarded as a traitor, but Boabdil withdrew his assurances and prepared to defend Granada.

Early Modern Wars
1500–1775

The Early Modern era was a transformative period in the history of warfare. Armies became larger and increasingly professionalized, while gunpowder weaponry introduced firearms and artillery into both naval and land warfare.

Ottoman Wars 1500–1775

◼ DIU, 3 FEBRUARY 1509

Aggressive Portuguese expansion in the Indian Ocean during the first decade of the sixteenth century threatened both the balance of power in the region and long-established Ottoman and Mamluk trading interests. This provoked an alliance between the Ottomans, Mamlûks, the Sultanate of Gujarat and the ruler of Calicut, who assembled a fleet of almost 120 vessels to oppose the 18 Portuguese warships under the Viceroy, Dom Francisco de Almeida, which were based at Fort Kochi, south-

west India. The Portuguese fleet comprised:

- Five large carracks or naus: *Flor de la mar* (Viceroy's flagship), *Espírito Santo* (Cap Nuno Vaz Pereira), *Belém* (Jorge de Melo Pereira), *Great King* (Francisco de Távora) and *Great Taforea* (Fernão de Magalhães). These were large vessels with high stern and forecastles and usually three masts. The foremast and mainmast were square-rigged, while the mizzenmast was lateen-rigged (triangular sail);

- Four smaller naus (each probably with three masts): *Small Taforea* (Garcia de Sousa), *Santo António* (Martim Coelho), *Small King* (Manuel

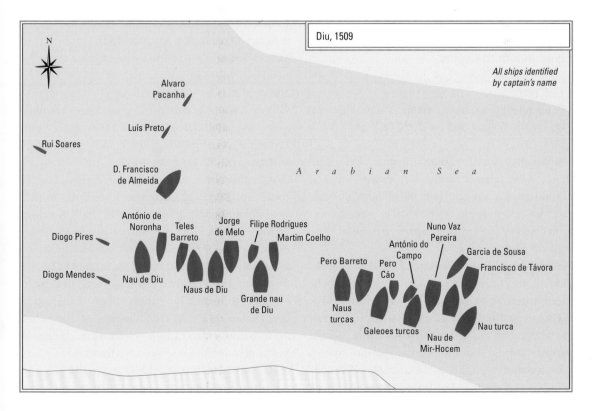

Diu, 1509

All ships identified by captain's name

Teles Barreto) and *Andorinho* (Dom António de Noronha);
- Four caravelas redondas, three-masted ships with a square foresail and lateen sails on the other two masts. They were probably up to 30m in length and averaged 50 tonnes (captains António do Campo, Pero Cão, Filipe Rodrigues and Rui Soares);
- Two caravelas Latinas (captains Álvaro Peçanha and Luís Preto);
- Two gales, probably two-masted, lateen rigged galleys with 25–30 oars per side, with three men to an oar. Like most galleys, a gale had only forward-firing guns, but could also carry up to 200 troops (captains Paio Rodrigues de Sousa and Diogo Pires de Miranda);
- One bergantim, a smaller, two-masted vessel with a square sail on the foremast and lateen-rigged on the other (captain Simão Martins).

The allied fleet commanded by Ottoman Adm Mir Hussein Pasha included approximately 100 vessels from Gujarat and Calicut, mainly small dhows of limited combat value. Its most effective warships were:
- Four naus from Gujarat
- Four Mamlûk naus
- Two caravelas
- Four galeotas (galliots), small galleys with two lateen-rigged sails and up to 20 oars per side
- Two gales.

Although heavily outnumbered, Almeida's ships were armed with far more effective cannon than even the best allied vessels, while the 1500 Portuguese troops that it carried were more heavily armed and better armoured than their opponents.

Adm Mir Hussein Pasha deployed the allied fleet in the inner harbour at Diu, covered by shore batteries, which he hoped would offset the superior firepower of the Portuguese vessels. He also relied on the protection given by the narrow channel leading into the harbour, which was notoriously difficult to navigate. However, Almeida captured a local fisherman who agreed

to pilot his ships through the harbour approaches. The battle began at about 11:00, when the prevailing winds and the incoming tide were favourable. The Portuguese initially concentrated their fire on the coastal batteries guarding the port and the allied fleet before turning on Mir Hussein Pasha's ships.

The technological superiority of the state-of-the-art European vessels became obvious as the Portuguese blasted the enemy vessels with cannon fire, before closing in to board, taking two Turkish naus, two Gujarati naus and the two Turkish gales. In addition, two Turkish naus, two Gujarati naus and two Turkish caravelas were sunk. By 17:00, the wind began to change and Almeida ordered his fleet – which had lost no ships – to leave the harbour with their prizes.

■ **CHALDIRAN, 23 AUGUST 1514**
Sultan Selim I's 60,000-strong Ottoman army defeated an Iranian army of 55,000 men commanded by Shah Ismail I at Chaldiran in north-western Iran. Selim lost 2000 men, but inflicted 5000 casualties on the Iranians.

■ **MARJ-DARBIK, 24 AUGUST 1516**
Sultan Selim I's 65,000-strong Ottoman army defeated a Mamlûk army of 80,000 men commanded by Sultan Al-Ashraf Qansuh al-Ghawri near Halab in Syria. The Mamlûk army was annihilated, losing 72,000 men, while Ottoman casualties totalled 13,000.

■ **RIDANIYA, 22 JANUARY 1517**
A Mamlûk force under Sultan Tuman Bay II took up a strong defensive position, which was stormed by Sultan Selim I's 20,000-strong Ottoman army. The Ottomans lost 6000 men, but inflicted 7000 casualties on the Mamlûks.

■ **BELGRADE II, 25 JUNE–29 AUGUST 1521**
Suleiman the Magnificent marched along the Danube followed by supply boats. Building a bridge across the Sava failed because of floods, but a bombardment and attack was launched. Belgrade surrendered when a tower was destroyed.

■ **RHODES, 26 JUNE–22 DECEMBER 1522**
An Ottoman army of 100,000 men commanded

by Sultan Suleiman I the Magnificent besieged the Knights Hospitaller's stronghold of Rhodes, which was defended by a garrison of 7500 men under Grand Master Philippe Villiers de L'Isle-Adam.

The Turks blockaded the harbour and subjected the city to repeated artillery bombardments, followed by almost daily infantry attacks. They also attempted to demolish key sectors of the fortifications by mining – on 4 September two mines were detonated under the bastion of England, bringing down a large part of the wall. The Turks stormed this breach, but a counter-attack by the English brothers under Fra' Nicholas Hussey and the Grand Master drove them back.

Further major attacks in September and November were also repulsed, but the city's supplies were running out and supplies were unable to get through. The Knights surrendered on 22 December after inflicting 50,000 casualties for the loss of 2000 men.

◼ MOHÁCS, 29 AUGUST 1526

The Ottoman Empire had been expanding into the Balkans for decades, capturing Belgrade in 1521. In 1526, Sultan Suleiman I the Magnificent advanced northwards towards Budapest with an Ottoman army of 55,000, including Turks, Balkan militia and at least 9000 elite Janissaries. Opposing this army was the Hungarian King Louis II – who was only 19 years old – with an army of 40,000 men consisting of Hungarians, Croatians, Bohemians, Austrians and various European mercenaries. Louis' field commander was Pál Tomori. The two armies met at Mohács, south of Budapest, to the west of the Danube River. Only part of the Hungarian army arrived on the field in time to take part in the battle, at least 10,000 reinforcements being too late to affect the outcome. Both armies included a mix of heavy and light cavalry, including mounted archers. Both armies also possessed a mix of light and heavy infantry, including some armed with

Rhodes, 1522

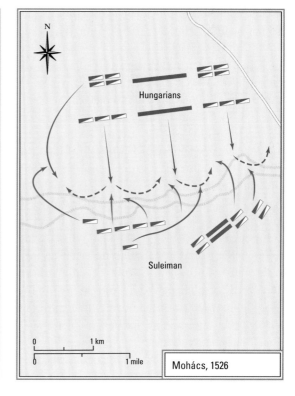

Mohács, 1526

early muskets in the form of arquebuses. The Ottomans had a significant edge in artillery with at least 160 cannon to 85 Hungarian cannon.

Both armies set up encampments, the Ottoman army with the Danube and marshy ground on their right flank, the Hungarian army facing south with the Danube on their left flank. It was late afternoon, but rather than wait for the next day King Louis decided to attack. Ottoman light cavalry manoeuvred towards the Hungarian right and the Hungarians launched a major attack with heavy armoured cavalry against Ottoman Rumelian light cavalry militia on the left of the Ottoman position. The Hungarian attack was successful, driving in the Ottoman left. The Hungarian cavalry then attempted to wheel in and attack the Ottoman centre, but ran into heavy fire from Ottoman artillery, firing stone projectiles for maximum anti-personnel effect. Elite Ottoman Janissaries, armed with arquebuses, provided close-range fire. Mounted Hungarian archers came close enough to fire at Suleiman in the Ottoman centre, one arrow glancing off of the Sultan's armour. However, the Hungarian attack had become overextended and the horsemen suffered heavy casualties from Ottoman firepower.

With the Hungarian right engaged and out of position, Suleiman attacked the Hungarian left with Turkish regular cavalry, supported by more Janissaries. Ottoman artillery fire aided the progress of this attack. Ottoman cavalry on the left flank rallied and the Hungarian army was soon enveloped on both flanks. Suffering heavy losses, elements of the Hungarian army began to fall back and Pál Tomori was killed while trying to rally the troops. Many Hungarian infantry were trapped in the centre, while mounted troops fled in disorder. King Louis, caught up in the rout, was thrown from his horse while trying to cross marshy ground and fell into a deep creek. Dressed in heavy armour, the young king was drowned. By nightfall the Hungarian army was completely defeated.

Estimates of Hungarian casualties vary, from 14,000 to 20,000 dead. Adding to controversy are estimates of 2000 prisoners executed by the Ottomans after the battle. Estimates of Ottoman casualties also vary, from 1500 to 7000 men. The decisive battle paved the way for the Ottomans to take Budapest and besiege Vienna within three years. Hungary did not exist as fully independent for nearly three centuries after the battle. The death of Louis without an heir meant that the Austrian Habsburg dynasty became the chief claimants to the throne of Hungary.

■ HUNGARIAN CAMPAIGN, 1527–28

Following the battle of Mohács, Sultan Suleiman the Magnificent was forced to withdraw his field army from Hungary to counter threats to other provinces of the Ottoman Empire. This gave Archduke Ferdinand of Austria an opportunity to attempt to enforce his claim to the Kingdom of Hungary. In 1527–28 he defeated John Zapolya, the Ottoman-backed claimant to the Hungarian throne and captured Buda (now Budapest), Győr, Komárno, Esztergom and Székesfehérvár.

■ BALKAN CAMPAIGN, 1529

Following Ferdinand I's daring assault on Ottoman Hungary, Suleiman launched an offensive to take Vienna. The 120,000-strong Ottoman army began its advance on 10 May 1529, taking Buda on 8 September and installing John Zapolya as King of Hungary. Suleiman went on to take Gran, Tata, Komoron and Raab, wiping out much of Ferdinand I's territorial gains of the previous two years, before besieging Vienna on 27 September.

■ VIENNA I, 27 SEPTEMBER–15 OCTOBER 1529

The Ottoman Empire had won a decisive victory at the battle of Mohács in Hungary in 1526 and controlled most of the Balkans. The Austrian Habsburg Ferdinand I contested the Ottoman Sultan Suleiman I the Magnificent for control of Hungary. Suleiman organized a huge Ottoman army in Bulgaria, consisting of Turks, elite Janissaries and various Balkan recruits in order to advance on the Habsburg capital of Vienna.

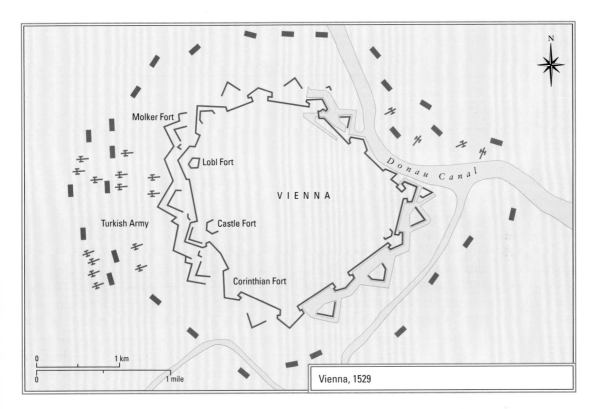

Molker Fort

Lobl Fort

VIENNA

Donau Canal

Turkish Army

Castle Fort

Corinthian Fort

N

0   1 km

0   1 mile

Vienna, 1529

The Ottoman army numbered at least 120,000.

With ample warning of the Ottoman advance, Ferdinand gave command of the Vienna garrison to Wilhelm von Roggendorf, who appointed Niklaus Salm to organize the defence of the city. Salm arrived in Vienna with German mercenary Landsknechts and Spanish musketeers, bringing the total garrison to 23,000. Suleiman's army was depleted by marches on the way to Vienna, giving an effective Ottoman force of over 80,000. Salm reinforced Vienna's walls with earthworks, which Ottoman cannon could not breach. The Ottoman besiegers dug mines under the walls to cause a collapse and broad breach. Ottoman mining efforts were detected and sorties at night were made by the garrison, successfully disrupting these efforts. One mine was completed and the Ottomans exploded gunpowder charges under the walls on 9 October, creating a breach. The garrison had detected the mine in time to have reserves of Landsknechts at the breach to meet and repel the Ottoman assault. The Ottoman army, suffering from lack of supplies and disease, launched a final assault in three columns on 14 October. This attack was repulsed and Suleiman decided to break off the siege, having lost 15,000 men. Vienna garrison casualties were light, most losses being among the civilian population.

■ Coron, 1533–34

The Ottoman fortress of Coron (now Koroni) in Messenia, Greece, was captured by Imperialist forces in 1532. The following year, it was besieged by an Ottoman army, which forced the surrender of its Spanish garrison.

■ Baghdad, 1534

Suleiman the Magnificent captured Baghdad from the Safavid Dynasty in a bloodless conquest, because its ruler had fled leaving the city undefended. It was a significant strategic and military gain for the ascendant Ottoman Empire.

▪ TUNIS, 1535

Holy Roman Emperor Charles V destroyed Hayreddin Barbarossa's fleet off Tunis after a costly yet successful siege at La Goletta. Tunis fell and a massacre of its inhabitants was carried out. Barbarossa managed to flee to escape to Algiers.

▪ PREVESA, 28 SEPTEMBER 1538

In 1537, Suleiman the Magnificent chose to besiege Corfu. Charles V's admiral, the Genoese Andrea Doria, was sent in pursuit of the Ottoman fleet. His approach made Suleiman the Magnificent abandon the siege and return to Constantinople, leaving Khaireddin Barbarossa in charge at Prevesa, the nearest Ottoman base to Corfu. Andrea Doria caught up with him in 1538, but he held back from fighting a decisive battle. Instead, an isolated Venetian galleon lay becalmed some distance from friendly galleys. The static vessel was then attacked by Ottoman galleys, but it managed to drive them off using superior broadside gunnery and took no damage from ramming. Doria's caution appeared justified, although his subsequent naval victory was due more to the weather; the pursuing corsair fleet was caught in a storm and many ships were wrecked off the coast of Albania.

▪ BACENTE, 1542

Cristóvão de Gama, son of Vasco de Gama, led a Portuguese army in Somalia against a Somali Muslim army. The enemy had taken possession of the strategic hill of Bacente to launch raids. De Gama believed that failing to engage them would make the natives abandon his troops. He won his first battle against the Somalis when he captured this strategic hill despite superior enemy numbers, losing only eight soldiers.

▪ SOKHOISTA, 1545

After an unsuccessful siege of the Georgian fortress of Oltisi, the battle of Sokhoista was fought between Ottoman and Georgian armies in what is now north-eastern Turkey. It was a decisive defeat for the Georgians.

▪ SIEGE OF EGER, 1552

Then called Erlau, Eger was defended by Istvan Dobo, who drove off the Ottomans for 38 days, sustained by wine – thought by the enemy to be bull's blood – and the resourceful women of the garrison.

▪ DJERBA, 9–14 MAY 1560

The naval battle of Djerba took place near the island of Djerba off Tunisia. The Ottoman fleet, under Piyale Pasha's command, defeated a large joint fleet composed mainly of Spanish ships. Half of the European ships were destroyed and thousands of men were killed, many of them oarsmen. The survivors took refuge in the castle of Djerba, which was then besieged and fell following surrender after three months of assault.

▪ MALTA, 18 MAY–11 SEPTEMBER 1565

In 1530 the Knights of St John were given the island of Malta by the Holy Roman Emperor Charles V and built modern fortifications mounting a total of 80 guns to protect key points on the island. These included Fort St Elmo on the Sciberras Peninsula dividing Marsamxett Harbour from the Grand Harbour, Fort St Angelo at Birgu and Fort

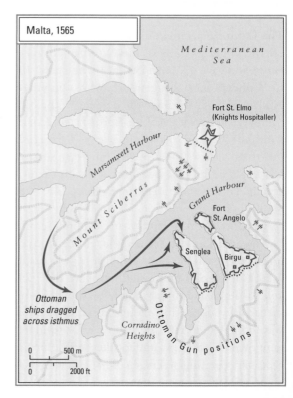

Saint Michael at Senglea. In 1565 Sultan Suleiman the Magnificent ordered an invasion of Malta to eliminate the threat posed by the Knights' constant raids on Ottoman shipping and harbours.

Suleiman gathered an invasion force of at least 32,000 men and up to 100 siege guns under Kızılahmedli Mustafa Pasha which landed at Marsaxlokk. The Grand Master of the Knights of St John, Jean de la Valette, commanded the island's defenders, but was badly outnumbered, having just over 6,000 men (including 500 knights). The invaders initially besieged Fort St Elmo, defended by a 1,500-strong garrison, which held out for over a month before being overrun. The capture of the fort had cost 6,000 Ottoman casualties, but Kızılahmedli Mustafa Pasha followed up this costly success with repeated assaults on Birgu and Senglea supported by artillery bombardments in which an estimated 130,000 round shot were fired. All these attacks were beaten off with heavy losses and by early September, both sides were exhausted. The deadlock was broken on 7th September when a 10,000-strong Spanish relief force under the Viceroy of Sicily, Don Garcia Álvarez de Toledo, landed at St Paul's Bay and routed the Ottoman army. Kızılahmedli Mustafa Pasha's force had inflicted 2,500 casualties on the island's defenders, but lost at least 10,000 men. An estimated 7,500 Maltese civilians died during the siege.

■ ASTRAKHAN, 1569

In 1569, Ottoman Sultan Selim II besieged Astrakhan, which had been Russian since 1556. The city on the Volga river held out, but was partially burnt down. A Russian relief army then broke the siege.

■ CYPRUS I NICOSIA, 1570

The operations of the Ottoman conquest of Cyprus fall into two distinct episodes. The first was the seven-week-long siege of Nicosia, which lasted from 22 July to 9 September 1570. The city, with its fine new angle bastions, had supplies and munitions for a two-year siege, but these were badly administered. The rivalry that existed between Nicosia and Famagusta also played its own part in compounding the tragedy, because there was actually a dispute over who should cut and store the crops that lay midway between the two cities. The lack of ammunition allowed the Ottomans entry. As panic spread through Nicosia many tried to escape, only to be cut down. The commander Dandolo dressed himself in his finest robe so that he would be recognized. He was beheaded, the most senior of the 20,000 to lose their lives.

■ CYPRUS II FAMAGUSTA, 1570–71

The defence of Famagusta, which held out for eleven months, was helped by the outstanding quality of its garrison commanders. The city only fell when ammunition and food supplies ran low and no relief came.

■ LEPANTO, 7 OCTOBER 1571

The Ottoman Empire dominated the eastern Mediterranean and, after capturing Cyprus, was in position with a huge galley fleet to project its power into the central and western Mediterranean as

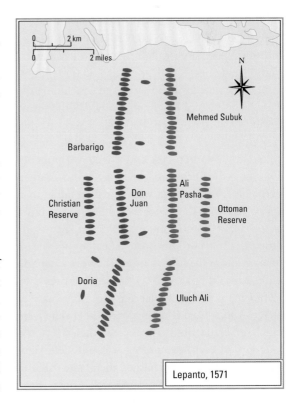

Lepanto, 1571

well. In response, several Catholic Mediterranean states created a Holy League and formed a fleet to oppose the threat from the Muslim Ottoman fleet.

The Ottoman fleet was commanded by Muezzinzade Ali Pasha and consisted of 280 galleys of various sizes – carrying 740 cannon – plus about 40 support vessels. The Ottoman crews included 22,000 Turkish soldiers, plus 10,000 elite Janissaries. In addition, the ships were manned by 10,000 skilled sailors of various nationalities, plus another 40,000 galley slaves. Ottoman crews were armed with composite bows, muskets and various edged weapons. Ottoman artillery traditionally used stone projectiles, which were designed to fragment upon impact, inflicting large numbers of personnel casualties.

The Holy League fleet was commanded by Don Juan of Austria, seconded by Colonna of Venice, Andrea Doria of Genoa, Barbarigo of Venice and Bazan of Spain. Galleys of the fleet were from Spain, Malta, Venice, Genoa, the Papal States and other Italian states, with the total number of galleys being 208, carrying 1300 cannon. Six of the ships were large galleases, able to carry extra cannon and crew. The fleet carried 23,000 soldiers from every state in the Holy League, including the elite Spanish Naval Regiment, in which the future author Cervantes served. The galleys were further crewed by 40,000 sailors and oarsmen, armed with crossbows, muskets and edged weapons. In contrast to the Ottoman fleet, many of the oarsmen of the Holy League fleet were free men rather than slaves. Another difference was that the cannon crews favoured iron cannonballs rather than stone projectiles. Finally, Don Juan had ramming beaks removed from the galleys, in order to place cannon in the forward bows with a clear field of fire.

The opposing fleets met off the west coast of Greece and advanced against each other drawn up in lines of battle. Both sides formed their fleets into four groups each, comprising a centre, left, right and reserve. The League pushed their large galleases forward and the iron cannonballs fired from

these sank dozens of Ottoman ships, disrupting the formations of the enemy fleet. In an effort to retrieve the situation, the Ottoman fleet tried to outmanoeuvre their opponents. The Ottoman left wing attempted to outflank the League fleet and Doria turned south to meet this threat. This created a gap in the League line, which Ottoman ships rowed into. Part of the Ottoman fleet also moved around the League left flank, in between the ships and the shore. The League centre and reserve groups moved into position successfully covering both flanks and the gap in the line.

The opposing fleets came into contact all along the line, with boarding parties clashing in fierce close combat. Barbarigo was killed by an arrow, and Cervantes was shot three times, losing the use of one hand. On board the Ottoman ships, many Christian galley slaves turned on their masters in the midst of battle. Spaniards boarded Ali's flagship and killed the Ottoman commander, as his fleet suffered decisive defeat. The Holy League sank 50 enemy ships, captured 137 more and liberated 10,000 slaves, while inflicting 20,000 casualties. Holy League losses included 17 ships and 7500 casualties.

■ SZIKSZO, 8 OCTOBER 1588

Szikszo was ransacked and burnt down several times, destroying even the strongest building of the town, the church. In 1588, there was a battle nearby when the outnumbered Hungarian Army defeated the Turks.

■ SISAK, 22 JUNE 1593

In 1593, a combined force of Croats with the Duchies of Carinthia and Carniola inflicted a defeat upon Ottoman forces under the Bosnian governor-general at Sisak, at the confluence of the rivers Sava and Drupa.

■ CĂLUGĂRENI, 23 AUGUST 1595

The battle of Călugăreni was one of the most important battles in the history of Romania, fought between the victorious Michael the Brave with his Wallachian army and Sinan Pahsa, who commanded the Ottoman forces.

■ KERESZTES, 24–26 OCTOBER 1596

Archduke Maximilian of Austria and Sigismund

Bathory of Transylvania risked everything in one huge battle with the Ottoman forces at Keresztes (modern Mezokeretses in eastern Hungary). Not only was their army a large one, but it was most unusual in its composition, being predominately cavalry. On the right, the Ottomans were driven back in disarray across the marsh. Their centre companies advanced to join them and destroyed a force of Janissaries.

■ **KHOTYN (CHOCIM), 2 SEPT–9 OCT 1621**
An Ottoman army of at least 120,000 men commanded by Sultan Osman II advanced from Constantinople and Adrianople into the western Ukraine. At Khotyn, it was confronted by a Polish army of 30,000 men under Grand Lithuanian Hetman Jan Karol Chodkiewicz, supported by 25,000 Cossacks commanded by Hetman Petro Konashevych-Sahaidachnyi. Chodkiewicz' forces had taken up strong defensive positions around the fortress of Khotyn, which were reinforced with extensive earthworks. Repeated Ottoman

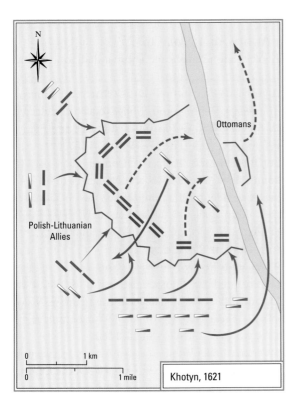

Khotyn, 1621

assaults were made over several weeks, but were all beaten off with heavy losses. The Sultan's efforts to cut Polish supply lines were more successful and Chodkiewicz was one of many who died from disease and malnutrition. His successor, Prince Stanisław Lubomirski, was forced to abandon his outer defences, but heavy losses on both sides (42,000 Ottoman and 14,500 Polish casualties) led to a compromise peace, the Treaty of Khotyn.

■ **ACTION OF 28 SEPTEMBER 1644**
An Ottoman convoy sailing from Constantinople to Alexandria was intercepted and defeated by a squadron of six Maltese galleys in a seven-hour action. Two Ottoman vessels were captured after inflicting 250 casualties on their opponents.

■ **ACTION OF 26 MAY 1646**
An Ottoman fleet of five galleases and 75 galleys under Kapudan Pasha Kara Musa Pasha attacked Tommaso Morosini's Venetian squadron of seven sailing ships that was in the mouth of the Dardanelles Strait. The action was inconclusive, but the Ottoman fleet withdrew.

CANDIA, 1 MAY 1648–27 SEPTEMBER 1669
An 80,000-strong Ottoman army under Grand Vizier Köprülü Fazil Ahmed forced the surrender of Candia (now Heraklion) on Crete after the longest siege in history. The Venetian garrison of 22,000 men were allowed to evacuate the island.

■ **FOCCIES, 12 MAY 1649**
A Venetian fleet of 19 sailing vessels under Giacomo Riva defeated an Ottoman fleet of 11 sailing ships, 10 galleasses and 72 galleys. The Turks lost nine sailing vessels, three galleasses and two galleys.

■ **ACTION OF 10 JULY 1651**
An Ottoman fleet of 55 sailing ships, 6 galleasses and 53 galleys under Kapudan Pasha Hosambegzade Ali Pasha was defeated off Naxos by Alvise Mocenigo's Venetian fleet of 28 sailing vessels, six galleasses and 24 galleys.

■ **DARDANELLES I, 16 MAY 1654**
Giuseppe Delfino's Venetian fleet of 16 sailing ships, two galleasses and eight galleys fought an

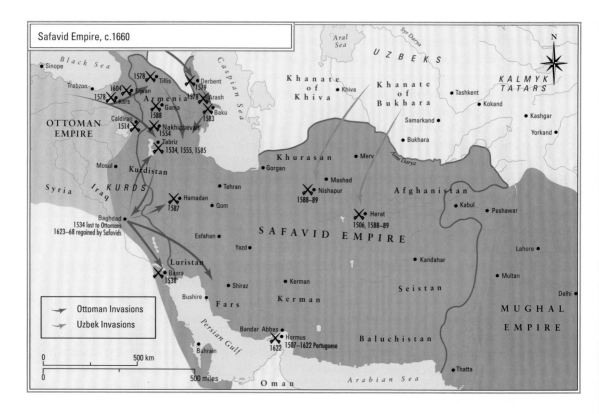

Safavid Empire, c.1660

Ottoman Invasions
Uzbek Invasions

indecisive action against an Ottoman fleet of 30 sailing vessels, six galleasses and 40 galleys. Each side lost four vessels.

■ DARDANELLES II, 21 JUNE 1655
An Ottoman fleet of 36 sailing ships, eight galleasses and 60 galleys was defeated by Lazzaro Mocenigo's Venetian fleet of 26 sailing vessels, four galleasses and six galleys. Mocenigo lost one ship, but destroyed 13 Ottoman vessels.

■ DARDANELLES III, 26 JUNE 1656
Lorenzo Marcello's Venetian fleet of 29 sailing ships, seven galleasses and 31 galleys defeated an Ottoman fleet of 28 sailing ships, nine galleasses and 61 galleys. The Venetians lost four ships, but destroyed 84 Ottoman vessels.

■ ACTION OF 3 MAY 1657
A Venetian fleet of six galleasses and 19 galleys defeated an Algerian squadron of nine vessels. All but one of the Algerian ships were captured or destroyed, while Venetian casualties totalled 117 killed and 346 wounded.

■ ACTION OF 18 MAY 1657
A Venetian squadron commanded by Lazaro Mocenigo comprising the *Capitana d'Algeri* (ex-Algerian *Perla*, captured earlier that year), *Arma di Midelborgo*, *Pomerlan* and *Arma di Cologia* defeated an Algerian and Ottoman squadron at Suazich.

■ DARDANELLES IIII, 17–19 JULY 1657
Topal Mehmed Pasha's Ottoman fleet of 18 sailing ships, 10 galleasses and 30 galleys defeated a Venetian fleet of 20 sailing vessels, seven galleasses and four galleys under Lazzaro Mocenigo, breaking the blockade of the Dardanelles.

■ ACTION OF 27 AUGUST 1661
A Venetian fleet of two galleasses and 20 galleys commanded by Giorgio Morosini defeated an Ottoman fleet of 36 galleys off the island of Milos in the Aegean. The Ottomans lost nine galleys.

■ ACTION OF 29 SEPTEMBER 1662
A Venetian fleet intercepted an Alexandria-bound Ottoman convoy of 58 vessels between the Aegean islands of Kos and Kalymnos. The convoy's escort

was defeated and a total of 32 Ottoman vessels were captured or sunk.

■ SZENTGOTTHÁRD, 1 AUGUST 1664

A 120,000-strong Ottoman army commanded by Grand Vizier Köprülü Fazıl Ahmed was defeated at Szentgotthárd (Saint Gotthard) in western Hungary by Raimondo Montecúccoli's Imperialist army of 40,000 men. The Imperialists lost 2000 men, but inflicted 16,000 casualties.

■ LWÓW (LESIENICE), 24 AUGUST 1675

An Ottoman army of 20,000 men commanded by Pasha Ibrahim Shyshman invaded Poland, advancing on the city of Lwów (now Lviv, western Ukraine). King Jan III Sobieski had only 6000 Polish troops to defend the region, which were attacked by an Ottoman advance guard of 10,000 men (largely Tatar cavalry). Sobieski made skilful use of the terrain to negate his opponents' numerical superiority, defeating the Ottoman force in a 30-minute action.

■ TREMBOWLA, SEPTEMBER–OCTOBER 1675

An Ottoman army of 10,000 men destroyed the town of Trembowla in the Ukraine, but were unable to take the castle, which was held by a garrison of no more than 80 dragoons and 200 civilians.

■ VIENNA II, 17 JULY–12 SEPTEMBER 1683

The Ottoman Empire had failed to take the Austrian Habsburg capital of Vienna by siege in 1529 and had disputed with the Habsburgs over control of Hungary for over a dozen decades. The Ottomans organized an army to try a siege of Vienna again. Kara Mustafa was given command of an Ottoman army of 200,000 Turks and Balkan auxiliaries, which reached Vienna with an effective strength of 150,000 for the siege. Habsburg Emperor Leopold I left Vienna with a garrison of 16,000 under the command of Count Starhemberg. As in 1529, cannon were not able to breach the walls of Vienna, so the Ottomans had to rely on digging mines under the walls in attempts to create breaches. Meanwhile, a Holy League was organized and Holy Roman Empire German states assembled an army to relieve Vienna. The Polish-Lithuanian Confederation joined the League and the Polish King Jan III

Sobieski took command of the relief army. Several Ottoman mining attempts were foiled during the siege, while other mines were successfully loaded with gunpowder and exploded. These created breaches in the outer works of Vienna, but the inner works remained intact. The Ottoman army continued assaults on the city even after Sobieski arrived just west of Vienna at Kahlenberg Hill with the relief army of 80,000 troops. League infantry engaged the Ottoman army, while Sobieski kept 20,000 cavalry in reserve. Sobieski then launched the cavalry in a decisive attack, personally leading the spearhead of 3000 Polish 'winged hussars'. The exhausted Ottoman army, having lost over 15,000 men, broke and fled, abandoning hundreds of cannon. League losses were 4500. For his failure, Kara Mustafa was executed in Belgrade.

■ BUDA, JUNE–SEPTEMBER 1686

Buda was besieged by a 75,000-strong army of the Holy League (the Holy Roman Empire, Poland and Venice). The Ottoman garrison of 7000 men repelled several assaults, but the city was stormed on 2 September.

■ MOHÁCS, 12 AUGUST 1687

A 60,000-strong Imperialist army commanded by Duke Charles of Lorraine and the Elector of Bavaria, Maximilian II, advanced into Hungary where they were confronted by an Ottoman army of similar size under the Grand Vizier, Sari Süleyman Paşa.

Although the Ottoman Army was deployed in well-fortified positions, the Grand Vizier ordered his 8000 Spahi cavalry to attack on the Imperialists' left flank which was held after fierce fighting. The two armies then disengaged for some hours, before each attacked simultaneously. The Ottomans' Janissary infantry made a frontal assault, again supported by Spahi cavalry which attempted to outflank the Imperialist line, but failed as they were unable to penetrate the broken terrain. Having beaten off this attack, the Imperialists advanced, breaking the demoralized Ottoman army, which sustained losses of 10,000 men and over 60 cannon. Imperialist casualties were less than 1000.

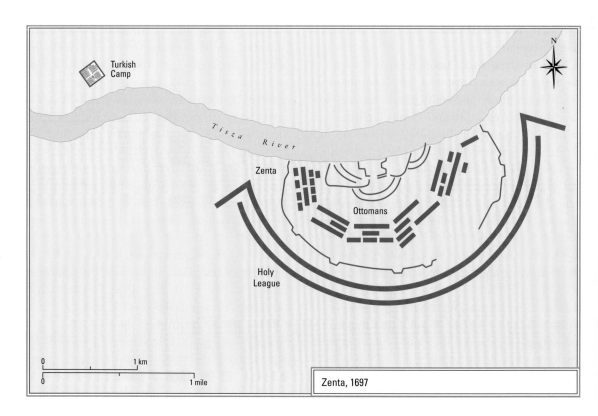

Zenta, 1697

■ **BELGRADE, 30 JULY–6 SEPTEMBER 1688**
A Holy League army commanded by the Elector of Bavaria, Maximilian II, besieged the Ottoman garrison of Belgrade. After prolonged bombardment, Maximilian stormed the city with the loss of 4000 men. Ottoman casualties totalled 5000.

■ **SLANKAMEN, 19 AUGUST 1691**
An Imperialist army of 50,000 men commanded by Louis William, Margrave of Baden-Baden, invaded Serbia, but was surrounded by an Ottoman army of 80,000 men under the Grand Vizier, Köprülü Fazıl Mustafa Pasha. By the time that the battle was fought, disease and desertion had reduced the armies to 33,000 and 50,000 men respectively. Despite being outnumbered, the Imperialists won a decisive victory, inflicting 20,000 casualties for the loss of 8000 men.

■ **OINOUSSES ISLANDS, 9 AND 19 FEB 1695**
Antonio Zeno's Venetian fleet of 21 sailing ships, five galleasses and 21 galleys was defeated with the loss of three vessels by an Ottoman fleet of 20 sailing ships and 24 galleys under Mezzo Morto Hüseyin Pasha.

■ **AZOV CAMPAIGN, 1695–1696**
Tsar Peter the Great's armies fought an epic campaign between 1695 and 1696 to capture the Ottoman fortress of Azov, which blocked Russian access to the Sea of Azov and the Black Sea. In 1695, a Russian army of 31,000 men unsuccessfully besieged Azov, which was held tenaciously by a garrison of 7000 men. The fortress finally fell on 19 July 1696, following attacks by a 70,000-strong Russian army and prolonged bombardments by the Tsar's newly built fleet.

■ **ANDROS, 22 AUGUST 1696**
Bartolomeo Contarini's Venetian and Papal fleet of 22 sailing ships, plus some galleasses and galleys fought an indecisive action off the Aegean island of Andros against an Ottoman fleet of 35 sailing ships and some galliots.

BOZCAADA SEA BATTLES, 6 JULY, 1 AND 20 SEPTEMBER 1697

A Venetian fleet of 29 sailing ships commanded by Bartolomeo Contarini was defeated in a series of three actions in the Aegean by an Ottoman fleet of 26 sailing vessels. One Venetian ship was lost.

ZENTA (SENTA), 11 SEPTEMBER 1697

An 80,000-strong Ottoman army commanded by Sultan Mustafa II was overtaken by the Austrians as it was crossing the river at Zenta and trapped and defeated by Prince Eugene of Savoy's Austrian Army of 50,000 men. The Ottomans lost all their artillery as well as the sultan's treasure box to the Austrians. It was a major victory for Austria. The Ottomans lost at least 20,000 men, while Austrian casualties totalled 500.

PODHAJCE, 8–9 SEPTEMBER 1698

A 6000-strong Polish army commanded by Field Crown Hetman Feliks Kazimierz Potocki defeated a 14,000 man Tatar force under Kaplan-Girey near Podhajce in the western Ukraine. Much of the Tatar force escaped the Polish pursuit.

SAMOTHRACE, 20 SEPTEMBER 1698

A Venetian fleet of 20 ships fought an inconclusive action against an Ottoman fleet of 25 ships, supported by a squadron of seven Tunisian and Tripolitanian vessels off the island of Samothrace in the northern Aegean.

PETERWARDEIN, 5 AUGUST 1716

An Ottoman army of 120,000 men under Silahdar Damat Ali Pasha besieged Peterwardein (Petrovaradin), which was defended by 8000 Serbian troops. The Ottomans were defeated with the loss of 6000 men by Prince Eugene's 83,000-strong Imperial Army.

MATAPAN, 19 JULY 1717

Kapudan Pasha Ibrahim Pasha's Ottoman fleet of 52 sailing ships and four galleys was defeated by the Count of Rio Grande's fleet of 33 sailing ships and 24 galleys, which included Portuguese, Venetian, Papal and Maltese vessels.

GROCKA, 22 JULY 1739

A 100,000-strong Ottoman army under the Grand Vizier İvaz Mehmet Pasha defeated Feldmarschall George Olivier's Austrian army of 56,000 men at Grocka near Belgrade. The Austrians were forced to retreat after losing 10,000 men.

STAVUCHANY, 28 AUGUST 1739

Field Marshal Count Burkhard Christoph von Münnich's Russian Army of 61,000 men attacked an Ottoman army of at least 80,000 men under Serasker Veli-pasha. The Ottoman army deployed on high ground protected by field defences near the village of Stavuchany in the Ukraine and used this as a base for repeated attacks on the Russian flanks and rear. All these attacks were beaten off and the Russians won a decisive victory.

KHESILI, 14 DECEMBER 1757

Ali Pasha's Ottoman Army of 61,000 men (including 10,000 Georgian auxiliaries) was defeated by a Georgian army of barely 16,000 men commanded by King Solomon I. The Ottoman force was almost annihilated, losing 45,000 men.

ASPINDZA, 20 APRIL 1770

A Georgian Army of 7000 men commanded by King Heraclius II defeated a 20,000-strong Ottoman army near Aspindza in southern Georgia. The Ottomans lost at least 4000 men, while Georgian casualties were insignificant.

LARGA, 7 JULY 1770

A Russian army of 38,000 men and 115 guns commanded by Field Marshal Pyotr Rumyantsev attacked and defeated a force of 65,000 Crimean Tatar cavalry, 15,000 Ottoman infantry and 33 guns under Kaplan Girey. The Russians lost no more than 100 men in the eight-hour battle, but inflicted 3000 casualties and captured 33 guns. Rumyantsev was awarded the Order of St George, First Class, in recognition of his victory.

KAGUL (CAHUL), 1 AUGUST 1770

A Russian army of 40,000 men commanded by Field Marshal Pyotr Rumyantsev attacked and defeated Grand Vizier Ivazzade Halil Pasha's Ottoman Army of 75,000 men near the River Kagul in Moldavia. (The Grand Vizier's army was theoretically supported by 80,000 Crimean Tatar cavalry, but these refused to take any part in the battle.) The Russians lost no more than 1500 men, while inflicting 22,000 casualties on the Ottoman forces.

■ ORLOV REVOLT, 1770

Russian agents began stirring unrest against Ottoman rule in the Mani region of the southern Peloponnese in the mid-1760s. The arrival of a Russian fleet of 14 ships of the line under Count Aleksey Grigoryevich Orlov in February 1770 prompted the region to flare up into rebellion, which spread across much of Greece. However, the Russian failure to land an army to support the rebels allowed Ottoman troops to crush the revolt.

■ VROMOPIGADA, 1770

A 7000-strong Maniot (southern Greek) rebel force commanded by Exarchos Grigorakis and his nephew, Zanet Grigorakis, defeated an Ottoman army of 16,000 men under Hatzi Osman, Pasha of the Peloponnese. The Ottomans lost 10,000 men.

■ ACTION OF 4 JULY 1773

Captain Kingsbergen's 16-gun Russian warships *Koron* and *Taganrog* encountered two Ottoman ships of the line, a frigate and a xebec, off Balaklava in the Crimea. The Russians drove off the Ottoman squadron despite being heavily out-gunned.

■ ACTION OF 3 SEPTEMBER 1773

Captain Kingsbergen's Russian squadron of three ships of the line and a frigate fought an inconclusive action in the Black Sea against an Ottoman squadron of three ships of the line and four frigates.

■ ACTION OF 20 JUNE 1774

An Ottoman fleet of five ships of the line, nine frigates and 26 galleys fought an inconclusive action against Vice Admiral Senyavin's squadron of three frigates, four 16-gun vessels, two bomb vessels and three smaller craft.

■ SZOLNOK CASTLE, 17TH–18TH CENTURIES

The castle of Szolnok was a key strongpoint in Ottoman Hungary between 1552 and 1685,

armed with 24 cannon and garrisoned by 2000 Ottoman troops. In 1685, the castle was retaken and modernized by the Imperialists.

Italian Wars 1495–1504

■ FORNOVO, 1495

In an attempt to exert his claim on the Kingdom of Naples in 1494, the French King Charles VIII marched his forces through Italy. His army was large and outfitted with the most up-to-date technology. Few contended against it, with the French entering Naples in February 1495. In response to the French invasion, Venice, Milan and the Papacy joined the Holy Roman Empire to create the Holy League. But Charles' army was devastated by disease, not warfare. Weakened, they slowly retreated, only to find armies of the Holy League blocking them at Fornovo. A bloody battle followed, leaving the Holy League barely in charge of the field,

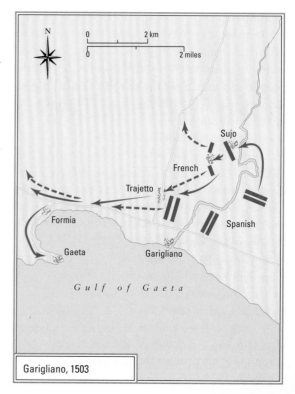

Garigliano, 1503

but they could not stop their men leaving the battle to loot the booty from the French League baggage train, meaning that the outcome was undecided at first. This is generally considered to be the first major engagement of the Italian Wars.

■ NOVARA, 1500

A French army, largely composed of Swiss mercenaries, besieged Novara, which was held by Ludovico Sforza's garrison of Swiss mercenaries. The garrison agreed to evacuate the city and Sforza was betrayed to the French.

■ RUVO, 23 FEBRUARY 1503

A Spanish force under Gonzalo Fernández de Córdoba had held a fortified camp at Barletta on the Italian Adriatic coast for several months against a larger French army commanded by Louis d'Armagnac, Duke of Nemours. Gonzalo seized the opportunity presented by the Duke's departure to storm the town of Ruvo, which was defended by a French garrison under Jacques de la Palice, taking 600 prisoners and capturing 1000 cavalry horses.

■ GARIGLIANO, 29 DECEMBER 1503

Gonzalo Fernández de Córdoba's 15,000 Spaniards attacked and defeated a French army of 23,000 men under Ludovico II, Marquess of Saluzzo on the River Garigliano. The Spanish lost 900 men, but inflicted 8000 casualties.

Indian and South-East Asian Wars 1500–1775

■ SUKHOTHAI, 1507

Because Chiang Mai (northern Thailand) was a smaller state than neighbouring Ayutthaya (south-central Thailand), its rulers maintained an aggressive stance of independence. In 1507, King Ratana of Chiang Mai attempted an invasion of Ayutthaya, but was defeated near Sukhothai.

■ PANIPAT I, 21 APRIL 1526

The first battle of Panipat was a major victory for Babur against Sultan Ibrahim Lodi, one that helped establish the Mughal Empire. Babur ordered his men to gather as many carts as they could find, which were lashed together using ropes, with enough space to place five or six mantlets. Babur's matchlock men were posted behind the mantlets. The defences were held and a victory resulted.

■ KHANWA, 17 MARCH 1527

A 25,000-strong Mughal army commanded by the Emperor Babur attacked and defeated a huge Rajput force of 140,000 men at Khanwa, near Agra. The victory allowed Babur to consolidate his rule in northern India.

■ GHAGHRA, 6 MAY 1529

A Mughal force of 30,000 men commanded by the Emperor Babur defeated a 150,000-strong Afghan and Bengali army under Sultan Mahmud Lodi and Sultan Nusrat Shah. Babur inflicted 12,500 casualties for the loss of only 200 men, in a one-sided victory.

■ PANIPAT II, 5 NOVEMBER 1556

A Rajput and Afghan army of 30,000 cavalry and 1500 war elephants commanded by Samrat Hem Chandra Vikramaditya (Hemu) – the Hindu Emperor from Delhi who ruled northern India – attacked a Mughal force of 10,000 men. The Mughal Army under Ataga Khan was on the point of defeat when Hemu was mortally wounded by an arrow and his disheartened men broke ranks. Following this victory, the Mughal Emperor Akbar reconquered Agra and Delhi.

■ NONG SARAI, 1593

At the battle of Nong Sarai, King Naresuan of Siam, who had been planning to attack Cambodia, foiled an invasion attempt by the Burmese. During a celebrated elephant-back duel, Naresuan killed the Burmese Crown Prince.

■ BALOCHPUR, 1623

Whilst his father, the Mughal Emperor Jahangir, was embroiled in a war against Persia, Prince Shahjahan raised a rebel army of dissident nobles, which was destroyed at Balochpur, south of Delhi, by loyalist forces.

■ SAMUGARH, 29 MAY 1658

The illness of the Mughal Emperor Shah Jahan

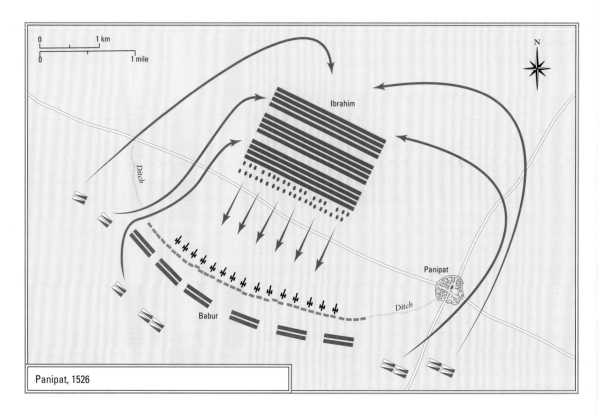

Panipat, 1526

in September 1657 led to a war between his sons, Dara Shikoh (the eldest and heir apparent) and his two younger brothers, Aurangzeb and Murad Baksh. Dara Shikoh had already been defeated by Aurangzeb at Dharmat, but still managed to assemble a 60,000-strong army with 80 cannon and 120 camel-mounted swivel guns. Aurangzeb and Murad Baksh commanded a force of 40,000 men supported by 60 cannon and 75 camel-mounted swivel guns. Aurangzeb's commander, Mir Jumla II, deployed many of his guns in concealed batteries to protect them from the initial bombardment of Dara Shikoh's more powerful artillery. This deployment was a key factor in Aurangzeb's victory, as his artillery inflicted a high proportion of the 30,000 casualties sustained by Dara Shikoh's army, while Aurangzeb lost no more than 2000 men.

■ KHAJWA, 5 JANUARY, 1659
After his victory at Samugarh, Aurangzeb deposed his father to become Mughal Emperor

and assembled an army of 90,000 men to attack his elder brother Shah Shuja, his most dangerous remaining rival. Shah Shuja was able to raise only 25,000 men, but employed European mercenary artillerymen and armed his infantry with the latest European muskets. Aurangzeb beat his brother in a hard-fought action, inflicting 9000 casualties for the loss of 11,000 men.

■ CHAMKAUR, 6 DECEMBER 1705
The Sikh Guru Gobind Singh and his 40-strong bodyguard held a fort near Chamkaur for almost 24 hours against a huge Mughal army. The Sikhs fought to the last man to allow the Guru to escape.

■ NADIR SHAH'S INVASION OF INDIA, 1738–39
An Iranian army of 55,000 men under Nadir Shah invaded the Mughal Empire and seized the frontier provinces of Ghazni, Kabul, Peshawar, Sindh and Lahore. Nadir Shah defeated the Mughal field army at the Battle of Karnal in February 1739, capturing the Emperor

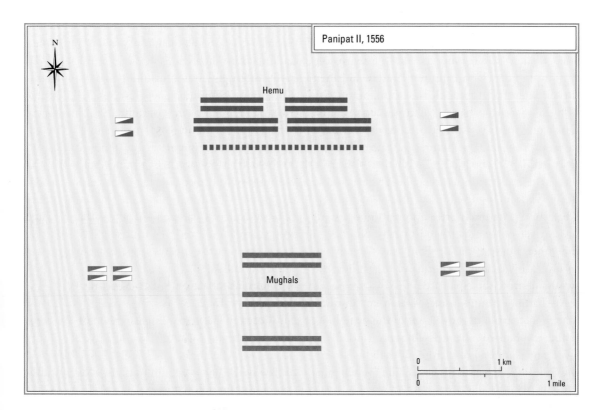

Panipat II, 1556

Hemu

Mughals

0   1 km

0   1 mile

N

Mohammad Shah and occupying Delhi. When rioting broke out, Nadir Shah ordered the sack of the city; the loot included the Peacock Throne of the Mughal Emperors.

■ AYUTTHAYA, 1767

Ayutthaya finally fell to the invading Burmese in 1767 after a long and brave siege. An extensive sack of the city was carried out, during which many works of art and historical records were destroyed.

War of the League of Cambrai 1508–1516

■ AGNADELLO, 14 MAY 1509

A French army of 30,000 men under Louis XII invaded Venetian territory in April 1509, opposed by a 25,000-strong army commanded by the Orsini cousins, Bartolomeo d'Alviano and Niccolò di Pitigliano. The French vanguard intercepted d'Alviano's 8000-strong detachment near the village of Agnadello, between Milan and Bergamo.

Initial French attacks were repelled, but Pitigliano refused to come to his cousin's aid and the Venetians were beaten with the loss of 4000 men.

■ PADUA, 15–30 SEPTEMBER 1509

Maximilian I's Imperialist army of 40,000 men besieged Padua, which was defended by a 15,000-strong Venetian garrison under Niccolò di Pitigliano. Maximilian raised the siege after his assaults were repelled, with the loss of 700 men.

■ POLESELLA, 22 DECEMBER 1509

A Venetian fleet moored in the River Po in preparation for an assault on the Duchy of Ferrara was defeated by a bombardment by Ferrarese artillery, which sank at least 15 galleys and inflicted 2000 casualties.

■ MIRANDOLA, 19 DEC 1510–20 JAN 1511

A Papal army commanded by Pope Julius II besieged Mirandola, which was held by a French garrison under Charles d'Amboise, Seigneur de Chaumont. The citadel fell when Papal forces launched an assault across the frozen moat.

■ **RAVENNA, 11 APRIL 1512**

In 1512, King Louis XII went on to the offensive. The French commander in Italy was young Gaston de Foix, who captured Brescia and then turned against Ravenna, the most important city still left in enemy hands. With the help of the Duke of Ferrara's artillery, breaches were made in the city's walls. But before the place could be stormed, de Foix had to deal with a Spanish army sent to relieve the situation. The Spanish dug a defensive trench and awaited the French attack. Theirs was a naturally strong position because it had a river on one flank and marshy ground on the other, but Gaston de Foix was determined to take it by assault. By means of his artillery he would destroy the Spaniards' field positions to leave barren ground across which to advance. The French artillery moved out of the siege lines, while the bulk of the French army forded the river. The planned bombardment then began, but the Spanish also had field pieces. The French guns

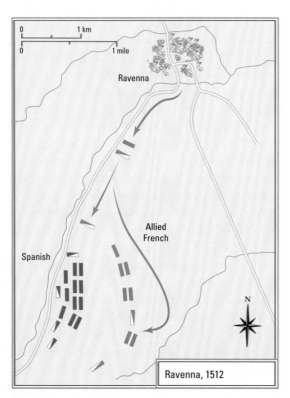

Ravenna, 1512

targeted the mounted Spanish knights, while the Spanish cannon created havoc among the French infantry. This short-range fire into densely packed ranks of knights was a turning point in the battle. One single cannon ball apparently killed 33 men. Knight charged against knight, breaking lances when they met. The Landsknechts in the French Army advanced, but here the trench came into its own by slowing their advance, allowing the Spanish sword and buckler men to slip under the points of the pikes and get in among them. The victorious French Army suffered huge losses, including its commander Gaston de Foix, while the losing Spanish Army was almost annihilated.

■ **BREST (BATTLE OF SAINT-MATHIEU), 10 AUGUST 1512**

Sir Edward Howard's English fleet of 25 ships defeated a Franco-Breton fleet of 22 vessels under René de Clermont, off Brest. The *Cordelière* accidentally blew up, sinking the *Regent*, after which the French withdrew.

■ **NOVARA, 6 JUNE 1513**

Swiss mercenaries captured Milan from Ludovico Sforza, but King Louis subsequently failed to pay them, so 6000 men from the Swiss troops crossed to Sforza's side at nearby Novara and vowed to recapture Milan for him. The pro-Sforza Swiss were then besieged in Novara by a French army. An armed confrontation was happily avoided by negotiation, although a plot to smuggle Sforza out was betrayed.

■ **GUINEGATE, 16 AUGUST 1513**

At Guinegate, English troops under Henry VIII and Imperial troops under Maximilian I surprised a body of French cavalry. So rapidly did the French retreat, the clash is called the Battle of the Spurs.

■ **FLODDEN FIELD, 9 SEPTEMBER 1513**

The Battle of Flodden Field was fought near the village of Branxton (an alternative name for the battle) in Northumberland between an English army commanded by the Earl of Surrey and an invading Scottish army under King James IV, who marched south with 30,000 men. The

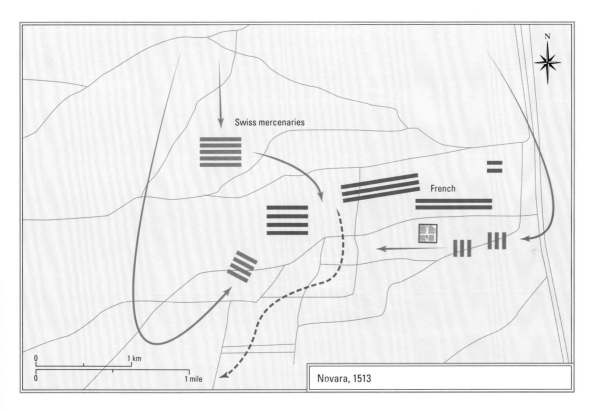

Swiss mercenaries

French

Novara, 1513

0   1 km

0   1 mile

Earl of Surrey placed himself across the Scottish route. The initial Scots attack was beaten off and the contest developed into a fierce hand-to-hand melee. King James IV got within a spear's length of Surrey before he was killed. Artillery was present on the Scottish side, but was little used. Archery also played a small part and Flodden is regarded as being a victory for the use of the bill over the pike, for which the conditions were not suitable. The death of their king meant that Flodden was a major defeat for the Scots.

■ LA MOTTA, 7 OCTOBER 1513

Also known as the battle of Schio, the battle of La Motta ended in a fine victory for a Spanish army over a Venetian army, whom they had pursued into the Veneto region of Italy.

■ MARIGNANO, 13–14 SEPTEMBER 1515

At Marignano, King Francis I of France defeated Swiss pikemen by using a combination of heavy cavalry and artillery. The Swiss reverse is regarded as ushering in a new era in the history of warfare.

4th Russian Lithuanian War 1512–22

■ ORSHA, 8 SEPTEMBER 1514

A 40,000-strong Muscovite army commanded by Boyar Ivan Chelyadnin invaded the Grand Duchy of Lithuania (modern Belarus) and attacked a combined Polish and Lithuanian force of 30,000 men under Konstanty Ostrogski, the Grand Hetman of Lithuania. The Muscovites failed to exploit their numerical superiority – their initial ill-coordinated attacks against the flanks of Ostrogski's force were beaten off and a Polish-Lithuanian cavalry counter-attack came close to breaking through the centre of Chelyadnin's over-stretched line. At the crucial moment the Grand Duchy's cavalry seemed to waver, before hastily retreating. The Muscovites pursued with all their remaining cavalry, but the fugitives suddenly wheeled aside to reveal massed artillery. The pursuers broke after a close-range bombardment and charges by the

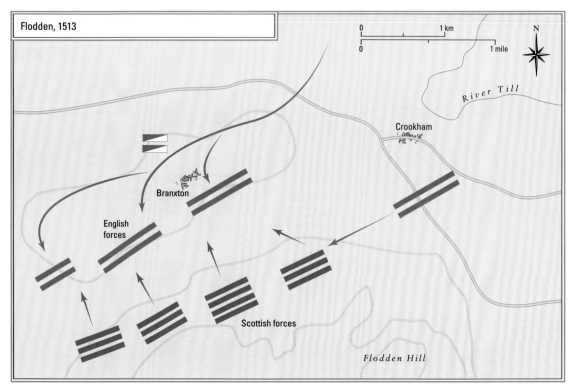

Flodden, 1513

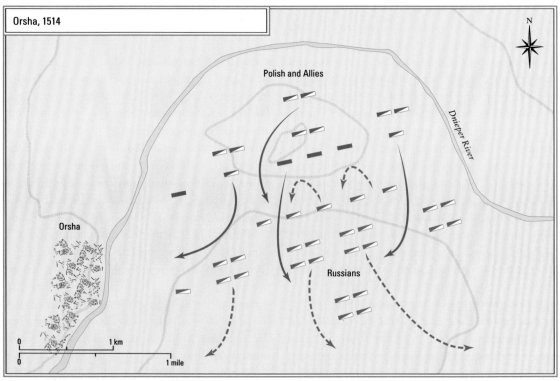

Orsha, 1514

Polish and Lithuanian reserves. The Muscovite Army was shattered – Chelyadin and at least 3,000 of his men were captured, together with 140 guns.

Slovenian Peasant Revolt 1515

■ **SLOVENIAN PEASANT REVOLT, FEBRUARY 1515**
Smouldering Slovenian peasant resentment against harsh landlords flared into open revolt in February 1515 and, within weeks, had spread throughout Slovenia. By the spring of that year, rebel forces numbered 80,000 men, who had taken effective control of the countryside. Many poorly defended castles were stormed and the alarmed local aristocracy raised an army, including a large contingent of mercenaries, which defeated the rebels near Celje, inflicting at least 2000 casualties.

Spanish Conquest of Latin America 1520–1680

■ **TENOCHTITLÁN, 1520**
The Spanish conquistador Hernán Cortés arrived in Tenochtitlán on 8 November 1519. Within a few months, the Spaniards became unpopular guests and a revolt began. During an Aztec festival, Pedro de Alavarado – a lieutenant of Cortés – armed with a small force slaughtered a large number of Aztec priests and nobles, fearing an uprising was about to occur. Cortés was at the time subduing a rival Spanish force, under Panfilo de Narvaez, sent out to arrest him by order of the Spanish governor in Havana. Cortés immediately returned to Tenochtitlán upon word from Alvarado. The Aztec Emperor Moctezuma tried to quell the anger of his subjects, but was stoned to death by the mob. Cortés decided to leave the capital before his force was overwhelmed by the Aztecs.

On 1 July 1520, the conquistadors exited the palace with their Indian allies close behind. They had muffled the horses' hooves and

carried wooden boards to cross the canals. The conquistadors were able to pass through the first three canals, the Tecpantzinco, Tzapotlan and Atenchicalco before, being detected by the Aztecs. The Aztecs attacked the fleeing conquistadors on the Tlacopan causeway from canoes, shooting arrows at them. The Spaniards returned fire with their crossbows and arquebuses. Many died as the conquistadors leaped into the water and drowned, weighed down by their armour and booty. A third of Cortés' men succeeded in reaching the mainland, while the remaining ones died in battle or were captured and later sacrificed on Aztec altars. The surviving conquistadors had little reprieve after reaching the mainland before the Aztecs appeared for an attack and chased them towards Tlacopan. The Spaniards finally found refuge in Otancalpolco, where they were aided by the Teocalhueyacans. This major Aztec victory is remembered as 'La Noche Triste', or 'The Night of Sorrows'.

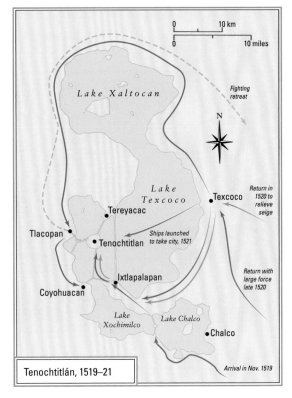

Tenochtitlán, 1519–21

Before reaching Tlaxcalan, the remaining force of conquistadors arrived at the plain of Otumba Valley where they were met by a vast Aztec force. The Aztecs intended to cut short the Spaniard's retreat from Tenochtitlán, but they had underestimated the value of the Spanish cavalry, as they had never seen them used in open battle on the plains. Despite the overwhelming numbers of Aztecs and the generally poor condition of the surviving conquistadors, Cortés snatched victory from the jaws of defeat when he spotted an Aztec commander in his distinctive colourful feather costume. He immediately charged him with several horsemen, killing the commander. The Spaniards suffered heavy losses, but were victorious. The Aztecs retreated. When Cortés finally reached Tlaxcala five days after fleeing Tenochtitlán, he had lost over 860 Spanish soldiers, as well as over 1000 Tlaxcalan allies. Cortés was able to regroup, then laid siege and conquered Tenochtitlán the following year.

■ **OTUMBA, 7 JULY 1520**

After the forced expulsion of the Spanish from Tenochtitlán, Cortes' forces arrived at the plain of Otumba Valley. Despite the overwhelming number of Aztec warriors, the Spanish prevailed in the battle and were able to reach Tlaxcalan to regroup.

■ **PUNTA QUEMADA, JANUARY 1525**

A brief encounter between a band of Spanish conquistadors and the warlike natives of Colombia. The conquistadors – under the command of Francisco Pizarro – fearing subsequent hostile encounters and unable to continue south by sea, chose to end the expedition at Punta Quemada.

■ **PUNÁ, APRIL 1531**

An engagement of Francisco Pizarro's conquest of Peru, which was fought in April 1531 on the island of Puná in Ecuador. The conquistadors decisively defeated the island's indigenous inhabitants.

■ **CAJAMACA, 16 NOVEMBER 1532**

A surprise attack on the Inca royal entourage

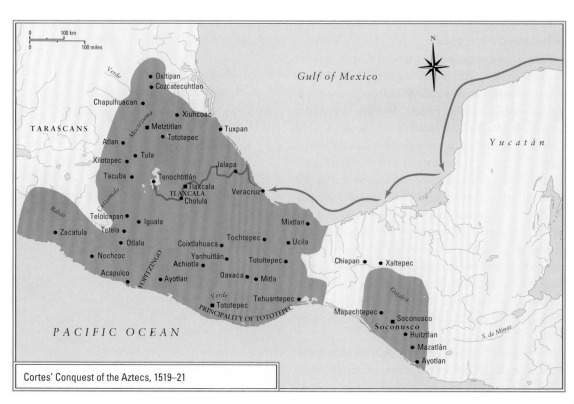

Cortes' Conquest of the Aztecs, 1519–21

orchestrated by Francisco Pizarro. The ambush achieved the goal of capturing the Inca (King) Atahualpa and claimed the lives of thousands of his followers.

■ Cuzco, 1533

After executing the Inca Atahualpa, the Spanish forces led by Francisco Pizarro marched to Cuzco, the Incan capital. The advance guard of 40 men fought a pitched battle with Incan troops in front of the city, securing victory.

■ Renoguelen (Reynogüelén), 1536

A battle between Spanish conquistadors and Mapuche warriors near the confluence of the Ñuble and Itata Rivers in Chile. The Spanish victory is usually taken as the beginning of the Arauco War.

■ Cuzco, 1536–37

A ten-month siege of Cuzco by Inca Emperor Manco Capac Yupanqui's forces against a garrison of Spanish conquistadors and their Indian auxiliaries under the command of Hernando Pizarro (Francisco's brother) between May 1536 and March 1537. After months of vicious fighting around Cuzco, with increasing low morale playing a factor and word of a Spanish relief force from Chile, Manco Capac decided to raise the siege at Cuzco and withdrew to Vilcabamba.

■ Manco Capac's Rebellion, 1536–44

After withdrawing from the siege of Cuzco, Manco Capac mounted a lengthy but ultimately unsuccessful rebellion against Spanish rule. The Incas moved to Ollantaytambo to wage a war of attrition against the conquistadors and later retreated to Vitcos. Manco Capac sided with Diego de Almagro against Pizarro when civil war broke out among the conquistadors. Seven of Almagro's followers managed to escape Pizarro and were given refuge by Manco Capac where they later assassinated the Inca in 1544.

■ Ollantaytambo, January 1537

A battle between the forces of Inca emperor Manco Capac and a Spanish expedition led by Hernando Pizarro in January 1537. To end the stand-off of the siege of Cuzco, the besieged mounted a raid against Manco Capac's headquarters in Ollantaytambo. The Incas defeated the Spaniards, but they did not pursue them to secure their victory because of the arrival of Spanish reinforcements to Cusco.

■ Abancay, 1537

After Diego de Almagro scattered the remnants of Manco Capac's army and seized Cuzco, a civil war broke out between him and the Pizarros. He defeated a Pazarrist army at the Abancay River in July 1537.

■ Las Salinas, 26 April 1538

A battle between the forces of Hernando and Gonzalo Pizarro against Diego de Almagro in April 1538. The engagement yielded a victory for Pizarro's forces with Almagro captured, the enemy routed and Cuzco in their possession.

■ Mixtón War, 1540–42

A war between the Spanish Conquistadors and their Aztec and Tlaxcalan allies against the Caxcanes and other semi-nomadic Indians of the area of north-western Mexico from 1540 until 1542. The war was named after an Indian stronghold in Zacatecas state in Mexico.

■ Chupas, 16 September 1542

Diego de Almagro II (El Mozo) continued to press claims as the rightful ruler of Peru. He gathered an army of supporters but was defeated outside Cuzco at Chupas in September 1542.

■ Anaquito, 1546

Spain had begun restricting the conquistadors' privileges, whereby the conquistadors revolted against the viceroy of Peru. Gonzalo Pizarro led the anti-royalist forces to victory at the battle of Anaquito, where the viceroy was murdered.

■ Chichimeca War, 1550–90

A conflict between the Spanish and their Indian allies against the Chichimeca Indians – one of the longest conflicts between the Spaniards and the Indians of New Spain within the history of the colony.

■ Quilacura, 11 February 1546

One of the battles in the long-running Arauco War, between the Spanish expedition of Pedro de Valdivia and a force of Mapuche warriors led by

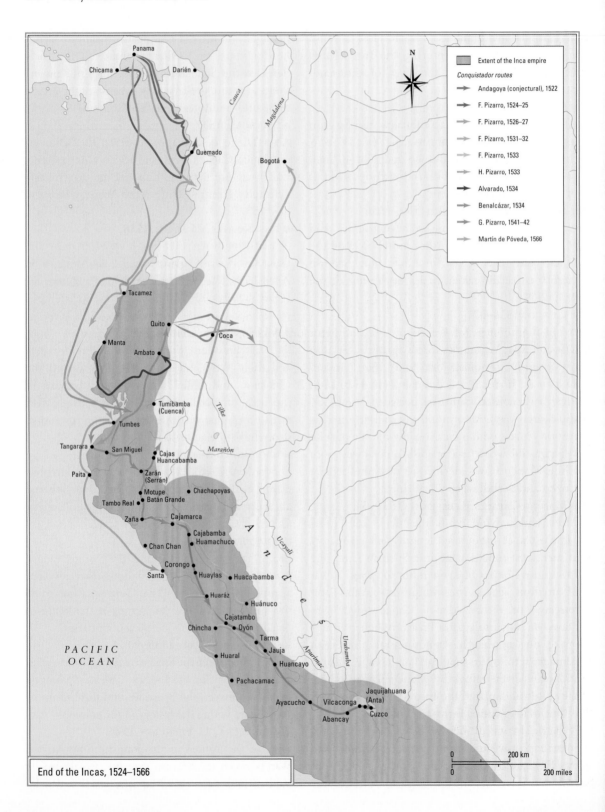

PACIFIC OCEAN

	Extent of the Inca empire
Conquistador routes	
→	Andagoya (conjectural), 1522
→	F. Pizarro, 1524–25
→	F. Pizarro, 1526–27
→	F. Pizarro, 1531–32
→	F. Pizarro, 1533
→	H. Pizarro, 1533
→	Alvarado, 1534
→	Benalcázar, 1534
→	G. Pizarro, 1541–42
→	Martín de Póveda, 1566

End of the Incas, 1524–1566

0   200 km
0   200 miles

Malloquete in February 1546. On the bank of the Bio-Bio river, the Spaniards defeated the Mapuche.

■ **HUARINA, 1554**
The new viceroy, Pedro de la Gasca, landed in Peru in 1547 and immediately began retaking areas taken by Gonzalo Pizarro. A contingent of viceroyalist troops, led by Diego Centeno, was severely defeated at Huarina by Francisco de Carvajal.

■ **ANGOL, 25 MARCH 1564**
A battle fought between the Mapuche and the Spanish conquerors in March 1564. The Spanish, under the command of Capt Lorenzo Bernal del Mercado, drove the Mapuche out of their defensive positions, pursued them down to the river bank and drove them into the river, where they were trapped. Approximately 1000 Mapuche forces were killed, including the Toqui Illanguelén and many more were wounded or captured.

■ **CONCEPCION, 1 FEBRUARY–1 APRIL 1564**
During the Arauco War, 20,000 warriors of the army of the Mapuche laid siege to the Spanish in the fortress of Concepcion, Chile On the first of April, the Mapuche army raised the siege and dispersed to their homes for the winter.

■ **CATIRAI, 7 JANUARY 1569**
A battle on a steep wooded hill in Catirai (Chile) between the Mapuche army of Toqui Llanganabal and the Spanish Army, led by Martín Ruiz de Gamboa, that resulted in a Mapuche victory.

■ **CURALABA, 21 DECEMBER 1598**
A battle between Spaniards led by Martín García Óñez de Loyola and Mapuche warriors led by Pelantaru at Curalaba (southern Chile) on 21 December 1598. The surprise night raid completely surprised Spaniards – killing the governor and nearly all of his soldiers – resulting in a rare victory for the Mapuche. This event marks the end of the 'Conquista' period in Chile's history, although the fast Spanish expansion in the south had already been halted in the 1550s.

■ **PUEBLO REVOLT, 10–21 AUGUST 1680**
An uprising of several pueblos of the Pueblo people against Spanish colonization in the province of Santa Fe de Nuevo México. Popé and a number of other Pueblo leaders planned and orchestrated the Pueblo Revolt. The day of the attack was ordered on 10 August. Meanwhile, Popé's insurgents besieged Santa Fe. On 21 August, the remaining Spanish settlers streamed out of the capital.

Spanish Conquest of the Yucatán
■ **FIRST EXPEDITIONS, 1517–18**
An expedition led by Francisco Hernández de Córdoba in search of slaves discovered the Yucatán Peninsula. The expedition was ambushed by Mayan warriors, forcing the Spaniards to return to Cuba and report of their discovery.

■ **FIRST CAMPAIGN, 1527–28**
Francisco de Montejo arrived in eastern Yucatán in 1527. As the Spanish advanced, they were first harried as they travelled and then openly attacked. There was no further success in subduing the country by 1528.

■ **SECOND CAMPAIGN, 1531–35**
Francisco de Montejo returned in 1531 to retake the Yucatán. Despite the brief occupation of Chichen Itza, Montejo was frequently besieged in his fort in Campeche, eventually forcing him to withdraw his forces to Veracruz in 1535.

■ **CONQUEST, 1540–46**
Francisco de Montejo 'the Younger' invaded Yucatán in 1540. He set up his capital in the Maya city of T'ho, which he renamed Mérida in 1542. The Xiu of Maní converted to Christianity, becoming a valuable ally of the Spanish that assisted in the conquest of the rest of the peninsula. The Spanish and Xiu defeated an army of the combined forces of the states of Eastern Yucatán in 1546, completing the conquest.

Italian Wars 1521–59

■ **FUENTERRABIA, 1521–24**
French and Basque forces held the fortress of Fuenterrabia in Navarre, in present-day northern Spain, repulsing repeated attacks by Spanish forces. Fuenterrabia was yielded to Spain by treaty in September 1524.

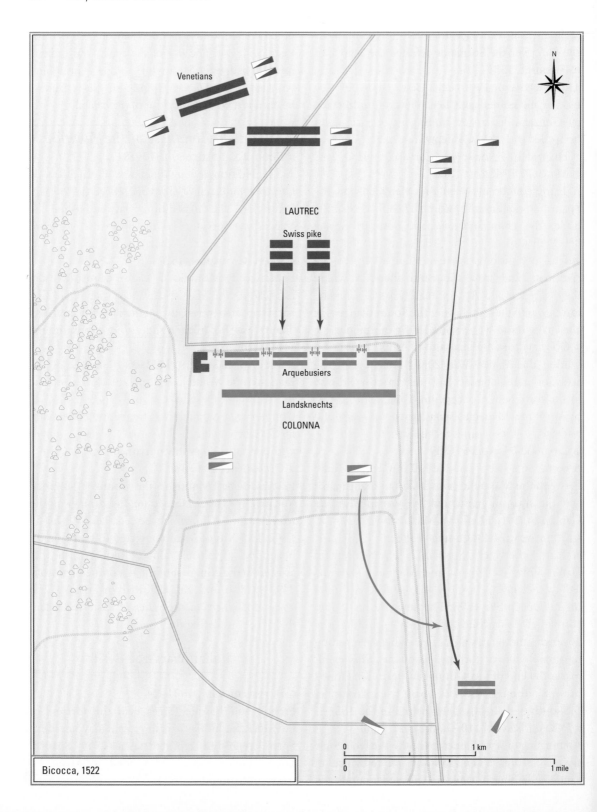

N

Venetians

LAUTREC

Swiss pike

Arquebusiers

Landsknechts

COLONNA

0 _____ 1 km

0 _____ 1 mile

Bicocca, 1522

■ MÉZIÈRES, 30 AUG–26 SEPT 1521

Bayard and Montmorency with 1000 Frenchmen successfully defended Mézières in modern-day western France against a besieging force of 35,000 Nassau troops, serving in Holy Roman Empire forces.

■ BICOCCA, 27 APRIL 1522

Vicomte de Lautrec led roughly 24,000 French troops, mercenary Swiss pikemen, Venetian troops and Italian 'Black Band' volunteers against Prospero Colonna's army, composed of Spanish troops, German Landsknechts and Milanese and Papal States forces. Lautrec hoped to manoeuvre Colonna out of Milan in northern Italy by a long strategic march around the city.

This plan could not be executed because Lautrec's 8000 Swiss mercenary pikemen demanded immediate battle or they would leave the army. The Swiss had not been paid and hoped that a quick capture of Milan would result in loot, so they volunteered to spearhead the attack on Colonna's defences. Colonna's troops numbered about 17,000 in a strong position, protected by earthworks and a sunken road running along the front, with the left flank protected by marshy ground and the right flank protected by an irrigation ditch.

Colonna posted artillery and Spanish arquebusiers behind the earthworks. Lautrec placed Montmorency in command of the Swiss pikemen, who advanced in two large columns. When Montmorency ordered a pause to let French artillery bombard the earthworks, the Swiss charged ahead anyway, confident of victory. The Swiss suffered devastating losses once they fell within range of the Spanish arquebuses, but advanced to the ramparts. Slowed by the sunken road and unable to climb the earthworks quickly, they were completely vulnerable to Spanish fire. The Swiss withdrew, having lost over 3000 men.

Meanwhile French cavalry had forced a crossing over the ditch on Colonna's right flank, but, with his front secure, Colonna was able to repulse this effort with his own cavalry and reserves. Lautrec withdrew his army, the surviving Swiss departing for home. Colonna's losses were light in comparison with Lautrec's.

■ SESIA RIVER, 30 APRIL 1524

A retreating French-Swiss army under Bonnivet was intercepted by a German-Spanish army under Lannoy at the Sesia River in Italy. Chevalier de Bayard was killed while commanding the French rear guard.

■ MIRABELLO, 21–22 FEBRUARY 1525

During the French siege of Pavia in northern Italy, Francis I had his fortified headquarters park at Mirabello. This park was raided and reconnoitered by Habsburg Germans before the battle of Pavia.

■ PAVIA, 24 FEBRUARY 1525

French King Francis I deployed 24,000 French troops and Swiss and German mercenaries during a siege of Pavia, northern Italy. Lannoy led 24,000 Spanish and Habsburg German troops

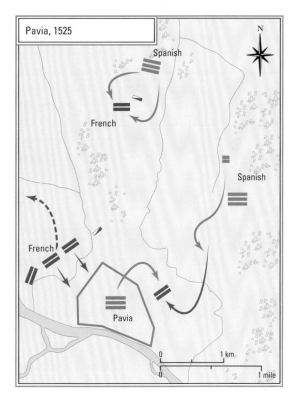

Pavia, 1525

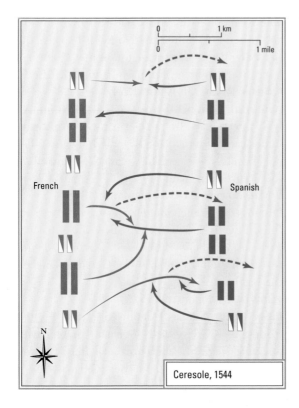

French

Spanish

Ceresole, 1544

to lift the siege. Another 9000 troops were in Pavia itself. Lannoy's main forces manoeuvred during the night towards the rear of Francis' army, skirmishing in predawn darkness. Francis led his elite cavalry to repulse enemy advance forces in the early morning. This was successful, but Francis and his cavalry were separated from other French forces. They were soon engaged on three sides by enemy cavalry and infantry, including Spanish arquebusiers firing into the rear of the French cavalry. Francis' horse was killed and he was surrounded and captured, the separated elements of his army defeated in detail, losing 10,000 casualties to Lannoy's losses of a 600 men.

■ NICE, 6 AUGUST–8 SEPTEMBER 1543
As part of Barbarossa's campaign, combined Turkish and French amphibious force besieged the Duchy of Savoy city of Nice, on the southern coast of present-day France. A Habsburg German relief force raised the siege.

■ CERESOLE, 1 OCTOBER 1544
A French-Swiss-Italian force under François de Bourbon – the Count of Enghien – fought an opposing force of German-Spanish-Italian army under d'Avalos at Ceresole in northern Italy. Enghien had about 13,000 infantry plus 2000 cavalry, while d'Avalos had about 17,000 infantry and 900 cavalry. Enghien's army faced east with the army of d'Avalos directly opposite, both armies putting their heaviest infantry forces in the centre. A French attack on the right pinned d'Avalos' Italian troops there. Opposing infantry of both armies in the centre advanced against each other, pikemen in the front rank, with arquebusiers immediately behind. The arquebusiers fired at point-blank range when the pikemen engaged, resulting in heavy casualties for both sides. French cavalry charged the disrupted German infantry in the centre, achieving a breakthrough. D'Avalos' army suffered heavy casualties while retreating, losing 6000 killed and over 3000 captured, Enghien losing 2000 men.

■ BOULOGNE, 19 JULY–18 SEPTEMBER 1544
English forces of 16,000 men under Henry VIII besieged Boulogne on the French coast of the English Channel. Defended by less than 2000 men, Boulogne finally capitulated.

■ SOLENT, 18–19 JULY 1545
A French fleet engaged an English fleet off the south coast of England before withdrawing. Neither fleet suffered serious damage, apart from the loss of the English carrack Mary Rose.

■ MARCIANO, 2 AUGUST 1554
An Italian-Sienese-French force of 15,000 was badly defeated, losing 8000 casualties inflicted by a Florentine-Spanish-Habsburg force of 18,500 at Marciano in the Tuscan region of Italy.

■ RENTY, 12 AUGUST 1554
A Spanish-Habsburg German army led personally by Emperor Charles V invaded northern France and was repulsed. Charles' losses were 2000 and French pursuit continued on 13 August.

War of the League of Cognac

■ SACK OF ROME, 6 MAY 1527

A German-Spanish Habsburg army of 20,000 had not been paid and attacked Rome, intending to loot it. The army commander, Constable Charles de Bourbon, was killed while leading the assault, but the army broke into the city and pillaged ruthlessly. The rampage continued for eight days, while 45,000 civilians were killed or fled the city.

■ FLORENCE, 1529–1530

A German-Spanish Habsburg force engaged in a lengthy siege of Florence, Italy, after that city overthrew the Medici Dynasty and declared a republic. The loose siege dragged on as the besiegers awaited additional artillery and reinforcements and the Florentines improved their defenses, with the artist Michelangelo pressed into service as design engineer. The defeat of a relief force at the battle of Gavinana finally convinced the Florentines to surrender.

■ GAVINANA, 3 AUGUST 1530

During the siege of Florence by Spanish-German Habsburg forces, a Florentine relief force under Ferruccio was intercepted and defeated. Both Ferruccio and the Habsburg commander, the Prince of Orange, were killed.

German Peasants' War 1524–25

■ FRANKENHAUSEN, 15 MAY 1525

A 6000-strong army commanded by Philip I, Landgrave of Hesse and George, Duke of Saxony defeated a rebel force of 8000 peasants under the radical theologian Thomas Müntzer. At least 6000 peasants were killed and wounded.

Scottish Internal Conflicts 1526–1603

■ LINLITHGOW BRIDGE, 4 SEPTEMBER 1526

The Earl of Lennox' 10,000-strong army advancing on Edinburgh was opposed by the Earl of Arran, who deployed his 2500 men in a strong position on Pace Hill overlooking Linlithgow and the River Avon. Lennox forded the river in an attempt to outflank and defeat Arran before he could be reinforced from Edinburgh. However, Arran's troops held out until reinforcements arrived and Lennox was defeated with the loss of 3000 men.

■ ALLTAN-BEATH, 1542

Clan Sutherland and Clan Murray, led by Hutcheon Murray of Abirscors, attacked and defeated the MacKays at Alltan-Beath in retaliation for raids on their lands. Donald MacKay was captured and imprisoned in Foulis Castle, Ross-shire.

■ THE SHIRTS, 15 JULY 1544

Clan Cameron and Clanranald forces totalling 500 men had plundered the country of Urquhart and Glenmorriston throughout the summer of 1544 before being intercepted by a 300-strong force under Hugh Fraser, the Third Lord Lovat, at the northern end of Loch Lochy. After each side's archers had fired off all their arrows, the opposing clansmen fought a fierce melee, which ended in stalemate as both sides were almost wiped out.

■ CORRICHIE, 28 OCTOBER 1562

The forces of Clan Gordon and Clan Brodie, commanded by the Earl of Huntly, were defeated by a force drawn from the Clans Fraser, Munro, Mackenzie, Mackintosh, Mackay and Cameron, under the Earl of Moray.

■ THE CHASEABOUT RAID, 26 AUGUST 1565

Infuriated by Mary Queen of Scots' (second) marriage to Lord Darnley, James Stewart, First Earl of Moray, was defeated after attempting to raise a rebellion with the support of the Earl of Argyll and Clan Hamilton.

■ CARBERRY HILL, 15 JUNE 1567

Led by Alexander Lord Home, Scottish nobles who resented Mary Queen of Scots' (third) marriage to the Earl of Bothwell raised an army that was confronted by royalist forces at Carberry Hill, near Musselburgh, east of Edinburgh. Neither side was willing to risk an all-out battle, but the Queen's army rapidly dwindled due to desertion, forcing her to surrender and to abdicate in favour of her infant son, James VI.

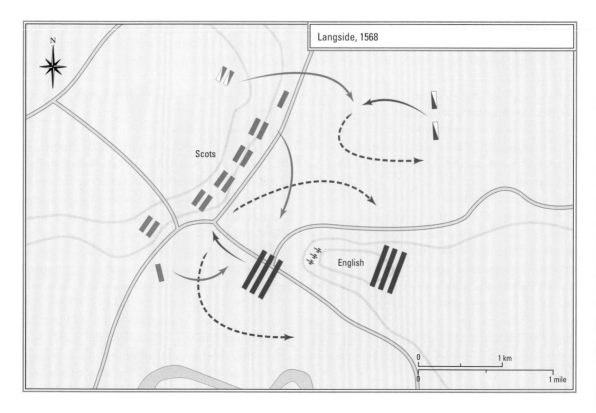

Langside, 1568

Scots

English

0   1 km

0   1 mile

■ Langside, 13 May 1568

In May 1568, Mary Queen of Scots escaped from house arrest at Loch Leven Castle and raised a 6000-strong army commanded by Archibald Campbell, 5th Earl of Argyll. Mary intended to establish a base at Dumbarton Castle from which she would gradually regain control of Scotland, but her forces were intercepted near Glasgow by Regent Moray's army of 4000 men. Moray's battlefield commander, Sir William Kirkcaldy of Grange, realized that Mary's forces were intent on keeping south of the Clyde to avoid action. He ordered a detachment to occupy the village of Langside to gain time for him to bring the rest of his forces into action. Argyll broke through the village's defenders, but was held by the Regent's pikemen until Kirkcaldy organized a counter-attack, which routed the royalists.

■ Bun Garbhain, 1570

The Clan Cameron defeated the Clan Mackintosh in a series of actions at Bun Garbhain near Loch

Arkaig. The chief of Mackintosh was killed in single combat by Donald 'Taillear Dubh na Tuaighe' Cameron.

■ Spoiling Dyke, May 1578

The Clan MacDonald of Uist barred the doors of Trumpan Church, trapping the congregation before setting it alight. One fatally injured girl raised the alarm, allowing the Clan MacLeod to intercept and defeat the MacDonalds.

■ Allt Camhna, 1586

In a typical Highland feud, William Mackay, commanding the combined forces of the Clan Gunn and the Clan Mackay, attacked the Clan Sinclair. The Sinclairs were defeated and lost 120 men, including their leader, Henry Sinclair.

■ Leckmelm, 1586

Shortly after their victory at Allt Camhna, the Clan Gunn were attacked and defeated by the combined forces of the Clans MacLeod, Mackay and Sutherland, commanded by William Sutherland, Niel Mackay and James MacLeod.

■ **TRAIGH GHRUINNEART, 5 AUGUST 1598**
A 1000-strong force from Mull led by Sir Lachlan Mor MacLean of Duart invaded Islay, but was defeated by the MacDonalds commanded by Sir James MacDonald, son of Angus MacDonald

■ **COIRE NA CREICHE (BENQUHILLAN), 1601**
A year-long feud between Clan MacLeod of Dunvegan and Clan MacDonald of Sleat culminated in a MacDonald victory at Coire Na Creiche, on the northern slopes of the Cuillin hills on the Isle of Skye.

■ **GLEN FRUIN, 9 FEBRUARY 1603**
Alasdair MacGregor of Glenstrae's 300 MacGregor clansmen attacked and defeated a 600-strong force of the Clan Colquhoun at Glen Fruin near Loch Lomond. The MacGregors inflicted 200 casualties for the loss of less than a dozen men.

Japanese Internal Conflicts 1526–55

■ **KAMAKURA, 1526**
During his campaign against the Hojo family, Satomi Sanetaka attacked Kamakura. Various retainers of Hojo Ujitsuna, including Ito and Ogasawara, engaged him, during which the famous Tsurugaoka Hachiman Shrine was set on fire and destroyed.

■ **OZAWAHARA, 1530**
At the battle of Ozawahara, Musashi province, Hojo Ujiyasu, greatest of the Hojo lords, fought his first battle at the age of 15. It was conducted against Uesugi Tomooki, of the Ogigayatsu branch of the Uesugi family.

■ **IDANO, 1535**
In December 1535, Matsudaira Kiyoyasu, whose grandson was to be the famous Shogun Tokugawa Ieyasu, was murdered by one of his vassals, Abe Masatoyo. Seven days later, both sides met at Idano in Mikawa province, with Matsudaira's forces victorious.

■ **SENDANNO, 1536**
Nagao Tamekage set out from Kasugayama castle to fight the Ikko-ikki of Kaga province.

At Sendanno he was defeated and killed, along with many of his men. Tamekage's son Terutora became the famous Uesugi Kenshin.

■ **UMINOKUCHI, 1536**
Takeda Nobutora attacked his enemy Hiraga Genshin at Uminokuchi, but was forced to retreat through snow and wind. He was saved by his 15-year-old son, the future Takeda Shingen, who came to his rescue.

■ **MUSASHI-MATSUYAMA, 1537**
During this action the Uesugi clan lost Musashi-Matsuyama castle to their Hojo rivals; they would regain it in 1563. At the 1537 siege, messages were sent out using letters attached to collars of dogs.

■ **KONODAI, 1538**
At the first of two battles, Hojo Ujitsuna defeated the forces of Satomi Yoshitaka and Ashikaga Yoshiaki. Another Hojo victory occurred in 1564; the armies were led by the sons of the same lords.

■ **UEHARA, 1542**
In one of the eariest victories of this period of expansion, Takeda Shingen crossed the border between Kai and Shinano provinces and captured Uehara castle from Suwa Yorishige, whose daughter he was soon to marry.

■ **ANKOKUJI, 1542**
A battle between the Takeda and the Takato. After losing Fukuyo castle, Takato Yoritsugu was himself defeated by Shingen's Gen Itagaki Nobukata at the battle of Ankokuji. Yoritsugu's younger brother, Yorimune, was killed there.

■ **AZUKIZAKA, 1542**
At this battle of Azukizaka in Mikawa province, Oda Nobuhide, father of the famous unifier Oda Nobunaga, fought and defeated Imagawa Yoshimoto. This was an important victory in the long rivalry between the two families.

■ **SEZAWA, 1542**
Takeda Shingen's most important gains were in Shinano province. In an attempt to stop his invasion, the local lords united and the combined forces of Ogasawara Nagatoki, Suwa Yorishige, Murakami Yoshikiyo and Kiso Yoshiyasu met him

in battle at Sezawa in March 1542. They gathered a force of 12,000, but Shingen defeated them all with just 3000 men. The Shinano forces suffered 3000 casualties, while Shingen lost about 500.

■ Kuwabara 1542

As part of his campaign against the Suwa, Takeda Shingen took Suwa Yorishige's Kuwabara castle. Yorishige was then taken to Shingen's capital on the pretext of safe conduct, but then treacherously forced to commit suicide.

■ Toda Castle 1542–43

Ouchi Yoshitaka tried to capture Toda castle belonging to Amako Haruhisa. Failing in his attempts, Yoshitaka withdrew to Yamaguchi where he was deposed by his retainer, Sue Harukata.

■ Nakakubo, 1543

Oi Sadataka, the keeper of Nakakubo castle, deserted Takeda Shingen for Murakami Yoshikiyo. As part of his drive into the Saku area, Shingen captured Nagakubo and sent Sadataka as prisoner to be executed in Kofu.

Kojinyama, 1544

Kojinyama was a further Tozawa possession in the Ina valley taken by Takeda Shingen. This allowed Shingen to increase his control of the Ina valley leading deep into the Shinano mountains.

■ Kawagoe, 1545

The two branches of the Uesugi family, the Ogigayatsu and the Yamanouchi, joined forces with Imagawa Ujichika and Ashikaga Haruuji to attack strategic Kawagoe castle, held for the Hojo by Hojo Tsunanari with a garrison of 3000 men. Hojo Ujiyasu led a relieving force of 8000 in a daring night march. At the battle, entirely fought in darkness, Hojo Ujiyasu defeated the coalition and Uesugi Tomosada was killed in action.

■ Ryugasaki, 1545

Ryugasaki was a satellite castle of Fukuyo. It fell to Takeda Shingen in 1545 after a fierce attack as part of his advance into Shinano province.

■ Takato, 1545

Takeda Shingen captured Takato castle in the Ina valley from Takato Yoritsugu when the latter was unable to obtain help from Ogasawara Nagatoki and Tozawa Yorichika. This was an important gain in a strategic area.

■ Odaihara, 1546

At the castle of Odaihara in Saku Takeda Shingen, who was besieging Shika castle at the time, detached part of the Takeda army and defeated Uesugi Norimasa. The victors collected many heads in the process.

■ Uchiyama, 1546

Uchiyama was one of many similar encounters fought by Takeda Shingen in his attempt to take over Shinano province. As in other engagements a frontal attack failed, so Shingen restorted to starving out the defenders.

■ Shika, 1547

Takeda Shingen besieged Kasahara Kiyoshige's Shika castle in 1547 and, to intimidate the terrified garrison, Shingen had the 300 freshly severed heads from the recent battle of Odaihara displayed in front of the castle walls.

■ Kanoguchi, 1547

Saito Toshimasa of Mino inflicted a defeat at Kanoguchi upon Oda Nobuhide and followed it up by the marriage of his daughter to Nobuhide's son Nobunaga, as one of the terms of the peace settlement.

■ Imizu, 1554

Imizu was like many similar encounters between rival lords (in this case Jimbo Nagamoto and Shiina Yasutane) were it not for including one of the few recorded single combats between rival leaders in Japanese history.

■ Oshikibata, 1554

The battle of Oshikibata was effectively a preliminary round to the battle of Miyajima. At Oshikibata Mori Motonari, with an army of 3000 men, defeated a retainer of Sue Harukata called Takagawa with an army of 7000 men.

■ Kannomine, 1554

In his advance down the Kiso valley, Takeda Shingen took Fukushima castle on the Kiso river from Kiso Yoshiyasu by starving out the garrison.

■ Kiso Fukushima, 1554

In his advance down the Kiso valley, Takeda Shingen took Fukushima castle on the Kiso river from Kiso Yoshiyasu by starving out the garrison.

■ Matsuo, 1554

Continuing down the Ina valley, Takeda Shingen captured Matsuo from Ogasawara Nobusada and, soon after, the nearby Yoshioka castle surrendered.

■ Miyajima, 1555

Sue Harukata had fortified the holy island of Miyajima in the Inland Sea. Taking advantage of a blinding rainstorm, the Mori launched a surprise attack. Mori Motonari and his two sons sailed round the northern tip of the island to land unseen on a beach to the rear of the Sue positions. At the same time, Mori's other son, Kobayakawa Takakage, sailed up the strait in view of the Sue castle, but then doubled back when out of sight and made a frontal assault at dawn, synchronized with his father's attack from the rear. By the victory of Miyajima, the Mori were raised to a pre-eminent position in this part of Japan.

Ethiopian–Adal War 1529–43

■ Antukyah, 1531

A 12,000-strong army of the Adal Sultanate commanded by Ahmad ibn Ibrihim al-Ghazi 'the Conqueror' invaded Ethiopia and decisively defeated an Ethiopian army of anything up to 100,000 men under Eslamu, Governor of Fatagar.

■ Amba Sel, 28 October 1531

A 12,000-strong army of the Adal Sultanate commanded by Ahmad ibn Ibrihim al-Ghazi attacked and defeated an Ethiopian army under Emperor Dawit II at Amba Sel on the River Walaqa. Ahmad's forces captured part of Dawit's imperial regalia.

■ Hill of the Jews, August 1542

A Portuguese expeditionary force commanded by Cristóvão da Gama supported the Ethiopian Emperor Gelawdewos in his war against the Adal Sultanate. The fire of the Portuguese arquebusiers was the decisive factor in this victory.

■ Wofla, 28 August 1542

Ahmad ibn Ibrihim al-Ghazi's men were reinforced by 2900 arquebusiers (2000 from Arabia plus 900 regular Ottoman infantry) and a handful of Ottoman cavalry. Ahmad was quick to exploit his newly gained superiority in numbers and firepower, attacking the Portuguese fortified camp that was held by Cristóvão da Gama and 300 arquebusiers. The Portuguese were overwhelmed. Although da Gama managed to escape with a few survivors, he was quickly captured and killed.

■ Wayna Daga, 21 February 1543

After victory at Wofla, Ahmad ibn Ibrihim al-Ghazi assumed that the Portuguese had been destroyed and retained only 200 Ottoman arquebusiers. However, a cadre of Portuguese troops – 60 cavalry and 70 arquebusiers – joined the Ethiopian Emperor Gelawdewos' army of 8000 infantry and 500 cavalry. Ahmad fielded a total of 14,000 infantry and 1200 cavalry and had almost defeated the Ethiopian/Portuguese forces when he was killed and his army routed.

Swiss Wars 1529–31

■ Kappel I, 1529

In 1529, tensions between the Catholic and Protestant Swiss cantons flared up into the first war of Kappel. Although both sides raised armies, open warfare was narrowly avoided by intensive diplomacy in the federal *Tagsatzung* (legislature).

■ Kappel II, 1531

Unresolved tensions from the first war of Kappel led to fighting, in which the Catholic cantons defeated their Protestant rivals, leading to the adoption of Catholicism and Protestantism as the official religions of the Swiss Confederation.

Polish–Moldavian Wars 1531

■ Gwozdiec, 1531

Voivode Petru Rareş of Moldavia invaded southern Poland in support of the Ottoman Empire. Grand Hetman Jan Tarnowski led the

Polish counter-offensive, attacking and defeating Petru's forces at Gwozdiec, near Kolmyrra, in the Ukraine.

■ OBERTYN, 22 AUGUST 1531

Voivode Petru Rareş's Moldavian Army of 17,000 cavalry and 50 guns was defeated at Obertyn in the Ukraine by a Polish force of 4800 cavalry, 1200 infantry and 12 guns commanded by Grand Hetman Jan Tarnowski.

Uprising in England 1536–37

■ PILGRIMAGE OF GRACE, OCTOBER 1536– FEBRUARY 1537

Henry VIII's break with Catholicism provoked an uprising in Yorkshire led by Robert Aske who raised a force of 40,000 men and occupied York. Henry negotiated a settlement, but subsequently had Aske arrested and executed.

Rebellion in Poland 1537

■ POLISH CHICKEN WAR, 1537

'Chicken War' is the popular term for an unsuccessful anti-royalist and anti-absolutist rebellion staged by the Polish nobility in protest against the reforms of King Zygmunt I 'the Old'. The name was coined by the King's supporters who claimed that the 'wars' only effect was the near-extinction of the local chickens.

Swedish Uprising 1542–43

■ DACKE WAR, 1542–43

Gustav I's high taxes and support of the Reformation caused resentment throughout Sweden, which culminated in June 1542 with a peasant uprising led by Nils Dacke. Gustav responded by sending an army in an unsuccessful attempt to crush the rebellion, following which royalist forces blockaded the rebel provinces. Gustav then raised a fresh army, including a large contingent of veteran landsknecht mercenaries, which defeated the rebels in March 1543.

Anglo-Scottish Conflicts 1542–1688

■ HADDON RIG, 24 AUGUST 1542

An English army of 3000 men under Sir Robert Bowes, Deputy Warden of the English East March, was attacked and defeated near Kelso by a 2000-strong Scottish force commanded by George Gordon, 4th Earl of Huntly.

■ SOLWAY MOSS, 24 NOVEMBER 1542

A Scottish army of between 15,000 and 18,000 men commanded by Robert, Lord Maxwell, the Warden of West March, invaded England, but encountered his English counterpart Sir Thomas Wharton, the Deputy Warden of the West March, with a force of 3200 men. Sir Thomas skilfully deployed his small force to give the impression of far greater numbers and rapidly demoralized the Scottish troops who surrendered to a few hundred English 'Border Horse'.

■ ANCRUM MOOR, 27 FEBRUARY 1545

An English army of at least 5000 men under Sir

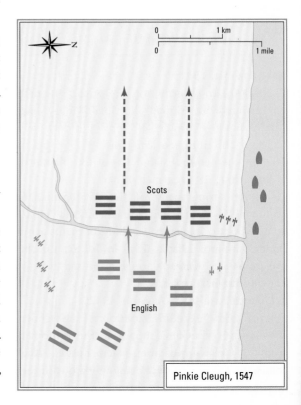

Pinkie Cleugh, 1547

Ralph Eure was attacked and decisively defeated at Ancrum Moor near Jedburgh by a 2500-strong Scottish force commanded by the Earls of Arran and Angus.

■ **PINKIE CLEUGH, 10 SEPTEMBER 1547**

A 23,000-strong Scottish army commanded by the Earls of Arran and Angus was defeated at Pinkie Cleugh near Musselburgh with the loss of 8000 men by the Duke of Somerset's English army of 17,000 men.

■ **RAID OF THE REDESWIRE, 7 JULY 1575**

A 'Day of Truce' – one of the regular meetings held between the English and Scottish March Wardens – flared up into open warfare. The Scots under Sir John Carmichael defeated Sir John Forster and his English borderers.

■ **MAOL RUADH, AUGUST 1688**

This was the last 'private' battle between Highland clans fought at Maol Ruadh in Lochaber, where the Mackintoshes and a detachment of government troops were defeated by an alliance of MacDonalds of Keppoch and Camerons.

Italian Wars 1542–46

■ **BONCHURCH, JULY 1545**

A detachment of 500 French troops commanded by Le Seigneur de Tais landed at Monk's Bay on the Isle of Wight, but were defeated by 300 English militiamen under Capt Robert Fyssher on St Boniface Down.

Schmalkaldic War 1546–47

■ **MÜHLBERG, 24 APRIL 1547**

A Spanish-Imperialist army of 29,500 men under the Emperor Charles V – with the Duke of Alba as his battlefield commander – invaded Saxony, a key member of the anti-Imperialist Protestant Schmalkaldic League. A League army of 15,000 men commanded by Elector John Frederick I of Saxony and Philip I of Hesse defending the line of the River Elbe was surprised and routed by Alba's veterans with the loss of 8000 men.

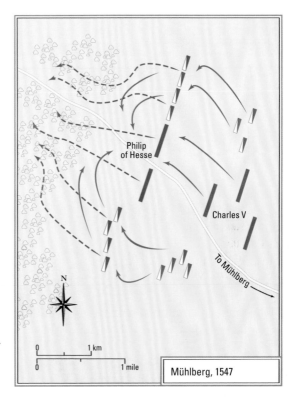

Mühlberg, 1547

■ **DRAKENBURG, 23 MAY 1547**

An Imperialist army of just over 6000 men commanded by the Duke of Calenburg was attacked and almost wiped out by an 8000-strong army of the Protestant Schmalkaldic League at Drakenburg in Lower Saxony.

Prayer Book Rebellion 1549

■ **CREDITON, 1549**

A revolt in Devon and Cornwall against the Protestant Book of Common Prayer led to an attempt to negotiate with the rebels at Crediton, but fighting broke out and the growing rebel force advanced on Exeter.

■ **EXETER, 1549**

A force of 2000 rebels besieged Exeter for five weeks after failing to persuade the mayor to surrender the city. During the siege, 'the famine was so sore, that the people were fain to eat horse-flesh'.

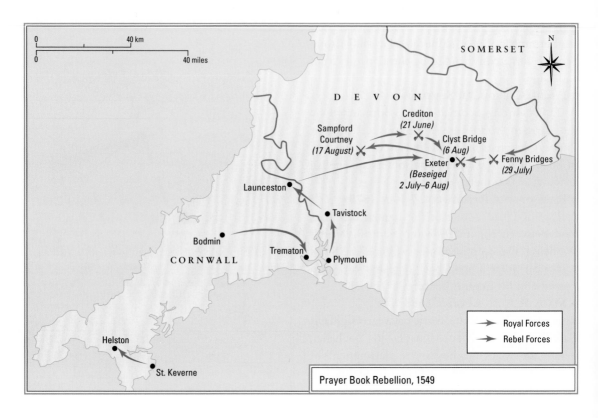

Prayer Book Rebellion, 1549

■ **FENNY BRIDGES, 28 JULY 1549**

A royalist army commanded by Lord John Russell attempting to raise the siege of Exeter was intercepted by a rebel force at Fenny Bridges. Each side lost roughly 300 men in an inconclusive battle.

■ **WOODBURY COMMON, 4 AUGUST 1549**

Lord John Russell's royalist army of 5000 men made a further attempt to relieve Exeter, but was intercepted by another 2000-strong rebel force. The rebels launched a dawn attack, which was beaten off with heavy losses.

■ **CLYST ST MARY, 5 AUGUST 1549**

A rebel force of 7000 men defended the village of Clyst St Mary, which was stormed by three assault columns of Lord John Russell's royalist army. His men inflicted 1000 casualties and took 900 prisoners.

■ **CLYST HEATH, 6 AUGUST 1549**

Enraged by Lord John Russell's massacre of the 900 prisoners taken at Clyst St Mary, 2000 rebels attacked the royalist camp on Clyst Heath and were virtually wiped out after a fierce all-day battle.

■ **EXETER, 1549**

Lord John Russell followed up his victory with the relief of Exeter. The lands of the rebel leaders were confiscated and many were transferred to the royalists Sir Gawen Carew and Sir Peter Carew.

■ **SAMPFORD COURTENAY, 17 AUGUST 1549**

Lord John Russell's 8000-strong royalist army defeated the remaining rebel forces in their fortified camp outside the village of Sampford Courtenay. After storming the camp, the royalists took the village, inflicting a total of 1300 casualties.

Russo-Livonian Wars 1554–1656

■ **ĒRĢEME, 2 AUGUST 1560**

A 12,000-strong Muscovite army under Vasily Ivanovich Barbashin invaded the Livonian Confederation. A small force of the Livonian Order,

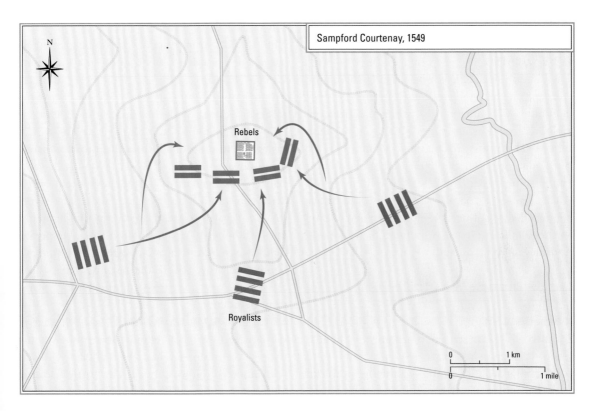

Sampford Courtenay, 1549

Rebels

Royalists

0   1 km

0   1 mile

totalling 330 knights and 500 auxiliaries under Philipp Schall von Bell, attempted to ambush a Muscovite detachment, but mistakenly attacked Barbashin's entire army. The Livonians succeeded in smashing through the Muscovite front, but were enveloped and destroyed. The Livonian Order was dissolved following the loss of more than 250 of its knights in this action.

■ NARVA, 1590

Swedish forces commanded by Pontus De la Gardie took Narva from its Russian garrison in 1581. During the Russo-Swedish War (1590–95), Russian attempts to re-take the city were repelled by Swedish forces under Arvid Stålarm.

■ DE LA GARDIE CAMPAIGN, 1609–10

A 15,000-strong Swedish army under Jacob De la Gardie and Evert Horn operated in alliance with the Russian commander Mikhail Skopin-Shuisky against the Poles in the Polish–Muscovite War (1605–18). Their forces left Novgorod late in 1609 and marched on Moscow, taking the city the

following year and suppressing the rebellion against Tsar Vasili IV. The army was decisively defeated by Polish forces at Klushino on 4 July 1610.

■ MOSCOW, 1612

Polish forces captured Moscow following their victory at Klushino, but the city's garrison was defeated by Prince Dimitri Pozharski (22–25 August 1612). The survivors withdrew into the Kremlin and were starved into surrender by 27 October 1612.

■ TIKHVIN, 1613

The small Swedish garrison of the fortified Bogorodichno-Uspenskij monastery at Tikhvin was expelled by a revolt of the townspeople. Jacob De la Gardie's Swedish army returned and unsuccessfully besieged the monastery before withdrawing in September 1613.

■ GDOV, 1614

The town was taken by Sweden in 1613, but was recaptured by the Russians within a few months. In 1614, a Swedish army under King Gustavus

Adolphus retook Gdov, which remained under Swedish control until 1621.

■ Pskov, 1615

The Swedish siege of Pskov began in 1615, but the Russian generals Morozov and Buturlin held their own until 27 February 1617, when the Treaty of Stolbovo ceded the province of Ingria to Sweden.

■ Riga, 21 August–5 October 1656

A Swedish garrison of 7500 men under Baron Simon Grundel-Helmfelt successfully defended Riga against a 35,000-strong Russian army commanded by Tsar Alexei Mikhailovich. The Swedes suffered minimal losses, but inflicted 14,000 casualties on the Russians.

Japanese Wars 1560–1615

■ Norada, 1560

South-central Japan started to become a battlefield when Rokkaku Yoshikata led his vassals and combined army to Kohoku against the powerful Asai clan and its allies, then led by Asai Hisamasa. The Asai and their allies offered battle at the Uso river, the Asai attacking unexpectedly. Under the confusion generated by Asai Nagamasa's successful diversion or by the sudden retreat of an Asai advance force, the Rokkaku army found itself driven back.

■ Marune, 1560

The arquebus assumed a central place in Japanese warfare when Tokugawa Ieyasu used firearms in quantity along with a powerful invasion force to reduce this frontier fortress of Oda Nobunaga.

■ Okehazama, 1560

Responding with unexpected ferocity to Imagawa Yoshimoto's invasion of his district, Oda Nobunaga launched a prompt counter-assault with greatly outnumbered forces. With Yoshimoto's army celebrating their initial successes in a narrow ravine, Nobunaga used dummies and banners to simulate a pending frontal attack, while his real army moved to the enemy's rear and deployed under cover of a thunderstorm. Their successful attack killed Yoshimoto, allowing Tokugawa Ieyasu to join Nobunaga.

■ Kawanakajima, 1561

The 20,000-strong army of Takeda Shingen launched a sudden assault upon the forces of Uesugi Kenshin with 13,000 men. Shingen bypassed the Uesugi army on Mount Saijo and reached Kaizu without opposition. Shingen followed Yamamoto Kansuke's plan of dividing his forces, leading smaller groups into a prepared position on the plain. Kosaka Masanobu and Baba Nobufusa's force found their intention to drive Kenshin off the mountain anticipated, with the Uesugi army instead launching a night attack upon Shingen's smaller command. Desperate fighting resulted in heavy casualties to Shingen's family and army before the balance of his force arrived to take and drive off the Uesugi army from behind.

■ Musashi-Matsuyama, 1563

Uesugi Kenshin's last redoubt was this castle, to which Takeda Shingen laid siege in a new alliance with his rival, Hojo Ujiyasu. The bastion forced Shingen to reduce it by undermining.

■ Second Azukizaka, 1564

The Ikko-ikki warrior monks posed a formidable obstacle to Tokugawa Ieyasu, facing him with armour arquebuses. Offering a personal challenge to combat, Ieyasu led a sudden charge that resulted in his narrow escape and victory.

■ Konodai, 1564

Hojo Ujiyasu near Konodai castle attacked the smaller force of Satomi Yoshihiro, which managed some success with a feigned retreat and ambush before being ground under a two-pronged attack by the Hojo army. Yoshihiro escaped.

■ Kuragano, 1565

Takeda Shingen twice laid siege to this formidable castle held by Kuragano Naoyuki during Shingen's efforts to complete the destruction of Uesugi Kenshin's hold on Kozuke Province. The undermanned castle fell to a small-scale siege.

■ Minowa, 1566

Takeda Shingen captured this castle from the family of Nagano Norimasa as Shingen mopped up remnant bastions still loyal to Uesugi Kenshin. The courage and skill of Kamiizumi Hidetsuna proved insufficient to save the castle.

■ TORISAKA, 1568

Mori Motonari had greatly expanded his clan's power in Shikaku and over the Inland Sea. The allied Kikkowa family adopted his second son Motoharu, who capably led them to this victory over the Utsunomiya clan.

■ HACHIGATA, 1568

Takeda Shingen's ongoing campaign of reducing the remaining citadels loyal to Uesugi Kenshin met with a check here, as this heavily-fortified castle on a defensible plateau resisted his attack under command of Kenshin's son, Uesugi Ujikuni.

■ MIMASETOGE, 1569

With Takeda Shingen's strength diminished by several sieges, the Hojo – under Ujiteru Ujikuni – sought to engage him in the narrows of the Mimase Pass with a large army. Shingen's army prevailed after desperate mountain fighting.

■ TATARAHAMA, 1569

The Otomo clan faced a sudden rebellion by the Mori clan. Negotiating an alliance with the Amako clan, they engaged the Mori, who fought Hetsugi Akitsura to a draw that forced a mutual retreat.

■ KANBARA, 1569

The Hojo and Kasahara Yasukatsu held this castle as Takeda Shingen continued reducing hostile bastions in the way of his ongoing conquests. Katsuyori and Nobushige led the Shingen in the successful storming of the fortification.

■ KAKEGAWA, 1569

Tokugawa Ieyasu received this castle on behalf of the Tokugawa when Asahina Yasutomo surrendered it under terms agreed upon between Ieyasu and Imagawa Ujizane, in return for guaranteeing the latter's safe return to Hojo territory.

■ TACHIBANA, 1569

The Mori clan had become quite powerful in the Inland Sea due to their use of Korean or Western-style cannon on wheeled gun carriages. They

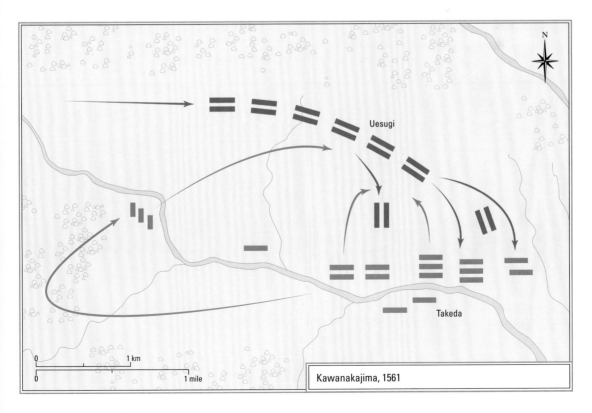

Kawanakajima, 1561

relinquished this castle back to the Otomo clan after Tatarahama.

■ ANEGAWA, 1570

Oda Nobunaga resumed his invasion of the Asai's territories in Omi province after Asai Nagamasa, his brother-in-law, had changed sides and forced his retreat. Taking a different route by Lake Biwa, Nobunaga made for Otani, headquarters of the Asai, who met him in force at this shallow river. Tokugawa Ieyasu and Toyotomi Hideyoshi commanded on Nobunaga's flanks while the Asai broke Nobunaga's centre. Reinforced from Yokoyama castle, Nobunaga's forces prevailed.

■ CHOKOJI, 1570

Rokkaku Yoshikata caught Shibata Katsuie at this castle with 400 men, next cutting the vital aqueduct. Smashing the castle's last water vessels, Katsuie led a death or glory charge that drove off the Rokkaku besiegers.

■ HANAZAWA, 1570

Takeda Shingen launched a series of sieges of the surrounding bastions hindering his expansion. Ōhara Sukenaga held Hanazawa castle for the Imagawa clan when Shingen, Nagasaka Tsuruyasu, and Hajikano Saemon stormed it after four days.

■ KANEGASAKI, 1570

Toyotomi Hideyoshi led out Nobunaga's forces to clean up the Asakura, here defending this fortress in the aftermath of Anegawa. Hideyoshi followed the bastion's reduction with a fighting retreat northwards out of the hostile province.

■ TONEGAWA, 1571

Uesugi Kenshin renewed hostilities with Takeda Shingen and laid siege to Shingen's outlaying garrison at Ishikura castle. Shingen's relieving force encountered Kenshin at the Tonegawa river. After a long and difficult struggle, both sides withdrew.

■ FUKUZAWA, 1571

Hojo Tsunanari held this castle in Suruga against Takeda Shingen's ongoing series of assaults upon surrounding hostile bastions. With no help coming from his clan, Tsunanari surrendered the fortress under terms and withdrew to Odawara.

■ MOUNT HIEI, 1571

The ancient monastery of Enryaku-ji on this mountain near Kyoto exerted sufficient prestige and military force against Oda Nobunaga's frontiers to provoke his all-out attack with 30,000 men. After surrounding the summit of the mountain at night, Nobunaga's soldiers moved upwards destroying every structure or person encountered.

■ NAGASHIMA, 1571

The Ikko-ikki military monks of Ishiyama Hongan-Ji were far more ready for Oda Nobunaga's sudden assault than had been their counterparts on Mount Hiei. Nobunaga's attack on their fortifications in the marsh against monks, well-trained in close-quarters combat, archery and the use of firearms, quickly stalled with heavy casualties. Finding the monks well supplied with food and weapons, Nobunaga called off the assault after heavy losses.

■ FUTAMATA, 1572

Takeda Shingen bypassed this bastion of Oda Nobunaga in his sudden descent on Kyoto,

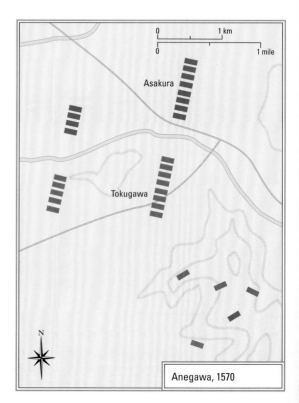

Anegawa, 1570

containing it with a force under his son Katsuyori. The Shingen smashed Futamata's water system with wooden rafts, forcing the town's surrender.

■ **MIKATAGAHARA, 1572**
With Uesugi Kenshin's path into his territory blocked by winter snows and Hojo Ujimasa neutralized with an alliance, Takeda Shingen found his rear areas secure enough to make his long-desired bid for the Shogunate with a sudden move upon Kyoto, led by his superb cavalry and experienced staff of generals. A force of 20,000 Takeda samurai and asigaru moved with 2000 Hojo towards the capital over a road dominated by Hamamatsu castle, under the command of Oda Nobunaga's best general, Tokugawa Ieyasu.

Ieyasu blocked the road with some 15,000 of his troops and Nobunaga's, his right flank anchored on the Magome river. In a snowstorm Shingen advanced, Ieyasu's right composed of 3000 newly-arrived troops collapsing. Ieyasu held the centre until Shingen's cavalry began blocking his retreat back to the castle, which he barely reached in time.

■ **ODANI, 1573**
Oda Nobunaga sought to eliminate his rival Asai Nagamasa by storming the Asai clan's mountain fortress. Strong support from the allied Asakura and a successful raid at night allowed the castle to withstand the siege.

■ **SIEGE OF NODA, 1573**
Takeda Shingen began his descent upon Kyoto by investing this castle in Tokugawa Ieyasu's command area. Listening to a sentry's flute playing, Shingen died at Komanba when a defender shot him.

■ **MAKINOSHIMA, 1573**
With the death of Takeda Shingen, Oda Nobunaga felt strong enough to depose the last Ashikaga Shogun, Yoshiaki. Yoshiaki resisted, fortifying a palace in Kyoto and losing skirmishes in this position before surrendering to Nobunaga.

■ **NAGASHIMA, 1573**
The well-trained and equipped military monks of Ishiyama Hongan-Ji faced a second assault in force by Oda Nobunaga's army, well equipped with arquebuses. Toyotomi Hideyoshi led a successful

diversionary assault while Nobunaga's main force drew up, preparing for a massive fusillade. The marsh-fortress survived when a sudden rainstorm drenched Nobunaga's matchlocks and the monks, who had kept their powder dry, launched their own attack that drove the Oda away in disorder.

■ **ODANI, 1573**
The mountain-top fortress of the Asai clan had withstood several fierce sieges, but Oda Nobunaga's overwhelming might proved too much for Asai Nagamasa who, with his son, committed suicide before Nobanaga razed the castle.

■ **ITANI, 1574**
Emulating Takeda Shingen's policy of reducing hostile bastions, Oda Nobunaga reduced this castle of the Miyoshi clan in Settsu province by using miners to excavate a tunnel leading down and under the castle's outer wall.

■ **NAGASHIMA, 1574**
Oda Nobunaga made a third, full-strength effort to annihilate the well-trained and well-supplied military monks of Ishiyama Hongan-Ji and their marsh fortress at Nagashima. Upon this occasion, he employed his fleet under Kuki Yoshitaka, who blockaded the monks and burned their wooden watch towers. Assaults on the outer fortifications forced the monks back into the central bastions of Nagashima and Ganshoji, which Nobunaga surrounded with wooden stockades, then burned.

■ **TAKETENJIN, 1574**
Takeda Tatsuyori hoped to continue his father's conquests, laying siege to this fortress of Tokugawa Ieyasu's district. Tatsuyori was only able to take the bastion after making the commander, Ogasawara Nagatada, governor of a province.

■ **ICHIJODANI, 1575**
Oda Nobunaga took vengeance upon the Asakura for their support of the allied Asai by laying siege to this clan fortress. Rather than resist to the end, Asakura Yoshikage abandoned the bastion, which Nobunaga burned.

■ **YOSHIDA, 1575**
Takeda Katsuyori did not possess his father Shingen's talents as a castle-taker. Tokugawa Ieyasu

preemptively reinforced this keep, which was commanded by Sakai Tadatsugo, the 6000 men of the garrison successfully withstanding all the Shingen's storming attempts.

■ NAGASHINO, 1575

The battle of Nagashino pitted the allied forces of Oda Nobunaga and Tokugawa Ieyasu (18,000), against Takeda Katsuyori (6000). This battle has achieved fame because it has been thought to be the first battle decisively influenced by marksmen shooting guns in groups of three. The name of the battle comes from Nagashino castle, which the Takeda were besieging two miles to the east, but the site of the battle was a place called Shitaragahara.

Takeda forces were separated from the combined Tokugawa and Oda armies by the narrow Rengo River. The Tokugawa occupied the low rising Danjō hills to the west, while the Oda had encamped at Cha'usu mountain, located further to the north-west of Danjō. The Takeda advanced from the east and strove to encircle Danjō, with the southern wing of their army circling to the south to keep the Tokugawa in place. Meanwhile, along the north, the right wing of the Takeda advanced to where Sakuma Nobumori commanded Oda troops. Nobumori fooled the Takeda into believing that he would join their cause during the battle. Instead, he led the Takeda into a trap, for the right wing were surprised and punished by fresh Oda reserves, located behind Danjō. The Takeda suffered 17 per cent casualties – including 37 prominent warriors – and later tried to incorporate more guns in their armies. However, contrary to common reconstructions, the Oda gunners were not lined up when firing, but were most likely scattered throughout the battlefield in groups of three. Bullets have been discovered to the east, south and west of the Danjō hills.

■ KIZUGAWAGUCHI, 1576

Oda Nobunaga's navy, victorious at Nagashima, established a blockade here under Adm Kuki Yoshitaka. The formidable Mori fleet rose to the challenge, aided by Western or Korean-style wheeled cannon and engaged and routed the Oda.

■ MITSUJI, 1576

Oda Nobunaga continued his pogrom against the Ikko-ikki military monks by personally leading the successful first attack against this remaining fortress. Himself wounded in the leg and stopped at the inner keep, Nobunaga eventually withdrew.

■ NANAO, 1577

Takeda Shingen's death allowed his rival Uesugi Kenshin to attack this castle of Hatakeyama Yoshitaka, who appealed to Oda Nobunaga for aid. However, disease killed Yoshitaka and a traitor opened the castle's gate before the Oda arrived.

■ TEDORIGAWA, 1577

Uesugi Kenshin, unobstructed by Takeda Shingen, besieged the Hatekeyama clan's castle of Nanao. Oda Nobunaga, along with Toyotomi Hideyoshi, advanced upon Kenshin's base at Masuto, lured into a night ambush that forced Nobunaga's retreat.

■ SHIGISAN, 1577

Oda Nobunaga's oldest son, Nobutada, along with Tsutsui Junkei, led part of his father's army against

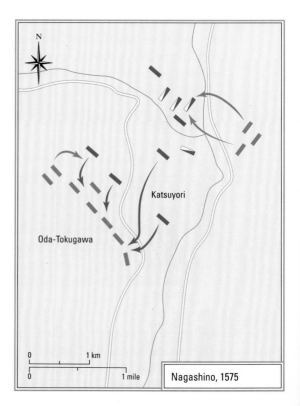

N

Katsuyori

Oda-Tokugawa

0   1 km

0   1 mile

Nagashino, 1575

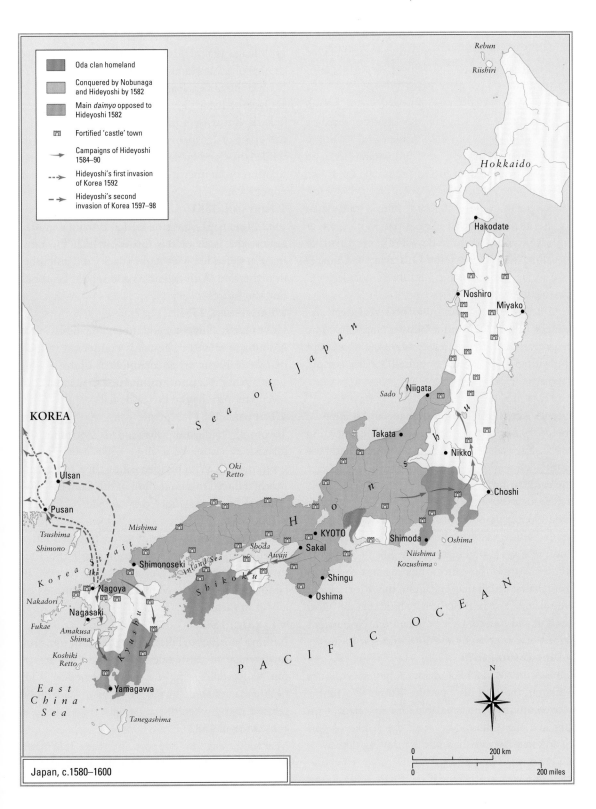

Legend:
- Oda clan homeland
- Conquered by Nobunaga and Hideyoshi by 1582
- Main *daimyo* opposed to Hideyoshi 1582
- Fortified 'castle' town
- Campaigns of Hideyoshi 1584–90
- Hideyoshi's first invasion of Korea 1592
- Hideyoshi's second invasion of Korea 1597–98

Japan, c.1580–1600

Map labels:

Rebun
Riishiri
Hokkaido
Hakodate
Noshiro
Miyako
Sado
Niigata
Takata
Nikko
Choshi
KOREA
Sea of Japan
Ulsan
Oki Retto
Pusan
Tsushima
Shimono
Mishima
H o n s h u
Shimoda
Oshima
Niishima
Kozushima
Ikki
Shimonoseki
Shoda
Awaji
KYOTO
Sakai
Inland Sea
Shikoku
Shingu
Korea Strait
Nagoya
Nagasaki
Nakadori
Fukae
Amakusa Shima
K y u s h u
Oshima
Koshiki Retto
East China Sea
Yamagawa
Tanegashima
P A C I F I C   O C E A N

N

| 0 | 200 km |
| 0 | 200 miles |

this defended castle, held by Matsunaga Hisahide and his son, Kojiro. The Matsunagas both killed themselves when the castle fell.

■ **MIMIGAWA, 1578**

The Christian Otomo family fought the rival Shimazu clan for control of Kyushu. Bombarding Takajo castle with Western artillery, the Otomo found their army drawn into ambushes and destroyed by the Shimazu, who responded in force.

■ **KOZUKI, 1578**

The Mori counter-attacked the Oda when Terumoto attacked this captured castle, under command of Toyotomi Hideyoshi's general, Amako Katsuhisa. So occupied, the Oda army was unable to stop the castle's fall and Katsuhisa's suicide.

■ **MIKI, 1578–80**

Oda Nobunaga built a more powerful fleet and besieged this castle under Bessho Nagaharu. The Oda took the outer defences while the Mori kept the stronger inner castle supplied. Finally cut off, the castle fell.

■ **OTATE, 1578**

Uesugi Kenshin willed his domains to his adopted son, Kagetora, and his nephew, Kagekatsu, starting a war. Kagekatsu attacked Kagetora at Otate, the latter's connection to the Hojo insufficient to save the castle or him.

■ **KIZUGAWAGUCHI II, 1578**

Oda Nobunaga built a large fleet including six of a new design of large ships, for his second bid to end the Mori's supremacy in the Inland Sea. Kuki Yoshitaka took these 'iron ships' against the Mori from bases in Sihma, engaging the Mori under Murakami Takeyoshi. So heavily built that the Mori cannon and musket balls bounced off, Nobunaga's behemoths overcame the Mori with few losses.

■ **MIMAOMOTE, 1579**

Chosokabe Motochika made a bid to conquer Shikoku when his vassal, Kumu Yorinobu, moved toward the formidable Doi Kiyonaga, who attacked the Chosokabe over the banks of this river. Yorinobu perished in the resulting defeat.

■ **OTATE NO RAN, 1579**

Uesugi Kakekatsu, having taken Otate castle, found the Hojo hostile after Kagetora's suicide. Worse, Oda Nobunaga pragmatically and ruthlessly exploited the fratricide and invaded, taking all lands west of Echigo province. The Uesugi never recovered.

■ **OMOSU, 1580**

Takeda Katsuyori's made for the Hojo at sea off the coast of Izu peninsula, met there by Ujimasa while the land armies moved to engage. The fighting on neither medium resulted in a decisive conclusion.

■ **HIJIYAMA, 1581**

Oda Nobunaga's invasion of Iga province crested against the walls of this fortress, which the ninja Iga-ryu defended with night attacks and ambushes near the gate. With defenders and supplies running out, the fortress burned.

■ **TAKATENJIN, 1581**

Continuing his long-term campaign, Oda Nobunaga moved against this conquered outpost of Takeda Katsuyori and brought it under a close siege. Okabe Naganori maintained the defence for several months before the castle fell.

■ **TOTTORI, 1581**

Toyotomi Hideyoshi abandoned storming this fortress in favour of a close siege lasting nearly seven months. With his men eating their horses and nearly reduced to cannibalism of the slain, Kikkawa Tsuneie finally surrendered by suicide.

■ **TAKAMATSU, 1582**

The fading Mori were not saved by the sudden news of Oda Nobunaga's death. With the Oda diverting nearby rivers to flood this fortress, its commander, Shimizu Muneharu, killed himself on a boat in surrender.

■ **TAKATO, 1582**

Nishina Morinobu, Takeda Shingen's fifth son, took final refuge in this castle against the Oda armies out to complete the Takeda's destruction. Oda Nobutada offered surrender, which Morinobu refused, dying when the castle fell.

■ **HONNO-JI, 1582**

Marching out in support of the Takamatsu siege, Akechi Mitsuhide suddenly attacked Oda Nobunaga in Honno-ji palace, Nobunaga's

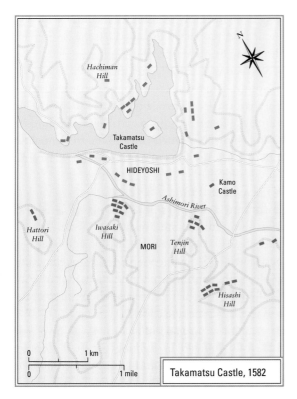

Takamatsu Castle, 1582

residence in Kyoto. His guards dead and severely wounded himself, Nobunaga killed himself, ending his remarkable career.

■ YAMAZAKI, 1582

Toyotomi Hideyoshi overtook Akechi Mitsuhide and his army here, Hideyoshi proclaiming himself Oda Nobunaga's avenger. With his army engulfed in vengeful soldiers, Mitshuide fled into the fields, where he was beaten to death by peasants.

■ KANAGAWA, 1582

The Hojo family took full advantage of the chaos caused by Oda Nobunaga's death and attacked the former Takeda territories of Takigawa Kazumasu. The large army overwhelmed Nobunaga's supporter, driving him into retreat.

■ TEMMOKUZAN, 1582

Takeda Katsuyori retained one last castle as Toyotomi Hideyoshi continued the Oda's destruction of the Takeda. Tokugawa Ieyasu led the final assault, with the last loyal Takeda retainers buying time for Katsuyori's suicide with their lives.

■ UCHIDEHAMA, 1582

Pursuing the heroic, and politically useful, vengeance of a murdered lord, Toyotomi Hideyoshi pursued the remnants of the slain Akechi Mitsuhide's army to this place. Their destruction completed the avenging of Oda Nobunaga's death.

■ SHIZUGATAKE, 1583

Shibata Katsuie was the first of Oda Nobunaga's generals to challenge Toyotomi Hideyoshi as Nobunaga's successor, advancing upon Kyoto through prepared defences. Hideyoshi's army arrived in overwhelming force. After his army collapsed, Katsuie committed suicide.

■ KOMAKI AND NAGAKUTE, 1584

Tokugawa Ieyasu posed the most formidable challenge among Oda Nobunaga's generals to Toyotomi Hideyoshi's sole possession of the shogunate. Hideyoshi's ally, Mori Nagayushi, advanced into Ieyasu's territory, prompting a strong response, which Nagayushi's forces endured until taken in the rear at Komaki by Sakai Tadatsugu. Both supreme leaders ordered the construction of extensive facing fieldworks, prompting a stalemate. Ikeda Nobuteru moved out from Nobunaga's lines only to find Ieyasu alerted and attacking that portion of the army. More of Nobunaga's forces moved to Nobuteru's aid, both forces resisting Ieyasu's advance at Nagakute. They then retreated back into the main body of Nobunaga's army, with Ieyasu's army moving directly into their centre, avoiding an effort to allow a flank attack. Hideyoshi's ally, Mori Nagayushi, perished early in the fighting, Ikeda Nobuteru soon thereafter stifling the response of Nobunaga's army. Fighting ceased.

■ KAGANOI, 1584

Oda Nobuo asserted his family's privilege against Toyotomi Hideyoshi's suzerainty and rallied his forces. Hideyoshi launched an attack upon Nobuo's ally Kaganoi Shigemochi's keep. Hideyoshi brought up artillery and the castle fell after severe bombardment.

■ TAKEHANA, 1584

Oda Nobuo's claim for his family's domination

over Nobunaga's territories received further rebuke when Toyotomi Hideyoshi moved against another Oda castle. Once again, a dam diverted a river into the fortification, which surrendered once flooded.

■ KANIE, 1584

Toyotomi Hideyoshi continued his efforts chastising Oda Nobuo's assertion of his family's rights against him. Maeda Tanetoshi defected and surrendered this castle only to find Hideyhoshi and the Oda reconciling, both successfully demanding his head.

■ SUEMORI, 1584

Sasa Narimasa moved against this allied castle of Toyotomi Hideyoshi, commanded by Okamura Sukie'mon, the post nearly falling despite Sukie'mon and his wife's defence. Having declared for Hideyoshi, Maeda Toshiie relieved his garrison, defeating Narimasa.

■ HITOTORIBASHI, 1585

Hatekyama Yoshitsugo had murdered Terumune Masamune at Nihonmatsu castle and faced his vengeful son, Date, in a decisive struggle for control of northern Japan. Despite a three-to-one disadavantage in numbers, Date achieved victory and revenge.

■ INVASION OF SHIKOKU, 1585

Chosokabe Motochika sought to maintain his family's grip on the island of Shikoku. Toyotomi Hideyoshi, his powerful navy and generals thought otherwise, hurling three separate invasion forces comprising 83,000 men onto Shikoku in 703 ships (600 of them capital units). Motochika sought to lift this force's siege of Ichinomiya castle, but eventually made terms and retained control of one province.

■ TOYAMA, 1585

Toyotomi Hideyoshi's control over vast areas allowed him to direct huge resources towards his objectives, such as Toyama castle, against which he sent 100,000 men. Sasa Narimasa's defeat there left Hideyoshi dominant in Etchu province.

■ OTA CASTLE, 1585

Toyotomi Hideyoshi flooded out his third bastion here, in which the Saiga Ikki military monks hoped to resist his pogrom. Difficulties with the inundation protracted the siege, but the bastion fell defending Samurai suicides.

■ SENDAIGAWA, 1587

Toyotomi Hideyoshi attacked the defiant Shimazu clan with a vast army. Finding a much smaller Shimazu force at the Sendaigawa, Hideyoshi nearly perished when the Shimazu launched a ferocious spoiling attack before Hideyoshi's hordes prevailed.

■ TAKASHIRO, 1587

Toyotomi Hideyoshi's invasion of Kyushu drove the Shimazu behind Takashiro castle, which Hideyoshi's half-brother, Hashiba Hidenaga, besieged. The Shimazu doubled back to relieve the castle, with dummies masking their movements, finally retreating before overwhelming numbers.

■ KYUSHU CAMPAIGN, 1587

The Shimazu clan's ability to resist Toyotomi Hideyoshi suffered in fighting the rival Otomo. Outnumbered, but seldom outfought, the Shimazu retreated further and further back until surrendering before their final redoubt at Kagoshima.

■ AKIZUKI, 1587

Akizuki Tanezane watched the army of Toyotomi Hideyoshi advance up Kyushu towards his castle of Oguma. Saving his army and himself by decamping secretly at night, Tanezane chose capitulation at daybreak with the castle occupied.

■ GANJAKU, 1587

Toyotomi Hideyoshi himself bypassed this bastion held for Akizuki Tanezane, offering gold pieces for the defenders' severed heads. Leaving (by lot) Gamo Ujisato to reduce it, Ujisato overwhelmed the castle with a sudden savage onslaught.

■ HACHIGATA, 1590

As he made ready for his final effort against the Hojo, Toyotomi Hideyoshi threw 35,000 men against this castle held by Hojo Ujikuni. The defenders resisted for a month, buying time for the inner defences.

■ ODAWARA, 1590

The Hojo were aware that their massive home castle of Odawara would be the target of Toyotomi

Hideyoshi's advance and poured 50,000 men and immense resources into its defence. Hideyoshi threw three rings of circumvallation and moats around the immense structure guarded by 200,000 troops and riotous camp followers. Hideyoshi enjoyed some success with mining and storming efforts, but the densely packed defenders only yielded after three months of mutual vigilance.

■ OSHI, 1590

With the fall of Odawara, Toyotomi Hideyoshi dispatched Ishida Mitsunari to clean up this Hojo bastion. Once more, the defenders held out until a diverted river flooded the bastion into submission.

SHIMODA, 1590

The Hojo's coastal fort of Shimoda in southern Honshu with 600 defenders held out for four months under a primarily naval assault by Toyotomi Hideyoshi's fleet and admiral, Kuki Yoshitaka, the attackers numbering 14,000 men.

■ SEKIGAHARA, 1600

Arguably the most decisive battle in Japanese history was fought between the 'eastern army' of Tokugawa Ieyasu and the 'western army' of Ishida Mitsunari. Surviving documents from the Kikkawa house reveal that projectiles inflicted 68 per cent of all wounds in 1600, with guns inflicting 80 per cent and arrows the remainder. Only a third of all wounds (32 per cent) were caused by shock weapons, almost all inflicted by pikes.

Divisions between five regents – who had been appointed by the hegemon Toyotomi Hideyoshi shortly before his 1598 death – propelled the conflict. These five, Tokugawa Ieyasu, Mōri Terumoto, Maeda Toshi'ie, Ukita Hide'ie and Uesugi Kagekatsu, likewise struggled with Ishida Mitsunari, the leader of five lower-ranking administrators (*bugyō*). Ultimately, armed hostilities broke out with Ishida Mitsunari getting Mōri Terumoto appointed the general commander of what became known as the western army. Tokugawa Ieyasu wrote letters to about half of Japan's daimyo to determine their allegiance and

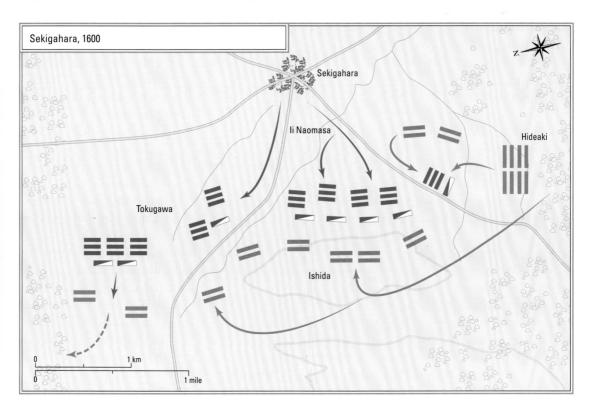

Sekigahara, 1600

the vast majority joined his cause. So bolstered, he departed his eastern base and arrived at Sekigahara, where he faced the western army.

The advantage would seem to be with Ishida's western forces, which occupied the high ground and outnumbered Ieyasu's army by 10,000 (84,000 to 74,000), but in fact, many western supporters wavered in their allegiance. Tellingly, the army's nominal commander, Mōri Terumoto, chose not to fight that day. Ishida had only about 35,000 reliable troops, which explains the ultimately decisive outcome of the battle.

The battle started around 08:00, with eastern army forces led by Ii Naomasa and Fukushima Masanori attacking the western army's Ukita Hide'ie and Konishi Yukinaga, who occupied the centre right and centre of their army's line. Kuroda Nagamasa then attacked Ishida's troops, located at the left wing of the western army, in a gruelling encounter that lasted for over four hours.

The forces of Kobayakawa Hideaki, a Mōri ally, occupied the right wing of the western army and Hideaki remained aloof from the fray, unable to decide where his loyalties lay. After four hours of battle, the Tokugawa forces fired upon his 15,000 men and Hideaki turned on their erstwhile allies. Some other members of the western army on the right wing, such as Kutsuki Mototsuna, sided with Hideaki, swelling his force to approximately 30,000 and they rolled up the western army. Forces in the centre of the line, such as those of Konishi Yukinaga and Ukita Hide'ie, were annihilated, while the left wing, under the command of Mitsunari, retreated. Most remarkably, the forces of Shimazu Yoshihiro, which occupied the centre left of the line, boldly attacked the centre of the eastern army, punishing Ii Naomasa's forces, before they escaped, collecting his relatives before returning to their homelands in Southern Kyushu. The western army suffered approximately 4–8000 casualties. After the battle, Ishida Mitsunari and Konishi Yukinaga were executed, Ukita Hide'ie was banished and supporters of the western army, including Mōri Terumoto, lost considerable lands. Only the formidable Shimazu

were largely spared from punishment. This battle laid the basis for Tokugawa's political hegemony, for Ieyasu bolstered the wealth and lands of his house, and collateral lineages. At the same time, the Mōri and Shimazu resented their treatment and, 267 years later, samurai from their domains would be instrumental in bringing down the Tokugawa.

■ Gifu Castle, 1600
In the aftermath of Toyotomi Hideyoshi's death, forces loyal to his son, Hideyori, sought to hold this castle and the pass it guarded against troops supporting the cause of Tokugawa Ieyasu. Surrounded, the castle fell.

■ Ueda, 1600
As fighting erupted between Ishida Mutsonari and Tokugawa Ieyasu over the shogunate, Ieyasu's son, Hidetada, besieged this hostile fortress held by Sanada Masayuki and his son Yukimura. Hidetada failed to take the strongly defended castle.

■ Fushimi, 1600
Torii Mototada held this indefensible castle for ten days in order to delay forces loyal to Toyotomi Hideyori from invading Tokugawa Ieyasu's lands. After a legendary defense, the castle fell by treachery.

■ Hasedo, 1600
Naoe Kanetsugu supported Ishida Mutsonari's bid against Tokugawa Ieyasu and laid siege to this fortified obstacle as he advanced. With a relieving army under Date Masakage in sight, Kanetsugu assaulted the castle, which successfully resisted.

■ Hataya, 1600
Naoe Kanetsugu, along with with 20,000 men, attacked this small castle held by under 300 men and Eguchi Gohei as Kantetsugu and his army moved toward Yamagata castle, held by Tokugawa Ieyasu's allies. Gohei finally was overwhelmed.

■ Kaminoyama, 1600
In support of Ishida Mutsonari against Tokugawa Ieyasu, Naoe Kanetsugu's general Honmura Chikamori – with Yokota Munetoshi and 4000 men – overwhelmed this bastion under Satomi Minbu, at the cost of Chikamori's own life.

■ Shiroishi, 1600
While Naoe Kanetsugu supported the cause

of Ishida Mutsonari, Date Masamune likewise advanced the cause of Tokugawa Ieyasu in the north by launching a successful attack upon this castle, held for Kanetsugu's ally Uesugi Kagekatsu.

■ **TANABE, 1600**

As the forces loyal to Ishida Mutsonari and Tokugawa Ieyasu marshalled for a decisive confrontation, a general respecting the aged Hosokawa Yusai Fujitaka laid a pro-forma siege with blank charges to the respected retainer's castle.

■ **UDO, 1600**

The struggle between Ishida Mutsonari and Tokugawa Ieyasu for the shogunate allowed the gratification of old feuds, such as here when Kato Kiyomasa – on behalf of Ieyasu – destroyed his rival Konishi Yukinaga and his castle.

■ **YANAGAWA, 1600**

Kato Kiyomasa joined Kuroda Yoshitaka in attacking this bastion held by Tachibana Muneshige after the battle of Sekigahara. Having been forbidden by Tokugawa Ieyasu to change sides and join his besiegers, Muneshige surrendered the castle.

■ **OTSU, 1600**

Tachibana Muneshige and Tsukushi Hirokado with 15,000 men attacked this castle under Kyogoku Takatsugu, a Tokugawa ally, as picnickers watched from nearby hills. With the besiegers' side defeated at Sekigahara, Takatsugo's surrender spared his men.

■ **KASHII, 1615**

The 5000 defenders of Wakayama castle attacked 3000 besiegers who had previously ambushed forces of Tokugawa Ieyasu en route to the years-long siege of Osaka castle. Suffering unexpected losses, the Toyotomi forces fled to Osaka.

■ **DOMYOJI, 1615**

Toyotomi Hideyori, Hideyoshi's son and heir, retained Osaka castle and his father's name and wealth. Tokugawa Ieyasu with 194,000 men attacked Hideyori's 100,000 defenders. Here, an effort to raise the siege failed with heavy casualties.

■ **TENNOJI, 1615**

Toyotomi Hideyori and his remaining garrison launched a death-or-glory attack from Osaka castle with two relieving armies hitting the besiegers'

rear. The messy attack resulted in a bloody repulse, the castle's fall and Hideyori's suicide.

■ **HARA, 1637**

The Christians of Shimabara revolted under persecution, perishing in this refuge after a long and bitter siege of the dilapidated castle. Starvation prevailed where mining, bombardment by a Dutch ship and multiple escalades had failed.

Sinhalese–Portuguese War 1562–1638

■ **MULLERIYAWA, 1562**

A 1600-strong Portuguese force under Dom Afonso Pereira de Lacerda and allied troops from Kotte were virtually annihilated in a prolonged battle by King Mayadunne's army of several thousand Sitawaka militia, supported by war elephants.

■ **RANDENIWALA, 25 AUGUST 1630**

A Kandian army of approximately 35,000 men, commanded by King Senarat Adahasin, defeated a Portuguese force under Dom Constantino de Sá de Noronha at Randeniwela near Wellawayain, in what is now Sri Lanka.

■ **GANNORUWA, 28 MARCH 1638**

A Portuguese army of 900 men and 5000 Sinhalese commanded by Diogo de Melo de Castro, the Portuguese CGen in Colombo, was annihilated by forces of the Kingdom of Kandy under Rajasimha II.

French Religious Wars 1562–1628

■ **DREUX, 19 DECEMBER 1562**

A French Catholic army intercepted and defeated a French Huguenot Protestant army marching towards Le Havre on the French coast. The Catholics, led by Montmorency, had about 18,000 troops and the Huguenots, led by Condé, about 15,000. Both sides included foreign mercenaries. The leader of each side was captured while leading cavalry charges and estimates for the bloody battle vary, but may have totaled 6000.

■ **VASSY, 1 MARCH 1562**

Francois de Guise led a troop of cavalry to confront

a Huguenot congregation at Vassy, France. The situation escalated until Guise ordered his troops to fire, killing or wounding about 200 civilians.

■ **ROUEN, 29 SEPTEMBER–26 OCTOBER 1562**
A large French Catholic force besieged and finally took the French coastal city of Rouen, which was defended by French Huguenots along with a small English force.

■ **SAINT DENIS, 10 NOVEMBER 1567**
A large French Catholic army of 20,000 fought a French Huguenot army of 3000 north of Paris. The Catholic commander Montmorency was killed and the Huguenots withdrew four days later.

■ **MEAUX, 25 SEPTEMBER 1567**
French Royal Catholics discovered a French Huguenot plot to seize the Royal court at Meaux to the east of Paris and marched Swiss Guards towards Paris to disrupt the plot.

■ **JARNAC, 13 MARCH 1569**
A small French Huguenot force was defeated by a French Royal Catholic force near the Charente River in west central France. The death of Condé was a significant Huguenot loss.

■ **LA ROCHE-L'ABEILLE, 25 JUNE 1569**
A French Huguenot army of 24,000 under Coligny inflicted a minor defeat on a French Royal Catholic army of 22,000 in south-central France.

■ **ORTHEZ, 11–24 AUGUST 1569**
French Huguenot forces besieged and took the Catholic town of Orthez in southern France. The town was sacked and burnt, with military leaders, priests and many other inhabitants killed.

■ **MONCONTOUR, 5 OCTOBER 1569**
A French Royal Catholic army defeated Coligny's French Huguenot army in western France before it could join forces with German allies. Coligny escaped, but with a badly damaged army.

■ **LA ROCHELLE, 1572–73**
The fortress city of La Rochelle on the west coast of France was a French Huguenot stronghold, with a garrison of 3200. A French Catholic army of 40,000 began a siege in December, but bombardments and assaults did not commence until March. By June, 29 assaults had failed and the siege army had lost

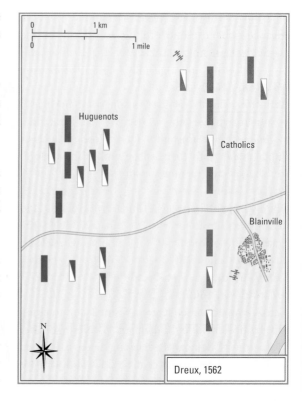

Dreux, 1562

22,000 men from combat and disease. The garrison lost 1300 before peace was negotiated.

■ **SANCERRE, 1572–73**
A French Royal Catholic army unsuccessfully besieged the French Huguenot stronghold of Sancerre in central France. The garrison resorted to eating horses, rodents and dogs. The siege was ended by negotiation.

■ **ST BARTHOLOMEW'S DAY MASSACRE, 24 AUGUST 1572**
French Catholics killed Adm Coligny and slaughtered 2000–3000 French Huguenots in Paris, who had gathered there for a royal wedding. Similar massacres occurred throughout France.

■ **COUTRAS, 20 OCTOBER 1587**
Henry of Navarre (the future King Henry IV of France) commanded a French Huguenot army of 6300 men at Coutras in south-western France. Opposing this was a French Royal Catholic force of 10,000 under Joyeuse. Henry put his army in a convex defensive position, with his left flank

secured by the Donne River and his right anchored in a wooded park and warren. Detachments of musketeers were on both flanks and also between his units of pikemen and cavalry. with three cannon positioned to cover the front.

Joyeuse used his superior numbers to attack, but they suffered heavy casualties from effective artillery and musket fire. Joyeuse was killed while leading a cavalry charge; Henry successfully counter-attacked the disorganized Royal Catholics, inflicting losses of 2500. Henry, victorious, lost 500 men.

■ VIMORY, 26 OCTOBER 1587

A French Royal Catholic army under Henry of Guise defeated a combined force of Protestant Swiss and German mercenaries near Vimory in north-central France. The mercenary army left France.

■ ARQUES, 15–29 SEPTEMBER 1589

Henry IV, King of France upon the death of Henry III, repelled 35,000 Catholic League troops with 8000 men near the Channel coast until reinforced by English and French troops.

■ IVRY-LA-BATAILLE, 14 MARCH 1590

Henry IV, King of France, not being recognized as such by the Catholic League, confronted them at Ivry, about 50km due west of Paris. Henry's French army included about 8000 infantry and 3000 cavalry. The League army, commanded by Mayenne, included 12,000 infantry and 4000 cavalry, thousands of these being Swiss and German mercenaries, plus Spanish cavalry and arquebusiers. Henry set up positions facing north-east, with Mayenne positioned directly opposite. Henry was on the right-centre with his heavy cavalry, telling his troops to always follow his white plume in the confusion of battle. Battle commenced, but Mayenne's mercenaries refused to advance, causing gaps along the line and on the flanks. Henry's attacks, him personally leading the cavalry charge, were successful. Mayenne's army fell apart, most being killed or captured.

■ EL LEON, 1 OCTOBER–19 NOVEMBER 1594

A Spanish garrison of 400 fought until they had

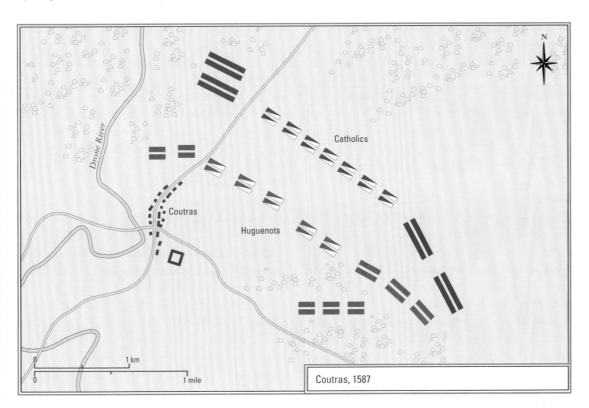

Coutras, 1587

only 13 survivors against a besieging force of 9000 English and French troops near the port of Brest, France.

■ FONTAINE-FRANCAISE, 5 JUNE 1595

King Henry IV foiled a Spanish invasion near Dijon, defeating the Spanish advance guard by recruiting peasants, making his army appear larger. The ruse worked and the invaders withdrew.

■ NEGREPELISSE, 10–11 JUNE 1622

The army of French King Louis XIII besieged and quickly took the Huguenot town of Negrepelisse in southern France. No quarter was given and the town was sacked and burnt.

■ BLAVET, 17 JANUARY 1625

A Huguenot fleet under Souhan broke through chain barriers, surprising and capturing 15 ships of the Royal Navy of France in the port of Blavet, near La Rochelle in Brittany, France.

■ LA ROCHELLE, 1627–28

French royal army and naval forces compelled the surrender of the Huguenot port of La Rochelle in western coast France, after the Huguenots held for fourteen months, with English support.

Northern Seven Years' War 1563–70

■ ACTION OF 30 MAY 1564 (NR BORNHOM)

Jakob Bagge's Swedish fleet of 35 ships was defeated in a two-day action by a Danish and Lübeck fleet of 36 vessels commanded by Herluf Trolle and Friedrich Knebel. Each side lost a single ship.

■ ACTION OF 12 JULY 1564

The Danish ships *Byens Løffue* (56), *Morian* (47) and *David* (42) defeated the Swedish ship *Hvita Falk*, under Capt Björnson off Warnemünde. After several hours of fierce fighting, Björnson blew up his ship to avoid capture.

■ ACTION OF 4 JUNE 1565

A fleet of 33 Danish and Lübeck ships under Herluf Trolle was defeated by Klas Horn's Swedish fleet of 49 vessels. The Danes withdrew to Køge Bay, where the wounded commander Trolle died on 25 June.

■ ACTION OF 7 JULY 1565

A Swedish fleet of 49 ships, commanded by Klas Horn, defeated a combined Danish and Lübeck fleet of 36 ships under Otto Rud. Horn lost two ships, but sank three and captured two more.

■ AXTORNA, 20 OCTOBER 1565

Daniel Rantzau's 7500 Danish troops defeated an 11,000-strong Swedish army commanded by Jacob Henriksson Hästesko at Axtorna, near Falkenberg in southern Sweden. Rantzau lost 1000 men, but inflicted 1500 casualties and captured the Swedish artillery.

■ ACTION OF 26 JULY 1566

Klas Horn's 60-strong Swedish fleet fought an indecisive action against a Danish and Lübeck fleet of 36 ships. However, two days later, 15 Danish and Lübeck ships were wrecked by a storm on the coast of Gotland.

Irish Internal Conflicts 1565–80

■ AFFANE, FEBRUARY 1565

A feud erupted between the Earl of Desmond, Gerald Fitzgerald and the Earl of Ormonde, Thomas Butler. After the death of the Countess of Ormonde, who married into the Desmonds and established a temporary peace, fighting over territory in Cork, Tipperary, Kilkenny and Waterford resumed. At Affane, 300 Desmonds under Fitzgerald were killed and Fitzgerald himself was captured.

■ GLENTAISIE, 2 MAY 1565

Under orders from Elizabeth I, the O'Neill clan, led by Shane O'Neill, attacked and destroyed the Scottish Clan Macdonald's holdings in northern Ireland. During the battle, leader James Macdonald was captured and died in captivity.

■ FARSETMORE, 8 MAY 1567

Clan O'Donnell fought, with English assistance, against Clan O'Neill for authority in Ulster. The O'Neills suffered more than 500 casualties including chieftain Shane O'Neill, who was assassinated by Clan Macdonald in reprisal for Glentaisie.

■ ATHENRY, 1572

The battle that began the Mac an Iarlas Wars between Richard de Burgh, 2nd Earl of Clanricarde, and his sons. The battle began as a title dispute, but following English intervention became a rebellion against the Crown.

■ GLENMALURE, 25 AUGUST 1580

Leading an army of 3000 men, Arthur Grey attempted to put down the Desmond rebellions. An Irish insurgent force led by Viscount Baltinglas ambushed the force, killing 350 men and forcing a retreat into Dublin.

■ CARRIGAFOYLE CASTLE, 1580

Fifty Irishmen and 16 Spaniards attempted to defend Carrigafoyle Castle against more than 500 Englishmen under the command of Lord Justice Sir William Pelham. The English shelled the castle, destroying it. The defenders were executed.

■ SMERWICK, 7–10 NOVEMBER 1580

Funded by Pope Gregory XIII, 500 Spanish and Italians landed in southern Ireland to assist the rebellion against the English. The force was cut off from the Irish and massacred by Earl Arthur Grey and his men.

Islamic invasion of India 1565

■ TALIKOTA, 23 JANUARY 1565

Despite rivalry between the Deccan Sultanates, Ali Adil Shah of Bijapur, Husain Nizam Shah of Ahmadnagar, Ali Barid Shah of Bidar and Ibrahim Qutb Shah of Golconda temporarily united against the Hindu Empire. Their army of 110,000 men defeated the forces of Vijayanagar commanded by Aliya Rama Raya, which totalled 150,000 men and over 100 war elephants. This defeat marked the beginning of the end of the Hindu Empire.

Persian Invasion of Georgia 1567

■ DIGOMI, 1567

The army of Georgian king Simon I of Kartli defeated the forces of his brother, Daud Khan, at Digomi, near Tbilisi.

Revolts in Philippines 1567–1601

■ DAGAMI REVOLT, 1567

Chief Dagami of Gabi organized and led a series of attacks against the newly established Spanish colonial regime on Cebu in the Philippines from 1565, until he was betrayed and executed in 1567.

■ BANKUSAY CHANNEL, 3 JUNE 1571

Tarik Sulayman of Macabebe led a force of warriors against a Spanish detachment of 280 men and 600 auxiliaries at Tondo, near Manila. Sulayman was defeated and killed, allowing the Spanish to consolidate their control of Manila.

■ IGOROT REVOLT, 1601

Spanish attempts to impose Christianity on the Igorot people of northern Luzon provoked a major revolt. Troops under Capt Aranda supressed the rebellion, but the Spanish were only able to establish nominal control of the region.

Revolt in Granada 1568

MORISCO REVOLT, 1568

Philip II's repression of Moorish culture provoked a rebellion in Granada. It was led by Ferag ben Ferag, a descendant of the royal house of Granada and Diego Lopez Ben Abu. They raised a 25,000-strong army and fought a three-year guerilla campaign with the support of Berber and Ottoman mercenaries. The rebels were defeated by veteran Spanish and Italian troops commanded by Don Juan of Austria.

Eighty Years' War 1568–1648

■ OOSTERWEEL, 13 MARCH 1567

Often seen as the first battle of the Eighty Years' War, a Spanish army under Gen Beauvoir defeated Calvinist rebels under Jan de Marnix. William the Silent, still under oath to Spain, did not intervene in the fighting.

■ HEILIGEREE, 1568

The first Dutch victory during the Eighty Years' War, Heiligeree was an ambush planned by Adolf and Louis of Nassau. The Dutch infantry played a major role, capturing seven cannon and killed almost 2000 men.

JEMMINGEN, 21 JULY 1568

The battle of Jemmingen was the Spanish Army's revenge for their defeat at Heiligerlee. Having failed to capture Groningen, Louis of Nassau was hounded by the Duke of Alva. The forces were evenly balanced when they engaged, but after three hours of skirmishing, Louis ordered an attack, abandoning the protection of earthworks. They were met by musket fire and Spanish cavalry and forced to retreat towards the River Ems.

EMS, LATE JULY 1568

The Duke of Alva pursued Louis of Nassau to Ems, driving the Dutch over the bridges and into the river, where many died by drowning. Louis stripped off his heavy armour and swam across.

JODOIGNE, 16 OCTOBER 1568

In a further defeat for the Dutch rebels, at Jodoigne the Spanish Army destroyed the rear guard of William the Silent's army, forcing

him to abandon his plans for an invasion of the Netherlands.

DAHLEN, 25 APRIL 1568

A Dutch rebel army under Joost de Soete, Lord of Villers, was defeated at Dahlen by a Spanish army under Sancho Davila y Daza, after having to withdraw from Roermond, under attack by William of Orange.

BRIELLE, 1 APRIL 1572

The capture of Brielle by the 'Sea Beggars' represented the first foothold on land for the rebels at a time when they were being defeated. It was a turning point in the Eighty Years' War.

HAARLEM, 1572–73

Haarlem was the site of a long and arduous siege, fought partly during the winter, that was to become a celebrated engagement in the Eighty Years' War. Bitter fighting took place across the walls, but, in March 1573, the Spanish Army took control of the Haarlemmermeer and began to starve the rebels out. A relieving army under William of

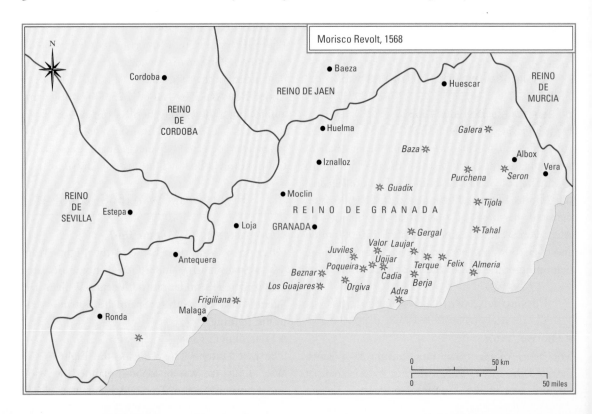

Morisco Revolt, 1568

Orange marched in support, but were defeated and Haarlem finally surrendered.

■ ALKMAAR, 1573

During the defence of Alkmaar the citizens drove off the Spanish, commanded by the son of the hated Duke of Alva, in a siege using boiling tar and burning branches dropped from their city walls.

■ LEIDEN, 1573

The first siege of Leiden by the Spanish Army was beaten off. The loose soil round the city prevented the Spanish from building siege lines and William of Orange's troops threatened to arrive with relief.

■ FLUSHING, 17 APRIL 1573

The naval battle of Flushing was fought near the city of Flushing and resulted in the seizure of five Spanish ships, while others escaped. Cannon fire from the city also played a part in the victory.

■ BORSELE, 22 APRIL 1573

Spanish ships sailed from Antwerp to supply the cities of Middelburg and Arnemuiden, which were under siege from the Dutch. They were intercepted at Borsele and most were forced to return home.

■ ZUIDERZEE, 11 OCTOBER 1573

This battle saw a Dutch fleet destroy a larger Spanish fleet. It was a successful attempt to hinder Spanish communication with Amsterdam. After initial reverses, the wind changed and the Dutch managed a surprise attack.

■ WALCHEREN, 1574

A naval battle off the island of Walcheren (also called Reimerswaal) resulted in a Dutch victory against a Spanish attempt to reinforce Middelburg, then besieged by the Dutch for over six months.

■ MOOKERHEYDE, 14 APRIL 1574

The battle of Mookerheyde was the final event in a series of Dutch disasters as they tried to relieve besieged Leiden. A mercenary army raised in Germany headed for Maastricht, but – before joining forces with William of Orange – many deserted, 700 were killed in a night attack and the rest mutinied for their pay. They were then defeated by a Spanish army, although the Dutch cavalry had been initially victorious.

■ LEIDEN, 1574

The siege and subsequent relief of Leiden in 1574 was one of the most celebrated Dutch victories in the Eighty Years' War. After many setbacks, a relieving army approached the city across the flooded countryside.

■ ANTWERP, 4 NOVEMBER 1576

The notorious sack of Antwerp in the 'Spanish Fury' caused the loss of 7000 lives and was sparked by the failure of the Spanish to pay their soldiers, who then took revenge on the city.

■ GEMBLOUX, 31 JANUARY 1578

The battle of Gembloux was a serious defeat for the Dutch rebels. Alexander Farnese, Duke of Parma, was pursuing a retreating Dutch army and observed that the boggy ground his enemy were traversing would make it unlikely for them to mount an ordered infantry defence. He led the Spanish cavalry in a devastating advance that broke the disordered Dutch infantry. The Spanish infantry never needed to engage in this battle.

■ RIJMENAM, 31 JULY 1578

At Rijmenam, a feint using musketeers and cavalry enticed the Dutch into leaving the safety of their entrenchments. But the positions were reversed when the Spanish discovered that they had been led into a trap.

■ DEVENTER, 3 AUGUST–19 NOVEMBER 1578

The siege of Deventer, which was held for the Spanish forces by a German mercenary army, was completed with a negotiated surrender when the defenders realized that the strategy of the besiegers made relief impossible.

■ MAASTRICHT, 12 MARCH–1 JULY 1 1579

The siege of Maastricht witnessed underground warfare when the Dutch defenders tried to countermine the Spanish attempts to dig into the city. Explosive mines were also used and after the capture a sack took place.

■ BREDA, 1581

Breda was entered by the Spanish after a sentry was bribed. Fighting continued in the streets and the Dutch surrendered when the Spanish promised not to sack the city, a promise that was not kept.

Union of Utrecht, 1579

Joined Union of Utrecht
by 1581

United Netherlands, 1609

To United Netherlands, 1648

Spanish Netherlands, 1648

Boundary of Holy Roman
Empire

Border in 1648

0   100 km
0   100 miles

N

Groningen
• Groningen

Friesland

Drenthe

R. Vecht

R. Ijssel

Overijssel

• Amsterdam

H o l l a n d

Zutphen •

Leiden •   • Utrecht   *Gelderland*

North   H O L   L   Y

Sea   • Rotterdam   Utrecht

R. Maas

R. Lippe

Zeeland

L a n d s   o f   t h e   G e n e r a l i t y

Upper
Gelders

R. Ruhr

Mörs

• Sluys   • Antwerp   R   O   M   A   N

Brugge •   B
                                            r   Cologne •
Ghent •   a
         R. Schelde   b   Maastricht
                                            a
         F l a n d e r s   Brussels   n   • Aachen
                                            t
Calais •   Limburg

R. Lys   Bishopric of Liège

Lille •   • Tournai   N a m u r   Liège •

Artois   • Namur

Arras •   E   *R. Sambre* M   P   I   R   E

         H a i n a u t   Bishopric of Liège

R. Somme   L u x e m b o u r g

                                                    • Trier

F   R   A   N   C   E   *R. Aisne*

                              Luxembourg •

R. Oise   *R. Saar*

                                            R. Meuse

• Reims   Verdun •   • Metz

Eighty Years' War, 1568–1648

■ **ANTWERP, 1584**

An important feature of the Spanish siege was the construction of a long pontoon bridge to cut off the city's access by water. Fire ships were used against it, but Antwerp eventually surrendered.

■ **ZUTPHEN, 22 SEPTEMBER 1586**

The battle of Zutphen involved the service of English soldiers who aided the United Provinces of the Netherlands against the Spanish. Among their ranks was Sir Philip Sidney, Robert Devereux, the 2nd Earl of Essex and Robert Dudley, Earl of Leicester. Sidney was mortally wounded during the battle and is remembered for having given his water bottle to another wounded soldier. In spite of bravery, the Spanish were eventually triumphant.

■ **BOKSUM, 17 JANUARY 1586**

When the Spanish invaded Frisia during the winter the frozen lakes allowed easy movement, but, when a thaw began, the Dutch rebels attacked them. The Spanish cavalry helped to aid the rebels' defeat.

■ **WERL, 3–8 MARCH 1586**

During the Cologne War of 1586, Protestant mercenaries tried to capture the well-defended city of Werl, but the arrival of a strong relieving force brought about a hasty withdrawal with a number of civilian hostages.

■ **BREDA, 1590**

Maurice of Nassau managed to infiltrate 70 men into Breda concealed within a delivery of peat. Their arrival allowed the city to be broken into, resulting in a speedy Dutch victory.

■ **TURNHOUT, 24 JANUARY 1597**

Dutch cavalry under Maurice of Nassau defeated a Spanish detachment near the largely unfortified Turnhout. Maurice, cautious in victory, did not follow up other than to burn part of the local castle.

■ **GROENLO, 11–28 SEPTEMBER 1597**

Maurice of Nassau laid siege to the city of Groenlo as part of a campaign to gain control of Spanish-held possessions. Groenlo fell and was held until it was lost to a Spanish attack in 1606.

■ **NIEUWPOORT, 2 JULY 1600**

At Nieuwpoort, the Dutch lay on top of a stretch of dunes, with guns covering both flanks with enfilade fire under Maurice of Nassau. The Spanish advanced, but two unruly mutineer regiments in the vanguard started the attack with a rash charge up the hill. They were repulsed in disorder, while the light cavalry – counter-charged by the Dutch cuirassiers – were routed. It was then time for the second line of the Spanish infantry to advance. The tercios on the Dutch right made quick progress against the Frisian regiment and Maurice sent his entire second line to protect that sector, stabilizing the front. Maurice then sent his entire cavalry against the Spanish flank, except for a small body of cavalry in the second line that he kept in reserve behind the infantry. The Dutch cuirassiers easily routed the lighter Spanish cavalry and the mutineer cornets that had just rallied fled the battlefield never to return. However, the Dutch were checked by the Spanish third line of infantry, supported by some guns, retreating with heavy losses. The English, well drilled in Maurice's new tactics, kept a rolling fire on the Spaniards and advanced up the slope at a steady pace, covered by a screen of skirmishing musketeers. The fight was even for a time, until it came to the push of pike. Maurice sent his reserve cavalry against them, only three cornets strong. Their well-timed charge was unexpectedly very successful. The Spaniards were thrown into confusion and started a slow retreat. Some English companies behind a battery joined the fight and were reinforced by the regiments in the third line that had finally arrived. The Spaniards, heavily assailed, retreated in disorder.

BANTEN (BANTAM) BAY, 27 DECEMBER 1601

A Dutch naval squadron of five vessels, intent on securing a monopoly of the spice trade with East India, defeated a Portuguese squadron of eight galleons and several light galleys off the coast of Java.

■ **SLUYS, 26 MAY 1603**

Adm Frederigo Spinola's squadron of eight Spanish galleys attempted to break the Dutch blockade of Sluys, but were defeated by a squadron of three ships and two galleys under VAdm Joost de Moor.

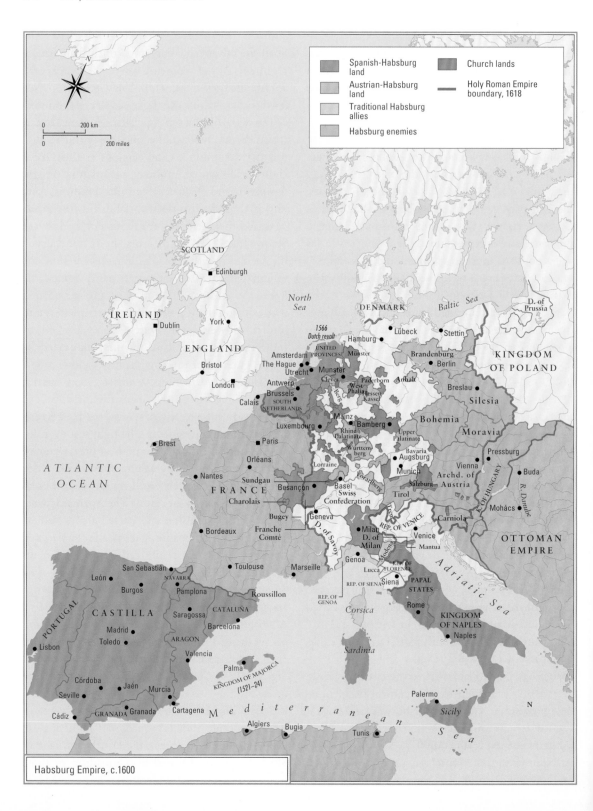

Legend:
- Spanish-Habsburg land
- Austrian-Habsburg land
- Traditional Habsburg allies
- Habsburg enemies
- Church lands
- Holy Roman Empire boundary, 1618

0   200 km
0   200 miles

SCOTLAND
Edinburgh

IRELAND
Dublin

North Sea

DENMARK

Baltic Sea

D. of Prussia

York
1566 Dutch revolt
Hamburg
Lübeck
Stettin

ENGLAND
Bristol
London
Calais

Amsterdam
The Hague
Utrecht
Antwerp
Brussels
SOUTH NETHERLANDS

UNITED PROVINCES
Münster
Münster
Cleves
West Phalia
Paderborn
Hessen Kassel
Anhalt

Brandenburg
Berlin

KINGDOM OF POLAND

Breslau
Silesia

Berg

Luxembourg
Mainz
Rhine Palatinate
Bamberg
Upper Palatinate
Bohemia
Moravia

Brest
Paris
Orléans

Württemberg
Bavaria
Augsburg
Munich

Pressburg
Vienna
Archd. of Austria

Buda

ATLANTIC OCEAN

Nantes
Sundgau
Besançon
Lorraine
Basel
Swiss Confederation

Vorarlberg
Salzburg
Tirol

K. OF HUNGARY

R. Danube
Mohács

FRANCE
Charolais
Bugey
Geneva
Franche Comté
D. of Savoy

Trent
REP. OF VENICE
Carniola

Bordeaux
Milan
D. of Milan
Venice
Mantua

OTTOMAN EMPIRE

Toulouse
Marseille
Genoa
Lucca
REP. OF FLORENCE
Modena
Siena
REP. OF SIENA

Adriatic Sea

San Sebastián
León
NAVARRA
Pamplona
Burgos
Roussillon
REP. OF GENOA
PAPAL STATES

PORTUGAL
CASTILLA
CATALUÑA
Saragossa
Barcelona
ARAGON
Madrid
Toledo
Valencia

Corsica

Rome

KINGDOM OF NAPLES
Naples

Lisbon

Córdoba
Jaén
Murcia
Seville
GRANADA
Granada
Cartagena
Palma
KINGDOM OF MAJORCA (1521–24)

Sardinia

Palermo
Sicily

N

Cádiz

Mediterranean Sea

Algiers
Bugia
Tunis

Habsburg Empire, c.1600

■ OSTEND, 5 JULY 1601–16 SEPTEMBER 1604

The Dutch had steadily improved the fortifications of Ostend since 1583 and, by the time that Archduke Albert's Spanish Army of over 20,000 men besieged the city, it was one of the most powerful fortresses in Western Europe. The 8000-strong Dutch garrison under Daniel de Hertaing and Sir Francis Vere put up a fierce defence before being forced to surrender after prolonged bombardments, which reduced much of the city to rubble. .

■ GIBRALTAR, 25 APRIL 1607

Dutch commander Adm Jacob van Heemskerk led a fleet of 26 ships in a bold attack on the island of Gibraltar, against a Spanish fleet of 21 vessels including 10 galleons commanded by Adm Don Juan Alvarez d'Avila. Both admirals were killed, though the knowledge of van Heemskerk's death was kept from his captains – hence these captains went on to achieve a stunning victory. The Spanish fleet was destroyed without the Dutch losing a ship.

■ BREDA, 28 AUGUST 1624–5 JUNE 1625

Don Ambrogio Spinola's 18,000-strong Spanish army besieged and took the city of Breda, inflicting 10,000 casualties on its Dutch garrison of 14,000 men under Justinus van Nassau. Spanish losses throughout the siege totalled 4000 men.

■ BAY OF MATANZAS, 7–8 SEPTEMBER 1628

A Dutch fleet of 31 ships commanded by Adm Piet Hein intercepted 21 vessels of the Spanish treasure fleet off the coast of Cuba. Hein captured 16 Spanish vessels carrying bullion valued at over 11,500,000 guilders.

■ SLAAK, 12–13 SEPTEMBER 1631

A Spanish fleet of 90 vessels and 5500 men under Count Jan van Nassau Siegen, attempted to seize the islands of Goeree and Overflakee, but were destroyed by a Dutch squadron of 50 ships.

■ PERNAMBUCO, 12–17 JANUARY 1640

Fernando de Mascarenhas' Spanish and Portuguese fleet of 30 galleons, 34 armed transports and 13 smaller vessels was intercepted and defeated off

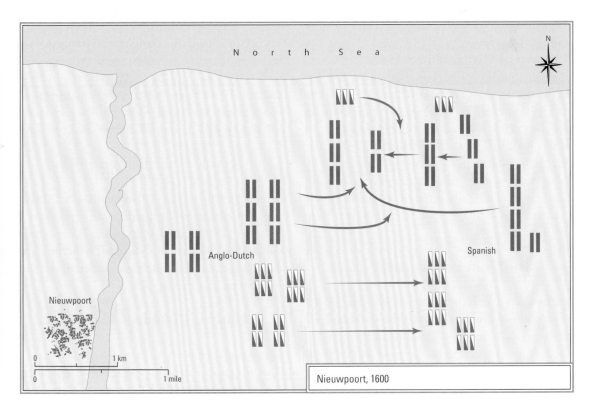

Nieuwpoort, 1600

Pernambuco, Brazil, by a Dutch fleet of 30 warships and 10 smaller vessels.

■ Hulst, October 1645

A Dutch army of 15,000 men and 20 guns under Frederick Henry, Prince of Orange, besieged Hulst in Zeeland in October. The town was held by a Spanish garrison of 2500 infantry and 250 cavalry. Henry attacked eastern defences, before working his way towards the centre of Hulst. The defenders surrendered after 28 days, having sustained over 1200 casualties, while the Dutch lost 1600 men.

■ La Naval de Manila, 15 Mar–4 Oct 1646

A Spanish squadron of only two, later, three Manila galleons, a galley and four brigantines decisively defeated a Dutch fleet of 18 warships in a series of five naval actions off the Philippines.

■ Dunkirk, 19 September–11 October 1646

A French army commanded by Louis II Duke d'Enghien attacked the key Spanish port of Dunkirk. Supported by a naval blockade by a Dutch squadron under Adm Martin Tromp, d'Enghien and his forces captured Dunkirk after a month-long siege.

■ Puerto de Cavite, 10 June 1647

A Dutch squadron of 12 ships attacked the harbour of Puerto de Cavite in Manila Bay, wrecking the fort at Porta Vaga. Fire from Spanish shore batteries sank two Dutch ships and drove off the rest.

■ San Juan de Ulúa, 23 September 1568

An English squadron of six ships commanded by John Hawkins and Francis Drake was defeated in San Juan de Ulúa harbour by four Spanish vessels. Hawkins and Drake escaped with only two ships still intact.

Revolt in England 1569–70

■ Rising of the North, Nov 1569–Jan 1570

A 4600-strong rebel force under the Catholic Earls of Westmorland and Northumberland attempted to depose Queen Elizabeth I in favour of Mary Queen of Scots. The revolt collapsed on the approach of a royalist army.

Unrest in Russia 1570

■ Novgorod, 1570

Reacting to rumours that the boyars of Novgorod planned to hand over the city to Polish forces, Tsar Ivan the Terrible led his 'secret police', the Oprichniki, in a massacre of up to 12,000 inhabitants.

Russo-Turkish War 1570–74

■ Molodi, 30 July–3 August 1572

A 120,000-strong horde of Tatars and Ottoman troops commanded by the Khan of the Crimea, Devlet I Giray, advanced on Moscow in an attempt to repeat their devastating raid of the previous year. Devlet I Giray hoped to take advantage of Tsar Ivan the Terrible's involvement in the Livonian War and was surprised to be intercepted by a Russian army of 60,000 men under Prince Mikhail Vorotynsky at Molodi near the River Lopasnya.

The Tatars were defeated with the loss of almost 100,000 men in a five-day battle, during which Russian firepower proved decisive. Their artillery was far superior to anything that the Tatars could deploy and their arquebusiers were well protected from Tatar archery by gulay-gorods ('mobile castles'). These were sections of prefabricated wooden walls fitted with firing ports, which could be locked together to form mobile strong-points.

Revolt in the Balkans 1573

■ Croatian-Slovenian Peasant Revolt, 1573

Harsh treatment by local landowners provoked a peasant revolt in Croatia and Slovenia led by Matija Gubec. The rebels were crushed with the loss of 3000 men in three decisive battles at Brežice, Samobor and Stubičko polje.

Mughal Conquests 1573–75

■ Tukaroi, 3 March 1575

The Mughal Emperor Akbar sent an army commanded by Munim Khan against Daud Khan, the Afghan ruler of Bengal. An indecisive battle was fought at Tukaroi, but the Afghans retreated to Katak in Orissa. This withdrawal allowed Mughal forces to capture Tanda, the capital of Bengal and Daud was forced to sign the Treaty of Katak, ceding the provinces of Bengal and Bihar to the Mughal Empire.

Danzig Rebellion 1577

■ LUBISZEWO, 17 APRIL 1577
A Polish force of 2500 men under Hetman Jan Zborowski attacked and defeated a 10,000-strong army raised by the city of Danzig. The Poles lost barely 200 men, but inflicted over 9000 casualties.

Portuguese Invasion of Morocco 1578

■ KSAR-EL-KEBIR/ALCAZARQUIVIR, 4 AUG 1578
King Sebastian I's Portuguese army of 18,000 men invaded Morocco with the support of the deposed Sultan Abu Abdallah Mohammed II, but was virtually annihilated by a 50,000-strong Moroccan army under Sultan Abu Marwan Abd al-Malik.

Struggles for the Portuguese Throne 1580

■ ALCÂNTARA, 25 AUGUST 1580
A Spanish army of almost 15,000 men under the Duke of Alba defeated King António I's 8500-strong Portuguese army at Alcântara, near Lisbon. Alba's veterans inflicted 4000 casualties on the Portuguese, while losing only 500 men.

Russian Campaign in Siberia

■ CHUVASH CAPE, 23 OCTOBER 1582
An 800-strong Cossack expedition under Yermak Timofeyevich invaded the Tatar Khanate of Sibir (Siberia). Tatar forces were decisively defeated by Cossack musketry on the River Irtysh, marking the start of the Russian conquest of Siberia.

Anglo-Spanish Wars 1587–96

■ CADIZ, APRIL 1587
Sir Francis Drake's squadron of 24 ships raided Cadiz to disrupt the Spanish Armada's preparations for the invasion of England. Drake destroyed or captured 24 Spanish ships and destroyed a vast quantity of naval stores.

■ THE SPANISH ARMADA, 21 JULY–21 SEPT 1588
Drake's raid on Cadiz imposed a crippling delay to the Armada as the lost ships and naval stores took months to replace. The strain was too much for its commander, the veteran Marquis of Santa Cruz, who died on 9 February 1588 and was replaced by the inexperienced Duke of Medina Sidonia. The Armada sailed from Lisbon on 28 May, but a combination of gales and rotten provisions forced it into Corunna to refit and resupply. It was not until 21 July that the Armada's 125 vessels carrying 17,000 troops finally sailed for England. The chances of a successful invasion were compromised from the beginning by Philip II's attempt to micro-manage the entire operation; Medina Sidonia was ordered to rendezvous with the invasion barges of the Duke of Parma's army at Dunkirk and escort them across the Channel. This lack of operational freedom was to prove crippling throughout the campaign.

On 29 July, an English scouting vessel spotted the Armada off the Lizard in Cornwall and alerted the main English fleet under Charles Howard, Lord Effingham, at Plymouth. Its 73 assorted ships had all put to sea by the following morning and the first serious action of the campaign was fought off Plymouth on 31 July. This set the pattern for most subsequent engagements; the more manoeuvrable English ships easily avoided the Spanish attempts to close and board, but their firepower proved to be inadequate to sink or cripple the Armada's major vessels at long and medium ranges. Although English gunnery was relatively ineffective, two ships, the *Nuestra Senora del Rosario* and the *San Salvador* suffered accidental damage and were captured. During the next week, the English fleet pursued the Armada up-

Legend:
- → Route of the Armada
- ⇢ Individual or small groups of ships blown off course
- ✕ Site of battles
- Spanish Empire
- Under English control

Faroe Islands

21 Aug.

Shetland Islands

24 Aug.

Orkney Islands

Alesund

Bergen

NORWAY

Stavanger

Outer Hebrides

12 Aug.

North Sea

SCOTLAND

Edinburgh

Newcastle

DENMARK

Ireland

Dublin

Wales

ENGLAND

Bristol

London

8 Aug.

Amsterdam

ATLANTIC OCEAN

Scilly Islands

Plymouth

Dover

6–7 Aug.

Netherlands

HOLY

20 Sept.

29 July

31 July

Calais

Brussels

ROMAN

English Channel

Brest

Le Havre

EMPIRE

17 Sept.

Rouen

Paris

Seine

Nantes

Loire

Bay of Biscay

La Rochelle

FRANCE

SWISS CONFED.

18 June – 21 July

Corunna

Gijon

23 Sept.

Bordeaux

Lyon

Santander

Bilbao

Rhône

Oporto

Ebro

Marseille

Valladolid

Portugal

Madrid

Zaragoza

Lisbon

Tagus

Barcelona

28 May

SPAIN

Valencia

Cordoba

Majorca

Sevilla

Cadiz

Gibraltar

from Naples and Sicily

Arrival of Portuguese galleons from Brazil

Tangier

Ceuta

Mediterranean Sea

Rabat

Oran

Algiers

Fez

ALGERS

MOROCCO

Spanish Armada, 1588

Channel, inflicting damage, but never enough to break its formation. By 6 August, Medina Sidonia had brought his ships to Calais Roads where it was decided to anchor and await Parma's invasion fleet. However, Howard was reinforced by Lord Henry Seymour's squadron from the Thames with desperately needed supplies and ammunition. As the Armada remained at anchor, Howard decided to expend some of his smaller vessels as fireships and eight merchantmen were hastily converted.

The fireship attack was launched during the night of 7–8 August and, although it failed to destroy any Spanish vessels, the Armada was forced to cut its anchor cables and scatter. This gave Howard his opportunity and, throughout 8 August, he fought a fierce close-range action, which damaged many Spanish ships, although only one, *La Maria Juan*, was sunk. By the end of the day, the Armada was still a potent fighting force and the English fleet was again desperately short of ammunition. Although Medina Sidonia was keen to renew the action, the wind and tides were against him, forcing his battered ships towards the dangerous sandbanks off the coast of Flanders. At the last minute, the wind changed, allowing the Spanish to claw their way out to sea, but also driving them north-eastwards into the North Sea. The prevailing winds forced the Armada to attempt to return to Spain by sailing around the Shetland Islands and skirting the west coast of Ireland. The Armada was ravaged by fierce storms, which wrecked many ships on the Irish coast and only 65 vessels finally returned to Spanish ports.

■ COUNTER-ARMADA, 1589

An English counter-offensive was launched to destroy the remaining Spanish warships, raise a Portuguese rebellion against Spanish rule and seize the Azores and the Spanish treasure fleet. The force was based on six royal galleons and 60 armed merchantmen, supported by 80 smaller craft and carried 19,000 troops under Sir Francis Drake and Sir John Norreys. The force failed to achieve its objectives and lost 30 ships and 11,000 men.

■ FLORES (AZORES), 30 AUG–1 SEPT 1591

Lord Thomas Howard's squadron of 22 ships was attacked by a Spanish fleet of 63 ships under Alonso de Bazán. All of Howard's ships escaped, except for the *Revenge*, which surrendered after an epic fight.

■ BLAYE, 18 APRIL 1593

A Spanish squadron commanded by Pedro de Zubiaur on its way to raise the Hugenot siege of the French Catholic port of Blaye defeated an English squadron of six ships, sinking two without loss.

■ CORNWALL, 2 AUGUST 1595

A 400-strong Spanish raiding party of musketeers and pikemen commanded by Carlos de Amésquita landed from the galleys *Capitana*, *Patrona*, *Peregrina* and *Bazana* at Mount's Bay. Most of the several hundred local militia fled, allowing the Spaniards to burn Penzance and the villages of Mousehole, Paul and Newlyn. The raiders also seized cannon from abandoned coastal artillery batteries before re-embarking without loss two days later.

■ SAN JUAN, 22 NOVEMBER 1595

Sir Francis Drake attacked San Juan (Puerto Rico) with 27 ships and 2500 men, but only destroyed one Spanish warship before being driven off by the town's garrison with the loss of 400 men.

■ CADIZ, 30 JUNE–15 JULY 1596

An Anglo-Dutch raiding force was formed to attack Cadiz. The fleet of 150 ships was led by Charles Howard, Earl of Nottingham, and carried 10,000 troops under Robert Devereux, Earl of Essex. The allied fleet attacked the 40 Spanish ships in the anchorage, capturing the galleons *San Andrés* and *San Mateo* and almost taking the *San Felipe* and *Santo Tomás*, which were scuttled to avoid capture. During the attack, 5000 Spanish troops arrived to reinforce the garrison, but these were mainly poorly armed, ill-trained conscripts. The defenders were so badly organized that the city was taken in a few hours by a small English landing party. The demoralized garrison of Fort San Felipe surrendered the following day. The city was looted, occupied for six weeks, then burned when the raiders withdrew.

■ ISLANDS VOYAGE, 1597

An English squadron commanded by Robert Devereux, Earl of Essex, made an unsuccessful raid on the Azores. The failure was attributed to his pursuit of the Spanish treasure fleet without first defeating its naval escort.

■ CADIZ EXPEDITION, 1–7 NOVEMBER 1625

An Anglo-Dutch attempt to repeat the successful 1596 raid on Cadiz was defeated by the 6300-strong Spanish garrison. The allies lost 62 of their 105 ships, while their 10,000 troops suffered 7000 casualties.

■ BATTLE OF THE DOWNS, 31 OCTOBER 1639

A Spanish fleet of 75 ships commanded by Antonio de Oquendo, carrying 13,000 reinforcements for the Spanish armies in Flanders, was intercepted by a Dutch squadron of 16 ships under Adm Maarten Tromp. On 16 September, the Dutch attacked and forced the Spanish to withdraw. A second attack on 18 September by a reinforced Dutch fleet forced Oquendo to flee into neutral English waters and seek shelter in the Downs between Dover and Deal. While a weak English squadron attempted to keep the two sides apart, the Dutch were resupplied and, on 31 October, attacked the Spanish fleet in English territorial waters. Tromp decisively defeated Oquendo's fleet, sinking or capturing 40 ships and inflicting 7000 casualties. The battle destroyed what remained of Spanish naval power, seriously weakened their position in Flanders and gave the Dutch undisputed naval supremacy.

■ SIEGE OF SANTO DOMINGO, 23–30 APRIL 1655

A 13,000-strong English army under MGen Robert Venables besieged Santo Domingo but was driven off by its Spanish garrison of 2400 men, despite the support of Adm William Penn's fleet of 34 ships.

■ CADIZ, 9 SEPTEMBER 1656

An English squadron of eight ships under Capt Richard Stayner intercepted a Spanis.h treasure fleet commanded by Don Marcus del Porto off Cadiz. Stayner captured two Spanish ships carrying cargoes that were valued at £1,250,000.

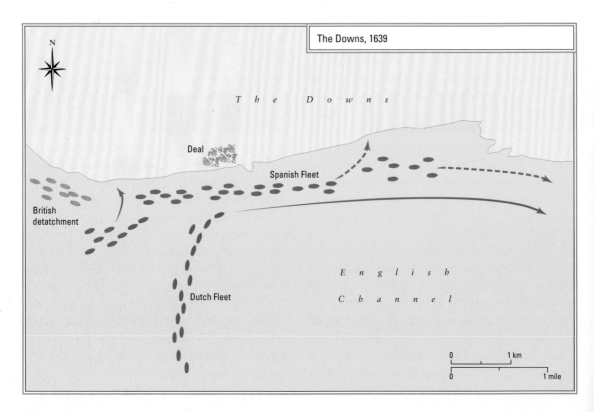

Japanese Invasion of Korea (Imjin War) 1592–98

■ DADAEJIN, 1592

Konishi Yukinaga, pretending to withdraw, filled the moat of this fortress near Pusan and stormed it after the governor Yun Heung-sin had refused Yukinaga's demand for its surrender. The Japanese butchered the garrison of 3000.

■ OKPO, 7 MAY 1592

Adm Yi Sun-sin began his unanticipated naval counter-offensive at this island, where a fisherman told him a Japanese fleet was loading loot. Yi's 26 ships at range obliterated the unprepared Japanese with artillery and incendiaries.

■ IMJIN RIVER, 17–18 MAY 1592

Korean gullibility allowed Japanese guile to breach this barrier to the advance north. With Korean archers blocking the only ford, the Japanese retreated and the Koreans crossed were butchered and the survivors on the far bank scattered.

■ SACHEON, 29 MAY 1592

Yi Sun-Sin's squadron of 23 ships and the three survivors of Won Kyun's ships bore down upon a Japanese fleet anchored below the heights at Sacheon as the Japanese loaded forage and other booty from the surrounding countryside. Yi's cultivation and protection of the local fisherman and refugees had provided him with excellent intelligence of the Japanese numbers and position. From his own long service in the region's waters, Yi understood that the onslaught of his combined fleet would necessarily come at the ebb of the local high tide, when the 12 largest Japanese warships would be either beached or in the shallows. Yi had to preserve his own vital fleet while luring the enemy into deep water where they could be utterly destroyed without hope of salvage.

Yi's previous victories over the Japanese at sea had left few survivors to disabuse the plundering Samurai of their contempt for the Koreans as warriors, with Won Kyun's flight and destruction of most of his own fleet a strong support for such thinking. Moreover, the Japanese were, as of this battle, still ignorant of telling differences in Korean versus their own naval technology. The Japanese atake-bune heavy fleet unit superficially resembled the Korean panokson; both were rowed vessels featuring high palisaded sides to protect their crews, but the stouter Korean ships featured advanced heavy cannon on wheeled carriages where the Japanese had only marines and arquebuses. Superior Korean casting technology produced four standardized types of naval artillery, the heaviest firing large iron arrows wrapped with combustibles that would prove to be devastating incendiaries.

The Japanese were also ignorant of a vessel Yi had constructed as the threat of invasion loomed, the kobukson, or 'turtle ship', based on an old Chinese design for a fast, protected ram. The first of these was present at Sacheon, Yi having improved upon the original model with a lightly armoured spiked turtle-back, camouflaged with straw and a bow shaped like a dragon from which heavy guns could

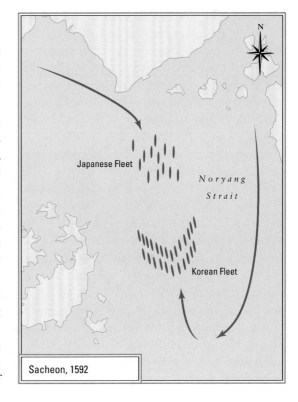

Sacheon, 1592

fire. Both the turtle ship and the panokson featured strong protection against the favoured boarding tactics of the Japanese. With his goal of luring the Japanese into deep water, Yi's ships first approached and then feigned a retreat as if put into panic by the mere appearance of the Japanese vessels, Yi's rapport with his subordinates allowing the Korean ships to fall into a semblance of disorder before resuming a tight crescent formation when safely out of Japanese observation. Rushing into their ships, the Japanese pursued in poor order, their ragged formation by twilight entering into a zone of which Yi was keenly aware, which was within range of the Korean cannon, but out of range of their own arquebuses.

Bursting out of Yi's crescent as the rest of the fleet reversed its retreat, the new and unfamiliar turtle ship startled the Japanese, attacking as the Japanese left the bay. The new vessels under the command of Yi's Flying Squadron Captain, Yi Mong-ku, shot flame, iron and smoke into the Japanese from its bow, stern and broadside ports, as it spread panic and destruction into the Japanese. Fire from the surrounding heights kept Yi from landing his own marines to exploit the victory, but the Japanese lost their 12 atake-bune and a number of smaller vessels burned or captured, while Yi had preserved his vital squadron for further severing of Toyotomi Hideyoshi's invasion's lifeline.

■ DONGNAE, 25–26 MAY 1592

This fortress north of Pusan held 20,000 infantry under Song Sang-hyon, who refused both surrender and safe passage to Konishi Yukinaga's army. The Koreans resisted for 12 hours, suffering 5000 casualties before the fortress fell.

■ PUSAN, 1 SEPTEMBER 1592

Toyotomi Hideyoshi, having united Japan, directed his people's warlike energies outward across the Tsushima Straits into Korea, which he intended to use as a staging area for a conquest of China. Japanese pirates had made the crossing for centuries when Hideyoshi dispatched 158,850 men in two army groups for the conquest of both coasts. The Japanese landing at Pusan received

unintended assistance due to the cowardly incompetence of the district admirals, Park Hong and Won Kyun, who at first mistook the invading fleet for a trading mission and then destroyed their commands and fled. Around 8000 soldiers under Chong Bal resisted to the last, but the port's two bastions collapsed under assaults by So Yoshitomo and Konishi Yukinaga. The Korean infantry with their flails and padded cloth armour fought bravely, but fell in scores to the fire of the Japanese massed arquebuses.

■ TANGPO, 1592

Yi Sun-sin and his fleet attacked 21 Japanese ships commanded by Kurushima Michiyuki in a large flagship. During a turtle-ship attack with cannon, ram and archery fire, Michiyuki perished. His fleet lost direction, being utterly annihilated during the attack

■ SANGJU, 1592

Yang Il raised an army of some 800 peasants, executing one local who warned him of the Japanese approach. The Koreans found their archery outranged by devastating arquebus fire and fled into a disastrous rout.

■ CHUNGJU, 1592

This fortress – vital to the defence of Seoul – guarded the pass of Choryong, from which Shin Nip and 16,000 men retreated before Konishi Yukinaga's advance and the news of Sangju. Advancing away from the fortress, Shin Nip deployed his cavalry on the neighbouring plain. He led the cavalry forth, his charge into the Japanese centre collapsing under withering fire from arquebuses on the surrounding heights. The fortress surrendered thereafter.

■ PYONGYANG, 1592

The Korean court fled north to their final defended city. A Korean attack across the Taedong river revealed the fords to the army of Konishi Yukinaga, Kuroda Nagamasa and So Yoshitomo, which captured the city.

■ CHONJU, 1592

Japanese savagery and resurgent Korean nationalism combined with forces under Yi Kwang to deal the Japanese a reverse in their advance up the

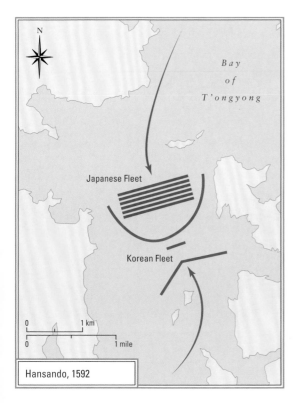

Hansando, 1592

Yi drew his fleet up in front of Hansan Island in a crescent formation, which invited the Japanese to advance forward into the awaiting arms of his line. In another feigned panic, the Koreans backed water. The Japanese charged forward at speed with confidence buoyed by past success and current numbers. For their part, Yi's men possessed great confidence in their leader and the Korean fleet reversed direction instantly upon the Admiral's sudden signal to cease backwatering and engage.

In the prolonged fighting, the Japanese managed to close and board, in their own accounts describing how the Samurai hacked into one of the turtle ships with their swords. The Koreans again employed their artillery, firing explosive shell from their heaviest cannon for the first time in the conflict. Yi sank 42 ships, capturing 12 and mauling Hideyoshi's personal flagship.

◾ CHINJU, 1592

Refugees were protected by 3800 Korean soldiers and the castle, from Hosokawa Tadaoki and 20,000 Japanese attacking with storming parties and cannon. Japanese signal fires, bombardments and round-the-clock assaults backfired upon the attackers, a guerilla army of some 8000 collecting and attacking the Japanese rear. A fixed siege tower and an escalade with 1000 ladders failed. The Japanese withdrew after a diversion allowed 2000 of the guerillas to enter and reinforce the garrison.

◾ HAEJONGCH'ANG, 1592

A grain depot attracted the Japanese. Han Kuk-ham – with cavalry and archers – surrounded the building and advanced on all sides. Arquebus fire from the barricaded Japanese forced withdrawal and a Japanese night attack routed the Koreans.

◾ PYONGYANG, 1592–93

Deciding it better to fight the Japanese in Korea, the Chinese crossed the Yalu and twice attempted to evict the Japanese from Pyongyang. The first effort failed, ambushed; the overwhelming second provoked a Japanese evacuation.

◾ HAENGJU, 1593

Kwon Jul was unlike his fellow Korean generals as he was willing to accept the assistance of any

Peninsula. Kobayakawa Takakage reversed march after the defeat and returned to Kumsan.

◾ HANSANDO, 1592

As Yi Sun-Sin's fleet continued to ravage his invasion's supply lines, Toyotomi Hideyoshi ordered his commanders to neutralize the Korean navy at sea, overlooking his army's ability to neutralize the Korean's vital off-shore naval bases. With no informed knowledge of Yi's fleet and tactics, Wakizaka Yasuharu put out with 82 vessels to search out and destroy Yi and his squadron. Yasuharu chose to rush his attack and to forego impending reinforcements, while Yi's squadron had grown to nearly 100 vessels, among them two more of the turtle ships that proved devastating at Sacheon.

Yi had carefully kept the movements and support bases of his fleet hidden from the Japanese, but a fleeing refugee informed him of Yasuharu's planned attack and decision to seek a decisive battle. Yi trained his sailors and concentrated his forces accordingly when the Japanese fleet hove into view.

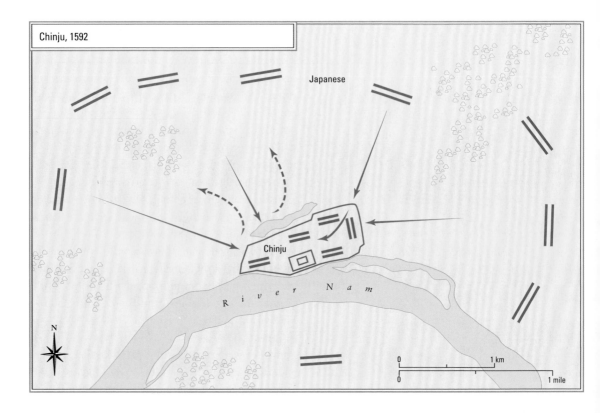

Chinju, 1592

Japanese

Chinju

River   Nam

N

0   1 km

0   1 mile

wishing to fight the invaders and defend Korea. With 9000 soldiers and 1000 warrior-monks, Kwon re-occupied and refortified this small mountain castle, the presence of so many Koreans threatening the Japanese grip on Seoul. Kwon – with 2300 soldiers and women – remained behind palisades defending the one side of the castle not protected by swampy ground. In response, Ukita Hideie launched an uphill attack with 30,000 men previously stationed in Seoul. The Japanese ranks ascended the castle's mount into the fire of rocket-carts (hwach'a – exploding fougasses made from mortar shells) and captured arquebuses. At closer range, tree trunks and thrown stones brought by the women in their aprons inflicted further casualties. Nine attacks carried the first Korean palisade before the Japanese withdrew with heavy losses.

■ JINJU (CHINJU), 1593

The previous year's repulse drew Ukita Hideie to storm the castle with 90,000 Japanese attacking 60,000 garrison under Hwang Jin and Kim

Cheon-il. With numbers enough to prevent relief, the Japanese prevailed after desperate fighting.

■ JAPANESE INVASION, 1597

The Japanese withdrew before a grinding Chinese advance into a perimeter of coastal forts (wajo) around the port of Pusan, harassed by rebuilding Korean forces and Yi Sun-Sin's fleet. During negotiations in 1597, Toyotomi Hideyoshi launched a second two-pronged invasion with 141,100 men out of Pusan, this time with different commanders, Yi Sun-Sin having been relieved and broken in disgrace by what proved to be Japanese disinformation and incompetent rivals.

■ ULSAN, 1597–98

A relieving Chinese army – eventually numbering 80,000 commanded by Yang Ho – laid close siege around Kato Kiyamasa and Asano Yukinaga in this post north of Pusan. The Japanese garrison shrank through fighting and starvation to 5000 as the Chinese cut off water and Korean irregulars poisoned nearby wells. The Korean navy allowed a relieving fleet under Konishi Yukinaga to deliver supplies, while a Japanese army drove off the Chinese.

■ **CHILCHONRYANG, 1597**

A catastrophic Korean naval defeat, in which Won Kyun with 200 ships sailed into an ambush by the larger Japanese fleet off Cholyongdo, the Koreans unable to fight at range due to Won's incompetence and a gale. The Japanese placed troops on nearby Kojedo Island and boarded the Koreans at Chilchonryang. Dispirited, the Koreans beached and lost all but 13 ships. Won and his crews were butchered by the Japanese.

■ **SIEGE OF NAMWON, 1597**

Anticipating the renewed Japanese advance, the Chinese and Koreans strengthened the defences of this plains town, with 6000 mixed garrison. Ota Kazuyoshi's Japanese filled the moat and stormed the town with over 3000 defenders killed.

■ **MYONGYANG, 1597**

Disaster restoring Yi Sun-Sin to command with a remnant of 13 ships, Yi took them into the heart of the anchored Japanese fleet of 133 and the turning tide, destroying many and killing the Japanese admiral.

■ **HWANGSEOKSANG, 1597**

The Koreans hastily manned this small mountain fortress as the Japanese resumed their northern advance with thousands of garrison, who fled with losses when the Japanese launched a moonlit night escalade and stormed the walls.

■ **SACHEON, 1598**

Having captured a smaller Korean castle on a neighbouring peak, Shimazu Yoshihiro and Tadatsune noted a small harbour with a defensible peninsula nearby and there constructed a castle on the harbour defended on three sides by the sea. Yoshihiro remained to hold it with 8000 garrison as the Japanese moved northward out of Cholla province. Ton Yuan moved to attack the two positions with a large army of 34,000 Chinese and 2000 Koreans. Murakami Tadatsune and 300 Japanese holding the nearby captured castle reached the new castle just before the attack. The new castle having been built with a rapid sally in mind, Yoshihiro suddenly attacked the Chinese and Korean lines with his entire force, catching the besiegers unawares. Unable to reform in the aftermath of the attack, the allies fled in great disorder, the Japanese inflicting extremely severe casualties.

■ **NORYANG, 1598**

Having rebuilt and re-manned the Korean fleet, Yi Sun-Sin resisted Chinese pressure to let the Japanese withdraw unmolested, the Japanese previously having returned to the offensive. Local fisherman informed Yi of 500 transports gathering in the Noryang strait. Yi personally led 83 panokson heavy vessels with 63 Chinese warships into the Japanese vessels. Leaving only 50 of these seaworthy, Yi himself perished when the Japanese escorts concentrated fire on his flagship.

Anglo-Irish Wars 1595–1602

■ **CLONTIBRET, 25–27 MARCH 1595**

An English force under Henry Bagenal, 1700 strong, was ambushed by 4000 Irish under Hugh O'Neill, Earl of Tyrone, on its way to relieve the besieged garrison at Monaghan. Bagenal's force took heavy losses and retired to Newry.

■ **CARRICKFERGUS, 1597**

A dispute between John Chichester, the English governor of Carrickfergus castle and the MacDonnell clan led to a battle. The English were worsted with 180 killed. A ceasefire was arranged between the garrison and the MacDonnells.

■ **YELLOW FORD, 14 AUGUST 1598**

An English column of 4000 under Henry Bagenal, marching to relieve the Blackwater Fort, was ambushed by the forces of Ulster Irish chieftains Hugh O'Neill and Hugh O'Donnell. The English force was routed and Bagenal and 900 of his men were killed. Many others deserted and the remainder were evacuated by sea from Newry to Dublin. The English defeat encouraged O'Neill's sympathizers and spread the rebellion across Ireland.

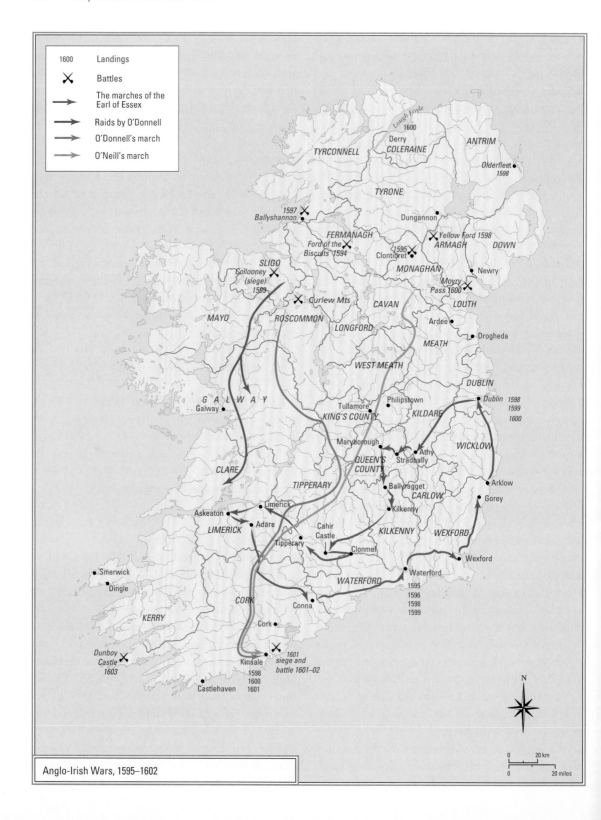

Legend:

- 1600 — Landings
- ✕ — Battles
- → — The marches of the Earl of Essex
- → — Raids by O'Donnell
- → — O'Donnell's march
- → — O'Neill's march

Anglo-Irish Wars, 1595–1602

Labels on map:

Lough Foyle 1600
Derry
COLERAINE
ANTRIM
TYRCONNELL
Olderfleet 1598
TYRONE
Dungannon
1597 Ballyshannon
FERMANAGH
Ford of the Biscuits 1594
Yellow Ford 1598
ARMAGH
DOWN
1595 Clontibret
MONAGHAN
Newry
SLIGO
Collooney (siege) 1599
Moyry Pass 1600
Curlew Mts
CAVAN
LOUTH
MAYO
ROSCOMMON
LONGFORD
Ardee
MEATH
Drogheda
WEST MEATH
DUBLIN
GALWAY
Tullamore
Philipstown
Dublin 1598 1599 1600
Galway
KING'S COUNTY
KILDARE
WICKLOW
Maryborough
Athy
Stradbally
CLARE
QUEEN'S COUNTY
Ballyragget
Arklow
TIPPERARY
Gorey
Limerick
CARLOW
Kilkenny
Askeaton
Adare
Cahir Castle
KILKENNY
WEXFORD
LIMERICK
Tipperary
Clonmel
Smerwick
Dingle
WATERFORD
Waterford 1595 1596 1598 1599
Wexford
CORK
Conna
KERRY
Cork
Dunboy Castle 1603
Kinsale 1598 1600 1601
1601 siege and battle 1601–02
Castlehaven

N

0   20 km
0   20 miles

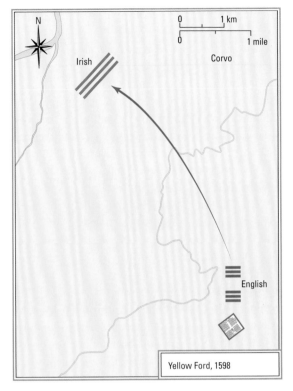

Yellow Ford, 1598

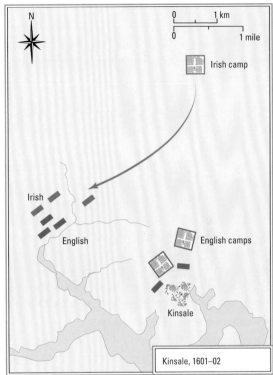

Kinsale, 1601–02

■ CAHIR CASTLE, 26–29 MAY 1599

English forces under the Earl of Essex besieged and took Cahir castle, held for Irish rebel forces by James 'Galdie' Butler. The castle commanded the Suir river, a strategic point for control of south-eastern Ireland.

■ CURLEW PASS, 15 AUGUST 1599

Hugh O'Donnell's Irish forces defeated an English force marching to raise the siege of Collooney castle. English commander Clifford and 500 of his men were killed. Collooney Castle surrendered.

■ MOYRY PASS, 20 SEPT–9 OCT 1600

Moyry saw 20 days of attritional fighting, as English forces under Mountjoy tried to break through prepared defences and into the territory of Hugh O'Neill. Both sides suffered several hundred casualties. Mountjoy left a garrison at Mountnorris.

■ KINSALE, 2 OCTOBER 1601–3 JANUARY 1602

A 3500-strong Spanish force, sent to aid Catholic Irish rebels, was besieged at Kinsale by 12,000 English troops under Mountjoy. Hugh O'Neill's Irish forces attempted to break the siege, but were routed in battle on 3 January 1602, with over 1000 killed. The Spanish then surrendered. Around 6000 English troops died of disease during the siege. The failure of the Spanish expedition broke the rebellion. Hugh O'Neill surrendered in 1603.

■ DUNBOY, 5–18 JUNE 1602

Dunboy castle, seat of Donal O'Sullivan Beare, was besieged and taken by English forces under George Carew, after O'Sullivan sided with the Spanish force that landed at Kinsale in 1601. O'Sullivan evacuated his dependants to rebel territory.

Revolt in Finland/Sweden 1596

■ THE CUDGEL WAR, 1596–97

Finnish peasants rebelled against harsh treatment by local nobility and landowners. The revolt was named after the variety of flails and clubs carried by the peasants, which proved to be highly effective against armoured opponents.

The rebels won several small-scale actions, but were decisively defeated by an army under Baron Klaus Fleming at Nokia and Ilmajoki. Over 2500 rebels were killed and their leader, Jaakko Ilkka, was captured and executed.

Polish–Swedish Conflicts 1598–1658

■ STÅNGEBRO (LINKÖPING), 25 SEPTEMBER 1598

Sigismund III of Poland inherited the Swedish crown on the death of his father, King John III, in 1592. The Catholic Sigismund was resented by the largely Protestant Swedes and eventually the regent, Duke Charles of Södermanland, staged a coup. Sigismund invaded Sweden with 5000 (largely mercenary) troops, but was defeated with the loss of 2000 men at Stångebro and Duke Charles was proclaimed as King Charles IX of Sweden.

■ KOKENHAUSEN, 23 JUNE 1601

Carl Carlsson Gyllenhielm's 4900-strong Swedish army was defeated near Koknese in Livonia (modern Latvia) by a Polish army of 3000 men under Krzysztof Mikołaj 'the Thunderbolt' Radziwiłł. Polish casualties totalled 200, but Gyllenhielm lost 2000 men.

■ KIRCHOLM, 27 SEPTEMBER 1605

An 11,000-strong Swedish army commanded by Charles IX was defeated by a Polish force of 3600 men under Jan Karol Chodkiewicz, Grand Hetman of Lithuania. Polish casualties were only 300, while the Swedes lost 5000 men.

■ WALLHOF, 7 JANUARY 1626

A Swedish force of 3100 men (2100 of them cavalry) under Gustavus II Adolphus ambushed and defeated Jan Stanisław Sapieha's Polish force of 7000 men at Wallhof in Latvia. Polish casualties totalled at least 500.

■ OLIVA, 28 NOVEMBER 1627

A Polish fleet of 10 ships commanded by Adm Arend Dickmann defeated Niels Göranson Stiernsköld's Swedish squadron of six vessels off Danzig (Gdansk). Both admirals were killed.

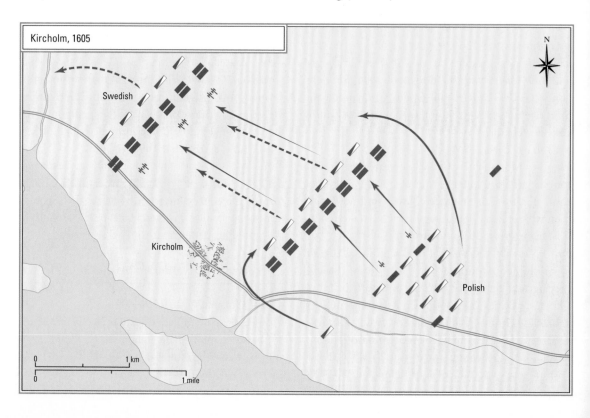

Kircholm, 1605

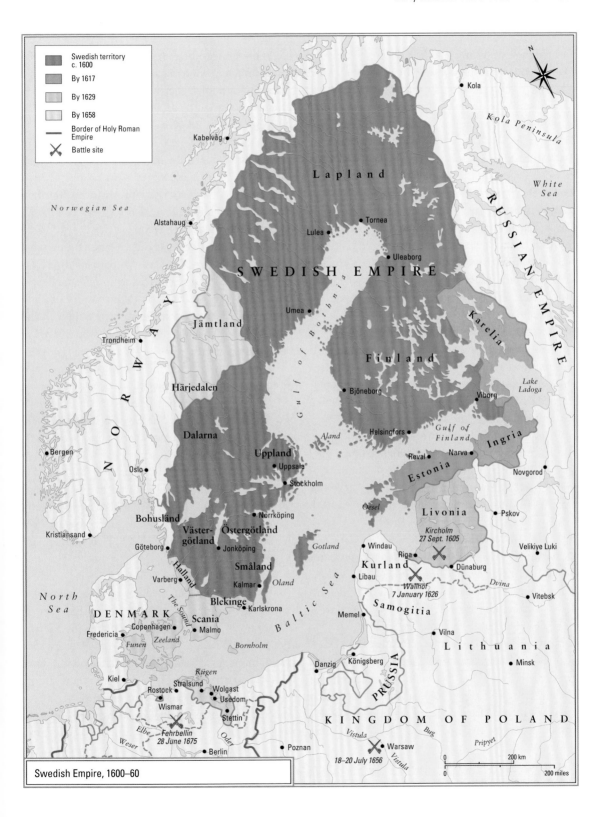

Swedish Empire, 1600–60

Legend:
- Swedish territory c. 1600
- By 1617
- By 1629
- By 1658
- Border of Holy Roman Empire
- Battle site

Map labels:

Norwegian Sea

Kabelvåg

Alstahaug

N O R W A Y

Trondheim

Bergen

Oslo

Kristiansand

Göteborg

North Sea

DENMARK

Frederica

Copenhagen

Kiel

Rostock

Stralsund

Wismar

Wolgast

Usedom

Stettin

Elbe

Weser

Fehrbellin 28 June 1675

Berlin

Lapland

SWEDISH EMPIRE

Jämtland

Härjedalen

Dalarna

Uppland

Uppsala

Stockholm

Norrköping

Västergötland

Östergötland

Jönköping

Småland

Kalmar

Bohusland

Varberg

Halland

Blekinge

Karlskrona

Scania

Malmö

Zeeland

Funen

Bornholm

Rügen

Oder

Tornea

Lulea

Uleaborg

Umea

Gulf of Bothnia

Finland

Björneborg

Åland

Helsingfors

Gotland

Oland

Oesel

Baltic Sea

Danzig

Königsberg

Memel

PRUSSIA

Kola

Kola Peninsula

White Sea

RUSSIAN EMPIRE

Karelia

Lake Ladoga

Viborg

Gulf of Finland

Reval

Narva

Ingria

Estonia

Novgorod

Livonia

Pskov

Kircholm 27 Sept. 1605

Velikiye Luki

Riga

Windau

Dünaburg

Kurland

Libau

Wallhof 7 January 1626

Dvina

Vitebsk

Samogitia

Vilna

L i t h u a n i a

Minsk

KINGDOM OF POLAND

Vistula

Bug

Pripyet

Warsaw

18–20 July 1656

Poznan

0   200 km

0   200 miles

■ **Danzig, 1655–56**

In 1655, Swedish forces under Charles X besieged Danzig (Gdansk) and captured the Danziger Haupt, a key fortress on the River Vistula. This alarmed the Dutch who saw a potential threat to their trading interests in the region, and in July 1656 a combined Dutch and Danish fleet arrived at Danzig, carrying 10,000 troops to reinforce the garrison. Charles raised the siege and recognized Danzig's neutrality by the Treaty of Elbing.

■ **Ujście, 24–25 July 1655**

Field Marshal Arvid Wittenberg's 17,000-strong Swedish army defeated a demoralized and ill-trained Polish army of 14,400 men under Krzysztof Opaliński and Andrzej Grudziński. The defeated army and its commanders then defected to the Swedes.

■ **Sobota, 23 August 1655**

A small Polish force commanded by King John II Casimir was routed by King Charles X Gustav's 25,000-strong Swedish army at Sobota near Łódź. After the battle, Charles marched on Warsaw, which surrendered on 29 August.

■ **Wojnicz, 3 September 1655**

A Polish army of at least 6000 men commanded by Field Crown Hetman Stanisław Lanckoroński and Grand Crown Hetman Stanisław 'Rewera' Potocki was defeated by a slightly smaller Swedish army under King Charles X Gustav.

■ **Arnów, 6 September 1655**

A Swedish army of 11,000 commanded by Count Magnus Gabriel de la Gardie and Count Gustav Otto Stenbock defeated King John II Casimir's 10,000-strong Polish army. Swedish casualties were negligible, but the Poles lost 1000 men.

■ **Nowy Dwor Mazowieki, 20 Sept 1655**

An 8000-strong Swedish force commanded by Count Gustav Otto Stenbock defeated Jan Kazimierz Krasiński's Polish army of 11,000 men at Nowy Dwór Mazowiecki near Pultusk. Swedish casualties were negligible, but the Poles lost 400 men.

■ **Kracow, 25 Sept 1655–13 Oct 1655**

Following the capture of Warsaw, Swedish forces besieged the city of Kracow, which was fiercely defended by a Polish garrison commanded by Field Hetman Stefan Czarniecki. Although he eventually had to surrender, he was allowed to evacuate the garrison.

■ **Jasna Góra, 28 Nov–27 Dec 1655**

A Swedish force of 3200 men under Gen Burchard Müller von der Luhnen unsuccessfully besieged the fortified monastery of Jasna Góra, which was defended by a garrison of just over 300 men (including 70 monks).

■ **Gołąb, 8 February 1656**

A 6000-strong Swedish cavalry force commanded by King Charles X Gustav, supported by 1700 allied Polish and Tatar cavalry, defeated Field Hetman Stefan Czarniecki's Polish cavalry of 2500 men in an encounter at Gołąb near Lublin in the south-east of Poland.

■ **Warka, 7 April 1656**

A Polish army of 7500 men commanded by Field Hetman Stefan Czarniecki decisively defeated a 2500-strong Swedish force under Margrave Frederick V of Baden. The Swedes lost over 1700 men, while Polish casualties barely numbered 200.

■ **Kłecko, 7 May 1656**

A Polish force of 12,000 cavalry commanded by Field Hetman Stefan Czarniecki was defeated by Prince Adolf Johan av Pfalz-Zweibrücken's 8000-strong Swedish army. The Swedes lost 500 men, but inflicted 1000 casualties on Czarniecki's cavalry.

■ **Warsaw, 28–30 July 1656**

A Swedish army of 10,500 men commanded by King Charles X Gustav, supported by an 8500-strong Brandenburg force under the Elector Frederick William I, marched on Warsaw, but were intercepted near the capital by King John II Casimir's Polish army of 36,000 men. Initial Swedish frontal assaults were beaten off, but a successful outflanking attack routed the Poles who lost 2700 men. Charles was wounded in action and lost 1300 men.

■ **Prostki, 8 October 1656**

A Polish force of 10,000 cavalry commanded

by Field Lithuanian Hetman Wincenty Korwin Gosiewski, supported by 2000 Tatars under Subhan Ghazi Agi, annihilated Prince Georg Friedrich of Waldeck's 7000-strong Swedish army near Prostken (modern Prostki).

■ Filipów, 22 October 1656

Count Gustaf Otto Stenbock's 9000-strong Swedish army defeated a Polish army of 8500 men under Hetman Wincenty Korwin Gosiewski at Filipów in north-eastern Poland. Swedish casualties were minimal, while the Poles lost 500 men.

■ Chojnice, 2–3 January 1657

A Swedish army under Charles X Gustav made a successful night attack inflicting 3000 casualties on a Polish force of 10,000 cavalry, which was attempting to break through to King John II Casimir in Gdansk.

■ Kolding, 25 December 1658

A 1000-strong combined Polish and Danish force under the command of Field Hetman Stefan Czarniecki defeated a Swedish army of 2000 men commanded by King Charles X Gustav at Kolding in southern Denmark.

African Wars 1599–1764

■ Djenné, 26 April 1599

Emperor Mansa Mahmud IV of Mali attacked the city-state of Djenné, a vassal of the Moroccan pashalik of Timbuktu. The city's garrison was reinforced by Moroccans, including arquebusiers who decisively defeated the Mali forces.

■ Feyiase, 1701

The king of Denkyira, Ntim Gyakari, became over-confident after driving Ashanti forces from Adunka, Aboatem and Aputuogya. This was exploited by the Ashanti ruler, Osei Tutu, who ambushed and destroyed the Denkyiran forces at Feyiase in Ghana.

■ São Salvador, 15 February 1709

The Kongo Civil War saw the rise of a heretical Catholic sect – the Antonians – which were founded by a noblewoman, Beatriz Kimpa Vita. The sect was a major political and military force in the civil war until a 20,000-strong orthodox Catholic army under King Pedro IV of Kongo decisively defeated Prince Kibenga's Antonian Catholic force at São Salvador (modern M'banza-Kongo in Angola). Prince Kibenga was killed and the heresy was crushed.

■ Atakpamé, 1764

In 1763, the Ashanti vassal state of Akyem made contact with the Kingdom of Dahomey while planning a rebellion with other dissidents within the Ashanti Empire, including the Kwahu and Brong. This provoked an Ashanti invasion of Dahomey, but the invading army was ambushed and defeated near Atakpamé (in what is now Togo) by a Dahomean force, including the kingdom's elite Ahosi corps of female soldiers and allied troops from Oyo.

Tunisia

■ Action of 29 June 1609

A Spanish fleet of eight galleons and three smaller vessels raided La Goulette, the port of Tunis, supported by three French ships. A total of 22 Tunisian and Algerian vessels were destroyed and two more were captured.

■ Action of May 1612

A force of 13 Sicilian and Neapolitan galleys made a night attack on Tunisian vessels at anchor in the port of La Goulette. Up to ten Tunisian ships were destroyed and several smaller vessels were captured.

■ Action of March 1616

A Spanish squadron under Francisco de Ribera in the 36-gun *San Juan Bautista* defeated a Tunisian fleet of 19 vessels off the harbour of La Goulette. .

■ Action of 14 April 1655

An English fleet of 16 ships commanded by 'General at Sea' (Adm) Robert Blake destroyed two shore batteries and nine Algerian ships in Porto Farina, the first time that shore batteries were silenced by naval bombardment alone.

Balkan Wars 1599–1600

■ Selimbar, 18 October 1599

Prince Michael the Brave of Wallachia led 36,000 men in an invasion of Transylvania, which was ruled by Prince Cardinal Andreas Báthory. Michael was supported by the Holy Roman Emperor, Rudolf II, who paid for 5000 mercenaries to strengthen his forces. The unpopular Báthory raised a 30,000-strong army, but many of his men deserted and Michael beat him decisively at Şelimbăr, inflicting 1500 casualties for the loss of 1000 men.

■ **Miraslau (Miriszló), 18 September 1600**
Michael the Brave's 22,000-strong Wallachian army was attacked and defeated near Miriszló in Transylvania by an Imperialist force of 30,000 men commanded by Giorgio Basta. The Wallachians inflicted 1000 casualties, but lost over 5000 men.

American Colonies/French and Indian War 1622–1774

■ **Virginia Colony, 1622**
The commercial success of tobacco cultivation at Jamestown resulted in the rapid expansion of the English plantations into surrounding Indian territory, provoking a large-scale attack and the massacre of 350 colonists by the Powhatan tribe.

■ **Kalingo (Kalinago), 1626**
Upon arriving at the British island of St Kitts, French settlers found the native Caribs resisting, with 4000 of the Kalingo tribe in arms. The French joined forces with the British to butcher them.

■ **Pequot War, 1634–38**
The expanding Massachusetts colony ground into the expanding Pequot tribe with bloody results. After the murder of an English trader by some of the tribe, indemnity negotiations broke down. Further incidents led to colonial punitive expeditions burning villages. Indian counter-attacks led to the cooperation of Connecticut with Massachusetts against a Pequot-Narragansett alliance. An amphibious assault upon two Pequot stockaded towns devastated the tribe, making the English dominant in New England.

■ **Iroquois Wars, 1640–98**
These were struggles between the Great Lakes tribes for control of the trade for European goods. The Iroquois Confederation combined the powerful Cayuga, Mohawk, Oneida, Onondaga and the Seneca tribes into a formidable body. The Iroquois desired control of the trade routes with the English settlements in New York and to increase their power and numbers decimated by multiple epidemics. The initial attacks were upon native rivals in the fur trade, which expanded to a full-scale attack upon the Hurons, through whose lands the trade went. Using European-supplied weapons, the Iroquois defeated the Hurons and went on to fight the Susquehannocks, who resisted successfully with weapons purchased from the Swedish along the Hudson and with the support of the English in Maryland and Delaware. Surrounded by hostile tribes, the Iroquois finally ceased their expansion.

■ **Kieft's War, 1643–45**
The Dutch Governor Willem Kieft turned a theft of pigs on Staten Island into warfare with previously friendly tribes. Reprisals on both sides led to widespread slaughter, ending when the Dutch imported English mercenaries and negotiated.

■ **Long Sault, 1660**
The Iroquois stormed this unprepared French fort at strategic portage on the Ottawa river. Joined by some 200 friendly Hurons, Adam Dollard and 54 French unsuccessfully resisted a powerful Iroquois force coming down the river.

■ **King Philip's War, 1675–76**
In terms of proportional casualties, this conflict remains North America's bloodiest Indian war. Alliance with the Pilgrims and subsequent Puritan settlements in and around Boston had made the Wampanoag tribe the most powerful in New England, but upon assuming leadership, Metacom, christened 'King Philip' by the Pilgrims, realized that English expansion would include his tribe's lands. Colonial efforts to disarm his tribe exasperated Metacom's fears and prompted his alliance with the Nipmuck and Narragansett tribe. The Wampanoags began killing English spies and raiding outlying farms, while the Massachusetts Bay Colony raised a militia and established new tribal alliances, slaughters taking place on both

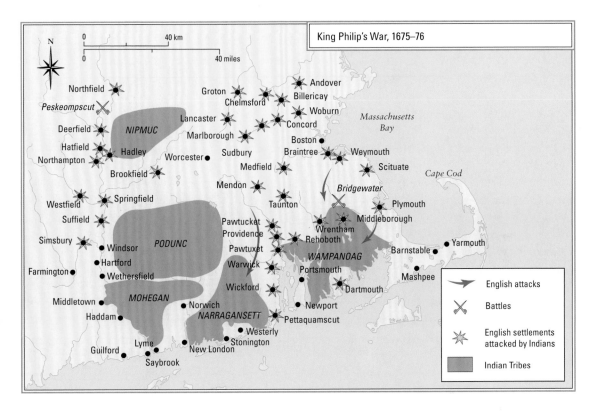

King Philip's War, 1675–76

Massachusetts Bay

Cape Cod

NIPMUC

PODUNC

MOHEGAN

NARRAGANSETT

WAMPANOAG

→ English attacks

✕ Battles

✳ English settlements attacked by Indians

█ Indian Tribes

Northfield — Groton — Andover — Billericay
Peskeompscut — Chelmsford — Woburn — Concord
Lancaster — Deerfield — Marlborough — Boston — Weymouth
Hatfield — Hadley — Worcester — Sudbury — Braintree — Scituate
Northampton — Medfield — Bridgewater — Plymouth
Brookfield — Mendon — Middleborough
Westfield — Springfield — Taunton — Wrentham — Yarmouth
Suffield — Pawtucket — Rehoboth — Barnstable
Simsbury — Providence — Pawtuxet — Portsmouth — Mashpee
Windsor — Warwick — Dartmouth
Farmington — Hartford — Wethersfield — Wickford — Newport
Middletown — Norwich — Pettaquamscut
Haddam — Westerly
Guilford — Lyme — Stonington — New London
Saybrook

sides. By the time a powerful colonial force had reduced the last of Metacom's strongholds and set Metacom's head on a pike, at least 2500 colonists plus an unknown, but larger number of Indians had perished.

■ BACON'S REBELLION, 1676

Virginia Governor Berkeley's policy of Indian conciliation provoked a strong reaction by planter Nathaniel Bacon, who led colonial attacks upon the Susquehannocks and Pamunkey tribes. Bacon lost support when he burned the capital at Jamestown.

■ LACHINE MASSACRE, 5 AUGUST 1689

With England suddenly at war with France, the allied Iroquois sacked this French village with 1500 warriors under cover of a hailstorm. The village's three blockhouses could not prevent the death or capture of 114 inhabitants.

■ LEISLER'S REBELLION, 1689

After the Glorious Revolution, protestant Jacob Leisler seized power in New York, seeking royal authorization for his measures against Catholics and Indians. Leisler's plan backfired and he was hanged after the return of British government and his enemies to power.

■ PORT ROYAL, 19 MAY 1690

This French bastion and naval base in Acadia became a target of the English colonists in King William's War. Sir William Phips led a Massachusetts regiment by sea against the town, which Governor Meneval surrendered.

■ APALACHEE MASSACRE, 25–26 JANUARY 1704

During the War of the Spanish Succession, Governor James Moore of British Carolina attacked the allied Apalachee tribe in Florida with colonists and native allies. The 1000 surviving Apalachees were taken as slaves back to Carolina.

■ DEERFIELD, 29 FEBRUARY 1704

The French and allied Indians attacked this western Massachusetts town, killing 41 villagers and taking 112 for ransom to Canada. The attackers scaled the ungarrisoned town's

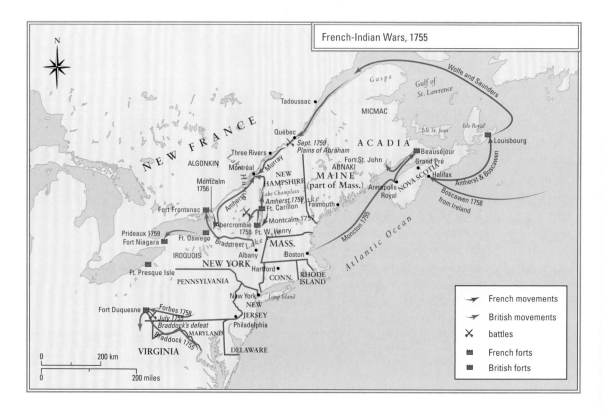

French-Indian Wars, 1755

stockades at night and captured the village's houses individually.

■ CARY'S REBELLION, 1707–11

Thomas Cary, governor of Carolina, disputed the claim of Edward Hyde to be his appointed successor. Sporadic fighting between associated religious factions ended when Royal Marines entered the capital, with Cary eventually acquitted of treason charges.

■ BLOODY CREEK, 1711

Acadian French and Abenaki Indians successfully ambushed 70 Massachusetts militia in three boats moving up the Annapolis river. The ambush killed 16 in the first boat and wounded nine of the others, capturing the surrendering survivors.

■ QUEBEC EXPEDITION, 1711

Buoyed by success in Nova Scotia, the Massachusetts colony sent 12,000 sailors and soldiers under Sir Hovenden Walker against French Canada. Eight transports in the Gulf of St. Lawrence grounded with 900 dead, Walker abandoning the campaign.

■ NICHOLSON EXPEDITION, 22 AUGUST 1711

Col Francis Nicholson led 2000 militia overland from Albany against French Canada, intending to rendezvous with Sir Hovenden Walker's forces sailing up the St. Lawrence. The troops from three colonies turned back when Walker retreated.

■ FORT NEOHEROKA, 1713

Governor James Moore of British Carolina advanced into Florida, attacking Tuscarora Indians retaliating for British incursions into their tribal lands. Moore's taking of this fort killed many, some Tuscaroras fleeing north to join the Iroquois.

■ VILLASUR EXPEDITION, 1720

Along with a mixed force of Spanish and allied Indians, Pedro Villasur moved from New Mexico up the Platte river to assert Spanish authority. French traders and their Indian allies attacked and killed Villasur in Nebraska.

■ CHICKASAW CAMPAIGN, 1736–40

The French and allied Choctaws had defeated the Chickasaws, Natchez and their British allies in the

Natchez Rebellion of 1729. The French, lacking resources to maintain their extensive claims in the Mississippi drainage, did not authorize the Choctaws to launch a surprise attack against the Chickasaws in 1734. A French gunpowder convoy opened fire upon encountering a large force of Natchez and Chickasaw, prisoners and the gunpowder ending up in the Indians' hands. Abandoning diplomatic settlement, Louisiana governor Jean-Baptiste Le Moyne de Bienville ordered the construction of Fort Tombeché in Alabama and employed mercenaries in invasions of the Chickasaws' lands.

Warfare with the Chickasaws by both the French and Choctaw proved difficult, because of both the Chickasaw's acquisition and skilled use of European muskets and their tradition of living in hilltop forts of considerable defensive strength. The Chickasaws also proved adept at throwing French grenades back at the Europeans in the gap between ignition and detonation.

Pierre d'Artaguette led a force of French and Indian allies into ambush attacking the Chickasaw village of Ogoula Tchetoka, with the Chickasaws burning the survivors. Meanwhile, Bienville, with a European-style column, assaulted a prepared Chickasaw position at Ackia, modern Tupelo. Efforts to employ siege equipment proved futile, and the French scorned the advice of the Choctaws witnessing their attack. The resulting disaster infuriated the Choctaws, who became increasingly disaffected at French ineptitude and disdainful of them as allies. The French withdrew, Bienville leaving his governorship in 1740. They then supplied their Choctaw allies with weaponry while securing passage for their Mississippi trade from the Chickasaws. French prestige among the Indians and, consequently, influence, entered into irreversible decline.

■ STONO REBELLION, 1739

Twenty colonists and 40 slaves perished in this uprising in South Carolina. A Spanish proclamation of emancipation for slaves escaping to their territory combined with a Yellow Fever outbreak to spark the revolt, which was soon crushed.

■ GULLY HOLE CREEK, 18 JULY 1742

The Spanish launched one major assault against the Georgia colonists, who were well-prepared with a fort and an ambush with allied Indians here. Fort Fredrica holding, the Spanish lost the resulting battle of Bloody Marsh.

■ KATHIO, 1750

The Chippewa attacked this large Lakota village, in retaliation (so Chippewa legends say) for the murder of four Chippewa travellers. Purchasing muskets and ammunition, the Chippewa mustered at Fond du Lac and drove out the Lakota.

■ PIMA INDIAN REVOLT, 1751–2

Efforts to Christianize south-western tribes conflicted with Spanish colonization and Indian resistance to wholesale changes in daily life. Pima resistance was sporadic and largely unfocused, complicating Spanish efforts at repression. In 1751, secular Spanish resentment of the Church's lands and efforts to protect the natives' land flared up when Oacpicagigua began killing Spanish settlers. The Spanish response was crushing and the revolt and the mission system in the area both collapsed from lack of support.

American Colonies/French and Indian War 1754–1774

As each nation's colonists expanded influence over North America, the inevitable conflict began between French fur traders and English farmers. French wiles and Indian alliances could not overcome superior British resources thrown into the fray.

■ FORT NECESSITY, 3 JULY 1754

Major George Washington led 150 Virginia militia investigating accurate reports of French entry into trans-Allegheny Virginia. Seneca allies led Washington to a French encampment. In the resulting skirmish, the Indians butchered all but 20 of what turned out to have been a diplomatic mission to the English, including the surrendering Ensign Jumonville. Washington began Fort Necessity in expectation of the French counter-attack, soon receiving 350 reinforcements and constructing a military road. French soldiers numbering 600 plus 100 Indians soon reached the uncompleted fort, which could not contain Washington's entire force. Their weapons and spirits soaked in two days' worth of heavy rain, the Virginians offered only ten hours of resistance to the French, who offered lenient terms that included Washington's unknowing admission that he had ordered Jumonville's death. The entire affair sparked a war raging for seven years from Canada to India.

■ BEAUSÉJOUR, 3–16 JUNE 1755

The Micmacs and French built this pentagonal stone bastion across the Missaquash river from British Fort Thomas in Acadian territory. With a traitor's aid, the British and colonials launched a strong siege, which the fort surrendered to.

■ MONONGAHELA RIVER, 1755

Gen Edward Braddock refused to recognize the differing nature of colonial warfare as he led a powerful column against the French forts in the Ohio valley. With a large supply train, the 2200 British regulars and militia moved slowly, road-building as they went, giving the French time to collect Indian allies and ambush Braddock at the crossing of the Monongahela river. Braddock and two-thirds of his command perished in the rout.

■ CROWN POINT EXPEDITIONS, 1755

Crown Point was a staging point for invasions south into British areas of North America. Gen William Johnson led several columns into the area, constructing a road and Fort William Henry to block further invasions.

■ LAKE GEORGE, 8 SEPTEMBER 1755

Gen William Johnson with 2000 militia and 200 Indian allies dug in to interdict a French invasion route. French Col Ludwig Dieskau routed a supply column, attacked the fort without Indian support and fell captive.

■ TALIWA, 1755

Expanding their territory southward, the Cherokee (under Oconostota) invaded the territory of their

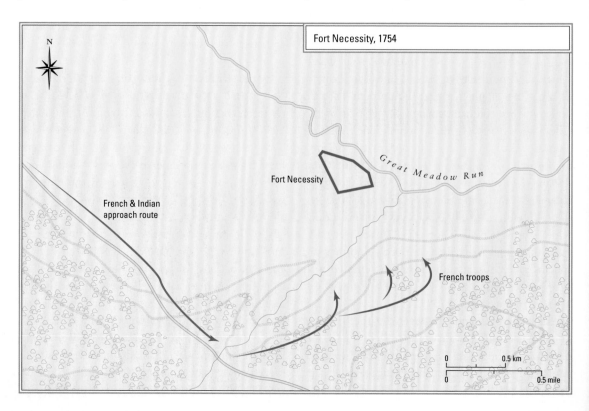

Fort Necessity, 1754

N

Fort Necessity

Great Meadow Run

French & Indian approach route

French troops

0   0.5 km

0   0.5 mile

long-term enemies, the Creeks. The outnumbered Cherokee defeated the Creek war-party and secured the territory north of the Chattahoochee.

■ Oswego, 10–14 August 1756
Advancing against French Fort Niagara, which controlled the portage-way around the namesake falls, Governor William Shirley of Massachusetts and British Gen William Pepperell ended their march at Fort Oswego, which they further fortified with a post – Fort Ontario – and garrisoned with 1600 men. The column's retreat that winter left Forts Ontario and Oswego insufficiently defended against French Gen Montcalm's advance and siege train, Ontario's fall leaving Oswego indefensible and having to surrender.

■ Fort Bull, 27 March 1756
The French followed up their victory at Fort Oswego by their winter attack on this small post further down the supply road from British territory. A total of 362 French, Canadians and Indians overwhelmed a colonial garrison of 60.

■ Fort William Henry, 3–9 August 1757
The French Marquis de Montcalm continued his policy of reducing the unsupported chain of British outposts meant to forestall French counter-thrusts down from Canada. A previous attack and difficulties in transport had left Fort William Henry damaged and with smaller artillery than those possessed by the French siege-train, which included mortars. LCol George Monro commanded 1500 regular and colonial garrison with 18 guns in the fort's defence.

Montcalm's forces included 6000 French and 2000 allied Indians, lured on by promises of glory and plunder. The fort's strength prompted Montcalm to begin a classic European-style siege of trenches and traverses as his artillery weakened the fort's walls and defenders, while allowing a message that reinforcements would not be forthcoming to reach Monro. Such tactics left Montcalm's Indians bored and angry as the siege wore on for six days. In keeping with European tradition, Monroe asked for terms when the French produced a breach in the fort's walls.

Montcalm granted honours of war and safe passage to British territory to the British, with the French retaining the fort and its stores. Indians out to profit from the campaign proceeded to do so on the night of the surrender, by taking the scalps of the British wounded left behind and, for the following two days, attacking and slaughtering as many as 184 of the departing garrison as they sought loot, scalps and prisoners to be held for profitable ransom. French efforts to stop the Indians proved ineffective, the massacre provoking an enduring storm of resentment among the English and colonists, since celebrated in literature. Montcalm burned the fort and retreated back into Canada, while the British began preparations for a massive counter-thrust.

■ Sabbath Day Point, 23 July 1757
British MGen Daniel Webb probed for Montcalm's advancing siege column in ignorance of the French numbers. Col John Parker lost 250 killed or captive when 450 French fired on his boats. Webb retreated.

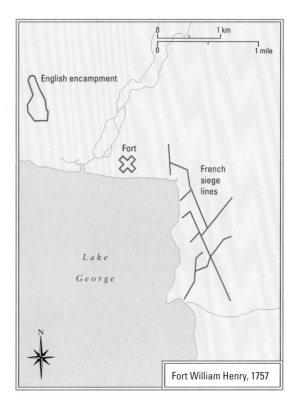

Fort William Henry, 1757

■ **FORT CARILLON, 6–8 JULY 1758**

Gen James Abercromby led a waterbourne British thrust towards the French forts along Lake Champlain towards this strong stone bastion, later Ticonderoga. Both a reconnaissance and six subsequent assaults failed with heavy casualties. Abercromby withdrew.

■ **LOUISBOURG, 8 JUNE–26 JULY 1758**

Having survived previous attacks, this French fortified port fell after a large-scale assault by 39 British ships and landings by 13,200 troops under Gen Jeffrey Amherst. Hard fighting by both arms finally carried the town.

■ **FORT FRONTENAC, 26–28 AUGUST 1758**

From the site of burned Fort Oswego, LCol John Bradstreet launched a successful amphibious attack against this vital French stone fort. Landing stealthily with 3000 men, Bradstreet gunners' bombardment startled the French into surrender.

■ **FORT DUQUESNE, 26–28 AUGUST 1758**

Gen John Forbes led a British force of 1600 regulars with several thousand Colonials against this southernmost French bastion (modern Pittsburgh), suddenly isolated by Fort Frontenac's fall. Forbes moved slowly, rebuilding Braddock's military road in preparation for Prime Minister Pitt's planned powerful thrust into Canada. Forbes carefully wooed the surrounding Indians away from their French alliances. With supplies and conditions eroding rapidly, the French finally burned the post and retreated north.

■ **FORT LIGONIER, 12 OCTOBER 1758**

This strong wooden stockade served as a supply depot for the British column moving against Fort Duquesne. Col James Burd and his garrison repelled an attack by 1200 French with Indian support, resulting in heavy losses.

■ **FORT TICONDEROGA, 26–27 JULY 1759**

Using his secured line of communications southward, Gen Jeffrey Amherst followed up previous inroads into Canadian French defenses with a build-up at the southern end of Lake George, his forces numbering 7000 soldiers. Taking forces and siege artillery up the lake, Amherst landed and

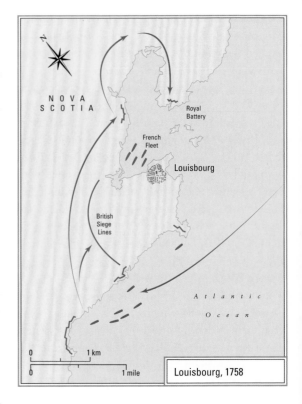

Louisbourg, 1758

positioned his cannon, the French taking advantage of the interval to evacuate the fort and fire its magazine, delaying further invasion of the Fort.

■ **FORT NIAGARA, 6–26 JULY 1759**

Capt Pierre Pouchot sent most of his garrison south against the British advance before Gen John Prideaux's army attacked. Pouchot surrendered after the British defeated a relieving column at the battle of La Belle Famille.

■ **BEAUPORT, 31 JULY 1759**

The British found this village the most strongly defended of the French positions around Quebec. Montcalm had anticipated a landing on the rising ground and Wolfe's men suffered badly before retreating back into the river.

■ **QUEBEC, 13 SEPTEMBER 1759**

Just as the Fort William Henry Massacre had steeled British resolve to take Canada, it also had made Marquis de Montcalm nervous about relying on Indian allies, weakening his ability to resist Prime Minister William Pitt's large-scale invasion

Ticonderoga, 1759

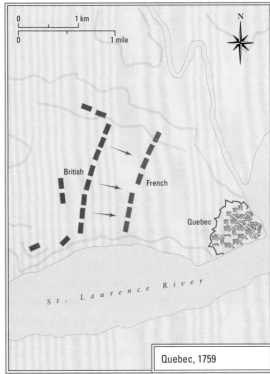

Quebec, 1759

of Canada. Both sides considered strongly fortified Quebec on its promontory the most likely site for a final decisive battle. Pitt's choice of command was Gen James Wolfe, who had distinguished himself in earlier battles.

The British sailed up the St Lawrence, where they established a heavy battery across the river and bombarded the city for seven weeks. In turn, the French tried fireships in vain against the British. Wolfe launched probing attacks after landings at Beaupre and Beauport, which failed. The length of the siege and intelligence that the French were expecting a supply train allowed Wolfe to employ pioneers to scale a height overlooking a cove near the city, where they dispatched Montcalm's sentries. Wolfe then secretly landed half of his force before advancing toward the city's walls.

■ PLAINS OF ABRAHAM, 13 SEPTEMBER 1759

After seven weeks of siege, Gen James Wolfe sent pioneers to scale cliffs overlooking this open area outside Quebec's walls to remove sentries placed

there by the Marquis de Montcalm, in expectation of an attempt to resupply his city. Surprise achieved, Wolfe moved 4500 men onto these plains and drew them up in view of the French with the support of two cannon.

It is difficult to understand Montcalm's decision to lead only 4000 men outside his defences against Wolfe's smaller force (his superiority in numbers or fear of the British fleet starving his city are both explanations). The approaching onset of winter favored the French. Wolfe took the time to entrench his men and position artillery as the French advanced towards them across the Plains of Abraham.

Montcalm put militia and allied Indians on his flanks and opened a bombardment on the British with three field guns. The French line, however, lost formation charging the British, while the British maximized shock with volleys of double-shotted muskets. When the French broke, the British artillery inflicted still further casualties, fatally wounding Montcalm while Wolfe, struck three times by musket fire, died shortly after securing his victory.

■ SAINTE-FOY, 28 APRIL 1760

With Wolfe dead, the defences breached and only Gen James Murray and 7300 men left to secure captured Quebec, escaping French forces rallied under Gen François-Gaston de Lévis and got ready to retake the city as the British garrison dwindled over a winter of scurvy and hunger. Lighter French ships could move in the St Lawrence before the British fleet escaped the frozen harbour. These ships landed 7000 French soldiers, militia and allied Indians upon this spot on Quebec's promontory near the Plains of Abraham. Murray led out the 3800 men still fit to bear arms, the French prevailing on this occasion when their superior numbers overwhelmed the British. Murray retreated into the city's remaining defences, which he held until the British fleet drove off the French and resupplied him. Lévis retreated to Montreal, where converging British armies forced his surrender.

■ RESTIGOUCHE, 3–8 JULY 1760

After Prime Minister Pitt's renewal of the blockade of Canada and with spring allowing movement in the St Lawrence, the British fleet bombarded French positions along the river and destroyed the French flotilla in this bay.

■ THOUSAND ISLANDS, 16–24 AUG 1760

The final stages of the British control of forts and regions captured during Prime Minister William Pitt's large-scale invasion of Canada depended upon the ability of the British navy to transport men and supplies up the St Lawrence river. Gen François-Gaston de Lévis nearly recaptured Quebec before the British could resupply the city's starving garrison. The French enjoyed some advantage in that their smaller river craft regained their mobility in the spring thaw before the ocean-worthy British vessels could move. Capt Pierre Pouchot with 400 men and two gunboats held a fortified position here in the St Lawrence archipelago. An arriving British fleet cleared the river and bombarded Pouchot's fort, reducing it after two days.

■ TACKY'S WAR, 1760

Jamaican slaves rose against their British masters under the leadership of Takyi, an enslaved Ghanan war chief intending to conquer the island. Several plantations fell before the authorities could organize and slaughter the rebel slaves.

■ SIGNAL HILL, 15 SEPTEMBER 1762

The French sought to secure a negotiating advantage with a landing and occupation of St Johns on Newfoundland. French and Irish infantry began systematically pillaging the island. A British force here ejected the raiders, with the French securing fishing rights.

■ HAVANA, 6 JUNE–13 AUGUST 1762

Spain's new king renewed an alliance with France, prompting the descent by a powerful British and colonial amphibious force upon this slackly defended port. The city fell, later to be exchanged by the British for Florida.

■ LOUISIANA REBELLION, 1768

The 1762 Treaty of Fontainebleu ceded French Eastern Louisiana to Spain in compensation for Spain's alliance in the Seven Years' War. Spanish governor Antonio de Ulloa found his effort to regulate New Orleans's trade opposed.

■ DUNMORE'S WAR, 1774

After the conclusion of hostilities in the French and Indian War, the British Crown issued the Proclamation of 1763 forbidding the colonists from further westward settlement, with the view of avoiding further expensive conflict with the powerful Trans-Appalachian tribes, such as the Mingos and Shawnee. With claims extending to the Pacific Ocean, the Western colonies reacted with fury and conflict between encroaching whites and responding Indians finally erupted into open warfare in 1774. The inability of the Iroquois Confederacy to compel non-conferated tribes to honour treaty obligations complicated the situation. With atrocities fuelling both sides' militancy, Virginia governor Lord Dunmore began sending strong forces into Ohio, striking at Shawnee and Mingo villages. The Shawnee-Mingo counter-attack upon Dumore's camp at Point Pleasant collapsed and both tribes eventually ceded land and made terms. Further British efforts to limit conflict provoked colonial resentment.

Dutch–Portugese War 1602–54

■ TABOCAS, 3 AUGUST 1645

A Dutch force of 1100 men under Hendrik van Haus was defeated by João Fernandes Vieira's 900-strong Portuguese force near Vitória de Santo Antão in Brazil. This was the first Portuguese victory in their reconquest of Brazil.

■ GUARARAPES, 19 FEBRUARY 1649

A Portuguese force of 2600 men under Francisco Barreto de Menezes decisively defeated Col Van Den Brinck's 3500-strong Dutch army at Jaboatão dos Guararapes in Brazil, inflicting over 1000 casualties for the loss of 250 men.

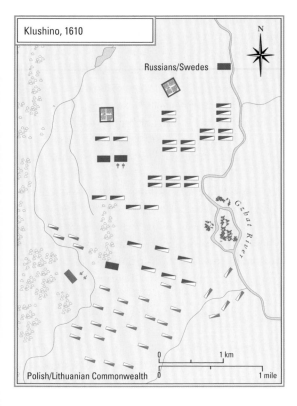

Klushino, 1610

Russians/Swedes

N

Gzhal River

0   1 km

0   1 mile

Polish/Lithuanian Commonwealth

Polish–Russian Conflict 1605–60

■ SMOLENSK, 1609–11

On 25 September 1609, a Polish army of 22,000 men and 30 siege guns commanded by King Sigismund III Vasa besieged Smolensk. The city was defended by Mikhail Borisovich Shein's 5000-strong Russian garrison and 200 guns. Initial Polish assaults were beaten off and Smolensk held out until 13 June 1611, when a mine breached the defences. The city was taken the same day after hours of fierce street fighting.

■ KLUSHINO, 4 JULY 1610

A 48,000-strong Russian army under Prince Dmitry Shuisky attempted to raise King Sigismund III Vasa's siege of Smolensk, but was intercepted by a Polish force of 12,300 men commanded by Field Crown Hetman Stanisław Żółkiewski.

Żółkiewski trapped a Russian advance guard of 8000 men under Hrihorij Walujew in their fortified camp at Tsaryovo-Zaymishche, but was well aware that the remainder of Shuisky's force was within a few days' march. Żółkiewski achieved complete tactical surprise when he split his force, leaving his infantry to blockade Tsaryovo-Zaymishche, while he attacked the main Russian force with his cavalry. Despite being heavily outnumbered, the elite Polish hussars broke Shuisky's cavalry after repeated charges and penned his remaining forces in their camp. Shuisky was thoroughly demoralized after losing 5000 men – Polish casualties were only 400 – and withdrew. The isolated Russian force at Tsaryovo-Zaymishche was forced to surrender.

■ SMOLENSK, JUNE–SEPTEMBER 1654

The Russian siege of Smolensk began in July 1654, but was threatened by Janusz Radziwiłł's 10,000-strong Polish force at Orsha until Prince Aleksey Trubetskoy defeated Radziwiłł at Shepeleviche. The isolated garrison of Smolensk surrendered on 23 September.

■ SHKLOW, 12 AUGUST 1654

A Polish force of 8000 men under Field Crown Hetman of Lithuania, Janusz Radziwiłł, defeated Prince Yakov Cherkassky's 40,000-strong Russian

Army as it crossed the River Dnieper, inflicting 3000 casualties for the loss of 700 men.

■ SHEPELEVICHE, 24 AUGUST 1654

Prince Aleksey Trubetskoy's 15,000-strong Russian Army defeated a Polish force of 8000 men commanded by Field Crown Hetman of Lithuania, Janusz Radziwiłł. Trubetskoy outflanked the Poles and inflicted 1000 casualties, losing only 100 men.

■ OKHMATIV (OCHMATÓW), 29 JANUARY 1655

A Polish and Tatar army of 53,000 men under Grand Crown Hetman Stanisław 'Rewera' Potocki and Khan Mehmed IV Giray fought an inconclusive action near Cherkasy against Vasily Borisovich Sheremetev's 34,000-strong Russian and Cossack army.

■ VILNIUS, 8 AUGUST 1655

A Russian and Cossack army defeated Polish forces commanded by Field Crown Hetman of Lithuania, Janusz Radziwiłł, taking Vilnius and looting the city for several days. An estimated 20,000 inhabitants were killed.

■ HORODOK (GRÓDEK JAGIELLOŃSKI), 29 SEPTEMBER 1655

Russian and Cossack forces under Vasily Borisovich Sheremetev and Bohdan Khmelnytsky defeated Stanisław 'Rewera' Potocki's Polish army near Gródek Jagielloński (now Horodok, Lviv Oblast, Ukraine). The Russians followed up their victory by besieging Lviv.

■ WERKI, 21 OCTOBER 1658

A Polish force commanded by Field Lithuanian Hetman Wincenty Gosiewski was surprised at Werki, near Vilna, by Prince Yuri Dolgorukov's Russian army. Gosiewski was decisively defeated and the Russians followed up their victory by sacking Vilna.

■ KONOTOP, 29 JUNE 1659

The advance of Prince Grigory Romodanovsky's 150,000-strong Russian army was delayed by the Cossack fortress of Konotop, giving time for Hetman Ivan Vyhovsky to assemble a Cossack, Tatar and Polish force, which decisively defeated the Russians.

■ LYAKHAVICHY, 23 MARCH–28 JUNE 1660

Lyakhavichy was a modern Polish fortress, which withstood all attacks during the Russo-Polish War of 1654–67, notably the siege by Ivan Andreyevich Khovansky's Russian army, which was raised by the Polish victory at Polonka.

■ POLONKA, 27 JUNE 1660

A 13,000-strong Polish army commanded by Field Hetman Stefan Czarniecki and Paweł Jan Sapieha defeated Ivan Andreyevich Khovansky's Russian army of 8500 men. The Poles lost 2000 men, but inflicted 3500 casualties on Khovansky's forces.

■ LYUBAR, 14–27 SEPTEMBER 1660

Vasily Borisovich Sheremetev's 18,000-strong Russian army and his 15,000 Cossack allies were defeated with the loss of 1000 men by a Polish and Tatar army of 30,000 men commanded by Grand Crown Hetman Stanisław 'Rewera' Potocki.

■ RIVER BASYA, 24 SEPT–10 OCT 1660

A Polish army of 24,000 men under Field Hetman Stefan Czarniecki fought a series of inconclusive actions against a 16,000-strong Russian force commanded by Yuri Dolgorukov. Both sides withdrew as they lacked supplies for a winter campaign.

■ SLOBODYSHCHE, 8 OCTOBER 1660

An 8000-strong Polish force commanded by Field Crown Hetman Prince Jerzy Sebastian Lubomirski defeated Hetman Yuri Khmelnytsky's Cossack army of 20,000 men, which was attempting to reinforce the Russian forces trapped in their camp near Chudniv.

■ CHUDNIV, 27 SEPTEMBER–2 NOVEMBER 1660

Following their defeat at Lyubar, Sheremetev's forces retreated into a fortified camp near Chudniv where they were attacked and finally forced to surrender by a 30,000-strong Polish and Tatar army under Grand Crown 'Rewera' Potocki.

Iranian Conflicts 1609–25

■ DIMDIM, 1609–10

In 1609, the ruined fortress of Dimdim was rebuilt by Amir Khan Lapzērīn, ruler of the

Kurdish principality of Barādūst. Shah 'Abbās I saw the rebuilding of Dimdim as a move that could threaten Safavid power in the region. The fortress was taken after a long siege led by the Safavid Grand Vizier Hātem Beg, which lasted from November 1609 to the summer of 1610, during which all the defenders were massacred.

■ **MARTQOPI, 25 MARCH 1625**

Giorgi Saakadze's 15,000-strong force of Georgian rebels decisively defeated an Iranian army of 30,000 men commanded by Qarciha-Khan near the village of Martqopi. The Georgians inflicted 27,000 casualties for the loss of 250 men.

■ **MARABDA, 1 JULY 1625**

An Iranian army of 60,000 men under Jesse of Kakheti was sent to invade Georgia and avenge the defeat at Martqopi. At Marabda, near Tbilisi, he defeated Giorgi Saakadze's 20,000-strong Georgian army, inflicting 10,000 casualties.

Kalmar War 1611–13

■ **KRINGEN, 26 AUGUST 1612**

Sweden recruited 300 Scottish mercenaries commanded by LCol Alexander Ramsay for its war against Denmark (the Kalmar War). The detachment landed in Norway (then ruled by Denmark) and began a cross-country march to join the Swedish Army. However, at Otta they were ambushed by 500 Norwegian militia under the local sheriff, Lars Gunnarson Hågå, who annihilated Ramsay's force, inflicting 280 casualties for the loss of fewer than 20 men in a one-sided battle.

The British in India, 1600–22

■ **SWALLY, 29–30 NOVEMBER 1612**

A squadron of four English East India Company galleons under Capt Thomas Best defeated a Portuguese squadron of four galleons and 26 smaller vessels off Swally (Suvali) near Gujerat. At least one Portuguese vessel was sunk.

■ **ORMUZ, 22 APRIL 1622**

The island of Ormuz (Hormuz) in the Persian Gulf had been held by the Portuguese since 1507, but was taken by an Anglo-Iranian force in 1622. An English East India Company (EIC) squadron of five warships and four pinnaces landed a 3000-strong Iranian army commanded by Imam-Quli Khan, which overran the island, taking the Fort of Our Lady of the Conception after a ten-week siege. Over 1000 Portuguese prisoners were taken during the battle.

Iceland 1615

■ **SLAYING OF THE SPANIARDS, 1615**

During the sixteenth century, Basque whalers regularly ventured far afield to Iceland and Labrador. In 1615, however, three Basque whaling vessels were wrecked on the coast of Iceland and the surviving crew members were massacred by the vengeful local population.

Venetian Naval Conflicts 1618–1700

■ **ACTION OF 24 JUNE 1618**

A fleet of 12 Dutch ships commanded by Melcior van den Kerchove, which had been hired by Venice and were flying Venetian colours, defeated a Spanish squadron of ten ships that were blockading the Strait of Gibraltar, demonstrating the skill of Venice's naval tactics.

■ **ACTION OF 26 MAY 1646**

Showing that Venice's navy could also fight defensively, a Venetian squadron of seven warships blockading the Dardanelles under the command of Tommaso Morosini beat off a series of attacks by Kapudan Pasha Kara Musa Pasha's Ottoman fleet of five galleasses and 75 galleys.

■ **ACTION OF 8 SEPTEMBER 1690**

An Ottoman and allied fleet of nine sailing ships and 49 other vessels fought an inconclusive action off Mytilene in the Aegean against a Venetian squadron of 11 warships commanded by Daniele Dolphin.

Thirty Years' War 1618–48

■ PILSEN, 1618

A Protestant army of 20,000 men under Ernst von Mansfeld besieged Pilsen, whose weak Catholic garrison commanded by Torquato Conti comprised 4000 militia and little more than 150 cavalry. The defenders were also short of powder, but managed to hold out from 19 September until 21 November, when the city was stormed after the besieger's artillery finally breached the walls. Mansfeld lost 1100 men, while the garrison's casualties totalled 2500.

■ SABLAT, 10 JUNE 1619

A 5000-strong Imperialist Army under Charles Bonaventure de Longueval, Count of Bucquoy, intercepted and defeated Mansfeld's force of 3200 men. Imperialist casualties totalled 650, but Mansfeld lost at least 1500 infantry and his entire baggage train.

■ HUMENNÉ, 23 NOVEMBER 1619

A force of 10,000 Polish Lisowczycy cavalry (irregular light cavalry) commanded by Walenty Rogawski defeated a 7000-strong Transylvanian army under Prince György Rákóczi I. The Poles lost 850, while Transylvanian casualties totalled 2100.

■ WHITE MOUNTAIN, 8 NOVEMBER 1620

A 30,000-strong Protestant army under Christian I, Prince of Anhalt-Bernburg, deployed at Bílá Hora, near Prague, in an attempt to defend the city against an Imperialist force of 27,000 men commanded by Johann Tserclaes, Count of Tilly. Much of the Protestant force was poorly trained, whereas Tilly's men included many veterans. Although initial Protestant attacks were successful, Tilly's cavalry charges quickly broke their opponents who fled with the loss of 4000 men.

■ WIESLOCH (MINGOLSHEIM), 27 APRIL 1622

Tilly's 28,000-strong Imperialist Army attacked a Protestant force of 12,000 men commanded by Mansfeld. The Imperialists defeated Mansfeld's rearguard, inflicting 2000 casualties, but were driven off by his main body with the loss of 800 men.

■ WIMPFEN, 6 MAY 1622

Margrave George Frederick of Baden-Durlach commanding a Protestant force of 14,000 men was trapped near Wimpfen in Baden-Württemberg by a 25,000-strong Imperialist army under Tilly and Gonzalo Fernández de Córdoba. The Protestants held a strong defensive position, beating off several attacks until an Imperialist bombardment detonated their magazine. Tilly then launched an attack that broke the Margrave's army, inflicting 12,000 casualties. The Imperialists lost 4000 men.

■ HÖCHST, 20 JUNE 1622

Duke Christian of Brunswick's 17,000-strong Protestant force took Höchst near Frankfurt am Main, but was defeated by an Imperialist army of 26,000 men under Tilly. Christian lost 2000 men, while Tilly's casualties were barely 100.

■ FLEURUS, 29 AUGUST 1622

A Protestant army of 14,000 men under Mansfeld and Christian of Brunswick attacked Gonzalo Fernández de Córdoba's 8000-strong Spanish force. The Protestants were routed after their cavalry were defeated, suffering 5000 casualties. Spanish losses totalled 1200 men.

■ STADTLOHN, 6 AUGUST 1623

Christian of Brunswick's ill-disciplined force of 15,000 men was the only major Protestant field army in Germany. As such, it was the primary target of Tilly's 25,000-strong Imperialist army, which pursued it towards the Dutch border. The Protestants were finally forced to give battle at Stadtlohn in Westphalia. Tilly attacked, sustaining 1000 casualties in a series of cavalry charges, but routed Christian's force, which lost 13,000 men.

■ DESSAU BRIDGE, 25 APRIL 1626

Albrecht von Wallenstein's Imperialist army of 20,000 men took Dessau and seized a bridgehead on the eastern bank of the River Elbe. Mansfeld's 12,000-strong Protestant army attacked, but was defeated with the loss of 4000 men.

■ LUTTER AM BARENBERGE, 27 AUGUST 1626

Tilly's Imperialist army of 20,000 men attacked a Danish force of similar size commanded by King Christian IV. The Imperial infantry broke through the Danish line on three occasions but were repulsed by cavalry counter-attacks. However, when the Danish artillery was overrun, panic set in and Christian's men retreated towards the town of Stade. Danish losses were approximately 6000 dead and 2500 prisoners, while the Imperialist casualties numbered only 200.

■ STRALSUND, 13 MAY–4 AUGUST 1628

Stralsund was besieged by Wallenstein's army after it ignored the Duke of Pomerania's orders to accept an Imperialist garrison. The 5000 defenders, reinforced by Danish and Swedish troops, beat off all assaults, forcing Wallenstein to withdraw.

■ WOLGAST, 2 SEPTEMBER 1628

A 7000-strong Danish army led by King Christian IV occupied Wolgast in Pomerania, but was defeated by an Imperialist force of similar size under Wallenstein. The Danes lost just over 2000.

■ MAGDEBURG, NOVEMBER 1630–20 MAY 1631

An Imperialist army of 24,000 men under Tilly and Gottfried Heinrich Graf zu Pappenheim stormed Magdeburg. The 2400-strong garrison inflicted 1900 casualties on the attackers, but was virtually wiped out and 20,000 inhabitants were massacred.

■ FRANKFURT AN DER ODER, 13–15 APRIL 1631

A Swedish army commanded by King Gustavus Adolphus successfully stormed Frankfurt an der Oder after a two-day siege with the loss of 800 men. The town was thoroughly looted and its Imperialist garrison sustained 3000 casualties.

■ WERBEN, 22 JULY 1631

Tilly's 23,000-strong Imperialist army attacked Gustavus Adolphus' force of 16,000 men entrenched around the town of Werben. Although the Swedes repelled the first assaults, they were eventually forced to retreat with the loss of 6000 men.

■ BREITENFELD I, 17 SEPTEMBER 1631

Tilly's Imperialist army of 32,000 men attacked a 42,000-strong Swedish-Saxon army commanded by Gustavus Adolphus and John George I, the Elector of Saxony. (The 24,000 Swedish troops formed on the right of the allied line, with the

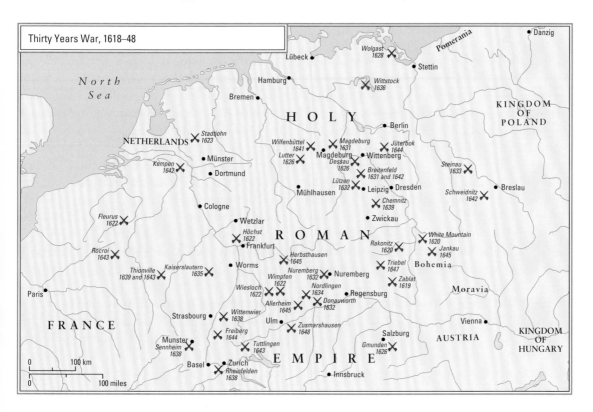

Thirty Years War, 1618–48

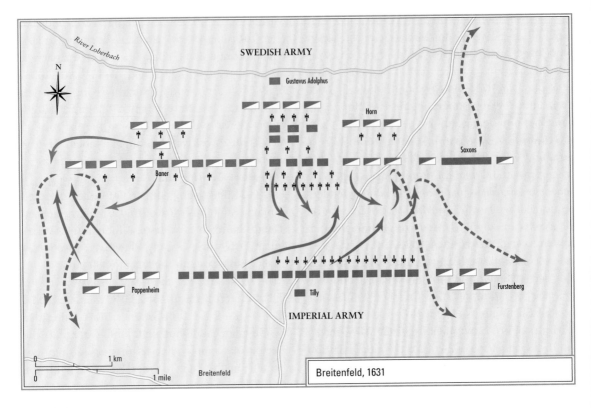

River Loberbach

N

SWEDISH ARMY

Gustavus Adolphus

Horn

Saxons

Baner

Pappenheim

Tilly

IMPERIAL ARMY

Furstenberg

0   1 km

0   1 mile

Breitenfeld

Breitenfeld, 1631

18,000-strong Saxon contingent to their left.)

The battle began around midday with a two-hour exchange of artillery fire, during which the more modern Swedish guns demonstrated their superior rate of fire. (This was especially true of the 42 'regimental guns' – lightweight 3-pounders – which provided close-range fire support.) Tilly seems to have intended a double envelopment of the Protestant forces. After the bombardment, Pappenheim's Black Cuirassiers charged the Swedish right seven times, but were consistently beaten back by steady musketry and carefully timed counter-charges by the Swedish cavalry. After three hours' fighting, Pappenheim's men finally broke.

While these actions were being fought, the Count of Fürstenberg's cavalry and the Imperial infantry advanced against the ill-trained Saxon units, which quickly broke, exposing the Swedish left flank. However, Tilly's disordered infantry were pinned by a series of Swedish cavalry

charges. These gained time for the infantry of the Swedish second line to form a new front facing the Imperialist advance.

Following the defeat of Pappenheim's cuirassiers, Gustavus led his right flank cavalry in an attack that overran the Imperialist artillery. The captured guns were quickly deployed to fire on Tilly's infantry, which were barely holding their ground against increasing Swedish pressure. This bombardment proved to be the final straw – Tilly was wounded and his army routed with the loss of 16,000 men, plus a further 3000 who were captured in the Swedish pursuit. The allied army's casualties totalled 4000, the majority from the shattered Saxon contingent.

■ RAIN (RIVER LECH), 15 APRIL 1632

Tilly deployed his 25,000-strong Imperialist army in a strong defensive position along the River Lech, near the Bavarian town of Rain. Gustavus Adolphus used his powerful artillery to cover an assault crossing of the Lech by his infantry, while the Swedish cavalry crossed the river 10km away to the south to trap the Imperialist army. Tilly was mortally wounded and his army routed with the loss of 3000 men.

■ ALTE VESTE, 9 SEPTEMBER 1632

Wallenstein's 40,000-strong Imperialist army occupied a fortified camp near Nürnberg. The Swedish army of 46,000 men was running out of supplies, forcing Gustavus to lead an assault on the camp, which was beaten off with heavy losses.

■ LÜTZEN, 16 NOVEMBER 1632

In the days immediately before the battle, Wallenstein was alarmed by reports of Gustavus Adolphus' advance with the Swedish field army He decided to detach forces to deal with these threats to Imperialist positions across Germany. He also deployed the remainder of his army around Leipzig where it could both counter any Swedish attack and find better shelter from an increasingly cold winter. News of these moves prompted Gustavus to attack Wallenstein's

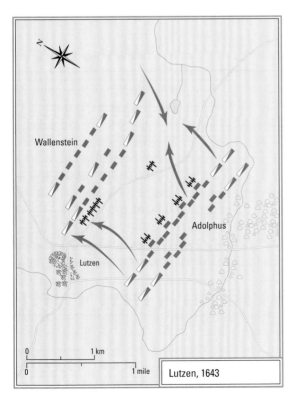

Lutzen, 1643

weakened main army with his 20,000 men, but the Swedish advance was delayed by a skirmish with a small force of Imperialist Croat light cavalry on the afternoon of 15 November at the Rippach stream, about 5km south of the small town of Lützen. This delay prevented Gustavus forcing a full-scale action on the 15th and gave just enough time for Wallenstein to recall Pappenheim's corps, the largest of his detachments.

Pappenheim received the order after midnight and turned his force around to rejoin Wallenstein. During the night, Wallenstein deployed his army in a defensive position along the main Lützen-Leipzig road, which he reinforced with trenches. He anchored his right flank on a low hill on which he placed his main artillery battery, with a further battery positioned on the left flank. (The left flank was the weakest part of the Imperialist line, covered by unreliable Croat light cavalry and even camp followers deployed to give the impression of formed infantry.)

Morning mist and the crossing of two small waterways – the Muhlgraben and the Flossgraben – delayed the Swedish advance, but, by 11:00, Gustavus had completed his deployment and was ready to attack. Initially, the battle went well for the Swedes, who quickly broke the Croat cavalry and camp followers and began to outflank Wallenstein's weak left wing. The Imperialists were unable to hold Lützen – threatened by the advance of the Swedish left wing – and set fire to the town to prevent its capture. However, Pappenheim now arrived with 2000 cavalry and shored up the crumbling Imperialist left flank, but was mortally wounded and, in his absence, the counter-attack collapsed.

Within the hour, Gustavus Adolphus was also dead. He had led a series of attacks on Wallenstein's left flank, but became separated from his men in a confused melee and was killed by a group of Imperialist cuirassiers. With his death, the Swedish advance on this flank petered out. At much the same time, the veteran Swedish infantry of the Yellow and Blue Brigades were decimated as they attacked the centre of the Imperialist line. It seemed that victory was now within Wallenstein's grasp. Most of the Swedish front line was in chaotic retreat, but the royal chaplain (Jakob Fabricius) and Gen Maj Dodo zu Innhausen und Knyphausen helped to prevent a complete disaster by rallying the survivors behind the Swedish second line well out of range of Imperialist artillery fire. By 14:00, the Swedish second-in-command, Bernhard of Saxe-Weimar, having learned of Gustavus' death, took command of the entire army. He restored morale and re-organized units so effectively that by 15:30 the Swedes were able to launch an all-out attack that overran the main Imperialist artillery battery with heavy losses on both sides. As darkness fell, Wallenstein decided to retreat; he had lost about 4000 of his 22,000 men, while Swedish casualties totalled 6000.

■ OLDENDORF, 8 JULY 1633

A Swedish army commanded by George, Duke of Brunswick-Lüneburg and Marshal Dodo zu Innhausen und Knyphausen attacked and defeated an Imperialist force under Jobst Maximilian von Gronsfeld, Count John of Merode and Lothar Dietrich Freiherr von Bönninghausen.

■ NÖRDLINGEN, 5–6 SEPTEMBER 1634

In 1634, a Protestant Saxon and Swedish army invaded Bohemia, threatening the Habsburg heartland. King Ferdinand of Hungary decided to attack the Protestant territories in southern Germany to draw the Swedish and German armies away from Bohemia. Both sides were aware that Spanish reinforcements under his cousin, the Cardinal-Infante Ferdinand, were en route from northern Italy. The Protestant commanders decided they could not ignore this threat and combined their two largest armies – the Swabian-Alsatian Army under Gustav Horn and the so-called Franconian Army under Bernhard of Saxe-Weimar – to give a combined force of 25,000 men. This force pursued Ferdinand in an effort to prevent the merger of the two Habsburg armies, but he maintained a sufficient lead to besiege the town of Nordlingen in Swabia, while

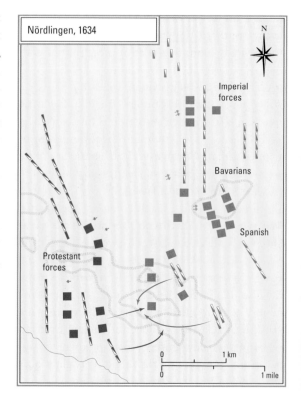

Nördlingen, 1634

awaiting the Cardinal-Infante who arrived on 2 September, three days before the Protestants caught up, bringing the strength of the combined Catholic forces up to at least 34,000 men.

Bernhard and Horn made the crucial mistake of believing that they had a distinct numerical superiority due to under-estimating the strength of the Spanish reinforcements. During the battle, almost anything that could go wrong went wrong for the Protestant forces. This was largely due to the veteran Spanish infantry, the 'Tercios Viejos' (Old Tercios). Fifteen assaults by Horn's right wing were repulsed by the Spaniards with the support of Ottavio Piccolomini's Italian cavalry squadrons. The left of the Protestant line under Bernhard of Weimar was steadily weakened to reinforce these attacks and quickly collapsed when it came under attack late in the day. Horn's remaining troops also broke and he was captured. Protestant losses were at least 12,000 men, while Catholic casualties totalled 2500.

WITTSTOCK, 4 OCTOBER 1636
Field Marshal Johan Banér's 18,000-strong Swedish army attacked and defeated an Imperialist force of similar size under Count Melchior von Hatzfeld and the Saxon Elector John George I. Banér lost 3100 men, while Imperialist casualties totalled 7000.

BREDA, 21 JULY–11 OCTOBER 1637
An 18,000-strong Dutch army commanded by Frederick Henry, Prince of Orange, besieged the city of Breda, which was defended by a Spanish garrison of 2000 men. The garrison surrendered after the Dutch stormed the city's outer defences.

RHEINFELDEN, 28 FEB & 3 MAR 1638
Bernhard of Saxe-Weimar's 12,000-strong Protestant army defeated an Imperialist army of 25,000 men commanded by Count Johann von Werth in two battles near Rheinfelden. Bernhard lost almost 2000 men, but inflicted 4000 casualties on the Imperialists.

BREISACH, 18 AUGUST–17 DECEMBER 1638
The 20,000-strong Imperialist garrison of Breisach, one of the strongest fortresses on the upper Rhine, surrendered after a four-month siege to a Franco-German army of 19,000 men under Bernhard of Saxe-Weimar and the Vicomte de Turenne.

CHEMNITZ, 14 APRIL 1639
Swedish forces under Johan Banér inflicted a crushing defeat on the Saxon and Imperial army commanded by John George I, Elector of Saxony, in broken country north of Chemnitz, after which the Swedes advanced into Bohemia.

LA MARFÉE, 6 JULY 1641
A French army of 13,000 men under Marshal Gaspard de Coligny attacked the 4000-strong forces of the Principality of Sedan, which were reinforced by 7000 Imperialist troops. De Coligny was defeated with the loss of 8500 men.

BREITENFELD II, 23 OCTOBER, 1642
A 15,000-strong Swedish force under FM Lennart Torstenson attacked and decisively defeated an Imperialist army of 25,000 men commanded by Archduke Leopold Wilhelm of Austria and his deputy, Prince-General Ottavio Piccolomini, Duke of Amalfi. The Imperialists suffered 15,000

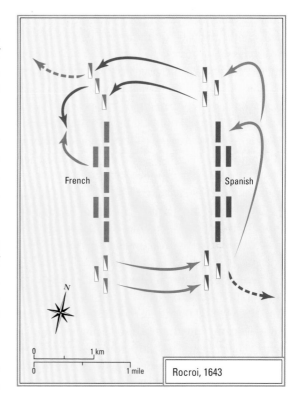

French

Spanish

0 ____ 1 km
0 ____ 1 mile

Rocroi, 1643

casualties, including 5000 prisoners and lost 46 guns. Swedish losses were 4000 killed and wounded, including Gen Torsten Stålhandske, commanding the elite Finnish Hakkapeliitta cavalry, who was seriously wounded.

ROCROI, 19 MAY 1643
A Spanish army of 27,000 men under CGen Francisco de Melo was besieging the town of Rocroi in the Ardennes when it was attacked by a 23,000-strong French force commanded by Louis, duc d'Enghien. Enghien's right wing cavalry defeated its opponents, but his left was repulsed by Isembourg's cavalry, which threatened the exposed French left flank. The Spanish advance was checked by French reserves, giving time for Enghien to swing his victorious cavalry behind de Melo's army and charge the rear of Isembourg's units, which were still fighting the French reserves. Unsurprisingly, this attack quickly routed the remaining Spanish cavalry, leaving their veteran infantry and artillery isolated. Despite this, de Melo's elite infantry fought

on for several hours under heavy artillery fire before defeat, inflicting 4000 casualties on Enghien's forces. Spanish casualties totalled 15,000.

■ TUTTLINGEN, 24 NOVEMBER 1643

A French army commanded by Marshal Josias Rantzau was surprised and defeated by a combined Spanish-Imperialist force under Franz Freiherr von Mercy near Tuttlingen in Baden-Württemberg. Rantzau and several thousand French troops were captured.

■ FREIBURG, 3–9 AUGUST 1644

A 20,000-strong French army under Louis, duc d'Enghien and the Vicomte de Turenne took a fortified position held by Franz Freiherr von Mercy's 16,500 Bavarian troops. French casualties totalled 7000, while von Mercy lost 2500 men.

■ JANKAU, 5 MARCH 1645

Torstenson's 16,000-strong Swedish army attacked and defeated an Imperialist army of similar size under Gen Melchior von Hatzfeldt near Jankau, 50 km south-east of Prague. Torstenson lost 1500 men, but inflicted 8000 casualties on the Imperialists.

■ MERGENTHEIM (HERBSTHAUSEN), 2 MAY 1645

Turenne led a French army of 11,000 deep into Germany, but was surprised and defeated in detail while encamped near Herbsthausen in Baden-Württemberg by a 6000-strong Bavarian force commanded by Franz Freiherr von Mercy.

■ NÖRDLINGEN II (ALLERHEIM), 3 AUGUST 1645

A Franco-German army of 17,000 men under Enghien and Turenne attacked a 14,000-strong Imperialist force commanded by von Mercy. The Imperialists took up a strong defensive position, with their right on a hill known locally as the Wennenberg. Their left flank was anchored on a hilltop castle, the Schloss Allerheim, while their centre held a low ridge running between the two hills. The Imperialist centre was partially protected by the village of Allerheim, which was held by a mixed force of Imperialist infantry and dragoons.

Enghien launched a frontal attack, but the Imperialist forces holding the Schloss Allerheim counter-attacked, breaking his right wing. The French left wing under Turenne stormed the Wennenberg and von Mercy was killed. In the confusion, the garrison of Allerheim thought that they were surrounded and surrendered. Both sides had lost 5000 men, but the Imperialists conceded defeat and withdrew.

■ ZUSMARSHAUSEN, 17 MAY 1648

An 18,000-strong Imperialist army commanded by Count Raimondo Montecúccoli was heavily defeated at Zusmarshausen near Augsburg by a Franco-Swedish army of 30,000 men under the Prince de Condé and FM Carl Gustav Wrangel.

■ PRAGUE, 25 JUNE–1 NOVEMBER 1648

Count Hans Christoff von Königsmarck's Swedish army besieged Prague and captured Prague castle. Swedish attempts to storm the Old Town failed and they withdrew on news of the Peace of Westphalia. which ended the Thirty Years' War.

Manchu Invasion of Korea, 1627

■ FIRST MANCHU INVASION, 1627

Korean support for the Ming in their fight against the Manchu tribes provoked the Manchu Khan Hung Taiji to order an invasion of Korea. The Korean Army was ill-prepared to counter the offensive effectively as it was still weakened by losses sustained in the Seven-Year War against Japan. The invasion force advanced deep into Korean territory before a peace was negotiated.

Vietnam 1627–1775

■ TRINH-NGUYEN WAR, 1627–73

In 1627, open warfare broke out between the Trinh and the Nguyen. After several months, the situation stabilized with the virtual partition of Vietnam into northern and southern regions, with the Trinh ruling the north and the Nguyen the south.

After the first offensives, the Nguyen built two massive fortified lines north of Hue near the city of Dong Hoi. These lines were defended against numerous Trinh assaults that continued until 1672, when the Trinh army made a final unsuccessful

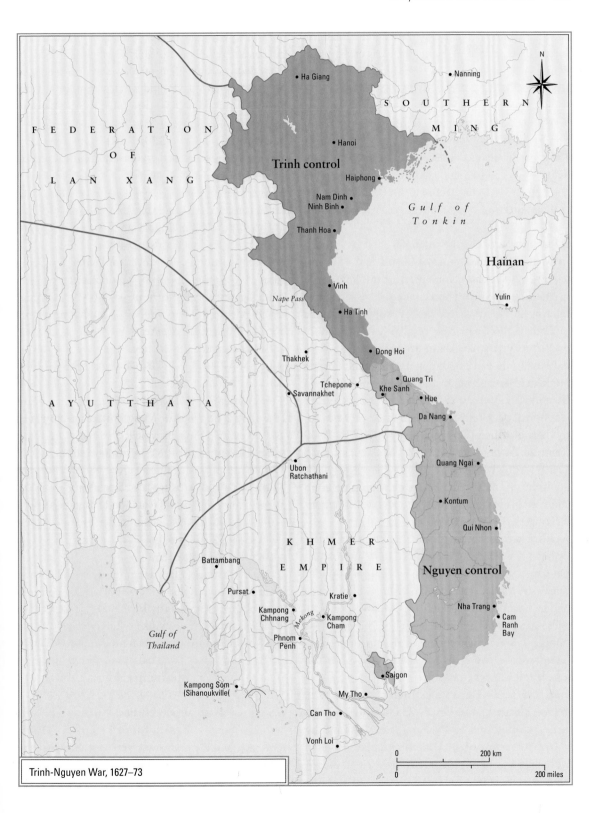

N

• Nanning

S O U T H E R N

M I N G

• Ha Giang

F E D E R A T I O N

O F

L A N   X A N G

• Hanoi

Trinh control

Haiphong •

Nam Dinh •
Ninh Binh •

Thanh Hoa •

Gulf of
Tonkin

Hainan

• Vinh

Nape Pass

Yulin
•

• Ha Tinh

• Dong Hoi

Thakhek •

• Quang Tri

Tchepone •   Khe Sanh •
Savannakhet •   • Hue

• Da Nang

A Y U T T H A Y A

• Quang Ngai

Ubon •
Ratchathani

• Kontum

K H M E R

• Qui Nhon

E M P I R E   **Nguyen control**

Battambang •

Pursat •   Kratie •   Nha Trang •
                                                                • Cam
Kampong •   Ranh
Chhnang   *Mekong* • Kampong   Bay
                        Cham
          Phnom •
          Penh

Gulf of
Thailand

• Saigon

Kampong Som •
(Sihanoukville(
                        My Tho •

                Can Tho •

        Vonh Loi •

                    0   200 km

Trinh-Nguyen War, 1627–73
                    0   200 miles

attack. A year later a treaty was agreed that the River Linh should become the border between Trinh and Nguyen provinces and the Lê King was recognized as the ruler of Vietnam.

■ **FALL OF HUE, 1775**

Trinh Sam, one of the last Trinh lords and ruler of the north, attacked the Nguyen on 15 November 1774. Their defence lines were overrun and, in February 1775, the Trinh captured the capital Hue.

Cossack Uprising 1630–59

■ **FEDOROVYCH UPRISING, 1630**

In March 1630, Ukrainian peasants and Cossacks led by Taras Fedorovych rebelled against Polish rule in the Ukraine. After three months of indecisive fighting, both sides agreed to a compromise peace settlement, the Treaty of Pereyaslav.

■ **ZHOVTI VODY, 29 APRIL–16 MAY 1648**

A Polish army of 12,000 men under Grand Crown Hetman Mikołaj Potocki and Field Crown Hetman Marcin Kalinowski was defeated by 8000 Cossack rebels led by Bohdan Khmelnytsky, Hetman of the Zaporozhian Cossacks, supported by 3000 Crimean Tatars under Tugay Bey. They surrounded a 3000-strong Polish detachment in its tabor, which gradually disintegrated as its Cossack units deserted and was finally destroyed for the loss of 150 rebels.

■ **KORSUŃ, 26 MAY 1648**

A Cossack rebel army of 15,000 men commanded by Bohdan Khmelnytsky, Hetman of the Zaporozhian Cossacks, supported by 3000 Crimean Tatars under Tugay Bey, attacked a 6000-strong Polish force under Grand Crown Hetman Mikołaj Potocki. The Poles beat off an initial assault on their fortified camp, but were then cut off as they attempted to withdraw and were decisively defeated with the loss of at least 4500 men.

■ **PYLIAVTSI, 23 SEPTEMBER 1648**

Prince Zasławski-Ostrogski's 25,000-strong Polish army was defeated at Pyliava in the Ukraine by a Cossack army of 30,000 men under Bohdan Khmelnytsky, Hetman of the Zaporozhian Cossacks, supported by 2000 Crimean Tatars.

■ **LOYEW, 31 JULY 1649**

A Cossack rebel army of 18,000 men under Stepan Pobodailo and Mykhailo Krychevsky was defeated by a 6000-strong Polish force commanded by Prince Janusz Radziwiłł and Wincenty Korwin Gosiewski. The Cossacks lost at least 3000 men.

■ **ZBARAZH, 10 JULY–22 AUGUST 1649**

A Polish garrison of 15,000 men commanded by Prince Jeremi Wiśniowiecki held the fortress of Zbarazh against repeated assaults by Cossack and Tatar forces under Bohdan Khmelnytsky, Hetman of the Zaporozhian Cossacks, and Tugay Bey.

■ **ZBORIV, 15–16 AUGUST 1649**

A 25,000-strong Polish army commanded by King John II Casimir fought an inconclusive two-day battle against a rebel force of 40,000 Cossacks and 20,000 Crimean Tatars under Bohdan Khmelnytsky and Khan İslâm III Giray.

■ **BERESTECHKO, 28–30 JUNE 1651**

King John II Casimir's 63,000-strong Polish army defeated a rebel force of 140,000 Cossacks and Tatars under Bohdan Khmelnytsky and Khan İslâm III Giray. The Poles lost 400 men, but inflicted 40,000 casualties on the rebels.

■ **BILA TSERKVA, 24–25 SEPTEMBER 1651**

Within months of his defeat at Berestechko, Bohdan Khmelnytsky raised a fresh Cossack force of about 50,000 men and fought a bloody but indecisive action against a Polish army under Grand Crown Hetman Mikołaj Potocki.

■ **BATOH, 1–2 JUNE 1652**

A 15,000-strong Polish army under Field Crown Hetman Marcin Kalinowski was decisively defeated by Bohdan Khmelnytsky's 45,000 Cossacks and Tatars. Kalinowski was killed while trying to escape and 8000 Polish prisoners were massacred.

Piracy, 1631

■ **SACK OF BALTIMORE, 20 JUNE 1631**

Muslim pirates under Murat Reis, a Dutch renegade, plundered this western Irish village at the culmination of a raiding voyage from North Africa. Over 200 raiders bore off 100 civilians into slavery.

Franco-Spanish War 1635–59

■ LES AVINS, 20 MAY 1635

A 35,000-strong French army commanded by Marshal Urbain de Maillé and the Comte de Coligny defeated the Prince of Carignano's Spanish army of 14,000 men. The French inflicted 4000 casualties for the loss of 260 men.

■ TORNAVENTO, 22 JUNE 1636

A French and Savoyard army of 10,400 men under the Marquis de Créquy and Duke Victor Amadeus I of Savoy defeated the Marquis of Leganés' 14,000-strong Spanish army, inflicting 1300 casualties for the loss of 3000 men.

GUETARIA, 22 JULY 1638

A French squadron of six warships and five fireships commanded by Henri de Sourdis defeated Lope de Hoces' Spanish squadron of 12 galleons off the port of Guetaria. All 12 Spanish vessels were destroyed.

■ TURIN, 22 MAY–20 SEPTEMBER 1640

A French garrison held the citadel of Turin against the Prince of Carignano who controlled the city. The Prince's men were in turn besieged and finally forced to surrender by a 13,000-strong French and Savoyard army.

■ HONNECOURT, 26 MAY 1642

Francisco de Melo's 19,000-strong Spanish army defeated a French army of 10,000 men under Antoine III de Gramont, Comte de Guiche, near Honnecourt-sur-Escaut in the Pas-de-Calais. The Spanish inflicted 7100 casualties and lost 500 men.

■ CARTAGENA, 3 SEPTEMBER 1643

A French fleet of 34 vessels commanded by the Marquis of Brézé defeated Martín Carlos de Mencos' Spanish squadron of 25 ships off Cartagena. One Spanish galleon was destroyed and two more were captured.

■ LENS, 20 AUGUST 1648

An 18,000-strong Spanish army under Archduke Leopold Wilhelm of Austria was defeated by the Prince de Condé's French army of 16,000 men

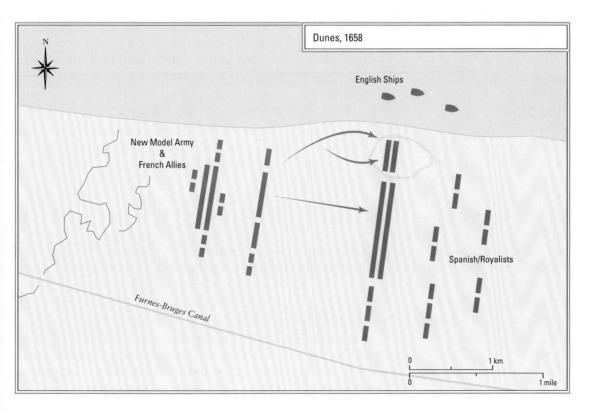

Dunes, 1658

English Ships

New Model Army & French Allies

Spanish/Royalists

Furnes-Bruges Canal

N

0   1 km

0   1 mile

near Lens in the Pas-de-Calais. Condé inflicted 8000 casualties for the loss of 3500 men.

■ **ARRAS, 23–25 AUGUST 1654**

The rebellious Prince de Condé led a Spanish army in an attempt to capture Arras, but was surprised and defeated by the night attack of a French relief force commanded by the Vicomte de Turenne.

■ **THE DUNES (DUNKIRK), 14 JUNE 1658**

The Vicomte de Turenne's 15,000-strong French army, supported by 3000 English troops from Cromwell's New Model Army, defeated a Spanish army of 13,000 men (including 2000 English Royalists) under Don Juan José de Austria.

Bishops' Wars 1639–40

■ **FIRST BISHOPS' WAR, 1639**

Charles I's attempts to impose Anglican doctrine on the Church of Scotland led to riots, which rapidly spread across Scotland. A 20,000-strong English army deployed near Berwick-upon-Tweed, while Alexander Leslie concentrated his 12,000 Scottish troops around Duns. After inconclusive skirmishes, the Pacification of Berwick was negotiated, under which it was agreed that the dispute should be referred to a General Assembly of the Church of Scotland or to the Scottish Parliament.

■ **SECOND BISHOPS' WAR, 1640**

Unresolved tension over religious doctrine led to more serious fighting in 1640. The Scots under Leslie and Montrose invaded England, overrunning all of Northumberland and County Durham against feeble resistance from a demoralized English army. Charles was forced to leave both counties in Scottish hands as a pledge for the payment of their expenses when he agreed to peace and signed the Treaty of Ripon in October 1640.

■ **NEWBURN FORD, 28 AUGUST 1640**

Lord Conway's ill-equipped 5500-strong English army was routed with the loss of 300 men by a Scottish army of 20,000 men commanded by Alexander Leslie. The Scots sustained barely 200 casualties.

The First English Civil War 1642–46

■ **HULL, 10 JULY 1642**

In 1642, Hull contained one of the largest arsenals in England, which had been established to equip English forces for the Bishops' Wars of 1639–40. As relations between Charles I and Parliament worsened in early 1642, both sides manoeuvred to secure the country's few sizeable arsenals. In January 1642, Parliament appointed Sir John Hotham as military governor of the mainly Royalist city of Hull, commanding a garrison of almost 1500 men. He closed the gates against the king when he tried to enter the city in April that year and subsequently supervised the despatch of large consignments of weapons to London for the armies being raised by Parliament. In early July, the king returned, besieging the city with an army of 3000 infantry and 1000 cavalry, but withdrew at the end of the month after his forces failed to breach the defences.

■ **POWICK BRIDGE, 23 SEPTEMBER 1642**

A Royalist force of 1000 cavalry commanded by Prince Rupert routed a similar detachment of Parliamentary cavalry at Powick Bridge near Worcester. The action helped make Prince Rupert's reputation as a daring cavalry commander.

■ **EDGEHILL, 23 OCTOBER 1642**

Charles I's 13,500 men won a narrow victory over the 15,000-strong Parliamentarian army commanded by the Earl of Essex at Edgehill, near Warwick. The Royalists followed up their success with an advance on London.

■ **AYLESBURY, 1 NOVEMBER 1642**

Royalist forces, under the command of Prince Rupert, attacked Aylesbury's Parliamentarian garrison at Holman's Bridge a few kilometres to the north of Aylesbury, resulting in a victory for the heavily outnumbered Parliamentarian forces.

■ **BRENTFORD, 12 NOVEMBER 1642**

A 4600-strong detachment of the Royalist army (predominantly cavalry and dragoons, but including one regiment of Welsh foot) under the command of Prince Rupert assaulted Brentford, which was

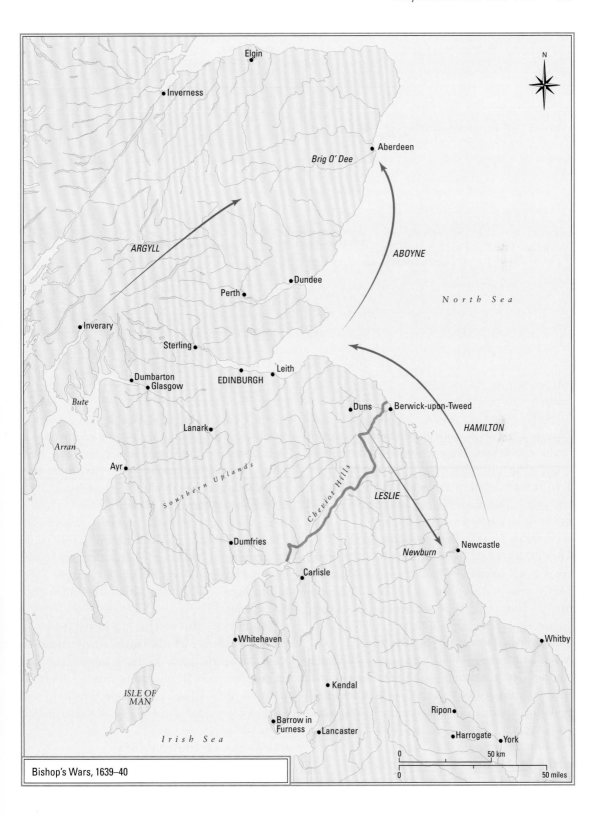

Elgin

• Inverness

Aberdeen

Brig O' Dee

ARGYLL

ABOYNE

• Dundee

Perth •

North Sea

• Inverary

Sterling •

Leith

Dumbarton •
• Glasgow   EDINBURGH

Bute

Duns •   • Berwick-upon-Tweed

HAMILTON

Arran

Lanark •

Ayr •

Southern Uplands

Cheviot Hills

LESLIE

• Dumfries

Newburn   • Newcastle

• Carlisle

• Whitehaven   • Whitby

*ISLE OF
MAN*

• Kendal

Ripon •

Irish Sea

• Barrow in
Furness   • Lancaster

• Harrogate   • York

0   50 km

Bishop's Wars, 1639–40

0   50 miles

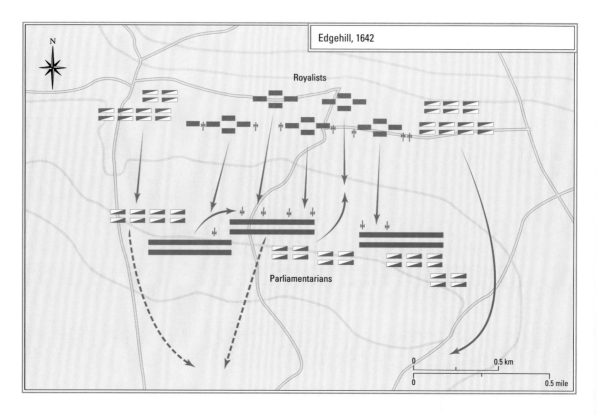

Edgehill, 1642

Royalists

Parliamentarians

0   0.5 km

0   0.5 mile

garrisoned by two Parliamentary infantry regiments totalling 1300 men. Rupert's cavalry and dragoons attacked the town under cover of a morning mist. The garrison repulsed the initial Royalist assault, but were driven from their defences by a second attack led by the Welsh infantry.

■ TURNHAM GREEN, 13 NOVEMBER 1642

The 13,000-strong Royalist army's advance on London was blocked by Parliamentarians totalling 24,000 men commanded by the Earl of Essex. After a short artillery bombardment, the heavily outnumbered Royalists withdrew to Oxford.

■ BRADDOCK DOWN, 19 JANUARY 1643

A Royalist force of 5000 men under Sir Ralph Hopton defeated a 4000-strong Parliamentarian army commanded by Col William Ruthven near Bodmin, inflicting 200 casualties and taking 1500 prisoners. The victory ensured Royalist control of Cornwall.

■ HOPTON HEATH, 19 MARCH 1643

The Earl of Northampton's 1200 Royalists fought an inconclusive action against a Parliamentarian force totalling 1500 men under Sir John Gell. The Earl was killed attacking the Parliamentarian infantry, but his men broke Gell's cavalry.

■ SEACROFT MOOR, 30 MARCH 1643

Lord Goring's Royalist cavalry caught Sir Thomas Fairfax's Parliamentarian army while it was on the march to Leeds. Fairfax's badly outnumbered cavalry were quickly scattered and his infantry broke, losing almost 1000 men (and 800 prisoners.)

■ BIRMINGHAM (CAMP HILL), 3 APRIL 1643

After defeating 300 Parliamentarian defenders, Prince Rupert's force of 1200 cavalry and 600 infantry stormed Birmingham. Parts of the town were burned in the ensuing street fighting and the story provided the basis for Parliamentarian propaganda.

■ READING, 13–16 APRIL 1643

Reading had been held for the Royalists since November 1642 by a garrison of 2500 men. On

English Civil War, 1642–43

Royalist campaigns

Parliamentarian campaigns

Battle

town captured, with date

Royalist areas by the end of 1643

Parliamentary areas by the end of 1643

SCOTLAND

Aberdeen 13 Sept. 1644

Tippermuir 1 Sept. 1644

Dundee

Invereray

Glasgow   Edinburgh

Berwick

Morpeth 28 Jan. 1644

Newcastle upon Tyne 3 Feb. 1644

Dumfries 15 April 1644

Sunderland 4 March 1644

Carlisle

Northallerton 15 April 1644

N

Marston Moor 2 July 1644

Scarborough

Bolton 28 May 1644

Tadcaster 6 March 1644

Liverpool 11 June 1644

York

Hull

Rowton Heath 24 Sept. 1644

Sheffield

Selby 11 April 1643

Chester

Beacon Hill 21 March 1644

Nantwich 25 Jan. 1644

Nottingham

Newark 22 March 1644

Kings Lynn

Shrewsbury

Leicester

Norwich

Montgomery

Lichfield

Northampton

WALES

Cropredy Bridge 29 June 1644

Cardigan

Worcester

Banbury

Colchester

Gloucester

Pembroke

Monmouth

Oxford

London

Newbury 27 Oct. 1644

Maidstone

Cheriton 29 March 1644

Taunton

Wardour Castle

Arundel

0   50 km

Tavistock 23 July 1644

Lyme Regis

Corfe Castle

0   50 miles

Lostwithiel 31 Aug. 1644

Plymouth

English Civil War, 1643–44

13 April, the town was besieged by a 13,000-strong Parliamentarian army and surrendered only three days later.

■ Sourton Down, 25 April 1643

This was a victory for MGen Chudleigh's Parliamentarian forces, which surprised Sir Ralph Hopton's Cornish army at Sourton Down on the edge of Dartmoor. It was one of very few Civil War night actions.

■ Grantham, 13 May 1643

A Royalist force commanded by Sir Charles Cavendish made a surprise attack on the Parliamentarian army, but were defeated by a charge led by Oliver Cromwell in his first independent action as a cavalry commander.

■ Stratton, 16 May 1643

Sir Ralph Hopton's 2500 infantry and 500 cavalry attacked a Parliamentarian army of 5400 men, which held a strong hill-top position near Stratton. Despite being heavily outnumbered, the Royalists broke the defenders in a 10-hour battle.

■ Chalgrove Field, 18 June 1643

Prince Rupert's raiding force of 1000 cavalry, 350 dragoons and 500 infantry was intercepted by Sir Philip Stapleton's 1150 Parliamentarian cavalry and dragoons. The prince led his bodyguard in a surprise attack that routed the enemy.

■ Adwalton Moor, 30 June 1643

A Parliamentarian army of only 4000 men under Lord Ferdinando Fairfax attempted to prevent the Earl of Newcastle's 10,000 Royalists from storming Bradford. After beating off several attacks from the cover of the hedged fields around Westgate Hill, the Parliamentarians unwisely advanced onto the open moor where Newcastle's numerical superiority proved to be decisive. Fairfax's army was routed and the Royalists gained control of Yorkshire, except for the port of Hull.

■ Lansdowne, 5 July 1643

Sir William Waller's Parliamentarian army of 1500 infantry and 2500 cavalry held Lansdown Hill near Bath to delay the eastward advance of Sir Ralph Hopton's forces totalling 4000 infantry, 2000 cavalry and 300 dragoons. Waller ordered his cavalry to charge to provoke a Royalist attack on his strong position. Hopton's men took the hill at the cost of heavy casualties, but Waller broke contact and retreated with his army intact.

■ Roundway Down, 13 July 1643

Following the battle of Lansdowne, Hopton's battered forces occupied Devizes where they were besieged by Waller who had received reinforcements from Bristol. A 1800-strong Royalist cavalry column under Lord Wilmot was sent from Oxford to raise the siege. Waller deployed his 2500 infantry and 2000 cavalry in a strong position on Roundway Down, but Wilmot defeated his cavalry and the Parliamentarian infantry surrendered when Hopton's 3000 men advanced from Devizes.

■ Bristol, 24–26 July 1643

After their victory at Roundway Down the Royalists advanced on Bristol, which was held by a Parliamentarian garrison of 1800 men. The city was taken, but the Royalists (especially their elite Cornish infantry) suffered heavy casualties.

■ Gainsborough, 28 July 1643

A Parliamentarian force under Oliver Cromwell and Sir John Meldrum defeated Sir Charles Cavendish's Royalists, but was forced to retreat from Gainsborough later that day by the approach of the Earl of Newcastle's main army.

■ Gloucester, 10 August–5 September 1643

The king led a 25,000-strong army in the siege of the city, which was garrisoned by 1500 men. The prolonged siege allowed the Earl of Essex to bring his army from London to relieve Gloucester.

■ Hull, 2 September–12 October 1643

Hull was besieged by a Royalist army of 12,000 infantry and 4000 cavalry under the Earl of Newcastle. The siege was abandoned after a series of raids by the garrison, which had been reinforced by sea.

■ Newbury I, 20 September 1643

After raising the siege of Gloucester, the Earl of Essex marched back towards London with his 10,000 infantry and 4000 cavalry, constantly harried by the king's army (8000 infantry and 6000 cavalry), which overtook him, blocking his path at Newbury. The Royalists routed the opposing cavalry, but failed to break the Parliamentarian infantry defending Round Hill. The battle ended in stalemate; the Royalists retreated to Oxford, while Essex withdrew to London.

■ WINCEBY, 11 OCTOBER 1643

Sir John Henderson's Royalist cavalry force of 1500 men marching to raise the siege of Bolingbroke castle was intercepted and defeated by Oliver Cromwell's Eastern Association cavalry. This victory enhanced Cromwell's reputation.

■ ALTON, 13 DECEMBER 1643

The Royalist garrison of 600 infantry and 400 cavalry at Alton was surprised by a 5000-strong Parliamentary army. The Royalist cavalry fled and their infantry surrendered after making a final stand in the Church of St Lawrence.

■ NANTWICH, 25 JANUARY 1644

A Royalist army of 1800 infantry and 2000 cavalry under Lord Byron was besieging Nantwich, when it was attacked and defeated by a Parliamentarian force of almost 7000 men commanded by Sir Thomas Fairfax.

■ LATHOM HOUSE, 27 FEBRUARY–27 MAY 1644

The Countess of Derby and a garrison of 300 men held Lathom House against repeated assaults by a 2000-strong Parliamentarian force commanded by Sir Thomas Fairfax until the arrival of Prince Rupert's relief force.

■ NEWARK, 21 MARCH 1644

A Parliamentarian army of 7000 men under Sir John Meldrum besieging Newark was attacked by Prince Rupert's slightly smaller relief force. Meldrum was forced to surrender after being trapped between the prince's army and the garrison.

■ BOLDON HILL, 25 MARCH 1644

This action was little more than a skirmish in which the Earl of Newcastle's Royalists drove off a Scottish army under the Earl of Leven, which had invaded England in support of the Parliamentarians.

■ CHERITON, 29 MARCH 1644

Lord Hopton's Royalist force of 3500 cavalry and 2500 infantry attacked Sir William Waller's Parliamentarian army of 3500 cavalry and 6500 infantry. The Royalists were defeated as Waller made good use of his numerical superiority.

■ SELBY, 11 APRIL 1644

The Royalist garrison of Selby was attacked by a Parliamentarian army of over 3000 men commanded by Sir Thomas Fairfax. The town was taken after fierce street fighting and 1600 Royalist infantry were captured.

■ YORK, 22 APRIL 22–30 JUNE 1644

York was besieged by a mixed Parliamentarian and Scottish force totalling 14,000 men. The Marquess of Newcastle's garrison of 6000 men beat off a series of assaults until Prince Rupert raised the siege on 30 June.

■ BOLTON, 28 MAY 1644

Prince Rupert's 2000 cavalry and 6000 infantry stormed Bolton, which was held by a Parliamentary garrison of 4000 men. The town was captured after fierce street fighting in which 1000 of the garrison were killed.

■ OXFORD, 28 MAY–8 JUNE 1644

A Parliamentarian army commanded by the Earl of Essex unsuccessfully probed the outer defences of Oxford (the Royalist 'capital'), but moved off to follow the king's field army when it broke out of the city.

■ CROPEDY BRIDGE, 29 JUNE 1644

The king's Oxford Army of 5000 cavalry and 4000 infantry faced Sir William Waller's Parliamentarian forces of equal strength across the River Cherwell. Waller attacked across Cropedy Bridge, but was beaten off with heavy losses.

■ TAUNTON, JULY 1644–JUNE 1645

The Parliamentarian garrison commanded by Col Robert Blake was besieged by Royalist forces under Lord Goring. A relief column broke through to the town on 11 May, but the Royalists maintained the siege until 14 June.

■ MARSTON MOOR, 2 JULY 1644

After raising the siege of York on 30 June, Prince Rupert interpreted the king's ambiguous instructions as a direct order to give battle to the combined Parliamentarian and Scottish (Allied) army that had been besieging the city. Accordingly, on the morning of 2 July, he moved his army to the west of York and took up a position north of the Long Marston–Tockwith road, where he was joined by the Earl of Newcastle's troops, bringing the total Royalist force to 11,000 infantry, 6500 cavalry and 16 guns. The Allied army totalling 18,000 infantry, 9000 cavalry and 25 guns deployed on the high ground south of the road. No action took place during the day, but the Allied commanders decided to attack in the evening under cover of a thunderstorm.

On the Allied left flank, Cromwell routed Lord Byron's Royalist cavalry, but on the other side of the battlefield, Sir Thomas Fairfax's Parliamentarian cavalry were broken by Lord Goring. In the centre, both sides' infantry were locked in fierce fighting. The initial Allied assault was held with difficulty, but a Royalist counter-attack, combined with charges by Lord Goring's cavalry, broke several Allied regiments. Only the stand of two Scottish regiments (the Earl

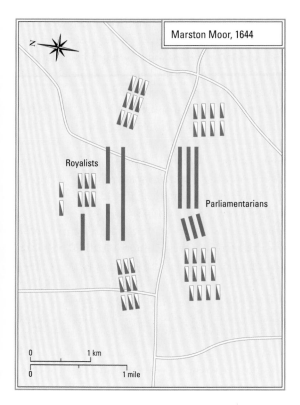

Marston Moor, 1644

Royalists

Parliamentarians

0   1 km

0   1 mile

of Lindsay's and Lord Maitland's) prevented a complete rout in the Allied centre. Sir Thomas Fairfax managed to make his way across the battlefield to warn Cromwell who led his cavalry in a charge that routed Lord Goring's men. They then attacked the disheartened Royalist infantry who broke and fled towards York.

Royalist casualties were 4000 dead and 1500 captured, while the Allies lost about 300 killed. York surrendered two weeks later, ending Royalist power in the north of England.

■ LOSTWITHIEL, 2 SEPTEMBER 1644

The king, with 16,000 men, trapped a 10,000-strong Parliamentarian force commanded by the Earl of Essex. The earl's cavalry broke out and he escaped by sea, but his 6000 infantry were forced to surrender.

■ NEWBURY II, 27 OCTOBER 1644

Charles' route back to Oxford from Lostwithiel was blocked at Newbury by a large Parliamentarian army commanded by the Earl of Manchester. The Earl planned to exploit his numerical superiority (19,000 Parliamentarians to 12,000 Royalists) to trap the Royalist forces by sending part of his forces in a wide flanking march. While this manoeuvre was successful, the king's army managed to beat off all the Parliamentarian attacks and the battle ended in stalemate.

■ OXFORD, 21 MAY–4 JUNE 1645

The capture of Oxford was one of the main Parliamentary objectives for 1645 and Sir Thomas Fairfax took reluctant command of the siege. The operation was abandoned following reports of the Royalist capture of Leicester.

■ LEICESTER, 30 MAY 1645

Prince Rupert's army of 5500 men stormed Leicester, which was defended by an 1800-strong Parliamentarian garrison in a successful attempt to provoke Sir Thomas Fairfax's New Model Army to raise the siege of Oxford.

■ NASEBY, 14 JUNE 1645

The king's army, totalling 4000 infantry and 5000 cavalry, deployed on Dust Hill near the village of Naseby where they faced Sir Thomas Fairfax's New

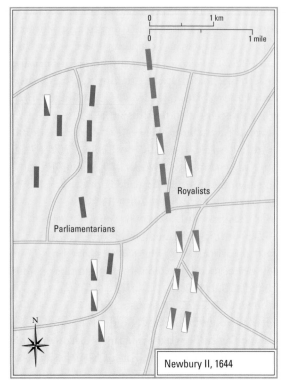

Newbury II, 1644

Model Army of 7000 infantry and 6000 cavalry. Both sides had their infantry in the centre with their cavalry on each flank, each backed by a small reserve. In addition, Fairfax deployed Col Okey's dragoons along hedges bordering the battlefield from which they could fire into the flank of Prince Rupert's cavalry as it advanced.

The battle began with successful cavalry charges by the right wings of both armies, but Prince Rupert's undisciplined troopers pursued their opponents off the battlefield and attempted to loot the Parliamentarian baggage train. In contrast, Cromwell kept his men under control, driving off Sir Marmaduke Langdale's Northern Horse before leading his second line in a series of charges against Lord Astley's veteran Royalist infantry who were forcing back the Parliamentarian centre. This was the crisis of the battle and the king brought his Lifeguard forward with Langsdale's rallied cavalry, intending to make what could have been a decisive charge against Cromwell's flank. At this crucial point, the Earl of Carnwath, who was riding next to him, seized his bridle and roughly pulled him away, creating panic and a general rout. Royalist casualties were 1000 killed and 5000 captured (many inflicted in the ruthless Parliamentarian pursuit), while the New Model's losses were no more than 400 killed and wounded.

The battle was one of the most important of the war; the Royalist Oxford army was shattered and all its artillery and stores captured. In particular, the loss of so many veteran infantry officers crippled the King's efforts to raise new field armies.

■ Langport, 10 July 1645

Following his victory at Naseby, Sir Thomas Fairfax marched into the West Country with 20,000 men and rapidly defeated Lord Goring's force of 7000, which was the last Royalist field army in the region.

■ Rowton Heath, 24 September 1645

After the loss of Bristol on 11 September, Chester was the only port held by the Royalists. The king attempted to raise the siege, but his 2500 cavalry were defeated by Sydnam Poyntz' 3500 Parliamentarian cavalry.

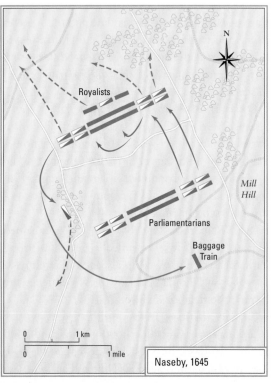

Naseby, 1645

■ **TORRINGTON, 16 FEBRUARY 1646**

Lord Hopton's 5000-strong Royalist garrison was attacked by Sir Thomas Fairfax with 10,000 men of the New Model Army. The initial Parliamentarian assault was held, but the town was finally taken after fierce street fighting.

■ **STOW-ON-THE-WOLD, 21 MARCH 1646**

Sir Jacob Astley commanded a scratch Royalist army of 3000 men drawn from various scattered garrisons, which was attempting to join the king in Oxford, but was intercepted and defeated by Sir William Bereton's forces.

■ **OXFORD III, 3 MAY–24 JUNE 1646**

The king escaped from Oxford in disguise on 27 April as the New Model Army under Sir Thomas Fairfax closed in. The city held out until generous terms for surrender were agreed in late June.

The Civil War in Scotland

■ **TIPPERMUIR, 1 SEPTEMBER, 1644**

This was Montrose's first success for the Royalists in Scotland. Commanding only 3000 infantry, most of them poorly armed, he defeated a force of 7000 men under Lord Elcho 5km west of Perth.

■ **ABERDEEN, 13 SEPTEMBER 1644**

Montrose led a Royalist force of 1500 infantry and 44 cavalry in a devastating attack on Lord Burleigh's Covenanter army of 2500 infantry and 500 cavalry. The Covenanters were routed, suffering at least 160 casualties.

■ **CARLISLE, OCTOBER 1644–25 JUNE 1645**

After storming Newcastle in October 1644, the Earl of Leven's Scottish army besieged Carlisle. The Royalist garrison only surrendered after all hopes of raising the siege were dashed by the Parliamentarian victory at Naseby.

■ **INVERLOCHY, 2 FEBRUARY 1645**

Pursued by through the Scottish Highlands by the Marquess of Argyll with a Covenanter army of 3000 men, Montrose took his force of only 1500 men on a long flank march across exceptionally difficult terrain to make a surprise attack. The plan worked perfectly and the Royalists deployed on the slopes of Ben Nevis.

The Covenanters formed up in front of Inverlochy castle, which was garrisoned by 200 musketeers. The Campbells of Argyll held the centre with the lowland militias on each flank. Montrose posted his 600 Highlanders in the centre with the Irish on their flanks.

The Royalists attacked at dawn; the Irish charged and routed the Lowlanders, while the Highlanders closed with the Campbells, who also broke. The small garrison of Inverlochy castle surrendered without a fight. Over 1500 Covenanters were killed, while Montrose only lost eight men.

■ **AULDEARN, 9 MAY 1645**

A 1500-strong Royalist Irish and Scottish forces under the Earl of Montrose defeated Sir John Urry's 3900 Sottish Covenanters at Auldearn near Nairn. Montrose' losses were insignificant, but his forces inflicted 1500 casualties on the Covenanters.

■ **ALFORD, 2 JULY 1645**

William Baillie's Covenanter army of 2000 infantry and 600 cavalry was attacked by Montrose with 2000 infantry and 300 cavalry as it crossed the River Don at Alford. The Covenanters were routed, losing 1500 men.

■ **KILSYTH, 15 AUGUST 1645**

A new Covenanter army of 7000 infantry and 800 cavalry commanded by William Baillie was attacked and routed by Montrose's 3000 infantry and 500 cavalry, while attempting a flank march around the Royalist position.

■ **PHILIPHAUGH, 13 SEPTEMBER 1645**

Many of Montrose's Highlanders left him after Kilsyth to pursue their clan feuds, while his cavalry was weakened by the loss of Lord Aboyne's Gordon troopers who resented the appointment of the Earl of Crawford as his LGen of Horse. His forces were reduced to 100 cavalry and 600 musketeers when he was surprised and defeated at Philiphaugh by Sir David Leslie's Covenanter army of 6000 cavalry and 1000 infantry.

■ **ANNAN MOOR, 21 OCTOBER 1645**

Lord Digby and Sir Marmaduke Langdale invaded Scotland with the Royalist Northern Horse to join forces with Montrose, but were routed by a Covenanter cavalry force under Col Sir John Browne at Annan Moor in Dumfriesshire.

■ **RHUNAHAORINE MOSS, 24 MAY 1647**

The remnants of the Scottish Royalist forces under Alasdair Mac Colla were defeated by a Covenanter army commanded by Sir David Leslie. The Covenanters then destroyed Largie castle at Rhunahaorine.

■ **MAUCHLINE MUIR, 12 JUNE 1648**

This action involved two rival Covenanter factions; the Engagers, who supported a secret treaty with Charles I to impose Presbyterianism on England and the Kirk Party who opposed the treaty. The Engagers were victorious.

■ **STIRLING, 12 SEPTEMBER 1648**

The Marquess of Argyll commanding a Kirk Party force totalling 1000 men occupied Stirling on 12 September, although the castle's Royalist garrison refused to surrender. An Engager army under the Earl of Lanark was in the vicinity and its advance guard commanded by Sir George Munro successfully stormed the city in a surprise attack. Lanark's casualties were minimal, while Argyll's force lost 200 dead and 400 prisoners.

■ **INVERCARRON (CARBISDALE), 27 APRIL 1650**

Montrose returned to Scotland in March 1650, but his 1200 infantry and 40 cavalry were surprised and destroyed at Invercarron by a Covenanter force of 230 cavalry, 40 musketeers and 400 Highlanders under LCol Strachan.

■ **DUNBAR, 3 SEPTEMBER 1650**

Sir David Leslie's Covenanter/Royalist army of 2500 cavalry and 9500 infantry were shattered by Oliver Cromwell's 3500 cavalry and 7500 infantry. English casualties were barely 100, while the Scots lost 800 dead and 6000 captured.

■ **INVERKEITHING, 20 JULY 1651**

Sir John Brown's Covenanter/Royalist army of 4500 men was defeated by an English force of similar size under Gen Lambert. The Scots lost 800 dead and 1400 captured, while English casualties were less than 200.

■ **DALNASPIDAL, 19 JULY 1654**

MGen Morgan's Parliamentarians surprised a

force of Royalist rebels commanded by the Earl of Middleton. The Royalist cavalry fled, followed by their infantry. This defeat marked the end of the Royalist uprising in Scotland.

Chinese Qing Dynasty Wars 1644–83

■ **GUALAR, 1639**

In December 1639, the Manchu Emperor Hung Taiji sent a large force to subdue the tribes of the Amur basin, which trapped and defeated a war band of 500 Solon-Daurs, led by the Solon-Evenk leader Bombogor.

■ **YASKA, 1640**

The Manchu Emperor Hung Taiji sent a further large force in an attempt to complete the conquest of the peoples of the Amur basin, which attacked and defeated the Solon, Daur and Oroqen tribes.

■ **BEIJING, FEBRUARY–APRIL 1644**

Li Zicheng's huge rebel army of possibly 1,300,000 men forced the surrender of Beijing's 250,000-strong Ming garrison. The Chongzhen Emperor (the last Emperor of the Ming Dynasty) committed suicide and 40,000 Ming officials were killed.

■ **YANGZHOU, MAY 1645**

After the fall of Beijing to the Manchus, Yangzhou remained loyal to the Ming regime of the Hongguang Emperor. Prince Dodo's Manchu army took the city after a short siege and massacred 800,000 inhabitants.

■ **ACHANSK, 24 MARCH 1652**

In September 1651, Cossacks led by Yerofey Khabarov built a fortified camp at Achansk on the banks of the River Amur. The following year, Fort Achansk was attacked by Manchu forces, but the Cossacks stood their ground in a day-long battle and even managed to capture the attackers' supply train. Once the ice on the Amur thawed in the spring of 1652, Khabarov's men destroyed their fort and sailed away.

■ **KOMAR, 13 MARCH–3 APRIL 1655**

A Manchu army of 10,000 men besieged the

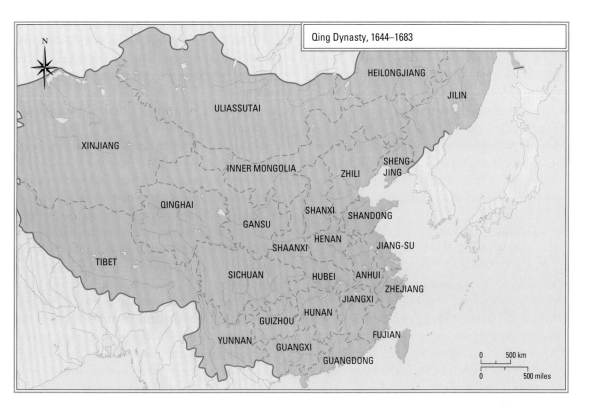

Qing Dynasty, 1644–1683

fortress of Komar, which was defended by a 500-strong Cossack garrison commanded by Onufriy Stepanov. The defenders repelled several assaults, forcing the much bigger Manchu army to abandon the siege.

■ HUTONG (SUNGARI), 1658
Byeon Geup's Manchu army of 3000 men, supported by a detachment of 150 Joseon (Korean) musketeers defeated a 500-strong Russian force at Hutong (on the lower reaches of the River Sungari, near present-day Yilan).

■ TAIWAN, 1661–62
The Ming commander Koxinga led a Chinese force of 25,000 men in the seizure of Taiwan, which was held by a Dutch East India Company garrison of 1200 men under Frederick Coyett.

■ WARS OF THE THREE FEUDATORIES, 1673
Three former Ming generals, Wu Sangui, Geng Jingzhong and Shang Kexi, were rewarded for their services in establishing the Manchu Dynasty with vast territories in southern and western

China. Wu rebelled against the Manchu Dynasty in December 1673 and Geng soon followed suit. However, Shang Kexi remained loyal to the Manchus and was imprisoned by his son, who joined the rebellion.

The rebels failed to mount any cooperative military effort, allowing the Manchu generals to defeat them individually. The revolt began to collapse with the surrenders of Geng in 1676 and Shang's son in 1677. In March 1678, Wu declared himself first emperor of the Great Zhou Dynasty, but died in October that year. His grandson Wu Shifan assumed command of the Zhou and continued the fight, but his armies were defeated in December 1681 and he committed suicide.

■ PENGHU (PESCADORES), 16–17 JULY 1683
The Manchu emperor Kangxi sent Adm Shi Lang with 100,000 men and 600 warships to invade the Kingdom of Tungning (Taiwan). Shi targeted the Penghu Islands (Pescadores), the main base of the Taiwanese fleet under Liu Guoxuan. Superior

Manchu firepower destroyed the Taiwanese fleet and Shi's 60,000-strong landing force defeated the 20,000 defending troops. Liu Guoxuan surrendered and the defeat prompted the surrender of Zheng Keshuang, the King of Tungning.

■ ULAN BUTUNG, 3 SEPTEMBER 1690

When Galdan Boshugtu Khan of the Zunghar Mongols threatened to establish an alliance with the Russians on China's northern border, the Kangxi Emperor led a large Manchu army north which defeated Galdan at Ulan Butong.

Indian and South-East Asian Wars 1646–1740

■ CAMPAIGNS OF SHIVAJI MAHARAJ, 1646–80

Shivaji was a Maratha aristocrat of the Bhosle clan who fought for independence from the Muslim Sultanate of Bijapur. He created an independent Maratha kingdom and successfully fought against the Mughals, frequently raiding their territories, notably the port of Surat in 1664 and 1670. He was crowned as Chhatrapati ('sovereign') of the Maratha Empire in 1674 and had conquered much of the Deccan by his death in 1680.

■ SIAMESE REBELLION, 1688

A revolt in the Kingdom of Ayutthaya (modern Thailand) overthrew King Narai. One of his commanders, Gen Phetracha, killed the king's Christian heir and expelled most foreigners, largely isolating the country until the nineteenth century.

■ BANGKOK, JUNE–NOVEMBER 1688

Following a coup d'état that ousted the pro-Western King Narai, 40,000 Siamese troops besieged Gen Desfarges' garrison of 200 French troops in Bangkok. The French finally negotiated a settlement under which they evacuated the country.

■ BHANGANI, 18 SEPTEMBER 1688

Sikh Guru Gobind Singh was attacked by the combined forces of the Rajas of the Sivalik Hills. The greatly outnumbered Guru's army won a

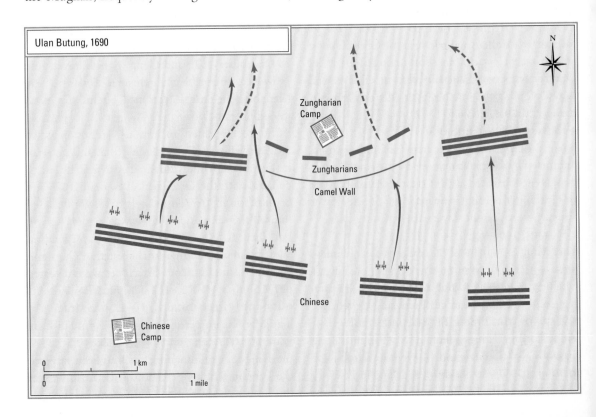

Ulan Butung, 1690

Zungharian Camp

Zungharians

Camel Wall

Chinese

Chinese Camp

0   1 km

0   1 mile

decisive victory near Bhangani, east of Paonta on the Jumna.

▪ Jajau (Agra), 12 June 1707

The Emperor Aurangzeb's death in March 1707 sparked off a civil war as Bahādur Shah, governor of Kabul, and his brother, Azam Shah, fought for the Mughal throne. Their armies, each of 100,000 men, clashed at Jajau near Agra. Bahādur Shah won a decisive victory largely due to his superior artillery and the desertion of part of the enemy army. Azam Shah and his son, Bīdār Bakht, were killed in action.

▪ Palkhed, 28 February 1728

A highly mobile 25,000-strong Maratha army commanded by Peshwa Baji Rao I out-manoeuvred and decisively defeated the Nizam of Hyderabad's slow-moving army of 80,000 men at the village of Palkhed, near the town of Vaijapur.

▪ Ta Chia-Hsi Revolt, 1731–32

Resentment at Manchu demands for forced labour provoked a rebellion by the Taiwanese Taokas tribe who were joined by other aboriginal tribes. The revolt was suppressed by Green Standard troops, supported by the An-li tribe.

African Colonial Wars 1647

▪ Kombi, 29 October 1647

A 400-strong Dutch force invaded the Portuguese colony of Angola in support of 8000 Ndongo warriors. The allies defeated a detachment of 600 Portuguese troops and 30,000 native auxiliaries near Masangano, inflicting 3000 casualties.

Second English Civil War 1648–51

▪ St Fagans, 8 May 1648

MGen Laugharne's Royalist army of 7500 infantry and 500 cavalry was badly defeated when it attacked a detachment of the New Model Army under Col Thomas Horton comprising 900 cavalry, 800 dragoons and 1000 infantry.

▪ Preston, 17–19 August 1648

The Duke of Hamilton's Covenanter/Royalist army of 16,000 infantry and 3600 cavalry was attempting to join forces with English Royalists when it was caught on the march by Oliver Cromwell with 6000 infantry and 3000 cavalry of the New Model Army. Hamilton's men were badly strung out and Cromwell was able to crush isolated detachments in turn. On 17 August, he attacked Sir Marmaduke Langdale, who had deployed 3000 infantry and 500 cavalry on Ribbleton Moor guarding the Royalist left flank. Hamilton failed to support Langdale's men who were defeated by sheer weight of numbers, while the main body of the Royalist army continued its southwards march. Cromwell then pursued Hamilton's rapidly disintegrating force. Most of its infantry were captured at Winwick, near Warrington, on 19 August, while Hamilton with 3000 cavalry was forced to surrender at Uttoxeter on 25 August.

▪ Rathmines, 2 August 1649

The Earl of Ormonde's army of 11,000 Irish Confederate Catholics and English Royalists attempted to take Dublin, but was defeated with the loss of 5000 men when LGen Jones' Parliamentarian garrison sortied from the city.

▪ Drogheda, 11 September 1649

Oliver Cromwell landed at Dublin on 15 August and moved swiftly to take the other ports on Ireland's east coast to secure his communications with England. The first to fall was Drogheda, which was held by a garrison of 3000 English Royalist and Irish Confederate troops, commanded by Sir Arthur Aston. After Cromwell's men stormed the town, the majority of the garrison and its Catholic priests were massacred on his orders.

▪ Wexford, 2–11 October 1649

After taking Drogheda, Cromwell besieged Wexford with a 6000-strong army. The town was held by an Irish Confederate force of 4800 men, but was successfully stormed and over 2000 killed.

▪ Worcester, 3 September 1651

Charles II with a largely Scottish force of 8000 infantry and 4000 cavalry was attacked by Oliver Cromwell commanding 18,000 infantry and 9000

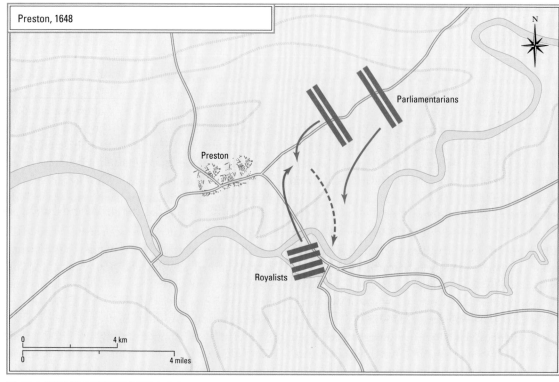

Preston, 1648

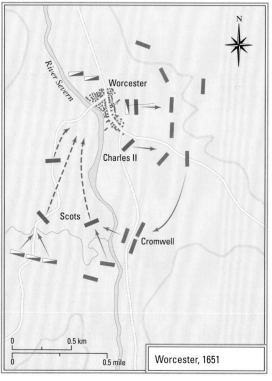

Worcester, 1651

cavalry. The Royalists' infantry contained the first attempt by the New Model Army to force a crossing of the Severn and its tributary, the Teme. Charles then launched two counter-attacks that came close to breaking Cromwell's right flank before it was reinforced. (These sorties might well have succeeded if they had been supported by the Royalist cavalry stationed to the north of Worcester.) The Parliamentarian reinforcements forced the Royalists back into the city and their retreat turned into a rout when Cromwell's men took Fort Royal (a redoubt near the city walls) and turned its guns on them. Charles just managed to escape, but Royalist losses were heavy (3000 dead and 7000 captured). Parliamentarian casualties were barely 300.

Revolt in Poland 1651

■ **KOSTKA-NAPIERSKI UPRISING, 1651**
Aleksander Kostka Napierski led a peasant uprising

in the Tatra Mountains that gained only limited support. The rebels seized Czorsztyn castle, but it was retaken by the Bishop of Kraków's forces and the revolt was crushed.

Anglo-Dutch Wars 1652–74

■ GOODWIN SANDS, 29 MAY 1652
The Commonwealth claimed sovereignty of the North Sea and Channel and therefore it required foreign vessels sailing in these waters to dip their flags to English warships as a mark of respect. This highly jingoistic policy did little but increase existing Anglo-Dutch tension over trade in these waters, leading to an action between a Dutch convoy escorted by 40 warships under LAdm Maarten Tromp and General-at-Sea Robert Blake's English fleet of 25 ships. Two Dutch vessels were captured.

■ PLYMOUTH, 26 AUGUST 1652
Cdre Michiel de Ruyter's Dutch fleet of 31 warships

was protecting a convoy of 60 merchantmen bound for the Mediterranean when it was intercepted by the 'Western Guard', an English squadron of 47 assorted vessels under General-at-Sea George Ayscue. The over-confident Ayscue concentrated his efforts on an unsuccessful attempt to capture the valuable convoy and was beaten off with almost 700 casualties and several ships damaged. Dutch casualties totalled 110.

■ ELBA, 28 AUGUST 1652
A Dutch squadron of 10 vessels commanded by Jan van Galen attacked and defeated four English warships under Capt Richard Badiley. The Dutch captured the 36-gun 'Phoenix', but sustained heavy casualties, including three of the ships' captains.

■ KENTISH KNOCK, 8 OCTOBER 1652
General-at-Sea Robert Blake's fleet of 68 warships attacked and defeated a 64-strong Dutch fleet commanded by VAdm Witt Corneliszoon de With in the North Sea. Two Dutch vessels were captured and a third blew up.

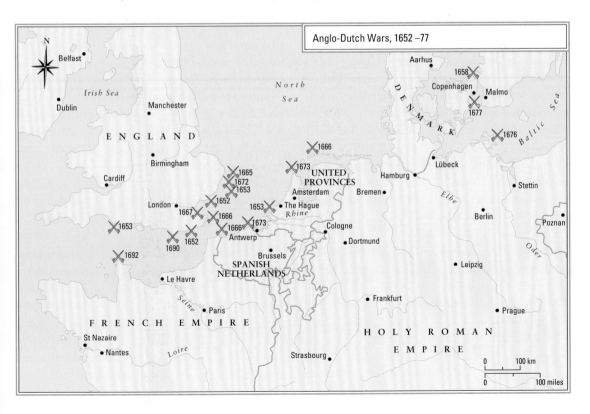

■ **DUNGENESS, 10 DECEMBER 1652**

General-at-Sea Robert Blake's fleet of 42 ships was attacked and defeated by a Dutch fleet of 88 warships under Lt Adm Maarten Tromp. Blake lost five ships with many more damaged. One Dutch vessel was destroyed.

■ **PORTLAND, 28 FEBRUARY–2 MARCH 1653**

LAdm Maarten Tromp's 75 warships escorting a convoy of 150 merchantmen were defeated by General-at-Sea Robert Blake's 80 vessels. The Dutch lost 11 warships and 40 merchantmen, while one of Blake's ships was captured.

■ **LEGHORN, 14 MARCH 1653**

Capt Henry Appleton's squadron of six ships was blockaded in Leghorn by a Dutch fleet of 16 ships under Cdre Johan van Galen. A second English squadron of eight vessels commanded by Capt Richard Badiley was based at Elba. The English commanders attempted to combine their forces, but Appleton sailed too soon and was intercepted by the Dutch, losing all but one of his ships before Badiley could join him.

■ **GABBARD SHOAL, 12–13 JUNE 1653**

LAdm Maarten Tromp's 98-strong Dutch fleet was defeated by an English fleet of 100 ships under Generals-at-Sea George Monck and Richard Deane near the Gabbard shoal off the Suffolk coast. Dutch losses totalled 17 ships.

■ **TEXEL (SCHEVENINGEN), 10 AUGUST 1653**

A total of 127 Dutch ships under LAdm Maarten Tromp and VAdm Witt de With attacked General-at-Sea George Monck's 120-strong fleet. Two English vessels were sunk, but the Dutch were defeated, losing 20 ships.

■ **LOWESTOFT, 13 JUNE 1665**

LAdm Jacob van Wassenaer Obdam's fleet of 103 ships was defeated by a slightly larger English fleet under James, Duke of York off Lowestoft. The Dutch lost 17 ships and only captured one English vessel.

■ **VÅGEN (BERGEN), 2 AUGUST 1665**

RAdm Sir Thomas Teddiman's 30 warships attacked a Dutch convoy of 50 armed merchantmen in the neutral Norwegian harbour of Vågen

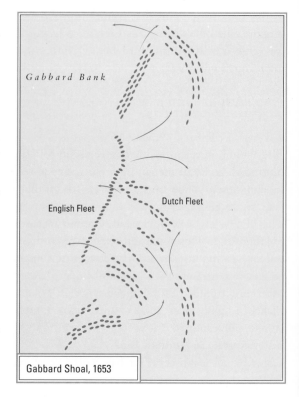

Gabbard Bank

English Fleet

Dutch Fleet

Gabbard Shoal, 1653

(Bergen). The attack was beaten off with the loss of almost 500 men.

■ **FOUR DAYS' BATTLE, 11–14 JUNE 1666**

In early 1666, France and Denmark declared war on England in support of the Dutch. The threat from three enemies greatly complicated English naval strategy and proved to be a decisive factor in the Four Days' Battle.

By the early summer of 1666, the Dutch fleet under LAdm Michiel de Ruyter had 84 ships and was opposed by the 79-strong English fleet commanded by Prince Rupert and George Monck, 1st Duke of Albemarle. Prince Rupert was dispatched with a squadron of 23 ships to counter a (non-existent) French fleet in the western Channel, leaving Monck badly outnumbered until he returned on the evening of the third day of the battle. In four days of fierce fighting, the English lost 10 ships, 3000 killed and wounded plus 1800 prisoners. De Ruyter lost four ships, together with 2800 killed and wounded.

■ **St. James' Day Battle, 4 August 1666**

LAdm Michiel de Ruyter's 89-strong fleet was defeated (with the loss of two ships and 1200 casualties) by an English fleet of similar size under Prince Rupert and George Monck, 1st Duke of Albemarle.

■ **Holmes's Bonfire, 19–20 August 1666**

RAdm Robert Holmes' squadron of eight warships carried out a highly destructive raid on the Vlie estuary. Two Dutch warships and 140 merchantmen were burnt, together with naval stores in the town of West-Terschelling.

■ **Medway, 9–14 June 1667**

A Dutch fleet of 60 ships under the nominal command of LAdm Michiel de Ruyter, bombarded and captured the town of Sheerness. Guided by two renegade English pilots, it then sailed up the Thames and Medway to Gravesend and Chatham, where much of the Royal Navy was laid up due to lack of funding. Dutch fireships destroyed three capital ships (HMS *Loyal London*, HMS *Royal James*

and HMS *Royal Oak*) and 10 lesser naval vessels, while the 42-gun HMS *Unity* and the 80-gun fleet flagship HMS *Royal Charles* were captured. (Approximately 30 other English warships were scuttled to avoid capture.) The Dutch fleet then briefly blockaded London before withdrawing with their prizes.

The raid led to a quick end to the Second Anglo-Dutch War and a favourable peace for the Dutch. It was the worst defeat in the Royal Navy's history.

■ **Sole Bay (Southwold Bay), 7 June 1672**

A Dutch fleet of 93 warships commanded by LAdm Michiel de Ruyter attacked a 95-strong Anglo-French fleet under James Duke of York and Adm Jean d'Estrées.

As the fleets manoeuvred for position, the 30 French warships broke away to the south, followed by a Dutch squadron of perhaps 25 vessels, which fought an entirely separate inconclusive long-range action. De Ruyter, with almost 70 ships, now had a superiority of two to

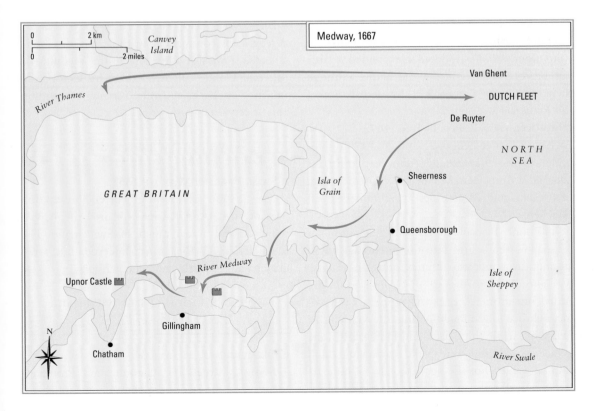

one over the Duke of York's division in the first part of the battle and the fighting was intense. The Duke of York's flagship, HMS *Prince*, was attacked by several vessels, including fireships and was so badly damaged that the duke was forced to transfer his flag to HMS *St. Michael*. When the latter also succumbed to severe damage, he and his staff were rowed through the thick of the action to HMS *London*. The main Dutch fleet and the two British squadrons fought in line-of-battle, a distinct change from the melee battles of the First Anglo-Dutch War.

The 100-gun HMS *Royal James* fought a fierce action with the much smaller *Groot Hollandia*, two fireships and the 82-gun *Dolphijn*. Eventually a third fireship grappled with the *Royal James*, setting her on fire in the action.

The battle ended in stalemate. The Dutch lost the 48-gun *Stavoren* (captured) and the 60-gun *Jozua* (sunk), sustaining roughly 1600 casualties. The English lost HMS *Royal James*, while HMS *Royal Katherine* was captured, but was soon retaken after the Dutch prize crew drank themselves insensible on the ship's brandy. British casualties were around 2500. Both sides expended a large number of fireships during the battle, although their only major success was the destruction of the *Royal James*.

■ **SCHOONEVELD, 7 AND 14 JUNE 1673**
An Anglo-French fleet of 91 ships and 42 fireships under Prince Rupert and Adm Jean d'Estrées attacked LAdm-Gen Michiel de Ruyter's fleet of 64 ships and 25 fireships at Schooneveld off Walcheren.

On 7 June, Prince Rupert sent a squadron of 35 shallow-draft ships into the anchorage in an attempt to tempt the Dutch out. De Ruyter was already preparing to put to sea and the Allied squadron fell back. After eight hours of inconclusive long-range fighting, the French lost two ships, while the British and Dutch lost none in action, although one badly damaged Dutch ship sank at anchor the next day. On 14 June, de Ruyter launched a second attack on the Allied

fleet, which was also indecisive, with no ships lost on either side. Dutch casualties totalled 500 and the Allies lost a similar number of men during the fighting.

■ **TEXEL, 21 AUGUST 1673**
LAdm-Gen Michiel de Ruyter's powerful fleet of 75 ships and 30 fireships drove off an Anglo-French fleet of 92 ships and 30 fireships under Prince Rupert and Adm Jean d'Estrées. Neither side lost any ships.

Revolt in Taiwan 1652

■ **GUO HUAIYI REBELLION, 7–11 SEPT 1652**
Guo Huaiyi, a farmer and militia officer, led a peasant revolt against Dutch rule on Taiwan, but his 15,000 rebels were defeated by the superior firepower of the 1000-strong Dutch garrison commanded by Governor Nicolas Verburg.

Rebellion in France 1652

■ **BLÉNEAU, 7 APRIL 1652**
A rebel army commanded by the Prince de Condé defeated a royalist force under the Vicomte de Turenne. Condé failed to exploit his victory and retreated to Paris, allowing Turenne to regroup and besiege Étampes.

Revolt in Switzerland 1653

■ **SWISS PEASANT WAR OF 1653**
A devaluation of Bernese currency caused a peasants' tax revolt led by Niklaus Leuenberger, which spread across much of Switzerland. The rebels besieged Bern and Lucerne, but were crushed at the battle of Wohlenschwil.

Internal Conflict in Switzerland 1655–1712

■ **VILLMERGEN I, 24 JANUARY 1656**
Tensions between the Catholic and Protestant Swiss cantons ran high throughout much of

the seventeenth century. In 1655, these tensions escalated into open warfare in which the Catholics defeated a Protestant Bernese army at Villmergen.

■ **VILLMERGEN II, 1712**

A dispute between Toggenburg's Protestants and St Gallen monastery over the construction of a road linking the central cantons with southern Germany flared up into civil war. Zurich and Bern supported the Toggenburgers and defeated the Catholics.

Northern Wars 1656–77

■ **KUSHLIKI, 4 NOVEMBER 1661**

A 14,000-strong Lithuanian army under pułkownik Kazimierz Żeromski beat off repeated attacks by Prince Ivan Andreyevich Khovansky's Russian army. The Russians were surprised and defeated by a Polish relief force commanded by King John II Casimir.

■ **FEHRBELLIN, 18 JUNE 1675**

A Swedish army of 12,000 men under Waldemar Wrangel invaded Brandenburg, but were surprised and defeated by a 15,000-strong Brandenburg army commanded by the Elector Frederick William and FM Georg von Derfflinger. Wrangel was trapped by a destroyed bridge over the River Rhin at the town of Fehrbellin and failed to secure the surrounding heights on which Derfflinger deployed his artillery. These guns badly disrupted the Swedish right flank and Frederick William exploited the damage by attacking this sector, breaking the Swedish cavalry and exposing their infantry to a flank attack led by Prince Frederick II of Hesse-Homburg. The Swedes just managed to hold until the bridge at Fehrbellin was repaired and Wrangel got much of his army across. Swedish casualties in the battle itself were only 600 (although many more were lost in the retreat), while Frederick William lost 500 men.

■ **BORNHOLM (JASMUND), 25–26 MAY 1676**

A Swedish fleet of 59 vessels commanded by Adm Lorentz Creutz fought an indecisive action against a combined Danish and Dutch fleet of 35 warships under Adm Niels Juel and RAdm Philips van Almonde.

■ **ÖLAND, 1 JUNE 1676**

A Dutch and Danish fleet commanded by Adms Cornelis Tromp and Niels Juel defeated a Swedish fleet of 57 vessels under Adm Lorentz Creutz. Five Swedish ships were sunk and six were captured.

■ **HALMSTAD, 17 AUGUST 1676**

A 6000-strong Swedish army commanded by Charles XI defeated MGen Jakob Duncan's Danish force of 4000 men near Halmstad in southern Sweden. The Swedes inflicted 3500 casualties for the loss of only 180 men.

■ **LUND, 4 DECEMBER 1676**

An 8000-strong Swedish army under Charles XI defeated Christian V's Danish army of 11,000 men, which was supported by a detachment of 1300 Dutch marines. The Swedes inflicted 8000 casualties for the loss of 2500 men.

■ **MØN, 31 MAY 1677**

Adm Erik Carlsson Sjöblad's Swedish fleet of 12 warships was defeated by a Danish fleet of 17 vessels under Adm Niels Juel. One Swedish ship was burned after running aground and seven more were captured.

■ **MALMÖ, 10–26 JUNE 1677**

A Danish army of 14,000 men commanded by Christian V besieged Malmö, which was defended by a 2000-strong Swedish garrison under Fabian von Fersen. Under cover of a bombardment by 28 siege guns and 27 mortars, the Danish engineers dug trenches towards the castle and the city's southern and eastern gates (Söderport and Österport). During the night of 25/26 June, a feint attack was made against the castle to divert attention from the main assaults on the Söderport and Österport. The attackers succeeded in storming the defences near the Österport, but the Danish guns had to cease fire to avoid hitting the assault troops who then came under devastating close-range fire from the Swedish artillery. The few Danes who broke in were captured or killed, bringing their total losses to at least 3000 men and the siege was eventually abandoned.

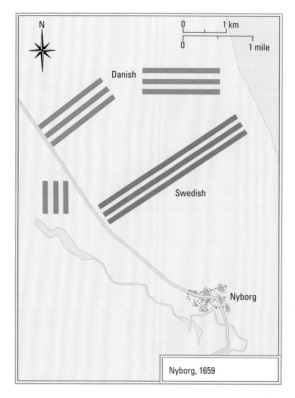

Nyborg, 1659

3000 men near Uddevalla in southern Sweden. De la Gardie ordered his cavalry to cover the Swedish infantry's retreat, but it fled when charged by the Danish cavalry. De la Gardie himself was almost captured and the rest of his force was routed with the loss of 500 men.

■ **JEMTLAND, 1677**

A 1700-strong Swedish force under Carl Larsson Sparre, governor-general of Västernorrland attempted to launch an offensive into Norway (then part of Denmark), but was defeated by a Norwegian attack that overran the border province of Jemtland.

Dano-Swedish War 1658–60

■ **COPENHAGEN, 1658–59**

Charles X's Swedish army of 10,000 men besieged Copenhagen in 1658, although the force was defended by an 11,000-strong Danish garrison under Frederick III. The outer defences were taken and an attempt was made to starve the city into surrender.

■ **SOUND, 8 NOVEMBER 1658**

Alarmed by the possibility of Sweden gaining control of the Baltic, the Dutch sent a fleet of 45 warships under Adm Jacob van Wassenaer Obdam to aid the Danes who seemed to be on the point of being routed by the aggressive Charles X of Sweden. Obdam decisively defeated the Swedish fleet of 45 vessels commanded by Carl Gustaf Wrangel, sinking four ships for the loss of two of his own.

■ **COPENHAGEN, 11 FEBRUARY 1659**

The battle of the Sound re-opened supply lines to Copenhagen and ended the chance of starving the city into surrender. Charles X ordered an unsuccessful assault on the night of 11/12 February and then raised the siege.

■ **FUNEN, MAY–JUNE 1659**

Swedish troops retreating from Copenhagen re-formed on the Danish island of Funen. An anti-Swedish alliance of Denmark, Brandenburg, Poland and Austria had now formed and allied

■ **KØGE BAY, 1–2 JULY 1677**

A Danish fleet of 34 ships commanded by Adm Niels Juel defeated a Swedish fleet of 45 vessels under Adm Henrik Horn in Køge Bay, south of Copenhagen. The Swedes lost a total of eight ships.

■ **LANDSKRONA, 14 JULY 1677**

Charles XI's Swedish army of 9000 men supported by 4000 peasants defeated a 12,000-strong Danish army commanded by Christian V near Landskrona in southern Sweden. The Swedes inflicted 2500 casualties for the loss of 650 men.

■ **MARSTRAND, 6–23 JULY 1677**

A Danish force of at least 1600 men commanded by Ulrik Frederik Gyldenløve besieged and took the port of Marstrand in southern Sweden, which was defended by a 600-strong Swedish garrison under Anders Sinclair.

■ **UDDEVALLA, 28 AUGUST 1677**

A 5600-strong Danish army commanded by Ulrik Frederik Gyldenløve attacked Count Magnus Gabriel De la Gardie's ill-trained Swedish force of forces made two unsuccessful attempts to retake Funen in May/June 1659.

■ **NYBORG, 24 NOVEMBER 1659**

Adm de Ruyter's Dutch fleet landed a 9000-strong allied army on Funen, which attacked a Swedish force of 5500 men near Nyborg. The Swedes held a strong defensive position with their flanks protected by a small lake on the left and a forest on the right. Initially their firepower and cavalry charges beat off allied attacks, but they finally surrendered after inflicting 1900 casualties.

Scottish-Covenanter Wars 1666–79

■ **RUILLON GREEN, 28 NOVEMBER 1666**

Scottish resentment at the imposition of episcopalianism provoked an uprising led by Col James Wallace of Auchens whose 900 rebels were routed by Gen Tam Dalyell's 3000 government troops at Rullion Green in the Pentland Hills.

■ **DRUMCLOG, 1 JUNE 1679**

A force of 1500 rebel Covenanters commanded by William Cleland was attacked by 150 dragoons under John Graham of Claverhouse. The Covenanters deployed behind a ditch and marshy ground, which forced the dragoons to dismount and advance on foot to within pistol shot. Claverhouse's men seemed to be gaining the upper hand in initial skirmishing when the rebels suddenly charged and the dragoons fled with the loss of 40 men.

■ **BOTHWELL BRIDGE, 22 JUNE 1679**

An ill-disciplined force of 6000 rebel Covenanters, under the nominal command of Robert Hamilton of Preston, were routed by the Duke of Monmouth's 5000 government troops. At least 600 rebels were killed and 1200 captured.

Mughal Empire 1671

■ **SARAIGHAT, 1671**

A Mughal army of at least 60,000 men invaded the Kingdom of Ahom (Assam), but after initial successes was decisively defeated on the Brahmaputra river by an Assamese army commanded by Lachit Borphukan.

The Franco Dutch War 1672–79

■ **MAASTRICT, 6–30 JUNE 1673**

French King Louis XIV with 45,000 troops and 58 cannon besieged a Dutch and Spanish force of 6000 under Fariaux in the fortress city of Maastrict in the Netherlands. This was the first siege conducted by Louis' fortification expert Vauban and his system of parallel trenches approaching the city proved highly effective. The city was forced to surrender after less than a month of siege.

■ **SINSHEIM, 16 JUNE 1674**

An Imperialist army of 9000 men under Count Aeneas de Caprara was defeated at Sinsheim near Heidelberg by the Vicomte de Turenne's 7500-strong French army. The French inflicted 2500 casualties for the loss of 1100 men.

■ **SENEFFE, 11 AUGUST 1674**

A 62,000-strong Dutch, Spanish and Imperialist army under William III of Orange fought an inconclusive action against the Prince de Condé's 45,000-strong French army. Condé lost 8000 men, but inflicted 11,000 casualties on the allied army.

■ **ENTZHEIM, 4 OCTOBER 1674**

The Vicomte de Turenne advanced along the Rhine after his victory at Sinsheim in June and captured Strasbourg before winning a narrow but costly victory at Entzheim against Prince Alexandre de Bournonville's Imperialist army.

■ **TURCKHEIM, 5 JANUARY 1675**

A combined Austrian and Brandenburg army of 50,000 men commanded by the Elector Frederick William invaded Alsace, but was forced to retreat after being surprised and decisively defeated by the Vicomte de Turenne's 30,000-strong French army.

■ **SASBACH, 27 JULY 1675**

The Vicomte de Turenne crossed the Rhine to prevent Prince Raimondo Montecuccoli's Imperialist army relieving Strasbourg. However, Turenne was killed by artillery fire at Sasbach and

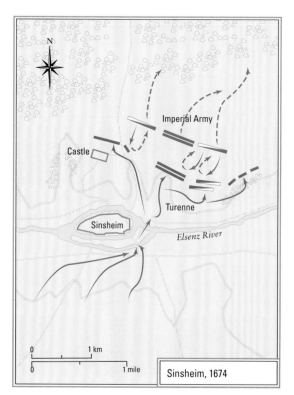

Sinsheim, 1674

Polish–Ottoman War 1672–76

■ **Kamianets-Podilskyi, 1672**
Köprülü Fazıl Ahmed Pasha's 150,000-strong
Ottoman army took the Polish city of Kamianets-
Podilskyi after a two-week siege. The city and the
province of Podolia were ceded to the Ottoman
Empire by the Treaty of Buchach.

■ **Khotyn, 11 November 1673**
A Polish army of 40,000 men commanded
by Grand Crown Hetman Jan Sobieski defeated
Hussein Pasha's 35,000-strong Ottoman
army near Khotyn on the River Dniester.
The victory led to Sobieski's election as King
of Poland.

■ **Żurawno, 25 September–14 October, 1676**
An Ottoman and Tatar army of 200,000 men under
Ibrahim Shetan fought a series of inconclusive
actions against King Jan III Sobieski of Poland
around his fortified camp at Zurawno (modern
Zhuravno), on the River Dniester.

Montecuccoli drove the demoralized French back
across the Rhine.

■ **Stromboli (Alicudi), 8 January 1676**
VAdm Abraham Duquesne's French fleet,
consisting of 20 ships of the line, fought an
indecisive action against Michiel de Ruyter's
Dutch and Spanish fleet of 19 ships of the line
and 12 smaller vessels.

■ **Augusta, 22 April 1676**
Despite the reputation of the Dutch commander,
Michiel de Ruyter's combined Dutch and Spanish
fleet of 27 ships of the line fought a further
indecisive action off Augusta, Sicily, against VAdm
Abraham Duquesne's French fleet of 29 ships of
the line.

■ **Mons (Saint-Denis), 14–15 August 1678**
A combined Dutch and Spanish army under William
III of Orange defeated Marshal Luxembourg's
French army at Saint-Denis. Despite inflicting 4500
casualties for the loss of 2500 men, Luxembourg
abandoned the siege of nearby Mons.

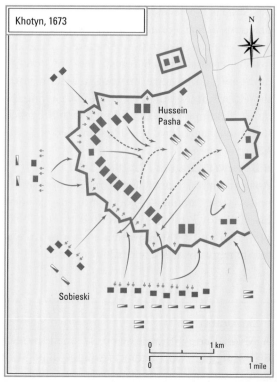

Khotyn, 1673

Lipka Rebellion

■ LIPKA REBELLION, 1672

Lipka Tatars had served in Polish armies since the fourteenth century, but were increasingly discriminated against during the seventeenth century. In 1672, resentment over arrears of pay provoked a mutiny by 3000 Lipka Tatar cavalry who defected to the Ottomans and served with them during the Polish-Ottoman War of 1672–76. However, these defectors gradually returned to Polish service following the election of their former commander as King Jan III Sobieski.

Russo-Turkish War 1676–81

■ CHYHYRYN, 1676

Petro Doroshenko, the pro-Ottoman former Hetman of the Ukrainian Cossacks, led 12,000 men. The force seized the city of Chyhyryn in central Ukraine, anticipating the support of an approaching Ottoman army. However, Russian forces besieged Chyhyryn and forced Doroshenko's surrender.

Streitsi Uprising 1682

■ MOSCOW, 1682

The Streltsi uprising was triggered by the death of Tsar Feodor III. The brothers of Tsarina Natalia Naryshkina had her 10-year-old son, Peter, proclaimed as Tsar. In retaliation, Sophia, daughter of the late Tsarina Maria Miloslavskaya, spread rumours that Peter's elder half-brother Ivan, had been strangled by the Naryshkins. The Streltsi's support allowed Sophia and her allies have Peter and Ivan proclaimed as joint tsars, with Sophia acting as regent.

Monmouth Rebellion 1685

■ SEDGEMOOR, 6 JULY 1685

The Duke of Monmouth's 3700 rebels made an unsuccessful night attack on a 2500-strong Royalist army under the Earl of Faversham. The Royalists lost 300 men, but they destroyed the rebel force, inflicting 1000 casualties.

War of the Glorious Revolution 1689–92

■ LONDONDERRY, 18 APRIL–28 JULY 1689

The exiled James II landed in Ireland in March 1689 with 6000 French troops and raised an Irish Jacobite army. This force besieged Londonderry until a naval relief force broke through from Lough Foyle.

■ KILLIECRANKIE, 27 JULY 1689

Viscount Dundee's Jacobite force of 2400 Highlanders attacked a government army of 3500 men under MGen Mackay. The Highlanders shattered their opponents, inflicting 2500 casualties for the loss of Dundee and 600 of his men.

■ NEWTOWNBUTLER, 31 JULY 1689

Viscount Mountcashel's 3000 ill-trained Irish Jacobites were routed by a government force of 2000 men commanded by Col William Wolseley. Government losses were low, but Jacobite casualties totalled 2000 killed and wounded, plus 400 prisoners.

■ DUNKELD, 21 AUGUST 1689

Col Cannon's 4,000 Jacobite Highlanders attacked the 1200-strong government garrison of Dunkeld under Col Cleland. The defenders barricaded themselves in the cathedral, successfully beating off a series of assaults and inflicting 300 casualties on the attackers.

■ CROMDALE, 30 APRIL 1690

MGen Buchan's 800 Jacobite Highlanders were attacked and routed by a detachment of the government garrison of Inverness commanded by Sir Thomas Livingstone. This defeat effectively ended the first Jacobite rebellion in Scotland.

■ BOYNE, 12 JULY 1690

The deposed James II, commanding a force of 19,000 Irish and 6000 French troops, was withdrawing towards Dublin when he was attacked by William III with an army of 36,000 men. William's forces included English, Scots, Irish Protestants, Dutch, Danes and French Hugenots, but most of the infantry were armed with modern flintlock muskets, in contrast to James' Irish troops who were mostly equipped with obsolescent matchlocks.

The battle itself was fought for control of a ford on the Boyne at Oldbridge, near Drogheda. William sent about a quarter of his men upstream to cross at Roughgrange, near Slane. James feared that he might be outflanked and sent half his troops, along with most of his artillery, to counter this move. However, neither side had realized that there was marshy ground and two deep, high banked ditches at Roughgrange that prevented the opposing forces in this sector from engaging and forced them to sit out the battle.

At the main ford at Oldbridge, William's infantry led by the Dutch Blue Guards forced their way across the river, using their superior firepower to slowly drive back the enemy, but were pinned

Boyne River, 1690

down when James' elite Irish cavalry counter-attacked. William was unable to resume the advance until his own cavalry managed to ford the river and fend off the Jacobite cavalry, which then retired in good order.

The outnumbered Irish units at Oldbridge finally broke and the bulk of the Jacobite army fled towards Dublin, covered by their remaining cavalry and the French infantry, which fought a series of effective rearguard actions. Overall casualties were surprisingly low; the death-toll in William's army was about 750 men compared to the Jacobite's 1500.

■ **AUGHRIM, 23 JULY 1691**

A government army of 20,000 men under the Dutch Gen Godert de Ginkell defeated the Marquis de St Ruth's 18,000-strong Franco-Irish Jacobite forces. Ginkell lost 3000 men, but inflicted 4000 casualties and took 3000 prisoners.

■ **LIMERICK, AUGUST–OCTOBER 1691**

The Jacobite forces that escaped from Aughrim reinforced the garrison of Limerick, bringing it to 14,000 men. However, their morale was low and the city surrendered after a two-month siege by Ginkell's 20,000-strong government army.

■ **GLENCOE, 13 FEBRUARY 1692**

In late January 1692, a 120-strong detachment of the Earl of Argyll's Regiment of Foot, under Capt Robert Campbell of Glenlyon, were billeted on the MacDonalds in Glencoe. This was the first stage of a plan to terrorize the Highland clans into submission to William III's government by a massacre of the MacDonalds. Early on 13 February, the troops turned on their hosts, killing 38 clansmen and their families.

Jacobite Rebellions 1715 and 1745–46

■ **SHERIFFMUIR, 13 NOVEMBER 1715**

The Earl of Mar raised a Jacobite army of 7000 men and was advancing towards Stirling when he was intercepted by 3500 Hanoverian troops, commanded by the Duke of Argyll. The right wing of both armies broke their opponents, but Mar failed to use his numerical superiority to crush the remaining Hanoverian forces and withdrew during the night. Argyll had suffered 700 casualties, while Jacobite losses were only 230 men.

■ PRESTON, 13–14 NOVEMBER 1715

Thomas Forster, MP for Northumberland, had raised a small Jacobite force in the county, which was reinforced by a detachment of 2000 Highlanders. Although there were initially few Hanoverian troops to oppose them, the Jacobite commanders were fiercely divided on the best course of action and wasted valuable time arguing before finally agreeing to march on to Liverpool and Manchester. This decision was resented by the Highlanders, many of whom deserted and, by the time the army arrived at Preston, its strength was no more than 3000 men. Forster's over-confidence led to him being trapped in the town by a Hanoverian force of 2500 men under the command of MGen Wills. The Jacobites beat off several attacks in fierce street fighting, inflicting 200 casualties for the loss of 42 men, but surrendered following the arrival of Hanoverian reinforcements.

■ PRESTONPANS, 21 SEPTEMBER 1745

Prince Charles Edward Stuart's 2500 men surprised and routed a 2200-strong Hanoverian army under Sir John Cope. The Jacobites inflicted 300 casualties and took 1500 prisoners for the loss of just over 100 men.

■ FALKIRK, 17 JANUARY 1746

Prince Charles Edward Stuart's 8000 men were besieging Stirling Castle, when they received warning that an 8000-strong Hanoverian army under LGen Hawley was advancing from Edinburgh to raise the siege. The Jacobite army quickly deployed to meet the expected attack, but Hawley showed no sign of advancing any further than Falkirk. After some debate, the Prince agreed to an attack on the Hanoverian camp, which achieved almost complete surprise as Hawley refused to believe reports of the Jacobites' advance. The Hanoverian forces hastily formed up and their three regiments of dragoons charged the Jacobite

infantry, but were shattered by close-range musketry and routed. The Highlanders counter-charged, sweeping away all but three Hanoverian infantry regiments, which were able to withdraw in good order. The Jacobites inflicted 350 casualties and took 300 prisoners for the loss of no more than 130 men.

■ CULLODEN, 16 APRIL 1746

The Duke of Cumberland advanced from Aberdeen towards the Jacobite base at Inverness with an army of 9000 men. Although his advisors advocated retreating to fight a guerilla campaign, Prince Charles Edward Stuart was determined to fight a decisive battle and deployed his 5400 men on Drummossie Moor, near the Culloden Park estate. The prince mishandled the action, allowing his men to stand inactive for over 30 minutes, while taking losses from the Hanoverian artillery bombardment and then abandoning any attempt at exercising command as the Highlanders made a series of uncoordinated charges, all of which were shattered by Hanoverian firepower. A charge by Cumberland's cavalry finally broke the dispirited Jacobites. The prince escaped, but 1500 of his men were killed and over 550 taken prisoner. In comparison, Hanoverian casualties were no more than 289 killed and wounded.

War of the Grand Alliance 1688–97

■ BANTRY BAY, 11 MAY 1689

A French fleet of 24 ships of the line, two frigates, some fireships and transports carrying weapons and supplies for James II's campaign in Ireland sailed from Brest commanded by the Marquis de Châteaurenault. The marquis managed to evade the Earl of Torrington's English fleet of 19 ships of the line off Kinsale and anchored in Bantry Bay to land 1500 reinforcements for James' army, together with money, arms and supplies. The English fleet appeared as the landing operation was under way and the Marquis set sail to protect the transports. A four-hour running battle ensued before the French broke off the action late in

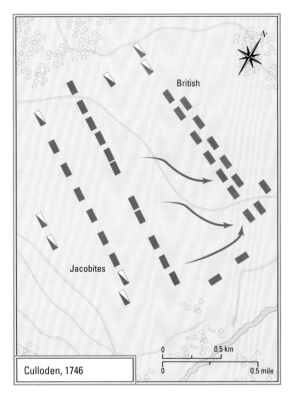

Culloden, 1746

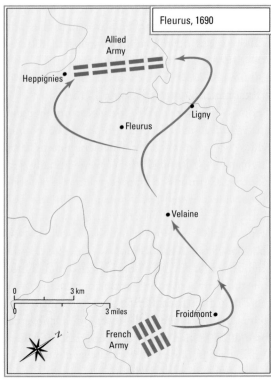

Fleurus, 1690

the afternoon and returned to the anchorage. Although the action was essentially a draw, the marquis was able to complete landing his troops and supplies without further interference from the badly battered English fleet.

■ WALCOURT, 25 AUGUST 1689

A French army of 24,000 men under the Duc d'Humières was defeated by the Prince of Waldeck's 35,000-strong army of Dutch, British, Imperialist and Spanish troops. Allied casualties totalled 300, while the French lost 2000 men.

■ FLEURUS, 1 JULY 1690

French Marshal Luxembourg with 35,000 troops attacked 38,000 Dutch, Spanish, and Habsburg troops under Prince Waldeck in the Spanish Netherlands (present-day Belgium). Waldeck's force was in defensive positions on high ground, with its left flank resting on the village of St Brice and the right flank on the village of Happignies.

Luxembourg crossed the Sambre and Orne rivers and decided to split his force in the face

of the enemy, in order to accomplish a double envelopment and attack both of Waldeck's flanks. The complicated manoeuvre was screened partly by terrain and partly by French cavalry. To pin Waldeck's forces in the centre, Luxembourg deployed 40 cannon with small infantry supports near the village of St Amant and another 30 cannon near the town of Fleurus.

Luxembourg gave command of the French left wing to Gournay, who successfully placed his troops on Waldeck's right flank. Meanwhile, Luxembourg, with the French right wing, reached positions on Waldeck's left flank. The French artillery in the centre opened fire at 10:00 with effect, simultaneously giving the signal for the attacks on both flanks. Gournay was killed while leading his cavalry in a charge, causing a temporary setback for the French on the left wing. Luxembourg's cavalry on the right, supported by infantry, attacked successfully and, when the French left renewed their attack, the envelopment was complete and Waldeck's troops were forced from their positions.

Waldeck reformed his troops further back, but the offensive momentum of the French army continued and further attacks routed Waldeck's forces. Waldeck's army retreated north-west towards Nivelles, having lost 6000 killed, 5000 wounded and 8000 prisoners. French losses were 3000 killed and 3000 wounded.

■ **BEACHY HEAD, 10 JULY 1690**

During the spring and summer of 1690, the French assembled a fleet of 75 ships of the line and 23 fireships, which sailed from Brest on 23 June under the Comte de Tourville. The French decisively defeated the Earl of Torrington's Anglo-Dutch Channel Fleet of 56 ships of the line off Beachy Head. Two of Torrington's ships were sunk, another was captured and Torrington had eight damaged vessels scuttled to avoid capture.

■ **STAFFARDA, 18 AUGUST 1690**

A French army of 12,000 men commanded by LGen Nicolas Catinat invaded Savoy and defeated the Duke of Savoy's 18,000-strong army at Staffarda, near Saluzzo. The French lost 2000 men, but inflicted 4000 casualties.

■ **LA HOGUE, 1–4 JUNE 1691**

Twelve French ships of the line that had escaped from the defeat at the battle of Barfleur were beached near the port of Saint-Vaast-la-Hougue in Normandy where the exiled James II was assembling an army for the invasion of England. The ships were protected by shore batteries and a flotilla of small craft, but all 12 were burned by boats from the Inshore Squadron of Adm Russell's Anglo-Dutch Channel Fleet.

■ **LEUZE, 18 SEPTEMBER 1691**

The Duc de Luxembourg sent a force of 28 squadrons of French cavalry to attack Prince Georg Friedrich of Waldeck's Anglo-Dutch cavalry, which were surprised and decisively defeated with the loss of 2000 men.

■ **STEENKERKE, 3 AUGUST 1692**

The Duc de Luxembourg's French army of 80,000 men defeated a botched surprise attack by William III's army, which included Dutch, British and Danish contingents. The French inflicted 10,000 casualties for the loss of 8000 men.

■ **LAGOS, 27 JUNE 1693**

An Anglo-Dutch convoy of 200 merchantmen escorted by 16 warships under Adm Sir George Rooke was intercepted by the Comte de Tourville's French fleet of 100 vessels off Lagos, Portugal. A total of 90 merchantmen were lost in the action.

■ **NEERWINDEN (LANDEN), 29 JULY 1693**

The Duc de Luxembourg's French army of 80,000 men attacked and defeated a 50,000-strong Anglo-Dutch army commanded by William III near Neerwinden (in modern Belgium). Luxembourg inflicted 19,000 casualties for the loss of 9000 men.

■ **MARSAGLIA, 4 OCTOBER 1693**

A 30,000-strong Savoyard-Spanish army commanded by Duke Victor Amadeus II was defeated by Marshal Nicolas Catinat's French army of 35,000 men near Marsaglia in Piedmont. The French inflicted 10,000 casualties for the loss of 1800 men.

■ **TORROELLA, 27 MAY 1694**

The Duc de Noailles' French army of 24,000 men defeated a slightly smaller Spanish army commanded by the Marquis of Villena-Escalona at Torroella near Girona, inflicting 3000 casualties for the loss of 500 men.

■ **TEXEL, 29 JUNE 1694**

A French squadron of seven Dunkirk privateers under Jean Bart recaptured the bulk of a French grain convoy of 120 vessels that had been seized by eight Dutch warships. (Three of the Dutch warships were captured.)

■ **NAMUR, 2 JULY–1 SEPTEMBER 1695**

William III's army of 58,000 men including Dutch, British and Imperialist contingents besieged Namur, which was garrisoned by 13,000 French troops. The garrison surrendered after inflicting 12,000 casualties for the loss of 8000 men.

■ **DOGGER BANK, 17 JUNE 1696**

A French squadron of seven Dunkirk privateers

under Jean Bart attacked a Dutch convoy of 112 merchant vessels escorted by five warships. All five escorts were captured, together with 25 of the convoy's merchantmen.

Chinese-Mongolian Conflict 1696

■ JAO MODO, 1696

The Kangxi Emperor led an 80,000-strong Manchu army against the forces of the Mongol Zunghar Khanate under Galdan Boshugtu Khan. Manchu artillery played a key role in defeating the Mongols at Jao Modo near Ulan Bator.

Persian Afghan Wars 1700–50

■ KHANDAHAR, 1711

Shah Husayn of Iran sent Khosru Khan, the governor of Georgia, to recover Kandahar from the Afghan rebel, Mir Weis. The rebels were defeated and besieged in Kandahar, but Weis decided to counter-attack, defeating and killing Khosru in the process.

■ GULNABAD, 8 MARCH 1722

Shah Mahmud's 20,000-strong Afghan army decisively defeated an Iranian army of at least 50,000 men commanded by Shah Husayn. The Afghans inflicted up to 15,000 casualties and began their conquest of the Safavid Empire.

■ ISFAHAN, FEBRUARY–OCTOBER 1722

After his defeat at Gulnabad, Shah Husayn and the remnants of his army fled to Isfahan. Husayn was urged to escape to the provinces to raise more troops, but he remained in the capital, which was rapidly encircled by Shah Mamud's forces. Lacking heavy artillery, the Afghans starved the city into surrender. Over 80,000 of its population had died when Husayn surrendered and abdicated in favour of Shah Mahmud.

■ ISFAHAN (KIEMEREH), NOVEMBER 1726

An 60,000-strong Ottoman army commanded by Ahmad Rahman Pasha invaded Iran, but was decisively defeated by Shah Ashraf at Kiemereh near Isfahan with the loss of 12,000 men.

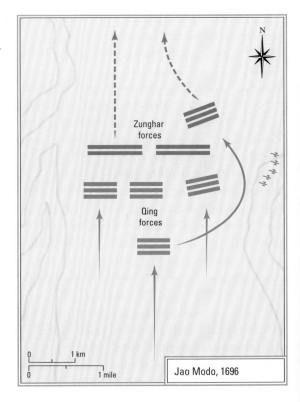

Jao Modo, 1696

■ MEHMANDOST, 1729

Shah Tahmasp II began the process of regaining control of Iran from its Afghan conquerors by taking the cities of Meshed and Herat. His general, Nadir Kuli, began this process by defeating the Afghan usurper Shah Ashraf at Mehmandost, east of Damghan.

■ HAMADAN, 15 SEPTEMBER 1731

An Ottoman offensive against Iran led by Ahmad Pasha took Kermanshah and threatened Hamadan. Shah Tahmasp II marched south to relieve Hamadan, but his army was routed and he had to accept a humiliating peace.

■ BAGHDAD, JANUARY–JULY 1733

Nadir Kuli deposed Shah Tahmasp II and declared himself Regent for the infant Shah Abbas III. Nadir then invaded Ottoman territory and besieged Baghdad after beating the forces of Ahmad Pasha at Adana.

■ KIRKUK (KARKUK), 19 JULY 1733

The Iranian Regent Nadir Kuli followed up his

victory at Adana by besieging Baghdad, but was then decisively defeated by an Ottoman relief force of 80,000 men under Grand Vizier Topal Osman Pasha at Kirkuk.

■ Delhi I, 28 March 1737

Peshwa Baji Rao I's 85,000-strong Maratha army defeated a Mughal army of 250,000 men under Amir Khan. Baji Rao's forces occupied Delhi, before evacuating the city on payment of 5,000,000 rupees by the Emperor Muhammad Shah.

■ Karnal, 13 February 1739

Nadir Shah's 55,000-strong Iranian army decisively defeated a Mughal army of up to 100,000 men under Emperor Muhammad Shah at Karnal in northern India. The Iranians inflicted 20,000 casualties for the loss of 2500 men.

Great Northern War 1700–21

■ Humlebæk, August 1700

Charles XII of Sweden defeated the Danish fleet off Humlebæk before landing a force of 10,000 men to threaten Copenhagen. The city paid a massive indemnity to avoid siege and Frederick was forced to make peace.

■ Narva, 30 November 1700

A Russian army of 32,000 besieged the Swedish-held city of Narva in present-day Estonia. Swedish King Charles XII led an army of 10,000 to relieve the city. Although the Russian army was entrenched and had a three-to-one numerical advantage, it was poorly trained, Tsar Peter I having barely begun military reforms. The Swedes attacked in two columns, covered by a strong blizzard blowing in the faces of the Russians. Charles led one column personally and both attacks broke through the defences. The Russian army fled, losing 8000 in killed and wounded, 20,000 prisoners and 180 cannon. Swedish losses were 1900. With this decisive victory, Charles left Russia to confront Tsar Peter's Polish and Saxon allies. Charles defeated these enemies and invaded Russia in 1708, but Peter had built an improved army by that time.

■ Dunamunde (The Duna), 9 July 1701

Charles XII's 7000-strong Swedish army attacked and defeated a Russian and Saxon army of 19,000 men under Augustus II of Poland and Saxony near Riga. The Swedes inflicted 2500 casualties for the loss of 500 men.

■ Erastfer, 9 January 1702

Gen Boris Sheremetev's Russian army of 12,000 men defeated a 2200-strong Swedish force under MGen von Schlippenbach near Erastfer (modern Erastvere in Estonia). The Russians inflicted 1000 casualties for the loss of 3000 men.

■ Kliszów, 19 July 1702

A Polish and Saxon army of 22,500 men under Augustus II of Poland and Saxony was defeated by Charles XII's 12,000-strong Swedish army near Kliszów. The Swedes inflicted 3700 casualties for the loss of 1200 men.

■ Pułtusk, 21 April 1703

A Saxon army of 3500 men under Generalfeldmarschall Adam Heinrich von Steinau

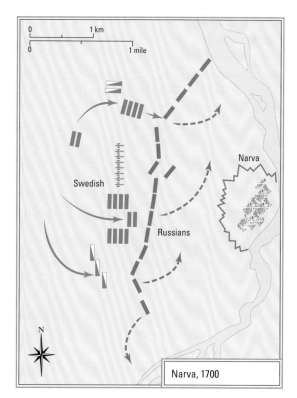

Narva, 1700

was defeated by Charles XII's 3000-strong Swedish army at Pułtusk, north of Warsaw. The Swedes inflicted 1000 casualties for the loss of 50 men.

■ THORN, MAY–SEPTEMBER 1703

Charles XII followed up his victory at Pułtusk by besieging Thorn (modern Torun) on the Vistula. The city surrendered after a long siege – which cost Charles fewer than 50 casualties – giving him effective control of Poland.

■ JĒKABPILS, 5 AUGUST 1704

A Russian and Polish army of 13,500 men under Grand Lithuanian Hetman Michał Wiśniowiecki, was defeated near Jēkabpils by Count Lewenhaupt's 5000-strong Swedish and Lithuanian army. The Swedes inflicted 2500 casualties for the loss of 250 men.

■ POZNAŃ, 9 AUGUST 1704

A Swedish force of just over 2000 men commanded by Johan August Meijerfeldt decisively defeated Count Johann Matthias von der Schulenburg's combined Saxon and Polish army of almost 6000 men near Poznań in Poland.

■ PUNITZ, 28 OCTOBER 1704

A force of 3000 Swedish cavalry commanded by Charles XII defeated Count Johann Matthias von der Schulenburg's 5000-strong Saxon army near Punitz (Poniec) in Poland. Charles inflicted 500 casualties for the loss of 300 men.

■ GEMAUERTHOF, 16 JULY 1705

Gen Boris Sheremetev's Russian army of 12,000 men was defeated by a 7000-strong Swedish army commanded by Count Lewenhaupt near Gemauerthof (modern Mūrmuiža, Latvia). The Swedes inflicted almost 5000 casualties for the loss of 1800 men.

■ WARSAW, 31 JULY 1705

A Swedish force of 2000 men under LGen Carl Nieroth, comprising three cavalry regiments and a detachment of 60 infantry, advanced boldly on Warsaw in support of Stanisław Leszczyński's claim to the Polish throne. They were opposed by a combined Polish and Saxon army of 3500 Saxon cuirassiers and 6000 Polish cavalry under the Saxon LGen Otto Arnold von Paykull. Although badly outnumbered and partially surrounded, LGen Nieroth decided to go onto the attack. His cavalry charges achieved complete tactical surprise and their demoralizing effect was enhanced by close-range volleys from his 60 infantry, who had been concealed by standing crops. Several of von Paykull's units were so badly shaken that they broke almost immediately and his army was decisively defeated. Swedish losses totalled roughly 150 dead and a similar number wounded, while von Paykull's casualties were 500 dead and 1000 wounded, plus a large number of prisoners.

■ GRODNO, JANUARY–MARCH 1706

A 20,000-strong Swedish army under Charles XII besieged Grodno, which was defended by FM Ogilvy's Russian garrison of 23,000 men. Charles cut off the city by forcing Gen Menshikov's cavalry back to Minsk and simultaneously forcing Augustus II with four Russian dragoon regiments to retreat into Poland. A total of 8000 Russians died during the siege and a further 9000 were lost during the retreat after the garrison's survivors broke out.

■ FRAUSTADT, 13 FEBRUARY 1706

A 9400-strong Swedish army under FM Carl Gustav Rehnskiöld defeated Count Johann Matthias von der Schulenburg's combined Saxon and Russian army of 20,000 men. The Swedes inflicted 15,000 casualties for the disproportionate loss of 1400 men.

■ KALISZ, 29 OCTOBER 1706

Gen Arvid Axel Mardefelt's 15,000-strong Swedish and Polish army was defeated by a Saxon, Russian and Polish army of 32,000 men commanded by Augustus II. The Swedes inflicted 750 casualties for the loss of 2500 men.

■ HOLOWCZYN 4 JULY 1708

Swedish King Charles XII invaded Russia and, at Holowczyn, defeated 38,000 Russians with 13,000 Swedes. The Russian army retired in good order, losing 1700 casualties. Swedish losses were 1300 men.

■ **MALATITZE, 31 AUGUST 1708**

MGen Carl Gustaf Roos' 4000-strong Swedish army fought an inconclusive action against a Russian army of 13,000 men commanded by Prince Mikhail Golitsyn. The Russians inflicted 800 casualties for the loss of 2700 men.

■ **LIESNA, 9 OCTOBER 1708**

A Swedish detachment of 13,000 under Lewenhaupt, which was escorting supply wagons during an invasion of Russia, was attacked by 18,000 Russians. The Swedes lost 3500 troops plus the wagons, the Russians losing 4100.

■ **POLTAVA, 27 JUNE 1709**

Swedish King Charles XII had defeated a Russian army at Narva in 1700 and then defeated Russia's allies Poland and Saxony. When Charles invaded Russia again in 1708, Tsar Peter I 'The Great' had completely rebuilt and modernized the Russian army. The Swedish Army failed to take Moscow, but survived through the winter. Charles moved

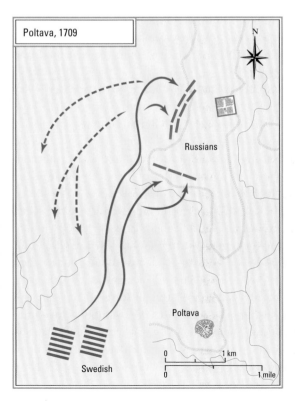

the Swedish Army into the Ukraine in 1709 and besieged the town of Poltava there. Peter moved the main Russian Army to Poltava in response.

Peter built breastworks and brought reinforcements to Poltava, where the Russians outnumbered the Swedish Army 49,000 to 24,000. Charles was wounded a few days before the battle – shot through the foot while reconnoitering the Russian position – and was largely incapacitated. Despite these disadvantages, Charles ordered an attack, underestimating the improved quality of the Russian Army since Narva nine years earlier.

Charles normally led his armies in person, but, confined to a stretcher, he gave executive command to Gen Rehnskjöld. Peter had built an additional line of redoubts perpendicular to his main line in order to channel any advance into two parts. The outnumbered Swedish Army advanced under fire from 100 Russian cannon. The Swedes did split into two main wings, capturing some Russian redoubts, but suffering heavy losses. The final Swedish attack was made with less than 7000 men. The attack was repulsed and at this key juncture Peter ordered a counter-attack with 40,000 troops. The Swedish Army was routed, losing over 9000 in the battle, with all but 1000 survivors captured within days afterwards. Charles escaped into Ottoman territory. Russian losses were 4600. Decisive victory at Poltava gained international prestige for Peter and Russia.

■ **KØGE BAY, 4–6 OCTOBER 1710**

GenAdm Count Gyldenløve's Danish fleet of 26 ships of the line was anchored in Køge Bay in readiness to support an invasion of Sweden by 6000 Russian troops from Danzig. However, on 4 October, Adm Wachtmeister's Swedish fleet of 21 ships of the line sailed into the bay.

The Danish fleet were surprised and struggled to form a battle line, but managed to hold their own, losing only the 94-gun *Dannebroge*, which caught fire and blew up. Two Swedish ships ran aground and were scuttled the next day to avoid capture. Bad weather prevented any major action on the 5th, but the next day, the Danish transports, which had been ordered back from Danzig without picking up the Russian invasion force, sailed straight into the Swedish fleet. A total of 24 Danish ships were captured, one destroyed and 14 ran aground.

■ HELSINGBORG, 10 MARCH 1710

Gen Magnus Stenbock's 14,000-strong Swedish army defeated a Danish army of similar size commanded by LGen Jørgen Rantzau near Helsingborg in southern Sweden. The Swedes inflicted over 5000 casualties for the loss of 3000 men.

■ ACTION OF 11 APRIL 1712

A Swedish squadron of seven ships commanded by Adm Erik Carlsson Sjöblad fought an inconclusive two-hour action against a Danish squadron of five ships under Adm Knoff, off Fladestrand in Jutland. The Danes sustained 44 casualties.

■ ACTION OF 31 JULY 1712

A Danish squadron of five ships commanded by VAdm Sehested fought an indecisive action off the Baltic island of Rugen against a Swedish squadron of at least eight vessels under Cdre Michael Henck.

■ GADEBUSCH, 9 DECEMBER 1712

Gen Magnus Stenbock's 14,000-strong Swedish army attacked a Danish army of 16,000 men commanded by Frederick IV, which was supported by Generalfeldmarschall Jacob Heinrich von Flemming's contingent of 3500 Saxon cavalry. Swedish artillery superiority caused heavy losses to the tightly packed Danish infantry, while a series of Swedish flanking attacks proved decisive in the defeat of Frederick's forces. Stenbock inflicted at least 6700 casualties for the loss of 1500 men.

■ BENDER, 1 FEBRUARY 1713

Charles XII and the remnants of his army escaped to Ottoman territory after their defeat at Poltava in 1709. In 1713, increasing tension led to fighting in which Charles was captured and 50 Ottoman troops were killed.

■ ACTION OF 22 JULY 1713

A Swedish squadron of three warships fought an inconclusive action off the island of Hogland in the Gulf of Finland against a Russian fleet of 11 vessels. One Russian ship was scuttled after running aground.

■ PÄLKÄNE, 17 OCTOBER 1713

Count Fyodor Apraksin's 14,400-strong Russian army defeated a Swedish army of 3700 men commanded by LGen Carl Gustaf Armfeldt at Pälkäne in Finland. The Russians inflicted 800 casualties for the loss of almost 700 men.

■ STORKYRO, 2 MARCH 1714

Prince Mikhail Golitsyn's 9000-strong Russian army defeated a Swedish army of 4500 men commanded by LGen Carl Gustaf Armfeldt at Storkyro in western Finland. The Russians inflicted 2500 Swedish casualties for the loss of 2000 men.

■ GANGUT (ARVENANMAA), 7 AUGUST 1714

A Russian fleet of at least 99 galleys commanded by Adm Fyodor Apraksin destroyed RAdm Nils Ehrenskiöld's Swedish squadron of one 18-gun prahm, six galley and two smaller vessels off Hanko in southern Finland.

■ STRALSUND, NOVEMBER 1714–22 DEC 1715

Charles XII of Sweden envisaged that Stralsund would act as a base for a renewed Swedish offensive against Russia and made an epic 15-day ride across Europe to reach the city on his escape from house arrest in Constantinople in 1714.

Stralsund had been under attack by Danish, Russian and Saxon forces since 1711, although they had been unable to effectively besiege the city. Charles' arrival in November 1714 led to the Swedish garrison being reinforced to a total strength of 17,000 men. Prussian troops joined the besiegers during the following year, after Frederick William I declared war on Sweden in April 1715. The allied army of 36,000 men gradually increased the pressure on the garrison throughout 1715. In November, surrender became inevitable after a combined Danish-Saxon-Prussian army took the island of Rügen north of the city. Charles escaped just before the surrender.

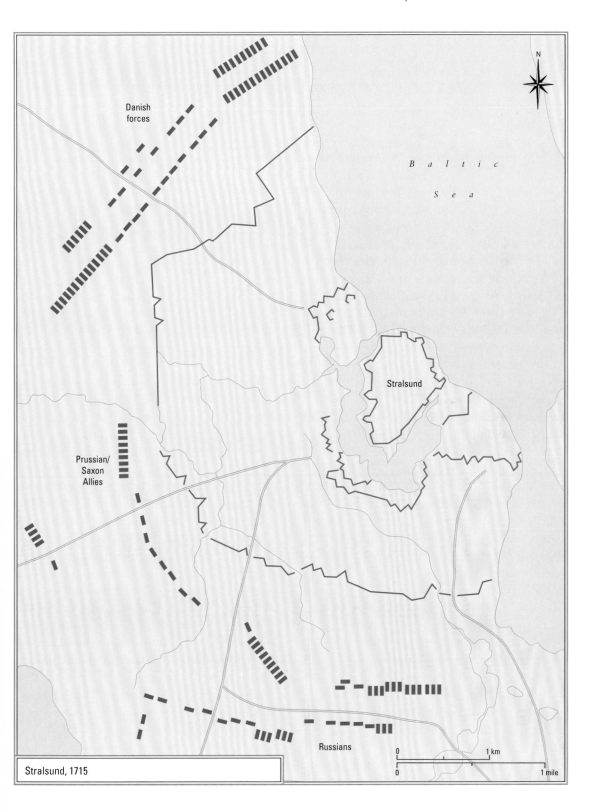

N

Danish
forces

B a l t i c

S e a

Stralsund

Prussian/
Saxon
Allies

Russians

Stralsund, 1715

0		1 km
0		1 mile

■ **ACTION OF 24 APRIL 1715**

In an action off Kolberg, a Danish fleet of 14 ships commanded by Adm Christian Carl Gabel defeated a Swedish squadron of six warships, capturing RAdm Hans Wachtmeister and four of his vessels.

■ **DYNEKILEN, 8 JULY 1716**

A Danish squadron of six warships commanded by VAdm Peter Tordenskjold decisively defeated RAdm Olof Strömstierna's Swedish flotilla of 15 small armed vessels, which was escorting a supply convoy in Dynekilen fjord.

■ **FREDRIKSHALD (FREDRIKSTEN), DEC 1718**

Charles XII's 40,000-strong Swedish army stormed the Norwegian town of Fredrikshald and besieged the nearby fortress of Fredriksten. The siege was abandoned after Charles was killed by artillery fire from the fortress on 11 December.

■ **ÖSEL ISLAND, 4 JUNE 1719**

A Russian squadron of seven warships under Cdre Naum Senyavin defeated Cdre Wrangel's Swedish flotilla of three vessels off Ösel (Saaremaa) Island. All three Swedish ships were captured at the cost of 18 Russian casualties.

■ **STÄKET, 13 AUGUST 1719**

Adm Fyodor Apraksin's Russian fleet landed 3000 troops at Baggensstäket near Stockholm, which were defeated by Col Rutger Fuchs' Swedish force of 1200 men. The Swedes inflicted 500 casualties for the loss of 100 men.

■ **GRENGAM, 7 AUGUST 1720**

VAdm Carl Georg Siöblad's Swedish squadron of 14 assorted vessels fought Prince Mikhail Golitsyn's Russian fleet of 61 galleys and 29 smaller craft. Four Swedish frigates were captured, but 43 Russian galleys were sunk.

War of the Spanish Succession 1701–14

■ **CARPI, 9 JULY 1701**

The first battle of the War of the Spanish Succession took place on 9 July 1701 between France and Austria. The Austrians under Prince Eugene of Savoy defeated the French forces commanded by Nicolas Catinat.

■ **CHIARI, 1 SEPTEMBER 1701**

The battle was fought on 1 September 1701 and was part of Austrian Prince Eugene of Savoy's campaign to seize the Spanish-controlled Duchy of Milan in the Italian peninsula.

■ **CREMONA, 1 FEBRUARY 1702**

The indecisive battle of Cremona was an engagement between France and Austria that took place on 1 February 1702. Prince Eugene of Savoy conducted a night attack that caught the French garrison, under Marshal François de Neufville, Duc de Villeroi, completely by surprise. The Austrians captured high-ranking French officers and approximately 1000 French soldiers were killed in the attack. However, the citadel held out and, as a relieving French army approached Cremona, Eugene was forced to withdraw.

■ **LANDAU, 29 JULY–12 SEPTEMBER 1702**

Led by Prince Louis of Baden, who crossed the Rhine and – from 29 July through to 12 September – besieged Landau. Bavaria joined the war on the French side in September and Prince Louis was forced back into Germany.

■ **LUZZARA, 15 AUGUST 1702**

A battle between Austria and France was fought on 15 August 1702, near Luzzara in Italy. The Prince of Savoy attacked the forces of Duc de Vendôme without any conclusion.

■ **CADIZ, 23 AUGUST–30 SEPTEMBER 1702**

The battle was an Anglo-Dutch attempt to seize the southern Spanish port of Cadiz during the War of the Spanish Succession and was fought in August/September 1702, ending in a Spanish victory.

■ **FRIEDLINGEN, 14 OCTOBER 1702**

A battle fought in 1702 between France and the Holy Roman Empire. The Imperial forces were led by Louis William, Margrave of Baden-Baden, while the victorious French were led by Claude Louis Hector de Villars.

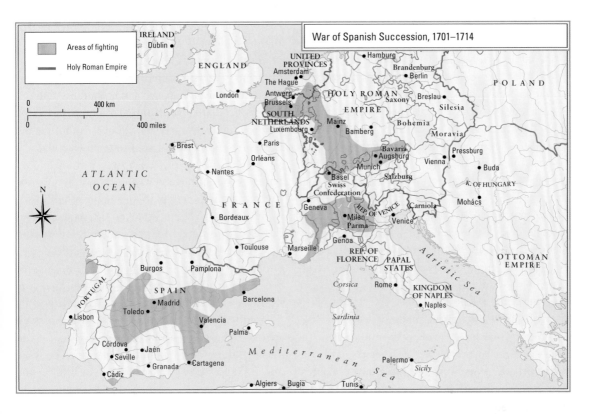

War of Spanish Succession, 1701–1714

▪ VIGO BAY, 23 OCTOBER 1702

The battle of Vigo Bay was a naval engagement that followed an Anglo-Dutch attempt to capture the Spanish port of Cádiz in September in an effort to secure a naval base in the Iberian peninsula. The engagement was an overwhelming naval success for the Allies.

▪ SAINT AUGUSTINE, 10 NOV–30 DEC 1702

English provincial forces from the province of Carolina and their native American allies fought against the fortress of Castillo de San Marcos at St Augustine, in Spanish Florida, between November and December 1702. The siege lifted when a Spanish relief force arrived from Havana in late December.

▪ CAP DE LA ROQUE, 22 MAY 1703

A naval battle that took place on 22 May 1703, between a French squadron under Alain Emmanuel de Coëtlogon and a Dutch convoy protected by Capt Roemer, during the War of the Spanish Succession.

▪ EKEREN, 30 JUNE 1703

The French surrounded a Dutch force, which barely avoided destruction, on 30 June 1703 and ended the hope of a decisive allied victory in the Spanish Netherlands in 1703.

▪ HÖCHSTÄDT, 30 SEPTEMBER 1703

The battle was fought on 30 September 1703, near Höchstädt in Bavaria and resulted in a French-Bavarian victory under Marshal Villars against the Austrians under Gen Limburg Styrum.

▪ SPIRA (SPEYERBACH), 15 NOVEMBER 1703

The battle of Speyerbach in November 1703 took place when a French army besieging Landau surprised and defeated a German relief army near Speyer.

▪ DONAUWORTH, 2 JULY 1704

The Duke of Marlborough, with an Allied force of British, Dutch, and Hapsburg Imperial troops totaling 22,000 men, attacked a French-Bavarian entrenched camp at Donauworth on the Danube in Bavaria. The French and Bavarian garrison numbered 13,000 troops under d'Arco. Marlborough reached the enemy camp at 17:00 and decided upon an immediate attack, rather than attempting a siege. Marlborough's initial attacks were against d'Arco's right. These attacks did not break through the strong French and Bavarian positions, but did draw off d'Arco's reserves. With part of the French-Bavarian line weakened, Allied forces under the Margrave of Baden attacked and broke through the fortifications. The French and Bavarians, caught with their backs to the Danube, suffered casualties of 5000 killed – including some drowned – plus 3000 captured. Only half of d'Arco's force escaped. Marlborough lost casualties totaling 5000.

■ Gibraltar, 3 August 1704

A small Spanish garrison surrendered Gibraltar to British Adm Rooke, commanding a British-Dutch fleet of over 50 vessels. The de facto British possession of Gibraltar was later confirmed by treaty.

■ Blenheim, 13 August 1704

The English Duke of Marlborough, commanding an Allied army including British, Danish, Hanoverian, Prussian and Hessian regiments, had marched into the territory of Bavaria, the ally of France. Marlborough had moved his army unexpectedly from the Netherlands in order to assist his Austrian allies against French and Bavarian forces. Marlborough's army was reinforced by a Habsburg, Prussian and Danish force under Prince Eugene of Savoy. Meanwhile, a French army under Tallard was reinforced by French and Bavarian forces under Marsin and the Elector of Bavaria near Blenheim, Bavaria.

Marlborough assembled 56,000 well-supplied troops north-west of Blenheim in attack positions. The Allied right wing was commanded by Prince Eugene. Tallard was not expecting a major attack, but had to set up defensive positions hastily as Marlborough advanced in nine large columns. Tallard deployed 52,000 French and Bavarian troops facing northwards, with their

right flank resting on the Danube and the town of Blenheim. The French left centre was anchored on the village of Oberglau. Tallard's defensive positions were protected in front by the Nebel river, a marshy tributary of the Danube. The left wing of Tallard's position was commanded by the Elector of Bavaria and Marsin, although the Bavarians and French here operated essentially as a separate army.

Marlborough began attacks at 12:30. Prince Eugene, though outnumbered against the Elector of Bavaria and Marsin, attacked them throughout the day, pinning down this larger force around the town of Lutzingen. Marlborough's main efforts were at the other end of the line, against the French right, nearest Blenheim and the Danube. The French here were commanded by Clérambault and, against them, Marlborough sent four brigades under the experienced Lord 'Salamander' Cutts, including British, Hessian, and Hanoverian regiments. Leading the

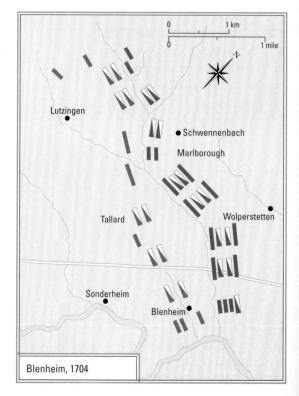

Blenheim, 1704

vanguard, Brigadier Rowe of the Scots Fusiliers was shot as he reached the French ramparts. Though Clérambault's troops repulsed Cutts' initial assault, the attacks continued. Without consulting his superior, Tallard, Clérambault called in reinforcements. By 14:00, the French had over 12,000 troops concentrated on their right, more than could be effectively deployed in the part of the line around Blenheim.

The diversion of French reinforcements to their right was an anticipated opportunity for Marlborough, as he massed reserves of cavalry and infantry in order to attack the French centre. Marlborough crossed the Nebel using bridges thrown across by his engineers. Allied troops attacked the town of Oberglau, which was fiercely defended by two French regiments and three Irish battalions in French service. Oberglau held, but the garrison was pinned. Marlborough was able to launch his attack in the centre at 17:00, with 81 squadrons of Allied cavalry and 18 infantry battalions. In the centre to oppose them the French had 64 cavalry squadrons and only nine infantry battalions.

Marlborough's well-prepared assault achieved a complete breakthrough and the Allied troops smashing through the centre swung to their left and advanced to the Danube, cutting off the French right wing and trapping it against the river. French forces were thrown into confusion and Tallard was captured while trying to rally his troops. Marsin and the Elector, seeing the disaster in the centre and right, withdrew, pressured by Prince Eugene. French and Bavarian losses included 20,000 killed and wounded, 14,000 captured and 60 cannon captured. Allied casualties totalled 13,000. Marlborough's victory removed the French threat to Austria, while the Allies occupied most of Bavaria.

■ MALAGA, 24 AUGUST 1704

After the British capture of Gibraltar, a French-Spanish fleet under Toulouse sailed against Rooke's British-Dutch fleet off the Spanish coast. Toulouse' fleet included 68 ships and 24 galleys, totaling 3522 guns and 24,275 men. Rooke's fleet had 65 ships with 3614 guns and 22,545 sailors. Rooke's losses were 2700 and Toulouse lost 1600. Toulouse claimed victory, but sailed back to port, leaving Gibraltar to Rooke.

■ MARBELLA, 10 MARCH 1705

This naval battle took place while a combined Spanish-French force besieged Gibraltar on 10 March 1705. The battle was an allied victory (consisting of English, Dutch and Portuguese), which effectively ended the Franco-Spanish siege of Gibraltar.

■ CASSANO D'ADDA, 16 AUGUST 1705

A hard-fought battle between the French and an Austrian/Prussian force in the Italian theatre of the War of the Spanish Succession in August 1705. The French were victorious with both sides suffering serious casualties.

■ BARCELONA, 14 SEPTEMBER–19 OCT 1705

The siege of Barcelona took place between 14 September and 19 October 1705, when an Allied army supporting the Austrian pretender to the Spanish throne led by Lord Peterborough captured the city from its Franco-Spanish Bourbonic defenders.

■ ELIXHEIM, 18 JULY 1705

On 18 July 1705, the English Duke of Marlborough punched through the French Lines of Brabant. Although the battle was inconclusive, the subsequent razing of the lines proved critical to the allied victory at Ramillies the following year.

■ CALCINATO, 19 APRIL 1706

A battle between the forces of Bourbon France and Spain and the forces of the Austrian Habsburgs fought on 19 April 1706 near Calcinato, Italy. The result ended in a victory for Marshal Vendôme's Bourbon French and Spanish army.

■ RAMILLIES, 23 MAY 1706

The English Duke of Marlborough commanded 62,000 British, Dutch, and Danish troops against 60,000 French, Bavarian and Spanish troops under

Villeroi at Ramillies, in present-day Belgium. Marlborough, facing westwards, bombarded Villeroi's encampment around Ramillies at 11:00. Villeroi, unprepared for battle, deployed in haste a long concave line, anchored from north to south by the villages of Autre Église, Offus, Ramillies and Taviers. Marlborough attacked both flanks from 14:00 to 15:30, then shifted 38 cavalry squadrons from his right to his centre. Marlborough, leading cavalry attacks, lost one horse killed under him and one aide, but successfully remounted. After 18:00, Marlborough shifted six infantry battalions from his right to the centre and finally achieved a breakthrough. Villeroi's army fled in disorder, losing 13,000 casualties and 70 cannon. Marlborough lost 3700 killed and wounded.

■ TURIN, 14 MAY–7 SEPTEMBER 1706

The Duke of Orléans and Marshal de la Feuillade laid siege against the Savoyard city of Turin between May and September 1706. After the French had invested the city for nearly five

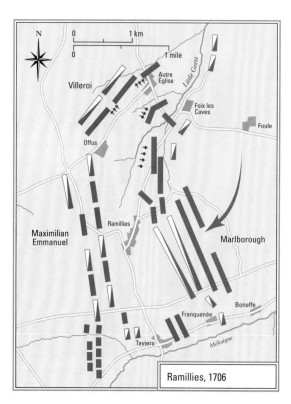

Ramillies, 1706

months, their army was attacked on 7 September by an Imperial relief column under Prince Eugene of Savoy and the Duke of Savoy and routed at the battle of the Stura, thereby lifting the siege of Turin. Following this, the retreat of French forces from northern Italy began.

■ CASTILIGIONE, 8 SEPTEMBER 1706

A French army defeated a Hessian army besieging Castiglione delle Stiviere on 8 September 1706. This defeat was a setback for the Allies who had won the battle of Turin the previous day, by which the French were chased from Milan and Savoy.

■ ALMANZA, 25 APRIL 1707

In April 1707, the Franco–Spanish army under Berwick soundly defeated the allied forces of Portugal, England and the United Provinces at Almanza, reclaiming most of eastern Spain for the Bourbons. With the main allied army destroyed, the victory was a major step in consolidating Spain under the Bourbons, thereby allowing Philip V of Spain to regain the initiative and take Valencia.

■ STOLLHOFEN, 23 MAY 1707

French Marshal Villars occupied the Stollhofen position on 23 May 1707. These defences were a massive system of trenches, redoubts and fortifications that prevented any incursion into Germany along the Rhine valley.

■ GAETA, JULY–AUGUST 1707

A three-month siege of the Italian city of Gaeta by Austrian forces under Wirich Philipp von Daun, which ended on 30 September 1707 with the destruction of the city's historic fortifications.

■ TOULON, 29 JULY–21 AUGUST 1707

A French and Spanish force defeated a combined force from Austria, the Dutch Republic, Savoy and Great Britain in a battle that was fought from 29 July to 21 August 1707, at Toulon, France.

■ LIZARD, 21 OCTOBER 1707

A naval battle that took place on 21 October 1707, near Lizard Point, Cornwall (in England) between two French squadrons under René Duguay-Trouin and Claude de Forbin and an

English convoy protected by a squadron under Cdre Richard Edwards. The victorious French naval commanders had caused much damage to the allied merchant fleet.

■ CARTAGENA, 8 JUNE 1708
The battle of Cartagena, also known as Wager's Action was a naval battle fought on 8 June 1708, between a British squadron under Charles Wager and the Spanish treasure fleet. The battle was a British victory.

■ OUDENARDE, 11 JULY 1708
This battle between the French and the forces of Great Britain, the Dutch Republic and the Holy Roman Empire at Oudenarde, Belgium, that resulted in a decisive victory for the allies.

■ LILLE, 12 AUGUST–10 DECEMBER 1708
The siege of Lille ran from 12 August to 10 December 1708 during the War of the Spanish Succession. The French garrison surrendered the city and citadel of Lille, commanded by Marshal Boufflers, to the forces of the Duke of Marlborough and Prince Eugene after 120 days of being besieged.

■ GHENT, DECEMBER 1708
After the loss of Lille and the disintegration of the French presence in northern Flanders, the Allies took Ghent from the French and Spanish forces in December 1708.

■ TOURNAI, 1709
The Allied siege (under command of the Duke of Marlborough) of the French-held fortified city of Tournai (commanded by the the Marquis de Surville-Hautfois) from 27 June to 3 September 1709. The French had taken 3800 casualties and had inflicted 5400 on the Allies, making this one of the bloodiest sieges of war.

■ MALPLAQUET, 11 SEPTEMBER 1709
The battle of Malplaquet was between the Bourbons of France and Spain against an alliance of the Habsburg monarchy, Great Britain, the United Provinces and the Kingdom of Prussia that was fought on 11 September 1709. The

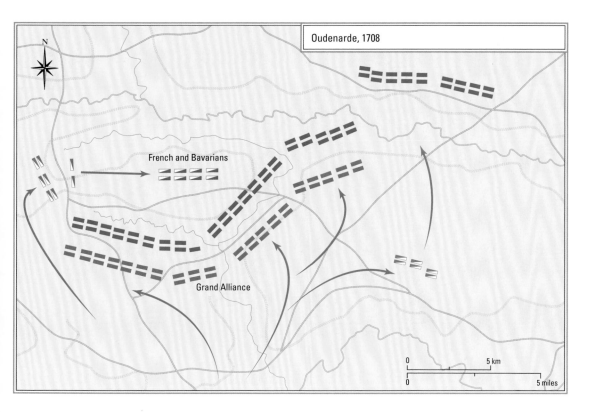

Oudenarde, 1708

Allied army was led by Marlborough and Prince Eugene of Savoy, while the French and a contingent of Bavarians were commanded by Villars and Marshal Boufflers. The Allies had suffered such huge casualties in their attack of the French that they could not pursue them upon their retreat. Despite the heavy losses on the side of the Allies, they are considered to be the Pyrrhic victors after the battle. The French were able to withdraw from the battlefield in good order and – most importantly – intact, leaving them to be able to fight another day.

■ **ALMENAR, 27 JULY 1710**

A battle between the troops of Phillip V and the Archduke Charles on 27 July 1710 where Philip V's army, having been defeated, was forced to evacuate Catalonia and regroup behind the Ebro.

■ **SARAGOSSA, 20 AUGUST 1710**

A battle between the Spanish-Bourbon army commanded by the Marquis de Bay and a multi-national army led by the Austrian commander

Guido Starhemberg took place on 20 August 1710. In this battle were present the two candidates to the Spanish Crown: Phillip, Duke of Anjou and Charles, Archduke of Austria. The battle ended with the victorious Habsburg Archduke Charles entering Saragossa the following day.

■ **BRIHUEGA, 8 DECEMBER 1710**

The battle of Brihuega took place during the allied retreat from Madrid to Barcelona on 8 December 1710. A Franco-Spanish army under the Duke of Vendôme cut-off and overwhelmed a British rearguard under Lord Stanhope.

■ **VILLAVICOSIA, 10 DECEMBER 1710**

A battle between the Franco-Spanish army led by Louis Joseph, Duke of Vendôme, and Philip V of Spain and the Habsburg-Allied army commanded by the Austrian Guido Starhemberg on 10 December 1710.

■ **BOUCHAIN, 9 AUGUST–12 SEPTEMBER 1711**

The Duke of Marlborough broke through the

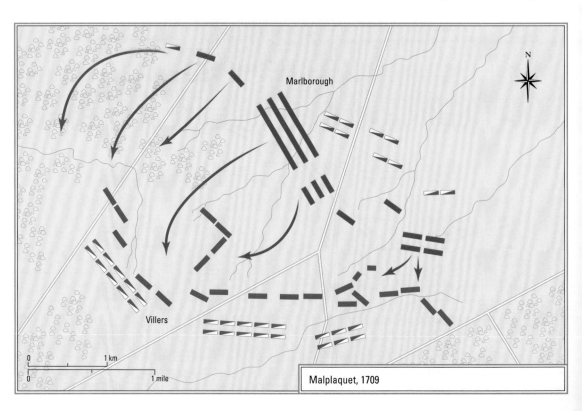

Malplaquet, 1709

French defensive lines of Bouchain without losing a man to enemy action and took the town after a siege that lasted over a month. The Siege of Bouchain was the last major victory of John Churchill, 1st Duke of Marlborough.

■ **RIO DE JANEIRO, 12–22 SEPTEMBER 1711**
A raid on the Portuguese port of Rio de Janeiro by a French squadron under René Duguay-Trouin in September 1711. The Portuguese defenders were unable to put up an effective resistance and the city had to pay a ransom to avoid destruction of its defences.

■ **DENAIN, 24 JULY 1712**
A battle that was fought on 24 July 1712 and resulted in a French victory under Marshal Villars against the Austrian and Dutch forces under Prince Eugene of Savoy.

■ **BARCELONA, 25 JULY 1713–11 SEP 1714**
A siege by the Bourbons against the Habsburgs, who held Barcelona, that lasted from 25 July 1713 to 11 September 1714, resulting in an eventual Bourbon victory. This battle marked the end of the War of Spanish Succession (1701–14).

Hungarian War of Independence 1705

■ **SAINT GOTTHARD, 13 DECEMBER 1705**
Hungarian resentment at their treatment by the Habsburgs flared up into a rebellion led by Prince Francis II Rákóczi. The uprising began in 1703 with French support and spread rapidly, gaining control of most of the Kingdom of Hungary, both east and north of the Danube. At the peak of its success, the rebel army decisively defeated the Habsburg forces at Saint Gotthard, almost succeeding in capturing the Emperor Joseph I.

Bulavin Rebellion 1707–08

■ **BULAVIN REBELLION (ASTRAKHAN REVOLT), 1707–08**
Peter the Great's attempts to control the Don Cossacks provoked a rebellion led by Kondraty Bulavin. Prince Yuri Dolgorukov, the commander

of Peter's punitive expedition, was assassinated before the uprising ended with Bulavin's death in 1708.

War of the Quadruple Alliance 1718–20

■ **CAPE PASSARO, 11 AUGUST 1718**
VAdm Don José Antonio de Gaztañeta's Spanish fleet of 26 warships, two fireships, four bomb vessels, seven galleys and several transports was intercepted off Cape Passaro in Sicily by a British fleet of 22 ships of the line and six smaller craft commanded by Adm Sir George Byng. The Spanish were decisively defeated by the British, losing a total of 16 vessels, including their flagship, the *Real San Felipe*, which blew up after being captured.

■ **MILAZZO, 15 OCTOBER 1718**
The Marquis of Lede's 9300-strong Spanish army defeated an Austrian army of 6000 men commanded by Count Wirich Philipp von Daun near Milazzo in Sicily. The Spanish inflicted 1800 casualties for the loss of 1700 men.

■ **FRANCAVILLA, 20 JUNE 1719**
The Marquis of Lede's 29,000-strong Spanish army defeated an Austrian army of 21,000 men commanded by the Comte de Mercy near Francavilla in Sicily. The Spanish inflicted 3100 casualties for the loss of 2000 men.

■ **CAPTURE OF VIGO, OCTOBER 1719**
Lord Cobham's force of 4000 British troops was landed on the Galician coast by RAdm James Mighels' squadron. They then seized the port of Vigo, which was held for ten days before the force re-embarked.

Jacobite Risings 1719–46

■ **GLEN SHIEL, 10 JUNE 1719**
A 1000-strong Jacobite force, including reinforcments by 200 Spanish troops, was defeated at Glen Shiel by a Hanoverian force of similar size under Gen Joseph Wightman. The

Jacobites inflicted 120 casualties for the loss of over 400 men.

■ **HIGHBRIDGE SKIRMISH, 16 AUGUST 1745**

Capt Scott's detachment of two companies of the Royal Scots – marching all the way from Fort Augustus to reinforce the garrison of Fort William – were attacked and forced to surrender by Jacobite clansmen at Highbridge on the River Spean.

■ **CARLISLE, NOVEMBER AND DECEMBER 1745**

Carlisle was taken by the Jacobites after a two-day siege in November 1745, but they didn't hold onto their new possession for long – their 400-strong garrison surrendered the city and castle to the Duke of Cumberland after a nine-day siege during the following month.

■ **CLIFTON MOOR, 18 DECEMBER 1745**

As the Jacobite army retreated from Derby, it came under increasing pressure from the Duke of Cumberland's pursuing Hanoverian forces. At Clifton in Cumbria, the Jacobite rearguard attacked and defeated a detachment of 500 Hanoverian dragoons.

■ **INVERURIE, 23 DECEMBER 1745**

A Jacobite force of 1100 men and five guns commanded by Lord Lewis Gordon, surprised and defeated Laird MacLeod of MacLeod's 1200-strong Hanoverian detachment near Inverurie in Aberdeenshire. The Jacobites inflicted at least 70 casualties.

■ **FORT WILLIAM, 20 MARCH–3 APRIL 1746**

MGen Cameron's force of 1500 Jacobites, supported by 200 French artillerymen, besieged Fort William, which was defended by a Hanoverian garrison of 3500 men. The siege was raised after several sorties destroyed the Jacobite siege guns.

■ **LITTLEFERRY, 15 APRIL 1746**

A force of 500 Jacobites commanded by George Mackenzie, 3rd Earl of Cromartie, were surprised and defeated by Ensign John Mackay of Moudale's company of the Sutherland militia, with the loss of at least 200 men.

War of the Polish Succession 1733–35

■ **KEHL, 14–28 OCTOBER 1733**

A French army of 33,000 men under the Duke of Berwick besieged and took the fortress of Kehl (in modern Baden-Württemberg), which was held by an Austrian garrison of 250 men supported by 1200 Swabian militia.

■ **DANZIG, 22 FEBRUARY–30 JUNE 1734**

Count Pyotr Petrovich Lacy's 12,000-strong Russian army besieged Danzig, which was held by a Polish garrison of 4500 troops under Stanisław Leszczyński. Both sides were gradually reinforced; Polish volunteers and a French contingent brought the garrison up to 17,500 men, while additional Russian units and a Saxon force raised the besiegers' strength to a total of 37,000 men. The city surrendered after a 135-day siege, during which the Russians lost 8000 men.

■ **GAETA, 8 APRIL–6 AUGUST 1734**

The well-fortified city of Gaeta, set on a promontory stretching towards the Gulf of Gaeta, was one of the last Austrian strongholds in southern Italy. Its garrison of 1500 men commanded by Count von Tattenbach held out against attacks by a 16,000-strong Franco-Spanish army under the Duke of Parma (the future Charles III of Spain) for almost four months. The Count surrendered after prolonged artillery bombardments breached the citadel.

■ **BITONTO, 25 MAY 1734**

The Duke of Montemar's 14,000-strong Spanish army defeated an Austrian army of 10,500 men commanded by the Prince of Belmonte near Bitonto in southern Italy. The Spanish inflicted 4500 casualties for the loss of 300 men.

■ **PHILIPPSBURG, MAY–JULY 1734**

The Duke of Berwick's 60,000-strong French army besieged and took the fortress of Philippsburg (near Karlsruhe in modern Baden-Württemberg), which was held by an Austrian garrison of 4200 men under Freiherr Gottfried Ernst von Wuttgenau.

■ **PARMA, 29 JUNE 1734**

Marshal Coigny's French army of 60,000 men defeated a 50,000-strong Austrian army commanded by the Count de Mercy at the village of Crocetta, near Parma. The French inflicted 6200 casualties for the loss of 4400 men.

■ **GUASTALLA (LUZZARA) 19 SEPTEMBER 1734**

A 49,000-strong Franco-Sardinian army commanded by Charles Emmanuel III of Sardinia defeated Dominik von Königsegg-Rothenfels' Austrian army of 40,000 men near Guastalla in northern Italy. The battle was close, with the Austrians inflicting 5600 casualties for the loss of 5800 men.

War of Jenkins' Ear 1739–48

■ **PORTOBELLO, 22 NOVEMBER 1739**

A British squadron of six ships of the line commanded by VAdm Edward Vernon attacked Portobello in Panama, which was defended by Francisco Javier de la Vega's 700-strong Spanish garrison. Landing parties of seamen and marines stormed the forts of Todo Fierro and Santiago, demoralizing the garrison, which surrendered the following day. Vernon sank one Spanish sloop and captured three other vessels for the loss of three killed and seven wounded.

■ **ST AUGUSTINE, 13 JUNE–20 JULY 1740**

Gen James Oglethorpe's British and colonial force of 1900 men – supported by over 1000 Creek warriors – besieged Fort Augustine in Florida, which was defended at the time by a 750-strong Spanish garrison commanded by Governor Manuel de Montiano. The attack was unsuccessful.

■ **ANSON EXPEDITION, 1740–44**

Cdre George Anson's British squadron of six warships: HMS *Centurion* (flagship), *Gloucester*, *Severn*, *Pearl*, *Wager*, and the sloop *Tryal*, plus two store ships – *Anna* and *Industry* – were sent to

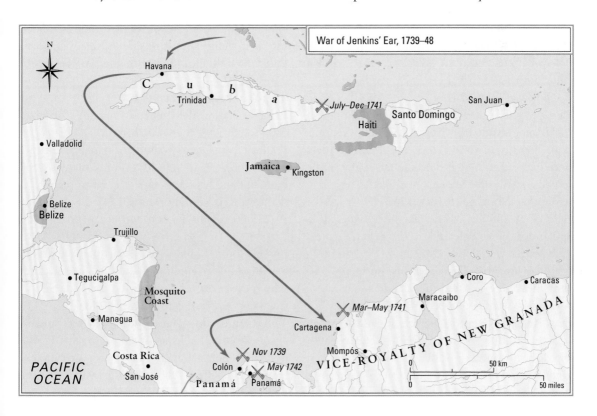

attack Spain's American colonies. When Anson reached the island of Juan Fernández in June 1741, only three of his six ships remained. In the absence of any effective opposition, he sacked the port of Paita in Peru (13–15 November 1741). Dwindling crew numbers and the poor state of his ships forced him to transfer all the survivors to *Centurion*. He docked at Macau in November 1742, before sailing again and taking an immensely rich prize, the *Nuestra Señora de Covadonga*, carrying 1,313,843 pieces of eight, on 20 June 1743. Anson took his prize back to Macau, sold her cargo to the Chinese and sailed for England, arriving on 15 June 1744.

■ CARTAGENA DE INDIAS, MARCH–MAY 1741

A British expeditionary force of 26,600 men and 186 ships under VAdm Edward Vernon was sent to capture the Spanish port of Cartagena de Indias in Nueva Granada (modern Colombia). MGen Thomas Wentworth's landing force of 12,000 men far outnumbered the port's 6000-strong garrison under Adm Blaz de Lezo. However, bickering between Vernon and Wentworth delayed operations and the attack failed with the loss of 17,000 men. (Spanish casualties totalled 2000.)

■ GEORGIA, JULY 1742

The Spanish governor of Florida, Manuel de Montiano, invaded St Simond's Island, Georgia, with an army of almost 2000 men. The invaders withdrew after being defeated at Gully Hole Creek and Bloody Marsh.

■ BLOODY MARSH, 18 JULY 1742

A force of 650 British regulars, colonial militia and Indian allies defeated a 200-strong Spanish detachment at Bloody Marsh on St Simond's Island, Georgia. The Spanish sustained 50 casualties and evacuated the island a week later.

■ HAVANA, 12 OCTOBER 1748

Don Andrés Reggio's Spanish squadron of six ships of the line and a frigate was defeated with the loss of two ships off Havana by RAdm Charles Knowles' British squadron of seven ships of the line.

War of the Austrian Succession 1740–48

■ MOLLWITZ, 10 APRIL 1741

Frederick the Great overran the Austrian province of Silesia, but was caught off-balance by an Austrian counter-offensive. His 22,000-strong army was intercepted by an Austrian force of 19,000 men commanded by Marshal Wilhelm Reinhard von Neipperg near Mollwitz (modern Małujowice in Poland).

The battle began disastrously for Frederick as six regiments of Austrian cavalry routed the Prussian cavalry covering his right flank, before turning on the exposed Prussian infantry. Frederick's second in command, Generalfeldmarschall Kurt Christoph Graf von Schwerin, persuaded him to leave his men to avoid probable capture on the battlefield. (Ironically, he was very nearly captured by Austrian hussars near Oppeln.) The Prussian infantry's sheer discipline and firepower won the battle; their volleys killed the Austrian cavalry commander Gen Römer and decimated his men before breaking the Austrian infantry, inflicting a total of 4000 casualties for the loss of 2500 men.

■ CHOTUSITZ, 17 MAY 1742

Prince Charles Alexander of Lorraine's Austrian army of 28,000 men was narrowly defeated by Frederick the Great's 30,000 Prussians at Chotusitz in Bohemia. Each side lost approximately 7000 men, but the Austrians were forced to retreat.

■ PRAGUE, JUNE–DECEMBER 1742

A 25,000-strong French force was trapped in Prague by an Austrian army of 70,000 men under Count Lobkowitz. Much of the garrison broke out in September and December, after which the remaining 6000 men surrendered.

■ CAMPO SANTO, 8 FEBRUARY 1743

The Comte de Gages 14,000-strong Spanish army was defeated by an Austrian force of 12,000 under Generalfeldmarschall Traun at Campo Santo in northern Italy. Spanish casualties were 4000, while the Austrians lost 1500 men.

War of the Austrian Succession, 1740–48

Holy Roman Empire
Main areas of fighting

*North
Sea*

Copenhagen • Malmö

Baltic Sea

DENMARK

• Königsberg

• Danzig

PRUSSIA

Hamburg •

• Stettin

HANOVER

• Berlin

• Warsaw

NETHERLANDS

POLAND

Austrian
Netherlands

SAXONY

• Cracow

Galicia

Aachen •

• Prague

Frankfurt •

• Paris

BAVARIA

Metz •

• Vienna

Munich •

AUSTRIA

• Buda

FRANCE

HUNGARY

SWITZERLAND

Geneva •

Lyon •

PIEDMONT

V E N E T I A N

• Belgrade

• Milan

Turin •

Venice •

O T T O M A N   E M P I R E

Genoa •

• Ravenna

Florence •

• Marseille

TUSCANY

PAPAL

STATES

*Adriatic
Sea*

Ragusa •

Corsica

Rome •

0   200 km
0   200 miles

KINGDOM OF NAPLES

PIEDMONT

Naples •

• Taranto

AND SICILY

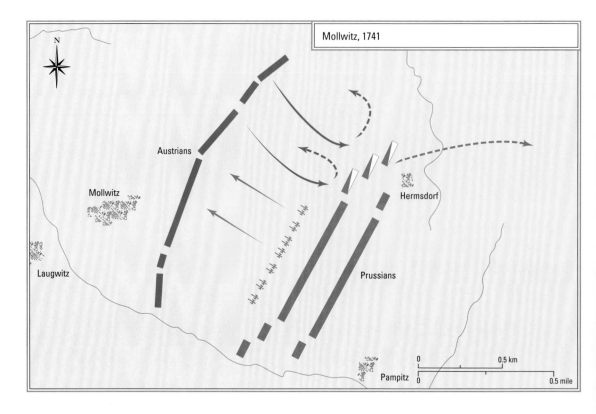

Mollwitz, 1741

Austrians

Mollwitz

Laugwitz

Hermsdorf

Prussians

Pampitz

0   0.5 km

0   0.5 mile

■ DETTINGEN, 27 JUNE 1743

An allied army of 35,000 men including British, German and Austrian contingents under the overall command of King George II defeated a 45,000-strong French force under the Duc de Noailles at Dettingen in Bavaria.

The Allied army was retreating along the northern bank of the River Main when it was faced by a French blocking force of 23,000 men under the Duc de Gramont in a strong defensive position around the village of Dettingen, supported by artillery batteries on the southern bank. Noailles intended that this force should fix the Allied army, while he sent a further 12,000 men across the Main at Aschaffenburg to attack the Allied rear. However, Gramont became impatient and attacked against orders, achieving some initial success before his men were routed by an Allied counter-attack. The French lost 4500 men, while Allied casualties totalled 2500.

■ TOULON, 22 FEBRUARY 1744

A Franco-Spanish fleet of 27 ships of the line under José Navarro and La Bruyere De Court defeated VAdm Thomas Mathews' British fleet of 30 ships of the line off Toulon. Ten British ships were damaged in a confused action in which the British failed to exploit their numerical superiority due to poor signalling. The Franco-Spanish fleet lost a single ship which was scuttled to prevent its capture.

■ VILLAFRANCA, 20 APRIL 1744

The Prince de Conti's Franco-Spanish army of 30,000 men attacked an 8000-strong Anglo-Sardinian force commanded by the Marquis of Susa near Villafranca, which had taken up strongly entrenched positions in the hills overlooking the town. Conti's men overran many of the Anglo-Sardinian positions, but were eventually driven off by a series of counter-attacks, losing 2800 men. The marquis and some 1800 of his men were captured, with a further 1500 killed and wounded.

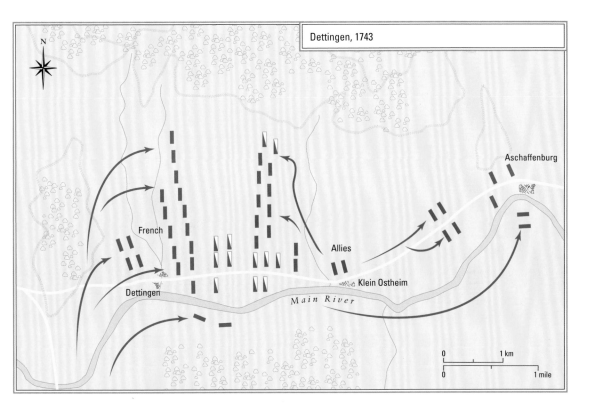

Dettingen, 1743

CASTELDELFINO, 18 JULY 1744

A French army of 5000 men under the Prince de Conti attacked a Sardinian force of only 2000 men commanded by King Charles Emmanuel III near the village of Casteldelfino in Piedmont. The Sardinians had deployed in strong defensive positions across mountainous terrain, which were reinforced with extensive field defences, but were defeated in a series of fierce actions with heavy losses. The French lost at least 1900 men.

VELLETRI, 12 AUGUST 1744

Prince Lobkowitz' 10,000-strong Austrian force was defeated by a Neapolitan and Spanish army of 12,000 men under King Charles VII of Naples. Each side lost 4000 men, but the Austrians were forced to retreat.

CUNEO (MADONNA DELL'OLMO), 30 SEPTEMBER 1744

The Prince de Conti's 26,000-strong Franco-Spanish army defeated a Sardinian army of 25,000 men under King Charles Emmanuel III near Cuneo in Piedmont. The Sardinians lost 4400 men, while inflicting 2700 casualties on Conti's forces.

PFAFFENHOFEN, 15 APRIL 1745

A 7000-strong French force commanded by the Comte de Ségur was defeated at Pfaffenhofen in Bavaria by Count Karl Josef Batthyány's Austrian army of 10,000 men. French casualties totalled 2400, while the Austrians lost 800 men.

FONTENOY, 11 MAY 1745

A 50,000-strong Allied army principally composed of British, Hanoverian and Dutch troops under the Duke of Cumberland was defeated by a French army of similar size commanded by Marshal Maurice de Saxe.

Cumberland was attempting to raise the French siege of Tournai, but found that Saxe had taken up a strong position south-east of the town which was protected by extensive field fortifications. After failing to make progress on the flanks – the Dutch on the left, Brigadier Ingolsby's brigade

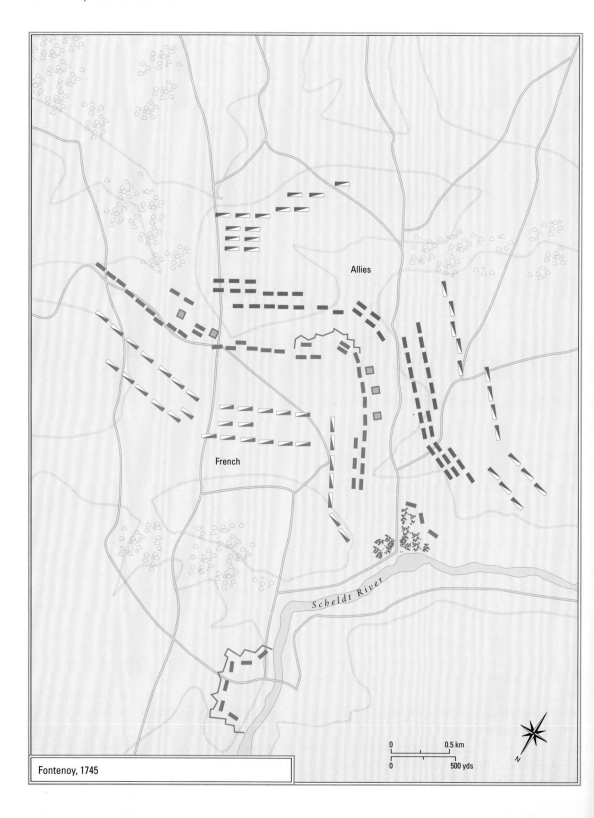

Allies

French

Scheldt River

0   0.5 km

0   500 yds

N

Fontenoy, 1745

on the right – Cumberland launched a frontal attack. Despite devastating flanking fire, the British and Hanoverian infantry broke through the French lines and came close to winning a decisive victory. However, Saxe scraped up just enough reinforcements to halt the Allied advance. Cumberland lost 11,000 men, but was able to retreat in good order, having inflicted 7500 casualties on the French.

■ **HOHENFRIEDBERG, 4 JUNE 1745**
Frederick the Great's 58,000 Prussians attacked an Austro-Saxon army of similar size commanded by Prince Charles of Lorraine near Striegau in Silesia. Frederick led his men on a night march intending to surprise the enemy in a dawn attack on their camp, but a clash with Saxon outposts robbed him of complete surprise. Despite this, he won a decisive victory, inflicting over 13,000 casualties for the loss of 4800 men.

■ **LOUISBOURG, 11 MAY–28 JUNE 1745**
A 4200-strong New England colonial force supported by a British fleet attacked Louisbourg, capital of the French province of Île-Royale (present-day Cape Breton Island). The French garrison of 1800 men surrendered after a six-week siege.

■ **BASSIGNANO, 27 SEPTEMBER 1745**
The Marquis de Maillebois' 70,000-strong Franco-Spanish army defeated a Sardinian army of 54,000 men under King Charles Emmanuel III at Bassignano near Alessandria. The Franco-Spanish army inflicted 1500 casualties for the loss of 500 men.

■ **SOOR, 30 SEPTEMBER 1745**
Frederick the Great's 22,500 Prussians were surprised by a 39,000-strong Austrian army under Prince Charles of Lorraine near the Bohemian village of Burkersdorf. The Prussians stormed the heavily defended Graner-Koppe hill that dominated the battlefield, before following up this success with an assault on Burkersdorf. The capture of the village led to the collapse of the Austrian army, which retreated with the loss of 7500 men; Prussian casualties totalled 4000 men.

■ **HENNERSDORF, 23 NOVEMBER 1745**
MGen Zieten's Prussian force of two regiments of hussars and two regiments of cuirassiers defeated a Saxon detachment of two infantry battalions and three cavalry regiments near Hennersdorf in Silesia, inflicting 2000 casualties.

■ **KESSELSDORF, 15 DECEMBER 1745**
A 32,000-strong Prussian force commanded by Leopold I, Prince of Anhalt-Dessau, attacked and defeated a Saxon army of 35,000 men under Gen Rutowsky at Kesselsdorf, near Dresden. The Prussians lost 5100 men, but inflicted 10,500 casualties.

■ **PIACENZA, 16 JUNE 1746**
A 40,000-strong Franco-Spanish army under the Comte de Gages was defeated by Prince Josef Wenzel's Austrian army of 45,000 men near Piacenza in northern Italy. The Comte intended to win the battle with powerful attacks on each flank, but the French contingent was trapped in a narrow valley as it attempted an outflanking manoeuvre and the Spanish were defeated by Austrian cavalry. Franco-Spanish casualties totalled 13,000, while the Austrians lost 3400.

■ **NEGAPATAM, 25 JUNE 1746**
Adm Bertrand-François Mahé de La Bourdonnais' formed an improvised squadron of seven French armed merchantmen fitted with numerous 'quakers' (dummy cannon) and one ship of the line. He was opposed by a far stronger British squadron of seven ships of the line commanded by Cdre Edward Peyton, who allowed himself to be intimidated by French attempts to close and board and broke off the action without serious losses on either side.

■ **ROTTOFREDDO, 12 AUGUST 1746**
A small Austrian force commanded by Antoniotto Botta Adorno attacked a Franco-Spanish army under the Marquis de Maillebois at Rottofreddo (now Rottofreno) in Piacenza, northern Italy. The Austrians were defeated, allowing Maillebois to retreat to Genoa.

■ **MADRAS, 7–9 SEPTEMBER 1746**
Adm Bertrand-François Mahé de La Bourdonnais'

squadron landed a French army under Joseph François Dupleix, which besieged Madras. The city's poorly constructed defences rapidly crumbled under bombardment and the 300-strong British garrison surrendered within 48 hours.

■ GENOA, SEPTEMBER 1746

An Austrian and Sardinian army commanded by Antoniotto Botta Adorno took Genoa with the support of a British squadron under Capt George Townshend. Adorno's harsh rule as governor of Genoa caused a successful revolt in December 1746.

■ ROCOURT (ROCOUX/RAUCOUX) 11 OCTOBER 1746

A French army of 120,000 men under Marshal Saxe attacked and defeated Prince Charles of Lorraine's 97,000-strong army composed of Austrian, British, Hanoverian and Dutch troops. Saxe inflicted 8000 casualties for the loss of 3500 men.

■ GENOA, 11 APRIL–9 JULY 1747

An Austro-Sardinian army under Count Schulenberg besieged Genoa, but French troops were able to break through to reinforce the garrison. The siege was raised by a Franco-Spanish relief force commanded by Marshal Belle-Isle and Gen Las Minas.

■ FIRST CAPE FINISTERRE, 14 MAY 1747

VAdm George Anson's fleet of 14 British ships of the line attacked a French 30-ship convoy with an escort of four ships of the line and three frigates commanded by Adm de la Jonquière in the Bay of Biscay. The British captured four ships of the line, two frigates and seven merchantmen in a five-hour battle. One French frigate, one French East India Company warship and the remaining merchantmen escaped.

■ LAUFFELD, 2 JULY 1747

The Duke of Cumberland's allied army of 60,000 men, which included British, Hanoverian, Austrian and Dutch contingents, advanced on

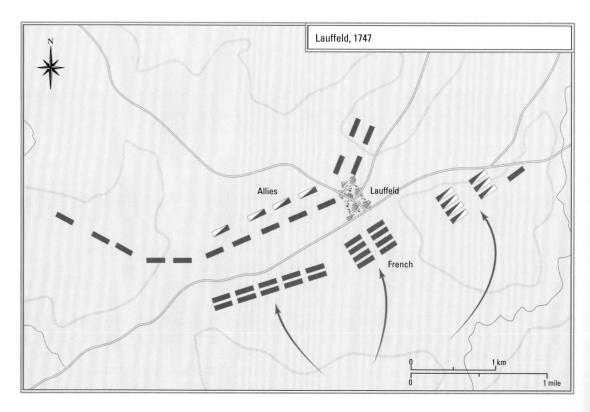

Lauffeld, 1747

Lauffeld near Maastricht, intending to trap an isolated detachment of the 80,000-strong French army commanded by Marshal Saxe. However, Saxe had deliberately deployed this detachment as bait to draw the allies out and force them into battle on the ground of his choosing.

Cumberland was beaten, largely due to ignoring advice to occupy and fortify a line of villages across the front of the Allied army. These were the targets of repeated French attacks and changed hands several times, until a major attack on Lauffeld forced out the 10,000 British and Hanoverian defenders. An Anglo-Dutch counter-attack failed and the French broke the centre of the allied line, forcing Cumberland to retreat with the loss of 8000 men. French casualties may well have been slightly higher.

■ **BERGEN-OP-ZOOM, JULY–SEPTEMBER 1747**

The survivors of the 10,000-strong Anglo-Dutch garrison of Bergen-op-Zoom surrendered when the city was stormed by a French army of 30,000

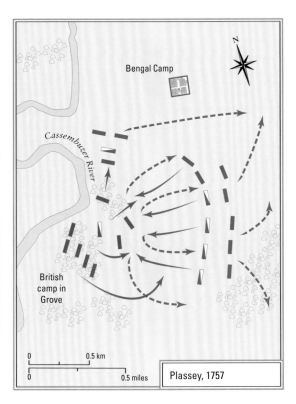

men commanded by the Comte de Lowendal. Each side lost almost 5000 men.

■ **ASSIETTA, 19 JULY 1747**

The Chevalier de Belle-Isle's 40,000-strong French army was routed when it attacked the Assietta Pass held by the Count of Bricherasio's Sardinian garrison of 7000 men. French casualties totalled 5000, while the Sardinians lost 127 men.

■ **MAASTRICHT, APRIL–MAY 1748**

A French army under Marshal Saxe forced the surrender of the Dutch garrison of Maastricht after a two-month siege. The city was returned to Dutch rule later that year by the Treaty of Aix-la-Chapelle.

Indian and South-East Asian Wars 1750–75

■ **ARCOT, 23 SEPTEMBER–14 NOVEMBER 1751**

Robert Clive's force of 200 British troops and 300 sepoys (Indian soldiers) successfully defended the fort at Arcot against a 50-day siege by almost 7500 Indian and French troops commanded by Chanda Sahib, Nawab of the Carnatic.

■ **CALCUTTA, JUNE 1756**

An Indian army of at least 35,000 men commanded by Siraj ud-Daulah, Nawab of Bengal, attacked Calcutta, which was defended by a garrison of little more than 500 men under the East India Company's governor, John Zephaniah Holwell. The 50-strong garrison of the East India Company fort at Cossimbazar surrendered after a two-day siege, while the city itself fell as soon as Fort William was stormed on 13 June.

■ **PEGU, MAY 1757**

Alaungpaya attacked the Mon King Binnya Dala, taking Ava, Prome, Rangoon and finally Pegu, where the king was captured. Alaungpaya founded a 120-year dynasty and Binnya Dala was executed in 1774 by Alaungpaya's son Hsinbyushin.

■ **PLASSEY, 23 JUNE 1757**

Following the capture of Calcutta by Siraj

ud-Daulah, Nawab of Bengal, the East India Company retaliated with an offensive led by Col Robert Clive, which recaptured the city in February 1757. Clive then assembled a force of 800 European troops and 2100 Indian sepoys – supported by eight guns – and attacked the Nawab's field army of 35,000 infantry, 18,000 cavalry and at least 53 guns near the village of Plassey (Palashi) in Bengal. The Nawab's artillery inflicted only a few casualties on Clive's forces before a tropical storm soaked much of the Indian army's ammunition, drastically reducing their firepower. Clive's forces had carefully protected their ammunition, which was relatively unaffected and exploited their advantage in firepower, destroying an Indian cavalry charge, before launching a counter-attack that broke Siraj ud-Daulah's army. Clive inflicted at least 500 casualties for the loss of 70 men.

■ SIAM, 1759–60

A Burmese army of 40,000 men commanded by King Alaungpaya invaded Siam (Thailand). The invasion force won several victories, but broke off the siege of the Siamese capital, Ayutthaya, due to Alaungpaya's terminal illness.

■ MASULIPATAM, 6 MARCH–7 APRIL 1759

Robert Clive sent Col Francis Forde from Calcutta against French forces under Herbert de Brienne, Comte de Conflans. Forde besieged the key port of Masulipatam, forcing Conflans to surrender with almost 3000 men.

■ WANDIWASH, 22 JANUARY 1760

The Comte de Lally's 2000-strong French army besieging Wandiwash was attacked by a British relief force of 1700 men under Col Eyre Coote. A French cavalry charge was repulsed and Lally then ordered an infantry attack. As this was also defeated, his army was demoralized by a chance British shot, which blew up an ammunition wagon. Coote won a decisive victory, inflicting at least 600 casualties for the loss of 200 men.

■ PONDICHERRY, 4 SEP 1760–15 JAN 1761

Col Eyre Coote followed up his victory at Wandiwash with a siege of the main French base at Pondicherry, supported at sea by a squadron commanded by RAdm Charles Steevens. Despite storm damage to the fleet, Coote maintained the siege and forced the surrender of the Comte de Lally's garrison, virtually ending the French presence in India. British casualties totalled 32 officers and 500 rank and file either killed or wounded.

■ PANIPAT, 14 JANUARY 1761

In 1758, the Marathas occupied Delhi, captured Lahore and drove out Timur Shah Durrani, the son and viceroy of the Afghan ruler, Ahmad Shah Abdali. This marked the peak of the Maratha Empire's power and provoked a counter-offensive by Abdali, who raised an army of 100,000 men, including contingents from the Rohillas and Shuja-ud-Daula, Nawab of Oudh. The Maratha army totalled 70,000 men, but was encumbered by anything up to 300,000 non-combatant camp followers and pilgrims.

The Afghan forces cut the Marathas' supply lines, forcing men and horses to live on reduced rations, which severely weakened the Marathas' formidable cavalry. In a hard-fought action, Afghan weight of numbers and the firepower of their 2000 *shutarnaals* – light camel-mounted swivel guns – proved to be decisive. The Marathas sustained 30,000 casualties and were decisively defeated, while the Afghans lost at least 20,000.

■ SIAM, 1765

King Hsinbyushin's Burmese army of 50,000 men invaded Siam (Thailand), winning several victories before taking the Siamese capital of Ayutthaya in April 1767 after a 14-month siege. The city was destroyed and Siam temporarily ceased to exist.

■ BURMA, 1765

Alarmed by the Burmese conquest of Chinese border territories, the Manchu Qianlong Emperor ordered an invasion of Burma. This offensive was repulsed and a settlement was only reached in 1769 after three further Chinese invasions.

CHENGAM (CHANGAMA), 3 SEPTEMBER 1767

A combined Mysore – Hyderabad army of 70,000 men under Hyder Ali – attacked the East India Company's outpost at Changama. Although heavily outnumbered, Col Joseph Smith's 7000-strong garrison beat off the assault, inflicting heavy casualties on the attackers.

TIRUVANNAMALAI, 26 SEPTEMBER 1767

After defeating Hyder Ali at Changama, Col Joseph Smith retreated to Tiruvannamalai for supplies and reinforcements. The Mysore-Hyderabad army attacked the city, but was again repulsed with heavy losses by the East India Company's garrison.

CAPTURE OF GWALIOR, 3 AUGUST 1780

Gen Thomas Goddard ordered Capt William Popham to take the Maratha fortress of Gwalior, near Lashkar. In a remarkable night-time assault – aided by treachery – Popham's small force scaled the walls and the surprised garrison quickly fell.

Seven Years' War 1756–63

MINORCA, 20 MAY 1756

A British squadron of 12 ships of the line and seven frigates under Adm Byng was sent to Minorca to support the island's garrison, but the fleet was intercepted by the Marquis de La Galissonière's fleet of 12 French ships of the line and five frigates. Byng was cautious, sticking rigidly to the Admiralty's fighting instructions and he broke off the action after several of his ships were damaged. This defeat led to the French capture of Minorca.

LOBOSITZ (LOVOSICE) 1 OCTOBER 1756

A 34,000-strong Austrian army commanded by Generalfeldmarschall Maximilian Ulysses, Reichsgraf von Browne, was defeated by Frederick the Great's 29,000 Prussians. Both sides lost 2900 men, but the Austrian retreat left their Saxon allies trapped in Pirna.

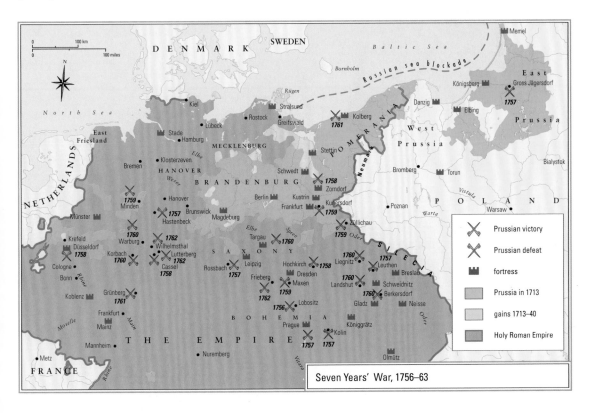

Seven Years' War, 1756–63

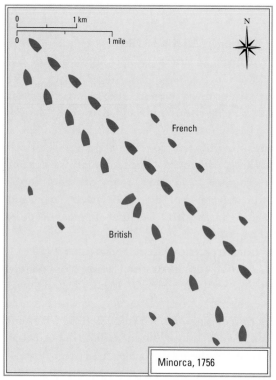

Minorca, 1756

REICHENBERG, 21 APRIL 1757

A Prussian corps of 16,000 men under August Wilhelm, Duke of Brunswick-Bevern, invaded Bohemia. Near Reichenberg (modern Liberec) he attacked and defeated a 10,500-strong Austrian force commanded by Count Christian Moritz von Koenigsegg und Rothfels.

PRAGUE, 6 MAY 1757

Frederick the Great's 67,000 Prussians attacked an Austrian army of 60,000 men commanded by Prince Charles Alexander of Lorraine. The Austrians held an exceptionally strong defensive position outside Prague and an initial Prussian attempt to outflank their line was repulsed with heavy losses. Further Prussian outflanking moves were more successful and Prince Charles ordered his forces to retreat into the fortifications of Prague. Austrian casualties totalled 16,500, while Frederick lost 14,300 men.

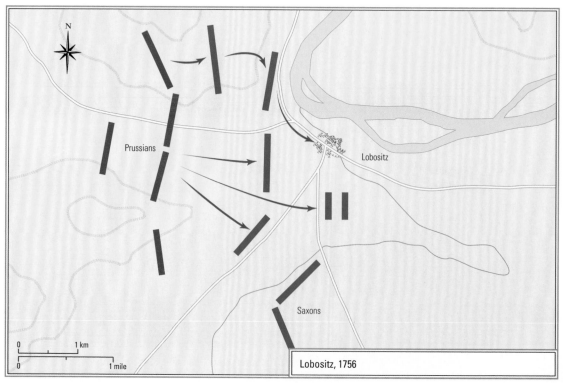

Lobositz, 1756

◼ KOLIN, 18 JUNE 1757

Generalfeldmarschall Count Leopold Joseph von Daun led a 44,000-strong Austrian Army to decisively defeat a Prussian force of 32,000 men under Frederick the Great. Frederick lost 14,000 men, while Austrian casualties were no more than 8000.

◼ HASTENBECK, 26 JULY 1757

A French army of 60,000 men commanded by Marshal Louis Charles d'Estrées defeated the Duke of Cumberland's 35,000-strong Hanoverian force at Hastenbeck, near Hamelin. The French suffered heavy losses from well-entrenched Hanoverian artillery, but were able to outflank Cumberland's position. His attempts to counterattack the outflanking force weakened the centre of his line, which was overrun by a frontal assault. The French lost 2200 men, while Cumberland's casualties totalled 1400.

◼ GROSS-JÄGERSDORF, 30 AUGUST 1757

A Prussian force of 28,000 men under GenFM

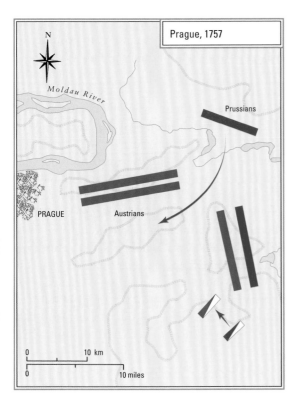

Prague, 1757

Hans von Lehwaldt was defeated by FM Stepan Fedorovich Apraksin's 55,000-strong Russian army at Gross-Jägersdorf in East Prussia. Prussian casualties totalled 3600, but Apraksin lost almost 6000 men.

◼ MOYS, 7 SEPTEMBER 1757

A 13,000-strong Prussian force commanded by Gen Hans Karl von Winterfeldt was defeated near Görlitz, in Upper Lusatia (present-day Zgorzelec in Poland) by an Austrian army of 26,000 men under Count Leopold Joseph von Daun.

◼ ROCHEFORT, SEPTEMBER 1757

A British force of 8000 men under Sir John Mordaunt landed on the French coast to raid the port of Rochefort. The Île d'Aix was taken, but Rochefort was not attacked and the force was withdrawn.

◼ ROSSBACH, 5 NOVEMBER 1757

A Franco-Austrian army of at least 41,000 men under Charles de Rohan, Prince of Soubise and Prince Joseph of Saxe-Hildburghausen invaded Saxony. Frederick the Great could only deploy 21,000 men to oppose them and both sides spent several days in indecisive manoeuvring for position.

On the evening of 4 November, the Prussian army camped around the town of Rossbach, close to the enemy's position. The next morning, Hilburghausen and Soubise decided to attack. Rather than making a frontal attack, they intended to screen their camp and move in column around the Prussian left flank, catching Frederick unawares. However, it took most of the morning for the French and Austrians to form up into three columns of march. These were headed by advance guards of Austrian heavy cavalry. French troops formed the first two Allied columns, while Hilburgshausen led the third.

Prussian reconnaissance indicated that several French battalions were screening the enemy camp, but that it was clearly the centre of great activity. Even when the Allied columns began to move southwards, Frederick believed that they were beginning to retreat, but rapidly changed

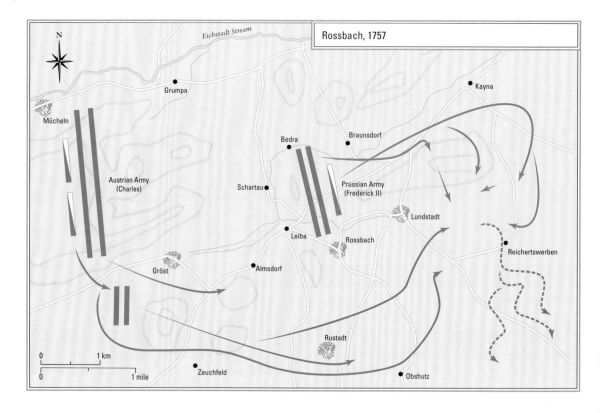

his mind as the columns began to swing around his left flank. He ordered Gen von Seydlitz, his cavalry commander, to take all the army's cavalry and head off the allied advance.

As Seydlitz led his cavalry away, Frederick redeployed the rest of the army, taking advantage of the local geography. The Janus Hill lay immediately behind his lines and to the flank of the Allied columns. He ordered a battery of 18 heavy guns to the crest, from which they bombarded the French as the 38 squadrons of Seydlitz' cavalry moved around the hill, surprising the allied cavalry, which was still in column. His devastating charge scattered the Austrian cuirassier regiments of Bretlach and Trautmansdorff and the Szecheny Hussars. French cavalry attempting to support the Austrians was also routed, after which Seydlitz quickly rallied his men and led them on their own wide flanking march to the French right, beyond the towns of Posendorf and Tagewerden.

Prussian infantry were now in position to make their attack from the Janus Hill. Only seven French battalions had time to deploy before the Prussian infantry attacked, shredding the heads of the Allied columns with disciplined volleys. The fire of the leading Prussian regiments of Kleist and Alt-Braunschweig was especially effective, inflicting heavy casualties on the French regiments of Piémont and Mailly. As the infantry attack developed, Seydlitz' cavalry emerged and charged the French right flank. This charge broke the already shaken French columns. Hilburghausen was luckier as the Austrians were in the rear, giving him time to bring his battalions into line to cover the French rout. Prussian musketry and artillery fire tore holes in Hilburghausen's line, but the Hesse-Darmstadt battalions stood firm under withering fire while covering the retreat. Seydlitz then reformed his cavalry for a further charge, which finally cracked Austrian morale. Hilburghausen was

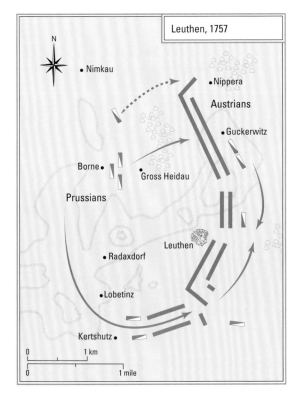

Leuthen, 1757

35,000 Prussians could not break even this over-extended enemy by a frontal attack and feinted against the Austrian right wing to cover a march around their left flank. The plan worked perfectly; an alarmed Prince Charles reinforced the forces on his right and remained completely oblivious to the real Prussian attack until far too late.

When Frederick's assault went in, the Austrian left wing disintegrated. Prince Charles rushed forces from his right and attempted to form a new line anchored on Leuthen to halt the Prussian advance. However, Frederick's infantry stormed the town and the Austrian army was routed with the loss of 22,000 men. Prussian casualties were less than 6500.

■ FORT ST DAVID, 1758

Fort St David was the principal British fortress in south-eastern India, which had been strengthened since its purchase by the East India Company in 1690. Despite these improvements, it was captured by the French in 1758.

■ CUDDALORE, 28 APRIL 1758

VAdm George Pocock's squadron of seven ships of the line and a frigate fought an indecisive action against a French squadron of eight ships of the line and a frigate under the Comte d'Aché.

■ OLMÜTZ (OLOMOUC) MAY–JUNE 1758

Frederick the Great invaded the Austrian province of Moravia in May 1758 and besieged the city of Olmütz (modern Olomouc). The destruction of a massive Prussian supply convoy at Domstadtl forced him to raise the siege.

■ RHEINBERG, 12 JUNE 1758

A French force under the Comte de Clermont attempted to block the advance of a Hanoverian army commanded by the Duke of Brunswick in an indecisive action that led to the battle of Krefeld.

■ KREFELD (CRÉFELD) 23 JUNE 1758

A 32,000-strong Hanoverian force under Duke Ferdinand of Brunswick attacked and defeated a French army of 47,000 men commanded by the Comte de Clermont. French casualties totalled 3000, while Ferdinand lost no more than 2200 men.

able to extract a few battalions from the general rout, but the Allied army was shattered, losing 3000 killed and wounded, plus 5000 prisoners. Total Prussian casualties were only 169 dead and 379 wounded.

The battle had lasted less than an hour and a half, with the last infantry fire-fight lasting no more than 15 minutes. Only seven Prussian infantry battalions had engaged the enemy, firing five to 15 rounds per man.

■ BRESLAU, 22 NOVEMBER 1757

The Duke of Brunswick-Bevern's 28,000 Prussians were defeated by an Austrian army of 84,000 men under Prince Charles Alexander of Lorraine. The Duke lost 6000 men, but his stubborn defence inflicted 5000 casualties on the Austrians.

■ LEUTHEN, 5 DECEMBER 1757

A 60,000-strong Austrian army under Prince Charles of Lorraine deployed on a front of almost 8km centred on the town of Leuthen in Silesia. Frederick the Great appreciated that his

■ **DOMSTADTL, 30 JUNE 1758**

By June 1758, the Prussian army besieging Olmütz (Olomouc) was rapidly running out of supplies and Frederick the Great ordered the formation of a massive resupply convoy of 4000 wagons and 2500 cattle, escorted by almost 11,000 troops. This convoy immediately became a priority target of an Austrian force of 12,000 men under MGen Ernst Gideon von Laudon.

The convoy first came under attack on 28 June. Although the Austrians withdrew after five hours, they inflicted considerable damage and, even with the help of 20,000 men under LGen von Ziethen who arrived several hours later, the convoy was unable to resume its journey for almost 48 hours. It had barely got under way when it was attacked again by an Austrian force of 12,000 men. Despite its 30,000-strong escort, the convoy was almost totally destroyed, forcing Frederick to raise the siege.

■ **NEGAPATAM, 3 AUGUST 1758**

VAdm George Pocock's squadron of seven ships of the line and a frigate fought another action against a French squadron of eight ships of the line and a frigate under the Comte d'Aché. Again, the action was indecisive.

■ **CHERBOURG, 7–16 AUGUST 1758**

A British raiding force under LGen Thomas Bligh defeated a 3000-strong French detachment and stormed the city of Cherbourg. After occupying the town for a week while its defences were destroyed, the force re-embarked and returned to Britain.

■ **ZORNDORF, 25 AUGUST 1758**

Frederick the Great's 36,000 Prussians attacked and defeated a Russian army of 42,000 men under Count Wilhelm Fermor in a confused battle of attrition. Prussian casualties exceeded 12,000, while the Russians lost at least 21,000 men.

■ **SAINT CAST, 11 SEPTEMBER 1758**

LGen Thomas Bligh's 10,000-strong raiding force was preparing to re-embark at Saint Cast in Brittany when it was defeated by 9000 French troops under the Marquis d'Aubigné. Bligh lost 2000 men, while French casualties totalled 300.

■ **TORNOW, 26 SEPTEMBER 1758**

A 6000-strong Prussian army under Gen von Wedel attacked and quite understandably defeated a Swedish force of only 600 men at Tornow, Brandenburg. Despite being heavily outnumbered, the Swedes inflicted 800 casualties for the loss of 100 men.

■ **HOCHKIRCH, 14 OCTOBER 1758**

An Austrian army of at least 78,000 men commanded by Marshal Leopold von Daun surprised and defeated a Prussian force of 30,000 men under Frederick the Great. Austrian casualties totalled 7300, but Frederick lost 9000 men.

■ **MADRAS, 14 DECEMBER 1758–16 FEBRUARY 1759**

The Comte de Lally's 8000-strong army besieged Madras, which was defended by a British garrison of 3900 men commanded by Col William Draper. Lally raised the siege on the arrival of a small relief force.

■ **BERGEN, 13 APRIL 1759**

Duke Ferdinand of Brunswick's 35,000-strong Hanoverian and British army advanced into Hesse against a French force of 28,000 men commanded by the Duc de Broglie. The French had taken up a strong defensive position around the fortified town of Bergen, but Ferdinand under-estimated their strength and ordered an immediate attack, which was beaten off after heavy fighting. French casualties totalled 1800, while Ferdinand lost almost 2400 men.

■ **LE HAVRE, 3–5 JULY 1759**

RAdm Rodney's squadron of five ships of the line, five frigates and six bomb ketches bombarded Le Havre for two days, destroying many of the barges being assembled for the planned French invasion of England.

■ **KAY, 23 JULY 1759**

A 28,000-strong Prussian force under Gen von Wedel was defeated after a reckless attack on a numerically superior Russian army of 47,000 men commanded by Count Pyotr Saltykov. Prussian casualties totalled 8300 and Saltykov lost 5000 men.

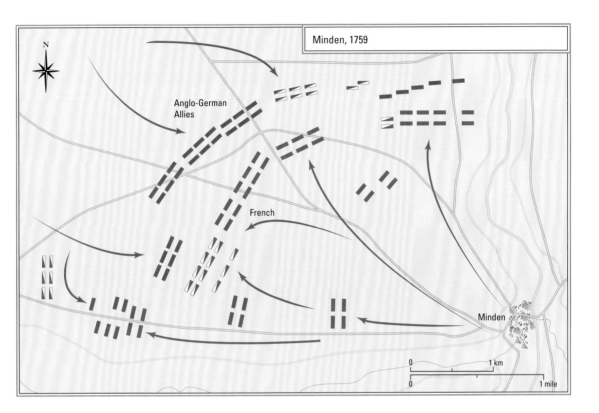

Minden, 1759

Anglo-German
Allies

French

Minden

0   1 km

0   1 mile

N

■ **MINDEN, 1 AUGUST 1759**

Duke Ferdinand of Brunswick's Anglo-German army of 42,500 men had retreated to Minden, pursued in the process by a 54,000-strong French force commanded by the Marquis de Contades. Due to misunderstood orders, six British and three Hanoverian infantry battalions advanced against the French cavalry forming the centre of Contades' line. They beat off three charges before the rest of Ferdinand's army attacked. The French finally broke under the pressure of the assault from the Anglo-German forces, with the loss of over 7000 men.

■ **KUNERSDORF, 12 AUGUST 1759**

A 60,000-strong Austro-Russian army under Count Pyotr Saltykov and MGen Ernst Gideon von Laudon was attacked by Frederick the Great, who had a force of 51,000 men at his disposal. The Prussians were defeated in this bloody clash, losing over 25,000 men, while allied casualties totalled 23,500.

■ **LAGOS, 18–19 AUGUST 1759**

A British squadron of 14 ships under Adm Boscawen intercepted and defeated Adm de la Clue's French squadron of 12 ships. Two French ships were destroyed and three were captured.

■ **MAXEN, 20 NOVEMBER 1759**

LGen von Finck's 14,000-strong Prussian corps was defeated in the battle of Maxen by an Austrian army of 32,000 men commanded by FM von Daun. The Prussians surrendered after sustaining 2000 casualties, while von Daun lost almost 1000 men.

■ **PONDICHERRY, 10 SEPTEMBER 1759**

On 10 September 1759, VAdm Pocock's squadron of nine ships of the line and a frigate fought an indecisive action against a French squadron of 11 ships of the line and two frigates under the Comte d'Aché.

■ **QUIBERON BAY, 1759**

The French realized that they would either match the British commitment of resources

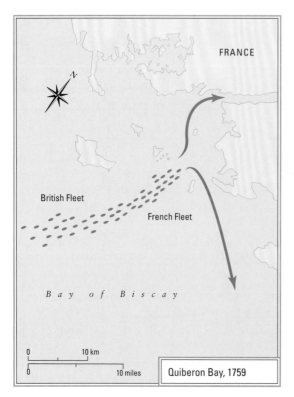

Quiberon Bay, 1759

to North America or forfeit their possessions there. Accordingly, 21 capital ships under Adm Conflans sought to break out from Brest and cross the Atlantic with much needed military support. British Adm Edward Hawke, who was blockading Brest, had stationed a frigate at this anchorage, which bore him word of the escaped French fleet's presence there. Despite the severity of the ongoing weather, Hawke bore down upon the French with 23 ships, ordering his captains to 'Just go at them' in the wind-swept confines of the narrow river sheltering the French. The storm and British cannon sank eight French ships, with the British finding at sunrise the next day that two of their own ships had been wrecked. A total of eight French ships were taken, two escaped and the rest were trapped in the river for the duration.

■ **HOYERSWERDA, 25 SEPTEMBER 1759**
A detachment of 3000 men under the command of Prince Henry of Prussia defeated an Austrian force of similar size under Gen Wehla near Hoyerswerda in Saxony. The Austrians lost 2400 men, but Prussian casualties were minimal in this one-sided engagement.

■ **MEISSEN, 4 DECEMBER 1759**
Prince Henry of Prussia's force of 26,000 men invaded Saxony, but was defeated by a 21,000-strong Austrian army commanded by FM von Daun. Prince Henry lost 7000 men, but Austrian casualties were barely 3000.

■ **LANDESHUT, 23 JUNE 1760**
A Prussian corps of 12,000 men under Gen Fouqué was attacked and defeated by a 28,000-strong Austrian army commanded by Gen von Laudon near Landshut in Silesia. Fouqué was captured and his corps lost 10,000 men.

■ **KORBACH, 10 JULY 1760**
Duke Ferdinand of Brunswick's 20,000-strong Anglo-German army was attacked and defeated by a French army of similar size commanded by the Duc de Broglie. Ferdinand lost 1000 men, but inflicted 800 casualties on the French.

■ **EMSDORF, 17 JULY 1760**
The Prince of Hesse-Kassel's 3000-strong Anglo-German force surprised and defeated a French detachment of similar size commanded by MGen Glaubitz. The French force was shattered, losing 2600 men. Allied casualties were no more than 200.

■ **WARBURG, 31 JULY 1760**
The 24,000-strong advance guard of Duke Ferdinand of Brunswick's Anglo-German army attacked and defeated a French corps of 21,500 men commanded by the Chevalier du Moy. Ferdinand lost 1200 men, but French casualties totalled 3000.

■ **LIEGNITZ, 15 AUGUST 1760**
Frederick the Great's army of 30,000 men was virtually surrounded in Silesia by Austrian and Russian forces. He attempted to breakout before he was completely surrounded, but, in doing so, collided with an Austrian army of similar size commanded by Gen von Laudon near Liegnitz (modern Legnica). The action was a confused night encounter battle in which Frederick

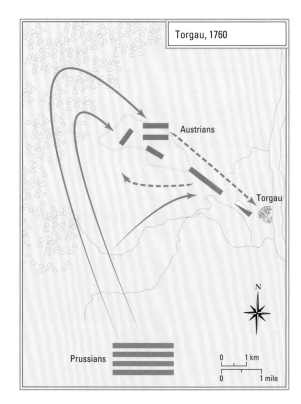

Torgau, 1760

Austrians

Torgau

N

Prussians

0   1 km

0   1 mile

decisively defeated the Austrians, inflicting a total of 10,000 casualties for the loss of just 1800 men.

■ KLOSTER KAMPEN, 15 OCTOBER 1760

The Duke of Brunswick's 20,000-strong Anglo-German force was defeated by a French army of 25,000 men commanded by the Marquis de Castries. Despite the defeat in battle, the Prince's force inflicted 3000 casualties for the loss of 1600 men.

■ TORGAU, 3 NOVEMBER 1760

A Prussian army of 50,000 men commanded by Frederick the Great attacked FM von Daun's 53,000-strong Austrian army. Frederick won a narrow victory, losing almost 17,000 men, while inflicting almost 16,000 casualties on the Austrians.

■ PONDICHERRY, 4 SEPTEMBER 1760– 15 JANUARY 1761

A British army commanded by LGen Sir Eyre Coote besieged Pondicherry, which was

defended by a French garrison under the Comte de Lally. The garrison only surrendered when on the verge of starvation.

■ VILLINGHAUSEN, 15–16 JULY 1761

Two French armies commanded by the Duc de Broglie and Prince de Soubise joined forces, intending to force Duke Ferdinand of Brunswick to abandon the important town of Lippstadt. Allied reinforcements under Gen Spörcken brought Ferdinand's forces up to 65,000 while the combined French armies numbered around 90,000. The French attacks were badly co-ordinated and were defeated with the loss of 5000 men, while Ferdinand's casualties were no more than 1400.

■ MARTINIQUE, 5 JANUARY–12 FEBRUARY 1762

The British invasion force comprising approximately 8000 men commanded by MGen Robert Monckton sailed from Barbados on 5 January, arriving off Martinique two days later. The island was defended by a French garrison of 1200 regular troops, 7000 local militia and 4000 privateers, but the invaders landed unopposed on 16 January, near the southern tip of the island about 5km from the capital of Fort Royal (now Fort-de-France). Monckton patiently constructed batteries for his main offensive, which was not launched until preparations were complete on 24 January. Under covering artillery fire, his men cleared on the steep slopes of Morne Grenier in fierce fighting. By 28 January, Monckton's lines were secure and he had established firing positions overlooking Fort Royal. The town surrendered on 3 February and the remainder of the island was secured by 12 February.

■ WILHELMSTHAL, 24 JUNE 1762

Duke Ferdinand of Brunswick's Anglo-German force of 50,000 men defeated a 70,000-strong French army commanded by the Prince Soubise and the Duc d'Estrées. Ferdinand inflicted at least 4500 casualties for the loss of only 700 men.

■ BURKERSDORF, 21 JULY 1762

A Prussian army of 40,000 men commanded by

Frederick the Great attacked and defeated FM von Daun's 30,000-strong Austrian army near Burkersdorf (now Burkatów) in Silesia. This defeat forced the Austrians to withdraw to the city of Glatz.

■ **HAVANA, 6 JUNE–13 AUGUST 1762**
LGen George Keppel's 12,000-strong landing force besieged and took Havana, which was defended by a Spanish garrison of 11,500 men under MGen Juan de Prado. A total of 13 Spanish ships of the line were captured during the engagement.

■ **MANILA, 24 SEPTEMBER–6 OCTOBER 1762**
A substantial British force of 10,300 men under the command of Brig William Draper made an unopposed amphibious landing in the Philippines and captured Manila, which was defended by a 9000-strong Spanish garrison commanded by acting Governor and Captain-General Archbishop Manuel Rojo.

■ **FREIBERG, 29 OCTOBER 1762**
Prince Henry of Prussia's 22,000-strong army attacked and defeated an Austrian army of 27,000 men commanded by Prince Stolberg near Freiberg in Saxony. Prince Henry lost 1400 men, but inflicted 7400 casualties on the Austrians.

■ **PORTUGAL, 9 MAY–24 NOVEMBER 1762**
A 45,000-strong Spanish army commanded by the Marquis of Sarriá invaded Portugal, supported by a French force of 12,000 men. The Spanish objective was Porto whose capture would cripple the Portuguese economy, but they made slow progress. This gave time for the 10,000-strong Portuguese field army to be reinforced by 8000 British troops under Wilhelm, Count of Schaumburg-Lippe, who defeated the invasion in a brilliant defensive campaign with minimal casualties.

Russo-Turkish War 1768

■ **CHESMA, 5–7 JULY 1770**
Count Alexei Grigoryevich Orlov's Russian squadron of nine ships of the line and 12 other ships defeated an Ottoman fleet of 16 ships of the line and 57 smaller vessels in Çeşme Bay, western Anatolia.

Koliyivshchyna Uprising 1768–69

■ **KOLIYIVSHCHYNA UPRISING 1768–69**
The Koliyivshchyna (named for the Ukrainian word for impaling) uprising began as a Ukrainian protest against Polish oppression, but rapidly became a racial campaign of extermination against Poles, Jews and non-Orthodox Ukrainians. The revolt was eventually crushed by Polish and Russian troops.

Prelude to American War of Independence 1770

■ **BOSTON MASSACRE, 1770**
Increasing resentment against British troops quartered in Boston culminated in the deaths of five colonists. Harassment of a sentry at the State House escalated into eight British soldiers firing their muskets into the large rock-throwing crowd.

Russo-Polish Conflicts 1771

■ **LANCKORONA, 23 MAY 1771**
A Polish force of 1300 men and 18 guns commanded by the French military envoy LCol Charles François Dumouriez was attacked and decisively defeated by Gen Alexander Suvorov's 4000 Russians at Lanckorona, near Kraków in southern Poland.

Pugachev's Rebellion 1774–75

■ **PUGACHEV'S REBELLION, 1774–75**
Yemelyan Pugachev claimed to be the deposed Tsar Peter III and led a revolt that spread from the Volga to the Urals before it was crushed by Gen Michelsohn's army at Tsaritsyn in January 1775.

Revolutionary Wars 1775–c.1815

The period of the Revolutionary Wars was a transformative age in human history. Not only did the conflicts of the late eighteenth and early nineteenth centuries change the nature of Western politics, but they also brought the power of mass citizenry to the battlefield, and further refined the use of gunpowder weaponry.

American War of Independence 1775–83

■ BOSTON, APRIL 1775–MAY 1776

With cannon captured from Ticonderoga posed on the surrounding heights, the British under Gen Thomas Gage made the rational decision to evacuate by sea, the Americans sparing the British and the city by withholding bombardment.

■ LEXINGTON AND CONCORD, 10 APRIL 1775

With both sides already poised on the brink of hostilities, Gen Thomas Gage sought to arrest colonial leaders John Hancock and Samuel Adams and to seize an American depot of weapons and ammunition at Concord, outside of Boston. Previous British forays had prompted the Americans to establish an early-warning system that alerted the surrounding countryside to the departure by sea of LCol Francis Smith of the 10th Regiment and Maj John Pitcairn of the Royal Marines with 700 men from Boston. At Lexington Common Capt John Parker with 130 'Minute Men' stood in line before the British column. An exchange of fire there began hostilities, with the British meeting much fiercer resistance at Concord Bridge and retreating under continuous attack with losses by land back to Boston. The American leaders escaped and the British failed to find the sought-for cannon.

■ FORT TICONDEROGA, 10 MAY 1775

Left useless since the French surrender in 1763, this post still contained 90 cannon and stores. At the commencement of hostilities, Ethan Allen and his Vermont militia surprised the garrison of 42 men. As George Washington and the Continental Army surrounded the British in Boston, Washington dispatched bookseller-turned-artillerist Henry Knox to Fort Ticonderoga to move the cannon south. Knox's brilliant improvisations in transporting the guns forced the British to withdraw.

■ CHELSEA CREEK, 27–28 MAY 1775

Hostilities commenced and the British raided islands in Boston harbour for livestock. Around 600 colonials sought to remove the animals across this creek, while 400 British regulars and the schooner *Diana* engaged the Americans, suffering casualties, including *Diana*, which was destroyed.

■ MACHIAS, 11–12 JUNE 1775

HMS *Margaretta* escorted two sloops loading timber for barracks at this Maine town as hostilities commenced. Patriots seized a sloop, sailing out and engaging *Margaretta*, taking her after a short pursuit and a sharp fight.

■ BUNKER (BREED'S) HILL, 17 JUNE 1775

At the commencement of open warfare, 20,000 New England militia mustered under Gen Artemis Ward and surrounded Boston. The Americans learned through spies that British governor and Gen Thomas Gage intended to occupy the Charlestown peninsula and strategic heights overlooking Boston. Two days before Gage's move, by the advice of Gen Israel Putnam, 1000 colonials under William Prescott and Richard Gridley with two small cannon constructed at night a redoubt on Breed's Hill. The position north of Boston lay in the line of the planned British advance and directly under British observation, the covert and necessarily hasty establishment of the position limiting the amount of food and ammunition the Americans had on hand. British ships commenced an ineffective bombardment at daylight, Gage and his generals deciding upon an immediate attack before the Americans could link the new fortification with their others. Tides, wind, shallows and the heights elevation hampered the British Royal Navy's efforts to assist the army's attack. The first British difficulty in launching an infantry assault upon the position was in securing enough water transport to land Gage's allotted force of 2600 men, the first British wave of 1000 troops digging in and prompting Ward to reinforce the American position to 1400 men, while Prescott frantically tried to firm up the resolution of his green troops and anchor his line on the Mystic river. The British failed to scout the line of their planned attack, which was crossed with stony ridges, long grass and fences. Gen Putnam did his best to solidify the American defenders, who wavered in some cases between fleeing before the attack or attacking outside of the defences.

Additional British forces landing in Charlestown came under American fire and retaliated by burning the town. The British plan, followed repeatedly in the course of the ensuing war, was to flank the Americans out of their position; in this case the British right found fences and a well-designed American position pouring an effective fire into their advance despite the British artillery bombardment. With the flanking movement failing, Charlestown in conflagration and evening approaching, Gage ordered his entire force into a headlong attack uphill.

The celebrated American order was, 'Don't fire 'til you see the whites of their eyes' and, with breastworks, walls and fences to steady them, the Americans obeyed it, maximizing the effectiveness of their minimal ammunition supplies. As the British force drew back with casualties, Gen Henry Clinton moved through burning Charlestown and launched another attack upon the American left, victorious so far, but now searching the fallen for ammunition.

British artillery finally cleared the American defenders and the British finally rolled up the American flank. Both sides resorted to the bayonet as the Americans slowly withdrew, suffering 310 casualties and 30 prisoners, having

inflicted 1053 British casualties. Despite the efforts of the British light infantry to exploit the Americans' withdrawal, sufficient resistance and reinforcements remained to halt further advance, leading to stalemate on the peninsula upon which the battle had been fought.

Both sides considered the engagement a classic 'Pyrrhic' victory, one not worth the costs to the victorious British side. The Americans found a battle cry and a sense of confidence from the clash, in which untried numbers had faced, fought and blooded the finest army in the world. The stage was set for more long years of sanguinary struggle.

■ FORT JOHNSON, JULY 1775
As revolution erupted, 100 patriots in Charleston launched an attack across the harbour and surrounding mudflats to seize this fort at the mouth of the harbour. The surrendering British had already removed the fort's cannon.

■ GLOUCESTER, AUGUST 1775
HMS *Falcon* under John Linzee seized a schooner returning to this port from the West Indies. A 'cutting out' expedition failed, Americans retook the prize, and Falcon withdrew after a desultory bombardment.

■ SAINT JOHNS, 17 SEP–3 NOV 1775
Anticipating the American invasion, British, Canadian and allied Indian land and water forces collected at this post, with about 1000 defenders wearing down Gen Richard Montgomery's 2000. The starving British surrendered after lengthy fierce fighting.

■ LONGUE POINTE, 25 SEPTEMBER 1775
Rapid action having secured him Fort Ticonderoga, Col Ethan Allen of the Vermont militia pressed swiftly up into Canada with 110 men, hoping to take Quebec unprepared. Surrounded here by some 250 defenders, Allen surrendered.

■ FALMOUTH, 18 OCTOBER 1775
Adm Samuel Graves made an example of this Maine town, retaliating for patriot attacks along the New England seaboard. After a warning, Capt

Henry Mowat and a small squadron burned the town, infuriating the colonies.

Kemp's Landing, 15 November 1775
Moving out of Norfolk, Virginia governor Lord Dunmore led a series of raids against patriot storehouses and posts. At this location, Dunmore's regulars routed 170 green militia, seizing the town and proclaiming Virginia in revolt.

Great Bridge, 9 December 1775
Virginia governor Lord Dunmore tried to seize the militia's stores of arms and ammunition as revolt loomed. Retreating to Norfolk, he offered freedom to slaves supporting the crown and raised the first loyalist forces, which defended Norfolk at this bridge with a wooden stockade. Col William Woodford took 900 men and established a position at the Virginia side of the bridge. The loyalists and regulars attacked, retreating with casualties.

Quebec, 31 December 1775
With the British withdrawing from Boston and the Americans hoping for a Continental revolution, a force moved northward under Gen Philip Schuyler and Col Benedict Arnold to drive the British out of their last stronghold of Quebec. Gen Richard Montgomery's 3000 men were to converge with Arnold's 1050 at Quebec after Montgomery reduced intervening British forts and captured Montreal. Matters progressed slowly, Arnold's depleted column rendezvousing with Montgomery's as winter started. The British and Canadians spotted Arnold's column and put the city into a state of defence. Arnold crossed the river and sought in vain to lure the British from the defences as Montgomery's force moved up and began a formal siege. Disease and cold weather reduced the Americans to 1700 against a 1200-strong British and Canadian garrison and a complicated American assault collapsed disastrously.

Norfolk, 1 January 1776
Great Bridge convinced Lord Dunmore and loyalist families in Norfolk to withdraw to the crowded British ships in the roadstead. As the Americans occupied the town, the British ships opened fire and the city burned.

Moore's Creek Bridge, 27 February 1776
Americans who remained loyal to the crown, 'Tories' to the patriots' 'Whigs', sought to support royal control of North Carolina. British Gen Donald MacDonald organized 1600 loyalists into a force of 'Highlanders', which encountered Col James Moore with 1100 patriot militia at this location. Charging across the defended bridge with bagpipes and broadswords, the loyalists collapsed under withering fire, losing 30 dead and 850 captured, along with vital military stores.

Rice Boats, 2–3 March 1776
Under threat of the city's destruction, a British fleet landed at this Georgia port to collect supplies for the war in the north while patriot forces mustered in response. Roughly 500 patriot militia moved the sought-for supplies on rice boats upriver to Hutchinson's Island. A British landing party of 300 secured 10 boats before the patriots ignited two with fire ships and forced the British to retreat with their haul.

Nassau, 3–4 March 1776
Capt Esek Hopkins with two ships, two brigs and a sloop led the Continental navy's first overseas descent upon this island city in the Bahamas, where the islanders turned over British cannon and stores bloodlessly.

Saint-Pierre, 25 March 1776
French Canadians joined both patriot and British armies during the American invasion of Canada and siege of Quebec. Alerted patriots, numbering 230, surprised and captured 46 loyalists here near Quebec after the American invasion faltered.

The Cedars, 18–27 May 1776
As the patriot invasion of Canada collapsed, the British counter-attack under Gens Carleton and Burgoyne, armed with 13,000 troops, followed up on the Americans' retreat from the areas around Quebec and Montreal. Indians allied to the British located a party of 400 patriots in this location west of Montreal, the British capturing both these troops and another 100 sent in a relief column before Gen Benedict Arnold arrived with the main patriot force.

■ **TROIS-RIVIERES, 8 JUNE 1776**

Gen William Thompson reconnoitered this region with 2000 men as the Americans withdrew from Canada. Led into a swamp, the Americans took fire from British vessels and infantry, losing Thompson, 235 prisoners and 40 dead.

■ **CHARLESTON I, 28 JUNE 1776**

A British fleet from Ireland combined with troops from New York to attack the southern port. Patriot defences and a botched landing on a tidal island produced a British debacle and retreat to New York.

■ **FORT MOULTRIE (SULLIVAN), 28 JUNE 1776**

William Moultrie commanded Fort Sullivan (walled with logs) with 435 men and 31 cannon protecting the mouth of Charleston harbour when a British fleet and landing force assailed the vital port. Supported by 750 infantry on Sullivan's island, the garrison survived a ten-hour bombardment by the British fleet, the soft logs and sand of their palisade absorbing British shot, while their own careful gunnery killed 225 British before the attackers withdrew.

■ **LONG ISLAND, 27 AUGUST 1776**

The Howes' coordinated invasion of New York began with a fleet-supported landing here opposite Manhattan. A total of 15,000 British troops repeatedly outflanked 9000 patriots, who, by stubborn fighting, kept their retreating army intact and escaped to Manhattan.

■ **HARLEM HEIGHTS, 16 SEPTEMBER 1776**

As the British Army and Royal Navy advanced out of lower Manhattan, Washington made his first stand, allowing his force of 2000 to collect their numbers and supplies. The Americans withdrew after bloodying the British advance guard.

■ **FORT HILL/LOOKOUT PLACE, 1776**

Gen William and Adm Richard Howe established this bastion on Staten Island, where arriving fleets collected 30,000 men including loyalists and supplies for the British assault upon New York City and the 23,000 patriot defenders.

■ **VALCOUR ISLAND/BAY, 11 OCTOBER 1776**

Gen Benedict Arnold fought and lost this three-day fleet action on Lake Champlain with 15 small vessels against 23 heavier British craft. Despite the loss of his flotilla, Arnold successfully delayed Gen John Burgoyne's invasion.

■ **PELL'S POINT/PELHAM, 18 OCTOBER 1776**

British and Hessian troops, numbering 4000, landed here against a strong delaying action fought by Col John Glover and 750 Continentals, who by retreating slowly and firing from multiple defensible lines safeguarded Washington's retreat from Manhattan.

■ **WHITE PLAINS, 28 OCTOBER 1776**

The patriot army of 14,500 – disordered and demoralized by the reverses at Long Island and Harlem Heights, Washington – along with Israel Putnam and William Heath, sought to draw up a defensible line across the Bronx river from which they could bloody the advancing British. Sir William Howe advanced with 13,500, including Hessians. The British succeeded in forcing Washington's withdrawal through a series of flanking movements, the patriots retreating in good order.

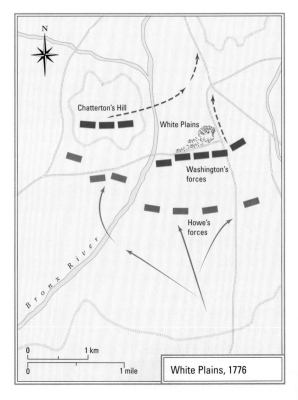

White Plains, 1776

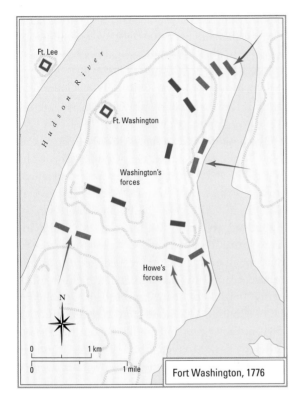

Fort Washington, 1776

FORT CUMBERLAND, 10–29 NOVEMBER 1776

Nova Scotia nearly joined the patriot cause when Col Jonathan Eddy and 400 militia attacked this post and 200 defenders under the British Joseph Goreham. Support from the locals prompted British retaliation when the patriots withdrew.

FORT WASHINGTON, 16 NOVEMBER 1776

Against its namesake's wishes, the garrison of 2800 held this Manhattan earthwork against the British Army and Navy. Howe struck with 11,000 men and captured fort and defenders before they could be reinforced or withdrawn.

FORT LEE, 20 NOVEMBER 1776

The American earthwork guarding the New Jersey side of the Hudson lasted until November, when Gen Charles Cornwallis and 4000 men attacked across the river. The Americans had sufficient warning for the garrison to escape.

IRON WORKS HILL, 22–23 DECEMBER 1776

Col Samuel Griffin, with 600 New Jersey militia, raided New Jersey, drawing Hessian Col Carl von Donop and 1500 men away from Trenton. The brief clash resulted in few casualties on either side.

TRENTON, 26 DECEMBER 1776

A characteristic of Washington's generalship was that he always left his army opportunities either to withdraw or attack. Winter's onset added to the misery of the patriots' retreat into Pennsylvania with depleted numbers after multiple defeats in the unsuccessful defence of New York City. Washington's ability to flee or menace the British forces received tremendously valuable assistance from the general's own intelligence network of spies and observers. Through these channels came the news across the Delaware that Col Johann Rall and 1600 Hessians held Trenton on the river's far bank as part of a chain of outlying posts screening the British continental beachhead in Manhattan. Some 6000 men remained to Washington, who felt any hope of prolonging the war rested upon a demonstration that the Continental Army could still prevail. The British had their own reports that Washington intended to attack New Jersey, but long quiescence and the previous defeats lulled Rall and his superiors into celebration of Christmas and their victories. Washington gathered boats capable of crossing the nearly frozen river and awaited his opportunity.

A snowstorm blinded Hessian sentries and chilled Washington's 2400 tattered soldiers as they crossed the Delaware. They sent out screening forces around Trenton and drew up in line before the barracks where the Hessians were digesting their Christmas dinner. Rall was killed trying to rally his befuddled men with a final spy's warning left unread in his vest pocket. Of the Hessians, 900 surrendered and 106 died. Two colonials were wounded. Not the least reward of the victory were the warm winter uniforms of the captured Germans, but the resulting legend raised patriot spirits and forced the British to forfeit control of the New Jersey countryside.

SECOND TRENTON/ASSUNPINK CREEK, 2 JANUARY 1777

After the successful surprise attack, Washington again moved his forces to Trenton, withdrawing

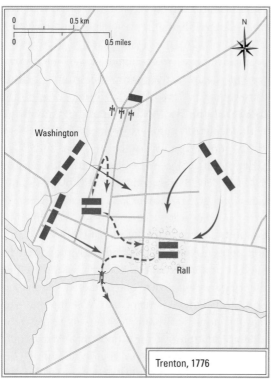

Trenton, 1776

before the advance of British Gen Charles Cornwallis and his 5000 regulars and inflicting heavy casualties here on the road from Princeton.

■ **PRINCETON, 3 JANUARY 1777**

The British withdrawal of the scattered units, such as the Hessians Washington had overwhelmed at Trenton, convinced Washington to re-cross the Delaware and link up forces already operating in New Jersey. In response, Gen Charles Cornwallis and 8000 British and Hessian troops advanced from Princeton toward Trenton, where Washington and 5000 Continentals were dug in. Expecting to crush Washington the following day, Cornwallis prepared his assault only to find that the Continental Army had decamped and moved around his flank to attack his rear guard of 1700 back in Princeton. Valiant fighting by LCol Charles Mawhood and a retreat through the university prevented collapse, but the British suffered some 130 captured, 28 killed and 58 wounded, while the American casualties totalled

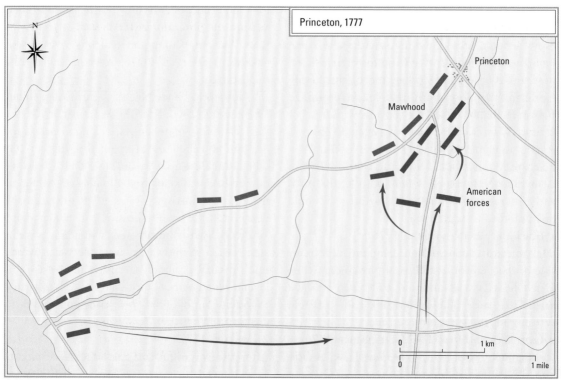

Princeton, 1777

44. Washington went into winter quarters at Morristown, from which he further weakened British control of New Jersey.

■ MILLSTONE/SOMERSET COURTHOUSE, 20 JANUARY 1777

Gen Philemon Dickinson, harassing the British, here with 500 Jersey militia successfully attacked a British foraging party on the patriot side of the Millstone river, capturing 40 wagons and 100 horses before the regulars retreated.

■ BOUND BROOK, 13 APRIL 1777

Gen Benjamin Lincoln avoided an American Trenton by leading 500 men out of an attack by 4000 Hessian Jaegers against his outlying camp. The Americans reoccupied the New Jersey post before Washington withdrew them.

■ DANBURY, APRIL 1777

Gen William Tryon and 1800 seaborne troops sought to capture a patriot arsenal here. The materiel there having been moved, Tryon's battered troops destroyed other supplies and escaped through Continental forces attempting to trap them.

■ RIDGEFIELD, 27 APRIL 1777

Gen William Tryon and 1800 regulars landed to destroy patriot stores in Connecticut, finding here Gen Benedict Arnold and 500 colonial militia across their line of retreat. The British outflanked the Americans and resumed their retreat.

■ THOMAS CREEK, 17 MAY 1777

Georgia militia cavalry under Col Samuel Elbert moved toward the British and Indians based at St Augustine, Florida. Planned naval support collapsing, the Americans fell into a costly ambush, losing some 30 taken captive and killed.

■ SHORT HILLS, 26 JUNE 1777

Gen William Howe sought a decisive battle with Washington's forces in New Jersey. At this place, his army attacked Lord Stirling's command, the Americans retreating into Washington's nearby army. Their flanks endangered, the British retreated.

■ FORT TICONDEROGA II, 2–6 JULY 1777

The British counter-attack out of Canada took the form of an invasion southwards along Lake Champlain with 8500 men under Gen John Burgoyne, planning to link with a force under Gen Charles Cornwallis moving up out of New York City and splitting New England from the rest of the colonies. The naval battle of Valcour Island delayed, but did not stop, the movement southward. Gen Arthur St. Clair and 3100 men garrisoned the stone fort blocking Burgoyne's route into New England. Ticonderoga had changed sides several times over its existence. In previous sieges, attackers had mounted siege cannon on Mount Defiance, a neighbouring height, which St Clair had neglected to defend. Burgoyne having followed that precedent, St Clair and his men abandoned the fort by night, following another precedent of the fort's past defenders. St Clair faced and survived court-martial.

■ HUBBARDTON, 7 JULY 1777

Burgoyne's advance guard of 1750 men overtook the retreating St Clair's exhausted rearguard of 1300 recovering bivouacked at this town. The British captured 200 Americans after a bitter fight that allowed St Clair's withdrawal.

■ FORT ANNE, 8 JULY 1777

British Gen John Burgoyne's advance guard of 190 moved towards this fort – in between Lake Champlain and the Hudson – into an ambush by its 550 militia garrison. The Americans then burned the fort and retreated.

■ FORT STANWIX, 2–22 AUGUST 1777

Col Barry St Leger led 1600 of Burgoyne's force through the Mohawk valley at this bastion, encountering Col Peter Gansevoort and 750 men. St Leger's allied Indians forced him to abandon his siege after losses.

■ ORISKANY, 6 AUGUST 1777

Gen Nicholas Herkimer led 800 men in a relief column for Fort Stanwix into an ambush by British Col Barry St Leger's Indians. A thunderstorm allowed the patriots to withdraw. St. Leger's advance completely stalled.

■ BENNINGTON, 16 AUGUST 1777

LCol Friedrich Baum led 1200 Hessians and Loyalists screened by Indians into Vermont, seeking horses for Burgoyne's invasion. Gen John Stark of

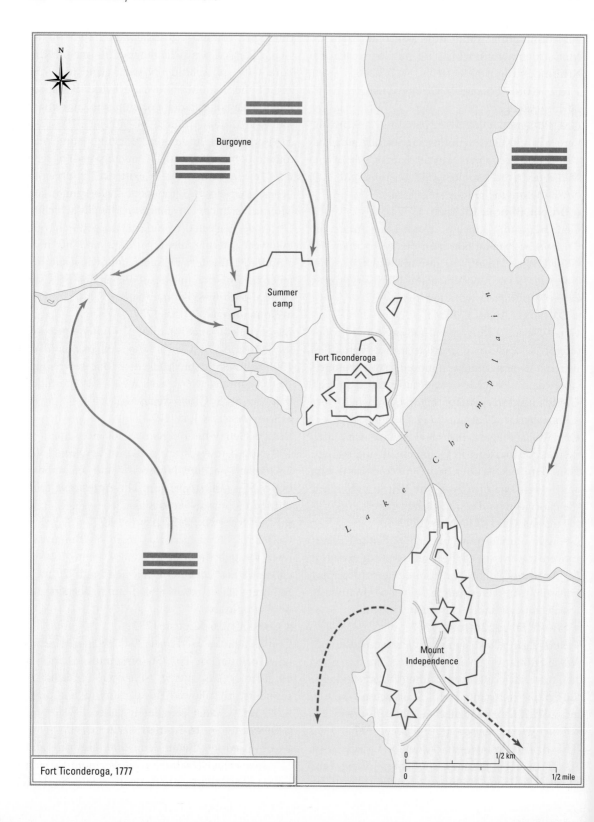

N

Burgoyne

Summer
camp

Fort Ticonderoga

Lake Champlain

Mount
Independence

0   1/2 km
0   1/2 mile

Fort Ticonderoga, 1777

Vermont collected 2000 militia and engulfed the invaders and a relief column.

■ STATEN ISLAND, 22 AUGUST 1777

Gen John Sullivan led 1000 militia from New Jersey in a raid upon this British base. Achieving surprise and some initial success against Tory forces, the Americans retreated before two British regiments, suffering 172 captured.

■ FREEMAN'S FARM (FIRST SARATOGA), 1 SEPTEMBER 1777

American resistance and several lost actions on the periphery of his advance had slowed, but not halted, Gen John Burgoyne's advance into New York from Canada. With 5500 regulars and 800 Tories and Indians, Burgoyne moved towards American Gen Horatio Gates's heavily fortified camp where 7000 Continentals prepared to resist him. In the namesake farm's fields, Burgoyne's army eventually prevailed with heavy losses against American attacks through the surrounding woods.

■ COOCH'S BRIDGE, 3 SEPTEMBER 1777

As the British moved to capture Philadelphia, Washington marched to Delaware where a screening force 700 strong blocked the British advance here. The British flanked the American force several times before Washington withdrew into Pennsylvania.

■ BRANDYWINE CREEK, 11 SEPTEMBER 1777

With the help of the newly arrived Marquis de Lafayette, Washington and the Continental Army ventured open battle to prevent Gen William Howe's thrust up from the Chesapeake to seize the American capital of Philadelphia. British forces numbered 13,000 men against Washington's 15,000, making this action the largest battle on the North American continent before the American Civil War.

American light infantry shadowed the British Army's approach to Washington's line across Chad's Ford through the namesake creek. Finding the Americans prepared to receive him, Howe dispatched light units and received intelligence from the local loyalists about the American positions. Howe decided upon a holding attack,

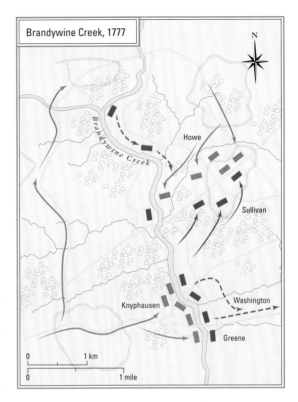

Brandywine Creek, 1777

with 5000 men under Gen Wilhelm von Knyphausen attacking at Chad's Ford, while Gen Charles Cornwallis took 8000 troops around Washington's right flank. The British forced the crossing, while Washington received a growing trickle of reports about a second British force to the north.

Washington sent troops to reinforce his right and ordered a defensive line prepared on Birmingham Meeting House, a half mile to his rear. With both American flanks slowly yielding to his attacks, Howe launched a bayonet charge into the American centre that collapsed Washington's line as other British units attacked frontally. Isolated American units slowed the British as the day drew on, while Gen Nathaniel Greene's command's determined resistance retreating from Birmingham Meeting House to Battle Hill frustrated British attempts to turn the defeat into a rout. Howe had cleared the way to Philadelphia, but his primary objective of Washington's army survived with 300

killed, 600 wounded and 400 captured against the
British losses of 100 dead and some 400 wounded.
The grimness of American resistance signalled a
fundamental shift in the war.

■ THE CLOUDS/WHITE HORSE TAVERN, 16 SEPTEMBER 1777

After Brandywine, Washington positioned his
army between the White Horse and Admiral
Warren taverns in the Pennsylvania countryside.
British Gen William Howe hoped to trap and
destroy the Continentals before severe rain allowed
Washington's retreat.

■ PAOLI, 20 SEPTEMBER 1777

Gen 'Mad Anthony' Wayne's command of 1500
in bivouac at this Pennsylvania town suffered 350
casualties before fleeing a night attack by British
Gen Charles Grey and 5000 regulars. The British
employed their bayonets heavily.

■ GERMANTOWN, 4 OCTOBER 1777

With the British now occupying Philadelphia,
Washington with 11,000 men launched a four-part

attack from the north of the city. Confusion, the
plan's complexity and unexpectedly stiff British
resistance eventually frustrated the assault.

■ SECOND SARATOGA, SEP–OCT 1777

British plans to sever New England by an invasion
south along Lake Champlain finally collapsed along
with Gen John Burgoyne's army in the second
most decisive battle of the American Revolution.
Foraging and scouting parties repeatedly fell
foul of American militia drawn to the line of his
advance, the defeats at Bennington and Oriskany
breaking off significant portions of Burgoyne's
army and reducing his ability to receive supplies
and information. Meanwhile, American generals
Horatio Gates, Philip Schuyler, Daniel Morgan and
Benedict Arnold were becoming used to Burgoyne's
tactics and capabilities as the British advance got
ever further from reinforcement or safe retreat.
Burgoyne continued southwards in the hope of
linking up with a force of some 3000 under Gen
Henry Clinton marching up from occupied New

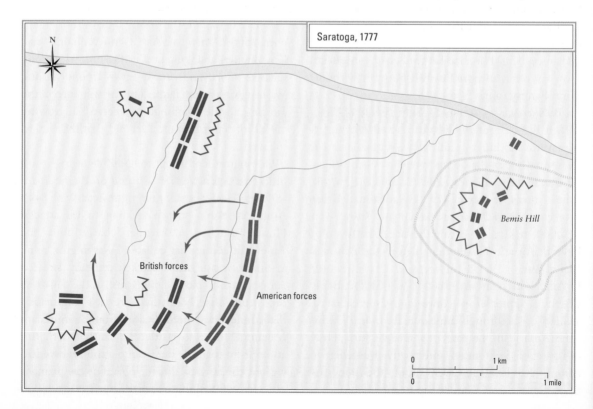

Saratoga, 1777

British forces

American forces

Bemis Hill

0   1 km

0   1 mile

York City, which had met and overcome American resistance at Forts Clinton and Montgomery and when attempting to close the Hudson.

As the British advance down the Hudson neared the namesake town, Gates collected all available forces in a large camp expertly fortified by Thaddeus Kosciuszko as Burgoyne's advance ground to a halt around 5km away. Burgoyne's probe towards Gates's fortifications ran into attacks by Morgan's troops from the surrounding woods, with Gens Friedrich von Riedesel, Simon Fraser and James Hamilton's troops holding the battlefield at Freeman's Farm. However, they were outnumbered and still some distance from the American camp on Bemis Heights. Burgoyne chose to rest his troops in trenches on the Freeman's Farm battlefield while the Americans brought up additional supplies of ammunition and constructed fortifications in the direction of Clinton's advance. Meanwhile, Burgoyne fortified posts near the Hudson to help the delivery of vital supplies from New York as his men went onto reduced rations. The stalemate lasted for three weeks, Burgoyne's forces dwindling to 5000.

Burgoyne broke out of his trenches and probed the Continental left on 7 October with 2100 men, the regulars and loyalists finding three American columns marching in response more than powerful enough to halt their advance and pressure the British on both flanks before the British withdrew. Fraser was mortally wounded and Benedict Arnold was wounded in the attack that broke the British centre. British casualties were some 400 men.

Arnold pressed the attack back upon Burgoyne's own fortifications constructed during the intervening weeks, carrying the strongest with 700 Hessians killed or captured against 150 Continental losses, the 1000 total casualties and silence from Clinton convincing Burgoyne to abandon his advance and retreat back to Fort Ticonderoga. Rains and mud slowed the speed of the disengagement, with Burgoyne finally constructing a camp overlooking the town of Saratoga, inviting Gates's attack. Instead, Gates

was content to leave the British starving as further troops arrived, swelling Continental numbers to some 20,000, while additional militia blocked Burgoyne's retreat. Clinton, who had relieved Gen William Howe in command of the war, had abandoned his advance after burning the town of Kingston in New York and declined to send reinforcements. Burgoyne now found his army trapped by the Americans, starvation and the Hudson river, with no hope of rescue. On 17 October, he surrendered 5895 men and himself to Gates and the Continental Army.

The consequences of the debacle extended beyond Howe's relief by Clinton and unpleasant political repercussions for Lord North's ministry in London. American resistance at Brandywine, Germantown and the victory at Saratoga had combined with Benjamin Franklin's canny diplomacy to secure an alliance between the American colonists and Louis XVI's France, which brought additional supplies, a potent navy and international consequences into the war.

■ **FORT CLINTON/FORT MONTGOMERY, 6 OCTOBER 1777**
These two unfinished American bastions protected a chain across the Hudson river intended to prevent British forces supplying Burgoyne's invasion from Canada. Gen Henry Clinton's river-borne forces stormed and captured both and destroyed the chain.

■ **BEMIS HEIGHTS, 7 OCTOBER 1777**
Polish engineer Thaddeus Kosciuszko fortified this camp overlooking the endpoint of the British advance, where American Gen Horatio Gates collected troops and dispatched forces defeated at Freeman's Farm and victorious at Saratoga.

■ **FORT MERCER/FORT MIFFLIN, OCT 1777**
Fort Mercer in New Jersey and Fort Mifflin, a Pennsylvania stone fort, blocked the Delaware even after British forces had seized Philadelphia. Bombarded by siege artillery and warships, Fort Mifflin's stubborn defenders succeeded in burning HMS *Augusta* and a brig before finally abandoning the ruins. Col Carl von Donop with

2400 Hessians failed to storm Fort Mercer, with 400 falling due to the abatis, ditch and resolute defenders who later evacuated the post.

■ **WHITEMARSH, 5–8 DECEMBER 1777**

British Gen William Howe launched a probing night attack towards Washington's first winter camp at this Pennsylvania town, encountering screening forces that resisted and fired as they retreated. Advised, Washington's strong position prompted Howe's retreat.

■ **MATSON'S FORD, 11 DECEMBER 1777**

British Gen Charles Cornwallis and 3500 regulars left Philadelphia seeking livestock for Gen William Howe's army. Pennsylvania militia repeatedly fought Cornwallis before the British advance, while Washington's army avoided engagement by crossing the Schuylkill elsewhere.

■ **VALLEY FORGE, WINTER 1777**

Washington set his winter quarters 40km from occupied Philadelphia, menacing the British and having the distance to respond to a surprise attack. Supplies unexpectedly lacking, Gen Friedrich von Steuben's drills hardened Washington's cold and hunger-tested troops.

■ *RANDOLPH* VS. *YARMOUTH*, 7 MARCH 1778

Continental Capt Nicholas Biddle had taken prizes in the frigate *Randolph*. HMS *Yarmouth*, twice *Randolph*'s size, demanded surrender and got a close hot action until *Randolph* suddenly exploded, killing Biddle and nearly all her crew.

■ **QUINTON'S BRIDGE, 18 MARCH 1778**

A powerful British scouting party received word from New Jersey loyalists of an American detachment 300 strong guarding this bridge some distance away. Col Charles Mawhood allowed a portion of his command to be seen by the Americans after placing the rest of his force in concealment and trapping Americans crossing in pursuit. The arrival of reinforcements allowed the Americans to fall back from the British ambush with light casualties.

■ **HANCOCK'S BRIDGE, 21 MARCH 1778**

British Col Charles Mawhood announced that he would leave New Jersey if the militia disbanded.

If they did not, he would attack militia leaders. Mawhood lived up to his threat by massacring a household full of civilians here.

■ **FREDERICA, 19 APRIL 1778**

Col Samuel Elbert discovered a British frigate, sloop and two supply vessels anchored in this Florida river. Four galleys of the Georgia navy attacked the becalmed ships at ebb tide, capturing all but the frigate.

■ **RAID ON WHITEHAVEN, 22 APRIL 1778**

John Paul Jones took the sloop *Ranger* to raid this familiar English port, retaliating for British depredations along the American coast. British reaction to the raid was vastly disproportionate to the slight amount of damage inflicted.

■ **NORTH CHANNEL/** *RANGER* **VS.** *DRAKE*, **24 APRIL 1778**

After the raid at Whitehaven, John Paul Jones, along with *Ranger*, greatly compounded British consternation by taking HMS *Drake* after a short, sharp, ship-to-ship combat. Jones' escape greatly embarrassed the Royal Navy in its home waters.

■ **CROOKED BILLETT, 1 MAY 1778**

Repeating the tactics of Paoli, 850 British surprised and drove the bivouacked three regiments of Gen John Lacey in disorder, inflicting some 92 casualties before the Americans escaped, with reports of atrocities against the wounded.

■ **FREETOWN, 25 MAY 1778**

A British landing from Newport at this Massachusetts town encountered unexpected resistance from local patriots, British marines and barges responding with grapeshot to patriot challenges and musket shot. The British set some fires and withdrew.

■ **COBLESKILL, 30 MAY 1778**

With the support of the Iroquois and British in Quebec, loyalist Joseph Brant and other Indians attacked and destroyed much of this small town in upstate New York, after routing and scattering the outnumbered defenders.

■ **MONMOUTH, 28 JUNE 1778**

Gen Henry Clinton, relieving William Howe as ground commander in the colonies, had to evacuate Philadelphia after France's open entry into the war on behalf of the Patriots. Moving his wounded and endangered loyalists by sea and his army by land, Clinton and the rest of the army moved out of Philadelphia. Washington chose to shadow the British march and wait for a favourable opportunity to bring them to battle. With the British tired from the march to Monmouth Courthouse, Washington engaged, ordering Gen Charles Lee to attack the British rear, while the bulk of the Continental army blocked the British advance. Lee's wavering delayed his attack, allowing the British to concentrate on the forces ahead. Washington and more decisive generals firmed up the Continental line, Clinton deciding to break off the engagement and complete his march towards New York.

■ ALLIGATOR CREEK (SWAMP), 30 JUNE 1778

American Gen Richard Howe led 3000 Continentals south against the British in Florida. Loyalist Col Thomas Brown's Rangers fled to

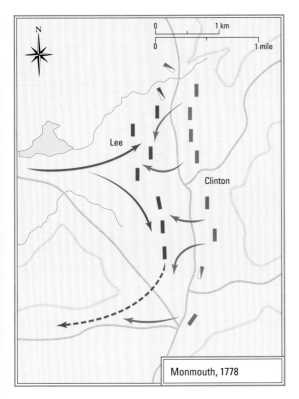

Monmouth, 1778

the British fort here, the patriots retreating with casualties. The invasion was soon abandoned.

■ GREAT RUNAWAY, JULY 1778

The Iroquois Confederation imploded as Oneidas attacked loyalist Mohawks in the aftermath of Oriskany. Fighting between the Indians and loyalists urged on by the British in Quebec prompted this whole-scale flight of the region's settlers.

■ ILLINOIS CAMPAIGN, JULY 1778–FEB 1782

George Rogers Clark launched an expedition into Kentucky against British outposts, encouraging the local tribes to attack patriot towns and settlements. Clark used intelligent diplomacy towards the Indian tribes. British LGov Henry Hamilton moved from Detroit to counter Rogers' efforts, but Rogers countered the British occupation of Vincennes and efforts to court the powerful Shawnee tribe. Clark's activities largely neutralized British efforts in the Trans-Appalachian west.

■ WYOMING MASSACRE (WILKES-BARRE), 3 JULY 1778

Loyalist John Butler and allied Seneca fell upon this Pennsylvania village and surrounding region for five days, burning eight forts and 1000 houses, killing 227 men and executing some prisoners, while securing cattle for British Fort Niagara.

■ USHANT I, 27 JULY 1778

With the bulk of the British fleet and army engaged in North America, the French decided on a direct assault upon the British Isles. Anticipating that, British Adm Augustus Keppel took 32 capital ships and engaged the Comte d'Orvilliers with the same numbers off the French coast. Keppel's difficulty in controlling his own squadron and the inexperience of the French produced no more than casualties before the French disengaged.

■ PONDICHERRY, 21 AUGUST–19 OCTOBER 1778

The British East India Company moved to prevent planned French incursions into India by deploying their company regiments against this French outpost. The city eventually fell after an arriving fleet drove off a defending squadron.

■ NEWPORT, 29 AUGUST 1778

The British occupied this Rhode Island town

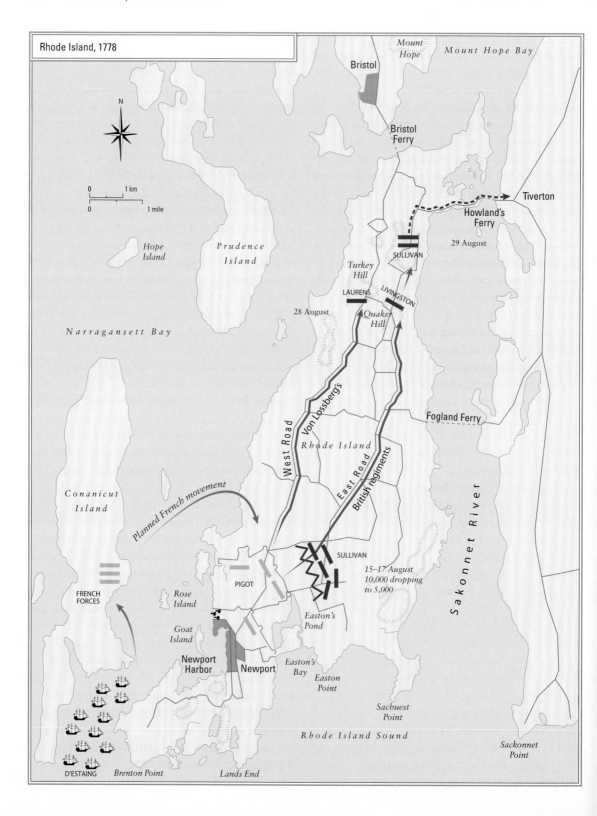

Rhode Island, 1778

as a fleet anchorage. The French fleet and army intended to clear the British in a combined assault with American Gen Philip Sullivan's army, weather producing a debacle.

■ RHODE ISLAND, 29 AUGUST 1778

The smallest colony held disproportionate laurels and action due to its vital ports and brave soldiers, both of which drew the attention of the British, who occupied the important port of Newport for three years from 1776. After the French alliance, Gen Philip Sullivan led 10,000 Continentals with the Comte de Rochambeau landing 4000 French with the goal of retaking the city. The British successfully counter-attacked during bad weather.

■ BOONESBOROUGH, 7–8 SEPTEMBER 1778

A French-Canadian engineer and Shawnee Indians sought to reduce Daniel Boone's namesake fortified town in Kentucky. The siege collapsed after determined resistance by the settlers and the collapse of a sapping tunnel due to rain.

■ GERMAN FLATTS, 17 SEPTEMBER 1778

A combined force of Loyalists and Iroquois under Joseph Brant ravaged this town in upstate New York. A scout's warning allowed the inhabitants to shelter in two forts, while the raiders sacked and burned the town.

■ BAYLOR OR TAPPEN MASSACRE, 27 SEP 1778

Col George Baylor and his dragoons, bivouacked away from the main Continental force, fell victim to a Loyalist-guided British night surprise attack. Gen Charles Grey could or did not spare many, bayoneting the surrending Americans.

■ CHESTNUT NECK (MINCOCK ISLAND), 6 OCTOBER 1778

American privateers operating from New Jersey's Little Egg harbour provoked a British landing here, which burned several ships, but failed to destroy a neighbouring ironworks. Col Patrick Ferguson's night attack upon houses produced several atrocity reports.

■ CARLETON'S RAID, 24 OCT–14 NOV 1778

Capt Christopher Carleton with soldiers, two warships and smaller craft destroyed patriot supplies, boats and mills and arrested male civilians along the coast of Lake Champlain. Driving off his captives' families, Carleton met little resistance.

■ CHERRY VALLEY MASSACRE, 11 NOV 1778

Col Walter Butler and Mohawk Joseph Brandt led 250 loyalists and 400 Iroquois against Fort Alden here. The Iroquois burned the town, killing 15 soldiers and 32 civilians. The fort held.

■ ST LUCIA, 15 DECEMBER 1778

A British fleet under Adm Samuel Barrington occupied part of this French Caribbean island after the outbreak of hostilities. The French fleet under Adm Jean-Baptiste d'Estaing began an amphibious counter-assault, but calm winds hampered d'Estaing's efforts. The French launched three failed attacks with 7000 marines upon improvised British fortifications before abandoning their efforts. The governor surrendered the entire island, from which the British harassed Martinique.

■ SAVANNAH I, 29 DECEMBER 1778

In an early effort at a 'Southern Strategy,' the British seized this important Georgia port, assisted by fugitive slaves, loyalists and a quarrel between the governor, John Houstoun, and the garrison commander, Gen Richard Howe.

■ PORT ROYAL ISLAND/BEAUFORT, 3 FEB 1779

A force of 200 regulars and loyalists moved to disrupt Continental supply routes at this South Carolina port. Col William Moultrie moved with 300 men in response, putting up sufficient resistance to send the British back to Savannah.

■ KETTLE CREEK, 14 FEBRUARY 1779

LCol Archibald Campbell moved with 3000 men in the South Carolina backcountry in the hope of rallying Loyalists. Around 500 Loyalists were encamped here when Andrew Pickens led 300 militia from surrounding colonies to attack the loyalist bivouac from three sides, killing the leaders and scattering the loyalists after initial resistance. This dramatic failure of the 'Southern Statregy' of reasserting British control in the south did not yet discourage the British.

■ VINCENNES, 23–25 FEBRUARY 1779

George Rogers Clark's Illinois expedition had taken this French trading town and protecting fort the previous summer, only to see them recaptured by a British expedition from Detroit, led by Col Henry Hamilton, named 'the Hair Buyer', from his employment of the Indians against the patriots. Clark moved back along the rivers with a stronger force, skilfully using his own knowledge of Indian mores to dissuade them from support of the British and also playing upon the French population's resentment of British control. With good intelligence about the size of Hamilton's force at Vincennes, Clark attacked, carefully keeping the British unaware of his actual numbers and Hamilton's French-Canadian militia informed of his support among their brethren. Caught at a loss, the British surrendered, Clark capturing Hamilton and making reprisals upon the captured Indians, greatly damaging Britain's control of the Trans-Appalachian west.

■ BRIAR CREEK, 3 MARCH 1779

Gen John Ashe with 2000 colonial militia moved in pursuit of LCol James Prevost's somewhat smaller force of Highlanders and Loyalists in upper Georgia, while the British at Savannah proclaimed the colony under royal control. Prevost used 900 men to launch a holding attack on Ashe's encamped force, which collapsed when the balance of Prevost's men attacked from the rear, solidifying British control of that part of the Colony.

■ ST. VINCENT ISLAND, 16–18 JUNE 1779

The Marquis de Bouillé, governor of Martinique, cooperated with Adm Jean Baptiste d'Estaing to seize this island bloodlessly with a light force before the British could respond in strength to France's entry into the war.

■ STONO FERRY, 20 JUNE 1779

Continental Gen Benjamin Lincoln sent 1200 of his command to flush out 900 Scots and Hessians at the redoubt British Gen Augustine Prevost constructed here. Unexpectedly tough resistance allowed the British to retreat unmolested further.

■ GRENADA, 2–4 JULY 1779

French Adm Jean Baptiste d'Estaing, with 25 ships of the line and supporting frigates, seized this island and prepared to defend it from a British squadron of 21 ships and a troop convoy. The British attacked immediately upon sighting the French, trying to form up into line as the French sailed out to meet them. Failure there and a need to guard the troop convoy resulted in a British disaster.

■ STONY POINT, 16 JULY 1779

The British established outposts to maintain their grip along the lower Hudson river valley. Getting control of Washington's elite force of Continental Light Infantry, Gen 'Mad Anthony' Wayne secured Washington's permission to use 1200 of these in a surprise assault upon the northernmost British post at Stony Point, which both Wayne and Washington had reconnoitered. Landing upriver, the Americans advanced through the British ditch and abatis under darkness with strict (and obeyed) orders not to fire. The Americans succeeded in catching the 500-strong garrison between the two prongs of their attack and overrunning the fortification, delivering an implicit rebuke to British conduct of previous similar operations by maintaining discipline and granting quarter to the surrendering enemy, despite Wayne himself being wounded. Taking prisoners, ordinance and supplies, the Americans levelled the post and withdrew before the British could respond.

■ PENOBSCOT, 24 JULY 24–12 AUGUST 1779

Capt Dudley Saltonstall had to scuttle 46 Continental ships with 500 casualties after the British Royal Navy trapped his force and marines in the Penobscot River, when the colonials tried to dislodge a landing in Maine.

■ PAULUS HOOK, 19 AUGUST 1779

Emulating the raid on Stony Point, Maj Henry 'Light-horse Harry' Lee launched a attack on this British post directly across from Manhattan. Mistaken for loyalists foragers, Lee and his men withdrew almost unscathed with 158 prisoners.

■ NEWTOWN, 29 AUGUST 1779

Gen John Sullivan and 5000 Continentals attacked the Iroquois in response to depredations in the Wyoming valley. Mohawk Joseph Brandt

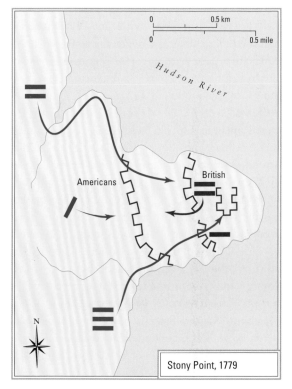

Stony Point, 1779

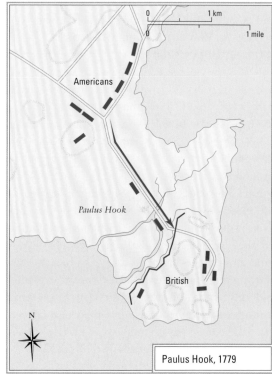

Paulus Hook, 1779

and loyalist William Butler with 700 Indians and loyalists failed to stop Sullivan's expedition here.

■ **BOYD AND PARKER AMBUSH, 13 SEP 1779**
Little Beard and his Seneca ambushed a scout of 23 men under Lt Thomas Boyd with Sgt Michael Parker. The Indians tortured and killed Boyd and Parker; seven Colonials escaped.

■ **BATON ROUGE, 12–21 SEPTEMBER 1779**
The Spanish, entering the war, immediately attacked and overwhelmed this British fort on the border between West Florida and previously ceded French Louisiana. Spanish governor Bernardo de Gálvez with 1000 Spanish, militia and allied Indians captured this and two other forts. Gálvez paroled the garrisons after heavily fortified Baton Rouge collapsed under a large-scale bombardment scientifically applied by Gálvez's large artillery train. The British defeats let Spain control the lower Mississippi valley.

■ **FLAMBOROUGH HEAD, 23 SEPTEMBER 1779**
John Paul Jones with an old Indiaman he named *Bonhomme Richard, Alliance* and *Pallas* encountered HMS *Serapis* under Capt Richard Pearson and *Countess of Scarborough* escorting the Baltic convoy off the north coast of England. The convoy scattered when Richard hotly engaged *Serapis*, while *Alliance*, under an insane captain, periodically attacked both ships. French *Pallas* captured *Scarborough* while Jones' sheer determination and heroic crew captured his second prize within sight of England, *Bonhomme Richard* sinking afterwards.

■ **SAVANNAH II, 16 SEP–20 OCT 1779**
Gen Benjamin Lincoln and the Continental Army, supported by the French fleet and marines of French Adm Jean Baptiste d'Estaing, bloodily failed to dislodge the British Army fortified here due to difficulties co-ordinating repeated attacks.

■ **SAN FERNANDO DE OMOA, 16 OCTOBER–29 NOVEMBER 1779**
With Spain's entry into the war, British 'Baymen' irregulars reinforced from Jamaica captured this fort on the Honduran coast. The Spanish soon

raised a powerful column of regulars and militia and counter-attacked, the British decamping.

■ CAPE ST VINCENT I (THE MOONLIGHT BATTLE), 16 JAN 1780

British Adm George Rodney with 22 ships of the line, 14 frigates and smaller craft escorted a large convoy of supply ships and troop transports for the relief of the British fortress at Gibraltar, under close siege since Spain's entry into the war. Off the southern Spanish coast, Rodney overtook a Spanish squadron of 11 ships of the line and two frigates and engaged at once, taking advantage of the speed-enhancing copper bottoms of his ships to keep the Spanish from disengaging and cutting off their course for Cadiz, as he brought up his superior numbers in good order. Less than an hour after fighting began, the *Santo Domingo* exploded and sank with all hands. By the time intervening darkness allowed the surviving four Spanish ships to escape, Rodney had captured six, with two driven ashore and one other later salvaged by Spain.

■ YOUNG'S HOUSE, 3 FEBRUARY 1780

Col Joseph Thompson with 250 Continentals sheltered here during a winter storm north of New York City. A force of 450 British, Hessian and Loyalist infantry, plus 100 dragoons learned of their location and killed 14, capturing 73.

■ CHARLESTON II, 29 MARCH–12 MAY 1780

Gen Benjamin Lincoln, with 5200 Continentals and militia and four Continental warships, defended this port against a second British attack by Gen Augustine Prevost with 10,000 troops, supported by the Royal Navy. The British bypassed the city's defending forts and launched a punishing bombardment that the Americans, weakened by illness, proved unable to endure. The British captured the garrison, port and ships. Much of South Carolina returned to British control.

■ FORT CHARLOTTE, 2–14 MARCH 1780

Marching eastward Spanish governor of Louisiana Bernardo de Gálvez continued his policy of reducing British outposts, this large brick fort with 300

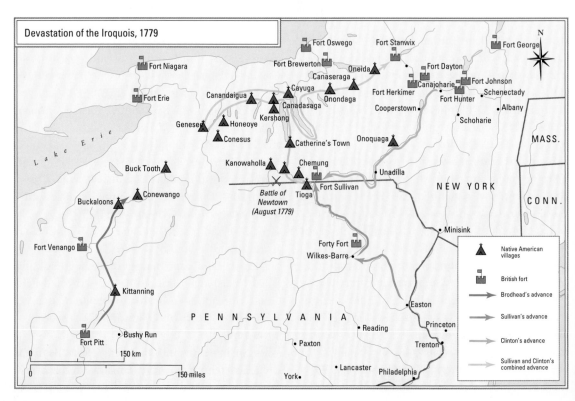

garrison and the village of Mobile soon falling to 2000 Spanish, plus Gálvez's powerful artillery train.

■ Monck's Corner, 14 April 1780

British LCol Banastre Tarleton defeated Gen Isaac Huger and 500 men here north of Charleston along the city's route of supply. Tarleton's dawn attack captured a Patriot wagon train and scattered Huger's command.

■ Lenud's Ferry, 6 May 1780

Continental Col Anthony White with 300 men captured a British foraging party during the siege of Charleston. LCol Banastre Tarleton, alerted by a Loyalist, scattered White's command here with 150 dragoons, freeing the captives.

■ St. Louis/Fort San Carlos, 25 May 1780

Spanish Louisiana's LGov Fernando de Leyba built a large stone tower that protected the town from an attack by British-allied Indians, prompted by British fur traders eager to gain control of the upper Mississippi.

■ Waxhaw Creek/Buford's Massacre, 29 May 1780

Continental Col Abraham Buford with some 350 men withdrew north after the fall of Charleston. LCol Banastre Tarleton moved in pursuit with 270 loyalist cavalry, overtaking Buford and killed 113, inflicting 203 further casualties.

■ Connecticut Farms, 7 June 1780

Hessian Gen Wilhelm von Knyphausen marched with 5000 men against this New Jersey town near Washington's winter quarters. Militia engaged Knyphausen in the village, while Washington brought up the main army, forcing a British retreat.

■ Mobley's (Gibson's) Meeting House, 8 June 1780

Despite British orders to disband, loyalists in South Carolina fought their own war against the patriots in the aftermath of Charleston. Patriot Maj Richard Winn rallied 100 scattered militia and dispersed a Loyalist concentration here.

■ Ramseur's Mill, 20 June 1780

With British money and success, Col John Moore rallied 1300 South Carolina loyalists here. Col Francis Locke, with 400 Patriot infantry and horses, defeated the loyalists in a pitched battle, both sides suffering 70 killed.

■ Springfield, 23 June 1780

Hessian Gen Wilhelm von Knyphausen's 5000 British here in New Jersey engaged Gen Nathaniel Greene's 1500 Continental regulars and militia, while Washington counter-marched. Greene slowly retreated to defensible heights and held out, prompting Knyphausen's retreat.

■ Huck's Defeat/Williamson's Plantation, 12 July 1780

Loyalist Capt Christian Huck favoured reprisals against Patriots' homes in South Carolina. During one such attack, a girl escaped to alert Patriot militia, who attacked from two directions, killing Huck and some 40 of his men.

■ Colson's Mill, 21 July 1780

Col William Davidson rallied North Carolina militia and assaulted 400 loyalists mustering here seeking to surprise the encampment with his 250 patriot partisans. Despite Davidson's wound early in the fight, his men scattered the Loyalists.

■ Rocky Mount, 1 August 1780

LCol George Turnbull with 300 New York and South Carolina loyalists held off three assaults by Gen Thomas Sumter with 500 men, who then ambushed a loyalist relief column, inflicting 60 casualties before withdrawing.

■ Hanging Rock, 6 August 1780

The British consolidated their hold on South Carolina with scattered outposts. Gen Thomas Sumter attacked this one with 800 militia and inflicted 200 casualties on the British defending force of 500 men, with much less loss.

■ Camden, 16 August 1780

Taking command in the south after Charleston, Gen Horatio Gates led 3000 Continentals against what Thomas Sumter had told him were 700 British. Lincoln's hasty march starved and weakened his army, while British Gen Charles Cornwallis reinforced Camden with 2400 men. Learning too late of Cornwallis's arrival, Gates' army fought desperately, but eventually disintegrated, with

Gates and the survivors hounded by LCol Banastre Tarleton's loyalist cavalry.

■ **FISHING CREEK, 18 AUGUST 1780**
British LCol Banastre Tarleton with 160 dragoons and double-riding infantry caught Gen Thomas Sumter's command of 500 partisans unprepared, inflicting 150 casualties and capturing 300. Tarleton also recaptured 44 supply wagons and 100 prisoners.

■ **MUSGROVE HILL, 18 AUGUST 1780**
South Carolina patriots rallied after Camden to lure a loyalist force into a prepared ambush behind previously constructed breastworks prepared here. Patriot cavalry drew on loyalist infantry who suffered 63 dead, 90 wounded and 170 prisoners.

■ **BLUE LICKS, 19 AUGUST 1780**
The powerful Shawnee tribe, led by Tory captain William Caldwell and loyalist renegade Simon Girty, dealt Patriot settlers in Kentucky a severe blow in an ambush here. A total of 77 colonists died; Girty burned seven alive.

■ **BLACK MINGO, 14 SEPTEMBER 1780**
Loyalist numbers swelling after Continental defeats, Continental Gen Francis Marion, the 'Swamp Fox', rallied remaining Patriot militia and, at this creek, defeated a Loyalist force under John Ball, some 50 men fighting on each side.

■ **WAHAB'S PLANTATION, 21 SEPTEMBER 1780**
Col William R. Davie with 150 cavalry and infantry surprised 300 loyalists here in North Carolina, with the infantry engaging, while the cavalry charged from the rear. The patriots killed 20 men, capturing 96 furnished horses.

■ **CHARLOTTE, 26 SEPTEMBER 1780**
Col William R. Davie sought here with 120 militia to impede British Gen Charles Cornwallis's advance into North Carolina, where Cornwallis sought to rally loyalists. Driven back with 30 casualties, Davie and his men inflicted 15 on the British.

■ **KINGS MOUNTAIN, 7 OCTOBER 1780**
British Maj Patrick Ferguson led 1000 picked loyalists into the North Carolina mountain country in an effort to force the locals to cease rebellion. When Ferguson threatened reprisals

against intransigents, Isaac Shelby and John Sevier rallied angry mountaineers, their ranks soon joined by militia from other states as they prepared to engage Ferguson and his force. Possessed of superb Pennsylvania rifles, many of the mountaineers were superlative shots. Ferguson moved south, seeking to overtake a retreating Georgia patriot band. Ferguson occupied the ridge of King's Mountain upon learning that patriot bands were converging on him from all directions. Rifle fire from surrounding trees cut down Ferguson and any British officer trying to lead a charge. Loyalists numbering 400 fell before the Patriots accepted the surrender of the surviving 600, some of those later executed after this blow to British prestige.

■ **ROYALTON RAID, 16 OCTOBER 1780**
After Burgoyne's defeat, the British and allied Indians ravaged New England to forestall Patriot attacks upon Canada. Lt Houghton, with 300 Mohawks, launched a raid in which they escaped with 26 captives and much property.

■ **FISHDAM FORD, 9 NOVEMBER 1780**
British Maj James Wemyss sought to kill Gen Thomas Sumter with a night attack upon his encampment. However, Wemyss was wounded with his men when silhouetted by the light of picket fires surrounded by alert, rifle-equipped sentries.

■ **BLACKSTOCK'S FORD, 20 NOVEMBER 1780**
Patriot Gen Thomas Sumter with 1000 militia prepared defences here against LCol Banastre Tarleton's onrushing 250 dragoons. Sumter attacked with horsemen when Tarleton hesitated, inflicting some 200 casualties on Tarleton's force, despite Sumter's wound.

■ **JERSEY, 6 JANUARY 1781**
The Channel Islands had become a nest of British privateers, against which the French sent a landing force of 1000 marines. Forces of 2000 regulars and island militia overwhelmed these, both the British and French commander perishing.

■ **MOBILE VILLAGE, 7 JANUARY 1781**
A small post here guarded the supply route to the Spanish occupying captured Mobile. Indian

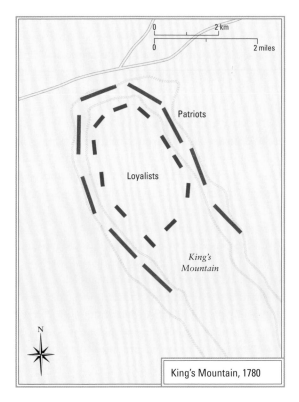

Patriots

Loyalists

King's
Mountain

N

King's Mountain, 1780

facing Tarleton's advance with his Continentals behind them, exacting from the former a promise to fire three volleys before they ran with the Continentals ready to enforce that guarantee. Too worn out for elaborate flanking manoeuvres, Tarleton's men marched forward as Continental riflemen picked off their officers. British efforts to flank or re-form collapsed under attack by Col William Washington's more numerous cavalry. The British line narrowed under pressure, while the Americans retreated before it, firing volleys as they fell back and re-formed. British artillery supporting the advance fell to a swift American rush. Washington's cavalry charged again as the British line collapsed, capturing guns, wagons and supplies. Tarleton suffered 800 casualties to 25 Americans killed and 125 wounded.

■ HAW RIVER/ PYLE'S DEFEAT, 25 FEB 1781
Col John Pyle with 400 mounted loyalists mistook Cols Henry Lee and Andrew Pickens with 900 cavalry for British troops under Banastre Tarleton, which wore similar uniforms. The American ruse resulted in 240 loyalist casualties.

■ WETZELL'S MILL, 6 MARCH 1781
Continental Gen Otho Williams with 1000 cavalry and infantry avoided British Gen Charles Cornwallis's effort to trap them between parts of the British Army by a fighting retreat in stages across the Reedy Fork here.

■ PENSACOLA, 9 MARCH–8 MAY 1781
Spanish governor Bernardo de Gálvez completed evicting the British from the Gulf of Mexico, this port attacked by an army from New Orleans and a Cuban fleet. Bombardment exploding Fort George's magazine, the British surrendered.

■ GUILFORD COURTHOUSE, 15 MARCH 1781
The defeats at King's Mountain and Cowpens galvanized British Gen Charles Cornwallis into launching a full-strength effort with 1900 troops against the resurgent patriot cause in the Carolinas. Gen Nathaniel Greene's brilliant strategy of allowing the British to chase his Continentals and alienate populations throughout the south had left Cornwallis with only brute

attacks having failed, the Spanish then resisted a British assault, sheltering with 40 casualties in a wooden blockhouse, inflicting 20 wounded.

■ COWPENS, 17 JANUARY 1781
Gen Nathaniel Greene moved the Continental army back into South Carolina, dispatching Gen Daniel Morgan to rally militia and threaten British outposts. LCol Banastre Tarleton with 1250 British regulars and loyalists moved in pursuit, while Morgan gathered forage and militia forces around his Continentals. Upon hearing of Tarleton's pursuit, Morgan consolidated his forces at this battlefield, which offered opportunities for both forage and retreat. Tarleton exhausted his own men in a rapid approach that failed to catch Morgan off guard. As more militia arrived, Morgan made the decision to engage the dreaded commander. Morgan had about 2000 men to face Tarleton's picked body.

Placing riflemen in the trees on his flanks, Morgan put his militia in the crescent front line force as a means to reassert British sovereignty. With his own forces elevated in numbers and morale, Greene carefully selected this battlefield and made ready for Cornwallis's assault, setting up his some 4440 Continentals and militia in three independent lines in the face of the British advance.

Fighting began with an inconclusive cavalry skirmish between Col Henry Lee's Legion and British LCol Banastre Tarleton's British Legion. The British line fanned out from the road, while light artillery supported their advance from the centre and heavier guns replied from the American third line. Cornwallis' line moved straight ahead, shifting sideways as the terrain necessitated and crumbled the North Carolina militia in Greene's first line, patriots retreating back to the flanks of their second line. The Virginia militia there held out longer, the British taking a steady amount of casualties as they advanced, their own artillery blasting both sides in the middle. Despite the collapse of the third line's Marylanders soon afterwards, Greene's forces withdrew 16km in good order and largely re-formed. American casualties were 79 killed, 260 wounded; British 93 dead, 213 wounded, a Pyrrhic victory.

■ FORT WATSON, 15–23 APRIL 1781

Riflemen in a wooden 'Maham Tower' allowed Gen Francis Marion and LCol Henry Lee's 400 Continentals and militia to reduce this South Carolina palisade and capture its 114-man garrison of regulars and loyalists.

■ PORTO PRAYA, 16 APRIL 1781

French Adm Pierre de Suffren with five ships in the Cape Verde Islands attacked seven British ships provisioning at anchor immediately upon sighting them, inflicting damage and escaping Cdre George Johnstone's efforts at pursuit.

■ HOBKIRK'S HILL, 25 APRIL 1781

Ignoring Gen Charles Cornwallis' march into Virginia after Guilford Courthouse, Continental Gen Nathaniel Greene moved into South Carolina with 1550 Continentals, most of his militia returning home. LCol Francis Rawdon

raised 900 regulars and loyalists, the latter certain of reprisals if the Continentals retook the South. Attacking Greene's army at the namesake Hill, Rawdon's regulars and loyalists succeeded in throwing the Continentals into disorder, but not stopping Greene's advance.

■ BLANDFORD, 25 APRIL 1781

Gen William Philips arrived with 2500 regulars and loyalists from New York to raid Virginia. Continental Gen Friedrich von Steuben and 1000 militia here fought a delaying action, reducing the damage of the British raid.

■ FORT ROYAL, 29–30 APRIL 1781

British Adm Samuel Hood, with 18 ships, sought to intercept French forces at sea meant for North America. The French Adm Comte de Grasse had 20 in escort of the supply ships and transports, the British appearing off the island of Martinique. De Grasse put out to sea with his convoy en route to this port. Hood tried to close, failed and, after an exchange of fire, withdrew.

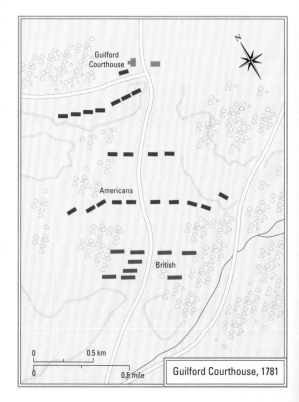

Guilford Courthouse, 1781

■ **FORT MOTTE, 8–12 MAY 1781**

Mrs Rebecca Brewton Motte's disapproval of British use of her South Carolina house as a supply depot extended to supplying Continental Gen Francis Marion with a bow to launch flaming arrows to burn the fort and her home, resulting in the British surrendering.

■ **FORT AUGUSTA/FORT CORNWALLIS, 22 MAY–6 JUNE 1781**

LCol Henry Lee continued Continental Gen Nathaniel Greene's policy of reducing isolated British outposts, this one in Georgia having changed hands repeatedly. A brisk two-week assault finally prompted the stubborn garrison to surrender.

■ **NINETY SIX, 22 MAY–19 JUNE 1781**

With less than 1000 men in his army, Continental Gen Nathaniel Greene employed it in reducing British outposts in South Carolina. The defences of this outpost and Col John Harris Cruger withstood a formal siege.

■ **TOBAGO, 24 MAY–2 JUNE 1781**

At the outbreak of hostilities with the Dutch, the British occupied this West Indies island. The French Marquis de Bouillé recaptured the island with an amphibious force at the cost of 50 wounded and 50 dead.

■ **CHARLOTTESVILLE, 1 JUNE 1781**

When British Gen Charles Cornwallis moved his army into Virginia, LCol Banastre Tarleton launched a two-pronged raid on the provisional Virginia capital here, burning stores and capturing seven of the legislature, the rest escaping.

■ **SPENCER'S ORDINARY, 26 JUNE 1781**

Having fought British Gen Charles Cornwallis' vanguard, Continental Gens Lafayette and Anthony Wayne attempted his rearguard here as Cornwallis' army occupied Williamsburg. Gen Richard Butler led an indecisive attack against an improvised British palisade.

■ **GREEN SPRING, 6 JULY 1781**

The vanguard of British Gen Charles Cornwallis's army and LCol Banastre Tarleton's cavalry caught Continental Gen Anthony Wayne's 500 with 3000 regulars. Wayne retreated until darkness, swamps and the Marquis de Lafayette saved him.

■ **FRANCISCO'S FIGHT, 9–24 JULY 1781**

By his own account in this unconfirmed rumour, Continental soldier Peter Francisco seized a sabre from one of British LCol Banastre Tarleton's raiders stealing his shoe buckles, killing three and dispersing the surviving six. Tarleton admitted to casualties.

■ **DOGGER BANK, 5 AUGUST 1781**

Dutch support of the colonists resulted in open war and this battle, in which British Adm Hyde Parker with eight ships engaged seven Dutch ships. Both fleets protected convoys and fought a fierce, drawn struggle.

■ **MINORCA, 19 AUGUST–5 FEBRUARY 1781–82**

The British had controlled this island off the southern coast of Spain since 1708, where the fortress of St Philip guarded the vital British naval base of Port Mahon. The island was a major objective of Spain once the latter country entered

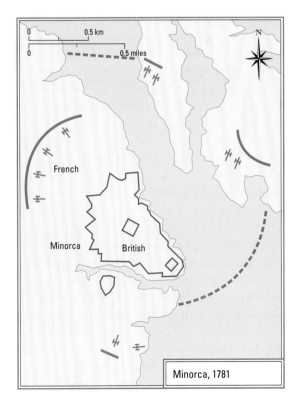

Minorca, 1781

the war in 1779. By 1781, combined French and Spanish forces were laying siege to Fort St Philip, their operations over the next six months hampered by the simultaneous siege of British Gibraltar and the success of the Royal Navy in capturing supplies meant for Minorca. The Allies were similarly successful in starving the garrison. Two British regiments under Gen James Murray were down to 680 emaciated survivors before Murray surrendered the island to the French Duc de Crillon and his 4000 troops and engineers. Minorca's fall allowed the British to divert intended supplies to Gibraltar, which held.

■ LOCHRY MASSACRE, 24 AUGUST 1781
Traveling to join Clarke's expedition in the Ohio valley, Col Archibald Lochry and some 100 Pennsylvania militia fell into Mohawk Joseph Brant's ambush, the Indians killing 40 after Lochry surrendered, the rest were held in Canada.

■ CHESAPEAKE BAY, 5 SEPTEMBER 1781
The supervisors of the French Navy had, from long experience of being beaten by the British fleet, raised their own level of ship design and armaments and, in some cases, achieved more than parity with their traditional rivals. The improvement of French technology and signaling came to fruition at this battle. Adm François de Grasse positioned 28 ships of the line across the mouth of Chesapeake Bay, having frightened off British Adm Samuel Hood with 14 ships seeking to preserve Gen Charles Cornwallis' army's route of evacuation or supply from the Yorktown peninsula. British Adm Thomas Graves with 19 ships moved to break the French blockade. De Grasse moved out to offer battle, both fleets having difficulties of co-ordination, but the British retreated when unable to penetrate De Grasse's formation. Cornwallis' trapped army was doomed.

■ NEW LONDON, 6 SEPTEMBER 1781
Former Continental Gen Benedict Arnold accepted a loyalist brigade and launched a destructive raid in 1780 up the James river, burning Colonial ships and barely failing to capture Virginia governor Thomas Jefferson. In 1781, Arnold turned against his native

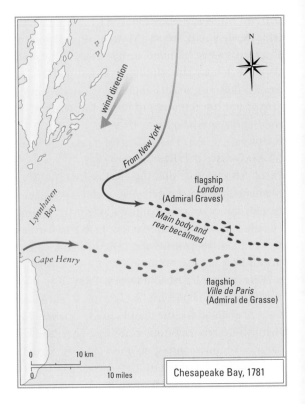

Chesapeake Bay, 1781

Connecticut with 1700 troops. Arnold's force sailed from New York and burned New London and Groton, overwhelming and butchering 80 of the 215 garrison of Fort Griswold near Groton before withdrawing.

■ EUTAW SPRINGS, 8 SEPTEMBER 1781
Continental Gen Nathaniel Greene with 2400 men sought decisive battle here with Col Alexander Stewart's 2000 men, worried that peace negotiations might leave the British with the Carolinas. Greene trusting to his cavalry to prevent a rout, his militia stiffly withstood British fire, both sides erring as the costly battle progressed. The British remained when Greene withdrew, but themselves retreated two days later to defensible positions, leaving the Carolinas to Greene.

■ YORKTOWN I, 28 SEP–19 OCT 1781
The final decisive major battle of the war, Yorktown established both the collapse of the British 'southern strategy' and Prime Minister Lord North's ability to prosecute the war further.

After a series of reverses and costly battles in the Carolinas, plus the hoped-for masses of loyalists not flocking in vast numbers to his army, British Gen Charles Cornwallis shifted his 7000 remaining troops into Virginia, having sent 2000 to the New York area in response to George Washington's plans to assault the main British foothold in the colonies.

Meanwhile, the French general dispatched to assist in the war, the Comte de Rochambeau, demurred at that objective, but offered the 7000 troops under his command to support operations against Cornwallis in Virginia. Washington had 2000 of his troops combined with the Marquis de Lafayette's 2000 Continentals in Virginia before British Gen Henry Clinton in New York was aware of their departure.

Cornwallis added the then British Gen Benedict Arnold's command to his own and moved the combined force into the Yorktown peninsula, a magnificent defensive position, in the reasonable assumption that the Royal Navy would maintain command of the sea. Across the peninsula's neck, Cornwallis employed his artillerymen and engineers in erecting a series of trenches and redoubts, with which he felt confident of repelling any conceivable Franco-American attack. Having forfeited the initiative, Cornwallis could only watch as Patriot troops clustered before his lines and French ships in the James river landed thousands of troops and, significantly, siege artillery. His entire strategy predicated upon the idea of support or evacuation by sea, Cornwallis found himself reft of both when the French fleet under Adm François de Grasse drove off a British relieving squadron in the battle of the Chesapeake Capes.

Washington and Rochambeau's combined forces numbered some 7000 Continentals, 4000 militia and 3100 French marines with 5000 regulars. Cornwallis' 65 cannon found themselves under the close-range fire of 92 guns under the expert command of Gen Henry Knox. The besiegers moved their lines to within 730m of the British and opened fire. Cornwallis gradually contracted his perimeter in the vain hope of yet another relief force from New York by sea, the allies pressing in each time and further limiting British opportunities for escape or forage. British sapping parties did at times capture or disable Allied batteries and positions, only to see them recaptured the next day by overwhelming counter-attacks that also began to capture the British redoubts. Smallpox and starvation joined the ranks of Cornwallis' enemies, even a simple lack of ammunition limiting his offensive ability.

An attempt to evacuate part of Cornwallis' army via boats to the neighbouring Gloucester peninsula collapsed under a sudden storm with severe losses. After a siege of some three weeks, Cornwallis offered to begin negotiating his surrender. Terms concluded upon the same day that Clinton finally arrived with 25 ships and 7000 relieving troops, which returned to New York at the news of Cornwallis' surrender. Slaves promised

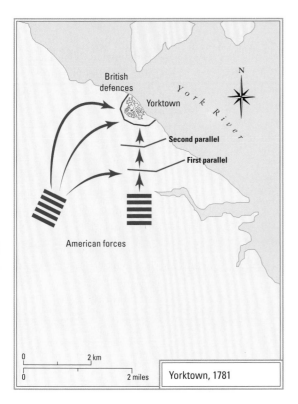

Yorktown, 1781

their freedom in the British lines returned to their master's control, while 8041 British and Hessian troops stacked arms. A total of 660 British had died and 478 of the allies. With the surrender and the transfer of the British and Hessian troops to prisoner camps, land combat in North America essentially ceased, while British Prime Minister Lord North finally resigned upon the news of a second large-scale surrender in the Colonies.

■ JOHNSTOWN, 25 OCTOBER 1781

A force of 670 loyalists, regulars and allied Indians from Canada raided this upstate New York town. Col Marinus Willett, leading 400 militia, engaged a small force attacking from the raiders' rear, prompting their withdrawal.

■ JERSEYFIELD, 30 OCTOBER 1781

Col Marinus Willett with 460 militia and Oneidas pursued 1000 British regulars, loyalists and Indians, led by Walter Butler, retreating to Canada from their raid upon Johnstown, New York. Butler died and the other raiders escaped.

■ USHANT II, 12 DECEMBER 1781

Successes in the Caribbean prompted the French to send additional support in the form of warships and supplies to the war in North America. Difficulties in securing and repairing both escort and transport ships and obtaining the supplies required delayed the convoy's sailing until December, when winter storms routinely churned the Bay of Biscay.

Adm Luc Urbain de Bouexic with 19 heavy warships was to escort the convoy out of the bay. Bouexic positioned his escort ahead of and to the convoy's lee. A smaller but powerful British force of 12 heavy warships and six lighter vessels under Adm Richard Kempenfelt fell upon the convoy's unprotected rear in the midst of a powerful storm, capturing 15 of the convoy while the rest scattered under the gale, only five transports and two French warships reaching North America, with the others returning to France.

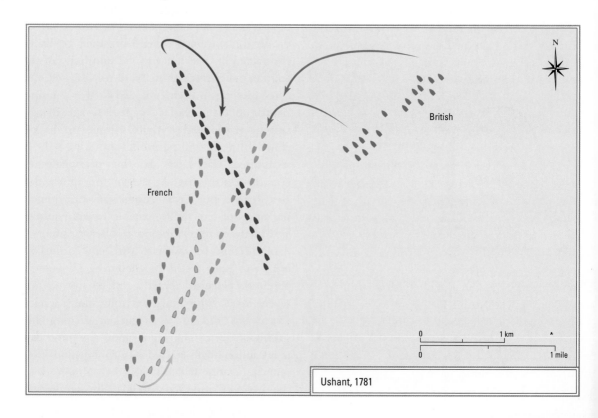

Ushant, 1781

■ **TRINCOMALEE I, 11 JANUARY 1782**

French Adm Pierre de Suffren with 14 heavy ships sailed out to meet British Adm Sir Edward Hughes with 12 somewhat lighter ships, after Suffren's capture of this port on Ceylon. Hughes sheered off upon finding Trincomalee taken, Suffren pursuing and finally bringing Hughes to battle 40km out to sea. In this encounter, the British proved the more adept at ship handling, with the French, once in position to engage, only managing to bring parts of their line into action against greater numbers of the British fleet. Hughes was able to disengage after inflicting disproportionate damage upon the French, but three of his captains perished and the prevailing monsoon drove his fleet to Madras, leaving the new French base at Trincomalee intact and able to repair the damage suffered by the ships of Suffren's fleet, which soon moved against India.

■ **MADRAS, FEBRUARY–SEPTEMBER 1782**

French Adm Pierre de Suffren with 12 ships captured a fleet of grain ships en route to this British Indian base. Sir Edward Hughes with nine ships could only watch as the French sailed past.

■ **SADRAS, 17 FEBRUARY 1782**

French Adm Pierre de Suffren's squadron of 10 heavy warships engaged Sir Edward Hughes' nine heavy ships capturing six French transports. Winds hampered both sides' tactics, the French inflicting slightly more damage upon the British.

■ **GNADENHUTTEN MASSACRE, 8 MARCH 1782**

The peaceful Moravian Christian Delawares of this settlement perished, caught between suspicious tribesmen and militia vengeful for other tribes' attacks. Despite their having offered no resistance, colonial militia butchered 96 and burned their settlement.

■ **ROATAN, 16 MARCH 1782**

This island off the coast of Honduras changed hands twice when the Spanish captured it from British 'baymen' timber thieves, a British force 1200-strong retaking it, despite resistance from 750 Spanish soldiers and militia.

■ **LITTLE MOUNTAIN/ESTILL'S DEFEAT, 22 MARCH 1782**

Kentucky Capt James Estill fell in a bloody combat having pursued a Wyandot raiding party discouraged from attacking Estill's Station by Monk, a captured slave, later freed. Seven of the 25 militia died, along with 17 Wyandots.

■ **LES SAINTES, 9–12 APRIL 1782**

British Adm George Rodney with 34 ships caught French Adm François de Grasse with 29 escorting a troop convoy to Jamaica. De Grasse and four of his fleet became Rodney's prizes after a bloody battle.

■ **PROVIDIEN, 12 APRIL 1782**

French Adm Pierre de Suffren's squadron of 10 warships here re-engaged Sir Edward Hughes' nine ships after both sides refitted at friendly ports. Hughes could not at first disengage from a bloody, but indecisive battle.

■ **CRAWFORD EXPEDITION, MAY–JUNE 1782**

Col William Crawford led 485 mounted militia into the Ohio river valley, shadowed by 200 Wyandot and Delaware tribesman enraged by past attacks and reinforced by 240 loyalists, including the infamous Simon Girty and two cannon. Brought to battle near the Sandusky, Crawford's command ran low on ammunition after refusing Girty's offer of quarter. Most of the expedition fought their way out; Crawford was captured and tortured to death.

■ **NEGAPATAM, 6 JULY 1782**

British Adm Edward Hughes with 11 heavy ships here caught French Adm Pierre de Suffren's 12 ships after storm damage and inflicted double his own casualties upon them in another engagement muddled by shifting winds.

■ **PIQUA, 8 AUGUST 1782**

After the Blue Licks disaster, George Rogers Clark led 1050 militia and a vengeful Daniel Boone in burning five Shawnee villages and a British trading post.

■ **CUDDALORE I, 1782**

The French joined their ally Hyder Ali of Mysore in capturing this Indian port, despite Gen Sir Eyre

Coote's defence of the British areas and capture of the Dutch East India Company's holdings.

■ **TRINCOMALEE II, 25 AUG–3 SEP 1782**
French Adm Pierre de Suffren quickly seized this fortified Bristish Ceylonese port with 600 men before Sir Edward Hughes arrived, securing a French naval base in the Indian Ocean for further operations against the British.

■ **COMBAHEE RIVER, 26 AUGUST 1782**
Cornwallis's departure and defeat and Nathaniel Greene's attacks had driven the British into Charleston, while French ships left them dependent upon local supplies. Patriot Gen Mordecai Gist moved approximately 300 infantry and cavalry against a strong British foraging party, out to retrieve supplies from Carolina loyalists. The British, observing colonial movements from boats, managed to ambush the colonists twice before retreating by river with no garnered supplies back into Charleston.

■ **ACTION OF 18 OCTOBER, 1782**
Off the coast of Hispaniola, the French '74' *Scipion* mauled HMS *London*, which was armed with 90 guns, pursuing her with HMS *Torbay*, also with 90. Seeking refuge in Samana Bay, *Scipion* hit a rock and foundered, her crew taken captive.

■ **CAPE SPARTEL, 20 OCTOBER 1782**
A British fleet of 34 heavy warships under Adm Richard Howe overshot the entrance to Gibraltar. A Franco-Spanish fleet of 49 sought battle here off Morocco. The faster British ships escaped after resupplying the Rock.

■ **CUDDALORE II, 20 JUNE 1783**
French Adm Pierre de Suffren appeared with 15 heavy ships as British Adm Sir Edward Hughes with 18 supported the siege of this French base. Suffren's survival of an indecisive battle drove off the British.

■ **GIBRALTAR, 1781–83**
The Royal Navy's repeated ability to resupply this nearly impregnable fortress frustrated a Franco-Spanish amphibious siege, involving as many as 30,000 men, fleets and floating batteries and lasting nearly 32 months. Less than 1000 British died.

Native American Wars 1763–1814

■ **BUSHY RUN, 5–6 AUGUST 1763**
The French defeat in North America greatly discommoded their allied Indians, the Ottawa chief Pontiac leading an uprising of the Great Lakes tribes against the British and colonists. British Col Henry Bouquet with 400 men marched from Fort Niagara to relieve Fort Pitt, under sporadic attack. Bouquet dug in here and lured attacking Indians into a gap in his lines, inflicting casualties enough to stop the attack and Pontiac's Rebellion.

■ **POINT PLEASANT, 10 OCTOBER 1774**
The powerful Shawnee tribe sent 1000 warriors and allies into Virginia against the camp of Col Andrew Lewis and 1100 Virginia militia here. The militia rallied after the initial surprise and eventually repelled the attack.

■ **HARMAR'S DEFEAT, 18 OCTOBER 1791**
Near here, Miami chief Little Turtle and his warriors attacked and defeated part of US BGen Josiah Harmar's 1300 regulars and militia riflemen while they marched in three columns, inflicting 300 casualties before withdrawing.

■ **WABASH, 4 NOVEMBER 1791**
Gen Harmar's defeat had prompted the American Gen Arthur St Clair's march into Ohio with all 600 US regulars and 1500 militia. Miami chief Little Turtle collected many warriors, who attacked St Clair's camp at this river. Neither St Clair nor his officers could establish any sort of order as the warriors inflicted 800 casualties in the worst defeat suffered by the Americans or British at the hands of Native Americans.

■ **FORT RECOVERY, 1794**
US Gen 'Mad Anthony' Wayne invaded Ohio, building this post at the end of his march into Little Turtle's territory near the Wabash battlefield and repelling a Miami attack upon his ready and better-trained troops.

■ **NICKAJACK EXPEDITION, 1794**
The Chickamauga Cherokee faction had settled near Nickajack Cave in Tennessee after rejecting

peace overtures before and after the revolution, launching sporadic attacks. With 15,000 militia mustered against them, the surrounded tribe surrendered and evacuated.

■ FALLEN TIMBERS, 20 AUGUST 1794

Into this tornado-struck clearing, US Gen 'Mad Anthony's Wayne with a mixed force of 3000 drove out Little Turtle and his warriors, often employing the bayonet. Anthony's mounted force collapsed Indian resistance and created a rout.

■ TIPPECANOE CREEK, 7 NOVEMBER 1811

Shawnee chief Tecumseh and The Prophet, with some British military support, rallied the neighboring tribes for a stand against white encroachments. US Gen William Henry Harrison, later president, marched into Ohio against the Shawnee capital of Prophetstown, emulating Anthony Wayne's earlier tactics on the march and likewise building defences along his line of supply. With his army attacked in camp here, Harrison burned Prophetstown after his dragoons eventually scattered the Indians.

Peoria War 1812–13

The impending War of 1812 between the British and the US created difficulties and pressures for the Peoria and Potawatomi tribes in Illinois. There were successes such as the burning of Fort Dearborn and the repulse of the first Hopkins punitive expedition in 1812, but even British support could not prevent the subsequent destruction of the tribes' homes and winter stores, leading to their submission and evacuation across the Mississippi.

Creek War 1813–14

■ BURNT CORN CREEK, 27 JULY 1813

The warring Red Stick Creeks, having obtained weapons from the British and Spanish in Pensacola, at first fled and then routed an ambush by Alabama militia. The 'Red Sticks' then attacked Americans and assimilated Creeks.

■ FORT MIMS, 30 AUGUST 1813

The warring 'Red Stick' drove assimilated 'Lower Creek' tribesmen and settlers to shelter at this weak and undermanned post in Alabama. A massacre of the garrison and sheltering civilians followed a costly Red Stick surprise attack.

■ TALLUSHATCHEE, 3 NOVEMBER 1813

A detachment of US Gen Andrew Jackson's 5000 Tennessee militia and some hundreds of allied Cherokee and assimilated 'White Stick' Creeks ambushed a 'Red Stick' domestic band here, killing 186 in retaliation for the earlier events at Fort Mims.

■ TALLADEGA, 9 NOVEMBER 1813

The Creek War partook something of the War of 1812 and a civil war between the assimilated 'White Stick' Creeks and the 'Red Stick' faction, pursuing their original culture and waging war against white settlers and their former fellow tribesmen. Perhaps 1000 Red Sticks besieging this White Stick Creek village suffered heavy losses, when US Gen Andrew Jackson marched quickly and raised their siege, killing some 290, suffering 15 losses.

■ EMUKFAW/ENOTACHOPO CREEK, JAN 1814

US Gen Andrew Jackson's advance into 'Red Stick' Creek territory with 1000 green militia met a check at Emukfaw Creek and began retreating, the Creeks overtaking them at Enotachopo Creek, where the militia effectively resisted.

■ HORSESHOE BEND, 22–24 JANUARY 1814

Hostile 'Red Stick' Creeks numbering 1200 had constructed a large and heavily fortified encampment, protected on three sides by the Tallapoosa river and on the fourth by a log and earthwork barricade 2.4m high with firing steps, with canoes left along the beach in case of evacuation. US Gen Andrew Jackson's force included 600 regulars, 1400 militia and 700 mounted troops as well as 100 'White Stick' assimilated Creeks and 500 allied Cherokees. Jackson's initial and overcome foes were the expiring enlistments of his militia and difficulties of supply. The attack on Horseshoe Bend began with a bombardment by Jackson's two cannon while the Cherokees swam the river to steal the

Red Sticks' canoes. Allied Indian archers fired on the encampment with incendiary arrows.

Jackson then sent his regulars with fixed bayonets directly against the earthwork across the peninsula's neck, there meeting, but overcoming stout resistance by the Red Sticks. Meanwhile, the balance of Jackson's force surrounded the peninsula across the river to prevent escapes, joining in the fight by crossing the Tallapoosa to the burning village, in which groups of Red Sticks maintained a 'hut to hut' fight, some employing captured settlers and slaves as human shields during the battle.

When the fighting stopped, some 800 warriors were dead, and some 350 surviving women and children captured and dispersed among 'White Stick' villages. Jackson's force lost 26 killed, the allied Indians 23. The latter had a shock five months later when Jackson, in negotiating the Treaty of Fort Jackson, held them as responsible for the war as the Red Sticks and forced all factions and the Cherokee to cede some 22 million acres of tribal land to the United States.

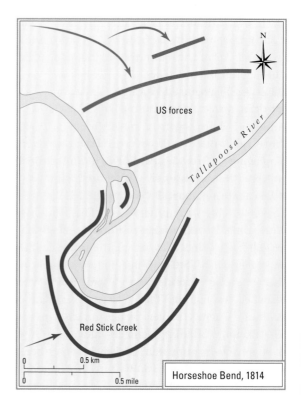

Horseshoe Bend, 1814

Ottoman/Turkish Wars 1770–1829

■ **ACTION OF 18 JUNE 1788**
In this action John Paul Jones' Russian fleet of 14 ships defeated Hassan el Ghazi's Ottoman fleet of 12 ships of the line, 13 frigates and numerous smaller craft in the Black Sea, sinking two or three Ottoman vessels.

■ **FIDONISI, 14 JULY 1788**
At Fidonisi RAdm Count Voynovitch's Russian fleet of 12 ships of the line and 24 smaller craft defeated Hassan el Ghazi's Ottoman fleet of 17 ships of the line and 32 other vessels, sinking one xebec vessel.

■ **FOCŞANI, 21 JULY 1789**
In this major confrontation in July 1789, a 25,000-strong Russian and Austrian army under FM Alexander Suvorov defeated Grand Vizier Koca Yusuf Pasha's Ottoman army of 30,000 men at Focşani in Romania. The allies inflicted 1600 casualties, losing 400 men.

■ **RYMNIK, 22 SEPTEMBER 1789**
FM Alexander Suvorov's 25,000-strong Russian and Austrian army defeated Grand Vizier Cenaze Hasan Pasha's Ottoman army of 60,000 men near Rymnik (modern Râmnicu Sărat). Suvorov inflicted 26,000 casualties, losing 700.

■ **KRUSI, 22 SEPTEMBER 1796**
The Albanian warlord Kara Mahmud Bushati of Shkoder (Scutari) had repeatedly attacked Montenegro since 1785, on one occasion burning the capital, Cetinje. In 1796, he led a 23,000-strong Ottoman army in a further invasion and again attempted to raid Cetinje. The Prince-Bishop of Montenegro, Petar I Petrović-Njegoš, had ample warning of the attack and raised an army of 6500 men, which was deployed in strong defensive positions around Mount Sađavce, on the right bank of the River Matica, with a detachment under the command of Jovan Radonjić positioned at Mount Busovnika near the village of Krusi. The Ottoman attack failed to penetrate the Montenegrin

defences and Bushati was killed in action. His head was taken as a trophy by Bogdan Vukov from the village of Zalaz. The Montenegrins inflicted 3500 casualties for the loss of less than 400 men.

■ LOPATE, OCTOBER 1796

Ottoman forces from Bosnia and Herzegovina invaded Montenegro and attacked Morača (Mount Lopatice, near Lopate), defended by clans of Trebješani, Morača and Rovci. Each side lost about 40 men in inconclusive skirmishing.

■ VARNA, 5 AUGUST–11 OCTOBER 1828

A Russian army of 23,000 men and 170 guns commanded by Prince Alexander Menshikov besieged the Black Sea port of Varna, which was held by 20,000 Ottoman troops. Omer Vryonis Pasha's Ottoman relief force attempted to break through the siege lines, but was defeated in fierce fighting. The garrison also made determined but unsuccessful sorties on 7 and 21 August; the city was eventually stormed on 11 October.

■ KULEVICHA, 11 JUNE 1829

A 50,000-strong Russian army under Count Hans Karl von Diebitsch defeated Reşid Mehmed Pasha's Otttoman army of 40,000 men at Kulevicha (modern Kyulevcha, Bulgaria). The Russians inflicted 5000 casualties, losing 1000.

Ottoman Invasions of Mani 1770–1826

■ OTTOMAN INVASION OF MANI, 1770

Ali Bey, with 10,000 Ottomans, invaded Mani in the southern Peloponnese in retaliation for the Russian-inspired Orlov Revolt. The Ottomans withdrew after their defeat at the battle of Vromopigada.

■ OTTOMAN INVASION OF MANI, 1803

Zanet Grigorakis's involvement in plots with France against Turkish rule in Greece provoked an Ottoman invasion in 1803, which attacked his fort on the island of Cranae. Zanet escaped and the Ottomans abandoned the siege.

■ OTTOMAN INVASION OF MANI, 1807

Zanet's cousin, Antony Grigorakis, was appointed Bey of Mani, but failed to halt Zanet's raids

on Ottoman territory. This provoked another Ottoman invasion that was abandoned after an unsuccessful siege of Antony's fort on Cranae.

■ OTTOMAN INVASION OF MANI, 1815

Maniot piracy in the Aegean provoked an Ottoman attack on Skutari, one of the main pirate bases. This was defeated by the townsmen who inflicted 115 casualties, losing 30.

■ OTTOMAN–EGYPTIAN INVASION OF MANI, 21 JUNE–28 AUGUST 1826

An Ottoman-Egyptian army of 17,000 men commanded by Ibrahim Pasha of Egypt invaded Mani, but was forced to withdraw after being defeated by the rebels at Vergas, Diros and Polytsaravo with the loss of 4000 men.

Austro-Turkish War 1788–91

■ KARÁNSEBES, 17–18 SEPTEMBER 1788

A 100,000-strong Austrian army was setting up camp around the city of Karánsebes (modern Caransebeş, in Romania) when a scouting detachment of hussars bought schnapps from local Romani. A drunken argument over the schnapps between the hussars and their supporting infantry became violent and shots were fired. Nearby units panicked, thinking that Ottoman forces were making a surprise attack and began firing on each other, inflicting up to 10,000 casualties.

Russo-Turkish Wars 1790–91

■ KERCH STRAIT, 19 JULY 1790

Hussein Pasha's Ottoman fleet of 10 ships of the line, 8 frigates and 36 other vessels was defeated by a Russian fleet of 10 ships of the line and 6 frigates under Fyodor Ushakov.

■ TENDRA, 8–9 SEPTEMBER 1790

Hussein Pasha's Ottoman fleet of 14 ships of the line and eight frigates was defeated off Tendra by a Russian fleet of 10 ships of the line and six frigates commanded by Fyodor Ushakov.

■ MĂCIN, 10 JULY 1791

Advancing up the Danube after taking Izmail, 40,000 Russians under Prince Nikolai Repnin and Gen Mikhail Kutuzov attacked and defeated

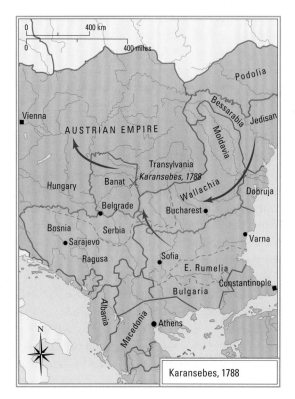

Karansebes, 1788

Grand Vizier Yusuf Pasha's Ottoman army of 100,000 men at Măcin (in modern Romania).

■ **CAPE KALIAKRA, 11 AUGUST 1791**

A Russian fleet of 15 ships of the line, two frigates and 19 other vessels commanded by Fydor Ushakov defeated Hussein Pasha's Ottoman fleet of 18 ships of the line, 17 frigates and 48 smaller craft.

Persian Expedition 1796

■ **PERSIAN EXPEDITION, 1796**

Catherine the Great sent a 13,000-strong force under Count Valerian Zubov against Shah Agha Muhammad Khān. The Russians stormed Derbent and overran much of Azerbaijan before withdrawing on Catherine's death.

Russo-Persian War 1804–13

■ **ASLANDUZ, 31 OCTOBER 1812**

A Russian force of 3000 men and six guns commanded by Gen Pyotr Kotlyarevsky defeated Prince Abbas Mirza's 30,000-strong Persian army at Aslanduz in Azerbaijan. The Russians inflicted 2000 casualties for the loss of 200 men.

Ottoman–Saudi War 1811–18

■ **YANBU, 1811**

Tusun Pasha's 10,000-strong Ottoman army landed at the Red Sea port of Yanbu in response to the conquest of Mecca by the Wahhabi Islamic fundamentalist movement and the House of Saud. The 70-strong Saudi garrison surrendered.

■ **AL-SAFRA, 1812**

Tusun Pasha's 8000-strong Ottoman army was defeated near Medina by a Saudi force of 10,000 men under Saud bin Abdul-Aziz bin Muhammad bin Saud. The Saudis inflicted almost 900 casualties for the loss of 800 men.

■ **MEDINA, 1812**

Tusun Pasha's Ottoman army of 20,000 men, 18 guns and three mortars took Medina, which was held by a 10,000-strong Saudi garrison. The Ottomans inflicted 600 casualties, losing 300.

■ **JEDDAH, JANUARY 1813**

Tusun Pasha was reinforced by an army under his father, Muhammad Ali Pasha. The combined Ottoman force of 25,000 men defeated the 2000-strong Saudi garrison of Jeddah, inflicting 800 casualties for the loss of 60 men.

■ **MECCA, JANUARY 1813**

Exploiting the demoralizing loss of Jeddah on the ill-disciplined Saudi forces, a 22,000-strong Ottoman army under Muhammad Ali Pasha and Tusun Pasha forced the surrender of Mecca's Saudi garrison of 1000 men.

■ **NEJD CAMPAIGN, 1817–18**

Ibrahim Pasha's 30,000-strong Ottoman army began the campaign against the Saudi heartland of the Nejd, which was defended by Abdullah bin Saud's 6000 men. The Ottomans inflicted 5000 casualties, losing 800.

■ **DIRIYAH, APRIL–SEPTEMBER 1818**

Ibrahim Pasha's 30,000-strong Ottoman army with 30 guns, besieged and captured the Saudi capital of Diriyah, defended by a garrison of 5000 men commanded by Abdullah bin Saud.

Maratha-British Wars 1776–1818

■ MAONDA AND MANDHOLI, 1776

Maharaj Jawahar Singh of Bharatpur's army was attacked by the forces of Sawai Raja Madho Singhji of Jaipur near the villages of Maonda and Mandholi. A total of 25,000 casualties were sustained in this indecisive battle.

■ POONA, 25 OCTOBER 1802

In a bloody war between rival factions of the Maratha Confederacy, Maharaja Jaswant Rao Holkar of Indore rapidly recovered from his defeat at Indore in October 1801. In a fierce battle outside Poona, he defeated the forces of Daulat Rao Sindhia of Gwalior and his ally Peshwa Baji Rao II. British demands to restore the deposed Peshwa led to the Second British-Maratha War, when Scindia changed sides to support Holkar.

■ ALIGARH, 1–4 SEPTEMBER 1803

Gen Gerard Lake's British force stormed the Maratha fort at Aligarh after a brief siege. The fort was one of the most formidable in India, having been greatly strengthened by a French officer, Pierre Cuillier-Perron.

■ DELHI, 11 SEPTEMBER 1803

A British East India Company army of 21,000 men commanded by Gen Gerard Lake attacked and defeated a 19,000-strong Maratha army under Louis Bourquin. Lake inflicted 3000 casualties for the loss of 1500 men.

■ ASSAYE, 23 SEPTEMBER 1803

MGen Arthur Wellesley's British army of 9500 men and 17 guns defeated the 41,000-strong army of the Maratha Confederacy commanded by the renegade Hanoverian Anthony Pohlmann near Assaye in western India. Although heavily outnumbered, Wellesley decided to attack immediately, believing that the Maratha army would soon move off. Both sides suffered heavily in the ensuing battle; the Maratha artillery caused heavy losses, but the vast numbers of irregular

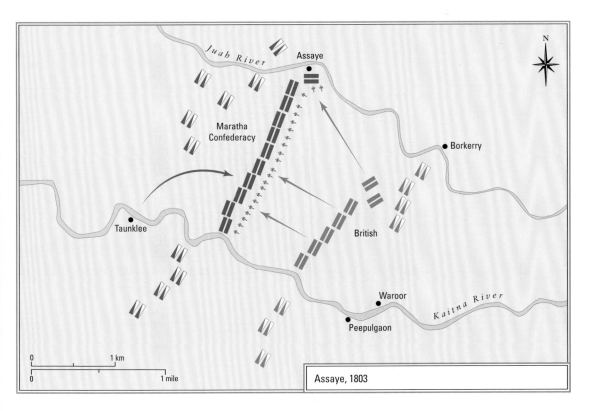

Assaye, 1803

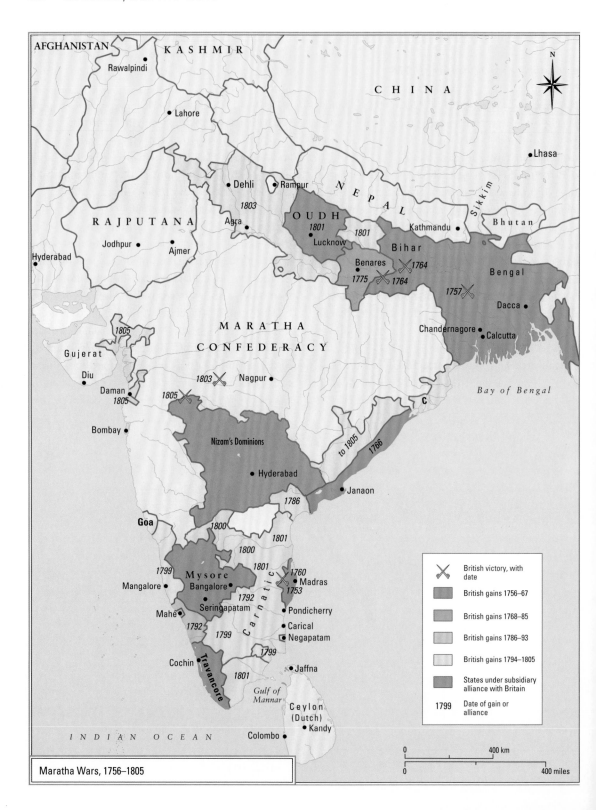

AFGHANISTAN
KASHMIR
Rawalpindi
CHINA
Lahore
Lhasa
Dehli
Rampur
NEPAL
1803
Sikkim
OUDH
Kathmandu
Bhutan
1801
RAJPUTANA
Agra
Jodhpur
Ajmer
1801
Bihar
Hyderabad
Lucknow
Benares
1764
1801
1775
1764
Bengal
1757
Dacca
MARATHA
Chandernagore
Calcutta
CONFEDERACY
1805
Gujerat
Bay of Bengal
Diu
1803
Nagpur
Daman
1805
1805
C
Bombay
Nizam's Dominions
to 1805
1766
Hyderabad
Janaon
1786
Goa
1800
1801
1800
1799
Mysore
1801
1760
Mangalore
Bangalore
Madras
1753
1792
Seringapatam
Pondicherry
Mahé
Carical
1792
1799
Negapatam
1799
Cochin
Travancore
Jaffna
1801
Gulf of
Mannar
Ceylon
(Dutch)
Kandy
INDIAN OCEAN
Colombo

✕	British victory, with date
	British gains 1756–67
	British gains 1768–85
	British gains 1786–93
	British gains 1794–1805
	States under subsidiary alliance with Britain
1799	Date of gain or alliance

Maratha Wars, 1756–1805

0   400 km
0   400 miles

Maratha cavalry proved largely ineffective against regular troops. A combination of disciplined close-range musketry, bayonet and cavalry charges eventually forced the Maratha army to retreat, but Wellesley's army was too battered and exhausted to pursue. Wellesley had lost 1600 men, but inflicted 6000 casualties on the Marathas and captured 98 of their 100 guns. The European-trained infantry and artillery that formed the core of the Maratha army had largely been destroyed.

■ LASWARI, 1 NOVEMBER 1803
Gen Gerard Lake's force of 10,000 men attacked a 14,000-strong Maratha army under Raghoji II Bhonsle at Laswari, near Alwar. The Marathas were defeated in a fierce action, sustaining heavy casualties and losing 72 guns.

■ ARGAON (ARGAUM), 29 NOVEMBER 1803
Two months after his victory at Assaye, MGen Arthur Wellesley inflicted a further defeat on Daulat Rao Scindia of Gwalior and Raja Raghuji Bhonsle of Berar at the village of Argaum, north of Akola.

■ GAWILGHUR, 15 DECEMBER 1803
MGen Arthur Wellesley pursued Raja Raghuji Bhonsle of Berar's defeated force to the hill fortress of Gawilgarh, east of Burhanpur. The fortress was successfully stormed after heavy bombardment, effectively ending the fighting in central India.

■ FARRUKHABAD, 14 NOVEMBER 1804
Gen Gerard Lake defeated Maharaja Yashwant Rao Holkar of Indore at Delhi on 2 November, before pursuing the remaining Maratha forces down the Ganges towards Farrukhabad in what is now Uttar Pradesh. Lake achieved complete tactical surprise by making forced marches of more than 97km in the preceding 24 hours and destroyed the Maratha cavalry. Holkar himself only just avoided being captured in the rout.

■ BHARATPUR, 2 JANUARY–22 FEBRUARY 1805
Gen Gerard Lake besieged Bharatpur, which was defended by Maharaja Yashwant Rao Holkar of Indore's Maratha garrison. Lake had insufficient siege artillery and abandoned the siege after four unsuccessful assaults cost him over 3000 men.

■ KIRKEE, 5 NOVEMBER 1817
Peshwa Baji Rao II of Poona's Maratha army of 26,000 men was defeated with the loss of over 500 men by a 2800-strong British force under LCol Charles Burr near Kirkee (modern Khadki).

■ SITABALDI FORT, 26 NOVEMBER 1817
Raja Appa Sahib of Nagpur's army of 22,000 men was routed by a surprise attack by three squadrons of Bengal cavalry under Capt Charles Fitzgerald, while attacking Fort Sitabaldi's garrison of less than 1500 men.

■ MAHIDPUR, 20 DECEMBER 1817
Peshwa Baji Rao II of Poona and his ally Mulhar Rao Holkar of Indore renewed war against the British in India. A 5500-strong British force commanded by LGen Thomas Hislop attacked the Maratha army of 35,000 men at Mahidpur on the Sipra. Despite their immense numerical superiority, the Marathas were routed by a fierce frontal attack, which inflicted heavy losses and captured large quantities of stores.

Mysore–British Wars 1780–99

■ POLLILURE, 10 SEPTEMBER 1780
Tipu Sultan's Mysorean army of 10,000 men and 18 guns intercepted and decisively defeated a British force of 4000 men commanded by Col William Baillie on its way to reinforce Sir Hector Munro's army.

■ PORTO NOVO, 1 JULY 1781
Hyder Ali of Mysore's army of 40,000 men was defeated by Gen Eyre Coote's 8000-strong British force at Porto Novo, just north of the British base at Cuddalore. Hyder Ali lost an estimated 10,000 men.

■ NEGAPATAM, 21 OCT–11 NOV 1781
A British army of almost 4500 men under Gen Hector Munro besieged and forced the surrender of the Dutch fortress of Negapatam, which was defended by Governor Reynier van Vlissingen's garrison of 8000 men.

■ **SEEDASEER, 6 MARCH 1799**

A Mysorean army of 20,000 men under Tipu Sultan was defeated at Seedaseer by LGen James Stuart's 6500-strong detachment of the Bombay Army. Stuart's forces inflicted 2000 casualties for the loss of 143 men.

■ **SERINGAPATAM, 5 APRIL–4 MAY 1799**

A British army of 50,000 men under LGen George Harris besieged Seringapatam, the capital of Mysore, which was defended by Tipu Sultan's 30,000-strong garrison. When the siege began, the River Cauvery, which surrounded the city, was at its lowest level of the year and could be forded by infantry – if an assault could be made before the summer monsoon. By 2 May, the siege batteries opened a practical breach in the outer wall and further bombardment detonated the mines that were hastily laid under the breach. The assault was made on 4 May by two columns commanded by MGen David Baird, which forded the river

and broke through the breach before fighting their way along the ramparts to take the city. Tipu Sultan was killed in action and his garrison sustained 6000 casualties, while British losses totalled 1400 men.

Hawaiian Unification 1781–95

■ **MOKUOHAI, JULY 1782**

When King Kalani'ōpu'u of Hawaii died, the island was divided between his son Kīwala'ō and his nephew Kamehameha, leading to war between the cousins. Kīwala'ō was defeated and killed at Mokuohai on the west coast.

■ **OLOWALU MASSACRE, 1790**

Capt Simon Metcalfe's trading expedition to Maui led to disputes with chief Kame'eiamoku, in which one of Metcalfe's crew was killed. In retaliation, Metcalfe's ship fired on local villagers, inflicting at least 100 casualties.

■ **KEPANIWAI, 1790**

Kamehameha I invaded King Kahekili's island of Maui with a force of 1200 men. Kahekili's son Kalanikūpule held the 'Īao valley with a similar-sized force and the two armies fought an indecisive action. Even Kamehameha's deployment of two cannon commanded by his British advisers John Young and Isaac Davis failed to break the stalemate, although there were so many dead that the stream was renamed Kepaniwai: damming of the waters.

■ **EAST HAWAII, 1790**

Kamehameha I was ambushed by his cousin, Keōua Kuahuula, at Paauhau, Hawaii, and fought an inconclusive action in which one of his cannon was captured, although Keōua lacked the ammunition and expertise to use it.

■ **KAWAIHAE, 1791**

Kamehameha I invited Keōua to a meeting. As he landed, one of Kamehameha's chiefs threw a spear at him. He dodged this, but was cut down by musket fire, together with his bodyguards.

■ **NU'UANU, MAY 1795**

Kamehameha I invaded Kalanikūpule's island

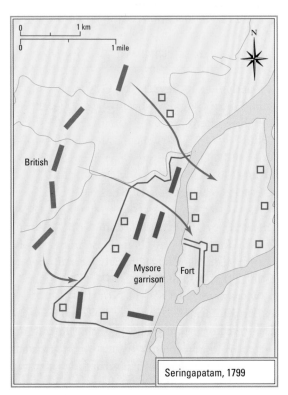

Seringapatam, 1799

of Oahu. Landing near modern Honolulu, Kamehameha destroyed his enemy at Nu'uanu Pali. Kalanikūpule fled (later captured and executed) and his ally Kaiana was killed.

Tây-Son–Siam War 1785

■ Rạch Gầm-Xoài Mút, 20 January 1785
A Siamese force of 50,000 men and 300 warships invaded Vietnam in support of Nguyễn Ánh's fight against the Tây-Son. The Tây-Son ruler, Nguyễn Huệ (Emperor Quang Trung), deployed infantry and artillery along the River Mekong (Rạch Gầm-Xoài Mút in the modern Tiển Giang province) and its islands. While the Siamese were distracted by negotiations, Nguyễn Huệ's forces launched a surprise attack, routing and virtually annihilating their opponents.

Wars in India 1790–1837

■ Patan, 20 June 1790
A Rajput and Mughal army of 50,000 men commanded by Ismail Beg was routed with heavy losses near Patan in Rajasthan by the disciplined firepower of Benoît de Boigne's European-trained 10,000-strong Maratha army.

■ Jamrud, 30 April 1837
The 600-strong garrison of the Sikh fortress Jamrud at the mouth of the Khyber Pass beat off attacks by a force of 23,000 Afghans under Amir Akbar Khan, forestalling an Afghan offensive to recapture Peshawar.

Haitian Revolution 1791–1805

■ Saint-Domingue Expedition, Dec 1801–Dec 1802
A 31,000-strong French expeditionary force under Gen Charles Leclerc attempted to suppress Toussaint L'Ouverture's rebellion in Haiti (then Saint-Domingue). The French were subsequently decimated by tropical diseases, with only 8000 survivors eventually evacuating in December 1802.

■ Ravine-à-Couleuvres, 23 February 1802
A 3000-strong French infantry division commanded by Gen Donatien de Rochambeau was attacked and defeated by Toussaint Louverture's 2800 Haitian rebels at the Ravine-à-Couleuvres. The defeat temporarily halted the French advance on the city of Gonaive.

■ Crête-à-Pierrot, 4–24 March 1802
Jean-Jacques Dessalines and his 1300 Haitian rebels defended the fort at Crête-à-Pierrot against a French army of 18,000 men under Gen Charles Leclerc. The garrison inflicted heavy casualties on Leclerc's army, but after a 20-day siege they were forced to abandon the fort due to lack of food and munitions. However, most of the rebels successfully broke through the French siege lines and escaped into the Cahos Mountains.

■ Vertières, 18 November 1803
Gen Jean Jacques Dessalines' Haitian army of 27,000 men attacked Gen Donatien Rochambeau's 2000-strong French force at Cap Francais (modern Cap Haitien). Haitian assaults on nearby Fort Vertieres were repulsed, but Rochambeau surrendered the following day.

■ Siege of Santo Domingo, March 1805
A garrison of some 2000 French troops commanded by Gen Louis Ferrand held the former Spanish capital of Santo Domingo against a three-week siege by a force of 21,000 Haitian troops led by the newly proclaimed Emperor of Haiti, Jacques I (the former Gen Jean Jacques Dessalines) and Gen Henri Christophe. The siege was raised by the arrival of a relief force carried in a squadron of six French frigates.

Russo-Polish War 1792

■ Mir, 11 June 1792
Russian forces under Mellin invaded the Polish-Lithuanian Commonwealth and defeated a small Lithuanian army under Judycki at Mir in modern-day Belarus. The Russians also captured a nearby castle as Judycki withdrew.

■ ZIELEŃCE, 18 JUNE 1792

A Polish army of 15,500 men with 12 cannon under Poniatowski, including a division under Kosciuszko, defended a position near Zieleńce (Zielencami) in modern-day Ukraine against a Russian force of 11,500 troops with 24 cannon under Morkov. The Russians under Morkov represented the advance guard of a larger Russian army of over 60,000, but had marched ahead beyond the possibility of immediate reinforcement, so Poniatowski, having consolidated his forces, decided to make a stand. Poniatowski positioned his infantry in the centre, with cavalry supporting both flanks. Morkov's force included 6000 infantry and over 4000 cavalry, including a brigade of Cossacks under Orlov.

Morkov attacked, employing his superior artillery to considerable effect. Some of Poniatowski's raw recruits panicked as the Russians, despite heavy losses, reached the centre of the Polish lines. Poniatowski personally rallied his troops and counter-attacked the Russians. A charge by Orlov's Cossack Brigade was repulsed by a converging charge of Polish cavalry. The battle was in flux as Morkov attacked the Polish left with the Ekatierinoslav Grenadier Regiment, which was driven back by the Potocki and Malczewski Polish regiments. The Russians were then driven from the field, having lost two flags and many prisoners. The Russians lost a total of about 2000 troops and the Poles lost about 1000, although the Russians had carried off three Polish cannons.

After the victory, Poniatowski's uncle, King Stanislaw August Poniatowski, instituted the Virtuti Militari medal, awarding it to both Poniatowski and Kosciuszko. The Polish army continued to retreat after the battle, as the main Russian army advanced. Poniatowski planned to gather forces near Warsaw in order to organize an effective defense, but, despite some successes

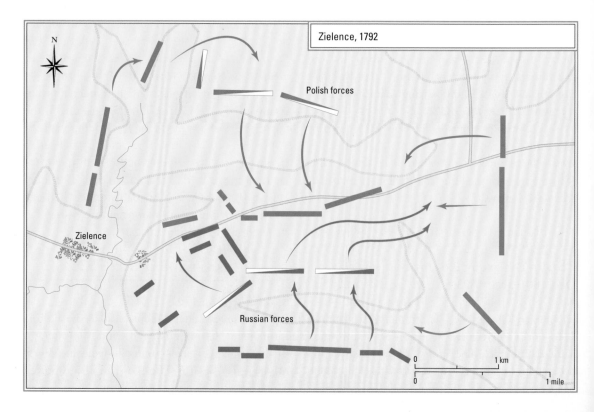

Zielence, 1792

Polish forces

Zielence

Russian forces

0   1 km

0   1 mile

in battle, King Stanislaw soon accepted Russian peace terms.

■ ZELWA, 4 JULY 1792

A small Polish force including a regiment under Dzialinsky fought a delaying action at Zelwa in north-eastern Poland against a secondary Russian invasion advancing through Lithuania, with light casualties on both sides.

DUBIENKA, 18 JULY 1792

Kosciuszko with 4000 Poles in strong positions on the Bug river in Poland fought a rearguard action against over 20,000 Russians under Kochowski. The Russians suffered losses of 4000 casualties in frontal attacks, the Poles losing a total of 900 men.

■ MARKUSZOW, 26 JULY 1792

Poniatowski, leading 12 squadrons of Polish cavalry in eastern Poland, attacked a large force of Russian cavalry advancing ahead of a Russian invasion. The Russians were repulsed with heavy losses.

Wars of the French Revolution/ Napoleonic Wars 1792–1815

War of the First Coalition 1792–1800

■ VERDUN, 20 AUGUST–2 SEPTEMBER 1792

A small French force fought an invading army of Prussians and fell back into the fortress in Verdun, France. The Duke of Brunswick then led 60,000 Prussians in a successful siege of Verdun.

■ VALMY, 20 SEPTEMBER 1792

A Coalition force of Prussians and Austrians under the Duke of Brunswick invading France was confronted by French forces under Kellermann and Dumouriez, astride the Coalition lines of communication. Brunswick moved west with 35,000 troops to attack the French positions. Many of the French units consisted of new recruits and partially trained volunteers. Kellermann commanded the French front line of 36,000 men

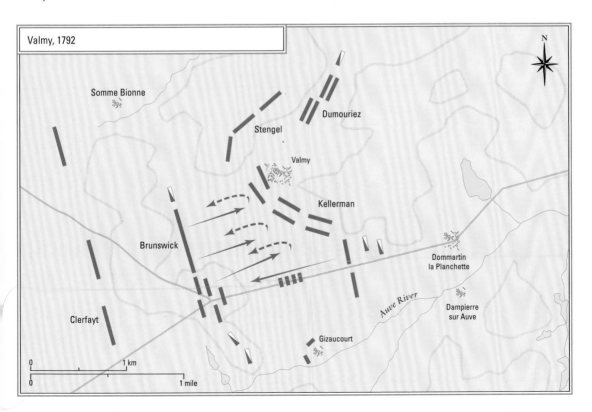

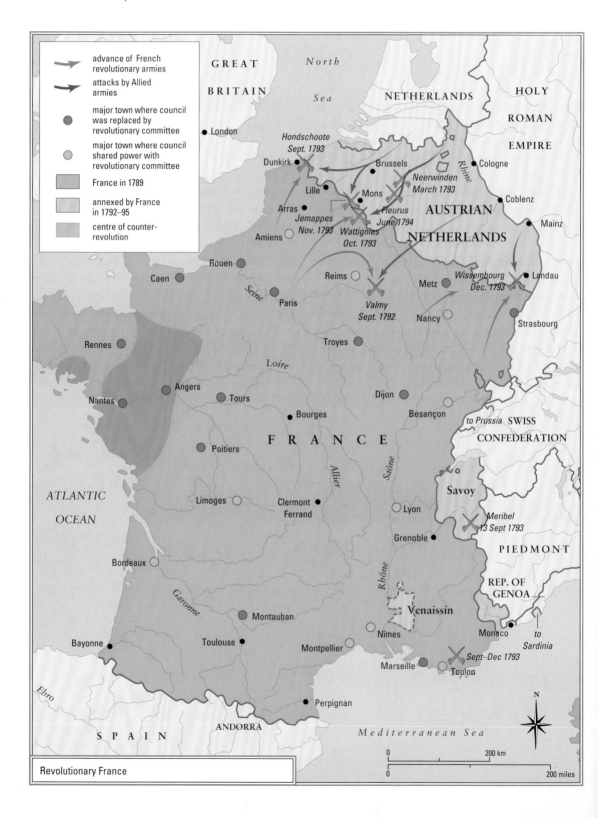

Legend

advance of French revolutionary armies

attacks by Allied armies

major town where council was replaced by revolutionary committee

major town where council shared power with revolutionary committee

France in 1789

annexed by France in 1792–95

centre of counter-revolution

GREAT
BRITAIN

North Sea

NETHERLANDS

HOLY ROMAN EMPIRE

London

Hondschoote Sept. 1793

Dunkirk

Brussels

Cologne

Lille

Mons

Rhine

Neerwinden March 1793

Coblenz

Arras

Amiens

Jemappes Nov. 1793

Fleurus June 1794

AUSTRIAN NETHERLANDS

Wattignies Oct. 1793

Mainz

Rouen

Caen

Seine

Reims

Metz

Wissembourg Dec. 1793

Landau

Paris

Valmy Sept. 1792

Nancy

Strasbourg

Rennes

Troyes

Loire

Angers

Tours

Nantes

Bourges

Dijon

Besançon

to Prussia SWISS CONFEDERATION

F R A N C E

Poitiers

Allier

Saône

Savoy

ATLANTIC OCEAN

Limoges

Clermont Ferrand

Lyon

Meribel 13 Sept 1793

Grenoble

PIEDMONT

Bordeaux

Garonne

Rhône

REP. OF GENOA

Montauban

Venaissin

Nîmes

Monaco

to Sardinia

Bayonne

Toulouse

Montpellier

Marseille

Sept–Dec 1793

Toulon

Ebro

Perpignan

N

S P A I N

ANDORRA

Mediterranean Sea

0   200 km

0   200 miles

Revolutionary France

on high ground, while Dumouriez was in reserve with another 18,000 French soldiers ready for action. French artillery at Valmy consisted of 40 cannon manned by veterans and exchanged fire with 54 Prussian cannon throughout the battle. Brunswick attempted two tentative infantry attacks, but halted them when the French troops held steady. Expecting an easy victory, Brunswick withdrew discouraged. The French victory saved Paris from threat of attack. French losses were 300, Prussian losses 184 men.

■ JEMAPPES, 6 NOVEMBER 1792

A French army under Dumouriez invaded the Austrian Netherlands (present-day Belgium) and attacked an Austrian army in defensive positions on heights near Jemappes. Dumouriez had 40,000 troops, many of them volunteers who had learned to attack in column formations by training on the march. The Austrians, commanded by Saxe-Teschen, numbered only 14,000, although in strong positions, reinforced with 56 cannon.

Dumouriez attacked at dawn on both flanks and the centre. One French column in the centre was led by Louis-Philippe, who would become king in 1830. The French had 100 cannon, but these were not well placed to fire with effect, so the attacks relied mainly on the infantry assaults. These eventually overwhelmed the Austrian defenders, who fell back by 14:00. French casualties were 2000 and the Austrians lost 1300, plus five cannon captured by the French.

■ NEERWINDEN, 18 MARCH 1793

Dumouriez with 45,000 French troops attacked 39,000 Austrian troops under Saxe-Coburg at Neerwinden in present-day Belgium. Dumouriez mistakenly thought that the northern part of the Austrian lines would be strongest, so put most of his strength against the southern part of their lines. The French took some positions, but Saxe-Coburg was able to hold most of his line. Dumouriez withdrew after losing 4000 troops, while the Austrians lost 2000.

■ SIEGE OF MAINZ, 14 APRIL–23 JULY 1793

A Coalition force of Prussians, Austrians and

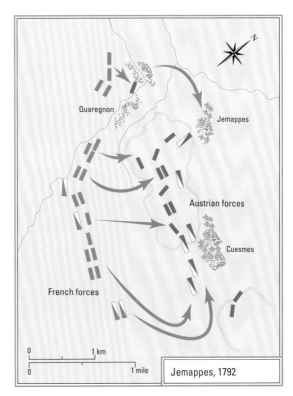

Jemappes, 1792

Hessians under Kalkreuth and Brunswick was reinforced to 44,000 while besieging 23,000 French troops under d'Oyre in Mainz on the Rhine in modern-day Germany. The garrison suffered 4000 casualties during the siege and the Coalition lost 3000 men. The garrison finally negotiated surrender terms, allowing them to return to France, where they were used against the Royalist insurrection in the Vendée.

■ FAMARS, 23 MAY 1793

Prince Saxe-Coburg, with 53,000 Austrian, Hanoverian and British troops attacked 25,000 French troops at Famars in northern France. The French withdrew during the night after losing 3300 casualties, while Coalition losses were 1100.

■ VALENCIENNES, 24 MAY–28 JULY 1793

The Duke of York with 25,000 Austrian, Hanoverian and British troops besieged 9000 French troops under Ferrand in Valenciennes, France. Ferrand surrendered with the honours of war after mines were exploded under French earthworks.

■ **ARLON, 9 JUNE 1793**

Houchard, with 10,000 French soldiers, attacked 8000 Austrians in strong positions at Arlon in modern-day Belgium. The Austrians were driven out, losses unknown, but including one company captured. French losses were 826.

■ **DUNKIRK, 23 AUGUST–8 SEPTEMBER 1793**

The Duke of York commanded 35,100 Austrian, Hanoverian, Hessian and British troops, besieging 10,000 French in the northern French port of Dunkirk. The siege was lifted due to the French victory at Hondschoote.

■ **TOULON, 7 SEPTEMBER–19 DECEMBER 1793**

Republican troops besieged the Royalist port of Toulon on the southern coast of France. The Royalists were supported by a British fleet, plus 20,000 British, Spanish and Neapolitan troops. French besieging forces were 32,000 under Dugommier. Napoleon Bonaparte commanded siege artillery and his plans were adopted by Dugommier. After Toulon fell, Napoleon was promoted to general.

■ **HONDSCHOOTE, 8 SEPTEMBER 1793**

Houchard with 40,000 French troops defeated a Coalition army of 24,000 Austrians and Hanoverians under Freytag at Hondschoote in northern France. Freytag was wounded and lost 4000 casualties, the French losing 3000.

■ **MERIBEL, 13 SEPTEMBER 1793**

A French force under Francois-Christophe Kellermann defeated a Savoyard-Sardinian force under Gordon at Meribel, France, near the modern Italian border, securing the former Duchy of Savoy as part of the French Republic.

■ **MENIN, 13–15 SEPTEMBER 1793**

Houchard with 30,000 French troops defeated 13,000 Dutch troops at Menin, modern-day Belgium, on the border of France. Two days later, Houchard was defeated by a large Austrian army under Beaulieu.

■ **WIESSEMBOURG, 13 OCTOBER 1793**

Carlenc's 51,000 French soldiers occupied entrenchments extending 20km along the present-day Franco-German border. The lines were breached at the northern end by Wurmser's concentrated attack with 42,000 Austrians and Hessians.

■ **WATTIGNIES, 15–16 OCTOBER 1793**

A French army of 45,000 under Jourdan and Carnot defeated an Austrian army of 23,000 under Saxe-Coburg at Wattignies in northern France. French losses were 1400, the Austrians losing 3000, including prisoners.

■ **KAISERSLAUTERN, 28–30 NOVEMBER 1793**

Hoche with 30,000 Frenchmen (outnumbered and in rough terrain) attacked 40,000 Prussians under Brunswick at Kaiserslautern in modern-day western Germany. Hoche finally withdrew, having lost 3000 casualties, Prussian losses being 1300.

■ **WOERTH, 18–22 DECEMBER 1793**

Separate columns from Hoche's French army of 35,000 defeated deployed detachments of Wurmser's Austrian, Prussian and Bavarian army of 35,000 in a series of actions from Froeschwiller to Woerth in Alsace, eastern France.

■ **GEISBERG, 26 DECEMBER 1793**

A French army of 35,000 troops under Hoche defeated 35,000 Austrian and Prussian Coalition soldiers under Wurmser at Geisberg in eastern France. Coalition cavalry counter-attacks failed and Hoche liberated Wiesembourg, France.

■ **ACTION OF 22 JANUARY 1794**

A British Royal Navy squadron, sent to protect merchant shipping through the Sunda Strait between Java and Sumatra, captured two French privateer ships that were raiding in the area.

■ **ATLANTIC CAMPAIGN, APRIL–JUNE 1794**

The British and French navies operated against each other across the Atlantic during April and May, from the Bay of Biscay to the Caribbean, without any major engagements. Each side captured some merchant vessels and small warships. Operations centred chiefly around the assembly of a large French merchant convoy of 117 ships on the coast of neutral United States.

The convoy loaded badly needed grain supplies to bring to France, which was experiencing near-famine conditions. This convoy had an escort of only five warships under Vanstabel. The main French fleet under Villaret at Brest was to meet the convoy as it crossed the Atlantic and drew closer to France. The main British fleet under Howe manoeuvred to intercept the main French fleet. These operations precipitated the battles of Ushant, which the British fleet won, but the convoy successfully reached France.

■ **SECOND ARLON, 17–18 APRIL 1794**

Jourdan with a French army of 20,000 moved against Beaulieu's Austrian army of 16,000 soldiers at Arlon in north-eastern France, near Luxembourg. The French assaulted the Austrian positions on high ground. Lefebvre's column became overextended and had to withdraw. The next day, Jourdan renewed the attack and Championnet's column turned the Austrian left flank. The Austrians were routed with losses of 900, French losses being over 200.

■ **VILLIERS-EN-CAUCHIES, 24 APRIL 1794**

An Austrian and British cavalry force under Otto routed 7000 French troops under Chapuis in northern France. Attacking the surprised French on the flank, Otto successfully charged with only 300 troopers.

■ **TOURCOING, 17–18 MAY 1794**

Coalition armies including 74,000 Austrians, British and Hanoverians were directed by Mack to converge in six columns and attack the French armies of Souham and Moreau near Tourcoing in northern France. French strength in the area was 80,000, but 70,000 were able to concentrate for the battle. Coalition attacks were repulsed. French counter-attacks were successful, inflicting 4000 casualties and capturing 1500 prisoners and 50 cannon. French losses were 3000.

■ **THIRD ARLON, 21 MAY 1794**

Austrian Gen Beaulieu, hoping to recapture the city of Arlon in north-eastern France near Luxembourg, marched with 20,000 Austrian troops to capture the city. Beaulieu began the

attack, not realizing that French Gen Jourdan was reinforcing Arlon, bringing the total of French troops to 45,000. Once the size of French forces became apparent, Beaulieu extricated his forces and withdrew towards Luxembourg. Casualties on both sides were light.

■ **TOURNAI, 22 MAY 1794**

Pichegru with 45,000 French soldiers attacked 30,000 Coalition Austrian, British and Hanoverian troops under Saxe-Coburg in strong positions at Tournai in modern-day Belgium. Pichegru withdrew; French losses were 6000 and Coalition losses 4000.

■ **USHANT, 28–29 MAY 1794**

The first two battles of Ushant involved elements of Howe's British Royal Navy fleet and Villaret's French fleet about 644km west of the French coast. Despite damage, neither side lost any ships sunk.

■ **GLORIOUS FIRST OF JUNE, 1 JUNE 1794**

A French merchant convoy of 117 ships assembled on the coast of neutral USA, loading grain supplies to bring to France, which was suffering from near famine conditions. The main French fleet under Villaret left Brest on the west coast of France to rendezvous with the grain convoy as it approached. The French had good ships, but suffered from a lack of trained officers and sailors due to the upheaval of the French Revolution.

The British Royal Navy Channel Fleet under Howe left port in search of Villaret's fleet and the convoy. The Royal Navy had excellent ships and sailors, but was very short on manpower, supplementing Royal Marine crews with the 29th Foot and Queen's Royal Regiment.

Villaret sailed westward, hoping to draw Howe away from the grain convoy. Howe contacted elements of Villaret's fleet in late May, 644km west of the port of Ushant. Partial engagements damaged ships of both fleets, setting the stage for a general engagement on 1 June. Howe deployed his 25 ships in a line facing northwards towards Villaret's 26 ships. Howe planned for each ship to sail directly at the French and pierce their line, crossing the bow of each opposing ship.

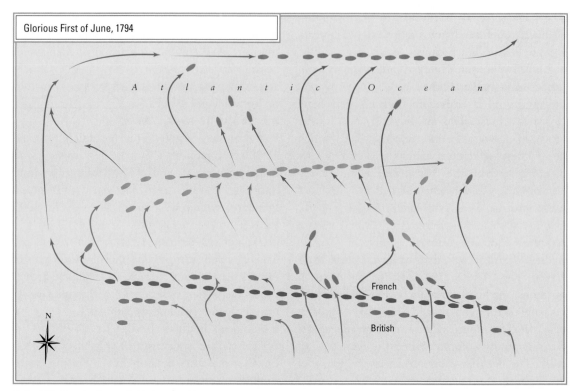

Glorious First of June, 1794

French

British

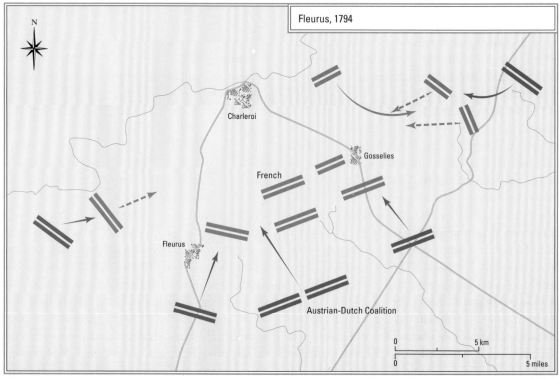

Fleurus, 1794

Charleroi

Gosselies

French

Fleurus

Austrian-Dutch Coalition

0   5 km

0   5 miles

This plan suffered in execution and the battle became a confused brawl, but British fire was far more effective. Ten French ships were dismasted and seven captured, while two British ships were dismasted and several others badly damaged. One captured ship, *Le Vengeur du Peuple*, sank. Villaret lost 4000 men killed and wounded and 3000 captured. British casualties were 1200. The grain convoy reached France safely.

■ **HOOGLEDE, 14 JUNE 1794**

Pichegru with 24,000 French soldiers defeated Clerfayt commanding 19,000 Austrian, Hessian and British troops at Hogledge in modern-day Belgium. French losses were 1300. Coalition troops lost 900, but were driven from the field.

■ **FLEURUS, 26 JUNE 1794**

An Austrian-Dutch army of 52,000 troops under Coburg attacked 70,000 French troops under Jourdan at Fleurus, in present-day Belgium. Jourdan formed his defense in a convex semicircle on high ground; Coburg formed five attack columns and attacked Jourdan's line for over 10 hours. The French used a balloon for reconnaissance during the battle. Coburg's forces were repulsed and retreated, each side losing about 5000 casualties.

■ **PLATZBERG, 13–14 JULY 1794**

Parts of Michaud's French army attacked Prussian positions in the Vosges, in eastern France. French troops under Gouvion St-Cyr captured the town of Johanniskreuz. Prussian losses included Gen Pfau killed.

■ **VOSGES, 13 JULY 1794**

Michaud's French army of 115,000 attacked a Coalition army of 70,000 Prussians, Saxons and Austrians, pushing them out of the Vosges Mountains in eastern France. Coalition losses were 3000, with French losses numbering 1000.

■ **BOXTEL, 14–15 SEPTEMBER 1794**

Pichegru's French army captured Boxtel in the Netherlands. A rearguard action north of the town by British forces under Ambercromby was the first combat for Wellesley, the future Duke of Wellington.

■ **DEGO, 21 SEPTEMBER 1794**

Gen Massena with 18,000 French troops defeated an Austrian-Sardinian army of 8000 under Wallis in modern-day north-western Italy. Casualties were light. The victory helped secure possession of the port of Nice for France.

■ **ALDENHOVEN, 2 OCTOBER 1794**

Gen Jourdan with eight French divisions attacked Coalition Austrian forces under Clerfayt (also spelled Clairfayt) at Aldenhoven, along the line of the Roer river in modern-day western Germany. Jourdan planned a three-pronged attack on a broad front and on both flanks. Although delays prevented some French columns from getting into action, Coalition troops were forced back at every point. Future marshals Ney and Bernadotte were distinguished in the victory.

■ **ACTION OF 6 NOVEMBER, 1794**

A French squadron of nine ships under Nielly intercepted HMS *Alexander* and HMS *Canada* in the Celtic Sea, west of Brest. HMS *Canada* escaped, but HMS *Alexander* was engaged and forced to surrender.

■ **LUXEMBOURG, 22 NOVEMBER 1794– 7 JUNE 1795**

The city of Luxembourg was held by 15,000 Austrian Empire troops under Bender during a siege by French forces of various strengths which lasted from 22 November 1794 until 7 June 1795, when surrender was negotiated.

■ **CROISIERE DE LA GRANDE HIVER, DECEMBER 1794–FEBRUARY 1995**

The French Navy attempted winter operations in the Atlantic, capturing some merchant ships, but suffering serious damage due to rough weather, including three warships sunk.

■ **GENOA, 14 MARCH 1795**

A British-Neapolitan fleet of 14 ships under Hotham fought a French fleet of 13 ships under Martin off the Genoan coast in north-western Italy. Distinguished in the battle was Nelson, commanding HMS *Agamemnon*. Several French ships were badly damaged and two were captured.

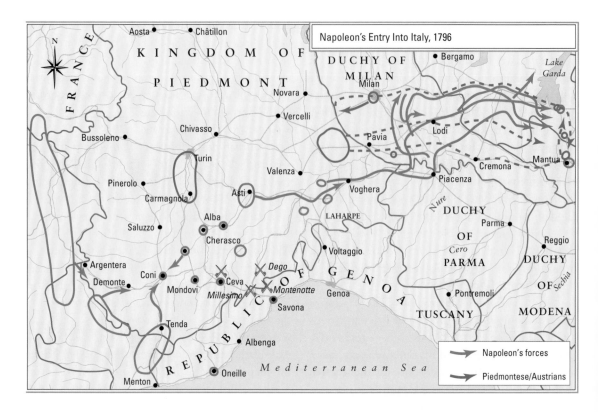

Napoleon's Entry Into Italy, 1796

HMS *Illustrious* was evacuated and burned after the battle. French losses were 1600 killed and wounded, British-Neapolitan losses being 358.

■ **GROIX, 23 JUNE 1795**
A British fleet of 14 ships under Bridport pursued a French fleet of 12 ships under Villaret off the Island of Groix off the western coast of France. Three French ships were captured.

■ **QUIBERON CAMPAIGN, 27 JUNE–22 JULY 1795**
British naval forces landed 5000 French Royalists on the Quiberon peninsula in western France, hoping they would lead local Royalists against the French Republic. Gen Hoche defeated them and British ships evacuated survivors.

■ **HYÈRES ISLANDS, 13 JULY 1795**
A British and Neapolitan fleet of 38 ships under Hotham pursued a French fleet of 23 ships under Martin off the southern coast of France. The French lost one ship before escaping.

■ **SECOND MAINZ, 29 OCTOBER 1795**
A French army of 33,000 men under Schaal,

attempting to retake Mainz in modern-day western Germany, set up preliminary siege positions near the city, but a relief force of Austrian, Hessian and Saxon troops under Clerfayt brought Coalition strength to 44,000. Clerfayt drove off the French, who lost 3000 killed and wounded and 1800 captured, the Coalition losing a total of 1400 killed and wounded.

■ **LOANO, 22–23 NOVEMBER 1795**
A French army of 25,000 under Scherer, with executive command by Massena, defeated an Austrian-Sardinian army of 18,000 under Wallis in this battle in modern-day north-western Italy. French losses were 3000 and Coalition losses were 7000.

■ **FRENCH EXPEDITION, 1796–97**
The French Directory was persuaded by Irish revolutionary Theobald Wolfe Tone to send an expedition to Ireland to aid the republican United Irishmen. A French fleet of 44 ships, containing up to 20,000 soldiers, approached the

south coast of Ireland, but was hit by a storm off Bantry Bay and wrecked. Over 2000 Frenchmen were drowned and 1000 captured. Twelve French ships were lost and the invasion was called off.

■ **MONTENOTTE, 11–12 APRIL 1796**

Napoleon Bonaparte led his French army into north-western Italy and manoeuvred to separate Austrian Empire forces under Beaulieu from their Sardinian allies under Colli. Napoleon sent two French columns totaling 8500 troops under Massena and Joubert, with supports nearby, against Argentau's corps of 9000 Austrians. Argentau's force was routed and scattered, losing 2500 men – mostly prisoners – and 12 cannon. Based on conflicting reports of the engagement, the French lost about 400 casualties.

■ **MILLESIMO, 13–14 APRIL 1796**

In a series of actions in modern-day north-western Italy, Napoleon Bonaparte's French army defeated elements of Colli's Sardinian army and Beaulieu's Austrian Empire army. Napoleon's objective after victory at Montenotte was to further separate the Sardinians and Austrians from each other and defeat them in detail. To that end, Bonaparte sent several columns through mountainous terrain to locate and defeat scattered enemy units; the Sardinians being mostly to the north-west and the Austrians being mostly to the north-east. The greatest difficulty was a unit of 1000 Austrians under Gen Provera who took position in castle ruins at Cossaria. Bonaparte's Italian Gen Joubert's French brigade assaulted unsuccessfully and Joubert was wounded in the attack. Menard's French brigade took Millesimo from the Sardinians, isolating Gen Provera who later surrendered. Meanwhile, Massena, with 10,000 French troops under him, captured 4000 Austrians near Dego. Coalition total losses were 5000, the French losing 1000.

■ **DEGO, 14–15 APRIL 1796**

Operating in north-western Italy, Napoleon sent Massena with 12,000 French troops to take the municipality of Dego, held by 5700 Austrians and Sardinians. This attack succeeded,

but French troops failed to post guards for the night. An Austrian column of 3500 under Vukassovich surprised the French and recaptured Dego. Napoleon sent 15,000 French troops and recaptured Dego a final time. Total losses were 2400 French and 4700 Coalition.

■ **CEVA, 16–17 APRIL 1796**

Augereau, with 8000 French troops operating in north-western Italy, attacked 6000 Sardinians under Count Vitali, in strong positions. The Sardinians later withdrew to their main army. French losses were 600 and Vitali lost 150.

■ **MONDOVI, 19–21 APRIL 1796**

Napoleon, having isolated the Sardinian army of 13,000 under Colli well away from their Austrian allies, attacked Colli's positions with 17,500 French troops. Colli withdrew after losing 1600 casualties, French losses being 600.

■ **FOMBIO, 7–9 MAY 1796**

Napoleon, having won initial victories in modern-day northern Italy, successfully crossed the Po river with 11,500 French soldiers, defeating 6600 Austrian Empire troops under Beaulieu. French losses were 450, Beaulieu losing 600.

■ **LODI BRIDGE, 10 MAY 1796**

Napoleon with 17,500 French, pursuing Austrian Empire forces in northern Italy, attacked the rearguard of 9500 troops, taking Lodi Bridge on the Adda River, with French losses of 500. Austrian losses were 2000.

■ **BORGHETTO, 30 MAY 1796**

Napoleon Bonaparte's French army with 28,000 soldiers defeated 19,000 Austrian Empire troops under Beaulieu in modern-day northern Italy. Beaulieu lost almost 600 casualties. The French took the field, losing 500.

■ **RASTATT, 5 JULY 1796**

Moreau with 34,000 French soldiers operating in modern-day southern Germany attacked 18,000 Austrian Empire troops under Latour and defeated them before they could receive reinforcements. Both sides lost about 500 casualties.

■ **RIVOLI, 29 JULY 1796**

Wurmser's 24,000 Austrian Empire troops

advanced southwards along the west coast of Lake Garda in modern-day northern Italy and drove back 15,000 French troops under Massena.

■ LONATO, 3–4 AUGUST 1796

Austrian Empire forces in northern Italy marched southwards to the west and east of Lake Garda to catch Napoleon Bonaparte's French army in a pincers movement. Napoleon, using his central position, detached Augereau's division to hold Wurmser's army approaching from the east, concentrated 20,000 Frenchmen against Quasdanovich's 15,000 troops west of Lake Garda and defeated them. Quasdanovich lost 5000 casualties and 23 cannon, French losses being 2000.

■ CASTIGLIONE DELLE STIVERE, 5 AUGUST 1796

Having defeated one wing of the Austrian Empire forces in northern Italy west of Lake Garda, Napoleon concentrated 28,000 French soldiers against 24,000 Austrian Empire troops under Wurmser advancing from the east. Elements of Napoleon's forces arrived as the battle progressed, attacking both of Wurmser's flanks and throwing him back with 3000 casualties and 20 cannon lost, while French casualties were 1500. An effective pursuit followed.

■ NERESHEIM, 11 AUGUST 1796

Moreau led a French army of 50,000 soldiers into modern-day south-eastern Germany and attacked 20,000 Austrian Empire forces under Archduke Charles. Charles lost 1600 casualties and retreated, although Moreau lost 2400 casualties.

■ SALDANHA BAY, 17 AUGUST 1796

A Batavian Republic (Dutch) flotilla of nine ships under Lucas, operating in Saldanha Bay in southern Africa, experiencing near mutiny, surrendered without firing a shot to a British fleet under Elphinstone.

■ THEININGEN, 22 AUGUST 1796

Bernadotte with 9200 French soldiers fought a rearguard action against 25,000 Austrian Empire troops under Archduke Charles in modern-day western Germany, giving the main French army under Jourdan time to retreat.

■ AMBERG-FRIEDBERG, 24 AUGUST 1796

Archduke Charles with an Austrian Empire army of 40,000 outflanked and defeated Jourdan's 34,000 Frenchmen at Amberg in modern-day southern Germany. Further south at Friedberg, Moreau's 40,000 French defeated 2500 Austrians.

■ WURZBURG, 3 SEPTEMBER 1796

Archduke Charles with an Austrian Empire army of 38,000 operated in modern-day southern Germany against two French armies, under Jourdan and Moreau. Charles had successfully concentrated against Jourdan and defeated him at Amberg on 24 August. After retreating, Jourdan assembled 30,000 men and turned to attack a small force at Wurzburg on the Main river. Jourdan was unaware that Archduke Charles was in position to reinforce Wurzburg rapidly with most of his army. Austrian reinforcements arrived as Jourdan assaulted and the French found themselves overextended and threatened on the flanks.

Jourdan had to retreat or be cut off and posted a rearguard under Grenier. This suffered heavy casualties as the rest of the French army escaped. French losses were between 3000 and 6000. Charles lost 1500 in this victory, which isolated Moreau's French army, forcing its retreat as well.

■ ROVERETO, 4 SEPTEMBER 1796

Austrian Empire forces operated in northern Italy in three groups. Napoleon concentrated 20,000 French troops against the westernmost group of 10,000 men under Davidovich, routing them. Davidovich lost 3000 men, Napoleon lost 750.

■ BASSANO, 8 SEPTEMBER 1796

Austrian Empire forces were divided into three groups in order to operate in northern Italy with the goal of relieving their troops besieged in Mantua and defeating Napoleon Bonaparte's French army. Davidovich was in the west on the Adige River. Wurmser with 8700 troops marched southwards along the Brenta river to link up with Meszaros's 10,700 troops at Bassano. Napoleon foiled these plans, first by

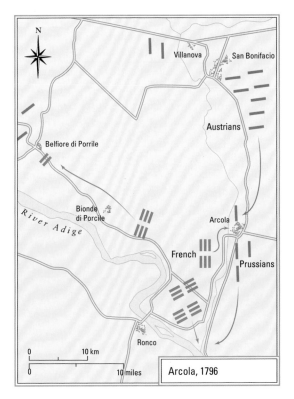

Arcola, 1796

decided to manoeuvre against the rear of the closer Austrian army of nearly 30,000 men under Alvinczy. Leaving 2600 men to cover Verona, Napoleon took 19,000 troops eastwards along the south bank of the Adige river. The French troops began crossing the Adige where the river turns southwards, at Ronco, on 15 November. There they had to march along narrow dikes through swampland between the Adige and its tributary, the Alpone. A French division advanced northwards to the village of Belfiore di Porcile and successfully engaged an Austrian detachment there. A French detachment trying to cross the Alpone across a bridge at Arcola ran into strong Austrian infantry and artillery defences and was driven back. Napoleon, flag in hand, attempted to rally his troops and lead them across the bridge. He was unhorsed and nearly captured. Napoleon pulled back to Ronco in the evening.

Alvinczy was unsure as to French dispositions on the 16th, but was worried about his communications through Villanuova. Napoleon repeated his attacks on the 16th, but could not get across the Alpone, so withdrew again to Ronco. Alvinczy began withdrawing to Villanuova and sent his baggage trains further east. Napoleon renewed his attacks on the 17th with better success. French troops outflanked the Austrian position at Arcola. Napoleon utilized a ruse de guerre with 30 of his mounted escorts and four trumpeters, fooling the Austrians near Arcola into thinking another French force threatened their rear. Alvinczy withdrew his army to the east. French losses were 4600 and Austrian losses were 6200 men.

concentrating against Davidovich at Rovereto and defeating him and then marching eastwards cross-country and falling upon Wurmser from the rear. Wurmser barely managed to form a line to face the onslaught of Napoleon's 20,000 men. Wurmser was badly beaten, losing 600 killed and wounded, 3000 taken prisoner, 30 cannon, two pontoon trains and eight flags, while the French lost 400 casualties. Wurmser and remaining forces joined the garrison in Mantua, instead of relieving it.

■ **CALLIANO, 6–7 NOVEMBER 1796**
Vaubois with 10,500 French troops attempted to hold off the advance of 19,500 Austrian Empire troops under Davidovich in northern Italy. Davidovich finally took the positions after losing 3600 casualties, Vaubois losing 4400.

■ **ARCOLA, 15–17 NOVEMBER 1796**
Gen Napoleon Bonaparte's French army in northern Italy held Verona, which was threatened by the advance of two Austrian armies. Napoleon

■ **MANTUA, 1796–97**
French forces besieged Austrian Empire forces in northern Italy from August 1796 to February 1797. The large garrison reached 29,000 with reinforcements under Wurmser. Napoleon's victories in northern Italy eventually compelled Wurmser's surrender.

■ **ACTION OF 13 JANUARY 1797**
British frigates HMS *Indefatigable* and HMS

Amazon engaged French ship of the line *Droits de l'Homme* in stormy seas off the west coast of France. *Droits de l'Homme* and HMS *Amazon* wrecked on the shore.

■ RIVOLI, 14 JANUARY 1797

Austrian Empire forces under Alvinczy marched southwards into northern Italy in a fourth attempt to relieve the fortress of Mantua and defeat Napoleon's French army. Napoleon began bringing his army to the plateau near Rivoli to block Alviczy's advance. Napoleon was familiar with this ground, which had been the scene of fighting the previous year. Alvinczy had 28,000 troops on hand for the attack and Napoleon began the fight with Joubert's 9700 soldiers, although more French were arriving throughout the morning. The rough terrain allowed Napoleon to form his army in a defensive convex semicircle and to plug enemy breakthroughs with reserves and arriving reinforcements. Alvinczy divided his troops into five columns to approach the French

through the semi-mountainous countryside around Rivoli, with the columns on either end assigned to get around both French flanks.

Napoleon took full advantage of his tactical central position and hit Alvinczy's centre columns under Knoblos and Ocksay as they arrived on the plateau, exposed to French artillery fire and limited cavalry counter-attacks. Alvinczy's centre was battered before his flank columns could develop a threat. The eastern column, under Lusignan, did advance along the Adige River and threaten the French right and rear, but French reinforcements under Massena arrived and repulsed Lusignan with heavy losses. The reinforcements brought French strength up to 23,000 and Alvinczy's attacks had been badly beaten into piecemeal elements. Napoleon's counter-attacks routed Alvinczy's men, who fled in disorder, having lost 3300 killed and wounded, plus 7000 taken prisoner and 40 cannon captured. French pursuit the following day bagged another

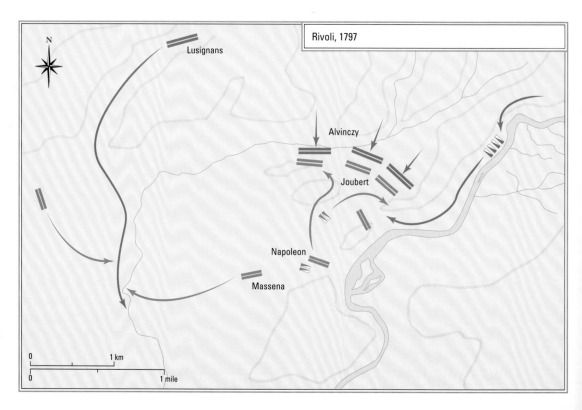

Rivoli, 1797

6000 prisoners. In comparison, French total losses were 3200. The victory secured the French strategic position in Italy, Mantua surrendering on 2 February.

■ **CAPE SAINT VINCENT, 14 FEBRUARY 1797**
An outnumbered British fleet under Jervis attacked a Spanish fleet under Cordoba off the coast of Portugal. The British surprised the Spanish in fog, inflicting great damage and capturing four ships.

■ **FISHGUARD, 22–24 FEBRUARY 1797**
Tate landed on the coast of Wales with 1400 French, largely irregulars. Most dispersed to loot the area. Meanwhile, Lord Cawdor gathered British militia and sailors and forced Tate to surrender.

■ **MALBORGHETTO, 23 MARCH 1797**
Archduke Charles, with 8000 Austrian Empire troops, counter-attacked Massena's 11,000 advancing French troops in north-eastern Italy and was repulsed. An Austrian supply train and 3000 troops under Bajalich were captured by the French.

■ **NEUWIED, 18 APRIL 1797**
Hoche with 35,000 French troops attacked Werneck's 15,000 Austrian Empire troops in western Germany. Werneck retreated, losing 3000 killed and wounded, 7000 prisoners and 27 cannon. French losses were 1000.

■ **DIERSHEIM, 20–21 APRIL 1797**
French Gen Moreau, in order to support victories in other theatres of the war, crossed the Rhine River at Diersheim in modern-day western Germany. He was opposed by Austrian forces under Sztaray. The Rhine crossing was notable for the use of boats to ferry 3000 troops across in two trips. This established a bridgehead, which held until the completion of a pontoon bridge, enabling the French army to cross.

■ **ACTION OF 16 MAY 1797**
A Danish flotilla of three ships under Capt Bille sailed into Tripoli harbour centre in modern-day Libya, successfully engaging the Tripolitan

forts and six ships. Negotiations with the Bey of Tripoli followed.

■ **CAMPERDOWN, 11 OCTOBER 1797**
A British fleet of 14 ships of the line plus 10 smaller vessels under Duncan attacked a Dutch fleet of 11 ships of the line and 15 smaller vessels under De Winter off the coast of Holland. Duncan manoeuvred aggressively, sailing directly at the Dutch line. The battle was fierce and bloody, as reflected in the Dutch losses, which included 1160 casualties and 11 ships captured. British losses were 825 killed and wounded.

War in the Pyrenees 1793–96
■ **TRUILLAS, 22 SEPTEMBER 1793**
Dagobert, with 22,000 poorly trained French troops, attacked 17,000 Spanish troops under Ricardos, formed in strong defensive positions in southern France. The French were repulsed, suffering 3000 casualties. Spanish losses were 2000.

■ **BOULOU, 29 APRIL 1794**
Dugommier with 30,000 French troops defeated 20,000 Spanish and Portuguese troops under Carvajal, at Boulou in southern France. Carvajal lost 3500 casualties and 140 cannon. French losses were 20 killed and 300 wounded.

■ **SAN LORENZO DE LA MUGA, 13 AUGUST 1794**
Carvajal led 20,000 Spanish and Portuguese troops in a failed assault against 10,000 French soldiers under Dugommier in strong positions in southern France. Carvajal lost 1400 casualties, the French losing 800.

War in the Vendée 1793–96
■ **THOUARS, 5 MAY 1793**
Lescure and others, leading 20,000 anti-revolutionary French, routed French Republicans in Thouars, western France and captured arms and munitions. The Republicans lost 600 killed and 3000 captured. The anti-revolutionaries lost 200 men.

■ **FONTENAY-LE-COMTE, 25 MAY 1793**
Lescure and 35,000 anti-revolutionary French Vendean peasants overwhelmed 14,000 French

Republican troops under Chalbos in western France. Chalbos lost 4000 casualties and 40 cannon. Lescure lost 1000 casualties.

■ **SAUMUR, 9 JUNE 1793**

Lescure and Cathelineau led 30,000 anti-revolutionary French against 12,000 French Republican troops under Menou in western France, continuing a string of victories by anti-revolutionary forces. The issue was in doubt when the anti-revolutionaries wavered under Republican artillery fire. Cathelineau personally rallied them and renewed the attack. About half the Republican force was killed or captured, with the anti-revolutionaries losing 400. Cathelineau was elected head of the 'Royal and Catholic Army'.

■ **LUCON, 28 JUNE 1793**

Royrand commanding 6000 anti-revolutionary French attacked 1800 French Republican troops outside Lucon in western France. The anti-revolutionaries retreated when troops of the former Provence Regiment switched sides, going over to the Republicans.

■ **NANTES, 29 JUNE 1793**

Cathelineau with 30,000 anti-revolutionary French attacked the city of Nantes, garrisoned by 12,000 French Republicans. The attack was repulsed with a loss of 132 killed, including Cathelineau. Republican losses were about 200.

■ **MONTAIGU, 16 SEPTEMBER 1793**

Beysser and 6000 French Republicans attacked 10,000 anti-Revolutionary French under Charette in western France. Kleber arrived with 2000 Republican reinforcements and the anti-revolutionaries retreated, losing 600 men. Republican losses were light.

■ **TIFFAUGES, 18 SEPTEMBER 1793**

Kleber, with an advance guard of 2000 veteran French Republican troops, moved against 20,000 anti-revolutionary French in western France. The anti-revolutionaries initially panicked and fled, but their own female family members in the field rallied them. Kleber was expecting significant reinforcements, but only received

4000 and had to retire from the field. The Republicans lost 200 killed and 800 wounded; the anti-revolutionaries lost at least 200 killed.

■ **CHOLET, 17 OCTOBER 1793**

Bonchamps and d'Elbee led 40,000 anti-revolutionary French against 26,000 French Republican troops north of Cholet in western France. The Republican forces were under Lechelle, with Kleber in executive command. Republican forces faced north, with both flanks anchored by buildings, but with the centre on low marshy ground.

The anti-revolutionaries, better drilled than earlier in the war, advanced in three lines, in good order and began to drive back the Republican centre and left in fierce fighting. Kleber committed French reserves on the left, hitting the flank of the advancing anti-revolutionaries and repulsing them. In the centre, the Republicans fell back past their massed artillery, which decimated the anti-revolutionaries attacking there.

The anti-revolutionaries were routed with losses of 7000, including Bonchamps, who was mortally wounded and d'Elbée wounded and captured. Their army reformed north of the Loire. Republican losses were 2000.

■ **GALERNE, 18 OCTOBER–23 DECEMBER 1793**

After their victory at Cholet, French Republican forces pursued anti-revolutionary French forces (including non-combatants) and attacked their towns, first north from the Vendee through Normandy, then southwards towards Brittany.

■ **ENTRAMES, 26 OCTOBER 1793**

The advance guard of Lechelle's French Republican army of 20,000 encountered a French anti-revolutionary force of 25,000 in western France. Hit on three sides, the advance guard was repulsed, losing 4000 men.

FOUGERES, 3 NOVEMBER 1793

A hastily formed French Republican force of 3500 attempted unsuccessfully to block the path of an anti-revolutionary French army of 30,000 marching through western France towards Saint-Malo. The Republicans lost 1000 men.

■ GRANVILLE, 14 NOVEMBER 1793

Having taken Fougères in western France, French anti-revolutionary forces attempted to take the port city of Granville, hoping to contact a British landing force. Granville was fortified and defended by 5500 French Republican troops. The anti-revolutionaries attacked with 25,000 men and took the suburbs, which caught fire. Unable to take Granville proper, the attackers retreated, having lost 600 men. The Republicans lost over 200 troops.

■ DOL, 20–22 NOVEMBER 1793

Anti-revolutionary French forces of 25,000 men defeated a French Republican army totaling 20,000 in a series of combats in western France. Casualties were 3000 for the anti-revolutionaries and 6000 for the Republicans.

■ ANGERS, 3–4 DECEMBER 1793

Rochejaquelein with 20,000 anti-revolutionary French soldiers made an unsuccessful assault on the French Republican stronghold of Angers, defended by a garrison of 4000 troops under Thevenet in western France. Rochejaquelein withdrew as a Republican relief force approached, but Marigny, leading the advance guard of the relief force, was killed in the action. The battle was a costly one for both sides – the garrison lost 400 total casualties, and the anti-revolutionaries lost at least 300 killed.

■ LE MANS, 12–13 DECEMBER 1793

A French Republican army of 20,000 troops utterly routed 15,000 anti-revolutionaries, who were accompanied by 20,000 non-combatants in Le Mans, in western France. The anti-revolutionaries, caught unprepared, lost over half their numbers.

■ SAVENAY, 23 DECEMBER 1793

After losses at Angers and Le Mans, anti-revolutionary forces lost many combatants and were scattered. One group under Fleuriot went to Savenay in western France with 6000 armed men, plus 6000 non-combatants. Kléber pursued them with a Republican army of 18,000 troops, taking up positions on three sides of Savenay.

The anti-revolutionaries made a dawn pre-emptive attack at the Touchelais woods outside Savenay. This surprised the Republicans, but Kléber counter-attacked with elite gendarmes. Republican forces then attacked all along the line, advancing into Savenay proper, with fighting moving into streets and houses. Anti-revolutionary women and wounded joined the desperate defense, while their artillery massed in front of the town church. The Republicans overwhelmed the defenders by 14:00, the anti-revolutionaries losing 7000 casualties, including non-combatants and prisoners later executed. Republican losses were 230, including wounded.

Kosciuszko Uprising 1794

■ RACLAWICE, 4 APRIL 1794

Denisov marched through southern Poland with 3000 Russian troops in an attempt to take Krakow, but his path was blocked at Raclawice by Kosciuszko with 2000 Polish troops. In addition, Kosciuszko was able to augment his force with 2000 peasants armed with scythes and pikes. The peasants captured 12 Russian cannon in a charge, and Denisov withdrew with a loss of 1100. Polish losses were 500.

■ WILNO UPRISING, 22 APRIL 1794

Poles and Lithuanians under the leadership of Jacob Jasinski in Wilno (Vilnius) in modern-day Lithuania mobilized in support of Kosciuszko's uprising. The Russian garrison quickly withdrew and neither side suffered casualties.

■ SZCZEKOCINY, 6 JUNE 1794

Russian and Prussian forces numbering 27,000 invading southern Poland attacked Kosciuszko's Polish army of 9000 regulars and 6000 militia. Kosciuszko's badly outnumbered force was defeated with heavy losses, successfully evacuating with 346 wounded.

■ CHELM, 8 JUNE 1794

Derfelden with 17,000 Russian and Prussian troops attacked a Polish force of 6000 regulars and 2000 militia under Zajaczek. The outnumbered Poles were defeated while losing 1500 casualties, Derfelden losing 200.

■ **GREATER POLAND UPRISING, AUGUST–DECEMBER 1794**

North-western Poland, claimed by Prussia since the 1793 partition, rose in support of Kosciusko's uprising in central Poland. However, a lack of coordination doomed the uprising, despite leadership by Niemojewski and Dabrowski.

■ **KRUPCZYCE, 17 SEPTEMBER 1794**

Sierakowski, with a large force of peasant militia, fought a delaying action in present-day Belarus against Suvorov's invading Russian army. Sierakowski disengaged and withdrew when Suvorov's cavalry moved around his flank.

■ **TERESPOL, 19 SEPTEMBER 1794**

Sierakowski with 8000 Polish cavalry and poorly-armed peasant militia failed to stop the advance of Suvorov's Russian army of 13,000 in modern-day Belarus. Sierakowski lost 5500 men, while Suvorov lost 1000.

■ **MACIEJOWICE, 10 OCTOBER 1794**

Kosciusko led 6200 Poles in an attempt to prevent the linkage of two Russian armies, totaling 24,500 soldiers. The Russian armies combined and defeated Kosciusko, who was wounded and captured. ·

■ **WARSAW, 4 NOVEMBER 1794**

Suvorov with 40,000 Russian troops advanced towards Warsaw, the Polish capital, which had repulsed a loose siege from July to September. Suvorov targeted the fortified suburb of Praga, across the Vistula River just east of Warsaw. Praga had a Polish garrison of 14,000 troops under Zajaczek, plus 3200 militia, including a Jewish regiment under Joselewicz.

Suvorov bombarded and deployed as if for a siege, but made plans for an immediate assault. The Russians reached the earthworks at night without detection and assaulted at 03:00, capturing the earthworks before the defenders were alerted.

Desperate fighting ensued, the Russians using captured artillery at close range to destroy pockets of resistance. Almost the entire Polish garrison was killed or captured. The Russians then looted Praga and killed thousands of civilians, contrary

to Suvorov's orders. Russian losses were 580 killed and 960 wounded.

■ **PRAGA, 4 NOVEMBER 1794**

Suvorov led 22,000 Russians assaulting the Polish town of Praga, on the east bank of the Vistula River, across from Warsaw. Polish forces under Zajaczek included 14,000 soldiers, a regiment of Polish Jews under Joselewicz and 3200 militia, many armed only with scythes. The Russians broke through the defences, losing 1500 casualties and killed many civilians, making total Polish casualties at least 26,000.

Anglo–Spanish War 1796–1808

■ **CAPE ST VINCENT, 14 FEBRUARY 1797**

British Adm Jervis with 15 ships of the line and five frigates intercepted a larger Spanish fleet under Cordoba off the coast of Portugal. Cordoba commanded 27 ships of the line and seven frigates, making for Cadiz in two lines, remaining unaware of the proximity of Jervis' fleet. Jervis aggressively sailed his fleet between the two groups of Spanish ships, taking advantage of an early fog and the superior speed and gunnery of the British ships.

Nelson, commanding HMS *Captain*, cut off the lead ships of the Spanish fleet. Despite losing all masts, he boldly boarded and captured two Spanish vessels, with soldiers of the 69th Foot serving as marines. Jervis' fleet captured four Spanish ships and 3000 prisoners, severely damaging several more, including Cordoba's flagship. Killed and wounded were nearly 1000 for each side.

■ **TRINIDAD, 18–21 FEBRUARY 1797**

A British fleet landed 10,000 soldiers and marines under Abercromby on the Spanish island of Trinidad in the Caribbean Sea. Some Spanish ships were scuttled and the island surrendered without a fight.

■ **SAN JUAN, 18 APRIL–2 MAY 1797**

A British fleet landed 6000 soldiers and marines under Abercromby near heavily fortified San Juan in Puerto Rico, held by 6000 Spanish

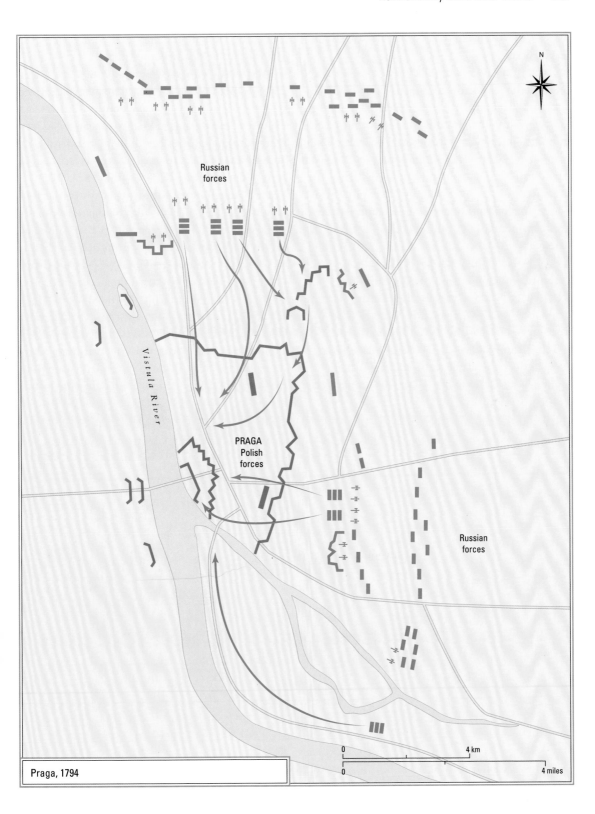

Russian
forces

Vistula River

PRAGA
Polish
forces

Russian
forces

0   4 km

0   4 miles

Praga, 1794

under Castro. Unable to take the city, the British re-embarked.

■ CADIZ, JULY 3–5 JULY 1797

During the blockade of the port of Cadiz by a British fleet under Lord Jervis, Adm Nelson led several launches and small bomb vessels into the inner port to bombard the city. They were engaged by Spanish launches, and Nelson participated in hand-to-hand fighting, his life famously being saved by coxswain Sykes. Three small Spanish boats were captured. Two bombardments of Cadiz produced fires and damage.

■ SANTA CRUZ, JULY 22–25 1797

Nelson, with nine ships and 4000 men, was repulsed at Santa Cruz in the Canary Islands, defended by 1700 Spaniards. Nelson lost 678 casualties, as well as the loss of his right arm.

■ ST GEORGE'S CAYE, 3–10 SEPTEMBER 1798

A Spanish force of 32 ships and 2500 men was repulsed at St George's Caye in modern-day Belize by 700 militia, 12 local vessels, plus the British ship HMS *Merlin*.

■ MINORCA, 7–15 NOVEMBER 1798

Twenty British ships under Duckworth carried 6000 soldiers and marines under Stuart and captured the Spanish Mediterranean island of Minorca, which surrendered after light skirmishing and no loss of life.

■ ALGECIRAS I AND II, 6–13 JULY 1801

French Adm Linois, with three ships of the line, was attacked by British Adm Saumarez, with six ships of the line at Algeciras Bay near Gibraltar. Linois had supporting fire from a Spanish fort at Algeciras. Linois suffered serious damage plus 160 killed and 300 wounded. British losses were 130 killed and 250 wounded, with HMS *Hannibal* captured. After this first battle, both sides repaired and received reinforcements.

Linois planned to run past the British and link up with the Spanish fleet at Cadiz. Meanwhile, five Spanish ships and one French ship joined

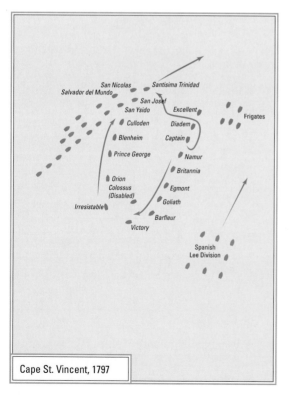

Cape St. Vincent, 1797

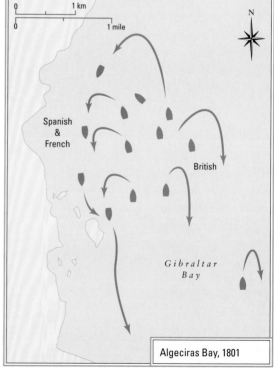

Algeciras Bay, 1801

Linois. Saumarez attacked Linois' fleet as it sailed. Fighting in darkness, two Spanish ships mistook each other for British and were destroyed by fire. One French ship was captured. The rest of Linois' fleet reached Cadiz.

■ Cape Santa Maria, 10 October 1804

British Cdre Moore with four frigates attacked four Spanish frigates under Guerra off Portugal's coast, destroying one and capturing the others. A renewed declaration of war by Spain followed.

■ Trafalgar, 21 October 1805

Napoleon had cancelled plans for an invasion of England, instead marching his army into central Europe against Britain's Coalition allies, but the naval forces of France and Spain still posed a strategic threat. The French-Spanish Combined Fleet under Adm Villeneuve was at Cadiz, Spain. Adm Nelson commanded a British fleet, purposefully planning to bring the Combined Fleet to battle and destroy it.

Villeneuve's new instructions from Napoleon were to sail the Combined Fleet into the Mediterranean for operations. This order brought Villeneuve into a confrontation with Nelson's fleet at Cape Trafalgar, Spain. Villeneuve ordered the fleet to turn back to Cadiz, putting the Combined Fleet in a long line along a north-south axis, sailing north.

Nelson boldly planned to form two columns perpendicular to the French-Spanish line. The two columns would sail straight at the enemy, cutting their forces into three sections, making it difficult for ships at either end to come to the assistance of the centre, where the British would have concentrated force. The risk involved being exposed to fire during the advance to attack. Nelson's fleet had 27 ships of the line and six smaller ships, with 18,500 men and 2148 cannon. The Combined Fleet totaled 33 ships of the line and seven smaller ships, with 27,000 men and 2632 cannon. It included the two largest ships in the world, *Santisima Trinidad* and *Santa Ana*. Nelson was unconcerned with enemy numerical superiority,

as British ships were more manoeuvrable, with vastly superior gunners. From his flagship *Victory* he signaled, 'England expects that every man will do his duty'.

Nelson led the northern attack column in *Victory* and Collingwood led the southern attack column in *Royal Sovereign*. Collingwood reached enemy lines just after noon, engaging *Santa Ana* and the *Fougeux*, as the rest of his column came up and engaged. Nelson reached the enemy line by 12:30 but already damaged in the approach, then raking Villeneuve's flagship *Bucentaure*, causing massive damage.

Victory then engaged the French *Redoutable*, the ships crashing together. French sailors and marines in the rigging and fighting tops of *Redoutable* swept the deck of *Victory* with musket fire and grenades. Nelson, conspicuous in full uniform, was mortally wounded and taken below deck at 13:15. Capt Lucas of *Redoutable* prepared to board *Victory*, but HMS *Temeraire* came alongside firing broadsides.

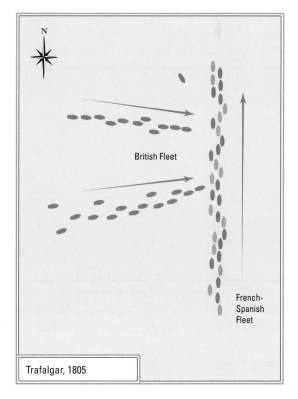

British Fleet

French-Spanish Fleet

Trafalgar, 1805

As more British ships came up, *Redoutable* was pummeled with cannonballs. Lucas, with most of his crew, himself included, killed or wounded, surrendered at 13:55.

Meanwhile, the battle continued much as Nelson had envisioned. British ships wrought destruction on opposing ships and crews alike. Spanish Adm Gravina was mortally wounded and ranking officers Galiano, Churruca and Bustamante were killed. French RAdm Magon was killed. Villeneuve surrendered aboard *Bucentaure*, dismasted and wrecked with 450 casualties. At 16:00, Nelson was informed the battle was won. He died at 1630.

British losses were 455 killed, 1243 wounded and no ships lost. French and Spanish losses were 3243 dead, 2538 wounded and 7000 prisoners, many rescued from the sea. The British destroyed four enemy vessels and captured 17, although only four were returned as prizes to England, the rest too badly damaged to survive the trip. Trafalgar ensured British naval supremacy for the rest of the Napoleonic Wars, and for many decades thereafter.

■ **INVASIONS OF RIO DEL PLATA, 1806–07**
Two British invasions of Spanish colonial Rio Del Plata in modern-day Argentina and Uruguay achieved temporary success, but were ultimately repulsed, followed by local political unrest.

■ **MONTEVIDEO, 3 FEBRUARY 1807**
Auchmuty with 6000 British troops captured Spanish Montevideo in modern-day Uruguay, losing 600 casualties and inflicting losses of 3500, including prisoners. Montevideo was evacuated by Whitelocke the following August.

Franco-American War (The Quasi-War) 1798–1800

US Presidents George Washington and John Adams considered the alliance with France terminated on Louis XVI's execution. The Directory authorized privateers to seize US ships and the US Navy engaged French warships.

■ **LA CROYABLE, 7 JULY 1798**
USS *Delaware* under the command of Stephen Decatur captured this French privateer schooner of 12 guns operating off New Jersey. She became USS *Retaliation*, later recaptured, then taken for good by the US.

■ **CONSTELLATION VS. VENGEANCE, 1 FEB 1800**
Secretary of War Henry Knox had urged the construction of frigates capable of outrunning what they could not out-fight. One of these, *Constellation*, under Capt Thomas Truxtun, found French frigate *Vengeance* about to return to France off Guadalupe. *Vengeance* surrendered after a fierce 12-hour battle. The escaped French ship became an American prize when *Constellation*'s mainmast collapsed. *Vengeance* absconded in darkness and limped back to France.

■ **SANTO DOMINGO RAID, MAY 1800**
Toussaint L'Ouverture became LGov of French Saint-Domingue as invading British and Spanish freed and armed French slaves, after which the French abolished slavery. Using fellow freed slaves, he conquered Spanish Santo Domingo without French authorization.

■ **USS *BOSTON* VS. *LE BERCEAU*, 12 OCTOBER 1800**
Boston, under Capt George Little, overhauled French ship *Le Berceau*, under Cdr Louis André Senes. The battle lasted until sunset, both ships damaged and losing manoeuvrability. *Boston* captured *Le Berceau* upon making repairs.

War of the Second Coalition 1798–1800

■ **ISLES DE SAINT-MARCOUF, 7 MAY 1798**
A British garrison occupying the Isles Saint-Marcouf off the coast of Normandy, France, repulsed a French amphibious assault by rowed vessels carrying infantry. French losses were over 1200 with seven vessels sunk.

■ **MALTA, MAY 1798–SEPTEMBER 1800**
French forces captured Malta in May 1798, leaving a garrison of 3000 troops under Vaubois. A Maltese uprising followed, later reinforced by

a British fleet under Nelson, which blockaded Malta, landing weapons for the Maltese and British and Portuguese marines. Vaubois held the fortress of Valetta from September 1798 to September 1800. With food supplies gone and 100 men dying each day, Vaubois finally surrendered.

■ ACTION OF 30 MAY 1798

Three British vessels under Laforey intercepted two French vessels under Pevrieux off the coast of Normandy, France. The damaged French frigate *Confiante* was beached and evacuated, then burnt by a British landing party.

■ ACTION OF 27 JUNE 1798

British Capt Foote in *Seahorse* captured the frigate *Sensible* in the Sicilian Straits. *Sensible* had been detached from the French fleet after the capture of Malta and was returning to Toulon.

■ PYRAMIDS, 21 JULY 1798

Napoleon with 21,000 troops defeated 26,000 Mamluks and militia in Egypt, inflicting 2000

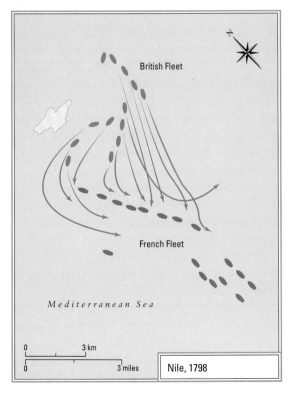

Nile, 1798

casualties. French losses were 29 killed and 260 wounded. The French then occupied Cairo.

■ NILE, 1–3 AUGUST 1798

Adm Brueys commanded the French fleet, which escorted Napoleon's army across the Mediterranean for an invasion of Egypt and then occupied Aboukir Bay, on the northern coast of Egypt. Adm Nelson with a British fleet targeted this French fleet for destruction.

Brueys positioned his fleet in a curved defensive line in the bay, running from south to north-west, the coast of the bay being to the west. The northern end of the line was furthest from shore, as Brueys assumed that the water on the landward side was rocky and impassable. This proved a fatal miscalculation. There was one battery for coastal defence. Up to one-third of crew strength was ashore at any time as foraging parties. The fleet comprised 13 ships of the line, plus four frigates, led by the flagship, the 120-gun *l'Orient*.

Nelson arrived from north-east with his British fleet of 13 ships of the line and two smaller vessels. Nelson ordered an immediate attack, despite approaching darkness. Nelson, although outgunned overall, planned to achieve local superiority. The British had the wind and the French were anchored. Working their way down the French line from north to south, the British could concentrate on one ship at a time, eliminating each in turn, while French ships at the southern end of the line could not aid the others. Nelson noted that Brueys had left gaps between his ships. Nelson's ships, with their mobility and excellent crews, could exploit these gaps, raking French ships bow and stern.

British ships *Goliath* and *Zealous* led the way, sailing to the point of the French line occupied by *Guerrier*, which opened fire along with *Conquerant* at 18:20. Capt Foley of *Goliath* used his initiative and passed to the landward side of *Guerrier*, taking advantage of Brueys's flawed deployment. Four more British ships followed, catching the French line from the landward side, while the rest of the British fleet hit the French from the seaward side. British ships lit signal lights by 19:00, while enveloping five ships in the French line. Nelson, in *Vanguard*, was gashed on the head by scrap iron fired from French cannon. Temporarily blinded by severe bleeding, he was taken below, returning to action after being well bandaged. By 21:25, four French ships had been wrecked and captured, with another out of action.

In the centre, Brueys aboard *l'Orient* bested *Bellerophon*. The damaged British ship drifted out of action, before *Swiftsure* and *Alexander* fell upon *l'Orient*, raking her from two directions. Brueys was wounded twice, but refused to surrender. He was wounded a third time, mortally, as *l'Orient* caught fire. Flames spread to the powder magazine and *l'Orient* blew up at 22:00, the massive explosion heard as far away as Cairo. By midnight, only Capt Thouars of the *Tonnant* still resisted. Thouars lost both legs and one arm but refused surrender, ordering the tricolor nailed to a mast so it could not be struck. He finally bled to death, before *Tonnant* was also taken.

Six French ships under Villeneuve attempted to sail away, four ultimately escaping. French losses were nine ships captured, two destroyed, casualties of over 2000 killed or wounded and 3000 prisoners. British losses were 218 killed, 677 wounded, with some ships damaged but none lost. Nelson's decisive victory established British naval supremacy in the Mediterranean.

■ ACTION OF 18 AUGUST 1798

The French ship *Généreux* pursued the smaller British ship *Leander* off the coast of Crete. After a fight of several hours, *Leander* finally surrendered, having been dismasted and with many wounded crew members.

■ ACTION OF 24 OCTOBER 1798

Capt King in the frigate *Sirius* captured two Batavian Republic ships 48km north of the Dutch coast. The ships were attempting to reach Ireland to support a rebellion there.

■ ACTION OF 14 DECEMBER 1798

Off the south-west coast of France, the French corvette *Bayonnaise* managed to ram and board the much larger British frigate *Ambuscade*. The French crew, including infantry serving as marines, captured *Ambuscade*.

■ SWISS AND ITALIAN EXPEDITION, 1799–1800

Russian expeditionary forces of over 30,000 under Suvorov, plus Austrian allies, launched a campaign against French troops in Italy. Suvorov defeated Moreau, pushing him out of Milan and Turin. A French army under MacDonald advanced northwards from Rome. Rather than being trapped, Suvorov concentrated against French general MacDonald, defeating him. Suvorov finally retreated through Switzerland because of French victories against other allied forces in the region.

■ EL ARISH, 10–20 FEBRUARY 1799

Reynier with 2150 Frenchmen besieged 1500 Turks on the northern Egyptian Sinai coast, defeating a Turkish relief force of 8000 on 15 February. Napoleon arrived with French reinforcements and the fortress surrendered.

■ SIEGE OF JAFFA, 3–7 MARCH 1799

Napoleon with 10,000 French besieged 5000 Turks in the fortress of Jaffa in present-day Israel. The fortress fell to the French and all the Turks were killed. French casualties were 250.

■ STOCKACH, 25 MARCH 1799

Archduke Charles with 72,000 Austrian troops attacked 35,000 French under Jourdan in present-day south-western Germany. Jourdan counter-attacked before withdrawing, having inflicted 6000 casualties for losses of 4000.

■ ACRE, 18 MARCH–20 MAY 1799

Napoleon with a French army of 13,000 unsuccessfully besieged 4000 Turks in the peninsula fortress in present-day Israel. A British flotilla under Smith supported the Turks. Napoleon withdrew after losses of 4500.

■ MAGNANO, 5 APRIL 1799

Kray, with 46,000 Austrian Empire troops, repulsed an attack by Schérer commanding 41,000 French troops in present-day north-eastern Italy. French losses were 8000; Austrian losses totaled 6000.

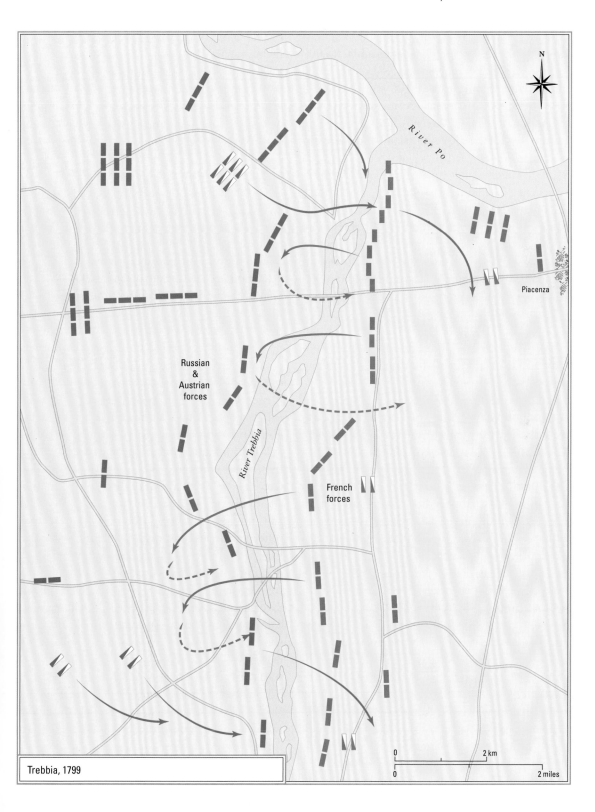

River Po

Piacenza

Russian
&
Austrian
forces

River Trebbia

French
forces

0		2 km
0		2 miles

Trebbia, 1799

■ **MOUNT TABOR, 16 APRIL 1799**

Kléber with 2500 French was attacked by 25,000 Turkish troops. Napoleon arrived with 3000 reinforcements and routed the Turks. Turkish losses were 6500, the French losing 62.

■ **CASSANO D'ADDA, 27 APRIL 1799**

Suvorov with 50,000 Austrian and Russian troops (25,000 actually engaged) defeated 27,000 French under Moreau. French losses were 5000, Coalition losses 4000.

■ **ZURICH, 2–5 JUNE 1799**

Archduke Charles with 40,000 Austrian Empire troops attacked 30,000 French troops under Masséna in Switzerland. Masséna, his position compromised, withdrew, having inflicted 3500 Austrian casualties. French losses were 1700.

■ **TREBBIA RIVER, 17–19 JUNE 1799**

Suvorov with 36,000 Russian and Austrian troops defeated MacDonald's French army of 35,500 in Italy. MacDonald lost 16,000 casualties including prisoners and Suvorov lost 5500.

■ **ABOUKIR, 25 JULY 1799**

A Coalition fleet landed a total of 18,000 Turkish troops on the Egyptian coast near Alexandria. The Turks built redoubts and awaited reinforcements. Napoleon with 7700 French, however, attacked the Turkish beachhead to preempt this threat. French infantry pushed themselves hard against the centre of the Turkish line, while cavalry under Murat exploited gaps between the redoubts. The Turkish army was driven into the sea, with losses of 15,000 killed, drowned and captured. French losses were 900.

■ **NOVI LIGURE, 15 AUGUST 1799**

Suvorov with 45,000 Russians and Austrians attacked Joubert's 38,000 French soldiers in northern Italy. Joubert was killed in action and the French retreated with losses of 9200. Coalition losses were 8500.

■ **HELDER EXPEDITION, AUG–NOV 1799**

A British and Russian invasion of the Netherlands, then known as the Batavian Republic, was unsuccessful and eventually evacuated. At maximum strength, the invasion numbered 40,000 effectives, but was defeated by French and Dutch forces.

■ **CALLANTSOOG, 27 AUGUST 1799**

A British amphibious landing was successfully made by 12,000 troops under Abercromby, defeating 10,000 Dutch troops defending the coast of the Netherlands. British losses were 450 and Dutch losses over 1000.

■ **VLIETER INCIDENT, 30 AUGUST 1799**

In this incident in the summer of 1799, a Dutch Batavian Republic fleet of 13 ships off the coast of the Netherlands surrendered without a fight to a British and Russian fleet. The surrender followed a near mutiny aboard the ships.

■ **KRABBENDAM, 10 SEPTEMBER 1799**

Gen Brune with 25,000 Dutch and French troops unsuccessfully attacked the British beachhead on the northern coast of the Netherlands, defended by Abercromby with 23,000 troops. Brune was compelled to withdraw with heavy losses.

■ **BERGEN-OP-ZOOM, 19 SEPTEMBER 1799**

French Gen Brune commanding 22,000 French and Dutch troops successfully defended his position in the Netherlands against a Russian and British expeditionary force of 30,000 under the overall command of the Duke of York. The Coalition force advanced in four columns, attempting to negotiate terrain cut up by canals and ditches. Coalition forces withdrew after suffering casualties of over 4000, mostly Russian. French and Dutch losses were over 3000.

■ **ZURICH II, 25–26 SEPTEMBER 1799**

Masséna commanding 75,000 French troops in Switzerland decisively defeated 60,000 Russians and Austrians under Korsakov. Coalition losses were 7000 killed and wounded, plus 6000 prisoners. Total French losses were 3000.

■ **ALKMAAR, 2 OCTOBER 1799**

The Duke of York with 40,000 Russian and British troops attacked 25,000 French and Dutch under Brune. Brune withdrew once his flank was turned. Both sides lost over 2000 casualties.

■ **CASTRICUM, 6 OCTOBER 1799**

The Duke of York with 27,000 British and

Russian forces was repulsed in the Netherlands by 25,000 French and Dutch troops under General Brune. York lost over 2500 casualties, Brune losing 1300.

■ ACTION OF 1 JANUARY 1800

Fourteen barges of Haitian pirates attacked a neutral American merchant flotilla of five ships off the coast of present-day Haiti. Two American merchant vessels were captured, but three pirate barges were sunk.

■ HELIOPOLIS, 20 MARCH 1800

Kléber with 9000 Frenchmen defeated an Ottoman army of 30,000, plus Egyptian insurgents, under Nassif Pasha in northern Egypt. Ottoman losses were 3000, the French losing 300.

■ GENOA, 20 APRIL–4 JUNE 1800

Masséna commanded 10,000 Frenchmen in the port of Genoa, besieged by 21,000 Austrians and bombarded by a British fleet. Masséna surrendered on terms, his surviving troops evacuating.

■ STOCKACH II, 3 MAY 1800

Lecourbe with 24,000 French troops defeated 12,000 Austrian Empire troops under Lothringen in present-day south-western Germany, capturing 4000 prisoners, while the main opposing armies fought at Engen, 16km further west.

■ ENGEN, 3 MAY 1800

Moreau's French army of 76,000 troops defeated Kray's 72,000 Austrians in present-day south-western Germany, inflicting losses of 2400 Austrians, against 2000 French casualties. The French also won at nearby Stockach.

■ MOERSCIRCH, 5 MAY 1800

At Moersrich Moreau with 50,000 French troops defeated Kray's 60,000 Austrian Empire troops at Moerscirch (also spelled Moskirch). Kray, despite a strong position, lost 5000 casualties; Moreau lost 3500.

■ ERBACH, 15 MAY 1800

Kray's 36,000 Austrian Empire troops attacked the 12,000 men of the French division of Sainte-Suzanne, in advance of Moreau's main army in present-day southern Germany. The French held successfully, despite the odds.

■ MONTEBELLO, 9 JUNE 1800

French Gen Lannes with 8000 troops crossed the Po river in present-day northern Italy and, despite being outnumbered, attacked 12,000 Austrian Empire troops under Gen Ott. Lannes received 6000 French reinforcements during the battle, while Ott was reinforced by 4000 troops. Ott withdrew after 11 hours of battle, but his rearguard under O'Reilly was cut off, resulting in a French victory. Austrian losses totaled 3000 killed and wounded plus 5000 prisoners, French losses totaling 3000.

■ MARENGO, 14 JUNE 1800

First Consul Napoleon Bonaparte had led the French Army of the Reserve across the Alps into northern Italy and manoeuvred into position to the east of an Austrian army under Gen Melas. Napoleon expected Melas to attempt an escape without fighting, but was surprised when the Austrians attacked instead.

Napoleon recalled detached troops he had sent marching south earlier, but until they could arrive on the battlefield the French were outnumbered, with under 23,000 men against an Austrian force of over 31,000. The French were slowly driven back until a division of 5300 Frenchmen led by Gen Desaix arrived in the evening and the tide of battle turned. Desaix was killed in action, but the Austrian army was thoroughly routed. French losses were 5600 killed, wounded and missing. Austrian losses were 9500, including 3000 captured.

■ HÖCHSTADT, 19 JUNE 1800

Moreau's 70,000 French defeated an Austrian army of 80,000 under Kray taking 5000 prisoners and driving the Austrians beyond Ulm. A temporary armistice followed this French victory.

■ DUNKIRK RAID, 7 JULY 1800

A British flotilla under Inman raided the northern French naval base of Dunkirk, which was already under blockade. The raid was conducted by stealth at night. Several small ships served as guides into the port, leading two frigates and the heavily armed experimental

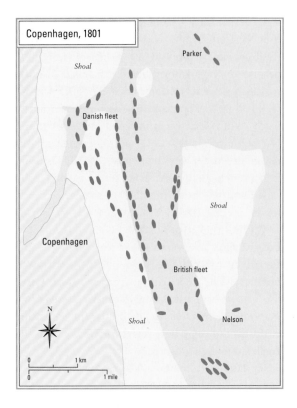

Copenhagen, 1801

Shoal

Parker

Danish fleet

Shoal

Copenhagen

British fleet

Shoal

Nelson

N

0   1 km

0   1 mile

sloop *Dart*. The British also launched four burning fire ships. One French frigate was captured and three others damaged.

■ **ACTION OF 4 AUGUST 1800**
British Capt Bulteel with one frigate and a large convoy of merchant vessels deployed in line of battle successfully captured two French frigates off the coast of Brazil, a third vessel escaping.

■ **HOHENLINDEN, 3 DECEMBER 1800**
Moreau with 56,000 Frenchmen decisively defeated 64,000 Austrians and Bavarians under Archduke John in present-day southern Germany. The Archduke lost 4600 killed and wounded, plus 9000 men captured. French losses were 3000.

■ **POZZOLO, 25 DECEMBER 1800**
A French army of 66,000 under Gen Brune defeated an Austrian Empire army of 50,000 under Gen Bellegarde at the Mincio river in Italy. Austrian losses were 8500, the French losing 4000.

■ **ABOUKIR II, 21–22 MARCH 1801**
Menou with 11,000 French troops made an unsuccessful night attack on a British force of 18,000 under Abercromby in Egypt. Abercromby himself was mortally wounded and lost 1300 casualties in the battle, with French losses being 3000 men.

■ **COPENHAGEN, 2 APRIL 1801**
The naval battle of Copenhagen resulted from complex diplomacy in Europe towards the end of the War of the Second Coalition. The Austrian Empire surrendered to France in February 1801 and Russia exited the Coalition. Russian Tsar Paul I organized the League of Armed Neutrality, designed to use force against Britain to protect the shipping of Russia, Sweden and Denmark. A British fleet was sent to the Baltic Sea to confront the League. Parker was in nominal command, but Nelson was tactical leader. Nelson successfully argued for an attack on the Danish fleet in port at Copenhagen, before it could be reinforced by Sweden or Russia. Nelson planned to attack the Danish line from south to north, characteristically achieving firepower superiority. Nelson led 30 ships into battle, including 12 ships of the line. The Danes had 36 ships, mostly not seaworthy, but drawn up in the port as a line of batteries, with strong shore batteries in support.

The engagement became fierce and obscured by smoke, so Parker hoisted a signal to Nelson to disengage. Nelson jokingly observed the signal through a telescope held to his blind eye and continued the battle. While British ships suffered casualties and damage, Danish losses were far worse, so the Danes used launches from shore to reinforce their ships. This weakened their shore batteries without strengthening their ships, most of which were too damaged to fight.

Nelson offered a truce, which Crown Prince Frederic took. The Danes lost 12 ships captured, three destroyed and 1700 casualties. British losses were 253 killed and 688 wounded, but with no ships lost.

WAR OF THE ORANGES, MAY–JUNE 1801

Spanish and French forces under Godoy invaded Portugal. After a brief campaign, Portugal agreed to the Peace of Badajoz, ceding border territories to Spain and part of northern Brazil to France.

Steklikrieg 1802

PILATUS, 28 AUGUST 1802

Swiss insurgents numbering 8000 under Bachmann defeated government troops of the Helvetic Republic. The government troops were unmotivated to fire upon their own people and soon retreated.

FAOUG, 3 OCTOBER 1802

Swiss insurgent forces defeated Helvetic Republic troops and the government collapsed, being replaced with a confederation of Swiss cantons. Napoleon subsequently occupied Switzerland and issued the Act of Mediation.

War of the Third/Fourth Coalition 1803–08

LINOIS IN THE INDIAN OCEAN, 1803–06

Napoleon sent Adm Linois with one ship of the line, *Marengo*, plus three frigates, to raid British shipping in the Indian Ocean. Using present-day Mauritius and other bases, Linois operated for three years.

PAULO AURA, 15 FEBRUARY 1804

Three French ships under Linois off the coast of present-day Malaysia aborted his attack on British merchant fleet of 29 ships under Dance, convinced by ruse that seven of the ships were actually warships.

VIZAGAPATAM, 15 SEPTEMBER 1804

Linois with three French ships attacked a British frigate and two merchant ships off the south-eastern coast of India, capturing one merchant ship and destroying the other, before eventually withdrawing.

BOULOGNE RAID, 2–3 OCTOBER 1804

A British flotilla under Lord Keith made a night raid on Napoleon's invasion barge concentration at Boulogne on the Channel coast of France.

American inventor Robert Fulton's experimental torpedo-catamarans and four explosion vessels (fireships) were launched. No French vessels were damaged.

TROUBRIDGE'S COMMAND, 1805–07

Furious when his Indian Ocean Command was split into two, he sailed for Cape Town in HMS *Blenheim*. Caught by a massive typhoon, his elderly vessel disappeared with all hands

DIAMOND ROCK, 25 MAY–3 JUNE 1805

Diamond Rock, an isolated pinnacle off the coast of Martinique was seized by Cdre Samuel Hood and manned with 100 sailors under Cdr James Maurice. They hauled 4 cannon to the top of the peak, which effectively blockaded the harbour of Port de France for 17 months. It was commissioned as a sloop named HMS *Diamond Rock* and controlled the harbour until the arrival of the Combined Fleet in May 1805. It was bombarded for four days, during which Cdre Cosmao-Kerjulien's Spanish vessel was damaged. The garrison surrendered when their water cistern was fractured by an earth tremor.

CAPE FINISTERRE, 22 JULY 1805

The French and Spanish Combined Fleet under Villeneuve left the West Indies and returned to Europe with some merchant prizes. A British fleet under Nelson had followed the Combined Fleet to the West Indies and had not yet returned, but a British blockading fleet under Calder was available. Calder with 15 ships of the line attacked Villeneuve's 20 ships of the line off the north-west coast of Spain. Heavy fog resulted in disorganized fighting. HMS *Malta*, captained by Buller, captured two Spanish ships. The battle was broken off after dark, British losses being 200 while the Combined Fleet lost 476, plus 1200 captured. Both commanders were later criticized for not renewing battle. Napoleon had wanted Villeneuve to link up with French ships at Brest, France, but instead Villeneuve took the Combined Fleet to Cadiz, Spain.

ALLEMAND EXPEDITION, 16 JUL–24 DEC 1805

French VAdm Allemand escaped from blockade

in Rochefort with 10 ships, plus one captured and incorporated into his flotilla. This 'Invisible Squadron' captured or destroyed three British naval vessels and 43 merchant ships.

■ **WERTINGEN, 8 OCTOBER 1805**

Lannes and Murat leading 15,000 French troops in present-day southern Germany surprised and attacked 5500 Austrians under Auffenberg, inflicting 400 casualties and capturing 3000. French losses were 200.

■ **HASLACH-JUNGINEN, 11 OCTOBER 1805**

Mack commanding 23,000 Austrian troops attacked 5300 Frenchmen under Dupont in present-day southern Germany. The French held successfully despite the odds, inflicting casualties of 5100, while losing 1000.

■ **ELCHINGEN, 14 OCTOBER 1805**

Marshal Ney leading 18,000 French troops badly defeated an Austrian Empire force of 17,000 under Riesch in present-day southern Germany. Riesch lost 6500 casualties and retreated to Ulm, Ney losing 1000 casualties.

■ **ULM, 15–20 OCTOBER 1805**

Rather than a battle per se, the military actions around Ulm, Bavaria, involved manoeuvres and skirmishes. Napoleon had marched most of his army in separate corps past and to the east of the main Austrian army under Gen Mack at Ulm, on the Danube River. Napoleon turned his various corps westwards to trap Mack. Mack had been abandoned by Archduke Ferdinand and 6000 troops before Napoleon's forces were concentrated. Another Austrian force of 5000 troops under Jellacic escaped to the south, leaving the total Austrian force under Mack in Ulm at 27,000. Napoleon had four corps around Ulm by the 15th, with his Imperial Guard, Reserve Cavalry and another army corps nearby, totaling nearly 150,000 troops.

Napoleon demanded the surrender of Austrian forces in Ulm on 15 October, but Mack refused. Napoleon continued to concentrate his forces, detaching only Murat and a large cavalry force to pursue an Austrian force under Werneck.

Mack wanted to pin Napoleon's main force for as long as possible in order to buy time for the Austrians and their Russian allies to organize. Instead, Mack's subordinate commanders staged what amounted to a mutiny and demanded that he surrender. Mack negotiated the surrender on 20 October. All 27,000 Austrian troops became prisoners of war, Napoleon's only concession in the negotiations being that Soult's IV Corps would remain immobile at Ulm until the 25th.

The French considered this decisive victory as having been won chiefly with marches, rather than with fighting. The capture of Ulm enabled Napoleon to march on and take the Austrian capital of Vienna and thereafter conduct his enormously successful Austerlitz campaign against Russian and Austrian forces.

■ **CALDIERO, 29–31 OCTOBER 1805**

Masséna commanding 37,000 French troops defeated 49,000 Austrian Empire troops under Archduke Charles in modern-day northern Italy. French losses were 3700 while Austrian losses were 9100, including 6500 prisoners, mostly isolated rearguard troops.

■ **CAPE ORTEGAL, 4 NOVEMBER 1805**

Four French ships that had escaped from the battle of Trafalgar were captured by eight British ships under Strachan off the north-western coast of Spain, after several hours of fierce fighting between the warring sides.

■ **AMSTETTEN, 5 NOVEMBER 1805**

Bagration commanded approximately 7000 Russians and Austrians in a rearguard action in Austria against 10,000 Frenchmen under Murat. Bagration withdrew at night with losses of 1100, French losses being 1000.

■ **DURENSTEIN, 11 NOVEMBER 1805**

Kutusov attacked with 18,000 Russians and Austrians against a French force of 5000 under Mortier, reinforced to 9900 during battle in Austria. The French forces held, both sides losing over 4000 casualties.

■ **OBERHOLLARBRUNN, 16 NOVEMBER 1805**

Bagration led a rearguard action in Austria by

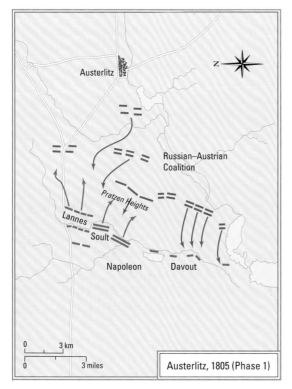

Austerlitz, 1805 (Phase 1)

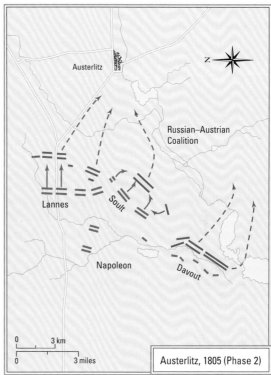

Austerlitz, 1805 (Phase 2)

7300 Russians and Austrians against a much larger army of 20,000 French troops under Murat. Bagration's force suffered 2400 casualties, but held until nightfall, then retreated. French losses were 1200.

■ L'Hermite's Expedition 1805–07

A French naval squadron of four ships under l'Hermite operated in the Atlantic, destroying several merchant vessels and one British naval vessel, later recaptured, and also lost one ship captured.

■ Austerlitz, 2 December 1805

Napoleon, Emperor of the French, having captured the Austrian imperial capital of Vienna in November 1805, was operating in Moravia against a Coalition army. The Coalition forces at Austerlitz totalled 86,000 men, including 70,000 Russian troops, with the remaining contingent being Austrian Empire troops. Tsar Alexander I of Russia had titular command of the Coalition army, although Kutusov was the senior Russian commander and the Coalition battle plan was

created by Austrian staff officer Weyrother. Napoleon's Grande Armée at Austerlitz was outnumbered, totaling 73,000 men.

Napoleon's plan was tactically ambitious. He had withdrawn his army to the west of Pratzen Plateau, abandoning the high ground in order to entice the enemy army to occupy it and then attack him. Napoleon further enticed an attack on his right flank by extending it and presenting it as the weakest part of his force. The Coalition plan was indeed to attack the French right and these attacks began at dawn on 2 December.

The French right was commanded by Marshal Davout, with only 10,500 troops essentially acting as both bait and holding force. Golbach Brook and buildings at Sokolnitz and Telnitz provided Davout's defensive positions. Coalition attacking forces against Davout eventually totaled nearly 40,000 and had to descend from the southerly end of Pratzen Plateau and extend the Coalition left. Meanwhile, early morning fog concealed most

Revolutionary Wars

of Napoleon's centre and left as they massed for attack. As the Coalition forces reinforced their attacks against Davout, they continually drew from and weakened their forces on Pratzen Plateau between 06:30 and 08:30. Seeing this anticipated enemy action, Napoleon launched his main attack.

The French corps of Marshal Soult advanced rapidly up Pratzen Plateau, with the corps of Bernadotte in close support on his left and the corps of Lannes on the French extreme left. French cavalry under Murat supported these forces. The unexpected French attack crushed the Coalition centre and French troops dominated Pratzen Plateau by 09:30. In desperation, the Russian Imperial Guard Cavalry was committed to battle and counter-attacked, driving back part of a French infantry division under Vandamme. The Russian Guards were in turn repulsed and defeated by Napoleon's Imperial Guard Cavalry, ending any chance for the Coalition to repair their broken centre.

With the Pratzen Plateau secured, Napoleon swung his main force to the right, onto the flank and rear of the Coalition troops attacking Davout. The massed Coalition forces were caught between the converging French forces and began to rout. Davout, having held until that point against much larger forces, counter-attacked as well. Some Coalition forces attempted to reform south of the Pratzen Plateau, but were broken up by French cannon fire and routed by French cavalry attacks. Coalition troops attempting to flee across frozen ponds were devastated by French artillery fire, causing the ice on the ponds to break.

Battered Russian forces commanded by Bagration on the northern portion of the battlefield finally withdrew. French victory was complete. French total battle losses were 2000 killed and 7000 wounded. Coalition forces lost 15,000 killed and wounded, plus 11,000 taken prisoner. The French also captured 180 cannon and 45 flags. The Russian army withdrew from the Austrian Empire following this defeat and the Austrian Emperor Francis II

sued for peace. The battle of Austerlitz, fought on the first anniversary of Napoleon's coronation, is generally considered his greatest victory.

■ BLAAUWBERG, 8 JANUARY 1806
A British expeditionary force of 7000 under Baird successfully attacked the Dutch possessions around Cape Town in southern Africa. Janssen commanded 2000 defenders, losing 350, before retreating. British losses were about 200.

■ CAPE TOWN, 9 JANUARY 1806
After defeating Janssen's defence force the previous day, Baird's British expeditionary force obtained the surrender of Batavian Republic Col Prophalow and occupied Cape Town proper. Janssen surrendered nine days later.

■ ATLANTIC CAMPAIGN, 1806
Despite the decisive defeat at Trafalgar in October 1805, in 1806, Napoleon ordered French naval activity in the Atlantic with a view to raid British shipping and stretch Royal Navy resources. Several French squadrons, none larger than eight ships, broke through the British blockade of the French coast to conduct operations, especially in the Caribbean. Several French ships were lost to a devastating combination of British action and a hurricane.

■ SANTO DOMINGO, 6 FEBRUARY 1806
Eleven British ships under Duckworth defeated eight French ships under Leissegues off the coast of present-day Dominican Republic. Three French ships were captured and two were destroyed. British ships suffered damage only.

■ LA MEILLERIE EXPEDITION, 23 FEBRUARY–28 JULY 1806
A French squadron of five ships under La Meillerie operated in the Atlantic, along the coast of Africa and in the Caribbean to raid British shipping. Two French ships were captured by the British.

■ WARREN'S ACTION, 13 MARCH 1806
Warren, commanding a British squadron of eight ships, intercepted two French ships under Linois west of the Canary Islands. After a fierce fight, Linois, wounded and outgunned, finally surrendered his ships.

■ MAIDA, 4 JULY 1806

When French forces occupied southern Italy, a revolt broke out in Calabria. The British Royal Navy landed an Anglo-Sicilian force of 5200 men under Gen Stuart to support the rebellion. French Gen Reynier with 6400 troops attacked Stuart's force near Maida.

Both sides advanced as the combat commenced, the French left and the British right coming into contact first. The French 1st Light Infantry, on order to attack with bayonet only, fired a volley too early and too high. Against them, a combined brigade of 11 light companies under Kempt advanced and fired a volley at point-blank range with devastating effect. This began a ripple effect down the line of battle. Reynier left the field with a loss of 2000, Stuart's loss being 330.

Stuart's force was evacuated after French forces under Masséna captured Gaeta.

■ ACTION OF 9 JULY 1806

The French privateer *Bellone* under Perroud, rather than surrender immediately as expected, fought a British ship of the line and a brig before surrendering off the coast of modern-day Sri Lanka.

■ ACTION OF 26 JULY 1806

A British frigate and brig under Elphinstone defeated and captured the Dutch frigate *Pallas*, plus two Dutch merchant vessels off the southern coast of Celebes (then in Dutch possession) in present-day Indonesia.

■ ACTION OF 25 SEPTEMBER 1806

Cdre Hood lost an arm, but won a battle, commanding three British ships against six smaller French vessels off the coast of France. The British ships suffered battle damage while capturing four French ships.

■ SCHLEIZ, 9 OCTOBER 1806

A French division of 4000 troops, part of Bernadotte's I Corps, defeated 2600 Prussians and Saxons under Tauenzien in present-day northern Germany. Murat commanded a pursuit and Tauenzien lost over 500 casualties.

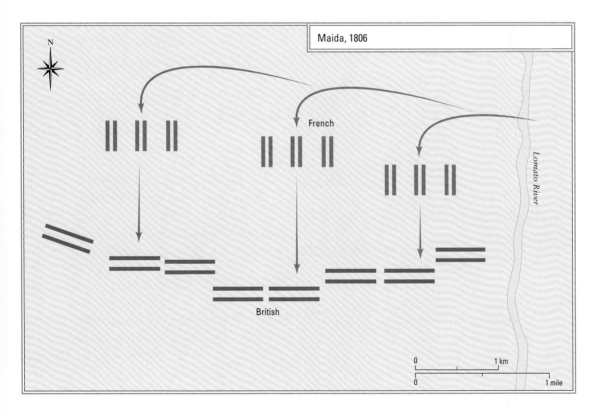

Maida, 1806

■ SAALFELD, 10 OCTOBER 1806

Lannes led 12,000 French troops, decisively beating 8300 Prussians and Saxons under Prince Louis, who was killed in this action in northern Germany. French losses were under 200, Coalition losses totaling over 1500.

■ JENA-AUERSTÄDT, 14 OCTOBER 1806

Napoleon had manoeuvred the various corps of his French Grande Armée through Saxony to the south and east of the main Prussian army. In response to the threat, the Prussian high command began a phased withdrawal, with their army divided into three groups. The result was two simultaneous battles of Jena and Auerstädt, fought about 21km apart.

Napoleon, with four corps, his Guard and part of the Reserve Cavalry, advanced through Jena against a Prussian and Saxon force of 38,000 under Hohenlohe. The Prussians occupied the Dornberg plateau north of Jena, which Napoleon attacked at dawn as his corps advanced through heavy fog and difficult defiles in order to deploy onto the plateau. Napoleon had 96,000 troops available, but could only get them into action piecemeal as the corps came into position, giving the Prussians time to mount counter-attacks. These attacks employed rigid, outdated formations and suffered crippling casualties from French musket fire. The French troops fought in a combination of skirmish formations and from behind cover, especially around the village of Vierzehnheiligen. Soult's French IV Corps deployed fully into position by 12:30, turning the Prussian left. Napoleon then attacked all along the line, driving Hohenlohe from the field in complete disorder by 14:30.

Another Prussian force of 13,000 under Rüchel arrived too late to reinforce Hohenlohe and was defeated separately. Only 40,000 of Napoleon's whole force had actually engaged in combat, but the forces of Hohenlohe and Ruchel were crushed, losing 11,000 killed and wounded, another 15,000 captured, plus the loss

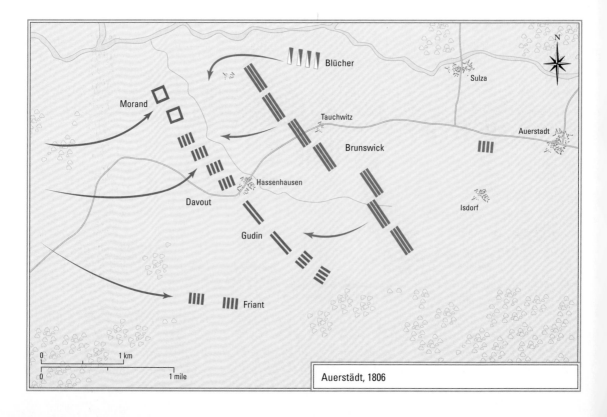

Auerstädt, 1806

of 200 cannon and 30 flags. Napoleon's casualties were 5000.

Meanwhile, the French III Corps numbering 26,000 under Marshal Davout, 13km to the north of Jena, confronted a Prussian army of 64,000 under the Duke of Brunswick, just north-east of Auerstädt. Davout's lead division under Gudin was attacked by masses of Prussian cavalry led by Blücher. The French formed squares and repulsed the Prussians with heavy losses. Another French division under Friant arrived on Gudin's right. Despite being outnumbered by over two to one, Davout manoeuvred to attack with local superiority, while the Prussians were not fully concentrated. Brunswick was mortally wounded, throwing the Prussian command into confusion. The King of Prussia, Frederick William, then took command.

Davout's division under Morand came up on Gudin's left and was attacked by large numbers of Prussians in tight formations. Morand's Frenchmen repulsed these attacks, utilizing flexible formations and firing at will. Davout then renewed his attacks, committing all troops available, including his company of engineers.

Pushing his 40 cannon forward on both flanks, Davout covered the Prussian forces with interlocking artillery fire. The Prussians were driven back slowly until the King decided to withdraw from the field and link up with Hohenlohe and Ruchel, unaware that they had already been defeated. Davout's outnumbered force had lost 8000 men, but had inflicted 12,000 killed and wounded on the Prussians, plus the capture of 3000 men and 115 cannon. Napoleon later awarded Davout the title Duke of Auerstädt.

Retreating troops from both Prussian defeats crossed paths, with further confusion and disorder resulting. Pursuit by French cavalry under Murat exploited the victories. The French had won without the I Corps under Bernadotte, who had marched between the battles, participating in neither. The victories enabled the French to capture Berlin, Davout's troops getting the honour of parading there first in October.

■ ACTION OF 18 OCTOBER 1806
British Capt Rainier with HMS *Caroline* captured the Dutch frigate *Maria Riggersbergen* in a fight off Dutch-controlled Batavia harbour, on the island of Java, in present-day Indonesia.

■ LÜBECK, 6–7 NOVEMBER 1806
French Marshals Bernadotte, Soult and Murat with 30,000 troops stormed the city of Lübeck in present-day northern Germany, which Blücher had occupied with 17,000 Prussian troops. Blücher lost 7000 killed or captured and escaped with part of his force, but was cornered the next day at the Trave river and forced to surrender. Over the two days, the French captured 13,000 prisoners and 80 cannon, losing 1500 casualties.

■ BATAVIA RAID, 27 NOVEMBER 1806
Pellew with a powerful British squadron, including four ships of the line, two frigates and a brig, attacked near the Dutch possession of Batavia on Java. The Dutch, with one frigate, some cutters and 20 merchant vessels, were hopelessly outgunned. In desperation, they ran their ships aground to prevent capture. Under cover of squadron cannon, British landing parties burned all the ships, except for two merchant vessels successfully captured.

■ PULTUSK, 26 DECEMBER 1806
Marshal Lannes with 20,000 French troops boldly attacked 40,000 Russians under Bennigsen in northern Poland. Bennigsen withdrew at night as French reinforcements arrived. Casualty estimates vary; over 3000 for each side is likely.

■ GOLYMIN, 26 DECEMBER 1806
Fought concurrently with the battle of Pultusk, 16km further south-east, 38,000 Frenchmen under Murat drove off 18,000 Russians under Galitzine, who withdrew in good order. Casualties were over 700 for both sides.

■ BUENOS AIRES, 1806–07
The British made two attempts to capture Buenos Aires against local defenders. The city was occupied temporarily in 1806, but the British withdrew and the 1807 attempt failed.

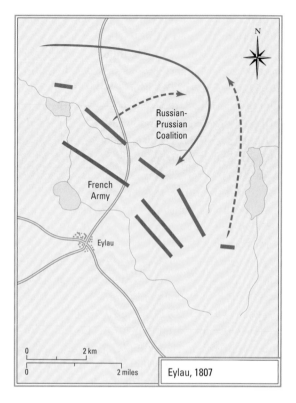

0   2 km

0   2 miles | Eylau, 1807

■ GREATER POLAND UPRISING, 1807

North-western and central Poland, which had been under Prussian occupation since the partitions of 1772–95, saw pro-French uprisings as Napoleon's French army defeated Prussian and Russian Coalition forces and entered Polish lands in late 1806. Dabrowski, a leader during the uprising of 1794, organized military units in Poznan, with other Poles organizing further uprisings in more remote areas. Later, Prince Poniatowski organized the army of the newly independent Duchy of Warsaw, created from Prussian-held Polish territory.

■ STRALSUND, 30 JANUARY–24 AUGUST 1807

The French twice besieged the Swedish fortress of Stralsund on the Baltic in present-day northern Germany. The first siege was conducted by Mortier with 13,000 men, the garrison numbering 15,000. An armistice on 29 April ended this siege. The Treaty of Tilsit notwithstanding, Sweden remained at war, with King Gustav IV taking command at

Stralsund. Brune besieged Stralsund on 24 July with 38,000 French troops. Stralsund surrendered a month later.

■ EYLAU, 8 FEBRUARY 1807

Napoleon, expecting reinforcements, brought 45,000 troops to the village of Eylau, in north-eastern Prussia. Opposing him was a Russian army of 67,000 under Bennigsen, later reinforced by 8000 Prussians under Lestocq. Napoleon was reinforced by Davout's corps of 15,000 troops, who attacked the Russian left. Davout drove back the Russian left until Lestocq's arrival stabilized the situation. A snowstorm during the battle caused a great deal of confusion on both sides. Augereau's French corps was decimated by the fire of 72 Russian cannon, unseen on their flank. A Russian attack exploited this success. Marshal Murat then led a massive French cavalry charge to counter the Russian advance. French reinforcements under Ney approached the field as night fell. Napoleon's losses were severe: 25,000 soldiers were killed and wounded. Russian losses were actually fewer at 15,000, but Bennigsen withdrew during the night.

■ OSTROLEKA, 16 FEBRUARY 1807

Essen with 25,000 Russians attacked 20,000 Frenchmen under Savary in modern-day north-eastern Poland. Essen's headlong attacks were repulsed, losing 2500 casualties. French losses were 900. Both armies subsequently went into winter quarters.

■ DANZIG, 19 MARCH–24 MAY 1807

At Danzig in March–May 1807 Lefebvre with 30,000 French and Polish troops successfully besieged 20,000 Prussians under Kalkreuth in the Baltic fortress of Danzig in northern Poland. Russian ships supported the garrison. Kalkreuth surrendered on generous terms.

■ KOLBERG, MARCH–JULY 1807

The Baltic fortress of Kolberg located in northern Poland was held by 6000 Prussian soldiers supported by Coalition naval forces and besieged by 14,000 French troops and Polish insurgents until the Treaty of Tilsit.

■ HEILSBURG, 10 JUNE 1807

A French army under Napoleon clashed with a Russian army under Bennigsen in eastern Prussia. The battle was bloody, each side losing about 8000 killed and wounded. As in the battle of Eylau, Bennigsen withdrew at night.

■ FRIEDLAND, 14 JUNE 1807

A Russian army of 60,000 under Bennigsen crossed the Alle river at Friedland in north-eastern Prussia to attack a French corps of 26,000 under Lannes. Lannes fought a delaying action for nine hours until Napoleon arrived with 54,000 additional French troops. French artillery fire destroyed bridges across the Alle, trapping most of the Russian army against the river when Napoleon launched attacks all along the line. Russian counter-attacks were driven off by French cannon fire. The Russian army was pushed against the river and many of the soldiers drowned trying to escape. French losses were about 10,000 wounded and 1400 killed. Russian losses were 30,000, including 11,000 dead on the field, plus 7000 wounded and large, but unknown, numbers drowned. This decisive defeat led Russian Tsar Alexander I to negotiate peace with Napoleon at Tilsit.

■ KOGE, 29 AUGUST 1807

Wellesley (later Duke of Wellington) with 8000 British defeated a poorly armed, poorly trained Danish militia force of 7600 near Copenhagen. Danish casualties were over 1500 including prisoners, and British casualties were 209.

■ COPENHAGEN, 16 AUGUST–7 SEPTEMBER 1807

A British expedition under Adm Gambier including 67 warships, 380 transports and 30,000 troops besieged Copenhagen from land and sea. The Danish garrison under Peymann numbered 13,000. The British demanded the surrender of the Danish fleet, which was rejected. A massive bombardment of Copenhagen followed from 3 September through the 5th. Danish casualties, including civilians, numbered over 5000. Following this, the Danes finally agreed to surrender their fleet, totaling 71 ships.

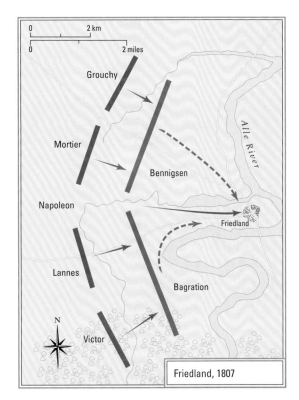

Friedland, 1807

■ CAPTURE OF THE JEUNE RICHARD, 1 OCT 1807

French privateer *Jeune Richard* attempted to capture the much smaller British vessel *Windsor Castle* in the Caribbean. British fire inflicted 54 casualties. Capt Rogers then boarded and captured *Jeune Richard*.

■ ACTION OF 10 NOVEMBER 1808

The French frigate *Thétis* was intercepted by British frigate *Amethyst* in the Bay of Biscay. Devastating close-range fire killed or wounded most of the French crew and their ship was boarded and captured.

Java Campaign 1806–07

■ GRIESSIE, 5–11 DECEMBER 1807

RAdm Pellew commanding eight British ships successfully raided the Dutch naval base at Griessie towards the eastern end of Java in present-day Indonesia. During the engagement he destroyed a shore battery, several vessels and some military supplies.

Gunboat War 1807–14

■ ADRIATIC CAMPAIGN 1807–14

British naval forces successfully contained and defeated French naval forces, plus naval forces of French satellite states Italy and Naples, which were operating in the Adriatic Sea and attempting to raid into the Mediterranean Sea.

■ ZEELAND POINT, 22 MARCH 1808

The only ship of the line in the Danish navy, *Prins Christian Frederik*, under Jessen, was operating off the coast of the main Danish island of Zeeland. A British flotilla under Parker cornered the Danish ship. Two British ships of the line engaged, driving *Prins Christian Frederik* onto a sand bar. The ship was burned the following day, British casualties being 54 and Danish 143.

■ ALVOEN, 16 MAY 1808

Five small Danish-Norwegian gunboats attacked the British frigate *Tartar* in a fog, off the coast of Norway. The frigate lost Capt Bettersworth and 11 more killed and withdrew.

■ ANHOLT, 27 MARCH 1811

A Danish amphibious attack on the British-held island of Anholt off Jutland failed, with two British frigates driving off supporting Danish gunboats. The Danish landing force lost 50 killed and 638 captured; British casualties numbered 32.

■ LYNGOR, 6 JULY 1812

A British flotilla under Steward attacked and destroyed Denmark's last remaining frigate, *Najaden*, off the south-east coast of Norway. British losses were 35, Danish losses being over 110. Three surviving Danish brigs withdrew.

War of the Fifth Coalition 1809–12

■ BASQUE ROADS, 11–13 APRIL 1809

A powerful British naval squadron under Gambier attacked the French naval base at Basque Roads on the western coast of France. Four French ships of the line and a frigate were destroyed.

■ SACILE, 15–16 APRIL 1809

Archduke John with 40,000 Austrian Empire troops defeated 37,000 French and Italian troops under Eugene in present-day north-eastern Italy. Eugene had underestimated the size of John's army by half and attacked across the Livenza river, only to be badly repulsed. Austrian numerical advantage in cavalry was decisive. Eugene lost 6300 casualties, John losing 4400. Eugene then retreated to the Adige River and gathered reinforcements, later resuming the offensive.

■ ABENSBERG, 20 APRIL 1809

Napoleon, moving south, successfully crossed the Danube with 90,000 French, Bavarian and Württemberger troops in present-day southern Germany. Napoleon then defeated 80,000 Austrian Empire troops under Archduke Charles. Napoleon pinned Charles' centre, while a French corps under Lannes turned the right flank, forcing Austrian Empire forces to withdraw post-haste. Napoleon's forces lost 3000 killed and wounded in action, while inflicting 2800 Austrian Empire casualties and capturing 4000 prisoners.

■ LANDSHUT, 21 APRIL 1809

Napoleon pursued Austrian Empire forces in present-day southern Germany with 36,000 French, Bavarian and Württemberger troops. He attacked 40,000 Austrian Empire troops under Hiller at Landshut on the Isar river. Hiller fell back, setting fire to the Isar bridge. Napoleon's aide Mouton led French troops across the burning bridge, breaking into Landshut proper. Following this, Hiller withdrew. Napoleon lost 780 casualties, while inflicting 1500 and capturing 6000 prisoners.

■ RATISBON, 19–23 APRIL 1809

Ratisbon, on the Danube in present-day southern Germany, was occupied by a single French regiment and retaken by 26,000 Austrian troops under Charles. Napoleon with 37,000 French troops defeated Charles and recaptured Ratisbon.

■ ECKMÜHL, 21–22 APRIL 1809

An Austrian Imperial army under Archduke Charles attacked French Marshal Davout's force in Bavaria at Eckmühl (also spelled Eggmühl). Davout initially held with 20,000 men, while

Charles added troops to the attack, eventually totaling 40,000. Davout held against stiff odds until Napoleon sent reinforcements on 22 April. Austrian attacks were repulsed as more troops under Marshal Lefebvre and Marshal Lannes came to the aid of Davout. Napoleon's forces, including French, Bavarian and Württemberger troops, amounted to 60,000 by the end of the day and Napoleon arrived on the field in the evening. Although Charles had fresh troops who had not been in the battle, he withdrew his army in good order. Charles had lost 7000 killed and wounded, plus 5000 prisoners. Napoleon's army suffered 6000 casualties. Napoleon awarded Davout the title Prince of Eckmühl.

■ ASPERN-ESSLING, 21–22 MAY 1809

Napoleon had captured Vienna, the Austrian capital, on 13 May. However, the Austrians still did not make peace. Consequently, Napoleon prepared to cross to the north bank of the Danube river to pursue the Austrian army commanded by Archduke Charles, unaware of the true proximity and size of Charles' army.

The French built two sets of bridges; one to cross to the Danube island of Lobau and another to cross from Lobau to the northern bank, at the villages of Aspern and Essling. Charles moved 96,000 troops towards the French river crossings, a development that Napoleon had not anticipated. The French IV Corps under Massena and cavalry under Bessieres crossed the bridges during 19/20 May, an operation complicated by the fact that the Danube was in flood stage after spring rains. The French bridges were broken repeatedly by rising waters and floating debris. Additionally, Austrians upstream launched rafts to damage the bridges.

Charles attacked on the afternoon of the 21st. The 30,000 French in the bridgehead were badly outnumbered by Charles' 96,000, but held until after dark, while being reinforced by Marshal Lannes. French forces were 45,000 by pre-dawn on the morning of the 22nd and Napoleon attacked, still unaware of the size of Charles' force. Successful French attacks could not be exploited or reinforced due to the destruction of their bridges by a floating mill launched by the Austrians upstream.

The French successfully defended Aspern and Essling against Charles' attacks while the bridges were again repaired. French cavalry counter-attacked throughout the day. The bridges were repaired, but Lannes was mortally wounded and Napoleon ordered evacuation to the island of Lobau. Charles's losses were 23,400 and French losses nearly 20,000.

■ RAAB, 14 JUNE 1809

Eugene with 40,000 French and Italian troops defeated 36,000 Austrian Empire troops under Archduke John in present-day Hungary. Eugene lost 2200 casualties, inflicting losses of 3700 and capturing 2400 prisoners.

■ WAGRAM, 5–6 JULY 1809

Napoleon – having captured Vienna, but subsequently suffering a repulse at Aspern-Essling in May – had reorganized his army on Lobau Island in the Danube river, just east of Vienna. The French army, reinforced with German and Italian satellite forces, numbered nearly 190,000. Archduke Charles commanded an Austrian army of 140,000 men, positioned across the Danube on the 'Marchfeld' parade grounds to the north-east of Vienna. During the night of 4/5 July, under cover of a heavy rainstorm, Napoleon utilized newly constructed bridges on the east side of Lobau Island to cross his army over to the open country of the Marchfeld to confront Charles' army. Napoleon left behind a garrison supporting heavy artillery positioned on Lobau Island. The massive opposing forces fought tentatively on 5 July, as Napoleon's forces deployed and advanced to contact with the Austrian army.

Charles' left was partly covered by Russbach Brook, while his centre was anchored on the town of Wagram. The French had captured the town of Aderklaa, just south-west of Wagram, late on the 5th. Charles planned to attack in the morning with his right against the French left, closest to the Danube, turning the French flank and cutting them off from their bridges and Vienna.

Charles launched his attack at 04:00 on 6 July and his plan initially met with great success as the Austrians drove back the French left. The town of Aderklaa changed hands twice in attacks and counter-attacks. French Marshal Bernadotte formed his Saxon troops into attack columns, but they came under heavy fire from Austrian artillery and were routed. Napoleon personally stemmed the rout and relieved Bernadotte of command. Napoleon then ordered Marshal Massena to retake Aderklaa. Massena, recovering from earlier injuries, could no longer ride and conspicuously led his troops from a carriage drawn by four white horses. Meanwhile, the successful advance of the Austrian right was halted by intense fire from the French heavy artillery on Lobau Island.

While Charles had attacked with his right, his left came under attack by the French III Corps, commanded by Davout. Davout's forces crossed the Russbach and began a steady advance against the Austrian left. Napoleon then shifted Massena's

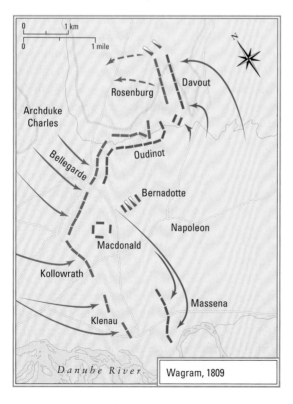

Wagram, 1809

troops to cover and stabilize the French left. Massena accomplished the difficult manoeuvre, supported by French cavalry charges launched by Napoleon to tie down the Austrians. Marshal Bessières was wounded leading these attacks. The Austrian offensive having stalled, Napoleon concentrated most of his army on the centre, while Davout continued attacks on the Austrian left.

Charles, wounded slightly, continued resistance largely on the chance that 12,000 Austrian reinforcements might arrive during the battle. Napoleon, also aware of this possibility, attacked vigorously in the centre. Napoleon's troops took Aderklaa a final time, while a French force under MacDonald formed a huge column of attack against the Austrian right centre. MacDonald advanced, covered by the fire of 112 French cannon, but in turn came under the fire of large numbers of Austrian cannon and was eventually halted by Austrian counter-attacks. By this time, Davout's attacks had driven back the Austrian left at a right angle to Charles' main line. This jeopardized the whole Austrian position and Austrian reinforcements had failed to arrive, so Charles decided to withdraw. The bloody battle had cost Austria a total of 40,000 casualties and Napoleon had lost 34,000. A truce followed a week after the battle and Austria sued for peace in October.

■ GRAND PORT, 23–26 AUGUST 1810

Duperré and Hamelin with four French vessels off the coast of Mauritius sank two British vessels and captured two more. French losses were 149, while inflicting 268 casualties and capturing 1600 prisoners.

■ LISSA, 13 MARCH 1811

British forces took the island of Lissa, off the coast of present-day Croatia, in 1807 and established it as a base in the Adriatic Sea. A French and Italian naval force of six frigates, plus supporting vessels, was assembled under Dubourdieu in order to capture the island. The British base was protected by four vessels under Hoste. Hoste arranged his ships in tight line formation, with bowsprits

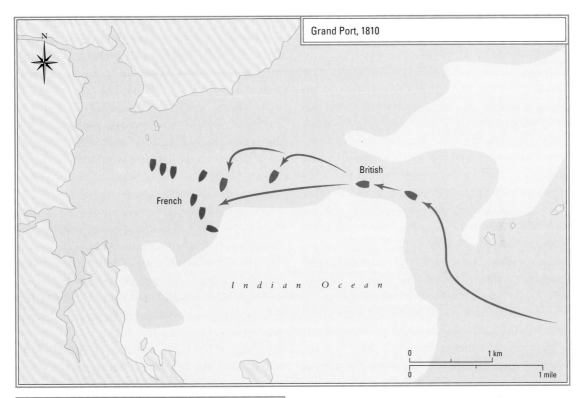

Grand Port, 1810

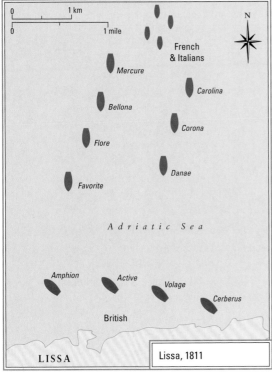

LISSA

Lissa, 1811

overhanging the sterns of each ship in front. This spoiled Dubourdieu's plan, as the French and Italian vessels attacked in two parallel columns, hoping to split Hoste's line.

Dubourdieu on *Favorite* attempted to board HMS *Amphion*, but close-range British fire wiped out the boarding parties and killed Dubourdieu. The French-Italian fleet was repulsed, losing three ships and 700 casualties, British losses being 200.

■ ACTION OF 29 NOVEMBER 1811

A British naval squadron under Maxwell intercepted a French convoy off the coast of modern-day Croatia. The British captured two ships and 300 prisoners in the action, with one French ship escaping.

■ ACTION OF 22 FEBRUARY 1812

In the Action of 22 February 1812 the French ship *Rivoli* was engaged in battle and captured by the British HMS *Victorious* under Talbot, in the northern Adriatic Sea off the coast of present-day Slovenia. French total losses were 400, British losses were 126.

Napoleon's Russian Campaign 1812

■ MOGILEV, 23 JULY 1812

Bagration with a Russian army of 46,000 attacked Davout's French I Corps of 28,000 men on the Dnieper river in present-day Belarus. Davout had been adequately forewarned and set up strong defensive positions. Of Bagration's force, only 20,000 Russians under Raevsky were effectivly engaged. Raevsky attacked gallantly, but was badly repulsed, losing over 4000 casualties. French losses were 1200. Bagration successfully disengaged and withdrew eastwards.

■ OSTROVNO, 25–27 JULY 1812

Murat, leading Napoleon's advance with 22,000 French, German and Italian troops, defeated 20,000 Russians under Ostermann-Tolstoy in present-day Belarus. Russian losses were 3800 casualties, Murat's losses numbering about 3300.

■ KLYSTITSY, 30 JULY–1 AUGUST 1812

Oudinot, commanding 23,000 French and Swiss troops, fought a bloody battle against 22,000 Russians under Wittgenstein in present-day Belarus. Oudinot withdrew, having lost over 5500 men. Russian losses were over 4500.

■ SMOLENSK, 17–18 AUGUST 1812

Napoleon's international Grande Armée had marched 644km into Russian territory, while outnumbered Russian forces withdrew in order to avoid being cut off. The Russian First West Army, under Barclay, with the Russian Second West Army, under Bagration, were in position to make a juncture at Smolensk. Napoleon's forces were already becoming depleted by hard marches and detachments, so the Russian commanders agreed to fight at Smolensk, even if only as a delaying action. Smolensk was astride the Dnieper river and had 5km of high brick walls. The combined Russian forces would number about 180,000, while Napoleon had nearly 200,000 within easy marching distance of Smolensk. A French corps under Davout, a French, Württemberger and

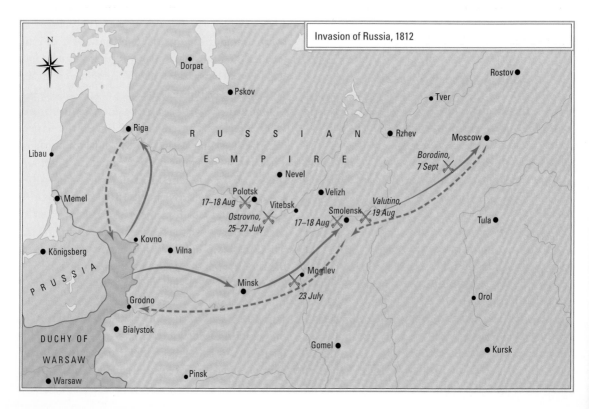

Portuguese corps under Ney and a Polish corps under Poniatowski, plus cavalry under Murat, reached the outskirts of Smolensk during 16–17 August. The Russian commanders, worried that Napoleon could cut them off from Moscow, decided that Bagration should cover Dorogobuzh, a crossing of the Dnieper 80km further east. Barclay's 150,000 men would remain in and around Smolensk.

Napoleon's forces attacked Smolensk beginning at 12:30 on the 17th, aiming for the gates. French artillery could not breach the walls, so howitzers were used to fire over them, causing the city to catch fire. Barclay began an evacuation of Smolensk at 23:00, despite the objections of subordinates. French forces entered the city on the 18th at 02:30, finding it deserted and burning. Ney crossed the Dnieper and Barclay counter-attacked, but most fighting on the 18th consisted of an artillery duel across the Dnieper. Barclay withdrew his army intact after suffering nearly 15,000 casualties. Napoleon's troops lost at least 9000.

■ POLOTSK, 17–18 AUGUST 1812

Napoleon detached portions of his international Grande Armée as he invaded Russia and sent Marshal Oudinot's II Corps, consisting of French, Swiss and Croatian troops, towards Polotsk, on the Dvina river. In support of Oudinot was Gen St Cyr commanding VI Corps, consisting of Bavarian troops.

On 17 August, Wittgenstein, commanding 28,000 Russians, attacked the positions at Polotsk. Although Oudinot and St Cyr combined had 35,000 troops in the vicinity, they were not completely concentrated. The Polota river, a tributary of the Dvina, separated the French reserves from the main line. Wittgenstein initially made his attack on the Bavarians on the right part of the line, near the village of Spas. The Bavarians held, despite suffering heavy casualties. The fighting developed all along the line. Oudinot, who had a reputation for conspicuous gallantry, was wounded badly in the shoulder, one of at least

21 wounds during his career. Unable to remain in the saddle, Oudinot notified St Cyr that he should take command. St Cyr pulled back slightly at nightfall, reorganizing the troops for action the next day. He also ordered an extra plank bridge built across the Polota.

On the morning of the 18th, St Cyr attacked suddenly, taking Wittgenstein by surprise. The Russians were driven back and the French captured seven cannon. In desperation, Wittgenstein launched a cavalry counter-attack, giving his troops a chance to rally. Wittgenstein then withdrew to positions about 32km north of Polotsk on the Drissa River. Estimates of French and Bavarian casualties vary, ranging from 2000 to 6000. Russian losses were at least 5500. St Cyr received the rank of marshal for his victory at Polotsk.

■ VALUTINO, 19 AUGUST 1812

After Napoleon's army took Smolensk in Russia, the withdrawal of the largest Russian army under Barclay only took them a few kilometres east and north-east of the city. Napoleon's French-Württemberger III Corps, commanded by Marshal Ney, ran into the Russian rearguard under Tutchkov at Valutino and attacked at 13:30. Tutchkov pulled back to better positions, while being reinforced by Cossacks and part of Barclay's army. Gen Junot, commanding Napoleon's VIII Corps, approached from the south-west, but did not engage the Russians.

Ney was reinforced by French cavalry under Murat and infantry under Gudin at 16:00. Gudin was mortally wounded in the final attacks beginning at 19:00 and the Russians were driven back by 23:30. The French had fought with 30,000 troops actually engaged in battle, the Russians fighting with 40,000, each side losing about 5000.

■ BORODINO, 7 SEPTEMBER 1812

A Russian army of 120,000 under Kutusov set up defensive positions at Borodino, 121km west of Moscow, to defend against Napoleon's Grande Armée of 130,000 troops. Napoleon's army included French, Polish, German and Italian soldiers and was complemented by 587 cannon.

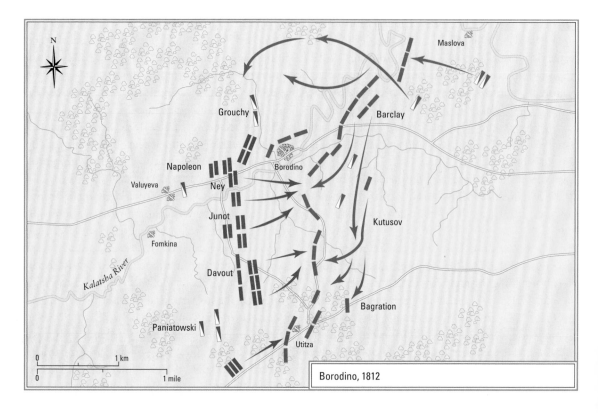

Borodino, 1812

The Russians had 640 cannon, some of which were in reserve and many of which were in defensive positions. Kutusov's right was behind the Kalatsha River, southward from the Moscova river, with part of the right centre garrisoning the town of Borodino across the Kalatsha. South of Borodino, the Russian centre and left was strengthened with a series of earthwork redoubts, to include the Great Redoubt just north of the village of Semyonovskaya and the 'Fleches'; three redoubts to the south of that village. The Russian left flank was set up in a wooded area around the village of Utitza. The Russian position overall was strong, but marred by its lengthy extent.

Napoleon's battle plans designated only a small cavalry screen north of Borodino, with the rest of the army focused against the Russian centre and left. Marshal Davout argued for a wider flanking attempt against the Russian left, despite the difficult wooded terrain there, but Napoleon rejected this idea. Poniatowski's Polish corps was to attack towards Utitza on the Russian left and Eugene's French and Italian corps were to attack Borodino in the centre. The extent to which Napoleon's ill health on the day of the battle affected his judgment and subsequent orders is a matter of much debate. Poniatowski's early-morning attack on the Russian left was slowed by the woods and French artillery was not effective at first, so was pushed further forward. Davout's corps attacked the Russian left-centre as the corps of Marshal Ney joined the attack on the northern end of the Fleches and the town of Semyonovskaya. French cavalry under Murat attacked with Davout and Ney. Eugene's corps took Borodino, but the Great Redoubt proved more difficult.

As most of Napoleon's morning attacks were on the Russian left, which was commanded by Bagration, the Russians shifted some troops away from the unthreatened right towards their beleaguered left. The Fleches changed hands several times in fierce attacks and counter-attacks. Bagration was mortally wounded and Davout was injured when his horse was killed. As more Russian troops massed on their left and centre, they came under the fire of the bulk of Napoleon's artillery and began to suffer extremely high casualties. Napoleon's assaulting troops also took heavy casualties.

Eugene's attacks against the Great Redoubt were stalled temporarily when Russian regular cavalry and Cossacks under Platov and Uvarov crossed the Kalatsha and threatened Napoleon's left. Eugene countered this move, resuming attacks on the Great Redoubt. French and Saxon cavalry attacked the Great Redoubt from the rear while infantry assaulted frontally, taking the position at 16:00. Meanwhile, the Russians were pushed back along their left, with Kutusov falling back 1000 paces to a ridgeline. Several officers had asked Napoleon to commit the Imperial Guard to ensure a complete breakthrough, but were refused.

Kutusov claimed victory, but withdrew during the night. Napoleon had won the field and went on to take Moscow a week later. One of the bloodiest Napoleonic battles, the French called the fight 'La Moscova'. The Russians lost at least 44,000 men and Napoleon's army about 30,000 soldiers.

■ TARUTINO, 18 OCTOBER 1812

Kutusov dispatched 36,000 Russians under Bennigsen to attack 26,000 French and Polish troops under Murat, about 48km south of Moscow. Russian Cossacks achieved initial surprise, driving back French cavalry outposts under Sebastiani. Murat, threatened with encirclement, was obliged to counter-attack and engage in a fighting withdrawal. Murat successfully escaped being cut off and retreated, but lost 4500 men and 38 cannon. Russian losses were over 1200.

■ MALOYAROSLAVETS, 24 OCTOBER 1812

The 20,000 French-Italian corps of Eugene fought a Russian force of 15,000, later reinforced by Kutusov with 10,000. Eugene won the field, losing 5000, while Russian losses were 6000.

■ CZASNIKI, 31 OCTOBER 1812

Marshal Victor assembled 36,000 French, Swiss and German troops against 30,000 Russians advancing under Wittgenstein in present-day Belarus. Neither side was able to engage effectively with all of their forces in the battle, the brunt of the fighting falling mostly on French II Corps. A Russian artillery bombardment was highly effective. Victor withdrew, having lost 1200 casualties. Wittgenstein, despite relatively low casualties of 400, did not pursue.

■ VYAZMA, 3 NOVEMBER 1812

Miloradovich with 26,500 Russian troops attacked a rearguard of 24,000 French, Italian and Polish troops, plus 13,000 stragglers and wounded under Davout. The rearguard lost 8000 men, Russian casualties being 1800.

■ SMOLIANI, 13–14 NOVEMBER 1812

Wittgenstein, with 30,000 Russians, repulsed 25,000 French, Swiss and German troops under Oudinot in present-day Belarus. Oudinot was unable to effectively engage all of his troops. Each side lost about 3000 casualties.

■ KRASNOI, 15–18 NOVEMBER 1812

During Napoleon's disastrous Russian Retreat, a Russian force of 80,000 under Kutusov blocked Napoleon's escape at Krasnoi. Napoleon's French army, suffering starvation and cold, included 40,000 organized troops and 40,000 stragglers, stretching back over many kilometres. Napoleon fought his way through over the course of four days, but lost almost 40,000 troops, including captured stragglers. Kutusov lost 5000 at most, but failed to destroy Napoleon's army.

■ BEREZINA RIVER, 26–29 NOVEMBER 1812

Napoleon's international army, suffering massive casualties due to starvation and cold during the Russian Retreat, was trapped by Russian forces at the Berezina river, near Borisov. Kutusov commanded 65,000 Russians. Napoleon had 49,000 organized troops, plus 40,000 stragglers. Napoleon feinted a river crossing at Borisov, but built bridges 13km upstream, enabling escape. Each side lost 15,000 in combats.

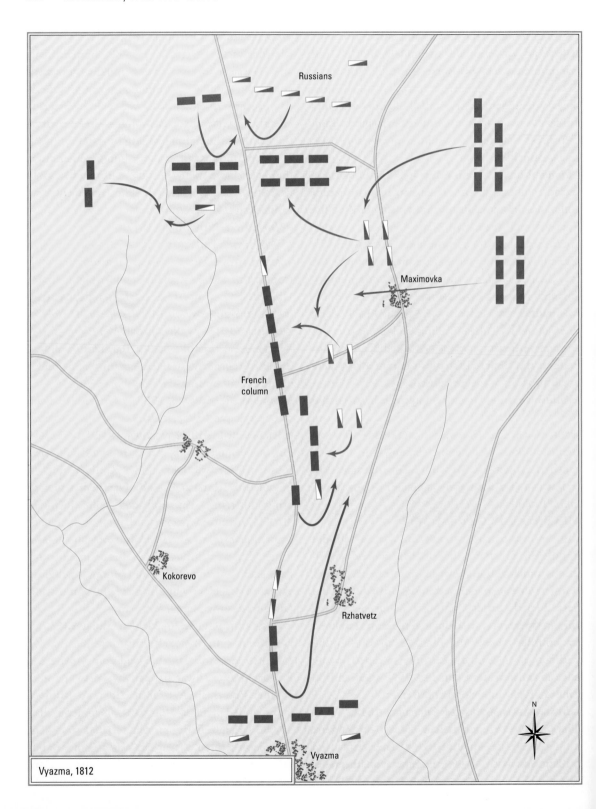

Russians

Maximovka

French
column

Kokorevo

Rzhatvetz

Vyazma

Vyazma, 1812

N

The Peninsular War 1808–14

■ Mutiny of Aranjuez, 17 March 1808

Spanish troops staged a coup against Charles IV of Spain and his unpopular chief minister, Manuel de Godoy. After Godoy's capture, Charles was forced to abdicate in favour of his son, who became Ferdinand VII.

■ El Bruc, 6 June & 14 June 1808

On 6 June, a force of 2000 Spanish regular troops and militia commanded by Gen Franch de Villafranca halted the advance of Gen Schwarz' 3800 French regulars at the pass of El Bruc, inflicting almost 1000 casualties for the loss of barely 100 men. On 14 June, the Spanish forces held the position against a further French attack, inflicting over 350 casualties for the loss of 65 men.

■ Cabezón, 12 June 1808

Gen Cuesta's 5000 men (largely ill-trained Spanish militia) attacked a French force of 9000 men commanded by Gen Lasalle. The veteran French cavalry broke Cuesta's forces, inflicting almost 1000 casualties for the loss of 50 men.

■ The Sieges of Saragossa, 15 June–13 August 1808 & 20 December 1808–20 February 1809

A Spanish garrison of 6500 under Gen Palafox held Saragossa against assaults by Gen Verdier's army of 9500 men. The French were repulsed after prolonged street fighting and abandoned the siege after sustaining 3500 casualties. Spanish losses totalled 5000.

In the second siege, Marshal Moncey's 44,000 men forced the surrender of Palafox' garrison of 32,400 after two months of fierce fighting. French casualties were 10,000, but Spanish military and civilian losses totalled 54,000.

■ Valencia, 24–26 June 1808

Marshal Moncey's 9000-strong army made several unsuccessful attempts to assault and take Valencia, which was held by a Spanish garrison of 19,000 men (1500 regulars, 6500 militia and 11,000 armed civilians). French casualties totalled 1100 men.

■ Medina del Rio Seco, 14 July 1808

Gen Cuesta commanding 21,000 infantry, 600 cavalry and 20 guns split his forces, posting a detachment under Gen Blake to his right front, but separated from him by more than a kilometre of virtually undefended ground.

Marshal Bessières with 12,200 infantry, 1200 cavalry and 40 guns seized the opportunity to defeat each part of the Spanish army in turn, attacking Blake's isolated forces, while sending a division to prevent Cuesta from intervening. He sent his cavalry into the gap between the two halves of the Spanish army, while concentrating his efforts against Blake's men, who broke and fled west across the River Sequillo.

Bessières then had to face an attack by Cuesta, which overran a French artillery battery before being routed by close-range musketry and a determined counter-attack. Spanish losses totalled over 3000 men and 13 guns, compared to barely 500 French casualties.

■ Bailén, 16–19 July 1808

Gen Dupont's Corps of 20,000 men was trapped at Bailén by a Spanish army of 35,000 under Gen Castaños. Dupont surrendered his entire Corps after confused fighting in which the Spaniards sustained almost 1000 casualties.

■ Roliça, 17 August 1808

Sir Arthur Wellesley with an Anglo-Portuguese army totalling 15,000 men attacked and defeated a French detachment of almost 5000 men commanded by Count Delaborde, inflicting a total of 700 casualties for the loss of just under 500 men.

■ Blockade of Barcelona, 20 August–17 December 1808

The French garrison of Barcelona under Gen Duhesme was blockaded by Gen Vives's Spanish forces totalling 30,000 men. The blockade was lifted by the victory of a relief force under Gen St Cyr at Cardadeu.

■ Vimeiro, 21 August 1808

Marshal Junot commanding the 13,000-strong French 'Army of Portugal' was defeated by Sir

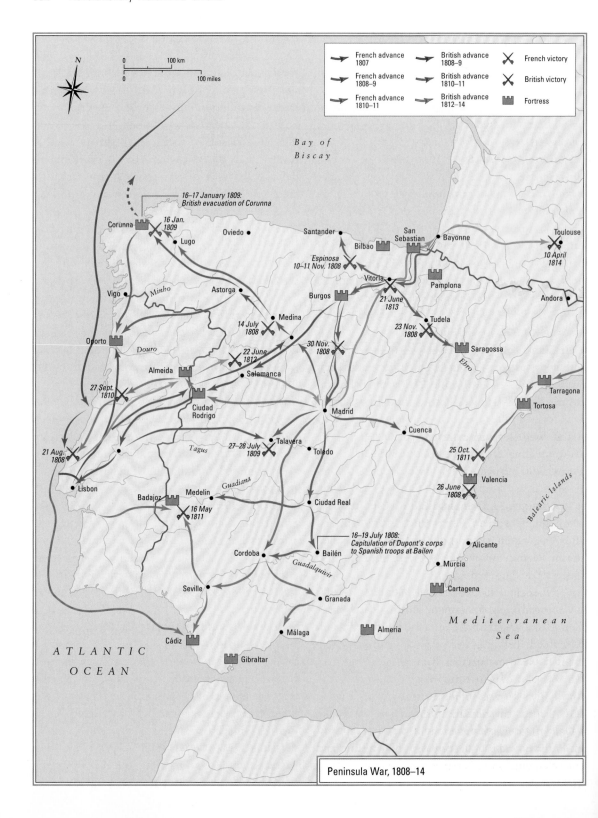

N

0   100 km

0   100 miles

French advance 1807	British advance 1808–9	French victory
French advance 1808–9	British advance 1810–11	British victory
French advance 1810–11	British advance 1812–14	Fortress

Bay of Biscay

16–17 January 1809: British evacuation of Corunna

Corunna
16 Jan. 1809
Lugo
Oviedo
Santander
San Sebastian
Bayonne
Toulouse
10 April 1814

Bilbao

Espinosa 10–11 Nov. 1808

Vitoria
21 June 1813
Pamplona
Andora

Vigo
Minho
Astorga
Burgos
23 Nov. 1808
Tudela

14 July 1808
Medina
Saragossa

Oporto
Douro
22 June 1812
30 Nov. 1808

Almeida
Salamanca

27 Sept. 1810

Ciudad Rodrigo
Madrid
Tarragona
Tortosa

Cuenca

21 Aug. 1808
27–28 July 1809
Talavera
Toledo
25 Oct. 1811

Tagus

Lisbon
26 June 1808
Valencia
Balearic Islands

Medelin
Guadiana

Badajoz
16 May 1811
Ciudad Real

16–19 July 1808: Capitulation of Dupont's corps to Spanish troops at Bailén

Alicante

Cordoba
Bailén
Murcia

Guadalquivir

Seville
Cartagena

Granada

Mediterranean Sea

Cádiz
Málaga
Almeria

Gibraltar

ATLANTIC OCEAN

Peninsula War, 1808–14

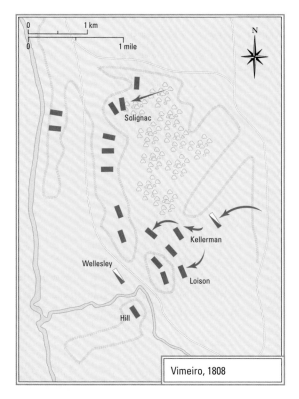

Vimeiro, 1808

Arthur Wellesley with a stronger Anglo-Portuguese army totalling 18,700 men. The French inflicted almost 700 casualties, but lost 3000 men and 13 guns.

■ PANCORBO, 31 OCTOBER 1808

Marshal Lefebvre's IV Corps totalling 24,000 men and 36 guns attacked and defeated the 19,000-strong Spanish Army of Galicia commanded by Gen Blake. The Spanish lost at least 600 men, while French casualties totalled 300.

■ VALMASEDA, 5 NOVEMBER 1808

Gen Blake's Spanish Army of Galicia had been reinforced, bringing its strength up to 24,000 men. Blake drew part of Marshal Lefebvre's IV Corps into a trap, in which Gen Villatte's 12,000-strong division was subjected to a surprise attack and forced to retreat. Although surrounded, Villatte refused to surrender, formed his troops into squares and fought his way out of the Spanish encirclement, losing 300 prisoners and one gun in the process.

■ BURGOS (GAMONAL), 10 NOVEMBER 1808

Marshal Soult's army of 18,000 infantry and 6500 cavalry was advancing on Burgos, the base of a 9000-strong Spanish army commanded by the Conde de Belveder. Incredibly, Belveder left Burgos, where he would at least have had some protection from the city's defences and advanced to the village of Gamonal, where he took up a weak position on an open plain. Soult decided to attack immediately, rather than to wait for his two remaining infantry divisions to reach the battlefield. His 5000 cavalry charged the Spanish right and centre, while the French infantry advanced through the woods to attack Belveder's left flank. Although elements of the Spanish Royal Guard and Walloon regiments fought a fierce rearguard action, the bulk of the raw, ill-trained Spanish army broke, losing 2500 killed and wounded, plus 900 prisoners. French casualties were no more than 200.

■ ESPINOSA, 10–11 NOVEMBER 1808

In this two-day engagement in November 1808 Gen Blake's 23,000-strong Army of Galicia was defeated by the 22,000 men of Marshal Victor's Corps. Victor was unable to make a breakthrough until 11 November, inflicting 3000 casualties for the loss of 1200 men.

■ TUDELA, 23 NOVEMBER 1808

Marshal Lannes' 31,000-strong III Corps defeated an over-extended Spanish force of 19,000 men under Gen Castaños, which was defending the line of the River Ebro. Lannes inflicted 4000 casualties for the loss of 650 men.

■ SOMOSIERRA, 30 NOVEMBER 1808

Gen San Juan deployed his 9000 Spanish infantry and 16 guns in strong positions in the Somosierra pass, blocking Napoleon's advance on Madrid. Napoleon had 45,000 men, but was unable to exploit his numerical superiority in such difficult terrain.

The French infantry attempted to outflank the Spanish defences, but were only able to make slow progress. Napoleon became impatient and ordered his Polish Chevaux-Légers to charge the Spanish artillery, which was firing down the pass. Despite intense fire, the Poles overran all four of the batteries, but were pushed back from the fourth battery on the crest of the ridge by a determined counter-attack. The situation was restored by a charge from the emperor's escort of Guard Chasseurs á Cheval, which succeeded in recapturing the guns. The disheartened Spanish troops abandoned their positions and fled back to Madrid, having lost 250 men and 3000 prisoners to the French.

■ SAHAGÚN, 21 DECEMBER 1808

Lord Paget's 400 men (10th and 15th Hussars) defeated a force of 800 French cavalry under Gen Debelle. The hussars inflicted 20 casualties and took over 300 prisoners for the loss of 25 men.

■ BENAVENTE, 29 DECEMBER 1808

At Benavente Gen Lefebvre-Desnouettes' 600-strong detachment of the Imperial Guard's Chasseurs á Cheval was defeated by a British cavalry force of similar size under Lord Paget. The French lost 128 men, with 50 British casualties.

■ CASTELLÓN, 1 JANUARY 1809

A 500-strong French battalion was attacked by a larger Spanish force under Gen Lazán. The French withdrew, but were trapped by a Spanish detachment, which blocked their line of retreat and lost almost 400 men.

■ UCLÉS, 13 JANUARY 1809

Marshal Victor's 16,000-strong IV Corps defeated an over-extended Spanish force of 11,000 men under Gen Venegas, which was defending the line of a ridge at Uclés. Victor inflicted 8000 casualties for the loss of 200 men.

■ CORUNNA, 16 JANUARY 1809

In late 1808, Gen Sir John Moore led a British army of 25,500 men into Spain to attack the French armies' lines of communication. Napoleon's arrival with reinforcements brought the number of French troops in Spain to over 250,000 men, which inflicted a succession of defeats on the Spanish armies. The isolated British force was compelled to retreat to Corunna for evacuation

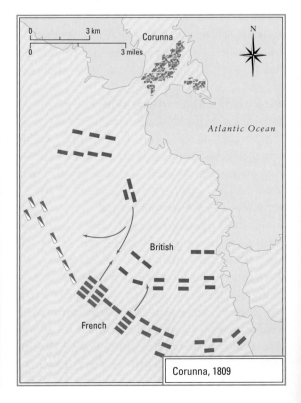

Somosierra, 1808

Corunna, 1809

by sea, pursued by Marshal Soult's Corps. Moore arrived at Corunna with 15,000 men on 11 January, but the delayed arrival of transport vessels gave time for Soult to attack with his 20,000 men. The village of Elvina formed a key part of the British position and was the focus of fierce fighting. Although it changed hands several times, the French were finally repelled with the loss of 2000 men. British casualties totalled roughly 2000, including Moore, who was mortally wounded during the action.

■ Villafranca, 17 March 1809

A force of 1500 Spanish troops commanded by José de Mendizábal attacked the 1000-strong French garrison of Villafranca, which retreated to the castle. The garrison surrendered when threatened with bombardment by a captured 12-pounder gun.

■ Cuidad-Real, 27 March 1809

The Conde de Cartaojal's 19,000-strong Spanish Corps defending the line of the River Guadiana was attacked and defeated by a French force of 12,000 men under Gen Sebastiani. Spanish casualties totalled 2000 killed and wounded.

■ First Porto, 28 March 1809

The 23,500 men of Marshal Soult's II Corps stormed Porto, inflicting 10,000 casualties on the 24,000-strong Portuguese defenders (5000 regulars, 10,000 militia and 9000 armed civilians). The French lost no more than 2100 killed and wounded.

■ Medellin, 28 March 1809

Marshal Victor's force of 17,500 men was attacked by Gen Cuesta's 23,000-strong Spanish Army of Estremadura. The Spanish were badly defeated with the loss of 10,000 men, while French casualties were no more than 1000.

■ Siege of Gerona, 6 May 6–12 Dec 1809

Gen Alvarez' 5600-strong Spanish garrison of Gerona was besieged by Marshal Augereau with 35,000 men. The city only surrendered after more than seven months, despite suffering a massive bombardment by 40 artillery batteries firing 80,000 rounds.

■ Second Porto, 12 May 1809

Sir Arthur Wellesley's 20,000-strong army attacked Porto, which was held by Marshal Soult's garrison of 11,200 men. Soult had destroyed the bridges over the River Douro, but Portuguese civilians ferried British infantry across the river in wine barges. These troops held a seminary against repeated French assaults. Soult was forced to withdraw as civilians ferried more troops across, losing 2100 men (300 killed and wounded, 1800 prisoners). British casualties totalled 125.

■ Alcañiz, 23 May 1809

Gen Suchet commanding an under-strength III Corps of just over 8000 men, attacked a 9000-strong Spanish force under Gen Blake, which was holding a strong position based on three hills around the town of Alcañiz. Suchet's main attack on the centre of the Spanish line was smashed by steady musketry and artillery fire, forcing him to retreat with the loss of 800 men. The Spanish had sustained only 300 casualties.

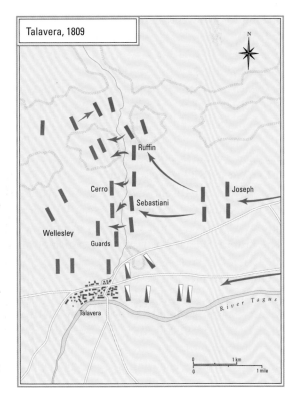

Talavera, 1809

■ **MARIA, 15 JUNE 1809**

A 14,000-strong Spanish army under Gen Blake was defeated by Gen Suchet with 8300 men. French losses were around 800 men, but Spanish casualties were 4000 men, plus 2000 deserters.

■ **TALAVERA, 27–28 JULY 1809**

Having driven Marshal Soult's forces from Portugal, Gen Sir Arthur Wellesley's 20,000-strong army advanced into Spain to join 33,000 Spanish troops under Gen Cuesta. They marched up the Tagus valley to Talavera, where they encountered a French force of 46,000 men under the nominal command of Joseph Bonaparte (In practice, the army was commanded by Marshal Jourdan.)

The raw Spanish troops held the right of the Allied line, while the British contingent held the more vulnerable left, including the key hill of Cerro de Medellin, which was almost taken by the French in a surprise attack on the night of 27/28 July.

Marshal Jourdan launched a further series of unsuccessful attacks on the British lines throughout 28 July, before withdrawing to block another Spanish force advancing on Madrid. Allied losses probably totalled 6500 men, while the French sustained 7200 casualties.

■ **ALMONACID, 11 AUGUST 1809**

A French force of 14,000 troops commanded by Gen Sébastiani defeated an over-extended Spanish army of 23,000 men under Gen Venegas. The French inflicted 3300 casualties and took 2000 prisoners for the loss of 2400 men.

■ **TAMAMES, 18 OCTOBER 1809**

The Duque del Parque's 21,500-strong Spanish army defeated Gen Marchand's weak VI Corps of only 11,000 men near the village of Tamames. The Spanish inflicted at least 1300 casualties for the loss of 670 men.

■ **OCAÑA, 19 NOVEMBER 1809**

Gen Aréizaga's 56,000-strong Army of La Mancha was intercepted near Madrid by Marshal Soult's force of 46,000 men. The Spanish army was shattered, sustaining a massive 18,000 casualties, while French losses were 2000 killed and wounded.

■ **ASTORGA, 21 APRIL–22 MARCH 1810**

The 2700-strong Spanish garrison of Astorga was besieged by Gen Junot's force of 12,000 men. The garrison surrendered after the town's defences were breached, having lost 160 killed and wounded. The French sustained 560 casualties.

■ **ALMEIDA, 25 JULY–27 AUGUST 1810**

Col Cox' 5000-strong Anglo-Portuguese garrison of Almeida was besieged by Marshal Masséna with 16,000 men. The fortress was forced to surrender after a French shell detonated the main magazine, killing and wounding 900 of the garrison.

■ **BUSACO, 27 SEPTEMBER 1810**

Wellington occupied the heights of Busaco (a 16km-long ridge near Luso in Portugal) with an Anglo-Portuguese force of 50,000 men (26,000 British and 24,000 Portuguese), where he was subjected to a series of attacks by Marshal Masséna's 60,000-strong army. Wellington had deployed his men on the reverse slope of the ridge, where they were largely hidden from French reconnaissance and were also virtually immune to fire from Masséna's artillery. The French assaults were made by Reynier's II Corps and Ney's VI Corps, both of which attacked in columns. While these formations allowed a rapid advance over difficult terrain, Wellington's well-trained men proved that they were highly vulnerable to close-range musketry and artillery fire. Every French attack was defeated after fierce fighting; Masséna inflicted a total of 1250 casualties, but was forced to concede defeat having lost 4500 men.

■ **FUENGIROLA, 15 OCTOBER 1810**

A 3500-strong British force commanded by MGen Lord Blayney landed near Fuengirola, intending to make a surprise attack on the weak French garrison of Málaga. He was joined by 1000 Spanish guerrillas, but discovered that Fuengirola's medieval fortress, the Castillo de Sohail, was garrisoned by 100 men of the Duchy of Warsaw's 4th Infantry Regiment. The garrison's commander, Capt Franciszek Młokosiewicz, refused to surrender and beat off an initial assault on the castle. Młokosiewicz was reinforced by about 300 men from the nearby Polish garrisons of Mijas and Alhaurín who had been alerted by the sound of the British artillery bombardment. Blayney was surprised and captured in a confused melee, after which his men hurriedly retreated to the beaches from which they were evacuated to Gibraltar. The Poles lost 120 men, but inflicted over 300 casualties on the Allied forces.

■ GEBORA, 19 FEBRUARY 1811

Marshals Soult and Mortier with only 7000 men attacked and defeated the 12,000-strong Spanish Army of Extremadura under Gen Mendizabal near Badajoz. Soult inflicted 5000 casualties for the loss of no more than 400 men.

■ BARROSA, 5 MARCH 1811

An Anglo-Spanish army of 15,000 men under Gen Manuel la Peña and LGen Sir Thomas Graham defeated Marshal Victor's force of 10,000 men. French casualties were 2400, while the Allies lost an estimated 1600 men.

■ ALMEIDA, 14 APRIL–10 MAY 1811

The 1400-strong French garrison of Almeida commanded by Brig Brenier was besieged by Wellington with an Anglo-Portuguese army of 13,000 men. Lacking siege artillery, Wellington was forced to blockade the town in an attempt to starve out the garrison. However, Brenier set delayed-action demolition charges in the fortifications and successfully broke out during the night of 10/11 May, eventually reaching French lines with the loss of only 360 men.

■ FUENTES DE OÑORO, 3–6 MAY 1811

The 46,000-strong French Army of Portugal commanded by Marshal Masséna was attempting to raise the Allied siege of Almeida when it was intercepted by Wellington's Anglo-Portuguese army of 36,000 men. Wellington deployed his forces along a line extending south from the ruins of Fort Concepcion to the village of Fuentes de Oñoro.

On 3 May, Masséna made repeated unsuccessful assaults on the village. The next day, both sides held their positions, while probing for weak points in the enemy lines. The French discovered that the Allied right flank was weakly held and, on 5 May, Masséna attacked this sector as well as launching renewed assaults on Fuentes de Oñoro. Although the French threatened to make a decisive breakthrough, all their attacks were eventually repulsed and Masséna was finally forced to withdraw with the loss of 2500 men to Wellington's 1500.

The 5th and 6th Divisions were stationed north of the village on the western heights of the ravine, through which flowed the River Dos Casas. The 1st, 3rd, 7th and Light Divisions, as well as Ashworth's Portuguese Brigade, held the high ground behind the village, while the village itself was garrisoned by 1800 light infantry, who were supported by 460 men of the 2/83rd. Further south, two battalions held Poço Velho, while Julian Sanchez's guerrillas occupied Nave de Haver.

In the early afternoon of 3 May, Masséna sent all ten battalions of Ferey's Division into a direct assault against Fuentes de Oñoro. Crossing the Dos Casas under heavy fire, the French forced their way uphill through the maze of alleyways in the village, reaching the church before being driven back by three battalions of the 1st Division. After being reinforced by four battalions from Marchand's Division, the French attacked again, but failed to regain a foothold on the western side of the stream. The casualties in the day's fighting amounted to 652 French and 259 British and Portuguese.

■ ALBUERA, 16 MAY 1811

An Allied army of 35,000 men under Gen Beresford intercepted Marshal Soult's 24,000-strong force at Albuera. Soult opened the battle with a feint attack on Albuera by Godinot's brigade supported by cavalry and artillery. Behind Godinot, Werle's brigade and two cavalry brigades threatened to attack Blake. Soult's real attack began when French cavalry, who were supported by the 19 infantry battalions of Girard and Gazan's divisions, moved against the Allied right, scattering Loy's cavalry.

To counter Soult's advance, Beresford ordered Blake to form a new line facing south, but, concerned at the threat posed by Werle's brigade, Blake only redeployed Zayas's division. Meanwhile, Beresford ordered Stewart's 2nd Division to support Blake, its place behind Albuera being taken by Hamilton's Portuguese division.

Zayas's men held off the French assault while the 2nd Division came up. Stewart had just ordered Colborne's brigade to attack the French left flank when a thunderstorm broke over the battlefield, making musketry almost impossible. Under cover of driving rain, Polish lancers charged the exposed flank of Colborne's brigade, which was deployed in line, virtually destroying three of its four battalions. Zayas's hard-pressed men were relieved by Hoghton's brigade of Stewart's division, which then fought a fierce action against Girard and Gazan's divisions.

Cole's division advanced against the French left. After beating off cavalry attacks, it fought a 20-minute action against Werle's brigade, which was subsequently forced to retreat. With the Soult's right flank now coming under fire from Abercrombie's brigade, the French assault disintegrated.

After four hours, the fighting ended in torrential rain. French losses are generally accepted to have totalled 8000 men, while the Allies sustained 6000 casualties (3500 of which were suffered by Colborne's, Hoghton's and Myer's brigades).

■ **Usagre, 25 May 1811**

A 2300-strong Allied cavalry force under MGen Lumley attacked and defeated 3500 French cavalry commanded by MGen Latour-Maubourg. inflicting almost 330 French casualties.

■ **Arroyo dos Molinos, 28 October 1811**

An Allied force of 9000 British, Portuguese and Spanish troops under MGen Rowland Hill trapped and defeated Gen Girard's division of 6000 men. Allied casualties were no more than 80, while Girard lost 2400 men.

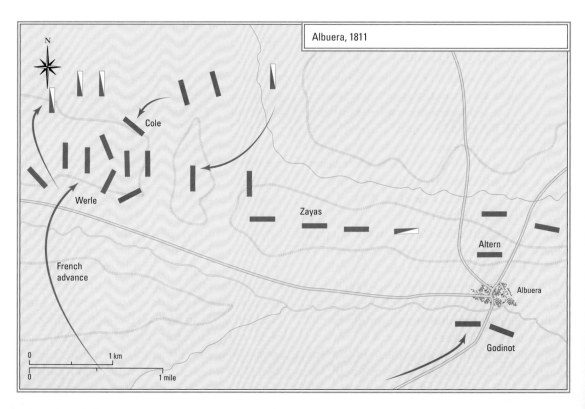

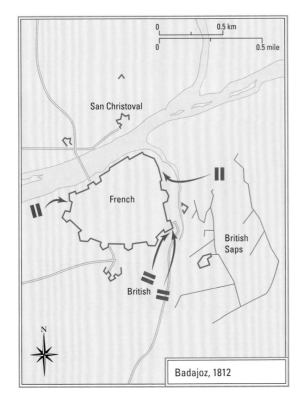

San Christoval

French

British
Saps

British

N

Badajoz, 1812

been reinforced with parts of the surrounding area being flooded and vulnerable sectors of the defences mined. Wellington's Anglo-Portuguese army totalled 27,000 men, but was hampered by the late arrival of its siege artillery, which left little time to thoroughly breach the town's defences before Marshal Soult could be expected with sufficient forces to raise the siege. Acutely conscious of the pressure to take the town quickly, Wellington ordered an assault on 6 April as soon as three practicable breaches had been made in the defences. The main assaults were all decimated by intense artillery fire and musketry, coupled with showers of grenades and kegs of gunpowder fitted with short fuses. Small groups of attackers managed to scramble up to the breaches, but were stopped by a mass of obstacles, including chevaux de frise (logs fitted with multiple wooden spikes or sword blades). In less than two hours, 2000 men were killed or wounded in repeated attacks on the main breach.

Finally, what had been intended as a diversionary attack on the castle by Picton's 3rd Division succeeded in breaking in and linking up with the 5th Division, which had also unexpectedly managed to scale the walls. As Allied troops poured into Badajoz, the garrison's survivors retreated to Fort San Christoval just north of the city, where they surrendered the following morning. The Allied troops then went on a drink-fuelled rampage for 72 hours before order was restored. Wellington's casualties totalled 4800, while the French lost 1500 killed and wounded, plus 3500 prisoners.

■ CIUDAD RODRIGO, 7–20 JANUARY 1812

Wellington's Anglo-Portuguese army of 10,700 men besieged Ciudad Rodrigo, which was held by a 2000-strong French garrison commanded by Brig Barrié. The besiegers deployed a total of 36 heavy guns, which fired over 9500 rounds to create two practicable breaches. These were successfully stormed during the night of 19/20 January, after which the garrison surrendered with the loss of 529 killed and wounded. Total Allied casualties were almost 1700.

■ CADIZ, 5 FEBRUARY–24 AUGUST 1812

The city's Allied garrison of almost 22,000 men was besieged by French armies under Marshals Victor and Soult totalling 60,000 men. Wellington's victory at Salamanca in July 1812 forced the French to abandon the siege.

■ BADAJOZ, 16 MARCH–6 APRIL 1812

By the spring of 1812, MGen Philippon's garrison of 5000 men had made Badajoz one of the most powerful fortresses in Spain. The town's walls had

■ VILLAGARCIA (LLERENA), 11 APRIL 1812

LGen Sir Stapleton Cotton's 1400-strong cavalry force trapped and defeated Brig Lallemand's 1100 hussars and dragoons in difficult terrain, after a premature attack that almost ended in disaster. Lallemand lost 53 killed and wounded, plus 136 prisoners, while British casualties totalled 51.

■ ALMARAZ, 18–19 MAY 1812

LGen Sir Rowland Hill led a 6000-strong Anglo-Portuguese force in a successful raid against the

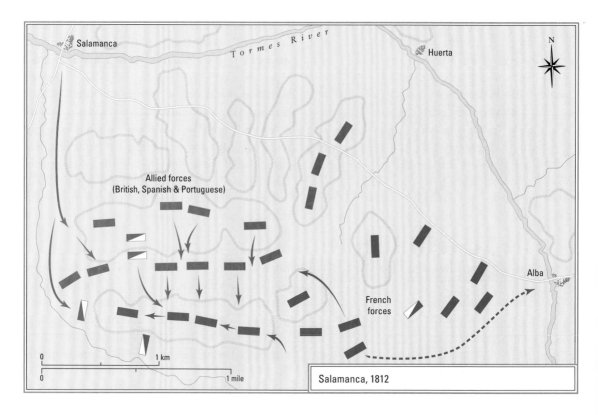

Salamanca, 1812

fortified French pontoon bridge over the River Tagus at Almaraz. The bridge formed a key link in the lines of communication between Marshal Soult's Army of the South and Marshal Marmont's Army of Portugal. Its destruction allowed Wellington to concentrate his forces to beat Marmont at Salamanca without fear of interference by Soult.

■ **MAGUILLA, 11 JUNE 1812**

A 700-strong British cavalry brigade commanded by the incompetent Brig John Slade was defeated with the loss of almost 160 men by two regiments of French dragoons of roughly equal strength under Brig Charles Lallemand.

■ **SALAMANCA, 22 JULY 1812**

As Wellington's Anglo-Portuguese army of almost 52,000 men advanced deeper into Spain, it was faced by an increasingly formidable Army of Portugal commanded by Marshal Marmont. By mid-July, reinforcements had brought Marmont's strength up to something in excess of 49,500

men and the two commanders were cautiously manoeuvring for position.

Throughout the morning of 22 July, the two armies were marching with sight of each other as had become commonplace. Wellington was close to ordering a retreat into Portugal as he had learned from intercepted French dispatches that Joseph Bonaparte had promised to bring a further 13,000 men to reinforce Marmont. Nonetheless, he continued to closely watch the French movements for any mistake that could be exploited. Suddenly, it became clear that Marmont had become over-confident; despite being unable to see the entire battlefield, he misinterpreted Allied movements and began an outflanking manoeuvre to cut off what he thought was their line of retreat. This was just the opportunity that Wellington had been waiting for and he immediately ordered Packenham's 3rd Division and D'Urban's Portuguese cavalry to attack the leading French division, which was surprised and routed with the loss of its commander, Gen Thomieres. Leith's 5th Division and Bradford's Portuguese brigade were launched against Maucune's division, which had formed squares on spotting advancing Allied cavalry. The French were decimated by the superior firepower of Leith's infantry who were deployed in line and, as they began to retreat, they were shattered by the charge of MGen Le Marchant's heavy cavalry. The next French division, commanded by Gen Brennier, was exhausted from rapid marches in the blazing heat and Le Marchant led his dragoons in a further charge, breaking Brennier's disordered first line. The second line had time to form squares and repelled the British cavalry, mortally wounding Le Marchant.

The French response to Wellington's attacks was slow as Marmont and his deputy, Gen Bonet, were both wounded by Allied artillery fire early in the action and there was a delay while Gen Clausel was able to assume command. Clausel acted quickly in a bold attempt to restore the situation. His division and that of Gen Bonet, supported by fire from a 40-gun 'grand battery', repulsed attacks by Cole's 4th Division and Pack's Portuguese brigade. The two French divisions and Gen Boyer's 1500 dragoons then launched a counter-attack against Cole's exhausted 4th Division, which was only contained by committing the 1st and 7th Divisions.

As the rest of the French army streamed away, Ferey's division fought a determined delaying action, repelling initial attacks by Clinton's 6th Division, until it too was broken by a concentrated artillery bombardment and a further assault. Foy's division covered the French retreat towards the bridge at Alba de Tormes, which should have been blocked by fortifications held by one of Major General D'Espansa's Spanish battalions. However, D'Espansa had withdrawn the unit without warning and the remnants of Marmont's army were able to escape.

Wellington's army had sustained 5200 casualties, but Marmont had lost 6000 killed and wounded, plus 7000 prisoners to the British. The victory greatly enhanced Wellington's reputation among his peers; Gen Foy wrote: 'It brings up Lord Wellington's reputation almost to the level of that of Marlborough. Up to this day we knew his prudence, his eye for choosing good positions, and the skill with which he used them. But at Salamanca he has shown himself a great and able master of manoeuvring.'

◼ GARCIA HERNANDEZ, 23 JULY 1812

Gen Foy's division was caught by a force of 1770 British cavalry under MGen Bock. As Bock's men charged, one of the French infantry squares was struck by a wounded horse, creating a gap that led to the collapse of the formation. On seeing this, a second square also broke and ran. Shortly after, Foy withdrew, having lost 200 men plus 1400 prisoners. Bock's casualties totalled 120 killed and wounded.

◼ MAJADAHONDA, 11 AUGUST 1812

MGen Treilliard's French cavalry division surprised and defeated Brig d'Urban's Portuguese cavalry brigade, which routed, causing the loss of 180 men. As Allied reinforcements came into action, Treilliard was forced to withdraw with the loss of 200 men.

◼ SIEGE OF BURGOS, 19 SEP–21 OCT 1812

Wellington's victory at Salamanca forced the French to evacuate Madrid and allowed him to advance towards the French frontier. His first objective was the castle at Burgos, which had been repaired and garrisoned by 2000 men under Brig Dubreton.

The siege began on 19 September, but was hampered by totally inadequate heavy artillery (three siege guns, with 1300 rounds and five howitzers). The lack of engineers was equally serious; Wellington had just five engineer officers and eight sappers. Although some parts of the outer defences were taken, progress was slowed by the garrison's fierce resistance and heavy rain, which flooded the besiegers' trenches. The news that Gen Souham's 53,000-strong French Army of Portugal was moving on Burgos forced Wellington to raise

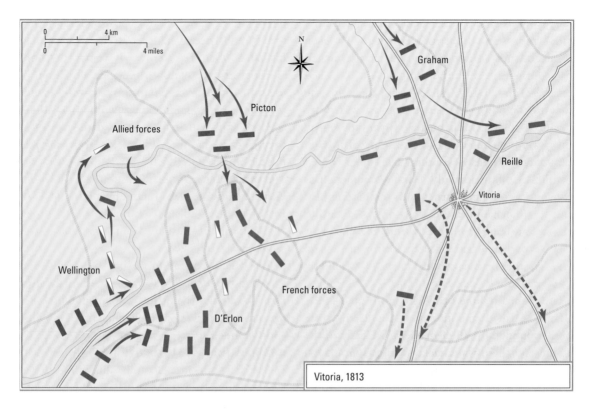

Vitoria, 1813

the siege on 21 October. Allied casualties totalled 2100, while the French lost over 600 killed and wounded, plus 60 prisoners.

■ CASTALLA, 13 APRIL 1813

LGen Sir John Murray's Allied force of 18,200 men, including British, Spanish and Italian contingents, was attacked by Marshal Suchet's 13,200-strong Army of Valencia and Aragon in Castalla, near Valencia, Spain. Murray deployed his forces in a strong position along the crest of a ridge, with their right flank protected by a swollen stream. Here he repulsed all the French attacks, inflicting 1300 casualties on Suchet's men. Allied losses were 440 killed and wounded.

■ TARRAGONA, 3–11 JUNE 1813

In June 1813 LGen Murray's 23,000-strong Anglo-Spanish force besieged the city of Tarragona, which was held by a French garrison of just 1600 men under Brig Bertoletti. Murray panicked at the approach of small French relief forces and withdrew, abandoning his artillery.

■ VITORIA, 21 JUNE 1813

Wellington's Allied army of 79,000 men attacked Joseph Bonaparte's 66,000-strong force west of the town of Vitoria. The French position was protected by the Heights of Puebla to the south and to the west and north by the River Zadorra, but none of the bridges had been destroyed. Joseph deployed his forces in three parallel lines facing west, the expected direction of attack.

Wellington's mutually supporting assault columns gradually forced the first two French lines back towards Vitoria throughout the clashes of the morning. The third line had to be hastily redeployed to counter an Allied flank attack, which threatened Vitoria from the north and cut the road to Bayonne. As Allied pressure increased during the afternoon, the French forces steadily retreated under cover of fire from their well-handled artillery, until they finally broke with the loss of 8000 men. Allied casualties totalled almost 5200 soldiers.

■ San Sebastián, 7 July–8 September 1813

Wellington's 18,000-strong Anglo-Portuguese army besieged San Sebastián, which was held by a French garrison of 3600 men under Brig Rey with 97 guns. After Allied siege guns battered a breach in the walls, an assault was launched on 25 July, but was repulsed with heavy losses. During the next few weeks, siege operations were effectively suspended as the Allies concentrated on halting Marshal Soult's offensive in the battle of the Pyrenees. The garrison made full use of the respite to reinforce the defences, building a new wall behind the hastily repaired breach.

The siege was resumed on 8 August and Allied heavy artillery opened fire against the repaired section of the defences on 26 August. After five days, the Allied forces had created a breach almost 90m wide in the south-east corner, as well as a smaller breach in the east wall. The British 5th Division repeatedly attacked the main breach, while Bradford's Portuguese brigade assaulted the east wall. Both attempts failed due to devastating close range musketry and artillery fire, which forced the surviving attackers to take cover amongst the rubble. In desperation, the siege guns concentrated their fire against the new inner wall, despite the risks to the Allied troops who were pinned down only a few metres from the target. This bombardment quickly breached the wall and renewed assaults broke through into the town.

Rey and the surviving members of the garrison retreated to the castle, which finally surrendered on 8 September after a bombardment by 61 guns and mortars. French casualties during the siege amounted to some 1400 men, while a further 1300 were taken prisoner when the castle fell. The Allies lost 2400 killed, wounded and missing during the assault.

■ Pyrenees, 25 July–2 August 1813

Marshal Soult's 79,000-strong army advanced into the Pyrenees to raise the sieges of Pamplona and San Sebastián. Wellington's 62,000 men halted the French at the cost of 7000 casualties and Soult withdrew having lost 12,500 men.

■ Maya, 25 July 1813

LGen Stewart's 7000-strong force was attacked by 21,000 men under Gen d'Erlon, which pushed back the British troops. D'Erlon retreated when British reinforcements arrived, having inflicted over 1300 casualties for the loss of 2000 men.

■ Roncesvalles, 25 July 1813

Gen Reille's army of 40,000 men attacked and defeated MGen Cole's 11,000-strong Anglo-Portuguese force defending the Roncesvalles Pass. Cole's force delayed Reille's advance for 11 hours, inflicting 200 casualties for the loss of 450 men.

■ Sorauren, 28–30 July 1813

Marshal Soult's 30,000-strong army attacked Wellington's 24,000 men. A series of French attacks were repulsed and Wellington counter-attacked on 30 July, forcing Soult to retreat with the loss of 4000 men. Allied casualties totalled 2600.

■ San Marcial, 31 August 1813

Marshal Soult made a final attempt to break through to San Sebastián, concentrating 55,000 men for the offensive. He was opposed by the 16,000 men of Gen Freire's Spanish Army of Galicia, which was deployed in a strong position on the San Marcial heights. The French made repeated attacks in column, all of which were defeated, meaning that Soult was forced to retreat after losing 4000 men. Spanish casualties totalled 2500.

■ Vera, 31 August 1813

The 5000 men of Gen Vandermaesen's division were trapped by a 100-strong detachment of the 95th Rifles under Capt Cadoux holding a bridge at Vera. The French finally broke through after losing over 230 men.

■ Bidassoa, 7 October 1813

Elements of Wellington's 89,000-strong Allied army defeated Marshal Soult's 62,000 men and established a bridgehead across the River Bidassoa, becoming the first Allied troops to enter France. Losses on both sides were equal, numbering 1600 men each.

■ NIVELLE, 10 NOVEMBER 1813

Wellington's 89,000-strong Allied army successfully assaulted a series of fortified positions defended by 60,000 men under Marshal Soult. Several garrisons abandoned their positions to avoid the prospect being cut off and Allied casualties were only 2450 compared to the more punishing losses of 4350 French.

■ NIVE, 9–13 DECEMBER 1813

Elements of Wellington's 64,000-strong Allied army were attacked by Marshal Soult's force of 62,000 men near Bayonne. All the French attacks were repulsed with the loss of 6000 men, while Allied casualties totalled 5000.

■ ORTHEZ, 27 FEBRUARY 1814

Marshal Soult's 36,000-strong force defending the hills north of Orthez was attacked and defeated by Wellington's veteran Anglo-Portuguese army of 44,000 men. The French inflicted just under 2100 casualties on Wellington's force for the loss of almost 4000 men.

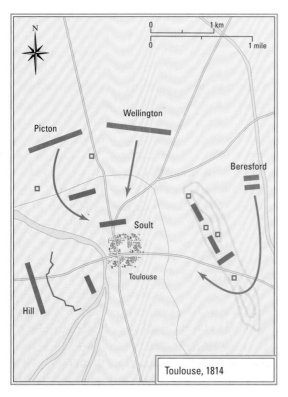

Toulouse, 1814

■ TOULOUSE, 10 APRIL 1814

Wellington's 50,000-strong Allied army attacked Toulouse, which was defended by Marshal Soult with some 42,000 men.

While recognizing the strength of the defences, Wellington saw no realistic alternative to storming the Heights of Calvinet overlooking the city from the east, which would make the defenders' position untenable. Marshal Beresford's 4th and 6th Divisions were given the unenviable task of moving against the Heights under heavy enemy fire for 3km, while Gen Hill would simultaneously attack the city's western suburbs in a diversionary assault.

Beresford's attack was slowed by thick mud, but made good progress, defeating a divisional-strength French counter-attack and establishing a foothold on the Heights. This allowed artillery to be brought up to deal with the French field defences and Soult was forced to withdraw with the loss of over 3200 men. Allied casualties exceeded 4600.

■ BAYONNE, 14 APRIL 1814

MGen Thouvenot's 14,000-strong garrison of Bayonne attacked an Allied force of 19,500 men under LGen Hope, which was besieging the town. The French were defeated, having lost 900 men, but inflicted over 830 Allied casualties.

Spanish Reconquest of Santo Domingo 1808

■ PALO HINCADO, 7 NOVEMBER 1808

This was the first action fought in the Spanish reconquest of Santo Domingo. Gen Juan Sánchez Ramírez's 2000 Dominican and Puerto Rican troops defeated a French detachment of 600 men commanded by Gen Louis Ferrand.

■ SANTO DOMINGO, 7 NOV 1808–6 JULY 1809

Gen Juan Sánchez Ramírez's 1850 Dominican and Puerto Rican troops, supported by a British expeditionary force, besieged and captured the city of Santo Domingo, which was held by a French garrison of 2000 men under Brig Dubarquier.

Napoleonic Wars outside the Peninsular Theatre 1809–12

■ **CAPTURE OF CAYENNE, 6–14 JANUARY 1809**

British ships supported a Portuguese invasion of French Guiana, employing colonial infantry and naval infantry recruited and organized in Brazil. A small French garrison and militia surrendered the capital of Cayenne.

■ **ACTION OF 22 JANUARY 1809**

The French frigate *Topaze* was engaged and captured by a British squadron off the coast of Guadeloupe in the Caribbean. Most of the crew were captured, although a few escaped and swam to shore.

■ **MARTINIQUE, 30 JANUARY–24 FEBRUARY 1809**

A British expedition of 29 ships and 10,000 troops landed on the French island of Martinique in the Caribbean. The garrison of 4900 soldiers surrendered after successful British sieges and bombardments.

■ **ACTION OF 10 FEBRUARY 1809**

The French frigate *Junon* was intercepted, engaged and captured in the Caribbean by a British naval squadron. French killed and wounded numbered 130, including Capt Rousseau, mortally wounded. British losses totaled 40 men.

■ **TROUDE'S EXPEDITION TO THE CARIBBEAN, FEBRUARY–MAY 1809**

Troude commanded a French naval squadron, which sailed from France in a futile attempt to supply Martinique in the Caribbean Sea. British forces captured Martinique before Troude could intervene. Withdrawing eastwards to Isle des Saintes, Troude was pursued by British naval forces under Cochrane. French ship of the line *Hautpoult* was captured, Troude's remaining force reaching France in May. Two frigates left behind by Troude were also later captured.

■ **WALCHEREN EXPEDITION, 1809**

A British army of 40,000 under Chatham was transported by 600 ships to invade the Netherlands, held by French forces. Walcheren Island was captured and used as a base of operations, but a severe malaria epidemic soon devastated British forces and there was little fighting. From August to December, more than 4000 British troops died and 12,000 were disabled by sickness. The expedition was withdrawn in December.

■ **ACTION OF 6 APRIL 1809**

The French frigate *Niéman* was intercepted, engaged and captured off the northern coast of Spain by a British naval squadron of three frigates under Seymour. French casualties were 110, British losses being 46.

■ **RASZYN, 19 APRIL 1809**

Poniatowski, with 14,000 Duchy of Warsaw Polish troops, defeated an Austrian Empire army of 29,000 under Archduke Ferdinand in modern-day Poland. Ferdinand lost 2300 casualties, Polish losses being nearly 1400 in total.

■ **TEUGEN-HAUSEN, 19 APRIL 1809**

Davout with 28,000 French troops defeated 28,000 Austrian Empire troops under Archduke Charles, fighting along a wooded ridge in present-day southern Germany. French losses were 4800 and Austrian Empire losses were 5000.

■ **ABENSBERG, 20 APRIL, 1809**

An Austrian army of 42,000, advancing into Bavaria under the Archduke Charles, was first halted and then defeated by a French and German army numbering 52,000 under the Emperor Napoleon in a series of running engagements. Napoleon mistakenly sent his main forces to pursue the retreating Austrian left, allowing the bulk of Charle's forces to escape. The French success gave Napoleon the initiative and led to the fall of Vienna.

■ **EBERSBERG, 3 MAY 1809**

Masséna with 22,000 French troops attacked 22,000 Austrian Empire troops under Hiller at Ebersberg, Austria. Taking the town in fierce street fighting, Masséna lost 3600 casualties, with Hiller losing over 6200, including prisoners.

■ **KOCK, 5 MAY 1809**

Berek Joselewicz, commanding his squadron of Polish Jews, was killed in a cavalry clash in present-day Poland, while fighting an Austrian Empire regiment of hussars during the Austrian invasion of the Duchy of Warsaw.

BERGISEL, 25 MAY–1 NOVEMBER 1809

Bergisel, a hill south of Innsbruck, Austria, was the site of four battles by Tyrolese insurrectionists who ultimately failed against Bavarian and French forces. Small forces of Austrian regulars assisted the Tyrolese.

■ **ACTION OF 31 MAY 1809**

The French frigate *Caroline*, commanded by Féretier, intercepted a lightly armed British merchant convoy in the Bay of Bengal. Two of the merchant ships were overtaken and captured, with one ship escaping.

■ **GEFREES, 8 JULY 1809**

Kienmayer, with 15,000 Austrian and Brunswick troops, repulsed a French and Bavarian force under Junot in present-day Germany near the Czech border. Junot suffered 2000 casualties, Kienmayer losing 400.

■ **ZNAIM, 10–11 JULY 1809**

After victory at Wagram, Napoleon sent Marmont to intercept the retreat of the Austrian Empire army under Charles, moving northwards. Marmont,

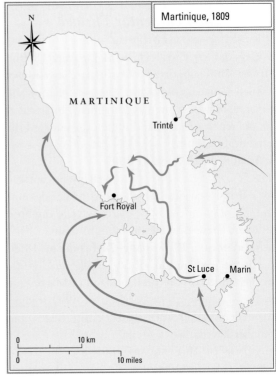

Martinique, 1809

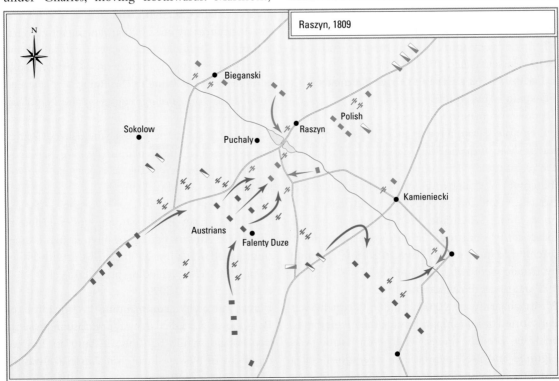

Raszyn, 1809

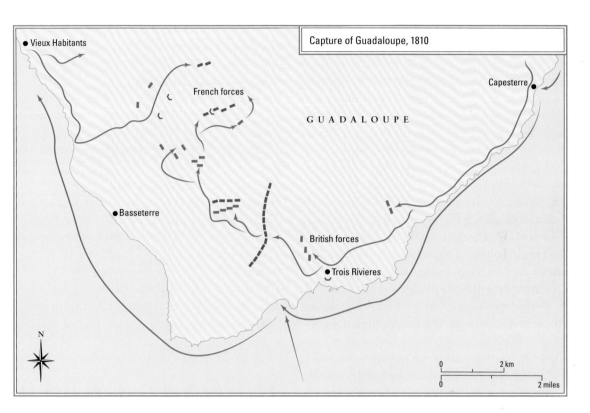

Capture of Guadaloupe, 1810

initially with 10,000 French troops, engaged 47,000 men present under Charles near Znaim in the present-day Czech Republic. Marmont was reinforced to 30,000 during the battle, with Napoleon arriving during the second day. Charles proposed an armistice, which Napoleon accepted. French losses were 3100, Charles losing 5300.

■ POLISH-AUSTRIAN WAR, 10 APRIL–14 OCTOBER 1809

The Polish Duchy of Warsaw, allied with Napoleon, resisted an Austrian invasion force of 35,000 led by Archduke Ferdinand. Active Polish forces under Poniatowski initially numbered only 15,000. Reinforced by 1350 Saxons, Poniatowski fought a successful delaying action at Raszyn on 19 April against Ferdinand's army, inflicting nearly 2500 casualties, while losing 1500. Despite this, Ferdinand's advantage in numbers dictated retreat and Warsaw fell.

Poniatowski subsequently manoeuvred southwards against Ferdinand's communications and invaded ethnic Polish territory claimed by the Austrian Empire in Galicia. Ferdinand evacuated Warsaw and pursued, but was unable to engage Polish forces successfully. Poniatowski took Lublin and captured Krakow in July. Polish forces grew to 45,000 troops by October. With Napoleon's victory against Austria's main army in the Wagram Campaign around Vienna, the Treaty of Schönbrunn included territorial gains for the Duchy of Warsaw in Galicia.

■ ACTION OF 18 NOVEMBER 1809

Hamelin, commanding a small French naval squadron, intercepted a convoy of lightly armed merchant ships of the British East India Company in the Bay of Bengal, capturing all three vessels.

■ ROQUEBERT'S EXPEDITION TO THE CARIBBEAN, 13 DECEMBER 1809

Roquebert commanded a small French squadron sent to supply Guadeloupe in the Caribbean. Roquebert destroyed the British ship *Junon*, leaving two ships at Guadeloupe then returning to France.

■ **MAURITIUS CAMPAIGN, 1809–11**

In 1809, modern-day Mauritius in the Indian Ocean included the French-held Isle Bonaparte and Isle de France. French naval raiders used the islands as bases and British naval and amphibious forces launched expeditions to eliminate these. After a severe setback at Grand Port, the British took the islands by the end of 1810. Not realizing the islands had fallen, a small French relief squadron approached in February 1811 and was repulsed.

■ **CAPTURE OF GUADELOUPE, 28 JAN–6 FEB 1810**

A British fleet landed 6700 troops and captured the French island of Guadeloupe in the Caribbean, the last French colony in the region. British casualties were 300, the French losing over 500.

■ **ACTION OF 3 JULY 1810**

A French naval squadron of three ships under Duperré operating in the Indian Ocean north-west of Madagascar engaged a British East India Company convoy of three ships, capturing two.

■ **CAPTURE OF ISLE BONAPARTE, 7–9 JULY 1810**

A British flotilla landed 3650 troops on Isle Bonaparte, present-day Réunion Island. A French regular force of 500-plus militia proved ineffective and the island was captured, along with one ship.

■ **ACTION OF 13 SEPTEMBER 1810**

Two French frigates temporarily captured a British frigate off the coast of Mauritius, but were driven off by three British ships. British losses were 163 and a merchant brig captured, French losses being 55.

■ **ACTION OF 18 SEPTEMBER 1810**

A British frigate off the coast of Mauritius was temporarily captured by two French vessels, but then rescued by another British frigate, a French frigate being captured at the end of the action.

■ **ISLE DE FRANCE, 29 NOV–3 DEC 1810**

A British fleet under Bertie successfully landed nearly 7000 soldiers, sepoys, marines and sailors under Abercromby on Isle de France, in present-day Mauritius, in order to eliminate the French base in the Indian Ocean. Governor Charles Decaen commanded the French garrison of 1300, plus 10,000 untrained militia. After a battle on 1 December, Decaen negotiated surrender on terms providing the repatriation of his regular troops to France.

■ **ACTION OF 29 NOVEMBER 1811**

Four British vessels under Maxwell intercepted a French convoy in the Adriatic Sea, with 60 British casualties and 100 French casualties being lost in the fight. The British captured two vessels and 300 prisoners.

■ **ACTION OF 3 FEBRUARY 1812**

British frigate HMS *Southampton* defeated a pirate flotilla loyal to renegade Haitian leader Borgella off the coast of Haiti. A large pirate frigate was captured and later turned over to Haitian authorities.

■ **ACTION OF 22 FEBRUARY 1812**

Also called the Battle of Pirano, two British vessels under Talbot captured a French ship of the line and destroyed a brig in the northern Adriatic Sea off the coast of present day Slovenia.

War of the Sixth Coalition 1812–14

■ **MÖCKERN, 5 APRIL–16 OCTOBER 1813**

Möckern in northern Germany was the site of two clashes in 1813. Wittgenstein with 32,000 Russian and Prussian troops fought skirmishes with 30,000 French under Eugene on 5 April. Eugene retreated, consolidating at Magdeburg. Möckern was part of the battlefield of Leipzig on 16 October, being the French northern flank under Marmont, attacked by Russians and Prussians under Blücher. French losses here were 7000, Coalition 9000.

■ **LÜTZEN, 2 MAY 1813**

A Coalition force of 73,000 including Russians under Wittgenstein and Prussians under Blücher, attacked a French force of 45,000 under Marshal Ney positioned south of the Saxon town of Lützen, at 11:45. Russian Tsar Alexander I and Prussian King Frederick William III were also present. Ney's badly outnumbered force held while suffering severe casualties until Napoleon arrived from the north with reinforcements. Napoleon arrived at 14:30, just as Ney's force

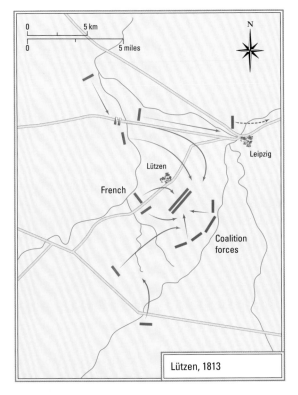

Lützen, 1813

at 18:30 in the centre with the Imperial Guard, as other French forces attacked all along the line. The Coalition army retreated, its centre beaten and its flanks threatened.

A lack of sufficient cavalry hampered Napoleon's pursuit. French casualties were 20,000, with the heaviest losses from Ney's force. The Coalition lost 18,000, their Chief-of-Staff Scharnhorst later dying of an infected wound.

■ BAUTZEN, 20–21 MAY 1813

Napoleon pursued the Russian and Prussian Coalition army eastwards through Saxony towards Prussia after his victory at Lützen on 2 May. The Coalition army of 96,000 took up defensive positions along the Spree River at Bautzen, their left centre anchored on the town, using heights along the river for the rest of the line. Tsar Alexander I was nominal Coalition commander, with Wittgenstein as field commander. Napoleon approached their strong positions with 115,000 men, intending to pin the Coalition, while Marshal Ney would come down on their right from the north with 85,000 more troops. This ambitious plan depended upon the timely arrival of Ney's forces, a difficult task as Ney had to march and concentrate five spread-out corps.

On 20 May, Napoleon used massed artillery to cover his advance across the Spree, as his troops built bridges and crossed the river under heavy Coalition fire. Napoleon's troops took Bautzen, and Wittgenstein pulled back to another line east of the Spree. Ney's forces had only begun to reach the battlefield as night fell. The Coalition army was intact and in position, but still vulnerable to Ney's flanking attack from the north.

On the 21st, there was intense fighting on the southern part of the battlefield. Napoleon hoped this would allow Ney's enveloping attack to develop, but Ney's forces came up piecemeal and uncoordinated. This allowed the Coalition forces to escape from the trap. Napoleon attacked in the centre with the Imperial Guard and Wittgenstein began an organized withdrawal before all of Ney's forces reached the battlefield. A combinaton of a

was falling back in disorder under the pressure of Coalition attacks. Napoleon personally rallied and led Ney's troops back into line, coming under enemy fire as he did so.

French, Italian and Württemberger forces under Marmont and Bertrand had marched on the battlefield from the west and additional forces under Macdonald and Latour-Maubourg approached from the north-east. The arrival of French forces from converging directions forced the Coalition army to form a convex line in order to protect their flanks. Napoleon's reinforcements eventually brought his numbers to 110,000. The Coalition was reinforced by 7000 Russian Guards and Wittgenstein committed a Prussian corps under Yorck to attack in the centre. Napoleon countered with a brigade of Young Guard. The villages of Gross Görschen and Rahna changed hands several times in attacks and counter-attacks, until Napoleon focused the fire of 70 cannon in the centre. Napoleon then attacked rainstorm and insufficient cavalry prevented French pursuit. Battle casualties totalled roughly 20,000 for each side.

■ LUCKAU, 6 JUNE 1813

Bülow, commanding 15,800 Russians and Prussians, defeated Oudinot leading 20,000 French troops in present-day northern Germany. Oudinot engaged only part of his force and withdrew, losing 2200 casualties, Coalition losses being 800.

■ GROSSBEEREN, 23 AUGUST 1813

Berndadotte commanding 80,000 Russians and Prussians defeated Oudinot commanding 60,000 French and Saxon troops in present-day northern Germany. Bernadotte lost 1000 casualties, Oudinot losing 4500, including Saxon prisoners who joined Prussian forces.

■ KATZBACH, 26 AUGUST 1813

MacDonald leading 80,000 French was defeated by 114,000 Russians and Prussians under Blücher in present-day western Poland. MacDonald was caught against the Katzbach river. French losses were 15,000, Blücher losing 4000.

■ DRESDEN, 26–27 AUGUST 1813

The Coalition Army of Bohemia with 158,000 Austrians, Russians and Prussians under Schwarzenberg attacked French Marshal St Cyr's force of 45,000 in fortified positions in Dresden, Saxony. St Cyr held while being reinforced by Napoleon. Napoleon arrived, building his forces to 120,000, while Schwarzenberg reinforced to 170,000. Napoleon attacked out of Dresden and drove back the Coalition forces, which lost 38,000. Napoleon's losses were 10,000.

■ KULM-PRIESTEN, 29–30 AUGUST 1813

Vandamme with 32,000 French troops was surrounded by 54,000 Russians, Prussians and Austrians in present-day Czech Republic. Part of Vandamme's force broke through. Vandamme was captured, losing 15,000 casualties, Coalition losses being 11,000.

■ DENNEWITZ, 6 SEPTEMBER 1813

A serious action between the French and Allied European armies. Ney detached Bertrand's division to mask Dennewitz, while he marched his main army along the road to Berlin. Bertrand was supposed to demonstrate and then move on, but he delayed so long that the action was joined and the French lost 10,000 men.

■ ALTENBURG, 28 SEPTEMBER 1813

Theilmann, commanding a mounted German Friekorps and Russian cavalry, raided behind French lines in northern Germany. French cavalry detachments and a brigade of Baden infantry were taken by surprise, with many captured.

■ LEIPZIG, 16–29 OCTOBER 1813

Also called the Battle of the Nations, the battle of Leipzig was the largest and bloodiest fought during the Napoleonic Wars, remaining the largest battle fought in modern European history until World War I.

Napoleon concentrated 177,000 French, Polish, German and Italian troops around the Saxon city of Leipzig on the Elster river. The Coalition Army of Bohemia with 205,000 Austrians and Russians under Schwarzenberg approached from the south-west on 16 October. Tsar Alexander I and Prussian King Frederick William III accompanied Schwarzenberg. The Prussian and Russian Army of Silesia under Blücher approached from the north-west with 54,000 troops, but had to march a greater distance. Consequently, Napoleon decided to attack Schwarzenberg, hoping to defeat the Army of Bohemia before Blücher could deploy all his forces. The Coalition armies planned to attack on all fronts and Schwarzenberg's offensive was underway before Napoleon attacked.

The Coalition attacks were repulsed and Napoleon attacked Schwarzenberg after 11:00. Much of the fighting revolved around the town of Wachau, near Schwarzenberg's left centre. French cavalry achieved breakthroughs in the centre, but Coalition cavalry counter-attacked. Blücher began attacking from the north at 14:00, resisted by Marmont's French corps and Polish forces under Dombrowski. Blücher's forces took the town of Möckern along the Elster towards evening and fighting ended for the 16th.

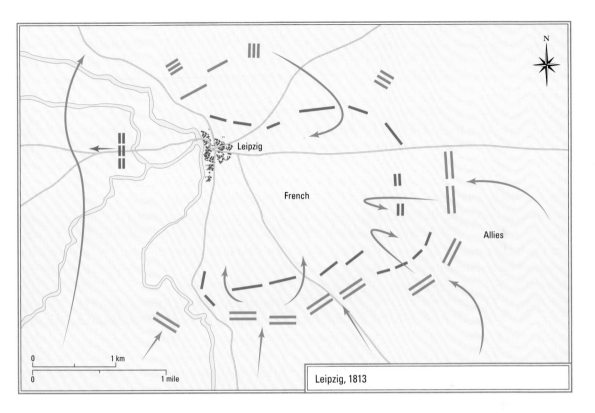

Leipzig

French

Allies

N

0   1 km

0   1 mile

Leipzig, 1813

Both sides agreed to a one-day ceasefire on 17 October. Meanwhile, Coalition forces were reinforced significantly, with Blücher's army reaching 125,000. Bennigsen reinforced Schwarzenberg with 70,000 troops. In addition, the Coalition Army of the North under Bernadotte with 85,000 Prussians, Russians and Swedes approached from the north-east. Napoleon received 18,000 reinforcements under Reynier, so his total forces numbered 195,000 with 700 cannon. However, these huge forces were badly outnumbered by the even more massive Coalition totals of 410,000, plus 1500 cannon. Making these numbers worse for Napoleon was the defection of his German satellite forces, some during the night of the 17th, while others would defect the next day.

For the battle of 18 October, Napoleon set up defensive positions in a large circle around Leipzig, securing a line of retreat westwards across the Elster river. The Coalition forces attacked all along the line, losing heavily in direct assaults on French positions in various Leipzig suburbs. Coalition attacks failed to make significant gains until about 16:30, when 4000 Saxon troops defected on the field of battle. Superior Coalition numbers began to push back the French.

Napoleon decided to withdraw and began to cross over the Elster. The withdrawal and the battle continued on the morning of the 19th. Polish troops under Poniatowski and French troops under Macdonald and Reynier were designated as the rearguard in a tight perimeter around Leipzig. The bridge across the Elster was prepared for gunpowder demolition to slow Coalition pursuit after the rearguard had crossed.

Engineer Col Montfort left a corporal in charge of the bridge. As the battle pushed into Leipzig, the bridge was blown up prematurely, a colossal mistake that left the rearguard trapped. Marshal Poniatowski was shot as he attempted to cross the Elster on horseback and died in the river, while Marshal Macdonald was able to swim across. The

Coalition lost 54,000 troops during the battle and Napoleon had lost 38,000 before the bridge incident cost him the loss of 30,000 more, turning the battle into a decisive defeat.

■ **HANAU, 30–31 OCTOBER 1813**

Napoleon, leading 20,000 French troops, broke through a blocking force of 43,000 Bavarians and Austrians under Wrede in present-day western Germany, inflicting 4000 casualties and taking 5000 prisoners. French losses were over 3000.

■ **BORNHOVED, 7 DECEMBER 1813**

Cederström, leading a Swedish cavalry regiment, defeated a Danish and Polish rearguard in far northern present-day Germany, inflicting 275 casualties and capturing some cannons. Swedish losses were 76 killed or wounded.

■ **SEHESTED, 10 DECEMBER 1813**

Pursued by Russian, Prussian and Swedish forces in northern Germany, 9500 Danes under Prince Frederik turned on the Coalition advance guard of 5000 and defeated it, inflicting 1220 casualties. Danish losses were 550.

■ **BRIENNE, 29 JANUARY 1814**

Napoleon with 30,000 men attacked Blücher's invading Coalition army of Prussians and Russians at Brienne in France, before he could fully concentrate his 53,000 troops and advance on Paris. Napoleon led the final attacks personally, as Coalition troops were driven back and Blücher was nearly captured. French RAdm Baste was killed while leading Young Guard troops. Coalition losses were 4000 and French losses were 3000.

■ **LA ROTHIÈRE, 1 FEBRUARY 1814**

Napoleon's 40,000 troops were outnumbered and defeated by 110,000 Prussians, Russians, Bavarians and Württembergers under Blücher. Napoleon fell back through Troyes, France. Each side lost about 6000 men.

■ **MINCIO, 8 FEBRUARY 1814**

Bellegarde with an Austrian Empire army of 35,000 invaded present-day north-eastern Italy. Thinking Eugene was still withdrawing his Italian and French forces, Bellegarde began crossing the Mincio river. Eugene, with 34,000 troops, had in fact halted and sent a flanking force to the west bank of the Mincio. Thus fighting raged on both sides of the river. Bellegarde withdrew, losing 4000 casualties, Eugene losing over 2500.

■ **CHAMPAUBERT-MONTMIRAIL, 10–11 FEB 1814**

Napoleon with 30,000 French troops defeated 40,000 invading Russians and Prussians under Olssufiev, Sacken and Yorck in Champagne. Coalition casualties were over 6000, including 2000 taken prisoner. Napoleon lost 2600.

■ **MONTEREAU, 18 FEBRUARY 1814**

Napoleon defeated 15,000 Austrians and Württembergers at the junction of the rivers Yonne and Seine, securing key bridges. Coalition losses were 5000 and Napoleon lost 2500 of roughly 12,000 engaged.

■ **BAR-SUR-AUBE, 27 FEBRUARY 1814**

Schwarzenberg, with 35,000 Austrian, Bavarian and Russian troops, defeated 18,000 French troops under MacDonald on the French Aube River. MacDonald, his forces split by the river, lost 3000 casualties, Schwarzenberg losing 2000.

■ **CRAONNE, 7 MARCH 1814**

Napoleon with 30,000 French troops attacked 30,000 Russians of Blücher's Army of Silesia. Blücher's forces were in good defensive positions on a plateau near Craonne, France. French Marshal Victor was wounded leading an attack by a corps of Napoleon's Young Guard. The corps advanced despite heavy casualties (including the 14th Voltigeur Regiment losing 650 of 920 soldiers and 30 of 33 officers). French Gen Grouchy was also wounded while leading his cavalry towards the Russian right flank.

Unsuccessful thus far, Napoleon gathered together a battery of 88 cannon and directed their fire at a corps of Russians under Woronzoff, posted in the Coalition centre. This proved decisive and Blücher ordered the troops at Craonne to fall back 10km to his main position at Laon. Blücher lost 5000 troops, while Napoleon lost 5400.

■ **LAON, 9–10 MARCH 1814**

Napoleon, commanding 47,000 French troops, unsuccessfully attacked 85,000 Prussian and

Russian troops under Blücher north of the Aisne river in France. French losses were 6000, Coalition losses being 2000.

■ REIMS, 13 MARCH 1814

Napoleon with 10,000 French troops surprised a Coalition force of 14,500 Russians and Prussians under St Priest in Reims, France. The French attacked at night, Gen Ségur leading a charge through the streets of the city itself. The Coalition force was completely routed, losing 6000 casualties, including the commander, St Priest, who was killed by a cannonball during the fight. French losses were about 700 men.

■ FÈRE-CHAMPENOISE, 25 MARCH 1814

French detachments of 20,000 men 121km east of Paris were overwhelmed and driven back by 200,000 Russian, Prussian and Austrian invading Coalition forces under Schwarzenberg and Blücher.

■ PARIS, 30 MARCH 1814

Marmont and Mortier with 42,000 French troops defended Paris against 110,000 Russian, Prussian and Austrian troops under Schwarzenberg and Blücher. Each side lost 9000 casualties. Paris was surrendered on 31 March.

■ ARCIS-SUR-AUBE, 20–21 APRIL 1814

Napoleon with 23,000 French troops moved eastwards along the south bank of the Aube river in Champagne towards Schwarzenberg's Army of Bohemia, which included Austrians, Bavarians and Russians. Schwarzenberg's invading army had been withdrawing, but then turned to attack. The French held throughout the 20th despite desperate odds, with Napoleon not yet realizing that Schwarzenberg had nearly 90,000 troops within marching distance of the battlefield. Napoleon exposed himself to great danger during the battle, having one horse killed under him by a howitzer shell. On the morning of the 21st, Napoleon received 10,000 reinforcements, but was still outnumbered nearly three to one. French reconnaissance finally confirmed that Schwarzenberg was concentrated. Consequently,

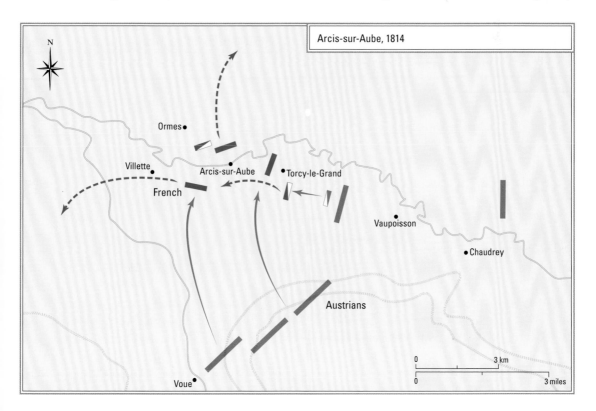

Arcis-sur-Aube, 1814

Napoleon fought a rearguard action, crossed to the north of the Aube, then blew up the bridge. Each army had lost about 3000 men.

■ **SWEDISH–NORWEGIAN NAVAL CONFLICT, JULY–AUGUST 1814**

Sweden invaded Norway in response to Norwegian attempts at political independence. Norway had only seven brigs and 150 small gunboats, while Sweden had five ships of the line supported by 70 gunboats. A Swedish amphibious force attacked the island of Hvaler off the south-eastern Norwegian coast near the Oslo Fjord. Norwegian gunboats withdrew, successfully evacuating troops from the island. A second Swedish amphibious landing was made on the coast.

Six Days' Campaign February 1814

■ **CHAMPAUBERT, 10 FEBRUARY 1814**

During the Coalition invasion of France, Napoleon leading 30,000 French troops surprised

and attacked a Russian corps of 4000 under Olssufiev, camping near a forest at Champubert. The Russians lost 1700 killed and wounded, with 1000 taken prisoner and nine cannon captured by the French. Olssufiev was captured by a French cavalry recruit. French losses were under 600 killed or wounded, out of 6000 actually engaged.

■ **MONTMIRAIL, 11 FEBRUARY 1814**

Napoleon with 30,000 French troops fought 36,000 Coalition Prussians and Russians under Sacken and Yorck near Montmirail, France. The battle initially commenced with advance guards, each side receiving reinforcements during the fighting. Napoleon's troops, including Imperial Guard regiments, drove the Coalition forces from the field. Coalition losses included 3000 killed and wounded. French forces captured 1000 prisoners, 17 cannon and six flags. French losses were 2000.

■ **CHATEAU-THIERY, 12 FEBRUARY 1814**

After defeating Coalition Prussian and Russian forces under Sacken and Yorck at Montmirail,

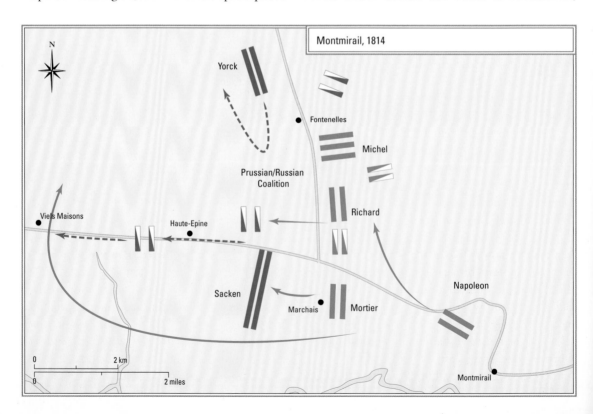

France, Napoleon pursued 30,000 Coalition troops with 22,000 French troops. Exposed to enemy fire, Napoleon attacked as Coalition forces retreated across the Marne River. Imperial Guard cavalry charges broke three Russian infantry squares. Coalition forces escaped across the Marne, losing 2700 men, nine cannons and their baggage train. French losses were 600.

■ **VAUCHAMPS, 14 FEBRUARY 1814**

Blücher, with 30,000 Coalition Prussians and Russians, attacked Napoleon's 20,000 French troops near Vauchamps, France. Napoleon counter-attacked before Blücher could fully engage all his troops and French cavalry under Grouchy outflanked Coalition positions. Attacks by French Imperial Guard troops routed Coalition troops, with Grouchy in pursuit. Blücher lost over 6000 men, 16 cannon and 10 flags and his army was disorganized. French losses were only 600.

Hundred Days Campaign June 1815

■ **LIGNY, 16 JUNE 1815**

Napoleon marched 125,000 French troops into Belgium hoping to defeat Blücher's Prussian army and Wellington's international army before they could invade France. Blücher marched 83,000 troops towards Napoleon, who concentrated 77,000 troops on Ligny, dispatching the rest under Ney against Wellington.

Blücher set up positions in Ligny and Sombreffe and Napoleon attacked from the south-west. Napoleon hoped part of Ney's force would join the attack on Blücher on his right flank, but this did not materialize. Failing reinforcements, Napoleon massed his artillery, Imperial Guard and IV Corps and broke through Blücher's centre, the rest of the French advancing on both flanks. Blücher himself was pinned under a fallen horse, barely escaping capture.

The defeated Prussians lost 34,000 men, while Napoleon lost 11,500. Ligny was Napoleon's last victory, but Blücher's army was still viable.

■ **QUATRE BRAS, 16 JUNE 1815**

Napoleon concentrated his forces against the Prussian army at Ligny in southern Belgium, sending Marshal Ney north on the Brussels road with part of the French army against Wellington and his British, Hanoverian and Dutch-Belgian forces. Wellington was not concentrated, deploying towards Nivelles, fearing being cut off from the sea. The army commanders had not yet appreciated the importance of the crossroads at Quatre Bras. Perponcher's Dutch-Belgian division occupied the crossroads and reinforcements began to arrive. The position was partly covered on the right by Bossu Wood. Ney, who had 21,000 troops available against 9000 Dutch-Belgians, delayed his attack until 14:00. Ney did not realize his advantage and, expecting reinforcements, committed only part of his force. Picton's British division arrived at 15:00, stemming the French advance before Wellington arrived, taking command. He was reinforced by Dutch-Belgian cavalry and the Brunswick division.

French cavalry under Piré repulsed the Dutch cavalry and damaged the 42nd Highlanders, who held in square. Ney renewed his attack, still expecting reinforcements. French infantry under Napoleon's brother, Jérôme, advanced in Bossu Wood, damaging the Brunswick division, with the Duke of Brunswick being killed in the fighting.

Key to Ney's plans was D'Erlon's Corps, but it never arrived. D'Erlon marched towards Ligny, then counter-marched back towards Ney. D'Erlons Corps, numbering 14,500 men, ultimately participated in neither battle.

Kellermann's brigade of cavalry arrived to reinforce Ney, who ordered the brigade to charge immediately. The charge was successful but nearly cut off, barely managing to return to French lines. Reinforcements had raised Wellington's numbers to 36,000 against Ney's 24,500. Wellington counter-attacked, with fighting ending at 21:00. With the Prussians defeated at Ligny, Wellington retired northwards in good order. Coalition losses were 4800, French losses being 4300.

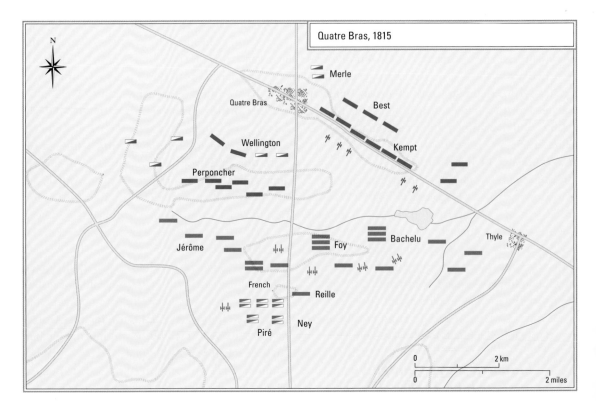

Quatre Bras, 1815

Merle

Quatre Bras

Best

Wellington

Kempt

Perponcher

Bachelu

Thyle

Jérôme

Foy

French

Reille

Piré

Ney

0   2 km

0   2 miles

▪ WAVRE, 18–19 JUNE 1815

Grouchy, leading 33,000 French troops, attacked Thielmann, commanding 17,000 Prussian troops on the Dyle river in Belgium. Grouchy had not been able to stay between Blücher and Wellington and so ended by attacking the corps of Thielmann, essentially a rearguard, while Blücher with 72,000 Prussians marched to the aid of Wellington at Waterloo. Grouchy defeated Thielmann, but too late to help Napoleon. Each side lost 2500 casualties.

▪ WATERLOO, 18 JUNE 1815

Napoleon's preemptive offensive into Belgium continued as he marched northwards towards Brussels after defeating the Prussian army at Ligny on 16 June. Blocking his path was Wellington's army of 68,000 British, Hanoverian, Dutch and Belgian troops. Wellington set up a defence in depth on a rise near Mont St Jean, 3.2km south of Waterloo. His right was strengthened by the walled chateau of Hougoumont and his centre was likewise screened by an advanced fortified

post at the farm of La Haye Sainte. Wellington had been promised support from Blücher's Prussian army, which was supposed to arrive from the east at some undetermined point in time.

Napoleon prepared to attack with 72,000 French troops. Heavy rains had created muddy fields, which hampered the deployment of French artillery and delayed any major attacks. By 11:30, Jerome Bonaparte's division attacked Hougoumont, Napoleon hoping to create a diversion on Wellington's right. Hougoumont's defenders held while Wellington sent reinforcements, including four companies of the Coldstream Guards.

Beginning after 13:00, Napoleon bombarded Wellington with 80 cannon focused on the centre and left. Wellington's troops were behind the crest of the rise as protection against artillery fire. Napoleon then sent D'Erlon's I Corps against Wellington's left. D'Erlon's massed column, an unwieldy formation, was met by British infantry under Picton, who was killed while leading his

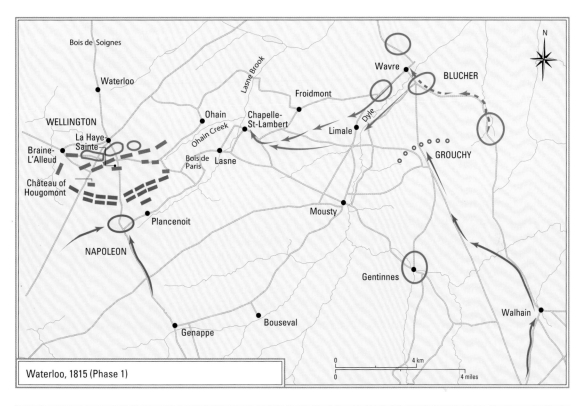

Waterloo, 1815 (Phase 1)

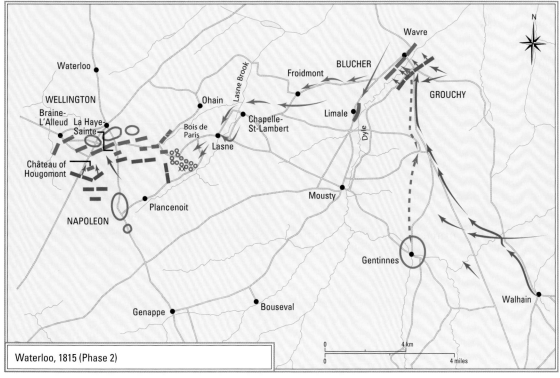

Waterloo, 1815 (Phase 2)

troops. British Household Cavalry and Union Brigade cavalry attacked I Corps and drove it back in disorder. French cavalry in turn attacked the British cavalry.

French officers had spotted Bülow's Prussian IV Corps advancing slowly from the east. Consequently, at 16:00, Napoleon positioned Lobau's corps to protect his right flank, although this drew off strength from the attack on Wellington. Meanwhile, French artillery increased their bombardment on Wellington, who pulled his troops back further behind the crest of the ridge. Seeing this, Marshal Ney assumed Wellington was in full retreat and led massed French cavalry at Wellington's left centre. Unsupported by infantry, several French cavalry charges were repulsed by Wellington's infantry in square formations.

After the failed cavalry charges, Napoleon ordered Ney to take La Haye Sainte in the centre. Ney took the place at 18:00 after savage fighting and Wellington's centre was driven back. Ney requested reserves to exploit the success, but Napoleon was occupied with the Prussians. Bülow had taken the town of Plancenoit, squarely on the French right flank. Napoleon sent in his Young Guard Division, plus two battalions of Old Guard and pushed the Prussians back. This threat temporarily averted, Napoleon gave Ney 11 battalions of Middle and Old Guard.

Ney personally led the Guard infantry in narrow columns at Wellington's right centre, rather than directly through La Haye Sainte. This exposed the Guards to artillery fire as they advanced. Taking heavy casualties, they were met by British Guards in their front and attacked on their flanks by Chasée's Dutch-Belgian Division, the British 52nd Foot and Adam's Brigade. The French Guards were slaughtered in the crossfire and fell back.

Meanwhile, Pirch's Prussian corps had joined Bülow in attacking Plancenoit again and Zeiten's corps also arrived on the French right, bringing Prussian strength to 50,000. Napoleon's now heavily outnumbered and exhausted army was routed. Rearguard fighting by the remaining Old Guard allowed Napoleon to escape. Napoleon's final battle was a disaster and led to his permanent exile. French losses were 44,000 men. Wellington lost 17,000 and Blücher lost 7000.

■ ROCHESERVIÈRE, 19–20 JUNE 1815
Lamarque with 6000 Frenchmen loyal to Napoleon defeated 8000 French Vendée Royalists in western France. Vendée leader Suzanne was killed, his forces losing over 500 casualties. Lamarque lost 70 casualties.

■ LA SUFFEL, 28–29 JUNE 1815
Rapp with 20,000 French made a successful spoiling attack against 40,000 Austrian and other Coalition troops in eastern France. Both sides lost nearly 3000 casualties. Rapp then took up positions at Strasbourg.

■ ROCQUENCOURT, 1 JULY 1815
Davout sent French cavalry under Excelmans to intercept a Prussian cavalry brigade under Sohr, operating near Versailles, south-west of Paris. Excelmans captured 400 Prussians after a brief fight, then returned to Paris.

■ ISSY, 3 JULY 1815
French infantry under Vandamme marched out of Paris towards Issy on the south-western outskirts of Paris. Prussians under Ziethen opposed the advance and Vandamme fell back, with peace negotiations being completed that day.

Neapolitan War, 1815

■ PANARO, 3 APRIL 1815
A 7000-strong detachment of King Joachim Murat's Neapolitan army defeated an Austrian force of 6600 men commanded by Gen Frederick Bianchi on the River Panaro, just south of Modena. The Neapolitans forced a crossing of the river at Castelfranco Emilia and turned the Austrian right flank, compelling Bianchi to retreat behind the line of the River Po. Murat's forces inflicted 461 casualties for the loss of 409 men.

■ FERRARA, APRIL 1815
King Joachim Murat followed up his victory at the Panoro by attacking Ferrara, but the Austrian garrison held out, tying down much of Murat's

force in a siege that was abandoned when the Austrians counter-attacked.

■ OCCHIOBELLO, 8–9 APRIL 1815

King Joachim Murat attempted to force a crossing of the River Po at Occhiobello with his 25,000 men as its bridge was only defended by a small Austrian detachment under the command of Johann Freiherr von Mohr. The first Neapolitan attack was repulsed by Mohr's outnumbered infantry, supported by a devastating artillery bombardment. Further attacks, including a charge by an entire dragoon regiment, were repulsed by the Austrian forces and the momentum behind the offensive eventually petered out as Neapolitan morale disintegrated.

The following day, Murat again attempted to force a crossing, but was finally compelled to retreat as he had lost heavily due to desertion, while Mohr's detachment had been reinforced, bringing its strength up to around 10,000 men. The Neapolitans had sustained over 2000 casualties during the fighting with thousands more deserting, but the Austrians lost only 400 men.

■ CARPI, 10 APRIL 1815

Gen Frederick Bianchi's Austrian force of 2500 men attacked the 5000-strong Neapolitan garrison of Carpi in the Duchy of Modena. Bianchi massed his artillery and began an intensive bombardment of the sector of the defences around the town's north gate. While the garrison's attention was focused on this sector, the Austrian assault broke through the south gate and took the town. Many demoralized Neapolitan troops deserted immediately after the battle.

■ CASAGLIA, 12 APRIL 1815

An Austrian force of 4500 men under Gen Johann Frimont attacked Gen Ambrosio's 7000-strong Neapolitan division, which was holding the villages of Ravale and Casaglia, north-west of Ferarra, Italy. The initial Austrian attack quickly routed the garrison of Ravale, but Gen Mohr's assault on the larger Neapolitan force holding Casaglia only succeeded after fierce street fighting. The Austrians inflicted 1000 casualties for the loss

of 230 men, but many more Neapolitans deserted after their defeat.

■ RONCO, 21 APRIL 1815

The 8000-strong Neapolitan rearguard under King Joachim Murat was defeated by Count Adam Albert von Neipperg's Austrian corps of 3000 men at the River Ronco. The Austrians inflicted a total of 1000 casualties for the loss of 150 men on their side.

■ CESENATICO, 23 APRIL 1815

A force of 600 Austrian hussars and jägers raided the town of Cesenatico on the Adriatic coast, which was held by a 3000-strong Neapolitan garrison. The Austrians inflicted 700 casualties for the loss of 50 men.

■ PESARO, 28 APRIL 1815

Repeating the tactics employed at Cesenatico, 400 Austrian hussars and jägers raided Pesaro on the Adriatic coast, which was held by a 3000-strong Neapolitan garrison. The Austrians inflicted 450 casualties for the loss of 25 men.

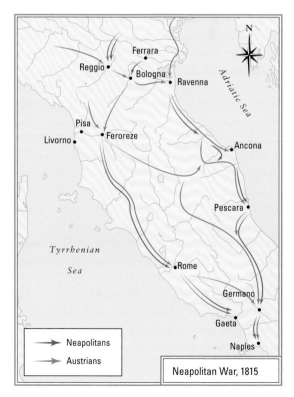

Neapolitan War, 1815

■ **SCAPEZZANO, 1 MAY 1815**
Count Adam Albert von Neipperg's Austrian corps of 15,300 men followed the retreating Neapolitan army along the Adriatic coast, while a 12,000-strong Austrian corps under Gen Frederick Bianchi marched on Foligno in central Italy to cut off Murat's line of retreat to Naples. Murat deployed Gen Carascosa's division at Scapezzano to halt von Neipperg while he defeated Bianchi, but, after limited skirmishing, Carascosa was forced to retreat to avoid encirclement.

■ **TOLENTINO, 2–3 MAY 1815**
King Joachim Murat's Neapolitan army of 25,500 men attacked a 12,000-strong Austrian force commanded by Gen Frederick Bianchi, which had deployed in strong defensive positions in and around the town of Tolentino.

Murat's initial attack achieved complete tactical surprise; Neapolitan troops managed to capture Gen Bianchi near Sforzacosta, but the general was almost immediately freed by a regiment of Hungarian hussars. The Austrian outpost at Rancia castle changed hands repeatedly during the first day, with Murat taking Monte Milone, but was unable to achieve a decisive breakthrough.

The second day started well for Murat as his men took Rancia castle and the hills of Cantagallo. However, further Neapolitan attacks against the Austrian flanks were repulsed and Murat was forced to retreat on receiving news of the defeat at Scapezzano, having inflicted 800 casualties for the loss of over 4000 men.

■ **ANCONA, 5–30 MAY 1815**
An Austrian detachment of 2300 men under MGen Menrad Freiherr von Geppert, besieged Ancona, which was defended by a Neapolitan garrison of 1500 men. The garrison lost 500 men before surrendering on 30 May.

■ **CASTEL DI SANGRO, 13 MAY 1815**
Gen Pignatelli Cerchiara's battered Neapolitan infantry division of 1900 men was defeated by a 2000-strong Austrian advance guard of hussars and jägers. The Austrians inflicted over 600 casualties for the loss of 15 men.

■ **SAN GERMANO, 15–17 MAY 1815**
King Joachim Murat's Neapolitan army of 15,000 men attacked Gen Laval Nugent von Westmeath's 8000-strong Austrian force and drove back Nugent's vanguard. However, Gen Frederick Bianchi's Austrian force of 25,000 men was now moving up and threatening to surround the Neapolitan position. Murat pulled back and attempted to take up defensive positions at San Germano (modern Cassino), but his demoralized forces panicked and broke with the loss of at least 4500 men.

South American Wars 1800–14

■ **COTAGAITA, 27 OCTOBER 1810**
In one of the first actions in the Argentine War of Independence, rebel forces under Antonio González de Balcarce advanced against an entrenched royalist position at Santiago de Cotagaita, south-east of Lake Poopo (in modern Bolivia), held by Spanish Gen José de Córdova y Roxas. Repeated assaults on the royalist defences were beaten off with heavy losses and the rebel forces retreated to Tupiza and then Suipacha.

■ **SUIPACHA, 7 NOVEMBER 1810**
A royalist detachment of 800 men and four guns under Gen José de Córdova y Roxas was defeated by de Balcarce's 600-strong rebel force supported by 10 guns on the River Suipacha.

■ **CALDERÓN BRIDGE, 17 JANUARY 1811**
A 6000-strong royalist army under Bdr Félix María Calleja del Rey decisively defeated Miguel Hidalgo's force of 100,000 ill-equipped Mexican rebels at Calderón Bridge. The royalists inflicted 13,000 casualties for the loss of 1200 men.

■ **FIGUEROA MUTINY, 1 APRIL 1811**
Spanish rule in Chile was destabilized by Napoleon's removal of Ferdinand VII from the Spanish throne in 1808. By 1811, the ruling Junta's moves towards independence provoked the Figueroa Mutiny, a royalist coup rapidly crushed.

■ **HUAQUI, 20 JUNE 1811**
A 4700-strong royalist force under Gen José Manuel de Goyeneche defeated Juan José Castelli's

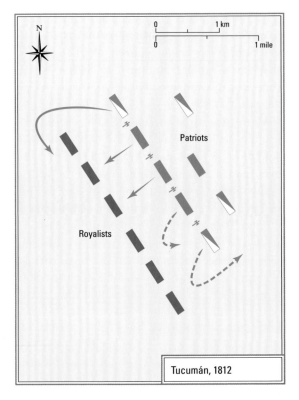

Tucumán, 1812

Argentinian rebel army of 5000 men, which was supported by 13,000 native auxiliaries. The rebels lost 1000 men and all their artillery.

■ **EL SALVADOR, NOVEMBER–DECEMBER 1811**
Spanish rule in San Salvador (modern El Salvador) was destabilized by Napoleon's removal of Ferdinand VII from the Spanish throne in 1808. By November 1811, unrest had escalated into open rebellion, led by José Matías Delgado, the vicar of San Salvador and his nephew, Manuel José Arce. The rebels retained control for nearly a month before the province was retaken by Royalist forces from Guatemala under Col Jose de Aycinena.

■ **TUCUMÁN, 24–25 SEPTEMBER 1812**
BGen Manuel Belgrano took command of the demoralized Argentinian rebel forces based at San Salvador de Jujuy following their defeat at Huaqui. He rapidly decided that the city was untenable in the face of advancing royalist forces and ordered a scorched-earth retreat, the so-called Jujuy Exodus

('Exodo Jujeño') in which the civilian population was forced to leave the city and retreat with the army, burning everything left behind to hinder the enemy's advance.

The retreat ended at Tucumán, where Belgrano decided to turn and face the royalists. The rebels' 1800 men were badly outnumbered by Juan Pío de Tristán's 3000 royalist troops, but a charge by Belgrano's lancers routed much of the royalist cavalry and infantry. The rebels inflicted over 1100 casualties for the loss of 280 men. Tristán retreated towards Salta, harassed by 600 men under Díaz Vélez.

■ **CERRITO, 31 DECEMBER 1812**
Argentinian rebels had besieged the royalist city of Montevideo as early as 1811, but were forced to raise the siege at the end of the year, following setbacks in Upper Peru. Gen José Rondeau's force of 1000 Argentinian rebels again besieged the city in October 1812 and defeated a sortie by the city's 2300-strong royalist garrison, commanded by Gaspar de Vigodet. The rebels inflicted 276 casualties for the loss of 130 men.

■ **SALTA, 20 FEBRUARY 1813**
Five months after his defeat at Tucumán, in north-western Argentina, royalist Gen Juan Pío de Tristán withdrew further north to the city of Salta, where he deployed his 3400 men and 10 guns in a well-entrenched position. BGen Manuel Belgrano's 3000-strong rebel army, supported by 12 guns, overran the royalist defences and forced the surrender of Tristán and his entire army. The rebels captured 10 guns and over 2000 muskets.

■ **YERBAS BUENAS, 27 APRIL 1813**
Bdr José Antonio Pareja's 6000-strong royalist army defeated a surprise attack by a smaller force of Chilean rebels commanded by Col Juan de Dios Puga at the village of Yerbas Buenas near Linares in central Chile.

■ **SAN CARLOS, 15 MAY 1813**
José Miguel Carrera's 4000-strong Chilean rebel army intercepted a royalist force commanded by Juan Francisco Sanchez as it retreated towards Chillán in central Chile. Carrera deployed with

his infantry in the centre and his cavalry well out on the flanks. An attack by unsupported rebel infantry broke down under close-range royalist artillery fire and the rebel cavalry were beaten off by royalist infantry, following which Carrera's demoralized force broke and ran.

■ **PEQUEREQUE, 19 JUNE 1813**
A detachment of 135 Argentinian rebel dragoons under Col Cornelio Zelaya defeated Col Pedro Olañeta's force of 200 royalist cavalry at Pequereque (in modern Bolivia). The rebels inflicted 30 casualties for the loss of 13 men.

■ **CHILLÁN, 27 JULY–10 AUGUST 1813**
A force of 5000 royalists commanded by Juan Francisco Sánchez and Brig José Antonio Pareja held the city of Chillán in central Chile against José Miguel Carrera's rebels. The siege began in the depths of winter, with conditions so bad that many of the rebels soon deserted. Carrera attempted to storm the city before his forces disintegrated, but was beaten off, losing over 500 men.

■ **LASTAGUANES (TAGUANES), 31 JULY 1813**
Advancing on Caracas in Venezuela, Simón Bolívar's rebel army intercepted 1200 royalist troops under Col Julian Izquierdo withdrawing towards Puerto Cabello. Bolívar defeated and killed Izquierdo in a night cavalry attack at Taguanes, south-west of Valencia.

■ **VILCAPUGIO, 1 OCTOBER 1813**
Joaquín de la Pezuela's 3500-strong royalist army defeated an Argentinian rebel force of 3400 men under Vilcapugio at Vilcapugio. The royalists inflicted 350 casualties for the loss of 200 men.

■ **EL ROBLE, 17 OCTOBER 1813**
José Miguel Carrera's Chilean rebel army of 800 men defeated a 1200-strong royalist army under Clemente Lantaño and de Luis Urrejola at El Roble. The rebels inflicted 80 casualties for the loss of 30 men.

■ **TAMBO NUEVO, 23–25 OCTOBER 1813**
Following his defeat at Vilcapugio, BGen Manuel Belgrano retreated to Santiago de Macha with the main rebel army, leaving a smaller detachment under Díaz Vélez to garrison Potosí. A royalist

cavalry force under Col Saturnino Castro seized the town of Yocalla, threatening the rebel's hold on Potosí. A rebel raiding force under Lt Lamadrid attacked a royalist outpost at Tambo Nuevo, panicking Castro into withdrawing and ending the threat to Potosí.

■ **AYOHUMA, 14 NOVEMBER 1813**
Joaquín de la Pezuela's 3500-strong royalist army defeated an Argentinian rebel force of 3400 men under Manuel Belgrano near the village of Ayohuma (in modern Bolivia). The royalists inflicted 900 casualties for the loss of 140 men.

■ **FIRST BATTLE OF TALCA, 3 MARCH 1814**
A royalist force of 300 men under Ildefonso Elorreaga successfully stormed the town of Talca in central Chile. The town was defended by a 300-strong rebel garrison under Col Carlos Spano, who was killed in action.

■ **EL QUILO, 19 MARCH 1814**
A Chilean rebel force commanded by Bernardo O'Higgins attacked and defeated a smaller, 400-strong royalist detachment under Col Manuel Barañao, which was holding a defensive position on the south bank of the River Itata.

■ **MEMBRILLAR, 20 MARCH 1814**
Bdr Juan Mackenna's Chilean rebel army defeated a royalist force under Bdr Gabino Gaínza near the village of Membrillar on the River Itata. The royalists made a disorganized assault on the rebel trenches near the village; this was repelled, but followed up by another unsuccessful attack, this time on the centre of the rebel line. Waves of royalist attacks and rebel counter-attacks continued until the battered royalist forces retreated.

■ **FIRST BATTLE OF CANCHA RAYADA, 29 MARCH 1814**
Manuel Blanco Encalada's 1400-strong Chilean rebel force was defeated by a royalist detachment of 450 men under the guerrilla leader Ildefonso Elorreaga at Cancha Rayada, near Talca in central Chile. The royalists took 300 prisoners.

■ **QUECHEREGUAS, 8 APRIL 1814**
Gabino Gaínza's royalist army advanced on the rebel capital of Santiago. A rebel force commanded

by Bernardo O'Higgins made a night march to block the road to Santiago and defeat the royalists at Quechereguas.

■ MONTEVIDEO, APRIL–JUNE 1814

The Argentine rebel fleet under Irish-born Adm William Brown blockaded Montevideo for several months. Following Brown's victory off Montevideo on 16 May, the city was surrendered by Gaspar Vigodet, the last Spanish viceroy of La Plata.

■ LA PUERTA, 15 JUNE 1814

Exhausted and nearly starving from the siege of San Mateo, Simon Bolivar's 3000-strong rebel army was routed by a royalist force, which included the lancers of the 'Infernal Legion' led by the warlord Tomás Rodríguez Boves.

■ LAS TRES ACEQUIAS, 26 AUGUST 1814

Disputes between Chilean rebel factions flared up into open warfare between the supporters of José Miguel Carrera and those of Bernardo O'Higgins. Carrera's 1600-strong force defeated O'Higgins' 600 men at Las Tres Acequias, near Santiago.

■ RANCAGUA, 1–2 OCTOBER 1814

Bernardo O'Higgins' 600-strong Chilean rebel force occupied Rancagua in an attempt to block the advance of Bdr Don Mariano Osorio's 5000-strong royalist army on Santiago. Osorio's second in command, Col Rafael Maroto, led his Queen's Talavera Regiment in an assault on the rebels' defences, which was beaten off with heavy losses. However, José Miguel Carrera and his brothers failed to support O'Higgins, who was forced to break out and retreat to Santiago.

Miscellaneous African Wars 1800–1900

■ DEBRE ABBAY, 14 FEBRUARY 1831

Rivalry between Ras Marye of Yejju, the Regent of Ethiopia and Sabagadis of Agame, the Governor of Tigray, flared up into open warfare. Their armies clashed at Mai Islami near Debre Abbay, Ethiopia, where the Regent was killed in action, although Sabagadis was defeated, largely due to his failure to fully exploit the superior firepower

of his matchlock musketeers against the Regent's cavalry. Sabagadis was captured and executed the following day.

■ DEBRE TABOR, 7 FEBRUARY 1842

An army of 30,000 men army commanded by Ali II of Yejju, Regent of Ethiopia, narrowly defeated a force of similar size under Wube Haile Maryam, the Governor of Tigray, capturing Wube and his son.

■ GUR AMBA, 27 SEPTEMBER 1852

The army of the Ethiopian Regent, Ras Ali II, was defeated by rebel forces led by Kassa Hailu. The victory marked the start of a campaign that led to Kassa becoming Emperor Tewodros II of Ethiopia.

■ AMBA JEBELLI, MARCH 1854

Kassa Hailu's army defeated the forces of the warlord Birru Goshu of Gojjam in northwest Ethiopia. Birru Goshu was captured and imprisoned, while Kassa Hailu was crowned as Emperor Tewodros II in February 1855.

■ SÉGOU, 10 MARCH 1861

El Hajj Umar Tall's Toucouleur army, equipped with European firearms, defeated the warriors of the Bambara Empire at Ségou in Mali. He then abolished the Bambara Empire, installing his son, Ahmadu Tall, as king of Ségou.

■ BASUTO GUN WAR, 1880–81

Attempts by the government of Cape Colony to disarm the Basuto tribes provoked a rebellion led by Chiefs Masopha, Lerothodi and Moletsane. A peace compromise was signed in September 1881, after a year of inconclusive guerilla warfare.

■ EKUMEKU WARS, 1883–1914

British attempts to control Nigeria were challenged by the Ekumeka warrior cult, which inspired numerous tribal uprisings between 1883 and 1914. These varied from small-scale guerilla campaigns to open warfare and were ultimately supressed by colonial forces.

First Barbary War 1801–05

■ TRIPOLI HARBOUR, 1804

Cdre Edward Preble assumed command of the US

Mediterranean Squadron in 1803 and blockaded Tripoli harbour to prevent raids by the Barbary pirates. The first significant action of the blockade came on 31 October, when the 36-gun frigate USS *Philadelphia* ran aground on an uncharted reef and was captured by Tripolitan gunboats together with its crew and Capt William Bainbridge. Although the frigate was unfit for sea, it was anchored in the harbour as a floating battery.

If the *Philadelphia* could be repaired, it would become the Barbary pirates' most powerful naval unit and its destruction was Preble's top priority. The defences of Tripoli harbour ruled out a conventional naval attack and it was decided that a night raid offered the best chance of success. On the night of 16 February 1804, a captured Tripolitan ketch renamed USS *Intrepid* disguised as a local merchant vessel sailed into the harbour under the command of Lt Stephen Decatur, Jr. He bluffed his way alongside the *Philadelphia*, allowing his detachment of marines hidden below decks to board the frigate and set her on fire. Despite heavy fire from the shore batteries, Decatur and his men successfully escaped in *Intrepid*.

In August 1804, *Intrepid* was converted into a 'floating volcano' to be sent into the harbour and blown up in the midst of the corsair fleet. The vessel was loaded with 100 barrels of powder and 150 shells, with their fuses set to burn for 15 minutes. On the evening of 4 September, *Intrepid* sailed into the harbour commanded by Master Commandant Richard Somers, but was hit by fire from shore batteries and blew up with the loss of all hands before reaching the enemy fleet.

■ **DERNA, 27 APRIL–13 MAY 1805**

Six months after failing to destroy the pirate fleet at Tripoli, American forces turned against Derna, which was attacked by a force from Alexandria, comprising a small detachment of US Marines and 500 Arab and Greek mercenaries under Capt William Eaton, Marine Lt Preston O'Bannon and the deposed Tripolitan ruler Hamet Karamanli. The USS *Nautilus*, the USS *Hornet* and the USS *Argus* were detailed to supply the force and provide

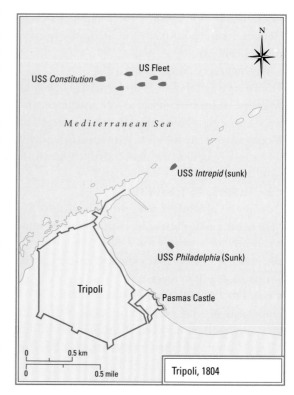

Tripoli, 1804

naval gunfire support. On 27 April, the three vessels bombarded the defences of Derna and Eaton's force successfully stormed the city, whose garrison fled after a short fight. The Pasha of Tripolitania, Yusuf Karamanli, had sent reinforcements to Derna, which arrived too late to prevent its capture. Nevertheless, they made several attempts to retake the city, all of which were beaten off with the loss of 2000 men.

Russia in the Americas 1804

■ **SITKA, OCTOBER 1804**

A 150-strong force of the Russian-American Company under Alexander Baranov, supported by Russian warships, attacked Chief K'alyaan's warband of 750 warriors of the Alaskan Tlingit tribe in retaliation for a Tlingit raid carried out on a Russian trading post in 1802. The Tlingit were well equipped with firearms obtained from British and American traders, but were decisively defeated, largely due to the Russians' destruction of the canoe, which had been carrying much of their ammunition.

Fulani Jihad 1804–08

■ Tsunta, December 1804

Following an assassination attempt by Yunfa, the ruler of the state of Gobir, the Islamic reformer Usman dan Fodio raised an army from the Fulani tribes. Yunfa defeated the Fulani at Tsunta, inflicting over 2000 casualties.

■ Alkalawa, October 1808

A year after their defeat at Tsunta, Usman dan Fodio's forces overran Kebbi and established a permanent base at Gwandu. Building on popular discontent, the jihadists continued to advance, taking Gobir's capital Alkalawa and killing the ruler, Yunfa.

First Serbian Revolution 1804–13

■ Ivankovac, 18 August 1805

Sultan Selim III sent Hafiz-Pasha, governor of Niš, with a 15,000-strong army to suppress the Serb rebellion. The Ottoman army attacked Duke Milenko Stojković's force of 2500 men, which was entrenched near the village of Ivankovac. The Serbs were reinforced, bringing their final strength up to 7500 men, enabling them to defeat a series of Ottoman assaults throughout the day. Hafiz-Pasha was mortally wounded and withdrew to the small town of Paraćin.

■ Mišar, 12–15 August 1806

A Serbian force under Karađorđe Petrović deployed in strong entrenched positions on the Sava at Mišar, near Shabatz west of Belgrade, where they defeated a series of attacks by an Ottoman army, inflicting 3000 casualties.

■ Deligrad, December 1806

A 55,000-strong Ottoman army commanded by Ibrahim Pasha was decisively defeated with heavy casualties and the loss of nine guns by Karađorđe Petrović's 37,000 Serbian rebels at Deligrad in Serbia. The Serbs lost 3000 men.

■ Belgrade 1806–07

In December 1806, the Serbian rebels besieged Belgrade. In response, an Ottoman army under Mehmed-beg Kulenović of Zvornik was sent to raise the siege, but this attempt ended in a devastating defeat and the city surrendered in March 1807. Governor Pasha Suleiman and his men were massacred following their surrender. Mehmed-beg Kulenović later made efforts to drive the Serbian rebels out of the western provinces, but was killed in action.

■ Čegar, 19 May 1809

A force of 5000 Serbian rebels commanded by Miloje Petrović was defeated by Hurşid Ahmed Pasha's 20,000-strong Ottoman army at Cegar, near Niš. The well-entrenched Serbs inflicted 15,000 casualties for the loss of 4000 men.

Russo-Turkish War 1806–12

■ Dardanelles, 22–23 May 1807

A Russian squadron of 10 ships of the line and a frigate under Vice Admiral Dmitry Senyavin defeated Kapudan Pasha Seyit-Ali's Ottoman fleet of eight ships of the line, six frigates and 55 smaller craft.

■ Arpachai, 18 June 1807

A 17,000-strong Russian army commanded by Count Ivan Gudovich decisively defeated an offensive by Yusuf Paha's Ottoman army of 24,000 men at Arpachai on the River Akhurian in Armenia. Gudovich was seriously wounded, losing an eye.

■ Mount Athos, 19–22 June 1807

Vice Admiral Dmitry Senyavin's Russian squadron of ten ships of the line defeated Kapudan Pasha Seyit-Ali's Ottoman fleet of nine ships of the line and 10 smaller craft. Seyit-Ali lost at least three ships of the line.

Finnish War 1808–09

■ Svartholm fortress, Feb–Mar 1808

Svartholm fortress was built between 1749 and 1764 on the shores of the Bay of Loviisa in southern Finland by Gen Augustin Ehrensvärd. Even when the Russians invaded Finland in 1808, Svartholm's fortifications were incomplete and only two-thirds of its artillery was emplaced. Although Russian siege guns caused only minor damage to the defences, the garrison commander, Carl Magnus Gripenberg, surrendered on 18 March 1808, after offering only token resistance.

■ PYHÄJOKI, 16 APRIL 1808

Deep snow hampered both sides in this skirmish in 1808, which was fought as the Swedish forces ended their retreat. The Russians had been following the Swedish army northwards, as it abandoned much of Finland to Russian occupation. MGen Georg Carl von Döbeln's Swedish force fought a fierce action against the Russian vanguard under MGen Yakov Kulnev, but Döbeln soon retreated in accordance with FM Klingspor's overall strategic plan.

■ SIIKAJOKI, 18 APRIL 1808

A 400-strong Swedish force under MGen Georg Carl von Döbeln and Carl Johan Adlercreutz defeated the Russian vanguard of 1000 men under MGen Yakov Kulnev, inflicting 200 casualties for the loss of 140 men.

■ REVOLAX, 27 APRIL 1808

Col Johan Adam Cronstedt's Swedish brigade of 2250 men defeated a 1800-strong Russian detachment under MGen Mikhail Bulatov, which had occupied the village of Revonlahti. Cronstedt divided his brigade into two assault columns and attacked in the morning. The right column, under LCol Gustav Aminoff, comprised two battalions of the Savolax Infantry Regiment, the Savolax Jaeger Regiment's third battalion and the Karelian Jaeger Corps' second battalion, supported by two 3-pounder guns. LCol Adolf Ludwig Christiern's left column consisted of two battalions from the Savolax Infantry Regiment, the Savolax Jaeger Regiment's first battalion and the Karelian Jaeger Corps' first battalion, again with two 3-pounder guns. The columns swept away the Russian outposts and advanced on the village, which was finally cleared after fierce fighting. The Swedes inflicted 600 casualties for the loss of 94 men.

■ BATTLE OF PULKKILA, 2 MAY 1808

Count Johan August Sandels' Swedish force of 1500 men marched eastwards to liberate those areas of Finland that were under Russian occupation. During the march they encountered Col Obuhov's 250-strong Russian detachment near the village of Pulkkila. The Russians were surrounded and attempted to break out, but were forced back to the village, where they were defeated in fierce fighting. Obuhov was forced to surrender, together with his entire force.

■ SVEABORG, 3 MAY 1808

Count Jan Pieter van Suchtelen's Russian army besieged Sveaborg after the fall of Helsinki in March 1808. After minimal fighting, the governor, VAdm Karl Kronstedt, surrendered the fortress with its 7500-strong garrison and 94 gunboats.

■ KUMLINGE, 1808

A Russian foraging detachment landed on Kumlinge, one of the Åland Islands off the Finnish

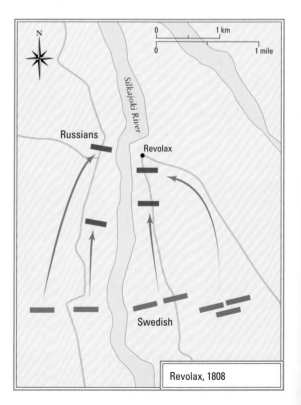

Revolax, 1808

coast, but was attacked and captured by a group of about a hundred local farmers. The prisoners were held at Kumlinge parsonage.

■ LEMO, 19–20 JUNE 1808

MGen Eberhard von Vegesack's Swedish force of 2500 men was defeated by LGen Karl Gustav von Baggovut's 3600 Russians. Both sides inflicted 200 casualties, but the Swedes were forced to retreat.

■ NYKARLEBY, 24 JUNE 1808

A Swedish army under Gen Carl Johan Adlercreutz attempted to trap the Russian army at Nykarleby as it retreated towards Vaasa. The Russians were able to escape by destroying the town bridge, slowing the Swedish pursuit.

■ VAASA, 25–26 JUNE 1808

Supporting the Swedish summer offensive down the west coast of Finland from Siikajoki, Col Johan Bergenstråhle landed with 1200 Swedish troops and four guns in an attempt to re-take Vaasa, which was held by MGen Nikolai Demidov's Russian garrison of at least 1700 men (two infantry battalions and 200 Cossacks). The Swedish force disembarked north of Vaasa in Österhankmo and advanced on the city. Already seriously outnumbered, Bergenstråhle launched his attack with only 1100 men, as small detachments had been left as flank guards. Despite the Russian numerical superiority, there was prolonged street fighting in which Bergenstråhle was wounded and captured before the Swedish forces were repelled and forced to retreat. The main Swedish army was unable to send reinforcements from Nykarleby and the outnumbered Swedes were evacuated by sea. The port was recaptured by Swedish forces within a few days.

■ RIMITO KRAMP, 30 JUNE–2 JULY 1808

RAdm Klas Hjelmstjerna's Swedish coastal forces totalling eight galleys, 15 gunboats and four sloops narrowly defeated a Russian fleet of 22 gunboats under Cap Selivanov. The Russians retreated to the shelter of shore batteries at Turku.

■ KOKONSAARI, 11 JULY 1808

Withdrawing from Vaasa, Russian forces under Gen Jegor Wlastoff turned on the pursuing Swedish army at Kokonsaari. Reinforced by Gen Ivan Fedorovich Jankovich's troops from Nykarleby, Wlastoff inflicted a sharp defeat on Gen Otto von Fieandt.

■ LAPUA, 14 JULY 1808

A Swedish army of 4700 men under Gen Carl Johan Adlercreutz decisively defeated a 4100-strong Russian force, commanded by MGen Nikolay Raevsky. The Swedes inflicted 2000 casualties for the loss of 500 men.

■ SANDÖTRÖM, 2–3 AUGUST 1808

RAdm Hjelmstjerna's Swedish squadron of 22 gunboats fought an indecisive action against Capt Hayden's Russian fleet of 50 gunboats off the island of Kemiö. A total of 35 Russian gunboats and 12 Swedish vessels were damaged.

■ KAUHAJOKI, 10 AUGUST 1808

The only important cavalry skirmish of the summer campaign was fought near Kauhajoki in western Finland. A patrol of Russian hussars were attacked and forced to retreat by a detachment of the Nyland Dragoon Regiment.

■ ALAVUS, 17 AUGUST 1808

A 3900-strong Swedish army under Gen Carl Johan Adlercreutz defeated a Russian force of 2400 men under Col Erikson near Alavus in western Finland. The Swedes inflicted 370 casualties for the loss of 200 men.

■ GRÖNVIKSSUND, 30 AUGUST 1808

A Swedish fleet of 35 gunboats commanded by LCol Johan Ludvig Brant defeated Capt Selivanov's Russian fleet of 24 gunboats off Kustavi. The Swedes sank nine Russian vessels for the loss of two gunboats.

■ SALMI, 1–2 SEPTEMBER 1808

A Swedish army of 11,600 men commanded by Gen Carl Johan Adlercreutz was forced to retreat by Count Nikolay Kamensky's 21,000-strong Russian army after a prolonged artillery duel at Salmi, north-west of Helsinki.

■ JUTAS, 13 SEPTEMBER, 1808

A 1500-strong Swedish force under MGen Georg Carl von Döbeln attacked and defeated a Russian force of similar size commanded by

Gen Kiril Fedorovich Kazatchovski, which was attempting to cut the Swedish line of retreat from Vaasa to Nykarleby. The well-deployed Swedish artillery (four six-pounder guns) halted the Russian advance and Döbeln then led a charge, forcing them to retreat. The Swedes inflicted 130 casualties for the loss of 43 men.

■ **ORAVAIS, 14 SEPTEMBER 1808**

A 5000-strong Swedish army under Gen Carl Johan Adlercreutz was defeated by Count Nikolay Kamensky's Russian army of 7000 men at Oravais in western Finland. The Russians inflicted 2000 casualties on their Swedish opponents for the loss of 1000 men.

■ **PALVA SUND, 18 SEPTEMBER 1808**

A Russian coastal fleet defeated a smaller Swedish squadron. Lt Otto Julius Hagelstam rallied the survivors and succeeded in holding an overwhelming Russian fleet at bay for a week, beating off daily attacks at Kahiluoto.

■ **KOLJONVIRTA (VIRTA BRIDGE), 27 OCT 1808**

A 1800-strong Swedish force under Count Johan August Sandels defeated LGen Nikolay Tuchkov's Russian army of 6000 men near Iisalmi in eastern Finland. The Swedes inflicted 1100 casualties for the loss of 300 men.

■ **HÖRNEFORS, 5 JULY 1809**

Count Johan August Sandels' Savolax Brigade camped at Hörnefors after the evacuation of Skellefteå. The brigade was surprised by a Russian attack and retreated, covered by a fierce rearguard action in which they sustained heavy casualties.

■ **SÄVAR, 19 AUGUST 1809**

A 6800-strong Swedish army under LGen Gustav Wachtmeister was attacked by Count Nikolay Kamensky's Russian force of 6000 men. Although his forces inflicted 1600 casualties for the loss of 850 men, the ultra-cautious Wachtmeister retreated.

■ **RATAN, 20 AUGUST 1809**

LGen Gustav Wachtmeister's remaining troops retreated to the coastal village of Ratan where they received naval gunfire support, which was crucial in driving off Count Nikolay Kamensky's forces. Each side lost roughly 150 men.

Pre-war of 1812

■ *CHESAPEAKE-LEOPARD* **AFFAIR, 22 JUNE 1807**

As US frigate *Chesapeake* (36 guns), Cdre James Barron, left Virginia, British frigate *Leopard* (50), Capt Salusbury Humphreys, ordered her to allow the British to search for deserters. Upon Barron's refusal, *Leopard* fired for 10 minutes at the completely unprepared Americans, *Chesapeake* surrendering after one shot. The British boarded and took four accused deserters, having killed three Americans and wounded 18. The US government was left furious.

War of 1812 (1812–15)

■ **MACKINAC ISLAND I, 17 JULY 1812**

British Capt Charles Roberts caught Lt Porter Hanks unaware that war had broken out with British artillery in position and his fort surrounded. Fearing that the British allied Indians might massacre his command, Roberts surrendered.

■ **BROWNSTOWN, 5 AUGUST 1812**

US Maj Thomas van Horne set out to escort a supply column to Hull in Detroit. Tecumseh had rallied the local Indians to support the British and ambushed van Horne here, capturing dispatches, frightening Hull.

■ **MAGUAGA, 9 AUGUST 1812**

US Gen William Hull sent 600 men under LCol James Miller to bring supplies to Detroit. Tecumseh and 400 British and Indians attacked Miller and each other in confusion, Miller retreated to Detroit.

■ **FORT DEARBORN, 15 AUGUST 1812**

Gen William Hull ordered this post, essentially a trading station, evacuated soon after the outbreak of hostilities with Britain and the fall of neighboring Fort Mackinac. Capt Nathan Heald led out 67 garrison with 27 women and children after destroying Dearborn's stores. Four hundred Potawatomi and Winnebago Indians attacked the column of evacuees, killing 38 garrison, two women and 12 children, selling the survivors to the British for ransom.

■ **DETROIT, 15–16 AUGUST 1812**

Gen William Hull received a commuted death sentence for cowardice after surrendering this bastion to British Gen Isaac Brock, after Brock warned that his Indians might massacre the garrison. Hull forbade his artillery to fire.

■ *CONSTITUTION* **VS.** *GUERRIERE*, **19 AUG 1812**

This frigate duel between *Constitution* (44 guns), Capt William Hull, and *Guerriere* (38), Capt Richard Dacres, featured British shot bouncing off 'Old Ironsides's' hull and the *Guerriere*'s dismasting, surrender and sinking in a stinging British defeat.

■ *CONSTITUTION* **VS.** *JAVA*, **19 AUGUST 1812**

'Old Ironsides' scored again when *Constitution* (44 guns), Cdre William Bainbridge, engaged and took HMS *Java* (38), Capt Henry Lambert. *Java*'s greater speed allowed her to pummel *Constitution* severely before *Constitution*'s strength and battery prevailed.

■ **FORT WAYNE, 5–12 SEPTEMBER 1812**

As hostilities erupted, Potawatomi and Miami Indians attacked this post in Miami territory, firing homes nearby and seizing two wooden cannon, almost prompting Capt James Rhea to surrender before his two lieutenants declared him unfit to command and took over the defence of the fort. before a relief column 2200 strong under Gen (later President) William Henry Harrison arrived. The resulting battle drove off the Miami, many of whom joined Tecumseh.

■ **QUEENSTON HEIGHTS, 13 OCTOBER 1812**

American plans for an invasion of Canada along the Niagara river frontier died along with British Gen Isaac Brock in this disastrous battle. With Gen William Hull's effort to launch an invasion in the Detroit area collapsing disastrously, Gen Stephen van Rensselaer led 6660 regulars and militia towards the Canadian town of Queenston, his officers quarrelling and his men exhausted by long marches and a previous crossing's failure in a rain storm. Brock was aware of the impending invasion with 2340 (mostly) regulars posted throughout

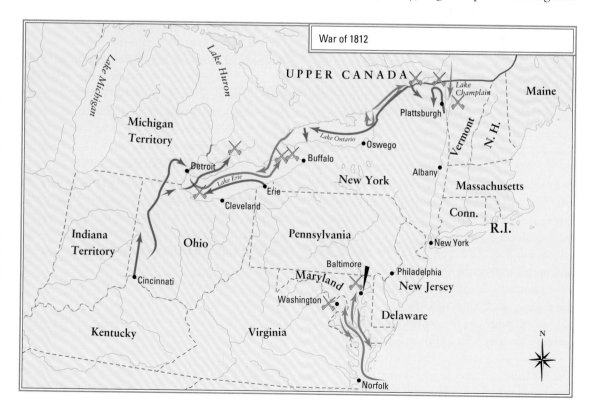

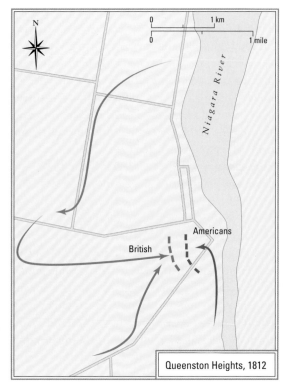

Queenston Heights, 1812

the threatened area. Van Rensselaer planned to ferry his remaining 4600 men over the river in 13 bateaux, with a battery covering the crossing. The boats became damaged or swept away during the many trips the landing required. Van Rensselaer himself had to be evacuated wounded when British Cap James Dennis launched a fierce attack on the US bridgehead. What American success there was came from Capt John Wool who led 100 regulars up Queenston Heights and captured a battery and the British camp there. Brock fell leading a charge up the heights, the British then falling back as American LCol Winfield Scott attempted to organize the 1350 Americans on the Canadian side of the river, while the British brought up additional units from Chippewa and sent allied Indians to harass Wool's position. There were no bateaux left to reinforce or rescue Scott's command, as Brock's replacement Gen Roger Sheaffe launched an attack that afternoon, which drove the exhausted Americans into flight. Scott

surrendered some 925 prisoners, as many as 200 Americans killed in the fighting and 20 British fell, mostly attacking Wool on the heights. Van Rensselaer resigned his commission. Winfield Scott was eventually exchanged.

■ **FORT HARRISON, 4–15 SEPTEMBER 1812**
Gen (later President) William Henry Harrison had built this powerful wooden bastion, but left it weakly garrisoned under the command of Cap (later President) Zachary Taylor. Emboldened by a series of American defeats, 600 Indians attacked the fort, which Taylor defended with 10 soldiers and sheltering civilians. The Indians continued to invest the fort until a relief column arrived. The desperately needed stand stemmed further Indian uprisings south into American territory.

■ *UNITED STATES* **VS.** *MACEDONIAN,* **25 OCTOBER 1812**
Weight of shot overcame rate of fire when frigate *United States* (44 guns), Captain Stephen Decatur, pummeled frigate HMS *Macedonian* (38), Captain John Carden, into surrender at long range. *Macedonian* became a gratifying US prize.

■ **WILDCAT CREEK, 22 NOVEMBER 1812**
Gen Samuel Hopkins with 1200 mounted militia and regulars moved south from Fort Harrison against Teumseh's Prophetstown and the Creeks. Destroying an abandoned Winnebago village here, Hopkins burned Prophetstown's homes and winter stores before withdrawing.

■ **MISSISSINEWA, 17–18 DECEMBER 1812**
The Miamis' failure to capture Forts Wayne and Harrison prompted LCol John Campbell's expedition down this river with 600 mounted troops, which enjoyed some success before bad weather and Miami counter-attacks prompted Campbell's withdrawal.

■ **FRENCHTOWN/RIVER RAISIN MASSACRE, 18–23 JANUARY 1813**
Gen James Winchester led 934 green militia north from Ohio. Col Henry Procter raised 1100 troops and Indians and overwhelmed the Americans here. Procter withdrew with his captives, the remaining Indians butchering 68 American prisoners.

■ **OGDENSBURG, 22 FEBRUARY 1813**
American raids across the St Lawrence river prompted this powerful British retaliatory raid in which LCol George Macdonell scattered Maj Benjamin Forsythe's defenders and captured and plundered mostly military stores from this New York town.

■ **YORK, 27 APRIL 1813**
An US force of 1800 under Gen Zebulon Pike landed at the Canadian capital and scattered 1100 British defenders under Gen Roger Sheaffe. During the occupation and plunder of the town, the Parliament buildings burned.

■ **FORT MEIGS, 28 APRIL–9 MAY 1813**
British Gen Henry Procter with Tecumseh led an army of 2000 to reduce this strong American bastion in Ohio. The fort's powerful earthworks held, with the worst of the American casualties occurring when 1200 militia attacked the British camp.

■ **FORT GEORGE, 25–27 MAY 1813**
This wooden fort at the north end of the Niagara river and its ruins changed hands twice during the war. Given its location along an invasion route, the British enlarged the bastion at the start of hostilities; however, the Americans succeeded in capturing it in mid-1813. Later, US Gen George McClure blew up the fort. By year's end, the returning British used the ruins as a base to capture US Fort Niagara.

■ **SACKET'S HARBOUR, 28–29 MAY 1813**
British Gen George Prevost and Cdre Chauncey Yeo launched an amphibious assault against this American naval yard on Lake Ontario. US Gen Jacob Brown grimly held the base's defences, the British successfully burning the naval stores.

■ **STONY CREEK, 6 JUNE 1813**
Advancing up from captured Fort George, 3400 US infantry under Gens John Chandler and William Winder retreated after British Gen John Vincent with 700 men surprised them in their encampment here, the British likewise withdrawing.

■ **CRANEY ISLAND, 22 JUNE 1813**
A British effort to 'cut out' the blockaded vessel USS *Constellation* in Norfolk failed after a British squadron in the Chesapeake landed as many as 3000 men in boats and barges to take Hampton and this island, upon which *Constellation's* own gunners manned a battery of cannon. Congreve rockets and the fall of Hampton could not overcome the fire of the battery and American gunboats, forcing a British retreat up the Chesapeake.

■ **BEAVER DAMS, 24 JUNE 1813**
After the fall of Fort George, LCol Charles Boerstler set out, armed with two cannon and 570 men, to strike a British outpost up the Niagara river country. Passing through Queenstown, the column alerted an expatriate loyalist, Laura Ingersoll Secord, who walked 32km in the darkness while Boerstler halted, to a camp of Indians allied to the British, one of whom led her to Lt James FitzGibbon, commanding troops skilled in forest warfare. Fitzgibbon joined with François Dominique Ducharme, an Indian agent, to post 400 allied warriors in especially thick brush in front of Boerstler's column here. The American cannon had no target and Boerstler's men could not get through the brush before the Indians arrived and fired upon them. Boerstler, under heavy attack, finally accepted FitzGibbon's proffer of surrender over the possible extinction of all his men by the Indians after 80 of his command had died.

■ **FORT STEPHENSON, 1 AUGUST 1813**
Withdrawing from Fort Meigs, Gen Henry Procter's siege train vainly attacked this Sandusky river bastion with cannon, Indians and gunboats. US Maj George Croghan and 160 garrison killed a quarter of Procter's regulars at close range.

■ **ST MICHAELS, 10 AUGUST 1813**
As the British fleet in the Chesapeake attempted to burn the shipyards in this Maryland town, a landing party overran the harbour cannon. The battery protecting the town repelled the attackers and saved the shipyard.

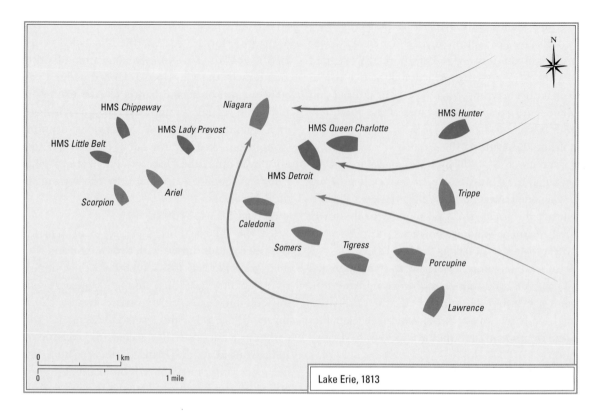

HMS Chippeway

Niagara

HMS Hunter

HMS Lady Prevost

HMS Queen Charlotte

HMS Little Belt

HMS Detroit

Trippe

Ariel

Scorpion

Caledonia

Somers

Tigress

Porcupine

Lawrence

N

0 — 1 km
0 — 1 mile

Lake Erie, 1813

■ LAKE ERIE, 10 SEPTEMBER 1813

Fighting on the Great Lakes was a matter of each side's confidence as a function of warships constructed. Royal Navy Cdr Robert Barclay repeatedly sought to lure his counterpart, Master Commandant Oliver Hazard Perry, into a battle when the British fleet was the stronger. Perry could not be rushed behind his defences at Preque Isle as he built up his own force into a powerful squadron.

Barclay decided to force the issue when the completion of HMS *Detroit* (11 guns), added her to *Queen Charlotte* (17), *Lady Prevost* (13), *General Hunter* (10) and two smaller ships. Barclay had stripped his own defending fort to secure cannon, with the result that his ships did not have a uniform weight of battery and were at times difficult to fire. Barclay was also short on supplies, and both sides faced a lack of skilled seamen.

Perry's two brigs, the *Lawrence* and *Niagara*, each mounted 20 short-range, but lethal 32-pound shot carronades, which could be reloaded rapidly. Seven smaller ships and gunboats made up the balance of Perry's fleet. When Barclay withdrew to make his own preparations for decisive battle, Perry moved his own fleet into deep water over a sandbar and sailed forth to engage Barclay. Shifting wind allowed Perry's nimble brigs to close range rapidly upon the British, *Lawrence* in the lead engaging the British line before the balance of the US fleet arrived. Perry had to abandon *Lawrence* two hours later in a near-sinking condition, rowing past the mauled British to *Niagara*, hanging back under the command of his disgruntled predecessor, Cdr Jesse Elliot. The undamaged *Niagara* plunged into the fight, the remaining American ships arriving and capturing the British squadron.

■ THAMES RIVER, 5 OCTOBER 1813

Having (despite Tecumseh's pleading) abandoned and partially burned Amherstburg after the defeat on Lake Erie, British Gen Henry Procter retreated along this river, burning ships and gunboats to forestall their capture. Procter finally made a stand with 430 soldiers and 600 Indians against US Gen William Henry Harrison's pursuing 3000 Kentucky militia, many of them mounted and vengeful. The British and surviving Indians retreated after suffering heavy casualties, including Tecumseh.

■ CHATEAUGUAY, 26 OCTOBER 1813

US Gen Wade Hampton, leading 4000 green infantry, moved down this river en route to Montreal. LCol Charles-Michel de Salaberry with 400 local troops in a series of defensive lines defeated Hampton in detail.

■ CHRYSLER'S FARM, 11 NOVEMBER 1813

Gen James Wilkinson's abortive advance into Canada foundered at Chrysler's Farm, during this attack in Ontario in November 1813, when 800 British regulars under LCol Joseph Morrison supported by gunboats repulsed the unco-ordinated advance of his 7000 men. Wilkinson's command errors prompted a court-martial into his actions.

■ LONGWOODS, 4 MARCH 1814

US dismounted dragoons numbering 164 under Capt Andrew Holmes, with the aid of an abatis and a height, defeated an effort by British Captain James Basden and 240 regulars and militia to evict them from Canada.

■ PORT DOVER, 14–16 MAY 1814

Lt John Campbell and 800 regulars and militia sailed to loot and burn the Canadian town in retaliation for British raids in Maryland and New York. The British used this attack to justify burning Washington DC

■ CHIPPEWA RIVER, 5 JULY 1814

British Gen Phineas Riall and 2000 regular soldiers blocked the advance from Fort Erie of Gen Jacob Brown with 4800 men. Gen Winfield Scott's regulars drew the British into a punishing crossfire, both sides afterwards retreating.

■ PRAIRIE DU CHIEN, 17–20 JULY 1814

British LCol William McKay led 650 regulars and allied Indians against US Fort Shelby, recently built here with 100 garrison. Under bombardment, a supporting American gunboat retreated, and Lt Joseph Perkins surrendered the fort.

■ LUNDY'S LANE, 25 JULY 1814

The British responding with 3000 men to Winfield Scott presence near the Niagara, US Gen Jacob Brown and British Gen Gordon Drummond fought a bloody and indecisive battle here in July 1814. A total of 81 British and 171 Americans perished.

■ MACKINAC ISLAND, 26 JULY–4 AUGUST

A US effort to retake this island in Lake Huron collapsed, when British LCol Robert McDouall with 200 soldiers at his disposal attacked the beachhead, capturing two American schooners, with US Col George Croghan retreating in the other three.

■ FORT ERIE, 4 AUGUST–21 SEPTEMBER 1814

Having seized this British post at the upper end of the Niagara, the US prepared to defend it in the aftermath of Lundy's Lane in what became the longest siege of the war. Gen Edmund Gaines enlarged the fort with batteries and entrenchments sheltering 2600 defenders. British Gen Gordon Drummond with siege artillery and 3000 regulars, militia and allied Indians surrounded the fort with batteries, but found the defenders, walls and trenches resistant to his bombardment. Several British efforts to storm the fort's bastions met with determined American resistance, while the besiegers were supplied by the river with less difficulty than the defenders via Lake Erie. Drummond finally withdrew when the Americans launched an attack with 2000 men against the British batteries, spiking cannon while inflicting and suffering heavy casualties. The Americans later abandoned and blew up the fort.

■ LAKE HURON, 13 AUGUST–6 SEPTEMBER 1814

A final series of American efforts to reassert control in the region of this lake generally did poorly in 1814. Five American schooners with 700 men landed and plundered an abandoned British base on St Joseph Island. The Americans next landed upon Mackinac Island, where a sudden British assault captured two of the schooners and prompted US Col George Croghan to abandon the effort to recapture the strategic island, which remained in British hands until the end of the war. The Americans next bombarded and destroyed a British fort protecting the supply base on Nottawasaga Bay. American foraging parties located schooner *Nancy*, which had been towed for safekeeping up the Nottawasaga River. The British had to destroy *Nancy*, the only British supply vessel on the lake, laden with winter supplies for the defenders, some of which they successfully concealed ashore. US Navy Capt Arthur Sinclair left schooners *Tigress* and *Scorpion* to patrol the northern Lake and intercept British traffic. Royal Navy Lt Miller Worsley, *Nancy*'s former commander, joined with army Lt Andrew Bolger and his Newfoundlanders in fitting out four bateaux with two cannon and sailing within 91m of *Tigress*, whose surprised gunners missed

their first defensive salvo. The British then rushed in and captured the American ship in a sudden boarding combat.

Setting her crew ashore, the British used the undamaged vessel, still flying the American colours, to seize *Scorpion* at 24km distance. The British then employed the two ships to ferry winter supplies and the prisoners to the British garrison on Mackinac Island. British plans to further secure their control of the lake with additional ship construction ended with the cessation of hostilities at the end of the year.

■ **BLADENSBURG, 24 AUGUST 1814**

After Napoleon's exile, Britain directed considerable resources into the ongoing war in North America. Around 2500 of Wellington's regulars joined a force of 20 warships in an attack up the Chesapeake Bay directly into the central United States. The American defences included a flotilla of gunboats and a few forts, the one at Mount Vernon being blown up by its own

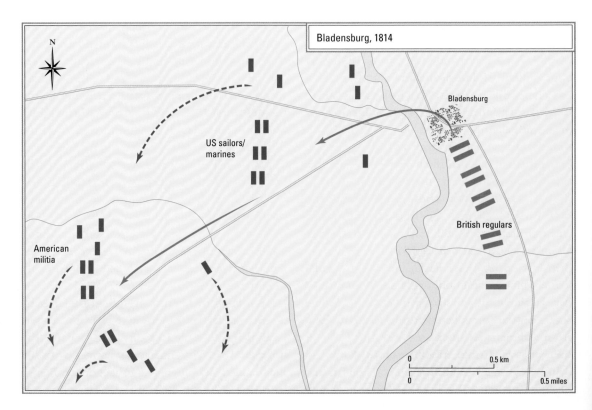

Bladensburg, 1814

garrison when the British approached. Adms Alexander Cochrane and George Cockburn sought profitable looting of Virginia tobacco, the crushing of Maryland privateering and the destruction of the US capital at Washington. American resistance varied from the heroic to the wildly incompetent, perfectly exemplified at this battle, when 4000 regulars marched through Maryland towards Washington. US Gen William Winder had 6000 green militia deployed at this town before the British advance, his positions changed at the last minute by Secretary of State James ·Monroe (later President) while President James Madison and most of his cabinet looked on.

Only 400 of US Cdre Joshua Barney's sailors and marines manning five navy cannon stood firm as the British approached up the pike, British Gen Robert Ross' Congreve rocket batteries scattering some militia, Winder ordering the remainder to retreat before they had engaged, while Madison and his cabinet escaped into the Maryland countryside. The British engulfed the sailors and marines, capturing the wounded Barney. About the only success in what later was known as the 'Bladensburg Races' was a day's time gained by the battle. The delay allowed First Lady Dolly Madison to evacuate some of the more important art and artefacts from the capital, which the British entered the following day and burned in a notorious action, ostensibly in retaliation for the burning of York and its parliamentary buildings in 1813.

■ **BURNING OF WASHINGTON, 24 AUGUST 1814**
British Adm George Cockburn planned and led this destructive and infamous raid on the US capital, the British regular soldiers under the command of Gen Richard Ross. Ross and Cockburn were methodical in their destruction, firing among other structures the Library of Congress, the executive mansion, the US Capitol, a ropewalk and the docks, the Washington Navy Yard burned by the Americans. A providential rainstorm extinguished the fires the day the British withdrew.

■ **ALEXANDRIA, 29 AUGUST–2 SEPTEMBER 1814**
The Virginia city of Alexandria drew ridicule for allowing British Adm Richard Cockburn to plunder their tobacco warehouses on the condition of sparing their homes. The citizens refused entry to Virginia militia attempting to repel the invaders.

■ **CAULK'S FIELD, 31 AUGUST 1814**
British Adm Alexander Cochrane sought to disperse American resistance during his fleet's raid up the Chesapeake estuary with diversions to draw the defenders away from his primary objective of Baltimore. Capt Peter Parker succeeded at the cost of his life when, on this farm, his force of 200 encountered Col Philip Reed and 174 militia, who had anticipated Parker's plan to attack their camp. At Parker's death, his men fled.

■ **HAMPDEN, 3 SEPTEMBER 1814**
A British amphibious expedition into undefended Maine and up the Penobscot river resulted in their long-term occupation of this and other coastal towns, plus the scuttling of the USS *Adams* (28 guns), to prevent capture.

■ **LAKE CHAMPLAIN, 6–11 SEPTEMBER 1814**
Guided by Perry's example at Lake Erie and his own considerable abilities as a leader and a sailor, US Cdre Thomas MacDonough – beginning in 1812 – constructed a powerful squadron upon the vital lake from green timber and imported fittings. British Cdre George Downie did likewise upon the lake's northern shore, with both sides mindful of the lake's potential role as a British invasion route from Canada. The British squadron numbered four large ships and 12 gunboats, the frigate *Confiance* (37 guns), the most powerful on the lake. MacDonough anchored his four large vessels and a total of ten gunboats across the mouth of Plattsburg bay. British firepower devastated the American ships, but when the British were within effective shot of MacDonough's carronades, they suddenly found themselves facing undamaged broadsides as MacDonough rotated his vessels by their anchor lines. Downie fell, his large ships captured.

■ **PLATTSBURG, 6–11 SEPTEMBER 1814**

British Gen George Prevost marched along the shore of Lake Champlain with 10,000 men, accompanied by a powerful fleet, as part of a plan to divide New England from the rest of the US. Prevost had reached this city in New York, where US Gen Alexander Macomb with 3400 resisted his attack until the news of the British fleet's destruction in the battle of Lake Champlain forced Prevost's retreat.

■ **NORTH POINT, 12 SEPTEMBER 1814**

The British sought to punish and plunder Baltimore, source of tobacco and privateers. British Gen Robert Ross and 4600 men landed here, the land assault ceasing after Ross fell to Gen John Stricker's militia riflemen.

■ **BALTIMORE, 12–15 SEPTEMBER 1814**

US Gen Samuel Smith poured 17,000 defenders into the city, the objective of the British fleet to raid the Chesapeake. Entrenched militia blunted a British landing force at North Point, while harbour batteries withstood British bombardment.

■ **FORT MCHENRY, 13–14 SEPTEMBER 1814**

This star-shaped brick fort's baptism of fire under the mortars, cannon and rockets of the British fleet became legendary in song. The fort's defenders grimly stuck to their cannon, blocking the harbour and managing to save Baltimore.

■ **FORT BOWYER, FIRST BATTLE, 14 SEP 1814**

A British naval squadron bombarded the Mobile Bay fort, while a detachment of Royal Marines attacked overland. The US garrison repulsed the attack and forced the British squadron to withdraw two days later.

■ **MALCOLM'S MILLS, 6 NOVEMBER 1814**

British efforts to forestall US Gen Duncan McArthur's cavalry raid into the Niagara river country prompted a force of 400 Canadians to fight here. McArthur's 700 troopers launched a holding attack that scattered the militia.

■ **FARNHAM CHURCH, 6 DECEMBER 1814**

A small detachment of British soldiers landing under the bombardment of a portion of the Chesapeake fleet failed to capture this coastal Virginia church, protected by rallying Virginia militia. Arriving defenders discouraged further British raiding.

■ **LAKE BORGNE, 14 DECEMBER 1814**

British forces in armed longboats and barges attacked an American gunboat flotilla. Despite the loss of the flotilla, the American gunboats delayed the British attack on New Orleans, allowing time to strengthen the city's defences.

■ **NEW ORLEANS, 23 DECEMBER 1814**

A 1800-man British vanguard landed 15km south of New Orleans. That night, the American defenders attacked the British. The failed attack halted the British advance, enabling the Americans to strengthen their defensive works.

■ **NEW ORLEANS, 8 JANUARY 1815**

After a weeklong artillery bombardment, the British attacked the American defences on 8 January 1815. Well-placed American artillery disrupted the initial attack. Subsequent attacks failed with most of the senior British officers, including the commanding general, among casualties. Consequently, the British failed to capitalize on the few battlefield successes they enjoyed. By the day's end, the British had suffered over 2000 casualties whereas the Americans had fewer than 100.

■ **FORT ST PHILIP, 9 JANUARY 1815**

British ships bombarding the fort were devastated by American artillery fire. Unable to silence the American batteries, the British withdrew after nine days, leaving the Americans in control of the Mississippi river.

■ **FORT PETER, 13 JANUARY 1815**

After seizing Cumberland Island, a British naval force sailed up the St Mary's river and captured the fort on 13 January 1815. A second British force advanced overland to St Mary's and occupied the town for 10 days.

■ **FORT BOWYER, SECOND BATTLE, 7 FEB 1815**

A 1400-strong British expedition attacked the fort, which surrendered after a five-day siege. Two days later, when news of the Treaty of Ghent arrived, the British postponed their attack on Mobile.

Wars of Empire and Revolt, 1815–1914

*Although the Napoleonic Wars ended in 1815, the world entered a new era of conflict.
Developments in weapons technology meant that by the beginning of World War I in 1914,
the potential for armies to unleash mass destruction was greater than ever.*

Second Barbary War 1815–16

■ ACTION OF 17 JUNE, 1815

With the War of 1812 concluded, the United
States' powerful and proven navy took the
opportunity to deal with resurgent Muslim piracy
in the Mediterranean, Congress declaring war
against the Bey of Algiers in 1815. Commodore
Stephen Decatur's squadron of nine ships arrived
before the news and USS *Guerriere* combined
with *Constellation* upon this day to maul and
capture frigate *Meshuda*, killing the pasha of the
Algerian Navy.

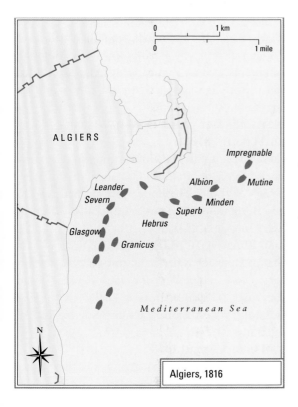

Algiers, 1816

■ ALGIERS, 27 AUGUST 1816

The United States made an example of the
Barbary pirates for preying upon American
shipping in the Mediterranean. Armed with
nine ships and a declaration of war, Commodore
Stephen Decatur had the orders and capability to
sweep every Algerian ship from the sea. The bey
renounced piracy against American shipping in a
treaty that was signed on 24 September 1816, on
the deck of Decatur's flagship. 1,083 Christian
slaves and the British Consul were freed.

South American Wars 1815–30

■ SANTA MARIA, 1815

General Simón Bolívar's liberation of Venezuela
received a check here, when a powerful Spanish
force – sent out from Europe under Viceroy Pablo
Morillo after Napoleon's surrender – defeated the
Venezuelans soundly, forcing Bolivar's temporary
exile to Jamaica.

■ SIPE-SIPE, 28 NOVEMBER 1815

José Rondeau's United Provinces Army of 3500
men was defeated at Sipe-Sipe (in modern
Bolivia) by a 5100-strong royalist army under
Joaquín de la Pezuela. The royalists inflicted 2000
casualties for the loss of 230 men.

■ CROSSING THE ANDES, 19 JAN–13 FEB 1817

The rebel Army of the Andes, totalling 4000
Argentine and Chilean troops and 1200
auxiliaries under José de San Martín and Bernardo
O'Higgins, made an epic 500km march across
the Andes from Argentina to Chile.

■ CHACABUCO, 12 FEBRUARY 1817

The Army of the Andes under José de San
Martín and Bernardo O'Higgins defeated Rafael

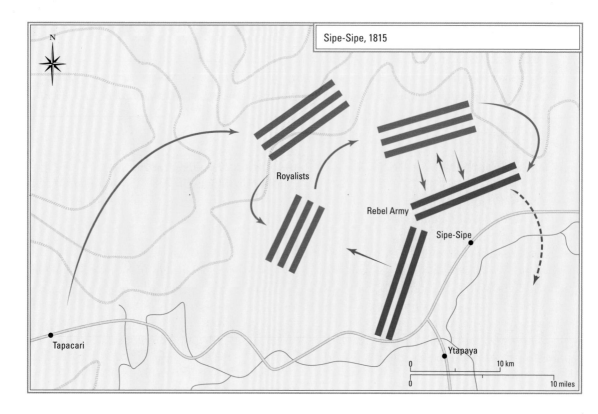

Maroto's 1500 royalists at Chacabuco near Santiago. The rebels inflicted 1100 casualties for the loss of 100 men.

■ PERNAMBUCAN REVOLT, 1817

The Portuguese province of Pernambuco in north-eastern Brazil had prospered during the War of 1812 between the United States and Britain, and opened markets for its cotton in Europe. However, as the Portuguese re-established control after 1815, they once again began to impose restrictions on Brazilian commerce. Tensions grew between Brazilians and Portuguese in Pernambuco, gradually developing into a full-scale movement to establish an independent republic in the region. The rebels formed a provisional government, which sought arms and diplomatic support from Argentina, Britain and the United States. Failing to get international help, the rebels sought support from Bahia and Ceará, but the governors of these regions remained loyal to the Portuguese crown.

The Pernambucan rebels abolished titles of nobility, class privileges and some taxes. Although insurgents from Paraíba and Alagoas joined those from Pernambuco, royalist forces quickly suppressed the rebellion.

■ SECOND BATTLE OF CANCHA RAYADA, 16 MARCH 1818

Don Mariano Osorio's 5000-strong royalist army decisively defeated the 7000 men of the rebel Army of the Andes under José de San Martín and Bernardo O'Higgins at Cancha Rayada near Talca in central Chile.

■ LA PUERTA, 16 MARCH 1818

Simón Bolívar's rebel army pursued the royalist forces of Pablo Morillo into Guarico and they met at El Semen, near La Puerta. Bolivar was routed in a bloody action with the loss of 1200 men.

■ MAIPÚ, 5 APRIL 1818

The 5000-strong rebel Army of the Andes commanded by José de San Martín and Bernardo

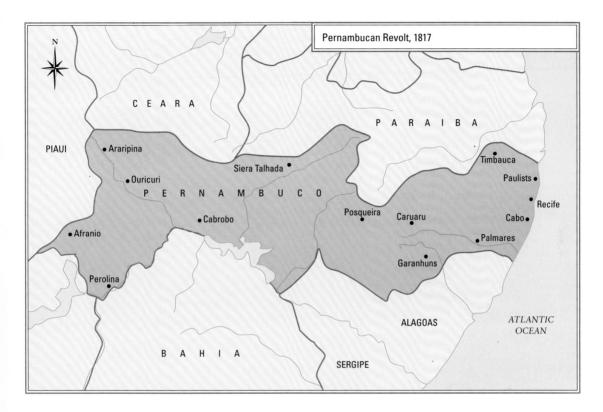

Pernambucan Revolt, 1817

O'Higgins attacked Don Mariano Osorio's royalist forces, also totalling roughly 5000 men, on the Maipú plains, near Santiago. The rebels won a decisive victory, inflicting 3000 casualties for the loss of 1000 men. The victory ended Spanish control of Chile and allowed Chilean and Argentine rebels to liberate much of Peru from Spanish rule.

■ LAS QUESERAS DEL MEDIO, 2 APRIL 1819

The cavalry vanguard of Simón Bolívar's rebel army comprising 153 men under José Antonio Páez, defeated the 1200 cavalry of Pablo Morillo's royalist army. The rebels inflicted 400 casualties for the loss of eight men.

■ BOYACÁ, 7 AUGUST 1819

Gen Simón Bolívar advanced with his rebel army of almost 3500 men on Bogotá, the capital of Gran Granada (modern Colombia). Anticipating this move, General José María Barreiro's 3000-strong royalist force marched to intercept the rebel forces.

Bolívar caught Barreiro's men as they were crossing the bridge at Boyacá (el Puente de Boyacá). Sending two-thirds of his men forward under Brigadiers Francisco de Paula Santander and José Antonio Anzoátegui, the Colombian, Venezuelan and British Legion troops successfully routed each half of Barreiro's army in turn. The infantry attacks were supported by effective cavalry charges against the Spanish rearguard, which completed the royalists' defeat.

Bolívar's forces only suffered 66 casualties, while the royalists lost 250 dead and wounded, plus 1600 prisoners including Barreiro and his second-in-command, Francisco Jiménez. Barreiro and 38 other royalist officers were later executed.

■ PÍLEO, 7 DECEMBER 1819

A foraging detachment of 50 Chilean cavalry under Capt Pedro Kurski was trapped and virtually wiped out by a 200-strong band of Vicente Benavides' royalist guerillas at Píleo, on the south bank of the Biobío river.

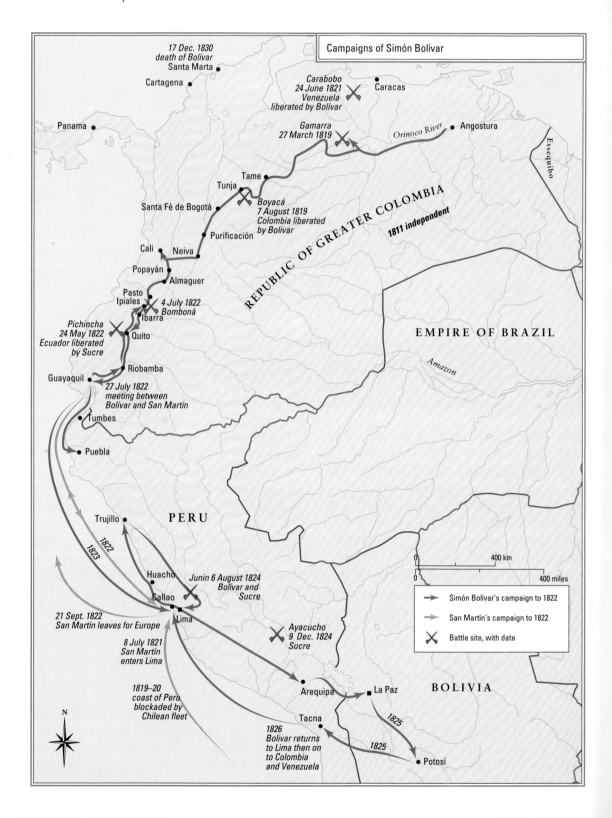

Campaigns of Simón Bolívar

17 Dec. 1830
death of Bolívar
Santa Marta

Cartagena

Carabobo
24 June 1821
Venezuela
liberated by Bolívar

Caracas

Panama

Gamarra
27 March 1819

Orinoco River

Angostura

Essequibo

Tame

Tunja

Santa Fé de Bogotá

Boyacá
7 August 1819
Colombia liberated
by Bolívar

Purificación

REPUBLIC OF GREATER COLOMBIA

1811 independent

Cali   Neiva

Popayán

Almaguer

Pasto
Ipiales

4 July 1822
Bomboná

Ibarra

EMPIRE OF BRAZIL

Pichincha
24 May 1822
Ecuador liberated
by Sucre

Quito

Amazon

Riobamba

Guayaquil

27 July 1822
meeting between
Bolívar and San Martín

Tumbes

Puebla

Trujillo

PERU

1822

1823

Huacho

Junín 6 August 1824
Bolívar and
Sucre

Callao

21 Sept. 1822
San Martín leaves for Europe

Lima

Ayacucho
9 Dec. 1824
Sucre

8 July 1821
San Martín
enters Lima

1819–20
coast of Peru
blockaded by
Chilean fleet

Arequipa

La Paz

BOLIVIA

1826
Bolívar returns
to Lima then on
to Colombia
and Venezuela

Tacna

1825

1825

Potosí

N

Simón Bolívar's campaign to 1822

San Martín's campaign to 1822

Battle site, with date

400 km

400 miles

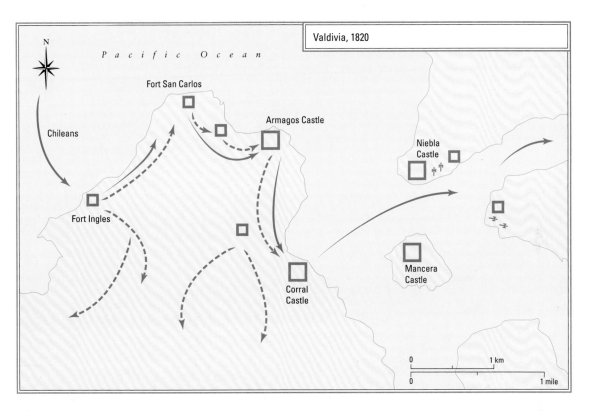

Valdivia, 1820

Pacific Ocean

N

Fort San Carlos

Chileans

Armagos Castle

Niebla Castle

Fort Ingles

Mancera Castle

Corral Castle

0   1 km

0   1 mile

■ VALDIVIA, 3–4 FEBRUARY 1820

Lord Cochrane, a former British naval officer who had commanded the Chilean Navy since 1818, led a 350-strong landing party that surprised and captured the heavily defended royalist port of Valdivia in southern Chile.

■ AGÜI, 18 FEBRUARY 1820

Lord Cochrane's squadron landed a 60-strong detachment of Chilean marines under William Miller in an unsuccessful attempt to capture Fort Agüi on the Chiloé archipelago, which was held by a royalist garrison under Antonio de Quintanilla.

■ EL TORO, 6 MARCH 1820

Jorge Beauchef, the Chilean governor of Valvidia, led a 140-strong detachment south against the remaining royalist forces. The Chileans defeated 300 royalists at the Hacienda El Toro, inflicting almost 150 casualties for the loss of 40 men.

■ TARPELLANCA, 26 SEPTEMBER 1820

Acting on forged orders, Pedro Andrés del Alcázar's 600-strong Chilean garrison of Los Angeles evacuated the town and was defeated by 2400 royalist guerillas under Vicente Benavides at the Tarpellanca ford on the Laja river.

■ CARABOBO, 24 JUNE 1821

Gen Simón Bolívar's 7500-strong rebel army (including roughly 1000 British Legion veterans of the Napoleonic Wars) attacked a royalist army of 5000 men under Miguel de la Torre that blocked the road to Puerto Cabello (in modern Venezuela). Bolívar attempted an outflanking manoeuvre across rough terrain that was initially beaten off. A further attack by the British Legion routed the royalist forces, inflicting 2900 casualties for the loss of 200 men.

■ PICHINCHA, 24 MAY 1822

Antonio José de Sucre's 3000-strong rebel army defeated 1900 royalists under Melchior Aymerich on the slopes of the Pichincha volcano, near Quito (in modern Ecuador). The rebels destroyed the royalist army for the loss of 340 men.

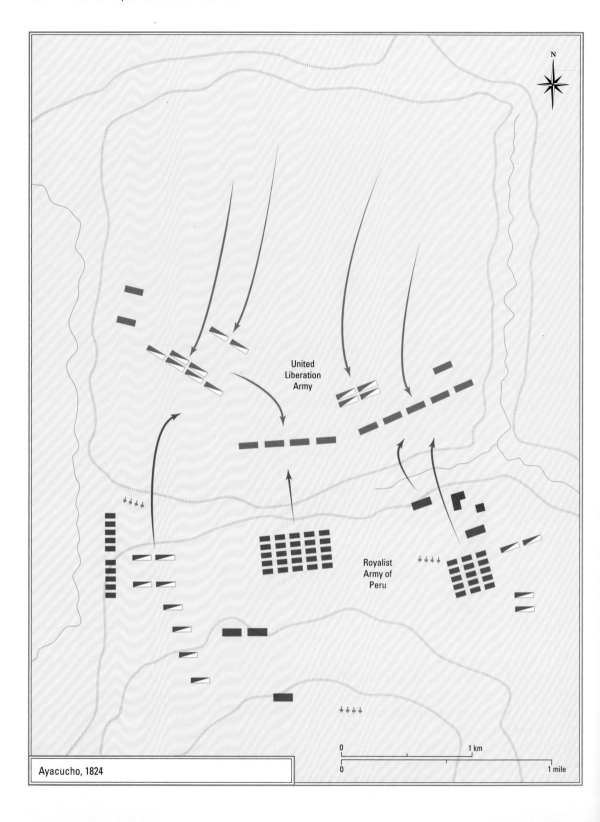

United
Liberation
Army

Royalist
Army of
Peru

0   1 km
Ayacucho, 1824
0   1 mile

N

◼ ACTION OF 4 MAY 1823

Expatriate British admiral Thomas Cochrane's services and long experience against Napoleon proved useful to more than one coastal South American country during the series of revolts that left Spain and Portugal at the end reft of their empires in the southern hemisphere. After service with Chile and Peru, Cochrane accepted an appointment as First Admiral of the Brazilian Navy in March 1823. Cochrane immediately experienced great difficulties with sub-standard ordnance and ammunition. A bigger obstacle was the insubordination of South American officers, who, during a revolt against Europe, became disgruntled with serving under a European and resentful of Cochrane's sudden superior rank. Cochrane faced a powerful Portuguese squadron comprising ships mounting 75, 50 and 44 cannon, with five smaller frigates and six lesser vessels. This flotilla took possession of Bahia on the Brazilian coast as the restored Portuguese government sought to reassert its control in Brazil. Cochrane's untried squadron of seven ships consisted of vessels mounting 74, 32 and fewer guns. Cochrane found his move to blockade Bahia countered by a sortie of the entire Portuguese squadron, which sailed forth to meet him in line. Nonetheless, in the largest vessel, the *Pedro Primiero*, Cochrane sailed Nelson-style through the approaching Portuguese, signalling to the rest of his squadron to support him in isolating and destroying the four vessels at the end of the enemy line. Instead, Cochrane found himself battling the entire enemy squadron when his subordinate commanders ignored his orders to engage. Defective munitions and unskilled gunners frustrated Cochrane's attempt to damage the nearest Portuguese, while the Portuguese serving in the magazines denied powder to the guns. Cochrane withdrew and launched a reformation of the Brazilian Navy into a capable fighting force.

◼ LAKE MARACAIBO, 24 JULY 1823

Adm José Prudencio Padilla defeated a royalist squadron under Capt Ángel Laborde on this Venezuelan lake, the rebel forces and royalists exerting considerable effort in what proved to be the last battle of Venezuela's liberation.

◼ JUNIN, 6 AUGUST 1824

Generals Simón Bolívar's and José Canterac's royalist cavalry employed lance and sabre in this battle in Argentina. Bolívar's hussars saved the day as Canterac's lancers drove the patriots back by attacking from the royalists' rear.

◼ AYACUCHO, 9 DECEMBER 1824

In this, the final, decisive battle for Spain's control over South America, Spain's last viceroy, José de La Serna e Hinojosa, led Spain's last effort to retain control of at least the southernmost portion of the New World in Peru. De La Serna and Antonio José de Sucre (Simon Bolívar's most talented subordinate) gathered their forces, the rebels securing some advantage by mustering in the Andean highlands and acclimatizing to the very high altitude. The two roughly even armies then manoeuvred against each other among the rivers and around the plateau of Ayacucho, each seeking geographic advantage. Both sides took their time in selecting a proper battlefield. The royalists occupied the proverbial high ground with well-equipped cavalry and artillery, factors that have determined more than one military victory for the side possessing them, while the rebels were the hardened veterans of a long succession of campaigns. Moreover, Sucre had the remnants of Bolívar's cadre of British and other European mercenaries (some veterans of the Napoleonic Wars) and experienced and well-motivated native officers of his own. A head injury incapacitated De La Serna early in the fighting. When the Spanish general José Canterac's detached artillery and cavalry forces got ready to make their assault downhill from the heights, Sucre launched a spoiling attack that negated the royalists' artillery, who were unable to fire into the melee. As the last royalist attack moved to flank Sucre's line, Gen William Miller, commanding a powerful if scratch reserve

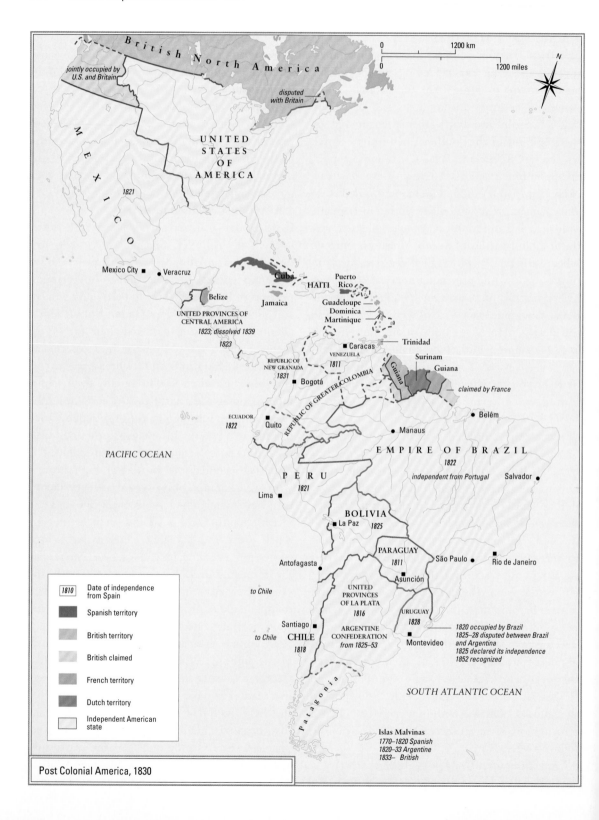

British North America

jointly occupied by
U.S. and Britain

disputed
with Britain

0   1200 km
0   1200 miles

N

M E X I C O

UNITED
STATES
OF
AMERICA

1821

Mexico City ■ ● Veracruz

■ Belize

Cuba

Jamaica

HAITI

Puerto
Rico

Guadeloupe
Dominica
Martinique

■ Caracas

Trinidad

Surinam

Guiana

UNITED PROVINCES OF
CENTRAL AMERICA
1823; dissolved 1839
1823

REPUBLIC OF
NEW GRANADA
1831   ■ Bogotá

VENEZUELA
1811

Guiana

claimed by France

ECUADOR
1822   ■ Quito

REPUBLIC OF GREATER COLOMBIA

● Belém

● Manaus

PACIFIC OCEAN

P E R U
1821

Lima ■

E M P I R E   O F   B R A Z I L
1822

independent from Portugal   Salvador ●

BOLIVIA
■ La Paz   1825

PARAGUAY
1811

São Paulo ●

Rio de Janeiro ■

Antofagasta ■

Asunción ■

to Chile

UNITED
PROVINCES
OF LA PLATA
1816

URUGUAY
1828

1820 occupied by Brazil
1825–28 disputed between Brazil
and Argentina
1825 declared its independence
1852 recognized

Santiago ■
to Chile   CHILE
1818

ARGENTINE
CONFEDERATION
from 1825–53

■ Montevideo

P a t a g o n i a

SOUTH ATLANTIC OCEAN

Islas Malvinas
1770–1820 Spanish
1820–33 Argentine
1833– British

1810   Date of independence
from Spain

Spanish territory

British territory

British claimed

French territory

Dutch territory

Independent American
state

Post Colonial America, 1830

of cavalry, launched a charge strong enough to defeat the long-maturing Spanish surprise attack toward the battle's end. De La Serna recovered and negotiated Spain's final withdrawal from South America, leaving Sucre with a complete and enduring victory.

Argentine–Brazil (Cisplatine) War 1827–28

■ JUNCAL, 8–9 FEBRUARY 1827

This naval battle took place between a squadron of ships from each country on 8–9 February 1827, at the Uruguay river near the Rio de la Plata. The Argentine Navy, under the command of Adm William Brown, was victorious, destroying or capturing 15 of 17 Brazilian ships from the Third Division of their fleet led by Cdr Jacinto Pereira, by using superior tactics and artillery.

■ MONTE SANTIAGO, 7–8 APRIL 1827

This naval battle occurred on 7–8 April 1827, between 12 Brazilian ships and four Argentine

ones. It resulted in a victory for Brazil and the loss of two Argentine ships that allowed Brazil's future domination of the Rio de la Plata.

■ IRISH–GERMAN SOLDIERS' REVOLT, 9 JUNE 1828

Revolt on 9 June 1928, by thousands of German and Irish immigrants to Brazil, who were falsely recruited as farmers, then forced into the Brazilian Army. The uprising was finally suppressed with the assistance of French and British marines.

Gran Colombia Peru War 1827–29

■ ITUZAINGO, 18 FEBRUARY 1827

A revolt by the Brazil province of Banda Oriental and the Argentine Army led to a battle near the Santa Maria river with Brazilian forces. The several thousand soldiers on each side fought to a stalemate on 18 February 1927.

■ TARQUI, 27 FEBRUARY 1829

The battle of Portete de Traqui took place on 27 February 1829, near Cuenca, Ecuador, between armies of about 4000 soldiers from the victorious Gran Colombia alliance of Colombia, Ecuador, Venezuela and Panama against Peru with hundreds of casualties.

■ SAN ROQUE, 22 APRIL 1829

A retreating federalist force in a defensive position at San Roque near Cordoba on 22 April 1829, was overrun by a Unitarian cavalry charge that followed an artillery bombardment. The Federalists fled leaving over 100 casualties.

Zulu War 1817–19

■ GQOKLI HILL, APRIL 1818

The Ndwandwe tribal army divided by a decoy manoeuvre twice attacked the Shaka-led Zulu Army in a defensive bull horn position on the hill in April 1818, leading to their defeat and loss of several thousand men.

■ MHLATUZE RIVER, 1819

While pretending to retreat from Gqokli Hill, the Zulu army attacked the Ndwandwe tribal forces when they crossed the Mhlatuze river in pursuit. The remnants of the Ndwandwe fled in disarray and their leader Zwide was killed shortly after. the attack.

Greek War of Independence, 1821–30

■ **TRIPOLITSA, APRIL–23 SEPTEMBER 1821**
A Greek rebel army of 15,000 men under Theodoros Kolokotronis began the blockade of Tripolitsa in April 1821, but failed to prevent reinforcements reaching the Ottoman garrison, which ultimately totalled 8000 Turkish and 3000 Albanian troops under Kâhya Mustafa Bey. Kolokotronis negotiated the evacuation of the garrison's Albanian contingent before the city was stormed and the remaining garrison troops were massacred, together with the entire Muslim and Jewish population.

■ **ALAMANA, 22 APRIL 1821**
An 8000-strong Ottoman army commanded by Omer Vrioni defeated a band of 1500 Greek rebels under Ioannis Dyovouniotis, Dimitrios Panourgias and Athanasios Diakos at the Alamana river (Spercheios) near Thermopylae. Diakos was captured and executed.

■ **GRAVIA INN, 8 MAY 1821**
After his victory at Alamana, Omer Vrioni headed south into the Peloponnese with an army of 9000 men. However, 120 rebels under Odysseas Androutsos blocked his advance at the village of Gravia, barricading themselves in a roadside inn. Vrioni ordered a series of frontal attacks on the inn, all of which were repelled before the rebels escaped into the surrounding hills, having inflicted 1100 casualties for the loss of six men.

■ **VALTETSI, 12 MAY 1821**
Following the outbreak of the Greek War of Independence in March 1821, the Greek rebels focused their efforts on the capture of the city of Tripolitsa (modern Tripoli) in the central Peloponnese. The veteran Greek warlord Theodoros Kolokotronis was proclaimed as rebel *Archistratigos* (C-in-C) and began to concentrate

his forces around the mountain village of Valtetsi near Tripolitsa. The 2300-strong rebel force was attacked by an Ottoman army of 5000 men under Kehayabey Mustafa. Although parts of the village were overrun, the Greeks held on, aided by the rocky terrain that was virtually impassable by the Ottoman cavalry. Effective flank attacks by a 700-strong force led by Theodoros Kolokotronis in person and a further Greek detachment under Dimitris Plapoutas forced the Ottomans to retreat, which rapidly became a rout. The rebels inflicted 650 casualties for the loss of 150 men.

■ **DOLIANA, 18 MAY 1821**
A 2000-strong Ottoman army that broke out from the besieged city of Tripolitsa (modern Tripoli) in the central Peloponnese was defeated with the loss of 300 men by 200 Greek rebels under Nikitas Stamatelopoulos.

■ **DRAGASHANI (DRĂGĂŞANI), 19 JUNE 1821**
A revolt in the Ottoman province of Wallachia (modern Romania) was exploited by the Greek nationalist secret society 'Filiki Eteria' ('Friendly Society'), who organized a military wing, the 'Sacred Band', from volunteers from the Greek communities around the Black Sea. Initially organized as a 500-strong unit, later expanding to 2000 men, it was annihilated by an Ottoman army of 7500 men at the village of Drăgăşani.

■ **SKULENI (SCULENI), 29 JUNE 1821**
Sultan Mahmud II's 5000-strong Ottoman army defeated a force of 500 Greek rebels under George Cantacuzenus and Giorgakis Olympios at the village of Sculeni in Moldova. Olympios blew himself up in the Secu Monastery rather than surrender.

■ **VASSILIKA, 25 AUGUST 1821**
A force of 800 Greek rebels under Ioannis Gouras ambushed and defeated an Ottoman army of 5000 men commanded by Behrem Pasha at Vassilika near Thermopylae. The Greeks inflicted over 1000 casualties and captured two guns.

■ **PETA, 4 JULY 1822**
A Greek rebel force of 2200 men commanded by Prince Alexandros Mavrokordatos and Markos

Botsaris was surprised and decisively defeated by Omer Vrioni's 7000-strong Ottoman army near the village of Peta in Epirus.

■ DERVENAKIA, 26–28 JULY 1822

Mahmud Dramali Pasha's 30,000-strong army of Ottomans was defeated by a Greek force of 10,000 irregulars under Theodoros Kolokotronis, Demetrios Ypsilantis, Papaflessas and Nikitas Stamatelopoulos. The Ottoman army sustained 20,000 casualties during the battle and was effectively destroyed.

■ KARPENISI, 8 AUGUST 1823

Markos Botsaris' band of 450 Greek rebels made a night attack on an Ottoman Army of 13,000 men encamped near Karpenisi. The Greeks inflicted 1000 casualties almost without loss, but retreated when Botsaris was killed.

■ KASOS MASSACRE, 7 JUNE 1824

The Pasha of Egypt, Mehmet Ali, invaded Kasos in retaliation for the islanders' raids on Egyptian shipping. After overcoming the defenders in two days of fighting, Egyptian landing parties massacred an estimated 7000 inhabitants.

■ SAMOS, 17 AUGUST 1824

A Greek squadron of 16 warships under Adm Georgios Sachtouris intercepted Koca Mehmed Husrev Pasha's Ottoman fleet of 22 vessels. An attack by Greek fireships sank three of the Ottoman vessels and the rest withdrew.

■ GERONTAS, 29 AUGUST 1824

An Ottoman fleet of 40 warships under Koca Mehmed Husrev Pasha approached the rebel-held island of Samos in July, but were forced to retreat by a Greek squadron of 21 vessels. Both sides were steadily reinforced until, by late August, Adm Andreas Miaoulis' Greek fleet of 70 ships faced an Ottoman fleet of 400 assorted vessels. An attack by Greek fireships destroyed at least 30 of the Ottoman vessels and the remainder eventually fled.

■ SPHACTERIA, 8 MAY 1825

The small Greek garrison of the island of Sphacteria was defeated by a force of 1500 Egyptian troops under Ibrahim Pasha. The Greek

Secretary of State, Alexandros Mavrokordatos barely managed to escape aboard the brig *Aris*.

■ MANIAKI, 1 JUNE 1825

Ibrahim Pasha's 6000-strong Ottoman army, largely composed of Egyptian troops, defeated 3000 Greek rebels under Papaflessas near the village of Maniaki in the Peloponnese. The Ottomans inflicted 1000 casualties for the loss of 400 men.

■ LERNA MILLS, 24 JUNE 1825

Ibrahim Pasha's 5000-strong Ottoman army, largely composed of Egyptian troops, unsuccessfully attacked a force of 350 Greek irregulars under Ioannis Makrygiannis and Konstantinos Mavromichalis. The irregulars were garrisoning the Lerna Mills, which were an important Greek supply point.

■ ARACHOVA, 18–24 NOVEMBER 1826

Greek rebels commanded by Georgios Karaiskakis and Dimitrios Makris trapped and defeated a force of 2000 Ottoman troops under Mustafa Bey and Kehagia Bey in the mountains near Arachova. No more than 300 Ottomans escaped.

■ KAMATERO, 27 JANUARY 1827

Reşid Mehmed Pasha's Ottoman army defeated 2800 Greek rebels at Kamatero near Athens. Vassos Mavrovouniotis and Panayotaki Notaras failed to support the attack by Col Denis Bourbaki's 800 men, who sustained at least 500 casualties.

■ NAVARINO, 20 OCTOBER 1827

A combined British, French and Russian fleet under VAdm Sir Edward Codrington, totalling 10 ships of the line, 10 frigates and six smaller craft, confronted an Ottoman fleet of three ships of the line, 17 frigates and 68 smaller vessels in Navarino Bay. Although the allied vessels had a total of only 1258 guns against the Ottoman 2180 guns, the British, French and Russian weapons were more modern and of markedly heavier calibre, giving them an overwhelming advantage in firepower. The confrontation flared up into open combat when the frigate HMS

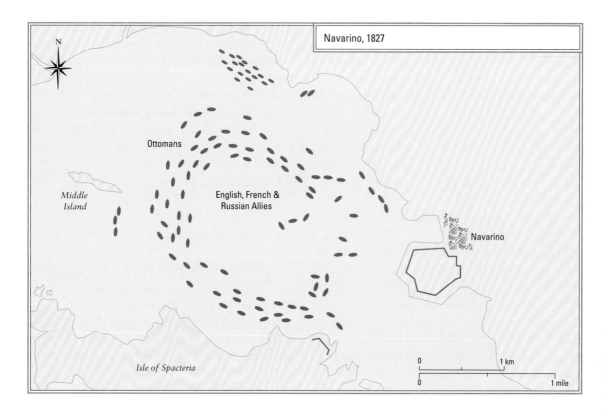

Navarino, 1827

Ottomans

Middle Island

English, French & Russian Allies

Navarino

Isle of Spacteria

0   1 km
0   1 mile

Dartmouth noticed an Ottoman fireship being prepared for action. *Dartmouth*'s captain dispatched a boat to negotiate, which was fired on and the firing rapidly escalated until a full-scale battle was in progress.

For four hours, the two fleets battered each other, with the allies' advantage in training and equipment becoming increasingly apparent.

The greatest threat to allied vessels in the confined waters of Navarino Bay was posed by the Ottoman fireships. One of these succeeded in grappling the French battleship *Scipion*, setting her rigging and upper gun deck ablaze before the fireship could be towed clear. This allowed *Scipion*'s crew to finally extinguish the fire, which had spread dangerously close to the forward magazine.

As the fighting died out, more than 75 per cent of the Ottoman fleet had been sunk, with no more than eight ships remaining operational: one dismasted battleship, two frigates and five corvettes. A total of six major allied vessels were badly damaged. The Russian battleships *Azov*, *Gangut* and *Iezekiil* were all disabled, while all three British ships of the line, *Asia*, *Albion* and *Genoa*, had to be sent to England for extensive repairs.

■ **PETRA, 12 SEPTEMBER 1829**

Demetrios Ypsilantis' 2000 Greek irregulars defeated an Ottoman army of 7000 men under Aslan Bey. The Greeks had prepared extensive field defences and Aslan Bey's forces lost over 1000 men in futile frontal assaults.

Spanish Civil War, 1820–23

■ **TROCADERO, 31 AUGUST 1823**

A French army under Louis-Antoine, Duke of Angoulême, decisively defeated Gen Rafael del Riego's force of Spanish rebels at the Trocadero Forts outside the city of Cadiz. The French inflicted a total of 600 casualties for the loss of 400 men.

Italian Wars of Independence, 1848–70

■ MILAN, 18–22 MARCH 1848

On 18 March, fighting broke out between Italian revolutionaries seeking independence from Austria and the 15,000-man Austrian garrison. After five days of intense street battles, FM Radetzky withdrew his army from the city to Verona.

■ PASTRENGO, 30 APRIL 1848

The Piedmontese under Charles Albert with 13,500 men attacked and defeated an Austrian force of 8000 near Peschiera. The victory opened the road to Verona and enabled the Piedmontese to lay siege to Peschiera.

■ SANTA LUCIA, 6 MAY 1848

FM Radetzky, with 26,000 men, engaged and repelled an attack by the Piedmontese Army of 20,000 men under Charles Albert just west of Verona. The Piedmontese withdrew toward Villafranca and observed Verona for the next several months.

■ VENICE, MAY 1848–AUGUST 1849

Daniele Manin led a revolution in Venice, forcing the Austrian garrison to withdraw to the mainland. Pressed by revolution and war in Lombardy-Venetia, Radetzky kept the city under siege until the summer of 1849. The city surrendered to the Austrians after the Piedmontese and Roman revolutions had been defeated.

■ GOITO, 30 MAY 1848

Austrian field marshal Radetzky, together with 40,000 men attempted to outflank the Piedmontese Army by marching north from Mantua. The Piedmontese, 28,000-strong under Carlo Alberto, counter-marched, catching the Austrians on the line of march at Goito, where they defeated them.

■ 1ST CUSTOZA, 19–22 JULY 1848

The Piedmontese under Charles Albert observed the fortress of Verona from their position between Villafranca and Custoza. Austrian field marshal Josef Radetzky took the initiative and attacked the Piedmontese to their front from Verona, while a second Austrian column from Mantua assailed the Piedmontese flank and rear. After two days of combat, Charles Albert retreated to Milan, where he signed an armistice ending the war.

■ ROME, 8 FEBRUARY–3 JULY 1849

After Pope Pius IX withdrew his support for the Italian revolutions of 1848, demonstrations against papal authority increased. The assassination of Pellegrino Rossi, the Minister of Justice, on 15 November, marked the beginning of the revolution. Pius IX fled Rome on 24 November, seeking sanctuary in the city of Gaeta, under the protection of Ferdinand II, the King of the Two Sicilies. In Rome, a republic was proclaimed in February 1849 and an executive Triumvirate established. Giuseppe Mazzini, the famed Italian revolutionary, arrived and was appointed to the new government. Giuseppe Garibaldi and volunteers from the north arrived several days prior to a French expeditionary force. Garibaldi was made co-commander of the army of the Roman Republic, along with General Roselli. Louis-Napoleon, the newly elected President of France, dispatched troops to restore Pius IX to the papal throne. Garibaldi and Roselli defended the city against a French Army of 10,000 men under Gen Charles Oudinot. Garibaldi repelled the first French attacks at the end of April. Oudinot withdrew his forces to Civitavecchia and requested reinforcements and a siege train. Louis-Napoleon sent another 10,000 men and artillery. Oudinot invested the city on 1 June. General Vaillant directed the siege of Rome and took the city after breaching the walls on the Janiculum (Giancolo) on 29 June. During the intervening two months between the first and second French assaults the Neapolitan army advanced upon Rome. Garibaldi defeated the Neapolitans at Palestrina on 9 May and again on 19 May at Velletri. After the city surrendered to the French, Garibaldi led his volunteers into the Apennines with the intention of reaching

Venice. Pursued by Austrian and Spanish troops, Garibaldi's forces eventually disintegrated. His wife Anita died during the retreat, and Garibaldi managed to avoid capture and flee Italy.

■ **NOVARA, 22–23 MARCH 1849**

King Charles Albert intended a second invasion of Lombardy in 1849. He concentrated 75,000 men in the Lomellina. Radetzky with 60,000 men, launched a pre-emptive offensive from Pavia. He flanked the Piedmontese positions at Mortara, pushing Charles Albert upon Novara. After two days of heavy fighting around Novara, the Piedmontese were defeated and Charles Albert abdicated in favour of Victor Emanuel II.

■ **BRESCIA, 26–31 MARCH 1849**

News of Charles Albert's war with Austria led Brescians to revolt. Generals Haynau and Nugent, leading Austrian forces, methodically cleared the Brescian revolutionaries from the suburbs, then the city, restoring Austrian control and relieving 4000 Austrians.

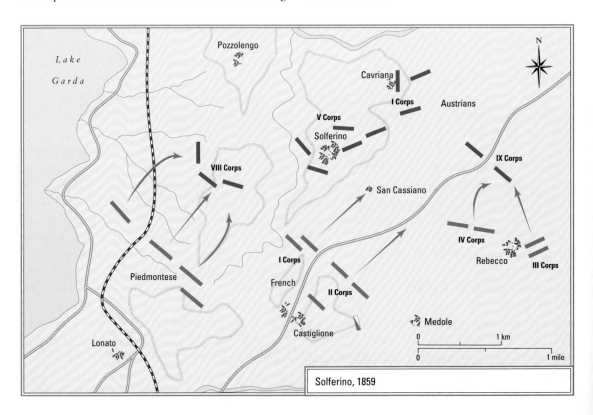

Solferino, 1859

■ MONTEBELLO, 20 MAY 1859

A French division under Gen Forey encountered an Austrian corps south of the Po near Montebello. Supported by Piedmontese cavalry, Forey held one Austrian division at bay, while the majority of his troops pushed the Austrians through Montebello and beyond. It was the first major engagement between French and Austrian forces in 1859.

■ VARESE, 26 MAY 1859

Giuseppe Garibaldi led the Cacciatori della Alpi, numbering some 3000 men, in the Alps during the 1859 campaign. He was attacked at Varese by an Austrian advanced guard of 4000 men. Medici's regiment held Garibaldi's centre and counter-attacked, while Cosenz's regiment assailed the Austrian left. The Austrians retreated, compelling the Austrian General Urban to withdraw his main force to the east.

■ PALESTRO, 30–31 MAY 1859

On 30 May, the Piedmontese under Cialdini attacked an Austrian brigade at Palestro. The following day, the Austrians counter-attacked in corps strength and engaged Cialdini, reinforced by Fanti's division and the III French Corps under Canrobert. The Austrian attacks were repulsed, thereby securing a bridgehead for the Franco-Piedmontese Army across the Sesia river.

■ MAGENTA, 4 JUNE 1859

The French Army under Napoleon III attacked the Austrian Second Army under Franz Gyulai. Four Austrian corps defended the approaches to Milan, but were assailed front and flank by three French corps. Gyulai withdrew his army by nightfall after heavy losses.

■ SOLFERINO, 24 JUNE 1859

Emperor Franz Josef led the Austrian First and Second Armies across the Mincio river in a counter-offensive against the Franco-Piedmontese under Napoleon III and Victor Emanuel II. The Austrian Army comprised seven corps and the cavalry reserve numbered some 134,000 men (111,000 engaged). The allied armies consisted of five corps, plus four divisions of Piedmontese, numbering 134,000 men (115,000 engaged). Franz Josef intended to achieve a decisive battle with the Franco-Piedmontese east of the Chiese river, near Castiglione. However, the allied armies began their movement in the middle of the night and encountered the Austrians west of Solferino early in the morning.

The battle of Solferino can be divided into three parts: the fighting for the town of Solferino and its environs; the battle south of Solferino on the Campo di Medole; and the fighting at Madonna della Scoperta and San Martino between the Piedmontese and the Austrian V and VIII Corps. At 05:00, the French divisions of Ladmirault and Forey from Baraguey d'Hilliers I Corps engaged Austrian brigades from Stadion's V Korps west of Solferino. After three hours of intense combat, the Austrians were pushed into the town and its walled cemetery. Fighting continued throughout the morning. By early afternoon, Austrian reinforcements from Clam Gallas' I Corps threatened French gains. Napoleon III committed the French Imperial Guard and Bazaine's division from I Corps. By late afternoon, the French had captured Solferino and the cemetery and the Austrians withdrew east of the town.

South of Solferino, MacMahon's II Corps with two divisions of cavalry attacked the Austrian VII Corps at San Cassiano. The fighting was indecisive until mid-afternoon when the French Imperial Guard Cavalry and La Motterouge's division broke the Austrian line toward Cavriana, but were stalled by Austrian reinforcements.

On the Campo di Medole, the French IV Corps under Niel, supported by part of Canrobert's III Corps, faced the Austrian, II, IX and XI Corps. Supported by three divisions of cavalry and massed artillery, Niel repelled numerous Austrian assaults until around 15:00. Reinforced by more of Canrobert's corps, Niel advanced toward Guidizzolo, but was halted by the arrival of fresh Austrian troops. Fighting continued until early evening. North of Solferino, two Austrian brigades from Stadion's V Corps held the town and heights of Madonna della Scoperta. The Piedmontese 1st Division under Durando assaulted the Austrian position throughout the day, finally taking it by early evening.

At San Martino, the Piedmontese 3rd and 5th Divisions ran into the Austrian VIII Corps under Benedek. The combat over San Martino heights raged throughout the day, as the Piedmontese brigades attacked as they arrived on the field and their initial success was tempered by Austrian reinforcements. After four assaults, plus reinforcements by a brigade from 2nd Division, the Piedmontese took the Cascina Contracania and the church at San Martino after 19:00.

Franz Josef decided to withdraw his army during the early evening while it remained in good order, albeit having suffered heavy casualties. Skirmishing continued through the evening until 22:00. The withdrawal of the army compelled Benedek to follow suit after losing his position on San Martino heights.

The Austrian defeat at Solferino led to negotiations between Franz Josef and Napoleon III that ended with the Peace of Villafranca on 11 July 1859. The inability of the respective armies to cope with the thousands of casualties inspired Swiss observer Henri Dunant to establish the Red Cross in 1863.

■ CALATAFIMI, 15 MAY 1860

Giuseppe Garibaldi and 1089 men ('the Thousand') engaged 2000 Neapolitans under Landi. The Garibaldini attacked uphill with the bayonet, forcing the Neapolitans to abandon their positions. The road to Palermo was opened.

■ MILAZZO, 17–24 JULY 1860

Garibaldi and Giacomo Medici attacked the Neapolitan forces under Bosco to secure the road to Messina. Bosco's disciplined troops inflicted heavy casualties upon the Garibaldini, but were outflanked. The Neapolitans withdrew to the castle of Milazzo, fending off successive assaults. Both sides suffered heavy casualties, but

after negotiations, Bosco was transported by sea to Messina, abandoning the castle.

■ CASTELFIDARDO, 18 SEPTEMBER 1860

Papal general Lamoricière attempted to reinforce Ancona prior to the city succumbing to a Piedmontese siege. The Piedmontese under Cialdini blocked the route on the north side of the Musone river. Lamoricière's army was decimated and only a small number reached Ancona.

■ ANCONA, 18–29 SEPTEMBER 1860

The Piedmontese under Cialdini laid siege to the city of Ancona held by a papal garrison. It was the only port capable of accommodating a relief force by sea. The Piedmontese naval squadron under Persano bombarded the city from the Adriatic, while Cialdini's siege guns fired from the land side.

■ VOLTURNO, 30 SEPTEMBER 1860

Giuseppe Garibaldi, with 27,000 men of the Southern Army, was attacked by the Neapolitan Army in roughly equal number. Garibaldi assumed a defensive posture on the south bank of the Volturno, observing Capua. His divisions held positions from Santa Maria to Caserta and Maddaloni. The Neapolitan Army attempted to conduct a double envelopment, but poor coordination led to piecemeal assaults. The attack on Garibaldi's right only partially materialized and was repelled by Bixio. Garibaldi moved reserves from Caserta to Santa Maria, assisting Medici and Milbiz. After repelling the Neapolitans at Santa Maria, a late assault on Caserta was repulsed with Medici's division redeployed from Garibaldi's left. The Neapolitan Army withdrew behind the walls of Capua. The battle sealed the fate of the Neapolitan kingdom and paved the way for the Piedmontese siege of Gaeta.

■ GAETA, 9 NOVEMBER 1860–13 FEBRUARY 1861

Francesco II and the remnants of his army took refuge in the fortress city after the defeat on the Volturno and the Piedmontese invasion of Naples from the north. The city was placed under siege by the Piedmontese Army under

Cialdini. The Neapolitan garrison comprised 12,000 men. The Piedmontese Navy could not effectively bombard the city, as the Neapolitan squadron in the harbour kept Adm Persano at bay. Until January 1861, the Piedmontese had few artillery pieces appropriate for a siege, but gradually assembled 166 siege guns, which permitted them to silence Neapolitan cannon on the outer works. The siege lasted 100 days. The surrender marked the conclusion of the Second War of Italian Unification and the creation of the Kingdom of Italy.

■ **ASPROMONTE, 29 AUGUST 1862**

Giuseppe Garibaldi with 3000 men crossed from Sicily to southern Italy. He led his force north with the cry 'Rome or Death!' He was intercepted by an Italian force of 3000 men and defeated. Garibaldi was wounded and captured, but later released.

■ **2ND CUSTOZA, 24 JUNE 1866**

Gen La Marmora crossed the Mincio into Venetia with 65,000 men, divided into two corps (I, III) and took up position on the heights from Sommacampagna to the Mincio, with Custoza at the centre. Archduke Albrecht, commanding 75,000 men of the Austrian Southern Army, attacked the Italian divisions spread along the line, permitting Albrecht to press the Italian flanks. Arrival of Italian reinforcements stalled the Austrian attacks, but La Marmora retreated by nightfall.

■ **LISSA, 20 JULY 1866**

The Italian fleet under Adm Carlo Persano sailed from Ancona, the main Italian naval base in the Adriatic, during the second week of July, with the intention of capturing the island of Lissa (Vis). The island held several strong forts and coastal batteries and an Austrian garrison of 2000 men. The Italian fleet comprised 34 warships, of which 12 were armoured, including the most advanced, *Affondatore*, which was built in England and possessed turrets and a ram. The Austrian fleet at Pola, under Adm Tegethoff, believed the Italian attack on Lissa was merely

a diversion. Persano had the freedom of almost a week of uninterrupted time to assault the island, but failed to effect a landing. Finally, Tegethoff led the Austrian fleet to intercept. On 20 July, Tegetthoff, with 27 warships, including seven armoured, attacked the Italians off Lissa. Both fleets were poorly prepared for the action, having spent little time on gunnery and fleet manoeuvres. Tegetthoff determined to arrange his ships in a wedge formation and break the Italian line. Naval tactics using armoured ships were still in their experimental stage; thus both fleets believed their armoured ships with rams could sink their enemies through collision. Tegetthoff directed the battle from the flagship *Ferdinand Max*, while Persano initially took post on the *Re d'Italia*. As the battle developed, Persano changed flags to the *Affondatore*, but neglected to inform his van and division commanders. Thus, the Italian captains were not clear on which ship to follow. Tegetthoff's flagship rammed the

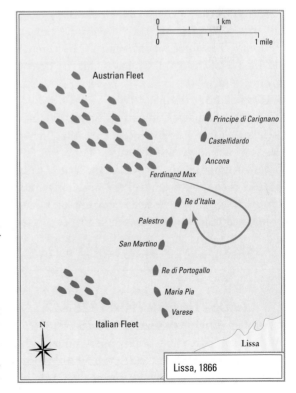

Lissa, 1866

Re d'Italia, which sunk. The *Palestro* took significant fire and exploded. The Austrians broke the Italian line, but the battle degenerated into a series of ship-to-ship actions and ramming. Two Italian warships were sunk and Persano ordered the fleet to withdraw to Ancona. Tegetthoff lost no ships.

■ **BEZZECCA, 21 JULY 1866**

Giuseppe Garibaldi led 40,000 men in an invasion of the Austrian-held Trentino. The Austrian forces comprised largely of elite Kaiserjäger and local battalions, inflicted heavy casualties on the Garibaldini during their offensive. At Bezzecca, 10,500 Austrians attacked the Garibaldinians in roughly equal number. The battle moved back and forth throughout the day, but significant Austrian casualties compelled General Kuhn to withdraw to contend with a flanking column led by Garibaldi's lieutenant, Giacomo Medici.

■ **MENTANA, 3 NOVEMBER 1867**

Giuseppe Garibaldi with 6000 men advanced upon Rome hoping to seize the city and unify it with Italy. A Franco-papal expeditionary corps of 9000 men intercepted Garibaldi's attack, defeating his force at Mentana. The French retained a garrison in Civitavecchia to defend Rome until 1870.

■ **ROME, 20 SEPTEMBER 1870**

The Italians under Cadorna with 50,000 men attacked Rome in September after the French garrison withdrew from the city. Pope Pius IX ordered Kanzler, the papal commander with 15,000 men, to surrender the city only after the walls were breached. The seizure of Rome completed Italian unification

Ottoman-Turkish Wars 1828–78

Russo-Turkish War 1828–29

■ **AKHALTSIKHE (AKHALZIC), 9 AUGUST 1828**

A Russian force of 9000 men under FM Ivan Fyodorovich Paskevich defeated Kios-Mahomet-Pasha's 30,000-strong Ottoman

Army at Akhaltsikhe in Georgia. The city was incorporated into the Russian Empire by the Treaty of Adrianople in 1829.

Egyptian Revolt against Turkey 1832–40

■ **KONYA, 21 DECEMBER 1832**

After overrunning much of Syria, Ibrahim Pasha's Egyptian Army of 15,000 men deployed just north of the Anatolian city of Konya, facing a 53,000-strong Ottoman army under the Grand Vizier, Reşid Mehmed Pasha. Persistent fog caused considerable problems for both sides and contributed to the capture of the Grand Vizier in a confused melee after which the Ottoman Army was routed. Ibrahim's forces inflicted 8000 casualties for the loss of 900 men.

■ **NIZIB (NIZIP), 24 JUNE 1839**

Ibrahim Pasha's 46,000-strong European-trained Egyptian Army defeated an Ottoman army of 80,000 men commanded by Hafiz Osman Pasha at Nizip near Aleppo. The Egyptians lost 4000 men, but inflicted far heavier casualties on the Ottoman forces.

■ **ACRE, 3 NOVEMBER 1840**

Adm Sir Robert Stopford's Mediterranean Fleet of eight ships of the line, six frigates and seven smaller warships bombarded the defences of Egyptian-occupied Acre until a magazine explosion forced the defenders to evacuate the city.

Russo-Turkish War 1877–78

■ **KIZIL-TEPE, 25 JUNE 1877**

A Turkish army of 55,000 men under Ahmed Mukhtar Pasha attacked Gen Mikhail Loris-Melikov's 60,000-strong Russian Army, which was besieging Kars. Both sides lost about 1000 casualties, but the Russians were forced to raise the siege.

■ **SVISTOV, 26–27 JUNE 1877**

MGen Mikhail Dragomirov's 4th Division attacked across the Danube at Svistov on 26 June. The Turkish fortress was taken the following day by MGen Mikhail Skobelev's troops at the cost of 800 casualties.

■ NIKOPOL, 16 JULY 1877

Baron Nikolai Kridener's 20,000-strong Russian IX Corps crossed the Danube and attacked the city of Nikopol, in the Ottoman Empire's Danubian Vilayet (modern Bulgaria). The city was held by a Turkish garrison of 7000 men who were expecting to be reinforced by Osman Nuri Pasha's 20,000-strong army. However, the Russian artillery battered the garrison into surrender before Osman could arrive and his army was forced to retreat to Plevna.

■ SHIPKA PASS, 17 JULY 1877–9 JANUARY 1878

The Shipka Pass in the Balkan Mountains was held by Suleiman Pasha's force of 4000 men with 12 guns, which repelled Count Iosif Gurko's initial attack from the north on 17 July and another from the south on the following day. Despite these successes, the Turks evacuated their strong position, which was occupied by the Russians on 19 July.

The first Turkish counter-attack was made on 21 August by Suleiman Pasha's 30,000-strong army on Major General Nikolai Stoletov's combined Russian and Bulgarian force of 7500 men garrisoning the pass. A series of attacks and counter-attacks were made during the following days until the battle ended in mutual exhaustion on 26 August, with the Russians and Bulgarians having inflicted 10,000 casualties for the loss of 3600 men. Despite their exhaustion, both sides held their ground, digging in around the pass.

The next major actions were fought several weeks later, when command of the Russian and Bulgarian garrison of 8000 men had passed to MGen Fyodor Radetzky. On 17 September, Suleiman Pasha's 25,000 men attacked after a four-day Turkish artillery bombardment, but were beaten off after breaking through the first line of trenches. The Turks inflicted 4000 casualties, but lost a further 10,000 men.

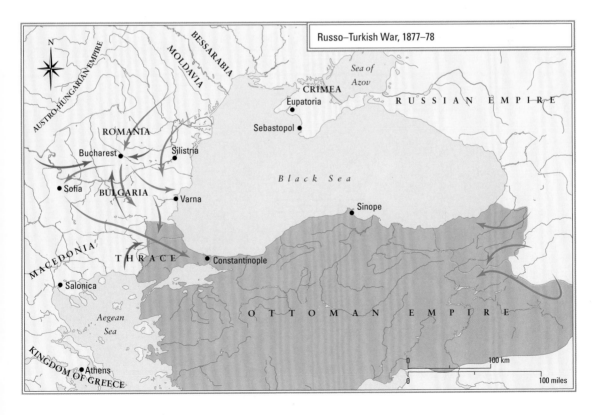

The fourth and final action began on 5 January 1878, after Russian forces in the area had been reinforced by units freed for redeployment by the surrender of Plevna. Count Iosif Gurko now had overall command of 65,000 men, facing a 40,000-strong Turkish army under Veissel Pasha. Radetzky's garrison attacked from the pass while two other Russian columns cut off the Turks' retreat, inflicting 4000 casualties for the loss of 5500 men and forcing the surrender of the 36,000 survivors.

■ PLEVNA, 20 JULY–10 DECEMBER 1877

A force of 110,000 Russian, Romanian and Bulgarian troops under the Grand Duke Nicholas and Prince Carol I of Romania defeated Osman Nuri Pasha's 40,000-strong Turkish garrison, but sustained an estimated 40,000 casualties.

■ LOVCHA, 1–3 SEPTEMBER 1877

Just after the siege of Plevna began, 15 battalions of Turkish infantry were assigned to reinforce Osman Nuri Pasha's garrison and were deployed

to defend the town of Lovcha (modern Lovech in Bulgaria), a key link in Plevna's supply chain. The Russians appreciated Lovcha's importance and the town was stormed by a force of almost 23,000 men under Gen Alexander Imerentinski. Three battalions of the garrison escaped to reinforce Plevna's defenders.

■ GORNI DUBNIK, 24 OCTOBER 1877

Count Iosif Gurko's 18,000-strong Russian Army stormed Gorni Dubnik, which was defended by a Turkish garrison of 4000 men under Ahmed Hifzi Pasha. Barely 200 of the garrison escaped after inflicting almost 3300 Russian casualties.

■ KARS, 17 NOVEMBER 1877

A Russian army of 28,000 men under Gen Mikhail Loris-Melikov sucessfully stormed the Turkish city of Kars in eastern Anatolia, defended by Hussein Hami Pasha's 24,000-strong garrison. The Russians sustained almost 2300 casualties.

■ TASHKESSEN, 28 DECEMBER 1877

Covering the Turkish withdrawal to Adrianople,

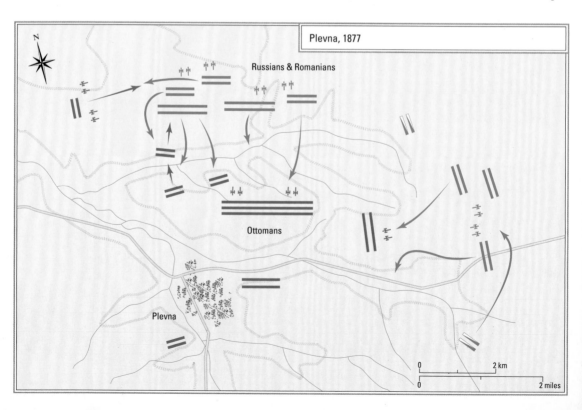

2000 men under Valentine Baker (a former British officer) made a stand at Tashkessen. Baker's force mauled Count Iosif Gurko's army, inflicting 1000 casualties for the loss of 800 men.

■ **PHILIPPOPOLIS (PLOVDIV), 17 JANUARY 1878**

Count Iosif Gurko's 12,000-strong Russian Army stormed the city of Philippopolis (modern Plovdiv, in Bulgaria). The city was defended by a Turkish garrison of 6000 men under Suleiman Pasha, which inflicted 1300 casualties on the attackers.

Ottoman–Montenegrin War 1876–78

■ **VUČJI DO, 18 JULY 1876**

A Montenegrin and Herzegovinian force commanded by Prince Nicholas I of Montenegro decisively defeated a larger Turkish army under Muktar Pasha. The prince's men inflicted 4000 casualties for the loss of under 200 men.

■ **FUNDINA, 2 AUGUST 1876**

A 5000-strong Montenegrin force under the warlords Ilija Plamenac and Marko Miljanov Popović defeated a Turkish army of 40,000 men under Mahmud Pasha. The Montenegrins inflicted at least 10,000 casualties for the loss of 600 men.

Anglo-Burmese Wars 1824–1905

■ **KEMMENDINE, 3 & 10 JUNE 1824**

After the capture of Rangoon, Gen Sir Archibald Campbell attacked the nearby fortress of Kemmendine. The assaults were initially beaten off with the loss of 120 men, but the fortress was successfully stormed on 10 June.

■ **RANGOON (YANGON), 30 NOV–16 DEC 1824**

When Burma conquered Arakan and threatened British India, Britain declared war and Gen Sir Archibald Campbell's force of 10,000 men occupied Rangoon in May 1824, fortifying the Shwedagon Pagoda compound. By late November, General Maha Bandula's 30,000-strong Burmese Army had surrounded the British garrison and

launched a series of unsuccessful frontal assaults on their defences. The poorly armed Burmese troops took heavy losses from British artillery and rocket fire, sustaining 23,000 casualties.

■ **PROME, 1–5 DECEMBER 1825**

Gen Sir Archibald Campbell's Anglo-Indian force of 5000 men defeated a 13,000-strong Burmese army under Gen Maha Ne Myo at Prome. Maha Ne Myo was killed in action and his army was virtually destroyed.

■ **MARTABAN, 5 APRIL 1852**

Gen Henry Godwin and Adm Charles Austen attacked Martaban, at the mouth of the Salween opposite Moulmein, held by 5000 Burmese troops. The city was successfully stormed and Godwin captured Rangoon a few days later.

■ **THIRD ANGLO-BURMESE WAR (IRRAWADDY CAMPAIGN), NOVEMBER 1885**

MGen Sir Harry Prendergast's 9000-strong Anglo-Indian force supported by 67 guns invaded Burma in a flotilla of 55 river craft.

	First Anglo–Burmese War, 1824–26
	Second Anglo–Burmese War, 1852
	Third Anglo–Burmese War, 1885

Burma 1830–1905

The Burmese surrendered after their defences at Minhla, Nyaung-U, Pakokku and Myingyan were destroyed.

Native American Wars, 1817–90

■ CLAREMORE MOUND, OCTOBER 1817

The Osage tribe lost this struggle with the Cherokee nation when the Cherokee overran and burned Chief Claremore's village in northern Oklahoma while the men were out hunting, killing some 80 old men, women, and children.

Arikara War 1823

This plains tribe sought to preserve their role in the fur trade by attacking traders in their territory. Col Henry Leavenworth joined with Lakota Sioux to bombard and attack Arikara villages along the Missouri river.

Winnebago War 1827

The Winnebago War was a limited war of a few skirmishes in June 1827, around Prairie du Chien, Wisconsin, by a large war party of Ho-Chunk warriors assisted by other tribes and a few civilians that eventually led to confrontation with a large contingent of US militia several hundred strong at Portage. Tribal leaders gave up six of their number – including the warrior Red Bird – who were imprisoned to avoid the battle.

Black Hawk War 1832

■ STILLMAN'S RUN, 14 MAY 1832

A detachment of 275 Illinois militia commanded by Maj Isaiah Stillman fled from a superior force of mainly Sauk warriors under Chief Black Hawk, leaving 12 dead behind on 14 May 1832, near a stream in Ogle County, Illinois.

■ SPAFFORD FARM, 14 JUNE 1832

On 14 June 1832, in Lafayette County, Wisconsin, a Kickapoo war party attacked and killed several farmers, including Spafford, while crossing the Pecatonica river in a prelude to the later battle of Horseshoe Bend.

■ HORSESHOE BEND, 16 JUNE 1832

On 16 June 1832, Col Henry Dodge and his militia attacked and killed an entire Kickapoo war party of 17 warriors at the battle of Horse Shoe Bend, also called Pecatonica or Bloody Lake.

KELLOGG'S GROVE, 16 JUNE 1832

The battle of Kellogg's Grove, Illinois, involved two skirmishes over several days on 16 June 1832, when a large band of warriors under Chief Black Hawk fought US militia with small losses on both sides.

■ WISCONSIN HEIGHTS, 21 JULY 1832

US militia commanded by Col Henry Dodge attacked and defeated a band of Sauk warriors under Chief Black Hawk on 21 July 1832, at Wisconsin Heights, in a static battle after a three-day chase.

■ BAD AXE, 1–2 AUGUST 1832

Chief Black Hawk led the Sauks and Fox back across the Mississippi into Illinois, counting on

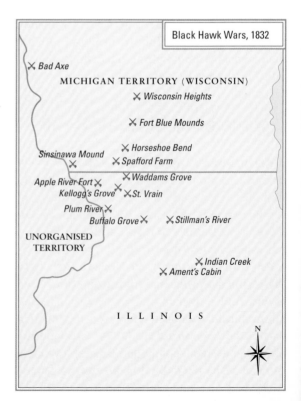

support from the British in Canada to regain lost territories as they attacked US settlements there and in Wisconsin. State militia, supported by Gen Henry Atkinson's Regulars, drove Black Hawk's 1500 back to the river. Black Hawk attempted surrender here, but some 200 men, women and children perished before the militia and soldiers relented.

Creek War 1836

The remnant of the Creek tribe in Alabama launched retaliatory raids when the state itself opened their treaty lands for settlement. After fierce fighting, troops eventually moved the rest of the Creeks to Oklahoma.

Comanche War 1820–75

■ **FORT PARKER, MAY 1836**
Members of a Baptist sect built this fort in north Texas, having concluded treaties with the neighbouring tribes and farmers. A considerable force of Comanche, Kiowa, Kichai, Caddo and Wichita warriors converged upon the unprepared bastion, which at the time had but five adult male defenders and wide open gates. Some of the women escaped, with Cynthia and John Parker being captured and spending most of their lives with the Comanches.

■ **STONE HOUSES, 10 NOVEMBER 1837**
Eighteen Texas Rangers chased around 150 Kichai across the Colorado river after the Indians raided Fort Smith. The Indians turned and overwhelmed the Rangers with numbers and a prairie fire, only eight walking to safety.

■ **NECHES, 15–16 JULY 1838**
The Republic of Texas moved against Cherokee Chief Bowl's settlement and the Indian presence in Easter, Texas, with 500 Texans overcoming around 600 Cherokee at this river crossing. The Cherokee retreated into Oklahoma.

■ **COUNCIL HOUSE, 19 MARCH 1840**
The Comanche tribe resisted Texas president Mirabeau Lamar's efforts to evict them, taking many captives in their raids. A smallpox

epidemic prompted Chief Muguara to lead a band of 65 chiefs and families into San Antonio to negotiate. The Texans had planned to hold the Comanche hostages against the captives' return. Half the Comanche died, the Indians reacting with fury to the treachery, launching more raids and executing their prisoners.

■ **GREAT RAID, 7 AUGUST 1840**
Comanche chief Buffalo Hump led this large-scale retaliatory raid upon San Antonio with careful planning and execution, avenging the Council House fight of three months ago. With the Texans' guard relaxed, 600 to 700 Comanche swept into the outlaying town of Victoria, killing the inhabitants found on the streets before the war party moved and slaughtered down the Guadalupe river into San Antonio's port of Linville. Once again, the Texans were caught unprepared, the survivors fleeing into boats or ships off shore as the Comanche plundered and burned their town. With a train of some 3000 pack animals, the Comanche set off with their loot, sufficiently slowly for Texas militia to collect and launch a running attack upon the band at Plum Creek. The Comanche escaped with most of their loot, the Texans suffering some 40 killed in the raid.

■ **BANDERA PASS, 1841**
A party of 50 Texas Rangers under John Hays fell into a Comanche ambush in this pass, the traditional boundary. With men unhorsed, Hays dismounted his troop, repelling the Comanche with rapid fire from revolvers.

■ **CAYUSE WAR, 1847–55**
Missionaries Marcus and Narcissa Whitman established their mission at Waiilaptu along what became the Oregon Trail, among the Cayuse tribe. The Whitmans taught the Cayuse farming techniques, but, as a trickle of white settlers along the trail became a stream, the Cayuse anticipated a takeover of their lands. When a measles epidemic broke out, in which Cayuse died while the whites recovered, the Cayuse leaders suspecting Whitman of poisoning their

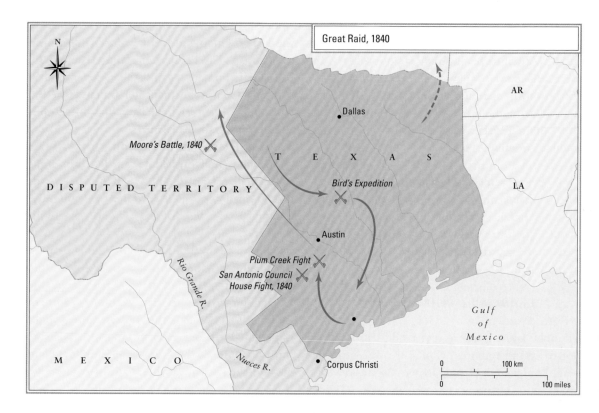

people. The response was the butchering of the Whitmans and 11 others in 1847. The Cayuse also took 60 hostages for ransom. Subsequently, American militia warred with hostile and non-hostile area tribes, the US Army eventually arriving and prompting the Cayuse to hand over five men involved in the Whitman massacre for execution. Sporadic fighting continued until, in 1855, the army removed the surviving Cayuse to the Umatilla Reservation in eastern Oregon.

■ CLARK MASSACRE, 30 AUGUST 1851
A Shoshone raiding party stealing horses attacked Thomas Clark and his wagon train in Idaho, killing two men and Clark's mother, leaving his sister for dead. The fleeing Indians resisted the train's efforts at pursuit.

Wakara War 1851–53

About 12 on each side died as Utah Mormons fought a series of skirmishes with Utes under Walker as the Mormons interfered with Ute horse raiding and trade with New Mexico. Negotiations ended the fighting.

The Jicarilla War 1854–55

■ CIENEGUILLA, 30 MARCH 1854
Hundreds of Jicarilla Apaches and Utes combined to ambush 60 US Cavalry under Lieutenant John Davidson. Nearly all of Davidson's command were killed or wounded before the survivors managed to escape the onrushing warriors.

■ OJO CALIENTE, 8 APRIL 1854
A punitive expedition of 300 US troops set out against the Utes and Apaches who had ambushed 60 cavalry in New Mexico. At this river, the soldiers and troopers scattered the Indians, many of whom froze to death afterwards.

■ GRATTAN MASSACRE, 19 AUGUST 1854
A dispute with the Brulé Sioux over a stray cow in Wyoming resulted in a botched parley in which a Sioux chief, 2nd Lt John Grattan and his entire command of 30 men perished.

■ **DIABLO MOUNTAINS, 3 OCTOBER 1854**
Some 200 Lipan Apaches drove a stolen cattle herd over this Texas range, pursued by Capt John Walker and some 40 Texas Rangers. Walker surprised the Apaches en route, scattering them and securing the cattle.

■ **MIMBRES RIVER, 4 DECEMBER 1860**
Thirty heavily armed miners surprised the slumbering camp of Chiricahua Apache chief Mangas Coloradas at this New Mexican river, killing four Apaches before withdrawing as more Indians rushed to the scene. The miners attacked to recover what they said were cattle stolen by the Apaches. Sporadic fighting throughout the region led to the arrest and death of Mangas Coloradas in 1863 when he came to negotiate terms of a peace treaty.

Puget Sound War 1855–56

■ **PORT GAMBLE, 1855**
A landing party from USS *Massachusetts* sought to remove Indian raiders from Victoria who occupied the port while attacking tribes in Washington. When the Indians resisted, the *Massachusetts* party killed 27 and destroyed their canoes.

■ **KLAMATH AND SALMON WAR, JAN–MAR 1855**
As more whites poured into the Pacific Northwest, the initially friendly Karok and Yurok Indian tribes began fighting using weapons and ammunition purchased from coastal traders. When the miners began arming to evict the Indians from this area in northern California, reprisals from both sides aggravated the situation. Army intervention finally pacified the violent Red Cap faction with the aid of non-hostile tribes, all moved to a reservation.

■ **ROGUE RIVER WARS, 1855**
Resentment over a treaty removing the Rogue tribes to a reservation resulted in raiding and punitive attacks by militia against villages in this region. Army effort to restore order failed, resulting in massacres and final pacification.

■ **KLICKITAT WAR, 1855**
Angered by treaties ignoring their own territorial claim, this tribe bought guns from the whites and launched raids against onrushing gold miners, prompting retaliation. Army probes met strong responses before the Indians relented.

■ **ASH HOLLOW, 3 SEPTEMBER 1855**
Vengeance for the Grattan Massacre came in an attack by Gen William Harney and 700 soldiers from Fort Leavenworth upon this Sioux village in Nebraska. Over 100 Sioux, including women and children, perished in the assault.

Yakima War 1855–58

■ **SEATTLE, 26 JANUARY 1856**
USS *Decatur* bolstered the defences of the Washington settlement as a coalition of hostile tribes collected for an attack upon the Americans there. Raids from the surrounding tribes had prompted the whites to construct a network of blockhouses in which they could shelter at need, two of these providentially in the settlement. With friendly tribes and their agents warning of attack, the whites organized a volunteer company while *Decatur* anchored where her shell-firing cannon could protect the blockhouses. Some 500 warriors worked their way into the forest close to the town, some within the town mixing with non-hostiles. *Decatur* landed marines and a boat howitzer as the Indians began a sporadic fire, answered by the settlers' guns and the warship's shells. An unknown number of Indians were killed before the attackers withdrew with booty collected from the outlaying houses.

■ **TINTIC WAR, FEBRUARY 1856**
Beliefs and practicality kept relations between the Mormons and the Utah Indian tribes fairly peaceful, but a drought and the disappearances of Mormon cattle led to some skirmishes in the area of this river valley.

■ **ANTELOPE HILLS EXPEDITION, 21 JANUARY–12 MAY 1858**
Texas Rangers renewed their offensive operations against Comanche and Kiowa villages, making an extended foray into this area of Oklahoma.

Their surprise attacks killed some 76 warriors and captured 16 prisoners and 300 horses.

■ **LITTLE ROBE CREEK, 12 MAY 1858**

In the course of one day, Texas Rangers from the Antelope Hills Expedition attacked three Comanche villages with the help of friendly Tonkawas. Chief Iron Jacket fell to the Rangers' powerful revolvers, the Comanche fleeing.

■ **FRASER RIVER WAR, 1858**

Settlers in search of gold in British Columbia clashed with the Thompson river Salish tribe as they moved up from the diggings in California. Upon the Salish killing three French miners in retaliation for a rape, the miners formed themselves into three armed companies at Yale and marched into the interior, where both villages and mining camps were anticipating mutual slaughter as the Indians mustered their own warriors. The more aggressive of the armed miners having wiped each other out by friendly fire, the captain of the 'Austrian Company', John Centras, and Captain Snyder of the New York Pike Guards travelled into the Salish camp at Camchin, at which the tribes had agreed to end the conflict before matters got out of hand. Governor James Douglas in Victoria later dispatched British soldiers who managed to keep the peace in the area.

Spokane-Coeur d'Alene-Paloos War 1858

■ **PINE CREEK, 17 MAY 1858**

LCol Edward Steptoe attempted a show of force that impressed the hostile tribes with only his vulnerability. Surrounded by warriors, Steptoe's command held out on a rocky knoll, abandoning supplies and escaping after darkness.

■ **FOUR LAKES, 1 SEPTEMBER 1858**

Steptoe's defeat prompted a harsher response when Col George Wright and 570 cavalry and an artillery train of six howitzers moved against the hostile tribes at this point near Spokane. Artillery and rifle fire decimated the Indians' charge upon the column, Wright's dragoons pursuing the

Indians, capturing 800 horses, which Wright slaughtered as punishment as he destroyed Indian food supplies. Wright executed 24 chiefs and imposed a peace treaty.

Mendocino War 1859

Slaughter of settlers' free-range cattle by Indians in need of sustenance resulted in open warfare, the whites making reprisals, attacking the nearest Indian community to the animals killed. Isolated California militia units would attack local Indians without any central command or authorization, several hundred Indians dying before the fighting ended. Captured young Indians were sold as labourers on white homesteads.

Other Wars 1859–1861

■ **BEAR RIVER EXPEDITION, 12 JUNE AND 18 OCTOBER, 1859**

An army detachment under Maj Porter investigated reports of an attack upon a California-bound wagon train by warriors of the Shoshone tribe. 2nd Lt Gay's company attacked a Shoshone camp, killing 20 Indians.

■ **PAIUTE WAR, 1860**

Rape and fatal retaliation upon Williams Station on the Carson river led to the combined Paiute tribe of Nevada to prepare for war as 105 ill-prepared Nevada militia rushed headlong into a running Paiute ambush at Big Bend, with half perishing. The debacle prompted California to dispatch 750 militia into Nevada, where they met and overcame the Paiute at the battle of Pinnacle Mountain, another 40 whites falling. Sporadic fighting continued until a ceasefire was negotiated.

■ **PYRAMID LAKE I AND II, 12 MAY 1860, 2–4 JUNE 1860**

The Paiute chiefs met here to debate war with onrushing miners. A subsequent militia attack upon the site having been ambushed and destroyed, a second attack forced the Paiutes' retreat and the end of the Paiute War.

■ **PEASE RIVER, 18 DECEMBER 1860**

The Texas Rangers under Capt Sullivan Ross

continued stalking and attacking outlaying Comanche villages, finding this one unprepared and rescuing some white captives in the midst of the resulting slaughter, including the unwilling Cynthia Parker.

■ FORT DEFIANCE, 30 AUGUST 1860

Pressured by American encroachments, some 1000 Navajo under Chief Manuelito gathered to attack this unwalled post in Arizona. Capt Oliver Shepherd and 150 regulars held out in the compound's central buildings until relieved.

■ BASCOM AFFAIR, 27 JANUARY 1861

US-Apache warfare began with a boy's kidnapping, provoking 2nd Lt George Bascom to capture and later execute the family of Chiricahua chief Cochise. Resulting hostilities did not entirely die down until Geronimo's surrender in 1886.

■ TUBAC, AUGUST 1861

This Arizona town came under siege from Mexican Banditos and Chiricahua Apaches, prompting Confederate militia to march to its rescue. The militia were able to evacuate the townsfolk before the raiders plundered and burned it.

■ COOKE'S CANYON, AUGUST 1861

After Confederate militia reached the besieged town of Tubac, the inhabitants chose evacuation rather than face annihilation by Apaches, who were vengeful after the murder of Chief Cochise's family. In the middle of this dangerous route, the Chiricahua Apaches attacked, moving up the canyon's slopes, firing upon the wagon train. The whites resisted the siege by means of mounted charges and fire from the wagons. The Apaches withdrew with the townsfolk's herds.

■ FLORIDA MOUNTAINS, AUGUST 1861

Confederate militia pursued the Apaches, who were retreating with animals taken from Tubac and Cooke's Canyon. Capt Thomas Mastin anticipated the Indians' route and dispersed the Apaches in a charge from ambush, recovering much of the livestock.

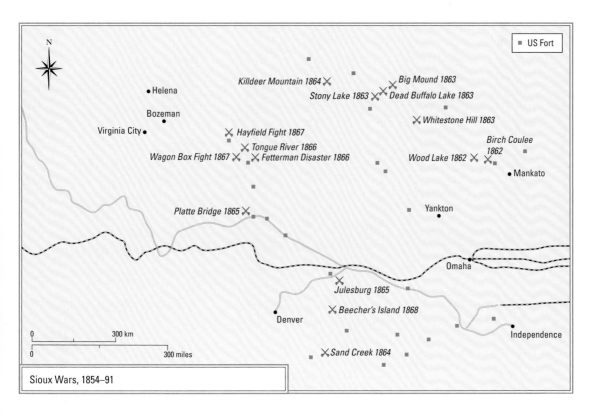

Sioux Wars, 1854–91

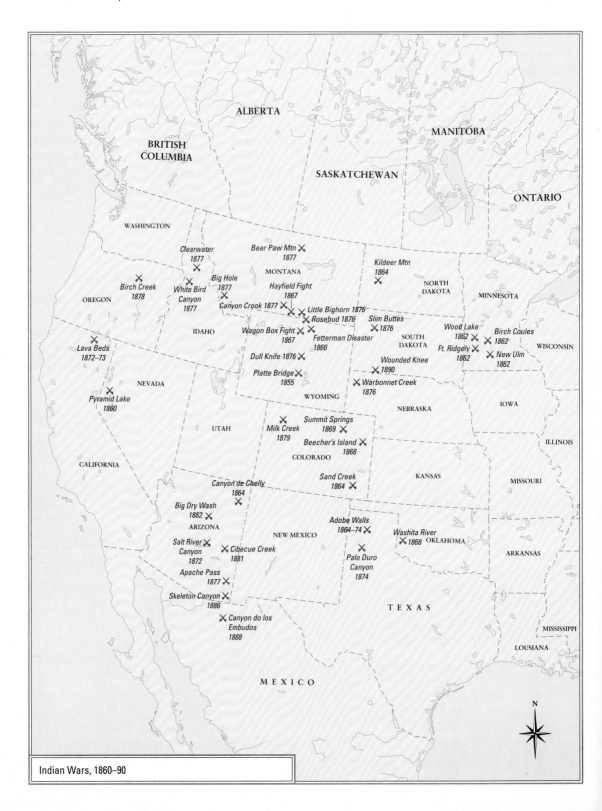

ALBERTA

MANITOBA

BRITISH
COLUMBIA

SASKATCHEWAN

ONTARIO

WASHINGTON

Clearwater
1877

Bear Paw Mtn
1877

Kildeer Mtn
1864

MONTANA

NORTH
DAKOTA

MINNESOTA

Birch Creek
1878

White Bird
Canyon
1877

Big Hole
1877

Hayfield Fight
1867

OREGON

Canyon Crook 1877

Little Bighorn 1876

IDAHO

Rosebud 1876

Slim Buttes
1876

Wood Lake
1862

Birch Coules
1862

Wagon Box Fight
1867

Fetterman Disaster
1866

SOUTH
DAKOTA

Ft. Ridgely
1862

New Ulm
1862

WISCONSIN

Lava Beds
1872–73

Dull Knife 1876

Wounded Knee
1890

NEVADA

Platte Bridge
1855

WYOMING

Warbonnet Creek
1876

Pyramid Lake
1860

NEBRASKA

IOWA

Summit Springs
1869

UTAH

Milk Creek
1879

Beecher's Island
1868

ILLINOIS

COLORADO

CALIFORNIA

Canyon de Chelly
1864

Sand Creek
1864

KANSAS

MISSOURI

Big Dry Wash
1882

ARIZONA

NEW MEXICO

Adobe Walls
1864–74

Washita River
1868

OKLAHOMA

Salt River
Canyon
1872

Cibecue Creek
1881

Palo Duro
Canyon
1874

ARKANSAS

Apache Pass
1877

Skeleton Canyon
1886

TEXAS

Canyon do los
Embudos
1888

MISSISSIPPI

LOUSIANA

MEXICO

N

Indian Wars, 1860–90

■ **GALLINAS MASSACRE, 2 SEPTEMBER 1861**
Four Confederate scouts watching for approaching Union troops fell afoul of a Chiricahua Apache band of more than 30, who killed three of the scouts after a running fight over several miles, the fourth scout escaping.

■ **PLACITO, 8 SEPTEMBER 1861**
A Confederate patrol under Lt John Pulliam moved to succor this New Mexico town under attack by Chiricahua Apaches. After reaching the town, the Confederates and townsfolk pursued the raiders into the desert, killing five.

■ **PINOS ALTOS, 27 SEPTEMBER 1861**
Chiefs Mangas Coloradas and Cochise continued their vengeance war with the Confederacy, 300 Chiricahua Apaches attacking this mining town in the New Mexico mountains in late September 1861. Capt Thomas Mastin with 15 Confederates reached the town in time, where the Confederates turned an ancient cannon filled with nails and buckshot upon the Indians, killing ten. Mastin led a charge as the Apaches retreated, with Mastin later dying and most of the town's inhabitants evacuating.

■ **PRYOR CREEK, 1861**
A large Crow band made their stand here after the Sioux, Cheyenne and Arapahoe combined against these hereditary enemies. The attack began in Wyoming, the Crow fighting at a river crossing, with both sides suffering losses.

Dakota War/ Minnesota Sioux Uprising 1862

■ **FORT RIDGELY, 20–22 AUGUST 1862**
Dakota chief Little Crow led 400 warriors against this post after the United States failed to provide support payments. The fort resisted two days' attacks by a total of 800 Sioux, who killed 21 soldiers.

■ **NEW ULM, 19–23 AUGUST 1862**
Wounded Dakota Sioux chief Little Crow with 400 warriors avenged undelivered promised annuities with a sudden attack on this hamlet. Part of the town burned and 100 settlers fell behind barricades repelling the vengeful Indians.

■ **BIRCH COULEE, 2 SEPTEMBER 1862**
After undelivered support drove the Minnesota Sioux into hostilities, Col Hastings Sibley sent part of his 1500 volunteers to bury the slain. Around 20 soldiers died with 60 wounded before the rest of Sibley's force arrived.

■ **WOOD LAKE, 23 SEPTEMBER 1862**
Col Hastings Sibley and a force of 1400 volunteers moved up the Minnesota river valley, pursuing some 2000 hostile Dakota Sioux who had attacked settlers after non-delivery of annuity payments. The drawn battle led to the Dakotas' surrender.

Arizona/New Mexico Apache War 1862–65

■ **DRAGOON SPRINGS, 5 MAY 1862**
Chiefs Mangas Coloradas and Cochise continued to fight the Confederacy, the Chiricahuas ambushing and killing four of a foraging party not far from Tucson, the Apaches capturing horse and cattle from the fleeing Confederates.

■ **APACHE PASS, 15–16 JULY 1862**
In response to the Confederate presence in Arizona and New Mexico and the ongoing fighting with the Chiricahua Apaches, US colonel Edward Canby asked for reinforcements. Around 700 infantry from the California militia under Gen James Carleton moved south through this pass, where Mangas Coloradas and Cochise had collected 500 Chiricahua and Mimbres Apaches in the hope of ambushing the soldiers while they were encamped in the defile. Instead, warriors attacked the vanguard as it entered the pass, Capt Thomas Roberts continuing the march and finding some shelter in an abandoned stone station house while the Apaches fired upon his men from the slopes. Roberts' two mountain howitzers bombarded the Indians, causing enough casualties for the desperate soldiers to reach a vital spring. By the time the approaching column arrived and relieved Roberts's command, the Apaches had withdrawn into the Dragoon Mountains.

■ **BEAR RIVER MASSACRE, 29 JANUARY 1863**
Friction between Mormon settlers moving into Idaho and the Shoshone tribe worsened with the departure of federal troops eastwards. Despite friction with the Mormons, California militia colonel Patrick Conner moved up the Bear river with 300 volunteers at the request of the Utah government. Conner's command surrounded and overran a fortified village here when the defending warriors' ammunition ran out, butchering some half of the village's 450 total population.

■ **BIG MOUND, 24 JULY 1863**
Attacks in retaliation for a murder resulted in this battle, in which Gen Henry Sibley's 3000 soldiers drove the Sioux from an entrenched position here after the Sioux fired upon him.

■ **DEAD BUFFALO LAKE, 26 JULY 1863**
Gen Henry Sibley's 3000 soldiers followed up their battle against Red Cap's band at Big Mound with an engagement at Dead Buffalo Lake two days later, inflicting more casualties upon the retreating Teton and Santee Sioux.

■ **STONY LAKE, 28 JULY 1863**
Sioux chief Red Cap's band of Santee and Teton Sioux continued its retreat, here linking up with a much larger body of Sioux warriors just as Gen Henry Sibley's 3000 soldiers reached this battlefield having rested for a day on their march. Sibley at once ordered his men to defend their column, the Sioux at first probing for weaknesses, then scattering in all directions, effectively ending Sibley's pursuit of Red Cap.

■ **WHITESTONE HILL, 3–5 SEPTEMBER 1863**
Gen Alfred Sully's scouting party encountered and attacked Sioux chief Red Cap's large village here with 300 men. The Sioux, caught unprepared, scattered soon after the initial attack, with Sully destroying their tipis and provisions.

■ **CANYON DE CHELLY, 12–14 JANUARY 1864**
Col 'Kit' Carson with allied Utes and Union troops devastated the stores of this New Mexico Navajo stronghold, with starvation forcing some 8000 of the tribe into a difficult march to Fort Sumner and harsh confinement.

■ **KILLDEER MOUNTAIN, 28 JULY 1864**
General Alfred Sully's 2200 regulars with artillery cleared away Sioux chief Red Cap's village on the slope of this North Dakota height. The Sioux attacked Sully's advance, scattering after 150 casualties from the artillery fire.

■ **ADOBE WALLS I, 25 NOVEMBER 1864**
Around 300 New Mexico militia under Col 'Kit' Carson fought a combined force of Kiowa and Comanche among these ruins of an abandoned trading post in north Texas. Carson's force retreated into the remaining walls when a larger Indian force engaged after Carson's attack upon a Kiowa village. Indian numbers and ferocity could not overcome the fire of Carson's mountain howitzers, which broke up the Indian attacks and saved his command.

■ **SAND CREEK, 29 NOVEMBER 1864**
Col John Chivington led 700 Colorado militia against Cheyenne chief Black Kettle's unprepared village and butchered some 148 men, women and children. The Indians were encamped upon an agreed-upon safe area and were not prepared for war.

■ **JULESBURG, 7 JANUARY 1865**
In the winter following the Sand Creek Massacre, some 1000 infuriated Cheyenne, Arapahos and Sioux twice laid waste to this Colorado transportation hub near Fort Rankin. Around 30 soldiers and civilians perished and the town itself burned.

■ **PLATTE BRIDGE, 26 JULY 1865**
Thousands of Sioux under Red Cloud and Cheyenne under Roman Nose moved to attack this isolated US post in Wyoming, annihilating cavalry under Lt Caspar Collins, but driven back from the post by artillery fire.

■ **POWDER RIVER EXPEDITION, 1 AUGUST–24 SEPTEMBER 1865**
The Bozeman Trail to the Montana goldfields bisected territory reserved to the Sioux,

Cheyenne and Arapahoe tribes. Gen Patrick Conner, with Jim Bridger as a guide, led three converging columns of US volunteers along the trail to chastise the war parties raiding the trail in consequence. For the most part, the troops only fought skirmishes, the expedition ending when the volunteers' terms of enlistments lapsed with the conclusion of the Civil War.

■ **TONGUE RIVER, 29 AUGUST 1865**
The Powder River Expedition fought its one major battle here against Arapahoe chief Black Bear's village. Gen Patrick Conner's 400 volunteers with two cannon attacked 500 Indians while more volunteers worked elsewhere, killing many Indian ponies.

Snake River War 1864–68

The Shoshone, Paiute and Bannock tribes of the Pacific Northwest, Nevada and Idaho united in sporadic raids to evict whites from their lands against the onrush of American settlers after the Civil War. Casualties on both sides were severe, with Indian raids resulting in white reprisals against uninvolved other natives, broadening the conflict. Army regulars freed after the Confederate surrenders eventually replaced state militia units and pacified the region.

Powder River War 1866–68

Despite a treaty recognizing Sioux possession of the lands, the US Army built a string of posts along the Bozeman Trail directly through the heart of this region to speed the passage of miners to the Montana goldfields out of a need for income in the aftermath of the Civil War. The construction of Forts Reno, C.F. Smith and Philip Kearney supported the trail and violated earlier agreements with the Sioux, who considered the region a prime hunting area. Negotiations with the Indians failed because of that fait accompli and Lakota Sioux chief Red Cloud began one of the most carefully waged wars ever fought by the Indians. Red Cloud's

Sioux, later joined by Cheyenne and Arapahoe with grievances of their own, ambushed supply trains and attacked farms, ranches and army work parties as they left the forts or moved along the trail, the raids forcing constant vigilance and inflicting noticeable physical and financial casualties. Red Cloud's tactics initially involved luring the whites into ambushes with small parties of warriors, then overwhelming small parties with much greater numbers of pre-positioned warriors before the whites could reload their weapons. Army logistics and the use of breechloading and repeating firearms made such ambushes more costly or futile, but the simple attrition of Red Cloud's tactics provoked the army into negotiations in 1867 on Red Cloud's terms. Red Cloud secured his conditions, including the abandonment of Forts Reno, C.F. Smith and Philip Kearney and the closing of the Bozeman Trail, all guaranteed and honoured by the Treaty of Fort Laramie.

■ **FETTERMAN MASSACRE, 21 DEC 1866**
Capt William Fetterman and 81 soldiers perished when Fetterman fell head-long into Lakota Sioux chief Red Cloud's carefully planned ambush outside Fort Philip Kearney. Fetterman chased a small party into 2000 Sioux who prevented retreat.

■ **KIDDER MASSACRE, 29 JUNE 1867**
US 2nd Lt Lyman Kidder, an Indian scout and 10 soldiers perished at the hands of a Northern Cheyenne and Sioux war party while bearing dispatches to Gen Custer along the Republic river in Nebraska.

■ **WAGON BOX FIGHT, 2 AUGUST 1867**
Lakota Sioux chief Red Cloud's ambush of Capt James Powell's 37 woodcutters fell afoul of the new breechloading M1866 rifle, with which Powell's command fought by their wagons until relieved from nearby Fort Philip Kearney, inflicting some 60 casualties. The Indian tactic had been to rush in while the soldiers reloaded. In 1868, the Army evacuated the fort under treaty, which the victorious Red Cloud then burned to the ground.

■ BEECHER ISLAND, 17–19 SEPTEMBER 1868

Northern Cheyenne chief Roman Nose had successfully led repeated raids in Colorado in retaliation for Sand Creek. Maj George Forsyth's 50 scouts took refuge here when Roman Nose and 500 Cheyenne, Arapahoe and Sioux trapped them near the Arikaree river in Colorado. Around 30 warriors, including Roman Nose, fell under the fire from the Scouts' repeating Spencer rifles before two messengers succeeded in bringing a relief column, which dispersed the Indians.

■ WASHITA RIVER, 27 NOVEMBER 1868

LCol George Custer and 800 7th Cavalry attacked Cheyenne chief Black Kettle's village here in Oklahoma, the Indians considered hostile by their presence outside of a reservation and tracked by their traces in the snow. Black Kettle and 100 of his people perished in the winter dawn attack, 20 of Custer's men dying when outraged warriors boiled up from surrounding encampments that Custer had failed to scout before he withdrew.

■ SUMMIT SPRINGS, 11 JULY 1869

Pawnee scouts led Maj Eugene Carr and 500 men to a large camp of Cheyenne Dog soldiers at the Platte river in Colorado. Caught unawares, the Cheyenne scattered as Carr took their camp and provisions.

■ MARIAS MASSACRE, 23 JANUARY 1870

After a period of quiescence, the Blackfoot tribe in Montana began resisting white incursions into their territory. Major Eugene Baker attacked Mountain Chief's winter village on the banks of the Marias with subsequent indiscriminate slaughter. 173 died (mostly women and children) and 140 women and children were captured.

■ CAMP GRANT MASSACRE, 30 APRIL 1871

1st Lt Royal Whitman's kindly treatment of surrendering Apaches at this post in Arizona resulted in more Apaches coming in to draw federal rations. As Apache raids upon Arizonan

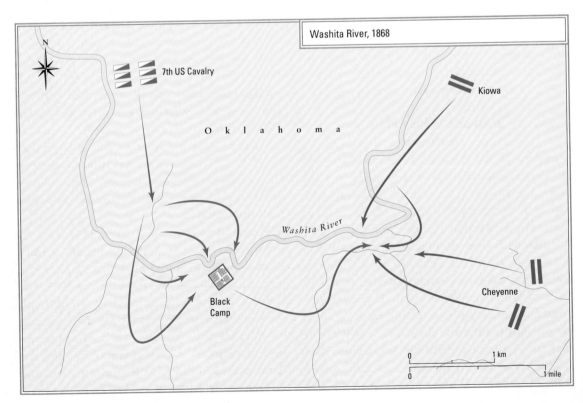

Washita River, 1868

civilians continued, the Papago tribe joined with a local militia in making preparations for an attack upon the Camp Grant Apaches, now 500 in number. The Papago and Arizona locals attacked the camp while the men were out hunting, butchering 144.

■ WARREN RAID, 18 MAY 1871

General of the Army William Tecumseh Sherman was touring the South-west when he encountered Henry Warren's wagon train delivering supplies to forts in western Texas. Warren ran into a large Indian raiding party, the Kiowas or Comanches torturing and killing seven teamsters and stealing the supplies, with five survivors able to describe the incident. Sherman sent out Col Ranald Mackenzie's command, which captured three of the chiefs considered responsible. Two were paroled and the other was killed while trying to escape.

■ BLANCO CANYON, 10 OCTOBER 1871

Colonel Ranald Mackenzie with 1000 regulars entered Comanche territory, encountering and defeating a large band, the army abandoning the pursuit as their animals wore out deep within areas previously considered a sanctuary for Comanche raiders.

■ GOING SNAKE MASSACRE, 15 APRIL 1872

Eight US marshals fell while attempting to remove an accused Cherokee murderer from tribal jurisdiction in Oklahoma for killing a white man. Four Cherokee perished defending the courthouse, with all charges in the affair later dropped.

■ NORTH FORK, 28 SEPTEMBER 1872

Col Ranald Mackenzie with 300 soldiers led by Tonkawa Scouts carefully probed Comanche territory in North Texas, here on the Red river encountering a large village. Mackenzie's force attacked, killing some 23 Comanches and taking many horses.

■ SALT RIVER CANYON, 28 DECEMBER 1872

Gen George Crook's reliance on allied Indian scouts and trains of pack mules in the place of cumbersome wagon trains paid off handsomely for the US Army in this successful campaign against the Yavapai in Arizona. Crook's ability to find and pursue bands of hostiles resulted in the Yavapai retreating into the fastnesses of this canyon, in which Skeleton Cave served as a fort for the hostiles. Crook approached the site with 130 cavalry led by 30 Apaches, surprising some 110 Yavapai at the cave mouth. When the hostiles refused surrender and retreated into the cave, Crooks' men fired at the cavern roof, killing many with ricocheted bullets and stone shards, while Crook and others of his command rolled stones down upon Indians attempting to escape. With 76 dead, including Chief Nanni-chaddi, the Yavapai surrendered, their tribe henceforth greatly weakened.

■ TURRET PEAK, 27 MARCH 1873

The Yavapai in Arizona considered this camp near the eponymous summit impregnable. Gen George Crook's Apache scouts and mule train convinced them otherwise when the US troopers attacked it, killing 57 of the hostile Yavapai.

■ CYPRESS HILLS MASSACRE, 1 JUNE 1873

Hostile Sioux fled to Canada after raids into the United States. Indians had stolen several horses from a party of Montana 'Wolfer' fur and buffalo hunters, who crossed the border, attacking an Assiniboine village, killing 23.

■ HONSINGER BLUFF, 4 AUGUST 1873

LCol George Custer's 7th Cavalry prepared to bivouac here when a party of Lakota Sioux under Chief Rain in the Face tried to lure it into an ambush, then killed veterinarian Honsinger and retreated.

■ MODOC WAR (LAVA BEDS), 1872–73

The Modoc Indians lasted as long as they had in California by mostly scratching out a living in areas unwanted either by neighbouring tribes or encroaching white settlers. Finally expelled to the Klamath Reservation in Oregon, 300 Modocs under Kintpuash (Captain Jack), returned to their old lands along Tule Lake and began raiding nearby whites. Efforts to negotiate and disarm the Modocs failing bloodily; in the resulting 'Modoc War', the tribe withdrew across the lake into 'the Stronghold', a natural fastness of the nearby lava beds. The Modocs killed 18 settlers and repelled subsequent army efforts to evict them, also capturing federal ammunition and supplies. Another 35 soldiers died attacking the Modocs in a heavy fog.

At President Grant's request, Gen Edward Canby headed a final effort at negotiations assisted by the Reverend E. Thomas, during which Kintpuash and other Modocs drew previously concealed firearms and murdered both men. Subsequently, overwhelming numbers of soldiers drove the Modocs out of the stronghold having cut off the Modocs' water supply. Kintpuash with 160 survivors fled into neighbouring lava caves, inflicting 17 dead upon an ambushed pursuing unit soon afterwards. Gen Jefferson Davis took over the war and encamped his forces at Dry Lake. There, the Modocs attacked them in the open, the army's charge defeating the Modocs and

driving them into retreat, the tribe fragmenting under the stress of the defeat and their worsening situation. A band under 'Hooker Jim', who had been active in the fighting, negotiated a separate peace with the army, agreeing to capture and hand over Kintpuash and the six others present at Canby's murder over to the US authorities. Kintpuash and four others were hanged, the survivors ended up in Oklahoma.

■ **ADOBE WALLS II, 27 JUNE 1874**

A new trading complex near the old battlefield provoked 700 Cheyenne, Comanche, Arapahoe and Kiowa warriors into an effort to extirpate some 28 professional buffalo hunters operating out of the post's stores, corral and smithy. Just after a supply train reached the post, the warriors under Comanche chief Quanah Parker and medicine man Isa-Tai ran off the post's cattle herd and settled down to a four-day siege, Isa-Tai having previously prophesied the hunters' destruction. However, the Indians had failed to

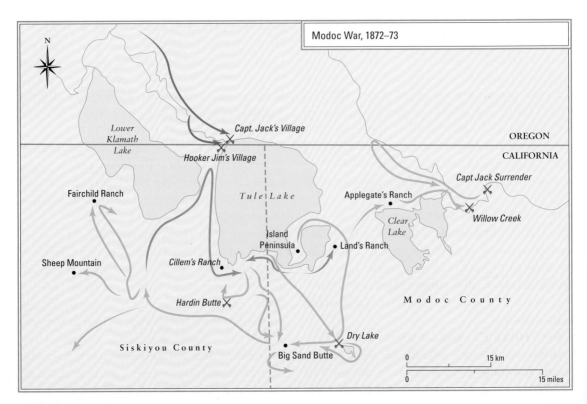

Modoc War, 1872–73

reckon with the extended accuracy and lethality of the hunters' long-range rifles, devastatingly employed against the buffalo and now against the warriors. The Indians abandoned their efforts on the fourth day in the face of 100 reinforcements, after hunter William Dixon with his Sharps rifle killed a warrior at a range later measured at 1406m distant.

■ BATES BATTLEFIELD, 1 JULY 1874
Capt Alfred Bates led 83 cavalry and Shoshone against a Cheyenne, Arapahoe and Sioux raiding party stealing horses from the Shoshone. An inconclusive fight cost both sides casualties and the Arapahoe a large horse herd.

■ PALO DURO CANYON, 28 SEPTEMBER 1874
Col Ranald Mackenzie concluded his destruction of the Comanche tribe. His scouts locating a large encampment, Mackenzie's regiment moved down the steep slopes of this canyon, scattering the Indians and capturing 1100 horses.

Black Hills War 1876–77
Rumours of gold in the Black Hills of South Dakota became a gold rush when LCol George Custer returned from the area confirming the accounts. The enraged Sioux nation, which claimed the region, joined with the Cheyenne and Arapahoe tribes in raids against the miners and settlements. In operations in Wyoming, Montana and the Dakotas, the army pursued the hostile bands under the general leadership of Sioux chiefs Crazy Horse and Sitting Bull. Indian successes at the Powder river augmented the hostiles' ranks to where they could blunt an army advance at the Rosebud and annihilate a third of the 7th Cavalry at Little Bighorn in 1876. That disaster prompted nearly half of the US Army's entry into the campaign, which continued until the winter of 1877 when the Indians' camps were much easier to locate and destroy.

■ ROSEBUD RIVER, 17 JUNE 1876
Gen George Crook's powerful column, consisting of 1050 regulars and 250 allied Crow and Shoshone Indians, encountered heavy resistance from the Sioux and Cheyenne under Chief Crazy Horse. The result was a brutal six-hour standing battle along the banks of this river, as the American column attempted to move north toward a planned rendezvous with Gen Terry's column and Custer's cavalry near the Bighorn river. Each side losing about 20 men, Crook withdrew.

■ LITTLE BIGHORN, 25–26 JUNE 1876
More than a third of LCol George Custer's 7th Cavalry perished along with their commander when Custer ignored the warnings of his Indian scouts and precipitately engaged 3000 Sioux and Cheyenne warriors along this river in Montana. The numerous and powerful Sioux tribes and the organized and militarily skilled northern Cheyenne left their reservations in the late spring of 1876, with the intention of resisting the US government's authority in response to past massacres and white incursions into the Black Hills of South Dakota, land which the Sioux considered theirs. The US Army's response took

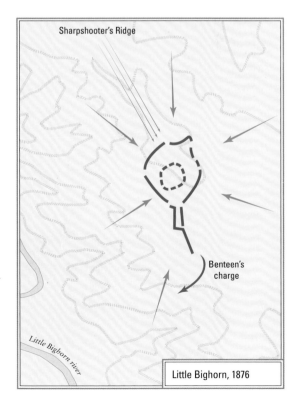

Little Bighorn, 1876

the form of a powerful force of nearly 3000 infantry and cavalry in three converging columns pursuing the departed Indians. Gen Terry (in overall command) and his subordinates were initially unaware that the total agglomeration of Indian warriors was of approximately equal numbers and more concentrated than the army's columns. Custer's orders and his desire for another successful engagement on the plains allowed him to rush into attack with less than a third of the army's total force, the result being the most resounding defeat the US Army ever suffered in the wars against the plains Indians.

Generals Terry and Crook sent Custer's 7th Cavalry ahead of their two columns to locate the village and vital pony herd of the missing tribes. Custer's Crow scouts returned and told him that they had located the largest single village and pony herd that they had ever seen, claims Custer dismissed as exaggerated, despite reports of Indians shadowing his regiment and

looting a fallen pack mule. Drawing closer to the village along the banks of the Little Bighorn, Custer divided his regiment of 647 men into four separate battalions, sending Maj Marcus Reno directly into the village, and Capt Frederick Benteen around the rear with the reserve ammunition, while moving his own two battalions toward the north, planning on containing and flanking the village against the river. Custer's final communication was an order to Benteen to bring up the ammunition quickly.

Reno's battalion moved directly into the village, where it encountered ferocious resistance, Reno taking casualties as he re-grouped in a clump of trees before making a disorganized retreat toward a nearby hill. There, his men dug in and resisted sporadic attacks for the next two days, joined by Benteen's column with the vital ammunition. Unaware of Reno's repulse to the south and with Custer forgetting his own promise to support Reno's thrust, Custer's

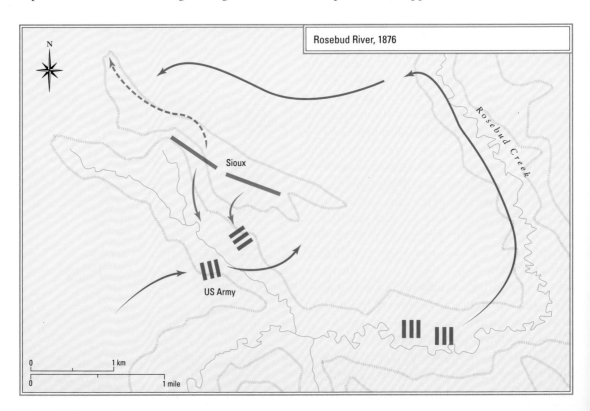

Rosebud River, 1876

individual companies attacked the village or encountered groups of Indians under their own war chiefs boiling out of the village in a fierce response that began to overwhelm Custer's 241 men.

Custer's command began to disintegrate as his movement north became a rout and then a headlong retreat away from Reno Hill. Individual units made their own 'last stands' while trying to escape destruction, their bodies found in situ by subsequent burial parties. Either because of Custer's death or due to his last order, his final remnant of the 7th stopped its flight on 'Custer Hill', where the warriors and their wives finished off the survivors, killing and mutilating the wounded in traditional fashion. Terry's column arrived and found Custer's body stripped, but otherwise untouched. The reinforcements informed Reno's and Benteen's dazed survivors of the fate of their comrades, with 268 perishing in total.

■ **WARBONNET CREEK, 17 JULY 1876**
Col Wesley Merritt with the 5th US Cavalry soon after Little Bighorn here intercepted several hundred Cheyenne as they attempted to leave the Red Cloud Agency to join the hostiles in the Black River War.

■ **SLIM BUTTES, 9–10 SEPTEMBER 1876**
Gen George Crook's column stumbled into a large village of the Miniconjou Sioux under Chief American Horse in South Dakota. Attacking immediately, the soldiers scattered the village and deprived the Indians of vital winter stores.

■ **CEDAR CREEK, 21 OCTOBER 1876**
Gen Nelson Miles' force moving up the Yellowstone river located Sitting Bull's village when the Sioux attacked its wagons near Spring Creek. Although the Sioux initially drove away the supply train, the wagons' escorts rallied and made the rendezvous with Miles. As the re-supplied column approached Sitting Bull's village, Sitting Bull began negotiations, but attempted to slip away the following morning. Nelson pursued, capturing much of the Indians' winter supplies.

■ **DULL KNIFE FIGHT, 25 NOVEMBER 1876**
Col Ranald Mackenzie led 1100 cavalry against a large northern Cheyenne village here celebrating in the aftermath of Little Bighorn. Mackenzie drove the Indians from their camp and captured ponies and vital winter stores.

■ **WOLF MOUNTAIN, 8 JANUARY 1877**
Crazy Horse led his band of Sioux and Cheyenne against the pursuing column of Gen Nelson Miles, some 500 warriors finding Nelson's 436 soldiers entrenched and ready for the assault. Weather and howitzers eventually drove Crazy Horse off.

■ **YELLOW HORSE CANYON, 18 MARCH 1877**
Black Horse's Comanche concluded their efforts against the buffalo hunters having set forth on a permitted hunting expedition, plundering camps, then torturing and killing one hunter who fell into their hands. An unofficial militia of 46 men set out in pursuit and tracked the Comanche band to a large camp in this canyon. Despite being outnumbered 12 to one, the hunters attacked the Comanche from three sides before being forced to retreat under the fire of women and the infuriated warriors, 12 of the hunters perishing. The Comanche set a prairie fire to camouflage their own movements and the hunters used a decoy bonfire that night to elude pursuit by the Indians. Black Horse and his band returned to the reservation after news that regular army units were en route against them, a brief skirmish serving to confirm that news violently.

Nez Perce War 1877

■ **WHITE BIRD CANYON, 17 JUNE 1877**
Nez Perce, when rejecting cessions in an 1855 treaty, began attacking white settlers. Capt David Perry's column of 150 men retreated after losing 32, the Indians capturing weapons and ammunition.

■ **CLEARWATER, 11–12 JULY 1877**
Nez Perce chiefs Joseph and Looking Glass combined their 300 warriors and moved

northwards, here in Idaho overtaken by Gen Oliver Howard's 350 soldiers. Mauled by Howard's artillery, the Nez Perce inflicted casualties and retreated.

■ Big Hole, 9–10 August 1877

The Nez Perce rested here, where US colonel John Gibbon surprised them with 206 men, the 200 warriors then rallying to protect their families and forcing Gibbon on the defensive, killing 32 soldiers; 52 Indians died.

■ Camas Creek, 20 August 1877

Gen Oliver Howard's 250 men, shadowing the Nez Perce here in south-eastern Idaho, suffered and inflicted some six casualties when the Nez Perce attempted to dismount the soldiers by stealing their horses, the Indians retreating.

■ Canyon Creek, 13 September 1877

The Nez Perce abducted and killed tourists in Yellowstone Park, pursued to this point by Gen Samuel Sturgis, who retreated from the fire of the Nez Perce holding a ridge. The Nez Perce

eluded pursuit, however, and disappeared into the wilderness.

■ Bear Paw Mountain, 30 September– 5 October 1877

The Nez Perce War ended when Gen Nelson Miles with 400 soldiers trapped 800 exhausted Nez Perce and blocked the escape route to Canada, with 200 Indians eluding the snare and escaping. The warriors dug in to defend their families, aiming in particular at Miles' officers, killing two officers and 21 enlisted men. Gen Oliver Howard arrived four days later with 120 reinforcements and two cannon with exploding shells. The Nez Perce endured for six days until a sniper killed Chief Looking Glass. Surviving chief Joseph ended his tribe's 2414km effort to escape the war when he left the beleaguered camp and made an impassioned speech of surrender to Howard, only 87 warriors and 331 women and children remaining with him. The army first shipped the captives to Kansas and

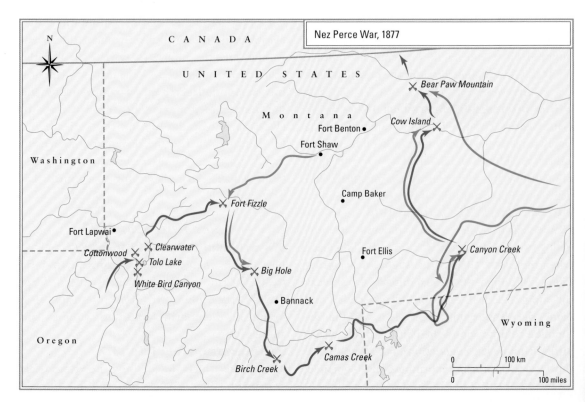

Oklahoma, although some later returned to central Washington.

Other Indian Wars 1878–90

■ **BUFFALO HUNTERS' WAR, 1877**
Commanche chief Black Horse led a final large raiding band out into the Staked Plains where they and allied Apaches plundered the camps of buffalo hunters. The hunters tracked and attacked the band, killing 35.

■ **STAKED PLAINS HORROR, 1877**
Black 'Buffalo Soldiers' and buffalo hunters under Capt Nicholas Nolan wandered for days while tracking Comanche in the Staked Plains region. Reported massacred by the Indians, most of the party actually managed to reach rescue.

■ **BANNOCK WAR, 1878**
The Bannock Shoshone vented their rage at settlers' destruction of their food supplies in an ongoing series of raids and murders, prompting Gen Oliver Howard and the army to move in pursuit of the hostile factions. Capt Reuben Bernard ambushed the group, killing 50, and 500 hostiles were beaten while attacking Capt Evan Miles' camp. The Bannocks next attacked the Umatilla Reservation; those Indians joined the army in tracking and capturing the survivors.

■ **CHEYENNE WAR, 1878–79**
Reservation conditions were poor enough to prompt Cheyenne chief Dull Knife and some 100 followers to leave Oklahoma for Montana. Captured and held at Fort Robinson, Nebraska, over half the Cheyenne died while attempting to escape.

■ **SHEEPEATER INDIAN WAR, 1879**
The army pursued north-western Indian holdouts called 'Sheepeaters' for the murder of seven people near the Salmon. The Indians defeated a badly led cavalry column in heavy winter snows before relentless army pursuit forced their surrender.

■ **WHITE RIVER WAR, 1879**
The Utes continued to resist the army and acclimatization to white culture along this

river in Utah and Colorado. After setbacks such as Milk Creek, increasing army numbers and pressure drove the Utes onto reservations.

■ **MILK CREEK, 29 SEPTEMBER–5 OCTOBER 1879**
Tensions with the Utes in Colorado resulted in this battle and the Meeker Massacre as Maj Thomas Thornburgh's 150 troopers were trapped for a week. Twice reinforced, the cavalry eventually drove the Utes into flight.

■ **ALMA MASSACRE, 28 APRIL 1880**
Chiricahua Apache chief Victorio led a raiding party against a silver mine and this town in New Mexico, killing three in town and three more while fleeing, then slaughtering 35 sheepherders before eluding army pursuit.

■ **FORT TULAROSA, 14 MAY 1880**
The 9th US Cavalry's black 'Buffalo Soldiers' here moved quickly to the relief of this New Mexican post when Chiricahua Apache chief Victorio and his 100 warriors attacked it and the civilians nearby. Arriving as the Apaches withdrew, having killed several settlers, the 9th's troopers worked to increase the town's defences, killing Apaches attempting to capture the settlers' cattle. The full regiment unsuccessfully gave chase to the Apaches when assembled.

■ **CIBECUE CREEK, 30 AUGUST 1881**
An Apache shaman's prayer to raise the dead and drive out the whites led to his arrest and death, plus the mutiny of army Apache scouts as Apaches throughout Arizona and New Mexico turned hostile.

■ **FORT APACHE, 1 SEPTEMBER 1881**
Apaches, infuriated by the death of a shaman at Cibecue Creek, attacked this post in Arizona, firing on the fort at long range, the army returning fire and suffering three dead before the Apaches disappeared.

■ **BIG DRY WASH, 17 JULY 1882**
Capt Adna Chaffee with 350 troopers overtook 54 Chiricahua Apache who planned an ambush. Informed, Chaffee launched a decisive holding attack, pinning the warriors while a part of his

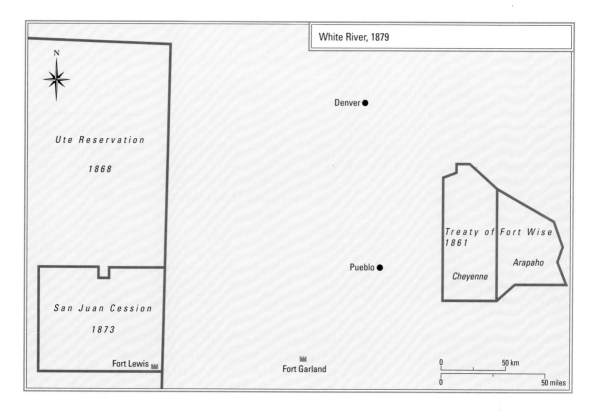

command attacked from the sides of this declivity to ambush the Apaches.

■ GERONIMO CAMPAIGN 1886

The last and perhaps grimmest of Indian leaders, Chiricahua Apache chief Geronimo resisted three campaigns and two generals' efforts to contain and catch him before his final surrender. Geronimo never forgave the Mexicans' slaughter of his wife and children. Having fought and learned in the campaigns of Mangas Coloradas and Cochise, Geronimo achieved fame after he led out several hundred Apaches from the barren San Carlos Reservation in 1882, undoing Gen George Crook's peace treaties with previous chiefs. Surrendering to Crook in 1884, Geronimo again rebelled and escaped in 1886, prompting the appointment of Gen Nelson Miles to command the campaign against him.

Repeated failures on the part of Miles and slaughters on the part of Geronimo forced Miles to adapt Crook's measures of employing mule trains and Apache scouts from rival bands to track the elusive Geronimo and his core band of highly seasoned followers. One of Geronimo's favourite tactics was to elude US or Mexican forces by crossing a border his pursuers could not cross without risking a diplomatic incident. For several years, he kept south-eastern Arizona and northern Mexico in turmoil. Around 5000 army with 500 native scouts participated in Miles' final campaign against Geronimo's camp in the Sonora Mountains. The pursuers took five months and 2647km of travel before Miles was able to convince Geronimo to surrender for a final time, the Apaches down to 16 warriors, 12 women and six children. Crook bitterly criticized Miles' broken promise that Geronimo and his followers would be allowed time to return to Arizona. Instead, Geronimo, his followers and Miles' own Apache scouts spent years in Fort Pickens, Florida, Geronimo eventually dying in Fort Sill, Oklahoma, in 1909.

■ WOUNDED KNEE CREEK (WOUNDED KNEE MASSACRE), 29 DECEMBER 1890

The spreading net of railroads completed the ability of white settlers and buffalo hunters to obliterate the plains tribes' way of life when the army returned to the plains after the civil war. Treaties, dependency upon government supplies and systematic military action forced the beaten Indians onto reservations, where some of the tribes turned to religion as their final hope to bring back better days still vivid in their memories.

Wovoka, a Paiute shaman, preached his vision of a Ghost Dance that would return the dead and the buffalo to the plains without additional outbreaks of fruitless violence. More aggressive Oglala Sioux in the band of Chief Big Foot claimed that a Ghost Dance shirt would protect against bullets, word of which quickly reached the nervous and scanty forces stationed to control and pacify the Indians.

Government unease and his stated support for the Ghost Dance led to the death of Chief Sitting Bull, when native police sought to arrest him despite the chief's long record of peaceful conduct since his role at Little Bighorn in 1876.

In another echo of that celebrated battle, Big Foot's band left their reservation and moved toward other militant bands in an unauthorized departure that prompted an army pursuit. With the Indians surrounded by soldiers on all sides at Wounded Knee Creek, members of the reconstituted 7th Cavalry moved into the crowd of Oglala Sioux on 15 December 1890 with orders to disarm the Indians. A resulting scuffle rapidly escalated into an outright and bloody slaughter, when jittery troopers outside the crowd turned Hotchkiss repeating cannon upon the surrounded Indians and other troopers still intermingled with the Sioux. Big Foot and 149 other Indians perished, along with 25 cavalry.

Northwest Rebellion 1885

Mixed-blood Metis of Alberta and Saskatchewan revolted against the Canadian government and attempted to enlist the support of the nearby tribes, with sporadic fighting. The Canadians ultimately employed cannon and Gatlings to suppress the revolt.

■ DUCK LAKE, 26 MARCH 1885

Louis Riel, an educated Metis with mixed Indian and trapper ancestry, proclaimed the Northwest Rebellion and did his best to enlist nearby Indian tribes in his movement. Around 100 mounted police and civilian militia rode toward the Northwest Rebellion capital at Duck Lake, intercepted nearby by the rebel Metis. Attempts at negotiation ended in gunfire and three dead, the government force retreating southwards back to Prince Albert amid mounting white panic.

■ FROG LAKE, 2 APRIL 1885

Wandering Spirit, a Cree war chief, joined the Northwest Rebellion and his band ordered a church congregation at this town to go to his camp. A scuffle broke out and the Cree killed nine townsfolk.

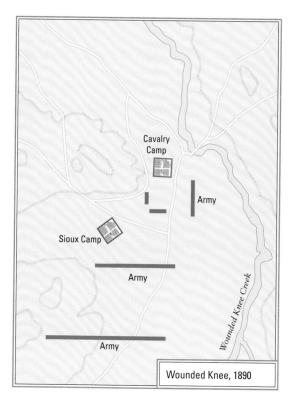

Wounded Knee, 1890

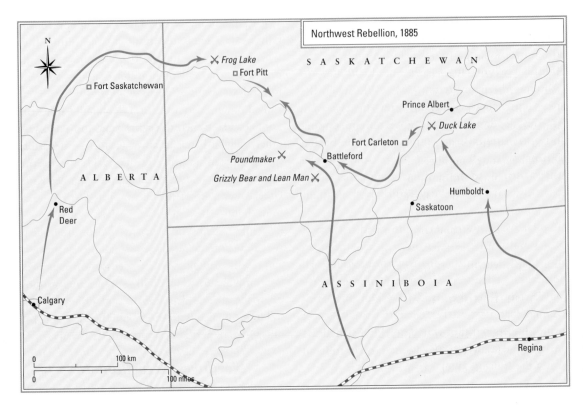

Northwest Rebellion, 1885

■ **FORT PITT, 2–15 APRIL 1885**

Chief Big Bear attempted to consolidate the Cree tribe at the outbreak of the Northwest Rebellion, his warriors attacking and taking this Northwest mounted police outpost after a raid on the town of Frog Lake and other towns. The Cree surprised an unfortunate police patrol, killing one constable – commander Francis Dickens – then surrendering the surprised fort. Big Bear released the remaining police and destroyed the fort, subsequently holding the townsfolk as hostages.

■ **FISH CREEK, 24 APRIL 1885**

Gabriel Dumont and 200 of the Metis and allied Indians killed 10 of the Alberta Field Force under Gen Frederick Middleton at this crossing, with the bulk of Middleton's force still on the far bank.

■ **CUT KNIFE, 2 MAY 1885**

Col William Otter's 50-man Battleford Column retreated from Chief Fine Day's some 350 Cree and Assiniboine warriors near the beleaguered town after firing his cannon upon the Indian camp, Otter losing eight, the Indians, six.

■ **BATOCHE, 9–12 MAY 1885**

Gen Frederick Middleton's 900-strong Alberta Field Force marched upon this Metis town, defended by Gabriel Dumont and some 250 militia from a series of rifle pits excavated on the town's approaches, while a government steamer moved up the river with additional riflemen. Dumont used the town's ferry cables to disable the steamer, while his rifleman stalled Middleton's advance and exploited the ground given up by his retreat. Middleton began a bombardment with his artillery, a Gatling gun preventing the Metis snipers from getting too close to the guns. On the second and third day of the battle, Middleton launched probing attacks against the Metis perimeter, which was weakening due to lack of defenders and ammunition. On the third day of the battle, a flanking force under

Col von Straubenzie suddenly fixed bayonets and stormed the town, utterly routing the Metis through determined action.

■ **FRENCHMAN'S BUTTE, 28 MAY 1885**
Gen Thomas Strange with 400 troops retreated from 200 Cree after the collapse of the Northwest Rebellion. Wandering Spirit entrenched his warriors in the way of Strange's advance and resisted Strange's bombardment.

■ **LOON LAKE, 3 JUNE 1885**
Maj Sam Steele and 47 mixed riders overtook a Cree war party retreating with white and Metis hostages. Surprised and short of ammunition, the Cree released their prisoners and scattered after fighting a delaying action.

South-East Asian Wars, 1825–1900

■ **DANUBYU, 7 MARCH–1 APRIL 1825**
A British force of 4000 men under Gen Sir Archibald Campbell defeated Gen Maha Bandula's 10,000-strong Burmese Army in its fortified camp at Danubyu. Bandula was killed by a mortar shell and his men abandoned the camp.

■ **JAVA WAR, 1825–1830**
Gen de Kock's 50,000-strong Dutch Army defeated a Javanese rebellion led by Prince Diponegoro. Rebel forces totalling 100,000 men were virtually wiped out after five years' fierce fighting, in which the Dutch lost 15,000 men.

■ **LAOTIAN INVASION OF SIAM, 1826**
King Chao Anouvong of Laos invaded Siam in an attempt to regain Laotian independence, but was defeated and forced to retreat. In retaliation, the Siamese Army sacked the Laotian capital of Vientiane. Anouvong returned with Vietnamese assistance, but was again defeated and captured. Vientiane was completely destroyed and Anouvong himself was brought to Bangkok as a prisoner. He was held in an iron cage until his death the following year.

■ **NONG-BONA-LAMP'ON, 1827**
Following King Chao Anouvong's unsuccessful attack on Siam, Laos was invaded by a Siamese army under Gen Sing Singhaseni. Anouvong was defeated at Nong-Bona-Lamp'on on the Mekong river and Vientiane was sacked.

■ **LE VAN KHOI REVOLT, 1833–35**
Le Van Khoi, the adopted son of Gen Le Van Duyet, led an unsuccessful revolt by southern Vietnamese, Vietnamese Catholics, French Catholic missionaries and Chinese settlers against Emperor Minh Mang. Up to 2000 rebels were executed.

■ **TOURANE (DA NANG), 15 APRIL 1847**
Two French warships, the *Gloire* and *Victorieuse*, which had been sent to Vietnam to negotiate the release of Catholic missionaries, were attacked by several Vietnamese vessels off Touane (now Da Nang). Four Vietnamese corvettes were sunk.

■ **COCHINCHINA CAMPAIGN, 1 SEPTEMBER 1858–5 JUNE 1862**
The campaign began as a limited Franco-Spanish punitive expedition and ended as a French war of conquest. The war concluded with the establishment of the French colony of Cochinchina, the starting point of almost a century of French colonial dominance in Vietnam.

Napoleon III was instrumental in establishing a French presence in the region. In 1858, he authorized a naval operation under Adm Rigault de Genouilly, which was initially intended to provide security for French and Spanish Catholic missionaries. The operation escalated and, by 1861, it had become an invasion. On 1 September 1858, France occupied Da Nang (Tourane). By 18 February 1859, they had conquered Saigon and three southern Vietnamese provinces: Biên Hòa, Gia Dinh and Dinh Tuong. Finally, on 13 April 1862, the Vietnamese Government was forced to cede those provinces to France under the Treaty of Saigon.

■ **TOURANE (DA NANG), SEPTEMBER 1858–MARCH 1860**
In September 1858, Adm Rigault de Genouilly's squadron landed a force of 2100 French and Spanish troops, which took Tourane. The city

was then besieged by a substantial Vietnamese army until the garrison was finally evacuated in March 1860.

■ **SAIGON, 17 FEBRUARY 1859**
A Franco-Spanish flotilla carrying 2000 troops commanded by Admiral Charner moved up the Saigon river, destroying several Vietnamese forts, before anchoring near the city of Saigon. The troops then landed and successfully managed to storm the city.

■ **SAIGON, MARCH 1860–FEBRUARY 1861**
In March 1860, the 1000-strong Franco-Spanish garrison of Saigon was besieged by a Vietnamese army of about 10,000 men. The siege was raised by the arrival of Gen de Vassoigne's relief force of 3500 men.

■ **MY THO, 12 APRIL 1861**
French gunboats carrying over 1000 French and Spanish troops fought their way along the Arroyo de la Poste creek towards the town of My Tho. Two forts at the mouth of the creek were stormed

and attacks by Vietnamese fireships were repelled as the force approached My Tho. The town was captured after being abandoned by its Vietnamese garrison, who fled when another French flotilla approached along the Mekong river.

■ **BIÊN HÒA, 16 DECEMBER 1861**
A Franco-Spanish force advanced on the city of Biên Hòa along the Dong Nai river. It stormed a fortified camp at My Hoa before taking Bien Hoa, which had been abandoned by its demoralized Vietnamese garrison.

■ **FIRST LARUT WAR, 1861–62**
The first conflict between Chinese secret societies in Malaya for the control of mining areas in Perak. Arguments over the watercourse to their mines led the Hai San Society to drive the Ghee Hin Society out of Klian Bahru. The governor of Straits Settlements, Col Cavenagh, intervened, ordering the Mentri Besar (chief state minister) of Larut, Ngah Ibrahim, to pay compensation of $17,447 to the Ghee Hin on behalf of the Sultan of Perak.

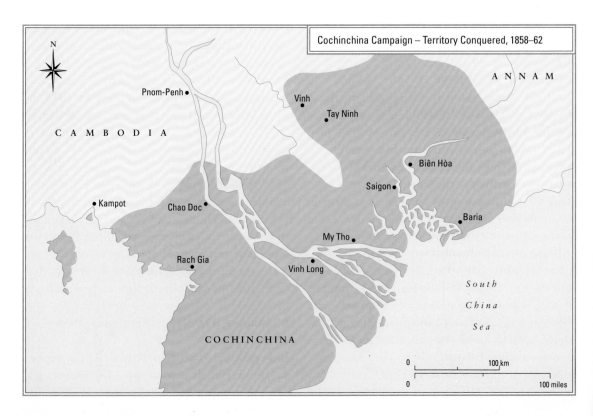

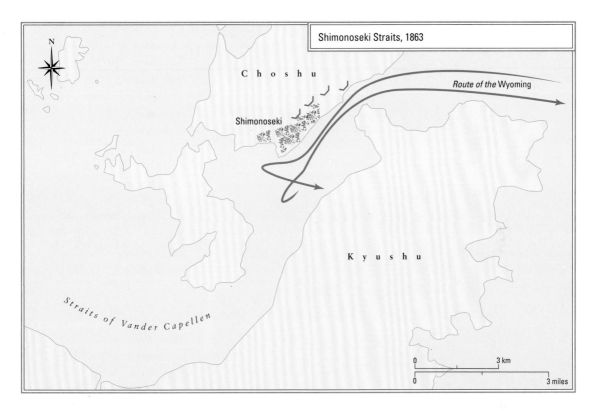

Shimonoseki Straits, 1863

Route of the Wyoming

C h o s h u

Shimonoseki

K y u s h u

Straits of Vander Capellen

0   3 km
0   3 miles

■ VINH LONG, 22 MARCH 1862

A Franco-Spanish force of 1000 troops under LCol Reboul was landed at Dinh Kao from two dispatch vessels and nine gunboats. The landing party stormed several artillery batteries protecting Vinh Long before taking the town.

■ KAGOSHIMA, 15–17 AUGUST 1863

Following an attack on British nationals by the *daimyo* of Satsuma's samurai, British warships were sent to enforce demands for compensation. Japanese shore batteries opened fire and the town of Kagoshima was bombarded in retaliation.

■ SHIMONOSEKI STRAITS I, JUNE–JULY 1863

In accordance with the Emperor Komei's 'Order to expel barbarians', the Shimonoseki-based Choshu clan under Lord Mori began to attack western shipping in the Shimonoseki Straits. During June and early July, Lord Mori's warships and coastal artillery fired on US, French and Dutch vessels. The USS *Wyoming* was then sent into the straits and was also attacked. It retaliated by bombarding shore batteries, sinking two Japanese warships and damaging another.

■ SHIMONOSEKI STRAITS II, 5–6 SEPT 1864

VAdm Sir Augustus Kuper led a fleet of nine British, four Dutch and three French warships to reopen the Shimonoseki Straits. The fleet bombarded the shore batteries, forcing the surrender of the Choshu clan.

■ FIRST CHOSHU EXPEDITION, SEPTEMBER–NOVEMBER 1864

The Tokugawa Shogunate led a punitive expedition against the Choshu Domain in retaliation for their attack on the imperial palace during the Hamaguri Rebellion. The expedition ended with the execution of the leaders of the Hamaguri Rebellion.

■ SECOND LARUT WAR, 1865–67

A gambling dispute between members of the Ghee Hin and Hai San Secret Societies flared up into serious fighting involving over 1000 men. In

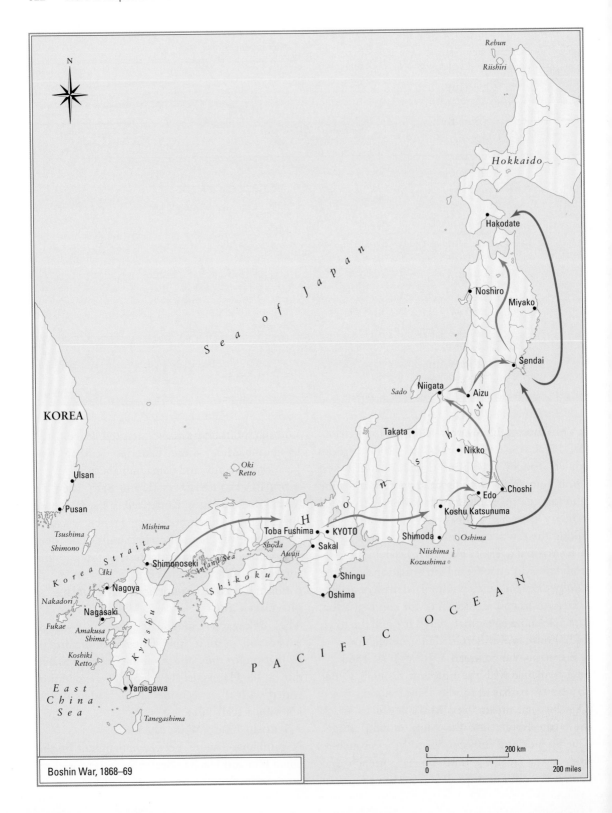

Boshin War, 1868–69

total, 14 members of the Ghee Hin were captured and all but one were subsequently murdered, despite attempts by local Chinese merchants to negotiate a settlement under the supervision of the Malay authorities. The sole survivor escaped to inform his clan and the Ghee Hin retaliated by sending a 400-strong raiding party to attack the Hai San village, razing it to the ground and killing 40 men in the process.

The Hai Sans fought back with the help of the local Malay headman and chief state minister of Larut, Ngah Ibrahim, who sent at least 200 armed Malay guards with light artillery support. They burned Klian Bharu and seized the Ghee Hin's stocks of tin ore. So Ah Chiang, the leader of the Ghee Hin, was captured by Ngah Ibrahim at Teluk Kertang (Port Weld) and executed. The 2000-strong Ghee Hin forces fled to Province Wellesley. The fight spread there and then on to Penang, where other Chinese secret societies aligned to the Hai Sans and the Ghee Hins were drawn into the conflict.

In 1867, fighting broke out on the streets of George Town, where it was known as the Penang Riot. This was a major nine-day battle that was only ended when British troops arrived from Singapore. By this stage, both sides had sustained heavy casualties and mutual exhaustion led to calls for a truce. An official enquiry was held, which resulted in the banishment of the leaders of the Ghee Hin and Hai San and each society being fined $5000 for causing a breach of the peace in Penang.

■ SECOND CHOSHU EXPEDITION, 1866

The Tokugawa Shogunate led a further punitive expedition against the Choshu Domain, but was defeated by the modern and better organized troops of Choshu. The new shogun, Tokugawa Yoshinobu, managed to negotiate a ceasefire.

■ FRENCH CAMPAIGN AGAINST KOREA, OCTOBER–NOVEMBER 1866

Korean persecution of French missionaries provoked a French punitive expedition of five warships and 800 troops commanded by RAdm Pierre-Gustave Roze. In October 1866, a landing party seized key points on Ganghwa Island off the Korean coast, which controlled access to Seoul along the Han river. Subsequent French attempts to seize a bridgehead on the Korean mainland failed in the face of stiffening Korean resistance and Roze evacuated the island.

■ KLANG WAR (SELANGOR CIVIL WAR), 1867–74

The tin-rich Klang District of Selangor in Malaya became a power vacuum on the death of the Sultan of Selangor in 1867 and was seized by Raja Mahdi, the son of a local chief. Prince Tengku Kudin was appointed viceroy by the new sultan and ordered to retake Klang. He gained British support following Raja Mahdi's attacks on British shipping, which enabled him to defeat the last enemy forces by 1874.

■ BOSHIN WAR, JANUARY 1868–MAY 1869

An alliance of southern samurai and court officials gained control of the Japanese imperial court and influenced the young Emperor Meiji against the Shogunate. Shogun Tokugawa Yoshinobu abdicated political power to the emperor, hoping that the house of Tokugawa's influence could be preserved. However, his opponents' continued enmity led Yoshinobu to launch a campaign to seize the imperial court at Kyoto. The campaign rapidly turned in favour of the smaller, but more thoroughly modernized imperial faction and Yoshinobu was forced to surrender. His supporters retreated to northern Honshu and later to Hokkaido, where they founded the Ezo republic. Defeat at the battle of Hakodate broke this last stronghold and ensured the supremacy of imperial rule throughout Japan, completing the military phase of the Meiji Restoration. A total of 120,000 men were mobilized during the conflict, of which 3500 were killed in the fighting.

■ UENO, 4 JULY 1868

Prince Arisugawa Taruhito's imperial army occupied Edo, but faced continued resistance by pro-Shogunate Shogitai rebels holding out in the city's Ueno temple district. Imperial General Omura Masujiro routed the rebels, who fled north towards Goryokaku.

■ TIANJIN (TIENTSIN) MASSACRE, 1870

Chinese resentment at the increasing influence of Catholic missionaries led to an attack on the Wanghailou Church's orphanage. The church and French consulate were destroyed in the riots. A total of 18 foreigners were killed.

■ THIRD AND FOURTH LARUT WARS, 1872–74

Simmering hostility between the Ghee Hin and Hai San Secret Societies flared up into open and bloody fighting involving 4000 Chinese mercenaries, which was only suppressed following the establishment of a British protectorate in Perak in 1874.

■ PERAK WAR, 1875–76

The Sultan of Perak and local chiefs were antagonized by the arrogant British resident, James W.W. Birch, who was murdered in November 1875. A British invasion deposed the sultan who was exiled to the Seychelles.

■ JEMENTAH CIVIL WAR, 1879

Following the death of Sultan Ali of Muar in 1877, disputes between his sons, Tengku Mahmood and Tengku Alam, flared up into civil war, which was suppressed by the Sultan of Johore aided by British troops.

Portuguese Civil War, 1828–34

■ PRAIA BAY, 28 AUGUST 1828

An invasion of Terceira Island in the Azores on 28 August 1828, by a Miguelite fleet of 22 ships, was repulsed by several loyalist-controlled forts and battery positions on the coast who took several hundred prisoners.

■ PONTE FERREIRA, 22–23 JULY 1832

During the siege of Porto on 22–23 July 1832, a Liberal expedition of three battalions and artillery was ambushed before a successful counter-attack at the Ponte Ferreira (bridge), with 460 casualties to greater losses by a fleeing enemy.

■ CAPE ST VINCENT, 5 JULY 1833

A Liberal squadron of six ships commanded by VAdm Napier attacked a superior force on 5 July 1833, engaging in close-combat boarding tactics, which caused enemy ships to change side. The attacking force suffered 30 dead to 300 enemies.

■ ASSEICEIRA, 16 MAY 1834

The last land battle of the Portuguese Civil War, fought on 16 May 1834, at the Asseiceira Hills, where Miguelite forces in a strong defensive position were overwhelmed by a cavalry charge leaving 1400 prisoners.

Central/South American Wars, 1830–1905

■ BUIN, 6 JANUARY 1839

Marshal Andrés de Santa Cruz' 6000-strong army of the Peru–Bolivian Confederation fought an indecisive action against a Chilean rearguard commanded by Gen Manuel Bulnes, which totalled 1500 men. The Chileans held a bridge across the Buin river, which was the only practicable crossing point for formed troops and prevented Santa Cruz from exploiting his numerical superiority. Santa Cruz inflicted 300 casualties for the loss of 70 men.

■ YUNGAY, 20 JANUARY 1839

Marshal Andrés de Santa Cruz, the President of Bolivia, seized power in Peru and created the Peru–Bolivian Confederation in October 1836, appointing himself as its Supreme Protector. The Confederation was resented in much of Peru, while Chile regarded it as a threat to its very independence, declaring war in December 1836. An initial Chilean invasion was defeated in 1837, but a further attack the following year was more successful.

After their inconclusive action at Buin, the armies fought the decisive battle of the campaign at Yungay in Peru, where a combined force of 5400 Chilean troops and Peruvian exiles under Gen Manuel Bulnes decisively defeated the Confederation's army of 6000 men commanded by Marshal Andrés de Santa Cruz. Bulnes inflicted 3000 casualties for the loss of just over 650 men and his victory marked the end of the Peru–Bolivian Confederation.

■ FAMAILLÁ, 19 SEPTEMBER 1841

A 2000-strong Argentine Unitarian army under Gen Juan Lavalle was defeated by Manuel Oribe's federal force of 2200 men at Famaillá in northern Argentina. The action was the last major battle of the Argentine Civil War.

■ INGAVI, 18 NOVEMBER 1841

A 3800-strong Bolivian force under President José Ballivián defeated an invading Peruvian army of 5200 men commanded by the Peruvian president Agustín Gamarra. The Bolivians inflicted 180 casualties for the loss of 160 men.

■ ARROYO GRANDE (URUGUAYAN CIVIL WAR), 6 DECEMBER 1842

A 12,000-strong conservative Blancos ('Whites') army commanded by Manuel Oribe defeated a liberal Colorados ('Reds') force of 7500 men under Fructuoso Rivera. Oribe's forces inflicted an estimated 3400 casualties for the loss of 300 men.

■ MONTEVIDEO, 1843–51

Oribe exploited his victory at Arroyo Grande by besieging the Colorados stronghold of Montevideo on 16 February 1843 with Argentine support. The siege lasted for eight years, with foreign volunteers coming to the city's defence, most notably the Italian patriot Giuseppe Garibaldi.

The defenders were also supported by British and French naval forces, which occupied parts of Uruguay and Martin Garcia Island at the mouth of the Uruguay River, besides blockading the Rio de la Plata between 1845 and 1849. However, both the French and British then withdrew after signing a treaty that represented a triumph for Juan Manuel de Rosas and his Federal Party in Argentina.

After the British and French withdrawal, it appeared that Montevideo would fall to Juan Manuel de Rosas and Oribe. However, an uprising against de Rosas changed the situation, forcing Oribe to abandon the siege.

■ VUELTA DE OBLIGADO, 20 NOVEMBER 1845

An Anglo-French naval squadron of 11 warships under François Thomas Tréhouart attacked Argentine positions along the Paraná river. The Argentines had blocked the river at Vuelta de Obligado with a boom covered by four artillery batteries mounting a total of 30 guns. Tréhouart's squadron broke through after a fierce action in which most of his ships were damaged. He destroyed the brigantine *Republicano* and inflicted 240 casualties for the loss of 123 men.

■ CASEROS, 3 FEBRUARY 1852

The Argentine dictator Juan Manuel de Rosas, commanding a force of 22,000 men, was attacked by Justo José de Urquiza's 24,000-strong army of Argentine dissidents, Uruguayans and Brazilians. Both sides suffered from poor morale and high rates of desertion, but after a three-hour action, Rosas' flanks collapsed and his forces were routed. Urquiza inflicted 8500 casualties for the loss of 600 men. Rosas fled to Britain and Urquiza took control of Argentina.

■ RIVAS, 29 JUNE 1855

The American filibuster William Walker invaded Nicaragua with a force of 55 Americans and 100 Indian allies in support of the Liberal Party in the Nicaraguan Civil War. His heavily outnumbered force was defeated near Rivas.

■ SANTA ROSA, 20 MARCH 1856

William Walker led the invasion of Costa Rica by a mercenary force. This was opposed by President Juan Rafael Mora's 9000 conscripts, who routed Walker's men in a 14-minute action at the hacienda of Santa Rosa.

■ SECOND BATTLE OF RIVAS, 11 APRIL 1856

William Walker was driven out of Costa Rica after his defeat at Santa Rosa. General José María Cañas pursued his men back to Rivas in Nicaragua where Walker was again defeated in fierce street fighting.

■ 'THE WATERMELON WAR', 15 APRIL 1856

A dispute in Panama City between a watermelon seller and a drunken American resulted in a shot being fired, which injured a bystander. The violence rapidly escalated into major rioting that was far beyond police control. A total of 15 Americans were killed and 16 wounded, while two Panamanians were shot dead and a further 13 wounded. Order was finally restored by armed railway staff, who were led by the Texan Randolph Runnels.

■ **GUAYAQUIL, 22–24 SEPTEMBER 1860**

The army of Gen Guillermo Franco, Supreme Chief of Guayaquil and Cuenca, was defeated by a 4000-strong force under Generals Gabriel García Moreno and Juan José Flores. The action marked the end of the Ecuadorian Civil War.

■ **PAVÓN, 17 SEPTEMBER 1861**

Gen Bartolomé Mitre led the 22,000-strong army of Buenos Aires against federalist Justo José de Urquiza's 17,000 men at Pavón. Mitre won a decisive victory and became the first constitutional president of a united Argentina.

■ **ECUADORIAN–COLOMBIAN WAR, 1863**

Tension between the United States of Colombia (modern Colombia and Panama) and the Republic of Ecuador flared up into open warfare. An Ecuadorian invasion of Colombia was defeated, but attempts to establish a Greater Colombia were abandoned.

■ **MATO GROSSO CAMPAIGN, 1864**

Paraguayan forces totalling 9000 men under the leadership of Colonels Vicente Barrios and Francisco Isidoro Resquin captured the Brazilian province of Mato Grosso, which was defended by only 200 troops, but were forced to evacuate the area in 1868.

■ **RIACHUELO, 11 JUNE 1865**

Capt Pedro Ignácio Meza's Paraguayan squadron of nine ships and seven armed barges, carrying a total of 45 guns, attacked a Brazilian flotilla of nine warships under Commodore Francisco Manuel Barroso at Riachuelo on the Paraguay river. The Brazilian flotilla mounted 58 guns, but the Paraguayans were supported by 22 shore-based guns and two Congreve rocket batteries. Barroso defeated the Paraguayans, sinking four ships and seven barges for the loss of a corvette.

■ **URUGUAIANA, AUGUST–SEPTEMBER 1865**

Col Estigarribia's Paraguayan force of 8000 men and eight guns captured the Brazilian town of Uruguaiana, but was besieged and forced to surrender by a combined Brazilian, Argentine and Uruguayan army of over 17,000 men.

■ **JATAI (YATAY), 17 AUGUST 1865**

Col Pedro Duarte's 3200-strong Paraguayan force was defeated by a combined Argentine, Uruguayan and Brazilian army of almost 8500 men under Gen Venancio Flores. The allies destroyed the Paraguayan force losing 340 men.

■ **TUYUTÍ (PASO DE PATRIA), 24 MAY 1866**

President Francisco Solano López' 23,000-strong Paraguayan Army was defeated by a combined Brazilian, Argentine and Uruguayan army of 32,000 men under Gen Bartolomé Mitre. The allies inflicted 12,000 casualties for the loss of 4000 men.

■ **CURUPAYTY, 22 SEPTEMBER 1866**

Gen José E. Díaz' 5000 Paraguayan troops supported by 49 guns defeated a combined Argentine and Brazilian army of 20,000 men under Gen Bartolomé Mitre. The Paraguayans inflicted 6000 casualties for the loss of 92 men.

■ **QUERÉTARO, 6 MARCH–14 MAY 1867**

In 1866, Napoleon III withdrew the French troops that had formed the cadre of the Emperor Maximilian's army. The weakened opposition allowed the Republican Mexican general Mariano Escobeda to advance south through San Jacinto and besiege the city of Querétaro, which was held by Emperor Maximilian and 20,000 men under Generals Tomás Mejía and Miguel Miramón. The emperor, together with Miramón and Mejía, was executed after the city was stormed.

■ **GRITO DE LARES, 23–24 SEPTEMBER 1868**

A revolt against Spanish rule in Puerto Rico planned by Ramón Emeterio Betances and Segundo Ruiz Belvis was thwarted by strong resistance from local Spanish militias. The ringleaders were exiled and the province was granted greater autonomy.

■ **ITORORO, 6 DECEMBER 1868**

Argentine, Brazilian and Uruguayan allies under Marshal Luís Aldes, Marquis of Caxias, defeated Gen Bernadino Caballero's Paraguayan force attempting to defend the Itororo river near Ypane. A total of 1200 Paraguayans and 3000 allied troops were killed.

■ **ITA YBATE (YPACARAI), 21–27 DEC 1868**

In a fresh offensive in central Paraguay against President Francisco Solano López, Marshal Luís Aldes, Marquis of Caxias, led Argentine, Brazilian and Uruguayan forces against Ita Ybate. Despite heavy allied losses, the Paraguayans were decisively defeated.

■ **CERRO CORÁ (AQUIDABAN RIVER), 1 MAR 1870**

Paraguayan president Francisco Solano López' 250-strong bodyguard was trapped and defeated at Cerro Corá in north-eastern Paraguay by a force of 4000 Brazilian troops under José Antônio Correia da Câmara. López was killed in action.

■ **TARAPACÁ, 27 NOVEMBER 1879**

A column of 2300 exhausted Chilean troops led by Gen Luis Arteaga recklessly attacked Gen Juan Buendía's 4500-strong Peruvian force at Tarapacá in southern Peru. The over-confident Gen Arteaga divided his outnumbered force into three assault columns and attacked without adequate reconnaissance. The isolated Chilean columns were defeated in detail, losing at least 750 men and all ten of their guns, while the Peruvian force sustained a total of more than 500 casualties.

■ **QUESTA DE LOS ANGELES, 22 MARCH 1880**

Chilean gen Manuel Baquedano's force of 4500 men defeated a 1400-strong Peruvian detachment under Col Andres Gamarra near Questa de Los Angeles, in southern Peru. Baquedano inflicted 145 casualties for the loss of 100 men.

■ **TACNA, 26 MAY 1880**

A 14,000-strong Chilean army under Gen Manuel Baquedano defeated Gen Narciso Campero's combined Bolivian and Peruvian army of 12,000 men near Tacna in southern Peru. The Chileans inflicted 5000 casualties for the loss of 2200 men.

■ **CHALCHUAPA, 2 APRIL 1885**

President Justo Rufino Barrios of Guatemala was determined to re-establish a Central American Confederation and invaded western El Salvador in alliance with Honduras. Barrios was killed in action at Chalchuapa and his army was routed.

■ **CHILEAN CIVIL WAR, 16 JAN–18 SEP 1891**

The war was fought between forces supporting Congress and those loyal to the president, José Manuel Balmaceda. The bulk of the Chilean Army sided with the president, while the Chilean Navy supported the Congress. The war ended with the defeat of the Chilean Army and President Balmaceda's suicide. More than 10,000 lives were lost and the total cost of the war exceeded the then enormous sum of £10,000,000.

■ **THE WAR OF CANUDOS, 1893–97**

Tensions between the Brazilian Government and a group of 30,000 dissident settlers led by Antonio Conselheiro based in the town of Canudos flared up into fighting in which 5000 troops and 20,000 settlers were killed.

■ **ARGENTINE REVOLUTION, 1905**

An uprising by Hipólito Yrigoyen's Radical Civic Union against the right-wing Argentine Government of Julio Argentino Roca's National Autonomist Party was suppressed by loyalist troops. The revolt prompted the government to begin a major social and political reform programme.

The November Uprising/ Polish Revolt, 1830–31

■ **STOCZEK, 14 FEBRUARY 1831**

A 3000-strong Russian detachment under Teodor Geismar was attacked by Gen Józef Dwernicki's 1000 Poles near the town of Stoczek Łukowski, on the Brest–Warsaw road. The over-confident Russians advanced without adequate reconnaissance and were surprised by the sudden appearance of Polish cavalry. As they tried to reform, the Russians were bombarded by Dwernicki's artillery and forced to retreat. The Poles inflicted 630 casualties and captured 11 guns for the loss of 90 men.

■ Białołęka, 24–25 February 1831

A 13,000-strong Polish force under Gen Jan Krukowiecki defeated Gen Ivan Shakhovsky's 11,000 Russians at Białołęka, near Warsaw. The Poles halted the Russian advance on the capital, inflicting 1070 casualties for the loss of 770 men.

■ Olszynka Grochowska, 25 Feb 1831

Gen Józef Chłopicki's Polish force of 36,000 men held dense woods east of Grochów, repulsing repeated attacks by a 59,000-strong Russian army under FM Diebitsch. The Poles inflicted 9500 casualties for the loss of 7300 of their men.

■ Iganie, 10 April 1831

Following their victories in February and March 1831, the Polish armies began a counter-offensive against the Russian invaders. An 11,000-strong Polish corps under General Ignacy Prądzyński advanced rapidly towards Siedlce, a major Russian munitions depot. At Iganie, west of Siedlce, the Poles encountered Gen Grigorij Rosen's Russian forces. Prądzyński launched an immediate attack in the belief that Polish reinforcements would soon arrive. The 16 guns of his horse artillery batteries commanded by Józef Bem quickly brought the village under fire. Their bombardment disorganized the Russian garrison, which was driven out by a Polish assault led by Prądzyński. A potentially dangerous Russian counter-attack was shattered by Ludwik Kicki's cavalry, which seized the only bridge over the Muchawka river and attacked Rosen's rear. The over-cautious Polish C-in-C, Gen Jan Skrzynecki, here failed to exploit Prądzyński's success.

■ Ostrołęka, 26 May 1831

Gen Jan Skrzynecki's 30,000-strong Polish garrison of Ostrołęka successfully defended the town against repeated assaults by a Russian army of 35,000 men and 148 guns, commanded by FM Hans Karl von Diebitsch.

■ Warsaw, 6–8 September 1831

After sustaining heavy losses at Ostrołęka, the Polish field army retreated to Warsaw, bringing its garrison up to 40,000 men and 200 guns under the overall command of Gen Jan Krukowiecki. By early September, a Russian army of 71,000 men and 360 guns under FM Paskevich had closed in on the city and attacked on the 6th, defeating the Polish forces.

French Conquest of Algeria, 1830–45

■ Algiers, 14 June–July 1830

A French force of nearly 40,000 men landed west of Algiers on 14 June 1830, at Sidi Ferruch and endured attacks by an Algerian army of 10,000 soldiers before laying siege to the Algiers fort of Sultan-Khalessi on 29 June 1830. The fort fell on 4 July, while their leader, Hussein Dey, capitulated the next day and was sent into exile. French losses were in the hundreds and Algerian casualties in the thousands.

■ Macta, 28 June 1835

Berber warriors attacked a French column of infantry and cavalry in retreat to resupply at the marshes of the Macta river on 28 June 1835. The French fled a vastly superior force leaving several hundred dead.

■ Mazagran, February 1840

Algerian irregular forces numbering in the hundreds attacked a garrison of 123 men at the French fort at Mazagran, in early February 1840, for several days. The well-armed and well supplied defenders repulsed the attack.

■ Smala, 16 May 1843

Several hundred French cavalry captured the camp of Algerian leader Abd Al-Qadir and valuable war booty with several thousand prisoners on 16 May 1843. Many of the warriors were away on a raid with Al-Qadir.

■ Sidi Brahim, 22–25 September 1845

Several thousand Algerian warriors attacked 450 French infantry east of Algiers at Sidi Brahim, initially reducing the defenders led by LCol

Montagnac to less than a hundred survivors. After taking up a defensive position, the French forces were besieged for several days with few supplies and little water, but did not surrender. A breakout bayonet charge by 80 men eventually left only 11 survivors to reach the French lines alive.

Belgian Revolution, 1830–31

Established after the Napoleonic Wars, the United Kingdom of the Netherlands incorporated the territory of modern Belgium and the Netherlands. Resentment at Dutch control led to an uprising in Brussels and the establishment of an independent Belgium.

■ **THE TEN DAYS' CAMPAIGN, 2–12 AUGUST 1831**

A Dutch army of 26,000 men under Prince William of Orange invaded Belgium and rapidly defeated both regular Belgian forces and the more poorly equipped Belgian militia. Dutch troops quickly occupied key points throughout Belgium for the small loss of less than 750 men, but then withdrew when a French army, under Marshal Gérard, invaded at the invitation of the Belgians. A ceasefire was arranged and the Dutch troops evacuated the country on 20 August 1831.

First Carlist War, 1834–39

■ **ALSASUA, 22 APRIL 1834**

Carlist forces led by Gen Zumalacarregui ambushed a Liberal column under Gen Vicente Quesada, travelling to Pamplona on 22 April 1834, near the town of Alsasua leaving the Cristinos with about 200 casualties. The column would have been destroyed but for the arrival of a rescue force. About 100 prisoners from this action except officers were offered execution or service with the Guias de Navarra unit with their distinctive red berets.

■ **ALEGRIA DE ALAVA, 27 OCTOBER 1834**

Also called the battle of Salvatierra, this was an ambush by two Carlist forces commanded by Gen Zumalacarregui of a Liberal convoy under Manuel O'Doyle on 27 October 1834, on the plains of Salvatierra near Alegria. The convoy was originally a division of several regiments including cavalry and artillery, but was dispersed to face feints by the Zumalacarregui forces in several areas. O'Doyle was left with two regiments as well as some cavalry and artillery, although still 2000–3000 strong. This depleted force reached Alegria and then moved east to the sounds of battle in the direction of Chinchetru. A Liberal vanguard led by their commander attacked the first Carlist force and was surprised by the second to the rear causing panic and decimation of the convoy, who scattered into the nearby countryside. Nearly 1000 defeated Liberals were killed, wounded or taken prisoner with any officers being executed.

■ **VENTA DE ECHAVARRI, 28 OCTOBER 1834**

The day after the battle of Salvatierra, a Liberal relief force under Gen Joaquin de Osma mistakenly took up a defensive position on a hill near Arrieta where they were outflanked and fled, leaving many weapons behind.

■ **MENDAZA, 12 DECEMBER 1834**

A fixed battle between 10,000 Carlist troops under Gen Zumalacarregui in the Berrueza valley facing an equal number. Premature movement of his line of skirmish exposed the Carlist forces to artillery fire and defeat.

■ **ARQUIJAS I, 15 DECEMBER 1834**

A Liberal column of several thousand soldiers under Gen Luis de Cordova successfully attacked a Carlist defensive position of equal strength under Gen Zumalacarregui at a river near Arquijas, but later relinquished their gain. A second flanking unsupported force of eight battalions with artillery under Gen Oraa was repulsed, leading to a stalemate. Both sides suffered about 1000 casualties. Gen de Cordova was relieved of his command after this action.

■ **ARQUIJAS II, 5 FEBRUARY 1835**

Several Liberal forces under Gen Espoz y Mina,

totalling nearly 10,000 men, attacked smaller Carlist forces a second time on the opposite bank of the Ega river under Gen Zumalacarregui, but were routed with heavy casualties.

■ **ATRAZA, 19–24 APRIL 1835**

Also known as the battle of Las Amescoas, this engagement was fought in the Valley of Las Amescoas during 19–24 April 1835, where a superior Liberal force travelling in difficult terrain faced repeated guerilla-style attacks by Gen Zumalacarregui, causing hundreds of Liberal casualties.

■ **MENDIGORRIA, 16 JULY 1835**

A Carlist force of more than 10,000 men retreated across a bridge over the Arga river when facing an attack by a superior force under the recalled Gen de Cordova on 16 July 1835. The Carlists were crowded into the narrow corridor by supporting forces.

■ **ARLABAN, 15–19 JANUARY 1836**

The Liberals advanced from Vitoria across Navarre in three columns between 15 and 19 January 1836, towards the Arlaban hills led by Generals Evans, de Cordova and Espartero. The centre force of five battalions, including two from the French Foreign Legion led by Gen de Cordova, had a series of skirmishes until nightfall when they captured a strategic position. The next day they were attacked, but repulsed a reinforced Carlist force with the arrival of a column under Gen Espartero. A British force under Gen Evans going towards Salvatierra faced repeated Carlist attacks by several battalions as they advanced into the village of Mendijur. There were several British cavalry charges and a bayonet charge at one point that ended well. The Liberal forces eventually withdrew back to Vitori in appalling weather, after both sides suffered casualties in the hundreds.

■ **TERAPEGUI, 26 APRIL 1836**

Two French Foreign Legion battalions under the Liberal banner repelled a much larger Carlist force near Terapegui on 26 April 1836. After inflicting substantial casualties, the French Foreign Legion battalions withdrew to Larrasoana.

■ **VILLARROBLEDO, 20 SEPTEMBER 1836**

A skirmish south of Villarrobledo on 20 September 1836 with Liberal cavalry resulted in the loss of several hundred casualties and supplies for Carlist general Damas, but was unable to stop his movement into Andalusia.

■ **MAJACIETE, 23 NOVEMBER 1836**

A Carlist expeditionary force led by Gen Miguel Damas was repelled by three Liberal divisions under Gen Ramon Narvaez y Campos at the Majaceite river, near the town of Arcos de la Frontera, on 23 November 1836.

■ **LUCHANA, 23–24 DECEMBER 1836**

During the siege of Bilbao, a riverine force attacked the Luchana bridge over the Asua river on Christmas Eve in 1836. After an extended battle of attacks and counter-attacks, the Liberal forces under Gen Espartero prevailed.

■ **HUESCA, 24 MAY 1837**

Carlist cavalry and infantry repeatedly attacked a Liberal expeditionary force until nightfall on 24 May 1837, imposing nearly 1000 Liberal casualties, including nearly half of the French Foreign Legion contingent with about half these losses to themselves.

■ **VILLAR DE LOS NAVARROS, 24 AUGUST 1837**

A superior force of Carlist cavalry in two columns ambushed a retreating Liberal expeditionary force of several divisions on 24 August 1837, near the towns of Villar de Los Navarros and Herrera. There were several Carlist flanking cavalry charges with small-arms fire that split the Liberal forces, causing 1500 casualties and prisoners, which included Brig Solana and nearly 100 other officers. Some of the Liberal divisions were completely decimated as a result of this battle.

■ **PENACERRADA, 20–22 JUNE 1838**

A Liberal force led by Gen Espartero crossed the Ebro river and made a successful attack on the Carlist defenders of the town of Penacerrada, with a timely cavalry charge producing several hundred casualties and many prisoners.

■ **RAMALES, 12 MAY 1839**

A Liberal attack of superior numbers on two

fronts commanded by Gen Espartero grew with a Carlist error to keep half of their forces in reserve on 12 May 1839. The attack included an extensive artillery barrage that forced an early withdrawal by the Carlist force from their fortification at Guardamino. The abandoned and destroyed town was renamed Ramales de la Victoria to commemorate the Liberal victory. Casualties on both sides were nearly 1000 in number.

Texan War of Independence/ Texas–Mexican Wars, 1835–43

■ VELASCO, 26 JUNE 1832
American settlers attempted to ship a cannon to Anhuac, where they objected to the local commander's conduct. When this fort fired upon the ship, the Texans stormed the post, but settled down after Mexican concessions.

■ GONZALES, 2 OCTOBER 1835
The Mexican government welcomed American settlers into the empty but fertile plains of Texas, but did not welcome slavery, which the Americans brought with them. Mexican instability joined with anti-Catholic sentiment to spark an uprising. Justified Mexican concern over the Texans' loyalty prompted Mexican soldiers to here demand the surrender of a cannon loaned to the settlers against Indian attack. Minor violence after the Texans refused began their revolt.

■ GOLIAD, 10 OCTOBER 1835
The port of San Antonio fell after Mexican general Martín Perfecto de Cos transferred most of the main garrison to San Antonio. A Texas party under Capt George M. Collinsworth surprised the remainder, killing three.

■ BÉXAR, 12 OCTOBER– 11 DECEMBER 1835
The garrison of Mexican general Martín Perfecto de Cos dwindled to 570 before 700 Texans finally stormed the town of Béxar (San Antonio). The Texans advanced house to house, while the

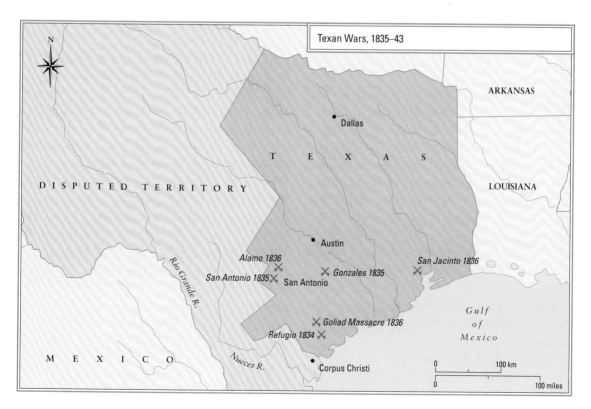

Texan Wars, 1835–43

desertion of his cavalry eventually prompted Cos to surrender.

■ CONCEPCIÓN, 28 OCTOBER 1835

Stephen Austin had led some 1700 families into Texas in the 1820s, but his – and his followers' – frustration with the Mexican Government (particularly after the Mexicans forbade further immigration from the United States) led to open warfare. The first shots were fired at Gonzales. Austin, when 400 Texan troops advanced upon the presidio in San Antonio, then called Béxar, and the nearest large concentration of Mexican troops. The town was then under the command of Mexican general Martín Perfecto de Cos, who with 750 men fortified the town's plaza and the adjacent Alamo mission across the San Antonio river. From here, the Texans were gathering their forces and scouting the town's outlaying ring of missions for defenders and their possible use in the revolt. Cos sent out 200 cavalry to dislodge a party of 90 men that Austin had sent out to establish a position near the town at this location, the mission of Nuestra Señora de la Purísima Concepción de Acuña. Around 275 Mexican infantry with two cannon moved out to support the cavalry against the Texans.

Capt James Bowie's party suffered the first casualty of the war as they advanced against the Mexican infantry. In response, Bowie's command opened rifle fire upon the Mexicans, inflicting casualties and capturing one of the cannon after repelling three charges by the Mexicans. The Mexican cavalry covered the retreat of the survivors back into San Antonio. A total of 200 East Texas reinforcements under Thomas Rusk prompted Austin to urge a full-scale attack upon the town, but the reluctance of his followers prompted Austin to settle into a siege over the winter, with his troops intercepting Cos' supplies and looking for weaknesses in the Mexicans' defences.

■ LIPANTITLAN, 4 NOVEMBER 1835

Approximately 90 Mexicans attempted to prevent the crossing of the Nueces river by 70 Texans under Ira Westover from this captured fort. The Texans established themselves in the riverside trees and killed 28 Mexicans as they approached.

■ GRASS FIGHT, 26 NOVEMBER 1835

As the siege of Béxar continued, Col Edward Burleson, commanding in Austin's absence, maintained pressure upon Mexican general Martín Perfecto de Cos in San Antonio. The Texans kept scouting parties out in anticipation of Col Domingo de Ugartechea's return with Mexican reinforcements. One of these returned with the news of Mexican cavalry escorting a pack train toward the city, which the Texans suspected might be carrying the garrison's pay. Around 40 Texan cavalrymen under James Bowie fought to delay the train, with another 100 engaging about 150 Mexican cavalry soon afterwards, supported by 50 infantry with cannon from the garrison. A sharp battle ensued, the Texans caught in a crossfire by the Mexican forces, but rallying to capture the pack train's 40 animals, killing three Mexicans. The train's burden proved to be cut grass fodder for the garrisons' animals within the town.

■ ALAMO, 23 FEBRUARY–6 MARCH 1836

The deceptive strength of the old mission's walls convinced James Neill, commander of captured Béxar, to repair and fortify the bastion with 21 cannon of various calibre, despite Texan general Sam Houston's misgivings that the mission would be both easy for the Mexicans to attack and difficult for the Texans to supply. Governor Henry Smith decided to hold the post as it and Goliad blocked the roads to the Texas interior, sending Maj Green Jameson to bolster the Alamo's defences. Green's promise to Houston that the repaired bastion could hold off ten times the number of the garrison would prove to fail.

James Bowie arrived and also supported maintaining the post as an outer barrier to the army of Mexican general, then-President Antonio López de Santa Anna (by coup), seizing power and proclaiming his intention of executing the rebel settlers of Mexico as pirates.

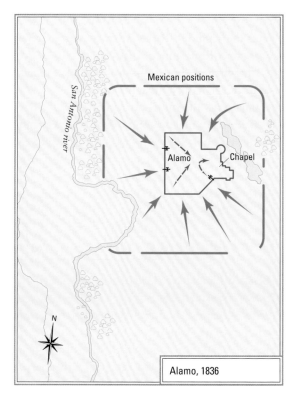

Alamo, 1836

LCol William Travis arrived with 30 cavalry to give the Alamo warning of a Mexican attack, while former US Congressman David Crockett with 30 Tennessee volunteers answered a call to defend the bastion. Neill's departure for family reasons left Travis in command and Bowie and his supporters disgruntled.

Santa Anna's assembled force numbered some 1800 picked soldiers, the Alamo's defenders totalling some 189 combatants after 32 scouts under George Kimbell slipped through Santa Anna's lines. Mexican artillery bombarded the mission over the 12 days of the siege, knocking holes in the walls and steadily lowering the morale of the doomed garrison. Santa Anna then ordered an assault, which soon crumbled under withering artillery and heavy rifle fire from the Texans. Approximately 600 Mexicans perished by the end of the second successful attack, with Santa Anna duly executing every surviving defender.

■ **SAN PATRICIO, 27 FEBRUARY 1836**
The Texans employed this town to corral horses for an expedition toward Matamoros. Gen José de Urrea attacked the post and an outlaying ranch at night, killing eight Texans and capturing 13, later executed at Goliad.

■ **AGUA DULCE, 2 MARCH 1836**
Some 60 Mexican cavalry under Gen José de Urrea overtook Dr James Grant and a foraging party of 27 volunteers here on their way to San Patricio with horses. Several Texans escaped, while Urrea captured six prisoners.

■ **REFUGIO, 12–15 MARCH, 1836**
Around 150 Texas troops from Goliad rode to this village under attack by the advance of Gen José de Urrea's army. After driving off the attackers, the Texans were overwhelmed, captured and executed by the Mexicans.

■ **COLETO, 19–20 MARCH 1836**
James Fannin with 300 men evacuated Goliad before the Mexican advance, but slowed his march with wagons. Gen José de Urrea overtook the Texans with eighty cavalrymen and 360 infantry, capturing and executing them all.

■ **BRAZOS SANTIAGO, 3 APRIL 1836**
Off this port on the gulf, the Texas schooner *Invincible* engaged the Mexican brig *Montezuma*, with *Invincible* slowly manoeuvring *Montezuma* into the shallows until it grounded on Brazos Island. *Invincible* then set the Mexican ship afire.

■ **SAN JACINTO (SAN JACINTO RIVER), 21 APRIL 1836**
As commander-in-chief of the Texas settlers' revolution against Mexico, Sam Houston kept his force in readiness and awaited his opportunity to strike against Mexico's final great effort to crush the rebellion. The ranks of the Texas Army were gradually increasing in reaction to Mexican slaughters of the rebels at the Alamo and Goliad. Houston's forces shadowed the Mexicans as Mexican president Antonio López de Santa Anna moved up the Texas coast in a campaign directed at strongholds and centres of the rebellion. On 21 April, Houston's scouts located

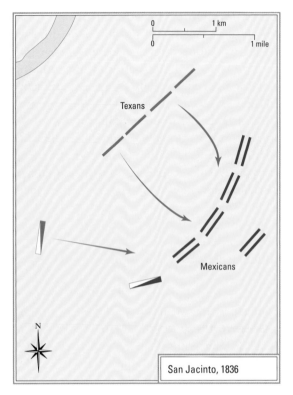

Texans

Mexicans

N

San Jacinto, 1836

an unwary Santa Anna and his army bivouacked on the Texans' side of the namesake river, near modern Houston. Houston with some 900 men moved stealthily against Santa Anna's fortified camp; 1360 Mexicans were caught taking their noonday meal while Santa Anna and his officers were engaged in making plans to attack and annihilate the Texans.

With two light cannon sent from Ohio, Houston's army initiated a headlong assault, with the Texans' cavalry on the flanks as they moved swiftly toward the Mexican encampment, the Texans' numbers and movements screened by riverside trees. 'Remember the Alamo! Remember Goliad!' was the first warning the Mexicans had of the onslaught, Santa Anna driven into flight without time to don his artificial leg. In a mere 16 minutes, 630 Mexicans had perished in disordered rout, with 200 more wounded, compared with only nine Texans falling. The pursuing Texans captured an additional 700 of the broken army over the

next day, among them Santa Anna. The Texans forced the captured Santa Anna to sign a treaty recognizing Texas' independence, which Mexico later repudiated, but took no further military action to re-conquer the rebel territory.

■ CAMPECHE, 30 APRIL–16 MAY 1843
Texas sloop *Austin* and brig *Wharton* joined with a small Yucatan squadron to engage Mexican steam warships *Moctezuma* and *Guadaloupe* and their consorts off this Yucatan port. The Mexicans withdrew, managing to escape the pursuing Texas ships.

French Intervention in Mexico 1838

■ BOMBARDMENT OF SAN JUAN DE ULUA, 27–28 NOVEMBER 1838
RAdm Charles Baudin's squadron of four French frigates, supported by brigs and bomb vessels, attacked the Mexican fortress of San Juan de Ulua, which protected the port of Veracruz. The fortress surrendered after an eight-hour bombardment.

Lower Canada Rebellion 1837–38

■ SAINT-DENIS, QUEBEC, 22 NOVEMBER 1837
When French Canadians in Quebec declared independence, a 300-strong detachment of British regular troops commanded by LCol Charles Gore marched against a force of 800 rebels under Wolfred Nelson at Saint-Denis, north-east of Montreal. Gore was repulsed with the loss of 70 men after inflicting fewer than 20 casualties in a badly handled action. His men were running short of ammunition and retreated on the approach of rebel reinforcements.

■ SAINT-CHARLES, 25 NOVEMBER 1837
Col George Wetherall's British detachment of 350 infantry from the 1st and 66th Regiments defeated 80 Canadian rebels under Thomas Storrow Brown at Saint-Charles, Quebec. The British inflicted 56 casualties for the loss of just 21 men.

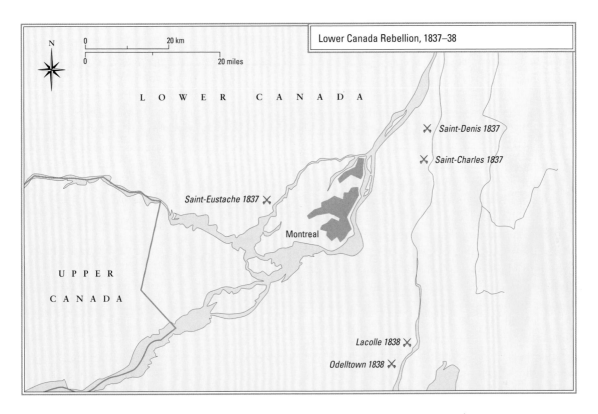

N

0   20 km

0   20 miles

Lower Canada Rebellion, 1837–38

L O W E R   C A N A D A

Saint-Denis 1837

Saint-Charles 1837

Saint-Eustache 1837

Montreal

U P P E R

C A N A D A

Lacolle 1838

Odelltown 1838

■ SAINT-EUSTACHE, 14 DECEMBER 1837

A group of 200 Canadian rebels under Jean-Olivier Chénier were defeated by MGen Sir John Colborne's force of 1280 British regulars and 220 militia. The British inflicted a total of 190 casualties for the loss of three men, in this unequal engagement.

■ LACOLLE, 7 NOVEMBER 1838

Major John Scriver's 400 Canadian loyalist militia defeated a force of 170 Canadian rebels under Colonel Ferdinand-Alphonse Oklowski at Lacolle in southern Quebec. Scriver's militia inflicted eight casualties for the loss of two men.

■ ODELLTOWN, 9 NOVEMBER 1838

The final conflict of the Lower Canada Rebellion of 1838 saw a force of 1000 Canadian loyalist militia commanded by Lewis Odell defeat Robert Nelson's group of 600 Canadian rebels at Odelltown in Quebec. The loyalists inflicted 25 casualties for the loss of 15 men.

Upper Canada Rebellion 1837–38

■ MONTGOMERY'S TAVERN, 7 DECEMBER 1837

After an initial skirmish days prior, 200 armed Canadian rebels faced off against 1000 loyalist troops at the Yonge Street tavern in Toronto on 7 December 1837. Artillery fire scattered the rebels and the tavern was destroyed.

■ PELEE ISLAND, 3 MARCH 1838

A combined British and loyalist force of more than 100 soldiers attacked and defeated a larger force of Canadian and American rebels on 3 March 1838, south of Pelee Island, with about 30 casualties on each side.

■ SHORT HILLS RAID, 21–23 JUNE 1838

Between 21 and 23 June, 50 Canadian and American rebels successfully attacked a smaller group of British soldiers near the Niagara river, but were tracked and attacked in turn by superior reinforcements, with over 30 of the men taken prisoner.

■ WINDMILL, 12–16 NOVEMBER 1838

A force of about 250 Canadian and American rebel members of a secret anti-British organization called the Hunter Patriots crossed the St Lawrence river on 12 November 1838, to land near the town of Prescott, but the invasion was repelled by loyalist soldiers. The rebel force then made a second landing east of Prescott at Windmill Point and took refuge in the nearby village of Newport, within a windmill built of thick walls that provided an ideal defensive position. The next day, a much larger loyalist force attacked the rebels, but was defeated with an equal small number of casualties on each side. Substantial loyalist reinforcements and artillery then arrived to lay siege with an extensive bombardment, which forced the rebels – by this time reduced by desertions – to surrender on 16 November 1838. The leaders among the nearly 200 prisoners were executed and the remainder were either exiled or released.

■ WINDSOR, 4 DECEMBER 1838

A rebel force of several hundred Hunter Patriots crossed the Detroit river on 4 December 1838 and proceeded to attack a small British garrison at Windsor before retreating from substantial reinforcements, leaving several prisoners who were summarily executed.

The Great Trek 1838

■ WEENEN MASSACRE, 17 FEBRUARY 1838

The massacre of hundreds of Voortrekker men, women and children with native workers at their camps along the Bushman river on 17 February 1838, by Zulu warriors. The massacre was named for a later town called Weenen, which is Afrikaans for 'weeping'.

■ ITALENI, 9 APRIL 1838

Two Voortrekker columns attacked Zulu warriors near Itala Mountain. One column, led by Cdr Uys, was ambushed by Zulu warriors on 9 April 1838, after the second column made a premature retreat, leaving ten Voortrekkers killed.

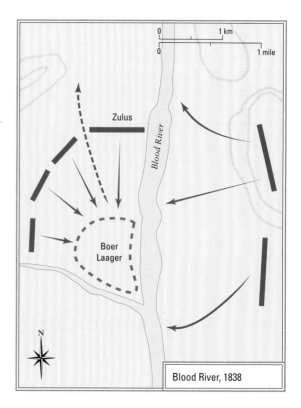

Blood River, 1838

■ BLOOD RIVER, 16 DECEMBER 1838

A Voortrekker Zulu settlement treaty was violently broken by Zulu king Dingane at a supposedly peaceful signing ceremony when the superstitious king killed their leader, Piet Retief and several others in February 1838. Later that year, nearly 500 desperate South African Voortrekkers commanded by Andries Pretorius fought several thousand Zulu warriors led by Gen Ndlela at the Ncome river in modern-day Kwa-Zulu Natal Province of South Africa, on 16 December 1838. The Voortrekkers formed up more than 60 interlocked wagons in a strategic square or laager with two sides against the steep river bank and adjacent dry river bed. The two remaining sides were each protected by cannon overlooking an open river flood plain. About half the Zulu force crossed the river at night to surround the temporary fort while making noises throughout to intimidate their foes, unsuccessfully.

At the first light of dawn, the Vortrekkers opened fire with muskets and cannon, which decimated the stationary Zulu warriors who were performing rituals for protection in battle. The Zulu began repeated attacks that were met by sustained rifle and cannon fire across the open space on two sides, while hundreds died from musket fire from above as they attempted to scale the steep river and gully banks. Blood from the wounded and dead Zulu gave name to the river battle. Pretorius unleashed his irregular cavalry during a lull in the battle, scattering the remaining Zulu warriors, who were killed in smaller groups.

First Opium War 1839–42

■ GUANGDONG OPERATION, 1840
Qing war-junks failed to break the blockade of the Pearl river in this province by 20 British warships, some of them steamers, as the trade war over British opium shipments to China escalated into fighting. Efforts by British and foreign ships to continue trading prompted Charles Elliot, superintending British trade, to order the blockade, as he tried to end the shipments of opium and consequent incidents with the Chinese.

■ BOGUE FORTS, 23–26 FEBRUARY 1841
The forts at either side of this narrow strait before Canton blocked British efforts to enter the port, the fire from a masked battery beginning hostilities. Cdre James Bremer landed parties to capture the forts.

■ NINGBO, 10 MARCH 1841
Having blockaded this city and the Pearl river, the British fleet under Cdre James Bremer landed marines, who seized first Chinhai and then Ningbo, beating off the attempt of 5000 Chinese to retake the city soon afterwards.

■ CANTON, 23–30 MAY 1841
Having earlier forced their way into Canton, months later the British found themselves under increasing pressure as the Qing court repudiated treaties negotiated with local officials

Ghazni, 1839

and dispatched additional troops toward the city. As the British evacuated the port, the civilians of Canton attacked the British, a rainstorm limiting the Westerners' fire. Maintaining order, the British reached the shelter of their fleet's cannon and completed their withdrawal with light casualties.

First Anglo-Afghan War 1839–42

■ GHAZNI, 23 JULY 1839
A 20,500-strong British force under Sir John Keane invaded Afghanistan and stormed the city of Ghazni, which was held by an Afghan garrison of 3500 men. The British inflicted 2100 casualties for the loss of 200 men.

■ JELLALABAD, 12 NOV 1841–13 APR 1842
An Afghan force of 5000 men under Amir Akbar Khan besieged the isolated fort at Jellalabad (now Jalalabad), about 130km east of Kabul, which was defended by BGen Sir Robert Sale's

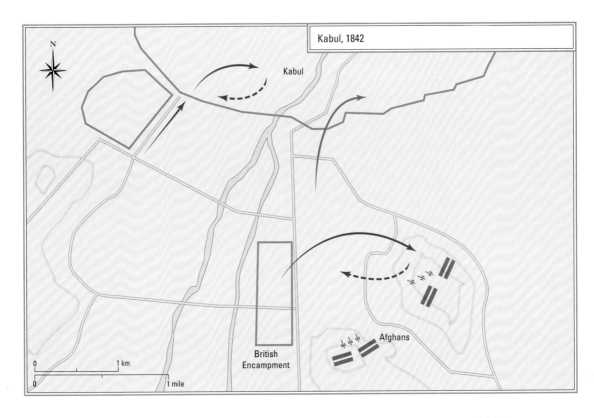

2000-strong British garrison. The half-ruined fortifications of the town had barely been repaired when the town was surrounded by Afghan tribesmen. Encouraged by the massacre of MGen Elphinstone's force during its retreat from Kabul in January 1842, the Afghans launched a series of attacks on the garrison. However, the British managed to beat off all the assaults and even captured 300 sheep from the besieging force when rations ran short. Eventually, after five months under siege, Sale mounted a major sortie against the besiegers, which overran their main camp and captured their baggage, stores, guns and horses. The demoralized Afghans fled to Kabul.

■ GANDAMAK, 13 JANUARY 1842

During the retreat of MGen Elphinstone's force from Kabul, a group of 65 British troops were surrounded and attacked by hundreds of Afghans. Only one member of the group, assistant surgeon William Brydon, escaped.

■ KABUL, AUGUST–OCTOBER 1842

Political pressure for revenge for the destruction of MGen Elphinstone's force led to the authorization of a punitive expedition of 13,000 men under Generals William Nott and George Pollock.

The expedition advanced in two columns. Nott's force moved off from Kandahar and defeated 10,000 Afghans at Khelat-i-Ghilzai, before taking and looting the city of Ghazni and occupying Kabul. In the meantime, Pollock's army, which was generally referred to as the 'Army of Retribution', advanced from Jellalabad (now Jalalabad) and defeated a force of 15,000 Afghans under Akbar Khan at Huft Kotal, before taking Kabul two days ahead of Nott's column.

The treatment of the British hostages taken by Akbar Khan from MGen Elphinstone's force improved as the punitive expedition advanced and they were able to bribe their guards to release them. With the hostages safe, a detachment from

Pollock's army laid waste to Charikar in revenge for the massacre there of an irregular Gurkha unit the previous November. Kabul's historic bazaar was also destroyed on Pollock's orders and the rest of the city was extensively looted.

On 12 October 1842, Pollock and Nott left Kabul with their troops and began the retreat to India via Gandamak, Jellalabad and Peshawar, destroying Jellalabad, Ali Masjid and many villages and towns on the way.

The expedition soon learned the truth of Wellington's comment that '… It is easy to get into Afghanistan. The problem is getting out again.' The Afghans harried the troops throughout their entire march, particularly through the gorges of Jugdulluk and the Khyber Pass. In the final actions, 60 of Nott's force were killed before the British reached Peshawar. Having learned a hard lesson about fighting in Afghanistan, it would be more than 35 years before British forces again entered the country.

Second Anglo-Afghan War, 1878–80

■ ALI MASJID, 21 NOVEMBER 1878
A 3800-strong detachment of the Peshawar Field Force under Gen Sir Samuel Browne bombarded and seized the fortress of Ali Masjid in the Khyber Pass, which was defended by an Afghan force of more than 4000 men.

■ PEIWAR KOTAL, 28–29 NOVEMBER 1878
MGen Sir Frederick Roberts' Anglo-Indian army of 4000 men defeated a 5000-strong Afghan force under Karim Khan at the Peiwar Kotal Pass near Kabul. Roberts inflicted 200 casualties on the superior Afghan force for the loss of 96 men.

■ SHERPUR CANTONMENT, 15–23 DEC 1879
LGen Sir Frederick Roberts' Anglo-Indian garrison of 7000 men was besieged in the Sherpur Cantonment at Kabul by Mohammed Jan Khan Wardak's 50,000-strong Afghan force. Despite the profound imbalance between the

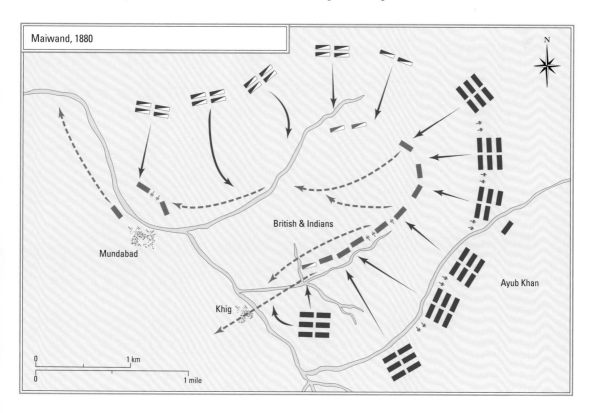

Maiwand, 1880

Mundabad

British & Indians

Khig

Ayub Khan

N

0   1 km

0   1 mile

two opposing sides, Roberts inflicted 3000 casualties for the loss of 33 men.

■ AHMED KHEL, 19 APRIL 1880

LGen Sir Donald Stewart's Anglo-Indian army of 7200 men defeated an Afghan force of 15,000 tribal warriors in a hard-fought and bloody action at Ahmed Khel. Stewart inflicted 1700 casualties on the Afghan force for the loss of 141 British men.

■ MAIWAND, 27 JULY 1880

A brigade of just under 2500 British and Indian troops commanded by BGen George Burrows was sent from Kandahar to support Afghan Government forces against Ayub Khan's uprising in western Afghanistan. Although his Afghan troops quickly deserted, the inexperienced Burrows took over their artillery and unwisely decided to carry on the campaign with his unsupported brigade.

At Maiwand, Burrows went into action against Ayub Khan's army of 25,000 men, in the mistaken belief that he was only faced by an Afghan advance guard. The truth was far more sobering. Ayub Khan's force included a cadre of 10,000 regular troops supported by 30 guns, some of which were modern high-performance Armstrong field guns. These gave the Afghans a marked advantage in firepower over the 12 British guns and were a very important factor in their victory. The Anglo-Indian force lost almost 1200 men, while inflicting 3000 casualties on the Afghans.

■ KANDAHAR, 1 SEPTEMBER, 1880

The survivors of Burrows' brigade retreated to the city of Kandahar, bringing its Anglo-Indian garrison up to a total strength of over 4300 men. On 8 August, Ayub Khan's forces besieged the city, but retreated on the approach of a 10,000-strong relief force under LGen Sir Frederick Roberts. The 12,800-strong Afghan Army took up strong defensive positions near the city, but were routed by Roberts with the loss of 1400 men.

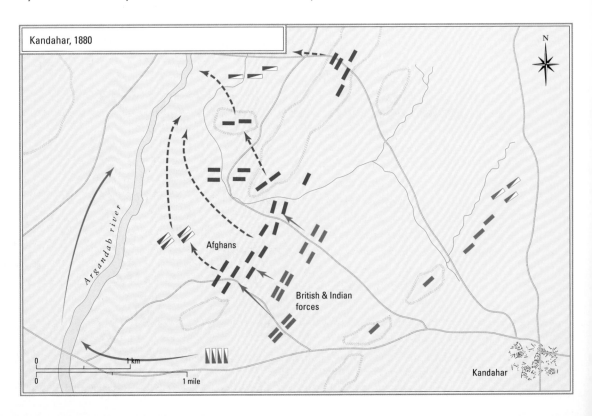

Kandahar, 1880

Argandab river

Afghans

British & Indian forces

Kandahar

0   1 km

0   1 mile

N

Anglo-Marri Wars 1840, 1880 & 1917

The Marri tribe of north-eastern Baluchistan took advantage of the First and Second Anglo-Afghan Wars to raid the supply lines of British forces in Afghanistan. In 1917, recruiting for the Indian Army provoked further clashes.

Indian–British Wars 1843–49

■ HYDERABAD, 15 FEBRUARY–24 MARCH 1843

When the Baluchi Amirs of Sind (now part of Pakistan) besieged the British residency at Hyderabad, Britain sent a relief force commanded by Gen Sir Charles Napier to raise the siege. The garrison, comprising the Light Company of the 22nd Foot under Maj James Outram, broke out and escaped aboard the Indian marine vessels *Planet* and *Satellite* to join Napier's relief force, having only lost two dead and four wounded in the engagement.

■ MIANI, 17 FEBRUARY 1843

Gen Sir Charles Napier's Anglo-Indian force of 2800 men routed Mir Nasir Khan Talpur's 22,000-strong army at the village of Miani just outside Hyderabad. Napier's troops inflicted 5000 casualties for the loss of 256 men.

DUBBA (DUBBO), 24 MARCH 1843

Sir Charles Napier's 5,000-strong Anglo-Indian army attacked and decisively defeated Emir Hosh Muhammad Sheedi's army of 20,000 men at Dubba near Hyderabad. Napier's forces inflicted at least 500 casualties for the loss of 267 men.

■ MUDKI, 18 DECEMBER 1845

A Sikh army of 20,000 men under Raja Lal Singh crossed the River Sutlej into British East Punjab where they attacked Gen Sir Hugh Gough's 10,000-strong British force at Mudki, south-east of Ferozepur. Gough defeated the Sikhs in a confused action, largely fought after nightfall, with a significant number of losses on both sides being incurred from 'friendly fire'. The British inflicted 3000 casualties for the loss of just under 900 men.

■ FEROZESHAH, 21–22 DECEMBER 1845

After the defeat of its advanced guard at Mudki, Lal Singh's Sikh army of at least 35,000 men with 88 guns deployed in a fortified camp near the village of Ferozeshah in the Punjab. Gen Sir Hugh Gough's army was exhausted following the fierce action at Mudki and had to recuperate and absorb reinforcements before going over to the offensive.

Gough's 18,000 men attacked at about 03:30 on the afternoon of 21 December under cover of a bombardment by his 65 guns. The advancing British and Indian troops suffered serious losses from the fire of the Sikh heavy artillery and attempted to rush the gun positions. Part of Gen Gilbert's division broke into the Sikh encampment, but his right flank was threatened by large numbers of Sikh irregular cavalry which were driven off by the 3rd Light Dragoons. As darkness fell, Sir Harry Smith's division attacked, taking several Sikh batteries and overran much

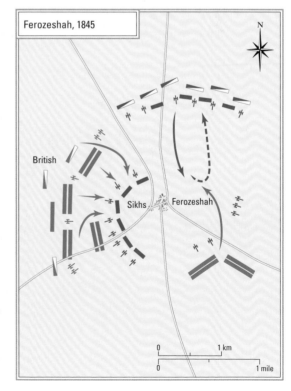

of the Sikh camp, before being driven back by counter-attacks. Fierce fighting continued until midnight and many casualties were caused on both sides by the explosion of a Sikh magazine.

By dawn on 22 December, Gough's men had captured most of the Sikh camp, together with 71 guns. The remainder of the camp was overrun during the morning, when Tej Singh's 30,000-strong Sikh army reached the battlefield and his 70 guns opened fire on the exhausted British and Indian troops, who were almost out of ammunition. Fortunately, Tej Singh mistook the withdrawal of some British artillery and cavalry for an outflanking manoeuvre and hastily withdrew. Gough narrowly won one of the hardest-fought battles of this era, inflicting at least 3000 casualties for the loss of just over 2400 men.

■ ALIWAL, 28 JANUARY 1846

Sir Harry Smith's Anglo-Indian division of 12,000 men attacked and defeated a 20,000-strong Sikh army commanded by Ranjodh Singh Majithia.

The British inflicted 3000 casualties for the loss of fewer than 700 men.

■ SOBRAON, 10 FEBRUARY 1846

Gen Sir Hugh Gough's Anglo-Indian army of 20,000 men with 65 guns attacked and defeated a Sikh force of 30,000 men and 70 guns commanded by Tej Singh. The Sikhs had deployed in a strong defensive position protected by extensive field fortifications around the village of Sobraon by the River Sutlej. Gough's artillery train included 35 siege guns to breach the Sikh defences, but these were short of ammunition and without their full gun crews. The start of the battle was delayed by thick fog, but as it lifted, the British siege artillery began a two-hour bombardment that did little damage to the Sikh defences. Two British divisions under Sir Harry Smith and MGen Sir Walter Gilbert then made feint attacks on the Sikh left. MGen Robert Henry Dick's division launched the main attack on the Sikh right, where the defences were weakest, but he was

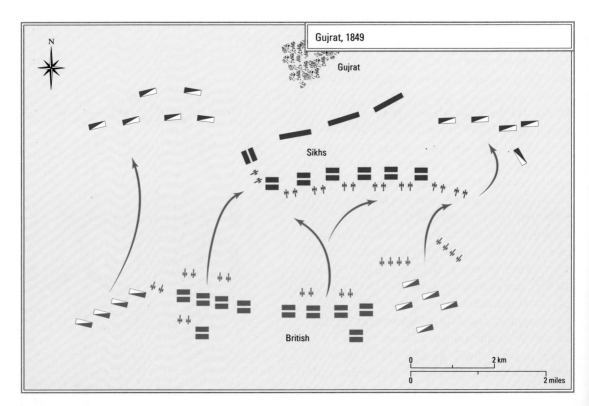

Gujrat, 1849

killed and his men were driven back by counter-attacks. Gough's men then renewed their attacks along the entire front and broke through on the vulnerable Sikh right, where engineers blew a breach in the fortifications. The 3rd King's Own Light Dragoons broke through in this sector, making a series of charges against the flank and rear of the defenders. At this stage, retreating Sikhs crowded onto their pontoon bridge across the River Sutlej; the bridge broke under their weight, trapping nearly 20,000 of Tej Singh's men on the east bank. Many of these trapped units fought to the death, whilst others tried to ford the river under close-range fire from British horse artillery. Gough's army inflicted 10,000 casualties on the Sikhs and captured 67 guns, but lost 230 killed and more than 2000 wounded.

■ MULTAN, 19 APRIL 1848–22 JANUARY 1849
Gen Whish's 32,000-strong Anglo-Indian army besieged the city of Multan, which was defended by a Sikh garrison of 12,000 men under Dewan Mulraj. The city was stormed and Mulraj surrendered the citadel on 22 January 1849.

■ RAMNAGAR, 22 NOVEMBER 1848
Gen Sir Hugh Gough's army of 15,000 men attempted to cross the River Chenab at Ramnagar, but was repulsed by the fire of the 60 guns supporting a 30,000-strong Sikh army under Sher Singh Attariwalla.

■ CHILLIANWALA, 13 JANUARY 1849
Gen Sir Hugh Gough's army of 13,000 men and 66 guns attacked a 30,000-strong Sikh army under Sher Singh Attariwalla near the village of Chillianwala in the Punjab. Gough allowed himself to be provoked into attacking without adequate reconnaissance or artillery support. In fact, his artillery was unable to operate effectively as advancing infantry masked its fields of fire for much of the action.

Gough's infantry overran part of the Sikh positions in confused fighting, but on the British right flank, the elderly and incompetent Brig Pope ordered a cavalry charge through thick scrub, a decision that disordered his entire brigade.

He then panicked and ordered a retreat in which the 14th Light Dragoons were routed. The Sikhs sustained 3600 casualties, but Gough had lost 2500 men and ordered a withdrawal, abandoning 40 captured guns, which were later recovered by the Sikhs.

■ GUJRAT, 21 FEBRUARY 1849
Gen Sir Hugh Gough's army of 24,000 men and 90 guns attacked a 50,000-strong Sikh and Afghan army with 60 guns under Sher Singh Attariwalla near the city of Gujrat in the Punjab. The Sikhs had again deployed behind field defences, but these were badly damaged and many of their guns destroyed in a preliminary two-and-a-half-hour bombardment by Gough's artillery.

Once the Sikh artillery was largely silenced, the British infantry advanced. There was desperate hand-to-hand fighting for the small fortified villages of Burra Kalra and Chota Kalra. However, the British guns advanced in successive 'bounds' to give constant fire support, and the Sikhs were forced back. Gough's horse artillery and cavalry pursued them for more than 19km, turning the retreat into a rout. The Sikhs inflicted almost 800 casualties, but lost over 2000 men.

Wars in New Zealand 1843–98

■ WAIRAU AFFRAY, 17 JUNE 1843
A dispute over land ownership between British settlers and the Maori chief Te Rauparaha escalated into a skirmish in which four Maori died and three others were wounded. British casualties totalled 22 dead and five wounded.

■ THE FLAGSTAFF WAR, 11 MARCH 1845–11 JANUARY 1846
The transfer of the capital of New Zealand from Russell (Okiato) in the Bay of Islands to Auckland provoked protests by the Maori chief Hone Heke and his uncle Te Ruki Kawiti over the impact of the transfer on the local Maori economy. These protests were ignored and the Maoris retaliated by repeatedly cutting down the flagpole near the

town of Kororareka and finally attacking the town. This marked the beginning of the Flagstaff War, which was characterized by the rebels' effective use of a new version of traditional Maori field fortifications, the gunfighter *pās*. These could be built in a few days, but their palisades, trenches and dugouts proved highly resistant to even siege artillery. After months of fighting, Heke and Kawiti negotiated a settlement with the loyalist chief, Tāmati Wāka Nene, who persuaded the governor to pardon the rebels.

■ OHAEAWAI, JULY 1845

The rebel Maori chief, Te Ruki Kawiti, provoked LCol Despard, commanding a 300-strong British force, into ordering a frontal attack on his *pā*, an attack that incurred almost 100 casualties. Kawiti then withdrew with minimal losses.

■ HUTT VALLEY CAMPAIGN, APR–AUG 1846

The Hutt Valley Campaign of 1846 was in many respects a sequel to the Wairau Affray. The cause was once again a series of dubious land purchases by the New Zealand Company, and the encroachment of settlers on to land whose ownership was still disputed. The campaign was largely a series of raids and skirmishes, but included a larger action at Battle Hill (6–13 August 1846) in which a British force of 250 men plus 150 loyal Maori warriors defeated a 300-strong rebel force. The British authorities had not realized that the elderly Maori chief Te Rauparaha, who had befriended settlers and the local administration, was at the same time orchestrating the Hutt attacks. When the military intercepted incriminating letters from Te Rauparaha he was captured in a surprise attack, which broke Maori morale and ended the campaign.

■ WANGANUI CAMPAIGN, APRIL 1846–FEB 1848

This conflict was caused by the Maori demand for *utu* (revenge) when one of the ringleaders of the Hutt Valley Campaign was hanged. The rebel Maoris were again pardoned after a series of raids and skirmishes.

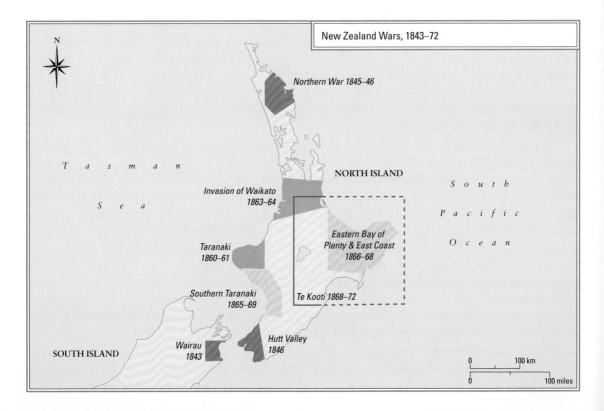

■ First Taranaki War, 17 March 1860–
18 March 1861

More than 3500 British troops from Australia, supported by volunteers and militia, fought a prolonged campaign against up to 1500 Maoris which ended in a compromise settlement. British forces inflicted 200 casualties for 238 losses.

■ Second Taranaki War, April 1863–
November 1866

The continuing confiscation of Maori lands provoked resentment, led to the rise of the anti-settler Hauhau religious movement and the outbreak of the Second Taranaki War, in which rebel Maori tribes were again defeated.

■ Invasion of Waikato, July 1863–April 1864

MGen Duncan Cameron conducted a careful and clever campaign against the rebel Waikato Maori, seeking always to minimize the casualties among both his own men and the enemy. Eventually the Maori, after 18 defeats in a succession of battles in Auckland, and the Waikato were forced to retreat into what is now The King Country, south of the Puniu river near Te Awamutu. Much of their lands were confiscated as reparations.

■ Defence of Pukekohe East,
13–14 September 1863

Eleven settlers and six militia men garrisoning an incomplete stockade around the Pukekohe East church held off a Maori war party of approximately 200 men for almost two days until the arrival of a relief force.

■ Rangiriri, 20 November 1863

MGen Duncan Cameron's force of 860 men successfully assaulted an earthwork fort at Rangiriri, which was defended by a garrison of 500 Maori rebels. The British inflicted 224 casualties for the loss of 131 men.

■ Tauranga Campaign, 21 January–
21 June 1864

MGen Duncan Cameron led 1700 troops in an offensive against rebel Maori tribes around Tauranga. A British assault on the Gate *pā* was beaten off with heavy losses, but the rebels were defeated at Te Ranga.

■ East Cape War, 13 April 1865–June 1868

There were at least three unrelated campaigns fought in the East Cape area during a period of relative peace between the main campaigns of the New Zealand land wars, which are collectively known as the East Cape War.

All of these conflicts stemmed from the arrival of the Hauhau movement, a version of the Pai Mārire religion, from the Taranaki region around 1865. Originally Pai Mārire was a peaceful religion, a combination of Christianity and traditional Maori beliefs, but its Hauhau form was a violent and vehemently anti-European (Pākehā) movement. The arrival of the Hauhau in the East Cape destabilized the whole region, causing great alarm among the settlers and also seriously disrupting Maori society because of its disregard of traditional tribal structures. The Hauhau were defeated in all three campaigns by a combination of British units, settlers and loyalist Maori tribes.

■ Te Kooti's War, 1868–72

Te Kooti, a Maori trader, was imprisoned for involvement in the Hauhau movement and founded a new religious cult, the Ringatū. In 1868, he escaped and led a rebellion which ended in his defeat four years later.

■ Titokowaru's War, June 1868–March 1869

Titokowaru, who had fought in the Second Taranaki War, led a rebellion as a priest and prophet of the extremist Hauhau movement. Despite his limited forces, highly effective attacks led to the withdrawal of most government military units from South Taranaki, giving Titokowaru control of the territory between New Plymouth and Wanganui. Although Titokowaru never lost a battle, his forces mysteriously dispersed after abandoning a strong position at Tauranga-ika *pā*.

■ The Dog Tax War, 1898

The introduction of a tax on dogs provoked a minor Maori revolt led by Hone Toia, who briefly captured the town of Rawene, before the rebels were persuaded to surrender by Hone Heke Ngapua, Hone Heke's great-nephew.

Dominican War of Independence 1844–49

■ CABEZA DE LAS MARÍAS AND LAS HICOTEAS, 13–18 MARCH 1844

A 10,000-strong Haitian army under the command of Gen Souffrand routed a smaller force of Dominican troops, forming part of the Army of the South, commanded by Gen Manuel de Regla Mota. The Dominican soldiers fled to Azua de Compostela

■ AZUA, 19 MARCH 1844

A force of 2200 Dominican troops, comprising a portion of the Army of the South, led by Gen Pedro Santana, defeated an outnumbering force of 10,000 troops of the Haitian Army led by Gen Souffrand.

■ SANTIAGO, 30 MARCH 1844

A force of some Dominican troops, a portion of the Army of the North, led by Gen José María Imbert, defeated an outnumbering force of troops of the Haitian Army led by Gen Jean-Louis Pierrot.

■ EL MEMISO, 13 APRIL 1844

A detachment of Dominican troops forming part of the Army of the South, commanded by Gen Antonio Duvergé, defeated a larger Haitian force under Col Pierre Paul near El Memiso (in present-day Azua Province, Dominican Republic).

■ TORTUGUERO, 15 APRIL 1844

Three Dominican schooners under the command of Juan Bautista Cambiaso intercepted a Haitian brigantine and two schooners which were bombarding shore targets. In the ensuring engagement, all three Haitian vessels were sunk, ensuring Dominican naval superiority for the rest of the war.

■ ESTRELLETA, 17 SEPTEMBER 1845

A force of Dominican troops, a portion of the Army of the South, led by Gen Antonio Duvergé, defeated a force of the Haitian Army led by Gen Jean-Louis Pierrot at the site of Estrelleta, near Las Matas de Farfán.

■ BELER, 27 NOVEMBER 1845

Dominican troops under Gen Francisco Antonio Salcedo defeated Gen Jean-Louis Pierrot's Haitian forces at Beler savannah. Salcedo was supported by Adm Juan Bautista Cambiaso's squadron of three schooners, which blockaded the Haitian port of Cap-Haïtien.

■ EL NÚMERO, 19 APRIL 1849

A 10,000-strong Haitian army under Gen Jean Francois Jeannot was defeated near Azua de Compostela by a smaller force of Dominican troops forming part of the Army of the South, commanded by Gen Pedro Santana.

■ LAS CARRERAS, 21 APRIL 1849

A detachment of Dominican troops forming part of the Army of the South, commanded by Gen Pedro Santana, defeated a larger Haitian force under Faustin Soulouque near Bani (in present-day Peravia Province, Dominican Republic).

US-Mexican War 1846–48

■ FORT TEXAS (FORT BROWN), 3–9 MAY 1846

Mexico had announced that US annexation of Texas would mean war, Texas entering the Union in 1845. Gen Zachary Taylor cemented the US claim to the Rio Grande boundary with Mexico by constructing this earthwork at the tip of the disputed area. The garrison returned fire from Mexican batteries at Matamoros across the river with their own four cannon, Maj Jacob Brown being killed by injuries from the Mexicans' fire.

■ PALO ALTO, 8 MAY 1846

Fighting began when Mexican cavalry crossed the Rio Grande, attacking a US patrol. Gen Mariano Arista crossed with 4000 infantry against US general Zachary Taylor's supply base at Port Isabel. Taylor moved 2200 troops toward Aras' line in this grassy plain. Taylor sent his 'flying artillery' batteries before his infantry's advance, the cannons' fire devastating the Mexicans. The Mexicans held their line until nightfall, suffering 400 casualties to Taylor's 55.

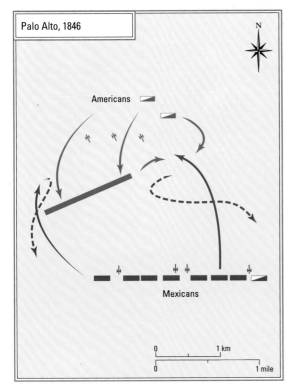

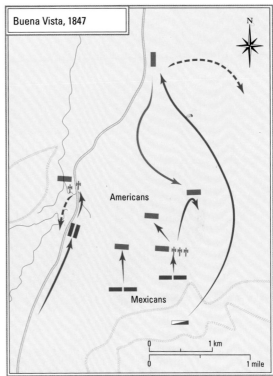

■ RESACA DE LA PALMA, 9 MAY 1846

US general Zachary Taylor followed up Gen Mariano Arista's retreat, the Mexicans establishing a defensive position in this ravine in the midst of heavy brush. US troops eventually captured Arista's artillery, the Mexicans then fleeing.

■ MONTERREY, 21–24 SEPTEMBER 1846

Zachary Taylor seized Matamoros, moving towards this city where Gen Pedro de Ampudia waited with 7000 men and 32 cannon. Taylor divided his 6000 regulars and volunteers for a simultaneous attack upon the city's fortified approaches. Mexican artillery from the fortifications could not prevent the US capture of artillery and barricaded houses, which they turned against the Mexicans. Ampudia surrendered the city with 370 casualties to Taylor's 500.

■ SAN PASQUAL, 6 DECEMBER 1846

Unaware of local conditions, Col Stephen Kearny collected 136 US troops after his journey from Santa Fe to California and engaged 76 Mexicans under Maj Andrés Pico here. Pico's troops vanquished the Americans, killing 21.

■ TUCSON, 16 DECEMBER 1846

The 500-man Mormon Battalion under LCol Philip Cooke occupied this Mexican outpost without a battle as Capt Antonio Comaduran and Cooke averted bloodshed. Comaduran's 100-strong garrison camped outside of town while the Mormons resupplied.

■ BUENA VISTA, 22–23 FEBRUARY 1847

Antonio López de Santa Anna, dictator of Mexico, personally took the field with 15,000 soldiers against US general Zachary Taylor's 4700 troops as they took position on the far side of this pass having countermarched before Santa Anna's army. Taylor made his preparations by ordering Gen John Wool to establish a defensive position on the heights overlooking the pass. Santa Anna left 5000 troops behind due to his forced march north in the hope of destroying Taylor's army, after President James Polk had transferred most

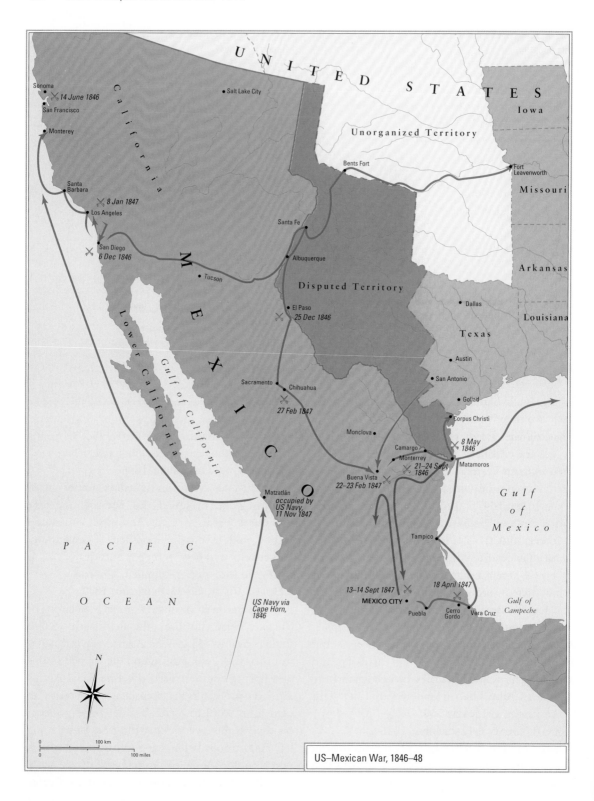

UNITED STATES

Iowa

Unorganized Territory

Sonoma
✕ 14 June 1846
San Francisco

California

Salt Lake City

Bents Fort

Fort
Leavenworth

Missouri

Monterey

Santa
Barbara

✕ 8 Jan 1847

Los Angeles

Santa Fe

MEXICO

Albuquerque

San Diego
6 Dec 1846
✕

Disputed Territory

Arkansas

Dallas

Louisiana

Tucson

El Paso
25 Dec 1846

Lower California

Gulf of California

Sacramento   Chihuahua
27 Feb 1847

Texas

Austin

San Antonio

Goliad

Monclova

Corpus Christi

Camargo   8 May
1846
Monterrey   21–24 Sept
1846
Buena Vista   Matamoros
22–23 Feb 1847

Gulf
of
Mexico

Matzatlán
occupied by
US Navy,
11 Nov 1847

Tampico

PACIFIC

OCEAN

US Navy via
Cape Horn,
1846

13–14 Sept 1847
MEXICO CITY   Puebla   Cerro
Gordo   18 April 1847
Vera Cruz

Gulf of
Campeche

N

0   100 km
0   100 miles

US–Mexican War, 1846–48

of it to Gen Winfield Scott's amphibious invasion of central Mexico. First demanding Taylor's surrender, Santa Anna expended his light infantry under Gen Pedro de Ampudia in a daylong assault upon the heights under the fire of US artillery and the breech-loading rifles of the regulars.

On the second day, Santa Anna launched a full-scale assault, his greater numbers having some success on the US flanks as Wool gradually refused his centre to reinforce them. Guards and reserve troops repulsed a Mexican cavalry attack upon the American's wagons in the rear. US artillery at the front of the lines suffered significant losses, but inflicted more as the Mexicans repeatedly struggled up the heights, capturing two cannon. Taylor's reserve line moved forward and halted a Mexican breakthrough late in the day, the Americans surprised the next morning to find that Santa Anna had withdrawn southwards to move against Winfield Scott. The Americans had suffered 267 dead, 456 wounded and 23 missing, while Santa Anna had lost 1800 missing, 1000 wounded and 600 dead. Santa Anna's retreat allowed Taylor and his volunteers to stand unmolested on the defensive in the north for the remainder of the war.

■ Sacramento River (Rio Sacramento), 28 February 1847

Col Alexander Doniphan led 924 mounted volunteers and their supply train south towards Chihuahua, defended here by Gen García Conde with 3400 infantry, militia and artillery on a plateau across Doniphan's advance. Doniphan ascended that from the rear, fending off Conde's cavalry behind his wagons. Doniphan then rapidly attacked the Mexicans' flanks and rear, dismounting his men behind his mobile artillery, killing 300 Mexicans, scattering the rest and capturing Chihuahua.

■ Vera Cruz (Veracruz), 9–29 March 1847

A brilliantly planned and executed amphibious invasion with 10,000 soldiers reduced this Mexican fortified port, US general Winfield Scott landing unopposed and eventually forcing the city's surrender with a long bombardment from landed naval artillery.

■ Cerro Gordo, 18 April 1847

Antonio López de Santa Anna with 12,000 troops blocked a defile on the National Road towards Mexico City. Gen Winfield Scott wanted to get his 8500 troops into the interior before the Yellow Fever season, and had scouts investigate the Mexican position. Capt Robert E. Lee discovered a trail leading to this village behind the Mexican left flank, Scott's columns attacking and flanking the Mexicans, killing 1000 and capturing 1000.

■ Contreras-Churubusco (Churubusco), 20 August 1847

Antonio López de Santa Anna counted on a vast lava field before Mexico City to channel US general Winfield Scott's advance into one of two roads running across it, and parcelled out his defending forces to guard both. Scott approached from the south, his engineers finding alternative routes though the lava that allowed the Americans to rout Gen Gabriel Valencia's 6000 men at Padierna, whom Santa Anna did not reinforce. Scott's army next attacked the bridge over the Churubusco river, defended by the 200 deserters of the San Patricio Battalion and 1800 Mexicans at a fortified convent. Very hard fighting there lasted until the doomed deserters and Mexicans collapsed under numbers and a flank attack from US forces that crossed another bridge. Scott's soldiers had opened the way to Mexico City at the cost of 1053 killed, 4000 Mexicans falling.

■ Molino del Rey, 8 September 1847

General Winfield Scott ordered these fortified buildings near Chapultepec castle captured, 4000 Mexicans with artillery fighting first before, then within, the buildings. Hard fighting cost the 3400 victorious Americans 800 casualties, the Mexicans 2000.

■ Chapultepec, 12–13 September 1847

Cadets defended the Mexican military academy here, 1000 defenders in the castle resisting behind 14,000 around the base. General Winfield's Scott's bombardment preceded an attack by select storming parties, who took the castle.

■ **PUEBLA, 14 SEPTEMBER–12 OCTOBER, 1847**
This post, under Col Thomas Childs with 400 men, protected the US supply line from the Mexican coast. Gen Joaquin Rea with 4000 men besieged Childs for four weeks before a relief column from Veracruz arrived.

Hungarian Revolt 1848–49

■ **SUKORO (PÁKOZD), 29 SEPTEMBER 1848**
On 11 September 1848, Lt FM Count Josip Jelačić's largely Croatian army crossed the River Dráva in an attempt to crush the Hungarian Revolt. Jelačić hoped that the imperial troops of the Hungarian Army would not be prepared to fight the Croatians, who were also serving under the imperial flag. He also thought that his numerical superiority would be sufficient to prevent any resistance, but a delegation of the Hungarian officer corps declared that they would fight. At Pákozd, Jelačić's army of at least 35,000 men and 99 guns attacked a 27,000-strong Hungarian force supported by 82 guns. Jelačić launched a frontal attack, which was halted by Hungarian artillery fire, and an attack on the Hungarian right wing was equally unsuccessful. Casualties on both sides seem to have been light and the battle ended in a truce and Jelačić's withdrawal from Hungary.

■ **SCHWECHAT, 30 OCTOBER 1848**
In the aftermath of the battle of Pákozd, Count Josip Jelačić's army was rapidly reinforced, bringing its strength up to 80,000 men and 210 guns. The Hungarians advanced to Schwechat near Vienna with a force of 30,000 men and 70 guns under János Móga in an attempt to support the anti-Hapsburg Vienna Uprising, but were decisively defeated by Jelačić, whose troops then helped to crush the uprising.

■ **KÁPOLNA, 26–27 FEBRUARY 1849**
An Austrian army of 30,000 men and 165 guns under Prince Windisch-Grätz defeated Gen Henryk Dembiński's 36,000-strong Hungarian army with 136 guns at Kápolna in northern Hungary. The Hungarians retreated and Dembiński resigned as C-in-C.

■ **TEMESVÁR, 9 AUGUST 1849**
A combined Austrian and Russian army of 90,000 men under Generals Ivan Paskievich and Julius von Haynau marched to raise the three-month Hungarian siege of Temesvár (now Timisoara, Romania). Gen Henry Dembinksi's 55,000-strong Hungarian army was routed with the loss of 10,500 men after inflicting almost 4500 casualties. On 13 August, Gen Artúr Görgey surrendered the remnants of the Hungarian army to Gen Rüdiger's Russian forces at Világos (now Şiria, Romania).

Minor Colonial Wars in Africa 1848–68

■ **BOOMPLAATS, 29 AUGUST 1848**
Several hundred Boer irregulars, angered by British annexation of territory, attacked a column led by the British governor of the region on 29 August 1848, but were repulsed by artillery and cavalry, leaving eight dead and 16 British killed.

■ **MEDINA FORT, APRIL 1857**
Thousands of Mali forces on a *jihad* led by Al-Haji Umar Tall in April 1857 unsuccessfully laid siege to a French fort at Medina for three months before being relieved by troops from the Senegal river.

■ **ABYSSINIA EXPEDITION, APRIL 1868**
Over 10,000 British soldiers led by LGen Sir Robert Napier travelled across Ethiopia to attack successfully the fortress of Emperor Tewodros at Magdala and release a small number of British hostages in April 1868.

First Schleswig War 1848–51

■ **BOV, 9 APRIL 1848**
A Danish army of 7,000 men commanded by Gen Hans Hedemann, supported by a naval squadron in Flensburg Fjord, defeated a slightly larger force of Gen Krohn's Schleswig-Holstein troops at Bov,

near Flensburg. Hedemann created a diversion on his left flank, while the right flank and the cavalry advanced and surrounded the disorganized and poorly deployed Schleswig-Holstein forces. The Danes inflicted almost 1100 casualties for the loss of 82 men.

■ HELIGOLAND, 4 JUNE 1849
Two Danish vessels that had been blockading the estuary of the River Weser fought an inconclusive action against a German squadron under Capt Karl Rudolf Brommy, comprising a steam frigate and two steam corvettes.

■ FREDERICIA, 6 JULY 1849
In May 1849, a force of 16,000 Schleswig-Holstein troops under Gen Eduard von Bonin besieged Col Lunding's 7000-strong Danish garrison of Fredericia on the east coast of Jutland. After several successful sorties by the garrison, a full-scale Danish offensive was launched by 24,000 troops under Gen De Meza in the early hours of 6 July. The attack broke the Schleswig-Holstein forces, inflicting 3000 casualties for the loss of almost 1900 men.

■ ISTED, 25 JULY 1850
Gen Gerhard Christoph von Krogh's 37,000-strong Danish army attacked and defeated a force of 26,800 Schleswig-Holstein troops commanded by Gen Karl Wilhelm von Willisen in a hard-fought action. Each side lost almost 3250 men.

■ LOTTORF, 24 NOVEMBER 1850
Two companies of the 11th Schleswig-Holstein Infantry Battalion attacked a 50-strong detachment of the Danish 3rd Reserve Jager Corps garrisoning the village of Lottorf. The attackers were beaten off and withdrew when Danish reinforcements arrived.

Taiping Rebellion 1850–64

■ JINTIAN UPRISING, 1850
The uprising, led by the charismatic leader of the 'God Worshippers' sect, Hong Xiuquan, marked the beginning of the Taiping Rebellion. His 10,000-strong rebel army commanded by Feng Yunshan and Wei Changhui routed government troops deployed in and around the town of Jintian (present-day Guiping, Guangxi). Hong's forces then defeated a series of imperial counter-attacks by skilfully conducted ambushes, allowing him to proclaim the establishment of his 'Taiping Heavenly Kingdom'.

■ CHANGSHA, 11 SEPTEMBER– 30 NOVEMBER 1852
Taiping general Xiao Chaogui attacked Changsha, held by imperial governor Luo Bingzhang. Xiao was killed leading the assault and, despite rebel reinforcements led by Hong Xiuquan, the city held out and the Taiping withdrew north towards Hankou.

■ NANJING (NANKING), 6–20 MARCH 1853
Taiping commander Shi Dakai, advancing down the Yangzi through Anqing with perhaps 100,000 men, reached Nanjing, held by Viceroy Lu Jianying and 60,000 imperial troops under Generals Fuzhu Hang'a and Xiang Hou. The rebels breached the walls with explosives and stormed the city, killing all three imperial commanders and 30,000 of their men after sustaining 10,000 casualties. At least 30,000 civilians were subsequently massacred and Nanjing became the Taiping capital.

■ NANJING (NANKING), 17–20 JUNE 1856
Gen Xiang Rong's 80,000-strong imperial army of poorly trained Green Standard Army troops was defeated near Nanjing by Taiping rebel forces totalling 460,000 men under generals Shi Dakai and Qin Rigang. The rebels inflicted 39,000 casualties.

■ SANHE, 7–18 NOVEMBER 1858
Li Hsu-pin's force of 6000 elite imperial troops drawn from the Hunan Army attacked the city of Sanhe, which was occupied by Taiping rebels. The rebel garrison held a strong defensive position, based on a newly constructed city wall, protected by an outer ring of nine forts.

Despite these formidable defences, the imperial troops attacked on 7 November, forcing the rebels to abandon all nine forts and retreat into the city itself. However, Taiping reinforcements totalling 100,000 men under Gen Chen Yucheng were gathering around the city and Li Hsu-pin's staff pressed him to retreat before his grossly outnumbered men were swamped by the rebel forces. Li refused, but agreed to pull his troops back from the city wall to the captured forts.

As the extent of the rebels' numerical superiority became apparent, Li was convinced that his only chance was to launch a pre-emptive offensive. Accordingly, he ordered a surprise attack on the night of 15/16 November, an attack that suffered 50 per cent casualties in a rebel ambush. The survivors were pinned down and Li personally led his remaining troops in a series of attacks which rescued some men, but incurred further heavy losses.

The remnants of the imperial forces retreated to the forts to await promised reinforcements of 15,000 Green Standard Army troops. However, these never arrived and the rebels quickly recaptured seven of the nine forts. Li led his surviving forces in a final desperate breakout attempt, but was killed in action, together with all his men. (Rebel losses are uncertain, but almost certainly totalled several thousand men.) The imperial defeat marked a major setback to operations against the Taiping rebels and the loss of 6000 elite troops was a blow to morale.

■ **NANJING (NANKING), 1–6 MAY 1860**
Taiping commanders Hong Rengan and Li Xiucheng led an attack on the Southern Imperial Barracks outside besieged Nanjing. Imperial commissioner He Zhou and General Zhang Guoliang were defeated and the siege of the Taiping capital was abandoned.

■ **ANQING, JUNE 1860–SEPTEMBER 1861**
As part of a major offensive in Anhui Province, the imperial commander Zeng Guofan recaptured Anqing from its Taiping garrison commanded by Li Xiucheng. The garrison was inexplicably permitted to withdraw, but the civilian population was massacred.

■ **SHANGHAI, JULY 1861–30 AUGUST 1862**
Taiping commander Li Xiucheng attacked Shanghai, which was held by a 9000-strong international force. This included British and French seamen and marines commanded by R Adm James Hope and French admiral Auguste Léopold Protet, together with American Frederick T. Ward's irregulars. The garrison was later reinforced by Gen Li Hongzhang's 60,000 imperial troops. After months of bloody fighting, a final Taiping assault led by Tan Shaoguang was repulsed and the rebels withdrew.

■ **CIXI (TZEKI), 20 SEPTEMBER 1862**
American adventurer Frederick T. Ward created the "Ever Victorious Army' (EVA) of Western-trained and equipped Chinese irregulars. When Taiping rebels seized Tzeki (modern Cicheng), the EVA drove the Taiping out, although Ward was fatally wounded.

■ **SUZHOU, 22 AUGUST–6 DECEMBER 1863**
Imperial commander Li Hongzhang besieged Suzhou and forced the retreat of Taiping forces under Gen Li Xuicheng. Tan Shaoguang, commanding the 200,000-strong garrison, was killed by a Taiping peace faction which surrendered the city.

■ **CHANGZOU, 19 DECEMBER 1863–
11 MAY 1864**
Li Hongzhang sent an imperial army under Liu Mingquan to besiege Changzhou, held by the veteran Taiping commander Chen Kunshu. Chen was defeated and captured after Li brought up reinforcements and led an assault on the city.

■ **NANJING (NANKING), 14 MAR–19 JULY 1864**
Imperial forces converged on Nanjing and by late 1863 Zeng Guoquan had encircled the Taiping capital, which was defended by Li Xiucheng's 30,000-strong rebel garrison. The first assault on the city itself was made on 14 March 1864, when Zeng's forces unsuccessfully attempted to storm the walls using scaling ladders. A second attempt used mines, but counter-mining and a hastily constructed inner wall prevented a breakthrough. On 3 July the imperial forces took Dibao castle. This position allowed them to beat off counter-attacks and to dig

new mines, which were detonated on 19 July, blowing large breaches in the city walls. Four assault columns broke into the city and defeated the defenders in fierce street fighting, at the cost of 9000 imperial casualties. The victors then went on the rampage, massacring the garrison's survivors and perhaps 200,000 of the city's civilian population.

■ **HUBEI POCKET, JULY–NOVEMBER 1864**
An imperial force of 440,000 Green Standard Army troops under Viceroy Guanwen and Sengge Rinchen trapped Lai Wenguang's 300,000 Taiping rebels in the Hubei Province of central China. A total of 60,000 rebels were killed in prolonged fighting, after which 200,000 surrendered. A remnant of 19,000 Taiping troops led by Lai Wenguang managed to break out and escape to southern Henan where they joined forces with 150,000 Nien rebels.

■ **FUJIAN POCKET, AUGUST 1864–JUNE 1865**
The 130,000-strong imperial Xiang Army

commanded by Zuo Zongtang, the Viceroy of Min-Zhe, trapped 280,000 Taiping rebels under Li Shixian in Fujian Province. The rebels were defeated largely due the superior firepower of Zuo's forces.

Crimean War 1853–56

■ **OLENTIA, 4 NOVEMBER 1853**
At the beginning of the Crimean War, hostilities commenced between Russia and the Ottoman Empire. Russian forces dispersed to guard all crossings along the lower Danube river in modern-day Romania. A large Ottoman army under Omar Pasha defeated the Russian IV Corps under Gen Dannenberg at the Danube crossing near Olentia (also spelled Olentsia), forcing the Russians to retire towards Bucharest to await reinforcements.

■ **SINOPE, 30 NOVEMBER 1853**
A Russian flotilla of 12 ships under Nakhimov

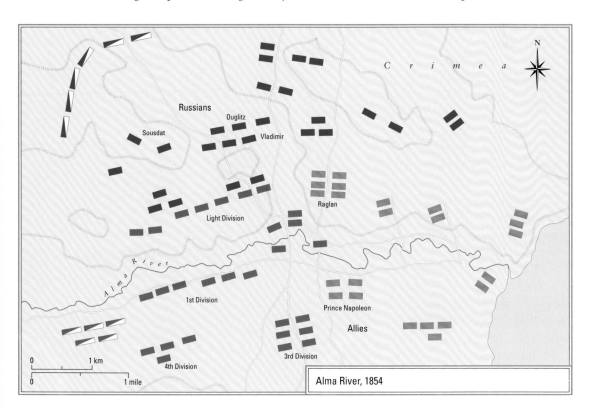
Alma River, 1854

attacked an Ottoman flotilla of 14 ships under Osman Pasha at Sinope, on the northern coast of modern-day Turkey. The Ottoman force also had support from shore batteries. Superior Russian gunnery and ammunition won a decisive victory. While Nakhimov suffered damage to three ships, the Russians destroyed the entire Ottoman flotilla and knocked out two shore batteries.

■ **SIEGE OF SILISTRA, 5 APRIL–22 JUNE 1854**

A Russian force of more than 50,000 troops besieged an Ottoman garrison of 12,000 in the fortress of Silistra in modern-day Bulgaria. The siege failed and the Russian force withdrew.

■ **KUREKDERE, 7 AUGUST 1854**

During the Crimean War, a Russian force of 20,000 defeated an Ottoman Empire force consisting largely of militia and totaling 40,000 men near Kurekdere in Armenia. Further Russian offensives followed.

■ **BOMARSUND, 8–16 AUGUST 1854**

A British and French naval and amphibious force of 32,000 besieged and took the Russian fortified base in the Aland Islands in the Baltic Sea during the Crimean War.

■ **PETROPAVLOVSK, 29 AUGUST– 7 SEPTEMBER 1854**

During the Crimean War, a British and French naval and amphibious force of 2600 men and six ships failed in their brief siege of the Russian Pacific port of Petropavlovsk.

■ **ALMA RIVER, 20 SEPTEMBER 1854**

A British force of 26,000 under Lord Raglan and a French force of 28,000 under Saint-Arnaud, operating jointly, advanced from north of the Alma river against a Russian army of 37,000 under Menshikov on the south bank of the river. The British and French also had the support of a Turkish force of 7000 troops The Russian position was very strong mainly because the south bank of the Alma consisted of steep cliffs and hills.

Menshikov anchored his line on Telegraph Hill on his left and Kourgane Hill on his right, strengthened further with two redoubts. The

French Army attacked the Russian left, while the British Army was to attack the Russian right. A French division under Bosquet successfully crossed the Alma on the far Russian left, and attacked the Russian flank. Bosquet's division took Telegraph Hill, forcing Menshikov to send reinforcements to his left. Two more French divisions were less successful attempting to cross the river and ascend the steep heights. The British then advanced under heavy fire directly against the Russians in their front.

Lord Raglan personally took up an observation position with the forward elements of Bosquet's French troops and ordered a fresh British advance at 15:00. The British First Division attacked the Russian right flank while the rest of the British force advanced directly on Kourgane Hill. The British suffered a temporary setback when an errant bugle call sounded the retreat and one brigade obeyed. British Guards and the Highland Brigade continued attacks and British artillery

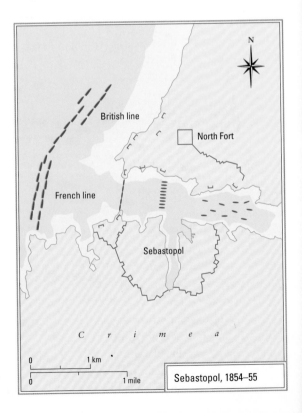

British line

North Fort

French line

Sebastopol

C r i m e a

0   1 km

0   1 mile

Sebastopol, 1854–55

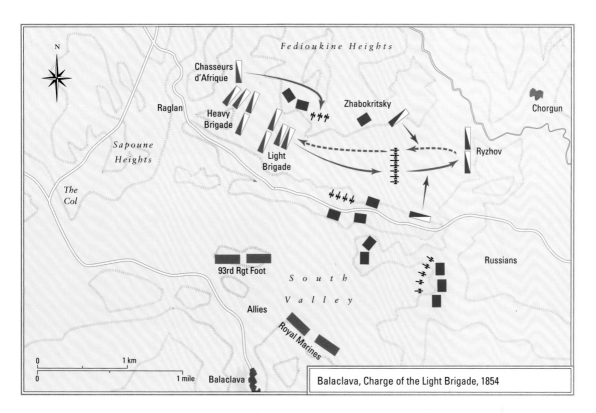

Balaclava, Charge of the Light Brigade, 1854

fire blew up a Russian ammunition wagon. Menshikov then ordered a withdrawal, having lost more than 5700 troops. British losses were 2000 and the French lost 1340.

■ Sebastopol, 2 October– 9 September 1854–55

The siege of the Russian naval base at Sebastopol (Sevastopol) in the Crimea was the longest and chief action of the Crimean War. French, British, Turkish and Sardinian land and naval forces took part in the siege against Russian forces. Both sides received reinforcements during the siege, and suffered casualties from bombardments and assaults, but disease caused by far the highest proportion of casualties.

The Russian garrison of 43,000 soldiers and sailors was initially commanded by Adm Kornilov, who was killed in a bombardment on 17 October, and replaced by Adm Nakhimov. The Sebastopol defences and entrenchments were improved throughout the siege by Russian Engineer

General Todleben, with the construction and repair of large fortifications. Todleben took direct command of the garrison after Nakhimov died from a bullet wound on 12 June. A Russian army of more than 40,000 under Menshikov remained in the Crimea during the siege, putting pressure on the besieging Allied army.

French besieging forces of 75,000 were commanded by Canrobert until 16 May, and by Pelissier thereafter. British forces totalling more than 35,000 were commanded by Lord Raglan until his death from illness on 29 June, and by Simpson thereafter. The Allied forces suffered severely during the winter, improving their supplies significantly in the spring. Assaults against Russian positions throughout the siege were costly failures until final assaults on 8 September. French infantry under MacMahon and Bosquet took the Malakoff fort, compromising the integrity of the entire Russian position. Russian forces evacuated the next day.

Total casualties from all causes during the siege cannot be calculatedly accurately separate from total deaths and wounds for the entire theatre, including over 70,000 French, 30,000 British and 102,000 Russians.

■ BALACLAVA, 25 OCTOBER 1854

French, British and Ottoman Empire troops had begun a siege of the Russian naval base in Sebastopol in the Crimean peninsula. Menshikov, commanding the Russian field army outside Sebastopol, decided to attack the British supply base at Balaclava, south of Sebastopol, in an effort to lift the siege and compel the allies to evacuate the Crimea. A Russian force of 25,000 infantry, 34 cavalry squadrons and 78 cannon was led by Gen Liprandi against the 4500 Allied troops at Balaclava. The Russians advanced onto Fedioukine Heights by 06:00 and bombarded the Allies to the south on Causeway Heights, consisting of a long ridge running east to west. Russian artillery fire concentrated on Ottoman forces, and Russian infantry and cavalry attacked. Three Ottoman Tunisian battalions retreated as the Russians advanced southwards across the valley and on to Causeway Heights.

The British commander Lord Raglan, observing from the east on Sapoune Heights, ordered reinforcements towards the valley south of Causeway Heights. The French commander Canrobert also sent for reinforcements. The Russian 6th Hussar Brigade attempted to complete the breakthrough and take Balaclava before allied reinforcements could arrive. Only the 93rd Highland Regiment barred the road to Balaclava, apart from a final reserve of 1200 marines. Rather than forming square, the 93rd remained in line (gaining fame as the 'thin red line') and repulsed the Russian cavalry with well-aimed volleys.

Allied reinforcements began to arrive and the British Heavy Brigade of cavalry charged into a large Russian cavalry force under Rijov. The Russian cavalry were quickly defeated and driven off. British artillery came into position to repulse

further Russian attacks. At 10:15 Raglan ordered the British cavalry commander Lucan to prepare to make further attacks if opportunity offered. Partly as a result of this directive, and in an effort to exploit the success of the Heavy Brigade, the British Light Brigade of cavalry under Cardigan attacked, resulting in one of the most famous blunders and displays of gallantry in military history, memorialized as 'The Charge of the Light Brigade'. Due to confusion regarding their instructions, the 670 troopers of the Light Brigade, rather than charging south of Causeway Heights, charged between Causeway Heights and Fedioukine Heights, into the infamous 'valley of death' lined with thousands of Russian infantry and 46 enemy cannon. Russian cavalry also counter-attacked the British cavalry. The Light Brigade (4th Light Dragoons, 8th King's Royal Irish Hussars, 11th Hussars, 13th Light Dragoons and 17th Lancers) lost more than 360 men and over 500 horses in their gallant charge, essentially crippling them as an effective unit for the rest of the war.

As the Light Brigade withdrew, 1500 mounted French Chasseurs d'Afrique troops under d'Allonville successfully charged Russian positions on the Fedioukine Heights, giving the Light Brigade survivors the opportunity to escape. Allied reinforcements were in place by this time, but the Russians were in good positions due to gains made in the early part of the battle. The Russians could not continue their advance on Balaclava with the Allied reinforcements facing them to the west, but Raglan risked no further attacks, and the Russians were left in possession of Causeway Heights. The Russians claimed that they had won the battle, but this limited success did not prevent the continuation of the siege of Sebastopol, so failed to achieve Menshikov's goals. Each side lost more than 600 men in the battle.

■ INKERMAN, 5 NOVEMBER 1854

British, French and Turkish troops were besieging the Russian naval base of Sebastopol in the Crimean peninsula, and Menshikov, commanding the Russian field army outside of Sebastopol, made plans to break the siege. Having failed to take the British supply base at Balaclava in October, Menshikov planned to concentrate an attack at one point along the overstretched Allied lines in the Crimea. Three Russian columns totalling 42,000 troops under Soimonov, Pavlov and Gorchakov were to attack the British 2nd Division in its positions. Even with nearby British and French reinforcements, Allied forces in the area numbered no more than 15,700. A fourth Russian column was to attack from Sebastopol, but this was not coordinated.

The Russians began their advance southwards toward allied lines at 02:00, attacking British positions by 06:00. The battlefield remained obscured by fog for most of the action. Soimonov advanced towards Home Ridge through Careenage Ravine, the rough and narrow approach largely negating his numerical advantage. As Russian attacks mounted, British 2nd Division commander Pennefather ordered counter-attacks. The battle developed as a confused melee as the British overall commander Raglan brought reinforcements forward. Soimonov and the British General Cathcart of the 4th Division were both killed in the fierce fighting. The Russian General Dannenberg took overall command of the assault columns in an effort to increase coordination, to no avail.

Forward of Home Ridge, the British Sandbag Battery became the focus of fighting, and changed hands several times as British Guards and Highland regiments joined the fight. French reinforcements under Bosquet arrived and helped drive back the final Russian attacks. Russian losses were about 11,000, British losses were about 2400 and French losses were 930.

■ EUPATORIA, 17 FEBRUARY 1855
A Russian army of 19,000 troops was repulsed at the Crimean port of Eupatoria by a Turkish force of 30,000 supported by French cavalry and British, French and Turkish ships.

■ CAPTURE OF KERCH, 24 MAY 1855
A British, French and Turkish fleet of 60 ships with a landing force seized and seriously damaged the Russian port of Kerch on the eastern end of the Crimean peninsula.

■ REDAN, 17 JUNE–9 SEPTEMBER 1855
The Redan was a strongpoint in Russian entrenchments during the siege of Sebastopol in the Crimea, attacked unsuccessfully by British forces, but evacuated by the Russians on 9 September.

■ KARS, 16 JUNE–29 NOVEMBER 1855
Some 50,000 Russian troops under Muraviev besieged 17,000 Turkish troops under British general Williams at Kars, in north-eastern Turkey. The garrison repulsed Russian attacks on 16 July, 7 August and 29 September, inflicting Russian losses of 7500, while suffering 6500 casualties. Relief forces failed to reach Kars, and the garrison was forced by starvation to surrender on honourable terms negotiated by Williams.

■ SVEABORG, 9 AUGUST 1855
During the Crimean War, a British-French fleet under Dundas bombarded the Russian naval base at Sveaborg in modern-day Finland, demolishing the Russian fortifications with no loss to the allied fleet.

■ CHERNAYA RIVER, 16 AUGUST 1855
A Russian army of 58,000 attempting to relieve Sebastopol in the Crimea attacked a French and Sardinian force of 37,000. The Russians were repulsed, losing 8000 troops while inflicting 2000 casualties.

■ TAGANROG, 19–31 AUGUST 1855
After taking the Russian port of Kerch in the eastern Crimea, a British and French force briefly besieged the Russian Azov Sea port of Taganrog, and withdrew to engage elsewhere.

■ MALAKOFF, 8 SEPTEMBER 1855
French, British, Turkish and Sardinian forces, after besieging the Russians in Sebastopol for nearly 11 months, prepared final assaults to carry the fortifications. Key to these fortifications was the Malakoff position, which was the target of the main French attacks. Intense bombardment by allied artillery for several days before the attack

caused severe Russian casualties, and French engineers brought approach trenches closer to the Malakoff. Gen Bosquet's French corps of 25,000 men attacked at midday; Bosquet was wounded while leading the assault. The French 1st Division, under MacMahon, reached the interior of the Malakoff within minutes, but had to fight the Russians hand-to-hand to secure the position. Allied attacks elsewhere along the line failed, but the capture of the Malakoff sealed the fate of the Russian positions, and Sebastopol was evacuated the next day.

■ KINBURN, 17 OCTOBER 1855

Towards the end of the Crimean War, after the fall of Sebastopol, a British and French fleet and landing force launched an attack on the Russian Black Sea port of Kinburn, near the mouth of the Dniepr river. The landing force included 6000 French and 4000 British, commanded by the French general Bazaine. The fleet included early examples of armoured vessels, and Kinburn fell quickly.

Second Opium War 1856–60

■ TAKU (DAGU) FORTS, 20 MAY 1858

The Chinese had extensively modernized the six forts protecting the estuary of the River Hai (Peiho) in the early 1850s. Each fort mounted three heavy guns with 20 small-calibre weapons for local defence, protected by multiple thicknesses of wood, brick and concrete. The six main forts were supported by additional field defences, but all were captured by landing parties from an Anglo-French naval force commanded by Adm Michael Seymour.

■ TAKU (DAGU) FORTS, 24– 26 JUNE 1859

RAdm Sir James Hope's Anglo-French squadron of 11 gunboats and four steamers attacked the Taku Forts, which were defended by a 4000-strong Chinese garrison. The assault was repulsed with the loss of six gunboats.

■ PALIKAO, 21 SEPTEMBER 1860

A 10,000-strong Anglo-French force under LGen Sir James Hope Grant and Gen Charles Cousin-Montauban defeated Sengge Rinchen's 30,000 Chinese at Palikao just outside Beijing. The Anglo-French inflicted 1200 casualties for the loss of 52 men.

Anglo-Persian War 1856–57

■ KHARG ISLAND, 4 DECEMBER 1856

Provoked by the Iranian capture of the Afghan city of Herat, a 5700-strong Anglo-Indian force under MGen Foster Stalker was sent to attack the Persian Gulf and captured Kharg Island on 4 December.

■ BUSHEHR (BUSHIRE), 10 DECEMBER 1856

After taking Kharg Island, a 5700-strong Anglo-Indian force under MGen Foster Stalker landed near the port of Bushehr and stormed the old fort at Rishahr. Bushehr was captured on 10 December after a short naval bombardment.

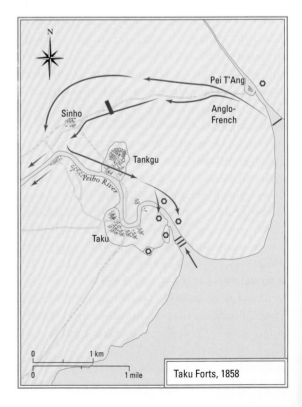

Taku Forts, 1858

■ **KHUSHAB, 7 FEBRUARY 1857**
MGen Sir James Outram's Anglo-Indian force of 4600 men and 18 guns defeated a 5000-strong Persian army under Khanlar Mirza at Khushab. The Anglo-Indians inflicted 800 casualties for the loss of 83 men.

The British in India 1855–95

■ **THE SANTHAL (SANTAL) REBELLION, 1855–56**
Exploitation by corrupt railway officials and moneylenders provoked a rebellion against British rule by 30,000 Santal tribesmen in northern Bengal. The rebels, led by the chiefs Sidhu and Khanu, were defeated in a year-long campaign.

The Indian Mutiny 1857–59

■ **CAWNPORE (KANPUR), 5–25 JUNE 1857**
At the outbreak of the Indian Mutiny, MGen Sir Hugh Wheeler held Cawnpore with a garrison of 300 British troops, aided by 600 British civilians. The garrison's four Indian regiments rebelled, joining forces with Nana Sahib who besieged the town with 4000 men. Wheeler surrendered after a siege of almost three weeks when Nana Sahib agreed to the evacuation of the survivors to Allahabad, but all except seven were later massacred.

■ **DELHI, 8 JUNE– 21 SEPTEMBER 1857**
Delhi was captured by mutineers on 11 May 1857 who proclaimed the 82-year-old Mughal Emperor, Bahadur Shah II, as their commander-in-chief and Emperor of India. Over the next few weeks, the city's garrison was reinforced, finally reaching a total strength of 12,000 regular sepoys and 30,000 irregular troops, supported by almost 100 guns.

A British detachment of 2500 men under MGen Sir Henry Barnard marched on Delhi and defeated a force of at least 3500 rebels at the village of Badli-ki-Serai just outside the city, inflicting 1000 casualties for the loss of fewer than 200 men. This victory allowed the British to occupy Delhi Ridge, which overlooked a long

sector of the city's defences. It was soon apparent that Delhi was too well fortified and strongly held to fall to a coup de main. Barnard ordered a dawn assault on 13 June, but the orders were confused and the attack had to be called off. After this, it was accepted that the odds were too great for any assault to be successful until the besiegers were reinforced.

Although a series of sorties from the city were beaten off, the besiegers were ground down by exhaustion and disease. Gen Barnard died of cholera on 5 July. His successor, MGen Reed, also contracted cholera and handed over command to Archdale Wilson, who was promoted to major-general. While the rebels were reinforced, British forces were also strengthened as units arrived from other areas, especially the Punjab. These included Brig John Nicholson's 'Flying Column' of 4200 men and siege artillery. The artillery arrived on 6 September and was a vital factor in supressing the fire of the rebels' guns and breaching the city's

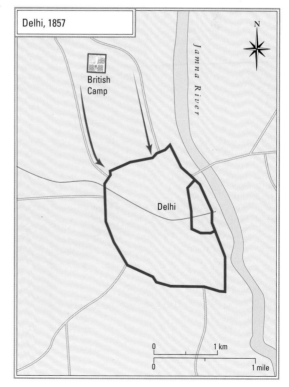

Delhi, 1857

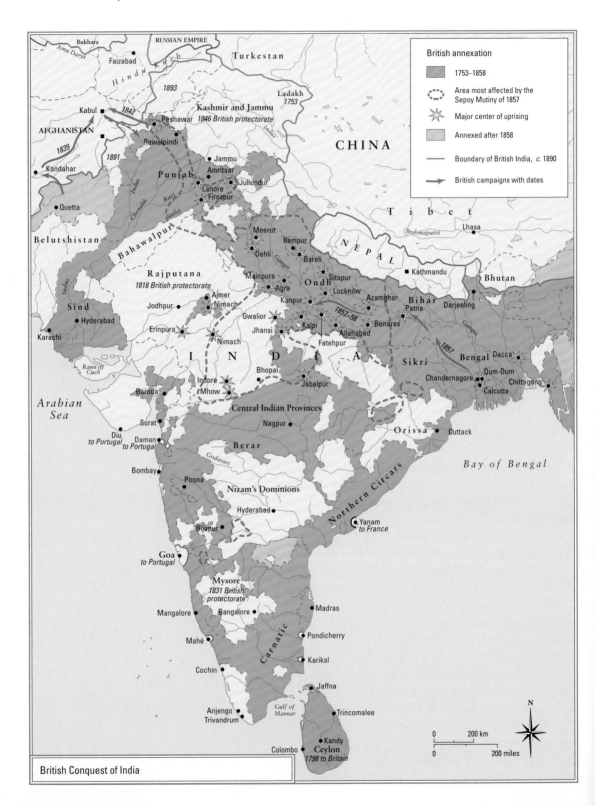

British annexation

	1753–1858
	Area most affected by the Sepoy Mutiny of 1857
	Major center of uprising
	Annexed after 1858
	Boundary of British India, *c.* 1890
	British campaigns with dates

Bukhara
Amu Darya
Faizabad
RUSSIAN EMPIRE
Turkestan
Hindu Kush
1893
Ladakh
1753
Kabul
1842
Peshawar   Kashmir and Jammu
1846 British protectorate
AFGHANISTAN
1839   Rawalpindi
Kandahar   *1891*
Quetta   Jammu
Punjab   Amritsar
Jullundur
Lahore
Firozpur
Indus
CHINA
T i b e t
Lhasa
Brahmaputra
Belutshistan   *Chenab*   *Ravi*   *Sutlej*
Bahawalpur
Meerut   Rampur
Dehli   Bareli
Ganges   NEPAL
Kathmandu
Bhutan
Rajputana   Mainpura   Sitapur
1818 British protectorate   Agra   Oudh   Lucknow   Azamgarh   Darjeeling
Ajmer   Kanpur   *1857–58*   Bihar
Sind   Nimach   Gwalior   Kalpi   Benares   Patna   *Ganges*
Jodhpur   Jhansi   Allahabad
Hyderabad   Erinpura   Fatehpur   *1857*
Karachi   Nimach   Sikri   Bengal   Dacca
I N D I A   Dum-Dum
Rann of Cuch   Bhopal   Chandernagore   Chittagong
Baroda   Indore   Jabalpur   Calcutta
Mhow
Central Indian Provinces
Arabian Sea   Surat   Nagpur   Orissa   Cuttack
Diu   Daman   Berar   *Godavari*
to Portugal   *to Portugal*   *Bay of Bengal*
Bombay
Poona   Nizam's Dominions   Northern Circars
Hyderabad
Bijapur   Yanam
to France
Goa
to Portugal
Mysore
1831 British protectorate
Mangalore   Bangalore   Madras
Mahé   Carnatic   Pondicherry
Karikal
Cochin
Jaffna
Anjengo   *Gulf of Mannar*   Trincomalee
Trivandrum

N

0	200 km
0	200 miles

Colombo   Kandy   Ceylon
1798 to Britain

British Conquest of India

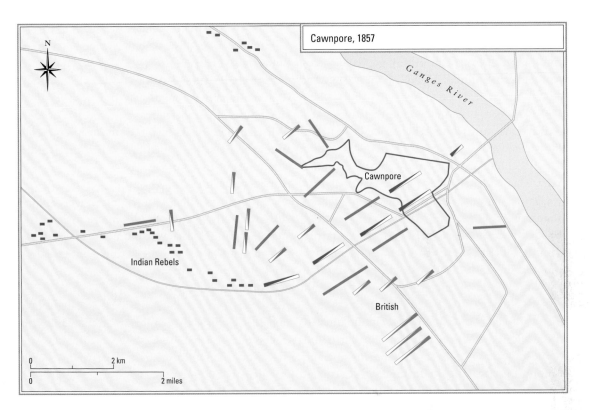

defences. After a week's bombardment, it was judged that enough had been achieved to allow an assault to be made with a reasonable chance of success.

A total of five assault columns were assembled during the night of 13/14 September. The attack was supposed to be launched at dawn, but the defenders had repaired some of the breaches overnight, and further bombardment was needed before the assault could be launched. The first column stormed through the breach in the Kashmir Bastion and the second through that in the Water Bastion, by the Jumna river. The third column attacked the Kashmir Gate on the north wall. Two engineer officers, Lieutenants Home and Salkeld (both of whom subsequently won the Victoria Cross), led a force that blew in the gate with demolition charges, allowing the third column to charge into the city.

Meanwhile, the fourth column encountered a rebel force in the suburb of Kishangunj outside the Kabul Gate before the other columns attacked, and was forced to retreat when Maj Reid, its commander, was seriously injured. The rebels followed up and threatened to attack the British camp, which had been stripped of its guards to form the assault force. The siege artillery batteries held them until cavalry and horse artillery could be brought up. Nicholson was mortally wounded and the British fell back to the church of Saint James, just inside the walls of the Kashmir Bastion. They had suffered 1170 casualties in the attack and Archdale Wilson almost ordered a retreat from the city, but was persuaded to hold on. A series of further attacks overran the remaining rebel positions and the city was finally captured on 21 September.

■ **Lucknow, June 1857–19 March 1858**

At the outbreak of the Indian Mutiny, the British Commissioner at Lucknow, Brig Sir Henry Lawrence, fortified the Residency and mobilized retired sepoys to strengthen the British 32nd Regiment of Foot which formed the city's peacetime garrison. Although rebel forces were gathering around Lucknow from late May, the full-scale siege only began in July when 5000 mutineers began attacking the improvised fortifications, now manned by a total of just over 1700 defenders.

On 19 September, a force of 3179 British troops, under Major-Generals Sir Henry Havelock and Sir James Outram, left Cawnpore to relieve the garrison. On the 23rd they encountered and defeated a force of 12,000 rebels at the Alambagh Palace near the city, capturing five guns. On the 25th the British forced the bridge at Charbagh and the main body broke through to the Residency after fierce street fighting. The British casualties during the operations totalled 535, while the garrison had lost 483 killed and wounded. Outram now took command and the reinforced garrison held out until 19 November, when it was relieved after Sir Colin Campbell's column of 4100 men captured the fortified villa and walled gardens at Sikandar Bagh. Campbell believed that the position was untenable as there were an estimated 30,000 rebel troops in the vicinity. He therefore ordered the evacuation of the city, although a strong garrison was left at the nearby Alambagh Palace complex, which held out until Campbell began an offensive to re-take Lucknow in early March 1858. His advance was aided by a large Nepalese contingent advancing from the north under Jang Bahadur. Campbell's carefully planned campaign drove the large but demoralized rebel forces from Lucknow with minimal British casualties.

■ FATEHPUR (FUTTEYPUR), 12 JULY 1857

As Gen Sir Henry Havelock marched out of Allahabad to recapture Cawnpore, the rebel leader Nana Sahib tried to intercept a detached column under Maj Sydenham Renaud, but found himself facing Havelock's entire force at Fatehpur. The rebels were decisively defeated, losing 11 guns, while not a single European in the British force

was killed. The British plundered Fatehpur before continuing their advance on Cawnpore via Aong and Pandu Nadi.

■ ARRAH, 25 JULY–3 AUGUST 1857

A British railway engineer, Mr Boyle, fortified his house in Arrah, which was held by 76 men who repelled attacks by three mutineer regiments until the siege was raised by a relief force under Maj Vincent Eyre.

■ ONAO, 28 JULY 1857

A 1500-strong British force under Sir Henry Havelock advanced from Cawnpore to raise the rebel siege of Lucknow. Mutineers blocked the advance at Onao, but were defeated with the loss of 300 men and 15 guns.

■ GORARIA, 23–24 NOVEMBER 1857

Brig Stuart's force of 3000 men defeated 5000 rebels at Goraria. British attacks on the 23rd were repulsed, but a renewed assault on the following day drove the mutineers from their defences with the loss of 1500 men.

■ SECOND BATTLE OF CAWNPORE, 19 NOVEMBER–6 DECEMBER 1857

British forces under the command of Gen Sir Henry Havelock recaptured Cawnpore on 17 July 1857, but were weakened by the need to send detachments to raise the ongoing siege of Lucknow. A garrison of 1500 men under Brig Charles Ash Windham was left to hold Cawnpore, the vital pontoon bridge across the Ganges, and the entrenchments constructed to protect it. Nana Sahib's general, Tatya Tope, led an army of 14,000 mutineers supported by 40 guns and seized Cawnpore in a surprise attack on 19 November, although Windham's garrison managed to hold the entrenchments.

Sir Colin Campbell's force from the siege of Lucknow returned on 27 November, bringing the total British strength up to 10,000 men and 65 guns. After careful preparations, Campbell and Windham attacked on 6 December, recapturing Cawnpore by exploiting the superior firepower of their artillery and inflicting a decisive defeat on the rebels.

■ Jhansi, 21 March–5 April 1858
MGen Sir Hugh Rose besieged the mountain fortress city of Jhansi, held by 12,000 rebels under the command of Queen Rani Lakshmibai, the Rani of Jhansi. On 1 April he took command of a detachment of 1500 men, who defeated Tatya Tope's 20,000-strong relief force at the River Betwa, inflicting a total of 1500 casualties on the rebels. Jhansi was stormed on 3 April, but the citadel held out until 5 April and the Rani managed to escape from the clutches of the British soldiers.

■ Gaulaui, 22 May 1858
A British column under MGen Sir Hugh Rose, decisively defeated a 20,000-strong rebel force under Tatya Tope and the Rani of Jhansi. The mutineers suffered heavy losses and Rose was able to retake Kalpi.

■ Gwalior, 20 June 1858
Despite their defeat at Kalpi, the rebel leaders Tatya Tope, Rao Sahib and the Rani of Jhansi led 12,000 men in an attack that seized Gwalior from the loyalist Maharajah Sindia. MGen Sir Hugh Rose organized a bold counter-offensive which beat the rebels at nearby Morar, killed the Rani at Kotah-Ki-Serai and finally stormed Gwalior. Tatya Tope and Rao Sahib fled, but both were eventually caught and hanged.

Umbeyla Campaign 1863–64
Attacks on British outposts in the Northwest Frontier of India by Pashtun and Bunerwal tribesmen provoked the dispatch of a 6000-strong punitive expedition commanded by Brig Neville Bowles Chamberlain. The British force was subjected to constant attacks by forces totalling 15,000 tribesmen, who were only defeated after months of fierce fighting in mountainous terrain. The British inflicted an estimated 3000 casualties for the loss of almost 1000 men.

Bhutan War 1864–65
Border disputes between the Himalayan kingdom of Bhutan and British India flared up into war in 1864. British forces initially encountered minimal opposition, but there was serious fighting before they annexed the disputed region in 1865.

■ The Panjdeh Incident, 30 March 1885
A 600-strong Afghan detachment, dug in along the west bank of the River Kushk near Panjdeh (now Serhetabat, Turkmenistan), was attacked and wiped out by a far larger Russian force commanded by Gen Alexander Komarov.

Chitral Expedition March–April 1895
The 500-strong Indian Army garrison of Chitral on the Northwest Frontier (modern Pakistan) were besieged by 5000 Chitrali, Afghan and Pathan tribesmen. The besiegers were driven off by MGen Sir Robert Low's 15,000-strong relief force.

Mexican Wars 1857–67

■ Calpulalpam, 22 December 1860
President Miguel Miramón took 8000 troops from Mexico City to meet the Liberal commander Jesús González Ortega's army of 15,000 men on the heights of San Miguel Calpulalpam. Miramón's forces were crushed and he fled to Europe.

■ Puebla, 5 May 1862
Gen Ignacio Zaragoza's 4500-strong Mexican force defeated a French army of 6500 men under MGen Charles de Lorencez near the city of Puebla. The Mexicans inflicted almost 800 casualties for the loss of 226 men.

■ Camarón (Camerone), 30 April 1863
The French Foreign Legion's 3rd Company commanded by Capt Jean Danjou formed the escort for an important convoy to Puebla with three million francs and supplies for the French forces besieging the city. By 01:00 on 30 April, the 3rd Company was on its way, with a total strength of three officers and 62 men. After covering 24km, it stopped at Palo Verde to rest.

Soon afterwards, a 2000-strong Mexican force (800 cavalry and 1200 infantry) was spotted. Danjou ordered the company into square and began a well-ordered retreat, repulsing several cavalry charges and inflicting heavy losses on the enemy.

Seeking a more defensible position, Danjou decided to make a stand at the Hacienda Camarón, an inn protected by a 3m-high wall. He intended to distract the Mexicans and hopefully prevent any attacks on the nearby convoy. Whilst the legionnaires barricaded the inn, the Mexican commander, Col Milan, demanded their surrender, emphasizing his enormous numerical superiority. Danjou went around to each of his men with a bottle of wine and made them all swear not to surrender.

At noon, Danjou was fatally wounded, but his men fought on under the command of 2nd Lt Vilain until his death in the late afternoon. By 17:00 only a dozen legionnaires remained in action, led by 2nd Lt Maudet. The last of their ammunition was fired at 18:00 and Maudet led the five remaining men in a desperate bayonet charge. All but two were killed and the deeply impressed Mexican commander released the survivors. Danjou's men had inflicted at least 400 casualties and their stand is still annually commemorated by the French Foreign Legion as 'Camerone Day'.

Spanish–Moroccan War 1859–60

■ TÉTOUAN, 4 FEBRUARY 1860

Gen Leopoldo O'Donnell led a 36,000-strong Spanish army supported by 65 guns against the forces of Sultan Muhammed IV in retaliation for Moroccan raids on the Spanish enclave of Ceuta in North Africa. Advancing south from Castillejos, the Spanish won a decisive victory near Tétouan, east of Tangier (largely due to their superior artillery), before taking the city on 6 February. The sultan sued for peace and O'Donnell was created Duke of Tétouan.

American Civil War 1861–65

■ PEA RIDGE, 7–8 MARCH 1861

MGen Earl Van Dorn launched an ill-planned attack against BGen Samuel Curtis' overextended lines at Elkhorn Tavern, Arkansas. The defeat forced the Confederates to retreat from Arkansas, surrendering the initiative there to the Federals.

■ FORT SUMTER, 12–14 APRIL 1861

Fort Sumter was a brick fort built on an artificial island in the middle of the main ship channel at Charleston, South Carolina. Even though South Carolina seceded on 20 December 1861, Federal commander Maj Robert Anderson refused to surrender his 84-man force. A weak Federal attempt to resupply and reinforce the beleaguered garrison by the unarmed *Star of the West* was turned back on 9 January 1861. In early March, BGen Pierre Gustave Toutant Beauregard arrived to assume command of the Confederate forces, and on 10 April he issued a demand that Anderson surrender or face bombardment. On 12 April, Beauregard commenced his attack. After a 34-hour bombardment of some 4000 shells, Anderson surrendered on 13 April and the Federals were evacuated to New York. The action compelled President Abraham Lincoln to call for volunteers to suppress the rebellion.

■ PHILIPPI, 3 JUNE 1861

As Confederate and Federal forces battled for control of western Virginia early in the war, a minor action was fought at Philippi. Federals commanded by Col Thomas Morris surprised Confederates under Col George Porterfield in a two-pronged attack before dawn. The Confederates suffered 26 casualties and retreated toward Huttonsville in what critics called the 'Philippi Races'. The Federals suffered four casualties. Philippi is sometimes credited as being the first battle of the war.

■ BIG BETHEL, 10 JUNE 1861

This Federal attack on a Confederate outpost north-west of Newport News, Virginia, was

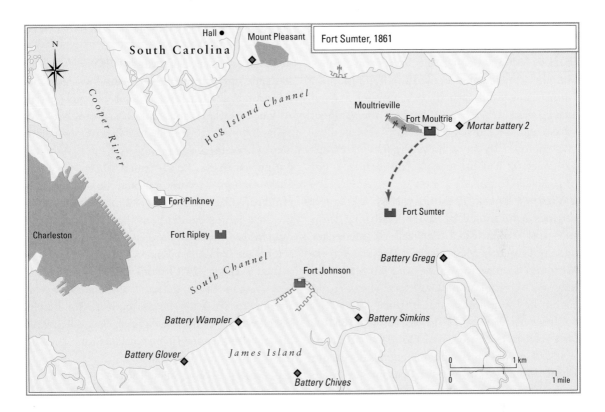

easily repulsed by Col John Magruder. Although a small action, at the time the battle was widely reported and elevated Magruder to the status of a minor celebrity.

■ **RICH MOUNTAIN, 11 JULY 1861**

MGen George McClellan attacked Confederate troops who had retreated from Philippi. The victory helped remove the Confederate presence from the north-western counties of Virginia. West Virginia was admitted to the Union as a new state in 1863.

■ **FIRST BULL RUN, 16–21 JULY 1861**

Under pressure from President Abraham Lincoln to act, BGen Irvin McDowell began moving his army toward Manassas Junction. Confederates commanded by BGen Pierre Gustave Toutant Beauregard soon ascertained the threat and requested reinforcements from Gen Joseph Johnston in the Shenandoah Valley. Johnston slipped away from MGen Robert Patterson, who had been ordered to hold him in place, and

Johnston moved by railroad to join Beauregard. On 21 July, McDowell launched a diversionary attack on the Confederate line at the Stone Bridge. A Confederate signal station noticed the flanking movement the attack had been designed to cover, and Col Nathan Evans moved to the southern slope of Mathews' Hill to counter this threat. Evans was joined by Confederate brigades commanded by BGen Barnard Bee and Col Francis Barlow but the Matthews' Hill position soon proved untenable, and the Confederates broke into a disorderly retreat back towards the Henry House. It seemed as if a Federal victory was at hand until BGen Thomas Jackson arrived with reinforcements from the Shenandoah Valley and took up a position on Henry Hill. The remnants of the other Confederate commands rallied around Jackson's line, prompting Bee to point to Jackson and declare he was standing there 'like a stone wall', giving Jackson the nickname he carried ever since. As the Confederates rallied,

McDowell was slow to renew his attack and he forfeited his numerical advantage by piecemeal attacks. After stopping the attack on Henry Hill, the Confederates focused their attention on Chinn Ridge and turned back another Federal attack there. Panic soon swept the Federal ranks, and McDowell chaotically retreated to Washington. By now, however, the victorious Confederates had also become disorganized and were unable to pursue.

■ WILSON'S CREEK, 12 AUGUST 1861

Federals commanded by BGen Nathaniel Lyon and Col Franz Sigel attacked Confederates under BGen Ben McCulloch at Wilson's Creek, Missouri. The victory gave the Confederates temporary control of south-western Missouri and encouraged secessionist sympathizers.

■ CHEAT MOUNTAIN, 12–15 SEPTEMBER 1861

Gen Robert E. Lee ordered Col Albert Rust to attack BGen Joseph Reynolds' Federals defending Cheat Mountain in western Virginia. A mere

Ball's Bluff, 1861

300 determined Federals held off Rust, and Lee withdrew to Valley Head.

■ COCKLE CREEK, 5 OCTOBER 1861

In spite of Virginia's secession, residents of Chincoteague Island were decidedly pro-Union. At Cockle Creek, the USS *Louisiana* sank the CSS *Venus*, helping secure the area from Confederate blockade runners and privateers.

■ NEW ORLEANS, 12 OCTOBER 1861

Cdre George Hollins attacked the remarkably unprepared Federal naval detachment commanded by Capt John Pope. Hollins's force included the ironclad *Manassas*. The Federals fled in what critics labelled 'Pope's Run.'

■ BALL'S BLUFF, 21 OCTOBER 1861

Col Nathan Evans defeated a bungled Federal attempt to cross the Potomac river. Col Edwin Baker was killed in the fighting and the overall Federal commander, BGen Charles Stone, became the scapegoat for the debacle.

■ BELMONT, 7 NOVEMBER 1861

Confederates commanded by MGen Leonidas Polk manned an observation post called Camp Johnston at Belmont, Missouri. BGen Ulysses Grant believed that Polk was planning to reinforce pro-Confederate forces under BGen Sterling Price in south-west Missouri. To prevent this move, Grant embarked from Cairo, Illinois, and landed a force of over 3000 men 3.2km above Belmont. As Grant advanced, he scattered Confederates commanded by BGen Gideon Pillow and then descended on Camp Johnson from two directions. While the Confederates withdrew, Grant lost control of his men as they celebrated and looted the camp. Polk then sent two steamers with reinforcements across the Mississippi river from Columbus, Kentucky, and threatened to surround Grant. Grant rallied his men and fought back to their transports and returned to Cairo, Illinois. Although a largely unnecessary battle, Belmont proved to be a formative experience for Grant.

■ MILL SPRINGS, 19 JANUARY 1862

Confederate MGen George Crittenden advanced from Mill Springs, Kentucky, and struck BGen

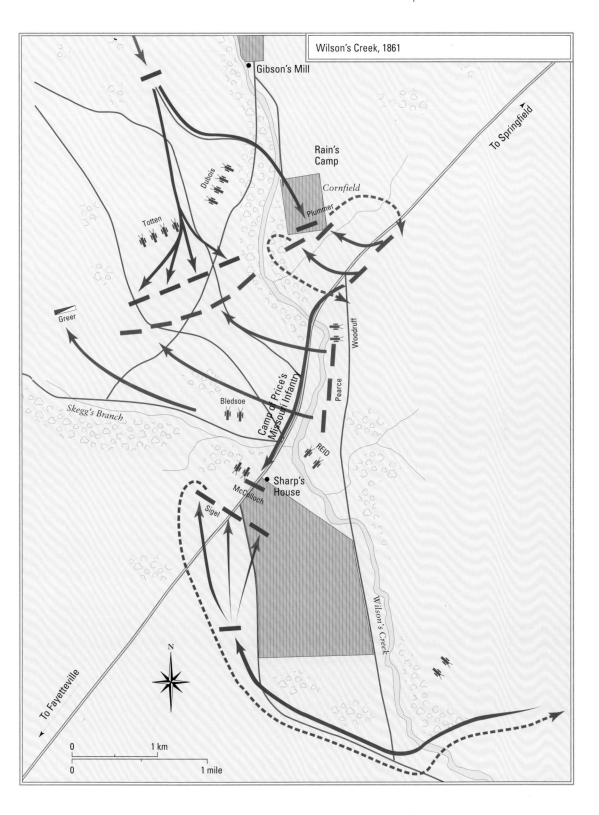

Wilson's Creek, 1861

Gibson's Mill

Rain's
Camp

Cornfield

Plummer

Dubois

Totten

Greer

Woodruff

Pearce

Skegg's Branch

Bledsoe

Camp of Price's
Missouri Infantry

REID

Sharp's
House

McCulloch

Sigel

Wilson's Creek

To Springfield

To Fayetteville

N

0   1 km

0   1 mile

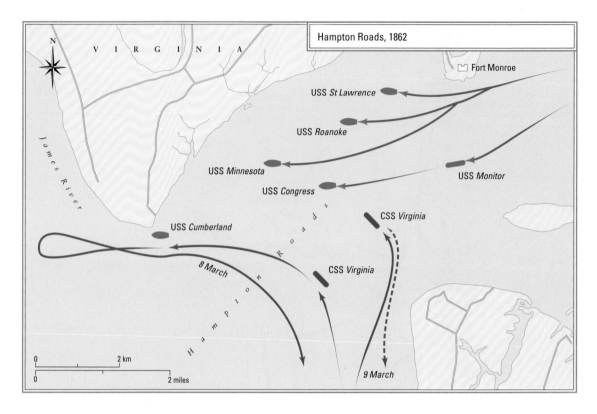

| Hampton Roads, 1862 |

George Thomas in a preemptive attack at Logan's Crossroads. Crittenden was forced to retreat to Murfreesboro, Tennessee. Confederate BGen Felix Zollicoffer was killed in the battle.

■ **FORT HENRY, 6 FEBRUARY 1862**

Fort Henry was a relatively weak Confederate position intended to guard the Tennessee river approach into the heart of Tennessee and north Alabama. In early February 1862 it was manned by a force of about 100 artillerymen under the command of BGen Lloyd Tilghman, who had sent the bulk of his force to Fort Donelson, a stronger position on the Cumberland river. BGen Ulysses Grant loaded 15,000 troops on to Flag Officer Andrew Foote's transports and headed up the Tennessee river. MGen Henry Halleck had previously rejected the plan, but when Foote lent his support, Halleck acquiesced. Grant landed a few miles below Fort Henry, while Foote steamed ahead to shell the position. After a brief bombardment, Tilghman surrendered. The

capture of Fort Henry opened the Tennessee river to Federal vessels as far as Muscle Shoals, Alabama and was a precursor to the capture of Fort Donelson.

■ **ROANOKE ISLAND, 7–8 FEBRUARY 1862**

BGen Ambrose Burnside and Flag Officer Louis Goldsborough brushed aside a weak Confederate force on this island off the North Carolina coast in what was the Federals' first major land victory east of the Alleghenies.

■ **FORT DONELSON, 13–16 FEBRUARY 1862**

A joint force commanded by BGen Ulysses Grant and Flag Officer Andrew Foote besieged this Confederate position on the Cumberland river. On 16 February, the Confederates surrendered, giving the Federals their first major victory of the war.

■ **HAMPTON ROADS, 9 MARCH 1862**

Confederate engineers raised the scuttled USS *Merrimack* and converted it into an ironclad rechristened as the CSS *Virginia*. On 8 March,

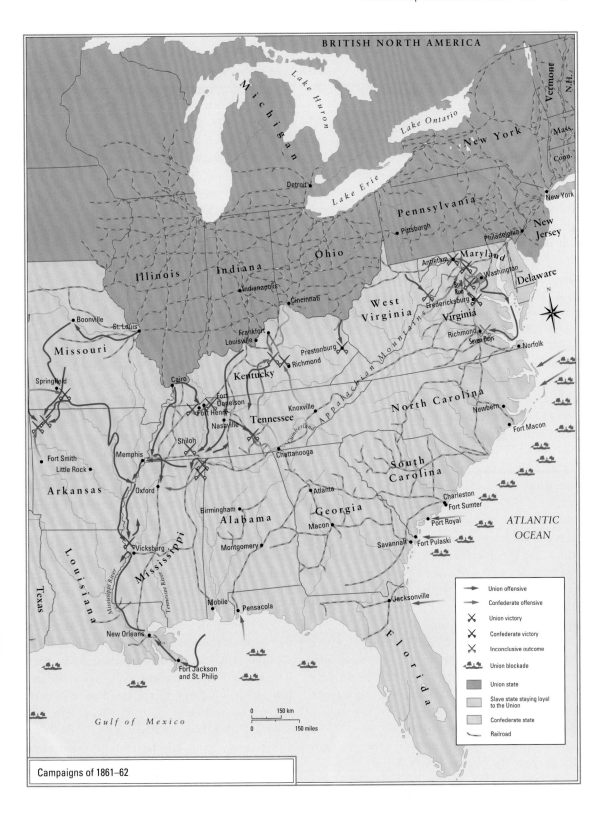

BRITISH NORTH AMERICA

Lake Huron

Michigan

Lake Ontario

Lake Erie

Detroit

New York

Mass.

Conn.

Pennsylvania

Pittsburgh

New Jersey

Philadelphia

New York

Ohio

Maryland

Antietam

Washington

Delaware

Indiana

Indianapolis

Bull Run

Illinois

Cincinnati

West Virginia

Fredericksburg

Virginia

Boonville

St. Louis

Frankfort

Louisville

Prestonburg

Richmond

Richmond

Seven Days

Norfolk

Missouri

Springfield

Cairo

Kentucky

Appalachian Mountains

North Carolina

Newbern

Fort Donelson

Fort Henry

Knoxville

Fort Macon

Fort Smith

Nashville

Tennessee

Little Rock

Shiloh

Cumberland

Memphis

Chattanooga

South Carolina

Arkansas

Oxford

Atlanta

Charleston

Fort Sumter

Birmingham

Georgia

Port Royal

Alabama

Macon

ATLANTIC OCEAN

Vicksburg

Montgomery

Savannah

Fort Pulaski

Louisiana

Mississippi River

Tennessee River

Mississippi

Texas

Mobile

Pensacola

Jacksonville

Florida

New Orleans

Fort Jackson and St. Philip

Gulf of Mexico

→	Union offensive
→	Confederate offensive
✕	Union victory
✕	Confederate victory
✕	Inconclusive outcome
⚓	Union blockade
	Union state
	Slave state staying loyal to the Union
	Confederate state
	Railroad

0   150 km

0   150 miles

Campaigns of 1861–62

the *Virginia* sailed into Hampton Roads off Norfolk, Virginia, and began destroying Federal ships anchored there. On 9 March, the *Virginia's* rampage was challenged when the Federal ironclad, the USS *Monitor*, arrived on the scene. Taking advantage of its superior manoeuvrability, the *Monitor* scored several hits on the *Virginia*, cracking its railroad iron armour but failing to penetrate its 60cm pitch pine and oak backing. The two combatants continued to duel indecisively for two hours, and then both ships withdrew for a half-hour respite.

In the second two-hour engagement, the *Virginia* made an attempt to ram the *Monitor*, but, having lost her ram-beak in the previous day's fighting, was unsuccessful. Then Lt Catesby ap Roger Jones, who had assumed command of the *Virginia* after Cdre Franklin Buchanan was wounded, tried to take advantage of his larger crew size and made several attempts to board the *Monitor*. The *Monitor* repulsed all efforts. Finally, Jones brought the *Virginia* to within 10m of the *Monitor* and struck her pilot house at point blank range with a 9in (28cm) shell. Stationed immediately behind the point of impact, the *Monitor's* commander, Lt John Worden, personally felt the full effect of this concussion and commanded his helmsman to sheer off. The *Virginia* had also taken a beating, and with the ebb tide running, she withdrew across Hampton Roads to Norfolk. After the battle, the *Virginia* was still a threat, but thanks to the presence of the *Monitor*, it no longer was able to thwart MGen George McClellan's developing Peninsula Campaign.

■ **NEW MADRID, 13 MARCH 1862**
Island No. 10 and New Madrid, Missouri, blocked Federal navigation of the Mississippi river. As BGen John Pope prepared to begin siege operations against New Madrid, the Confederate force there withdrew.

■ **KERNSTOWN, 23 MARCH 1862**
MGen George McClellan was eager to shift forces from the Shenandoah Valley to help him with his Peninsula Campaign. Confederate MGen

Stonewall Jackson's mission was to prevent that from happening. Col Turner Ashby reported Federal troops were preparing to join McClellan, and Ashby skirmished with Federals commanded by BGen James Shields on 22 March. At about 14:00 on 23 March, Jackson met Ashby at Kernstown, 6.5km south of Winchester. Jackson's men were tired from marching and the pious Jackson was reluctant to fight on the Sabbath, but he could not afford to let reinforcements slip away to McClellan. Jackson launched a disjointed attack and suffered a tactical defeat with 718 casualties compared to 568 for the Federals. Strategically, however, Kernstown was a huge Confederate victory. Jackson's presence and aggressive action caused Federal authorities to halt plans to shift forces to McClellan.

■ **SHILOH, 6–7 APRIL 1862**
Stinging from MGen Ulysses Grant's victories at Forts Henry and Donelson in February 1862, Gen Albert Sidney Johnston withdrew from Tennessee and concentrated his Confederate forces at Corinth, Mississippi. At the same time, Grant assembled some 45,000 men at Pittsburg Landing, Tennessee, about 32km north-east of Corinth, where he waited for the arrival of MGen Don Carlos Buell's Army of the Ohio from Nashville. Perhaps 2km south-west of Pittsburg Landing was Shiloh Church, the feature that would give the upcoming battle its common name. Grant arranged his command in a largely administrative camp configuration while he waited for Buell to join him to conduct a combined attack on Corinth. Grant never considered Johnston might launch his own offensive, and was caught by surprise when Johnston marched from Corinth and attacked before dawn on 6 April. The Confederates attacked with MGen William Hardee's Third Army Corps and MGen Braxton Bragg's Second Army Corps deployed in line, followed by MGen Leonidas Polk's First Army Corps and then BGen John Breckinridge's Reserve Corps advancing in column formation.

The Confederate attack hit the part of the

Federal line occupied by BGen Benjamin Prentiss' 6th Division, whose stubborn defence of the 'Hornet's Nest' bought time for Grant to reorganize his force. When Johnston was killed leading an attack through a peach orchard just to the right of the Hornet's Nest, Gen Pierre Gustave Toutant Beauregard assumed command and launched a series of frontal assaults that eventually forced Federals to withdraw back to Pittsburg Landing. Although initially caught off guard, Grant used Prentiss' stubborn defence to organize the stragglers into units and form a new defensive line that ran inland at a right angle from the Tennessee river above Pittsburg Landing north-westwards towards Owl Creek. There he held on until reinforcements from Buell's 35,000-man army began arriving at 19:00. In spite of the early Confederate success, the tide of the battle was beginning to turn in favour of the Federals. Still, Beauregard believed the Confederate attack had carried the day and stopped the pursuit,

declaring 'the victory is complete'. Beauregard was later subjected to much historical scrutiny for missing what became known as the 'Lost Opportunity' to destroy Grant's army. For his part, Grant continued to receive reinforcements and resolved to counter-attack the next day. Striking before dawn and taking advantage of the numerical advantage gained by the arrival of Buell, the Federals enjoyed quick success. Grant easily recaptured most of the ground he had earlier lost, and by 14:30, Beauregard decided to withdraw back towards Corinth. Grant's men were too exhausted to effectively pursue.

The battle of Shiloh was the biggest battle fought in North America to that date. Of the 62,000 Federals engaged, 13,047 were killed, wounded or missing. The Confederates suffered 11,694 casualties from their 44,000-man army. The Confederate forces in the west were now committed to an unwinnable war of attrition.

■ Island No. 10, 7 April 1862

BGen John Pope dug a canal to allow his boats to bypass the Confederate defences and ferried four regiments across the Mississippi river, cutting off the Confederate line of retreat. BGen William Mackall surrendered 3500 Confederates while another 500 escaped through the swamps. The victory opened the Mississippi river to Fort Pillow, Tennessee, and enhanced Pope's reputation enough that he became commander of the Army of Virginia two months later.

■ New Orleans, 25 April 1862

Adm David Farragut attacked New Orleans, the South's largest city and a key port and shipbuilding centre, shortly after midnight on 24 April 1862. After the Federals forced their way past the ram *Manassas* and Forts St Philip and Jackson, Confederate commander MGen Mansfield Lovell retreated. The city was in panic, and as Farragut pulled alongside, he hammered it with broadsides. He then dispatched his marines to take possession of the Federal mint, post office and customs house and replace the

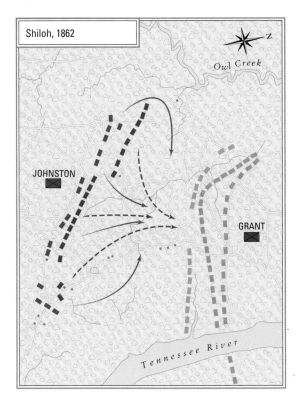

Shiloh, 1862

Confederate flag with the Stars and Stripes on all public buildings. Capt Theodorus Bailey worked his way through an angry mob and demanded the city's surrender, but the mayor claimed to be under martial law and without authority. When Farragut threatened a bombardment, the mayor and Common Council declared New Orleans an open city. On 1 May, MGen Benjamin Butler and the army began a controversial occupation of New Orleans.

■ FORT JACKSON AND FORT ST PHILIP, 25–28 APRIL 1862

Forts Jackson and St Philip guarded the Mississippi river approaches 120km south of New Orleans. On 18 April, Adm David Porter began a two-day mortar bombardment of the forts that failed to cause them to surrender. After Adm David Farragut captured New Orleans, Porter subjected the forts to additional shelling. Confederate morale waned and at midnight on 27 April, the troops refused to continue resistance. BGen Johnson Duncan was left with no choice but to surrender his forces to the enemy.

■ YORKTOWN, 3 MAY 1862

Late in the afternoon of 5 April, a Federal force commanded by BGen Erasmus Keyes came under fire at Lee's Mill as it marched up the Virginia Peninsula. Based on this small contact, Keyes reported that the Confederate position was too strong to be carried by assault. MGen George McClellan decided to reduce Yorktown by a siege which lasted until 3 May when the Confederates abandoned Yorktown and withdrew up the peninsula.

■ WILLIAMSBURG, 4–5 MAY 1862

After abandoning Yorktown, Gen Joseph Johnston withdrew up the Virginia Peninsula, hoping to retreat rapidly to the immediate vicinity of Richmond before MGen George McClellan could get there first. Johnston withdrew along two roads which came together 18km past Yorktown and 3km short of Williamsburg.

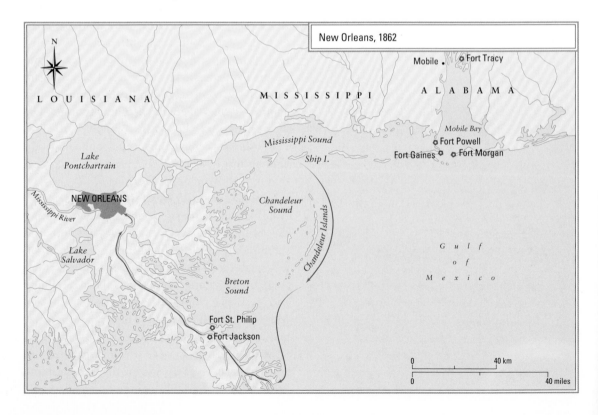

BGen Jeb Stuart's cavalry provided the rearguard, and on 4 May, Federal troops caught up with Stuart. Johnston then ordered MGen James Longstreet to fight a delaying action to allow the remainder of the Confederate force to continue withdrawing along the single road from Williamsburg to Richmond. In a sharp battle on 5 May, the Federals committed their forces piecemeal, allowing Longstreet to halt their advance, and then break contact and rejoin the Confederate retreat. Longstreet's successful delay was essential in allowing the Confederates to reorganize to defend Richmond.

■ McDowell, 8 May 1862

Leaving MGen Richard Ewell to hold MGen Nathaniel Banks in place, MGen Stonewall Jackson clandestinely moved to McDowell where he defeated MGen John Frémont, preventing him from uniting with Banks.

■ Plum Rum Bend, 10 May 1862

The Confederate River Defense Fleet guarded Mississippi river approaches to Memphis, Tennessee. An eight-ship flotilla attacked Federal ships at Plum Rum Bend. During the action the CSS *General Sterling Price* rammed the USS *Cincinnati* and sank it.

■ Front Royal, 23 May 1862

Aided by hard marching, deception and intelligence from the legendary spy Belle Boyd, MGen Stonewall Jackson concentrated 16000 men against about 1000 Federals at Front Royal, Virginia. Jackson inflicted 904 Federal casualties while losing fewer than 50 of his own men. The Confederates also captured some $300,000 worth of supplies. However, when the Federals counter-attacked on 30 May, the commander Jackson left to guard the supplies panicked and withdrew towards Winchester.

■ Winchester, 25 May 1862

After the Confederate victory at Front Royal, MGen Nathaniel Banks withdrew to Winchester. MGen Stonewall Jackson attacked and routed the Federals there, but was unable to conduct an effective pursuit.

■ Fair Oaks, 31 May 1862

On 30 May, Gen Joseph Johnston learned that two Federal corps were south of the Chickahominy river, making MGen George McClellan's army vulnerable to an attack. Johnston developed a plan to use a series of three roads emanating from Richmond to conduct a double envelopment against the isolated corps. The plan quickly began to unravel when MGen James Longstreet marched down the wrong road and became entangled with troops belonging to BGen Charles Whiting and MGen Benjamin Huger. The ensuing confusion delayed Johnston's attack by some five hours, and resulted in MGen D. H. Hill attacking alone. Longstreet attacked later, but of the 29,500 men in the three divisions under his command, he managed to get only 12,500 into the battle. Confederate efficiency was further hamstrung by the fact that an unusual combination of atmospheric conditions precluded Johnston from hearing the sounds of the firing from his headquarters, and he was late in learning the battle was under way. Towards nightfall, Johnston was severely wounded in the chest and thigh from fragments from an artillery shell and was succeeded by MGen Gustavus Smith who was quickly overwhelmed by his responsibilities. The Confederates launched a weak attack on 1 June which was stopped by Federal reinforcements that had moved from north of the river during the night. At about 14:00, Gen Robert E. Lee, who previously was serving as President Jefferson Davis' military advisor, assumed command of the Confederate forces. After midnight on 2 June, the Confederates retreated to the west. The Confederates lost 6134 killed, wounded or missing and the Federals 5031 during the battle. Its most significant outcome was Lee's rise to command of what became the Army of Northern Virginia.

■ Memphis, 6 June 1862

After the Federals occupied Corinth, Mississippi, Gen Pierre Gustave Toutant Beauregard ordered the Confederate troops to withdraw from Fort Pillow and Memphis, Tennessee. Federal troops

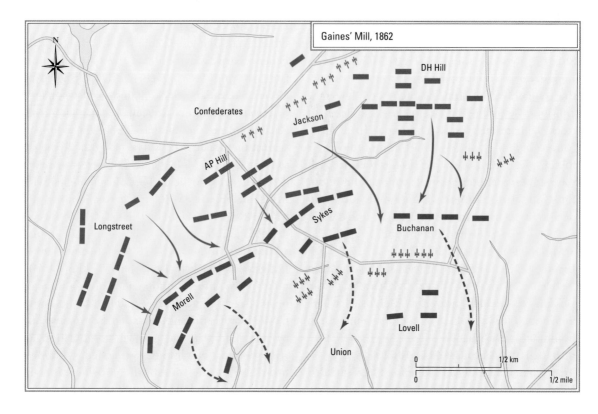

Gaines' Mill, 1862

occupied Fort Pillow on 4 June, and Flag Officer Charles Davis left one gunboat there in support. Davis and Col Charles Ellet then launched a naval attack on Memphis early on 6 June. Although Ellet and his Ram Fleet were authorized to operate independently of the navy, he and Davis achieved a working arrangement that involved surprisingly little friction. During the hour-and-a-half battle, the Federals sank or captured all vessels of the Confederate River Defense Fleet except for the *General Van Dorn*, the fastest of the Confederate gunboats. Memphis surrendered and was occupied by Federal forces. Ellet was severely wounded in the fighting and he subsequently died a few days later.

■ CROSS KEYS/PORT REPUBLIC, 8–9 JUNE 1862
After avoiding a Federal attempt to trap him at Strasburg, MGen Stonewall Jackson positioned MGen Richard Ewell at Cross Keys and stationed his own men at Port Republic. On 8 June, Ewell easily repulsed MGen John Frémont's attack and then withdrew to assist Jackson at Port Republic.

Jackson and Ewell defeated BGen James Shields while Frémont watched helplessly from the far side of a bridge Ewell's men had burned.

■ SEVEN DAYS' BATTLES, 25 JUNE–1 JULY 1862
MGen Stonewall Jackson reinforced Gen Robert E. Lee after Jackson's Shenandoah Valley Campaign. Lee then went on the offensive, and, in a series of battles collectively known as the Seven Days, forced MGen George McClellan to abandon his Peninsula Campaign.

■ MECHANICSVILLE, 26 JUNE 1862
Gen Robert E. Lee's planned envelopment was thwarted by MGen Stonewall Jackson's uncharacteristic slowness. Instead MGen A.P. Hill launched four separate unsuccessful frontal attacks against MGen Fitz John Porter's formidable Beaver Dam Creek positions.

■ GAINES' MILL, 27 JUNE 1862
After Mechanicsville, MGen George McClellan ordered MGen Fitz John Porter to fall back to a defendable position covering the Chickahominy

river bridges. Porter occupied an excellent defensive position at Turkey Hill about a 1.5km from Gaines' Mill. Porter's line was finally broken by an assault spearheaded by BGen John Bell Hood. The loss caused McClellan to announce his plans to abandon the Peninsula Campaign and shift his base to Harrison's Landing.

■ SAVAGE'S STATION, 29 JUNE 1862

After Gaines' Mill, Gen Robert E. Lee realized MGen George McClellan was in full retreat. Lee hoped to intercept McClellan using a network of four roads that fanned out to the east and south from Richmond. Leading the immediate pursuit was MGen John Magruder, whom Lee hoped could overtake the Federal rearguard and force it to turn and fight. Magruder caught up with BGen Edwin Sumner at 09:00 on 29 June at Allen's Farm, 3.2km short of Savage's Station. Both Magruder and Sumner fought cautiously, with Sumner delaying back to Savage's Station. Neither general engaged the majority of his force. Darkness and a thunderstorm brought an end to the stalemated fighting, and the Federals withdrew across White Oak Swamp, having lost 1038 men compared to 473 for the Confederates.

■ FRAYSER'S FARM, 30 JUNE 1862

Gen Robert E. Lee missed an excellent opportunity to cut off MGen George McClellan from the James river, in part due to MGen Stonewall Jackson's continued slowness. Instead McClellan continued his retreat.

■ TAMPA, 30 JUNE–1 JULY 1862

Capt J.W. Pearson's Osceola Rangers turned back a weak attack by the Federal gunboats *Sagamore* and *Ethan Allen* and refused a small landing party's demand to surrender. Neither side suffered any casualties, and the Federals withdrew.

■ MALVERN HILL, 1 JULY 1862

After Frayser's Farm, MGen George McClellan retreated to Malvern Hill, another formidable defensive position. There the Federal artillery defeated a Confederate attack, enabling McClellan to complete his withdrawal to Harrison's Landing and entrench.

■ BATON ROUGE, 5 AUGUST 1862

MGen John Breckinridge led Confederate forces from Camp Moore in an attempt to regain the Louisiana capital city. Breckinridge anticipated assistance from the ironclad CSS *Arkansas*, but the vessel had repeated engine problems, could not participate in the attack and ultimately was destroyed to prevent capture. Without the support of the *Arkansas*, Breckenridge's force was subjected to shelling by Federal gunboats, and his attack failed to carry the Federal works.

■ CEDAR MOUNTAIN, 9 AUGUST 1862

Hoping to attack Federal forces moving towards Culpepper, MGen Stonewall Jackson was instead attacked by MGen Nathaniel Banks. MGen A.P. Hill rescued Jackson, who suffered 1338 casualties compared to 2353 for Banks.

■ SECOND BULL RUN, 29–30 AUGUST 1862

Once Gen Robert E. Lee determined MGen George McClellan was withdrawing from the Virginia Peninsula, Lee ordered MGen Stonewall Jackson to cut MGen John Pope's line of communication along the Orange and Alexandria Railroad, threatening Washington in the process. Pope was commander of the newly formed Army of Virginia and in his address to his officers and men upon assuming command he crowed, 'Let us understand each other. I have come to you from the West, where we have always seen the backs of our enemies; from an army whose business it has been to seek the adversary, and to beat him when he was found; whose policy has been attack and not defense.' Pope's boast alienated his men, many of whom remained devoted to McClellan, and also reflected an overconfidence that did not serve Pope well in the upcoming battle.

While Pope was making his grand pronouncements, Jackson marched 92km in two days, descended upon the railroad, destroyed the Federal supply depot at Manassas Junction and occupied a strong defensive position a few kilometres west of Manassas. Still, Pope had 62,000 men compared to Jackson's 20,000, and on 29 August at about 07:00 the Federals attacked.

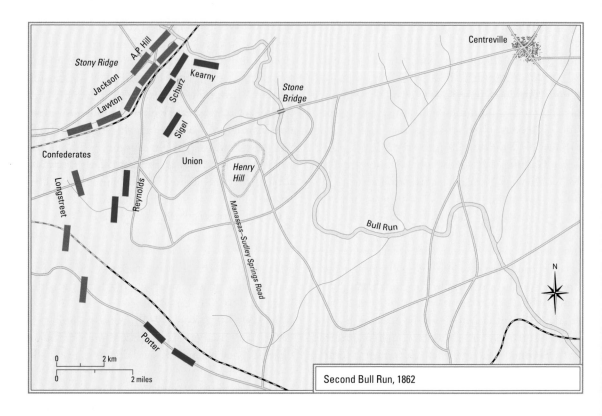

Second Bull Run, 1862

Fighting continued off and on throughout the day, but Jackson was able to absorb the series of piecemeal and uncoordinated frontal assaults from behind the protection of a railroad cut. MGen James Longstreet arrived on Jackson's right flank at about 11:00, but did not attack. Instead he brought his corps next to Jackson's, giving the Confederate line the shape of an open V along a 6.5km front facing the enemy to the east. Throughout the day, Pope had at least four opportunities to follow up a tactical success with a concerted attack. Each time he failed to send reinforcements, and Jackson held on.

Pope, who did not fully realize Longstreet was on the scene, thought Jackson had been weakened in the first day's fighting and attacked again on 30 August. Pope was unknowingly entering a trap and as Pope attacked the Confederate left, Longstreet would be able to envelop the weakened Federal left with five divisions. Pope would be caught between Jackson's anvil and

Longstreet's hammer. Adding to the Confederate firepower was the well-placed artillery of Col Stephen Lee that was able to engage the Federals throughout the attack.

By 15:00, the Federals were directly to Jackson's front, and Jackson requested General Lee to send reinforcements. Lee ordered Longstreet forward in a massive counter-attack against the exposed Federal left. Desperately, Pope threw together a makeshift defence that bought the Federals enough time to save his army. The fighting raged along Chinn Ridge for over an hour until the Federal line began to give way at about 18:00. By then, however, Pope had been able to create another line on Henry House Hill. The retention of this position allowed the Federals to escape across Bull Run via the Stone Bridge and nearby fords. By now it was getting dark, and Longstreet ended his attack. Pope withdrew his demoralized force north-east towards Washington, having suffered 14,500 casualties compared to 9500 for

Lee. The battle of Bull Run cleared northern Virginia of any major Federal presence and shifted the momentum in the eastern theatre to the Confederates. With Pope defeated and McClellan's army withdrawn behind the defences of Washington, Lee saw an opportunity to carry the war into Northern territory and began planning his Antietam Campaign.

■ GROVETON, 28 AUGUST 1862

As MGen Stonewall Jackson moved against MGen John Pope's line of communications outside Washington, Jackson fought a sharp skirmish with BGen Rufus King's division. As a result, Pope mistakenly thought Jackson was withdrawing towards the Shenandoah Valley.

■ RICHMOND, 29–30 AUGUST 1862

On 29 August, the day after Gen Braxton Bragg began moving towards Kentucky, MGen Edmund Kirby Smith ran into Federal skirmishers who withdrew to Richmond, Kentucky, after a brief engagement. The next day, Smith attacked the town and sent the Federals in full retreat. The Federals suffered 206 killed, 844 wounded and 4000 captured. Smith lost only 78 killed and 372 wounded. This important victory left Smith virtually unopposed in the territories of eastern Kentucky.

■ CHANTILLY, 1 SEPTEMBER 1862

After Second Bull Run, Gen Robert E. Lee kept the pressure on the Federals, causing MGen John Pope to withdraw to the defences of Washington. MGen Philip Kearny was the most notable Federal casualty.

■ HARPER'S FERRY, 12–15 SEPTEMBER 1862

As Gen Robert E. Lee began his Antietam Campaign, he expected the Federals to abandon their 13,000-man garrison at Harper's Ferry. Instead, they remained in place, forcing Lee to send MGen Stonewall Jackson to deal with this threat. Jackson reached Harper's Ferry on 13 September and encircled the position, but Col Dixon Miles, the Federal commander, did not surrender until 15 September. Jackson then marched to join Lee at Sharpsburg.

■ CRAMPTON'S GAP, 14 SEPTEMBER 1862

Although the Federal forces under BGen William Franklin forced the Confederate defenders from this South Mountain pass, MGen Lafayette McLaws succeeded in preventing Franklin from relieving the besieged Federals at Harper's Ferry.

■ SOUTH MOUNTAIN, 14 SEPTEMBER 1862

MGen George McClellan attacked defences at South Mountain and suffered 1813 casualties compared to 2685 for the Confederates. The slowness of McClellan's attack allowed Gen Robert E. Lee to concentrate at Sharpsburg.

■ ANTIETAM, 17 SEPTEMBER 1862

After his victory at Second Bull Run, Gen Robert E. Lee hoped to offer some relief to the Virginia countryside, influence European intervention and capitalize on Confederate sympathies by invading Maryland. On 4 September he led his 45,000 men across the Potomac river. Opposing him were some 85,000 Federals commanded by MGen George McClellan.

In the preliminary actions, Lee escaped close calls after having to divide his force to reduce Harper's Ferry and having his campaign plan accidentally fall into Federal hands. McClellan's slow responses to these opportunities allowed Lee to concentrate his force at Sharpsburg and establish a defensive line that stretched across the angle formed by the junction of the Potomac river and the Antietam Creek. The terrain favoured the defence and would allow Lee to use interior lines to move forces from one threatened location to another. McClellan's plan was to attack both Confederate flanks in a risky double envelopment and then use his reserve to attack the centre.

The Federal attack began around daybreak with MGen Joseph Hooker's striking the Confederate left. MGen Stonewall Jackson parried each of Hooker's uncoordinated assaults and Lee used the delays between attacks to reposition forces. By the time MGen Joseph Mansfield launched his echeloned attack next to Hooker's attack, Hooker's men were spent, having withdrawn to the cover of the Federal batteries in front of

Antietam, 1862

East Woods. BGen George Greene's division pierced the Confederate line, only to be stopped in front of the Dunker Church. In the centre, MGen Edwin Sumner's attack also ground to a halt as MGen John Sedgwick's division was caught in an ambush by Jackson in West Woods and BGen William French's brigade ran into strong Confederate defences in the Sunken Road, the first thousand yards of which became known as the 'Bloody Lane'. The defenders were eventually forced to withdraw from the Sunken Road, exposing a huge gap in the Confederate line. However, rather than pressing the attack, McClellan foolishly kept MGen William Franklin's and MGen Fitz John Porter's corps idle. The Federal attack had broken down into a series of piecemeal and uncoordinated assaults.

Still further to the left was perhaps the most notable example of Federal mismanagement of the battle. There, at the Rohrbach Bridge, just 550 Confederates commanded by BGen Robert

Toombs delayed 11,000 Federals under MGen Ambrose Burnside. In the nick of time, MGen A.P. Hill's hard-marching 3000-man division arrived from Harper's Ferry, having covered the 27km in seven hours. Hill attacked through a cornfield owned by John Otto, breaking the far left of Burnside's force and causing the Federals to retreat. Hill lacked the numbers to pursue, and by 17:30, the battle was over. Over the course of 12 hours of fighting, 12,400 Federals and 10,300 Confederates were casualties. It was the bloodiest single day in American military history. On the night of 18 September, Lee was forced to abandon his invasion of Maryland and retire across the Potomac.

While the battle of Antietam itself was a tactical draw, the fact that Lee was forced to withdraw back to Virginia made it effectively a strategic victory for the Federals, and that was enough to give President Abraham Lincoln the opportunity he had been waiting for to issue the Emancipation

Proclamation, a document that changed the fundamental nature of the war and made the European intervention the Confederacy hoped for highly improbable.

■ **IUKA, 19 SEPTEMBER 1862**

LGen Ulysses Grant attacked MGen Sterling Price at Iuka, hoping to trap him in a pincer between MGens William Rosecrans and E.O.C. Ord. Price escaped, suffering 1516 losses compared to 782 for the Federals.

■ **CORINTH, 3–4 OCTOBER 1862**

In early October 1862, Confederate commander MGen Earl Van Dorn attacked Federals under MGen William Rosecrans, hoping to seize Corinth's railroad junction. Van Dorn was forced to withdraw after suffering 4467 casualties, compared to 3090 for the Federals.

■ **PERRYVILLE, 7–8 OCTOBER 1862**

Climaxing Gen Braxton Bragg's invasion of Kentucky, Perryville cost the Federals 4211 casualties compared to 3396 for the Confederates. Although Bragg won a tactical victory, he was forced to withdraw from Kentucky, ending the campaign.

■ **PRAIRIE GROVE, 7 DECEMBER 1862**

MGen Thomas Hindman launched an offensive that was defeated by the combined Federal forces of BGens James Blunt and Francis Herron. The loss ended any Confederate hopes of regaining northern Arkansas. Both sides lost slightly over 1000 men.

■ **FREDERICKSBURG, 13 DECEMBER 1862**

On 7 November 1862, President Abraham Lincoln replaced MGen George McClellan with MGen Ambrose Burnside as commander of the Army of the Potomac. Within a week of assuming command, Burnside launched a new 'On to Richmond' campaign. The plan was to slide past Gen Robert E. Lee's right flank and cross the Rappahannock river at Fredericksburg, about 80km north of Richmond. Burnside would have to cross the Rappahannock quickly before the Confederates could oppose him in force. In order to cross the river, Burnside needed to build a pontoon bridge, but the necessary materials

did not arrive until December. By then Lee had plenty of time to concentrate in and around the town. This development made Burnside's plan obsolete, but he continued with it anyway.

On 11 December the Federals began crossing the river. Lee did not contest the town, leaving just BGen William Barksdale and 1600 Mississippians there to slow the Federal advance while the main Confederate defence was based on the nearly impregnable positions on Marye's Heights just west of Fredericksburg. There Lee had some 20,000 men under MGen James Longstreet behind a stone wall at the crest of the ridge.

On 13 December, Burnside made six major assaults against Marye's Heights. All failed, but the constricted battlefield prevented Lee from counter-attacking the weakened Federal army. The Federals lost more than 12,500 men while the Confederates fewer than 5500. After the defeat, Burnside attempted to move upstream and cross at Banks' Ford on 23 January 1863, but heavy rains produced a two-day 'Mud March' that stymied the offensive. Amid mounting complaints from his subordinates, Burnside returned to camp near Fredericksburg.

■ **CHICKASAW BLUFFS, 27–29 DECEMBER 1862**

While Confederate cavalry raids forced MGen Ulysses Grant to turn back his supporting attack, MGen William Sherman was repulsed in a front assault in this effort to reach Vicksburg. Sherman lost 1776 casualties, compared to 187 for the Confederates.

■ **STONES RIVER, 31 DECEMBER 1862–2 JANUARY 1863**

After withdrawing from Kentucky, Gen Braxton Bragg established a position alongside the Nashville to Chattanooga railroad line at Murfreesboro, Tennessee. MGen William Rosecrans replaced MGen Don Carlos Buell as the Federal commander and slowly built up his readiness. After amassing a huge logistical base at Nashville, Rosecrans finally began advancing on 26 December. On the night of 29 December the two armies of 44,000 Federals and 37,000

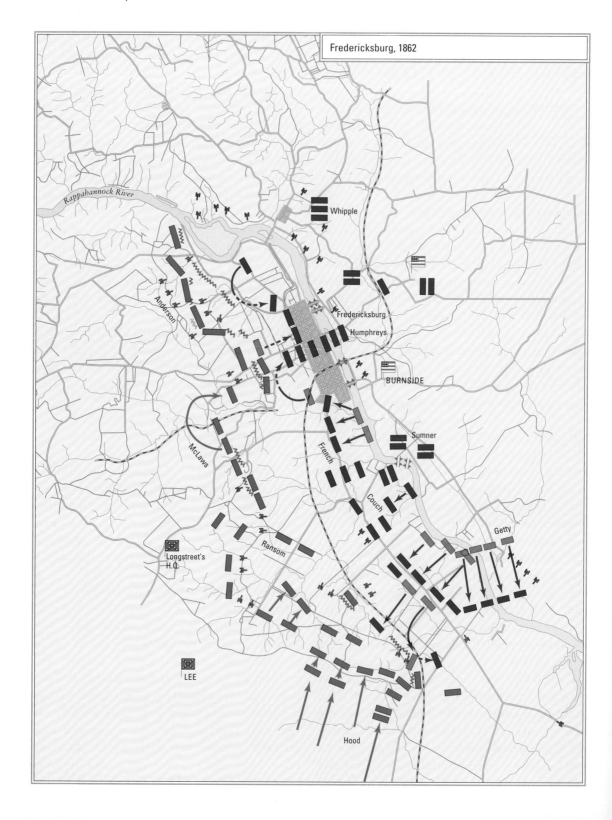

Fredericksburg, 1862

Confederates were camped within earshot of each other. Rosecrans had ordered an attack at 07:00, after his men finished breakfast, on 31 December, but before he could put the plan in motion, Bragg struck the Federal right flank in a surprise attack. The Federals repulsed two Confederate attacks, but a third attack succeeded in enveloping the Federal flank. BGen Philip Sheridan counter-attacked and re-established a new Federal line, but a fourth attack all along the Federal front eventually forced Sheridan to withdraw. However, subsequent Confederate attacks were all turned back. Fighting was especially fierce in the Round Forest, where MGen John Breckinridge's Confederates battled Col William Hazen's Federals in an area that became known as 'Hell's Half Acre'.

Both armies were silent on 1 January, and then Bragg renewed the attack, hitting the Federal left on 2 January. The Confederate attack was slow in developing and was defeated by the massed fire of 58 Federal artillery pieces, which had been posted by Maj John Mendenhall. Confederate losses were 11,739 out of a total of 34,739 engaged, while the Federals suffered 12,906 casualties out of 41,400 soldiers engaged. Although Bragg had scored a tactical victory, his army was physically exhausted, and he fell back 50km to Tullahoma. Rosecrans also was spent and did not resume operations until June.

■ ARKANSAS POST, 10–11 JANUARY 1863

A land and naval attack by MGen John McClernand and Adm David Porter forced the surrender of this Confederate strongpoint 80km up the Arkansas river from Vicksburg. Most of the 5000 Confederate defenders were captured.

■ CHARLESTON, 27 APRIL 1863

Adm Samuel Du Pont's plan to run past the in-depth defences of Charleston Harbor was foiled by Confederate obstacles and fire. The failure led Du Pont to conclude Charleston could not be taken by naval action alone.

■ PORT GIBSON, 1 MAY 1863

MGen Ulysses Grant began an unopposed crossing of the Mississippi river at Bruinsburg on 30 April.

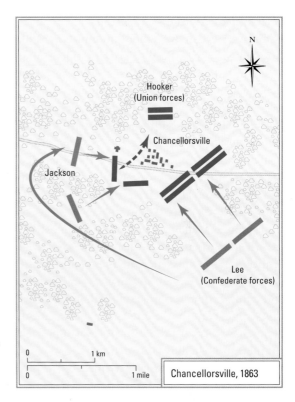

Chancellorsville, 1863

BGen John Bowen attempted to halt Grant's advance inland, but Grant brushed this small force aside and established a foothold at Port Gibson.

■ CHANCELLORSVILLE, 1–4 MAY 1863

After receiving a report from MGen Jeb Stuart that MGen Joseph Hooker's 'flank was in the air', Gen Robert E. Lee sent LGen Stonewall Jackson on a 17km route to the Federal flank. When Jackson attacked, the Federal line collapsed, causing Hooker to panic and withdraw north of Chancellorsville. Lee inflicted 17,000 casualties while suffering 13,000 himself, but among the Confederate losses was the invaluable commander Stonewall Jackson.

■ SALEM CHURCH, 3–4 MAY 1863

In the midst of LGen Stonewall Jackson's success at Chancellorsville, MGen John Sedgwick defeated MGen Jubal Early at Fredericksburg and began moving west. BGen General Cadmus Wilcox and an ad hoc Confederate force stopped Sedgwick at Salem Church.

■ **VICKSBURG, 19 MAY–4 JULY 1863**

After a series of five failed attempts to break through to Vicksburg between December 1862 and March 1863, MGen Ulysses Grant marched south down the Louisiana side of the Mississippi river and made an unopposed crossing at Bruinsburg on 30 April. Grant's forces closed on Vicksburg on 19 May after a brilliant campaign of manoeuvre that included victories at Port Gibson, Raymond, Jackson and Champion Hill. After two failed assaults on 19 and 22 May, Grant began a siege of Vicksburg. Grant and Confederate commander LGen John Pemberton had similarly sized armies, but the presence of the Federal navy gave Grant a decided advantage. On 25 June and 1 July, Federal troops exploded mines under the Confederate positions, but made no more general assaults. Instead, the city was subjected to incessant shelling throughout the 47-day siege. The Confederate surrender on 4 July gave the Federals control of the Mississippi river and served to split the Confederacy into eastern and western halves.

■ **JACKSON, 14 MAY 1863**

On May 13, MGen Ulysses Grant sent commanders William Sherman and James McPherson on two separate axes toward Jackson. The Federals attacked the next day, capturing the city with little resistance and destroying anything of military value.

■ **CHAMPION HILL, 16 MAY 1863**

During this decisive battle of the Vicksburg campaign, MGen Ulysses Grant forced LGen John Pemberton to retreat to the defences of Vicksburg and surrender initiative to Grant. Grant suffered 2441 casualties compared to 3851 for Pemberton.

■ **BIG BLACK RIVER, 17 MAY 1863**

After his defeat at Champion Hill, LGen John Pemberton retreated to the east side of the Big Black River. MG John McClernand attacked Pemberton, but the Confederates escaped to the defences of Vicksburg.

■ **PORT HUDSON, 27 MAY–9 JULY 1863**

This Confederate stronghold withstood repeated land and naval attacks and finally surrendered after a siege. The capture of Port Hudson, along with the earlier victory at Vicksburg, left the Federals in complete control of the Mississippi.

■ **FRANKLIN'S CROSSING, 5 JUNE 1863**

MGen Joseph Hooker ordered reconnaissance to determine Gen Robert E. Lee's location as Lee began his Gettysburg campaign. The Federals suffered 41 casualties and captured 35 prisoners in forcing the Confederates from this site.

■ **BRANDY STATION, 9 JUNE 1863**

After his victory at Chancellorsville, Gen Robert E. Lee pushed north for his Gettysburg campaign behind MGen Jeb Stuart's cavalry screen. In order to determine Lee's dispositions, MGen Joseph Hooker dispatched a cavalry reconnaissance led by MGen Alfred Pleasonton. Pleasonton attacked across the Rappahannock River at 04:00 in two columns. MGen John Buford struck Confederates under BGen W.E. 'Grumble' Jones from across Beverly Ford. Some 10km downstream at Kelly's Ford, BGen David Gregg also attacked. Although Stuart was initially surprised, a counterattack by MG Wade Hampton helped the Confederates maintain control of the battlefield. The Confederates were also helped by the fact that Col Alfred Duffie, a Frenchman who was supposed to attack with Gregg, was delayed in a fight with Confederates at Stevensburg, 9km to the south. Duffie did not reach Brandy Station in time to participate in the battle. Although Federal infantry was on the field and Confederate infantry was moving to it, Brandy Station was predominantly a cavalry battle. In fact, it was the biggest cavalry battle of the war. Overall, the battle of Brandy Station was tactically inconclusive, with the Confederates suffering 523 losses compared to 936 for the Federals. However, Pleasonton had succeeded in learning the Confederate whereabouts, and Stuart had failed his screening mission. It was a humiliation for Stuart, and many consider his ill-advised extended reconnaissance at Gettysburg to have been an attempt to repair his reputation after this setback. The battle is also considered a turning point at which Confederate cavalry no longer dominated their Federal counterparts in the Eastern Theatre.

■ Winchester, 13–15 June 1863

As the Army of Northern Virginia moved north on the Gettysburg campaign, MG Richard Ewell soundly defeated MGen Robert Milroy. The Federals lost 4443 in the disaster, compared to just 269 for Ewell.

■ Gettysburg, 1–3 July 1863

Building on the momentum of his victory at Chancellorsville, Gen Robert E. Lee launched a second invasion of Northern territory. In the meantime, President Abraham Lincoln replaced MGen Joseph Hooker with MGen George Meade on 28 June. Lee advanced north into Pennsylvania virtually unopposed, but because MGen Jeb Stuart, Lee's eyes and ears, had gone on an ill-advised raid around the Federal army, Lee was ignorant of the Federal dispositions. By 30 June, Lee had gathered most of his army in the area of Chambersburg, Cashtown and Heidlersburg. Meade had been pushing his army north, staying to the east of Lee's army in order to protect Washington and Baltimore. On 30 June, Meade advised MGen John Reynolds that it seemed Lee would concentrate his forces near the small town of Gettysburg. Reynolds thus sent BGen John Buford and two cavalry brigades toward Gettysburg to find Lee.

On 1 July, Buford encountered a Confederate brigade that had marched to Gettysburg in search of some shoes reported to be there. A meeting engagement ensued in which both Lee and Meade competed to rush forces to the location. Because the Confederates were closer, Lee was able to gain the upper hand. However, MGen Oliver Howard wisely occupied Cemetery Hill for the Federals. This hill on the north end of Cemetery Ridge dominated the approaches to Gettysburg and would be key to any defensive effort. Receiving

only a discretionary order from Lee, LGen Richard Ewell did not attack the position, giving the Federals a critical piece of terrain.

Lee wanted to press the advantage he had gained in the first day's fighting, and, over the objections of LGen James Longstreet, who favoured assuming a strong defensive position, Lee ordered an attack against the left of the Federal line in the vicinity of the Little and Big Round Tops on 2 July. Longstreet did not attack until 16:30 and by then Meade had rushed defenders to Little Round Top. After hard fighting, the Federals retained the key hill and the second day of the battle ended in a stalemate.

Having struck the Federal right the first day and the left the second, Lee now resolved to attack the Federal centre on 3 July. At 13:00 the Confederates initiated a 172-gun pre-assault bombardment, but most of the rounds sailed over the heads of the Federal defenders on Cemetery Ridge. With the Federal line still largely intact, MGen George Picket began his charge at about 13:45. His men met a devastating fire from the Federal artillery, and gaps soon appeared in the Confederate line. BGen Lewis Armistead led his men to the 'High Water Mark of the Confederacy', but MGen Winfield Scott Hancock repulsed the attack, and the scattered remnants of 'Pickett's Charge' staggered back across the field. The attack had caused 54 per cent losses to the Confederates. As Pickett's beaten men fell back, Lee said, 'It's all my fault.'

Although Meade had defeated Lee, it had been a close call, and Meade was in no mood to press his victory. Both sides had been badly hurt, with Lee suffering 28,063 losses and Meade 23,049. In spite of urgings by President Lincoln, Meade allowed Lee to withdraw back into Virginia, ending his second invasion of the North. The defeat cost Lee manpower he could ill-afford to lose and ended his ability to launch further offensives.

■ Fort Wagner, 10 & 18 July 1863

The Federals launched multiple attacks on this position guarding the land approach to Charleston

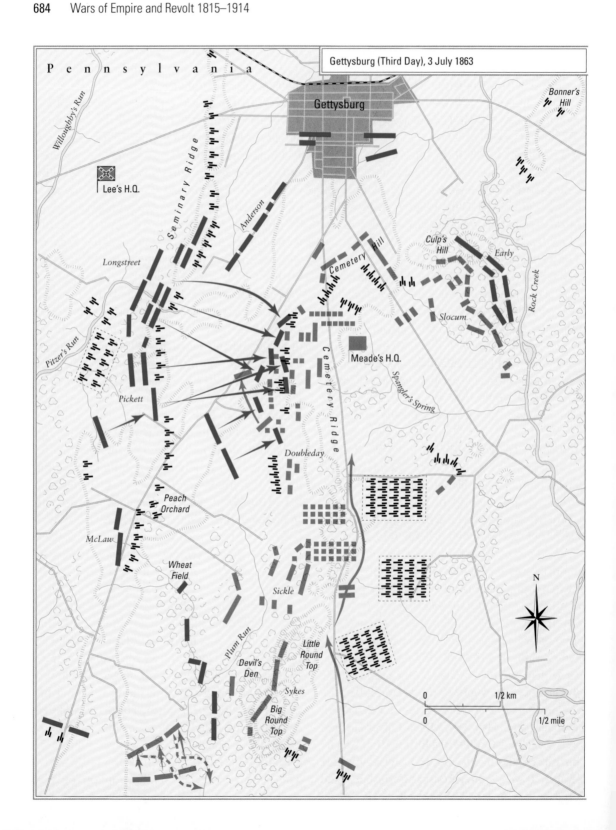

Gettysburg (Third Day), 3 July 1863

Pennsylvania

Bonner's Hill

Gettysburg

Lee's H.Q.

Seminary Ridge

Anderson

Longstreet

Culp's Hill

Early

Cemetery Hill

Rock Creek

Slocum

Pitzer's Run

Cemetery Ridge

Meade's H.Q.

Spangler's Spring

Pickett

Doubleday

Peach Orchard

McLaw

Wheat Field

Sickle

N

Plum Run

Little Round Top

Devil's Den

Sykes

Big Round Top

0   1/2 km

0   1/2 mile

from Morris Island. In the famous 18 July attack, the Federals suffered 1515 casualties compared to 174 for the Confederates.

■ **CHICKAMAUGA, 19–20 SEPTEMBER 1863**
Enjoying the rare advantage of numerical superiority, Gen Braxton Bragg inflicted 16,170 casualties on MGen William Rosecrans while suffering 18,454 of his own. Then, instead of aggressively pursuing, Bragg laid siege to Rosecrans in Chattanooga.

■ **BULLTOWN, 13 OCTOBER 1863**
Confederates led by Col William Jackson attempted to capture the small fort overlooking the Little Kanawha river in West Virginia. Jackson was repulsed after suffering light casualties. The Federals were commanded by Capt William Mattingly.

■ **BRISTOE STATION, 14 OCTOBER 1863**
Misinterpreting the size of the Federal force, LGen A.P. Hill was soundly defeated by Federal forces defending behind the Orange and Alexandria Railroad embankment. The Confederates lost 1428 men compared to 446 for the Federals.

■ **CHATTANOOGA, 23–25 NOVEMBER 1863**
In a pivotal campaign in which the Federals lost 5800 and the Confederates 6700, MGen Ulysses Grant forced Gen Braxton Bragg to retreat to Dalton, Georgia, opening the gateway to the heartland of the Confederacy.

■ **ORCHARD KNOB/INDIAN HILL, 23 NOVEMBER 1863**
BGen Thomas Wood and MGen Philip Sheridan drove in Confederate outposts on Orchard Knob, a low ridge between Chattanooga and Missionary Ridge. Gen Braxton Bragg then reinforced the extreme right of his line.

■ **LOOKOUT MOUNTAIN, 24 NOVEMBER 1863**
MGen Joseph Hooker attacked the Confederate left at Lookout Mountain to the south of Chattanooga. MGen Carter Stevenson commanded the defence. Hooker won this 'Battle above the Clouds', suffering 710 casualties and inflicting 521 on the Confederates.

■ **MISSIONARY RIDGE, 25 NOVEMBER 1863**
MGen Ulysses Grant ordered MGen George

Thomas to create a diversion in the centre of the Confederate defence outside Chattanooga to allow MGen William Sherman to continue making progress to the left. Thomas's attack was supposed to be just a limited one, but individual soldiers seized the initiative and turned the operation into a full-scale attack. Gen Braxton Bragg was forced to withdraw, ending the siege of Chattanooga.

■ **KNOXVILLE, 17 NOVEMBER–5 DECEMBER 1863**
After a rearguard action at Campbell's Station, MGen Ambrose Burnside withdrew to the fortifications around Knoxville, Tennessee. LGen James Longstreet began a siege which he abandoned after the Federal victory at Chattanooga.

■ **OLUSTEE, 20 FEBRUARY 1864**
After an unopposed landing at Jacksonville, Florida, BGen Truman Seymour advanced inland to Baldwin where he was joined by MGen Quincy Gillmore. Seymour met little resistance until approaching BGen Joseph Finnegan's 5000 Confederates entrenched near Olustee. After driving in Finnegan's outposts, Seymour incurred heavy losses as Finnegan launched several attacks. Seymour retreated back to Jacksonville, having suffered 1860 casualties. Finnegan, who had lost 946 of his own men, did not pursue.

■ **SABINE CROSSROADS/PLEASANT HILL, 9 APRIL 1864**
MGen Nathaniel Banks advanced some 240km up the Red river, forcing LGen Richard Taylor to withdraw to defensive positions 5km southeast of Mansfield, Louisiana, at Sabine Crossroads. Taylor was an independent-minded subordinate, and, without coordinating with his commander Gen Edmund Kirby Smith, he attacked Banks' advancing force at Mansfield on 8 April. Although Taylor was unsuccessful in his effort to turn the Federal right, he did force Banks to withdraw to Pleasant Hill, where Taylor attacked him the next day. Although Taylor was outnumbered, he expected the Federals to be demoralized and cautious after the fighting at Mansfield. He attacked at 17:00, hoping to fix the Federals with

a frontal attack while another attack led by BGen Thomas Churchill enveloped the left flank and Taylor's cavalry blocked the escape route on the right. Churchill succeeded in breaking the Federal left, but as he pressed on to attack the Federal centre from the rear, his right flank came under attack. Taylor ordered BGen C.J. Polignac's reserve brigade forward to stop the Federal counter-attack, but Polignac did not arrive in time. Instead, Polignac acted as a covering force while Churchill retreated. In spite of this victory, Banks began withdrawing from west Louisiana, abandoning his objective of capturing Shreveport for fear of suffering further damage to his army. Although he had repulsed Banks, Taylor complained that Smith's unwillingness to concentrate his forces prevented the annihilation of the Federal army. The Federals suffered 2000 losses compared to 1100 for the Confederates. After the battle, the Confederates left a cavalry force to screen Banks's men entrenched at Grand

Ecore and began moving against MGen Frederick Steele in Arkansas.

■ **FORT PILLOW, 12 APRIL 1864**
MGen Nathan Bedford Forrest surrounded this position in Lauderdale County, Tennessee, and, when the Federals refused to surrender, Forrest attacked. During the overwhelming Confederate victory, Forrest's men were accused of massacring black soldiers after they had surrendered.

■ **ALEXANDRIA, 1–8 MAY 1864**
In a series of actions, Confederate forces, including BGen J.P. Major's cavalry, harassed MGen Nathaniel Banks during his Red river campaign, destroying five Federal boats and blocking the Red River between 4 and 13 May.

■ **WILDERNESS, 5–7 MAY 1864**
As part of his comprehensive strategy to press the Confederacy on all fronts, LGen Ulysses Grant crossed the Rapidan river on 4 May 1864, into an area of Virginia appropriately called the Wilderness. Neither side knew the other's exact

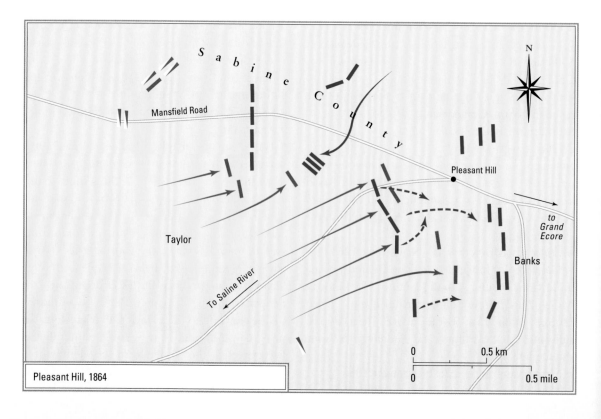

Pleasant Hill, 1864

location until 5 May, when the Federals made contact with LGen Richard Ewell's corps and launched a hasty attack which the Confederates halted. When the fighting resumed the next day at 05:00, Gen Robert E. Lee used the restrictive terrain to offset Grant's numerical advantage. The thick vegetation made the battle a small-unit fight. At one point, Lee vowed personally to lead BGen John Gregg's Texas Brigade into the fray, only to be dissuaded by the men's passionate pleas of 'Lee to the rear'. Although Lee scored a tactical victory, inflicting 17,000 Federal casualties compared to 10,000 of his own, the Confederacy could ill-afford the lost manpower.

■ SPOTSYLVANIA, 7–12 MAY 1864

In spite of his defeat at the Wilderness, LGen Ulysses Grant continued to keep pressure on the Confederates. Grant began a march to flank Gen Robert E. Lee and cut him off at Spotsylvania Courthouse. Lee ascertained Grant's intentions

and narrowly beat Grant to the strategic location. Once there, Lee established a defence, the flanks of which Grant probed on 9 and 10 May without success. During the attack on 10 May, Grant took notice of a technique used by Col Emory Upton to attack in column formation against a salient in the Confederate line known as the 'Mule Shoe'. Upton had not been able to hold his original gains because of a lack of troops, but Grant saw promise in the new tactic. He decided to send MGen Winfield Scott Hancock's entire corps against the Mule Shoe. On 12 May at 04:30, a massed attack of 20,000 Federals advanced, and in just 15 minutes they were pouring through gaps in the Confederate lines. Hancock captured 4000 Confederate prisoners. In a desperate attempt to restore the breach, Lee counter-attacked and succeeded in completing a new line of entrenchments across the base of the salient. For nearly 20 hours the ferocious fighting continued almost without pause. The contested

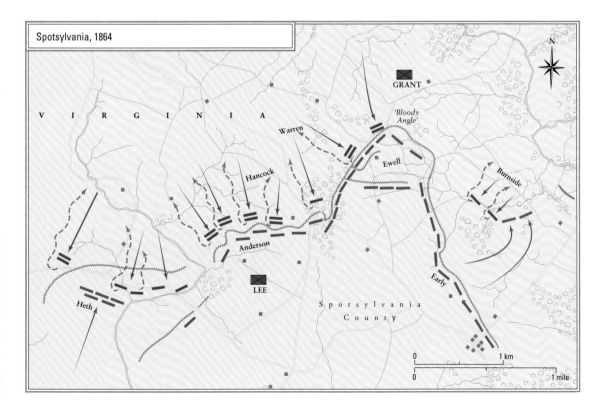

Spotsylvania, 1864

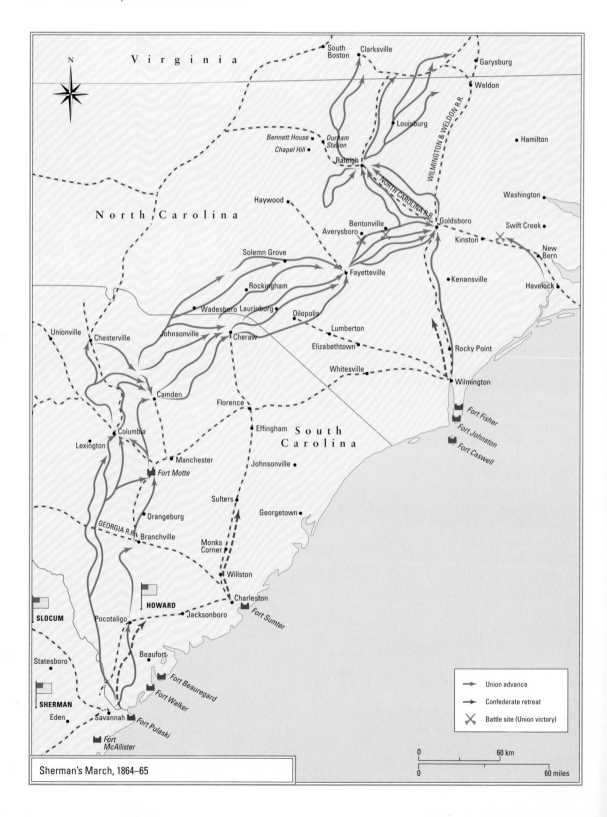

Sherman's March, 1864–65

area became known as 'the Bloody Angle'. There was more inconclusive fighting on 18 and 19 May, but the Confederate line held. Fighting mostly behind the protection of entrenchments, Lee suffered just 12,000 casualties compared to Grant's 18,000. Among the Federal losses was MGen John Sedgwick. Lee withdrew on 20 May to a new position at Hanover Junction, thwarting another attempted turning movement by Grant.

■ YELLOW TAVERN, 11 MAY 1864

MGen Jeb Stuart attempted to block MGen Philip Sheridan's raid toward Richmond. Sheridan overran the Confederates, but decided to move to the James river rather than continuing to Richmond. Stuart was mortally wounded in the fighting.

■ RESACA, 13–16 MAY 1864

As MGen William Sherman began his Atlanta campaign, Gen Joseph Johnston withdrew from Rocky Face Ridge to the hills to the north and west of Resaca before becoming decisively engaged. Sherman attacked Johnston's new position, and the fighting was inconclusive until Sherman sent a force across the Oostanula river at Lay's Ferry that threatened Johnston's railroad communications with Calhoun. Johnston then withdrew, having suffered 2800 casualties compared to 2747 for Sherman.

■ NEW MARKET, 15 MAY 1864

MGen Franz Sigel's advance up the Shenandoah Valley was challenged by MGen John Breckinridge whose force included a battalion of cadets from the Virginia Military Institute. Sigel was forced to retreat to Strasburg.

■ DREWRY'S BLUFF, 16 MAY 1864

MGen Benjamin Butler landed at Bermuda Hundred and began advancing towards Richmond. Gen Pierre Gustave Toutant Beauregard attacked, forcing Butler to withdraw and leaving him 'bottled up' on the peninsula between the Appomattox and James rivers.

■ NORTH ANNA RIVER, 23–27 MAY 1864

Although Gen Robert E. Lee's novel defensive

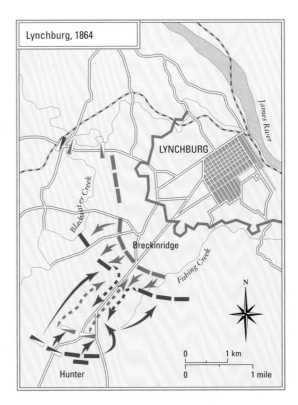

configuration forced LGen Ulysses Grant to split his army in three places, Lee was unable to capitalize on this advantage and Grant withdrew across the North Anna river.

■ NEW HOPE CHURCH, 25–27 MAY 1864

MGen William Sherman marched around Gen Joseph Johnston's left flank, heading towards Dallas. Johnston intercepted Sherman at New Hope Church. Thinking Johnston had only a token force, Sherman attacked and was easily repulsed.

■ COLD HARBOR, 3 JUNE 1864

LGen Ulysess Grant outnumbered Gen Robert E. Lee 108,000 to 59,000, but the Confederates delivered enfilading fire from carefully prepared trenches. Grant lost 7000 men in a disastrous frontal attack while Lee lost only 1500.

■ PIEDMONT, 5 JUNE 1864

MGen David Hunter replaced MGen Franz Sigel after Sigel's defeat at New Market and renewed the Federal offensive in the Shenandoah Valley. As

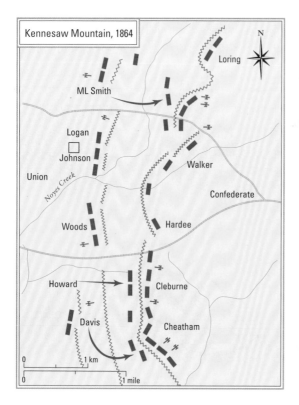

Kennesaw Mountain, 1864

Loring

ML Smith

Logan

Johnson

Union

Walker

Confederate

Noyes Creek

Woods

Hardee

Howard

Cleburne

Davis

Cheatham

0   1 km
0   1 mile

Hunter advanced, he divided his force to avoid BGen W.E. 'Grumble' Jones's defensive position en route to Staunton. In order to prevent the two Federal columns from reuniting, Jones attacked Hunter, only to be driven back to defensive positions at Piedmont, about 11km south-west of Port Republic. Amid attacks and counter-attacks, the Confederates were routed and Jones was killed. Hunter entered Staunton unopposed the next day. After he was joined by BGen George Crook, Hunter marched to Lynchburg, destroying much military and public property as he went. Among the targets of Hunter's rampage was the Virginia Military Institute, which he ordered burned on 12 June. Federal losses at Piedmont were 875 compared to 1500 for the Confederates.

■ Brice's Crossroads, 10 June 1864

LGen Nathan Bedford Forrest soundly defeated BGen Samuel Sturgis, inflicting 2610 casualties compared to just 495 of his own. In spite of the defeat, Sturgis succeeded in distracting

Forrest from MGen William Sherman's lines of communication.

■ Trevilian Station, 11–12 June 1864

LGen Ulysses Grant hoped to create a diversion and draw off the Confederate cavalry while he crossed the James river to attack Petersburg. He ordered MGen Philip Sheridan to cut the Virginia Central Railroad. Gen Robert E. Lee sent MGen Wade Hampton to meet this serious threat. Fighting on 11 June was inconclusive, but when Sheridan attacked the next day, he was repulsed with heavy losses and forced to abandon his campaign.

■ Lynchburg, 17–18 June 1864

After his victory at Piedmont, MGen David Hunter advanced to the important rail centre at Lynchburg. Gen Robert E. Lee dispatched LGen Jubal Early to the Shenandoah Valley to reinforce MGen John Breckinridge. The Confederate forces defeated Hunter's attack on Lynchburg, preventing him from joining MGen Philip Sheridan for Sheridan's Trevilian Raid. After the defeat, Hunter withdrew to West Virginia, opening the way for Early's advance into Maryland.

■ Petersburg, 19 June 1864–13 April 1865

Unable to turn Gen Robert E. Lee's flank and break through to Richmond, LGen Ulysses Grant decided to shift his line of advance south of the James river and use the river as his line of supply for an advance on Petersburg, about 32km south of Richmond. Petersburg was a shipping port as well as a rail centere and many of the supplies headed for both Richmond and Lee's army passed through there, making it critical to the survival of the Army of Northern Virginia. Once Grant decided to shift his line of advance, he got a jump on Lee, crossing the James river and reaching Petersburg while it was still defended by only a skeleton Confederate force. Grant launched an uncoordinated attack with his entire army on 18 June 1864, but was repulsed. By then Lee had arrived with reinforcements. The next day Grant began what would become the longest siege of the war.

During the siege, Grant built up a huge logistical base at City Point that benefited from outstanding rail and water communications. Grant had access to excellent supply, repair and medical facilities to help sustain his force. The result was that as Lee weakened inside Petersburg, Grant grew stronger outside. Pressing this advantage, Grant kept extending his lines to the west. When MGen Philip Sheridan joined Grant from the Shenandoah Valley, Grant gave him an infantry corps and told him to break Lee's western flank. In the ensuing battle of Five Forks on 1 April 1865, Sheridan pressed Lee, and Grant then ordered a general attack all along the Petersburg front. Faced with this threat, Lee was forced to abandon Petersburg, and the city fell on 3 April. Grant's men suffered 42,000 casualties compared to 28,000 for Lee.

■ KENNESAW MOUNTAIN, 27 JUNE 1864

MGen Sherman deviated from his series of turning movements en route to Atlanta and was soundly defeated by Gen Joseph Johnston in a disastrous frontal attack. Sherman lost about 3000 compared to 1000 for Johnston.

■ MONOCACY, 9 JULY 1864

With LGen Jubal Early advancing on Washington, MGen Lew Wallace rushed a hastily organized defence to Monocacy Junction, Maryland. Although the Federals suffered 1880 casualties compared to just 700 for the Confederates, the threat to the capital subsided.

■ TUPELO, 13–15 JULY 1864

Attempting to prevent LGen Nathan Bedford Forrest from interfering with MGen William Sherman's Atlanta campaign, MGen Andrew Jackson Smith was engaged by the combined forces of Forrest and LGen Stephen Lee and forced to withdraw towards Memphis.

■ PEACHTREE CREEK, 20 JULY 1864

Exasperated by Gen Joseph Johnston's failure to make a stand north of Atlanta, President Jefferson Davis replaced him with the combative LGen John Bell Hood. With Sherman closing in from the north and east, Hood ordered an attack as MGen George Thomas crossed Peachtree Creek.

After a series of failed assaults, Hood was forced to withdraw to the defences of Atlanta, having suffered 4796 casualties compared to 1710 for the Federals.

■ ATLANTA, 22 JULY 1864

As part of LGen Ulyssess Grant's coordinated strategy for the spring of 1864, MGen William Sherman was directed 'to move against [Confederate Gen Joseph] Johnston's army, to break it up, and to get into the interior of the enemy's country as far as you can, inflicting all the damage you can against their war resources.' Atlanta, with its vital supply, manufacturing and transportation assets, was such an objective. Johnston fought a retrograde battle from Dalton, Georgia, to the outskirts of Atlanta until he was relieved by President Jefferson Davis and replaced with the more aggressive and impulsive LGen John Bell Hood. In a desperate attempt to keep Sherman from taking Atlanta, Hood launched the battle of Peach Tree Creek on 20 July. Repulsed, Hood attacked again on 22 July. All told, Hood suffered 8499 casualties and failed to break the Federal line. MGen John McPherson was among the 3641 Federal casualties.

■ KERNSTOWN, 23–24 JULY 1864

LGen Jubal Early attacked a weakened Federal force commanded by BGen George Crook after Early withdrew from the outskirts of Washington on 12 July. Crook suffered 1200 casualties and was forced to retreat across the Potomac river.

■ CRATER, 30 JULY 1864

In a bungled attempt to break the stalemate at Petersburg, LGen Ulysses Grant detonated an explosion under the Confederate position. The Confederates inflicted 5300 casualties on the Federals while suffering just 1032.

■ MOBILE BAY, 5 AUGUST 1864

Adm David Farragut's attack on one of the few Confederate ports still open to blockade runners was challenged by a series of well-placed forts, the ironclad CSS *Tennessee* and a dangerous minefield. When Farragut's ironclad *Tecumseh* struck a torpedo and went down swiftly, Farragut famously

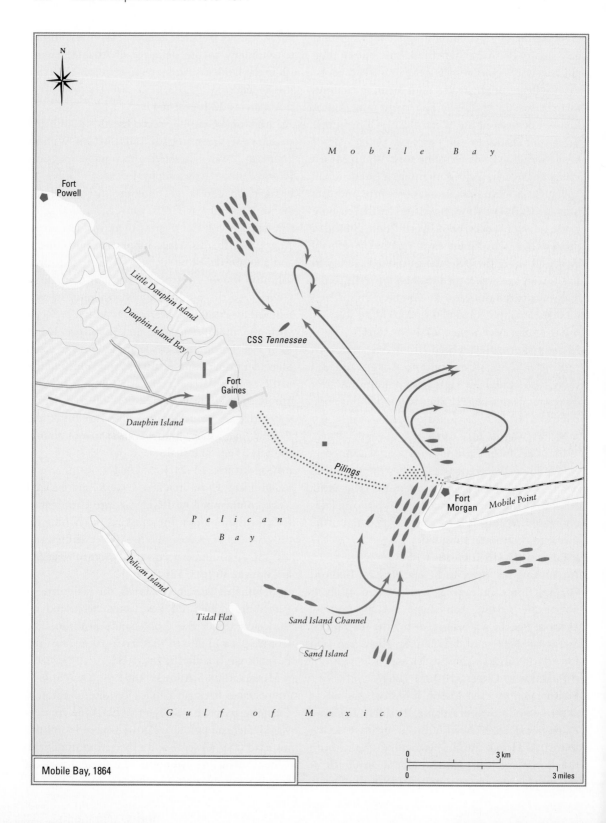

Mobile Bay, 1864

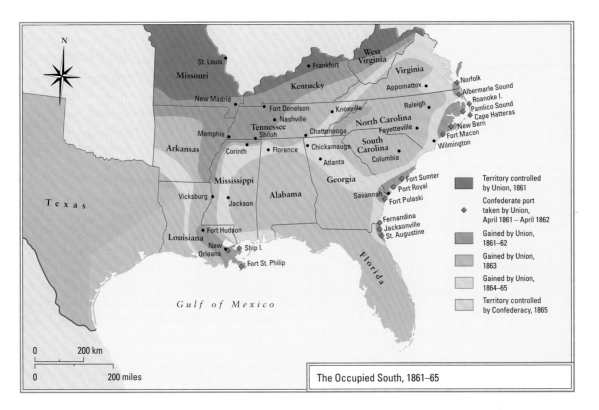

The Occupied South, 1861–65

Territory controlled by Union, 1861	
Confederate port taken by Union, April 1861 – April 1862	
Gained by Union, 1861–62	
Gained by Union, 1863	
Gained by Union, 1864–65	
Territory controlled by Confederacy, 1865	

declared, 'Damn the torpedoes! Full speed ahead.' As the Federal fleet pressed forward, its starboard batteries unloaded on Fort Morgan. The Confederates hit some of the ships, but Farragut was able to complete his run past the fort. His main threat now was the *Tennessee*, commanded by Adm Franklin Buchanan. The Tennessee withstood repeated Federal broadsides, but with only six hours of coal left, Buchanan was forced to attack. As Buchanan approached, Farragut ordered his fleet to descend on the *Tennessee*, and after a spirited fight, Buchanan was forced to surrender. The Federals suffered 319 casualties in the brief naval battle, including 93 who drowned when the *Tecumseh* sank. The percentage of Confederate naval personnel lost was much higher with 312 casualties of the 470 engaged.

The Confederate forts held out only slightly longer against Federals commanded by BGen Gordon Granger. The Confederates abandoned tiny Fort Powell, blowing it up as they departed.

Fort Gaines mustered a faint-hearted show of resistance and then surrendered the next day on 8 August. Fort Morgan was a stronger defence, but BGen Richard Page had only 400 men to oppose Granger's 5500. After receiving a siege train from New Orleans, the Federals began a heavy land and naval bombardment. The Confederate defenders raised a white flag over Fort Morgan on 22 August. The Federals captured 1464 prisoners.

■ WINCHESTER, 19 SEPTEMBER 1864
MGen Philip Sheridan used some 40,000 men to attack LGen Jubal Early's 11,500 Confederates positioned to the north and east of Winchester. The Federals suffered 5020 casualties compared to 3610 for the Confederates. Early then withdrew past Strasburg.

■ FISHER'S HILL, 21–22 SEPTEMBER 1864
After Winchester, LGen Jubal Early took up a defensive position south of Strasburg, which he was forced to abandon when MGen Philip Sheridan attacked. The battle opened the

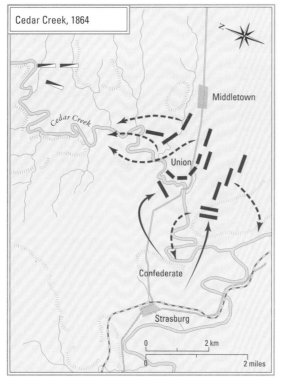

Cedar Creek, 1864

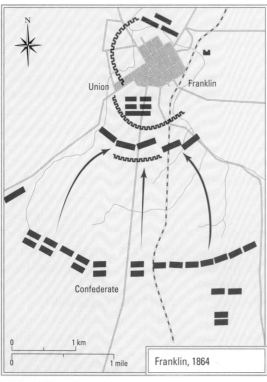

Franklin, 1864

unfortunate Shenandoah Valley to Sheridan's scorched-earth tactics.

■ **CENTRALIA, 27 SEPTEMBER 1864**

'Bloody Bill' Anderson, a notorious Confederate bushwacker, unleashed a massacre on this Missouri town 80km north of Jefferson City. Anderson captured a train and murdered 24 unarmed soldiers. He also defeated a Federal attack 5km from the town.

■ **CEDAR CREEK, 19 OCTOBER 1864**

After his success in the Shenandoah Valley, MGen Philip Sheridan began preparing to join LGen Ulysses Grant against Gen Robert E. Lee. While Sheridan was at a conference in Washington, LGen Jubal Early crossed the Shenandoah river at Fisher's Hill and attacked the surprised Federals along Cedar Creek. Sheridan rushed back from Washington and reversed Early's initial success. The Federals suffered 5665 casualties and the Confederates 2910.

■ **SPRING HILL, 29 NOVEMBER 1864**

Gen John Bell Hood missed his best chance to damage MGen John Schofield's army as it moved from Columbia to Franklin. Instead, Hood made his disastrous attack on Franklin the next day.

■ **FRANKLIN, 30 NOVEMBER 1864**

LGen John Bell Hood evacuated Atlanta on 1 September 1864, and the Federals moved in to occupy the city the next morning. Hood then marched north into Tennessee, hoping to recover middle Tennessee and force MGen William Sherman to abandon Atlanta by threatening his communications. Rather than following Hood in force, Sherman dispatched only MGen George Thomas' corps. Contrary to LGen Grant's desire that he attack, the methodical Thomas opted to delay Hood, who succeeded in turning MGen John Schofield's position near Columbia, Tennessee. By 30 November, Schofield had taken up a position at Franklin, about 50km south of Nashville. The wisest course would have been to execute another turning movement, but instead the impetuous Hood attacked in a disastrous frontal assault. Hood lost more than 6000 men, as well as whatever limited offensive capability he had once had. He withdrew his 30,000 men to the outskirts of Nashville, a place occupied by 70,000 entrenched Federals.

■ NASHVILLE, 15 DECEMBER 1864

MGen George Thomas launched a massive flank attack from his entrenched position that overwhelmed the Confederates. After suffering 4500 casualties, Gen John Bell Hood retreated to Tupelo, Mississippi, and asked to be relieved of command.

■ SAVANNAH, 21 DECEMBER 1864

MGen William Sherman reached Savannah on 10 December on his famous March to the Sea campaign. After LGen William Hardee evacuated it on 20 December, Sherman presented Savannah as a 'Christmas present' to President Abraham Lincoln.

■ FORT STEDMAN, 25 MARCH 1865

MGen John Gordon attacked this strongpoint in the Petersburg siege line in hopes of threatening the Federal supply depot at City Point. It was not to be – a Federal counter-attack forced Gordon to retreat from his early gains after suffering 2900 losses.

■ FORT FISHER, 12–15 JANUARY 1865

MGen Alfred Terry replaced MGen Benjamin Butler after Butler's failed attack in December 1864. Supported by an accurate naval bombardment from the offshore guns of Adm David Porter, Terry attacked Fort Fisher with a force of 8000 men. Col William Lamb's force of just 1500 Confederate soldiers defended stubbornly, but the superior Federal numbers captured the fort. With the loss of Fort Fisher, Wilmington, the last remaining Southern port was closed, completing the Confederacy's isolation from overseas goods.

■ BENTONVILLE, 19 MARCH 1865

Bentonville was the last time Gen Joseph Johnston could muster the strength to fight MGen William Sherman as the Federals advanced through North Carolina. Johnston asked for an armistice on 14 April and surrendered on 26 April.

■ FIVE FORKS, 1 APRIL 1865

After his success in the Shenandoah Valley, MGen Philip Sheridan joined LGen Ulysses Grant in the siege of Petersburg, Virginia. Grant gave Sheridan an infantry corps and told him to break the Confederate western flank. Gen Robert E. Lee had anticipated this move and dispatched MGen George Pickett with 19,000 infantry and cavalry towards Five Forks. However, when Sheridan attacked, Pickett and MGen Fitzhugh Lee were away at a shad bake north of Hatcher's Run. Pickett raced back to Five Forks and joined the battle in progress, but there was little he could do.

Once Grant learned of Sheridan's success, he ordered a general attack all along Lee's front. The loss of Five Forks made it impossible for Lee to maintain the Southside Railroad as a link to Gen Joseph Johnston in North Carolina, and Lee was forced to abandon Petersburg.

■ SAYLER'S CREEK, 6 APRIL 1865

Moving west from Aemlia Corthouse, nearly one fourth of Gen Robert E. Lee's retreating Confederate army was cut off by MGen Philip Sheridan's cavalry and two corps. Most of the Confederates surrendered, including LGen Richard Ewell.

■ APPOMATTOX RIVER, 6–7 APRIL 1865

While other Federal forces fought at Sayler's Creek, MGen E.O.C. Ord advanced his Army of the James on a parallel route to the south towards Burke's Junction. LGen Ulysses Grant ordered Ord to burn the Appomattox river bridges at Farmville and High Bridge to block Gen Robert E. Lee's line of retreat. However, BGen Thomas Rosser attacked BGen Theodore Read as Read approached High Bridge, capturing about 780 Federals. After LGen James Longstreet crossed the Appomattox, MGen William Mahone failed to burn High Bridge promptly and the wagon bridge that ran under and alongside it. BGen Francis Barlow was able to capture the wagon bridge and push across while Col Thomas Livermore led a party of pioneers who extinguished the fire on High Bridge. By crossing these bridges, the Federals were able to continue pursuing Lee to Farmville.

January Uprising (Poland), 1863

■ CIOŁKÓW, 22 JANUARY 1863
In the first skirmish of the January Uprising, Aleksander Rogaliński's 100 Polish rebels occupying a manor house near the village of Ciołków (now Ciółkowo) defeated a detachment of the Russian Murom Regiment under Col Kozlaninov.

■ STASZÓW, 17 FEBRUARY 1863
Gen Marian Langiewicz' 600-strong force of Polish rebels occupied Staszów in south-eastern Poland on 14 February in an attempt to out-maneouvre a Russian force commanded by Co Zagriashko. The Russians attacked three days later, but were unable to achieve a decisive victory. However, Langiewicz believed that his position was untenable and withdrew from the town the following day. Polish homes and businesses were thoroughly looted when Russian troops re-occupied Staszów.

■ MAŁOGOSZCZ, 24 FEBRUARY 1863
A force of 2600 Polish rebels under Gen Marian Langiewicz fought an inconclusive action against Col Dobrowolski's 3000 Russians supported by six guns near Małogoszcz in southern Poland. During the battle the Poles captured 500 rifles and two guns.

Second Schleswig War, 1864

■ EVACUATION OF THE DANNEVIRKE, FEB 1864
The Dannevirke (Danevirk), an earthwork defence line dating back to the Dark Ages, was a potent symbol of Danish nationalism, but was evacuated on the orders of the Danish C-in-C, Gen Christian Julius de Meza.

■ SANKELMARK, 5 FEBRUARY 1864
Austrian forces, following up the Danish retreat from the Dannevirke, were temporarily halted by a counter-attack near Sankelmark on the road between Schleswig and Flensburg. The Danish infantry brigade was commanded by Oberst Max Müller.

■ RÜGEN (JASMUND), 17 MARCH 1864
Throughout the Second Schleswig War, the Danes exploited their naval superiority by blockading the Prussian Baltic coast. The Prussian Navy could not successfully challenge the far more powerful Danish warships in a fleet action, but was pressured into making a sortie.

A Prussian squadron of two corvettes, an armed paddle-steamer and six gunboats under Capt Eduard Jachmann was ordered to attack the Danish vessels blockading Swinemünde (present-day Swinouscie in Poland). Jachmann's preliminary reconnaissance on 16 March identified the Danish frigate *Sjaelland* together with the corvettes *Hejmdal* and *Thor*. However, the balance of forces was dramatically altered by the subsequent arrival of the Danish screw ship of the line *Skjold*. When Jachmann sortied next day, he found himself badly out-gunned and was forced to turn and run for Swinemünde at full speed. All of the vessels engaged were damaged, but none were sunk.

■ DYBBØL, 7–18 APRIL 1864
Prince Friedrich Karl of Prussia's 37,000 men defeated an 11,000-strong Danish army under Gen George Gerlac despite intensive bombardment by the Danish ironclad *Rolf Krake*. The Prussians inflicted almost 5000 casualties for the loss of 1200 men.

■ HELIGOLAND, 9 MAY 1864
An Austro-Prussian naval squadron consisting of two screw frigates, an armed paddle steamer and two gunboats under the Austrian commodore Wilhelm von Tegetthoff was, in this engagement, defeated by Cdr Edouard Suenson's Danish squadron of two screw frigates and a screw corvette. Tegetthoff's flagship *Schwarzenberg* was set alight by accurate Danish shellfire and he was eventually forced to run for shelter in British territorial waters off Heligoland (then a British

naval base.) His squadron escaped to Cuxhaven that night.

■ Als, 29 June 1864

A Prussian army of 23,000 men under Gen Herwarth von Bittenfeld captured the island of Als, which was defended by Gen Steinmann's 10,000-strong Danish garrison. The Prussians inflicted almost 3000 casualties for the loss of 372 men.

■ Lundby, 3 July 1864

LCol Beck, with 160 men of his 1st Infantry Regiment's 5th Company, advanced against the village of Lundby, which Beck believed was held by a Prussian patrol. The 124 men of Captain von Schlutterbach's company of Niederschlesisches Infanterieregiment 50 actually held a strong defensive position behind an earth dyke, but Beck ordered a reckless bayonet charge which was repulsed with heavy losses. During the clash, the Prussians inflicted 70 casualties for the loss of just three men.

Chincha Islands War, 1864–66

■ Papudo, 26 November 1865

The Spanish armed schooner *Virgen de Covadonga* was intercepted off Valparaíso by the Chilean corvette *Esmeralda*. The *Esmeralda's* superior firepower forced the schooner to surrender after a 30-minute action in which 26 Spaniards were killed or wounded.

■ Abtao, 7 February 1866

Two Spanish steam frigates attacked a combined Chilean/Peruvian squadron of a frigate, two corvettes and a schooner off the island of Abtao. Accurate Spanish gunnery damaged several enemy vessels, but the action was indecisive.

■ Valparaiso, 31 March 1866

A Spanish squadron commanded by Cdre Casto Méndez Núñez attacked the undefended Chilean port of Valparaiso. The three-hour bombardment sank 33 ships and caused damage estimated at $10,000,000 (equivalent to $224,000,000 at current values).

■ Callao, 2 May 1866

A Spanish squadron of an ironclad, five frigates and a corvette under Cdre Casto Méndez Núñez bombarded the defences of the Peruvian port of Callao, driving off the defending squadron of two small ironclads and three gunboats.

The Seven Weeks' War, 1866

■ Custoza, 24 June 1866

Archduke Albrecht's 75,000-strong Austrian army defeated the 120,000-strong Italian Army of the Mincio under Gen Alfonso Ferrero La Marmora at Custoza near Verona in northern Italy. The Austrians inflicted 8100 casualties for the loss of 5650 men.

■ Langensalza, 27 June 1866

A 19,000-strong Hanoverian army under Gen von Arentschildt defeated Gen von Flies' Prussian force of 9000 men near Langensalza in Saxony. The Hanoverians inflicted at least 1700 casualties for the loss of 1400 men.

■ Nachod, 27 June 1866

The advance guard of Gen Karl Friedrich von Steinmetz's Prussian V Corps occupied advantageous high ground near Nachod in Bohemia to cover the Prussian advance from Silesia. From this position, they repelled repeated attacks by elements of the Austrian VI Corps under Gen von Ramming. These actions decisively demonstrated the superiority of the Prussian infantry's breech-loading Dreyse needle-gun over the muzzle-loading Austrian Lorenz rifles. (The needle-gun's rate of fire was roughly triple that of the Lorenz, and the needle-gun was also highly accurate.) This advantage was especially marked as von Ramming rapidly lost control of his units and the Austrian infantry were committed piecemeal to a series of bayonet charges in vulnerable assault columns. Although the Austrian cavalry held their own in action against their Prussian counterparts, the discrepancy in infantry firepower was too great and the Prussians inflicted at least 5700 casualties for the loss of 1100 men.

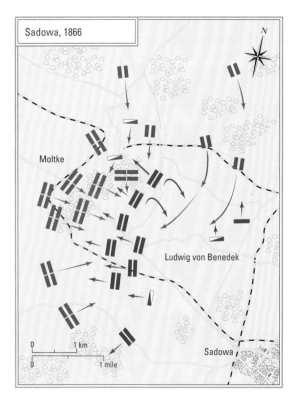

Sadowa, 1866

N

Moltke

Ludwig von Benedek

0   1 km

0   1 mile

Sadowa

■ TRAUTENAU (TRUTNOV), 27 JUNE 1866

The Austrian V Corps under Baron Ludwig von Gablenz repulsed FM Adolf von Bonin's I Prussian Corps at Trautenau in Bohemia (now Trutnov, Czech Republic). The Austrians inflicted 1400 casualties for the loss of 4,800 men.

■ MÜNCHENGRÄTZ, 28 JUNE 1866

Prince Friedrich Karl of Prussia's 14,000-strong army defeated an Austrian force of 20,000 men under Count Eduard Clam-Gallas at Münchengrätz, Bohemia. The Prussians inflicted 2000 casualties for the loss of 341 men.

■ GITSCHIN (JIČÍN), 29 JUNE 1866

An Austrian and Saxon force commanded by Count Eduard Clam-Gallas and Crown Prince Albert of Saxony was defeated by Prince Friedrich Karl's 85,000-strong Prussian First Army at Gitschin in Bohemia (present-day Jičín, in the Czech Republic).

■ SADOWA (KÖNIGGRÄTZ), 3 JULY 1866

Dismayed by his losses in the first actions of

the war, the Austrian C-in-C, Gen Ludwig von Benedek, ordered a withdrawal and advised the Emperor Franz Josef to make peace as the only way to save the army from a 'catastrophe'. When this was refused, and an ambiguous sentence of the imperial telegram was interpreted as ordering a final stand, Benedek deployed his forces by the Elbe between Sadowa and Königgrätz.

The 240,000-strong Austrian army initially faced two Prussian armies, Gen Herwarth von Bittenfeld's Army of the Elbe with 39,000 men and Prince Friedrich Karl's 85,000-strong First Army. Crown Prince Frederick's 100,000-strong Second Army was marching to join forces with them, but it was uncertain whether he could arrive in time to prevent them being defeated in detail. The battle began at dawn in rain and mist as Prussian forces formed up west of the Bystřice river. Shortly before 08:00, the Austrian artillery opened fire, pinning down the Prussian right flank under Herwarth von Bittenfeld. The Austrians' Saxon allies on the left fell back in good order, and prevented any further advance by von Bittenfeld's forces.

The Prussian centre, spearheaded by the 7th Division under Gen Eduard Friedrich Karl von Fransecky, advanced into Swiep Forest, where it fought a fierce action against two Austrian corps. The Prussians methodically cleared the villages of Austrian defenders and the First Army was ordered across the river to support Fransecky. Sadowa was captured, but a fierce battle ensued in the nearby forest. The Austrian artillery halted the Prussian advance by a heavy bombardment which decimated their 4th and 8th Divisions. However, Benedek refused to order a massed cavalry charge which might have won the battle.

At 11:00 the Austrian centre began a flank attack on the Prussian 7th Division, which had held off nearly a quarter of the Austrian army. This counter-attack forced the 7th Division back to the edge of the forest and threatened the entire First Army. Benedek's corps commanders pleaded with him to launch a counter-attack to destroy the Prussian First and Elbe Armies before the Second Army arrived, but Benedek refused and the opportunity was lost.

Crown Prince Frederick finally arrived at 14:30 with the bulk of his 100,000 men and hit the Austrian right flank retiring from Swiep Forest while the Prussian artillery pounded the Austrian centre. By 16:00 the last counter-attacks by the Austrian I and VI Corps were broken and LGen Friedrich Hiller von Gärtringen's 1st Prussian Guards forced the retreat of the Austrian artillery, which had played a key role in holding Benedek's line.

The Second Prussian Army broke through, taking Chlum behind the centre of the Austrian line. The Army of the Elbe, which had barely held its positions after its heavy losses early in the day, attacked and broke through the Austrian left flank. Benedek ordered a general retreat at 15:00, which was covered by a series of cavalry charges. These succeeded in keeping the bridges over the Elbe open for the withdrawal, but at a terrible cost: 2000 men and almost as many horses were killed, wounded or captured in the action. (It was later established that the Prussians had inflicted 44,100 casualties for the loss of 9000 men.) Benedek himself crossed the Elbe at 18:00 and several hours later informed the emperor that the catastrophe which he had anticipated had indeed occurred.

Ethiopian (Abyssinian) Wars 1867–72

■ AROGEE, 10 APRIL 1868

The 5000-strong advance guard of Gen Sir Robert Napier's Anglo-Indian army were attacked by an estimated 10,000 Ethiopian warriors under their chieftain Fitaurari Gabri near the Beshlio at Arogi whilst on a punitive expedition against Emperor Theodore (Tewodros). Napier inflicted a decisive defeat on the Ethiopians, who were demoralized by the Naval Brigade's rocket fire, losing 700 killed and about 1200 wounded. British losses

during the one-sided engagement were no more than 20 wounded.

■ MAGDALA, 15 APRIL 1868

After his victory at Arogee, Sir Robert Napier advanced on Emperor Theodore's capital of Magdala. The 33rd Regiment of Foot stormed the defences under cover of an intense artillery bombardment and the emperor committed suicide in response.

■ ABYSSINIAN CIVIL WAR, 1869–72

In 1868, Wagshum Gobeze proclaimed himself Emperor Tekle Giyorgis II of Ethiopia. His brother-in-law Kassai refused to recognize his title, despite being honoured by the emperor. This defiance provoked an attack by Tekle Giyorgis in 1871, but he was defeated by Kassai's well-trained and better-equipped forces near Adowa on 11 July 1871. He was captured and deposed and Kassai was crowned as Emperor Yohannes IV on 12 January 1872.

■ EMBABO, 6 JUNE 1882

Shewan forces of Negus Menelik II defeated Negus Tekle Haymanot's Gojjame army in a battle for control of the wealthy Oromia region. The Gojjame forces were defeated, but Emperor Yohannes IV imposed a compromise peace.

■ CHELENQO, 9 JANUARY 1887

A force of 400 men under Emir Abd Allah II of Harar made an unsuccessful surprise attack on the army of Shewa under Negus Menelik II. The Shewans routed the Emir's men and captured Harar.

■ DOGALI, 26 JANUARY 1887

A 7000-strong Ethiopian army commanded by Ras Alula Engida ambushed and virtually wiped out Col Tommaso De Cristofori's Italian force of 500 men which was attempting to raise the Ethiopian siege of Sahati.

■ GALLABAT (METEMMA), 10 MARCH 1889

An Ethiopian army of 130,000 infantry and 20,000 cavalry under the Emperor Yohannes IV was narrowly defeated by Zeki Tummal's 85,000-strong Mahdist army at Gallabat in the Sudan. Each side lost an estimated 15,000 men.

■ Adowa, 1 March 1896

Having advanced into Ethiopia in enforcement of the Treaty of Wuchale in late 1895, a small Italian expedition had been stopped at Amba Alagi and was forced to retire to defensible positions at Tigray. The Ethiopian and Italian armies remained in position until late February when the supplies of both sides started to dwindle and cause logistical problems.

The Italian commander, Gen Oreste Baratieri, hoped to attack the vastly more numerous Ethiopian forces of Emperor Menelik as they suffered from mounting desertions, and came under pressure from the Italian government to make a decisive action. Holding council with his subordinates on the evening of 29 February, Baratieri ordered an attack the next day.

The Italian army in the Ethiopian theatre was comprised of four brigades, numbering just over 14,000 effective soldiers and 56 guns. One of the brigades consisted of Ethiopians under the command of Italian officers. Many of the troops were inexperienced conscripts and armed with old-model rifles. Facing the Italians were at least 70,000 Ethiopians, with large numbers being mounted and one quarter being armed only with spears. The Ethiopians, however, also possessed Russian advisors and guns. Menelik was also aware of the desperate situation and ordered his own men forward as the Italians advanced in three separate columns.

The Italians failed to surprise the Ethiopians, who were intelligently positioned to receive them on the high ground above the Adowa Valley. In the hot, inhospitable terrain, the Italian troops were cut up and cut off during the course of the harrowing day, suffering from the overwhelming numbers of the enemy. In a shock outcome for the Europeans, by the end of the day the Italian army had been routed, losing more than half its number and almost all its firearms. Ethiopian losses were also high, at perhaps 12,000 men. The defeat gained Ethiopia its independence.

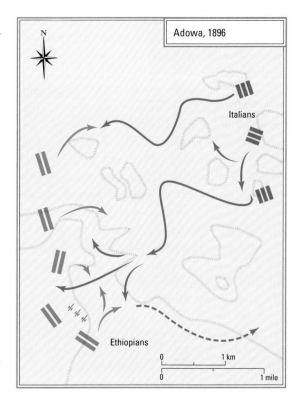

Adowa, 1896

Cuban Wars of Independence 1868–95

■ Ten Years' War, 1868–78

A declaration of independence from Spain by Cuban planter Carlos Manuel de Cespedes on 10 October 1868 led to insurrection in Oriente, Camaguey and Las Villas provinces. Cuban forces in the low thousands were mostly led by former Spanish officer Maximo Gomez, with fighters including the young José Martí, The Cuban troops had the advantage of being immune to the yellow fever that decimated Spanish soldiers during the conflict. There were several victories, defeats and attempts at reconciliation on both sides without initial result. Spaniard Gen Blas Villate and Capt Valeriano Weyler herded Cubans into concentration camps and conducted extensive summary executions, including of students, in a war of attrition. Cespedes was killed by Spanish soldiers on 27 February 1874. Hundreds of

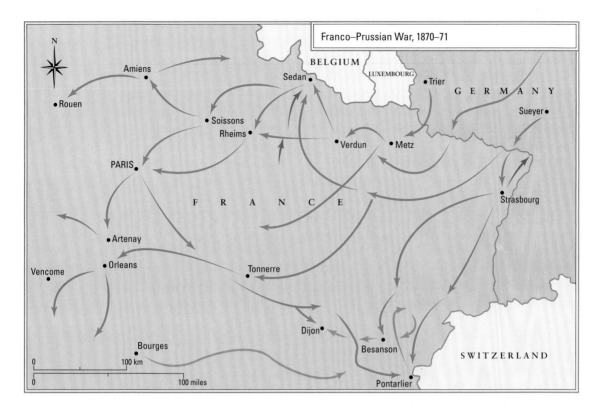

Franco–Prussian War, 1870–71

thousands of Cubans perished before the war ended in an uneasy truce negotiated over a protracted period.

■ LITTLE WAR, 1879–80

The Little War was a year-long insurgency, declared by a group of revolutionaries outside of Cuba against Spain. It was led by Gen Calixto Garcia and started on 26 August 1879, but petered out due to lack of local and material support.

■ DOS RIOS, 19 MAY 1895

Rearguard skirmish between Cuban rebels and Spanish forces during a doomed expedition led by the Maceo brothers on 19 May 1895 near Santiago. Dos Rios became prominent as the place José Martí was killed in a pointless charge.

Franco-Prussian War 1870–71

■ SAARBRÜCKEN, 2 AUGUST 1870

The border town of Saarbrücken was selected as the French objective for the opening offensive of the Franco-Prussian War, as it was defended by a single division (the Prussian 16th Infantry Division), which had the unfortunate honour of being faced by the entire French Army of the Rhine. Accordingly, on 31 July 1870 the army advanced to the River Saar in a confident push to to seize the city.

Gen Frossard's II Corps and Marshal Bazaine's III Corps crossed the German border on 2 August, and forced the 16th Infantry Division's 40th Regiment from the town by a series of forceful direct attacks. While the French hailed the invasion as the first step towards the Rhineland and Berlin, Gen Le Bœuf and Napoleon III were receiving alarming reports from foreign news sources of Prussian and Bavarian armies massing to the south-east in addition to the forces already identified to the north and north-east.

■ WISSEMBOURG (WEISSENBURG), 4 AUG 1870

On 3 August 1870, Gen Abel Douay led the 8600-strong 2nd Division of Marshal MacMahon's

I Corps into Wissembourg in Alsace. Faulty intelligence indicated that there was no major Prussian force in the vicinity, when in fact 60,000 men of Crown Prince Friedrich Wilhelm's Third Army were closing in. At 08:30 the next day, the Crown Prince's forces attacked and defeated Douay's division, inflicting 2200 casualties for the loss of 3500 men.

■ WÖRTH (FRÖSCHWEILER), 6 AUGUST 1870

In this major clash in August 1870, Crown Prince Friedrich Wilhelm's 81,000-strong Third Army defeated the 37,000 men of Marshal MacMahon's French I Corps around Wörth and Fröschweiler in Alsace. The Prussians, showing their skill at arms, inflicted around 20,000 casualties for the loss of 10,640 men.

■ SPICHEREN, 6 AUGUST 1870

Elements of Gen Karl von Steinmetz' First Army and Prince Friedrich Karl's Second Army totalling 37,000 men attacked the 29,000-strong French II Corps under Gen Charles Auguste Frossard near Spicheren in Lorraine. The French held a strong defensive position and beat off the initial Prussian assaults, but their counter-attacks were ineffective. Frossard was finally defeated by Prussian flank attacks after inflicting almost 4900 casualties for the loss of 4000 men.

■ BORNY-COLOMBEY, 14 AUGUST 1870

Marshal Bazaine's 83,500-strong French army, attempting to withdraw from Metz, won a tactical victory over Gen Karl von Steinmetz' First Army of 67,500 men. The French inflicted 6100 casualties for the loss of 3900 men.

■ STRASBOURG, 15 AUGUST– 28 SEPTEMBER 1870

LGen August von Werder's 40,000 Württemberg and Baden troops besieged Strasbourg, which was defended by a 17,000-strong French garrison under Gen Uhrich. The city surrendered, however, following its receipt of news of the French defeat at the battle of Sedan.

■ TOUL, 16 AUGUST–23 SEPTEMBER 1870

German forces besieged Toul until Frederick Francis II, Grand Duke of Mecklenburg-Schwerin, arrived with a 64-gun siege train. The city surrendered after being subjected to an intensive nine-hour bombardment in which 2433 shells were fired.

■ MARS-LA-TOUR, 16 AUGUST 1870

At Mars-la-Tour two Prusso-German Corps fought a day-long meeting engagement against the bulk of the French Army of the Rhine. The stiff Prussian resistance convinced the French that their withdrawal was blocked, so they retired on the fortress at Metz.

■ GRAVELOTTE-ST-PRIVAT, 18 AUGUST 1870

This engagement was the largest battle of the Franco-Prussian War, with roughly 188,000 Prussians facing 112,000 French. Although the Prussians sustained heavy losses, they achieved a strategic victory, driving the French Army of the Rhine into Metz.

■ METZ, 19 AUGUST–27 OCTOBER, 1870

Having been defeated and blocked from escape, the French Army of the Rhine withdrew into the defences of the fortress-city of Metz. Surrounded by the Prussian Second Army, the surrender of the city yielded 186,000 French prisoners.

■ NOISSEVILLE, 31 AUGUST–1 SEPTEMBER 1870

Marshal Bazaine's 190,000-strong French army attempted to break out from Metz, but was defeated by Prince Friedrich Karl's Second Army near Noisseville in Lorraine. The Prussians inflicted more than 3500 casualties for the loss of almost 3000 men.

■ BAZEILLES, 31 AUGUST–1 SEPTEMBER 1870

The French 'Blue Division' (Division d'Infanterie de Marine) defended the town of Bazeilles against Gen von der Tann's I Royal Bavarian Corps. The French were driven out after inflicting 5200 casualties for the loss of more than 2600 men.

■ SEDAN, 1 SEPTEMBER 1870

With the French Army of the Rhine under Marshal Bazaine besieged in Metz, the last hope for France rested with the 120,000-strong Army of Châlons, commanded by Marshal Patrice MacMahon. The marshal's options were either to move east to Bazaine's aid or to retreat westwards and fight a defensive battle based on the strong fortifications around Paris. Military considerations dictated a retreat to the west, but MacMahon was under great political pressure from the Empress Eugénie and her advisors. Furthermore, the Emperor Napoleon III himself was with MacMahon's army and retreat would have seriously destabilised the Empire. The Army of Châlons accordingly marched east.

To counter this threat, the Chief of the Prussian General Staff, Field Marshal Helmuth von Moltke, split his forces into four armies. Leaving two to keep Bazaine contained in Metz, he ordered the other two to head west and find MacMahon. German reconnaissance reported that the Army of Châlons was moving north-east, hugging the Belgian border. The obvious conclusion was that they were attempting to reach Metz via Sedan and Thionville. However, there was a real risk in simply pursuing the French – if MacMahon's move was a feint, Moltke would be inviting him to attack his left flank. On the other hand, if the French were about to retreat to Paris, the Germans would lose as much as a week in redeploying, giving them ample time to bolster the defences of Paris. Moltke took a calculated risk and ordered the two armies to turn north to intercept MacMahon. After a series of forced marches, the Germans caught up with the French on 31 August, halting the Army of Châlons at the town of Sedan, a few kilometres from the Belgian border.

The French were now trapped in a triangular pocket and the Germans wasted no time, attacking in strength on 1 September. MacMahon was seriously wounded early in the action, but there was confusion over his successor – he appointed Gen Auguste Ducrot as acting commander; however, a recently arrived more senior general, Emmanuel Wimpffen, refused to take orders from Ducrot and insisted that he was now in charge. The two commanders disagreed over which direction the army should attempt to breakout.

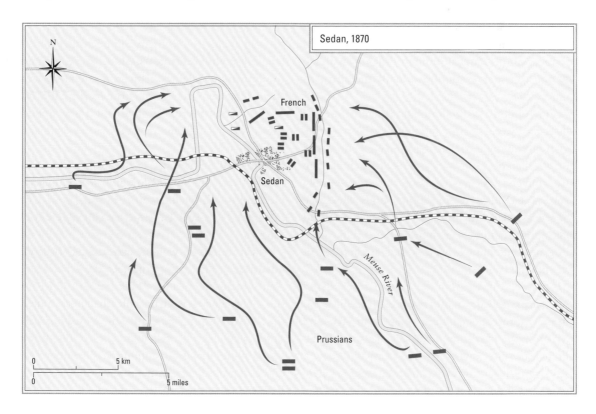

Sedan, 1870

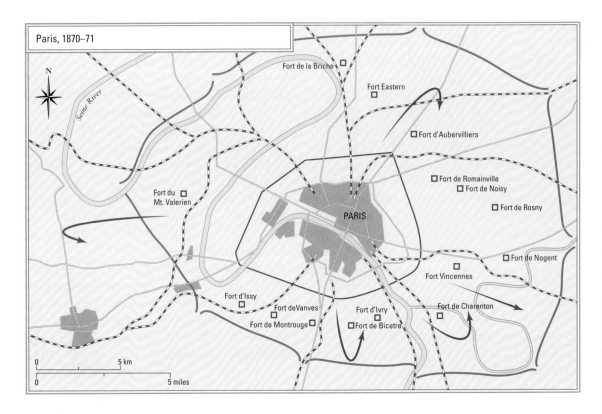

Paris, 1870–71

Ducrot advocated a breakout to the west and a retreat towards Paris; Wimpffen ordered an attack to the east and a continuation of the drive to relieve Metz.

Both options were doomed to failure as the besiegers were steadily tightening their martial grip on the town. German artillery was deployed on the heights above Sedan and its accurate fire was inflicting heavy casualties on the densely packed defenders. A few French units were able to work their way through the siege lines and escape to neutral Belgium, where they were interned, but the rest were killed or captured in the bloody engagement.

By the end of the day, the French had suffered 3000 men killed, 14,000 wounded and 21,000 more captured, including Napoleon III and MacMahon; over the next few days, the total French prisoner count reached nearly 100,000, a devastating total. The Germans' total losses – killed, wounded and missing – were no more than 9000,

the vast majority of which had been incurred by a few ill-advised infantry assaults by commanders too impatient to let the artillery do their work for them. The epic defeat at Sedan marked the end of the French Second Empire and it also opened the road to the French capital for the victorious German armies.

■ **Paris, 19 September 1870–28 January 1871**
LGen Leonard von Blumenthal commanded German forces totalling 240,000 men. They were besieging Paris, which was defended by Gen Louis Jules Trochu's 400,000-strong garrison. Half of this garrison, however, were poorly trained National Guardsmen. The city was protected by the 'Thiers wall' which stretched for a total of 33km and a ring of 16 detached forts, all of which had been built in the 1840s. Although these defences were actually obsolescent, they were sufficient to discourage von Blumenthal from attempting to storm the city, and prolonged German bombardments of the fortifications were largely ineffective.

Throughout the siege the French launched several major sorties which achieved localized successes, but the ground gained was quickly retaken by German counter-attacks. The garrison was finally starved into surrender after inflicting 12,000 German casualties. French losses totalled 24,000 dead and wounded, plus 146,000 prisoners and 47,000 civilian casualties.

■ ARTENAY (ORLEANS) 10 OCTOBER 1870

Baron Ludwig von der Tann's Bavarian Corps of 28,000 men defeated the French Army of the Loire under Gen Joseph Edouard de la Motterouge at Artenay north of Orleans and took the city the following day.

■ BELLEVUE, 18 OCTOBER 1870

Marshal Bazaine launched a major sortie towards Bellevue to resupply his army besieged in Metz. The French inflicted almost 1800 casualties for the loss of just over 1200 men, but were driven back to Metz empty-handed.

■ BELFORT, 3 NOVEMBER 1870– 18 FEBRUARY 1871

The fall of Strasbourg on 28 September 1870 allowed the German XIV Corps of 40,000 men under General August von Werder to move south against Belfort. Col Denfert-Rochereau, commander of the 17,000-strong French garrison, began building field defences around the city to supplement its seventeenth-century fortifications. These allowed the garrison to hold out until the end of the war, inflicting 8000 casualties for the loss of 4700 men.

■ COULMIERS, 9 NOVEMBER 1870

Gen Ludwig von der Tann's I Royal Bavarian Corps of 20,000 men was defeated by Gen Louis d'Aurelle's 70,000-strong French Army of the Loire. The French inflicted more than 2100 casualties for the loss of 1500 men.

■ HAVANA, 9 NOVEMBER 1870

The German gunboat *Meteor* fought an inconclusive action against the French sloop *Bouvet* off Havana, Cuba. The battle ended when the *Bouvet*'s engines were damaged and she was forced to retreat into neutral Cuban waters.

■ AMIENS, 27 NOVEMBER 1870

Gen Edwin von Manteuffel's First Army defeated the French Army of the North under Gen Jean-Joseph Farre at Villers-Bretonneaux near Amiens, inflicting almost 2400 casualties for the loss of 1300 men. Amiens was captured the following day.

■ BEAUNE-LA-ROLANDE, 28 NOVEMBER 1870

Konstantin Bernhard von Voigts-Rhetz' 10,000-strong Prussian X Corps defeated an attack by at least 31,000 men of the French XX Corps under Gen Crouzat. The Prussians inflicted over 8000 casualties for the loss of 850 men.

■ VILLEPION, 1 DECEMBER 1870

Gen Antoine Chanzy's French XVI Corps of 15,000 men defeated the 7000-strong I Royal Bavarian Corps under Gen Ludwig von der Tann. The French inflicted at least 1000 casualties for the loss of 600 men.

■ LOIGNY-POUPRY, 2–3 DECEMBER 1870

Gen Antoine Chanzy's XVI Corps and the XVII Corps under Louis-Gaston de Sonis attacked a 35,000-strong Prussian detachment under Frederick Francis II, Grand Duke of Mecklenburg-Schwerin near Loigny. The ill-equipped and poorly trained French conscripts were defeated despite being reinforced by elements of the Army of the Loire, which brought their strength up to 90,000 men. The Grand Duke's forces inflicted 11,000 casualties for the loss of just over 4,000 men.

■ BEAUGENCY, 10 DECEMBER 1870

Frederick Francis II, Grand Duke of Mecklenburg-Schwerin, retook Orleans after his victory at Loigny-Poupry before attacking Gen Antoine Chanzy's Army of the Loire near Beaugency. The outnumbered Germans took Beaugency despite a costly initial repulse.

■ HALLUE, 23–24 DECEMBER 1870

Gen Louis Faidherbe's 40,000-strong French Army of the North launched a mid-winter offensive on the Somme in an attempt to recapture Amiens, deploying to the north-east of the city on the River Hallue. He repulsed an attack by the Prussian 1st Army of 22,500 men under Gen

Edwin von Manteuffel, inflicting almost 1000 casualties for the loss of 2300 men. The approach of German reinforcements forced Faidherbe to withdraw towards Arras.

■ **BATTLE OF BAPAUME, 3 JANUARY 1871**
The Prussian First Army of 18,000 men under Gen Edwin von Manteuffel defeated Gen Louis Faidherbe's 33,000-strong French Army of the North near Bapaume. The Prussians inflicted more than 1600 casualties for the loss of 800 men.

■ **VILLERSEXEL, 9 JANUARY 1871**
A 20,000-strong detachment of Gen Charles Denis Bourbaki's French Army of the East drove Gen August von Werder's Prussian XIV Corps from the village of Villersexel. The French inflicted almost 600 casualties for the loss of 1350 men.

■ **LE MANS, 10–12 JANUARY 1871**
Prince Friedrich Karl's 50,000-strong Prussian Second Army defeated the 150,000 ill-equipped French conscripts of Gen Antoine Chanzy's Army of the Loire near Le Mans. The Prussians inflicted 25,000 casualties for the loss of 9400 men.

■ **LISAINE, 15–17 JANUARY 1871**
Gen Charles Denis Bourbaki's 100,000-strong French Army of the East was defeated by the 52,000 men of Gen August von Werder's Prussian XIV Corps. The Prussians inflicted 6000 casualties for the loss of just under 2000 men.

■ **ST QUENTIN, 19 JANUARY 1871**
Gen Louis Faidherbe's 40,000-strong Army of the North had operated with great effect by striking at isolated enemy forces before retreating behind the belt of fortresses around the Pas-de-Calais. However, in January 1871, the Minister of War, Leon Gambetta, ordered Faidherbe to launch an all-out offensive in an attempt to raise the siege of Paris. By this time the Army of the North was weakened by supply problems and Faidherbe himself was suffering from ill-health as a result of his years of service in West Africa. Nonetheless, he attacked the Prussian First Army of 33,000 men under Gen August Karl von Goeben near St Quentin, but his ill-trained and poorly equipped troops were defeated in a seven-hour action after

inflicting 2400 casualties for the loss of 12,500 men. The defeat led to the surrender of the garrison of Paris on 28 January.

US Expedition to Korea, 1871

■ **GANGHWA, 10–11 JUNE 1871**
Taewongun, Regent of Korea, resisted all external efforts to open the kingdom to trade. When two Korean forts fired upon two American ships of RAdm J. Rodgers' squadron, the Americans landed and destroyed both.

Egyptian and Sudanese Wars, 1875–1900

■ **GUNDET, 16 NOVEMBER 1875**
As the Ottoman Empire sought to expand Islamic rule, the Christian Abyssinians under Walad Michael and the Ethiopians under King John, using captured rifles, defeated 2000 Egyptians under Col Adolph Arendrup near the town of Gundet.

■ **ALEXANDRIA, 11–13 JULY 1882**
The construction of the Suez Canal, completed in 1869, catapulted Ottoman Egypt into a position of supreme importance in British imperial policy. Chastened by the French occupation of 1798 to 1801, the Ottoman Empire poured a considerable amount of its dwindling resources into securing modern defences for the vital port at the end of the Nile. An Ottoman general, Urabi Pasha, championed Islam and Egyptian nationalism in defiance of Turkish desires to maintain good relations with Britain, which supported the Ottomans against Russian encroachments. Rioting in Alexandria and the deaths of several Europeans drew a Franco-British fleet of 15 vessels and a landing force of around 3000 intended to protect the Suez Canal. Facing them were the harbour forts with some modern cannon manned by Urabi's gunners. A British ultimatum to cease construction of harbour emplacements provoked Egyptian fire, prompting the shore bombardment

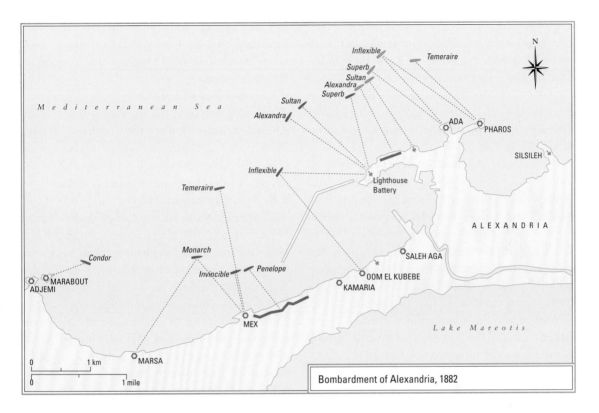

Bombardment of Alexandria, 1882

by the British fleet since 1855. Steam, armour and improved naval gunnery allowed the Europeans to complete the reduction of the port's defences, the landing force going ashore and establishing order by means which included an armoured train mounting hand-operated machine guns fitted out under the command of then captain of HMS *Inflexible*, John Arbuthnot Fisher.

The French fleet left after helping to deliver the punishing bombardment, leaving the British to continue. With Turkish authority ostensibly restored, Urabi withdrew from the city and interdicted interior communications while he collected nationalist forces with the goal of evicting the Europeans. Meanwhile, a British force under Sir Garnet Wolseley of some 40,000 troops arrived off the coast, while Urabi's army of some 60,000 nationalists mustered in opposition, Wolseley's force remaining at sea until August, Urabi's forces spread thin in guarding all possible landing sites.

■ **KASSASSIN (QASSASIN), 28 AUGUST 1882**
Near the Suez Canal, British general Gerald Graham and his force here twice repelled attacks by Egyptian forces under Ahmed Urabi, the first an infantry attack, the second a larger onslaught supported by artillery fire.

■ **TEL-EL-KEBIR, 13 SEPTEMBER 1882**
The British bombardment and capture of Alexandria in July followed the Ottoman Government's repudiation of the Egyptian nationalist uprising led by Urabi Pasha, whose personal popularity and call of Islamic struggle against infidel invaders drew thousands to his banner. With Alexandria secure as a base of supply and line of retreat, British general Garnet Wolseley held his expeditionary force of some 40,000 troops at sea, prompting Urabi Pasha to parcel his own army of some 60,000 nationalists throughout the Nile delta against the possibility of a sudden landing. Wolseley finally landed a strike force of 13,000 troops and artillery

midway along the Suez Canal at Ismailia. The British marched inland along a freshwater canal toward Kassassin, repulsing an Egyptian stand at Mahuta. Urabi Pasha meanwhile collected 24,000 Egyptians in entrenchments supported by his field artillery around a slight height at Tel-el-Kebir. The Egyptians expected more troops to arrive while the British advance halted in the face of two attacks by Egyptian artillery, supported by infantry and cavalry, at Kassassin. British field artillery and the Bengal Lancers prevailed in both conflicts and allowed Wolseley to make a sudden night march directly upon Tel-el-Kebir, taking the Egyptians by surprise with an attack the following dawn, launched from a mustering point on a hill 8.8km distant. The British employment of bayonets exclusively in the opening attack prolonged the surprise, while Wolseley's rapid advance allowed the Egyptians no time to regroup as their casualties mounted to some 2000 killed.

The subsequent arrival and employment of

Wolseley's cavalry and artillery drove the surviving Egyptians south toward Cairo, which they were unable to hold against the continuing British advance.

■ KAFR-EL-DAWWAR, 1882

The strong fortifications of this town, held by Ahmed Urabim with 6000 soldiers, delayed British general Garnet Wolseley's advance upon Cairo for five weeks, until Wolseley shifted his advance to the Suez canal to capture Cairo.

■ EL TEB, 4 FEBRUARY 1884

The Mahdi's Ansār in the Sudan under Osman Digna routed 3500 Egyptian troops under Pasha Valentine Baker, the Egyptians breaking under the first rush and being slaughtered by Mahdist cavalry. A relief force under Sir Gerald Graham, 4500 British troops, maintained their square against the Ansār's attacks, British artillery and machine guns prevailing over captured Mahdist cannon. Some 2000 of the Ansār perished, Graham recapturing the city of Tokar from the Sudanese.

■ TAMAI, 13 MARCH 1884

British general Gerald Graham routed 10,000 Ansār under Osman Digna, killing 4000. The 4500 British prevailed despite the celebrated breaking of one of their two squares and the jamming of their machine guns. A total of 221 British soldiers fell during the action.

Gordon Relief Expedition (Nile Expedition) 1884–85

In August 1884, British/Egyptian general Charles 'Chinese' Gordon busied himself defending besieged Khartoum and embarrassing the British Government in the final months of his life. Gordon's hatred for slavery had destroyed the economy in the Sudan and drawn thousands of Islamist Ansār to the *jihad* of the Mahdi, a Muslim mystic, against the Anglo-Egyptian presence in the country. Gordon's insistence on holding Sudan's chief city against the Mahdi's army defied the British Government's order for Gordon to supervise the evacuation of all Westerners from the country, which Gordon refused, citing his

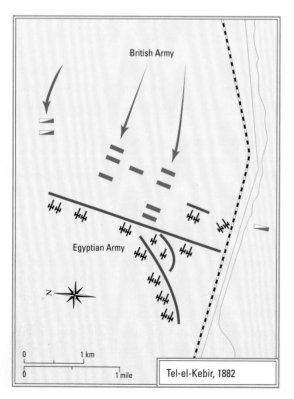

British Army

Egyptian Army

0   1 km
0   1 mile

Tel-el-Kebir, 1882

role as an Egyptian pasha. British prime minister William Gladstone grudgingly dispatched the 'Nile Expedition' under the proven Gen Garnet Wolseley to Gordon's aid.

Wolseley, a friend of Gordon, carefully led his outnumbered force southward along the Nile. Outlaying Egyptian mounted patrols surrounded and screened his central force, which consisted of a slow infantry column of some 5400 infantry and cavalry, some marching overland, and others supported by a river fleet of cargo and specially constructed gunboats with machine guns designed for operation in the Lower Nile, Wolseley's column finding itself short of supply due to difficulties navigating the river. Canadian river pilots guided the gunboats through the shallows. The expedition, with difficulty, overcame both Ansār attacks and the desert. The Mahdi himself kept informed of its progress as he drove his followers to press the siege before the British column could relieve Khartoum and the dwindling garrison of Egyptian soldiers, originally 6000, still fighting under Gordon's brilliant and inspiring leadership. The lead ships of the river flotilla arrived at Khartoum two days after Gordon's decapitated head became the Mahdi's trophy, the news conveyed mutely by the Mahdi's flag flying over the smouldering city.

■ ABU KLEA, 16–18 JANUARY 1885

As the Nile Expedition moved south, the vanguard found 3000 Ansār guarding wells here; opening fire on the British from a ravine, the Ansār charged and broke the British square, killing 71. Half the Mahdists died.

■ KIRBEKAN, 10 FEBRUARY 1885

The Nile Expedition's march toward beleaguered Khartoum found a Mahdist force lined up on these heights, which opened fire and then charged as the British approached. The British cross-fire killed some 2000; British losses were 60 men.

■ KHARTOUM, 13 MARCH 1884–
26 JANUARY 1885

British/Egyptian general Charles 'Chinese' Gordon with 3000 Egyptian troops entered

this principal city of the Sudan under orders to evacuate all Westerners in the face of an Islamist uprising under the Mahdi, commanding some 20,000 men. The Egyptian and British Governments ignored Gordon's requests for reinforcements, heartening the Ansār as they drew a ring around the city, employing rifles and artillery bought or captured from European and American sources to blast breaches in Khartoum's walls. The siege went on for 317 days, Gordon dispatching accounts out through the besiegers' lines of Muslim efforts inside the city to set fires and explode his magazines while Gordon's own steamers fought to keep the Nile open. The impending arrival of the relief column prompted the Mahdi to storm the city's remaining defences, Gordon's death resulting.

■ TOFREK, 22 MARCH 1885

The Mahdi's army pursued the British after the fall of Khartoum prompted the Nile Expedition's withdrawal. Another fierce attack broke the British

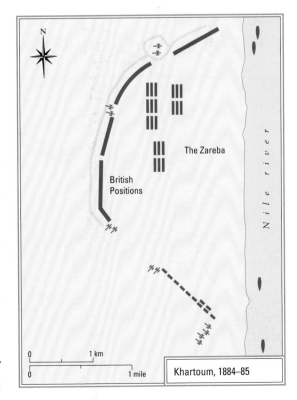

Khartoum, 1884–85

square, but the formation's resilence repelled the attackers, allowing the British to continue.

■ Ginnis (Gennis), 30 December 1885

An Anglo-Egyptian garrison held a fort here, the fort being besieged by some 5000 Ansār with cannon. After a month a relief column arrived including Egyptians with better training and equipment and British artillery, which dispersed the Mahdists.

■ Dufile, 28 November 1888

One of Gordon's forts on the Ugandan border, garrisoned by 1200 of the Khedive's soldiers, withstood an assault by 1400 Ansār, the Egyptians having time to consolidate local forces within the walls. Some 250 Ansār died.

■ Suakin, 20 December 1888

Osman Digna and the Ansār continued probing the southern frontier of Egypt in the aftermath of the Mahdi's death. British general Francis Grenfell's forces defending this port killed 1000 Ansār, Osman Digna losing an arm.

■ Gallabat, 9–10 March 1889

The Khalifa invaded Abyssinia with 70,000 Ansār, fortifying this position with a thorn stockade and artillery. King John massed a corresponding number of defenders, the king himself dying in the assault that broke the Ansār.

■ Toski, 3 August 1889

The Khalifa invaded north into Egypt, Abd al-Nujumi commanding 5000 Ansār as British general Francis Grenfell with 2000 men moved down the Nile in response, while Anglo-Egyptian cavalry slowed al-Nujumi's advance and the Ansār were weakened by supply difficulties. Al-Nujumi accordingly sought to avoid battle, retreating into the hills with Grenfell's force attacking, British artillery shelling each position held by the Ansār. The Mahdists finally collapsed, pursued by cavalry, 1200 men and al-Nujumi falling.

■ Kassala, 17 July 1894

At Kassala a total of 2400 Italian and Abyssinian troops, moving along the borders of Abyssinia,

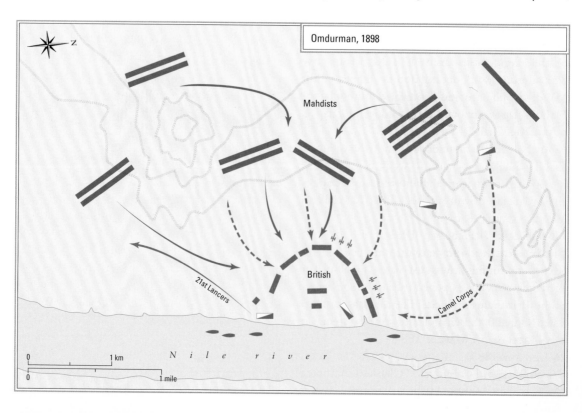

fought and annihilated an Ansār force of some 3000, the Mahdist raiders retreating into this town on the Adbara river, where they had artillery.

■ **FERKEH, 7 JUNE 1896**

Kitchener's Anglo-Egyptian Army surprised 4000 Ansār entrenched on the hills near this village in Sudan. Assisted by artillery, British and Egyptian infantry resisted Mahdist sorties and drove the defenders from their trenches, some 800 dying.

■ **ATBARA RIVER, 8 APRIL 1898**

A force of 13,000 Ansār under Osman Digna in a fortified camp blocked British/Egyptian general Herbert Kitchener's 12,000-strong expedition at this crossing. British artillery and Maxim guns opened an assault that killed 3000 Ansār, the rest retreating.

■ **OMDURMAN, 2 SEPTEMBER 1898**

The slow speed of General Herbert Kitchener's advance toward Khartoum had given the Khalifa time to rally a force of some 50,000–60,000 warriors to protect the tomb and capital of the Islamic Empire's founder. Such preparation was in accordance with Kitchener's strategic plan, the British desiring as many of the Ansār present as possible for a decisive battle of technology-assisted annihilation. With his artillery transported and landed by his river flotilla, Kitchener encamped his 12,000 infantry and horse and camel cavalry in a large fortified camp on the banks of the Nile, the perimeter guarded during the night by the searchlights and machine guns of his gunboat fleet. Kitchener opened his assault with the fire of long-range howitzers that soon damaged the Mahdi's tomb in Khartoum. Osman Digna's Army of the Green Flag, 20,000 strong, moved towards the British as they formed up before the camp. The Mahdists charging into a hail of machine-gun fire, suffering tremendous losses.

The 21st Lancers, including a young Winston Churchill, and the Camel Corps took a position on Kerreri Ridge to protect the British flank. The mounted troops withdrew before the onslaughts of Osman Digna's personal force of 15,000 riders. Slowed by their wounded, the horsemen and camel corps were saved when the gunboat *Melik* devastated the Sudanese with its machine guns and howitzers as the Mahdists neared the river. Other gunboats and Maxim guns spread destruction along the whole of Osman Digna's line when Osman Digna's reserve of some 15,000 fell upon the British rear. Kitchener once again allowed the Ansār time to reform, then the 21st Lancers charged the remnant of the Mahdist cavalry. Artillery then breached the walls of Khartoum., and the city was taken. A total of 10,000 Ansār perished in the battle.

■ **UMM DIWAYKARAT, 24 NOVEMBER 1898**

Khartoum now in Kitchener's hands, the Khalifa fled south and east to the Abyssinian border with his remaining 25,000 followers dwindling to 10,000 in the year after Omdurman. Kitchener dispatched Gen Reginald Wingate with 8000 troops from Khartoum, the Anglo-Egyptians locating and destroying a Mahdist supply depot, advancing to the Khalifa's camp here. The Ansār again charged machine guns, the Khalifa and his generals perishing as the surviving Mahdists scattered.

Zulu–British War, 1879

■ **ISANDHLWANA, 22 JANUARY 1879**

Shaka Zulu had formalized his tribe's weaponry and tactics with devastating military effect before his assassination in 1828, his troops employing the short Zulu spear called an *iklwa*, or *assegai*, and the small war shield called *umbhumbluzo*. As tensions between the British in South Africa and the Zulus rose, Col Anthony Durnford and LCol Henry Pulleine led 1200 British regulars, African troops and the Natal Native Horse as one of five columns intended to converge on Zulu chief Cetawayo's capital at Ulundi. On this hillside, approximate 12,000 Zulus led by Ntshingwayo and kaMahole Khoza closed with Durnford's and Pulleine's camp before the British had time to prepare a strong defence. At close quarters, the Zulus obliterated the British and levies, Durnford just having time before his death to release some of his mounted Africans, the sole survivors.

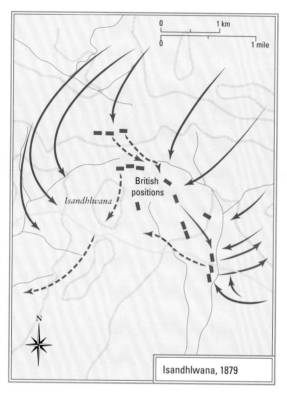

0   1 km

0   1 mile

British
positions

Isandhlwana

N

Isandhlwana, 1879

■ RORKE'S DRIFT, 22–23 JANUARY 1879

The celebrated defence of this mission station immediately after the British disaster at Isandhlwana exemplifies the utility of a contracting perimeter and interior lines, as well as the ferocity of men fighting for their lives with no chance of surrender. Lieutenants Gonville Bromhead and John Chard, the latter an engineering officer, assisted by Commissary James Dalton, a retired staff sergeant, received the news from two survivors of the battle of the destruction of the main column just 10km distant. Prince Dabulamanzi kaMpande, in disobedience of Chief Cetawayo's orders, took the Zulu Undi Corps, a total force of some 4500 trained warriors and the reserve from Islandhlwana, to destroy the hospital and depot at Rorke's Drift and sever the British lines of reinforcement or retreat. The final defenders at Rorke's Drift numbered one company of the 24th Foot – 141 men – some 200 Natal Native Horse, and Native Contingent

territorial cavalry withdrawing as the main Zulu force bore down upon the station. Some 30 of the defenders were hospital patients.

Chard's engineering expertise and Dalton's experience led to the decision to fortify the post with the materials at hand, the officers agreeing that any effort to flee the pursuing Zulus offered less hope of survival than such a defence, the post fortunately containing 20,000 rounds of ammunition for the regulars' breech-loading Martini-Henry rifles, 19,100 of which were expended during the battle. Consequently the defenders employed heavy sacks of maize to link the hospital, the stone cattle kraal and the store house into an oblate perimeter, Chard later ordering a wall of boxes built to form an inner redoubt in front of the kraal and storehouse. The British employed windows and loopholes picked through the buildings' mud walls as firing positions.

Given the unauthorized nature of his attack, Dabulamanzi launched multiple smaller assaults in an effort to minimize his casualties and probe for weaknesses in the British defence while such warriors as he had with rifles and the skill to use them put fire upon the defenders. The initial Zulu charge at the post's south wall set the pattern for much of the battle – the designated Zulu formation would rush toward the walls at a run, the British opening fire with their rifles at roughly 450m, the Zulus' stabbing weapons only inflicting casualties at point-blank range while the British fired over the walls and through the loopholes. The most prolonged and successful part of the Zulus' onslaught overran the defenders of the hospital, Zulu warriors scaling the walls, taking over the British loopholes and hacking their way through the roof to leap down upon the defenders and patients inside. The hospital's defenders escaped by 'mouseholing' through the interior walls and fleeing into the inner yard as the building burned, by its destruction forming yet another obstacle to the attacking Zulus. Attacks also continued along the entire perimeter, Zulus crouching near the walls of bags and trying to grab the soldiers' rifles as they levelled them

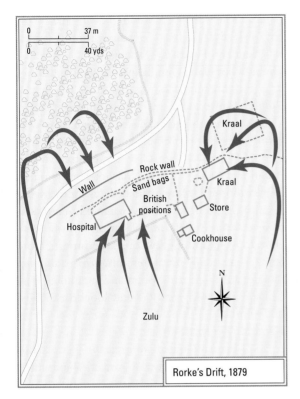

Rorke's Drift, 1879

over the improvised parapet. As night fell, the Zulus increased the numbers and ferocity of their attacks, finally taking the stone cattle kraal as the British retreated behind their inner wall of boxes, having also been driven back from the north wall of the perimeter. The Zulus had withdrawn by dawn. Some 351 Zulus died in the course of the assaults, and 17 of the British, five from the Zulus' gunfire.

■ GINGINDLOVU, 1 APRIL 1879

Lord Chelmsford, ignoring his supersession and peace overtures by Chief Cetawayo, moved 5600 British and African troops into Zululand. A total of 11,000 Zulus found Chelmsford's alerted camp anticipating their attack with cavalry and Gatlings, 1000 Zulus dying in the action.

■ ULUNDI, 4 JULY 1879

British Lord Chelmsford's reorganized army sent all the troops he could supply, some 17,000, into Zululand against Chief Cetawayo's capital here. Chelmsford ignored General Garnet Wolseley's

appointment to relieve him and telegraphed commands. Chelmsford's central column of 4200 British, a Gatling company and 10 cannon supplemented by 1000 African troops advanced on Ulundi disregarding Cetawayo's efforts to negotiate. Notwithstanding, the Zulu chief restrained his warriors from harrying the British invasion. Some 3000 Zulus tried to ambush Chelmsford's cavalry vanguard, Chelmsford consolidating his army into the hollow square formation and continued moving forward the following day. More than 12,000 Zulus advanced in their 'Buffalo' crescent formation, the British machine guns and artillery opening up as the two armies drew together. Intense prepared fire from the infantry kept the Zulus from closing, 500 Zulus being found dead around the British formation. Ten British perished.

■ BAMBATHA REBELLION, 1906

The Zulus of South Africa rose up at the imposition of a poll tax designed to bring the outlaying Zulus into the province's economy. Chief Bambatha kaMancinza launched attacks, his army being crushed with some 3000 killed.

War in the Pacific, 1877–1883

■ PACOCHA, 29 MAY 1877

The *Amethyst* and *Shah* of RAdm Algernon de Horsey's British Pacific Squadron fought an inconclusive action against the Peruvian ironclad *Huáscar*, which had been attacking British shipping after being seized by Peruvian revolutionaries.

■ TOPÁTER, 23 MARCH 1879

A detachment of 554 Chilean troops under Col Eleuterio Ramírez invaded Bolivia, defeating a force of 135 Bolivian troops and militia at the River Topáter. The Chileans inflicted 47 casualties for the loss of 13 men.

■ CHIPANA, 12 APRIL 1879

The Peruvian corvette *Unión* and gunboat *Pilcomayo* intercepted the Chilean corvette *Magallanes* on its way to Iquique. After a two-hour action, *Unión's* engine problems forced the Peruvians to abandon the pursuit and *Magallanes* escaped with minor damage.

■ PUNTA GRUESA, 21 MAY 1879

The Chilean armed schooner *Virgen de Covadonga* was pursued by the far more powerful Peruvian broadside ironclad *Independencia* for more than three hours. The ironclad was scuttled after running aground whilst attempting to ram the schooner.

■ IQUIQUE, 21 MAY 1879

The Peruvian ironclad turret ship *Huáscar* broke the Chilean blockade of the port of Iquique, sinking the wooden corvette *Esmeralda* by repeated ramming attacks. The Chilean captain, Arturo Prat, was killed whilst leading a vain boarding attempt.

■ ANGAMOS, 8 OCTOBER 1879

After Iquique, the entire Chilean fleet of two armoured central battery ships, the *Almirante Cochrane* and the *Almirante Blanco Encalada* (both British-built and more modern than *Huáscar*), two cruisers and two wooden gunboats concentrated on catching *Huáscar*. It was finally trapped off Punta Angamos in Bolivia by the Chilean fleet. Its steering was disabled by one of the first salvoes; then another hit penetrated the armoured bridge, killing Adm Grau and most of his officers. The *Huáscar* sustained a total of 76 direct hits in the two-hour battle, including two that disabled its turret, forcing it to rely on secondary armament. The surviving crew attempted to scuttle the ship, but the Chileans were able to board in time to save her. *Huáscar* was incorporated into the Chilean \ Navy, serving in various roles until 1934 when it was re-commissioned as a museum ship.

■ PISAGUA, 2 NOVEMBER 1879

A Chilean landing force of 2100 men under Gen Erasmo Escala defeated Gen Juan Buendía's 1700-strong combined Peruvian and Bolivian force defending the port of Pisagua. The Chileans inflicted 210 casualties for the loss of 180 men.

■ SAN FRANCISCO, 19 NOVEMBER 1879

Following the Chilean occupation of the Peruvian port of Pisagua, the combined forces of Peru and Bolivia were supposed to surround the invading Chilean forces in an ambitious pincer manoeuvre. However the Bolivian contingent commanded by President Hilarión Daza suddenly withdrew, leaving Gen Juan Buendia's 9000 Peruvian troops to face the 6500-strong Chilean force under Col Emilio Sotomayor.

The outnumbered Chileans were deployed in strong defensive positions on and around the hills of San Francisco, Tres Clavos and San Bartolo. Additional cover was provided by the mining installations at Dolores. Although crippled by the absence of the Bolivian contingent, the Peruvians made a series of determined assaults which came close to overrunning the Chilean position before being beaten off. After fierce fighting, Peruvian morale collapsed and Buendia's men fled. The Chileans inflicted over 4000 casualties for the loss of 200 men.

■ ARICA, 7 JUNE 1880

A 5000-strong Chilean force under Col Pedro Lagos stormed the Peruvian port of Arica, which was defended by Col Francisco Bolognesi's garrison of 1900 men. The Chileans inflicted 1000 casualties for the loss of 474 men.

■ SAN JUAN AND CHORRILLOS, 13 JANUARY 1881

Gen Manuel Baquedano's 23,000-strong Chilean Army defeated a Peruvian army of 19,000 men under the 'Supreme Commander-in-Chief', Nicolás de Piérola near Lima. The Chileans inflicted 8000 casualties for the loss of just over 3100 men.

■ HUAMACHUCO, 10 JULY 1883

A 1500-strong Chilean detachment under Col Alejandro Gorostiaga defeated Gen Andrés Avelino Cáceres' Peruvian force of 1400 regular troops supported by several hundred guerillas. The Chileans inflicted 1100 casualties for the loss of 160 men.

South African Wars, 1880–1902

First Boer War 1880–81

■ BRONKHORSPRUIT, 20 DECEMBER 1880

A column of 300 British soldiers was ambushed by an equal Boer force on 20 December 1880 when the stalled convoy received a hail of fire after the convoy refused to surrender, leaving over 150 British casualties.

▪ LAING'S NEK, 28 JANUARY 1881

On 28 January 1881 a British convoy of over 1000 soldiers travelling to the Transvaal confronted a larger Boer force in several defensive positions on a ridge in the Drakensberg foothills. After a small artillery bombardment the British made an attack on two fronts that was repulsed by sustained small-arms fire from Boer positions. The British retreat left nearly 200 casualties to a small number of Boer losses.

▪ SCHUINSHOOGTE, 8 FEBRUARY 1881

A British column of infantry, cavalry and artillery was attacked and pinned down with accurate rifle fire near the Ingogo river until nightfall and rain allowed their escape with nearly 150 casualties.

▪ MAJUBA HILL, 27 FEBRUARY 1881

Three overlapping Boer attack groups forced, with precise shooting, a panicked British retreat and prevented a British attempt to occupy Majuba Hill on 27 February 1881. British commander MGen Colley was killed alongside more than 200 casualties.

Second Boer War 1889–1902

▪ JAMESON RAID, 29 DECEMBER 1895– 2 JANUARY 1896

This 500-strong raid with artillery into the Transvaal by British activist Leander Jameson was aimed at forming an insurrection among local British residents. It failed after a few skirmishes and surrender on 2 January 1896.

▪ KRAAIPAN, 12 OCTOBER 1899

The battle of Kraaipan was an attack on a British garrison, railway siding and armoured train by several hundred Boers under Gen Koos de la Rey on 12 October 1899, resulting in the capture of substantial amounts of arms, artillery and ammunition.

▪ MAFEKING, 13 OCTOBER 1899–17 MAY 1900

In September 1899, Col Baden-Powell occupied the town of Mafeking (now called Mafikeng) on

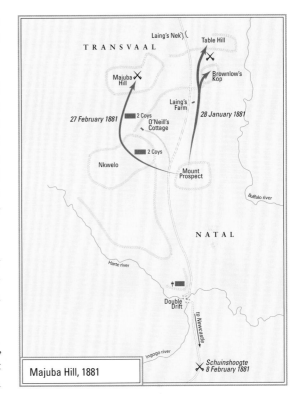

Majuba Hill, 1881

the banks of the Molopo river near the modern -day border with Botswana. He assembled a mixed band of 2000 soldiers, police, citizens, youths and African natives to defend the city from an anticipated Boer attack. Supplies were accumulated and defensive construction started with extensive perimeter fences, trenches and gun positions, in time for the start of a siege on 13 October 1899.

Gen Piet Cronje led an 8000 Boer force in a 217-day siege that began with a demand for surrender after cutting all communication to the town. The surrender was refused and the defending force began a series of deceptions, involving moving searchlights and cannon, setting up imaginary obstacles and laying imitation mines to increase their perceived force. Boer forces faced a series of small forays and probing attacks to keep them unsettled, but all enjoyed a regular Sunday truce for social activities. That November half of the Boer force was deployed elsewhere when it

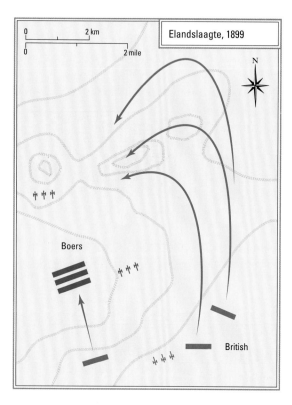

was decided to maintain the siege but not take the town. There were several attacks and counter-attacks with two notable events during the siege. A British armoured train was able to run up rails (those not destroyed by the besieging Boers) to make an attack on the Boer camp, whereupon it returned safely to the town. As relief forces neared the town a Boer force of 250 breached the perimeter on 12 May 1900 and burned an African village before being split up and surrounded. Most of the Boer attackers were killed or captured. On 17 May a relief force led by Col B.T.Mahon arrived at the town.

■ KIMBERLEY, 14 OCT 1899–15 FEB 1900

The siege of Kimberley began on 14 October 1899, shortly after the declaration of the Second Boer War and encirclement by several thousand Boers and artillery under Cdr Cornelius Wessels. The De Beers company had created defensive plans that included storage of supplies and arms, but the arrival of owner Cecil Rhodes forced

British attention and resources for the town along with his commercial interests. Water and rail links were severed before artillery attacks started on 7 November 1899, following a refusal to surrender by LCol Robert Kekewich. The bombardment continued daily for most of the 124 days of the siege, except on Sundays, interspersed with many small distraction attacks by the British. The town was relieved on 15 February 1900 by a force of 7500 British cavalry under MGen John French that broke through Boer lines at Klip Drift.

■ ELANDSLAAGTE, 19–21 OCTOBER 1899

A Boer force of about 1000 men under Gen Johannes Kock captured the railway station at Elandslaagte on 19 October 1899, to isolate Ladysmith and force a British intervention. Three times their number of British troops with artillery and cavalry led by MGen John French arrived from Ladysmith by train. On 21 October an extensive artillery bombardment preceded the British frontal infantry assault, supported by flanking attacks that eventually captured the Boer position in poor light and rain. In confused circumstances, a Boer counter-attack led by their commander initially succeeded, but they were then driven back and Gen Kock killed. The defeated Boers retreated on horseback, but many were cut down by British cavalry in pursuit. British and Boer casualties approximated nearly 300 men, and Boer artillery pieces were also captured.

■ TALANA HILL, 20 OCTOBER 1899

Two Boer forces moved near the town of Dundee, occupied by a British brigade, with matching numbers of troops in the low thousands. One force occupied nearby Talana Hill. On 20 October 1899, the British then attacked with artillery fire followed by a charge up the hill slowed by extensive and accurate Boer fire that caused more than 200 British casualties, including LGen Sir William Symons. The British captured the hill and the Boers retreated.

■ NICHOLSON'S NEK, 30 OCTOBER 1899

During the siege of Ladysmith, on 30 October 1899, a detachment of British troops sent to secure a strategic pass failed to reach their objective at night. Severe Boer fire caused hundreds of casualties, including many men taken prisoner.

◼ LADYSMITH, 2 NOVEMBER 1899– 28 FEBRUARY 1900

LGen Sir George White led a British force of several thousand to join other forces at this army base town on the banks of the Klip river in present-day KwaZulu Natal Province. On 29 October 1899 a large Boer force almost of equal size under the command of Gen Petrus Joubert arrived east of the town and set up their 155mm French Cruesot (Long Tom) guns that had a range in excess of 8km greater than any available British artillery on Pepworth Hill. The British commander felt compelled to attack, he did so with a force of three columns. The main force of four battalions attacked Pepworth Hill supported by another force that pursued capture of Long Hill on the flank. These thrusts were supported by a reserve force of cavalry and a fruitless artillery barrage. The flanking force, assisted by cavalry, had assembled near Lombard's Kop, but heavy Boer fire halted any advance. The main attack faltered under sustained artillery and small-arms fire at the same time that the Boer Long Tom artillery opened fire on Ladysmith, but British artillery was unable to deliver effective counter-fire on the Long Tom position using smokeless ammunition. LGen White called off the attack and there was a costly retreat under artillery cover with over 1000 British casualties and prisoners. The town was besieged by the Boer forces for 118 days until 28 February 1900, during which time there were sorties by both sides without result. The first relief attempt ended in disaster at the battle of Colenso. Gen Redvers Buller VC was finally able to break through Boer lines with coordinated use of artillery and infantry.

◼ BELMONT, 23 NOVEMBER 1899

A convoy of several thousand British infantry, cavalry and artillery attempted a night march that left them exposed to concentrated Boer fire. Several skirmishes resulted in hundreds of British casualties.

◼ MODDER RIVER, 28 NOVEMBER 1899

A Boer force of about 8000 men faced an equal British force from prepared trench positions along the river on 28 November 1899 causing several hundred casualties when the British advanced on the open unprotected plain.

◼ STORMBERG, 10 DECEMBER 1899

After Boer forces seized a railway junction at Stormberg, a British response force of 2000 infantry and cavalry attacked on 10 December 1899 when Boer artillery and mounted irregulars forced a retreat, with several hundred prisoners taken.

◼ MAGERSFONTEIN, 11 DECEMBER 1899

A 15,000-strong British relief force under LGen Lord Methuen moved up a railway line to confront a Boer force half its size under Gen Koos de la Rey. The Boers were laying siege to the diamond-rich town of Kimberley, occupying positions near a series of hills south of the town. The Boer forces were arranged in a defilade along the base of the hills, which offered the men in camouflaged trenches protection from artillery strikes. The Boer line extended for several kilometres but the main trench lay in front of Magersfontein Hill. The British scouting parties were hampered by wire fences and harassing sniper fire that kept them from a detailed inspection of the area. Following standard British tactics at the time, the soldiers kept close formation to maintain contact with each other and advanced towards the Boer trenches at night for an early-morning assault but dawn found them within range of Boer rifles and still grouped together. The first Boer volleys killed hundreds of soldiers and nearly all the officers, including Gen Wauchope. British attempts to flank the line failed and a flanking counter-attack by Boer general Piet Cronje forced the commitment of reserves and stalled the main attack. An afternoon truce arranged by the Boer command allowed the recovery of British wounded, despite some mistaken British artillery fire, that saved many British soldiers. Later a general British retreat was made under Boer artillery fire to their Modder river camp. Total British casualties ran to a thousand, with the majority from the Scottish Highland Brigade that led the attack all day under fire. Their opponents suffered only a quarter of that number.

■ COLENSO, 15 DECEMBER 1899

The Boer blockade of a road and railway to Ladysmith resulted in two battles with British forces at a loop in the Tugela river and near Colenso on 15 December 1899, causing 1000 British casualties and the loss of many artillery pieces. British forces c-in-c Gen Sir Redvers Buller made a frontal assault at Colenso after extensive artillery bombardment on 13 December 1899. He faced Gen Louis Botha, who entrenched troops along an extensive front that provided clear view of the open plain.

MGen Fitzroy Hart assembled several hundred British troops tightly near a loop in the Tugela river, but an extended Boer attack of rifle and

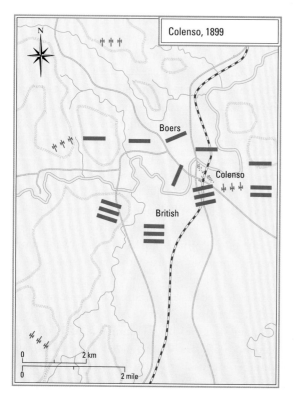

Colenso, 1899

artillery fire caused several hundred casualties. British artillery and ammunition was abandoned near Colenso in a rushed retreat under fusillades of rifle and artillery. British casualties were near to a thousand, including several hundred prisoners, including officers.

■ SPION KOP, 23–24 JANUARY 1900

The Ladysmith relief force under Gen Redvers Buller VC, having failed at Colenso, then decided to cross the Tugela river by attacking at two points with the main force of nearly 15,000 infantry, cavalry and artillerymen led by Gen Charles Warren, fording at Trichardt's Drift. A second and smaller diversionary force under MGen Neville Lyttelton crossed at Potgieter's Drift. Delay and slow movement by Gen Warren allowed Boer forces to keep them under observation and reinforce their positions. A forward cavalry force under LGen Dundonald successfully attacked some Boer forces on the flank, but were recalled. The British advance was met by entrenched Boer lines in the Rangeworthy or Tabanyama Hills, in the middle of which stood the tallest hill in the immediate area, Spion Kop or Spioenkop (meaning 'lookout hill'), which at about 450m could provide a good artillery position against the Boer forces.

On 23 January, Warren dispatched a part of his force under MGen Edward Woodgate to take the hill in what was expected to be a short sortie. An advance party of irregular local troops under LCol Alexander Thorneycroft, without the benefit of a proper map, attacked a skeleton Boer position successfully at night in fog, capturing what was believed to be the top. By morning the barely entrenched and exposed position of more than 1500 troops faced a steady stream of rifle fire from more elevated Boer positions, along with a sustained Boer artillery barrage from positions in the Tabanyama Hills. Shallow trenches in the rocky terrain provided little cover with many soldiers and most of the officers, including MGen Woodgate, killed, making Thorneycroft the de facto commander. At the repeated urging of Gen Louis Botha, a Boer force of less than a hundred men under Cdr Hendrik Prinsloo climbed up the hill and made an assault, which resulted in severe close combat and hundreds of casualties while initially securing a position, but no further advance. The Boer advance had stalled without support from surrounding units, but the British continued to receive punishing small-arms fire and artillery strikes from Boer positions at nearby Aloe Knoll, Conical Hill and the Twin Peaks. Thorneycroft intervened in an attempted surrender by some British troops and managed to prevent many from being captured. Several British counter-attacks under the remaining troops led by LCol Thorneycroft failed to shift the Boer line, while the British artillery failed to fire on Boer positions due to an error of command judgement.

Throughout 24 January both sides endured a stalemate and suffered from lack of water, ammunition and reinforcements. A British reinforcement rifle brigade diverted to the Twin Peaks and broke the Boer line just before nightfall, but was later ordered to withdraw. Despite receiving some reinforcements and messages of promised support, the replacement commander LCol Thorneycroft retreated during the night from the hill, having sustained some 1500 casualties. The Boer force under Cdr Opperman also began a substantial retreat that night, having suffered more than over 300 casualties, but Gen Botha intervened and in the early-morning hours the deserted position was finally occupied by Boer forces. The shallow trench full of dead British soldiers was used as a mass grave. A flanking British attack during this time had managed to secure nearby Bastion Hill. Prominent among those present at this battle was Winston Churchill, who acted as a courier, and medical attendant Mahatma Ghandi.

■ VAAL KRANTZ, 5–7 FEBRUARY 1900

A third series of repeated assaults by a British relief force, intended to break through Boer lines to Ladysmith, failed against entrenched Boer hill

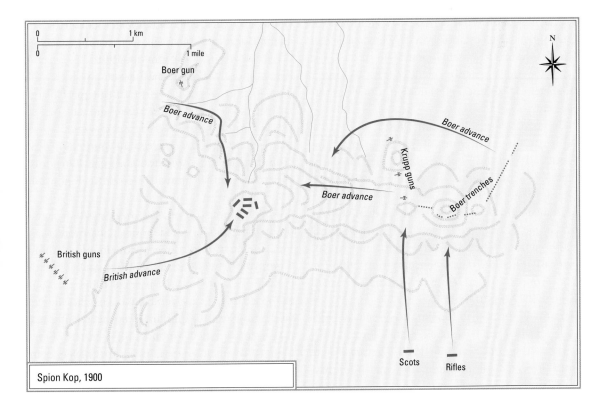

Spion Kop, 1900

positions commanded by Gen Louis Botha, with more than 300 British casualties.

■ Paardeberg, 18–27 February 1900

During February 1900, British forces confronted a Boer convoy crossing the Modder river. The convoy resisted a siege for several days before surrender. Each side suffered more than 300 dead and wounded, with the 4000 Boer prisoners including Gen Piet Cronje.

■ Bloody Sunday, 18 February 1900

A British frontal assault on 18 February 1900 ordered by Field Marshal Kitchener against an entrenched Boer position at the Modder river during the battle of Paardeberg. The attack resulted in 1000 British casualties.

■ Poplar Grove, 7 March 1900

More than 5000 Boer soldiers under Gen Christiaan de Wit failed to contain a British advance on 7 March, and withdrew from defensive positions having inflicted over 50 British casualties to only two Boer losses.

■ Dreifontein, 10 March 1900

A delaying action was fought on 10 March 1900 at Dreifontein by Gen Christiaan de Wets against the British advance to Bloemfontein. The action took place at a ridge near the Modder river, causing a Boer retreat and several hundred casualties on each side.

■ Bloemfontein, 13 March 1900

A British force originally of 50,000 men led by C-in-C FM Lord Roberts, who had recently replaced Gen Buller, occupied the capital of the Orange Free State on 13 March 1900 without resistance from Boer forces, who were demoralized by Cronje's earlier surrender. The Boer political leadership, including President Marthinus Steyn, had earlier fled the city. A concentration camp for Boer women and children was constructed nearby.

Karee, 29 March 1900

Boer forces threatened Bloemfontein railway links and were attacked by a mixed British force near a railway siding on 29 March 1900. They retreated from protected hill positions after causing nearly 200 British casualties.

■ Sanna's Post, 31 March 1900

A prepared ambush attack by Gen Christiaan de Wet near the Modder river caused more than 150 British casualties, took 400 prisoners and captured valuable artillery pieces and the Bloemfontein water supply, all for few Boer casualties.

■ Johannesburg, 31 May 1900

A large British northerly advance continued, despite small sorties by dispersed Boer forces, and crossed the Vaal river. Boer forces attempted a line of defence, but were outflanked and the city was occupied on 31 May 1900.

■ Bergendal, 21–27 August 1900

20,000 British troops successfully attacked a third of their number on 21–27 August 1900, with the main assault on a small hill that received extensive artillery bombardment before an overwhelming infantry assault.

■ Bothaville, 6 November 1900

A dawn attack by 600 British forces under LCol P. Le Gallais on an 800-strong Boer camp left more than 50 Boers dead and 100 prisoners taken. A skilful rearguard defence, however, enabled most of the Boers to escape.

■ Leliefontein, 7 November 1900

Also called Witkloof, this Boer attack at the Komati river was made on the rearguard of a large British convoy under the command of MGen Horace Smith-Dorrien, from a garrison at Belfast that had previously engaged in Boer farm and crop destruction. The Royal Canadian Dragoons, along with artillery, provided cover some distance from the convoy.

While waiting for the convoy to reach a safe point, the artillery force was surprised by a superior Boer unit from the Ermelo and Carolina Commando, who attacked using guerilla-style tactics. The initial attack was resisted by a small group led by Lt Hampden Cockburn, who allowed safe withdrawal of the artillery pieces although they were all killed, wounded or captured. Three of the Canadians, including Lt Cockburn, were awarded the Victoria Cross for their actions that dramatic day.

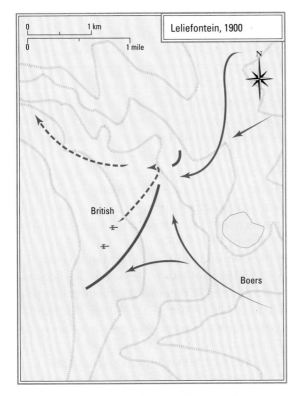

0   1 km
0   1 mile
Leliefontein, 1900

N

British

Boers

NOOITGEDACH, 13 DECEMBER 1900

A combined Boer commando of 2000 men under Gen Koos de la Rey attacked a smaller British brigade under MGen R. Clements camped at Nooitgedach, with the loss of more than 500 British casualties and prisoners.

BLOOD RIVER POORT, 17 SEPTEMBER 1901

Led by Gen Louis Botha, this flanking attack by 700 Boer horsemen on a smaller British force, attempting ambush at Buffalo river, caused over 50 British casualties, took 200 prisoners and captured British artillery pieces.

ELANDS RIVER/MODDERFONTEINM, 17 SEPTEMBER 1901

A couple of hundred mounted Boer commando under Cdr Jan Smuts were pursued across the Cape Colony by British forces under MGen John French to Stormberg Mountain. The Boers encircled a British camp of Lancers at Elands River Poort Pass near Modderfontein Farm on 17 September 1901, causing 70 casualties before

the British surrendered and the Boers captured much-needed supplies and horses. Artillery and equipment not required were destroyed before the Boers left.

BAKENLAAGTE, 30 OCTOBER 1901

In bad weather, a superior Boer force under Gen Louis Botha attacked the rearguard of a British column tasked with Boer farm destruction on 30 October 1901, inflicting over 200 casualties, including their commander.

GROENKOP, 25 DECEMBER 1901

On Christmas Day 1901, a Boer commando unit of several hundred soldiers, capably led by Cdr Christiaan de Wet, stormed a British camp at Groenkop, causing 500 casualties.

TWEEBOSCH, 7 MARCH 1902

Gen Koos de la Rey ambushed a British column under LGen Methuen at Tweebosch on 7 March 1902, causing 200 casualties and capturing an equal number of prisoners (including Gen Methuen) plus artillery pieces.

ROOIWAL, 11 APRIL 1902

A superior entrenched British force in the course of encirclement repulsed a frontal charge by more than 1500 mounted Boer forces in the Rooiwal valley on 11 April 1902, causing over 200 casualties including Cdr Ferdinandus Potgieter.

Sino-French War, 1883–85

NAM DINH, 27 MARCH 1883

Capitaine de vaisseau Henri Rivière's 600-strong French force took Nam Dinh in northern Vietnam which was defended by a garrison of 6800 Vietnamese and Chinese troops. The French inflicted 200 casualties for the loss of four men.

GIA CUC, 27–28 MARCH 1883

Chef de bataillon Berthe de Villers' French force of 360 men defeated Prince Hoang Ke Viem's 6000-strong Vietnamese Army at Gia Cuc in northern Vietnam. The French inflicted 1000 casualties for the loss of four men.

Sino-French War, 1883–85

CHINA

Zhenhai Bay, 1 Mar 1885

Shipu, 14 Feb 1885

Fuzhou, 23 Aug 1884

Taiwan

Taiwan Campaign Aug 1884– March 1885

Sino–French campaign Aug. 1884–April 1885

VIETNAM

South China Sea

0   200 km

0   200 miles

■ BATTLE OF CAU GIAY (PAPER BRIDGE), 19 MAY 1883

A French force of 550 marines and seamen under Capitaine de vaisseau Henri Rivière attacked a strong position known as Paper Bridge held by 1,500 Chinese Black Flag troops near the village of Cau Giay west of Hanoi. After initial successes, Rivière's men were almost surrounded and only just managed to regroup and fall back to Hanoi. The French inflicted just over 100 casualties for the loss of 87 men.

■ BATTLE OF THUAN AN, 20 AUGUST 1883

Adm Amédée Courbet's squadron comprising the ironclads *Bayard* and *Atalante*, the cruiser *Châteaurenault* and the gunboats *Lynx* and *Vipère* covered an assault by 1000 men, who took the Thuan An forts protecting the Vietnamese capital of Hue.

■ BATTLE OF PALAN, 1 SEPTEMBER 1883

Gen Alexandre-Eugène Bouët's French force of 1350 men and six gunboats defeated 4200 Vietnamese and Chinese troops under Liu Yongfu at Palan near Hanoi. The French inflicted several hundred casualties for the loss of just 59 men in total.

■ SON TAY CAMPAIGN, DECEMBER 1883

Adm Amédée Courbet's 9000 men of the French Tonkin Expeditionary Corps attacked the heavily fortified city of Son Tay in northern Vietnam. The city was defended by a garrison of 12,000 Chinese and Vietnamese troops under Liu Yongfu, Prince Hoang Ke Viem and Tang Zhiong. Son Tay was finally taken after a series of hard-fought actions in which the French inflicted 1,900 casualties for the loss of 403 men.

■ BAC NINH CAMPAIGN, 6–24 MARCH 1884

A French force of 10,000 men under Gen Charles-Théodore Millot captured Bac Ninh in northern Vietnam, which was defended by Xu Yanxu's 23,000 Chinese troops. The French inflicted 500 casualties for the loss of 48 men.

■ CAPTURE OF HUNG HOA, 12 APRIL 1884

Gen Charles-Théodore Millot's French force of 10,000 men took Hung Hoa in northern Vietnam, which was defended by a 3000-strong detachment of Liu Yongfu's Black Flag Army and 6000 Vietnamese troops under Hoang Ke Viem.

■ BAC LE AMBUSH, 23–24 JUNE 1884

Wan Zhongxuan's 4,600 Chinese troops ambushed LCol Alphonse Dugenne's 450 French regulars and 350 Tonkinese auxiliaries at Bac Le in northern Vietnam. The French withdrew after inflicting 300 casualties for the loss of 92 men.

■ FUZHOU, 23 AUGUST 1884

Elements of Adm Amédée Courbet's French Far East Squadron destroyed the Chinese Fujian Fleet under Zhang Peilun, which was defending the Mawei Arsenal and shipyard. The Fujian fleet consisted of the wooden corvette *Yangwu* (the flagship), the scout-transports *Chenhang*, *Yongbao*, *Fupo*, *Feiyun* and *Ji'an*, the paddle steamer *Yixin*, the wooden gunboats *Zhenwei* and *Fuxing*, and the 'flatiron' gunboats *Fusheng* and *Jiansheng*.

The 13 vessels of the French squadron were technically far superior to their Chinese opponents

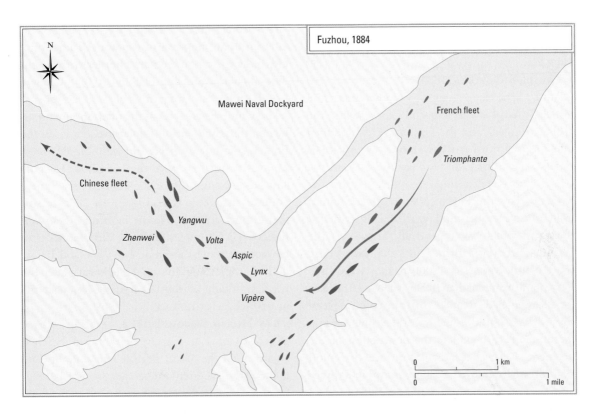

Fuzhou, 1884

N

Mawei Naval Dockyard

French fleet

Triomphante

Chinese fleet

Yangwu

Zhenwei   Volta

Aspic

Lynx

Vipère

0   1 km

0   1 mile

– notably Coubet's two ironclads, *Triomphante* and *La Galissonnière*, whose firepower and protection far outclassed those of any of Zhang Peilun's ships. As the action began, the Chinese flagship *Yangwu* ran aground after a successful spar torpedo attack by Torpedo Boat No. 46 (Lieutenant de vaisseau Douzans). The dispatch vessel *Fuxing* was unsuccessfully attacked by Torpedo Boat No. 45 (Lieutenant de vaisseau Latour), but was then crippled by a torpedo from Courbet's flagship, the cruiser *Volta*, and was carried by boarding. However, it was so badly damaged that it sank after being abandoned by the French prize crew.

Meanwhile the French cruisers and the ironclad *Triomphante*, which joined the squadron just before the battle began, rapidly destroyed the rest of the Chinese fleet. *Chenhang, Yongbao, Feiyun, Ji'an, Fusheng* and *Jiansheng* were either sunk or set alight by shellfire from the cruisers *Duguay-Trouin, Villars* and *d'Estaing*. Only *Fupo* and *Yixin* survived the battle without serious damage, by escaping

upriver before the gunboats *Lynx, Aspic* and *Vipère* had a chance to engage them. *Zhenwei* was blown up by a single shell from *Triomphante*. The French sank nine Chinese vessels and damaged at least ten others – only two of Courbet's ships, the *Volta* and *La Galissonnière*, were damaged.

■ **KEELUNG CAMPAIGN, AUG 1884–MAR 1885**
LCol Jacques Duchesne's 4500-strong French Formosa Expeditionary Corps fought an inconclusive campaign on Taiwan against Liu Mingchuan's 35,000-strong Chinese Army. The French withdrew after inflicting several thousand casualties for the loss of almost 1000 men.

■ **KEP CAMPAIGN, 2–15 OCTOBER 1884**
Général de brigade François de Négrier's 2800-strong French force defeated a 6000-strong detachment of the Chinese Guangxi Army under Wang Debang and Pan Dingxin in actions at Lam, Kep and Chu in northern Vietnam, inflicting 4500 casualties for the loss of 145 men. The Chinese retreated to Bac Le and Dong Song, while de

Négrier established forward positions at Kep and Chu to threaten the Guangxi Army's base at Lang Son.

■ Tamsui, 8 October 1884

RAdm Sébastien Lespès, commanding the ironclads *La Galissonnière* and *Triomphante*, the cruiser *d'Estaing* and the gunboat *Vipère*, arrived off Tamsui in northern Taiwan on 1 October. His orders from Adm Courbet were to bombard the Chinese forts protecting the port, destroy the barrage across the Tamsui river and seize Tamsui itself. On 2 October the French squadron shelled the forts, which were generally known as the 'White Fort' (Fort Blanc) and the 'New Fort' (Fort Neuf). More than 2000 rounds were fired in a bombardment that finally silenced the two forts. After bad weather had imposed several days' delay, Lespès ordered a 600-strong landing force ashore to complete the destruction of the defences. However, the assault force was driven off by 1000 well-deployed Chinese troops in a three-hour action. The French inflicted 300 casualties for the loss of 66 men.

■ Yu Oc, 19 November 1884

Col Jacques Duchesne's French force of 700 men defeated 2000 men of Liu Yongfu's Chinese Black Flag Army at Yu Oc in northern Vietnam. The French inflicted several hundred casualties for the loss of 47 men.

■ Tuyen Quang, 24 November 1884– 3 March 1885

Chef de battalion Marc-Edmond Dominé's 630-strong French garrison held Tuyen Quang in northern Vietnam against a siege by 12,000 Chinese troops under Tang Jingsong. The French inflicted 3000 casualties for the loss of 274 men.

■ Nui Bop, 3–4 January 1885

A French column of 2000 men under Général de brigade François de Négrier defeated Wang Debang's 12,000-strong Chinese force at Nui Bop in northern Vietnam. The French inflicted 600 casualties for the loss of 84 men.

■ Lang Son Campaign, 3–13 February 1885

Général de division Briere de l'Isle led the 7200-strong French Lang Son expeditionary column in an offensive to capture the important city of Lang Son on Vietnam's border with China. The French were opposed by 20,000 Chinese troops under Pan Dingxin.

The Chinese made use of the often mountainous terrain to fight a series of defensive actions as the French column advanced on Lang Son. The most important of these were the actions at Ha Hoa and Dong Song on 5 and 6 February, a Chinese counter-attack at Deo Quao on 9 February, and Pho Vy and Bac Vie on 11 and 12 February respectively. None of these did more than temporarily slow the French advance and Briere de l'Isle took Lang Son on 13 February after the Chinese fought a token rearguard action at the nearby village of Ky Lua.

■ Tay Hoa, 4 February 1885

When LCol Paul-Gustave Herbinger botched an attack on the 'Great Fort', Général de brigade François de Négrier ordered in the 3rd Foreign Legion Battalion, which attacked up steep mountain paths and captured the fort.

■ Bac Vie, 12 February 1885

In a costly but successful assault, Col Giovanninelli's Turcos and marine infantry stormed the Chinese defences. The battle was fought in thick fog, allowing the Chinese to mount a dangerous counter-attack that inflicted 218 French casualties.

■ Shipu, 14 February 1885

Adm Amédée Courbet's French squadron trapped the Chinese frigate *Yuyuan* and the sloop *Chengqing* in Shipu Bay. A night spar torpedo attack sank the *Yuyuan* whilst the *Chengqing* was sunk by wildly inaccurate Chinese fire.

■ Dong Dang, 23 February 1885

A 2000-strong detachment of Général de brigade François de Négrier's French 2nd Brigade defeated 6000 Chinese troops under Pan Dingxin and Feng Zicai at Dong Dang on the Vietnamese–Chinese border. French units then raided into southern China.

■ Zhenhai, 1 March 1885

Adm Amédée Courbet's French squadron found

the Chinese cruisers *Kaiji*, *Nanchen* and *Nanrui* in Zhenhai Bay, together with four other warships. The entrance to the bay was blocked by sunken junks and was also defended by two new forts. Courbet took the cruiser *Nielly* inshore and came under fire. The cruiser returned fire, damaging the shore batteries before rejoining the squadron which blockaded the bay until the end of the war.

■ **HOA MOC, 2 MARCH 1885**
The reinforced French 1st Brigade of 3400 men under Col Laurent Giovanninelli defeated Liu Yongfu's force of 6000 Chinese and Black Flag troops. Liu Yongfu's men held three lines of trenches with their flanks resting on the Clear river to the east and on impassable mountain terrain to the west. The French had no option except to launch frontal assaults and their sole advantage lay in their artillery, which was deployed on hilltop positions from which the guns could fire down into the enemy trenches. The first two French attacks were repulsed with heavy losses, but a third assault succeeded in taking much of the Chinese front line. Liu Yongfu launched a counter-attack during the night of 2/3 March, but when this was beaten off he withdrew his remaining forces. The French inflicted 3000 casualties for the loss of 484 men.

■ **PHU LAM TAO, 23 MARCH 1885**
Chef de bataillon Simon's 1st Battalion of the 1st Zouave Regiment attacked the village of Phu Lam Tao but was repulsed with the loss of 35 men by a strong force of Chinese and Black Flag troops.

■ **BANG BO (ZHENNAN PASS), 24 MARCH 1885**
Général de brigade François de Négrier ordered a cross-border raid by 1500 men against the Guangxi Army in retaliation for a Chinese attack on a French outpost at Dong Dang. LCol Herbinger botched the assault on the Chinese position and the 7000-strong detachment of the Guangxi Army launched a counter-attack that forced the French to retreat to Lang Son. The French inflicted 1650 casualties for the loss of 287 men.

■ **PESCADORES CAMPAIGN, 29– 31 MARCH 1885**
Adm Amédée Courbet's French Far East Squadron bombarded Chinese coastal defences on

the Pescadores before landing 600 marines who routed the 2400 Chinese defenders. The French inflicted 800 casualties for the loss of 17 men.

Colonial Serbo–Bulgarian War, 1885

■ **SLIVNITZA, 17–19 NOVEMBER 1885**
Prince Alexander's 32,000-strong Bulgarian Army defeated an invasion by a Serbian force of 40,000 men under King Milan I at Slivnitsa in western Bulgaria. The Bulgarians inflicted 2100 casualties for the loss of 1800 men.

Colonial Wars, 1890–1911

■ **FIRST FRANCO-DAHOMEAN WAR, FEBRUARY– OCTOBER 1890**
Just over 700 French troops, supported by 500 men from the allied territory of Porto Novo, defeated the 8000-strong army of the Kingdom of Dahomey. The French inflicted more than 1000 casualties for the loss of 100 men.

■ **JENNÉ, 24 FEBRUARY 1891**
French forces under LCol Louis Archinard seized the capital of Ahmadu Tall on the Bani river. Almami Ahmadu was deposed, and Umar Tall's son Agibu was enthroned as a puppet ruler.

■ **SECOND BATTLE OF JENNÉ, 11–12 APRIL 1893**
A French force under LCol Louis Archinard defeated the Tukulor Empire, forcing Ahmadu Tall to flee to the Sokoto Caliphate in what is now Nigeria. The battle marked the end of the Tukulor Empire.

■ **FIRST MATABELE WAR, OCTOBER 1893– JANUARY 1894**
In 1893, a British South Africa Company force of 750 men and 700 allied tribesmen under Dr Starr Jameson, one of Cecil Rhodes' lieutenants, invaded Matabeleland (in modern Zimbabwe), defeated King Lobengula's 100,000-strong Ndebele (Matabele) Army, and annexed the territory. British firepower (especially the new Maxim machine guns) proved to be decisive and by the end of the war, the British had inflicted

10,000 casualties for the loss of 100 men.

FIRST RIF WAR, 9 NOV 1893–25 APRIL 1894

In October 1893, the Spanish enclave of Melilla on the Moroccan coast was attacked by 6000 Rif tribesmen who were beaten off by the Spanish garrison of 400 regular troops supported by a local militia. The city was then besieged by a force that ultimately numbered 40,000 tribesmen. Spanish reinforcements of 25,000 men commanded by General Martínez-Campos finally defeated the tribesmen with the aid of naval gunfire support.

SHANGANI PATROL, 3–4 DECEMBER 1893

All but three men from a 37-man patrol of British South Africa Company troops were killed by 3000 Ndebele (Matabele) warriors near the Shangani river, Matabeleland (modern Zimbabwe). The patrol inflicted 400 casualties on the Ndebele.

FRANCO-SIAMESE WAR, 1893

Auguste Pavie, French vice-consul in Luang Prabang and subsequently resident minister in Bangkok, was the driving force in furthering French interests in Laos, which was then a vassal state of Siam. His intrigues led to the outbreak of the Franco-Siamese War, in which overwhelming French naval power quickly defeated the Siamese who were forced to cede Laos to France. The new protectorate greatly expanded the territory of French Indochina.

ANGLO-ZANZIBAR WAR, 1896

The succession of Khalid bin Barghash as Sultan of Zanzibar without British permission led to 'the shortest war in history' – a 45-minute bombardment by RAdm Harry Rawson's squadron of three British cruisers and two gunboats. The shelling inflicted 500 casualties, sank the sultan's royal yacht and destroyed a shore battery. (Return fire wounded one British seaman.) The sultan was forced to abdicate in favour of a British nominee, Hamud bin Muhammed.

SECOND MATABELE WAR, MARCH 1896– OCTOBER 1897

An Ndebele (Matabele) revolt inspired by Mlimo, a tribal spiritual leader, broke out in March 1896 against the rule of the British South Africa Company. The rebellion was well timed as the Administrator General for Matabeleland, Leander Starr Jameson, had been captured with most of his men in the ill-fated Jameson Raid. The revolt was finally suppressed in October 1897 after much hard fighting and 400 British and 50,000 Ndebele deaths.

BENIN EXPEDITION, 1897

A British punitive expedition of 1200 men under Adm Sir Harry Rawson attacked Benin in response to the defeat of a previous invasion force. Rawson's troops captured and looted Benin City, destroying the Kingdom of Benin.

TIRAH EXPEDITION, 1897–98

A 35,000-strong Anglo-Indian force under LGen Sir William Lockhart fought a fierce campaign against an estimated 50,000 Afridi and Orakzais tribesmen. Never defeated, the tribes were subdued at the cost of 1150 Anglo-Indian casualties.

MALAKAND, 26 JULY–2 AUGUST 1897

A force of 10,000 Pashtun tribesmen besieging the Anglo-Indian outposts of Malakand and Chakdara in the Swat valley was defeated by a 9000-strong relief force (the Malakand Field Force) under MGen Sir Bindon Blood.

FIRST MOHMAND CAMPAIGN, 1897–98

In August 1897 Mohmand tribesmen besieged the fort at Shabkadr, whose police garrison held out until a relief force arrived from Peshawar. The attack provoked a punitive expedition, the Mohmand Field Force, which burned several villages.

SARAGARHI, 12 SEPTEMBER 1897

A detachment of 21 men of the 36th Sikhs defended the fortified signal station at Saragarhi against attacks by 10,000 Afridi and Orakzais tribesmen. The Sikhs were wiped out after inflicting 450 casualties on their attackers.

FASHODA INCIDENT, 18 SEPTEMBER 1898– 21 MARCH 1899

Fashoda was a diplomatic crisis caused when rival French and British missions both arrived at a strategically located oasis in modern-day Sudan. As the two local commanders, Jean-Baptiste Marchand and Horatio Kitchener, wined and dined one another, nationalists and sensationalist newspaper editors in London and Paris began to demand war. Diplomats on both sides, however, realized the foolishness of war over so insignificant a piece of territory. French diplomat Paul Cambon worked out a deal to give Fashoda to Great Britain in exchange for British recognition of a French protectorate over Morocco. Both sides got something they wanted without having to resort to armed conflict. In the end, the Fashoda crisis made the British and French realize that they had significant strategic interests in common and helped lay the groundwork for the Entente Cordiale in 1904.

■ WAR OF THE GOLDEN STOOL, MARCH–SEPTEMBER 1900

Sir Frederick Hodgson, the Governor of the Gold Coast, provoked an Ashanti uprising by demanding their sacred Golden Stool. The revolt was finally suppressed at a cost of 1000 British and 2000 Ashanti casualties.

■ KOUSSÉRI, 22 APRIL 1900

The Sudanese warlord Rabih az-Zubayr's 10,000-strong army was defeated by a French force of 700 men under Maj Amédée-François Lamy, supported by 800 allied tribesmen. The French inflicted 4500 casualties for the loss of 100 men.

■ ANGLO-ARO WAR, 1901–02

Tension between the Aro Confederacy and British colonial authorities in Nigeria led to a British invasion of the confederacy's territory. The British force of just over 1600 men defeated the 7500-strong Aro Army and destroyed the confederacy.

■ BRITISH EXPEDITION TO TIBET, 1903–04

A 10,000-strong Anglo-Indian expeditionary force under Brig Sir James Macdonald and Francis Younghusband invaded Tibet to forestall a

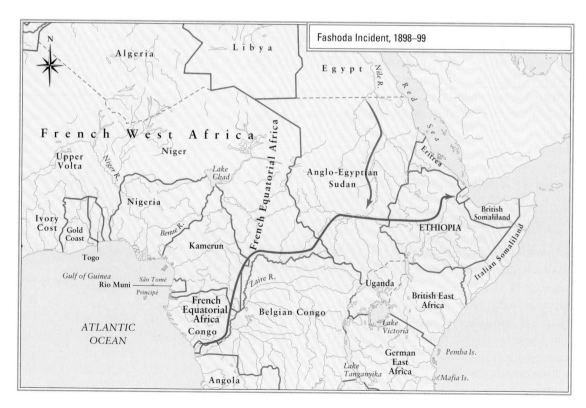

Fashoda Incident, 1898–99

perceived Russian threat to occupy the country. The force defeated poorly equipped Tibetan peasant conscript armies and occupied Lhasa.

■ Maji Maji Rebellion, 1905–07

Ruthless colonial rule in German East Africa (modern Tanzania) provoked a rebellion led by Kinjikitile Ngwale, a medium who gave his followers holy water (*maji*), which he claimed would protect them from German bullets. The governor, Gustav Adolf von Götzen, brought in reinforcements that crushed the uprising after prolonged guerilla warfare in which the insurgents sustained an estimated 200,000 casualties. Almost 400 German *askaris* (native troops) were killed, together with 15 Europeans.

■ Second Rif War, 1909–10

Spanish attempts to extend the perimeter of the enclave of Melilla to exploit mines around the city were met with fierce resistance by Rif tribesmen, who defeated the poorly trained Spanish conscripts in skirmishes at the Alfer and Lobo Canyons. In the aftermath of these defeats the garrison's strength was increased to 35,000 men with massive artillery support. This force defeated the Rif at the cost of 2500 Spanish casualties.

■ Wadai War, 1909–11

In 1909 France invaded the Wadai (Ouaddai) Empire, a region in eastern Chad and central Sudan. The empire was annexed after a campaign in which French troops inflicted 8000 casualties for the loss of 4000 men.

Sino-Japanese War, 1894–1895

■ Pungdo, 25 July 1894

RAdm Tsuboi Kozo's Japanese cruiser squadron intercepted the Chinese cruiser *Jiyuan*, which together with the gunboats *Kwang-Yi* and *Tsao-kiang* was escorting the troop-transport *Kowshing*. The Japanese sank the *Kowshing* and *Kwang-Yi* and captured the *Tsao-kiang*.

■ Seonghwan, 28–29 July 1894

MGen Oshima Yoshimasa's 4,000-strong

detachment of the Japanese 1st Army defeated a slightly smaller force from the Chinese Beiyang Army under General Nie Shicheng. The Japanese inflicted 500 casualties for the loss of 88 men.

■ Pyongyang, 15 September 1894

The Imperial Japanese Army's I Corps under Field Marshal Yamagata Aritomo decisively defeated Ye Zhichao's 13,000 Chinese troops at Pyongyang in Korea. The Japanese inflicted 6000 casualties for the loss of less than 600 men.

■ Yalu River, 17 September 1894

Adm Sukeyuki Ito's Japanese fleet intercepted the Chinese Beiyang Fleet under Adm Ding Ruchang, which was covering the landing of 4500 troops and 80 guns in the estuary of the Yalu river. The Beiyang Fleet deployed two battleships, nine cruisers, four gunboats and six torpedo boats, whilst Adm Ito commanded 10 cruisers, a gunboat, an armed merchantman and a flotilla of torpedo boats.

Adm Ding attempted to form his fleet into a line

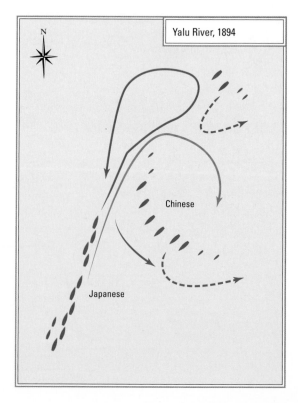

Yalu River, 1894

Chinese

Japanese

abreast with the strongest ships (the German-built battleships *Dingyuan* and *Zhenyuan*) in the centre. However, due to poor signalling and the differing speed of his ships, the formation disintegrated into a loose wedge shape. The well-trained Japanese fleet deployed in line-ahead formation and cut across the bows of the Chinese. Much of the Japanese fire was directed at the two battleships, which sustained several hundred hits during the action. Many of these were from small-calibre weapons that failed to penetrate the ships' armour, but the cumulative damage was considerable. Chinese return fire was relatively ineffective due to inaccurate gunnery and defective ammunition. (Corrupt officials had sold off explosives and issued shells filled with cement. Endemic embezzlement also resulted in many Chinese ships going into action with unsafe 13-year-old propellant charges for their guns.)

Although both Chinese battleships survived, Adm Ding's fleet lost five vessels with three more damaged and sustained 1350 casualties. Four Japanese ships were damaged and the fleet lost a total of 290 men. The remnants of the Beiyang Fleet sailed to Lüshunkou for repairs, but as the Japanese closed in on the port, the ships were withdrawn to the heavily defended naval base at Weihaiwei before any significant work could be completed.

■ JIULIANCHENG, 24 OCTOBER 1894

Elements of Gen Yamagata Aritomo's Japanese First Army totalling 10,000 men defeated the 15,000-strong Chinese Beiyang Army under Gen Song Qing on the Yalu river. The Japanese inflicted 2,000 casualties for the loss of 144 men.

■ PORT ARTHUR (LÜSHUNKOU), 21 NOVEMBER 1894

The Chinese naval base of Lüshunkou (Port Arthur) was a major fortress protected by hilly terrain and powerful artillery. It was a prime Japanese objective as it was the only base capable of carrying out major repairs to the warships of the Beiyang Fleet. MGenl Nogi Maresuke's 15,000 Japanese troops stormed the base, which

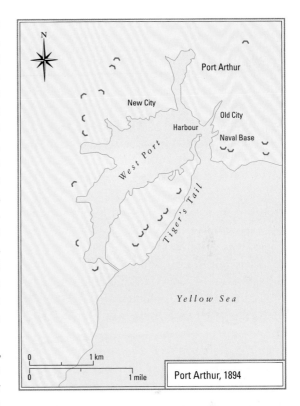

Port Arthur, 1894

was defended by a 13,000-strong Chinese garrison, inflicting 4500 casualties for the loss of 262 men.

■ WEIHAIWEI, 20 JANUARY–12 FEBRUARY 1895

The remnants of the Chinese Beiyang Fleet, including the battleship *Dingyuan*, two protected cruisers and 13 torpedo boats, assembled at the naval base of Weihaiwei. The anchorage was protected by powerful shore batteries, but these were stormed by Gen Oyama Iwao's Japanese Second Army on 30 January, allowing Japanese naval forces to attack the Beiyang Fleet. The Chinese surrendered on 12 February after inflicting 250 casualties for the loss of 4000 men.

■ YINGKOU, 4 MARCH 1895

Gen Nozu Michitsura's Japanese 5th Division defeated demoralized Chinese forces under Gen Liu Kunyi near Yingkou in Manchuria. The Japanese captured large quantities of supplies and inflicted almost 2600 casualties for the loss of 105 men.

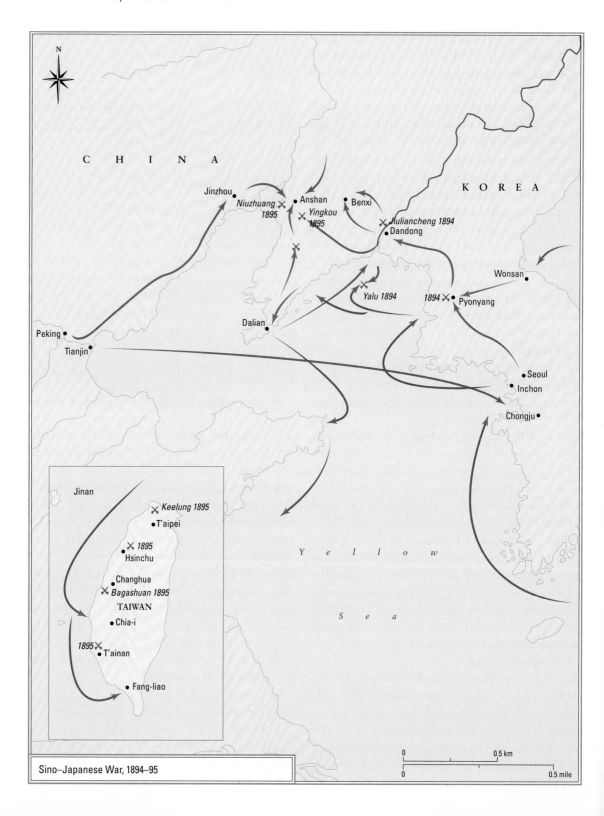

N

C H I N A

K O R E A

Jinzhou
Niuzhuang 1895
Anshan
Benxi
Yingkou 1895
Jiuliancheng 1894
Dandong
Wonsan
Yalu 1894
1894
Pyonyang
Peking
Tianjin
Dalian
Seoul
Inchon
Chongju

Y e l l o w

S e a

Jinan
Keelung 1895
T'aipei
1895
Hsinchu
Changhua
Bagashuan 1895
TAIWAN
Chia-i
1895
T'ainan
Fang-liao

Sino–Japanese War, 1894–95

0   0.5 km
0   0.5 mile

Japanese Invasion of Taiwan, 1895

■ PESCADORES CAMPAIGN, 23–26 MARCH 1895
A 5500-strong Japanese expeditionary force overran the Pescadores, which were defended by 5000 Chinese troops. The majority of the demoralized Chinese garrison surrendered and the Japanese captured 18 guns, 2663 rifles and 1,000,000 rounds of ammunition.

■ KEELUNG, 2–3 JUNE 1895
Japan's annexation of Taiwan and the Pescadores after the First Sino-Japanese War provoked the establishment of the short-lived Republic of Formosa. A 7000-strong Japanese force under Prince Kitashirakawa Yoshihisa landed near the port of Keelung in northern Taiwan. With the aid of highly effective naval gunfire support, the Japanese defeated the 12,000 demoralized Taiwanese defenders in a matter of 24 hours, inflicting 250 casualties for the loss of 29 men.

■ JAPANESE OCCUPATION OF TAIPEI, 7 JUNE 1895
The Taiwanese troops of the Taipei garrison mutinied on 7 June 1895 and began looting the city. Alarmed at the chaos, local businessmen, including the influential Koo Hsien-jung, sent three representatives of the city's foreign community to urge Japanese forces to enter Taipei to restore order on the streets. The Japanese commander immediately ordered an advance to occupy the city and the first Japanese troops entered Taipei on 7 June, and suppressed the riots within 48 hours.

■ JAPANESE OCCUPATION OF TAMSUI, 7–8 JUNE 1895
Extensive rioting and looting broke out in Tamsui following the Taiwanese defeat at Keelung. The unopposed arrival of two Japanese warships and an 18-strong Japanese cavalry patrol restored order and took the surrender of several hundred Chinese troops.

■ HSINCHU CAMPAIGN, 11 JUNE–2 AUGUST 1895
Guerilla warfare spread rapidly amongst the local people after the Japanese occupation of Taipei, and it became clear that all Taiwan's main towns would have to be captured. On 11 June the Imperial Guards Division advanced from Taipei and captured Hsinchu almost unopposed on 22 June. However, it was then embroiled in a series of actions against guerillas, inflicting over 600 casualties for the loss of 82 men, before the region was pacified in early August.

■ BAGUASHAN, 27 AUGUST 1895
The next major Japanese objective was the walled city of Changhua, where the Taiwanese were reported to have massed their forces to fight a major defensive battle. The Taiwanese commander, Liu Yung-fu, was said to have reinforced the local militia with a number of elite Black Flag units from his southern army. The defences of Changhua were formidable – the heights of Baguashan, to the north of the city, were fortified and defended by a strong artillery position, the Bagua Battery, and the Japanese made careful preparations for what they expected to be the decisive battle of the campaign.

The Japanese resumed their advance from Miaoli on 24 August, occupying the large village of Koloton the same day. On 25 August, as they continued their advance towards the Toa-to-kei river to the north of Changhua, the Japanese were ambushed by a large insurgent force in the fortified village of Tokabio, which was not completely cleared until the morning of 26 August. That evening, the 15,000-strong Japanese force closed up to the Toa-to-kei river and prepared to assault the Formosan positions around Changhua. The Japanese commander, Prince Kitashirakawa Yoshihisa, rashly insisted on making a personal reconnaissance – he and his staff soon came under fire from the Bagua Battery's four modern 120mm Krupp guns, which wounded him and killed his second-in-command.

During the night of 26/27 August, the Japanese crossed the river undetected, and at dawn their assault columns attacked the Bagua Battery, which was quickly taken. The 5000 Taiwanese defenders were totally surprised, but rallied and made two unsuccessful counter-attacks in an attempt to recapture the battery. As the final counter-attack was defeated, the Taiwanese forces broke and Changhua was taken without resistance.

■ **TALIBU, 5– 6 SEPTEMBER 1895**

During the night of 5/6 September, the Japanese attacked the walled city of Talibu. An assault force scaled the walls and opened the gates for its comrades. The Taiwanese fled and the city was taken by 5a.m.

■ **CHIAYI, 9 OCTOBER 1895**

A 3000-strong Taiwanese force defended the city of Chiayi, deploying cannon and machine guns on the city walls. After a preliminary artillery bombardment the Japanese scaled the walls and took the city, inflicting 200 casualties.

■ **CHIATUNG, 11 OCTOBER 1895**

Two Japanese infantry companies defeated Taiwanese militia holding the fortified village of Ka-tong-ka (Chiatung) after driving the defenders out by setting fire to the houses. The Japanese inflicted 70 casualties for the loss of 77 men.

■ **TAKOW, 13 OCTOBER 1895**

The forts protecting the southern Taiwanese port of Takow were silenced in a 30-minute bombardment by the Japanese cruisers *Yoshino*, *Naniwa*, *Akitsushima*, *Hiei*, *Yaeyama* and *Saien*. A naval landing force then occupied the town without any resistance.

■ **SHAU-LAN, 19 OCTOBER 1895**

The Japanese 17th Infantry Regiment trapped a force of 3000 Taiwanese insurgents in Shau-lan and stormed the fortified village. The Japanese inflicted almost 1000 casualties for the loss of 30 men, including three officers.

■ **TAINAN, 21 OCTOBER 1895**

By late October, the Taiwanese commander, Liu Yung-fu, realized that the Japanese were on the point of overrunning the whole of Taiwan. He left Tainan during the night of 19/20 October and escaped to Amoy aboard a British merchant vessel. His departure demoralized the remaining Taiwanese forces and local merchants surrendered the city, urging the Japanese to send troops quickly

to maintain order. Tainan was occupied without resistance on 21 October.

Greco-Turkish War, 1897

■ **TYRNAVOS (MATI), 22–23 APRIL 1897**

Edhem Pasha assembled a 9000-strong Ottoman force near Mati to oppose Crown Prince Constantine's Greek Army of 13,000 men. The Ottomans outflanked and defeated the Greek Army, which fled south through Larissa to Velestino and Farsala.

■ **LARISSA, 27 APRIL 1897**

The Greek Army was demoralized by its defeat at Tyrnavos and the shaken Crown Prince Constantine and his staff hastily abandoned their HQ at Larissa, retreating to a new defence line near Farsala in southern Thessaly.

Spanish–American War, 1898

■ **MANILA BAY, 1 MAY 1898**

The destruction of the Spanish fleet in Manila Bay and the reduction of the harbour forts allowed the US squadron to blockade the Spanish capital in the Philippines, despite the lingering presence of other foreign warships. Some 10,000 nationalist Filipino forces, led by Gen Emilio Aguinaldo, completed the landward investment of the city. US general Wesley Merritt arrived in June with the beginning of land forces eventually totalling 10,800 men by August. Adm Dewey maintained US control of Manila Bay over the intervening months with increasing difficulty, particularly as a reinforced German cruiser squadron under RAdm Otto von Diederich committed several violations of recognized procedures in the blockaded port. US policy was to avoid all formal terms of alliance with the Filipino rebels against Spain's rule. Notwithstanding, Merritt and Aguinaldo cooperated in trapping Fermin Jaudenes, Governor-General of the Philippines, and his 13,000 troops within Manila's walls while two monitors mounting large cannon suitable for

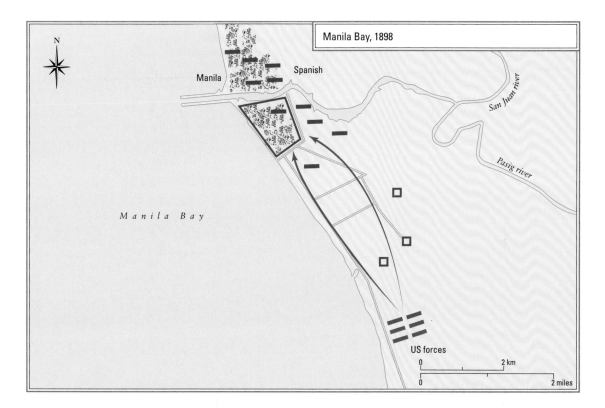

N

Manila Bay, 1898

Manila

Spanish

San Juan river

Pasig river

M a n i l a   B a y

US forces

0   2 km

0   2 miles

shore bombardment joined Dewey's squadron. At the start of August, Merritt delivered an ultimatum to Jaudenes, offering a chance to evacuate non-combatants before the reduction of the city. The Spanish refused, citing the hostility of the Filipinos as justification.

On 13 August, the American forces attacked Manila, the Spanish resisting until the following day, when Jaudenes formally surrendered the city. Even as their own forces attacked and entered Manila, the Americans denied entry to the surrounding Filipino troops, setting a stage for additional months of fighting as the United States asserted control over a fierce native force set upon independence for the Philippines. The formal end of the Spanish-American War had come with the signature of the Treaty of Paris some two months before Manila's fall.

■ CARDENAS, 11 MAY 1898
The US torpedo boat *Winslow* twice entered here trying to lure Spanish armed tugs away from the

port's defences. On the second run shore batteries killed five aboard, while seven Spanish died from US fire.

■ CIENFUEGOS, 11 MAY 1898
Three naval skirmishes took place outside this Cuban harbour as Spanish gunboats and shore batteries engaged American ships taking prizes or cutting cables near the harbour, American fire damaging the gunboats and destroying the lighthouse.

■ SAN JUAN, 12 MAY 1898
With the Spanish blockaded in Santiago, Adm William Sampson took two battleships, four cruisers and two monitors to bombard Puerto Rico's chief city, hampered by rough seas and winds. Two Americans and two Spanish died.

■ GUANTANAMO BAY, 6–10 JUNE 1898
The American authorities decided that this location in Cuba would make a good base for operations against neighboring Santiago. The US Navy cleared away Spanish ships, then 623 Marines were landed at Fisherman's Point, where

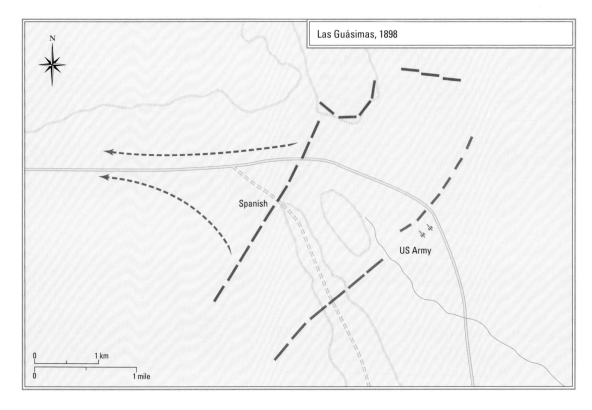

Las Guásimas, 1898

Spanish

US Army

0   1 km

0   1 mile

there were 5000 defenders in blockhouses and a fort at Cayo del Toro.

The surprised Spanish left the fortifications nearest the landing, but launched harassing attacks against the Marines, who lacked artillery and machine guns. Cuban rebels cleared the brush and Spanish snipers away from the position, while naval gunfire supported the landing. With the assistance of Cuban rebels and naval fire coordinated by flag signals, the Marines destroyed the well supplying the Spanish attackers, killing 68 soldiers while driving the Spanish back from the beachhead. The Spanish retreated back to the inland city of Guantanamo, which they fortified in expectation of an attack. The Americans instead employed the base on the bay.

■ GUAM, 20–21 JUNE 1898

In a rather benign engagement, the USS *Charleston*'s opening bombardment was taken for a salute, prompting negotiations and a bloodless surrender of 54 soldiers to the cruiser's captain

by the island's governor Juan Marina, previously unaware of the outbreak of war.

■ SECOND SAN JUAN, 22 JUNE 1898

The converted liner USS *Saint Paul* under Capt Charles Sigsbee prevented Spanish destroyer *Terror* and old cruiser *Isabel II* from escaping this blockaded harbour in Puerto Rico. *Terror*, having left Cervera's squadron for repairs in the port, attempted to torpedo *Saint Paul* while *Isabel II* disengaged, *Terror* abandoning its attack when *St Paul*'s shot disabled her rudder and left it unable to manoeuvre effectively. *Terror*, with two dead, beached herself on the Spanish shore, later being repaired.

■ LAS GUÁSIMAS, 24 JUNE 1898

Gen Joe Wheeler overtook Spanish retreating into Santiago at this ridge, sending Gen Leonard Wood's brigade to attack the Spanish flank. The Spanish resumed retreating after a two-hour holding action, the Americans suffering 16 killed.

■ **Third San Juan, 28 June 1898**

Spanish blockade runner *Antonio Lopez* slipped past USS *Yosemite* with a munitions cargo for the blockaded port. *Yosemite* drove *Lopez* aground despite fire from ships and forts in the harbour, the Spanish salvaging Lopez's cargo.

■ **I Manzanillo, 30 June 1898**

Three US gunboats escorted a prize past this harbour, Spanish gunboats, pontoons and field artillery engaging and disabling USS *Hornet*.

■ **Tayacoba, 30 June 1898**

A small US landing party attempting to supply Cuban rebels fighting against the Spanish ran afoul of Spanish scouts, the landing party retreating under fire on the beach only to find themselves trapped on there with their boats destroyed by Spanish artillery. After the first four efforts to rescue the wounded Americans failed under heavy Spanish fire from the surrounding jungle, boats from USS *Florida* offshore finally rescued the party.

■ **El Caney, 1 July 1898**

Gen William Shafter's army moved inland after landing unopposed at Daiquri. Gen Henry Lawton with 6653 men attacked blockhouses, his artillery at first ineffective before Lawton finally ordered his gunners to concentrate on individual targets, the most important being El Viso. Firing from their loopholes, the Spanish inflicted disproportionate losses before artillery cracked their strongpoints. The US lost 81 dead; the Spanish had 235 casualties, and 125 taken prisoner.

■ **Aguadores, 1 July 1898**

Some 274 Spanish in a fortified position on the western side of the San Juan river killed two Americans trying a diversionary attack supported by naval bombardment during the main assault on San Juan ridge.

■ **II Manzanillo, 1 July 1898**

The Spanish continued to accumulate smaller armed vessels in this defended harbour, three

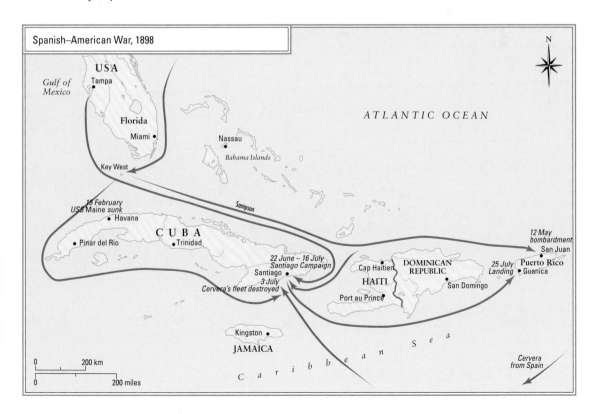

American gunboats entering and inflicting some damage until repelled by the combined fire of the gunboats inshore, troops and clustered shore batteries.

■ SAN JUAN (KETTLE) HILL, 1 JULY 1898

The San Juan Ridge was the last obstacle to the complete investment of Santiago, the principal port on the southern coast of Cuba. This hill was just off the southern end of the ridge, crowned by a strong blockhouse with 750 Spanish defenders. They were led by Gen Arsenio Linares and armed with Model 1893 Mausers, which reloaded from a stripper clip. After waiting under fire for the troops from El Caney, Gen Samuel Sumner ordered his Dismounted Cavalry Division up the hill, supported by the fire of Gatling guns, while the infantry moved up San Juan Ridge and its own blockhouse, taking casualties from accurate Spanish fire.

Leading the charge mostly on horseback was former Assistant Secretary of the Navy Theodore Roosevelt and his 'Rough Riders', a volunteer cavalry regiment equipped with Winchester repeating carbines. Alongside them were the African–American 'Buffalo Soldiers' of the 9th US Cavalry. The Spanish withdrew from the blockhouse, and the dismounted cavalry on Kettle Hill supported the attacks upon San Juan Ridge and higher San Juan Hill behind the ridge, although the Spanish resisted stubbornly. The Americans' field guns and some rifles fired black powder, which obscured the battlefield, while the more modern Spanish artillery fired smokeless charges more rapidly. The Spanish on San Juan Hill continued firing from the trenches as the US infantry moved forward. Linares kept most of his garrison within the walls of Santiago, taking the Americans under fire and launching one attack to retake San Juan Hill, which fire from the American Gatlings on Kettle Hill repulsed. For the eventual US victory, casualties on Kettle Hill were 35 US dead, a total of 170 infantry perishing

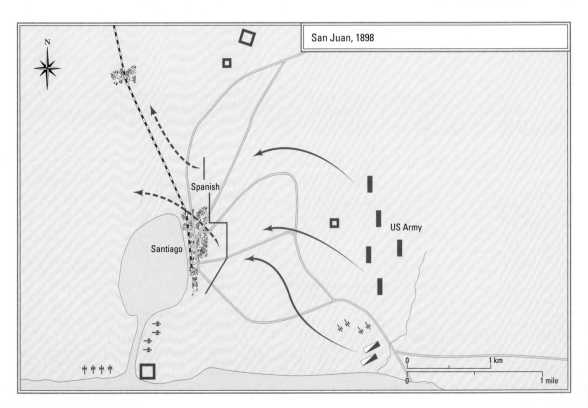

San Juan, 1898

in the assault on San Juan Ridge and Hill. Fifty-eight Spanish were also killed.

■ Santiago de Cuba, 3 July 1898

Spanish admiral Pascual Cervera slipped his fleet of four cruisers and two torpedo boats into harbour here despite US efforts at interdiction. Upon the location of Cervera's ships in the protected harbour, the US Navy moved to blockade the harbour while Cervera sought to coal his ships and make them ready for sea. Adm William Sampson arrived with the US North Atlantic Squadron and bombarded the harbour fort, an attempt to sink a blockship in the channel mouth failing. Cdre Winfield Schley added the fast cruisers of the Flying Squadron as US Army troops landed and surrounded Santiago. With *Massachusetts* coaling and Sampson taking *New York* for a meeting, Cervera sortied, Schley in *Brooklyn* interfering with the pursuit as the Spanish cruisers burst forth. All the Spanish ships were sunk in the resulting chase, *Oregon* overhauling the fastest, *Vizcaya*.

■ III Manzanillo, 18 July 1898

The battle of Santiago freed three cruisers and two gunboats of the US fleet to obliterate the shipping and defences at this port. The Spanish lost four gunboats, three merchant steamers and three floating batteries.

■ Nipe Bay, 21 July 1898

Three US gunboats and an armed yacht attacked the Spanish sloop *Juan Jorge*, clearing this Cuban harbour for use against Puerto Rico. A Spanish gunboat was scuttled upriver, *Juan Jorge* was sunk and the harbour forts were damaged.

■ Rio Manimani, 23 July 1898

An American force of 250 infantry supported by a gunboat came ashore near Havana to deliver supplies to Cuban rebels operating against remaining Spanish resistance. Spanish cavalry located and fired upon the party, which withdrew.

■ Manila, 25 July–13 August 1898

US general Wesley Merritt with 10,800 men and Filipino general Emilio Aguinaldo with 10,000 nationalist troops invested the landward defences of the Spanish provincial capital. The Spanish surrendered 13,000 troops after a token defence.

Philippine–American War, 1899–1902

■ Zapote River, 13 June 1899

Philippine nationalist leader Emilio Aguinaldo collected 5000 nationalist troops at the bridge over this river in Luzon and entrenched them in the path of American troops moving from Manila into the Philippine countryside, as General Henry Lawton advanced north with 3000 regulars. Fire from gunboat *Helena* allowed the Americans to turn the Filipino position while US field and naval artillery combined with machine guns to rout the nationalists. A total of 150 died.

■ San Jacinto, 11 November 1899

With war joined in earnest between US occupying forces and Philippine nationalist troops under the leadership of Emilio Aguinaldo, US general Elwell Otis made large-scale preparations to subdue the area of Luzon north of Manila around Malolos, proclaimed by the rebels as capital of their Philippine Republic. His first move was against the nationalists' supply line, dispatching Gen Lloyd Wheaton toward Laguna de Bay in a campaign that successfully rendered those territories in south-eastern Luzon unable to support the rebel army. Gen Arthur MacArthur took 9000 men north along the rail line from Caloocan, two brigades in the main advance, a third 'flying brigade' intended to trap the Filipino Army of Liberation in between the two columns. Aguinaldo's army avoided that trap, but despite the Americans' slow progress through the Luzon jungle, the nationalists had to burn and abandon their new capital before MacArthur's advance.

Summer rains forced a halt in the campaign. The pause allowed Aguinaldo to rally as many as 80,000 Filipinos to the nationalist cause. When the rains ceased in the autumn, Lawton's objective was to capture Aguinaldo and scatter the Army of Liberation, the US force moving north along the

Rio Grande de Pampanga, driving the nationalists 160km through rough terrain. The battle of San Jacinto occurred when Wheaton, with his flying column, moved by sea to the Lingayen Gulf, where 2500 men with artillery landed at San Fabian after a preparatory bombardment by the US fleet. There they faced a Filipino force under the command of Manuel Tinio; the Americans scattered the force as they united the flying column to MacArthur's main body, capturing Aguinaldo's mother and infant son, but not the nationalist leader.

■ **TIRAD PASS, 2 DECEMBER 1899**
Emilio Aguinaldo's aide Gregorio del Pilar undertook to hold this narrow passage with 60 men against 500 US Marines pursuing Aguinaldo's retreating forces moving into the Concepcion highlands. Pilar's life bought them five vital hours.

■ **PAYE, 19 DECEMBER 1899**
Filipino resentment of the US occupation of the Philippines expressed itself in this ambush, in which 200 Filipino snipers killed Gen Henry Lawton and 13 of his command, the survivors retreating back into San Mateo.

■ **CAGAYAN DE MISAMIS, 7 APRIL 1900**
Mindanao Filipino general Nicolas Capistrano's surprise dawn attack upon this large town on Mindanao island failed with 52 dead, when a native warrior gave his battle cry while killing an American sentry, alerting the US troops. Three more Americans were killed.

■ **SIEGE OF CATUBIG, 15–19 APRIL 1900**
Hundreds of Filipino nationalists on Samar gathered to attack a US post at this port garrisoned by 31 volunteers. The barracks burned and the 12 entrenched survivors were rescued two days later. Some 150 Filipinos perished.

■ **AGUSAN HILL, 14 MAY 1900**
US captain Walter Elliot and 80 men surprised Col Vincente Roa's 500 nationalists in this Mindanao village, killing Roa and 38 men and capturing stores of rifles and ammunition for the loss of two killed.

■ **MAKAHAMBUS HILL, 4 JUNE 1900**
Col Apolinar Velez had heavily fortified this

position on a steep height in Mindanao, with rocks and logs ready to roll down upon attackers as well as pits filled with punji sticks waiting as Capt Thomas Millar's company attacked. Nine Americans fell in the assault for the loss of only one Filipino. As the Americans retreated, Velez' troops captured a prisoner and a number of rifles.

■ **PULANG LUPA, 13 SEPTEMBER 1900**
Filipino colonel Maximo Abad on the island of Marinduque ambushed Capt Devereux Shields and 54 US troops with his 250 nationalists assisted by a hostile island population. Shields was wounded, and his force surrendered, having taken four casualties.

■ **MABITAC, 17 SEPTEMBER 1900**
Filipino general Juan Cailles' troops dug in behind a mud flat and successfully resisted LCol Benjamin Cheatham's assault upon their position with 300 men and support from a gunboat offshore. The Americans lost 21 soldiers.

■ **DOLORES RIVER, 12 DECEMBER 1900**
US lieutenant Stephen Hayt commanded 38 Philippine Constabulary in a patrol here through Cebu. Some 1000 Pulajan religious extremists suddenly attacked the contingent, killing all but Hayt after the constables killed large numbers of the attackers.

■ **LONOY, MARCH 1901**
Capt Gregorio Caseñas planned to ambush US troops en route to attack his camp at this location on the island of Bohol, imitating the success of earlier Filipino commanders by constructing a network of pits and trenches in the expected line of the Americans' advance. Instead, a local betrayed the ambush to the Americans, who on Easter Sunday circled around and attacked the entrenched Filipinos from behind, killing some 400.

Boxer Rebellion, 1899–1901

■ **PEKING, 20 JUNE–14 AUGUST 1901**
An involuntarily international force defended the American, British, German, Italian, Japanese,

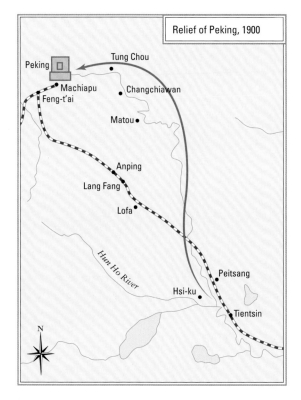

countered Chinese snipers and artillery, while 2800 Chinese Christians who had fled into the compound previously assisted with the defence. Lacking a unified command, the Boxers and Qing Army had difficulty coordinating a strong enough attack to overwhelm the defenders, who were fighting literally for their lives and making forays outside the compound to destroy hostile emplacements. The Boxers established roadblocks, burned railway stations and severed telegraph communication between the compound and the outside world as an international relief column of some 50,000 troops moved from Tientsin to rescue the diplomats. Fifty-five of the defenders and 13 civilians within the compound died before the relief column arrived on 14 August and scattered the armed Chinese, the foreign troops then plundering Peking for days.

Russo-Japanese War, 1904–05

■ PORT ARTHUR, FEB 1904–2 JAN 1905

The Russo-Japanese War began with a successful Japanese naval pre-emptive strike in February 1904 against the Russian fleet anchored at Port Arthur. By May 1904, Gen Baron Nogi Maresuke's 90,000-strong Japanese Third Army had surrounded Port Arthur, which was held by a Russian garrison of almost 50,000 men and 506 guns under Gen Baron Anatoly Stoessel. Initial Japanese frontal assaults were beaten off with heavy losses as their artillery bombardments failed to suppress well-entrenched Russian machine guns protected by extensive barbed wire entanglements. In desperation, Nogi launched a series of night attacks which were equally unsuccessful as Russian searchlights effectively illuminated the battlefield, allowing the garrison to decimate the 'human wave' assaults.

The Japanese attempts to storm the city had failed with the loss of 16,000 men and Nogi was forced to adopt the less costly tactics of siege warfare whilst awaiting heavy artillery to crack the Russian defences. By the autumn,

French, Austro-Hungarian and Russian legations in the Legation Quarter in Peking for 55 days. A Chinese nationalist movement calling itself 'The Fists of Righteous Harmony', known as the 'Boxers' in the West, formed a powerful force that began attacking Westerners, Japanese and Chinese Christians throughout China in an effort to reassert Chinese internal sovereignty, eroded for the half century following the Opium Wars. Drought conditions swelled the Boxers' ranks with recruits from the barren countryside. Sensing an opportunity to strike back against Western encroachments, on 20 June the Qing Empress's own army joined the Boxers in an attack on the diplomatic compound. Within the compound's walls were some 500 diplomats and 405 guards who had taken shelter as anti-foreign riots broke out throughout the city. Some 150 embassy personnel joined the armed defenders, among whom numbered future US president Herbert Hoover. Two cannon and three machine guns

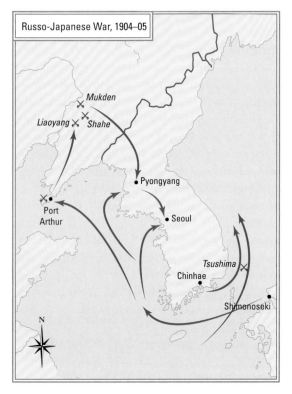

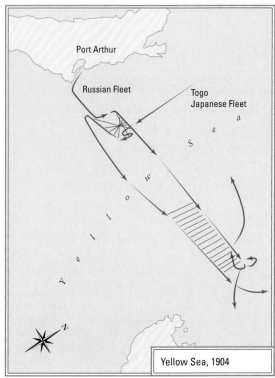

Nogi finally received several batteries of Krupp 280mm howitzers, whose 227kg shells at last began to destroy the Russian fortifications. More than 35,000 of these shells were fired against Port Arthur during the siege, together with a further 1,400,000 rounds from 450 lighter artillery pieces. Japanese bombardments became increasingly effective as techniques were developed for centralized fire control by a small number of HQs, each connected by miles of telephone lines to every battery under its command. These bombardments gradually sank most the remaining Russian warships in the harbour and, together with mines tunnelled under the defenders' positions, destroyed several key fortifications. Stoessel finally surrendered on 2 January 1905 with over 24,000 men, 15,000 of whom were wounded, having inflicted almost 58,000 casualties on Nogi's forces.

■ CHEMULPO BAY, 9 FEBRUARY 1904

The Russian protected cruiser *Varyag* and the gunboat *Korietz* were scuttled after being trapped in Chelumpo Bay, Korea, by a Japanese squadron of an armoured cruiser, five protected cruisers, a corvette and eight torpedo boats.

■ YALU RIVER, 30 APRIL–1 MAY 1904

Gen Kuroki Tamemoto's 42,000-strong Japanese First Army defeated the Russian 'Eastern Detachment' of 25,000 men under LGen Mikhail Zasulich on the Korean–Manchurian border. The Japanese inflicted 2000 casualties, for 1000 losses.

■ NANSHAN, 25–26 MAY 1904

A Japanese force of 35,500 men under Gen Yasukata Oku attacked and defeated Col Nikolai Tretyakov's 3800 Russians at Nanshan Hill in Manchuria. The Japanese inflicted 1600 casualties for the loss of over 4800 men.

■ TE-LI-SSU, 14–15 JUNE 1904

Gen Yasukata Oku's 40,000-strong Japanese Second Army defeated a Russian force of 33,500 men under LGen Georgii Stackelberg near Te-li-Ssu in Manchuria. The Japanese inflicted almost

3600 casualties for the loss of 1100 men.

■ MOTIEN PASS, 27 JUNE 1904

Gen Fedor Keller's 25,000-strong Russian force was defeated at the Motien Pass in Manchuria by 11,000 men of the Japanese First Army under Gen Kuroki Tamemoto. The Japanese inflicted 1200 casualties for the loss of 355 men.

■ TASHIHCHIAO, 24–25 JULY 1904

A 20,000-strong Russian force from I and IV Siberian Corps defending the rail junction at Tashihchiao in Manchuria was defeated by Gen Yasukata Oku's 34,000-strong Japanese Second Army. Each side lost an estimated 1000 men.

■ YELLOW SEA, 10 AUGUST 1904

Closely connected to the coterminous Japanese Army's land siege of Port Arthur, the battle of the Yellow Sea was a Russian attempt to join together two fleets. The Japanese Navy had bottled up six Russian battleships, four cruisers and 14 destroyers in Port Arthur. The Russian viceroy, himself a former admiral, urged the Russian commander, Adm Wilgelm Vitgeft, to push through the Japanese blockade and link up with the Russian Vladivostok Fleet then out on the high seas. By doing so, they could concentrate their power and avoid the inactivity that was their inevitable future as long as the Japanese blockaded Port Arthur. Vitgeft, however, preferred to remain at anchor and not challenge the four battleships, 10 cruisers, 18 destroyers, and other smaller craft under Adm Heihachiro Togo. The viceroy appealed to Tsar Nicholas II, who agreed and ordered Vitgeft to leave harbour.

Although both sides suffered damage, the better gunnery of the Japanese fleet won the day. All six Russian battleships were damaged, and Vitgeft himself was killed, leaving command confusion in the Russian fleet. One Russian ship, the *Retvizan*, bravely charged into the Japanese battle line, but it was too little to change the outcome of battle. The Russian fleet headed back to the relative safety of Port Arthur. It had scored some impressive tactical victories but it failed in its mission to get out of Port Arthur and

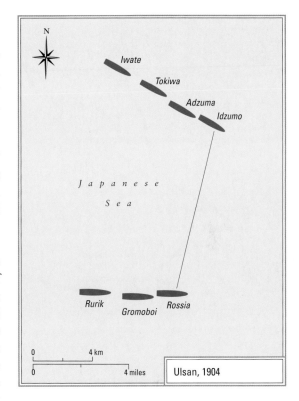

Ulsan, 1904

link up with the Vladivostok Fleet. It had also lost its commanding officer and 330 other sailors killed or wounded. The Japanese had lost 226 killed and wounded, but had successfully parried the Russian move. The Russian fleet remained in Port Arthur for the remainder of the war.

■ ULSAN, 14 AUGUST 1904

RAdm Karl Jessen's squadron of three Russian armoured cruisers, *Rossia*, *Gromoboi* and *Rurik,* was defeated by VAdm Hikonojo Kamimura's four Japanese armoured cruisers and two protected cruisers. *Rurik* was scuttled to avoid capture.

■ LIAOYANG, 24 AUGUST–4 SEPTEMBER 1904

FM Oyama's Japanese force of 127,000 men attacked the rail junction at Liaoyang in Manchuria. The Russian c-in-c, Gen Alexei Kuropatkin, failed to exploit the numerical superiority of his 158,000-strong armies and, although his men beat off a series of attacks, Japanese forces began to bypass the city. Fearful

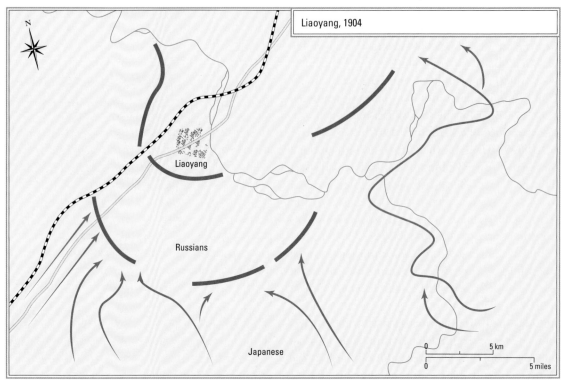

Liaoyang, 1904

Liaoyang

Russians

Japanese

0   5 km
0   5 miles

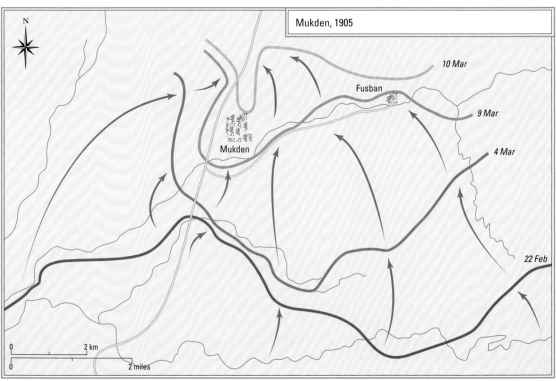

Mukden, 1905

10 Mar

Fusban

9 Mar

Mukden

4 Mar

22 Feb

0   2 km
0   2 miles

of being cut off, Kuropatkin ordered a retreat to Mukden. The Japanese inflicted 15,500 casualties for the loss of 23,600 men.

■ Sha-ho River, 5–17 October 1904

Gen Alexei Kuropatkin's 210,000 Russians fought a series of indecisive actions against FM Oyama's 170,000-strong Japanese armies along the Sha-ho river in Manchuria. The Russians inflicted over 20,000 casualties for the loss of 40,000 men.

■ Sandepu, 25–29 January 1905

Gen Alexei Kuropatkin's 285,000 Russians fought a series of indecisive actions near Sandepu in Manchuria against Japanese armies totalling 220,000 men under FM Oyama. The Russians inflicted 9000 casualties on their opponents for the loss of 14,000 men.

■ Mukden, 20 February–10 March 1905

A series of engagements fought over three weeks, the battle of Mukden in Manchuria was one of the largest land battles fought before World War I and the climactic battle of the Russo-Japanese War. Despite a series of set-backs the Russian commander in the East, Gen Alexei Kuropatkin, had slowed the Japanese advance against the strategically vital city of Mukden. Short of troops and fearful of the impact the arrival of the Russian Baltic Fleet might have, Japanese commander FM Oyama Iwao looked to force a decisive engagement.

Aware of the Japanese threat, Kuropatkin had deployed his 330,000 men in a 145km defensive line to the south of Mukden. His disposition was strictly defensive. In the approach Oyama formed his forces to move against the front and left of the Russians, using three armies, while a fourth army under Gen Nogi was to sweep wide around the Russian lines once the battle began and encircle them, eliminating the possibility of retreat. The initial Japanese attacks suffered heavy losses, but pinned the Russians as Nogi's Third Army swept left. The Japanese frontal assaults suffered horribly against the entrenched Russian machine-gun positions. Attempting to block this move, Kuropatkin's transfer of forces from his own

line, to the East, lead to confusion which Oyama exploited with a general assault.

The Russian order to retreat on 9 March quickly degenerated into a rout, resulting in nearly 90,000 casualties and the loss of most of their guns and ammunition, effectively ending resistance. Japanese losses were high as well at 75,000, with a higher percentage of dead in battle than the Russians. Losses were severe enough that there was no further large-scale ground fighting in the war.

■ Tsushima, 27–29 May 1905

During 27–29 May 1905, the Japanese and Russian fleets clashed in a major naval battle in the Straights of Tsushima, the narrow passage between Korea and Japan. During this encounter the Japanese Navy inflicted a crushing defeat over their adversaries.

The war had commenced on 8 February 1904, after a decade of expansionist rivalry over Korea and Manchuria, when Japanese warships attacked the Russian naval bases at Port Arthur, Dalny and Chemulpo. Subsequently, bitter naval and ground campaigns ensued between the Japanese and Russian forces. The clash at Tsushima originated in early autumn 1904, when Russian Tsar Nicholas II ordered his Baltic Sea Fleet to steam 29,000km round the world to Port Arthur. The Russians thus hoped to wrest back control of the seas in the theatre, thus buying time for Russian troop reinforcements to arrive via the Trans-Siberian Railway.

On 15 October 1904, Adm Sinovie Rozhestvensky's 2nd Pacific Squadron left Russian waters. Its 33 vessels included five modern and two old battleships, seven cruisers, nine destroyers and various support vessels. By the time the fleet reached Madagascar in January 1905, the Japanese had captured Port Arthur, but the Fleet continued with its mission. Meanwhile, the five obsolescent capital ships of RAdm Nebogatoff's 3rd Pacific Squadron had left the Baltic to reinforce Rozhestvensky's fleet. During April the two Russian squadrons joined up and

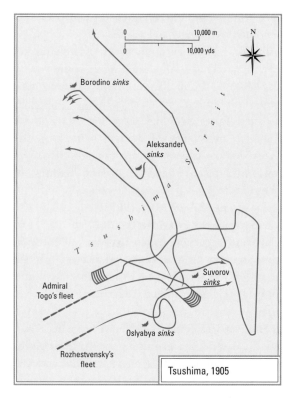

Tsushima, 1905

On the morning of 28 May the Japanese fleet again sighted and engaged what remained of Nebogatoff's fleet; at 10:34 Nebogatoff surrendered his four remaining ships. Elsewhere that day, Japanese cruisers and destroyers hunted down and sank most of the remaining Russian warships that had become detached from the main fleet.

The battle of Tsushima was a truly stunning Japanese success. For the loss of just three torpedo boats sunk, together with 118 personnel killed and 583 wounded, the Japanese Navy had devastated the Russian fleet. The latter suffered terrible personnel losses, including 4380 dead, 5917 captured and 1862 interned, together with thousands of wounded.

The Japanese fleet sunk 20 out of the 38 Russian warships, including all but one of their eight battleships, and captured a further seven vessels, including the remaining battleship; a further six warships were interned in neutral ports. Just three vessels made it back to the Vladivostok and one back to the Baltic. The annihilation of the Russian fleet at Tsushima was a devastating blow against Russian imperial pride, and it had far-reaching political effects. It prompted the Russians to sue for a humiliating peace, a settlement that ended their expansionist ambitions in the Far East.

Moro Rebellion, 1906

■ **BUD DAJO, 5–7 MARCH 1906**
MGenl Leonard Wood's US force of 790 men defeated 1000 Moro rebels at Bud Dajo on Jolo Island in the Philippines. Wood's force virtually wiped out the rebels for the loss of 96 men.

Albanian Revolt, 1911

■ **DEÇIQ, 6 APRIL 1911**
A force of almost 3300 Albanian rebels under Ded Gjo Luli and Pretash Zeka Ulaj defeated a larger Ottoman force commanded by Shefqet

subsequently these 38 vessels steamed through the South China Sea and into the Straits of Tsushima. At 14:05, 27 May, the main Japanese fleet, which comprised four modern battleships, eight new armoured cruisers, 16 cruisers and 21 destroyers, opened fire on the Russian squadron, which was now in a disorganized two-column formation. By 16:00 a deluge of accurate Japanese fire had caused the Russian fleet to disintegrate into isolated groups of vessels, many of them badly damaged. At 17:30 hours Nebogatoff assumed command after the wounded Rozhestvensky became incapacitated.

In the early evening continuing accurate Japanese fire sank three of the five modern Russian battleships. Throughout that evening and night, as well as the following morning, 21 Japanese destroyers and 37 torpedo boats also attacked the Russian fleet as it fled north towards Vladivostok; these attacks sank two old battleships and two ancient armoured cruisers.

Turgut Pasha at Deçiq Mountain near the town of Tuzi in Montenegro.

Italo-Turkish War, 1911–12

■ TOBRUK, 22 DECEMBER 1911
Mustafa Kemal's 1000-strong Ottoman force, supported by 200 Libyan tribesmen, defeated an Italian detachment of 2000 men under Major Gen Carlo Caneva near Tobruk in Libya. The Ottomans inflicted 200 casualties for the loss of 20 men.

■ BEIRUT, 24 FEBRUARY 1912
RAdm Paolo Thaon di Revel's Italian armoured cruisers *Giuseppe Garibaldi* and *Francesco Ferruccio* trapped the Ottoman corvette *Avnillah* and the torpedo boat *Angora* in Beirut harbour. The Italian cruisers were relatively modern vessels, massively out-gunning both the ancient *Avnillah* which had been completed in 1869 and the tiny *Angora*. The outcome was inevitable – the

corvette was sunk by a single torpedo and the *Angora* was destroyed by close-range fire from the *Francesco Ferruccio*.

Balkan Wars, 1912–13

■ SARANTAPORO, 22 OCTOBER 1912
Crown Prince Constantine's 80,000-strong Greek Army of Thessaly defeated Hasan Tahsin Pasha's Ottoman VIII Provisional Corps of 25,000 men at the Sarantaporo Gorge. The Greeks inflicted 1500 casualties for the loss of 1200 men.

■ KUMANOVO, 23–24 OCTOBER 1912
On 19 October, the 132,000-strong Serbian First Army under Crown Prince Alexander invaded the Ottoman province of Macedonia. It was opposed by Zeki Pasha's Vardar Army of 58,000 men which was preparing for its own offensive. The, Ottoman force was better concentrated and enjoyed local numerical superiority in its initial attacks on the Serbian right flank which

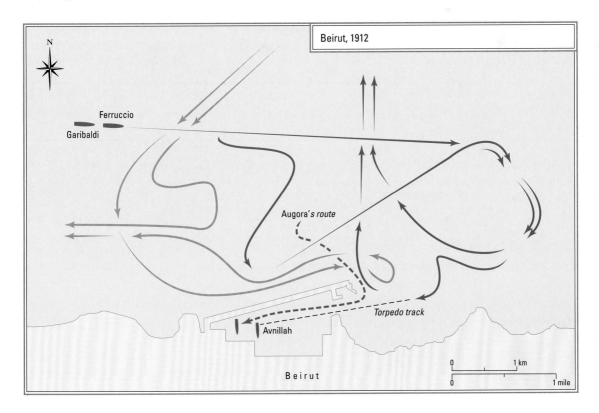

Beirut, 1912

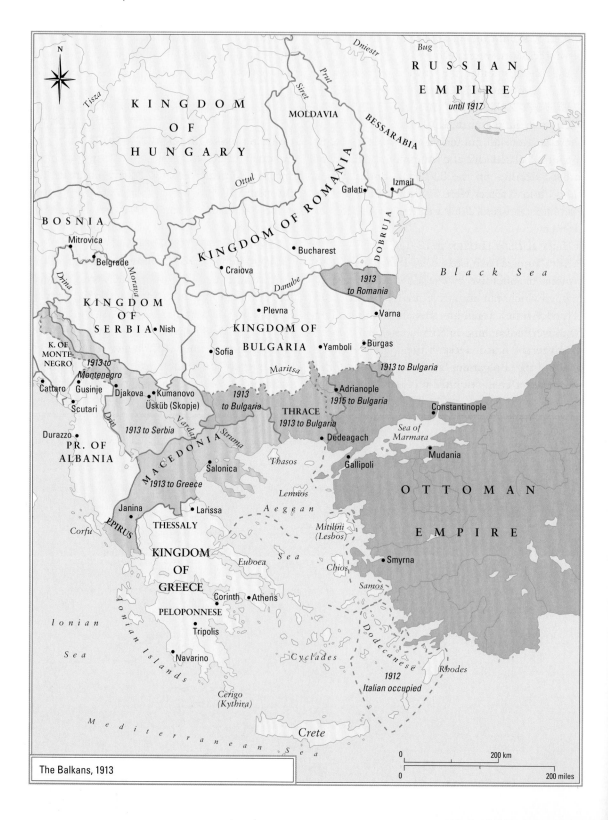

The Balkans, 1913

inflicted significant casualties. However, Serb reinforcements were steadily arriving and these were able to stabilize the situation in a series of actions throughout 23 October.

Although Zeki Pasha's men had at least held their own in the first day's fighting, the Serbs' increasing overall numerical superiority, coupled with the belated arrival of much of their artillery, proved decisive on the 24th. By the afternoon, the Ottoman forces were in retreat and the Serbs had inflicted over 12,000 casualties for the loss of 4500 men.

■ KIRK KILISSE (LOZENGRAD), 24 OCT 1912

The Ottoman Minister of War, Nizam Pasha, ordered an offensive by the 105,000-strong First Army, which ran into the Bulgarian First and Third Armies totalling almost 154,000 men, who were advancing on Kirk Kilisse (Lozengrad) in eastern Thrace. Despite poorly coordinated attacks, the Bulgarians decisively defeated the Ottoman forces, capturing Kirk Kilisse and

the forts protecting the town. The Bulgarians inflicted 4500 casualties on the Ottomans for the loss of just over 5700 men.

■ LULE BURGAS, 28 OCTOBER–3 NOV 1912

The Bulgarian First and Third Armies totalling 108,000 men defeated the 130,000-strong Ottoman First and Second Armies near Lule Burgas (modern Lüleburgaz, Turkey.) The Bulgarians inflicted almost 43,000 casualties for the loss of 19,500 men.

■ SCUTARI (SHKODËR), 28 OCTOBER 1912– 23 APRIL 1913

Hasan Riza Pasha's 15,000-strong Ottoman garrison held the city of Scutari (Shkodër) against 25,000 Montenegrin and 30,000 Serbian troops under Crown Prince Danilo. The garrison finally surrendered after inflicting 18,000 casualties on the besieging forces.

■ YENIDJE (GIANNITSA), 2 NOVEMBER 1912

Crown Prince Constantine's 80,000-strong Greek Army of Thessaly defeated Hasan Tahsin Pasha's

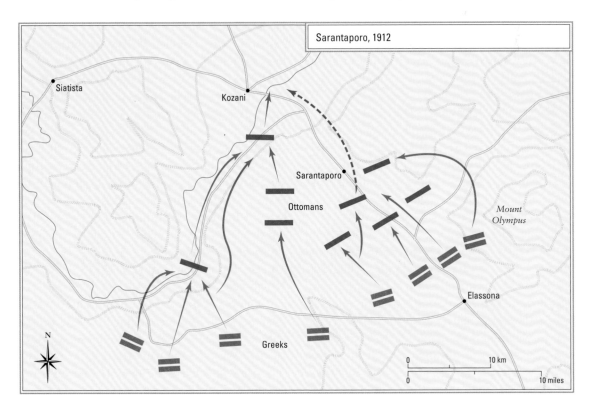

Kumanovo, 1912

SERBIA

N

Serbian First Army

Pristina

Vranja

BULGARIA

Kumanovo

Kiratova

Uskab

Kotchana

Veles

OTTOMAN EMPIRE

Ottoman VIII Provisional Corps of 25,000 men at Yenice-i Vardar (now Giannitsa, Greece). The Greeks inflicted 1500 casualties for the loss of 1000 men.

■ Prilep, 3–5 November 1912

The Serbian First Army under Crown Prince Alexander defeated Kara Said Pasha's Ottoman V Corps near Prilep in Macedonia. The Serbs lost 2000 men in a series of costly frontal attacks whilst inflicting 1050 casualties.

■ Sorovich, 3–6 November 1912

Following the battle of Sarantaporo, the bulk of the Greek Army marched north along the Aegean coast towards Thessaloniki, while Col Dimitrios Matthaiopoulos' 5th Infantry Division was detached to advance on Monastir (modern Bitola). However, during its advance the division was surprised near Banitsa (modern Vevi) by the Ottoman VI Corps (forming part of the Vardar Army together with the 16th, 17th and 18th Nizamiye Divisions), which was retreating after

the battle of Prilep. The Greeks, shaken, isolated and outnumbered by the counter-attacking Turks, fell back towards Sorovich (modern Amyntaio), leaving Monastir to be captured by the Serbs. The 5th Infantry Division lost 168 dead, 196 wounded and 10 prisoners. The Ottomans followed its retreat and launched further attacks on 4 November which were initially repelled, but the next day the division was forced to withdraw further south to Kozani.

■ Adrianople (Edirne), 3 November 1912– 26 March 1913

LGen Nikola Ivanov's 106,000-strong Bulgarian Second Army, supported by 47,000 men of the Serbian Second Army, took the city of Adrianople (Edirne) which was defended by an Ottoman garrison of 75,000 men under Mehmed Şükrü Pasha.

■ Pente Pigadia (Beshpinar), 5 November 1912

LGen Konstantinos Sapountzakis' 8000-strong Greek Army of Epirus defeated the Ottoman Yanya Corps of 14,000 men under MGen Mehmed Esad Pasha. The Greeks inflicted heavy casualties for the loss of barely 250 men.

■ Monastir, 16–19 November 1912

After its defeat at Kumanovo, the Ottoman Vardar Army regrouped around Monastir (modern Bitola). The Serbian First Army's advance on the city was initially halted by heavy Ottoman artillery fire, but when its own guns arrived the Ottoman artillery was quickly suppressed by Serbian counter-battery fire. This paved the way for a Serb offensive that inflicted 8600 casualties for the loss of 3000 men. The Serbs occupied Monastir on 19 November.

■ First Battle of Çatalca, 17–18 November 1912

The combined Bulgarian First and Third Armies totalling 176,000 men under LGen Radko Dimitriev, were defeated by Nazim Pasha's 140,000-strong Ottoman Çatalca Army. The Ottomans inflicted more than 12,000 casualties for the loss of 5000 men.

■ KALIAKRA (ATTACK OF THE DRAZKI), 21 NOVEMBER 1912

Under Capt Rauf Orbay's dynamic command, the British-built light cruiser *Hamidiye* became the most effective ship in the Ottoman Navy. During the night of 20/21 November 1912, whilst operating off Varna with two destroyers, it was attacked by the Bulgarian torpedo boats *Letyashti, Smeli, Strogi* and *Drazki* under the overall command of Cdr Dimitar Dobrev. The first three boats' torpedoes missed, but Warrant Officer Georgi Kupov's *Drazki* fired her three torpedoes at close range and scored a single hit on *Hamidiye's* bows. The 450mm torpedo tore a 3m hole in the starboard bow and killed eight men. The cruiser's bow compartments were badly flooded, but it managed to return to Constantinople for repairs under her own steam. (The Bulgarians reported that all the torpedo boats returned safely to Varna, whilst Orbay claimed to have sunk two of his attackers.)

■ ELLI, 16 DECEMBER 1912

RAdm Pavlos Kountouriotis' Greek squadron of an armoured cruiser, three coast defence battleships and four destroyers blockading the Dardanelles defeated an Ottoman fleet under Adm Remzi Bey comprising four battleships, an armoured cruiser and four destroyers.

■ LEMNOS, 18 JANUARY 1913

RAdm Pavlos Kountouriotis' Greek squadron of an armoured cruiser, three coast defence battleships and seven destroyers defeated a further attempt by Adm Remzi Bey's Ottoman fleet of three battleships, a cruiser and five destroyers to break the Greek blockade of the Dardanelles. All three Ottoman battleships, *Mesudiye, Barbaros Hayreddin* and *Turgut Reis*, were badly damaged by the fire of the armoured cruiser *Georgios Averof* and the battleships *Hydra* and *Psara*.

■ BULAIR, 26 JANUARY 1913

MGen Georgi Todorov's 10,000-strong Bulgarian 7th Infantry Division defeated the Ottoman Bulair Army of 50,000 men under Fethi Bey near Bulair in the Gallipoli peninsula. The Bulgarians

inflicted 16,000 casualties for the loss of 520 men.

■ ŞARKÖY, 9–11 FEBRUARY 1913

Gen Stiliyan Kovachev's Bulgarian 2nd Infantry Division, reinforced by the Rodopi Detachment, defeated Ottoman forces under Enver Pasha near Şarköy on the Sea of Marmara despite bombardment by Ottoman warships. The Bulgarians inflicted almost 1500 casualties.

■ BIZANI (IOANNINA), 4–6 MARCH 1913

Crown Prince Constantine's 41,000-strong Greek Army of Epirus decisively defeated the Ottoman Yanya Corps of 35,000 men commanded by MGen Mehmed Esad Pasha. The Greeks inflicted 11,400 casualties for the loss of 284 men.

■ BREGALNICA, 30 JUNE–8 JULY 1913

An offensive by Gen Mihail Savov's Bulgarian Fourth and Fifth Armies totalling 130,000 men was defeated by the 190,000-strong Serbian Operational Group South. The Serbs inflicted 20,000 casualties for the loss of over 16,600 men.

■ KILKIS–LAHANAS, 1–3 JULY 1913

Gen Nikola Ivanov's 40,000-strong Bulgarian Second Army retreated to a strong defensive line between Kilkis and Lahanas after the failure of its initial attack on Greek forces in Macedonia. The Greek counter-offensive had the advantage of overwhelming numerical superiority (almost 118,000 men), but was faced by powerful defences, including multiple trench lines and captured Ottoman guns. The Kilkis sector was defended by the Bulgarian 3rd Division, less its 1st Brigade, which was attacked by 38 Greek battalions supported by 100 guns. The Greeks finally broke through the Bulgarian defences around Kilkis after three days of fierce fighting. At the same time, the Greek 1st and 6th Divisions also captured the Lahanas sector despite accurate Bulgarian artillery fire. Although the Bulgarians inflicted almost 9000 casualties for the loss of 9500 men, it was their most serious defeat of the Second Balkan War.

■ KALIMANCI, 18–19 JULY 1913

Gen Mihail Savov's Bulgarian Fourth and Fifth Armies defeated an offensive by the Serbian Third

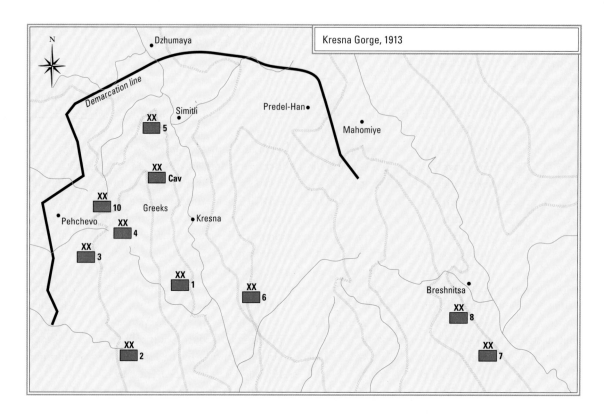

Army, which had been reinforced by a Serbian division. Each side lost approximately 8000 men in the clash, but Bulgaria was saved from Serbian invasion.

■ KRESNA GORGE, 21–31 JULY 1913
The Greek Army under the nominal command of King Constantine crossed the River Strymon (Struma) and invaded Bulgaria. The combined Bulgarian armies (the 79,370-strong First Army under Gen Vassil Kutinchev and Gen Saravov's Second Army of 122,748 men), launched attacks on both flanks of the Greek forces, pushing them down the valleys of the Strymon and Mesta rivers. The Greeks deployed six infantry divisions (1st, 2nd, 4th, 5th, 6th and 7th) and the Cavalry Brigade under the field command of MGen Emmanuel Manusoyannakes. A further series of Bulgarian attacks hit the weak centre of the Greek line held by 6th Infantry Division, followed by an offensive by the entire Second Army against the Greek 3rd, 8th and 10th

Infantry Divisions. The Greek line held until the armistice which ended the war. Each side lost around 10,000 men.

Mexican Revolution, 1912–18

■ RELLANO, 24 MARCH & 22 MAY 1912
On 24 March 7000 Mexican revolutionaries under Pascual Orozco beat Gen Salas' government force of similar size. In the second battle, Orozco was defeated by government forces which inflicted 600 casualties for the loss of 140 men.

■ TIERRA BLANCA, 23–25 NOVEMBER 1913
Francisco (Pancho) Villa was repulsed at Chihuahua but then circled north to capture Ciudad Juárez. He then marched south to defeat a federal army under José Inés Salazar on the plains of the Tierra Blanca.

■ VERACRUZ, 21 APRIL–25 NOVEMBER 1914
As the United States became more and more

involved in the fallout from the Mexican Revolution of 1911, tensions between the two countries grew. In April, the Mexican Government arrested nine American sailors for trespassing into off-limits areas. At the same time, the Wilson administration learned of an expected delivery to Veracruz of German weapons for Victoriano Huerta, the president Wilson sought to remove from power.

In fact, the weapons were American, and they had been transported through Germany so the manufacturer could skirt an American embargo. Nevertheless, the United States responded forcefully by sending sailors and Marines to seize the customs house, the railroad station, the telegraph and telephone exchanges, the post office, and any weapons they found. They took up positions as bewildered residents watched, at first impassive.

Soon, however, cadets at the Veracruz Naval Academy and local residents began to form opposition to the Americans. The senior American official, Adm Frank F. Fletcher, sent in more sailors in the hopes of calming the situation, but it only led to more violence. Fletcher looked for a local authority with whom he could negotiate, but found no one. He then expanded the mission to the occupation of the entire town. He also called for reinforcements which included five battleships and a battalion of Marines from Panama. Within three days the Marines had restored order, but the incident had been violent. More than 150 Mexicans and 22 Americans died. Among the former was José Azueta, who became a hero for his defence of the Mexican Naval Academy against American Marines. President Huerta cut all diplomatic ties to the United States and Mexican–American relations worsened even further. American forces remained in the city until November.

■ ZACATECAS, 23 JUNE 1914

Francisco (Pancho) Villa's 20,000 Mexican revolutionaries defeated a substantial government force of 12,000 men under Gen Luís Medina Barrón and took the mining town of Zacatecas. Villa inflicted 7000 casualties for the loss of 1000 men.

■ CELAYA, 13 APRIL 1915

A 12,000-strong government force under Álvaro Obregón defeated Francisco (Pancho) Villa's 8000 Mexican revolutionaries near Celaya in central Mexico. Obregón fought a skilful defensive action and inflicted 3000 casualties for the loss of 600 men.

■ AGUA PRIETA, 1 NOVEMBER 1915

A 6500-strong Mexican Government force under Gen Plutarco Elías Calles defeated Francisco (Pancho) Villa's 15,000 revolutionaries at Agua Prieta on the Mexican–US border. Calles' well-dug-in machine guns inflicted particularly heavy casualties on Villa's cavalry.

■ COLUMBUS, 9 MARCH 1916

Following his defeat at Celaya, Francisco (Pancho) Villa's Mexican revolutionaries were increasingly short of supplies. Desperate after months of foraging with little success in northern Mexico, Villa raided the US border town of Columbus, New Mexico. The town was defended by a 330-strong detachment of the 13th Cavalry which beat off the attack by 500 of Villa's men. US forces inflicted 90 casualties for the loss of 26 men.

■ CARRIZAL, 21 JUNE 1916

Francisco (Pancho) Villa's attack on Columbus provoked the USA to organize a punitive expedition under MGen John J. Pershing to capture Villa. A 100-strong US detachment drawn from C and K troops of the 10th Cavalry attacked what was thought to be 150 of Villa's men at Carrizal. The Mexicans were in fact government infantry who drove off the cavalrymen, inflicting 35 casualties for the loss of 67 men.

■ BEAR VALLEY, 9 JANUARY 1918

Yaqui tribes fighting to maintain their autonomy within Mexico raided US border ranches for food. A group of 30 Yaqui was defeated by a detachment of the US 10th Cavalry at Bear valley, Arizona.

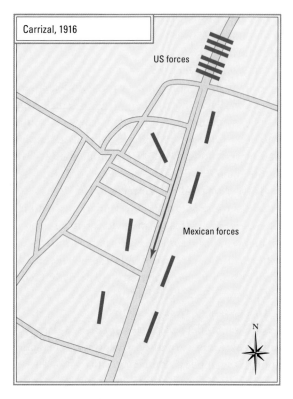

Carrizal, 1916

US forces

Mexican forces

N

AMBOS NOGALES, 27 AUGUST 1918

A minor incident at Nogales on the US–
Mexican border became a clash between an
800-strong US detachment and 600 Mexican
troops. US forces inflicted 400 casualties for the
loss of 35 men.

Miscellaneous Wars and Battles, 1783–1913

BAHRAIN, 1783

Taking advantage of civil war, the Bani Utbah
tribal federation launched an invasion of Bahrain
from the port of Zubara. Although victorious in
the internal conflict Sheikh Nasr Al-Madhkur
was overthrown by the invaders.

KETTLE WAR, 1784

More properly termed an international incident
than a war, the 'Kettle War' was a brief conflict over
access to the ports of Antwerp and Ghent, which
were blockaded by barriers on the River Scheldt.

Demanding that the barriers be dismantled, the
Holy Roman Emperor dispatched three ships
from Antwerp. This sortie was aborted by a
single shot from a Dutch warship, which hit a
soup kettle aboard the flagship.

REVOLT OF HOREA, CLOCSA AND CRISAN, 1784–85

Beginning in Zarand County in Transylvania,
a serfs' rebellion spread throughout the region
until rebel forces were sufficient to defeat an
Imperial army in late 1784. The rebel force was
defeated early the following year.

SHAYS' REBELLION, 1786–87

Former Revolutionary War officer Daniel Shays
was one of several commanders in an uprising
against the Massachusetts state government.
Initially bloodless, the rebellion escalated into
skirmishing before being put down early in 1787.

CONSPIRACY OF GOA, 1787

A conspiracy to overthrow Portuguese rule
in Goa arose mainly out a feeling of injustice
regarding the treatment of local religious figures.
The plot was betrayed and pre-emptively crushed
by the authorities.

SERB REBELLION, 1788

Assisted by Austrian forces, a popular uprising
led by Koca Andjelkovic succeeded in taking
control of Serbia from the Ottoman Empire.
Serbia was an Austrian territory for only three
years before Habsburg forces were withdrawn
and the region was returned to Ottoman rule,
with many Serbs fleeing in fear of reprisals. The
events of this uprising, and Ottoman responses,
heavily influenced later Serbian uprisings against
the Ottoman Empire.

TURNHOUT, 27 OCTOBER 1789

With the southern Netherlands in revolt against
Austrian rule, the city of Turnhout was hotly
contested. Austrian forces were able to enter
the city, but were ambushed and defeated by
the rebels.

MINAS CONSPIRACY, 1789

Opposition to a new tax and independence
from Portugal were among the few concepts the

various conspirators could agree on, resulting in a disjointed plot that was betrayed to the authorities and resulted in the arrest of the leaders.

■ MENASHI–KUNASHIR WAR, 1789

The indigenous Ainu people of north-eastern Hokkaido, increasingly marginalized by their Japanese overlords, rose in rebellion against their treatment by Japanese officials and merchants. The Ainu launched attacks against Japanese holdings on Kunashir Island and the Menashi District, and harassed sea traffic. The rebellion was a fairly small-scale affair, with about 70 Japanese casualties, and was put down swiftly. Defeat was followed by execution of the rebel leaders.

■ KHARDA, FEBRUARY 1795

The Maratha Confederacy demanded tribute from the Kingdom of Hyderabad, precipitating war when this was refused. Hyderabad was decisively defeated at the battle of Kharda and forced to pay a large indemnity.

■ MUIZENBERG, 7 AUGUST 1795

A British naval force landed approximately 1400 troops and supported their advance towards Cape Town with gunfire. The Dutch defenders were driven from their initial positions, but were nonetheless able to hold out until a larger British force arrived.

■ KRTANISI, 8–11 SEPTEMBER 1795

Seeking to reverse Georgian gains in the Transcaucasus region, a Persian army invaded Georgia and advanced on the capital, Tblisi. The vastly outnumbered Georgians managed to fight the invaders to a standstill at Krtanisi, but were defeated by a renewed attack.

■ THE DIAMOND, 21 SEPTEMBER 1795

Ongoing violence between Protestant and Catholic factions in County Armagh, Ireland, escalated into a bloody incident known as the Battle of the Diamond. The resulting Protestant victory led to the creation of the Orange Institution.

■ WEXFORD REBELLION, 1798

The United Irish Rebellion was most successful in County Wexford, in south-eastern Ireland. The rebels there had a victory over British forces at Enniscorthy in May. Attempts to spread the rebellion into neighbouring counties were defeated at Arklow and New Ross. The main rebel force was defeated at Vinegar Hill on 21 June by forces under Needham. Massacres of prisoners and civilians were committed on both sides.

■ FLEMISH PEASANTS' WAR, 1798

Having changed hands between France and Austria several times, Belgium revolted against French rule in 1798. Some of the rebels acted prematurely, warning the French of what was to come and permitting an effective response. The rebels themselves were ill armed and untrained, but hoped to benefit from British intervention. Attempts to land British troops at the mouth of the Scheldt failed, resulting in a series of defeats after which the rebellion collapsed.

■ COUP 18 BRUMAIRE, 1798

Tasked with protecting the French Revolutionary Government from a coup, Gen Napoleon Bonaparte instead used his troops to gain control of it, forcing three of the five Directors to resign. Faced with resistance from the Council of Five Hundred, Napoleon's brother Lucien ordered his troops to clear the chambers forcibly. The government was dissolved and replaced with one which Napoleon, as First Consul, exerted direct control over.

■ FRIES' REBELLION, 1799–1800

Led by John Fries, Pennsylvania Dutch farmers resisted attempts to collect new taxes levied on their holdings. Assessors were intimidated by armed bands and attempts to arrest tax resisters met with violence.

■ SURINAME, 5 MAY 1804

Despite difficulties imposed by operating in shallow water, a British naval squadron silenced Dutch forts protecting the colony of Suriname. Troops were landed to take possession of the island, which was accomplished with few casualties on either side.

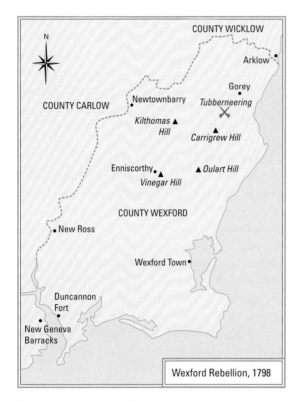

COUNTY WICKLOW

N

Arklow •

Gorey •

COUNTY CARLOW   Newtownbarry •   Tubberneering ✕

Kilthomas ▲
Hill   Carrigrew Hill ▲

Enniscorthy •▲   ▲ Oulart Hill
Vinegar Hill

COUNTY WEXFORD

• New Ross

Wexford Town •

Duncannon
Fort •
New Geneva
Barracks •

Wexford Rebellion, 1798

■ WALTON WAR, 1804

An ongoing dispute over the boundary between North Carolina and Georgia resulted in the death of a North Carolina official. North Carolina's militia entered the area to make arrests, which passed off more or less bloodlessly.

■ VELLORE MUTINY, 10 JULY 1806

Indian Sepoy troops at Vellore Fort rebelled and killed most of the Europeans stationed there. The rebellion was put down and the survivors rescued by reinforcements summoned by an enterprising officer who had escaped the initial violence.

■ RUM REBELLION, 26 JANUARY 1808– 1 JANUARY 1810

Troops of the New South Wales Corps forcibly deposed Governor William Bligh, bringing about a confused situation which was not resolved until a new governor arrived in 1810. The incident was only peripherally connected with the trade in rum.

■ BOYD MASSACRE, 1809

Enraged by the flogging of a Maori chief's son by the crew of the *Boyd*, a ship upon which he was working passage, Maori warriors boarded the vessel and massacred almost everyone aboard.

■ PERSIAN GULF CAMPAIGN, SEPTEMBER– DECEMBER 1809

British efforts to suppress piracy in the Persian Gulf met with limited success. Although many pirate vessels were destroyed, along with some bases, the long-term effect of the campaign was merely a reduction of the threat to shipping.

■ GERMAN COAST UPRISING, 8–10 JAN 1811

The German Coast region near New Orleans had a complex political situation, with French and Spanish influences and a large free black population in addition to a high proportion of slaves working the sugar plantations. Discontent among the latter resulted in a revolt that began in January 1811 after a period of plotting among the slave populations. Although the rising was violent, with considerable destruction of property, only two white people were killed. The rebels armed themselves as best they could, but had few firearms and were joined by only a small proportion of the slave population on the plantations they passed. They were met by militia and federal troops, and a short and one-sided battle ensued. The rebels, whose numbers have been postulated at anywhere between 200 and 500, suffered heavy casualties and scattered. The survivors were hunted down and recaptured.

■ SLACHTER'S NEK REBELLION, 1815

Hans Bezuidenhout, brother of a Cape Colony farmer who had died while resisting arrest, organized a rising against the British. Most of the rebels dispersed or surrendered to British forces. Bezuidenhout was killed after refusing to surrender.

■ SEVEN OAKS, 19 JUNE 1816

A dispute between the Northwest Company and the Hudson Bay Company over the export of pemmican resulted in a brief armed clash, in which the Northwest Company was overwhelmingly victorious.

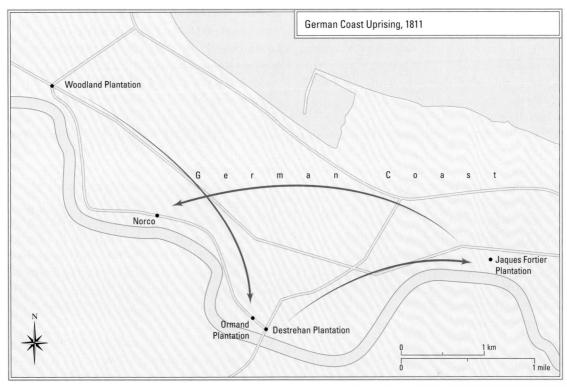

German Coast Uprising, 1811

Woodland Plantation

G e r m a n   C o a s t

Norco

Jaques Fortier
Plantation

Ormand
Plantation

Destrehan Plantation

N

0   1 km

0   1 mile

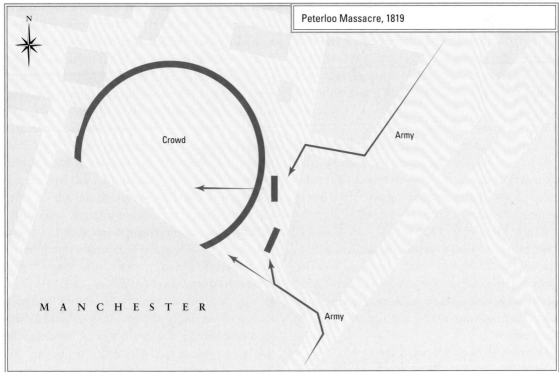

N

Peterloo Massacre, 1819

Crowd

Army

Army

M A N C H E S T E R

■ **AMELIA ISLAND, 13 SEPTEMBER 1817**
Amelia Island, off the coast of Florida, was taken and controlled by a succession of military adventurers in 1817. US naval forces then captured the island as part of the annexation of Florida.

■ **UVA REBELLION, 1817–18**
A rebellion began in Uva against British colonial control of what is today the island of Sri Lanka. The revolt was initially successful, but was put down and followed by harsh reprisals by the colonial authorities.

■ **CHUGEV UPRISING, 1819**
Conditions in the military settlement of Chugev caused its regiment and the population of nearby villages to revolt and demand reforms. The rebellion was put down by force after several weeks of fighting.

■ **PETERLOO MASSACRE, 16 AUGUST 1819**
A crowd estimated to possibly be as large as 80,000 individuals assembled at St Peter's Field, Manchester, UK, to hear radical speakers and to demand governmental reforms. Local authorities requested military assistance to arrest the leaders, resulting in an attempt to disperse the assembly with cavalry. Surrounded by a hostile crowd, the cavalrymen struck out with their sabres. Several people were killed and hundreds injured.

■ **WALLACHIAN UPRISING, 1821**
An initially successful revolt against Ottoman rule in Romania captured Bucharest but collapsed due to internal conflicts between its leaders. The rebel army largely dispersed, allowing the Ottomans to resume control with little opposition.

■ **CHIOS MASSACRE, 1822**
The island of Chios joined the Greek War of independence against the Ottoman Empire. Ottoman troops put down the revolt on Chios, devastating the island and massacring the population, of whom most had not taken part in the conflict.

■ **DESTRUCTION OF PSARA, 1824**
Invaded by Ottoman Turks in response to their participation in the Greek War of Independence, the island of Psara was quickly overrun. The defenders blew up their fort rather than surrender to the Ottoman forces.

■ **FRANCO-TRARZAN WAR, 1825**
Responding to an attempt by the Emirate of Trarzan to gain control over the Senegal river region, a French expeditionary force defeated the army of Trarzan. This paved the way for French expansion in the area.

■ **FREDONIAN REBELLION, 21 DECEMBER 1826–31 JANUARY 1827**
The Republic of Fredonia was proclaimed by settlers wishing to secede from Mexican rule. A small military intervention and diplomacy with nearby native American tribes restored the region to Mexican control, forcing the rebels to flee.

■ **JULY REVOLUTION, 1830**
After a motion of no confidence in the French Chamber of Deputies, Charles X dissolved parliament and became increasingly alienated from the populace. Attempts to strengthen the royal position included censorship of newspapers, resulting in a confrontation between police and disaffected workers on 26 July. This provided the spark for a revolution that had been threatened for some time. The next day saw clashes between royalist troops and citizens all over Paris, and on the 28th the violence escalated as the revolutionaries armed themselves and began to seize key areas of the city, including government centres. The poorly led and unprepared army could not contain the situation, and after a third day of violence the revolutionaries controlled Paris. A new government was formed, causing Charles X to abdicate in favour of a cousin from the house of Orleans.

■ **SOUTHAMPTON INSURRECTION, 1831**
Led by Nat Turner, a force of around 70 slaves embarked on a rampage of indiscriminate killing in Southampton County, Virginia, resulting in the largest number of non-slave fatalities in any American revolt.

■ Baptist War, 25 December 1831– 4 January 1832

Inspired by Baptist missionaries, slaves in Jamaica embarked upon what was essentially a strike, demanding better conditions and pay. The Jamaican Government and plantation owners responded with considerable brutality, killing about 200 slaves in suppressing what they saw as a dangerous revolt and executing a larger number afterwards. Only a handful of non-slaves were killed in the violence, although a great deal of property damage was caused.

■ June Rebellion, 1832

The new French constitutional monarchy, brought about by the July Revolution of 1830, was challenged by an uprising that very briefly gained control of much of Paris. It was crushed with military force.

■ Malê Revolt, 1835

Forewarned of a slave revolt, Brazilian Government forces were able to secure critical areas before the rebels could capture them. The revolt was crushed by government cavalry, which broke up the disorganized slave army.

■ Toledo War, 1835

A dispute between Ohio and Michigan over what is now the Toledo Strip resulted in militias being raised and deployed. Despite hard words and some warning shots there was no actual fighting, and a settlement was eventually agreed.

■ Myall Creek Massacre, 1838

A group of (mostly convict) stockmen rounded up around 35 Australian Aboriginals, claiming that they intended to 'frighten them'. The Aboriginals were then taken to a secluded area and massacred. Several of the murderers were sentenced to death.

■ Waterloo Creek Massacre, 1838

Ongoing conflict between Australian stockmen and Aboriginal people led to a police expedition to arrest several Aboriginals. An incident at the Namoi river resulted in a three-week pursuit that ended with the patrol being ambushed. The

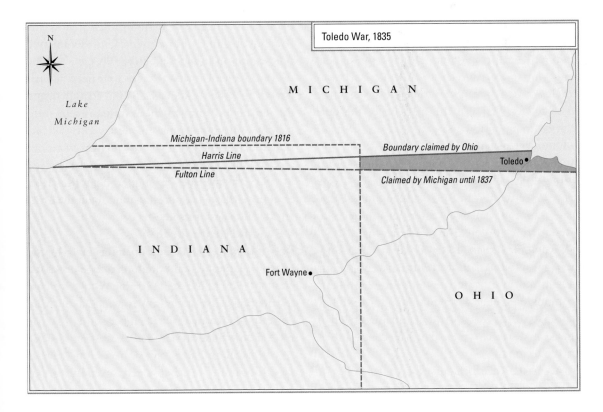

Toledo War, 1835

N

Lake Michigan

MICHIGAN

Michigan-Indiana boundary 1816

Harris Line

Boundary claimed by Ohio

Toledo

Fulton Line

Claimed by Michigan until 1837

INDIANA

Fort Wayne

OHIO

attack was beaten off and the attackers pursued to Waterloo Creek, where a confused and inconclusive engagement took place. Casualties have been estimated at anywhere between a handful and more than 70.

■ AROSTOOK WAR, 1839

Confusion and tension over the exact location of the border between Maine and what was then British North America resulted in a confrontation between British and US troops. The issue was settled through negotiation, with no recourse to armed force.

■ HONEY WAR, 1839

A dispute over the exact location of the Iowa–Missouri border arose from different interpretations of treaties with the Native American population and other legal documents, resulting in a bloodless standoff between poorly armed militias. The war got its name from the only casualties – some trees which were cut down to seize beehives in an attempt to collect taxation. The issue was eventually resolved by legal means, resulting in the current Iowa–Missouri border.

■ ZURIPUTSCH, 6 SEPTEMBER 1839

Outraged at the religious policies of the city leadership in Zurich, a large force of conservative rebels stormed the city and forced its government to surrender. This was the first use of the term 'Putsch' in a political context.

■ DORR REBELLION, 1841

Abandoning efforts to obtain electoral reform through legal channels, Thomas Dorr led a brief armed insurrection in the state of Rhode Island. The rebellion collapsed after an unsuccessful attempt to secure the Providence arsenal.

■ WARRIGAL CREEK, 1843

A series of killings, of both Australian Aboriginal people and immigrants, resulted from resistance to immigrant encroachment. Angus McMillian, who had seized tracts of Aboriginal land, led an attack at Warrigal Creek that killed upwards of 150 Aboriginals.

■ GREATER POLAND UPRISING, 1846

Between 1772 and 1795 Poland was gradually partitioned between Austria, Prussia and Russia, until it ceased to exist as an independent state. In the early 1800s, the Duchy of Warsaw was set up by Napoleon, but this too was partitioned between Prussia and Russia after his defeat. Partition did not prevent the Poles from desiring nationhood, and in 1846 a series of coordinated uprisings was planned. Although several highly active pro-Polish groups were involved, agendas varied and in general the rebels received little support from the general populace. In some areas local people assisted the authorities in dealing with rebel forces, and the risings quickly failed.

In the Free City of Kracow, there was some fighting but control was quickly reasserted by local police and Austrian troops stationed in the city; Kracow was annexed by Austria as a result. More widespread fighting took place in Galicia, but the rebels were no match for the Austrian Army, whose cavalry quickly dispersed their forces. In some areas the rebellion never really started; in Poznan, the revolutionaries were betrayed to the authorities a fortnight before the launch date, and were arrested. This decapitated one section of the rising before it began.

Over 250 of the revolutionaries were tried for high treason in Prussia. About half were acquitted, and the remainder were sentenced to imprisonment; a handful were condemned to death. The political situation was such that these sentences were not carried out, and the revolutionaries were freed in 1848 during the 'Spring of Nations'. Most promptly returned to Poland and joined the 1848 Greater Poland Uprising.

■ KRACOW UPRISING, 1846

Part of the Greater Poland uprisings of 1846, the Kracow Uprising, although briefly successful, was put down by the Austrian Army. Kracow lost its Free City status and became an Austrian possession governed from Lemberg.

■ GALICIAN SLAUGHTER, 1846

Polish peasants in Galicia rose up against their overlords and massacred several hundred members of the nobility, looting or destroying many estates. Austria supported the rising as a means to suppress an anti–Habsburg insurrection among Polish nobles.

■ SONDERBUND WAR, 3–29 NOVEMBER 1847

The Swiss cantons had traditionally been loosely organized, but in the 1840s there was a move towards a more centralized government. This alarmed Catholics, as the dominant factions were acting against the Catholic Church. In 1845, seven of the cantons formed the Sonderbund, or 'separate alliance', in order better to resist the centralization of power. This was in direct violation of the Federal Treaty of 1815.

In 1847, the Sonderbund was ordered to dissolve and refused, resulting in armed conflict between its forces and those of the Swiss Confederation. The Sonderbund struck first and achieved some limited successes, but its member cantons were defeated one by one in a short campaign during November 1847. The conflict was characterized by great restraint on the Federal side, and the

first use of a dedicated ambulance corps. It also removed the last obstacles to the centralization of power in Switzerland.

■ MATALE REBELLION, 1848

Disaffected with British colonial rule, peasants in Ceylon rebelled and named Gongalegoda Banda their king. After a brief and unsuccessful insurrection, Gongalegoda Banda was captured, tried and subsequently deported. This brought the rebellion to an end.

■ MAY UPRISING, DRESDEN, 3–9 MAY 1849

Revolutionary agitators attempted to force Frederick Augustus II of Saxony to accept a new constitution, at which point he dissolved parliament and thereby triggered a revolt. The poorly armed and outnumbered rebels were defeated by Prussian and Saxon troops.

■ ERIE GAUGE WAR, 1853–54

Opposition to an attempt to standardize the gauge of railways passing through Erie, Pennsylvania resulted in a campaign of destruction against

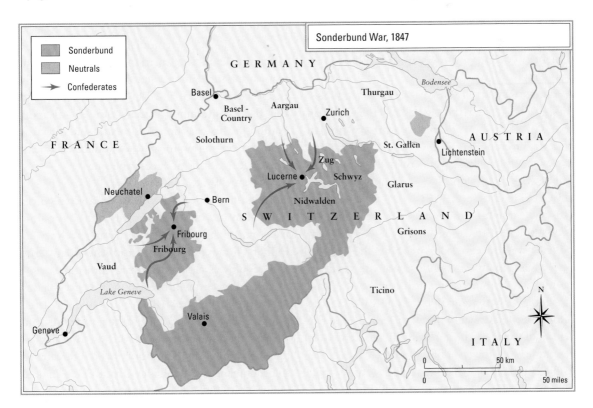

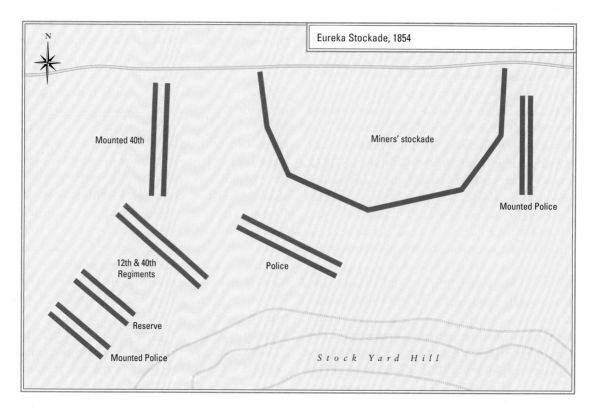

N

Eureka Stockade, 1854

Mounted 40th

Miners' stockade

Mounted Police

12th & 40th
Regiments

Police

Reserve

Mounted Police

Stock Yard Hill

new railway lines being laid, and occasional violence. Although shots were fired there were no fatalities.

■ EPIRUS REVOLT, 1854

Taking advantage of the outbreak of the Crimean War, Greeks in Epirus rebelled against Ottoman rule and attempted to join Greece. Despite some early success the rebels were crushed by Ottoman forces, with British and French support.

■ EUREKA STOCKADE, 1854

Growing resentment among the gold miners of Ballarat, Australia, against local government policies was brought to a head by the trial of one James Bentley. Bentley was accused of murdering a miner, but acquitted by a trial suspected of being corrupt. A large gathering of miners burned down his hotel in reprisal, and the arrests of some of those involved caused further resentment. As the level of violence escalated, the miners built themselves a makeshift camp which became known as Eureka Stockade and declared

their defiance of the colonial authorities.

The stockade was surrounded by police and troops, and for a time a standoff ensued. Eventually the stockade was stormed by the authorities and the badly outgunned miners quickly overrun. Although the rebellion was swiftly put down it had far-reaching political consequences, not least due to accusations of excessive force.

■ MAHTRA WAR, 1858

A peasant uprising on the Mahtra Estate near Tallin, Estonia, broke out mainly due to the slow pace of agricultural reforms. It was put down by military force after a short and one-sided fight. The revolt was suppressed using the regular army; 14 peasants were wounded and 10 were killed.

■ MCGOWAN'S WAR, 1858

Conflict between factions in the town of Yale, British Columbia, resulted in almost farcical feuding and abuses of authority, which threatened to become more serious. The situation was restored by the arrival of British officials escorted by troops.

■ **PIG WAR, 1859**

Confusion over the sovereignty of the San Juan Islands near Vancouver became an international incident when an American farmer shot a pig belonging to a British citizen. The resulting dispute escalated into an armed confrontation between British and US troops which went on for several years. The matter was resolved diplomatically without any conflict between the military forces; the only casualty in this 'war' was the pig.

■ **LEBANON, 1860**

Large-scale conflicts along religious lines pitted Christians, Druze and Muslims against one another. Casualties in this bitter and internecine conflict were very high and massacres took place until the conflicts were suppressed by international intervention.

■ **BEZDNA UNREST, APRIL 1861**

Peasants in several villages around Bezdna in the Khazan Governate, Russia, revolted in protest over what they saw was incorrect implementation of the emancipation reforms. The rebellion was put down by military force, with no casualties on the government side.

■ **MORRISITE WAR, JUNE 1862**

Convinced that the Apocalypse was nigh, Joseph Morris collected followers and occupied Kingston Fort, Utah Territory, imprisoning some former converts who tried to leave. The situation escalated into a clash with government militia, and the Morrisites were scattered.

■ **EGG WAR, 1863**

A commercial dispute over control of the lucrative egg-collecting trade on the Farallon Islands resulted in clashes between armed bands. The Pacific Egg Company eventually ran off its competitors and enjoyed a monopoly over the industry for some years.

■ **MORANT BAY REBELLION, 1865**

Unrest among the black population of Jamaica, resulting from perceived injustices, alarmed the white-dominated authorities. A protest march was fired upon by militia, sparking a riot that

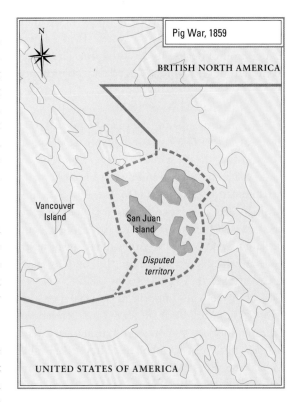

Pig War, 1859

in turn resulted in an indiscriminate rampage by government forces.

■ **RIDGEWAY, 2 JUNE 1866**

Fenian troops launched an incursion into Canada and engaged local militia near Ridgeway. The battle was characterized by skirmishing until the Canadian force became disorganized and was routed by a bayonet charge.

■ **FORT ERIE, 2 JUNE 1866**

Canadian militia, attempting to cut off the retreat of Fenian forces after the battle of Ridgeway, occupied the town of Fort Erie but were ultimately swept aside by a much larger body of Fenian militia.

■ **BAIKAL UPRISING, 1866**

A large band of Poles, exiled to Siberia, revolted and seized arms from their guards. Most were recaptured, and those that fought were defeated by overwhelming numbers of Russian troops.

■ **RED RIVER REBELLION, 1869**

Colonists at Red river formed a provisional

government, prompting the new Canadian government to dispatch the Red River Expedition to deal with the situation. The rebels eventually agreed to join Canada as the province of Manitoba.

■ **ECCLES HILL, 25 MAY 1870**
A Fenian force, raiding into Canada, was met by local militia at Eccles Hill. After a period of skirmishing, the Canadians were reinforced by cavalry, which charged and scattered the Fenians.

■ **REPUBLIC OF PLOIESTI, 1870**
A small group of revolutionaries were able to take control of key facilities in Ploiesti, and declared a republic. The coup melted away when government soldiers arrived in the town by train.

■ **CAVITE MUTINY, 20 JANUARY 1872**
Objecting to the imposition of taxes, which had to be paid both in cash and in labour, Filipino soldiers at Fort San Philipe, at Cavite in the Philippines, rebelled. They were able to take control of the fort after killing several Spanish officers, and began firing rockets. This was intended as a signal for a more general uprising, which they hoped would follow, but was misinterpreted as a celebration and was not acted upon.

  Fearing widespread mutiny, the authorities reacted vigorously and with purpose, sending reliable troops with artillery to besiege Fort San Philipe. With no possible assistance from elsewhere and no sign of a general uprising, mutineers were forced to surrender and were fired upon as they did so. All Filipino troops were disarmed as a precaution, and many were executed for harbouring sympathies with the mutineers.

■ **BROOKS-BAXTER WAR, 15 APRIL– 15 MAY 1874**
After a legal challenge over the result of the election of Arkansas state governor failed, the losing candidate attempted to take over by force. The result was a series of skirmishes between militias until the Federal government was forced to intervene.

■ **REVOLT OF THE MUCKERS, 1874**
Jacobina Mentz Maure, a religious leader in the German community in Brazil, proclaimed the Apocalypse and ordered her followers, known as Muckers, to kill various opponents. The majority were killed along with their leaders in a police raid.

■ **HERZEGOVINIAN REBELLION, 1875**
Aided by arms and reinforcements from Montenegro and Serbia, Herzegovinian peasants rebelled against their Ottoman overlords. The revolt also spread to Bosnia and elsewhere, precipitating the Great Eastern Crisis and drawing the attention of the rest of Europe.

■ **READING RAILROAD MASSACRE, 1877**
Depressed economic conditions resulted in a financial crisis for many US railroad companies, which had previously been enjoying a boom period. Wage cuts and job losses also resulted in resentment among the railroad workers, many of whom rioted or prevented rail traffic from moving. At Reading, Pennsylvania, state militia attempted to free a train blocked by rioters and were attacked. Shots fired by the militia resulted in several deaths among the rioters.

■ **SAN ELIZARIO SALT WAR, 1877**
Several attempts were made to exert private control over the salt-extraction industry near San Elizario, Texas, gradually replacing the traditional system whereby the salt lakes were considered to be communal property. This led to an ongoing feud between factions in the town, which was mainly political, legal and economic in nature and was mostly fought using those means.

  The situation changed when Charles Howard filed a legal claim of ownership to the salt lakes. This brought him into conflict with his former political ally Louis Cardis, who championed the idea of communal ownership. The local population were also concerned about the situation and made plans to disregard the pro-private ownership county government and set up their own local committees.

  Howard used his legal position to have some

local men arrested for planning to extract 'his' salt, which outraged the community sufficiently that he was taken captive and held for several days. During this time Howard agreed to relinquish his salt rights but instead shot and killed his rival Cardis before fleeing to New Mexico.

The situation in San Elizario was apparently calmed by negotiation. The local population agreed to respect the county government. In return, Howard was to be brought back to San Elizario to face trial. A force of 20 new Texas Rangers was raised for the purpose of returning him.

The Rangers brought Howard back to San Elizario, but were immediately attacked by the townsfolk. The Rangers, and Howard with them, were besieged in the town church and, after two days, surrendered to the townsfolk. Most of the Rangers were disarmed and expelled from the town. Two, and Howard, were murdered by the mob. The situation was restored by deploying a force of cavalry to nearby Fort Bliss.

■ Lincoln County War, 18 February– 19 July 1878

Rivalry over the dry goods trade in Lincoln County, New Mexico, grew into a range war between competing factions, in which both sides made use of legal measures as well as recruiting outlaws to fight the gunmen of the opposing side. The flashpoint was the murder of rancher John Tunstall, who was shot by a posse sent to seize his assets in what was ostensibly a legal move. In revenge, members of the original posse were murdered after surrendering. Their murderers were the Regulators, a group formed to arrest Tunstall's killers – again, supposedly in accordance with a legally issued warrant.

As the violence escalated, political and legal machinations resulted in the Regulators being outlawed when their faction's legal sponsor, Justice of the Peace John Wilson, was dismissed from his post. Pursued by an increasingly large force, some of the Regulators were killed and others exchanged fire with US troops, drawing Federal forces into what had thus far been a local dispute.

The Regulators were eventually forced to take up defensive positions in the town of Lincoln, where they held out for three days. Federal reinforcements, equipped with artillery, forced the Regulators to attempt an escape from one of their positions. Some of the Regulators were able to escape but remained in the general area.

The final Regulator stronghold caught fire, forcing the last of the gang to flee. Some were shot as they came out of the building, and others were killed in a close-quarters fight with Federal troops who attempted to arrest them. Others were able to link up with those who had escaped earlier and fled the area. Notable among those who escaped was the outlaw Billy the Kid.

■ Skeleton Canyon Massacre, 1879

A party of Mexican Guardia Rural (mounted police), pursuing cattle rustlers into Arizona

Lincoln County, 1878

despite this being a border violation, were ambushed in Skeleton Canyon. Skeleton Canyon is located in the Peloncillo Mountains (Hidalgo County), which straddle the modern Arizona and New Mexico state line border. Most of the Mexicans were killed in the attack or were murdered after surrendering.

■ **Second Skeleton Canyon Massacre, 1881**

Hearing that Skeleton Canyon was used as a route to smuggle silver from Mexico into the United States, a party comprising several men who had taken part in the original Skeleton Canyon massacre staged another ambush, killing all 19 smugglers.

■ **Guadeloupe Canyon Massacre, 1881**

US outlaws, who had been rustling cattle across the US–Mexican border, were ambushed as they camped in Guadeloupe Canyon. The majority were killed in the fierce attack, which was probably carried out by Mexican Guardia Rural personnel. It is known that Mexican personnel were in the area, commanded by an officer who had survived the 1879 Skeleton Canyon attack. Those killed in the ambush included perpetrators of the 1879 incident.

■ **Warsaw Pogrom, 25–27 December 1881**

A false accusation of thievery triggered numerous vicious attacks on Jewish homes and businesses in Warsaw. Although there were only two fatalities, hundreds of families suffered financially, triggering a wave of emigrations and further inflaming tensions.

■ **Kapsin Coup, 1882**

In an attempt to force through reforms in Korea, a coup was launched with Japanese support. Despite capturing the royal palace, the coup was put down by the Korean Government with assistance from Chinese troops.

■ **Imo Incident, 1882**

Military personnel, later joined by civilians, rioted and destroyed the Japanese Legation in incheon, Korea forcing its staff to flee. Various causes have been suggested, from bad rations and

delayed pay to subversion by Japanese agents. Whatever its causes, violence did erupt and the incident produced unplanned consequences.

■ **Hosay Massacre, 1884**

Having refused permission for the annual Hosay processions to enter San Fernando on the island of Trinidad, the British authorities read the riot act and then ordered troops to fire on the processions, causing numerous fatalities.

■ **Can Vuoung, 1885–89**

Having been driven from Hue by French forces, the Vietnamese emperor launched the Can Vuoung (variously translated as 'Loyalty to the King', or 'Aid to the Emperor') movement which was directed at driving the French from Vietnam. In the meantime the French installed a puppet emperor, who sent troops to fight against the rebellion. The Can Vuoung movement struggled on until 1895, but French control over the region was not broken.

■ **Abushiri Revolt, 1888–89**

German colonial expansion in East Africa met with significant local opposition, notably from the forces of the Sultan of Zanzibar. British influence initially helped contain the situation, but high-handed actions by German officials in the town of Pangani resulted in a revolt. By consequence, the German East Africa Company was largely driven from its holdings before the situation was restored. A naval blockade and operations by land forces supported by the British put down the rebellion.

■ **Revolution of the Park, 1890**

Ill-equipped rebels succeeded in taking control of the Buenos Aires artillery park, but were soon defeated by government forces. The revolution did, however, indirectly achieve its goal of bringing down the Argentine president.

■ **Johnson County War, 1892**

Conflict over land and water rights in Wyoming began after the harsh winter of 1886, with many smaller ranchers driven off by their more powerful neighbours. Allegations of cattle rustling were often used as an excuse for violence against the ranchers. This led to the existence of two rival organizations, the well-established Wyoming Stock Growers Association (WSGA) and the newly formed Northern Wyoming Farmers and Stock Growers Association (NWFSGA), which was created to protect the interests of newer and less powerful ranchers. Under the pretence of eliminating cattle rustling, the WGSA sent an armed band known as the Invaders into Johnson County. The Invaders attacked the ranch of Nate Champion, leader of the NWFGSA, and killed him as he tried to flee his burning home. They were then intercepted by a posse from Johnson County and a protracted skirmish ensued before US cavalry arrived and arrested the Invaders.

■ ENID-POND RAILROAD WAR, 1893–94

A dispute between railroad companies and the US Department of the Interior escalated into violence as citizens of towns where trains refused to stop began to attack the railroad infrastructure and even the trains themselves.

■ DONGHAK PEASANT REVOLUTION, 1894

Disaffection with governmental corruption resulted in a peasant uprising beginning in Gobu, Korea. The initial government response to the revolt was weak and disjointed, and as a result the rising gained in strength rather than being crushed at the outset. After a period of rapid expansion, the rebellion was met with more effective government measures and the peasants' forces heavily defeated.

Recovering from this setback, the resilient rebels were able to inflict several defeats on government forces and advanced on Seoul, causing the government there to request Chinese aid. This was furnished and enabled a settlement with the rebels to be negotiated, but the action alarmed Japan, which also sent troops into the situation. A second rebellion then broke out, this time targeted against the Japanese intervention. The ill-equipped peasant army was soundly defeated by superior Japanese firepower, after

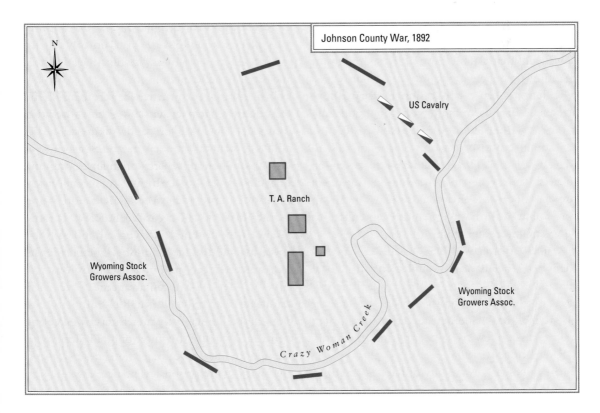

Johnson County War, 1892

which the rebellion was finally crushed by a vigorous military pursuit.

▪ UGEUMUCHI, 1894

Over several days, Donghak rebels attempted to attack strong positions held by a joint Korean–Japanese force. Japanese artillery proved decisive, and the peasant army was unable to make any headway despite heavy casualties.

▪ INTENTONA DE YAUCO, 1897

Intending to overthrow the Spanish colonial government in Puerto Rico, a rebel force marched on Yauco but encountered well-prepared government forces and was scattered. Other rebel bands were similarly defeated, bringing the revolution to an end.

▪ HUT TAX WAR, 1898

British attempts to impose a 'hut tax' on dwellings in Sierra Leone resulted in a guerilla war led by Bai Bureh, who led a successful resistance against heavy odds until his capture, which spelled the end of the revolt.

▪ CZESTOCHOWA POGROM, 1902

A relatively trivial incident in the town of Chenstokhov, Russian Empire, sparked an anti-Jewish riot that claimed several lives, though for the most part the rioters were more concerned with looting. On this occasion Russian troops attempted to protect the Jewish community.

▪ ILINDEN–PREOBRAHENIE UPRISING, 1903

A coordinated rising against Ottoman rule in Macedonia and Thrace achieved some initial success, but the overwhelming Ottoman response soon retook lost territory. The revolt was followed by savage reprisals intended to deter any future uprising.

▪ KISJINEV POGROM, 1903

Malicious accusations published in local Bessarabian newspapers resulted in a three-day riot directed at Jews and their property. Little or no attempt was made by the authorities to halt the attacks and few arrests were made afterwards.

▪ KIEV POGROM, 1905

In the troubled Russian city of Kiev, accusations that Jews were the cause of many social and economic ills resulted in a riot that caused enormous property damage as well as many casualties. This was one of many such pogroms that year, and as was often the case the authorities did little to halt the violence. Jewish communities began forming self-defence units of volunteers. Emigration from Russia also increased as a result of the pogroms.

▪ RUSSIAN REVOLUTION, 1905

The causes of the Russian Revolution were complex, including disaffection with the Tsarist regime, poverty and near-starvation in the countryside, and exploitative business practices that resulted in poor and miserable industrial workers. Although attempts were made to improve the situation, there were no real results and the practice of arresting dissenters merely created more unrest.

Early in 1905, a workers' delegation was fired upon by troops guarding the Winter Palace in St Petersburg. This precipitated a general strike, while defeat in the Russo-Japanese War increased unrest in the military. Naval mutinies took place throughout the year, notably aboard the battleship *Potemkin* in the Black Sea Fleet, at Sebastopol and Vladivostok.

Civil unrest also increased throughout the year, despite harsh measures by the authorities. Although demoralized and disaffected, the military generally obeyed the government and fired upon dissenters on many occasions. The closure of universities to reduce political agitation simply added the student population to the strikers, and Russia gradually became paralysed by dissent. With virtually no railways operating and industry almost at a standstill, the Tsar was forced to grant major concessions.

In October 1905 the Tsar agreed to accept a manifesto that reduced imperial authority and granted the Duma vastly increased power. Voting rights and civil liberties were granted, along with the right to form political parties. These measures met with widespread acceptance, causing the collapse of the revolution in many areas. Some hard-line groups had to be suppressed by armed force, and in some areas disaffected soldiers joined with the revolutionaries to take control of an area. By the end of the year, however, the revolution was more or less over, though strikes and minor acts of rebellion continued.

■ Revolution in Poland 1905–07

The 1905 Russian Revolution spilled over into the Russian-controlled regions of Poland, beginning with demonstrations and large-scale strikes. Many Poles saw the internal troubles in Russia as an opportunity to reassert Polish national identity, though economic troubles also caused significant unrest. Despite some concessions from St Petersburg, the unrest escalated and government response became violent, leading to gun battles between rebels and government forces in some major cities.

Russian efforts to contain the revolution drew in thousands of troops, and the revolution gradually lost impetus through 1906–07. The revolution came to an end in 1907 with concessions from St Petersburg. Among these was a reduction in efforts to 'Russify' Poland through its education system, and this in turn led to an increase in nationalistic sentiment which, over time, would set the stage for new efforts to achieve Polish independence.

■ Lodz Insurrection, 1905

Strikes in Lodz escalated into violence, with rebels seizing weapons from police and military patrols and barricading the streets. The insurrection was disorganized, with no central leadership, and was gradually crushed by government forces.

■ Theriso Revolt, 1905

Cretan rebels seeking union with Greece embarked upon an armed insurrection centred on Theriso. After numerous skirmishes and interventions by several major powers, a settlement was agreed whereby order was restored in return for governmental reforms.

■ Atlanta Race Riot, 1906

Racial tensions in Atlanta, Georgia, were increased by competition for jobs and concerns that black voters might upset a political situation that favoured the white population. The situation was inflamed by newspapers running a series of false reports claiming that white women had been assaulted by black men. As a result, an angry mob of white men, possibly numbering in the thousands, ran riot and attacked black-owned homes and businesses.

■ Bialystok Pogrom, 1906

Attacks on Christian processions were falsely blamed on the Jewish population of Bialystok, triggering widespread looting of Jewish property. Russian troops as well as civilians engaged in street fighting against Jewish militias trying to defend their homes.

■ Sveaborg Rebellion, 1906

Triggered by poor treatment and also the disastrous Russo-Japanese War, Russian soldiers rebelled at Sveaborg and planned to march on St Petersburg. The revolt ended with the surrender of the rebellious soldiers after less than three days.

■ Romanian Peasants Revolt, 1907

Tensions over landowners' exploitation of the peasants who worked the land led to a widespread revolt which caused the collapse of the government. Several thousand peasants were killed when the insurrection was put down by the army.

■ Santa Maria School Massacre, 1907

Striking miners, seeking improved working conditions, gathered at Domingo Santa Maria school in Iquique, Chile. After ignoring an ultimatum to disperse they were fired upon by the army, killing hundreds of miners and their families.

■ Marraketch, 1908

The rulership of Morocco was disputed between brothers Abdelaziz and Abdelhafid, with both for a time maintaining separate capitals. Defeating his brother in battle at Marraketch, Abdelhafid became Sultan of Morocco; he ruled over the country until 1912.

■ Ruse Blood Wedding, 1910

Ethnic tensions in Bulgaria caused by opposition to the wedding of a Bulgarian and a Turk resulted in a bloody clash between civilians and military personnel. The fighting caused around 100 casualties including 24 fatalities. Initially the police attempted to cover up the story by restricting communications to and from Ruse, but it soon became the top news all over the country.

■ SHIRAZ BLOOD LIBEL, 1910

Accusations that a Muslim child had been ritually murdered by the Jewish population of Shiraz, Iran, led to an outbreak of mob violence which was led by troops supposedly sent to protect the Jewish population.

■ AGADIR, 7 JULY–4 NOVEMBER 1911

The second of two diplomatic crises over Morocco, this clash began when French troops put down a riot in Fez. Technically the French action violated the terms of a previous treaty and Germany decided to support the sultan. German dispatch of a small warship to Agadir heightened political and military tensions,

Agadir Crisis, 1911

as did the overblown rhetoric of a few nationalist hotheads.

Britain offered diplomatic support to France, most notably in David Lloyd George's Mansion House speech. Both sides, however, realized that Agadir was not worth an escalation of tensions and they opened negotiations that resulted in a face-saving compromise for all. Although nationalists in Paris and Berlin claimed that their side had been cheated by the outcome, almost everyone was satisfied with the result. Agadir seemed to show that the great powers could resolve their differences peacefully, an image to be shattered just three years later.

■ HUANGHUAGANG UPRISING, 1911

Rebels in Guangzhou, China, launched an attack against the governor, who escaped by climbing over a wall. The rebels were heavily outnumbered by government forces, and their attack ended in complete failure.

■ THAI PALACE REVOLT, 1912

A group of army officers plotted to kill King Vajiravudh of Thailand, though their aims were confused and the plot was somewhat vague. The officer selected to assassinate the king instead betrayed the conspirators to the authorities.

■ CHAVES, 8 JULY 1912

Royalist rebels launched an attack into Portugal, hoping to spark a revolution against the new republican government. The resulting skirmish near Chaves was turned into a Republican victory by the arrival of government reinforcements with artillery.

■ OTTOMAN COUP, 1913

From 1908 until 1912, the Committee of Union and Progress (CUP) was a dominant force in the government of the Ottoman Empire. Its fortunes declined in 1912, but with the empire weakened by internal divisions and suffering from a loss of prestige after the Balkan Wars, the CUP took the opportunity to launch a coup in early 1913. The CUP outlawed all other political groups in order to cement its power.

The Era of World Wars 1914–45

The two world wars of the twentieth century were amongst the most convulsive events in human history. As well as costing millions of lives, they changed the nature of warfare itself, placing the advantage with manoeuvre and firepower.

World War I 1914–18

Western Front

■ **Liège, 5–16 August 1914**

Liège was one of the most powerful fortress complexes in the world in 1914, comprising a dozen interlocking strongpoints. The German Second Army needed to neutralize it quickly to secure the rail and road network of Belgium. The Germans used every weapon in their arsenal, including Zeppelins and custom-designed 420mm artillery guns. The fortresses held out long enough to slow the German advance and provide something of a moral victory for the Allies. Ludendorff became a hero in Germany when he pounded on the door of the citadel with his sword to demand Liège's surrender. Its capture allowed the Germans to continue their aggressive 1914 war plans.

■ **Mulhouse, 7–10 August 1914**

The 45,000 troops of France's VII Corps, under Gen Louis Bonneau, failed to seize Mulhouse from the 30,000-strong German XIV and XV Corps, led by Gen Josias von Heeringen. About 7000 French soldiers died.

■ **Haelen, 12 August 1914**

German Uhlan light cavalry and infantrymen were unable to outflank the Belgians across the River Gete. The Germans' poor tactics, lacking artillery support, together with strong response from Belgian infantry and cavalry, decided the day.

■ **Lorraine, 14–25 August 1914**

France's ill-starred offensive failed to recover Alsace-Lorraine. The French First and Second Armies were defeated by the German Sixth Army, under Bavarian Crown Prince Rupprecht, and the Seventh Army, under von Heeringen.

■ **Namur, 20–23 August 1914**

At the confluence of the Sambre and Meuse rivers, German FM Karl von Bülow's Second Army, and elements of the Third Army, under Gen Max von Hausen – comprising 107,000 men in total – besieged the garrison at Namur fort and 37,000 soldiers of the Belgian 4th Division, under LGen Michel. German and Austrian siege artillery proved decisive, with 304mm mortars and the 420mm 'Big Bertha' siege howitzer smashing the ill-prepared fortress and Belgian entrenchments.

■ **Charleroi, 21 August 1914**

Von Bülow's Second Army pushed south across the Sambre, driving into French Gen Charles Lanrezac's Fifth Army. A flank attack by von Hausen's Third Army, threatening encirclement, forced the French withdrawal. The French lost 30,000 men, the Germans 11,000.

■ **Ardennes, 21–23 August 1914**

Having misperceived German moves north of the Meuse, France's Gen Joseph Joffre ordered Gen Pierre Ruffey's Third Army and Gen Fernand de Langle de Cary's Fourth Army on a disastrous attack into the Belgian Ardennes. Their defeat cost France the vital Briey coalfield.

■ **Mons, 23 August 1914**

Deployed on the French left flank, the British Expeditionary Force (BEF), comprising two infantry corps and one cavalry division (70,000 men), was under the command of FM Sir John French. In its first fight of the war, the BEF faced the German First Army (160,000 men), under GenOb Alexander von Kluck, which attempted to envelop the Allied armies in the west. With 600 guns supporting, the German juggernaut advanced. The BEF's defence cost von Kluck 5000 casualties.

■ Le Cateau, 26 August 1914

British Gen Sir Horace Smith-Dorrien's 55,000 troops of the BEF II Corps withstood 140,000 Germans of von Kluck's First Army. A gallant artillery duel checked the German advance long enough for BEF infantry to escape the encirclement.

■ Guise (St Quentin), 29 August 1914

With the French withdrawing south to the Marne, Lanrezac's Fifth Army counter-attacked, slowing the advance of von Bülow's Second Army south of the Oise. The fighting cost 10,000 French and British casualties, and 7000 Germans.

■ Moselle River, 4–9 September 1914

The French First and Second Armies, under Gens Castelnau and Dubail, held the eastern end of Gen Joffre's line against Bavarian Crown Prince Rupprechet's Sixth and Seventh Armies (Bavarians) advancing on Nancy. Frustrated by their repulse, the Germans shelled the city before withdrawing.

■ Ourcq River, 5–9 September 1914

French Gen Michel-Joseph Maunoury's Sixth Army held ground against von Kluck's First Army advancing on Paris. The delaying action helped widen the gap between the First and von Bülow's other four German armies.

■ Marne River I, 6–12 September 1914

The culminating battle of the opening campaign of WWI, the First Battle of the Marne was then the largest battle ever fought. After moving through Belgium and northern France, the German First Army was supposed to move to the west of Paris as part of a giant encirclement. Their aim was to cut the city off from support and supplies, in theory, forcing its quick surrender. Without Paris, the Germans presumed that the French and British would surrender, allowing them to move the bulk of their forces east to face the Russians. The plan demanded much from inexperienced soldiers and left little room for the inevitable fog and friction of war. Due to the unexpected stiff resistance of the Belgians, German forces could not match the pace that their pre-war planners had set for them.

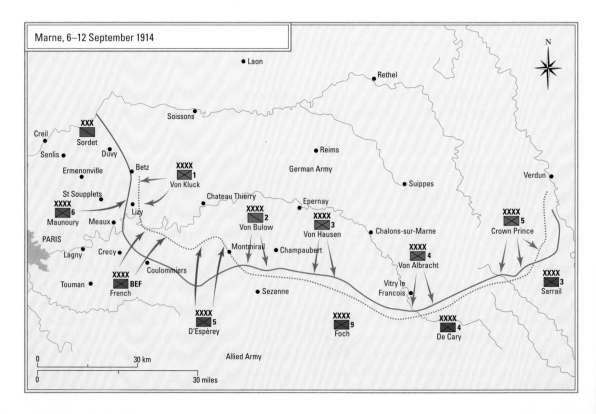

Marne, 6–12 September 1914

After several weeks of fighting they were unable to complete the manoeuvre as designed, although they had managed to place leading elements within 50km of Paris. Their success was sufficient to chase the French Government to Bordeaux and to force the British commander, Sir John French, to consider a withdrawal of his battered forces out of the line. Only strong pressure from the French and from the British Secretary of State for War, Lord Kitchener, convinced Sir John to return his weary troops to the fight. Instead of executing the risky manoeuvre west of Paris, the Germans opted instead to send the First Army east of the city as part of a proposed double envelopment of the Allied armies. Both sides had extended their lines from Paris to Verdun, a distance of almost 240km. The Germans hoped to pressure the Allies from both sides, forcing them in upon themselves and destroying them in one campaign.

Allied aviators detected the German maneuvre and the resulting exposure of the First Army's right flank. Quick work by French commander Joseph Joffre and Paris district commander Joseph Gallieni put Allied forces in a position to pressure the German flanks. A renewed effort by the BEF and a French Ninth Army commanded by Ferdinand Foch attacked the centre of the extended German line while the Allied right held around the fortresses of Verdun. The German attempt had failed. On 9 September, fearful that the Allies could move quickly into a gap that had opened up between the German First and Second Armies, Gen Helmuth von Moltke ordered his forces to retreat to the Aisne river and entrench. There were more than 250,000 casualties on each side. The Germans had suffered twice as many casualties as they had in the entire Franco-Prussian War. Trench warfare had begun.

▪ AISNE RIVER I, 12 SEPT–3 OCTOBER 1914

Von Bülow made his stand on the plateau north of the river. His armies constructed the first of what would become an elaborate system of entrenchments. Initially, their line extended from Verdun in the east, west across the Aisne to Noyon on the Oise. The British and French attempted a frontal assault but soon dug their own defensive trenches against fierce German resistance.

▪ ARTOIS I, 27 SEPTEMBER–10 OCTOBER 1914

As the situation along the Aisne became static, both sides attempted to flank one another north of Noyon. The French Eighth Army and the BEF eventually outmaneuvered the German Fourth Army, led by GenFM Albrecht, Duke of Württemberg, in this 'race to the sea'.

▪ ANTWERP, 28 SEPTEMBER–10 OCTOBER 1914

German artillery systematically battered down the city's great forts and dykes, inundating the outer line of Belgian entrenchments. France and Britain sent reinforcements, including 2000 Royal Marines, but they could not halt the German advance for long.

▪ YPRES I, 8 OCTOBER–20 NOVEMBER 1914

This was the opening of the Flanders Campaign, during which 4.4 million Allied soldiers confronted 5.4 million Germans. The major Central Powers forces were the Duke of Württemberg's Fourth Army, with Gen Erich von Falkenhayn's reserves, and Bavarian Crown Prince Rupprecht's Sixth Army. Gen Foch commanded the French Tenth Army and a detachment of Belgians. FM French led the BEF. Foch and French repulsed von Falkenhayn's attack at great cost: almost 20,000 Germans and as many as 85,000 Allies were killed.

▪ CHAMPAGNE I, 20 DEC 1914–17 MARCH 1915

The battlefront having stalemated in Flanders, both sides made probing attacks throughout the winter. Gen Fernand Langle de Cary's French Fourth Army advanced into the Champagne-Ardennes, sparking a battle that pinned down German reserves and cost each side more than 90,000 casualties.

▪ NEUVE CHAPELLE, 8–15 MARCH 1915

Decimated after Ypres, the BEF was rebuilt at Neuve Chapelle with fresh troops from Britain and India. A sustained British artillery barrage preceded the attack. The battle cost more than 11,600 British and Indian casualties, and 12,000 Germans.

▪ YPRES II, 22–25 APRIL 1915

German commander Erich von Falkenhayn began the second of three major battles in the Ypres sector

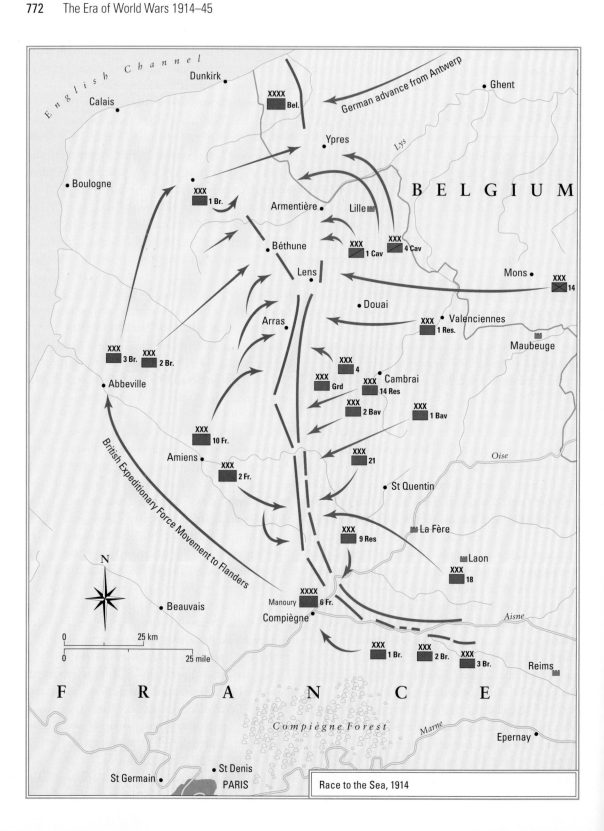

English Channel

Dunkirk

Calais

Ghent

XXXX
Bel.

German advance from Antwerp

Boulogne

Ypres

Lys

BELGIUM

XXX
1 Br.

Armentière

Lille

Béthune

XXX
1 Cav

XXX
4 Cav

Lens

Mons

XXX
14

Douai

Valenciennes

Arras

XXX
1 Res.

Maubeuge

XXX
3 Br.

XXX
2 Br.

XXX
4

XXX
Grd

Cambrai

Abbeville

XXX
14 Res

XXX
2 Bav

XXX
1 Bav

XXX
10 Fr.

Oise

Amiens

XXX
21

XXX
2 Fr.

St Quentin

British Expeditionary Force Movement to Flanders

La Fère

XXX
9 Res

Laon

XXX
18

N

Aisne

Beauvais

Manoury

XXXX
6 Fr.

Compiègne

XXX
1 Br.

XXX
2 Br.

XXX
3 Br.

Reims

0   25 km

0   25 mile

F   R   A   N   C   E

Compiègne Forest

Marne

Epernay

St Germain

St Denis

PARIS

Race to the Sea, 1914

Neuve-Chapelle, March 1915

of Belgium to cover his preparations for a massive offensive on the Eastern Front at Gorlice-Tarnow. Falkenhayn wanted to distract British and French attention and prevent them from providing material assistance to the Russians, his main target for 1915. With so many resources going east, however, Falkenhayn lacked the troops and equipment needed for a major breakthrough in Ypres, where the Germans had failed the previous autumn.

The Germans introduced poison gas to the Western Front. Although the Russians had used small amounts of gas in the east and although both sides had gas stockpiles, Ypres saw the first large-scale use of gas as a weapon. On the first day of the battle, the Germans used 168 tons of chlorine gas carried in more than 5000 cylinders. The introduction of gas allowed the Germans to minimize their use of artillery, helping to achieve surprise. A greenish cloud of gas covering 6.4km drifted towards a part of the line held by French Algerian and territorial troops. The Germans had

targeted a sector north of Ypres near the town of Langemarck. Of the 10,000 Allied troops who faced the first wave of gas, more than half died of asphyxiation within a few minutes. More than 2000 soldiers surrendered, while the rest panicked and fled. The Germans were as surprised as the Allies that the gas had opened such a major hole Lacking adequate reserves and protecting their troops with only the most primitive respirators, the Germans faced an unusual situation: they had their enemy on the run but could do little to exploit their success.

The Allies were surprised, but they began to respond, deducing that the gas cloud was chlorine based. British and Canadian engineers devised emergency counter-measures, including advising troops to breathe through cloth masks soaked in urine, whose ammonia mitigated the effects of the chlorine. A second gas attack on 24th April was less successful in the face of a heroic defence by Canadian troops. The battle resulted in the Germans gaining pieces of high ground of minor significance, but little else. Casualties were high, with 69,000 Allied (mostly British and Canadian) casualties against 35,000 Germans. Once the Allies recovered from the initial setbacks caused by the gas, the casualty numbers evened out. The Second Battle of Ypres opened the Pandora's Box of gas warfare.

■ CHAMPAGNE II, 23 SEP–2 OCTOBER 1915
The French Second Army, under Gen Pétain, and the Fourth Army, under Gen Langle de Cary, attacked the German Sixth Army, under Bavarian Crown Prince Rupprecht. After initial success, the French fell back losing 145,000 casualties to the Germans' 72,500.

■ ARTOIS II, 25 SEPTEMBER–15 OCTOBER 1915
Having failed to take Vimy Ridge in the spring, the French Tenth Army, under Gen Auguste Dubail, attacked again at Artois, facing the well-prepared German Sixth Army, led by Bavarian Crown Prince Rupprecht. In the new offensive, Joffre sought to exploit the Allies' numerical advantage, having deployed 132 divisions contrasted with the Germans' 102 divisions. After four days of artillery preparation, the French attacked through the

German first line to occupy the ridge. However, their thrust stalled against the German second line. The failure cost 48,000 French and more than 50,000 German casualties. Meanwhile, FM Sir John French's BEF, under the tactical command of Gen Sir Douglas Haig, attacked at Loos. That action, which marked the first British use of poison gas and direct aerial support of infantry, ended with the loss of 50,000 BEF soldiers and as many as 25,000 Germans.

■ Verdun, 21 February–18 December 1916

For much of 1916, the 220,000 troops of the German Fifth Army battled hard to capture the French fortress-town of Verdun in the face of bitter resistance from the 180,000 soldiers of the French Second and Third Armies. The Chief of the German General Staff, Gen Erich von Falkenhayn, hoped that by attacking the city of Verdun-sur-Meuse in north-eastern France (a location of huge symbolic importance) he would compel the French to defend the city fanatically. This would enable the Germans to 'bleed the defenders white' through massed artillery firepower. In January 1916, the French frontline in north-western Lorraine bulged north-east into the German lines along the Verdun sector. This created a large three-sided salient around the city, which had just one main road and one railway line that connected it to the rest of France. Given its strategic significance, Verdun was well fortified by an outer ring of 18 fortresses, all sited on dominating ground, including Forts Douaumont, Souville and Vaux. However, these forts were not the potent obstacles they might have been, as many of them had depleted garrisons and armaments. On 24 December 1915, the German High Command ordered that the offensive against Verdun should begin on 12 February 1916, but bad weather forced a postponement until the 21st. By then, the German Fifth Army's 72 battalions and 1300 artillery pieces outnumbered the French Third Army's 34 battalions and 300 guns. That day, the German artillery delivered one million rounds onto the French positions along the Brabant-Ornes sector, located north of Verdun. Although

this bombardment killed, wounded or stunned many defenders, the Germans still had to fight determinedly to secure their advance. Nevertheless, by the 25th the Germans had pushed forward as much as 8km into the French lines. Moreover, that day the Germans infiltrated into Fort Douaumont and captured it without a shot being fired. As a result, French reinforcements from Gen Philippe Pétain's Second Army poured into the Verdun salient, as did copious supplies, while Pétain himself assumed command of the sector. In the face of this strengthened French defence, the German offensive gradually ground to a halt. On 6 March, the Germans initiated an assault against the Forges-Haucourt sector, north-west of Verdun, and subsequently captured Hill 304 and Dead Man's Hill. During 22–25 May, however, the French unsuccessfully counter-attacked toward Fort Douaumont. The Germans resumed the offensive on 1 June, striking from Douaumont toward Fort Vaux; the battle for the fort's underground corridors raged for six days before the defenders surrendered. Subsequently, the Germans pushed south-west toward Fort Souville, which overlooked Verdun, but here French resistance halted their advance. Subsequently, the French counter-offensive recaptured Fort Douaumont on 24 October and Fort Vaux on 2 November. Over the ensuing five weeks, the continuing French counter-attacks slowly drove the Germans back north. By 18 December the French had in places closed to within 2km of the original February 1916 frontline. With their troops exhausted, supplies dwindling, and winter approaching, the French counter-offensive petered out, ending the battle of Verdun. The offensive was a German failure; most of their 12km advance had been lost to French counter-attacks and, while the French Army had been heavily damaged, so had the Germans. Around 160,000 French and 140,000 German military personnel died.

■ Fort Douaumont, 21 Feb–24 October 1916

Imperial Crown Prince Wilhelm's German Fifth Army attacked Fort Douaumont, the largest of the 19 forts protecting Verdun, leading with a heavy

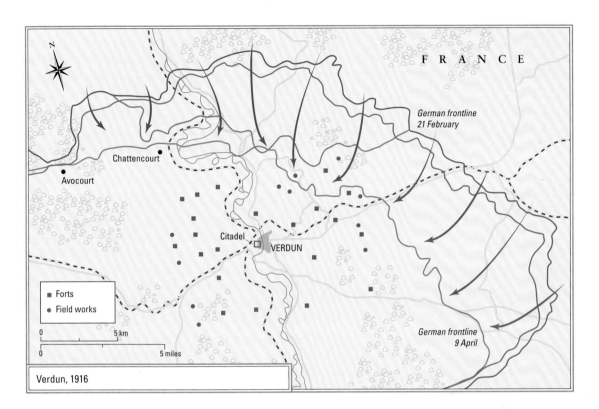

German frontline
21 February

FRANCE

Chattencourt

Avocourt

Citadel

VERDUN

- Forts
- Field works

0   5 km
0   5 miles

German frontline
9 April

Verdun, 1916

bombardment that included the 420mm siege howitzer. This strong point on the Meuse was key to conquering the medieval fortress city beyond. The fortress, largely disarmed and with only a small garrison, was infiltrated and fell to the Germans in February. It was briefly recaptured by the French in May, before finally being crushed in October.

■ FORT VAUX, 8 MARCH–3 NOVEMBER 1916

At Vaux, the German artillery barrage was blunted by the modernized fortress's reinforced concrete shelters. A small French garrison, led by Maj Sylvain-Eugene Raynal, repelled several assaults by elements of the Imperial Crown Prince's German Fifth Army. However, on 7 June the bastion finally succumbed as its garrison exhausted their potable water and ammunition. French general Robert Nivelle, having replaced Joffre as commander-in-chief, counter-attacked in October with heavy guns, driving the Germans out and reoccupying the fort.

■ THE SOMME, 1 JULY–18 NOVEMBER 1916

At the end of 1915 it was agreed that the French and British would mount a combined attack in the following year. The battle of Verdun gradually reduced available French troops, so it was Gen Sir Douglas Haig's British troops who eventually bore the main burden. Haig sought to break through the positions held by Gen von Below's German Second Army and reopen mobile warfare, but understood that 'Plan B' might be a battle of attrition. After a seven-day bombardment, Rawlinson's Fourth Army attacked on 1 July. In the northern sector, the assault achieved little success in return for heavy losses. It was the same story with a diversionary attack by Allenby's Third Army on Rawlinson's left flank. The Fourth Army did better in the southern sector, while the French on the right flank made a major advance with light casualties. Rawlinson failed to take advantage of the opportunity by reinforcing the south. The BEF suffered losses of 57,500 men on 1 July, including 19,000 dead.

After the first day of battle, the main focus of the British offensive was in the south, with the French

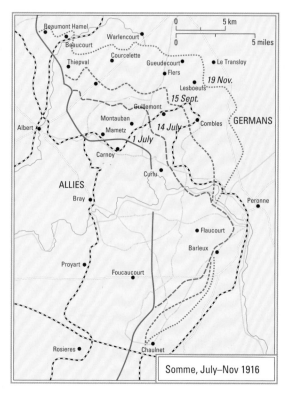

Somme, July–Nov 1916

continuing to fight in the River Somme sector. It was an attritional struggle, with the Germans constantly counter-attacking. On 14 July, Fourth Army captured Bazentin Ridge, but this was a rare clear-cut success. More typical was the seesaw fighting for High and Delville Woods, eventually captured by the British at a very high price. In the north, Gough's Reserve Army came into action, with the 1st Australian Division capturing Pozières on 23 July. The French also made progress, although not at the same rate as earlier in the battle, and coordination between the Allies was often poor. But the relentless Allied pressure caused alarm in Germany and Erich von Falkenhayn, the *de facto* commander-in-chief, was replaced on 29 August by the team of FM Paul von Hindenburg and Gen Erich Ludendorff.

In mid-September, the Allies launched another major push. The BEF's contribution, known as the battle of Flers-Courcelette, saw the debut of the tank. The attack made some ground but once again

failed to make a clean breakthrough. Joffre, his deputy, Gen Ferdinand Foch, and Haig continued to believe that the Allies should continue to hammer away at the Germans, and the battle lasted until mid-November, with the last spasm being the partially successful Ancre battle launched by Gough. Casualties were very high on both sides. Some 420,000 British and 200,000 French soldiers became casualties, and likely German losses amounted to between 450,000 and 600,000 men. In spite of a maximum advance of about 11km, the Somme was a strategic success for the Allies. The balance of attrition favoured the Allies, the BEF had gained much experience and learned how to fight more effectively and the pressure on Verdun was relieved. German High Command recognized that on land the pendulum had swung in favour of the Allies.

■ ARRAS, 9 APRIL–17 MAY 1917

Arras was envisioned as the British part of French Gen Robert Nivelle's grand plan to achieve a Western Front breakthrough. Two British armies targeted German forces near the strategically vital French city of Arras while the French attacked along the Aisne river. In the first phase, British forces gained air superiority over the Arras sector and also dug tunnels into the chalky soil of the region. Nearly 3000 artillery guns fired three million shells in support of the infantry. One of the British armies (the Third, commanded by Gen Edmund Allenby) succeeded in advancing and disrupting German lines, but the other army (the Fifth, commanded by Gen Hubert Gough) failed. Therefore, the Germans were able to focus their reserves on one section of the front only, and force the British to stop their attacks on 11 April. The British attacked again on 23 April, in part to relieve the French who had failed miserably on the Chemin des Dames. Too hastily planned and organized, these attacks failed. The British paused to refit and plan before attacking again near Bullecourt on 3 May. This attack also failed, forcing the British to call an end to the campaign in order to focus efforts on Sir Douglas Haig's planned

Vimy Ridge, 1917

Vimy was a success, cementing the reputation of Byng and his Canadians, but it was designed as only one part of the larger operational scheme developed by French general Robert Nivelle. As a result, there were too few reserves ready to exploit the Vimy success. When Nivelle's offensive on the Chemin des Dames failed the seizure of Vimy Ridge lost much of its strategic purpose. Still, the ridge remained in Allied hands for the rest of the war and Vimy had shown a model of tactical success that the Allies would repeat in 1918, with the Canadians again in the lead.

■ AISNE RIVER II, 16 APRIL–9 MAY 1917

Nivelle attacked along an 80.4km front, involving 800,000 men and 7000 guns against 650,000 Germans. The failed thrust cost 130,000 French and over 160,000 German casualties.

■ MESSINES, 7 JUNE 1917

The Messines Ridge sat on the southern edge of the Ypres salient. As long as it was in German hands, the British could not attack out of the salient itself.

offensive in Flanders. The Arras Campaign showed some clear signs of tactical improvements, but at the cost of 84,000 casualties to the Germans' 75,000 casualties. The British seized little ground of great value other than the simultaneous Canadian seizure of Vimy Ridge. Arras also increased Anglo-French tensions, as some British officers claimed that they had had to fight a battle under deteriorating tactical conditions to rescue their French allies.

■ VIMY RIDGE, 9–15 APRIL 1917

Vimy Ridge, a strategically important piece of high ground, was the target for a British offensive to be led primarily by the Canadian Corps. Four divisions assaulted the ridge on Easter Sunday supported by a well-designed artillery barrage. The Canadian commander, Julian Byng, had trained his men carefully for the mission and had demanded appropriate air and staff support from the British. The Canadians succeeded in capturing two lines of the German position in less than an hour despite a snowstorm. By 12 April they held the entire ridge.

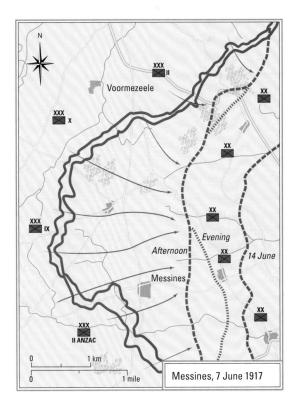

Messines, 7 June 1917

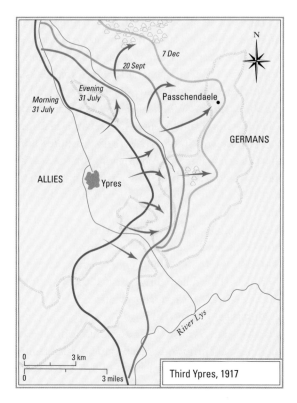

Third Ypres, 1917

British forces devised a plan to dig 22 mines under the ridge and blow it up from underneath. Months of painstaking work then ensued, including the digging of 8000m of underground tunnels. On 7 June, the British detonated 19 of the mines, setting off an explosion forming several craters over 60m deep. Surprise was total and an estimated 10,000 Germans were killed. A massive artillery bombardment then supported an infantry assault in capturing what was left of the ridge. Despite this, Haig moved too slowly to take advantage of the success and the opportunity slipped away.

■ YPRES III, 31 JULY–6 NOVEMBER 1917

FM Sir Douglas Haig planned a massive offensive in Belgium to accomplish three goals. First, he believed that the French Army had been badly shaken by its failures in the Chemin des Dames offensive in April. That failure, he argued, rendered the French Army unable to assume the offensive, just as the Bolshevik Revolution was paralyzing Russian forces. With the Americans still unable to contribute, Haig believed

that the burden of combat had to fall to the British. Second, he hoped to dislodge the Germans from their submarine pens along the Belgian coastline at a time when the submarine menace was a primary strategic concern of British leaders. Third, believing that the Germans had suffered terrible losses in 1916 and 1917, Haig looked for a chance to achieve a breakthrough into open country, away from the trenches of the Western Front. His plan envisioned preliminary operations against the high ground near Messines, to the south of Ypres. Once successful in neutralizing that threat, British forces would drive out of Ypres and link up with a force landed by the Royal Navy on the Belgian coast. Under pressure from politicians and his fellow generals, Haig dropped the amphibious plan but maintained his faith in the ability of British forces to break the German lines, despite intelligence showing the strength of enemy positions.

The first phase of the operation worked well, supported by a massive explosion of a series of large mines under the Messines Ridge on 7 June, which were loud enough to be heard in London. The few German survivors surrendered, leaving the ridge in British hands. Haig then moved inexplicably slowly, changing field commanders and debating operational aims with his chief subordinates. Preliminary artillery barrages began on 16 July, but were hampered by a series of problems, including poor weather and deep German defences. British ground attacks moved forward slowly amid torrential rainstorms that only exacerbated the already daunting drainage problems of Flanders. Despite heavy losses for both sides, Haig was encouraged by highly exaggerated intelligence reports suggesting an imminent collapse of German morale. He was also unable to resolve the debates among his army and corps commanders about the ultimate purpose of the campaign; some wanted to break through German lines, while others argued for smaller 'bite and hold' operations that asked less of British soldiers. In October, his subordinates recommended shutting the campaign down as the weather worsened, but Haig pressed on until

November. The British (including Canada and ANZAC) suffered 310,000 casualties and the Germans suffered 250,000.

■ PASSCHENDAELE, 12 OCTOBER 1917

British and Commonwealth troops, including Australians, New Zealanders and Canadians, attacked north of Ypres. Advance patrols reached the Belgian village, but returned to their starting positions after bloody fighting. The muddy terrain had neutralized British artillery preparation.

■ CAMBRAI, 20 NOVEMBER–3 DECEMBER 1917

Cambrai is best known for the British Army's innovative use of tanks. Previously used piecemeal and in small numbers, at Cambrai more than 120 tanks arranged in teams of three attacked along a 10km front. Planners, including J. F. C. Fuller, hoped that tanks could avoid the need for massive artillery bombardments that signalled an attack to the enemy and chewed up the ground for the infantry. At first, the plan seemed to work, as the Germans were indeed surprised. An 8km gap in the lines opened

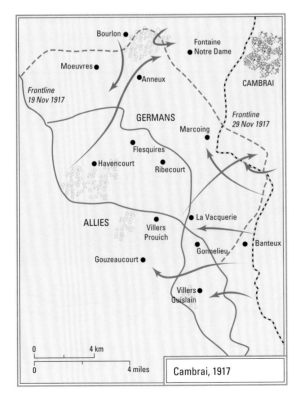

0   4 km

0   4 miles   Cambrai, 1917

up at minimal cost in lives, but the British could not exploit it. The Third Ypres Offensive denied the British infantry reserves and too many tanks had broken down at Cambrai to permit a mechanized exploitation. Nevertheless, sensing victory and a chance to recover the momentum lost at Ypres, FM Haig ordered the offensive continued despite a rapid German recovery. The Germans eventually counter-attacked, surprising the British and driving them back to their original lines. Cambrai thus revealed the potential of mechanized warfare, but also its limitations. The failure to fully coordinate infantry and armour showed that tanks were not yet ready to make a decisive impact on the battlefield, but they did point to a new way of providing fire support to the infantry. Mechanical problems and command challenges also limited the impact of the tanks, but Cambrai was a glimpse into the future.

■ SOMME RIVER II, 21 MARCH–5 APRIL 1918

German Gen Erich Ludendorff attacked the British Third and Fifth Armies along an 80.4km front south of Arras. The Germans endured 239,000 casualties, the British more than 177,700.

■ LYS RIVER (YPRES IV), 9–29 APRIL 1918

Ludendorff's offensive shifted to Flanders, where the German Fourth and Sixth Armies attacked the British First and Second. The Germans wanted the ports of Calais and Dunkirk, but the thin red line held at the cost of 120,000 German and a similar number of Allied casualties.

■ AISNE RIVER III, 27 MAY–3 JUNE 1918

Forty-one German divisions, supported by 6000 guns, attacked the Allied line on the Chemin des Dames, quickly capturing several bridges over the Aisne. British and French troops rallied and stopped Ludendorff at the Marne.

■ CHÂTEAU-THIERRY, 1–4 JUNE 1918

Having captured and held Cantigny in May, the American Expeditionary Force (AEF) helped the French to check the advance of German Gen Bruno von Mudra's First Army and Gen Max von Boehn's Seventh Army. The 3rd American Division, under Gen John Dickman, held the line at the Marne against Ludendorff's exhausted and

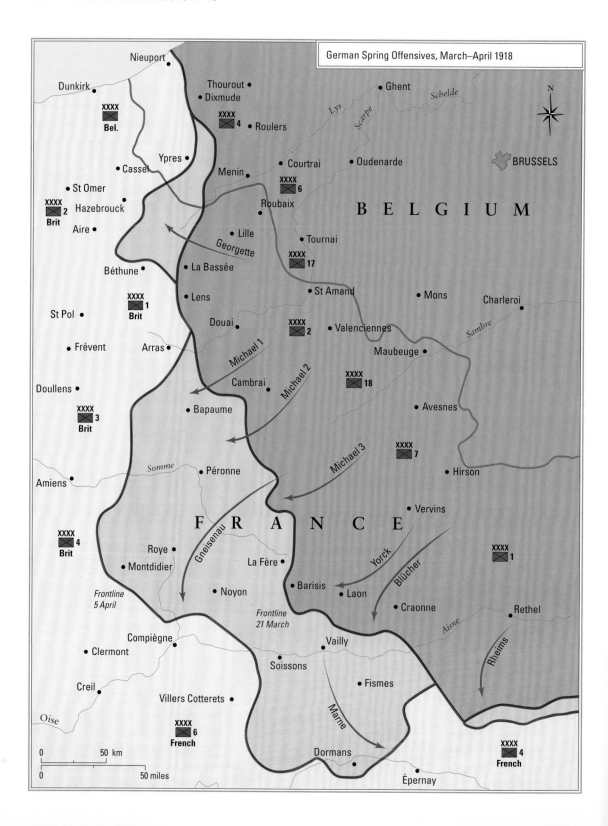

German Spring Offensives, March–April 1918

overextended troops. The success of the 'Rock of the Marne' complemented the 2nd American Division's victory at Belleau Wood.

■ Belleau Wood, 6–26 June 1918

'Retreat hell, we just got here.' So – supposedly – called out an American marine when told by a French counterpart that the fight for the small forest was lost. The American 2nd Division fought for three weeks as part of an effort to stop the German momentum during their 1918 offensives. The Americans suffered almost 10,000 casualties to take back the wood against heavily defended German positions. The Americans fought hard, but at times recklessly, including an open charge across a wheat field swept by German machine guns. The Marine Corps lost more men on the first day of battle than any other day in their history up to that point.

■ Marne River II, 15 July–6 August 1918

Ludendorff's gamble against Paris had failed (at the cost of over 800,000 German casualties during five offensives). FM Foch ordered a massive counter-attack, involving three French armies, two American divisions and British and Italian support. This marked the beginning of the drive north to reach the Armistice line by 11 November.

■ Champagne-Marne River, 15–17 July 1918

Three German armies attacked the French in the vicinity of Reims. After pushing a short distance across the Marne, Gen von Boehn's Seventh Army crashed into the French Ninth Army and the American 3rd Division. The attack cost 139,000 German and 133,000 Allied casualties.

■ Aisne–Marne Rivers, 18 July–6 August 1918

The French Tenth, Sixth and Fifth Armies, supported by American, British and Italian divisions, thrust into the German salient. Allied armored cavalry, including 350 new tanks, helped roll the Kaiser's troops back across the Marne.

■ Amiens, 8–12 August 1918

On the opening day of the Hundred Days Offensive Allied forces advanced over seven miles, one of the greatest advances of the war, with the British Fourth Army playing a decisive role. Total German losses were estimated to be 30,000, leading

Erich Ludendorff to describe the first day of the battle as 'the black day of the German Army'. The battle was a turning point in the war.

■ St Mihiel, 12–16 September 1918

The first major operation by the independent US Army targeted the St Mihiel salient just south of Verdun. It involved the largest air armada ever assembled at that time: 1481 airplanes from all of the Allied nations under the unified command of American Col William 'Billy' Mitchell. Having held the ground largely unopposed since 1914, German defenses in the region were formidable, but German leaders saw the precariousness of their position. They began to evacuate units as soon as they deduced that a major attack was imminent. Still, the campaign posed challenges. Terrain features, including lakes, forests and hills, canalized the movement of the infantry, creating a complex battlefield. The Americans assembled 550,000 troops, alongside 110,000 French troops, for the attack.

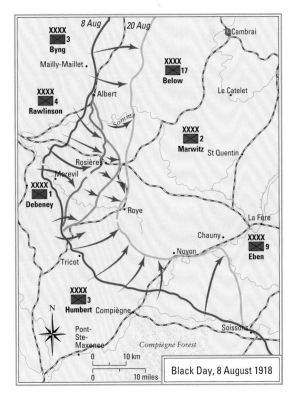

Black Day, 8 August 1918

St Mihiel was the largest US military operation since 1865. It targeted the southern and eastern parts of the salient with a supporting attack to the west. It achieved all of its first-day goals, disrupting German movements and pinching off the salient near the town of Hattonchâtel. The American capture of the heights near Montsec broke open crumbling German defences and cleared the way forward. By 16 September, the entire salient was in Allied hands and the threat to Allied communications in the Champagne area had been neutralized. The operation had been a big success. The Americans took 7000 casualties but captured more than twice that number of enemy soldiers.

■ MEUSE RIVER-ARGONNE FOREST, 26 SEPTEMBER–11 NOVEMBER 1918

Gen Henri Gouraud's French Fourth Army and Gen 'Black Jack' Pershing's American First Army successfully attacked the German Fifth Army's lines east of Reims. This was the AEF's largest battle of the war, involving more than half a million Allied troops and approximately 200,000 Germans.

■ CAMBRAI-ST QUENTIN, 27 SEPT–9 OCT 1918

The attack on the Cambrai-St Quentin sector was intended as the British portion of a joint offensive all along the Western Front. French marshal Ferdinand Foch, the architect of Allied strategy, wanted attacks on the entire length of the front to prevent the Germans from focusing their dwindling resources in one area only. The British attempt, in tandem with the American attack in the Meuse-Argonne sector and French attacks to the north, aimed to force the Germans out of the powerful set of fixed defences known as the Hindenburg Line. If the Allied armies could unhinge that line, they would face no insurmountable obstacles to the Rhine river. Breaking the line before winter afforded the Germans a chance to pause and refit could produce victory before the end of the year.

Although primarily a British operation, the forces dedicated to breaking the Hindenburg Line in the Cambrai sector included one French army, the Australian Corps, and the American II Corps. Preliminary assaults on German positions along the Canal du Nord succeeded in forcing the Germans back almost 6.4km, a huge achievement by WWI standards. The attack also produced 10,000 German prisoners of war, an indication that the enemy's morale might be breaking. Nevertheless, the American/Australian attack on the St Quentin Canal on 29 September at first fared poorly, in part due to American inexperience. The 'Yanks' tended to advance too far too fast, failing to neutralize German positions in their rear. Surviving German troops could then fire into the backs of advancing American troops. Staff coordination between British and American officers was also imperfect, leaving the Americans with inadequate artillery support.

Another reason for the setback emerged from the strength of well-planned German positions. The Germans had emptied a key tunnel of the St Quentin Canal and turned it into a mini-fortress, complete with field kitchens, hospitals and barracks. Once inside the tunnel, troops were well protected from Allied artillery barrages. The Germans had also carefully defended the approaches to the canal with barbed wire, interlocking machine-gun positions and pre-registered artillery pieces. The canal tunnel thus represented part of one of the most formidable defensive systems to be found anywhere in 1918. Despite their initial setback, the Americans regrouped and assaulted the canal again. Two raw and inexperienced American National Guard divisions attacked with support from British heavy artillery and tanks. Driving forward, the Americans captured the critical part of the German trench system around the present-day American military cemetery of Bony. Then, alongside the Australians, they attacked both ends of the St Quentin tunnel simultaneously, trapping the Germans inside and winning an important victory. That success allowed the British to press on towards the strategic road juncture of Cambrai, which Canadian troops took on 9 October. The conditions of the pillaged town and the demoralized state of German prisoners of war convinced the Allies that the end of the war might indeed be in sight. Meanwhile, at the German resort town of Spa, the German High Command had come to the same conclusion. They therefore began preparations to sue for peace.

Eastern Front

■ STALLUPOENEN, 17 AUGUST 1914

German Gen Hermann von Francois' I Corps (40,000 men) attacked elements of Gen Paul von Rennenkampf's Russian First Army. The Germans won, inflicting more than 5000 casualties on the poorly organized Russians, while enduring nearly 1300 casualties of their own.

■ GUMBINNEN, 20 AUGUST 1914

Against orders from Berlin, Gen Max von Prittwitz' German Eighth Army attacked von Rennenkampf's 200,000 advancing troops. Russian artillery proved decisive, routing the Germans. Berlin replaced von Prittwitz and von Francois with Gens Paul von Hindenburg and Erich Ludendorff, who would turn the tide at Tannenberg.

■ GALICIA, 23 AUGUST–12 SEPTEMBER 1914

Austro-Hungarian Gen Count Franz Conrad von Hoetzendorf campaigned against the Russians in Poland, north of the Carpathians. Although initially successful, the Austro-Hungarians would eventually be driven out of Galicia, at the cost of almost 400,000 men.

■ KRASNIK, 23–25 AUGUST 1914

In the first move of the Galicia Campaign, Austro-Hungarian Gen Viktor Dankl's First Army attacked the Fourth Russian Army under Baron Anton Saltza, north of Lublin. Austro-Hungarian forces drove Saltza back, with losses of 20,000 Russians and 15,000 of their own.

■ LEMBERG I, 23 AUGUST–12 SEPTEMBER 1914 & 17–22 JUNE 1915

Three Austro-Hungarian armies clashed with four Russian armies in Galicia, the territory of which is now divided between Poland and Ukraine. After initial success, the Austro-Hungarians, fighting without German support, went on the defensive

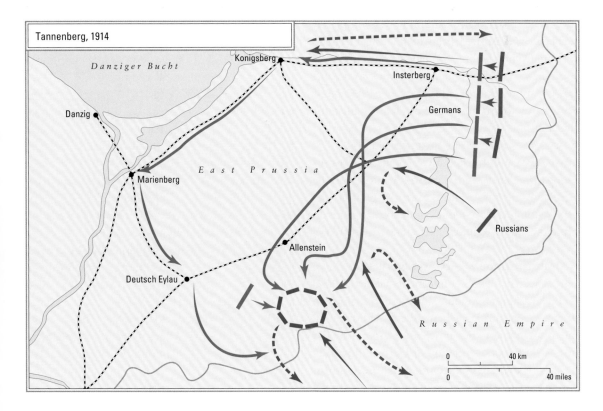

Tannenberg, 1914

against Russian forces that were larger and quicker than anticipated. In 1914, the Russians crossed the Gnila Lipa and conquered Lemberg, seizing control of the province. In the summer of 1915, Austrian and German forces recaptured the city.

■ GNILA LIPA RIVER, 26–30 AUGUST 1914

The Russian Third Army, under Gen Nikolai Ruzski, and the Eighth Army, under Gen Nikolai Brusilov, attacked Galicia unexpectedly from the east, along the northern bank of the Dniester river. The Austro-Hungarians fell back.

■ TANNENBERG, 27–28 AUGUST 1914

Following a Russian victory at Gumbinnen, the German High Command called on Paul von Hindenburg and Erich Ludendorff to turn the tide on the Eastern Front. The two agreed a plan to divide German forces in the face of two Russian armies. The larger portion would fall on the Russian Second Army of Alexander Samsonov before it could move west of the Masurian Lakes and link with the Russian First Army. The plan was daring, but succeeded spectacularly. Samsonov was completely surprised and isolated from help. The Germans surrounded him before he could respond effectively. Of the 150,000 men under Samsonov's command, 30,000 were killed and 95,000 surrendered. Stunned by the magnitude of his defeat, Samsonov shot himself.

■ RAVA RUSSKAYA, 3–11 SEPTEMBER 1914

Off-balance after the loss at Gnila Lipa, the Austro-Hungarian First and Fourth Armies became separated on retreat. The Russians exploited the gap, routing their enemies and costing Austria-Hungary up to 350,000 men and over 161km of territory.

■ MASURIAN LAKES I, 9–14 SEPTEMBER 1914

Russian First Army commander General Pavel Rennenkampf responded slowly to the Russian defeat to his north at Tannenberg. Although he ordered a retreat to better defensive ground, he did not detect the concentration of German forces on his flanks and lines of communication. German commanders attacked aggresively, inflicting heavy

casualties and forcing the Russians to move out of East Prussia. Russia lost 125,000 men at the battle. Nevertheless, the Russians could replace the manpower losses, meaning that even two huge defeats did not force Russia out of the war or solve Germany's two-front dilemma. The Russians counter-attacked at the end of the month and regained much lost ground.

■ PRZEMYSL, 24 SEPTEMBER–11 OCTOBER 1914 & 6 NOVEMBER 1914–22 MARCH 1915

Russia's Gen Radko Dimitriev's Third Army besieged this fortified outpost on the Hungarian border, commanded by Austro-Hungarian Gen Hermann Kusmanek. German relief columns helped to stall the first attempt, but the garrison surrendered in the spring of 1915.

■ VISTULA RIVER–WARSAW, 29 SEPT–31 OCT 1914

Hindenberg's German Ninth Army and Austro-Hungarian First Army attacked Warsaw. Initially successful on crossing the Vistula, the Central Powers' advance faltered. The Russians forced them

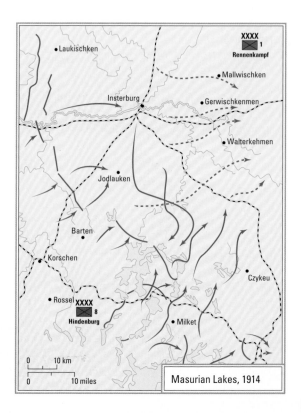

Masurian Lakes, 1914

back at the cost of 140,000 German and Austrian and 65,000 Russian casualties.

■ LODZ, 11 NOVEMBER–6 DECEMBER 1914

Three Russian armies (the First, Second and Fifth) battled Gen August von Mackensen's Ninth Army, which attempted to flank their march on Silesia. In deep cold winter fighting, the Germans were forced into a fighting retreat.

■ MASURIAN LAKES II, 7–22 FEBRUARY 1915

The German Eighth and Tenth Armies clashed with the Russian Tenth and Twelfth Armies as Hindenberg enacted his strategy to break out of East Prussia, advance east of the Vistula and force the Russians to terms. After a series of setbacks, including the loss of a corps to a German encirclement, Russian Gen von Plehve counter-attacked and halted the advance. The campaign cost the Russians more than 156,000 casualties and the Germans more than 16,000.

■ GORLICE-TARNOW, 2–10 MAY 1915

With Gen von Mackensen in command, the German Eleventh Army, with heavy artillery support, broke through the Russian line. The victory precipitated the 'Great Retreat' of the three Russian armies in the Carpathians, leading to the recapture of Przemysl and Lemberg.

■ WARSAW, 13 JULY–5 AUGUST 1915

As the Russians retreated from Galicia, Mackensen's Eleventh Army and the German Twelfth Army, under Gen Max von Gallwitz, crossed the Vistula and advanced through Russian Poland. Russian Grand Duke Nicholas' armies fell back, abandoning the city without a siege. Still the Germans advanced east, capturing the Novo-Georgievsk fortress. By the end of September, the new battle line extended from the Baltic to the Romanian frontier.

■ NAROCH LAKE, 18–26 MARCH 1916

To relieve pressure on the Allies at Verdun, the Russian Second Army, with 300,000 soldiers and as many as 5000 guns, unsuccessfully attacked Hermann von Eichhorn's German Tenth Army. Russia suffered 100,000 casualties before calling off the offensive.

■ KOVEL-STANISLAV (BRUSILOV), 4 JUNE–20 SEPTEMBER 1916

Russian Gen Alexei Brusilov launched a massive attack along a 322km front, involving 200,000 soldiers and almost 1000 guns. Surprised Austro-Hungarians and Germans fell back, but rallied. Each side lost more than one million men.

■ LEMBERG II (KERENSKY), 1–19 JULY 1917

In the Tsar's last offensive of the war, Russian War Minister Alexander Kerensky ordered three armies to break Austro-German lines in Galicia. Behind a heavy artillery barrage, the Russians gained ground. But fierce counter-attacks led to heavy casualties, which stalled the advance.

■ RIGA, 1 SEPTEMBER 1917

With Russian morale broken after heavy losses in the Brusilov and Kerensky offensives, and the Bolshevik Revolution looming, German forces easily drove the Russians from Riga. The Kaiser won an important port and extended the northern end of his battle front across the Daugava.

Italian Front

■ ISONZO, JUNE 1915–OCTOBER 1917

Italy expected its entry into World War I to bring high rewards at relatively low costs. Alliances with Great Britain and France meant secure coasts and lines of maritime communication that would ensure supplies of coal, food and industrial goods. More importantly, Italy could concentrate on just one front – its north-eastern frontier – while its principal enemy, Austria-Hungary, had to fight a simultaneous war against the massive Russian Army. Despite this, the war went poorly for Italy, partly because of material shortcomings and because of the dysfunctions of its high command. Instead of walking to Vienna, as Italian commander Luigi Cadorna had promised, the Italians found themselves stuck in the Julian Alps and the Isonzo river valley in modern-day Slovenia. High altitudes, heavy snowfalls and long supply lines combined to make the Isonzo theatre a difficult one for both sides. Cadorna's lack of original operational or tactical ideas doomed the Italians to repeated frustrations yet he pushed on, convinced that his enemy was breaking. Austria-Hungary's men were highly motivated to defeat the Italians for both political and ethnic reasons. Austro-Hungarian forces were led by Svetozar Boroevi, who made use of high ground, river crossings and other terrain features to hold the Italians at bay with minimal manpower, most of which was needed elsewhere. Nevertheless, successive Italian attacks wore down Austro-Hungarian power and morale in a theatre that turned increasingly savage. Fearful that the Austro-Hungarians might not withstand a 13th Isonzo battle, the Germans sent forces to the region to plan and lead the Caporetto Offensive.

■ Asiago, 15 May–10 June 1916

With the Italian Marshal Luigi Cadorna's offensives along the Isonzo having failed, Austro-Hungarian Gen Conrad von Hotzendorf launched a punitive counter-attack of his own. Blasting through Italian lines and threatening the Venetian Plain, the Austro-Hungarians were forced to withdraw after the success of Russia's Kovel-Stanislav Offensive.

■ Caporetto, 24 Oct–12 November 1917

Concerned that their Austro-Hungarian allies were being worn down by the battles on the Isonzo river, the Germans planned a major offensive to relieve the pressure. They used new 'storm troop' tactics to attack the Italian Second Army, whose capable commander, Luigi Capello, was incapacitated by illness. Bypassing main Italian positions and disrupting command and control systems, the German attack led first to retreat then to panic. German forces, one of whose units was led by a young Erwin Rommel, used mass and surprise to defeat a larger Italian force. The battle showed the power of the new German tactical system, although the German and Austro-Hungarian forces did not have sufficient supplies to sustain the attacks for longer than a few days. Of the Italian forces, 40,000 men were killed and 275,000 made prisoners of war compared to total Central Powers losses of

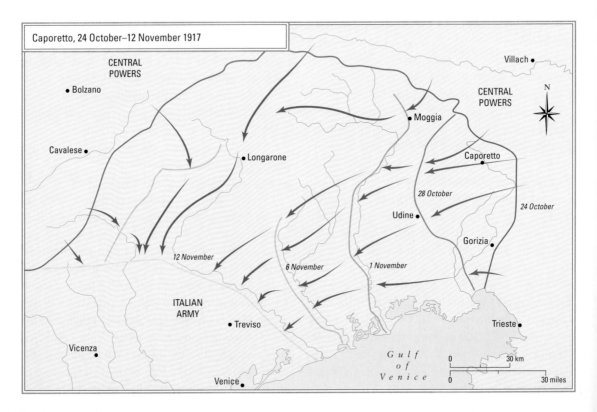

Caporetto, 24 October–12 November 1917

under 20,000 men. The Second Army's collapse led to the more orderly retreats of the neighbouring Third and Fourth Armies. Italian forces retreated to the Piave river and begged the British and French to send men and equipment. Caporetto was one of the most lopsided battles of the war. However, the Italians were not finished. They replaced Cadorna with Armando Diaz and welcomed back tens of thousands of men who had deserted during the rout. Thus the operational success at Caporetto did not lead to the defeat of Italy or the salvation of Austria-Hungary.

■ PIAVE RIVER, 15–23 JUNE 1918

Austro-Hungarian Baron Svetozan Borojevic von Bojna and Gen von Hotzendorf launched simultaneous attacks at Piave and Trentino, respectively. Allied troops under Italian Gen Armando Diaz, with the advantages of better terrain and armor support, repelled the attack with heavy casualties.

■ VITTORIO VENETO, 24 OCTOBER–NOVEMBER 1918

Following the disaster at Caporetto, the Italian Gen Armando Diaz, had reformed and rebuilt the Italian Army. Three French and two British divisions, hurriedly dispatched to Italy, had also been preparing to resume the offensive. A successful Italian defence of the Piave river line in June suggested that the efforts to reconstruct the Italian Army had paid dividends. Additional training efforts and the deteriorating political condition of the Austro-Hungarian Empire led Diaz and his allies to order an offensive across the Piave river aimed at Vittorio Veneto. Ignoring the military principle of concentration of forces, Allied armies separated their attacks to place maximum pressure on Austro-Hungarian forces. Fifty-one Italian and five Allied divisions attacked, crossing the Piave in several places then turning on the collapsing Austro-Hungarian Fifth Army. On 30 October, Allied forces reached the communication node of Sacile, splitting Austro-Hungarian forces in two. Italian reserves widened the gap in the days that followed while another Allied army advanced on

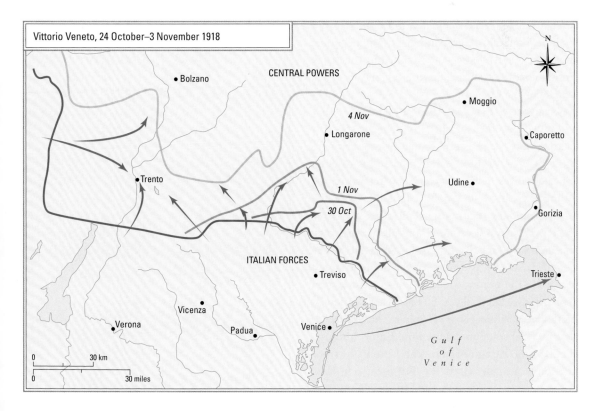

Vittorio Veneto, 24 October–3 November 1918

Trento. The pressure was too much for the Austro-Hungarians, who collapsed. More than 300,000 Austro-Hungarians became prisoners of war. Vittorio Veneto proved that even a defeat as massive as Caporetto had not destroyed the Italian Army. It also proved the value of inter-allied cooperation and coalition planning. Most importantly, the battle effectively ended Austro-Hungarian combat power. The day after the capture of Trento, Austria-Hungary signed an armistice. Soon the state itself dissolved as its army had.

Balkan Front

■ JADAR RIVER (CER), 12–21 AUGUST 1914

Gen Oskar Potiorek ordered the Austro-Hungarian Second and Fifth Armies (200,000 troops) to attack toward Valjevo. The Austro-Hungarians quickly secured bridgeheads and advanced. Although poorly equipped, the Serbs counter-attacked, temporarily halting the invasion.

■ RUDNIK RIDGES (KOLUBRA), 3–15 DEC 1914

A third Austro-Hungarian attack on Belgrade forced Serbian Marshal Radomir Putnik's troops into the mountains. Gen Potiorek's troops occupied the city. Later, having been resupplied by the Allies, Putnik counter-attacked, driving the invaders back across the Danube.

■ GALLIPOLI, 9 FEBUARY 1915–9 JANUARY 1916

Frustrated by the inability to achieve strategic victories on the Western Front, British planners, most notably Winston Churchill, began to look for alternatives. Then serving as First Lord of the Admiralty, Churchill sought a theatre where the British could use their most powerful military asset, the Royal Navy. Therefore, Churchill, supported by the aggressive First Sea Lord Adm Sir Jackie Fisher, designed a scheme to send what was then the largest armada in the history of the Mediterranean region through the Dardanelles Straits. Britain's newest battleship, a battlecruiser, 16 older battleships, 20 destroyers, and support ships would move through the Dardanelles and pressure the Ottoman capital at Constantinople. Both the Russians, who had their eye on picking apart the Ottoman Empire if

and when it collapsed, and the French gave their approval to the plan.

The British armada ran into problems from Ottoman defences that included 11 small coastal forts and 373 mines. Special German crews helped to bolster the defensive capabilities of the Ottomans, bringing with them 150mm howitzers designed to threaten British ships. Churchill and Fisher then convinced the British Army to land a force on the Gallipoli peninsula to neutralize the forts from the ground. On 25 April 1915, a British force that relied heavily on the ANZAC (Australia and New Zealand) Corps landed at Gallipoli, with a French force landing on the Asian side as a diversion. The operation experienced problems from the start, including troops landing in the wrong spots. The main force ran into a Turkish unit commanded by Mustafa Kemal, then a Lcol. He heroically rallied his retreating troops and held the high ground. British and ANZAC forces had enough strength to hold the beaches at Gallipoli, but not enough to

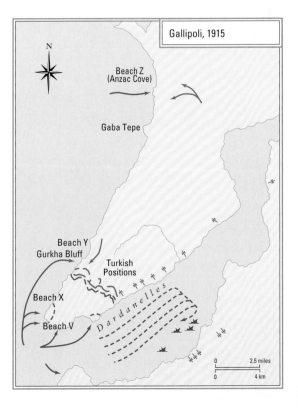

push Turkish troops out of their positions. Gallipoli thus became another example of the very trench warfare stalemate it was supposed to avoid. Not having planned for a long campaign, British supplies and staff arrangements soon proved inadequate. Another landing at Suvla Bay in August also failed, leaving both sides to fight a static war in a brutal Mediterranean summer that all too quickly turned into an equally brutal winter.

British and Australian politicians scrutinized and criticized the campaign. The British sent Gen Charles Monro to Gallipoli to provide a fresh assessment. Monro advocated a withdrawal, infuriating Churchill, but Churchill and Fisher were no longer influential voices: Fisher resigned in May and Churchill lost his job at the insistence of the Conservatives. Miraculously, the British executed a nearly flawless withdrawal of 83,000 men with virtually no manpower losses. The campaign, however, had cost the Allies 250,000 casualties.

■ SERBIA, OCTOBER–DECEMBER 1915

Twenty-three divisions of the German, Austro-Hungarian and Bulgarian Armies invaded Serbia from the north and east. Their combined force included more than 300,000 men and 1000 pieces of artillery. They were opposed by 200,000 soldiers and 300 guns of the Serbian Royal Army. The Austrian Third Army and the German Eleventh Army joined in the main attack on Belgrade. The Bulgarian First and Second Armies attacked from the east. Fewer than 140,000 surviving Serbs fled west to the Adriatic, completing the Central Powers' victory.

■ SALONIKA, 6 OCT 1915–29 SEPTEMBER 1918

Having landed in Greece at Thessaloniki, the Allies established a new front in Macedonia. From west to east, French Gen Franchet d'Esperey deployed the Armée d'Orient, the Serbian First and Second Armies, and the British XVI Corps. Opposite were Gen Friedrich von Scholtz' German Eleventh Army, with the Bulgarian First, Second and Fourth Armies. Battles at Monastir, Dobro Pole and Doiran stalemated. The Vardar Offensive broke the deadlock as the Allies knocked Bulgaria out of the war.

■ ROMANIA, AUGUST 1916–DECEMBER 1917

Joining forces with the Russians against the Central Powers, Romania campaigned to win territory in Transylvania, opposed by Austro-Hungarian, German, Bulgarian and Turkish armies. With Russian withdrawal in 1917, the king capitulated. More than 200,000 Romanians died in the fighting.

Middle East

■ SARIKAMISH, 22 DEC 1914–17 JANUARY 1915

The Russian Caucasus Army, under Gen Aleksandr Myshlayevsky, invaded Turkey. The Ottoman Third Army, under Enver Pasha, counter-attacked, pursuing their foes into the mountains. Bad weather and bitter fighting defeated the Turks, who endured more than 60,000 casualties before withdrawing.

■ KUT-AL-AMARA I, 28 SEPTEMBER 1915

To guard against a Turkish threat to the petroleum trade with Persia, the British sought to drive the Ottomans out of Mesopotamia. MGen Charles Townshend's Indian 6th Division (11,000 men) defeated Turkish commander Nureddin Bey, to seize this important town on the Tirgis.

■ CTESIPHON, 22–25 NOVEMBER 1915

Townshend's Indian Expeditionary Force advanced on Baghdad. At Ctesiphon, Nureddin Bey's second line proved impregnable to the British-Indian frontal assault, at the cost of between 6000 and 9000 casualties. Townshend withdrew to Kut, where he would endure a disastrous siege.

■ KUT-AL-AMARA II, 7 DEC 1915–29 APR 1916

The Sixth Ottoman Army (30,000-40,000 troops), under German Gen Colmar von der Goltz, besieged the 30,000 troops of the British Indian garrison at Kut-al-Amara. Despite several relief expeditions and the first military airdrop, Townshend surrendered. Of his remaining 10,000 troops, half died as POWs.

■ ERZURUM, 10 JANUARY–6 FEBRUARY 1916

The Russian Caucasus Army (165,000 men), under Gen Nikolai Yudenich, attacked the 50,000 Turkish combat troops in and around the city. After three days of heavy fighting, the Turks retreated. The Russians went on to crush Kerim Pasha's Ottoman Third Army at Bayburt and Erzincan.

■ SINAI (KATIA), 23 APRIL 1916

The Ottomans launched a campaign to seize the Suez Canal. Led by German Gen Friedrich von Kressenstein, the first action came in April as a column of 3000 Turks defeated 1500 troops of the British 5th Mounted Yeomanry Brigade, part of the 50,000 troops garrisoning Katia.

■ ROMANI, 3–5 AUGUST 1916

Kressenstein's large Turkish, German and Austrian force attacked the prepared and well-supplied troops of the Egyptian Expeditionary Force. Two days of fighting resulted in the first victory of the war for British and Commonwealth infantry and cavalry. The Central Powers endured approximately 8000 casualties, the British, 1200.

■ BAGHDAD, 5–11 MARCH 1917

After two years, the British finally captured Baghdad, and with it, controlled Mesopotamia. 46,000 British-Indian troops, under Gen Sir Frederick Maude, drove Khalil Pasha's Sixth Army out of the city, capturing 9000 Turks.

■ GAZA I, 26–27 MARCH 1917

To build on their success in the Sinai, the British attempted to dislodge Kressenstein's Turkish troops from this stronghold in Palestine. German air superiority and poor communication on the British side proved decisive. The British suffered 4000 casualties for their efforts.

■ GAZA II, 17–19 APRIL 1917

British Gen Charles Dobell attempted a frontal assault against a reinforced Turkish line comprised of 18,000 men, 100 artillery pieces and as many machine guns. The ensuing catastrophe cost the British another 6000 casualties.

■ RAMADI, 28–29 SEPTEMBER 1917

Preparing the way for an advance on the Mosul oilfields, the British 15th Indian Division attacked the Turks at Ramadi, on the Euphrates west of Baghdad. British cavalry successfully flanked Ahmad Bey's garrison and forced his surrender.

■ GAZA III, 31 OCTOBER–7 NOVEMBER 1917

British Gen Sir Edmund Allenby broke the Turkish hold on Gaza. A charge by the Australian 4th Light Horse Brigade captured Beersheba and its vital water supply. The British XX and XXI Corps then shattered Kressenstein's weakened lines at Gaza.

■ MEGIDDO, 19–25 SEPTEMBER 1918

At the apex of Britain's Palestinian campaign, Allenby's Egyptian Expeditionary Army, supported by the RAF's Palestine Brigade and Emir Faisal's Bedouin insurgents (advised by T.E. Lawrence), routed and annihilated a Turkish force of more than 33,000 men.

■ SHARQAT, 23–30 OCTOBER 1918

LGen Sir William Marshall's III Indian Corps advanced on the Mosul oilfields. The British-Indian force outflanked Hakki Bey's Tigris Group, of the Ottoman Sixth Army, forcing the surrender of 18,000 Turks.

■ DAMASCUS, 30 SEPTEMBER–1 OCTOBER 1918

With the successful campaign of the British Egyptian Expeditionary Force in Palestine, the way was clear for Faisal's Arab Revolt to seize Damascus. The demoralized Ottoman armies retreated on all fronts. Australians entered the city first, but Faisal's Bedouin fighters took the right of conquest.

Africa

■ WINDHOEK, JANUARY–MAY 1915

A British armed South African force of 40,000 led by Gen Louis Botha invaded German South West Africa (present day Namibia) in four columns to capture the capital of Windhoek. Despite delaying actions by a smaller German force, Windhoek was captured on 12 May 1915 with the entire colony surrendering a few months later.

■ RUFIJI RIVER, 11 JULY 1915

British naval forces blockaded the German light cruiser *Königsberg* at the Rufiji river in present-day Tanzania and attacked with artillery fire on 11 July 1915, disabling the ship, which was later scuttled.

China

■ TSINGTAO, 17 OCTOBER–7 NOVEMBER 1914

Having failed to break a Japanese and British naval blockade, the colony's German and Austro-Hungarian defenders prepared for a siege. On 31 October, Japanese artillery commenced a week-long bombardment of the port. The city's beleaguered, 3600-man garrison faced an invasion force of 25,000 allied troops. Short of supplies, the Kaiser's troops faced impossible odds. During a night attack on 6 November, the Japanese and British force finally overwhelmed the last German defences and seized the city.

Naval

■ HELIGOLAND BIGHT, 28 AUGUST 1914
British attack on German coastal patrols resulted in battlecruiser action, drawing German forces towards VAdm Beatty's battlecruisers. Germany lost three light cruisers (*Köln*, *Mainz* and *Aridane*) and one destroyer.

■ CRECY-CLASS CRUISERS, 22 SEPT 1914
On 22 September 1914, three obsolescent British armoured cruisers of the Crecy class were patrolling at slow speed off the Dutch coast. *Aboukir* was torpedoed by the German U-boat *U-9* (Capt LCdr Otto Weddigen). Her captain believed she had hit a mine and ordered *Cressy* and *Hogue* to pick up survivors; these ships were also torpedoed. All three ships were sunk with the loss of 1459 men.

■ CORONEL, 1 NOVEMBER 1914
Battle fought off Chile where the modern German armoured cruisers *Scharnhorst* and *Gneisenau* under VAdm Maximilian von Spee sank the older British cruisers *Good Hope* and *Monmouth* under Rear Admiral 'Kit' Cradock.

■ FALKLAND ISLANDS, 8 DECEMBER 1914
After the battle of Coronel, the armoured cruisers *Scharnhorst* and *Gneisenau* steamed into the South Atlantic to raid British commerce. On 8 December they attacked the base at Port Stanley, but were met by the fast battlecruisers *Invincible* and *Inflexible*, sent from Britain under VAdm Sir Frederick Doveton Sturdee to intercept them. *Scharnhost* and *Gneisenau* sought to escape but were chased down and sunk, along with the light cruisers *Leipzig* and *Nürnberg*.

■ DOGGER BANK, 24 JANUARY 1915
German battlecruiser raid agaifnst British light forces patrolling the Dogger Bank on 24 January 1915. Code breaking by Room 40 allowed the British battlecruisers to intercept; *Blücher* was sunk and *Seydlitz* badly damaged.

■ U-BOAT WAR, 1915–17
The use of submarines against merchant ships was unexpected because 'prize rules' meant that U-boats had to give a warning before attacking, making them vulnerable. There were some early surprise attacks by German U-boats, but international law was generally respected. However, when the planned quick victory on land was not achieved, some officers and politicians urged unrestricted submarine warfare, seeing maritime trade as Britain's key vulnerability. In February 1915, Germany threatened to attack any merchant ship in British waters, but US pressure forced them to exempt neutrals. Many ships were sunk by torpedoes or mines, among them several neutrals including the passenger liner *Lusitania*. It was sunk in May by *U-20* (commanded by Walter Schwieger), killing 1200 civilians, after which restrictions were tightened and then in September, fully reimposed. The second, limited U-boat campaign continued until February 1917. Restrictions fluctuated and the number of sinkings fell, but remained high in the Atlantic and the Mediterranean, as the U-boat force increased in numbers and quality. Countering this new threat proved difficult. Hydrophones were introduced to detect submerged submarines (Asdic/sonar came too late for operational use), then explosive sweeps and depth charges (in service only in 1916) were brought in. Merchant ships with concealed guns ('Q-ships') were used to ambush U-boats. Nets and minefields were laid to hinder U-boat access to the oceans and their bases were repeatedly attacked. There was a serious shortage of escorts, though numbers gradually increased. Aircraft were used; although they lacked the ability to sink U-boats, they could force them to dive and break contact, and could also call up warships. The Royal Navy resisted introducing a system of convoy and escort, seeing it as being too defensive and concentrating the U-boats' targets for them.

The German Navy continued to press for a resumption of unrestricted attacks, but some in the

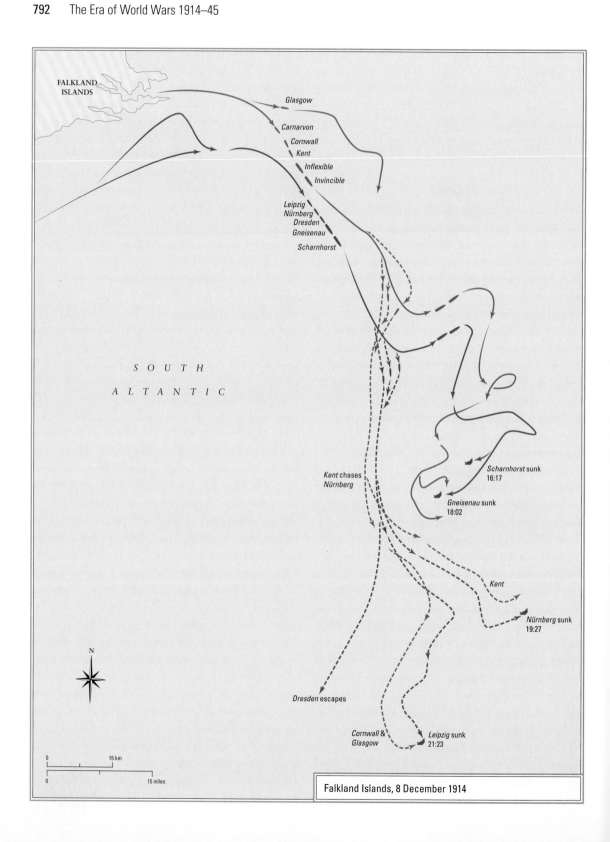

FALKLAND
ISLANDS

Glasgow

Carnarvon

Cornwall

Kent

Inflexible

Invincible

Leipzig
Nürnberg
Dresden
Gneisenau

Scharnhorst

S O U T H

A L T A N T I C

Kent chases
Nürnberg

Scharnhorst sunk
16:17

Gneisenau sunk
18:02

Kent

Nürnberg sunk
19:27

Dresden escapes

N

Cornwall &
Glasgow

Leipzig sunk
21:23

0   15 km

0   15 miles

Falkland Islands, 8 December 1914

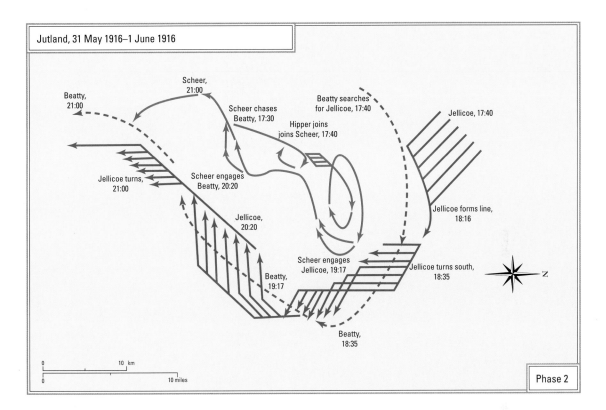

Jutland, 31 May 1916–1 June 1916

Beatty, 21:00

Scheer, 21:00

Beatty searches for Jellicoe, 17:40

Jellicoe, 17:40

Scheer chases Beatty, 17:30

Hipper joins joins Scheer, 17:40

Jellicoe turns, 21:00

Scheer engages Beatty, 20:20

Jellicoe, 20:20

Jellicoe forms line, 18:16

Scheer engages Jellicoe, 19:17

Beatty, 19:17

Jellicoe turns south, 18:35

Beatty, 18:35

0   10 km

0   10 miles

Phase 2

government resisted for fear of provoking the US into entering the war. The failure of the German Navy to defeat the British Grand Fleet and thereby break its crippling blockade of Germany, together with the strain of the prolonged war on land, led to a policy change. Unrestricted submarine warfare began again in February 1917 – the risk of the USA declaring war was accepted because its military power was limited and, it was believed, Britain would be defeated in five months. The U-boat fleet (111 strong and growing) inflicted heavy losses, as high as 860,000 tons in April 1917, the largest monthly figure in either world war.

The Allies now had more merchant hulls, escorts and aircraft (especially after the predicted entry of the USA into the war), the number of depth charges available was increasing, more and better mines were available, and administrative measures improved the efficiency of shipping. The key change was the eventual reconsideration of convoy, which was introduced in the summer of 1917 after a series

of promising experiments. Losses fell dramatically as the convoy system spread; U-boats found it difficult to locate merchant ships and if they did, they faced attack. By October more U-boats were being sunk than were built, with experienced crews being killed. In contrast, by April 1918, fewer Allied merchant ships were lost than were launched, although sinkings continued to the end of the war. The U-boats were contained rather than truly defeated.

■ DARDANELLES, 1915

Dardanelles saw an unsuccessful attempt in February–March 1915 to force the straits by naval forces alone. The outer Turkish forts were silenced but the inner defences of mines and artillery sank the pre-dreadnoughts *Bouvet* (French), *Ocean* and *Irresistible* (British).

■ JUTLAND, 31 MAY– 1 JUNE 1916

The only clash of the main opposing battlefleets occurred with both sides seeking to ambush the other. The German plan was for Hipper's five

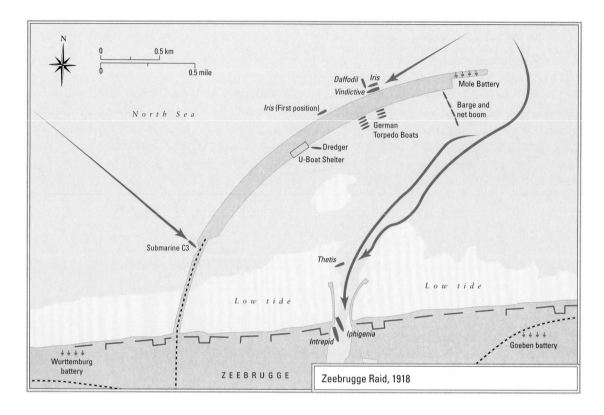

N

0   0.5 km
0   0.5 mile

North Sea

Daffodil   Iris
Vindictive
Iris (First position)

Mole Battery

Barge and
net boom

German
Torpedo Boats

Dredger
U-Boat Shelter

Submarine C3

Thetis

Low tide

Low tide

Iphigenia
Intrepid

Goeben battery

Wurttemburg
battery

ZEEBRUGGE

Zeebrugge Raid, 1918

battlecruisers to attack British patrols, drawing Beatty's Battlecruiser Fleet (six battlecruisers, four dreadnoughts) onto the High Seas Fleet (16 dreadnoughts, six pre-dreadnoughts) of Adm Reinhard Scheer. Forewarned by Room 40's code-breaking, Adm John Jellicoe's Grand Fleet (24 dreadnoughts, three battlecruisers) was already at sea. At the initial contact around 14:00 on 31 May, Beatty chased Hipper in the 'run to the south', losing the battlecruisers *Indefatigable* and *Queen Mary* but seriously damaging several German battlecruisers. On encountering the main German fleet, Beatty reversed course and led them towards Jellicoe in the 'run to the north'. As the main bodies closed (around 18:00) the battlecruiser *Invincible* exploded after inflicting fatal damage on the battlecruiser *Lützow*. The British fleet then twice 'crossed the T' of the High Seas Fleet, which narrowly escaped disaster by using the well-drilled 'battle about turn' under the cover of a destroyer torpedo attack, causing the risk-averse Jellicoe to turn away. During the night,

the High Seas Fleet escaped and reached port. The British suffered heavier losses of three battlecruisers, three armoured cruisers and eight destroyers, with a total of 6000 men killed, compared to one battlecruiser, one pre-dreadnought, four light cruisers, five destroyers and over 2500 men. Yet the Royal Navy achieved strategic victory: the High Seas Fleet had not broken the British economic blockade, which continued to choke the German war effort.

■ **OTRANTO STRAIT, 14–15 MAY 1917**
The attack by Austria-Hungary on British, French and Italian forces blockading the strait of Otranto. One French and one Italian destroyer and more than 12 light anti-submarine drifters were sunk.

■ **ZEEBRUGGE AND OSTEND, 1918**
Raids against the canals allowed Bruges-based U-boats to reach the sea. An assault on the Zeebrugge mole from *Vindictive* diverted the defences, allowing blockships to reach the canal. They blocked it temporarily but boosted Allied morale.

Russian Civil War 1917–20

■ **KAZAN, 5–10 SEPTEMBER 1918**
A White Russian army numbering approximately 10,000 troops under Gen Vladimir Kappel, supported by two battalions of Czechoslovaks, surrounded the city and routed the Red Guard.

■ **ARCHANGELSK, MARCH 1918–JULY 1919**
Under the so-called Northern Russia Expedition, more than 13,000 Allied soldiers occupied important Russian ports along the Barents and White Seas. Seizing Murmansk in March and Arkhangelsk in August 1918, the Allies attempted unsuccessfully to expel 14,000 Bolshevik troops from the area.

■ **OREL, 11 OCTOBER–18 NOVEMBER 1919**
Falling back before the White Russian advance, the Bolshevik Thirteenth and Fourteenth Armies made a stand at Orel-Kromy. Although the Whites captured Orel on 13 October, the Reds routed them on 20 October.

■ **ST PETERSBURG, 13 OCTOBER–NOVEMBER 1919**
The White Army attacked Red-held St Petersburg. Reaching the outskirts of the city on 19 October, the White Army hit strong resistance. Making effective use of the Moscow–St Petersburg Railway, the Seventh and Fifteenth Red Armies counter-attacked, driving their opponets back to Estonia by November.

Greek-Turkish War 1919–23

■ **IZMIR, 15 MAY 1919**
Supported by an Allied naval force, 20,000 Greek troops landed at Smyrna. The occupation, part of a controversial Allied partitioning of the defeated Ottoman Empire, was one of the sparks that ignited the Turkish National movement.

■ **SAKARYA RIVER, 23 AUG–13 SEPTEMBER 1921**
Some 120,000 Greek soldiers under Constantine I attacked more than 96,000 Turks, led by Mustafa Kemal, at the Sakarya Line. Strong entrenchments and heavy gunfire absorbed the Greeks' assault, and Constantine was forced to withdraw. Almost 6000 Turks and 4000 Greeks died in the fighting.

Polish-Lithuanian War 1920

■ **WARSAW, 12–25 AUGUST 1920**
As the Poles lost ground in their war with the Soviets, the Lithuanians seized the opportunity to occupy territory promised by treaty with Moscow. At Warsaw, Polish Gen Jozef Piłsudski's troops turned the tables against Russian Gen Mikhail Tukhachevsky's Red Army. The defensive line at Modlin Fortress held and the Polish counterstroke forced the Soviets to withdraw over the Niemen river. In the territorial dispute that followed, new fighting erupted between Poles and Lithuanians.

■ **AUGUSTOW, 28 AUGUST 1920**
Having defeated the Russians at Warsaw, the Poles sought to pursue their enemy through ostensibly neutral Lithuanian territory. Gen Edward Rydz-Smigly led Polish forces in the seizure of Augustow, surprising a Lithuanian garrison in the opening move of a campaign into the strategically important Suwalki region.

■ **SUWAŁKI, 30–31 AUGUST 1920**
Frustrated by a growing political impasse, the Poles moved against their former Lithuanian allies, driving them out of Suwalki by the end of August. The Lithuanians retreated and regrouped, forming a force of 7000 soldiers in 11 battalions to attempt to hold their border against the Poles.

■ **SEJNY, 13 SEPTEMBER 1920**
The Lithuanian battle plan called for recapturing the line of territory from Augustow to Lipsk and Hrodna. The Lithuanians were initially successful, taking Sejny and Lipsk and reaching Augustow by 4 September. The Poles counter-attacked, but ultimately the Lithuanians held Sejny.

■ **GIBY, 14 SEPTEMBER 1920**
After being pushed back by a Polish attack at the beginning of the month, by mid-September the Lithuanians had retaken Giby.

■ **KALWARIA, 15–18 SEPTEMBER 1920**
The site of ceasefire negotiations between the Poles and Lithuanians. While politically undermining the Lithuanians in the League of

Nations, the Polish armies planned their flanking manoeuvre against the Soviets by pushing round them through the Suwalki region.

■ **NIEMEN RIVER, 15–25 SEPTEMBER 1920**
Four large Polish armies, backed by Ukrainians, launched one of the largest offensives in their wars against the Soviets and the Lithuanians. The advance of more than 96,000 Polish troops overwhelmed the Lithuanians, who lost 1700–2000 captured. The Polish juggernaut pushed back a large Soviet force of nearly one million men, east of the Niemen river. At Druskininkai and Merkine, the Poles outflanked the Russians, forcing their retreat.

■ **VILNIUS, 8 OCTOBER 1920**
Gen Lucjan Zeligowski led a revolt of ethnic Poles, who captured Vilnius and declared the area the 'Republic of Central Lithuania', which was later absorbed by Poland. The Lithuanians were unable to recapture their city before both parties signed a ceasefire on 29 November.

Japanese Invasion of Manchuria 1931–32

■ **JAPANESE OCCUPATION, 18 SEPT 1931–27 FEB 1932**
Frustrated over economic problems at home, Japanese military commanders in the Kwangtung Garrison disobeyed their political leaders and sought new solutions through military expansion. At Mukden, a force of 500 Japanese easily defeated a garrison of 7000 Chinese conscripts. Allegedly, the Chinese had attacked the vital South Manchurian Railway line. In fact, the Japanese had staged the attack as a pretext for an outright invasion of the territory. More than 500 Chinese died in the fighting at Mukden. In the weeks that followed, between 30,000 and 60,000 Japanese troops of the Kwangtung Army invaded.

■ **NENJIANG BRIDGE, 4 NOVEMBER 1931**
From Heilongjiang Province, Chinese Gen Ma Zhanshan's 2500 troops resisted the Japanese advance. As approximately 800 Japanese soldiers and Chinese collaborators attempted to repair the Nenjiang

Bridge, Ma attacked unsuccessfully, losing 120 men to accurate Japanese rifle fire.

■ **JIANGQIAO CAMPAIGN, 4–18 NOVEMBER 1931**
During the first half of November, the Chinese fought several bold skirmishes, harassing the Japanese as they sought to consolidate their gains along the vital Manchurian railways. At Tsitsihar, the last holdout of Jiangqiao's three provincial capitals, Gen Ma's army made a desperate stand against a combined arms attack by Japanese Gen Jiro Tamon's 3500 crack troops. Although the city was defended by 8000 Chinese, Japanese firepower and tactics proved superior. Tamon's aircraft and artillery provided deadly support for his infantry, turning the tide against Ma's infantry and horsemen. Tamon broke Ma's lines on 17 November and occupied the city the next day. Retreating under the harsh winter weather to Baiquan and Hailun, Ma endured as many as 3000 casualties.

■ **CHINCHOW OPERATION, 21 DEC 1931–3 JAN 1932**
Advancing from Mukden, Japanese Gen Shigeru Honjo deployed 10,000 soldiers with plentiful air support. As the column marched to within 30km of Chinchow, the Japanese political leadership called off the operation while negotiations for a ceasefire continued at the League of Nations.

■ **HARBIN, 25 JANUARY–4 FEBRUARY 1932**
In Kirin Province, Chinese Gen Ting Chao's 30,000 soldiers attacked the forces of the Japanese-backed Manchukuo government. Ting faced Gen Xi Qia and Japanese LGen Jiro Tamon's 2nd Infantry Division. After 17 hours of fighting, and thousands of casualties, Ting's army eventually collapsed under pressure from the Japanese air force and artillery.

Italo-Abyssinian War 1935–36

■ **ADIGRAT, 5–7 OCTOBER 1935**
Italian Gen Emilio de Bono led 125,000 troops into Abyssinia. They were pursuing Mussolini's dream of a greater Italian Empire, one that would eventually lead the country to disaster in WWII. The Italian I Corps accepted the surrender of 1200 men under Dejazmach Haile Selassie Gugsa,

a nobleman whom the Italians had persuasively encouraged to defect.

◼ ADWA, 6 OCTOBER 1935

The II Corps avenged the Italians' humiliating defeat at this city in the first Italo-Abyssinian War (1896). The Italians began their attack with a two-day bombardment, which drove off the Ethiopian garrison. Emperor Haile Selassie ordered most of his troops to withdraw in the face of the Italian advance. With no resistance, de Bono's troops entered Adwa.

◼ DEMBEGUINA PASS, 15 DECEMBER 1935

The Ethiopians launched a major Christmas offensive. One hundred and ninety thousand Ethiopians confronted 125,000 Italian and Eritrean troops. At Dembeguina, 3000 Ethiopians surrounded and killed more than half the force of 1000 Eritreans, in the process commandeering nine Italian light tanks.

◼ GENALE DORIA, 12–20 JANUARY 1936

In southern Abyssinia, Ras Desta Damtu led 20,000 Ethiopian soldiers in a 322km march against 20,000 Italian troops of the 29th Infantry Division, led by Gen Rodolfo Graziani. The Italian Air Force used mustard gas to halt the advancing Ethiopians.

◼ TEMBIEN, 20–24 JANUARY 1936

At Tembien, each side fielded armies of approximately 70,000 men. Marshal Pietro Badoglio commanded a force that comprised the Italian I and III Corps, the 2nd Blackshirt Division and the Eritrean Corps. The Ethiopian commanders, Ras Kassa and Ras Seyoum, drove back the invaders and besieged the garrison at Warieu Pass. An Eritrean column, supported by Italian airpower, lifted the siege. A notable element of the battle was that the Italian Air Force used chemical weapons (mustard gas) against the Ethiopians.

◼ AMBA ARADAM, 10–19 FEBRUARY 1936

The Italian I and III Corps (70,000 men) encircled Amba Aradam, closing a vice on Ras Mulugeta's 80,000 Ethiopian troops. Italian artillery and airpower proved decisive. 6000 Ethiopians and 800 Italians died in the fighting.

◼ ENDERTA, 10–19 FEBRUARY 1936

With victory in hand across Enderta Province, Badoglio's air units pursued Ras Mulugeta's routed force. The air force annihilated the Ethiopian army, by bombing. strafing and attacking with chemical weapons, killing Mulugeta and his son.

◼ TEMBIEN II, 27–29 FEBRUARY 1936

The Italian III Corps with the Eritrean Corps attacked Ras Seyoum's 40,000 men amid the mountainous terrain and forests of central Ethiopia. Italian commandos seized the high ground of Amba Work. Poorly armed Ethiopian human-wave attacks broke against the invaders' rifle and machine-gun fire. Although Italian artillery could not be brought to bear, airpower once again proved deadly in the battle, and 8000 Ethiopians and 600 Italians died during the fighting.

◼ SHIRE, 29 FEBRUARY–2 MARCH 1936

At Shire Marshal Badoglio's II and IV Corps (47,000 Italian soldiers) defeated Ras Imru's army of 23,000. Badoglio deployed his air force to break up and destroy the retreating Ethiopians. Approximately 4000 of Imru's men died.

◼ MAYCHEW, 31 MARCH 1936

Emperor Haile Selassie led an advance of 31,000 men (including the elite Imperial Guard) against the Italian I Corps and the Eritrean Corps. Italian defence repelled determined Ethiopian human wave attacks. Between 1000 and 8000 Ethiopians died.

◼ OGADEN, 14–25 APRIL 1936

Italian Gen Rodolfo Graziani advanced in bad weather against 30,000 Ethiopians under Ras Nasibu. The conflict raged for 10 days, with Italian colonial troops backed by armour and heavy weapons against human-wave assaults by the Ethiopians. The invaders endured 2000 casualties while routing Nasibu's army.

Spanish Civil War 1936–39

◼ GIJÓN, 19 JULY–16 AUGUST 1936

In the province of Asturias, the rebel Nacionales movement faltered against strong opposition from loyal militias. Although poorly armed, a

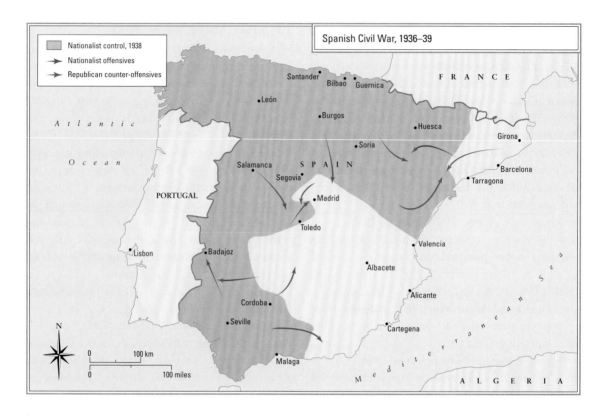

government-backed mob successfully besieged and wiped out the small Nationalist force that had seized the Guardia Civil barracks.

■ **TOLEDO, 21 JULY–27 SEPTEMBER 1936**

Nationalist troops of the Army of Africa, led by Gen Francisco Franco, arrived to lift the Republican siege of the Alcazar. After the Nationalist rebels declared a state of war, the government of the Second Spanish Republic dispatched a powerful force of 8000 leftist militiamen to recapture the historically significant fortress. A rebel force of 1000, including 800 men of the Guardia Civil, endured the siege until relieved by a victorious Gen Franco. The Alcazar was almost totally destroyed in the fighting, along with 65 Nationalists and an unknown number of Republican dead and wounded.

■ **BILBAO, SEPTEMBER 1936–19 JUNE 1937**

The capital of the Republican-backed autonomous Basque Country became a key objective for the Nationalists in their northern war. A total of 60,000 rebels, supported by 15,000 Italians and

the Nazi Legion Condor, finally broke the city's fortifications, the vaunted *el cinturón de hierro* (the iron ring).

■ **MADRID, 8 NOVEMBER 1936–28 MARCH 1939**

In November 1936, Gen Franco's rebels mounted an all-out assault on the Spanish capital city of Madrid, a Republican government stronghold. Some 20,000 Nationalists, backed by armour and air support from fascist Italy and Nazi Germany, smashed into the government entrenchments at the Carabanchel district and the Casa de Campo park. Under the stirring rallying cry of *No pasarán!* (they shall not pass) Republican government troops and the International Brigades bogged down Franco's advance in three years of bitter urban fighting.

■ **CORUNNA ROAD, 13 DEC 1936–15 JANUARY 1937**

As his advance on Madrid stalled, Gen Franco cut a vital roadway between the capital and the northwest; 17,000 Nationalists attacked 20,000 Republicans. Foreign armour (German and Soviet) featured on both sides, more than 30,000 died.

■ Jarama River, 6–27 February 1937

In a futile attempt to penetrate government lines east of Madrid, 25,000–40,000 Nationalists, including troops of the Spanish Legion and the Army of Africa, clashed with 30,000 Republicans. Among the thousands killed were members of the British Battalion and the American Abraham Lincoln Brigade, indicating what a truly international conflict the Spanish Civil War had become.

■ Malaga III, 3–8 February 1937

With support from 5000–10,000 'Blackshirts' of the Italian Corpo Truppe Volontarie, the Nationalist Army of the South overwhelmed this Republican stronghold on the Mediterranean coast. The government troops were routed after suffering 3000–5000 casualties.

■ Guadalajara, 8–23 March 1937

Buoyed by their success at Jarama river and Malaga, the Nationalists and their allies in the Italian Corpo Truppe Volontarie launched an ill-fated fourth offensive at Madrid. Mussolini's Gen Mario Roatta attacked with 50,000 troops, artillery support and more than 100 tanks and aircraft. Republican Gen José Miaja had 20,000 troops and one company of Soviet-built T-26 light tanks. Though outnumbered and outgunned, the Republicans halted and rolled back the Italians' advance in the government's last major victory of the war.

■ Brunete, 6–25 July 1937

The Republican government sought to lift the siege of Madrid by diverting rebel strength from the north and threatening this vital link on the supply route west of the capital. Gen José Miaja commanded the government's V and XVIII Army Corps, comprising 50,000–85,000 troops, with air support coming from a total of 100–300 aircraft. Nationalist Gen José Varela's I and VII Army Corps fielded 65,000 soldiers and more than 100 planes. After heavy fighting both sides gained some ground, at the cost of more than 20,000 Republican casualties and 17,000 Nationalists.

■ Santander, 14 August–1 September 1937

Having conquered the capital of the Basque Country, the Nationalist Army of the North (90,000 men, including 25,000 men of the Italian Corpo Truppe Volontarie) attacked mountainous Cantabria. The Republican Gen Adolfo Prada's XIV Army Corps and Gen Garcia Vaya's XV Army Corps assembled 80,000 government soldiers, supported by Soviet fighter, bomber and ground-attack aircraft, to oppose the rebels. German and Italian air superiority, coupled with the rebel Nationalists' stronger artillery and equipment, proved decisive in the engagement.

■ Belchite/Saragossa, 24 Aug–7 September 1937

The Republicans organized several Marxist and anarchist militias into the new 80,000-man Army of the East. They attacked the outer defences of Saragossa, the vital communication hub in Aragon, but succeeded neither in taking the city nor slowing the Nationalists' northern offensive.

■ Teruel, 15 Dec 1937–22 Febuary 1938

At this remote provincial capital in Aragon, a narrow salient surrounded by Republican territory, the Nationalists maintained a garrison of between 4000 and 10,000 men under Col Domingo Rey d'Harcourt. Unable to resist a massive Republican attack from 40,000–100,000 troops, and hampered by bitter winter weather, Rey d'Harcourt surrendered to government troops and was executed. The Nationalists counter-attacked savagely. Franco's victory over the Republicans was a major turning point in the war, and it was a battle in which more than 140,000 died.

■ Vinaroz, 15 April 1938

Having routed the Republicans at Teruel, Gen Franco launched his Aragon offensive in March, focusing on conquering territory in the east and dividing the remaining government enclaves. Nationalists quickly occupied this town on Valencia's Mediterranean coast.

■ Ebro River, 25 July–16 November 1938

Gen Franco mobilized more than 100,000 Nationalist troops for his decisive push across Aragon and into Catalonia. The Republicans had approximately 80,000 men in arms in the region, and set their sights on Gandesa. Franco defended the town vigorously with artillery and airpower, checking the attacking force and grinding it down in a ghastly battle of attrition. The International Brigades withdrew from the war during this battle, and Gen Franco effectively split the government-held portion of Spain, dividing Castile from Catalonia.

■ **BARCELONA, 16–18 MARCH 1938**
The Nationalists' Italian allies applied one of their countrymen's ideas of total war to the reduction of the Catalonian capital. Before WWI, Gen Giulio Douhet had theorized that airpower alone could be decisive in war. Mussolini ordered his bombers to attack the city. In the ensuing devastation, the bombs killed more than 1000 people before Gen Franco suspended the attack.

Soviet-Japanese Border War 1938–39

■ **LAKE KHASAN, 29 JULY–11 AUGUST 1938**
Almost 23,000 Soviet troops clashed with approximately 7000 Japanese over disputed high ground on the Manchurian border, overlooking Japanese-held Korea. After the Japanese demanded Russian troops withdraw from two key hills along the border, the Kwangtung Army laid plans to attack. The Russians' repelled the first sortie, but a few days later, the Japanese 19th Division drove off the Soviet XXXIX Rifle Corps. The Russians counter-attacked with armour and artillery. Marshal Vasily Blyukher moved the First Coastal Army into the region, overwhelming the Japanese and reclaiming the border.

■ **KHALKIN GOL, 11 MAY–16 SEPTEMBER 1939**
The battle was the culmination of tensions between Japanese forces in Manchuria and Soviet forces in Mongolia. Japan asserted the Khalin Gol river as the boundary, a claim the Soviets vigorously disputed. The clash in 1939 involved 57,000 Soviet troops under the command of Georgy Zhukov, who went on to become the USSR's most effective general of WWII. In August Zhukov inflicted a devastating defeat on the Japanese (who had 38,000 troops). Both sides knew that they had more important strategic aims than the borders in Mongolia so they signed a ceasefire, leaving the Soviets free to invade Poland in September 1939 and the Japanese to consolidate their hold on China. The battle is significant because it did not lead to a Soviet–Japanese war, which would have greatly changed the complexion of WWII.

Slovak-Hungarian War 1939

■ **HUNGARIAN ATTACK, 23 MARCH 1939**
Hitting the Slovak Army hard in a surprise attack, the Hungarian VII Corps, led by MGen Andras Littay, penetrated eastern Slovakia. Slovak officers attempted to rally their troops and assemble forces for a counterstroke.

■ **NIZNA RYBNICA, 24 MARCH 1939**
Supported by the machine guns of five OA vz 30 armored cars, Slovak soldiers advanced into a Hungarian artillery barrage. Attacking the Hungarian frontline beyond Nizna Rybnica, the shelling routed the inexperienced Slovaks.

■ **MICHALOVCE, 24–25 MARCH 1939**
The Slovaks attempted to regroup at Michalovce, adding four armored cars, three light tanks and a 37mm anti-tank gun to a formation of 15,000 troops. Their counter-attack never materialized, however, as a German-brokered ceasefire ended the war.

Italian Invasion of Albania 1939

■ **ITALIAN INVASION, 7–12 APRIL 1939**
A force of 100,000 Italian soldiers quickly overwhelmed the Kingdom of Albania's 15,000-strong army in April 1939. Italian 'advisors' helped to sabotage Albanian equipment, including artillery and ammunition, leaving the small nation virtually defenceless against a large expedition of Italian infantry, air and naval forces. The hottest fighting lasted less than two full days, before Tirana fell on 8 April. As many as 160 Albanians and 25 Italians died.

World War II 1939–45

Poland and Finland 1939

■ GERMAN INVASION OF POLAND, 1 SEPT– 6 OCT 1939

On 1 September 1939, 1.7 million German troops, organized into 53 divisions and backed by 2050 aircraft, invaded Poland. Striking from three directions, these forces engaged the Polish ground forces, organized in 43 divisions and brigades, backed by just 435 aircraft. The German Army Group North thrust east through the Polish Corridor to link East Prussia with Germany; then subsequently it attacked south-east towards Warsaw. Simultaneously, Army Group South thrust east and north-east from Silesia towards Warsaw and Lublin, while also attacking north-east from Slovakia. By 16 September these advances had encircled dozens of Polish divisions in several large pockets. On the 17th, as pre-arranged, Soviet forces invaded the lightly defended eastern Polish border. Overwhelmed by this two-front onslaught, Poland capitulated on 6 October. For the cost of 47,000 casualties and 675 tanks lost, the Germans inflicted 199,600 Polish casualties and took 587,000 prisoners.

■ WARSAW, 8–27 SEPTEMBER 1939

After their invasion of Poland, eastward-advancing German forces reached the Polish capital of Warsaw on 8 September, where they were repulsed. When German forces advancing from the north-east reached Warsaw on the 15th, 170,000 troops surrounded the city. The 125,000 defenders fought off repeated assaults, but surrendered on the 27th. Polish losses included 6000 troops killed, 16,000 wounded, and 103,000 surrendered, plus 70,000 civilian casualties. The Germans lost 3000 killed and 5000 wounded, plus 200 tanks destroyed.

■ KUTNO-LODZ (THE BATTLE OF THE BZURA) 9–19 SEPTEMBER 1939

During 9–15 September, two Polish armies outflanked in the Kutno-Lodz region west of the River Bzura, counter-attacked southward into the German flank. Having surrounded the Poles, relentless German attacks during 16–19 September finally forced a Polish capitulation on the 19th.

■ SOVIET INVASION OF POLAND, 17 SEPT– 6 OCT 1939

On 17 September 1939, 17 days after the German invasion of Poland, Soviet forces – as secretly agreed in the August 1939 Molotov-Ribbentrop pact – invaded eastern Poland. By then, most Polish forces were committed to attempting to resist the German onslaught. The 800,000 Soviet troops of the White Russian and Ukrainian Fronts quickly overran the meagre Polish defensive screen of 25 battalions, undermining the Polish intent to resolutely defend south-eastern Poland. As a consequence, Poland finally capitulated on 6 October.

■ SOVIET INVASION OF FINLAND, 30 NOVEMBER 1939–13 MARCH 1940

Called *Suomen Talvisota* in Finnish, the Winter War was fought amid impassable forest terrain during one of the coldest winters on record. Forty-five divisions of the Soviet Red Army, with 1500 tanks and 3000 aircraft, launched an unprovoked attack on the numerically inferior but determined defenders of Finland's 'Mannerheim Line'. Baron Carl Gustaf Emil Mannerheim led the Finnish army, fielding nine divisions (approximately 135,000 troops), with 30 tanks and 100 aircraft. Along Finland's 1300km border with Russia, Mannerheim mounted a successful guerilla campaign using *motti* ('cord wood') tactics, in which highly trained and mobile troops chopped the invaders into smaller and more easily defeated units. The Soviets, led by Voroshilov, Meretskov and Timoshenko, suffered significant losses before breaking the Mannerheim Line, taking Vyborg and threatening Helsinki. In the peace, Finland kept its sovereignty but lost 10 per cent of its territory and 20 per cent of its industrial capacity.

■ SUOMUSSALMI, 7 DEC 1939–8 JANUARY 1940

Mannerheim's *motti* tactics enabled agile, lightly armed forces to envelop and neutralize larger

Suomussalmi, December 1939

and heavier opponents. At Suomussalmi *kunta*, (municipality) three Finnish infantry regiments cut off and destroyed two retreating Soviet Red Army divisions, capturing an armored brigade's vehicles and weapons. Col Hjalmar Siilasvuo led his *Jägers* of JR-27 to victory against the Russian 163rd and 44th Divisions, elements of the Soviet Ninth Army under Gen Ivan Dashitsev.

■ CONTINUATION WAR, 25 JUNE 1941– 19 SEPTEMBER 1944

Aligned with the Third Reich by 1941, Finland again found itself in strategic opposition to the Soviet Union. As Hitler launched Operation *Barbarossa*, Russian warplanes struck German and Finnish positions in Lapland and to the south, to blunt a perceived threat to the Soviet northern flank. In the *Jatkosota*, or 'Continuation War', the Finns counter-attacked, sending 400,000 well-equipped troops 160km into Soviet-held Karelia to reclaim lost territory. The Finns dug in against a counter-offensive that devolved into trench

warfare from 1942 to 1943. In 1944, with the Germans reeling from their defeat at Stalingrad, the Soviet Air Force bombed Helsinki and other cities. On the Karelian peninsula, the Red Army pushed Mannerheim's force back beyond the 1940 armistice line. In September 1944, to forestall an imminent Soviet invasion, the Finns turned on the 150,000 German troops stationed in their territory.

Norway 1940

■ INVASION OF NORWAY, 9 APRIL–10 JUNE 1940

The German invasion of Norway began on 9 April 1940 and was one of the first major combined operations by air, land and naval forces. Although the German attack went well as a whole, British and French expeditionary forces assisted the Norwegian resistance, albeit in a largely ill-judged campaign that had little chance of defeating the German invasion. Norwegian troops finally surrendered on 10 June.

■ **BERGEN, 9 APRIL 1940**

A *Kriegsmarine* squadron of two light cruisers, an escort ship and two torpedo boats attacked Bergen. Fort Kvarven's batteries damaged the *Königsberg*, later sunk by British warplanes. Nevertheless, a landing force of 1900 Germans conquered the town.

■ **TRONDHEIM, 9 APRIL 1940**

The heavy cruiser *Hipper* and four destroyers engaged the batteries guarding Trondheim Fjord. German troop transports, disguised as merchantmen, landed 1700 soldiers. Occupied Trondheim, like Bergen, became a key U-boat base during the Battle of the Atlantic.

■ **NARVIK, 9 APRIL–9 JUNE 1940**

Narvik, a strategic link to Scandinavian iron mines, was a key objective of Operation *Weserübung*, the conquest of Denmark and Norway. Hitler's invasion force included the battlecruisers *Gneisenau* and *Scharnhorst* and 10 destroyers, which sank two Norwegian coastal defence cruisers, *Eidsvold* and *Norge*. After the Germans landed 2000 troops, the Norwegian commander, Col Sundlo, surrendered. On 10 April, Royal Navy Capt Warburton-Lee attacked, sinking two German destroyers, damaging three others, and sinking eight cargo ships. Five other German destroyers counter-attacked and sank two of Warburton-Lee's ships, killing him. On 13 April, a British squadron, including the battleship *Warspite* and planes from the aircraft carrier *Furious*, defeated the remaining *Kriegsmarine* units in the Ofotfjord. *Warspite* then shelled Narvik ahead of Allied troop landings. Despite initial success by British, French and Norwegian troops re-taking Narvik, the Allies withdrew as the Western Front collapsed onto Dunkirk, France.

Low Countries 1940

■ **EBEN EMAEL, 10–11 MAY 1940**

Initiating the 10 May German invasion of the west, 11 gliders landed Storm Detachment Koch's 78 paratroopers on the roof of the strategically vital Belgian fort of Eben Emael. Using hollow-charge explosives the paratroopers blasted their way into the fort. Bitter combat raged for the next 24 hours until, after advancing German infantry had arrived, the fort surrendered. For the cost of six dead, Koch's forces captured over 1,000 Belgian troops.

■ **FALL OF BELGIUM, 10–27 MAY 1940**

During the May 1940 German invasion of the West, German armour raced through south-eastern Belgium and northern France to the Channel coast on the 21st. Meanwhile, on 10–14 May the 900,000-strong Army Group B invaded eastern Belgium and pushed the 600,000-strong Belgian Army, augmented by French and British forces, back to the River Dyle. Outflanked by the Panzer dash to the coast and the Dutch surrender, Belgian forces withdrew west until they were overwhelmed, capitulating on 27 May.

■ **ROTTERDAM, 14 MAY 1940**

Following their 10 May invasion, by the 14th the Germans had overrun the Netherlands save for 'Fortress Holland'. Despite negotiations over Rotterdam's surrender, the Germans failed to halt a devastating aerial strike that killed 1000 civilians and left 85,000 homeless.

France 1940

■ **GERMAN INVASION OF FRANCE 1940**

The declaration of war upon Germany by Britain and France in 1939 did not lead to major combat operations between the two sides, resulting in the period between the autumn of 1939 and the spring of 1940 being labelled 'the Phoney War'. While the Allies expected an attack not dissimilar to the invasion of 1914, which saw Germans pass through Belgium, the Germans in fact adopted a more daring plan to attack France through the wooded area of the Ardennes, bypassing the much-vaunted defensive fortifications of the Maginot Line. The original German plan did not win favour with Adolf Hitler. Several leading generals agreed with him, seeing it as little more than an unsophisticated frontal assault that would result in heavy casualties and perhaps stalemate. The commander of Army Group A, Gen Gerd von Rundstedt, along with his chief of staff, GenLt Erich von Manstein, took the view that the German attack should

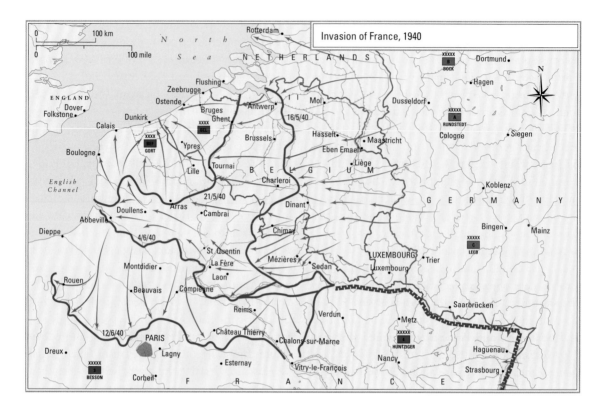

focus around Sedan, allowing the encirclement and destruction of Allied forces. With advice on the use of armor provided by GenLt Karl-Heinz Guderian, the leading proponent of armoured operations, Manstein presented an alternative plan. The Germans would attack towards Sedan, with the bulk of the German armoured forces driving on to the English Channel, in a bid to dislocate the Allied forces and bring about a swift collapse. This plan was much more to Hitler's liking, and despite the opposition of other senior officers, he approved the plan, code-named *Fall Gelb*, in January 1940.

The invasion was preceded by the German occupation of Luxembourg on 9 May 1940, and the following day saw German forces launch a major attack on Belgium and the Netherlands. The French responded by moving a significant number of their best troops forward into Belgium, which would later hamper their defence against the main thrust of the German attack. The Germans enjoyed air superiority, enabling Stuka dive-bombers to operate most effectively in support of the advancing armoured and infantry forces. The rapid collapse of the position in Belgium was accompanied by the German attack through the Ardennes, which proved to be almost inexorable.

The Germans attacked at Sedan on 12 May and the French position collapsed with surprising rapidity, notably in the face of air attack against positions on the western banks of the River Meuse. The capture of the Meuse bridges, despite desperate (and unsuccessful) Allied air attacks against them, enabled the Germans to drive past Sedan and into the rear of the Allied armies. By 20 May, the leading elements of the German forces were in sight of the Channel. On 26 May, the British began to evacuate their forces from Dunkirk, aided by an order from Hitler, who halted his armour in a bid to allow the *Luftwaffe* to destroy the British force. The evacuation of Dunkirk was completed by 3 June, leaving the French on their own. Under their new commander, Gen Maxime Weygand, the French Army managed to put up increased resistance to the German assault as it approached Paris, but it was too late. Paris was declared an open city on 10 June, and fell four days later. Prime Minister Reynaud resigned on 16 June, and was succeeded by Marshal Philippé Petain, who announced his intention to seek an armistice. Fighting continued until 25 June when France formally surrendered.

■ LAON, 19 MAY 1940

German Gen Heinz Guderian's *Blitzkrieg* advance to Arras having cut the Allied armies in two, the French 4th Armoured Division, under Gen Charles de Gaulle, made a futile counter-attack against the 10th Panzer Division at Laon.

■ ARRAS, 21 MAY 1940

As German armour charged through northern France toward the Channel, the British armoured Frankforce counter-attacked their exposed northern flank near Arras. Although the Germans repulsed the attack, it led them to halt on the 24th, making the miracle of Dunkirk possible.

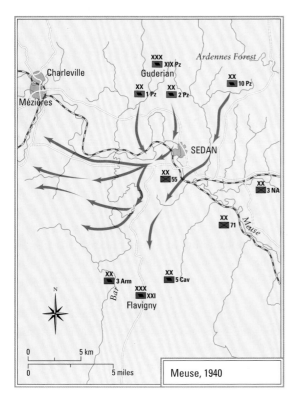

Meuse, 1940

■ DUNKIRK, 26 MAY–4 JUNE 1940

The advancing German Army pushed the British Expeditionary Force and allied French units back towards the Channel coast, but failed to press the advantage and complete their victory. Britain launched Operation *Dynamo*, organized by VAdm Bertram Ramsay, to evacuate as many troops as possible. Initial estimates were that the operation might last two days and could rescue up to 45,000 men.

Strong resistance by the rearguard, an increasingly effective organization at Dunkirk and the resilience of the naval crews allowed the Royal Navy – with the assistance of Allied navies and the 'little ships' – to conduct an evacuation over nine days (26 May–4 June) which, despite heavy air attacks, rescued 338,226 men (including 123,000 French), albeit without their heavy equipment. Most were taken from the harbour, but 30 per cent were lifted from the beaches to the east of Dunkirk.

■ DIEPPE, 19 AUGUST 1942

Operation *Jubilee* of August 1942 was a raid against the French port of Dieppe conducted by 6000 troops (mainly Canadian soldiers, with 1000 British commandos and 50 US Rangers) supported by over 250 warships and craft – but no battleships or cruisers – and Allied air forces. The aim was to test Allied amphibious warfare techniques against a 'live' target and to probe the German Channel defences.

Except for the commandos on the western flank, the raid was a failure, with few troops and no tanks making it off the beaches of Dieppe. Many soldiers were evacuated, but losses among the landing force were 60 per cent, plus one destroyer, 30 landing craft and more than 100 aircraft. German losses were less than 600 troops and 50 aircraft. The operation, although costly, resulted in many useful lessons for the Allied commanders. Controversy has raged over whether these were worth the casualties or were due to errors that could have been avoided.

Battle of Britain 1940

■ First Phase, 10 July 1940

Although there is some dispute as to the starting date of the Battle of Britain, it is generally held to be 10 July 1940. On this date, the Germans began a series of air attacks against coastal convoys in the English Channel, with the aim of probing British defences and interdicting shipping heading towards London. The convoy battles saw multiple engagements between RAF Fighter Command and the *Luftwaffe*. The *Luftwaffe* enjoyed numerical superiority, and the raids placed considerable strain upon the RAF's fighter force because of the need for standing patrols over the shipping. Known to the Germans as the *Kanalkampf* (Channel Battle), the opening phase also saw limited attacks against other targets in the United Kingdom. It drew to a close at the end of the first week of August 1940 as the Germans broadened the scope of their targeting in a bid to destroy Fighter Command, thereby gaining control of the air over Britain.

■ Second Phase, 8–23 August 1940

The second phase of the Battle of Britain saw an increase in German attacks on Channel convoys, but more notably the bid to destroy RAF Fighter Command began in earnest. Bad weather delayed the main German assault, codenamed *Adlerangriff* (Eagle Attack), with *Adler Tag* (Eagle Day) being pushed back to 13 August. The main attack was preceded by a bid to destroy British radar stations on 12 August, but three of the four stations attacked were back on the air within a matter of hours. This helped the Germans arrive at a pessimistic assessment of how difficult it was to destroy radar stations, and although attacks were to continue against this target for some days to come, there was increasing scepticism on the part of the *Luftwaffe* (particularly its commander Herman Göring) about the value of such attacks. *Adler Tag* began on 13 August, with an increasing German air effort against radar and airfield targets, particularly the aerodromes on the south coast of England. Extremely heavy fighting occurred on 18 August, subsequently branded 'the hardest day'

of the battle, as the Germans moved their focus towards the inland fighter aerodromes. The fighting on 18 August saw just over 30 British fighters destroyed in combat, while the Germans lost a total of around 70 aircraft. The phase concluded with growing British concerns over pilot losses. The Germans were equally concerned and, in a revision of tactics, the attacks on radar stations were abandoned, while Göring issued orders demanding increased close escort of bomber formations, thus hindering the effectiveness of German fighter sweeps. Bad weather led to a lull in the fighting, which resumed in earnest from 24 August.

■ Third Phase, 24 August 1940

The critical phase of the Battle of Britain began on 24 August 1940, with renewed and repeated heavy attacks on British aerodromes. British fighter losses increased, and the drain on experienced pilots became a serious issue. By early September, British concerns about the rate of attrition among Fighter Command pilots and airframes had grown considerably. However, a change in targeting policy by the Germans gave Fighter Command respite and helped to swing the balance of the battle once more.

■ Final Phase, 7 September 1940

On 7 September 1940, the *Luftwaffe* shifted its attacks from airfields to London. This returned the advantage to the RAF, and a combination of rising losses, poor weather and a desire to preserve forces for an attack on the USSR saw the battle peter out by the end of October.

■ The Blitz, 7 Sept 1940–10 May 1941

Increasing bomber losses during the Battle of Britain raised concerns among the German High Command about the effect upon the *Luftwaffe*'s ability to support the invasion of the USSR in 1941. This saw a move towards night-time raids from 7 September 1940. London was bombed for 76 consecutive nights, while other major industrial cities and ports were attacked. A particularly heavy raid against Coventry on 14–15 November 1940 caused widespread destruction, while the raid on London on 29 December became known as

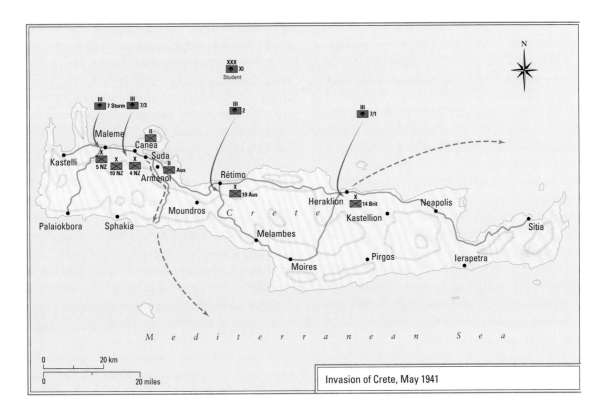

Invasion of Crete, May 1941

'The Second Great Fire of London', such was the destruction caused by fires raised by the bombing. Poor weather, reduced aircraft availability and the failure of the Blitz to bring about any British moves seeking peace saw the campaign draw to a close in May 1941, as the Germans prepared for the invasion of the Soviet Union.

The Balkans 1940–41

■ INVASION OF YUGOSLAVIA, 6–17 APRIL 1941

In 1940–41 Germany desired a peaceful Balkans that would not disrupt its preparations for its spring 1941 invasion of the Soviet Union. However, on 28 October 1940, Germany's Italian Axis allies invaded Greece from Albania, prompting German fears of British military intervention. Next, on 27 March 1941, a coup in Yugoslavia installed a pro-Allied regime. These events prompted Hitler to order a hasty German-led Axis invasion of both Yugoslavia and Greece commencing on 6 April. On 6–11 April, 42 German, Italian and Hungarian

divisions attacked Yugoslavia from Italian, Austrian, Hungarian, Rumanian, Bulgarian and Albanian soil. The Axis forces made rapid progress on all fronts, aided by the defection of Croat units to the newly declared Pro-Axis Croat Nationalist state. German forces captured the Yugoslavian capital Belgrade on 12 April. By the 13th, the Yugoslav Army had collapsed, and an armistice was signed on 17 April.

■ INVASION OF GREECE, 6–30 APRIL 1941

On 6 April 1941, the German Twelfth Army's 15 divisions struck south from south-western Bulgaria to invade northern Greece and west to invade southern Yugoslavia. During 1940–41, the Italian–Greek war and the presence of 40,000 British Commonwealth forces on Greek soil jeopardized the German build-up for their planned spring 1941 invasion of the Soviet Union, and so Hitler decided to conquer Greece. During 6–9 April, Twelfth Army battered its way through the Greek Metaxas Line defences in eastern Macedonia, while its armour charged through southern Yugoslavia and advanced into Greece to reach the coast at Thessaloniki. During 14–27 April the German forces, reinforced with divisions used to conquer Yugoslavia, advanced south to reach Athens on the 27th, by which time many Commonwealth troops had evacuated to Crete and Egypt. On the 30th, the remnants of the Greek Army in the Peloponnese peninsula in southern Greece capitulated.

■ INVASION OF CRETE, 20 MAY–1 JUNE 1941

Although German forces had overrun all of mainland Greece by 30 April, 35,000 Greek and Commonwealth forces – many just evacuated from the mainland – continued to hold the island of Crete. On 20 May the 11,000 troops of the German 7th Airborne Division began landing by parachute and glider onto Crete's three main northern coastal airfields at Maleme, Rétimo and Heraklion. Subsequently, 8000 troops of the German 5th and 6th Mountain Divisions arrived by sea and by transport aircraft once the airfields were secured. The paratroopers met ferocious resistance and suffered heavy casualties, but had secured all three airfields by the 27th. Subsequently, the Allied forces withdrew back to the southern port of Sphakia, where 3000 troops were evacuated by sea during 28–31 May to Egypt. The German forces suffered 6900 casualties, including 4000 dead; Allied casualties were 23,900, including 17,000 captured.

The Eastern Front 1941–44

■ OPERATION BARBAROSSA, 22 JUNE–5 DEC 1941

The German invasion of the Soviet Union, codenamed Operation *Barbarossa*, began on 22 June 1941. The Soviets were caught by surprise, and the opening phases of the invasion saw the Germans make considerable territorial gains all along the front. The German assault saw much of the available strength of the Red Air Force destroyed, while hundreds of thousands of Soviet prisoners were taken. By the end of the first week of operations, the three German army groups had taken most of their objectives, although fierce

fighting continued around Bialystok and Minsk. As the German infantry forces caught up with the fast-moving armoured formations, the second phase of the operation began on 3 July. Some delays were caused by poor weather, and the brief pause permitted the Soviets to launch a major counter-attack against Army Group Centre on 6 July. This was beaten back with heavy Soviet losses, and the German advance resumed. Attempts to encircle Soviet formations enjoyed some success, but a significant number of Red Army troops were able to escape a number of German pincer attacks and fall back on Moscow.

Hitler's assessment of the early phase of the invasion led to his decision to swing towards the oilfields of the Caucasus, the Donets Basin and the industrial centre of Kharkov. This meant a concomitant loss in the strength available for the advance on Moscow and protestations from his senior commanders about the weakening of the thrust towards the Soviet capital went unheeded. Although the forces advancing on Moscow were weakened, success continued, with the Soviets suffering major losses as the Uman pocket was closed off and Kiev falling under German control after heavy fighting during the last week of September. Meanwhile, German forces advanced towards Leningrad, which Hitler ordered besieged and forced into submission, rather than being captured via a major assault.

Following the fall of Kiev, the Germans launched Operation *Typhoon*, a drive on Moscow. The operation initially enjoyed considerable success and by 13 October, German forces were within 160km of the Soviet capital. The advance was conducted in deteriorating weather conditions, which made movement increasingly difficult. By 31 October, the Germans were forced to pause to deal with the problems created by the transportation difficulties. This gave the Soviets the opportunity to regroup, bringing in forces from the eastern regions of the USSR. The German assault resumed on 15 November 1941 as the ground hardened after increasingly heavy frosts. A week later, the Soviets launched a massive counter-

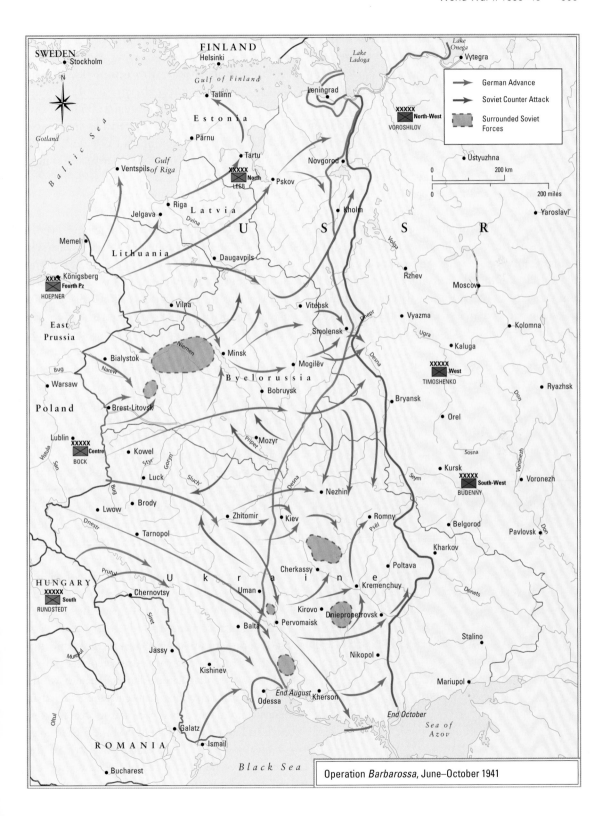

Operation *Barbarossa*, June–October 1941

attack, which enjoyed considerable success in some sectors, but did not stem the advance overall. By December, lead elements of German forces were within 8km of Moscow, but the first blizzards of winter arrived, changing the situation dramatically. The Germans were unequipped for operations in the harsh Russian winter, and the advance ground to a halt. Equipment froze and the *Luftwaffe* was grounded, giving the Soviets the opportunity to plan a counterstroke. On 5 December, the Soviets launched another huge counter-attack, utilizing more troops brought in from elsewhere. The Germans fell back in the face of the onslaught, with the Soviets driving the enemy back some 322km by the time their counter-attack ended in early January 1942. Operation *Barbarossa* cost both sides enormous numbers of casualties, setting the tone for the sanguinary nature of the war on the Eastern Front.

■ MINSK, 22 MAY–5 JUNE 1941

During 22–23 May, the first 48 hours of the

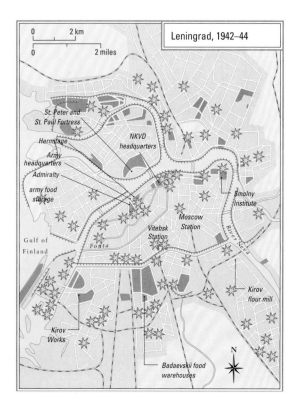

German invasion of the Soviet Union, two armoured groups spearheading Army Group Centre's advance along the central axis toward Moscow smashed through the Soviet frontier defences. Audaciously advancing 320km east, these armoured groups developed a double-pincer encirclement that linked up east of Minsk on 27 May. Of the 350,000 Soviet personnel caught in the Bialystok-Minsk pocket, 310,000 had surrendered by 5 June.

■ SMOLENSK, 5 JUNE–3 AUGUST 1941

Having successfully closed the Bialystock-Minsk pocket, between 5 June and 24 July the two armoured groups spearheading Army Group Centre's advance conducted a 330km-deep double-envelopment to reach Smolensk, netting 300,000 enemy troops in a pocket. It took the Germans another 10 days to liquidate this pocket. During the rest of August, however, Soviet counter-attacks, German logistical problems and bickering among senior commanders meant that the Germans did not advance any closer towards Moscow.

■ KIEV, 23 AUGUST–26 SEPTEMBER 1941

Between 23 August and 16 September 1941, the German Second Panzer Army from Army Group Centre struck south from the Smolensk area behind the Soviet forces that protected Kiev. Meanwhile, First Panzer Army from Army Group South thrust east to the River Dnieper before turning north to meet Second Army at Lokhvitsa (195km behind Kiev) on the 16th, trapping 590,000 Soviet troops in the Uman-Kiev pockets; by 26 September the Germans had liquidated the pocket, taking 550,000 prisoners.

■ LENINGRAD, 1941–1944

The capture of Leningrad was one of the key objectives of the German invasion of the Soviet Union, although Hitler decided that the city would be brought to surrender through siege rather than assault. The siege developed as rail connections between Leningrad and the rest of the USSR were cut on 30 August 1941, while a week later, the Germans reached Lake Lagoda, severing the last land communications. The city was bombarded with artillery and aircraft, causing heavy civilian casualties. With the Soviet defences holding out, and little inclination on Hitler's part to launch an all-out assault on the city, the two sides settled down to a siege, although it is unlikely that either side realized how long it would last.

The initial Soviet response to the siege was uncoordinated; a number of poor planning decisions meant that supplies for the city's population were limited from the outset. This problem was to reach almost unimaginable proportions as the siege drew on. Aware that the citizens of Leningrad faced considerable privations, the Soviets sought to lift the siege as soon as was practicable, although the military situation in late 1941 and early 1942 was such that this objective was unlikely to be realized quickly. Although some supplies could be taken into the city across Lake Lagoda, there was insufficient shipping available to meet the demands of the population. As no evacuation plan had been drawn up after the German invasion, the number of people in Leningrad remained high, and the number of people who could be evacuated by boat was relatively small. Furthermore, Stalin did not wish to see the city abandoned as this would represent a major propaganda triumph for Hitler, in addition to the loss of the significant industrial capacity within Leningrad.

As the winter arrived, an ice road was established across the lake, and supplies taken in by lorry. However, this did not become operational until late November 1941 and, in the interim, conditions in the city had deteriorated in the face of enemy bombardment and a lack of basic provisions. The road was frequently bombed and shelled by the Germans and, although it made a notable contribution to keeping the city alive, the amount of material that could be taken across remained inadequate to meet the city's requirements. The suffering of the population increased as a result of the lack of food supplies and fuel. This prompted the Soviets to plan an offensive to break the blockade, but it was not possible to attempt this until the Sinyavino Offensive, which began on 27 August 1942.

The offensive began with a number of Soviet successes, but a German counter-attack meant that the Soviets were unable to achieve their aim of lifting the encirclement of the city, which remained cut off by land and only accessible by air and water-borne transport. Finally, on 12 January 1943, the Red Army's Leningrad and Volkhov Fronts launched Operation *Iskra*, which saw fierce fighting from the outset. The Soviets took the German positions south of Lake Lagoda and the two fronts met on 18 January 1943. This created a narrow land corridor through which supplies could be taken, although it remained vulnerable to German bombardment. The siege was finally lifted following another major Russian offensive in January 1944, which drove the Germans back from the outskirts of the city.

■ MOSCOW, OCTOBER 1941–JANUARY 1942

As the capital of the Soviet Union, Moscow was the most important objective in Hitler's conception of Operation *Barbarossa*, since he believed that capturing the city would bring about the collapse of all Soviet resistance. Army Group Centre was tasked with capturing the city as part of Operation *Typhoon*.

The initial phases went well, with the Soviets suffering major reverses at the Vyazma and Bryansk pockets. In both cases, Russian resistance was fierce, and a significant number of troops were able to escape the encirclement and fall back towards Moscow. By 7 October, the German advance had been slowed by poor weather making roads impassable, but the threat to Moscow was still great enough to prompt Stalin to order the evacuation of the capital, which was turned into a fortress under the command of Marshal Zhukov. By 15 November, winter frosts had hardened the ground, allowing the Germans to resume their advance. However, in the interim the Soviets had been able to bring in more troops from eastern regions, particularly Siberia, and although some reconnaissance units from the German forces

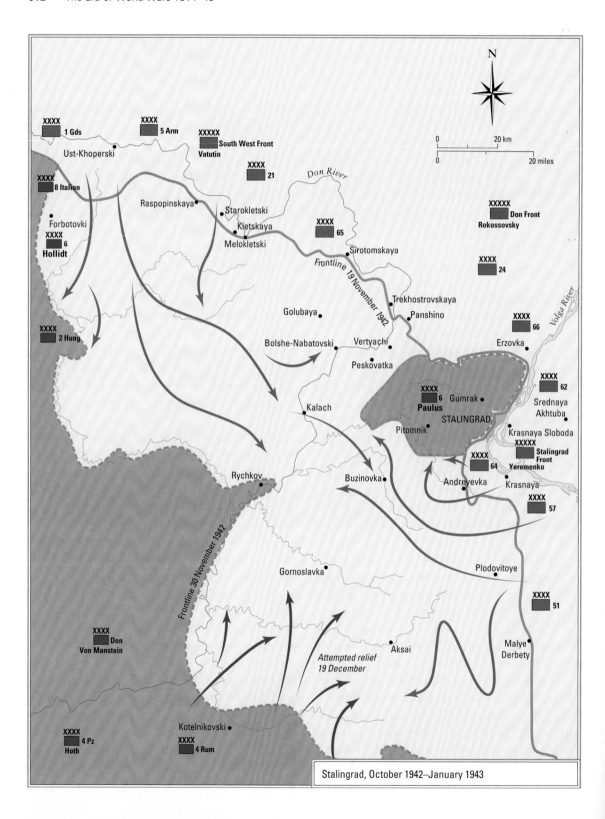

Stalingrad, October 1942–January 1943

came within 8km of Moscow by 2 December, the bulk of the German Army was stopped short by a massive Soviet counter-attack on 5 December. The Germans were forced to fall back, despite orders from Hitler that they were to fight to the last man. Although the Soviet advance in the central front was slower than on the flanks, the overall effect was to drive the Germans away from Moscow by January 1942. The Soviets then paused to regroup, preparing for a new offensive during the spring, although this ultimately stalled at Rzhev.

■ SEVASTOPOL, 30 OCT 1941–4 SEPTEMBER 1944

The German advance through the Ukraine isolated the Crimean peninsula, which included the key port of Sevastopol, in late August 1941 and the 70,000-strong German Eleventh Army began the siege of this fortress-port on 30 October. However, the city did not fall until 4 July 1942, when 80,000 prisoners from the 118,000-strong garrison were taken. Soviet counter-offensives in turn retook the city on 4 September 1944.

■ STALINGRAD, 23 AUG 1942–2 FEBRUARY 1943

One of the turning points of WWII in Europe, the battle of Stalingrad saw the Soviets and Germans contest control of the city of Stalingrad. The political significance of capturing 'Stalin's City' was an irresistible temptation for Hitler, who saw the capture of Stalingrad as an integral part of the drive on the Caucasus and its oil supplies. Originally, the German Army Group South was to conduct an offensive with the oilfields being the key objective, but Hitler intervened and instead ordered that the forces in Army Group South be split into two, the second formation tasked with taking Stalingrad. The assault in the south started at the end of June 1942, and by the end of July, the Germans had crossed the River Don. German Sixth Army, under Gen Friedrich Paulus, advanced quickly towards Stalingrad, but it was delayed when Hitler ordered Fourth Panzer Army to join the advance, an order that created massive traffic jams and which in fact delayed the march on Stalingrad. Fourth Panzer Army was redeployed, and by the end of July 1942, was to the south of Stalingrad, in a position

to turn north to aid Sixth Army's assault.

As the German advance progressed, it became clear that Stalingrad was one of their objectives, and the Soviets began to remove some vital supplies from the city. Stalingrad's factories, notably those producing tanks, continued to function, although much of the industrial capacity of the city was destroyed in the opening air attacks by the *Luftwaffe*. The German offensive against the city itself was met with fierce Soviet resistance, led by 62nd Army under LGen Vasily Chuikov, and drawing upon the efforts of numerous groups of Workers' Militia, established in a bid to ensure that almost every able-bodied citizen of Stalingrad was involved in the defence. The Germans advanced into Stalingrad, but soon became bogged down in the ruins of the city and the battle turned into a multitude of small unit actions as the fighting went from house to house. Although the Germans took control of much of the city, Soviet defenders remained resolutely in control of positions to the west bank of the River Volga.

It became clear to the Soviets that the German offensive was running out of steam, and the lack of preparedness for fighting in Soviet winter conditions that had dogged the German efforts during the winter of 1941–42 were again exploited. On 19 November 1942, the Soviets launched Operation *Uranus*, designed to relieve the pressure on Stalingrad. The offensive fell upon the Romanian and Italian forces that were covering the flanks of German Sixth Army, and as these forces were routed Sixth Army was encircled in Stalingrad. Attempts to relieve Sixth Army failed, as did an attempt to keep the city supplied from the air.

A follow-up Soviet offensive, Operation *Little Saturn*, ensured that Sixth Army – now starving and running out of ammunition – could not be relieved. When Soviet forces advanced on Paulus' headquarters on 1 February 1943, he bowed to the inevitable and surrendered and the remnants of Sixth Army capitulated the next day. Following Stalingrad, the Germans gained no victories of strategic significance on the Eastern Front for the remainder of the war.

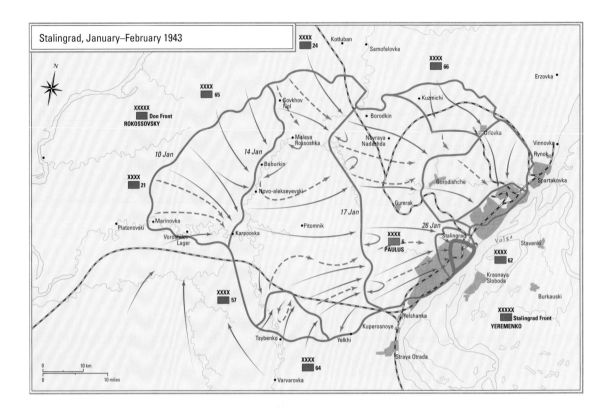

Stalingrad, January–February 1943

CAUCASUS, 28 JUNE 1942–31 JANUARY 1943

On 28 June 1942 the German Army Group South's 1.4 million troops initiated Operation *Blue*, aiming to capture the vital Soviet north Caucasian oilfields around Maikop, while also capturing Stalingrad as a secondary objective. After advancing south-east across the Don river between 25 July and 20 August, the 22 divisions of the newly created Army Group A advanced 485km south-east deep into the Caucasus, capturing the oilfields and reaching Mount Elbrus on the 20th. The overstretched German advance subsequently stalled, as efforts to capture Stalingrad absorbed forces, although Ordzhonikidze, the most southerly point of the Axis advance, was captured on 2 November. However, during late November and December, Soviet counter-offensives at Stalingrad and along the Don threatened to isolate Army Group A in the Caucasus. In January 1943, Army Group A's forces retreated back to the Don around Rostov and into the Kuban peninsula opposite the Crimea.

KHARKOV, 16 FEBRUARY–16 MARCH 1943

After the German surrender at Stalingrad, Soviet offensives advanced south-west until by 17 February they were just 160km short of the Azov coast. Amid this crisis the new SS-Panzer Corps withdrew from Kharkov on the 16th against Hitler's explicit wishes. During 28 February–5 March, FM von Manstein's counter-offensive smashed the Soviet advance. Exploiting this success during 6–16 March, the SS-Panzer Corps advanced to recapture Kharkov. During these battles, the Germans suffered 18,000 casualties and the Soviets 74,000.

KURSK, 5–23 JULY 1943

The end of the 1942–43 winter campaign in Russia ended with the Soviets holding a large salient around Kursk. This appeared to be vulnerable to attack and, in a bid to derail the expected Soviet summer offensive, the Germans planned to launch an assault to cut the salient off. The Soviets were fully apprised of the German plans thanks to

Sumy

Trostyanyets

Akhtyrka

Bogodukhov

Lyubotin — Kharkov

Merafa

Belgorod

Poltava

Krasnograd

Balakleya

Kupiansk

Chuguyev

Isyum

Lozoyaya

Slaviansk

Novomoskorsk

Kramatorsk

Druzhkovka

Dnepropetrovsk

Konstantinovka

Yasinovataya

0   100 km

0   100 miles

N

XXXXX
VORONEZH FRONT
GOLIKOV

XXXX
SOUTHWEST FRONT
VATUTIN

XXXXX
ARMY GROUP DON
MANSTEIN

Third Battle of Kharkov, February–March 1943

various intelligence sources. However, the date of the offensive could not be satisfactorily determined as Hitler repeatedly postponed the start, partly to permit the new Panther tank, in which he placed much faith, to be available in meaningful numbers.

In the interim, the Soviets prepared significant defensive positions to meet the German attack, and the scale of the resultant operation saw somewhere in the region of 1.3 million Soviet troops facing more than 750,000 Germans.

Some preliminary fighting occurred on 4 July 1943, when German units from Fourth Panzer Army sacrificed tactical surprise in a bid to take Soviet defensive positions as a precursor to the main advance the next day. The Soviets responded with an artillery barrage along the front during the early morning of 5 July. The offensive, codenamed *Citadel*, began in earnest on 5 July. The German advance was blunted by stiff Soviet resistance. The northern sector of the German pincer manoeuvre made little headway and sustained heavy losses as it

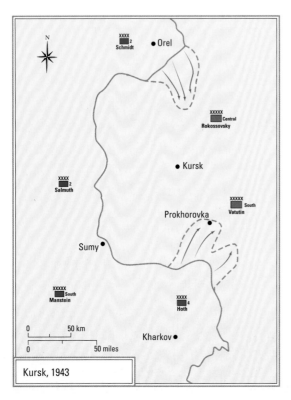

Kursk, 1943

went. To the south, German forces under FM von Manstein drove through the Soviet Sixth Army, but then began to run into the Soviet reserve as the advance continued.

A week after the offensive began, the German and Soviet tank forces met near the railhead at Prokhorovka, in what was to be the largest tank battle in history. In the course of eight hours of fierce fighting, Soviet forces blunted the German attack. The pincer movement in the northern sector was all but over by this point, but the position in the south appeared more propitious; the Germans had broken through the first two Soviet defensive lines and were making steady progress, even though the speed of advance and the depth of penetration slowed each day.

The large number of casualties sustained by the German forces in both arms of the pincer movement was a growing threat to their ability to continue, and a further complication arose following the Anglo-American-led invasion of Sicily on 9–10 July 1943.

The threat presented by the invasion prompted Hitler to send the entire SS-Panzer Corps to Italy, and he ordered that the Kursk offensive be halted. He was persuaded to allow the Offensive to continue for a few more days, but the Soviets launched a counter-attack in the northern sector on 12 July, while losses sustained in fighting to the south prompted the Germans to withdraw to their start lines on 16 July. The next day saw Hitler call off the offensive. A combination of numerical superiority on the part of the Soviets, plus much better command and control of the Red Army meant that the German offensive faced formidable obstacles from the outset. Improved tactics on the part of the Soviets further contributed to their success in blunting the German attack. The end of the offensive left both sides in need of a period of recovery and regeneration after the heavy losses both had sustained, but the Soviets were far better placed to recover and embark upon a new round of offensive operations, which they did from August 1943.

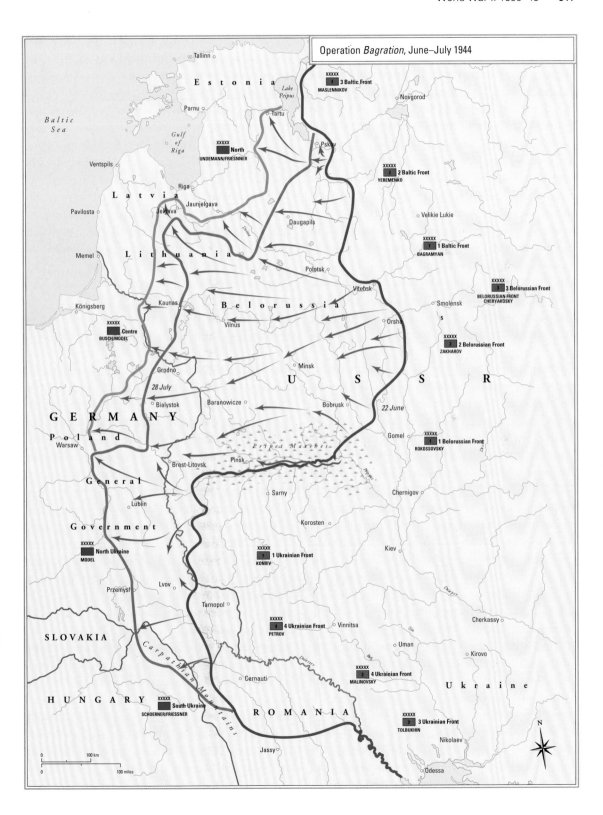

Operation *Bagration*, June–July 1944

■ **OPERATION *BAGRATION*, 22 JUNE–19 AUG 1944**
A major Soviet offensive of 1944, *Bagration* saw German forces cleared from Belorussia and eastern Poland between 22 June and 19 August 1944. The first phase of Soviet operations broke through the forward German defences, enabling the Red Army's sizable operational reserves to exploit the breakthrough, maintaining the momentum of the advance and with the aim of breaking the German cohesion. German army groups were to be encircled en masse with the aim of destroying them in situ (aided by Hitler's imprecations that German troops were not to withdraw), before the advance moved on. The links between Army Group North and Army Group North Ukraine were cut, and they were forced to fall back extremely quickly as manpower was poured into Army Group Centre in a vain bid to stem the Soviet advance. A series of relentless offensive operations shattered the German positions and, by 4 July 1944, Army Group Centre had been destroyed in the pocket around Minsk, representing the greatest single defeat of the German Army during the entire war.

A third phase of operations following the victory at Minsk ended with the Soviets having reconquered the western USSR. *Bagration* represented probably the largest and arguably the most significant Soviet victory of the war. The Germans could not properly recover from the enormous losses sustained during the offensives, leaving them perilously vulnerable to future offensive operations. The German Army lost around 25 per cent of its strength on the Eastern Front with Army Group Centre's almost total destruction, while losses in aircraft, armour and vehicles were similarly heavy. The offensive concluded with the Russians holding bridgeheads over the Vistula and territory in both Poland and Romania, which left them poised to strike into Germany itself in the course of subsequent operations.

■ **POLAND–EAST PRUSSIA, AUGUST 1944–MAY 1945**   During August 1944–February 1945, 1.9 million Soviet troops advanced west to overrun Poland and most of East Prussia. The remaining 150,000 Germans troops trapped in the Vistula Delta and Hela peninsula held out until 8 May before capitulation.

■ **WARSAW, 1 AUGUST–2 OCTOBER 1944**
With the Soviets advancing toward Warsaw, the Polish Home Army rose up against German occupation on 1 August. After 32,000 insurgents had seized control of the city by the 4th, the Germans massed 25,000 police and SS personnel. During the next two months' brutal fighting, the Germans liquidated the uprising. The insurgents suffered 16,000 casualties and 15,000 capitulated, plus 100,000 civilian casualties and the Germans 22,000 casualties. The Germans destroyed much of the city during and after the uprising.

■ **VIENNA, 2–13 APRIL 1945**
During 2–8 April 1945, four Soviet armies from the Third Ukrainian Front surrounded Vienna (the Austrian capital) which was defended by elements of the German Sixth SS-Panzer Army. Between 6 and 10 April, Soviet forces fought their way forward into the southern, western and northern suburbs. Finally, during 11–13 April the Soviet forces overran the city centre. The Germans suffered 25,000 casualties in the battle, plus 40,000 captured and the Soviets 26,000.

■ **BERLIN, 20 APRIL–2 MAY 1945**
The battle of Berlin (not to be confused with the air offensive of 1943–44 also given that appellation) began on 20 April 1945, and concluded on the morning of 2 May as Soviet forces brought about the final defeat of Nazi Germany by taking the capital city. A three-day assault on the Seelow Heights outside Berlin from 16 April by the Soviet 1st Belorussian Front under Marshal Georgy Zhukov was followed on 20 April by a Soviet artillery barrage against the city centre. Soviet Fifth Shock Army drove into the city on 23 April and, by the following evening reached the north side of the Tetlow Canal. On 26 April, Soviet forces pushed into the south of the city. Fighting was particularly heavy, with considerable numbers of casualties

on both sides. By 29 April, the Soviets were ready to attack Berlin city centre, aiming for the Reichstag. Again, the fighting was particularly heavy, and the Soviet advance was slow. However, by the morning of 30 April, it was clear that the German position was utterly hopeless; in addition to the losses in Berlin, German Ninth Army had been destroyed at Halbe, ending the unlikely possibility of a successful counter-attack. That afternoon, Hitler committed suicide in his bunker beneath the Reich Chancellery garden. An attempt by the remnants of the Berlin garrison to break out on the night of 1–2 May failed, and both the Reichstag and Reich Chancellery fell to the Soviets early on 2 May, prompting the final surrender of the survivors of the Berlin garrison.

■ **PRAGUE, 5–9 MAY 1945**

On 5–8 May 1945, as Soviet forces advanced toward Prague from the east, resistance forces rose up against German occupation. A ceasefire was agreed on the 8th and Soviet forces reached the city on the 9th.

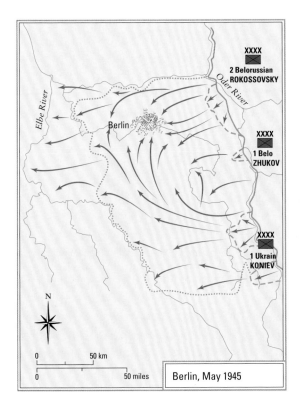

Berlin, May 1945

Italian Front

■ **SICILY, 9 JULY–17 AUGUST 1943**

During 9–10 July 1943, and following victory in North Africa (see below), as part of Operation *Husky*, 140,000 Western Allied troops invaded the Italian island of Sicily. Seventh US Army's three divisions landed at Licata-Scoglitti on the southern coast and the British Eighth Army's one Canadian and three British divisions landed at Pachino-Cassibili on the south-eastern coast, supported by airborne landings. By the 13th, the Allies had driven the defending Italian/German Axis troops back 55km to form a secure lodgement that included the port of Syracuse. Between 14 July and 6 August, American forces cleared western Sicily and the British the central-eastern quadrant, pushing the defenders back to the Etna Line that protected the north-eastern peninsula. During 7–17 August, Allied amphibious landings outflanked the Axis defences and during 10–17 August, 130,000 Axis troops evacuated Sicily from Messina at the island's north-eastern apex. The Allies suffered 24,500 casualties and the Axis 165,000, including 140,000 Italian prisoners.

■ **SOUTHERN ITALY, 3–16 SEPTEMBER 1943**

US Gen Clark's Fifth Army and British Gen Montgomery's Eighth Army faced 100,000 Germans of GenFM Kesselring's Tenth Army in the contest for Italy. Mussolini capitulated, leaving the Germans to fend for themselves. The invasion began with British landings at Calabria on 3 September. On 9 September, the US Fifth Army came ashore at Salerno. The Germans then withdrew northward. On 1 October, 190,000 Allied troops liberated Naples, and by 6 October, the Allies controlled the Campanian plain.

■ **SALERNO, 9 SEPTEMBER–6 OCTOBER 1943**

On 9 September 1943, 55,000 British/American troops of the US Fifth Army landed at Salerno on Italy's western coast south of Naples. During 3–9 September, British forces had invaded the 'toe' and 'heel' of Italy, while on the 8th, the Italians surrendered and the Germans had taken control of the country. During 10–13 September, the Allies consolidated the beachhead as German reserves arrived. German counter-attacks during 14–17 September sorely pressed the Allied line, though it ultimately held. With 160,000 troops in the beachhead on 19 September, the Allies attacked north toward Naples and captured the port on 1 October. By 6 October, the Allies had reached the eastward-running line of the River Volturno, 50km to the north. In the meantime, the British Eighth Army had advanced up Italy's Adriatic coast to the River Biferno, thus linking up with Fifth Army. The latter suffered 5,000 casualties and the Germans 7,000.

■ GUSTAV-CASSINO LINE, NOV 1943–MAY 1944

The Gustav (or Winter) Line was a German defensive position constructed in late 1943 across Italy from Gaeta, south of Rome, through Cassino, the Apennine Mountains and onto the Sangro estuary on the eastern coast. It took the Western Allies four offensives to break this position. The

optimal Allied route of advance to Rome was through the Liri valley, but the Gustav defences blocked this route around Cassino, particularly on the Monte Cassino heights, topped by its ancient monastery. In the first battle of Monte Cassino (17 January–11 February 1944), X Corps' three British divisions attacked across the River Garigilano close to the western coast, while three Fifth US Army divisions attacked Cassino. Subsequently, Allied forces landed behind the Garigliano at Anzio. The Allies closed on the monastery before being halted. During the second battle (15–18 February), one New Zealand and one Indian division attacked the Cassino defences to assist the beleaguered Anzio beachhead. Despite incurring high casualties and destroying the monastery, the Allies again failed to capture Monastery Hill. In the third battle (15–26 March), three Allied divisions attacked Cassino from the north-east, but the Allied advance was again halted short of the monastery. In the fourth battle (11–25 May), Operation *Diadem*, US Fifth

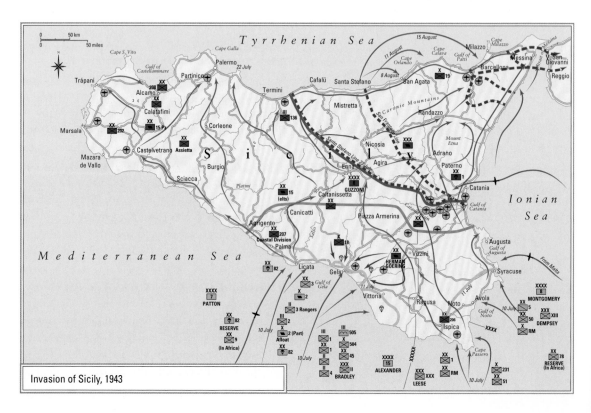

Invasion of Sicily, 1943

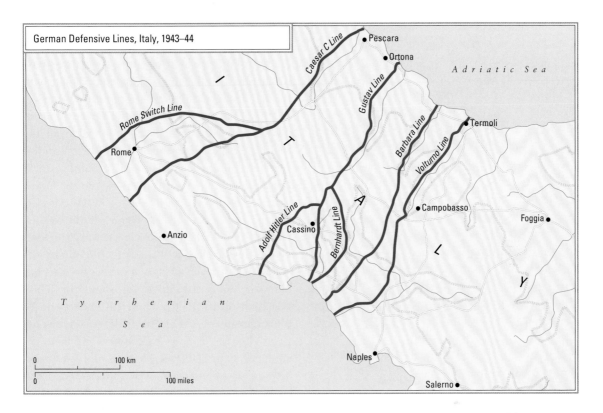

German Defensive Lines, Italy, 1943–44

Army and British Eighth Army forces attacked the Gustav Line's western sector in a large-scale offensive. While the US II and French I Corps assaulted across the Garigliano and US VI Corps broke out from the Anzio beachhead, Polish II and British XIII Corps assaulted the Cassino position. This offensive broke through Cassino and, by late May, the German forces were in full retreat north beyond Rome. The Allies suffered 55,000 casualties in these operations, while the Germans took 35,000.

■ ANZIO, 22 JANUARY–4 JUNE 1944

On 22 January 1944, as part of Operation *Shingle*, 36,000 Anglo-American troops of the US VI Corps landed virtually unopposed at Anzio on the western Italian coast, 40km south of Rome and 55km behind the main German Gustav Line defences. The aim was to unhinge the German main line, facilitating an offensive from Cassino north towards Rome. Once ashore, the Allied units dug in instead of advancing, enabling 40,000 German

Fourteenth Army troops to rush to the beachhead and seal it off. The 69,000 Allied troops in the beachhead attacked on 28 January, but the ensuing German counter-attacks during 3–20 February (there were now 100,000 German troops in the area) nearly overran the beachhead. By late February a stalemate had emerged. On 23 May, VI Corps broke out of the beachhead in conjunction with Operation *Diadem* (the Allied offensive against the Gustav Line) and on 4 June Rome fell.

■ GOTHIC LINE, 25 AUG–17 DECEMBER 1944

During August 1944, German forces in Italy retreated north to the Gustav Line defences that stretched from the western coast near Pisa through to Pesaro in the eastern coast. During 25 August–29 September, the British Eighth Army offensive against the line's eastern flank advanced 77km to the River Uso. Concurrently in the centre, during 12 September–15 October, US Fifth Army fought its way 51km forward toward Bologna, before poor weather halted operations.

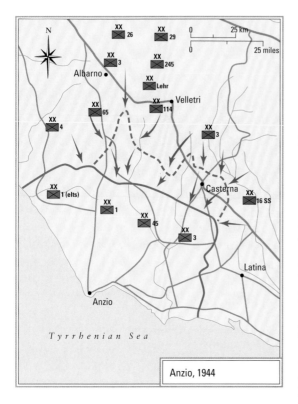

Anzio, 1944

■ **PO VALLEY, 6 APRIL–2 MAY 1945**

During April 1945, 600,000 Western Allied troops smashed through the defensive positions held by 430,000 German/Italian forces, crossed the River Po and pushed 250km north to the Alps by 2 May, when the collapsing Axis forces in Italy surrendered.

Western Front 1942–45

■ **STRATEGIC AIR CAMPAIGN , MARCH 1942–APRIL 45**

Before WWI, the Italian Gen Giulio Douhet had championed the role of strategic airpower in war. He had advocated the legitimacy of bombing an enemy's population as well as its military. Nevertheless, by the time WWII broke out, neither the Allies nor the Axis powers fully embraced Douhet's concept. In Nazi Germany, the *Luftwaffe*, under Reichsmarschall Hermann Göring, developed tactical bombing proficiency. The Ju 87 Stuka could carry one 250kg bomb

beneath its fuselage and four 50kg bombs beneath its wings. Stukas typically worked in concert with fighters to provide close air support to fast-moving mechanized troops on the ground. Such joint formations swept the *Wehrmacht* to early success in the *Blitzkrieg* of 1939–41 against Poland, France, Norway and parts of the Soviet Union. During the Battle of Britain, Ju 88s and He 111s, capable of carrying hundreds of kilograms of bombs, struck London and other British cities. Yet the Nazis had not developed large fleets of heavy bombers capable of mass attacks deep within enemy territory, as Douhet had envisioned a generation before. This oversight would prove costly, as the Allies, out of reach of the German war machine, built air forces capable of smashing the Third Reich to pieces. In the United Kingdom, under the leadership of AM Sir Arthur Travers Harris, the British Royal Air Force's Bomber Command re-equipped with Halifaxes, Sterlings and Lancasters. These four-engine planes were capable of carrying large payloads (between 5897kg and 6340 kg) on long missions. The Area Bombing Directive of 14 February 1942 gave Harris the authority to unleash his 'heavies' on Axis civilian, as well as military and industrial, targets. At Lübeck on the Baltic, British bombers applied the new strategy, releasing 400 tons of bombs and setting the city ablaze. More than 300 Germans died. Göring responded with air raids on historic British towns. Later in the war, Hitler augmented his bomber force with first-generation ballistic missiles (V-2) and glide bombs (V-1), which were deployed as terror weapons in reprisal for the Allied advance on the Western Front. Meanwhile, the British continued to hone their conventional strategic bombing capabilities. Some Lancasters were modified to carry the massive 10,000kg Grand Slam bomb, which Harris used to 'great effect' against the Third Reich's viaducts, railways and U-boat pens. Advances in radar and bomb sight technologies helped to increase the effectiveness of the joint US 8th Air Force/Bomber Command Combined Bomber Offensive (June 1943–April 1945). American B-17

Flying Fortresses were capable of carrying between 2000kg and 7800kg of bombs; B-24 Liberators could take between 1200kg and 3600kg. Hundreds of these planes participated in mass attacks on Germany's industrial base. In total, the Anglo-American offensive released more than 2.8 million tons of bombs in over 1.4 million bomber sorties. The raids played havoc with Axis industry at target sites like Schweinfurt and Regensburg. But success came at a cost. More than 22,000 Allied bombers were lost and almost 160,000 American and British aircrew were killed. The civilian toll was heavier, with estimates of between 300,000 and 600,000 German deaths. The Nazis' strategic bombing raids killed almost 61,000 in Britain.

■ NORMANDY LANDINGS, 6 JUNE 1944

The initial British–American landing in Normandy (Operation *Neptune,* the first stage of Operation *Overlord*), aimed 'to secure a lodgement on the continent from which further offensive operations can be developed'. Many preconditions

had to be met before the cross-Channel operation could be contemplated: vast American forces had to be transported to Britain, requiring the defeat of the U-boats and the availability of huge amounts of shipping; a high degree of command of the sea and air in the relevant area had to be achieved; enormous amphibious forces had to be built up and trained. Normandy was chosen because of the suitability of its beaches for landings and of the hinterland for the subsequent breakout, and because an assault here, rather than the Pas de Calais, would be unexpected. Careful intelligence preparation went alongside a meticulous campaign of deception to keep the defenders' attention focused on the Pas de Calais and Norway, allowing the Allies to achieve the surprise that was essential for success. The staggering logistical requirements would be guaranteed by two 'Mulberry' artificial harbours, together with undersea oil pipelines and supplies landed over the beaches. Gen Dwight D. Eisenhower was Supreme Allied Commander, with

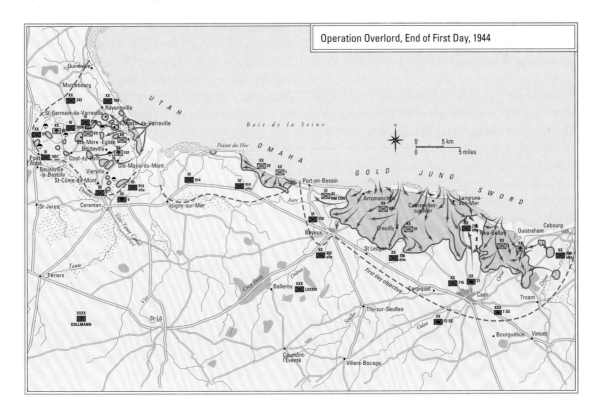

Operation Overlord, End of First Day, 1944

the bulk of the planning being conducted by the naval commander, Adm Sir Bertram Ramsay.

The initial plan envisaged three divisions landing on three beaches over a 48km front, though this was later revised to five divisions assaulting five beaches along a 96km front. This extended the landings to the Cotentin peninsula, allowing an earlier push for the port of Cherbourg. From the Allied left to right: in the east, British airborne forces took key bridges across the canals and protected the flank, British forces (with one unit of French commandos) landed on Sword Beach, British and Canadian at Juno, British at Gold, and US troops at Omaha and Utah, with US airborne forces dropping on the western flank. The Allied forces conducting the operation included 1213 warships from battleships to midget submarines, some 4125 amphibious ships and craft as well as hundreds of merchant ships, over 11,000 aircraft and 130,000 soldiers with 2000 tanks and 12,000 other vehicles. Atrocious weather caused Eisenhower to take the option of a 24-hour postponement; the decision to go ahead on 6 June was marginal, but while the continuing bad weather caused considerable problems for the airborne and amphibious forces, it also helped the landings to achieve surprise.

German forces had heavily defended the beaches with underwater obstacles, barbed wire and minefields backed by fortified artillery, machine-gun and infantry bunkers, with supporting defensive positions inland. Armoured reserves, with which Germany planned to push the invaders back into the sea, were mainly held back some distance from the beaches. The Allies sought to defeat these defences by heavy preliminary naval bombardment and bombing, airborne and commando assaults against key batteries, then by use of combat engineers, amphibious tanks and – on the British and Canadian beaches – specialist engineering vehicles known as 'Hobart's funnies'. The defensive positions put up stout resistance for a time, especially at Omaha where the landings came closest to failure, but they were eventually isolated and overwhelmed. The Allies suffered 10,300 casualties but managed to land 132,000 men by the end of D-Day. Although the breakout would take longer than expected, the Allies had successfully breached Germany's Atlantic Wall.

■ SAINT-LÔ, 2–19 JULY 1944

A crossroads on the Vere river, Saint-Lô was crucial in wresting Brittany and Normandy from German control. By 19 July, the US First Army had pushed the German Seventh Army out into the Falaise Gap, setting the stage for the liberation of France.

■ CAEN, JULY 1944

A key objective for the first day of the Allied invasion of Normandy, German resistance at Caen led to a month of hard fighting, including an attack by heavy bombers from RAF Bomber Command that destroyed much of the city on 7 July 1944 as a precursor to the final assault (Operation *Charnwood*). The bombing was followed by a full assault on 8 and 9 July, in which British and Canadian forces finally removed the Germans from the city.

■ FALAISE-ARGENTAN POCKET, 25 JULY–23 AUGUST 1944

Between 25 July and 5 August, the US First Army broke the western German front in Normandy, and American forces raced south to the apex of the Normandy peninsula, enabling further advances west into Brittany, south toward the River Loire and east toward the River Seine. The abortive 6–7 August German armoured counter-attack to seal off the American penetration simply pushed German forces west and deeper into an emergent pocket forming in the Condé-Falaise-Argentan area. On 19 August, the Canadian-Polish advance south from Falaise linked up at Trun-Chambois with the northward American advance from Argentan, trapping 100,000 German troops in a pocket. As II SS-Panzer Corps struck from outside the pocket at the eastern-facing Allied 'plug' of the Trun-Chambois pocket, the desperate forces trapped inside struck the plug's western face. In the ensuing breakout 40,000 German troops escaped, although they were forced to leave their heavy equipment and many of their vehicles behind.

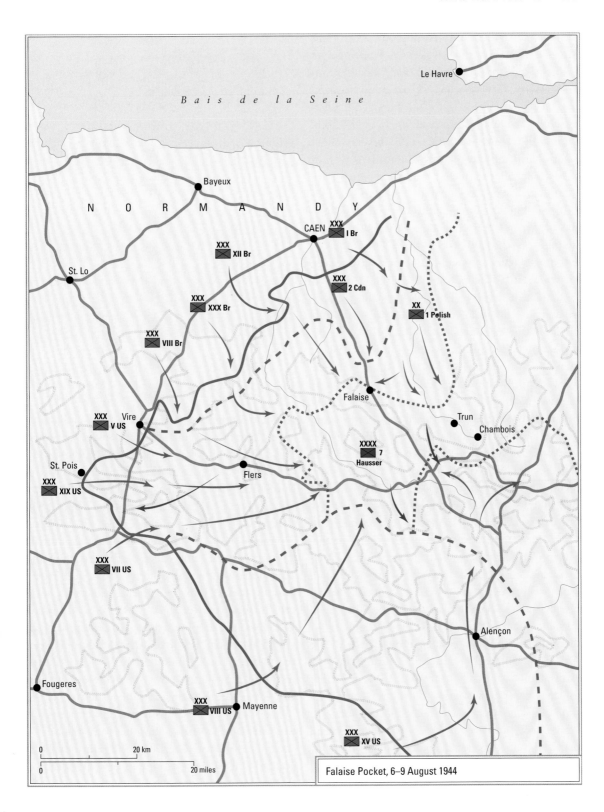

Le Havre

Bais de la Seine

Bayeux

N O R M A N D Y

St. Lo

CAEN

XXX 1 Br

XXX XII Br

XXX 2 Cdn

XX 1 Polish

XXX XXX Br

XXX VIII Br

Falaise

Trun

Chambois

XXX V US

Vire

XXXX 7 Hausser

St. Pois

Flers

XXX XIX US

XXX VII US

Alençon

Fougeres

XXX VIII US

Mayenne

XXX XV US

0   20 km

0   20 miles

Falaise Pocket, 6–9 August 1944

■ **SOUTHERN FRANCE, 15 AUGUST–11 SEPT 1944**

On 15–16 August 1944, American–French forces landed on France's south-eastern Mediterranean coast. With Army Group G's defenders reduced to 90,000 by drafts sent to Normandy, the Allies established an 80km-deep bridgehead by the 18th. During 19 August–11 September, 150,000 Allied troops pursued the withdrawing German forces up the Rhône valley until the latter linked up with the German front in north-eastern France. The Allies incurred 17,000 casualties, the Germans 157,000, including 130,000 trapped in south-western France.

■ **PARIS, 19–25 AUGUST 1944**

Beginning with a general strike and an uprising by the French Resistance, the liberation of Paris concluded with Free French armies and the US 4th Infantry Division entering the city to capture 12,800 German troops.

■ **SIEGFRIED LINE, 12 SEPT 1944–10 MAR 1945**

Between 12 September 1944 and 10 March 1945, Western Allied troops fought their way through the German Siegfried Line defences, which stretched for 635km along Germany's western border near Nijmegen down to the Swiss border at Basle.

■ **HÜRTGEN FOREST, 14 SEPT 1944–10 FEB 1945**

Between 14 September 1944 and 10 February 1945, 90,000 US First Army troops were locked in a protracted battle with 80,000 German troops from Army Group B, deployed in the Siegfried Line defences within the 130km² area of the Hürtgen Forest, which was located close to the German border with Belgium. The main American objective was to reach the German dams astride the Roer river. The Americans suffered 29,000 combat casualties, and the Germans 27,000 casualties.

■ **ARNHEM, 17–21 SEPTEMBER 1944**

On 17 September 1944, the Anglo-Canadian 21st Army Group and the First Allied Airborne Army initiated Operation *Market Garden*, an audacious ground offensive augmented by the dropping of three Allied airborne divisions into the German rear. The plan envisaged that as XXX Corps thrust rapidly north, Allied airborne forces would land in the Zon-Veghel, Nijmegen-Groesbeek, and

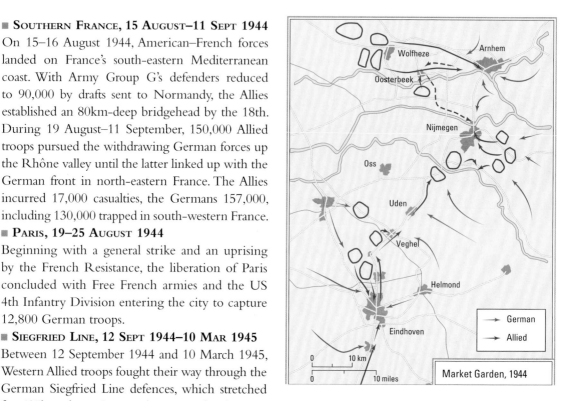

Market Garden, 1944

Arnhem-Oosterbeek areas in southern Holland to secure key bridges, including that over the Rhine bridge at Arnhem. The German Army Group B reacted swiftly to these landings, redeploying numerous battlegroups of garrison troops, backed by the 5000 survivors of the elite II SS-Panzer Corps. That day, the British 1st Airborne Division began landing at Oosterbeek, north-west of Arnhem. Subsequently, the 1st Parachute Brigade advanced on Arnhem, with LCol Frost's 2nd Parachute Battalion pushing south to seize the northern end of the key Rhine road bridge. However, the improvised SS battlegroups *Krafft* and *Spindler* blocked 1st Brigade's advance from reinforcing Frost's positions at the bridge. The next morning, Frost's unit destroyed an SS recce battalion that stormed the bridge, and then dug in, waiting in vain for XXX Corps to arrive. In the meantime, the Germans had rushed another 10 battalions to the Arnhem-Oosterbeek area, and a further 24 to contain the American landings and block XXX Corps' advance. During 19–20 September, II SS-

Corps units repeatedly attacked Frost's positions, inflicting severe casualties. Eventually, at noon on 21 September, after four days of heroic resistance, these attacks overwhelmed Frost's few remaining unwounded soldiers; XXX Corps was then still 16km south of Arnhem bridge. Subsequent German attacks forced 1st Airborne Division's remnants at Oosterbeek to withdraw, ending *Market Garden*. The German and British forces suffered 4000 and 7500 casualties respectively in the Arnhem-Oosterbeek area.

■ **AACHEN, 2–21 OCTOBER 1944**

During 2–21 October 1944, 70,000 US First Army troops battered through the German Siegfried Line defences that protected Aachen, manned by 19,000 LXXXI Corps troops. Captured on the 21st, it was the first German city overrun by the Western Allies.

■ **ARDENNES (BATTLE OF THE BULGE), 16 DEC 1944–15 JAN 1945**

On 16 December 1944, the beleaguered German forces on the Western Front launched a surprise counter-offensive in the hilly and forested Ardennes region; the area's unsuitability for armoured warfare meant that the Americans only deployed four divisions in this sector. At Hitler's insistence, the counter-offensive's objective was to advance 150km to seize the vital port of Antwerp. This was far too ambitious given the limited German resources available (particularly the lack of fuel) and the size of Allied reserves that could be committed to stop the attack. Three armies from GenFM Walther Model's Army Group B commenced the counter-offensive on the 16th amid bad weather that would keep Allied tactical air power grounded. SS-Oberstgruppenführer Dietrich's Sixth Panzer Army attacked in the north, while Panzer Gen Hasso von Manteuffel's Fifth Panzer Army struck in the south. Gen Erich Brandenburger's Seventh Army mounted limited subsidiary attacks to protect Manteuffel's southern flank. In the north, Battlegroup *Peiper* spearheaded the advance of the 1st SS-Panzer

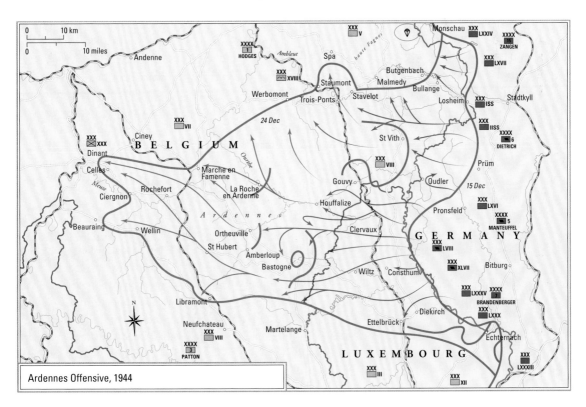

Ardennes Offensive, 1944

Division *Leibstandarte*. During 17–20 December, this battlegroup fought its way 40km forward to Stoumont, but Allied counter-attacks encircled and all but destroyed the unit. With this, Dietrich's advance in the north stalled. In the south, the Fifth Panzer Army enjoyed greater success, with the 2nd Panzer Division advancing by 23 December to within 6km of the River Meuse bridges. By then, its tanks had virtually run out of petrol, having failed to capture Allied fuel dumps. However, later that day, American reinforcements launched large-scale counter-attacks against the German salient or 'Bulge' as it became known. The widening Allied counter-offensive gradually drove the Germans back until, by mid-January 1945, they were back at their 16 December starting positions.

St Vith, 16–24 December 1944

A key objective for the Germans during the Battle of the Bulge in 1944, St Vith fell after several days of hard fighting. This unhinged the German timetable for their offensive. The town was recaptured by the Allies in January 1945.

■ Bastogne, 20–27 December 1944

The site of a major arterial road link in Belgium, Bastogne was a critical initial objective for the Germans during the Ardennes Offensive of 1944. As the Germans converged on Bastogne after overcoming stiff resistance from isolated American formations, Gen Dwight D. Eisenhower dispatched the 82nd and 101st Airborne Divisions to Bastogne to bolster the defences. From 20 December, the Germans besieged Bastogne, outnumbering the encircled paratroopers. On 22 December, a German demand for the Americans to surrender was famously turned down by BGen Anthony McAullife, the acting commander of 101st Airborne, with a single word – 'Nuts'. From 23 December, improved weather conditions enabled aerial resupply of the town as well as attacks on the Germans. On 27 December, lead elements of the American 4th Armoured Division broke through

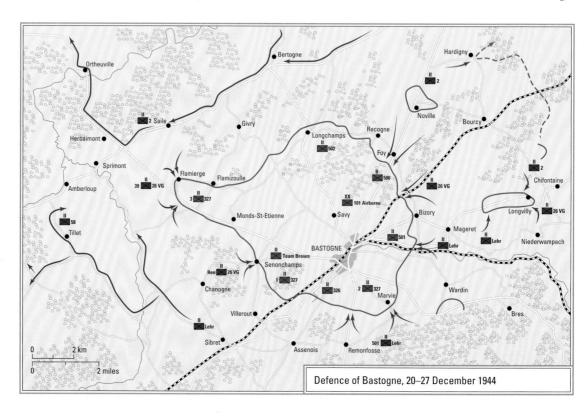

Defence of Bastogne, 20–27 December 1944

German lines and established a corridor to the town, lifting the siege.

■ **CELLES 1944, 25 DECEMBER 1944**

On Christmas Eve 1944 the German 2nd Panzer Division reached Celles, Belgium. This was the high-water mark of Nazi westward penetration during the Battle of the Bulge. The US First Army's VII Corps retook Celles and halted the German advance.

■ **RHINELAND, 8 FEBRUARY–10 MARCH 1945**

During February and March 1945, the 850,000 troops of Canadian First and US Ninth Armies pushed back the 400,000 troops of the German First Parachute Army from the River Maas to the Rhine at Wesel.

■ **REMAGEN, 8–23 MARCH 1945**

On 7 March 1945, American forces reached the sole remaining bridge across the River Rhine, located at Remagen. The defenders detonated demolition charges, but despite a massive explosion the bridge remained obstinately intact. American forces quickly captured the bridge and poured reinforcements across to form a bridgehead. Despite facing fierce counter-attacks, the American forces burst out of the bridgehead on 23 March, crushing the German attempt to halt the Allied advance along the Rhine.

■ **WEST GERMANY, 8 MARCH–8 MAY 1945**

During March 1945, 3.6 million Western Allied troops smashed the Germans' River Rhine defences. Between late March and early May, the Anglo-Canadian 21st Army Group advanced rapidly north/north-eastward to liberate most of the Netherlands and northern Germany up to Schleswig-Holstein. Meanwhile, two American army groups thrust east to reach the Elbe and link up with the westward Soviet advance, as well as thrust south/south-east into northern Italy, northern Austria and western Czechoslovakia by Germany's 8 May capitulation

■ **RUHR POCKET, 23 MARCH–18 APRIL 1945**

During 23 March–1 April, two American armies surrounded Army Group B's 360,000 troops in a 115km-deep pocket around the key Ruhr

industrial zone in the German heartland. The last of the 330,000 Germans to surrender did so on 18 April.

Africa and Middle East 1940–43

■ **NORTH AFRICA, 10 JUNE 1940–13 MAY 1943**

From 10 June 1940 (fascist Italy's declaration of war) to 13 May 1943 (the surrender of Axis forces in Tunisia), British, Commonwealth and Allied forces fought the Axis for control of colonial North Africa. Due to the conditions, the desert war was a challenging course for the leadership, training and technology of both sides' armies. Fortune often favoured better tactics and weaponry against superior numbers. Italy's 500,000-strong Libyan Army expected to crush easily the 50,000 troops garrisoning British Egypt. In fact, from December 1940 to February 1941, the British caused 130,000 casualties and routed Mussolini's troops. However, the British broke off pursuit to re-deploy for the disastrous defence of Crete. The German Afrikakorps seized this opportunity to buttress the collapsing Italian front, turning the tide for two years until the US Army arrived to help open a new front in the western North Africa.

■ **MALTA, JUNE 1940–NOVEMBER 1942**

Malta, situated at the intersection of British communications between Gibraltar and Suez, and Axis communications between Europe and North Africa, was pivotal to British control of the sea and air in the Mediterranean and hence was the key to the Middle East campaign. Italy and Germany looked to neutralize Malta by heavy bombing (an airborne invasion was planned but never carried out) but the besieged population held out, earning a collective George Cross for gallantry. A series of convoys fought through to supply the vital island, suffering heavy losses, notably Operation *Pedestal* in August 1942 in which five of 14 merchant ships reached Malta, including the tanker *Ohio*. Royal Navy warships and submarines, with Fleet Air Arm (FAA) and Royal Air Force aircraft operating from the island attacked Axis supply lines, inflicting increasing losses that severely limited the supplies reaching Rommel.

■ **EAST AFRICA, AUGUST 1940–DECEMBER 1941**
Following Italian entry into WWII in June 1940, Mussolini sought to take possession of various British colonies in East Africa. The Italians seized British Somaliland between 3 and 19 August 1940. A British counter-offensive began in January 1941, and over the course of the next 11 months, British forces drove the Italians out of East Africa, regaining lost territory, taking over Italian colonies and liberating Ethiopia.

■ **WEST AFRICA SEPTEMBER–NOVEMBER 1940–43**
The British and Free French fought the Vichy government at Dakar and Libreville to control these French colonies. At Dakar, the Royal Navy and Free French were repulsed. They succeeded at Gabon, with Gen de Gaulle winning all French Equatorial Africa.

■ **DAKAR, 23–25 SEPTEMBER 1940**
This Vichy-French controlled port and air base in West Africa was the target of a show of force by Britain with the Free French, aiming to coerce the colony into joining the Allied side. The attempt failed conspicuously – Vichy forces remained defiant.

■ **SIDI BARRANI, 13 SEP–11 DECEMBER 1940**
Italian Marshal Graziani's 10 divisions expected an easy victory over the British Egyptian garrison of 36,000 troops. During Operation *Compass*, a British counter-attack at Sidi Barrani cost the Italians 38,300 troops, 237 guns and 73 tanks.

■ **BARDIA, 3–5 JANUARY 1941**
The Australian 6th Division, supported by Matilda II infantry tanks of the British 7th Royal Tank Regiment, captured the Italian fortress of Bardia, Libya, killing 1000 enemy soldiers and taking 36,000 prisoners.

■ **TOBRUK I, 6–22 JANUARY 1941**
The Australian 6th Division, supported by the British 7th Armoured Division, surrounded Tobruk in the drive to oust fascist Italy from North Africa. On 21 January, the Allies, under MGen

Iven Mackay, attacked under a withering artillery barrage and airstrikes. Australian infantry, backed by British tanks and machine guns, breached the Italian perimeter and conquered the city on 22 January. Mussolini's army lost 25,000 men, who were captured, killed or wounded.

■ **BEDA FOMM, 5–7 FEBRUARY 1941**
During Operation *Compass*, British and Commonwealth forces, under MGen Sir Michael Creagh, caught and destroyed the retreating Italian Tenth Army at Beda Fomm on the Libyan coast. An ad hoc combined arms group under LCol John Combe led the attack with 500 riflemen, a tank squadron and a few field guns. 'Combe Force' decimated LGen Ferdinando Cona's 20,000-strong Italian army, including several medium tank battalions.

■ **HABBANIYA, APRIL 1941**
A *coup d'etat* in Iraq by pro-German elements in April 1941 led to the major British base at Habbaniya being besieged. The British forces there, using a motley assortment of training aircraft, drove the Iraqi forces back to Fallujah, where they were defeated by British reinforcements.

■ **TOBRUK II, 10 APRIL–10 DECEMBER 1941**
Outnumbered and outgunned, British, Commonwealth and Allied forces successfully held the Libyan seaport against a siege by LGen Erwin Rommel's Afrikakorps and the Italian XXI Infantry Corps. The fierce fighting cost a total of 8000 Axis and 3000 Allied killed and wounded.

■ **SOLLUM-HALFAYA PASS, MAY–NOVEMBER 1941**
The Afrikakorps held the ancient Roman port of Sollum, on the Libyan-Egyptian border, against a series of British thrusts to relieve Tobruk. Dug in at the Halfaya Pass, Rommel's deadly anti-tank artillery earned it the nickname 'Hellfire Pass'.

■ **SIDI REZEGH, 21–22 NOVEMBER 1941**
Although outnumbered and low on fuel, Rommel's 15th and 21st Panzer Divisions decisively defeated the British 7th and 22nd Armoured Brigades and infantry to recapture the vital airfield at Sidi Rezegh, 32km from Tobruk.

■ **GAZALA, 27 MAY–21 JUNE 1942**

At dawn on 27 May, an Axis force of approximately 90,000 men and 560 tanks attacked the British Eighth Army line south of Gazala. Rommel's 21st Panzer Division flanked the Allies' line at Bir Hacheim, but was halted by the Free French 1st Brigade. On 4 June, an Eighth Army counter-attack failed, costing two infantry brigades and four artillery regiments. Rommel encircled Tobruk and drove the remnants of the British XIII Corps east toward the Egyptian frontier.

■ **TOBRUK III, 20–21 JUNE 1942**

MGen Klopper, of the South African 2nd Division, attempted to hold Tobruk with four infantry brigades, supporting artillery and a few tanks. Isolated, the garrison fell to a combined arms attack by Axis land and air forces.

■ **METSA MATRUH, 22–28 JUNE 1942**

The British Eighth Army withdrew toward El Alamein, Egypt. On 26 June, German armour penetrated defences at Metsa Matruh. By 28 June, the Axis advance had overrun the 29th Brigade of the Indian 5th Division, which defended X Corps' retirement south.

■ **FIRST EL ALAMEIN, 1–27 JULY 1942**

The first battle of El Alamein saw the British Eighth Army check the second advance into Egypt by the German Afrikakorps under GenFM Erwin Rommel.

■ **ALAM EL HALFA, 30 AUGUST–5 SEPTEMBER 1942**

Fought between the British and the Germans, Alam el Halfa was an attempt by Rommel to envelop the British and defeat them before the Allies could reinforce North Africa. Under Gen Bernard Montgomery, the British deployed on Alam el Halfa Ridge in a strong defensive position. Unable to break through, and with his logistics breaking down, Rommel withdrew, his ability to launch future offensives now fatally compromised.

■ **SECOND EL ALAMEIN, 23 OCT–11 NOV 1942**

After the success of the battle of Alam el Halfa, Montgomery planned to go on the offensive with Eighth Army against the Afrikakorps. He sought to fight a setpiece battle that would enable him to drive German forces out of Egypt and end any possibility of them taking that country, with the ultimate aim of setting conditions for future operations, leading to the defeat of Rommel's Afrikakorps. After several weeks of planning and preparation, the second battle of El Alamein began with Operation *Lightfoot* on the night of 23–24 October 1942 with a massive artillery barrage. An infantry attack was sent in, followed by engineers who were to clear a path through the extensive minefields in front of the German positions, thus enabling British armour to advance. Although this was done successfully, the pace at which lanes were cleared was slower than planned and there were several delays caused by tanks breaking down and blocking the route. Therefore, the first phase of the attack fell short of its intended objectives and the attacking infantry had to dig in and consolidate.

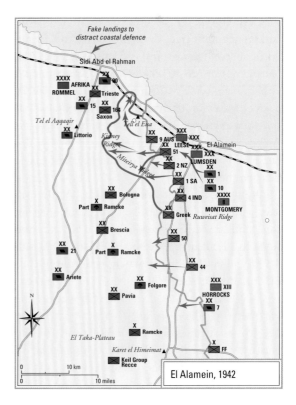

El Alamein, 1942

The attack continued over the next few days as part of what Montgomery referred to as the 'crumbling' of the Axis positions. Fighting was hard and progress slow, causing anxiety among the British War Cabinet that the offensive was about to stall. Rommel, who had been on sick leave in Italy when the battle began, returned to North Africa and launched a counter-attack against the British positions in the north of the battle area. Again, the fighting was hard and progress was slow going. Montgomery became concerned that the offensive was losing momentum and therefore made alterations to his plan, thinning out the frontline so as to create a mobile reserve which could attack elsewhere along the front. The attrition of the opening three days of battle upon the Axis forces was significant. As well as losses in men, armour and aircraft, their supplies were now becoming critical. The fighting continued over the next few days, with little signs of a decision being reached.

On 2 November, Montgomery launched Operation *Supercharge*, with the aim of forcing the Axis troops out of their defensive positions and seizing their lines of supply. The attack began with a seven-hour-long air attack against the German positions at Tel el Aqqaqir and Sidi Abd el Rahman, followed by a further heavy artillery barrage. After more intense fighting, notable for the loss of many British tanks, particularly 9th Armoured Brigade (which lost 102 of its 128 tanks), Eighth Army broke through the last major German positions.

Rommel now concluded that the battle was lost, and prepared to fall back on Fuka (despite the familiar orders from Hitler to stand and fight to the death). During the course of 3 and 4 November, the Eighth Army began the pursuit of the now-retreating Germans. Over the next week, a series of small actions followed as the Panzer Army Afrika made a fighting withdrawal. On the British side, a combination of bad weather and the need to allow British logistical reorganization led to the pursuit slowing. By 11 November 1942, Axis forces were clear of the Egyptian border, bringing the battle to its climax and beginning the inexorable retreat of German forces to the west..

■ **MEDENINE, 6 MARCH 1943**
Rommel's last battle in North Africa: three divisions of the Fifth Panzer Army, supported by the Italian First Army, unsuccessfully engaged the British 7th Armoured Division in a dawn attack. British artillery fire proved decisive.

■ **THE MARETH LINE, 19–31 MARCH 1943**
A major assault by Allied forces on a natural defensive position held by the Axis forces, which culminated in the Germans falling back on Akarit after their position became untenable.

■ **OPERATION *TORCH*, 8TH–16TH NOVEMBER 1942**
The invasion force of Operation *Torch* comprised 107,000 American, British and Free French troops, who landed in Vichy-held Morocco and Algeria. The Allies were up against a force of 120,000 Vichy troops and their German masters, although whether the French would long resist the Allies was a major unknown. The invasion plan called for the amphibious landing of three task forces at Algiers, Oran and Casablanca. Off the latter target, American naval gunfire and air support sank a French cruiser, six destroyers and six submarines, as well as disabling an unfinished French battleship.

The Vichy troops put up stiff resistance at Oran, until forced to surrender by heavy British naval gunnery and the US 1st Ranger Battalion. The US 509th Parachute Infantry Regiment executed the Americans' first combat airdrop of the war, landing inland to capture airfields south of Oran. At Algiers a successful coup by the French Resistance, coupled with a swift Allied landing, silenced the Vichy guns.

■ **TUNISIA, 17 NOVEMBER 1942–13 MAY 1943**
Following the American landings in Morocco and Algeria in 1942, the Allies had amassed 253,213 troops with which to conquer North Africa. After a fierce defeat, the Axis suffered 200,000 casualties, with 275,000 captured.

KASSERINE PASS, 19–25 FEBRUARY 1943

During 19–22 February 1943, two Panzer divisions from the German–Italian Panzer Army counter-attacked the 30,000 troops of US II Corps who had occupied the Kasserine Pass through the Atlas Mountains in west-central Tunisia. The Germans inflicted a heavy defeat, pushing the Americans 80km north-west to Tébessa, although the threat to their rear posed by the British Eighth Army's advance led them to withdraw from the pass by the 25th; the Germans suffered 2000 casualties, the Americans/British 10,000.

Atlantic, Mediterranean and North Sea 1939–45

ROYAL OAK, 14 OCTOBER 1939

The *Royal Oak* was a British battleship of 29,150 tons with eight 15in guns, launched in 1914, which fought at the battle of Jutland (1916). On 14 October 1939, it became the first Royal Navy battleship to be sunk in WWII when Günther Prien, commanding the U-boat *U-47*, managed to navigate into the anchorage at Scapa Flow in the Orkneys and torpedo the warship. More than 830 of its crew were killed.

GRAF SPEE, 17 DECEMBER 1939

Admiral Graf Spee was a German 'pocket battleship' – a misleading name since with 11in guns it were better armed than cruisers but no match for a major battleship. Used as a commerce raider, it was run to ground in December 1939 at the battle of the River Plate, by the cruisers *Exeter*, *Ajax* and *Achilles*. Its captain took refuge in neutral Montevideo then, confronted by a larger British force, scuttled his ship.

U-BOAT WAR, 1939–44

Despite the Treaty of Versailles prohibiting the Germany Navy from possessing U-boats, a covert programme kept the skills alive for rebuilding and, at the outbreak of war, the U-boat force was 57 strong, of which 39 were available for operations. The campaign began in 1939 with minelaying as well as direct attacks on merchant ships; initially 'prize rules' were followed but these scruples lasted little more than a month. Overall, international law was not allowed to be the hindrance it was in WWI.

The campaign began slowly as U-boat production was not yet a priority. From mid-1940 – a period referred to by U-boat crews as the 'happy time' – the losses inflicted on shipping began to increase for several reasons. First, although the Allies introduced a convoy system from the outset, it was far from comprehensive and there were few escorts available, giving the gradually increasing force of U-boats plenty of targets. Second, the U-boats tended to attack on the surface (which negated the Asdic/sonar on which British anti-submarine planning had relied) and at night (which made visual detection very difficult). Third, the fall of France allowed U-boats to be based on the French Atlantic coast. This, with the occupation of Norway, made the passage of U-boats from their bases

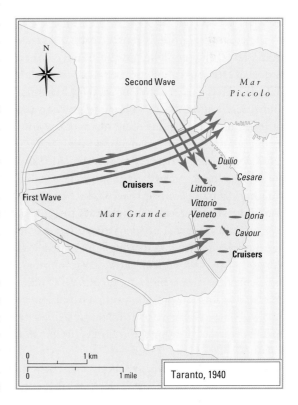

Taranto, 1940

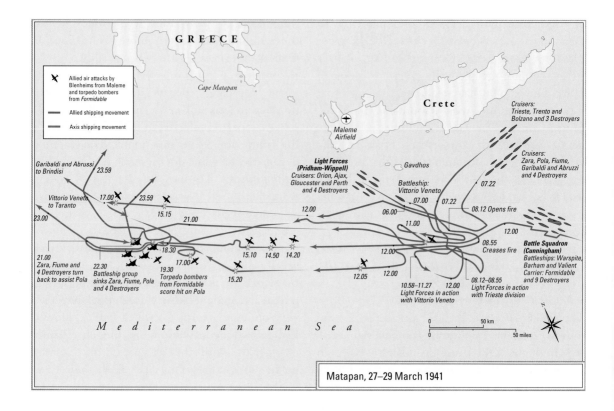

Matapan, 27–29 March 1941

to their hunting grounds much easier and faster (and meant they could avoid the heavily mined Straits of Dover); it also let them spend longer on patrol and reduced the time needed for rearming and repair. The result was a huge increase in the number of boats operational at any one time, even before higher production took effect. The conquered territory also provided bases for long-range aircraft that spotted convoys for the U-boats. Fourth, the U-boats began to use 'wolfpack' tactics, which Adm Karl Dönitz, who commanded the campaign, had devised in the interwar years. These sought to defeat the convoy system by concentrating large numbers of U-boats to overwhelm its escorts and inflict devastating losses rather than simply sinking one or two ships. German codebreaking helped to locate convoys, although the ability to do this eventually lapsed.

Gradually, the campaign tipped against Germany. The number of escorts available to their enemies steadily increased, as did their effectiveness. The Allies also had the priceless advantage of Ultra signals intelligence, which – apart from a dark period through much of 1942 – allowed them to route convoys away from patrolling U-boats. Allied counter-measures improved, notably with radar fitted to warships and aircraft, which could detect surfaced U-boats. The U-boats inflicted heavy losses during 1942, not least during Operation *Drumbeat* off the American coast, when they took full advantage of the remarkable unpreparedness of the USA following its entry into the war. November 1942 saw the highest losses of shipping inflicted throughout the war, leading to shortages of fuel, food and raw material in Britain. During 1943, however, there were fewer successful attacks by each U-boat, while their own losses increased (killing off experienced commanders), as the escorts – particularly escort carriers – became more numerous and effective, and as the Atlantic 'air gap' was closed. In May 1943, Dönitz effectively admitted defeat by withdrawing his U-boats from the North Atlantic. The campaign continued, but the escorts were increasingly dominant. The U-boat war saw over 14.5 million tons of merchant shipping sunk, for the loss of 785 of the 1100 U-boats.

■ MERS EL KEBIR, 3 JULY 1940

After the fall of France, Britain feared French warships falling into German hands and was unwilling to trust French or German assurances. Adm Marcel Gensoul, commander at the Mers el Kebir base in Algeria, declined a range of options to neutralize his fleet so on 3 July 1940, Force H, under VAdm James Somerville, opened fire, sinking the battleship *Bretagne* and immobilizing the battleships *Provence* and *Dunkerque*, killing nearly 1300 French sailors.

■ CONVOY SC-7, 16–19 OCTOBER 1940

A Canada-to-Britain convoy of 35 merchant ships escorted by six warships, in October 1940. German U-boats sank 17 of the merchant ships and damaged three more, demonstrating the effectiveness of their 'wolfpack' tactics of concentration.

■ TARANTO, 11–12 NOVEMBER 1940

The Mediterranean naval balance was precarious after the fall of France and the declaration of war by Italy, with the Royal Navy facing not only German naval and air forces but also the apparently powerful Italian fleet. The latter seemed reluctant to give battle, and after some early successes the commander-in-chief of the British Mediterranean fleet, Adm Andrew B. Cunningham, sought to deal a decisive blow to his enemy. He ordered Operation *Judgement*, a long-considered attack by carrier aircraft on the main Italian fleet in its well-defended base at Taranto, on 11–12 November 1940. It was carefully planned using photographs taken by Malta-based RAF reconnaissance aircraft; the original plan envisaged two carriers, but battle damage ruled out *Eagle*, though some of its aircraft and aircrews strengthened the air group of *Illustrious*. The attack took place at night due to the deficiencies of British naval aircraft, and involved 21 Swordfish torpedo biplanes (the main striking force was 12 torpedo-bombers). Some dropped flares, others bombed defences and alternative targets. Attacking in two waves and flying very low to avoid balloon defences and heavy anti-aircraft fire, the British aircraft achieved several hits on the anchored battleships – silhouetted against the flares – using torpedoes specially modified to operate in the shallow water of a port (an innovation pioneered by the Japanese Navy). Three battleships were sunk: *Littorio*, *Caio Duilio* and *Conte Di Cavour*; the last was never repaired and the other two were out of commission for up to six months. The Fleet Air Arm lost two aircraft in total, an impressively low rate of casualties considering the objectives. The result was to shift the material – and the psychological – naval balance in the Mediterranean. More broadly, it confirmed the strike potential of the aircraft carrier.

■ MATAPAN, 27–29 MARCH 1941

In March 1941, Italian cruisers supported by the battleship *Vittorio Veneto*, under Adm Angelo Iachino, sortied to attack Allied convoys to Greece. Four British light cruisers narrowly escaped this force, but the battleship came under attack from carrier aircraft. Lacking air cover, Iachino felt compelled to withdraw.

Further air strikes damaged *Vittorio Veneto* but did not slow it as Adm Andrew Cunningham – forewarned by signals intelligence – brought up his main force into the attack. The heavy cruiser *Pola* was torpedoed by an aircraft from *Formidable* and left immobilized. Unaware of the proximity of British capital ships, Iachino sent a surface force to assist it. They were taken by surprise in a night engagement by the powerful battleship force of *Barham*, *Warspite* and *Valiant*, resulting in the loss of three heavy cruisers (*Pola*, *Fiume* and *Zara*) and two destroyers. The Royal Navy lost one torpedo bomber in the action, making Matapan a signal success for the Allies.

■ HMS *HOOD,* MAY 1941

Hood was a British battlecruiser (eight 15in guns),

Sinking the *Bismarck*, 1941

GREENLAND

Limit of solid ice

Denmark Str

Norwegian Sea

0400
23.05.41
2332
2132
1250
1300
1420
1821
2037
2148
2338
0047
24.05.41
0532
0620
0724
Hood
1100
1345
1814
2230
25.05.41

ICELAND

Prince of Wales
withdraws

Faroe Is

Shetland Is

1800

1237

Orkney Is
Scapa Flow
Gulf of Moray

NORTH
ATLANTIC
OCEAN

North Sea

North Sea

Belchen
U93
U43
U46
U557
U66
U94
2
spy ships

Torpedo attack
by *Victorious*

2400
22.05.41

0200
21.05.41

Skagerrak Str

DENMARK

Baltic Sea

Departs from
Gotenhafen (Gdynia)
2130
18.05.41

POLAND

GERMANY

NETH

BELGIUM LUX

CZECHOSLOVAKIA

0617
0700

Course correction
1400

Route of
Prinz Eugen

2400
26.05.41

1030
26.05.41 1155

1620

Bismarck
respotted by plane

UNITED KINGDOM

IRELAND

St. Georges Channel

English Channel

U73
U556
U96
U97
U48

Bismarck
U552

FRANCE

SWITZ

HUNGARY

YUGOSLAVIA

Esso Hamburg
tanker

2400
31.05.41

0700

1500

2000

03.00

2400
1.06.41

Bay of
Biscay

ANDORRA

Corsica

Sardinia

ITALY

ALB

Spichern
tanker

Azores Is

PORTUGAL

SPAIN

Balearic Is

Mediterranean Sea

Malta

TUNISIA

ATLANTIC
OCEAN

Madeira Is

Strait of Gibraltar

MOROCCO

Breme

Canary Is

Ifni to
Spain

ALGERIA

LIBYA

WESTERN SAHARA

0   500 km

0   500 miles

launched in 1920 and well known because of its peacetime international deployments. On May 1941, with the battleship *Prince of Wales* it fought the modern German battleship *Bismarck*. The latter hit *Hood* with a shell that penetrated its inadequate deck armour – the curse of battlecruisers engaging battleships. The magazine exploded and *Hood* sank with the loss of all but three of her 1420-man crew.

■ BISMARCK, MAY 1941

A modern German battleship of 42,000 tons, completed in 1940 – fast, well armoured and carrying eight 15in guns – *Bismarck* was one of the most powerful warships afloat. With the heavy cruiser *Prinz Eugen,* she sortied to attack Atlantic shipping in May 1941, commanded by VAdm Günther Lütjens. Britain received intelligence warnings of their intended breakout; they were spotted by air and naval patrols and were intercepted. On 24 May in the battle of the Denmark Strait, they fought the newly commissioned battleship *Prince of Wales* and the obsolescent battlecruiser *Hood*. *Bismarck* sank the latter but suffered damage to her fuel tanks that compelled her to head south-east to return to port in France, shadowed by the Royal Navy, which concentrated forces to eliminate this serious threat to Allied shipping. Air patrols and signals intelligence revealed that *Bismarck* was heading for France and carrier air strikes were launched to slow her down. A minor hit by an aircraft from *Victorious* reduced her speed, while on 26 May a second torpedo attack by Swordfish from *Ark Royal* – closing in from Gibraltar with the battlecruiser *Renown* – to block the route to Brest – slowed her further, damaged her steering and left her unmanoeuvrable. After overnight harassing torpedo attacks by destroyers, on the morning of 27 May, *Bismarck* was caught by the battleships *King George V* and *Rodney*. She fought this unequal battle until all her main armament was knocked out and was finally sunk by torpedoes from the cruiser *Devonshire* (and, according to some accounts,

scuttling by her crew). Only 115 of her crew of 2200 survived. This action effectively ended the use of major German surface warships against Atlantic shipping.

■ ATLANTIC CONVOYS, 1942–45

When confronted once again by a submarine campaign in WWII, Britain avoided the great error of WWI by immediately instituting the convoy and escort system. However, it was far from comprehensive, with independently sailing merchant ships suffering high losses. Its effectiveness was further reduced by the shortage of escorts. This shortfall was worsened by the continued practice of using 'hunting groups', which dispersed anti-submarine vessels that could have been better used escorting convoys. Moreover, during the interwar period much expertise had been lost and few resources were devoted to anti-submarine warfare, partly due to complacency resulting from confidence in Asdic (sonar) – the effectiveness of which was negated by U-boats attacking on the surface. The Royal Navy, with the Royal Canadian Navy, were terribly over-stretched in the early stages of the war, a situation greatly worsened by the fall of France, which provided the U-boat fleet with bases far closer to the shipping lanes. Winston Churchill's acknowledgement that 'the only thing that ever really frightened me during the war was the U-boat peril' can be easily understood.

The campaign would not be won quickly but several factors helped to turn the situation around, slowly reducing losses of shipping while increasing the number of U-boats sunk. First, the number of escorts grew as vessels were freed from other tasks and more were built, especially small corvettes and trawlers, followed by escort carriers, which took airpower to meet the U-boats in mid-ocean. Equally important was the training and experience, which rapidly improved the effectiveness of captains and crews. As more warships became available, the escorts protecting individual convoys could increase, then additional Support Groups were formed that could come to the assistance of a convoy under attack, continuing to prosecute contacts as the convoy moved on. Second, many technological innovations helped combat the threat. Radar fitted to warships allowed them to detect U-boats even when they attacked on the surface at night. More effective depth charges were produced, with launchers that could throw them forward, allowing Asdic contact to be maintained during an attack. Third, aircraft became a far more deadly anti-submarine weapon than they had been in WWI, especially when fitted with radar, searchlights and depth charges. The stubborn reluctance of RAF Bomber Command to provide long-range aircraft to Coastal Command was eventually overcome, and the mid-Atlantic air gap shrank and finally closed.

A crucial advantage for the Allies was the signals intelligence provided by Ultra, especially after the May 1941 capture of a U-boat Enigma machine and code books by a Royal Navy destroyer. Although never leaving German signals completely open or readable – and sometimes suffering periods of blackout – this priceless intelligence allowed convoys to be routed away from U-boats.

Losses remained high during 1942, with November seeing the highest monthly losses of merchant shipping (over 800,000 tons), but the following month Enigma was cracked after a long period during which signals could not be decrypted, and the tide began to turn in the Allies' favour. By the early summer of 1943, the balance of advantage had shifted decisively and, in May, Dönitz recalled the U-boats from the North Atlantic. The Allies lost more than 2800 merchant ships to the U-boats and some 30,000 merchant sailors were killed. The battle of the Atlantic was a close-run thing, but unlike in WWI, the U-boats were eventually comprehensively defeated.

■ CHANNEL DASH, 11–13 FEBRUARY 1942

The battlecruisers *Scharnhorst* and *Gneisenau*, and heavy cruiser *Prinz Eugen*, were repeatedly bombed in Brest so they were ordered back to Germany. Their carefully planned voyage began on 11 February 1942, with strong surface and fighter escorts. Britain was taken by surprise by their passage of the Dover Straits in daylight. Poorly coordinated air and surface attacks failed to inflict significant damage, though both battlecruisers suffered minor damage hitting mines.

■ CONVOY PQ-17, 27 JUNE–10 JULY 1942

One of the Arctic convoys from Iceland to Russia, was timed for June – when ice would force it close to German bases in Norway and constant daylight would worsen the risk of attack – but Russia had to be supplied. The convoy consisted of 36 merchant ships escorted by eight destroyers, two anti-aircraft ships, four corvettes and two submarines, together with close cover of four cruisers and distant cover of two battleships and an aircraft carrier. Working with imperfect information, the Admiralty became (wrongly) convinced that heavy German warships including *Tirpitz* were about to attack and ordered the covering forces to withdraw and the convoy to scatter, making it more vulnerable to air and U-boat attack. Only 11 ships reached Murmansk, with 23 sunk (one grounded and one turned back earlier on).

■ CONVOY ONS-5, 29 APRIL–6 MAY 1943

This Britain-to-Canada convoy was attacked by 41 U-boats; 12 out of 42 merchant ships were lost, but seven U-boats were sunk and five damaged, showing Allied progress in the battle of the Atlantic.

■ DODECANESE ISLANDS, SEPTEMBER 1943

Churchill pushed for action in the Aegean Sea despite the shortage of forces available. In September 1943, British troops landed from warships and took Cos, Leros and other islands. However, Allied commanders would not divert aircraft from Italy, allowing the *Luftwaffe* to retain local air superiority. This made resupply difficult, though naval forces continued to support the garrisons and evacuated them when Germany retook the islands in October and November.

■ *TIRPITZ*, 1943–44

The sister ship of *Bismarck*, commissioned in 1941, *Tirpitz* was a powerful modern battleship (42,000 tons, eight 15in guns). In January 1942, it was moved to Norway to defend against the British invasion that Hitler was convinced would occur. While actually deployed with some caution – it fired on an enemy target only once (when it bombarded Spitzbergen in September 1943) – it remained a potential threat against convoys to Russia. It was joined in Norway by other major German surface ships and their continued presence caused much disruption (including the decision to scatter Convoy PQ-17) and either the Allied deployment of heavy covering forces or, when these could not be spared, a suspension of the Arctic convoys. A succession of operations was

mounted against *Tirpitz*. In 1942, the St Nazaire dock was successfully attacked to hinder any attempted sortie into the Atlantic. Operation *Source* in September 1943 saw *Tirpitz* attacked and immobilized by six 'X-Craft' – midget submarines purpose designed for the task – allowing the Arctic convoys to resume. In April 1944, when Ultra intelligence revealed that the ship's repairs were nearing completion, it was attacked and hit repeatedly by Barracuda bombers from the carriers *Victorious* and *Furious*, keeping it out of action for another three months. Further raids by the Fleet Air Arm and RAF Bomber Command were frustrated by smokescreens or bad weather. In September, Lancasters operating from Russia caused further damage, which compelled Germany to relocate *Tirpitz* to Tromso, for use as a floating defensive battery. On 12 November, a final Lancaster raid achieved several hits and near misses with 5454kg bombs and finally sank her.

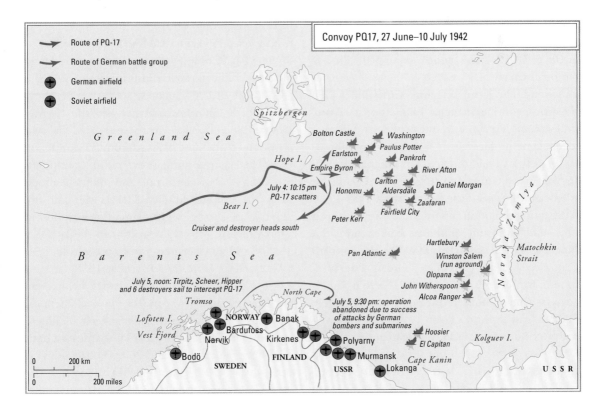

Second Sino-Japanese War 1937–45

■ MARCO POLO BRIDGE, 7 JULY 1937

By 1937, in accordance with the 1901 Boxer Protocol, the Imperial Japanese legation controlled a large area of territory around Peking with 7000–15,000 troops. Japanese military manoeuvres in the region, however, alarmed the Chinese. Tension boiled over in a bloody skirmish on the strategically important Marco Polo Bridge at the walls of Wanping. The bridge linked that city with Peking, and territory to the south controlled by 'Generalissimo' Chiang Kai-shek's National Revolutionary Army.

■ PEKING- TIENTSIN, JULY–AUGUST 1937

Japanese LGen Tashiro's two regiments of infantry and one of artillery, supported by tanks and cavalry, defeated warlord Sung Cheyuan's Twenty-Ninth Army to capture Tientsin and Peking in the opening moves of full-scale war between the two nations.

■ SHANGHAI, 13 AUGUST–26 NOVEMBER 1937

The battle at Shanghai involved almost one million troops, thousands of aircraft and hundreds of tanks in a three-month struggle that cost as many as 350,000 lives. The poorly equipped Chinese nationalist army was well led by Gens Cheng and Zhizhong. The Japanese Tenth Army under Gen Yanagawa and the Shanghai Expeditionary Army under Gen Matsui were surprised by Chinese stubbornness. However, Japanese amphibious landings threatened to encircle Shanghai, forcing the exhausted Chinese to retreat toward Nanking.

■ TAIYUAN, 1 SEPTEMBER–8 NOVEMBER 1937

Attempting to cut off supply and communication lines and push the Chinese armies into the North China Sea, the Japanese sent their North China Area Army to reduce Taiyuan. The two-month battle cost the National Revolutionary Army's 2nd Military Region approximately 100,000 casualties.

■ PINGXINGGUAN, 24–25 SEPTEMBER 1937

Lin Bao's 115th Division of the communist Eighth Route Army destroyed several vehicles, equipment, and killed more than 400 men of the ill-fated Japanese 5th Division's supply column. The narrow Pingxing Pass in China's Shanxi Province provided excellent cover for the ambush.

■ NANKING, 9 OCTOBER–13 DECEMBER 1937

The Japanese Central China Area Army, under Gen Matsui Iwane, fell upon Nanking, capital city of the Chinese Republic. As the Japanese approached, Chiang Kai-shek relocated the government to Wuhan. Warlord Tang Shengzhi commanded the Nanking garrison. On 10 December, the Japanese launched their final assault. Two days later, the Chinese commander ordered a retreat. In the weeks that followed, the Japanese army murdered hundreds of thousands of Chinese in the 'Rape of Nanking'.

■ TAIERZHUANG, 22 MARCH–15 APRIL 1938

In a key battle fought during the Japanese advance to Xuzhou, the Chinese National Revolutionary Army scored its first major success. German-made anti-tank artillery and Russian-made attack aircraft both played roles in this important victory.

■ XUZHOU, 15 APRIL–1 MAY 1938

Some 64 Chinese divisions, approximately 600,000 soldiers, proved insufficient to stop the advance of 240,000 Japanese soldiers at Xuzhou. The North China Area Army and the Central China Expeditionary Army, supported by two armoured battalions, attacked from the south and west. The Japanese outmanoeuvred and outfought the Chinese, but could not prevent their escape from the conquered city. The battle cost the combatants dearly, with the Chinese suffering approximately 100,000 casualties to the Japanese 30,000, and much materiel lost on both sides.

■ WUHAN, 11 JUNE–27 OCTOBER 1938

An important early Japanese victory in the war, the Japanese used airborne tactics and chemical weapons to rout a numerically superior Chinese army under Chiang Kai-shek. The battle cost both sides between 225,000 and 250,000 casualties.

■ NANCHANG, 17 MARCH–9 MAY 1939

By 27 March, the Japanese had penetrated

Nanchang's defences and defeated the National Revolutionary Army there. A counter-attack by Xue Yue's Chinese troops faltered against the Japanese use of air attacks and its timely application of infantry reinforcements.

■ SUIXIANG-ZAOYANG AND SUIZAO-HUIZHAN, 20 APRIL–24 MAY 1939

Three Japanese divisions – approximately 110,000 troops – attacked 220,000 Chinese here. Despite initial gains, the Japanese Eleventh Army retreated as the National Revolutionary Army recaptured the two cities. The battles cost Japanese Gen Yasuji Okamura 13,000 of his men.

■ CHANGSHA I, 17 SEP–6 OCTOBER 1939

In the first of four battles fought for control of the capital of Hunan Province between 1939 and 1941, the Japanese 101st and 106th Divisions attacked. Chinese Nationalist defenders, led by Gen Bai Chongxi, had a two-to-one numerical advantage over the invaders. The Japanese began their attack by shelling Chinese positions with toxic gas. Gen Yasuji Okamura then advanced with a precariously thin battleline, a tactical error that the Chinese fiercely exploited. After inflicting some 40,000 casualties in a counter-attack (costing the Japanese almost half their force), the Chinese routed their opponents. The battle was the first major reversal for the Japanese, whose advance across northern, central and southern China had been unchecked. The Chinese victory came as another in a series of setbacks for the Japanese, who had recently lost to the Soviets the battle of Nomonhan, Manchuria.

■ SOUTH KWANGSI, 15 NOVEMBER 1939–30 NOVEMBER 1940

The Japanese Twenty-First and Twenty-Second Armies landed along the Gulf of Tonkin, invading Kwangsi Province and capturing Nanning. Costly Chinese counter-attacks eventually drove the invaders out.

■ KUNLUN PASS, 18 DECEMBER 1939–11 JANUARY 1940

The National Revolutionary Army's mechanized 200th Division attacked and destroyed a Japanese brigade in the Kunlun Pass, along the main supply route to Chunking. The victory came at the high price of 27,000 Chinese casualties.

■ HUNDRED REGIMENTS OFFENSIVE, 20 AUGUST–5 DECEMBER 1940

In summer 1940, 400,000 soldiers of the communist Eighth Route Army, under Gen Peng Dehuai, confronted more than 800,000 soldiers of the Japanese North China Area Army, under Japanese LGen Hayao Tada. Tada provoked the confrontation by launching campaigns to eliminate communist resistance in central China. The Japanese defined the battlefield by building a fortified road network to compartmentalize the countryside. This network, along with Japanese-held railways and industrial sites, became the targets of Chinese guerillas, beginning with coordinated surprise attacks on the night of 20 August. The communists killed as many as 20,000 Japanese, and another 20,000 Chinese who supported the occupiers. Peng's army suffered at least 20,000 casualties. The battles led to a severe crackdown by the Japanese, who instituted a new policy called 'Three Alls: kill all, burn all, destroy all'.

■ SHANGGAO, 14 MARCH–9 APRIL 1941

Three Japanese divisions of the Eleventh Army, under Gen Korechika Anami attacked the Chinese Nineteenth Army's headquarters. Over 100,000 Chinese troops proved to be more than a match for Anami's 65,000, with both sides suffering more than 20,000 casualties before the Japanese retreated.

■ SOUTH SHANXI, 7–27 MAY 1941

Six divisions of 100,000 Japanese attacked 180,000 troops of the nationalist Fifth Group Army in their mountain fortifications. The Japanese won, inflicting as many as 42,000 casualties and capturing up to 35,000 prisoners.

■ CHANGSHA II, 17–30 SEPTEMBER 1941

Japanese troops of XI Corps, under Gen Tadaki Anan and numbering 120,000, comprising the 3rd, 4th, 6th and 40th Divisions, made their second attempt to seize the capital of Hunan Province.

Ably led by Gen Hsueh Yueh, the Chinese Ninth War Area Army, comprising the Nineteenth and Thirtieth Army Groups and 11 independent corps, successfully halted the Japanese advance. The Japanese lost more than 10,000 of their troops in bitter house-to-house fighting before retreating to Yueyang.

■ CHANGSHA III, 23 DECEMBER 1941– 15 JANUARY 1942

Japanese Gen Yuiki Anami's XI Corps launched a third attack on Changsha, initially to block the Chinese from reinforcing Hong Kong. Once again, 300,000 Chinese under Gen Yueh held their line and pushed the Japanese back across the Luoyang river.

■ WEST HUBEI, 12 MAY–3 JUNE 1943

After enduring as many as 60,000 casualties, Chinese Gen Chen Cheng's 14 army groups forced the withdrawal of Gen Isamu Yokoyama's Japanese, who suffered 25,800 killed and wounded. The Curtiss P-40 Warhawks of American Col Claire Chennault's 'Flying Tigers' supported the Chinese.

■ CHANGDE, 2 NOVEMBER–20 DECEMBER 1943

Japanese Gen Isamu Yokoyama attacked the city with chemicals and bubonic plague. Chinese defenders under Gen Sun Lianzhong withdrew but later reoccupied Changde. However, the Japanese had successfully prevented Chinese reinforcements from reaching other fronts.

■ HENAN-HUNAN-GUANGXI, 19 APRIL– 31 DECEMBER 1944

In the opening move of *Ichi Go* (Operation *One*), 17 divisions successfully split continental China from north to south, by means of three major battles fought in these provinces. China's American allies began to lose confidence in Chiang Kai-shek.

■ CHANGSHA-HENGYANG, MAY–AUGUST 1944

During Operation *One* (the Japanese campaign to conquer territory linking Manchuria in the north with Indochina in the south), 360,000 Japanese troops of the Eleventh Army invaded Hunan Province. One of the campaign's battles involved the fourth attempt to take Changsha. Changing tactics, the Japanese successfully outflanked the Chinese and took the city. Gen Chiang Kai-shek's government found the Chinese Commander at Changsha – Gen Zhang Deneng – guilty of incompetence.

■ GUILIN-LIUZHOU, 16 AUGUST–24 NOVEMBER 1944

In the last phase of Operation *One*, the Japanese sought to consolidate their gains and seize air bases used by China's American ally. Japanese troops numbering 150,000 routed 400,000 Chinese to capture the city after a 10-day battle.

■ WEST HUNAN, 6 APRIL–7 JUNE 1945

In the last major battle of the Second Sino-Japanese War. China's Third, Fourth and Tenth Army Groups, with support from the American Fourteenth Air Force, defeated the Japanese Twentieth Army as the fortunes of war turned irreversibly against the Chrysanthemum Throne.

The Pacific 1941–42

■ PEARL HARBOR, 7 DECEMBER 1941

The surprise Japanese attack on the United States Pacific Fleet at Pearl Harbor on Oahu in the Hawaiian Islands, on 7 December 1941, initiated WWII in the Pacific. During 1930–41, Japanese military and economic expansionism into China and South-east Asia led to significantly deteriorating relations with the USA. Many Japanese leaders felt that America would prevent Japan from acquiring the colonies in British Malaya and the Dutch East Indies it required to assume Japan's rightful place near the top of the league of states. Strategic planning by the Japanese military concluded that Japan was unlikely to win a war with America, given the USA's immense economic and military potential. As this level of disparity in military and economic potential was only likely to increase in future years, some military commanders advocated the immediate initiation of hostilities against the USA. If a surprise and sudden Japanese strike could place the enemy

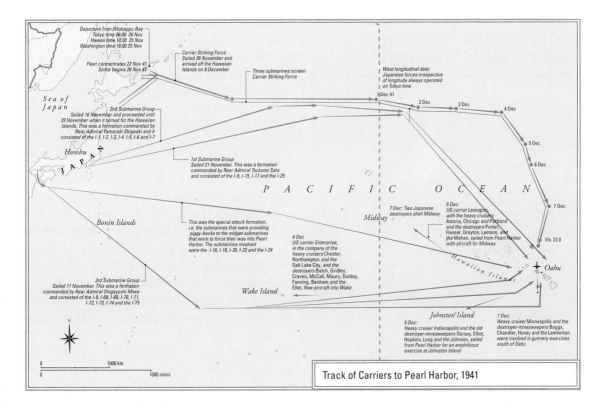

Track of Carriers to Pearl Harbor, 1941

on the back-foot, Japanese forces might be able to exploit this by capturing Malaya and the East Indies, thus gaining additional economic resources and altering the course of the war in Japan's favour.

Japan thus decided to use carrier-based naval aircraft to mount a surprise strike on the American Pacific Fleet as it sat in anchor at Pearl Harbor. The operation's main aims were to destroy the three American fleet carriers *Enterpise*, *Lexington* and *Saratoga*, as well as the rest of the American fleet. On 26 November, Adm Isoroku Yamamoto's Combined Fleet set sail from Japan; this included an escort force of two battleships, three cruisers and nine destroyers, plus Adm Chuichi Nagumo's strike force of six carriers with 408 aircraft on board.

By early morning on 7 December, the fleet had reached a point north of Oahu. At 07:38 the first wave of 183 aircraft, mainly torpedo- and dive-bombers, left the carriers and attacked the

American fleet. Subsequently, the 171 aircraft of the second wave attacked, concentrating on enemy airfields. Simultaneously, five Japanese submarines each launched a single midget submarine, but these operations achieved little. Just after the first attacks had commenced, the Japanese ambassador in Washington issued the Japanese declaration of war.

By the end of the day, the Japanese aerial strike on Pearl Harbor had been a stunning success, in what was probably the greatest feat of naval aviation witnessed in any war. The Japanese attacks sank four battleships and two destroyers, and severely damaged three battleships, three cruisers and four other vessels. The attacks also wrecked 188 aircraft and damaged a further 153, and caused significant personnel casualties, amounting to 2402 killed and 1282 wounded. The Japanese suffered only light casualties, including 29 aircraft and five midget submarines lost, together with 66 personnel casualties.

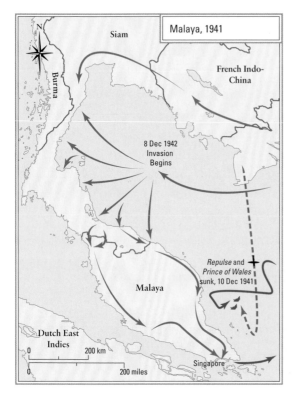

Malaya, 1941

The only sour note in the day's triumph, from the Japanese perspective, was that the critical American aircraft carriers had not been in Pearl Harbor that day.

The failure to destroy America's naval air capability would come to haunt the subsequent Japanese war effort. Although the attack and the scale of the losses suffered exerted a massive psychological effect on the USA this steeled the American nation to avenge the setback, rather than undermining American will and determination. Over the ensuing months and years, the US gradually gained the upper hand in the Pacific War.

■ HONG KONG, 8–25 DECEMBER 1941

MGen Christopher Maltby's 14,000 defenders faced an overwhelming attack by 52,000 soldiers of the Japanese Tweny-Third Army. After 18 days of street fighting, Hong Kong governor Sir Mark Young surrendered on the date now known as 'Black Christmas'.

■ MALAYA, 8 DECEMBER 1941–31 JANUARY 1942

The Japanese launched a determined campaign to defeat British and Commonwealth forces and complete their imperial conquest of South-east Asia. They faced LGen Arthur Percival, who commanded 88,600 men of the British Malaya Command (including the Indian III Corps and the Australia Imperial Force). With the Royal Navy occupied elsewhere, the Japanese established a beachhead at Kota Bharu. There, the Twenty-Fifth Army, under LGen Tomoyuki Yamashita, landed 70,000 soldiers (including the crack Imperial Guards Division and 200 light tanks). The troops quickly advanced down the Malay peninsula, successfully employing close air support, bicycle infantry and fast armour tactics to overwhelm the defenders and capture Kuala Lumpur. By the end of January 1942, Malaya Command had suffered devastating losses. Australian LCol Charles Anderson led the survivors in a desperate fight to cover the withdrawal to Singapore.

■ WAKE ISLAND, 8–23 DECEMBER 1941

Within hours of the air attack on Pearl Harbor, the Japanese pounced on Wake Island, an outpost in the North Pacific and a strategic link in the chain connecting the mainland with American possessions in the Philippines. The US Marine garrison repelled the first landing. However, the Japanese returned with 2500 infantry (including 1500 marines). The landing force overwhelmed the defenders and captured the atoll, which the Japanese held until the end of the war.

■ GUAM I, 8–10 DECEMBER 1941

After air raids softened Guam's defences, nine Japanese transport ships brought ashore 5900 troops of the South Seas Detachment and Special Naval Landing Forces. Within hours, the invaders overwhelmed the garrison of US marines, sailors and Guam Insular Force Guards.

■ PHILIPPINE ISLANDS, 8 DECEMBER 1941–46 JANUARY 1942

On 22 December, after several feints, the Japanese Fourteenth Army, under Gen Masaharu Homma, landed in force at Lingayen on Luzon. Building up approximately 130,000 troops, the Japanese confronted around 150,000 defenders, including more than 30,000 soldiers of US Army MGen Jonathan Wainwright's Philippine Division (the 23rd Infantry Brigade and supporting units). Blasting through five defensive lines en route south to Manila, the Japanese bottled up the defenders on the Bataan peninsula.

■ *PRINCE OF WALES/REPULSE*, **10 DECEMBER 1941**
'Force Z' – the battleship *Prince of Wales* and the battlecruiser *Repulse* – sailed to oppose the Japanese invasion of Malaya and Singapore; on 10 December 1941, lacking air cover, both warships were sunk by air attack.

■ **DUTCH EAST INDIES, 8 DECEMBER 1941–12 MARCH 1942**
After the Nazi conquest of the Netherlands (10–17 May 1940), the Free Dutch Government, exiled in London, faced the Axis invasion of its colonies in the East Indies (today's Indonesia). The Japanese war machine sought fuel (after the Americans had cut access to more than 90 per cent of its supply) and to consolidate its territorial gains in South-east Asia. The Dutch East Indies were an attractive target because of the islands' wealth of oil, rubber, quinine and other resources. Using an effective combined-arms strategy, Japanese sea, air and land forces, under FM Count Hisaichi Terauchi and Adm Ibo Takahashi, quickly seized Borneo, Celebes and Sumatra. Relentless attacks overwhelmed the air and naval forces of Gen Sir Archibald Wavell's American–British–Dutch–Australian (ABDA) Command. Following fierce fighting on Java, the last Dutch land forces, under Gen Hein ter Poorten, surrendered.

■ **BATAAN-CORREGIDOR, 7 JAN–6 MAY 1942**
The Japanese Eleventh Air Fleet had destroyed the US Far East Air Force on the Philippines. The Imperial Japanese Navy's 3rd Fleet and Gen Masaharu Homma's Fourteenth Army had successfully landed on Luzon, advancing south to the capital. Outmanoeuvred, Gen Douglas

MacArthur, commander of US Army Forces Far East, gave up Manila and ordered his American and Filipino troops to fight a delaying action at the Bataan peninsula and on the island fortress Corregidor. Supported by heavy artillery fire and aerial bombardment, the Japanese reduced Bataan's defences on 9 April. Corregidor held on for another month, until MGen Wainwright surrendered on 6 May. The Japanese took 15,000 American and 60,000 Filipino prisoners, many of whom would perish under harsh treatment (e.g. the 'Bataan Death March'). MacArthur withdrew to Australia to organize a counter-offensive. Adm Thomas Hart, commanding the US Asiatic Fleet, joined in the futile defence of the Dutch East Indies.

■ **BURMA I, JANUARY 1942–MAY 1943**
Four divisions of the Japanese Fifteenth Army, under LGen Shojiro Iida, advanced from occupied Thailand into southern Burma. British LGen William Slim's defence force comprised 13,700 British, 37,000 Indian and 12,300 Burmese troops. A Chinese expeditionary force, under Gen Lin Wei, was deployed to defend the Burma Road, the last overland route into the Republic of China. Nevertheless, outnumbered and outmanoeuvred by the Japanese, Slim ordered a fighting retreat to the Indian border, abandoning the indefensible Rangoon.

■ **SINGAPORE, 8–15 FEBRUARY 1942**
Three Japanese divisions of the Twenty-Fifth Army, comprising 36,000 troops under LGen Yamashita, confronted more than three times their number in the final battle of the Malay campaign. Thanks to determined rearguard action by the brigades of the Australian 8th Division, British and Indian forces had crossed the narrow Johore Straits, blown the causeway and taken defensive positions on Singapore Island. Despite determined resistance, the Japanese successfully landed under fire and advanced. In the air, they overwhelmed the Royal Air Force's Brewster Buffalo and Hawker Hurricane Mk II fighter squadrons to gain supremacy.

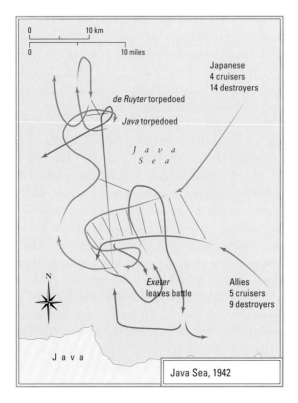

Java Sea, 1942

Finally, after a week's bitter fighting, LGen Percival presided over the surrender of more than 130,000 troops in what Winston Churchill described as 'the largest capitulation in British history'. Yamashita's troops became infamous for their murders of prisoners during the city's conquest.

■ DARWIN, 19 FEBRUARY 1942

After the fall of Singapore, four Japanese aircraft carriers launched more than 200 aircraft to strike Australian and US military and naval forces stationed at the port city. The raids killed or wounded several hundred and sank 10 Allied ships.

■ JAVA SEA, 27 FEBRUARY–1 MARCH 1942

As the Japanese grip on Java tightened, the Allies fought a series of disastrous naval engagements. RAdm Takeo Takagi's invasion fleet included two heavy cruisers, two light cruisers and 15 destroyers. Dutch RAdm Karel Doorman commanded a squadron of two heavy cruisers,

three light cruisers and nine destroyers. In addition to superior numbers, the Japanese ships had more 200mm heavy guns, outranging and hitting harder than their opponents. Despite his disadvantages, Doorman attacked, manoeuvring to intercept the Japanese landing ships. The initial exchange of gunfire disabled the British heavy cruiser HMS *Exeter* and sank two Allied destroyers, plus damaged one Japanese destroyer. Later that night, the Japanese sank the Dutch light cruisers HNMS *de Ruyter* and HNMS *Java*, killing Doorman and scattering his squadron. The Japanese hunted down most of the remaining units, sinking the cruisers USS *Houston*, HMAS *Perth* and HMS *Exeter*.

■ CEYLON RAID, 31 MARCH–10 APRIL 1942

In this engagement Japanese VAdm Chiuchi Nagumo's six aircraft carriers and four battleships attacked the British at Ceylon. He sank the light carrier HMS *Hermes* and two cruisers, countering the Royal Navy's Far East Fleet's supremacy in the Indian Ocean.

■ DOOLITTLE RAID, 18 APRIL 1942

The aircraft carrier USS *Hornet* launched 16 US Army B-25 medium bombers within 1200km of Japan. After the largely symbolic raid succeeded, American President Franklin D. Roosevelt facetiously told his people the mission had originated in the mythical Himalayan kingdom of 'Shangri La'.

■ MADAGASCAR, MAY 1942

Concerned that Japan might bully Vichy France into conceding bases on Madagascar, in May 1942, Britain launched Operation *Ironclad*, an innovative and ultimately successful amphibious operation to capture Diego Suárez.

■ CORAL SEA, 7–8 MAY 1942

Notable as the first naval engagement in which the opposing surface fleets never saw one another, this battle was fought entirely by carrier-based planes. As such, it clearly signalled the shift in naval warfare from the importance of the 'big gun' battleships and cruisers, to aircraft

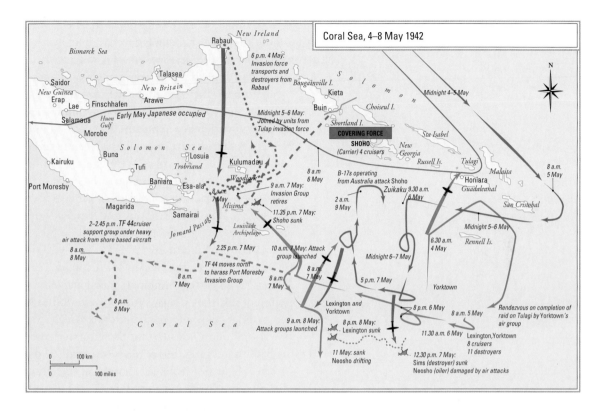

Coral Sea, 4–8 May 1942

carriers. Both the American and Japanese fleets were attempting to gain control of the area around Port Moresby, Papua, which was critical to the defence and resupply of Australia. The Japanese hoped to use three aircraft carriers to draw the Americans toward two of their heavy cruisers, showing that they still prioritized surface warfare. The American Pacific Fleet, taking advantage of radio decrypts, was able to avoid the trap. The Americans had two carriers, the *Yorktown* and the *Lexington*, which they planned to use to disrupt Japanese landings at Port Moresby, but poor weather and poor navigation placed them in an exposed position.

On 8 May the two fleets' reconnaissance aircraft located one another in the vast ocean. Each side had approximately 120 aircraft, although the Japanese planes were qualitatively superior and had a better range of offensive options. The Americans nevertheless did well. They sank the Japanese carrier *Shoho* and

damaged the *Shokaku* badly enough to force it to withdraw to the north, thus tilting the odds towards the Americans. That advantage soon dissipated, however, when the Japanese sunk the *Lexington* and badly damaged the *Yorktown*. The Japanese nevertheless abandoned efforts to take Port Moresby, handing the Americans a strategic victory despite their severe losses. The *Yorktown* was so badly damaged that the Japanese counted it as sunk; although limping, it did take part in the battle of Midway later that summer. Coral Sea showed the wisdom of the American decision to base its naval power around aircraft carriers rather than battleships.

South Pacific 1942–45

NEW GUINEA, 3 FEBRUARY 1942–22 JANUARY 1943

At the beginning of 1942, the Japanese had established at Rabaul, New Britain, a major base from which their air forces and navy could

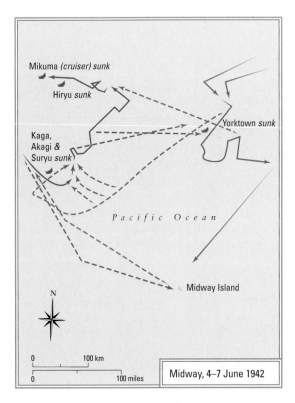

Mikuma *(cruiser) sunk*

Hiryu *sunk*

Kaga, Akagi & Suryu *sunk*

Yorktown *sunk*

Pacific Ocean

Midway Island

N

0   100 km

0   100 miles

Midway, 4–7 June 1942

WWII, inflicting a blow upon the Japanese from which they never fully recovered. The battle's origins lay in the decision of Adm Yamamoto to attempt to lure the US Navy's major units into a trap where they could be destroyed by the Japanese fleet. Yamamoto's plan was predicated on faulty intelligence about the status of the US Navy's aircraft carriers in the Pacific (erroneously believing that only two were likely to be available), and further undermined by American signals intelligence breaking the Japanese code and being able to work out the basis of the enemy plan.

Yamamoto intended to launch an attack on Midway Atoll as the means of bringing the Americans to battle,: the Americans, cognizant of his intentions, duly obliged. Adm Chester Nimitz, commander-in-chief, Pacific Ocean Areas, was able to call upon not two, but three carriers after the badly damaged USS *Yorktown* was made fit for service. The major damage sustained at the battle of the Coral Sea was rectified in 72 hours, with further work being carried out while *Yorktown* was under way to join the carriers *Enterprise* and *Hornet*.

The day before the battle, on 3 June, USAAF B-17 bombers operating from Midway attacked the Japanese fleet's transport group and bombed it without result. On 4 June, the Japanese launched their carrier aircraft to attack Midway, which was hard hit, but not put out of action. The Japanese then learned of the presence of an American carrier thanks to air reconnaissance, and Adm Nagumo, commanding the Japanese carriers, decided to launch an attack on the American fleet. By this point, the Americans were well aware of the location of the Japanese carriers, and launched aircraft from *Enterprise* and *Hornet* to attack. The first attacks were conducted by TBD Devastator torpedo-bombers from Torpedo Squadron 8; all of them were shot down as they attacked. Their sacrifice was not in vain, however, since they drew the Japanese defensive fighters out of position,

check the Allied advance through the Solomons, especially in the contest for Guadalcanal. From New Britain, Japanese land forces also deployed to New Guinea and sought to take Port Moresby, over the Owen Stanley Range in Papua. The naval battle of the Coral Sea prevented a direct Japanese landing at Port Moresby. As a result, MGen Tomitaro Horii's 144th Infantry secured a beachhead at Buna, on Australian New Guinea, in order to attempt an overland conquest of Papua. Although this was initially successful, the Australian 7th Division eventually checked the Japanese advance at Kokoda. By 22 January 1943, six months of bloody fighting had cost Australia almost 5700 casualties and the USA almost 3000. The Japanese lost more than half of Horii's force of 20,000 before withdrawing survivors for employment elsewhere.

■ MIDWAY, 4–7 JUNE 1942

The battle of Midway (4–7 June 1942) was a major turning point in the Pacific Theatre during

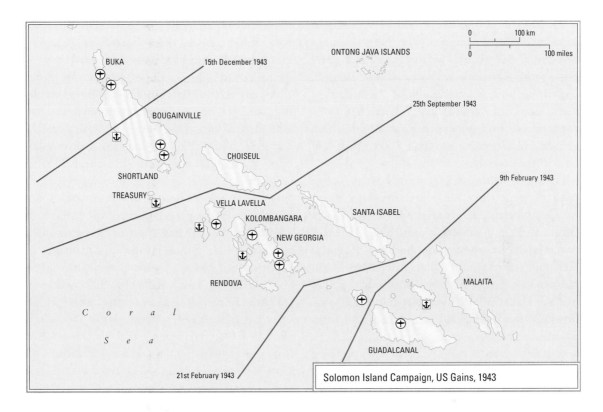

15th December 1943

ONTONG JAVA ISLANDS

0   100 km
0   100 miles

BUKA

BOUGAINVILLE

25th September 1943

CHOISEUL

SHORTLAND

9th February 1943

TREASURY

VELLA LAVELLA

KOLOMBANGARA

SANTA ISABEL

NEW GEORGIA

RENDOVA

MALAITA

C o r a l

S e a

GUADALCANAL

21st February 1943

Solomon Island Campaign, US Gains, 1943

leaving the carriers *Kaga*, *Akagi* and *Soryu* vulnerable to three squadrons of approaching American SDB Dauntless dive-bombers. The dive-bombers hit all three carriers, leaving *Kaga* and *Soryu* ablaze, while *Akagi* sustained serious damage to its rudder and flight deck. All three Japanese carriers were out of action, leaving just the fourth Japanese carrier, *Hiryu,* capable of operations.

Hiryu's air group then launched a major counter-attack, badly damaging the *Yorktown* and putting that ship out of action. The remaining two American carriers were untouched, however, and upon the discovery of the *Hiryu* by a scout-plane, they launched a further dive-bomber assault on the Japanese ship. The attack set the *Hiryu* ablaze from bow to stern, and it sank the following day, another crushing loss to the Japanese Navy. As darkness fell on 4 June, the Americans had knocked out four Japanese carriers in exchange for the *Yorktown* being

badly damaged. There was little fighting on 5 June, but over the course of the next 48 hours, the Americans managed to sink the Japanese cruiser *Mikuma* in another air strike. Yamamoto finally decided that he must withdraw. A Japanese submarine found the *Yorktown* and hit it with two torpedoes, which caused the ship to sink on 7 June 1942.

■ OWEN STANLEY RANGE, 21 JULY–16 NOVEMBER 1942

MGen Horii's 144th Infantry had seized the strategically important airfield at Kokoda. To repel the Japanese advance, the Australian 7th Division and the US 126th Infantry fought a difficult campaign along rugged mountain tracks, north to Buna.

■ SOLOMON ISLANDS, 7 AUGUST 1942–25 DECEMBER 1943

By April 1942, the Japanese line extended from the Burma–India border, east to the Philippines, New Britain and the Solomon Islands. Air and naval bases at Bougainville and New Georgia supported their campaign on New Guinea. To check and isolate Japanese air and naval power, the Allies planned a counter-offensive, beginning with the amphibious conquests of Tulagi and Guadalcanal. By 9 February 1943, the Japanese had been expelled from both places at tremendous cost: more than 7000 Allied and 30,000 Japanese lives.

The naval battles nearby were equally costly, with so many ships sunk in the passage north of Guadalcanal that it earned the sobriquet 'Iron Bottom Sound'. Countering Japanese naval power in the region became a central challenge throughout the campaign. Adm Yamamoto's powerful fleet outnumbered that of Adm Halsey. While often tactically successful, however, the Japanese ultimately suffered from attrition, unable to replace lost ships, aircraft and experienced personnel. Both sides suffered setbacks, including the loss of the carriers

Ryujo and USS *Hornet*. The American industrial base could absorb these losses; the Japanese, increasingly, could not.

The second phase of the campaign, Operation *Cartwheel*, included the conquest of Bougainville, the largest island in the archipelago. By Christmas 1943, US Destroyer Squadron 23 had sunk more than half the Japanese resupply effort, in the battle of Cape St George. Ashore, US Marines had wiped out the Japanese 23rd Infantry at the battle of Piva Forks. Soon the heart of Japanese power in the region, the base at Rabaul, New Britain, was to be surrounded and isolated, though fighting would continue in the area until 1945.

By the end of the war, the Solomon Islands campaign had cost the Allies more than 10,600 dead, along with 40 ships and 800 aircraft and the Japanese had lost more than 80,000 men, 50 ships and 1500 aircraft.

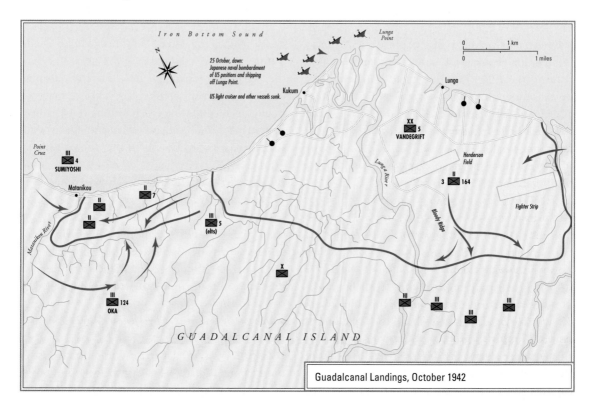

Guadalcanal Landings, October 1942

■ **GUADALCANAL, 7 AUGUST 1942–8 FEBRUARY 1943**

With information that the Japanese had started airfield construction on Guadalcanal, the Americans landed 19,000 Marines there, driving the Japanese troops away from the airfield (known to the Americans as Henderson Field). The Japanese responded by sending a task force of cruisers to the area, the force defeating an Allied naval group in the battle of Savo Island on 9 August. This success did not create conditions with which to dislodge the Marines, and the Japanese continued attempts to drive the Americans out throughout August, September and October. A final attempt by the Japanese to land their 38th Division in early November 1942 ended with their transport ships being sunk by air attack and 38th Division left with just 2000 men. This marked the turning point in the battle, and by February, the final Japanese soldier had been withdrawn.

■ **SAVO ISLAND, 9 AUGUST 1942**

Japanese VAdm Gunichi Mikawa's Eighth Fleet attacked Allied warships screening the Guadalcanal landings. Within an hour of night fighting, the Allies lost four heavy cruisers (three US and one Australian) and more than 1000 sailors and had damaged three Japanese cruisers. Both sides had made mistakes. Prior to the battle, American VAdm Frank Fletcher moved his task force's carriers, depriving the Allies of air cover. Mikawa failed to exploit his victory, leaving the Allied landing force unmolested.

■ **EASTERN SOLOMONS, 24–25 AUGUST 1942**

American carrier task groups, including USS *Enterprise* and USS *Saratoga*, attacked the Japanese carriers *Shokaku*, *Zuikaku* and *Ryujo*, which were screening a supply column bound for Japanese troops on Guadalcanal. Neither side's warships sighted the other's in this battle, fought entirely by opposing air wings. American aircraft from Henderson Field on Guadalcanal, along with seven USAAF Boeing B-17 bombers from Espiritu Santo, also joined in the fracas. VAdm

Nagumo's intention was to destroy the American carriers and deliver 1400 fresh troops to recapture the island's important airfield. *Saratoga*'s dive-bombers sank *Ryujo*. The Japanese strike force crippled *Enterprise* but it survived the battle. While indecisive, the fight enabled the Americans to slow, though not to halt, Japanese resupply and reinforcement. More significant for Japan was the loss of some of its most experienced aviators, who were irreplaceable.

■ **CAPE ESPERANCE, 11–12 OCTOBER 1942**

American RAdm Norman Scott's Task Force 64 surprised Japanese Cruiser Division 6, led by RAdm Arimoto Goto, on a night sortie to Guadalcanal. The heavy cruiser USS *San Francisco* and light cruisers USS *Salt Lake City*, USS *Boise* and USS *Helena*, together with five destroyers, 'crossed the T', bringing all guns to bear on the Japanese. Goto's flagship, *Aoba*, quickly lost communication and fire control and was forced to retire. US fires sank the cruiser *Furutaka* and three Japanese destroyers. Goto himself was mortally wounded when armour-piercing shells struck *Aoba*'s bridge.

■ **BISMARCK SEA, 1–3 MARCH 1943**

US Gen George Kenney's Allied Air Force, Southwest Pacific, carried out a devastating attack on Japanese merchant and naval shipping, sending eight transports and eight warships to the bottom and killing more than 3000 enemy troops in the process. The three-day battle, carried out by 335 American and Australian aircraft, with US Navy motor torpedo boats supporting, targeted a Japanese convoy bound for New Guinea. Allied bombers skilfully surprised the Japanese with low-level attack runs, evading the convoy's high-flying fighter escort. The attacking planes 'skipped' their bombs along the wave crests into their targets' hulls, puncturing the vessels close to or below the waterline. At the battle of Bismarck Sea, the Allies also destroyed 20–30 Japanese aircraft, in the air and at Lae. After the battle, the Japanese abandoned large supply missions to New Guinea, hastening its re-conquest by the Allies.

New Georgia, 20 June–25 August 1943

During the summer of 1943, the US invaded the islands of New Georgia, the next important objective after Guadalcanal. Despite unopposed landings and overwhelming numerical superiority (30,000 US troops to 9000 Japanese) the American advance stalled. At Bairoko Harbor, the 1st and 4th US Marine Raider Battalions, with two US Army infantry battalions, attempted to seize Japanese naval facilities. The attack failed at the price of 50 US and 30 Japanese lives before the Americans withdrew. In July, the US attacked Munda Point, where the Japanese had built and fortified an airfield. Adding that facility to the Allies' growing network of bases was an important objective for LGen Millard Harmon, commander of US Army Forces Pacific. The Americans used flamethrowers and explosives to envelope and destroy the last Japanese positions. With the airfield captured, the remaining Japanese forces evacuated the island.

Kula Gulf, 6 July 1943

US RAdm Ainsworth's cruiser-destroyer Task Group 36 attacked Adm Akiyama's Third Destroyer Group at night in the 8km gulf between Kolobangara and New Georgia. The Americans sank the destroyer *Nizuki* and drove *Nagatsuki* aground. In return, the Japanese sank the light cruiser USS *Helena*.

Vella Lavella, 15 August–9 October 1943

The US 25th and New Zealand 3rd Divisions crushed a Japanese garrison on Vella Lavella, west of New Georgia. In mid–August 1943–January 1944, the island's airbase hosted the Vought F4U Corsairs of US Marine Corps VMF-214 – Col 'Pappy' Boyington's 'Black Sheep' squadron.

Markham Valley, 5–15 September 1943

The US 503rd Parachute Infantry Regiment made the first American airborne landing of the Pacific War, seizing an airfield at Nadzab in the Markham river valley, New Guinea With

the Australian 25th Infantry Brigade, the Allies forced the Japanese to abandon the city of Lae.

Huon Peninsula, 22 Sept 1943–1 Mar 1944

The Australian 9th Division's superb amphibious landing captured Finschhafen, bottling up the Japanese 20th Division in eastern Papua. In a series of battles on the peninsula, the Japanese lost approximately 3000 soldiers while the Australians lost 1028.

Bougainville, 1 Nov 1943–21 August 1945

Bougainville, largest and most westerly of the Solomons, was an important campaign objective. Adm Halsey's plan included an amphibious landing at Empress Augusta Bay on 1 November 1943. Within the first day, US Marines had established and fortified a 4000m beachhead. Later, the US Army's XIV Corps, including the Americal and 37th Divisions, landed. The beachhead put Japanese airfields on Bougainville and at Rabaul within reach of Allied attack planes. More than 62,000 American troops dug in to await a counter-attack by 19,000 Japanese troops of Gen Harukichi Hyakutake's Seventeenth Army. The two sides bitterly contested the island's central ridgeline. By November 1944, the Americans had the upper hand. However, the Japanese continued to fight Australian and Commonwealth replacement troops until 21 August 1945. Final victory cost more than 1200 Allied and more than 20,000 Japanese lives.

Rabaul, 1943–44

After a crippling US air raid on Rabaul in 2 November 1943, which inflicted severe damage on the port, the Allied forces surrounded and strangled Japanese-held bases on New Britain by seizing airfields and naval facilities at Cape Gloucester, the Green Islands and the Admiralty Islands.

Cape Gloucester, 26 December 1943–22 April 1944

During Operation *Cartwheel*, the US 1st Marine Division landed on New Britain to seize the airfields at Cape Gloucester. Opposed by the Japanese 17th Division, the Marines used their new M4A1 Sherman tanks to overwhelm the defenders.

■ ADMIRALTY ISLANDS, 29 FEB–18 MAY 1944

In the final phase of the Allied effort to isolate the critical Japanese-held port of Rabaul, 35,000 troops of the US Cavalry Division attacked a Japanese Garrison of 4000 men during Operation *Brewer*. The fighting cost 3280 Japanese and 326 American lives.

■ AITAPE, 22 APRIL 1944

After a two-hour naval barrage on 22 April, troops from the US 41st Infantry Division, together with Australian engineers, landed at Aitape, New Guinea. The Allies easily overwhelmed a Japanese garrison of 2000 men. Nearby Tadji airfield became a base for Allied fighters.

■ HOLLANDIA, 22 APRIL 1944

Covered by carrier air strikes, a landing force of 80,000 US troops (a total of two divisions) seized this Japanese air base on New Guinea's north coast. Gen MacArthur's success isolated

the Japanese force at Wewak, although the victory cost 4000 American casualties.

■ BIAK, 29 MAY–13 JUNE 1944

Northwest of New Guinea, Biak was a battleground between the US 41st Division and the Japanese 222nd Infantry. After a grinding combat that annihilated more than 6000 Japanese and 400 Americans, US troops captured the Mokmer airfield.

■ MOROTAI, 15 SEPTEMBER–4 OCTOBER 1944

On the southern approach to the Philippines, this island in the Dutch East Indies was the scene of an unopposed landing by the US 31st Infantry Division. The island's topography made the landing and subsequent air and naval base development challenging.

■ LEYTE, 17 OCTOBER 1944–1 JULY 1945

The US Sixth Army, under LGen Walter Krueger, confronted Japanese LGen Shiro Makino's 16th Division. The Japanese took 70,000 casualties and lost irreplaceable aircraft and ships in this

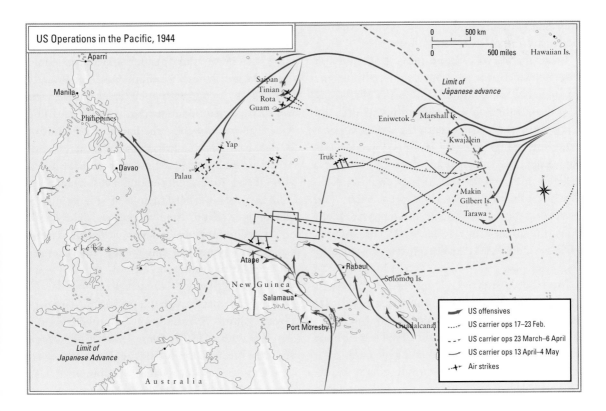

decisive battle of the American re-conquest of the Philippines.

■ LEYTE GULF, 24 AND 25 OCTOBER 1944

In terms of tonnage of warships deployed, the battle of Leyte Gulf is the largest naval battle ever fought, engaging 282 vessels as well as 180,000 sailors and pilots. The Imperial Japanese Navy (IJN) hoped to use the battle to destroy the US Third and Seventh Fleets outside the Philippine Islands, then isolate the US ground forces invading the Philippines themselves. The Japanese plan, developed by Adm Soemu Toyoda, envisioned amassing the Japanese fleet from disparate bases then dividing it into two in the waters off the Philippines. A decoy fleet of four carriers would steam to the north-east of the islands and attract the attention of the carriers of the US Third Fleet before running off to the north-east. Given that these carriers had few airplanes or pilots owing to Japan's earlier defeats, Toyoda did not believe that they could do much more. If, however, they could distract the US carriers, then the Japanese battleships coming from the west could even the odds against the US Seventh Fleet.

Aware that Leyte was possibly the last major engagement Japan was capable of fighting, the Japanese Navy committed almost everything it had, including its two enormous 72,000 ton battleships, the *Yamato* and the *Musashi*. Five other battleships and 16 cruisers joined them, supported by land-based planes on Japanese airfields in the Philippines. If they could lure the US Seventh Fleet away from the carriers and perform a pincer movement, the Japanese might deny the Americans access to the Philippines, giving them the major strategic victory they needed.

The battle of Leyte Gulf involved four related engagements in the gulfs and straits of the Philippines. Gen Douglas MacArthur's landing of the Sixth Army on the island of Leyte drew both navies toward Leyte Gulf like a magnet and made it the centre of gravity for the subsequent battle. Neither side had one admiral in overall command

of the entire engagement and confusion therefore reigned from beginning to end. With the clash spread out over hundreds of miles, it was nearly impossible for the commanders to develop a sense of the entire battle as it unfolded. Superior intelligence and quick decision-making gave the Americans a fundamental geographic advantage, although the Americans did initially fall for the carrier bait and divide their forces.

The decision to chase the decoys limited the power the Americans could bring to bear, although in fairness it must be noted that the Americans had no way of knowing how depleted of aircraft the Japanese decoy carriers really were. The Americans thus might have scored even greater triumphs at Leyte Gulf had they concentrated their ships, but they won a major victory nevertheless.

The Japanese Navy suffered devastating losses of all four decoy carriers, three battleships, 10 cruisers and nine destroyers. Most of the other capital ships the Japanese engaged were damaged and they also lost more than 500 airplanes. Perhaps most crucially, some 10,000 irreplaceable pilots and sailors died in the battle. Japan could not make good these losses, and was forced to rely increasingly on poorly trained replacements, who were virtual cannon fodder for the Americans. The American losses were three light carriers (out of 16 deployed), two destroyers, and 200 aircraft, but American industry could more than make good these losses. American personnel losses equalled 2800 men, about half of them from suicide attacks that previewed the deadly *kamikazes*. The battle of Leyte Gulf effectively destroyed Japanese naval power and opened the way for the American re-conquest of the Philippines.

■ SURIGAO STRAIT, 25 OCTOBER 1944

During the battles for Leyte Gulf, Japanese VAdm Shoji Nishimura's Southern Force clashed with US RAdm Jesse Oldendorf's Seventh Fleet. Despite having been observed in enemy-controlled waters, Nishimura's task force proceeded. The Americans ambushed and

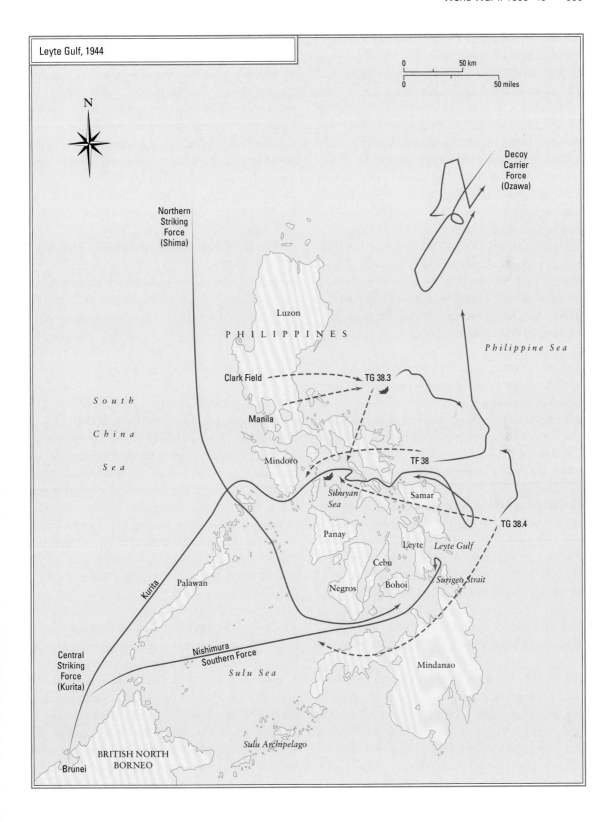

Leyte Gulf, 1944

0   50 km

0   50 miles

N

Decoy
Carrier
Force
(Ozawa)

Northern
Striking
Force
(Shima)

Luzon

P H I L I P P I N E S

Philippine Sea

Clark Field

TG 38.3

Manila

Mindoro

TF 38

*Sibuyan
Sea*

Samar

TG 38.4

*South

China

Sea*

Panay

Leyte

Leyte Gulf

Kurita

Palawan

Cebu

Negros

Bohoi

Surigeo Strait

Central
Striking
Force
(Kurita)

Nishimura
Southern Force

Sulu Sea

Mindanao

Sulu Archipelago

BRITISH NORTH
BORNEO

Brunei

successfully 'crossed the T' of their adversaries, raking Nishimura's line mercilessly with torpedoes and heavy gunfire, which decimated the Japanese fleet. Nishimura went down with his flagship, the Fuso-class battleship *Yamashiro*. This was the last large-scale surface engagement between battleships in the Pacific War.

■ Cape Engano, 25–26 October 1944

VAdm Jisaburo Ozawa's Northern Force baited Adm Halsey's Third Fleet into a risky pursuit. Ozawa commanded four aircraft carriers, making him an attractive target. But the depleted Japanese force actually had fewer than 30 aircraft. Halsey's 64 warships and more than 300 planes caught them up, sinking all four carriers in a crushing defeat. Halsey was later criticized for leaving the San Bernardino Strait unguarded.

■ Samar, 25 October 1944

In the San Bernardino Strait, six US escort carriers of task unit 'Taffy 3' attacked the mighty Japanese Central Force. Badly outgunned, Taffy 3 sank three Japanese cruisers at the cost of more than 1000 American sailors, two destroyers and two escort carriers, including one sunk by *kamikaze* attacks.

■ Wewak, mid-December 1944–10 May 1945

Allied amphibious operations at Hollandia and Aitape had isolated the Japanese Eighteenth Army in northern New Guinea. After five months' hard campaign, the Australian 6th Division took Wewak, at the cost of 451 killed. More than 7000 Japanese died.

■ Luzon, 9 January–15 August 1945

On the Philippine island of Luzon, the Japanese force included 152,000 soldiers of LGen Yamashita's Shobu Group, 30,000 soldiers of MGen Tsukada's Kembu Group (near Bataan) and 80,000 soldiers of LGen Yokoyama's Shimbu Group (along the Bicol peninsula). US Sixth Army commander, LGen Walter Krueger, landed 175,000 troops along a 40km beachhead between Lingayen and San Fabian. MacArthur ordered them to capture Manila, Bataan and Corregidor. In February, the US 37th and 1st

Cavalry Divisions raced toward the capital. Although lightly garrisoned, by 4 March Manila was razed to the ground in the most intense urban combat of the Pacific War. US amphibious and airborne landings then seized Bataan and Corregidor, leaving the Allies firmly in control of Subic Bay. Fighting continued in the centre and north. At the end of the war, the Americans had killed or captured almost all of the approximately 230,000 Japanese on Luzon. US casualties were 47,000 (killed and captured).

■ Southern Philippines–Borneo, 1 may–1 August 1945

Between 1943 and 1944, Borneo had provided 40 per cent of Japan's fuel oil and as much as 30 per cent of her crude oil. Having landed, the Australian 9th Division (with US and Dutch support) defeated the Japanese Thirty-Seventh Army to seize these vital resources.

Central Pacific 1943–45

■ Tarawa-Makin, 20–24 November 1943

Operation *Galvanic* was the first joint US Army and US Marine Corps amphibious operation of the Central Pacific Campaign. This represented a shift in the Americans' regional strategy from defence to offence. US Adm Chester Nimitz, Commander-in-Chief, Pacific Ocean Areas, and Marine LGen Holland Smith, V Amphibious Corps, ordered the plan to seize Makin Atoll, a Japanese seaplane base, and Tarawa Atoll, a fortified airfield.

Naval Task Force 52 landed the army's 27th Infantry Division on Makin, where they faced fewer than 800 defenders. Nevertheless, MGen Ralph Smith met fierce resistance. His soldiers shot dead 395 Japanese while suffering 218 casualties. On 23 November, Smith radioed his superiors: 'Makin taken'. Tarawa was a different scene. There, Task Force 53 had put the Marines' amphibious tractors (amtracs) ashore amid withering enemy artillery and automatic weapons fire. MGen Julian Smith's 2nd Marine

Division faced 4800 well-entrenched Japanese. The battle for Tarawa was one of appalling ferocity, as the Japanese soldiers fought to the death. By the time the smoke cleared on 24 November, nearly all the defenders were killed and the American had suffered more than 3000 casualties.

■ KWAJALEIN-ENIWETOK, 31 JANUARY–3 FEBRUARY / 17 FEBRUARY–23 FEBRUARY 1944

The American 4th Marine Division and 7th Infantry Division sought to break Japan's 'outer ring' defences. At Roi and Namur, northernmost islands of the Kwajaleien Atoll, they wiped out almost the entire Japanese garrison of 3500 men.

■ TRUK, 17–18 FEBRUARY 1944

Almost 600 US aircraft, from 12 carriers, attacked Japan's large naval base at Truk. The Americans destroyed 15 Japanese warships, more than 30 freighters and almost 300 aircraft. The Japanese shot down 25 US planes.

■ MARIANA ISLANDS 15 JUNE–1 AUGUST 1944

The Mariana Islands offered many benefits as a base for the Americans, particularly as a location for bomber airfields from which to attack Japan directly. The US Joint Chiefs of Staff decided to take the islands, and preparations began with a heavy air and sea bombardment of Saipan, Tinian, Guam and Rota on 11 June 1944. Adm Marc Mitscher's Task Force 58 launched fighter sweeps from its carriers; these destroyed over 150 Japanese aircraft. This was the beginning of what became known as 'The Great Marianas Turkey Shoot'. US carrier airpower was to inflict huge losses upon the Japanese Army and Naval Air Forces on the islands over the course of the battle. The invasion force landed on 15 June and, despite significant Japanese resistance which inflicted heavy casualties on the attackers, the beachhead was firmly established by the end of the day; the island was under American control by 9 July.

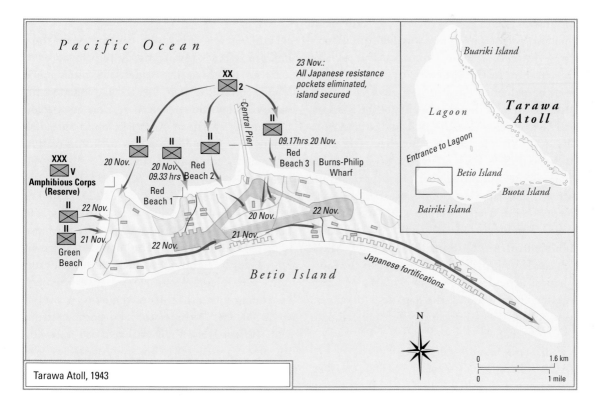

Tarawa Atoll, 1943

The arrival of the Japanese fleet in the area forced the Americans to send their ships to fight the battle of the Philippine Sea on 19–20 June. The need to fight this battle delayed the assault on Guam, which was attacked on 21 July, but this delay was the only success for the Japanese, whose aircraft losses reached around 600 machines by the end of the battle. Japanese resistance on Guam was heavy, and casualties significant, but the island was under American control by the end of the month. The last island, Tinian, was assaulted on 24 July. American casualty figures were low in comparison with the attacks on Saipan and Guam and most of the island was under American control in the space of four days, finally being declared secure on 1 August 1944.

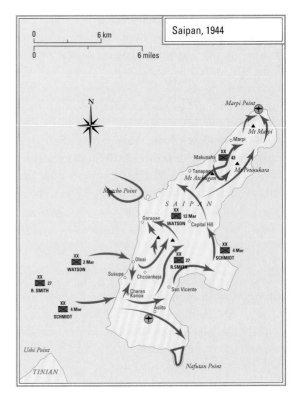

■ SAIPAN 15 JUNE–9 JULY 1944

Capturing the Mariana Islands would provide air bases for long-range air raids on the Japanese homeland by US Boeing B-29 Superfortress bombers. On Saipan, 25,000 troops of MGen Yoshitsugu Saito's 43rd Division and 6000 Japanese naval infantry had fortified the island's caves and cliffs. Cut off from resupply by the American victory in the battle of the Philippine Sea, the defenders made a desperate last stand. After a two-day bombardment, 8000 Marines of LGen Holland Smith's 2nd and 4th Marine Divisions hit the western beaches. The next day, the US Army's 27th Infantry Division came ashore and drove north to capture Aslito airfield. The Japanese fought tenaciously, with deeply entrenched machine-gun and mortar teams. American 'Satan' tanks (M3 Stuarts, modified to fire the Canadian 'Ronson' Mk 1 vehicle flamethrower) helped burn out the most fanatical defenders. After three weeks of bitter fighting, nearly all of the Japanese defenders were killed. The Americans suffered more than 14,000 casualties.

■ PHILIPPINE SEA 19–20 JUNE 1944

VAdm Jisaburo Ozawa's Mobile Fleet, comprising five aircraft carriers and their screen

of cruisers and destroyers, sortied from their Philippine bases toward the American invasion force in the Mariana Islands. US intelligence reports indicated that Ozawa had divided his force to draw the American carriers away from the landing at Saipan. Adm Raymond Spruance ordered his Fifth Fleet forces to hold position covering the amphibious squadron and await the Japanese attack.

The action came at 1000hrs on 19 June, 966km west of Saipan, as VAdm Marc Mitscher's Task Force 58 intercepted the first wave of Japanese fighters and bombers. The navy's Grumman F6F Hellcat fighters mauled the Mitsubishi A6M Zeros and Aichi D3 Val dive-bombers, destroying more than 40 of the first 68 aircraft by 11:00. TBF Avenger torpedo-bombers from USS *Belleau Wood* then attacked and sank the Japanese carrier *Hiyo*. To the Americans, the one-sided fracas became known as 'The Great Marianas Turkey Shoot', in which they downed

385 of Ozawa's 545 planes and sank three Japanese carriers (two by submarine torpedo strikes). American losses were comparatively light – 54 casualties and 26 aircraft. Despite this success, Spruance was criticized for his decision not to close with the Japanese fleet. Both he and Mitscher had wanted to deal the Japanese Navy a decisive blow. However, an offensive sortie could have left the amphibious operation at Saipan vulnerable to air and naval attack, had Ozawa divided his force as the Japanese had done at the Aleutians, Midway and in the Solomons. Six of Ozawa's nine 'flat-tops' escaped the battle. However, the Japanese naval air force, already battered after Guadalcanal and the Solomons, never recovered from the crushing blow it suffered over the Philippine Sea.

■ Guam II, 21 July–10 August 1944

From fortified dugouts and caves, the Japanese fought an invasion by MGen Roy Geiger's 3rd Marine Division and US Army's 77th Infantry. Americans re-captured the island after three weeks of intense battle, resulting in the deaths of more than 18,000 Japanese and 1700 American troops, some from 'friendly fire'.

■ Tinian, 24 July–1 August 1944

For the conquest of Tinian, which lay almost 6km south of Saipan, the US Army and Marine Corps divided their labours: Army soldiers would take the roles of artillery and engineer support, while Marines would be on the point as infantry. Less than one week after Saipan fell, the US Army faced its artillery batteries south and commenced a massive bombardment during which they fired thousands of shells by the end of the battle. LGen Harry Schmidt led the 2nd and 4th Marine Divisions, crossing the strait from Saipan in boats and amphibious tractors. The most important objectives were the island's three airfields, which were taken after a nine-day battle that cost more than 8000 Japanese and more than 300 American lives. Tinian became a base for US long-range bombers, including the B-29 'Enola Gay', which on 6 August 1945 famously left the island to carry out the atomic bombing of Hiroshima.

■ Peleliu-Angaur, 15 September–27 November 1944

In their conquest of Peleliu and Angaur islands, the 1st Marine Division, together with the US Army's 81st Infantry, faced bitter opposition. They killed almost all of the Japanese 14th Division's 11,000 men, while suffering 1700 casualties.

■ Iwo Jima, 19 February–26 March 1945

As 1944 drew to a close, the American High Command concluded that there were strong grounds for seizing the Japanese island of Iwo Jima. The most prevalent operational consideration was the need to provide a suitable base from which USAAF fighter aircraft could reach Japan, thus enabling the provision of escorts for B-29 bombers raiding the enemy homeland. Iwo Jima also had two airfields, one of which was large enough to accommodate B-29s.

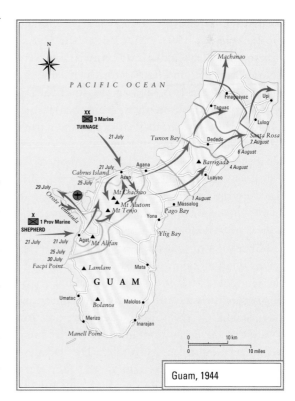

Guam, 1944

This offered an ideal emergency landing ground from the outset, as well as a permanent base for the bombers in due course. A final potent factor was that the Japanese viewed Iwo Jima as part of their home territories, and taking it would have a potent psychological effect on the enemy.

The Japanese were aware of the significance of Iwo Jima and set about boosting the defences in late 1944, sending reinforcements and constructing fortified defensive positions. By the end of 1944, a huge network of tunnels had been built, with the aim of sheltering the defenders from the inevitable massive bombardment that would precede an attack. The value of the trenches was proved from late November, when American air and sea bombardments began.

The invasion itself occurred on 19 February 1945. The American landing forces faced little opposition until they made their way inshore, where they encountered vigorous resistance from fanatically motivated defenders. Hand-to-hand fighting ensued as the US Marines cleared the defensive positions one by one and broke through.

By nightfall, around 30,000 Americans were ashore and surrounding Mount Suribachi, the highest point on Iwo Jima, in the south of the island. Four days of intense fighting then ensued as the Marines sought to clear the Japanese from Mount Suribachi. The last Japanese positions on Suribachi were cleared by late afternoon of 23 February, accompanied by the raising of the US flag atop the mountain; a flag was in fact raised twice, the second occasion being captured by a press photographer and becoming one of the iconic images of the war.

This symbolic moment, however, was far from the end of the battle. A vicious, bunker-to-bunker attritional clash ensued as the Americans were forced to fight from one defensive position to another, invariably finding that the Japanese defenders would not surrender. The Japanese exploited the tunnel system to the full, often attacking the Americans from behind, and the

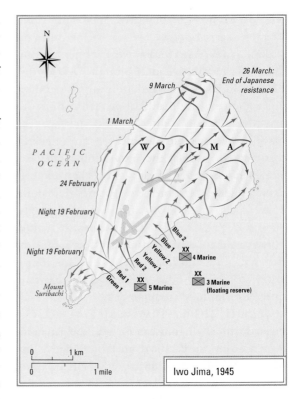

Iwo Jima, 1945

Americans made ever greater use of close air support, artillery and flamethrowers to clear the defenders from their positions. The Japanese met the Americans with a *kamikaze* attack on a number of ships during 21 February, and a number of massed frontal assaults on the American positions during the hours of darkness. One such attack on Hill 362 in the north of the island cost the Japanese more than 75 per cent of the attacking force.

Casualties were horrendous for both sides. By the tenth day of the battle, many American units were down to half strength, and the Japanese had sustained even higher casualties. On the night of 25–26 March, the surviving Japanese troops, estimated to number around 300 men, launched a suicidal human-wave charge against the Marines in the final counter-attack and were wiped out. In total, 23,000 Japanese died, and only 216 survived; the Marines lost 6281 killed and more than 18,000 wounded in what constitutes the bloodiest operation in the Marine Corps' history.

■ OKINAWA, 1 APRIL–21 JUNE 1945

The American attack on Okinawa began on 1 April 1945, the largest amphibious assault in the Pacific during the war. Although the landings met with little opposition to begin with, once the Americans had advanced further into the island, resistance was heavy. The Japanese launched a number of *kamikaze* attacks on the American ships, while the abortive *Ten-Go* operation saw the destruction of the Japanese battleship *Yamato*. Tenacious resistance made the American advance slow, and it was not until 21 June that Okinawa finally fell.

The battle had been an enormously bloody one for both sides. There were 62,000 American casualties, 12,000 of whom were fatalities, making this the most costly battle for the Americans in the Pacific campaign. The Japanese lost 94,000 killed, along with a considerable number of civilian fatalities. The casualties on Okinawa, and previously at Iwo Jima, helped influence the decision to use the atomic bomb.

Northern Pacific 1943

■ ALEUTIAN ISLANDS, 3 JUNE 1942–15 AUGUST 1943

Adm Isoroku Yamamoto believed the invasion of the Aleutians would draw the US Navy away from Midway, Japan's primary objective after Pearl Harbor. VAdm Boshiro Hosogaya's Northern Area Fleet landed troops unopposed on 6–7 June 1942. By November, there were 4000 Japanese on Kiska and another 1000 on Attu. Removing this enemy foothold on American soil became a psychologically important US war objective. At the battle of the Komandorski Islands, the US Navy had checked Japan's attempts to resupply their troops on the Aleutians. By January 1943, Alaska Command had 94,000 soldiers and a base on Amchitka Island within 80km of the

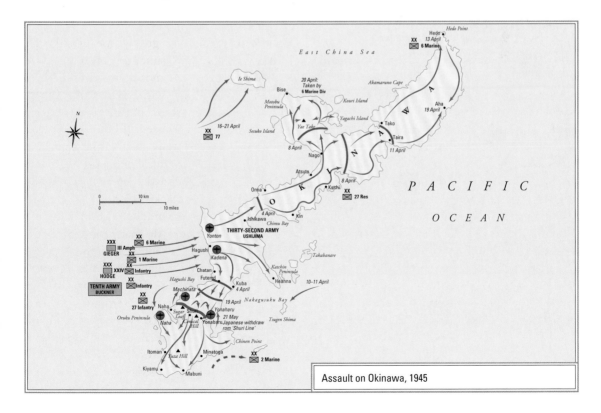

Assault on Okinawa, 1945

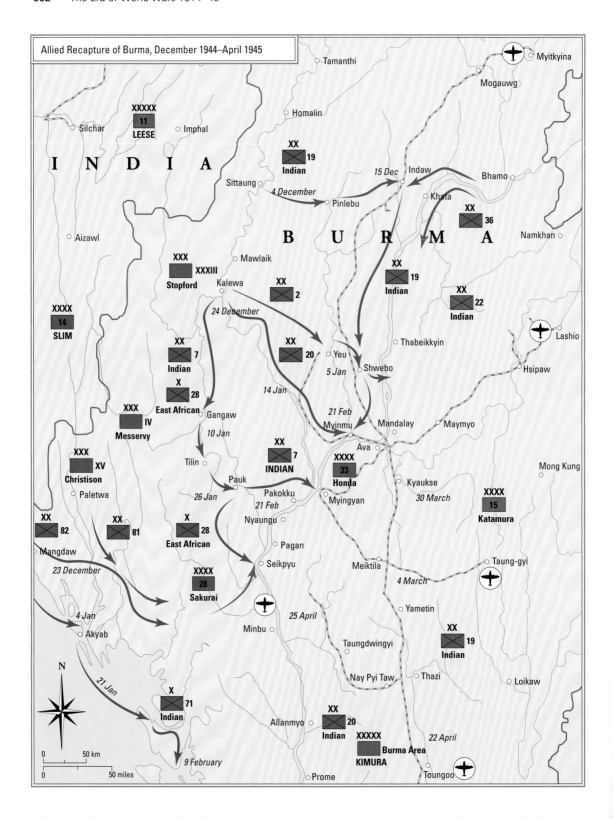

Allied Recapture of Burma, December 1944–April 1945

Japanese occupation force. Anticipating strong resistance on Kiska, the Americans landed 3500 soldiers on Attu. Battling harsh terrain and dangerous weather as much as the Japanese, the Americans drove north to Chichagof Harbor, where Col Yasuyo Yamasaki led his men on a suicidal final assault.

■ ATTU, 11–30 MAY 1943

In one of the costliest amphibious assaults of the war, the US 7th Division defeated the Japanese 301st Battalion, which had held the island since June 1942. More than 3000 Japanese and American soldiers died, many in the 'banzai' charge at Chichagof Harbor.

South-east Asia 1943–45

■ BURMA CAMPAIGN, 1942–1945

Following the cessation of the Japanese offensives of 1942 as the result of the monsoon, the Allies rebuilt their forces for future operations, although they were often constrained by the demands placed upon supplies by the war in Europe and the Middle East. In 1943 the Allies launched a failed offensive in the Arakan, and a long-range attack on Japanese communications in Burma by the 77th Infantry Brigade – better known as the Chindits – but 1943 was mainly a year of reorganization for the Allies. In 1944, the Japanese invaded India, but after fierce fighting at Imphal and Kohima they were forced to withdraw to the Chindwin river. A series of offensives by the Allies followed during 1944 and 1945, driving the Japanese deeper into Burma. By the end of April 1945, Rangoon had fallen, and the Burma campaign was effectively over.

■ FIRST ARAKAN, DECEMBER 1942–APRIL 1943

In late 1942, British forces began a limited offensive into Burma. General Noel Irwin's Indian Eastern Army was given the task of retaking the Mayu peninsula and Akyab Island. On 21 December 1942, 14th Indian Division advanced to Donbaik, where a small Japanese force in well-founded defensive positions blocked them, causing heavy casualties. A Japanese counter-attack on 3 April 1943 unhinged the Eastern Army's defences and forced them back to the Indian border.

■ KOHIMA, 4 APRIL 1944–22 JUNE 1944

Fought between 4 April and 22 June 1944, the battle of Kohima was the turning point in the Japanese invasion of India. The opening phase of the battle saw the Japanese attempt to take the Kohima Ridge, followed by a British counter-attack on 18 April. The Japanese were driven from the ridge, but retained control of the Kohima–Imphal road until forced to retreat on 22 June.

■ IMPHAL, MARCH–JULY 1944

Along with the simultaneous battle at Kohima, Imphal was another turning point in the Burma campaign. As part of the Japanese *U-Go* offensive, Imphal was besieged from 29 March 1944, but was kept resupplied from the air. Bitter fighting ensued for several months, but when British forces broke out from Kohima and met up with the defenders of Imphal at Milestone 109 on the Kohima–Imphal road, the battle was at an end.

■ MYITKYNIA, MAY–AUGUST 1944

The strategically important town of Myitkynia, was besieged by Allied forces under Gen Joseph Stilwell from 17 May 1944. After heavy fighting over the next two and a half months, the town fell into Allied hands on 3 August 1944.

■ MEIKTILA, FEBRUARY–MARCH 1945

The battle of Meiktila began on 28 February 1945, when the Indian 17th Division, part of British Fourteenth Army, launched an attack on the town. The Japanese forces defending the town belatedly became aware of the scale of the attack, and were still attempting to dig in when the four-pronged attack fell upon them. After three days of fighting the town was captured. The Japanese responded by attempting a counter-attack to retake the town. They surrounded the town, and supplies had to be air-dropped to 17th Division after the suspension of flights into the nearby airfield. The Japanese proved unable to breach the defences, however, and the advance of the Indian 5th and 7th Divisions eventually reopened communications to the beleaguered 17th Division. The Japanese were unable to take the town, and the deteriorating situation in central Burma compelled them to withdraw on 28 March.

■ MANDALAY, 8–21 MARCH 1945

The Burmese city of Mandalay was stormed by Gurkha troops of the British Fourteenth Army on 8 March 1945. Japanese troops had withdrawn by 21 March, and the battle marked the point at which Japanese resistance in Burma was effectively broken.

Allied Air Campaign Against Japan

■ TOKYO, 9–10 MARCH 1945

US MGen Curtis LeMay ordered his squadrons to fly low-altitude night attacks with incendiaries against Japan's dispersed wartime industrial base and cities. On the first mission, American bombers burned almost 41.4km² of Tokyo, killing 85,000 people in history's most destructive conventional air attack.

■ HIROSHIMA, 6 AUGUST 1945

Nazi Germany had surrendered in May 1945, freeing the Allies to turn their full attention to winning the Pacific War. By mid-summer, the Japanese were militarily defeated in the Philippines, on Iwo Jima and Okinawa. Despite LeMay's relentless aerial bombardment of the Japanese homeland, gutting 68 of its cities and smashing much of the war industry there, the Imperial Government ignored the 26 July Potsdam Declaration demanding its unconditional surrender.

The then US President Harry S. Truman, advised by the scientists of the Manhattan Project (America's atomic weapons programme) and War Secretary Henry L. Stimson, authorized the use of atomic bombs to finally break Japan's will to fight. Truman and his War Cabinet hoped to end the conflict without a costly invasion of the Japanese homeland. Although the technology had

been successfully demonstrated in July at New Mexico's Alamogordo Bombing and Gunnery Range, many critics inside the US Government questioned the reliability of the project, which only had enough fissile material to produce two weapons that summer.

Initially, the list of possible targets included the military and industrial centres of Kokura, Hiroshima and Niigata. Kyoto was not on the list, thus sparing the traditional Imperial capital from what Truman warned would call 'a rain of ruin from the air, the like of which has never been seen on this earth'. The first weapon, code-named 'Little Boy', was a gun-type fission device fuelled by 60kg of enriched uranium. Airmen of the 393rd Bombardment Squadron loaded it aboard a B-29 Superfortress called 'Enola Gay', which in the early hours of 6 August launched from Tinian Island with two wingmen. The bombers flew more than six hours to their objective: the naval embarkation port of Hiroshima. Enola Gay released the weapon at 08:15 local time, from just below 9800m altitude. Forty-three seconds later, approximately 600m above the city's centre, the bomb detonated, releasing a force equivalent to 13 kilotons of TNT. Although inefficient (little more than 1 per cent of the weapon's fissile material had released its energy), the blast and the resulting firestorm totally destroyed almost 13 km², killing as many as 80,000 people.

■ NAGASAKI, 9 AUGUST 1945

Three days after 'Little Boy's' burst etched a human shadow into the stone steps of Hiroshima's Sumitomo Bank, another B-29 bomber, 'Bockscar', released the second atomic bomb over Nagasaki. Code-named 'Fat Man', Nagasaki's bomb was an implosion-type weapon with a fissile core of 6.1kg of plutonium, similar to the 'gadget' used during the Trinity Site test. On 14 August, Japan surrendered. America's strategic aerial bombardment, including the two atomic bombs, had levelled all of Japan's major cities, causing 800,000 casualties.

Modern Wars 1945–Present

Even as the last shots of World War II were being fired, new conflicts were springing up around the globe. The wars that followed 1945 ranged from minor insurgencies through to full-blown conventional conflicts, and they have changed the political and social map of the world while creating millions of casualties and refugees.

Chinese Civil War 1945–49

■ **SHANTUNG, 10 SEPTEMBER–12 OCTOBER 1945**
Shanxi, in central China's mountainous north-west, had been a centre of communist power before the Second Sino-Japanese War. With the surrender of Japan in 1945, the region became the scene of renewed hostilities with the government. In the autumn, 35,000 Guomindang government troops, under warlord Gen Yan Xishan, attacked the People's Liberation Army (PLA) stronghold in the Shangdang Prefecture of southern Shanxi. More than 80,000 communist soldiers, including 50,000 militiamen loyal to Liu Bocheng, confronted the government army. Well armed, the nationalists seized Changzhi city, but could not dominate the surrounding countryside. For their part, the communists could not penetrate the city's defences. The campaign stalemated until the nationalists, under Shi Zebo, attempted a breakout and were defeated at the Peach river. Both sides had approximately 4000 troops killed, although the communists captured more than 30,000 government troops.

■ **MUKDEN (SHENYANG), MARCH 1946**
The Soviets withdrew in the spring of 1946 from Manchuria. In the opening moves of the renewed Chinese Civil War, Guomindang government troops of Gen Liu Yuzhang's Twenty-Fifth and Fifty-Second Armies moved in to occupy Shenyang. PLA general Lin Biao unsuccessfully tried to oust his former classmate, Liu. Despite the setback, the communists marched on elsewhere in north-eastern China. By the end of April, they had occupied Siping, and captured Changchun and Harbin.

■ **FIRST SIPING, 15–17 MARCH 1946**
In January 1946, bandit militias loyal to the Guomindang government attempted to drive a communist occupation force from this important Manchurian railway depot. The PLA counter-attacked in the spring, defeating Siping's 3000-man nationalist garrison.

■ **SECOND SIPING, 17 APRIL–19 MAY 1946**
Government troops again besieged the communist occupation force at Siping. The veteran New First and Seventy-First Armies, under Gen Du Yuming, drove the PLA out after a month of heavy fighting.

■ **FIRST CHANGCHUN, 17 APRIL–19 MAY 1946**
Controlling Manchurian railway lines and surrounding municipalities were strategic objectives for the Guomindang government. At Changchun, the PLA had violated a 10 January ceasefire, driving out government troops on 15 April. With former Japanese armaments, the communists had fortified themselves against a siege. As Gen Du Yuming's nationalist troops moved against Changchun, their mechanized units became precariously over-extended and bogged down, unable to penetrate Gen Biao's PLA defences.

■ **SUNGARI SONGHUA RIVER, 17 DECEMBER 1946–1 APRIL 1947**
In the Linjiang campaign, 19 Guomindang government divisions attempted four futile offensives to seize communist bases south of the Songhua river. Each of the nationalists' thrusts failed, resulting in more than 40,000 casualties (killed and captured).

■ **THIRD SIPING, 11 JUNE 1947–13 MARCH 1948**
Now on the defensive in Manchuria, three government divisions attempted unsuccessfully to defend the city against a siege by Gen Biao's 60,000 PLA troops. The communists finally overwhelmed Siping, killing more than 30,000 of its defenders.

■ **JINAN, 16–24 SEPTEMBER 1948**

In September 1948 90,000 PLA troops under Gen Chen Yi attacked the weakly fortified capital of Shantung. Gen Wang Yao-wu held the ancient, three-walled city with 50,000 troops. As Communist batteries opened fire, LGen Wu Huawen, commanding the government's 84th Division assigned to the city's south-western front, defected along with many of his men. These helped seal the communist victory. More than 22,000 nationalists died, with another 60,000 captured.

■ **MUKDEN (SHENYANG)-JINZHOU, 12 SEPTEMBER–12 NOVEMBER 1948**

More than 200,000 PLA troops besieged Mukden for 10 months. An American diplomat said the campaign was among 'the … final … military debacles for nationalist arms'. Mukden fell. Five Guomindang armies defected to the communists.

■ **HWAI HAI, 6 NOV 1948–10 JANUARY 1949**

As Lin Biao completed his conquest of Manchuria, Chen Yi's East China Field Army (ECFA) and Liu Bocheng's Central Plains Field Army (CPFA) launched two major offensives aimed at linking communist gains and destroying nationalist combat power in important eastern and central Chinese provinces. These operations evolved into the decisive campaign of the war. On 6 November, the CPFA moved north. At the same time, government troops were redeploying to buttress Xuzhou. The Seventh Army, slowed by a narrow crossing over the Grand Canal at Yaowan, attempted to reposition itself east of the city. Meanwhile, a mass defection of government troops in the Third Pacification Area emboldened the communists. By 11 November, the CPFA had blocked and surrounded the Seventh Army, 30km east of the city. Still, the nationalists held on, until the Seventh Army finally collapsed on 23 November. As many as 3000 soldiers escaped east of Xuzhou, but the communists had killed 25,000 and captured another 80,000. In the second major operation of the campaign, on 12–16 November, the CPFA besieged and captured Suxian, cutting the railway supply line for the Second, Thirteenth and Sixteenth Guomindang Armies at Xuzhou.

Bloody combat ensued, with the PLA annihilating the Twelfth Army on 15 December. The defeat cost the nationalists 46,000 dead and as many as 50,000 captured. The communists also seized much of the government's American-made equipment, vehicles, weapons and supplies. The remnant of the nationalist force limped away south and the campaign came to an end. In all, the communists had killed or captured 500,000 government troops, comprising five of the best-trained and best-equipped Guomindang armies. From this point, the government was on the back-foot against the PLA's inexorable advance on the Yangtze river delta.

■ **BEIJING–TIANJIN, 29 NOV 1948–31 JAN 1949**

In the first move of its campaign to seize the ancient cities of Beijing and Tianjin, the PLA encircled Zhangjiakou, a walled city north of the ancient capital. On 15 January, the communists took Tianjin, destroying two Guomindang armies, approximately 130,000 soldiers. The PLA command hesitated over whether to wrest Beijing from the government by force. Nationalist Gen Fu Zuoyi's two armies finally withdrew on 21 January. Ten days later, the communists entered the city unopposed.

■ **YANGTZE INCIDENT, 20 APRIL–30 JULY 1949**

The frigate HMS *Amethyst,* ordered to Nanking to relieve HMS *Consort* as guard ship for the British mission, came under fire by communist artillery on the north bank of the Yangtze. Despite *Amethyst* flying the colours of a neutral nation, two PLA batteries fired on the ship, badly damaging it and driving it aground. Rescue attempts by *Consort* and two other British ships failed. *Amethyst* escaped on 30 July. Twenty-two British sailors had been killed; 31 others were wounded.

■ **GUNINGTOU, 25–27 OCTOBER 1949**

In October 1949 a PLA amphibious expeditionary force attacked the Quemoy archipelago. Waiting until after the PLA's troops had landed, Guomindang air and naval forces destroyed the communists' transport ships. Thousands of Mao Zedong's stranded soldiers were defeated and captured.

Indochina 1945–54

■ **SIEGE OF HUE, DECEMBER 1946–FEBRUARY 1947**
Responding to the French colonial government demands to disarm, the communist Viet Minh attacked major cities in the north of Vietnam, including Hue. By February 1947, a French battalion had successfully resisted a six-week siege to maintain control of the ancient imperial capital. The Viet Minh withdrew after ransacking portions of the city. Consolidating their successes, the French launched an offensive drive north to the Chinese border.

■ **FORT CAO BANG, 3–7 OCTOBER 1950**
Gen Vo Nguyen Giap's Viet Minh attacked the French colonial garrisons at Cao Bang and Dong Khe, north of Hanoi. Gen Marcel Carpentier evacuated the posts, retreating via 'Route Colonial 4' (RC4). Attacked all the way, the French lost more than 4000 troops.

■ **VINH YEN, 13–17 JANUARY 1951**
To solidify communist gains in the north, Gen Giap's 20,000 Viet Minh attacked French forts between Hanoi and the Gulf of Tonkin. Fighting on open ground and from bunkers, French troops under Gen Jean de Lattre held back all but the most determined of Giap's human-wave assaults. These the French turned with air strikes, using napalm. Although successful in capturing some positions, Giap's divisions ultimately suffered 6000 casualties before withdrawing.

■ **DIEN BIEN PHU, 20 NOV 1953–7 MAY 1954**
Recognizing the deficiencies of the Vietnamese People's Army in training and materiel, Gen Giap's strategy was to use guerilla warfare to overcome France's military advantages. By striking at targets less well defended than Hanoi, Giap hoped to isolate the France's combat units and negate their weapons superiority. For his part, French Gen Henry Navarre wanted to break the stalemate that had left the Viet Minh in control of the north, and isolated French power at Hanoi and along the Red river delta. Against Giap's 125,000 communist soldiers, Navarre had 178,000, including French

and Vietnamese colonial troops, as well as 200,000 troops of the Vietnamese National Army (VNA). To change the situation, Navarre planned to go on the offensive. By using small-unit tactics behind enemy lines, he hoped to turn the Viet Minh's asymmetric advantage against it. Additionally, the French sought to lure the main body of Giap's army into a pitched battle where his weaknesses could be exploited. Learning of a Viet Minh supply route to Laos, Navarre deployed forces to Dien Bien Phu valley to put his strategy into action. He reinforced the garrison with an airborne landing on 20 November 1953, with forces arrayed in five camps (each given a woman's name). By 13 March, the French had deployed almost 11,000 troops to the area around the Dien Bien Phu airfield, under the command of Brig Christian de Castries. However, the French had not secured the surrounding hillsides. Seeing an opportunity to use the terrain against his foe, Giap moved a large force of almost 50,000 troops into the valley, placing his own guns on

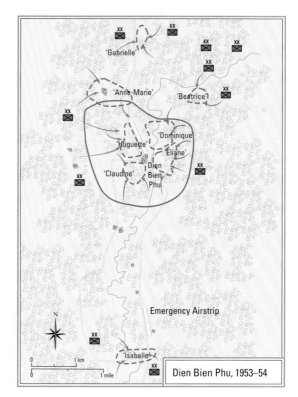

Dien Bien Phu, 1953–54

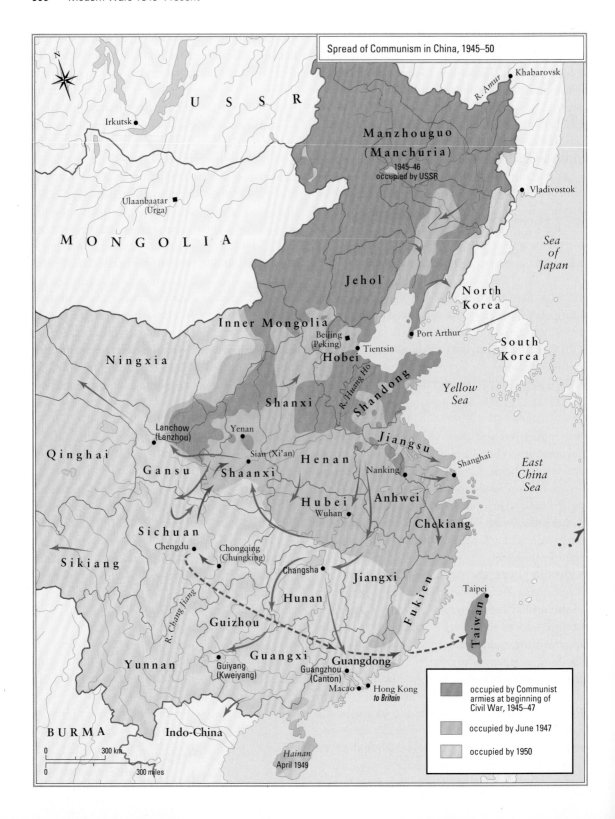

Spread of Communism in China, 1945–50

occupied by Communist armies at beginning of Civil War, 1945–47

occupied by June 1947

occupied by 1950

Indochina War, 1946–54

Map legend:
- Viet Minh control 1946–50
- Viet Minh control 1950–54
- French garrison

However, Viet Minh counter-attacks eventually seized the airfield, driving the French back onto the defensive. Despite the arrival of airborne reinforcements, the French withdrew to camp 'Isabelle'. Giap planned to complete his victory with a mass attack on 1 May. Counter-battery fire finally silenced the French artillery and the camp's fate was sealed. After a week of hand-to-hand combat, 'Isabelle's' defences collapsed and de Castries was overrun. The colonial government had understated Viet Minh combat strength and their will to fight at great cost: 25,000 Vietnamese and more than 1500 French dead. As Dien Bien Phu fell, so did French rule in Indochina. The day after Navarre's force was defeated, Paris agreed with Ho Chi Minh to partition Vietnam, setting the stage for the Second Indochina War, involving the United States from 1965 to 1975.

Indo-Pakistan War 1947–48

■ **OPERATION GULMARG, 22 OCTOBER 1947**
Pakistan-backed Muslim Pathan tribesmen rose up in Jammu and Kashmir ahead of the states' accession to India. By 25 October, 5000 guerillas had defeated Brig Rajinder Singh's state forces to threaten the strategically important Sringar airfield. On 26 October, the Hindu Maharaja agreed to accession and the Indian Army counter-attacked.

■ **MIRPUR, 25 NOVEMBER 1947**
Pakistani artillery fire breached Mirpur's walls, allowing Pathan tribal Lashkars to enter the city and drive out the state forces. There were thousands of civilian casualties in the looting that followed.

■ **JHANGER, 18 MARCH 1948**
Operation *Vijay*, spearheaded by India's Jammu and Kashmir (JAK) Division of paratroops and infantry, sought to reverse gains made by Pathan tribesmen in the previous autumn. The 19th Infantry Brigade recaptured and held Jhanger village.

■ **INDIAN SUMMER OFFENSIVE, 18 MAY–23 JULY 1948**
By the first of the year, the Indian Army had deployed three brigades in Jammu (50th Para,

the higher ground and in individual dugouts among the trench lines his engineers had dug around the French encampment. In the opening attack, Giap's 308th Division assaulted the French camps 'Gabrielle' and 'Beatrice,' both of which fell after two days of intense fighting. Viet Minh anti-aircraft fire – much more powerful than the French anticipated – helped to check French warplanes' attempts to support the defenders. Giap's guns shot down 12 French aircraft during the first phase of the battle. Communist artillery fire also closed the airfield and restricted French resupply missions to imprecise, high-altitude air drops. Meanwhile, under covering fire by communist mortar and machine-gun teams, Giap's engineers continued to dig their way toward the French perimeter. Navarre stepped up air strikes, using tens of thousands of litres of napalm, with little effect on the Viet Minh will to fight. Some sorties by French troops proved successful, in one instance capturing several of Giap's guns.

80th and 268th Infantry) and one in the Kashmir valley (161th Infantry). Meanwhile, the Pakistani army had deployed five brigades in support of local 'Azad Kashmir' forces, militias comprised mostly of Pathan tribesmen. MGen Kodendera Thimayya, Indian Army, planned an offensive drive to Domel with two brigades. By 23 May, the Indians had captured Chowkibal and Tithwal but, by June, had bogged down in their attempt to seize Domel. With Pakistani materiel support, tribal Lashkars had taken Skardu (Kharphocho) Fort on 18 April. They conquered Kargil, and threatened Leh, capital of Ladakh. Pakistani troops captured Pandu on 23 July. The summer offensive ended in a stalemate. The situation persisted until the ceasefire agreement on 1 January 1949.

Arab–Israeli War 1948–49

■ MISHMAR-HAEMEK, 4–12 APRIL 1948
Preceded by a Syrian artillery barrage, 1000 soldiers of Fawzi al-Qawuqji's Arab Liberation Army (ALA) assaulted Mishmar Haemek kibbutz in western Galilee. Troops of Yitzak Sadeh's Palmach force counter-attacked, burning several Arab villages before driving off the ALA on 12 April.

■ JERUSALEM, 15 MAY–18 JULY 1948
After the Mandate for Palestine ended on 14 May, Jewish militants seized former British outposts and Jewish neighbourhoods in central and west Jerusalem. More than 5000 Arab troops from neighbouring states invaded Israel. With them came 4500 troops of the 'Arab Legion', Transjordanian soldiers under the command of former British officers. By 28 May, the Arab Legion was firmly in control of East Jerusalem and the Old City. Arab armies blockaded Jewish-held West Jerusalem in a military stalemate.

■ LATRUN, 23 MAY–18 JULY 1948
In a series of failed attacks, the Hagana's 7th Brigade failed to dislodge the Arab Legion and ALA forces holding the heights of Latrun. Unable to conquer the old police fort, the Israelis developed an alternate route to resupply Jerusalem: the 'Burma Road'.

■ ISDUD, 29 MAY–3 JUNE 1948
In Operation *Pleshet*, 45 Israeli Defence Forces (IDF) soldiers and as many as 15 Egyptians of the 2nd Brigade died fighting over Isdud village. The Egyptians had repulsed an Israeli attack, but the Arabs' advance on Tel Aviv had been checked.

■ LYDDA AND RAMLE, 11–14 JULY 1948
With Arab Legion troops having withdrawn on 11–12 July, the IDF attacked the towns, killing some civilians. The Jewish troops then expelled most of the Arab population, creating 70,000 refugees.

■ OPERATION DEKEL, 9–18 JULY 1948
In its largest offensive in northern Israel, the IDF's 7th Armored Brigade, with air support, attacked lower Galilee. The brigade drove ALA forces from the region and captured 15 Arab villages, including Nazareth, which fell on 16 July.

■ OPERATION KEDEM, 16–17 JULY 1948
The IDF, supported by Jewish militants, made a futile frontal assault on the Old City. The Arab Legion drove off the attack, killing 83 Jewish soldiers.

■ OPERATION YOAV, 15–22 OCTOBER 1948
IDF air and land units attacked Egyptian forces at Hatta-Karatiya, opening a route to the Negev Desert. IDF aircraft bombed el-Arish, grounding the Egyptian Air Force. On 22 October, the IDF 8th Armoured Brigade broke through to capture Beersheba.

■ OPERATION HIRAM, 28–31 OCTOBER 1948
Four IDF brigades expelled a substantial Arab force from the Galilee region, including Fawzi al-Kaukji's 3000–4000 ALA troops. Israel gained all of Galilee except for the Syrian-held Mishmar Hayarden pocket. The Arabs suffered 400 dead and more than 500 captured.

■ OPERATION HOREV, 19 DECEMBER 1948–7 JANUARY 1949
Israeli troops attacked Egyptian bases in Gaza and seized territory in the Sinai. The IDF also shot down five British Spitfire fighters, prompting outrage from the UK and the USA. Israel agreed to a ceasefire on 7 January.

Costa Rican Civil War 1948

■ CARTAGO, 12 APRIL 1948

Having defeated government troops at the battle
of El Empalme, José Figueres Ferrer's 'National
Liberation Army' (NLA) was able to seize the
mountainous regions of Dota and Pereze Zeledon.
From these heights, the rebels successfully assaulted
Cartago, 19km from the capital San Jose.

■ PICADO SAN JOSE, 24 APRIL 1948

Having taken the heights of Ochomogo, the NLA
threatened San Jose with direct bombardment.
Costa Rican President Teodoro Picado Michalski
sued for peace. The 44-day civil war cost 2000 lives.

Tibet 1950–51

■ CHAMDO, 19 OCTOBER 1950

Forty thousand PLA soldiers entered Tibet,
defeating a pro-independence force of fewer
than 9000 men. The Chinese XVIII Corps
overwhelmed the poorly trained and equipped
militia and negotiations were then concluded with
Lhasa to re-establish Chinese sovereignty.

Korean War 1950–53

■ NORTH KOREAN INVASION, 25 JUNE–15 SEPTEMBER 1950

In 1950, the North Korean People's Army
(NKPA) had built up a fighting force that included
approximately 135,000 soldiers in 10 infantry
divisions, supported by artillery and an armoured
brigade equipped with Soviet-supplied, WWII-
vintage T-34/85 tanks. On the eve of the invasion,
the Republic of Korea Army (ROKA) comprised
95,000 men, most of whom would be routed within
a week of the invasion. On the morning of 25 June,
NKPA soldiers and 150 tanks crossed the 38th
Parallel and drove south in darkness. Overwhelmed,
the South Korean defensive line collapsed on Seoul.
ROKA commanders prematurely demolished the
bridges north of the capital, stranding much of their
army and its equipment. On 28 June, NKPA 3rd

and 4th Divisions captured Seoul and prepared
for a final push south to destroy what remained of
ROKA. As the situation worsened, US President
Harry Truman authorized Gen Douglas MacArthur
to send combat troops to assist the South Koreans.

MacArthur ordered MGen William F. Dean, of
the US 24th Infantry Division (based in Japan)
to airlift 500 men into the war zone as a delaying
force, while the US Navy brought the rest of the
division across in troop ships. LCol Charles B.
Smith commanded the 1st Battalion of the 21st
Infantry Regiment. On 5 July, Task Force Smith,
with artillery support, dug in near Osan. The NKPA
4th Division struck hard, its tanks defeating the
Americans' inadequate anti-armour weaponry. The
North Koreans successfully flanked the Americans
and cut Smith's force in half. By 19 July, Allied
troops had withdrawn to fight at Taejon, using new
3.5in rockets to defeat some of the NKPA's T-34s.
However, the communists' strong frontal attacks
and successful flanking manoeuvres carried the day,

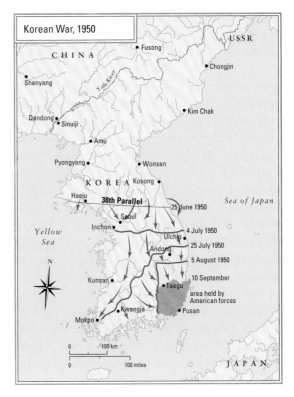

driving the defenders back to a 230km defensive line north and west of Pusan on Korea's southern coast. The NKPA captured MGen Dean and inflicted 30 per cent casualties on the 24th Division.

■ PUSAN PERIMETER, 4 AUGUST–15 SEPTEMBER 1950

By 1 August, the United Nations force in South Korea (largely comprised of American and ROKA combat units) numbered 92,000 soldiers, including more than 500 US tanks, the 24th and 25th Divisions, the 1st Cavalry Division, and five ROKA divisions. This force, led by LGen Walton Walker's US Eighth Army, held the vital port at Pusan. Seeking a knock-out blow that would drive the UN into the sea, 98,000 NKPA troops attacked unsuccessfully along four axes: Masan, Miryang, Taegu and Kyongju. Allied air power and artillery helped hold the line.

■ INCHON, 15–19 SEPTEMBER 1950

With the North Korean invasion halted, the US X Corps, led by MGen Edward M. Almond, had the task of planning an amphibious landing in the rear of the NKPA advance. Gen MacArthur wanted to relieve pressure from LGen Walker's Eighth Army, ROKA and UN troops at Pusan. The generals selected Inchon, a Yellow Sea port 41km west of Seoul, and the vital roads and railway hubs that linked the NKPA's troops in the south with their supply lines in the north. MacArthur's strategy was for a surprise landing at Inchon (codenamed Operation *Chromite*) to flank the communists and threaten to cut off their armies, even as the Eighth Army led a breakout from the Pusan Perimeter and pushed north. The landing force included more than 8000 South Korean augmentees, as well as the 1st Marine Division and the US Army's 7th Infantry Division, stationed in Japan. The ROKA 17th Regiment was in reserve, with no other reinforcements available in case the landing was strongly opposed. The gamble was serious, as it required the UN to commit its only combat-ready reserves to an operation fraught with difficulties. McArthur's plan roused the objections of some of his staff, particularly the naval warfare experts of Task Force 77, who

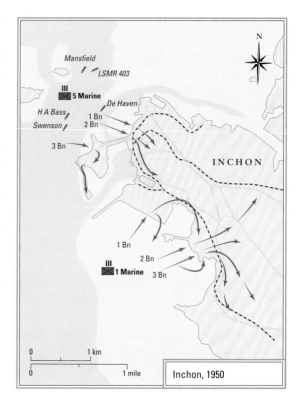

Inchon, 1950

noted the Yellow Sea's hazardous 9.1m tides, coastal sandbars and mudflats, and the difficulty of mounting a full-scale amphibious landing into an urban area with a high seawall. Complicating the plan, North Korean attacks had pinned down the Eighth Army's divisions, blunting the strength of the Pusan breakout. Walker was forced to delay his push north until after the landing force had established the Inchon beachhead. Meanwhile, informed by spies on Yonghung Do Island on the Inchon approaches, the UN task force knew it confronted an NKPA force totalling approximately 2000 men. Keystones to the area's defences were the fortifications on Wolmi Do Island (planned site for the landing operation's Green Beach). US Marine Corps' F4U Corsairs attacked with double loads of napalm (43,091kg in total), burning out the western half of the island. On the morning of 15 September, the initial wave of a 70,000-man invasion force completed the first major amphibious assault since the WWII landing at Okinawa (1 April

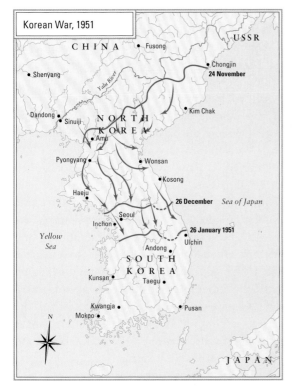

Korean War, 1951

Korean War, 1953

1945). The Marines of 3rd Battalion, 5th Marine Regiment, 1st Marine Division, supported by nine M26 Pershing tanks, overwhelmed Wolmi Do's garrison of approximately 400 NKPA marines and artillerymen. By 08:00, the UN task force had seized Wolmi Do and the causeway connecting it to Inchon. Two other assault waves, involving 500 landing craft, carried the 1st and 5th Marine Regiments to Red and Blue Beaches on the north and south of the city. Naval artillery from the cruisers HMS *Jamaica* and USS *Rochester* battered the communists as the UN troops hit the beach. At Red Beach, 5th Marines clambered over the seawall and overcame stiff resistance to capture the high ground of Cemetery Hill and Observatory Hill. At Blue Beach, naval rockets silenced an NKPA mortar team that had destroyed one of the landing craft. Subsequently, 1st Marines seized the main road to Seoul.

With the beachhead established, a major logistical operation got underway. By the seventh day, the task force had landed 53,882 people, 6629 vehicles and 25,512 tons of cargo. The battle had cost the UN 222 casualties, including 22 killed. The North Koreans, taken completely by surprise, endured more than 1350 casualties.

■ **BREAKOUT FROM PUSAN PERIMETER, 16–23 SEPTEMBER 1950**

With US X Corps at Inchon, LGen Walker's Eighth Army broke out from the 230km Pusan Perimeter. There, 92,000 UN troops faced the 70,000-man North Korean invasion. They attacked north and west, fighting bloody battles for the high ground against a deeply entrenched and determined foe. By 23 September, the NKPA in the south had disintegrated. The fighting cost 790 American and several thousand North Korean lives. UN forces captured 23,000 communist soldiers.

■ **PYONGYANG, 15–19 OCTOBER 1950**

On 27 September, US Gen Douglas MacArthur had crossed the 38th Parallel to destroy the remnant of the NKPA and unite Korea under President

Syngman Rhee. LGen Walker's I Corps, comprising the US 1st Cavalry, 24th Infantry and South Korean 1st Divisions, formed up at Kaesong. Battling through a series of fortified positions en route to the North Korean capital, the 5th Cavalry Regiment and South Korean 1st Division captured the city.

■ First Chinese Offensive, 25 October–30 November 1950

Although Gen MacArthur had not expected Chinese intervention, 200,000 soldiers of the newly re-designated 'Peoples Volunteer Army' (PVA) crossed the Yalu river into North Korea. A dangerous gap had opened between LGen Walker's American troops and allied South Korean units. The Chinese exploited this weakness, driving back the South Korean II Corps and pressuring the US I Corps. At Unsan, PVA attacks broke the South Korean 15th Infantry Regiment and US 8th Cavalry Regiment. On 1–2 November, the PVA 348th Regiment decimated the 8th Cavalry's 3rd Battalion. The fighting cost more than 1000 American, 500 South Koreans and 600 Chinese lives. As the PVA advance slowed, the US Eighth Army reorganized with the intention of attacking north of the Chongchon river. At that time, UN forces comprised three main bodies of troops, including I Corps (with the US 24th Infantry, South Korean 1st Infantry Divisions and the British 27th Commonwealth Brigade); IX Corps (with the US 2nd and 25th Infantry Divisions and the Turkish Brigade); and the South Korean II Corps (with the 6th, 7th and 8th Infantry Divisions). LGen Walker had placed in reserve the US 1st Cavalry Division, the 187th Regimental Combat Team (Airborne) and the British 29th Infantry Brigade. On 25 November, the Chinese resumed their offensive, crushing the South Korean II Corps and exposing the Eighth Army's right flank. By 28 November, plans for an offensive to the Yalu river had been abandoned and all US and South Korean forces were in retreat. The fighting at the Chongchon turned the tide, costing South Korean and UN forces thousands of dead and wounded, and forcing the Eighth Army to withdraw from North Korea.

■ Chosin Reservoir, 27–29 November 1950

The US X Corps, comprising the 1st Marine Division, the 3rd and 7th Infantry Divisions, and 41 Commando British Royal Marines, together with the South Korean I Corps, were moving north on the east side of the Korean peninsula. At the Chosin Reservoir, the Chinese 79th and 89th Divisions attacked US Marines deployed to the west at Yudam-ni. At the same time, the PVA's 80th Division hit a task force of UN soldiers on the eastern side, effectively splitting X Corps in two. Hand-to-hand night combat in frigid weather ensued. Hundreds of Chinese died in human-wave assaults. Nevertheless, low on ammunition and with hundreds of wounded men to evacuate, the UN task force withdrew south to link up with the other part of X Corps at Hagaru-ri. The Chinese set roadblocks and attacked the retreating column. The task force suffered more than one-third casualties. One Chinese division had been nearly annihilated.

■ Kunu-ri, 28 November 1950

The Chinese 42nd and 38th Armies flanked the US Eighth Army, threatening its retreat. At Kunu-ri, the PVA mauled the US 2nd Infantry Division and the Turkish Brigade, with the Americans suffering 4500 casualties and losing 64 guns and other equipment to the Chinese.

■ Second Chinese Offensive, 26 December 1950–22 January 1951

The Chinese attacked UN and South Korean forces guarding Seoul. Faced with a collapsing front as two of the three South Korean divisions broke, newly arrived Eighth Army commander, LGen Matthew Ridgway, ordered a withdrawal to positions south of the Han river. The British 27th Commonwealth Brigade took casualties in the fighting. On 15–16 January, the 25th Infantry Division conducted a reconnaissance south of Osan, where they made contact with the PVA. The division lost three men and caused 1380 Chinese casualties

■ Operation Ripper, 7–22 March 1951

The South Korean 1st Division and US 3rd Division liberated Seoul on 15 March. IX and X

Corps pushed north, capturing Hongchon and Chunchon. However, the UN had failed in one of its objectives: to destroy the PVA and North Korean armies in a pitched battle.

■ IMJIN RIVER, 21–25 APRIL 1951

China's Gen Peng Dehuai launched a major offensive to regain the initiative from UN forces north of the 38th Parallel, and drive south to capture Seoul. On the night of 21–22 April, in the sector held by the British 29th Infantry Brigade, 27,000 Chinese troops attacked across the Imjin river. The 29th Brigade included 1st Battalion the Gloucestershire Regiment, under LCol James P. Carne. Along a 15km front, the Chinese swept the UN troops south, isolating Carne's battalion, inflicting heavy casualties and forcing him into a defensive position on Hill 235. There, the Glosters made an heroic last stand: 11,000 Chinese held at bay for two days by 700 British soldiers, until they were overrun. The Chinese captured the remnant of two of the battalion's companies and Carne, who earned the Victoria Cross for his bravery and leadership. The UN renamed Hill 235 in honor of the Gloucestershire Regiment's sacrifice, which saved Seoul from conquest.

■ PORK CHOP HILL, 6–11 JULY 1953

During the last major communist offensive of the war, two Chinese divisions attacked the defenders of an outpost near Cheorwan. On 11 July, Eighth Army commander LGen Maxwell Taylor ordered UN troops to withdraw from the hilltop position. Within two days, six PVA divisions attacked the South Korean II Corps line at Kumsong but their offensive bogged down. The UN made a cursory attempt at regaining lost territory ahead of the 27 July armistice.

Laotian War 1953–75

■ FIRST NORTH VIETNAMESE INVASION, APRIL 1953

Forty thousand Viet Minh troops, under Gen Giap, joined by 2000 Pathet Lao communist guerillas, entered northern Laos. Ten thousand Lao and 3000 French troops eventually halted the communist advance on Luang Prabang and the Plain of Jars.

■ SECOND NORTH VIETNAMESE INVASION, 28 JULY 1959

The People's Army of Vietnam (PAVN) crossed the 'Ho Chi Minh Trail' to attack Royal Lao Army units along Laos' mountainous eastern border. With Pathet Lao guerillas in tow, the communists one again advanced on Laos' capital.

■ US AIR WAR AGAINST LAOS, 14 DECEMBER 1964–29 MARCH 1973

Embroiled in the struggle against North Vietnam's expansion, the US and its regional allies sought to counter sympathetic communist insurgencies, including the Pathet Lao movement, against the Kingdom of Laos. Under a covert program (Operation *Barrel Roll*), the Central Intelligence Agency (CIA), the US Air Force (USAF) and Navy carried out reconnaissance, forwarded air control, close air support and air mobility missions against Laotian and Vietnamese communists, centred geographically on the Plain of Jars. *Barrel Roll's* special missions included working with the fiercely anti-communist Hmong tribes to build secret airstrips and install aerial navigation beacons atop Laotian hills. From 1965 to 1968, the Americans also conducted Operations *Steel Tiger* and *Tiger Hound*, which attacked the North Vietnamese supply route through south-eastern Laos. These included Arc Light B-52 bombing missions.

■ NAM BAC, 13 JANUARY 1968

Pathet Lao and PAVN troops annihilated the Royal Lao Army reserve strength in a multi-division attack at the Bam Nam Bac airfield. Outgunned and outmanoeuvred, one-third of the Royal Lao defenders fled, leaving the rest of the garrison to be overwhelmed.

■ CU KIET CAMPAIGN, 23 MAR–SEPTEMBER 1969

With US air support from Operation *Barrel Roll*, the Royal Lao Army advanced on communist positions. During the summer, the Pathet Lao and the PAVN 174th Vietnamese Volunteer Regiment counter-attacked and, by September, recaptured lost territory in the Plain of Jars.

Cuban Revolution 1953–59

■ MONCADO BARRACKS, 26 JULY 1953

Fidel and Raul Castro led an attack by 135 communist rebels on the headquarters of Cuba's Antonio Maceo Regiment. Col Alberto del Rio Chaviano's troops outnumbered the rebels, who bungled their initial advance on the gated compound. Eighteen Cuban troops and nine rebels died. Government troops pursued the fleeing guerillas, executing 56 and capturing 99 (including the Castro brothers). After serving time in prison, the Castro brothers went into exile in Mexico, where they plotted the downfall of the Cuban president, Fulgencio Batista.

■ GRANMA LANDING, 2–5 DECEMBER 1956

Having acquired the yacht *Granma*, 82 rebels (including the Castros and Che Guevara) made a seven-day crossing to Niquero. The rebels reached Cuba's Sierra Maestra Mountains, but were attacked and nearly annihilated by government troops.

■ STORMING PRESIDENTIAL PALACE, 13 MAR 1957

At Havana, an anti-communist rebel group, the 'Directorio Revolucionario', led by Jose Echeverria, attacked Batista's Presidential Palace and a radio station in Havana. Most of the rebels died skirmishing with police and government soldiers. On 14 March, the USA imposed an arms embargo in response to Batista's brutality. Nevertheless, his 30,000–40,000-strong military and police forces used increasingly harsh tactics to put down rebel uprisings in the capital and throughout rebel strongholds, such as the mountains and foothills of Oriente Province.

■ LA PLATA, 11–21 JULY 1958

In Operation *Verano*, 12,000 Cuban soldiers advanced into rebel-held territory, where they were defeated in a series of gunfights with Castro's handful of guerillas. At La Plata, the rebels crushed a Cuban battalion and captured 240 soldiers.

■ GUISA, 20–30 NOVEMBER 1958

Having defeated Operation *Verano* and captured

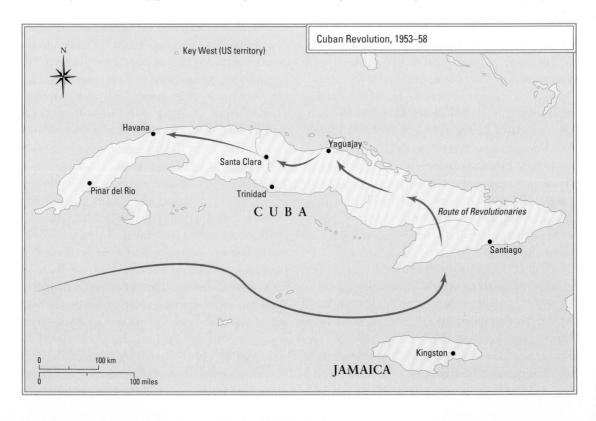

government weapons and equipment, Castro's rebels counter-attacked in Oriente Province. At Guisa, 200 rebels overwhelmed government troops.

■ YAGUAJAY, 19–30 DECEMBER 1958

Near Santa Clara, capital of Las Villas Province, two rebel columns, under Che Guevara and Camilo Cienfuegos, attacked a 250-man Cuban Army garrison. Resisting all efforts by the rebels, the soldiers fought until they exhausted their ammunition and were forced to surrender.

■ SANTA CLARA, 28 DEC 1958–1 JAN 1959

In the decisive final combat of the revolution, Che Guevara led two rebel columns in a successful siege. The communists captured an armoured troop train and forced the surrender of the city's garrison. Twelve days after the battle, Batista fled Cuba.

Algerian War of Independence 1954–62

ALGIERS 30 SEPTEMBER 1956–24 SEPTEMBER 1957

The Algerian National Liberation Front (FLN) carried out a campaign of bombings and ambush attacks against French Algerian police and French Army troops. As French and Algerian separatists negotiated secretly in Europe, reactionary French Algerian and FLN terrorist units carried out an escalating series of deadly attacks throughout the colony, including civilian targets in the city. During the battle, FLN fighters were responsible for more than 800 attacks each month through the first half of 1957.

The French authorities responded with overwhelming force, breaking a Muslim general strike and destroying the FLN organization in the city. Although the French regained control of the city, the FLN's campaign had been productive in compelling negotiations with the French Government and in gaining political support from sympathetic organizations including the French Communist Party. The FLN's tactics had succeeded in provoking a strong response from the French Government and military, which launched a brutal counter-insurgency campaign that hastened the loss of the 'hearts and minds' of Algerians and abroad. By September 1956, Paris had sent more than 400,000 French troops under Gen Raoul Salan. The force structure had been determined by France's analysis (based somewhat on its experience in Indochina) of how many soldiers would be required to secure Algeria's villages. Rebel groups had approximately 29,000 fighters throughout the country with 8000 assembled in the areas around Algiers, especially Kabylia to the east. Both sides became locked in a bloody eight-year war as the French Government tried – ultimately unsuccessfully – to conduct a punitive campaign against the rebels while retaining political control of the colony's Arab and Kabyle population. On 19 March 1962, the Algerian War ended with French withdrawal. The conflict had cost more than 153,000 Algerian and over 25,600 French lives.

Hungarian Revolution 1956

■ BUDAPEST, 23 OCTOBER–10 NOVEMBER 1956

Two hundred thousand students and citizens demonstrated for government reform outside the parliament building. The Hungarian Government condemned the protesters, who tore down a large bronze statue of Soviet leader Josef Stalin. Hungarian security forces fired on the crowd. Hungarian Army troops, deployed to quell the uprising, mutinied on the side of the protesters as the demonstration became increasingly violent.

On 24 October, Soviet soldiers and tanks crossed the border to restore Soviet authority in the country. The insurgents fought back with determination, using petrol bombs plus small arms seized during earlier clashes with the security services. After a lull in the fighting, the Soviet Eighth Mechanized and Thirty-Eighth Armies encircled Budapest. Then, on 4 November, Russian troops moved into the city to crush the rebellion. In Moscow, the Politburo argued that Soviet action was legitimate assistance for the Hungarian people fighting to reverse a violent counter-revolution. More than 2500 Hungarians and 700 Soviet soldiers died.

Political changes

- Social revolution
- Reformism
- Populism
- Christian democracy
- Unreformed militarism
- Guerilla movements
- Establishing or re-establishing democratic rule
- Cuban-inspired guerilla movements 1959–68
- US intervention 1965–94

Los Angeles

New York

Washington

UNITED STATES OF AMERICA

NORTH ATLANTIC OCEAN

N

MEXICO

Cuban Revolution 1959

Havana

Mexico City
Puebla Veracruz

CUBA

■ *Zapatista revolt 1994*

DOMINICAN REP.

■ *Civil conflict 1960–96*

BELIZE
HONDURAS

JAMAICA HAITI

Puerto Rico

GUATEMALA
Guatemala City

Tegucigalpa

■ *Civil war 1979–92*

EL SALVADOR

■ *Sandinista revolution, 1979–90,*
■ *US-backed Contras, 1981–89*
□ *Democratization, 1990*

NICARAGUA

Managua

GRENADA

Cartagena

Port of Spain

TRINIDAD & TOBAGO

COSTA RICA

San José

Caracas

GUYANA

Panama City

VENEZUELA

Georgetown
Paramaribo

■ *Rural insurgence from c. 1963*

PANAMA

SURINAM Fr. Cayenne
G.

■ *Democratization 1959*

Bogotá

COLOMBIA

Macapá

Belém

■ *Intermittent militarism to 1978*
□ *Democratization from 1979*

Quito

Manaus

Fortaleza

■ *Radical militarism 1968–75*
■ *Sendero Luminoso from 1980*
■ *Return to civil rule 1980*
(President Fujimori suspends constitution 1992)

ECUADOR Guayaquil

Piura

B   R   A   Z   I   L

Salvador (Bahia)

Trujillo

PERU

Huanuco

■ *João Goulart 1961–64*
■ *Modernizing militarism 1964–84*
■ *Civilian rule, 1985 and eventual democratization*

Callao
Lima

Cuzco

Brasília

■ *Bolivian revolution 1952–64*
■ *Che Guevara (killed 1967)*
■ *Military rule mainly, 1964–82*
□ *Democratization from 1982*

PACIFIC OCEAN

BOLIVIA

Arequipa

La Paz

Sucre

Belo Horizonte

Rio de Janeiro
São Paulo Santos

PARAGUAY

■ *Stroessner dictatorship 1954–89*
□ *Democratization from 1989*

Antofagasta

Asunción

Florianópolis

Copiapó

Tucumán

■ *Military 1974–84*
■ *Tupamaros highpoint 1967–72*
■ *Civilian rule and redemocratization 1985*

Córdoba
Santa Fe

Pôrto Alegre

Valparaíso

Mendoza

Fray Bentos

URUGUAY

Rio Grande

Santiago

Buenos Aires

Montevideo

Concepción

■ *Eduardo Frei 1964–70*
■ *Salvador Allende's Marxist programme 1970–73*
■ *Pinochet dictatorship 1973–89*
■ *Democratization 1989*

Valdivia
Osorno

Bahía Blanca

■ *Juan Domingo Perón 1946–55; 1973–4*
■ *Montoneros and the People's Revolutionary Army 1970s*
■ *Military 1976–83; the 'Dirty War' 1976–79*
■ *Democratization and civilian rule 1984*

CHILE

Rawson

Comodoro Rivadavia

ARGENTINA

Falkland Is.

1982: Invaded by Argentina British military task force recaptures the islands

Form of Government 1945–95

- Military support
- Democratic
- Socialist

South American Conflicts and Revolutions

Suez Crisis 1956–57

■ OPERATION *KADESH*, 29 OCT–6 NOV 1956

The Egyptian Government under Nasser had declared a blockade of the Tiran Straits at the Suez Canal, prompting a crisis response from Britain, France and the United States. Israel claimed before the United Nations that Nasser's actions leading up to the blockade had broken the Israel–Egypt Armistice Agreement of 1949, resulting in deadly clashes with Egyptian troops along the Sinai frontier. Israel determined to go to war. Its plan had four objectives: Sharm el-Sheikh and access to the Red Sea, al-Arish, Abu Uwayulah and the Gaza Strip. Israeli paratroops, under Gen Moshe Dayan, made an assault landing near Mitla Pass near the Suez Canal and, by 5 November, had overwhelmed the Egyptian garrison at Sharm el-Sheikh. Israel had control of the entire Sinai peninsula and the Gaza Strip. Soviet and American pressure at the UN later compelled the Israelis to withdraw to their pre-invasion border. As many as 3000 Egyptians and 231 Israeli soldeirs had died in the fighting.

■ JEBEL HEITAN, 29–31 OCTOBER 1956

At the mountainous Mitla Pass, Ariel Sharon's 202nd Paratroop Brigade attempted to seize the high ground at Jebel Heitan. Well-entrenched Egyptian forces sprung the trap, inflicting 38 casualties. The Israelis counter-attacked, killing more than 200 Egyptians and routing the others.

■ ANGLO-FRENCH INVASION 1956

Britain and France reacted furiously to President Nasser's nationalization of the Suez Canal and, while they pursued a diplomatic solution, they also prepared Operation *Musketeer*. These military plans were hindered by the lack of readiness of the two countries' armed forces (not least concerning landing craft) and their military commitments elsewhere. The operation began on 31 October with air attacks against the Egyptian Air Force. These strikes were conducted partly by bombers based in Cyprus and Malta but, because other airfields were either out of range or their use was denied for political reasons, heavy reliance was placed on the British carriers *Eagle*, *Albion* and *Bulwark* and the French *Arromanches* and *Lafayette*, especially for the more effective fighter-bombers. Air superiority was achieved within two days. One version of the plan had aimed to force Egypt's capitulation by bombing alone, but it was realized that this was not practical. On 5 November, British and French paratroopers dropped to capture an airfield and key bridges for the subsequent advance and, on 6 November, there followed an amphibious landing at Port Said. Two Royal Marine Commando units backed by tanks assaulted beaches west of the Suez Canal, while a third was landed ashore from the carriers *Theseus* and *Ocean* in the first ever helicopter-borne amphibious assault. French forces landed east of the canal. The landings, which encountered limited opposition, were supported by naval gunfire and carrier aircraft. While the British and French forces were well on their way to achieving their objectives, US diplomatic and financial pressure caused the two governments to end the operation.

Congo Crisis 1960–66

■ OPERATION *RUMPUNCH*, 28 AUGUST 1961

United Nations forces set out to disarm Katangan troops and expel foreign advisors and mercenaries. Canadian UN soldiers arrested 338 of the 442 European officers in the Gendarmerie. However, many mercenary troops later returned to the area.

■ OPERATION *DRAGON ROUGE*, JUL–NOV 1964

During the 'Simba Rebellion', Congolese tribesmen from Kivu and Orientale Provinces held some hostages at Stanleyville's Victoria Hotel. Under Col Charles Laurent, 350 Belgian paratroopers mounted a rescue. All but 60 of the hostages escaped.

Bay of Pigs Invasion 1961

■ BAY OF PIGS, 17–19 APRIL 1961

A CIA-backed invasion failed to unseat Castro's communist regime in Cuba. Preceding the landing, Cuban exile pilots made diversionary attacks near

Havana. At the invasion site 150km south-east of the capital, 1400 Cuban exile troops of Brigade 2506 came ashore. Cuban military and militia units, including tanks and artillery, counter-attacked and crushed the invasion force, killing 118 invaders, capturing more than 1000 and losing 176 of their own.

Invasion of Goa 1961

■ AIR WAR, 18 DECEMBER 1961

A dozen Indian Air Force Canberra bombers attacked the Portuguese air base at Dabolim, holing the runway but leaving structures intact. Indian fighter-bombers attacked a radio station at Bambolim as well as Portuguese artillery positions and supply depots.

■ NAVAL WAR, 18–19 DECEMBER 1961

The Indian Navy covered a landing by marines to secure Anjidiv Island. At Mormugao harbour, three Indian frigates attacked and crippled the Portuguese sloop *Afonso de Albuquerque*. The Indian cruiser INS *New Delhi* battered the Portuguese at Diu Fort with naval gunfire.

■ LAND WAR, 17 DECEMBER 1961

India's 17th Infantry Division, with 50th Para and 63th Infantry Brigades supported by artillery and tanks, advanced across Goa. Portuguese Army units withdrew to the south, forming for a final stand at Mormagao and Daman Fort, with its vital airfield.

Eritrean War of Independence 1961–91

■ BARENTU, APRIL 1977–JULY 1978

The Eritrean People's Liberation Front (EPLF) and the Eritrean Liberation Front (ELF) besieged an Ethiopian garrison. Soviet military advisors took direct action: Russian MiG 21 and MiG 23 fighters attacked ELF and EPLF fighters, breaking the siege.

■ MASSAWA, 23 DECEMBER 1977–JANUARY 1978

The EPLF attacked 6000 Ethiopian occupation troops, fighting two battles at this strategically important port city. In a futile attack across open

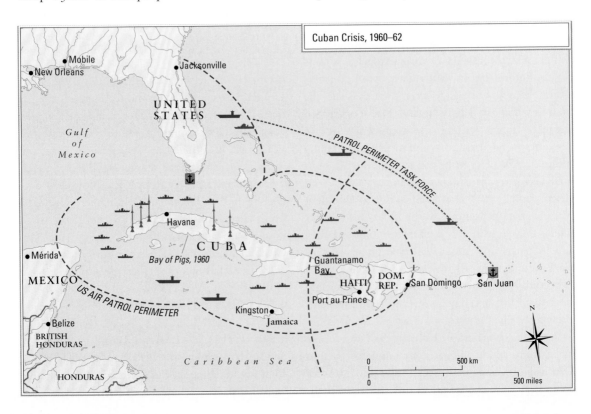

ground, 3000 EPLF troops came under fire by Soviet warships assisting the Ethiopians.

■ AFABET, 19 MARCH 1988

The EPLF captured this important Ethiopian military intelligence centre and supply depot. The rebels seized 50 tanks and a number of rocket artillery vehicles, outgunning the 300,000-strong Ethiopian occupation force for the first time.

Sino-Indian War 1962

■ CHINESE INVASION OF INDIA, OCTOBER 1962

Following a number of disputes between India and the People's Republic of China, (PRC) particularly over the ownership of the Arunachal Pradesh and Aksai Chin regions, the Chinese launched an invasion of the disputed territories on 20 October 1962. The invasion was notable for being conducted in areas more than 1000km apart. The Chinese made significant gains and then sought to negotiate. A peace proposal on 24 October from the Chinese was rejected, leading to a continuation of the fighting. The Chinese made further gains before declaring a unilateral ceasefire on 20 November 1962, then pulling back from the disputed territories, as the objective of securing its borders had been achieved.

■ SE LA AND BOMBDI 17–20 NOVEMBER 1962

Se La and Bombdi were the locations of two heavily fortified Indian positions in the North-east Frontier Agency during the 1962 Sino-Indian War. Se La was cut off and Bombdi fell to Chinese attacks between 17 and 20 November 1962.

■ REZANG LA, 18 NOVEMBER 1962

A bloody battle on 18 November 1962 during the Sino-Indian War, in which 114 out of 123 troops from the Indian Army's Kumaon Regiment died attempting to defend the Rezang La Pass.

Dhofar Rebellion 1962–75

■ OPERATION JAGUAR, OCTOBER 1971–SUMMER 1972

After communist rebels ousted the Sultan of Muscat and Oman, the British government authorized the deployment of special forces to train Oman's military in counter-insurgency tactics. Operation Jaguar was to seize the province's eastern highlands and establish a base of operations there. Omani soldiers and militia units, backed by British Special Air Service (SAS) G and B Squadrons, drove the rebels from their strongholds.

■ MIRBAT, 19 JULY 1972

After overrunning an Omani government outpost, a force of 250 communist rebels called Adoo attacked the British Army Training Team compound at the old frankincense trading port of Mirbat. Nine SAS troopers, led by Capt Mike Kealy, held their ground. British machine-gun and mortar fire took a toll on the rebels. Attacking in waves, the Adoo concentrated their fire on a QF 25-pounder gun emplacement, manned by SAS SSgt Talaiasi Labalaba. Although wounded in the face, the Fijian trooper and his comrades successfully beat back several determined thrusts at the position, firing the heavy gun from point-blank range. After seven hours of battle,

Sino-Indian War, 1962

Omani Air Force BAC 167 Strikemaster jets and a relief unit from G Squadron SAS helped to drive off the rebels. One Omani government soldier and two British troopers, including Labalaba, and more than 80 Adoo died. For his gallantry, Labalaba was posthumously awarded a Mention in Dispatches.

North Yemen Civil War 1962–70

■ RAMADAN OFFENSIVE, FEBRUARY 1963
FM Abdel Amr commanded 20,000 Egyptian and Republican mechanized troops to envelop royalist rebels at Jawf in north-east Yemen. The Egyptians captured the Marib supply depot, interdicting royalist support from Saudi Arabia and forcing a UN-backed ceasefire.

■ HARADH OFFENSIVE, SUMMER 1964
LGen Murtagi launched a conventional offensive against the royalists. On 12 June, Egyptian and Republican mechanized troops attacked north and west from Sanaa, and south and east from Haradh. Prince al-Badr's rebels successfully ambushed their tanks, stalling the campaign.

■ ROYALIST OFFENSIVE, DEC 1964–SUMMER 1965
Prince al-Badr counter-attacked, capturing nearly all of northern, eastern and central Yemen by autumn 1965. Having developed effective guerilla tactics battling off the two Egyptian offensives, the rebels were inflicting 10 casualties to every one they suffered.

■ SIEGE OF SANAA, NOVEMBER–DECEMBER 1967
Following a coup that unseated President as-Sallal, Prince Mohammed bin Hussein led 56,000 Royalist and tribal troops in a siege that captured the airport and highway to the coast, cutting the Republican rebels' Soviet supply route.

Sand War (Algeria–Morocco) 1963

■ TINDOUF/FIGUIG, SEPTEMBER–NOVEMBER 1963
Along the Saharan frontier, Algeria and Morocco fought over an ill-defined, post-colonial border. When the shooting actually started, Algerian troops quickly occupied the former French forts at Zegdou and Meridja. At Hassi Beida and Tinjoub,

on the hamada along the Tiznit–Tindouf route, the rivals battled for two weeks. The Moroccans controlled these points at the Ethiopian-brokered ceasefire in November. Algeria held Ich and the high ground at Figuig.

Guinea-Bissau War of Independence 1963–74

■ OPERATION GREEN SEA, 22 NOVEMBER 1970
Portuguese and Guinean soldiers made an amphibious assault at Conakry. Their plan to capture Amilcar Cabral, leader of the African Party for the Independence of Guinea and Cape Verde (PAIGC), failed, but they successfully rescued 26 Portuguese prisoners at Camp Boiro.

Mozambique War of Independence 1964–74

■ OPERATION GORDION KNOT, 10 JUNE 1970
BGen Kauzla de Arriaga launched a seven-month campaign, involving 10,000 Portuguese and native troops, to oust the Liberation Front of Mozambique (FRELIMO) guerillas from northern Mozambique. Gen de Arriaga's tactics included well-coordinated combined arms attacks and effective use of heliborne air assault to attack and destroy guerilla bases along the Tanzanian frontier. Colonial troops killed between 400 and 650 guerillas and captured more than 1800, and 132 Portuguese soldiers died in the fighting.

Rhodesian Bush War 1964–79

■ SELOUS SCOUT RAID, 9 AUGUST 1976
The Rhodesian Army's elite Selous Scouts attacked a base used by the Zimbabwe African National Liberation Army (ZANLA). Disguised as a rebel supply convoy from Mozambique, the Scouts gained access to the base and formed their vehicles on its parade ground. When the ZAMLA guerillas approached, the Scouts opened fire, killing more than 1000 and capturing 14. No Rhodesians died.

■ **Mapai, 30 May 1977**
With ZANLA fighters massing across the border at Mapai in Mozambique, the Rhodesian Army sent 500 troops on a 'hot pursuit' mission. Rhodesian soldiers, with air support, killed 32 ZANLA.

■ **Umtali, 7 September 1978**
At the Rhodesian border town Umtali, 450 ZANLA guerrillas undertook a 10-minute bombardment. They fired more than 24 82mm shells at civilians, injuring one. The Rhodesians retaliated, launching Canberra bombers and Hawker Hunter fighter jets to hit targets in Mozambique.

Colombian Civil War 1964–

■ **Colombian Palace of Justice, 6 Nov 1965**
Thirty-five M-19 guerillas attacked the Palace of Justice, taking 300 hostages and sparking a siege by Colombian military and police. During the ensuing gun battle, the building caught fire, killing more than 100 people and destroying important legal records.

■ **Las Delicias, 30 August 1996**
In a night attack, 400 FARC guerrillas overran a rural Colombian military base. The rebels carried out a 15-hour siege, killing 34 and capturing 60 government soldiers. The FARCs' success inspired a wave of similar attacks in remote areas.

Vietnam War 1963–75

■ **Ap Bac, 1963**
South Vietnamese forces attacked dug-in elements of the Viet Cong 261st Main Force Battalion south of Saigon. Instead of a predicted easy victory, the South Vietnamese suffered heavy losses and the Viet Cong (VC) slipped away at night.

■ **Gulf of Tonkin, August 1964**
On 2 August, three North Vietnamese torpedo boats launched an unsuccessful attack on the USS *Maddux*, which was engaged in surveillance missions off the North Vietnamese coast. On the night of 4 August, Capt John Herrick, of the USS *Turner Joy*, judged a second attack to be under way. President Lyndon Johnson used the incidents to obtain passage of the Gulf of Tonkin Resolution, allowing him a free hand to take military action in Vietnam.

■ **Bien Hoa, 1 November 1964**
VC forces attacked the American aircraft and crews at the Bien Hoa air base outside Saigon, destroying six B-57s, damaging more than 20 other aircraft, killing five Americans and two South Vietnamese.

■ **Binh Gia, 28 December 1964**
Two VC battalions attacked and occupied the village of Binh Gia. South Vietnamese forces sent to retaliate fell into an ambush fighting ensued, killing 200 South Vietnamese and 250 VC.

■ **Rolling Thunder 1965–1968**
This US–South Vietnamese bombing campaign against North Vietnam opened on 2 March 1965, designed to intensify military pressure in an effort to persuade the North to stop its support of the VC insurgency. Attacks, emanating from aircraft carriers offshore and from bases in South Vietnam and Thailand, initially focused on North Vietnamese airfields, military bases and storage depots. It was the desire to defend US air bases in South Vietnam that prompted Gen William Westmoreland's initial request for intervention by US combat troops. The slow escalation of bombing proceeded through five phases, reaching a crescendo in 1966 and 1967 with concentration on North Vietnamese petroleum facilities, power generation capability and industrial targets. Bombing targets, however, remained strictly limited, especially in sensitive border areas with China and around Hanoi and the port of Hai Phong, out of fear of escalation of the conflict. Although bombing pauses initially were built in to the programme, *Rolling Thunder* had little discernible impact on the war. The North did not choose to negotiate, and traffic down the Ho Chi Minh Trail increased during each year of the bombing. On 31 March 1968, President Lyndon Johnson, in part to spur the beginning of peace talks, limited the area of bombing in North Vietnam to below 19 degrees north latitude, and all bombing was halted on 31 October 1968. In *Rolling Thunder*, US and South Vietnamese aircraft dropped more than 600,000 tons of bombs on North Vietnam, destroying an

estimated 65 per cent of the country's petroleum storage capacity and power-generating capabilities. During the campaign, the US lost nearly 900 aircraft, resulting in the capture of more than 300 prisoners of war.

■ DON XOAI, 9 JUNE 1965

Elements of two VC regiments attacked the US Special Forces camp at Dong Xoai on 9 June and ambushed South Vietnamese relief forces. Losses supported the belief that South Vietnam could not survive without greater US commitment.

■ IA DRANG VALLEY, 14–18 NOVEMBER 1965

After a North Vietnamese attack on the Plei Me Special Forces Camp, on 14 November, 1st Battalion 7th Cavalry air assaulted into Landing Zone X Ray at the Chu Pong Massif near the Cambodian border, resulting in a running series of battles with the North Vietnamese 66th Regiment. US losses of 305 killed against enemy losses of more than 3000 dead helped convince Westmoreland of the wisdom of an attritional strategy.

■ OPERATION MARKET TIME, 1965–1972

Market Time was a US–South Vietnamese naval and air operation to interdict seaborne supplies to communist troops in South Vietnam. Carried out by Task Force 115, under the command of Naval Forces Vietnam (NAVFORV), *Market Time* consisted of three barriers against communist maritime infiltration.

An air barrier consisted of reconnaissance overflights by US Navy aircraft, which reported enemy activity to one of five Coastal Surveillance Centers. An outer ship barrier, stretching from the demilitarized zone (DMZ) on the North/South Vietnam border to the Cambodian border, was made up largely of Coast Guard cutters and destroyer escorts that operated within 64km of the South Vietnamese coastline to detect and interdict larger communist supply ships.

An inner ship barrier of South Vietnamese junks and US Swift boats operated within 19km of the South Vietnamese coast. This barrier searched the vast amount of Vietnamese coastal traffic and also took part in river raiding operations.

■ OPERATION CEDAR FALLS, 8–26 JANUARY 1967

Two US and one South Vietnamese infantry division swept through the Iron Triangle area north of Saigon from 8 to 26 January 1967. Allied forces lost 83 killed against more than 700 communist deaths, but most VC forces escaped.

■ OPERATION JUNCTION CITY, 22 FEBRUARY–14 MAY 1967

Operations from February through May by four South Vietnamese and 22 US battalions to destroy the VC 9th Division in War Zone C. After more than 2000 were killed against 282 US/South Vietnamese losses, the Viet Cong moved their headquarters to Cambodia.

■ HUE, 30 JANUARY–3 MARCH 1969

As part of the Tet Offensive of 1968, the VC and North Vietnamese dedicated two regiments to the seizure of the imperial capital of Hue. On the morning of 31 January 1968, the North Vietnamese 6th Regiment attacked the walled citadel north of the Perfume river, while the 4th Regiment attacked the new city south of the river. Hue was defended by minimal South Vietnamese and US forces, who were fixated more on the fighting in the countryside. In the initial fighting, the communists seized most of the city, except for the headquarters of Gen Ngo Quang Truong's 1st ARVN Division in the citadel and a small MACV compound south of the river. Numbering only a few hundred men, both outposts held out against heavy communist assaults. Initially concerned more with the fighting at nearby Khe Sanh, US and South Vietnamese commands were slow to respond to the threat and sent minimal reinforcements. Once the threat had become clear, troops from the 1st Cavalry and the 101st Airborne worked to cut off communist supply lines outside Hue against elements of three North Vietnamese divisions that US planners had thought were engaged at Khe Sanh. In Hue, three battalions of US Marines made their way to the new city south of the Perfume river and nearly 11 South Vietnamese battalions fought their way into Truong's embattled defences in the citadel. When the situations both south and north of the Perfume river were secure, US and South Vietnamese forces took the offensive in a street-to-street and house-to-house urban battle. Realizing that keeping their flag above the fabled citadel and imperial palace had immense psychological value, communist forces fought tenaciously. The fighting on both fronts moved very slowly, with very heavy losses until 12 February, when South Vietnamese I Corps commander Gen Hoang Xuon Lam gave permission to use whatever firepower was necessary to clear the city. Communist forces fought with desperation, resulting in artillery and air strikes levelling much of the city and the citadel to blast out communist resistance. With less organic heavy weapon support, South Vietnamese forces in the citadel were augmented by the 1st Battalion, 5th Marines. On 21 February, the 1st Cavalry Division closed off communist supply lines to Hue after heavy fighting and, on 24 February, the Second Battalion, 3rd ARVN Regiment overran the southern wall of the citadel. They took down

the VC flag that had been flying there for nearly a month. The next day South Vietnamese troops recaptured the imperial palace, heralding an end to the battle. In the fighting, US forces suffered more than 200 dead, while the South Vietnamese lost nearly 400 killed. North Vietnamese and VC losses exceeded 5000 dead. More than half of the city was destroyed in the fighting, leaving 116,000 civilians homeless of a population of 140,000. After the fighting, US and South Vietnamese began to unearth mass graves in the areas of Hue that the communists had once held, especially the Gia Hoa district outside the citadel. During their rule over Hue, the communists had swept through the city bearing lists of those who had aided the 'puppet government' of South Vietnam. Nearly 3000 bodies were discovered, but some estimates suggest that the communists summarily executed as many as 6000 civilians during the fighting.

■ **KHE SANH, 21 JANUARY–8 APRIL 1968**

Khe Sanh combat base, built on a hilltop located

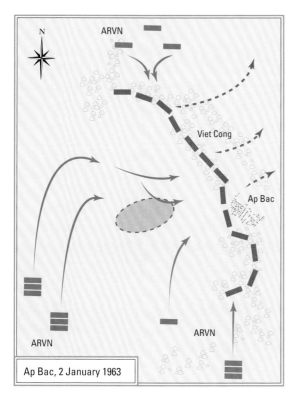

Ap Bac, 2 January 1963

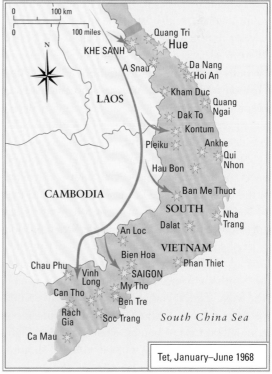

Tet, January–June 1968

10km from the Laotian border, was the westernmost in a line of Allied defences south of the DMZ designed to prevent communist infiltration into South Vietnam. By 1968 Khe Sanh combat base was occupied by 3000 US Marines of the 3rd Marine Division, while a further 3000 Marines were stationed on four nearby hilltop positions surrounding the base, positions that had been the subject of heavy fighting during 1967. That fighting not only had demonstrated a sizable enemy build-up in the area, but also prompted Gen William Westmoreland to believe that Khe Sanh was tenable even in the face of a heavy enemy siege, especially given that it housed a runway capable of landing C-130s. As part of their planning for the Tet Offensive, North Vietnamese forces began to stream into the area around Khe Sanh in November 1967. They eventually totalled as many as 40,000 troops, especially of the 325th Division and the 320th Division, cutting US ground contact with the Marines at Khe Sanh. Communist planners, led by Gen Vo Nguyen Giap, hoped by attacking Khe Sanh to draw American attention from the cities of South Vietnam, which were the real targets of the coming Tet Offensive. On 21 January 1967, North Vietnamese forces simultaneously attacked two of the outlying Marine hilltop positions and launched a massive artillery strike on Khe Sanh combat base, opening the siege of Khe Sanh. Fearing a defeat reminiscent of the French at Dien Bien Phu in 1954, President Lyndon Johnson kept a close eye on the fighting at Khe Sanh, receiving hourly reports and even having a mock-up of Khe Sanh constructed in the basement of the White House. Hoping that he had drawn North Vietnamese forces into what might prove to be a climactic battle, Westmoreland ordered the Marines to hold firm and launched Operation *Niagara*, a series of bombing strikes on the North Vietnamese troop concentrations around Khe Sanh. Tactical bombers flew more than 16,000 sorties in defence of the Marines, delivering more than 31,000 tons of bombs, while B-52 Arc Light strikes delivered nearly 60,000 tons of bombs, making Operation *Niagara* one of the heaviest

bombing campaigns in the history of warfare. At the beginning of February 1968, as the Tet Offensive raged throughout South Vietnam, fighting around Khe Sanh combat base intensified. On 7 February, a North Vietnamese assault involving 12 tanks overran the Special Forces camp at Lang Vei, west of Khe Sanh on Route 9. Bitter fighting also took place on the Marine hilltop outposts surrounding Khe Sanh, with Hill 861 being overrun by mid-February. By late February, the North Vietnamese artillery barrage on Khe Sanh combat base strengthened and, on 29 February elements of the North Vietnamese 304th Division stormed the base, but were driven off with major losses. Under heavy pressure from the air, and with the failure of the wider Tet Offensive, North Vietnamese forces began to withdraw from the Khe Sanh area in early March. By early April, US forces in Operation *Pegasus* reopened ground communication with Khe Sanh and the siege was at an end. During the fighting, the Marines lost 205 killed and 1600 wounded, while

Khe Sanh, 1968

97 US and 33 South Vietnamese were killed in the relief efforts. The North Vietnamese lost as many as 15,000 casualties during the siege of Khe Sanh.

■ SAIGON, 30 JANUARY–7 MARCH 1968

On 31 January a force of more than 35 North Vietnamese and VC battalions attacked targets in Saigon during the Tet Offensive, in efforts designed to seize key military and governmental targets, including the Tan Son Nhut air base and the presidential palace. One platoon of sappers struck the US embassy. In most areas, the communist attacks were repulsed, except for the Cho Lon district, where fighting lingered until early March.

■ OPERATION *MENU*, 18 MARCH 1969–28 MAY 1970

Codename for the secret bombing of Cambodia, which dropped more than 100,000 tons of bombs but failed significantly to disrupt the Ho Chi Minh Trail or to destroy the VC command in the South.

■ OPERATION *TAILWIND*, 11–13 SEPTEMBER 1970

Hoping to disrupt communist activity in Laos, US and Montagnard special forces made a covert raid that overran a regional headquarters and obtained significant intelligence. The force was then extracted by helicopter.

■ OPERATION *LAM SON* 719, 8 FEBRUARY–25 MARCH 1971

On 8 February, a South Vietnamese force invaded southern Laos with the goal of severing the Ho Chi Minh Trail at Tchepone. Expecting light resistance, the South Vietnamese, under heavy US air cover, seized hilltop fire support bases to guard an armoured thrust down Route 9. Predicting such an assault, the North Vietnamese gathered as many as 60,000 men to face the 17,000 South Vietnamese attackers. Amid command indecision at the highest levels, the South Vietnamese armoured thrust ground to a halt at A Luoi, not half-way to its objective, as North Vietnamese troops massed to assault the isolated South Vietnamese flanking positions. On 1 March, a South Vietnamese helilborne assault seized Tchepone, but found little of military value. During the withdrawal phase, several of the isolated South Vietnamese fire support bases were overrun and

were reliant on US airpower for defence and US helicopters for extraction. More than 100 US aircraft were lost, with over 250 Americans killed. The North Vietnamese lost an estimated 13,000 dead.

■ QUANG TRI CITY, 30 MAR–16 SEP 1972

A South Vietnamese offensive to retake Quang Tri City and citadel, which had been lost during the Easter Offensive. South Vietnamese troops of I Corps, commanded by Gen Ngo Quang Truong, entered Quang Tri in mid-July, fighting against six North Vietnamese divisions. After two months of fighting, Quang Tri fell to the South Vietnamese on 16 September, with the loss of nearly 3000 North Vietnamese killed in action.

■ AN LOC, 13 APRIL–20 JULY 20 1972

The South Vietnamese 5th Division was besieged in An Loc by elements of three North Vietnamese divisions from April to June during the Easter Offensive. The South Vietnamese lost 2000 dead, inflicting 10,000 casualties on the North Vietnamese.

■ KONTUM, 26–27 MAY 1972

Elements of three North Vietnamese divisions launched failed assaults on the Central Highlands road junction town of Kontum as part of the Easter Offensive. North Vietnamese forces suffered an estimated 15,000 casualties.

■ PHUOC BINH, 12 DEC 1974–6 JAN 1975

On 12 December 1974, North Vietnamese forces attacked Phuoc Binh Province in part to discern whether or not US forces would intervene. With no US reaction, the provincial capital fell on 6 January, emboldening the North Vietnamese.

■ CAMPAIGN 275, 10–11 MARCH 1975

North Vietnamese assault into South Vietnam through the Central Highlands, commanded by Gen Van Tien Dung. With the fall of Ban Me Thuot, South Vietnamese President Nguyen Van Thieu decided to abandon the Central Highlands.

■ XUAN LOC, 9–21 APRIL 1975

Battle at a critical road junction north of Saigon, in which the South Vietnamese 18th Division held for two weeks against the entire North Vietnamese IV Corps. Xuan Loc's fall on 23 April left the road to Saigon clear.

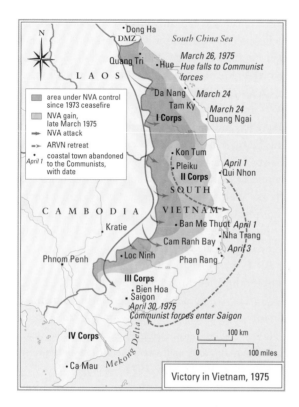

Victory in Vietnam, 1975

■ FALL OF SAIGON, 30 APRIL 1975

The North Vietnamese unleashed their final offensive against Saigon, the Ho Chi Minh Campaign. By 29 April, North Vietnamese units were pushing into the suburbs of the city before the Americans belatedly launched Operation *Frequent Wind* to evacuate at-risk South Vietnamese personnel. The chaotic evacuations were halted by the fall of Saigon on 30 April, leaving many of the South Vietnamese population that had supported the US behind to face North Vietnamese revolutionary justice.

US Occupation of the Dominican Republic 1965–66

■ OPERATION *POWER PACK*, 28 APRIL 1965– SEPTEMBER 1966

On 24 April, leftist guerillas deposed the elected government and began an intense campaign of intimidation against security forces in Santo

Domingo. Five hundred US Marines, two battalions from the Army's 82nd Airborne Division, and Special Operations Forces deployed to the island. Their mission was to secure the capital's power station at the Duarte Bridge. Forty-four US soldiers died, but between 6000 and 10,000 Dominicans may have died in the fighting.

Indo-Pakistani War 1965

■ INDIAN INVASION, 6–23 SEPTEMBER 1965

Provoked by Pakistan's August incursions across the 1949 ceasefire line in Jammu and Kashmir (JAK), the Indian Army made a three-pointed riposte into western Pakistan. The five-week war marked the first all-out war on the subcontinent since independence from Britain and partition in 1947. As had been the case in 1948–49, the territorial dispute over JAK lay at the heart of the conflict. Pakistan had launched the clandestine Operation *Gibraltar*, aimed at fomenting rebellion against Indian rule among the region's majority Muslim population. When an open incursion by Pakistani troops followed, the Indian Army enacted its own war plan and crossed the border for the first time. India's war plan called for the XI Corp's three divisions to attack through the Ravi–Sutlej Corridor toward the strategically significant Pakistani city of Lahore. The Indian divisions included mounted infantry supported by armour, in the form of Sherman, Centurion and AMX-13 tanks from the army's cavalry regiments.

On the night of 5–6 September, these units crossed the border with the infantry. Opposing were three Pakistani divisions in the Ravi–Sutlej Corridor, with the 10th Division responsible for the defence of Lahore, and the 7th Infantry and 1st Armoured Divisions in reserve. As the land war got under way, the Indian Air Force launched 26 attack sorties on Sargodha, the base for half the Pakistani Air Force, on 7 September. The Indians destroyed some targets on the ground, losing five aircraft in the process. By the ceasefire, India had lost approximately 60 aircraft, while Pakistan had lost 20. In the land war, the win–loss ratio was more in India's favour. At the ceasefire, India held approximately 1838km² of Pakistani territory, while Pakistan took approximately 648km² of Indian land, mostly at Khem Karan.

■ OPERATION GRAND SLAM, 28 AUGUST–5 SEPTEMBER 1965

Pakistan's Operation *Gibraltar*, to infiltrate and foment rebellion among Jammu and Kashmir's Muslim population, had failed, costing approximately 4000 casualties among Pakistani troops. Islamabad then sent the 12th Infantry Division (6000 men), supported by two regiments of M-48 Patton tanks, into Chaamb. The plan was to seize the Akhnur Bridge and cut off India's 25th Division. Although the Pakistanis initially were successful, the Indian I and XI Corps counter-attacked across the border toward Lahore, forcing the invaders to re-deploy.

■ LAHORE, 6 SEPTEMBER 1965

India's XI Corps launched a counter-offensive aimed at Lahore and Sialkot. The 15th Infantry Division was to attack on the Amritsar–Lahore axis, the 7th Infantry Division from Khalra to Lahore, and the 4th Mountain Division from Khem Karan to Kasur. At the Ravi river, Pakistan's 22nd Brigade successfully counter-attacked along the Ichhogil Canal, throwing the Indian 15th Division into chaos. The Indian 96th Brigade and 50th Para Brigade re-deployed to stabilize the situation.

■ ASSAL UTTAR, 10 SEPTEMBER 1965

At Assal Uttar, the Indian 4th Mountain Division blocked Pakistan's 1st Armoured Division. The clash involved hundreds of tanks. In the Valtoha area, the Pakistani 4th Cavalry became trapped, with all of its tanks destroyed or captured.

■ AIR WAR, 1–22 SEPTEMBER 1965

Indian Air Force (IAF) FB Mk 52 Vampires attacked Pakistani ground forces during Operation *Grand Slam*. But Pakistan's Air Force quickly balanced the scales. PAF B-57 Canberra bombers attacked Indian ground targets in Kashmir, while Pakistani F-86 Sabre jet fighters shot down four of India's slower De Havillands in their first encounter. Both sides raced more capable aircraft to the frontlines, including IAF Gnats and Pakistani F-104 Starfighters.

Six-Day War 1967

■ OPERATION FOCUS, 5 JUNE 1967

Operation *Focus* (*Moked* in Hebrew) was launched on 5 June 1967 by the Israeli Air Force (IAF) against the airfields of a number of Israel's Arab neighbours, most notably those of the Egyptian Air Force (EAF). Concerned that the Arab nations were about to launch an attack, the Israeli Government authorized a pre-emptive strike. The Egyptian airfields in the Sinai peninsula were particularly hard hit, with the Israelis benefitting from a piece of luck that saw Egyptian air defences unwilling to open fire for fear of bringing down an aircraft taking the Egyptian chief of staff on a visit to troops in the Sinai. The Israeli aircraft launched another two waves of attacks and, within less than three hours, most of the EAF had been destroyed or damaged on the ground and airfields rendered inoperable. The Syrian, Jordanian and Iraqi air forces carried out some limited retaliatory strikes against Israel, prompting the Israelis to conduct attacks on Syrian and Jordanian airfields, with similar levels of success.

■ ABU AGHEILA, 5–6 JUNE 1967

An initial Israeli attack was thwarted by stronger-than-expected resistance. A second, more closely coordinated attack by infantry and armour was launched. Striking from several directions, this assault was successful in driving the Egyptians from their positions.

■ JORDAN VALLEY, 6–7 JUNE 1967

Jordanian armoured forces were defeated by their Israeli counterparts, and reinforcements interdicted by air power. This opened the way for a drive into the Jordan valley, creating a natural defensive line to protect Israel's eastern flank.

■ JERUSALEM, 7 JUNE 1967

Following Jordanian attacks on targets in Israel on 5 June 1967, the Israelis responded with an assault on Jordan the following day. After heavy fighting over the next two days, the Israelis arrived outside Jerusalem. Despite lacking cabinet authority, the defence minister, Moshe Dyan, ordered IDF troops to take the city and, on 7 June, Israeli paratroopers

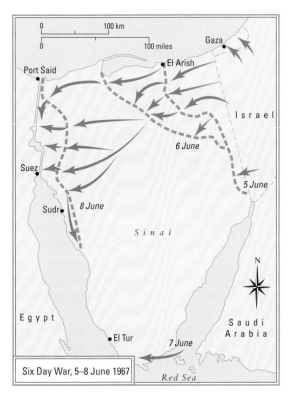

0 ——— 100 km
0 ——— 100 miles

Gaza
El Arish
Port Said
Israel
6 June
Suez
5 June
8 June
Sudr
Sinai
N
Egypt
Saudi
Arabia
El Tur
7 June
Six Day War, 5–8 June 1967
Red Sea

entered Jerusalem and seized the city after street-to-street fighting with the Jordanian army.

■ **GOLAN HEIGHTS, 9–10 JUNE 1967**

The Syrian Government was encouraged to join the Six-Day War by President Nasser of Egypt, who claimed that the Israeli pre-emptive air strike had been a disastrous defeat for Israel. The Syrians responded by carrying out air raids and some shelling into northern Israel. The Israelis in turn responded by destroying most of the Syrian Air Force on the ground. A Syrian ground offensive was rebuffed, with many of the Syrian's key reserve forces unable to reach the frontline due to Israeli air attacks. After some debate, the Israeli leadership decided to attack the Golan Heights on 9 June 1967. Although the fighting took place on difficult, defensible terrain, by nightfall on the 9th, the Israelis had broken through Syrian lines and consolidated their position during the course of the next day.

Cambodian Civil War 1967–75

■ **CAMBODIAN CAMPAIGN, 29 APRIL–22 JULY 1970**

Attempting to remove communist bases from Cambodia, US and South Vietnamese forces made several forays into Cambodian territory. Opposition mostly took the form of skirmishes and contacts between patrols as the communist troops were ordered to fall back in the face of major attacks. Significant resistance was dealt with by airpower and artillery bombardment. The operation uncovered a vast quantity of concealed military equipment intended for use by the communist forces.

■ **OPERATION *CHENLA II*, 20 AUGUST–3 DECEMBER 1971**

Launching a new offensive against communist forces, the Cambodian Army was initially successful but fighting eventually bogged down in the face of counter-attacks. An attempt to restart the campaign was decisively defeated by the communists.

■ **OPERATION *FREEDOM DEAL*, 19 MAY 1971–15 AUGUST 1973**

Freedom Deal was initially launched as an attempt to interdict supply routes to communist forces near the Mekong river. The area and scope of the mission expanded into a huge bombing campaign against communist forces and their logistics chain in Cambodia. As the communists overran Cambodia, increasing numbers of missions were flown in direct support of Cambodian troops. However, these failed to prevent the fall of Phnom Penh.

■ **PHNOM PENH, 1 APRIL 1975**

Government forces were gradually driven into a perimeter around the capital, Phnom Penh. Supply lines to the city, which was full of refugees, were cut by the communist forces, who then launched a final successful assault.

Nigerian Civil War 1967–70

■ **NIGERIAN OFFENSIVE, 1967**

With the secession of Biafra from Nigeria, the

majority of the former Nigerian Army's experienced officer class sided with Biafra, but the bulk of heavy equipment remained in Nigerian hands. The better-led Biafran forces advanced into Nigeria itself, but were forced back by a major offensive headed by Nigeria's few armoured vehicles. Nigeria also employed airpower and steadily crushed the secessionist forces.

Czechoslovakia 1968

■ PRAGUE SPRING, 20 AUG–20 SEP 1968

After government reforms brought by First Secretary Alexander Dubcek failed to meet popular expectations, a student-led uprising gripped Czechoslovakia, threatening to move the government away from its Soviet alignment. Under the guise of restoring order, 200,000 Soviet Union and Warsaw Pact troops, supported by 2000 tanks, entered the city. Soviet paratroops captured Ruzyne International Airport. While condemning the action politically, the USA – committed to the war in Vietnam – and NATO remained passive during the invasion. Although the civilian population put up no organized armed resistance, 108 Czechs and Slovaks were killed in clashes with the invasion force. Warsaw Pact troops withdrew from the country on 3 August, but set up bases along the frontier. The invasion prompted outrage from the world's press. On 17 April 1969, the Soviet-aligned Gustav Husak replaced Dubcek as First Secretary, ending the crisis.

Football War 1969

The Football War was a brief conflict fought between El Salvador and Honduras following tensions concerning emigration from El Salvador to Honduras. These tensions coincided with rioting during the second North American qualifying round of the 1970 FIFA World Cup.

■ AIR CAMPAIGN, 14–18 JULY 1969

With an air force comprised of 22 WWII and Korean War-vintage piston engine aircraft, including F-51 Mustang fighters and C-47 Skytrain transports jury-rigged as bombers, El Salvador attacked Honduran airfields, military units and civilian targets. Honduras, equipped with 38 planes of similar vintage, including F4U Corsairs, retaliated.

■ SALVADORAN OFFENSIVE, 14–18 JULY 1969

Hours after exchanging air strikes, Salvadoran troops invaded Honduras, capturing Nueva Ocotepeque and, on the eastern frontier, Goascoran. After their initial success, the invaders pressed on to capture San Juan Guarita, Valladolid, La Virtud, Caridad and Aramecina. Their offensive stalled at Cabanas, where Honduran troops put up stiff resistance. Both armies included about 5000 infantry soldiers, and neither possessed tanks or artillery. Under an Organization of American States-brokered ceasefire, Salvadoran troops withdrew from Honduras on 2 August.

Sino-Soviet Border Conflict 1969

■ ZHENBAO ISLAND, 2–15 MARCH 1969

Three hundred Chinese soldiers engaged a Soviet mechanized unit in two gun battles that left casualties on both sides. Each claimed that the other had fired first. In the aftermath, the 48 Soviet divisions stationed in Siberia, Outer Baikal and the Far East remained on high alert.

Indo-Pakistani War 1971

■ DHALAI, 31 OCTOBER–3 NOVEMBER 1971

India's 2nd (Mooltan) Battalion, the Jat Regiment, together with 7th Battalion (Rajputana Rifles), attacked the entrenched Pakistani 30th Battalion Frontier Force at this tea and rice plantation. After four days of intense combat, the Indians made an advance of 3–4km.

■ GARIBPUR, 20–21 NOVEMBER 1971

Before the war began, India's 14th Punjab Battalion, with 14 PT-76 tanks from the 45th Cavalry, crossed into East Pakistan and seized this strategic village. Pakistan's 107th Infantry Brigade, with M24 Chaffee tanks, failed to recapture it.

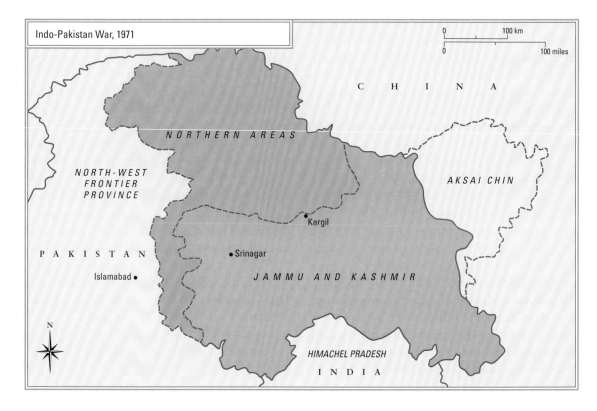

Indo-Pakistan War, 1971

BOYRA, 22 NOVEMBER 1971

Above the Boyra salient, four Gnats of No. 22 Squadron, Indian Air Force (IAF), clashed with four F-86s of No 14 Squadron, Pakistan Air Force (PAF). In the ensuing fracas, the IAF shot down two PAF Sabres and chased a damaged third back to Dhaka.

HILLI, 22 NOVEMBER–11 DECEMBER 1971

Pakistan's 205th Brigade attempted unsuccessfully to hold the line against a determined attack by four Indian infantry brigades of the 20th Mountain Division. Supported by the tanks of the 3rd Armoured Brigade, 20,000 Indian troops overwhelmed BGen Hussain's 3500 men.

KUSHTIA, 9 DECEMBER 1971

The Indian II Corps (two infantry divisions, two squadrons of PT-76 tanks from 45th Cavalry Regiment, and one squadron of T-55 tanks from the 63rd Cavalry Regiment) divided Pakistan's 9th Division. Cutoff and outnumbered, the two Pakistani brigades with one squadron of M24 Chaffee tanks fought before succumbing.

Yom Kippur War 1973

Sinai Front

EGYPTIAN CROSSING OF SUEZ CANAL, 6–9 OCTOBER 1973

On 6 October 1973, Egyptian and Syrian forces simultaneously launched twin surprise assaults on the Israeli-occupied territories of the former Egyptian-held Sinai peninsula and the former Syrian-held Golan Heights. In the Sinai, five Egyptian infantry divisions assaulted across the Suez Canal and struck the Israeli Bar-Lev Line defences in an intricately planned and well-executed operation. In total, the Egyptian campaign in the Sinai involved 500,000 troops, 2150 tanks, 150 surface-to-air missile (SAM) batteries, 2280 artillery pieces and 545 aircraft. The Bar-Lev Line, in contrast, was just a weak outpost position along the canal's eastern bank, defended by 9000 soldiers with 100 tanks and 30 guns in support. The line's purpose was merely to slow any attack while Israeli reserves mobilized for a counter-attack. During 6–7 October, the Egyptian assault achieved remarkable success. For the cost of just 208 fatalities, the Egyptians crossed the canal, overran the Bar-Lev Line and established a 16km-deep bridgehead in the Israeli-occupied Sinai.

Along this line the Egyptian forces dug in, with the entire bridgehead remaining under the protection of their static SAM batteries located on the canal's western side. Into this bridgehead, the Egyptians moved forward numerous anti-tank guns and Sagger anti-tank missile teams to block the counter-attacks soon to be mounted by Israel's two reserve armoured divisions, located in central Sinai. As predicted, the Israel armoured divisions charged headlong into the massed Egyptian anti-tank defences, while the SAM umbrella prevented the IAF from providing effective support. During the repeated counter-attacks mounted on 7–9 October, the Israeli armour suffered appalling casualties. By midnight on 9 October, the limited Egyptian incursion across the Suez Canal into the Sinai seemed to be a comprehensive victory.

■ SUEZ CANAL 10–25 OCTOBER 1973

On 14 October 1973, Egypt's two reserve armoured divisions struck deep into Sinai, beyond the SAM and anti-tank defences. Israeli all-arms armoured ripostes, backed by effective air support, decimated the Egyptians. During 15–17 October, the Israelis counter-attacked west and crossed the Suez Canal. By the ceasefire on the 25th, Israeli armour had advanced west and south to capture Suez on the Red Sea coast, thus trapping the Egyptian forces still holding the bridgehead on the canal's eastern (Israeli-held) bank.

■ CHINESE FARM, 15–17 OCTOBER 1973

The 'Chinese Farm' in question was an agricultural station in the Sinai peninsula. The battle began when the Israelis attempted to cross the Suez Canal, attacking the Egyptian forces around the Chinese Farm area so as to establish a secure corridor to the canal, which would enable the

canal to be bridged without enemy interference. The Egyptians put up fierce resistance, forcing the Israelis to put considerable numbers of tanks into the field. Despite the arrival of armoured forces, the Israelis found it heavy going and further reinforcements were required on 16–17 October. An Egyptian armoured counter-thrust failed on 17 October, forcing them to fall back, leaving the Israelis in control of the routes to the Suez Canal.

■ ISMAILIA, 18–22 OCTOBER 1973

The battle of Ismailia occurred between 18 and 22 October 1973. The Israelis sought to capture Ismailia, but vigorous Egyptian defence prevented this before a ceasefire came into effect. After the ceasefire that nominally ended the Yom Kippur War, the Israelis marched on Adabiya on the Bay of Suez, encircling the Egyptian Third Army. Superpower pressure ensured that the Israelis ended operations on 24 October 1973 without pressing home their advantage.

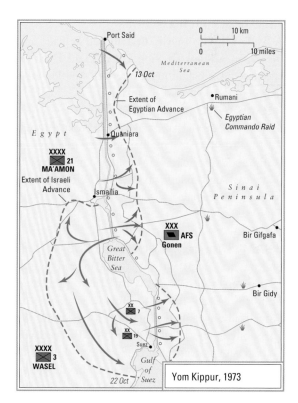

Yom Kippur, 1973

Golan Front

■ **Syrian Offensive, 6 October 1973**

On 6 October 1973, Syrian armed forces attacked Israeli positions in the Golan Heights. The Syrians broke through the post-1967 ceasefire line and seized the key position of Mount Hermon with a heliborne assault. The Israelis managed to bring reserves forward very quickly and, although the Syrians made limited gains in the course of four days' heavy fighting, the Israelis managed to stabilize their defences, allowing them to counter-attack.

■ **Mount Hermon, 6–22 October 1973**

During the 1973 Yom Kippur War, Mount Hermon saw heavy fighting in three distinct battles. The first battle of Mount Hermon occurred on 6 October, when a heliborne assault by the Syrians captured the Israeli outpost on the mountain. The second battle on 8 October, an Israeli counter-attack, failed to retake the position. Finally, on the night of 21–22 October, a third battle occurred in which the Israelis retook their outpost and drove the Syrians from their positions on the mountain.

■ **Amadiye, 7 October 1973**

A battle between Israeli 7th Armored Brigade and the Syrian 3rd Tank Division. The 3rd Tank Division attempted a breakthrough, but was rebuffed in a sharp engagement west of Amadiye.

■ **Rafid, 6–7 October 1973**

The Syrian 5th Mechanized Division broke through the Israeli 188th Armored Brigade near the town of Rafid, inflicting massive casualties. The defenders bought enough time for reserves to be brought up to halt the Syrian attack

Air War

■ **SAM vs Israel, 6–25 October 1973**

During the 1973 war, the Egyptian and Syrian forces employed static SAM batteries – purchased from the Warsaw Pact – to provide cover for the limited advance of their ground forces from the attentions of the effective Israeli Air Force (IAF). This strategy initially proved effective, with the IAF suffering heavy casualties. However, after Egyptian armour was decimated, having moved beyond this

SAM 'umbrella', the Israelis went on to secure significant success in the ground war.

■ **Israeli offensive against Syria, 9–25 October 1973**

From 9 October 1973, the Israeli Army recaptured the Golan Heights and continued advancing north-east towards the Syrian capital, of Damascus. They were ably supported by Israeli air attacks on Syrian SAM batteries, ground forces and industrial targets.

■ **Israeli Offensive, 8–23 October 1973**

The arrival of Israeli reserves in the Golan Heights area enabled the IDF first to stablize its defensive line and then, from 8 October 1973, to begin a counter-attack to push the Syrians back. The Israelis were determined to regain the Heights, since possession of them prevented Syrian bombardment of Israeli towns beneath the high ground, which prompted determined efforts to dislodge the Syrians. Heavy fighting ensued, but by 10 October the last Syrian troops had been forced off the Heights. The Israelis then decided to strike into Syria itself, beginning on 11 October. The Israeli attack reached Sassa and Damascus was shelled by IDF artillery. The Jordanian and Iraqi governments sent troops to assist the Syrians, which helped prevent further Israeli advances. A planned Syrian counter-attack did not take place after the acceptance of the UN ceasefire on 23 October.

Naval War

■ **Latakia I, 6 October 1973**

In history's first missile-boat-on-missile-boat combat, five Israeli Saar-class vessels sank five Syrian patrol boats in a night patrol, despite the latter being equipped with longer-range weapons. Making effective use of manoeuvre and counter-measures, the Israelis evaded eight Syrian Styx missiles.

■ **Damietta/Baltim, 8 October 1973**

Off the Egyptian coast, four Osa-class missile boats attacked a squadron of six Israeli Saar vessels. Firing from maximum range, the Egyptians fled. Israeli counter-measures proved superior to the Styx missiles. A salvo of 12 Gabriel missiles sank three of the attackers.

■ **Port Said/Latakia II, 10 October 1973**
Seven Israeli Saars attacked the Syrian harbour of Port Said. Five Syrian vessels counter-attacked, taking cover behind merchant vessels. In the exchange of missile fire, two civilian ships went down, along with two Syrian Osas. The Syrians scored no hits.

■ **Nile Delta Tartus, 11 October 1973**
Five Israeli boats attacked Syrian shore facilities, including oil storage tanks and gun emplacements. Two Osas counter-attacked from behind merchant vessels. Israeli Gabriel missiles sank both Syrian craft as well as a Russian freighter. Once again, none of the Syrian Styx missiles had found their marks.

Turkish Invasion of Cyprus 1974

■ **Operation *Attila*, 20 July and 14 August 1974**
Turkish paratroopers landed near Turkish Cypriot enclaves near Nicosia, while an amphibious assault landed at Kyrenia and moved inland. Turkish soldiers engaged 5000 Greek Cypriot national guardsmen in a two-day battle that left the invaders in control of 10 per cent of the island by 25 July. To consolidate their position, the Turkish Army deployed a force of 30,000 in two infantry divisions, with two special forces brigades, 120 pieces of artillery and more than 400 armoured fighting vehicles.

Angolan Civil War 1975–2002

■ **Bridge 14, December 1975**
At the Nhia river, a South African Defence Force (SADF) battlegroup attacked Cuban-backed left-wing guerrillas of the Exercito Popular de Libertacao de Angola (EPLA). Forward spotters directed SADF artillery fire onto EPLA formations and Sagger missile sites.

■ **Huambo, January–February 1976**
The SADF-backed, right-wing National Union for the Total Independence of Angola (UNITA) declared Huambo a separate republic in 1967.

Newly designated People's Armed Forces for the Liberation of Angola (FAPLA) government troops, backed by 12,500 Cubans and Soviet weapons, recaptured the city on 8 February.

■ **Cuban Offensive, November–December 1976**
Cuban and FAPLA troops launched a five-week campaign along several fronts. North of Luanda, at the battle of Quifangondo, they drove back the FNLA advance and secured the oil resources of Cabinda. From 9 to 18 December, at the Salazar Bridge north of Mussende, the Cubans relied on heavy artillery to defeat South African armour. By 1977, the Movement for the Liberation of Angola (MPLA) government controlled Angola's southern cities.

■ **Shaba Invasions, 8–15 March 1977 and 11 May 1978**
Angolan and Congolese rebels opposed to the violent, interventionist policies of Zaire's Mobutu Sese Seko twice invaded the former Belgian colony. In March 1977, 2000 National Front for the Liberation of Angola (FNLA) bicycle infantry crossed from Angola into the Shaba Province. In 1978, more than 3000 Front for the National Liberation of the Congo (FNLC) troops infiltrated from Zambia.

■ **South African Invasion, 23 August–1 November 1981**
Following air strikes against air defence radar sites, mechanized SADF columns crossed into Angola's Cunene Province during Operation *Protea*. The battles to seize Humbe, Xangongo, Ngiva and Cahama inflicted more than 1000 casualties on FAPLA and South West Africa People's Organization (SWAPO) units and their Soviet and Cuban advisors. The SADF followed up with an attack at Chitequeta. By November, they had seized tens of thsouands of square kilometres of Angolan territory. In response, Cuba deployed 7000 more troops to Angola.

■ **Cuito Cuanavale, 9 September 1987–23 March 1988**
More than 11,500 FAPLA government, SWAPO and Cuban troops sought to crush a similarly sized

force of SADF-backed UNITA rebels in a decisive battle. The rebels bested the government, but the SADF, under international pressure, began to withdraw from Angola.

■ **Huambo, December 1992–9 November 1994**
UNITA battled government troops in a successful 55-day siege for control of the city. Ten thousand died in the fighting. Refugees fled in to the heavily mined countryside. In August 1994, government troops returned to drive UNITA out

Lebanese Wars 1975–90

■ **Aishiya, 19 October 1976**
Palestinian Liberation Organization (PLO) fighters attacked the Christian village of Aishiya. Israeli 175mm artillery fire helped to slow the attack. The PLO ousted the Christian population of the village and made it a base of operations until 1982.

■ **Beirut, 6 June–21 August 1982**
Israel launched a campaign to expel the PLO from its base of operations against Galilee. The invasion began in response to a provoked PLO artillery attack on northern settlements. The Israel Defence Forces (IDF) deployed 75,000 soldiers, 1250 tanks and 1500 armoured fighting vehicles. On the opposing side were 30,000 Syrian troops (with 600 tanks) in the Bekaa valley and along the road to Damascus. In the city itself were 20,000 Palestinian/Arab fighters with approximately 100 tanks and 100 heavy cannon. Syria's 85th Mechanized Infantry Brigade was deployed to West Beirut. On 4 August, Gen Ariel Sharon shelled the area for 20 hours before marching toward the city centre. Fierce battles erupted in PLO-held neighbourhoods. On 19 August, Israel allowed a multinational peacekeeping force to assist the evacuation of more than 14,600 PLO militants. The battle's death toll numbered 5676 civilians and 1100 combatants, including 88 IDF soldiers.

■ **Sabra and Shatila, 14–18 September 1982**
On 23 August, Lebanon elected Bashir Gemayel, head of the Phalange Party of Christians opposed to the PLO, as its next president. On 14 September,

Bashir was assassinated by a Syrian terrorist, prompting a savage response from his 8000-man militia. The IDF troops who had deployed around the Palestinian camps Sabra, Shatila and Burj al-Barajinah allowed the Phalangists to enter. On the night of 17 September, Bashir's fighters murdered hundreds of civilians.

■ **Syrian Operation, June 1990**
During the siege, 2300 Syrian troops deployed in south-western Beirut, taking advantage of open ground to protect their tanks from infantry attacks. South of the airport, the Syrian brigade deployed on the Damascus Highway clashed violently with IDF troops advancing from the coast.

Cambodian-Vietnamese War 1975–89

■ **Tho Chu Island, 10–25 May 1975**
Cambodian leader Pol Pot's Khmer Rouge soldiers attacked the disputed island, Tho Chu, allegedly murdering 500 civilians. A Vietnamese force counter-attacked, capturing 600 Cambodian fighters and re-occupying the island.

■ **Vietnamese Invasion of Cambodia, 21 December 1978–7 January 1979**
Amid ongoing territorial disputes and enduring repeated incursions by the Khmer Rouge, 200,000 troops (13 divisions) of the Peoples' Army of Vietnam (PAVN) invaded Cambodia. The Vietnamese drove into Cambodia along Routes 13 and 14 to seize Kracheh, and along Route 19 to take Stoeng Treng.

The scene of heaviest fighting was in Svay Rieng Province, in the area known as the 'Parrot's Beak'. The true focus of the offensive was Phnom Penh at the Mekong river, which the Vietnamese reached by 5 January 1979. From there, Hanoi's invasion force pursued the Khmer Rouge west toward the Thai border where, after fierce fighting, they routed the Cambodians. The Vietnamese had destroyed the Cambodian government's military strength. Thus defeated in direct confrontation, the Khmer Rouge returned to its roots as a guerilla movement, launching an insurgency against Hanoi's puppet regime at Phnom Penh.

■ **PHNOM PENH, 5–7 JANUARY 1979**

After a failed attempt to infiltrate the city ahead of the main invasion force, two PAVN columns surrounded Phnom Penh. Airstrikes broke the back of Phnom Penh's defences and the PAVN marched into the capital.

■ **CAO BANG/LANG SONG, FEB–MAR 1979**

China opened a second front in 1979 invading Vietnam with a total of 85,000 troops. The Vietnamese 346th Division was beaten back at Cao Bang, as was the 3rd Division at Lang Song, which fell on 4 March. Having 'taught Vietnam a lesson', China withdrew.

Indonesian Invasion of East Timor 1975

■ **OPERATION *SEROJA*, 1975**

Indonesian forces landed by sea and air at East Timor's largest towns, arriving in such overwhelming numbers that the defenders were forced to retreat to the countryside to fight a guerilla war.

Libyan–Egyptian War 1977

■ **SOLLUM, 1977**

A Libyan protest march was prevented from entering Egypt by border guards, increasing tensions to the point where Libyan artillery shelled Sollum. A raid by Libyan armoured forces was then driven back with heavy losses.

Ogaden War 1977–78

■ **SOMALIAN INVASION, 1977**

Somalia invaded the Ogaden region of Ethiopia with a view to annexing it. The resulting war was characterized by shifting alliances due to the influence of Cold War politics and of outside parties. Ethiopia, which had received military aid from the USA in the past, was offered similar support from the Soviet Union. When the Soviets abandoned their previous support for Somalia, however, the USA stepped in. The invasion was ultimately repelled after heavy fighting.

■ **DIRE DAWA, 1977**

Somalian forces made a major effort to capture the port at Dire Dawa, an action that if successful would have crippled Ethiopia. The assault was eventually driven off after intense fighting, with heavy casualties on both sides.

■ **JIJIGA, 1977**

A Somalian assault on the city of Jijiga succeeded in driving the Ethiopian defenders out. The Somalis were unable to exploit their victory, however, due to a combination of poor road conditions and Ethiopian air interdiction.

Ugandan–Tanzanian War 1978–79

■ **LUKUYA, 1978**

Advancing Libyan forces fought an encounter battle with Tanzanian troops near Lukuya. The Tanzanians were defeated but the situation was reversed by a counter-attack the following night. Libyan forces pulled out of the conflict soon afterwards.

Chadian–Libyan Conflict 1978–87

■ **FAYA-LARGEAU, 1978**

Pro-Libyan insurgents of the People's Armed Forces (FAP) launched an offensive to demolish the last vestiges of the government in northern Chad. Victory at Faya-Largeau gave FAP and their Libyan allies control of the region.

■ **N'DJAMENA, 1980**

Libyan and Islamic League forces occupied Faya as a staging post, then advanced against rebel forces who had taken control of the capital at N'Djamena, which was riven by internecine fighting among rival warlords. The Libyans overwhelmed rebel forces and remained in the city for a year.

■ **MASSAGUET, 1982**

Forces of the Transitional Government of National Unity (GUNT), were decisively defeated at Massaguet in Chad by the FAP. With the power of GUNT broken, FAP was able to take control over the capital as the de facto government.

■ GUNT OFFENSIVE, 1983

A new Government of National Unity (GUNT) was formed in Chad, with Libyan support. The government was repeatedly attacked at its stronghold in Bardai by forces loyal to rival groups, but managed to go over to the offensive in mid-1983. Libya provided supporting troops and artillery for an initially successful campaign. The newly formed Chadian National Armed Forces (FANT), however, inflicted a series of crushing defeats against the Libyans, and thus gained control over much of the country.

■ OPERATION *MANTA*, 10 AUG–10 NOV 1983

Libya deployed 5000 mechanized troops to support Chadian rebels. France responded with 3500 of her own troops, including the Foreign Legion and several squadrons of Jaguar fighters. Both sides agreed to withdraw, an arrangement the Libyans circumvented.

■ OPERATION *EPERVIER*, 13 FEBRUARY 1986

GUNT rebels renewed their offensive, backed by 5000 Libyan troops and Gaddafi's air force. France redeployed 2500 soldiers to Chad and carried out a successful bombardment of Libya's Ouadi Doum airbase and countering Libyan attacks. France maintained 1200 troops at N'Djamena.

■ TOYOTA WAR, 1987

The breakdown of relations between GUNT and Libya deprived GUNT of much of its foreign support, permitting the president and leader of FANT, Hissène Habré, to attempt a final reunification of the country. FANT forces made extensive use of Toyota pick-up trucks for transport and as 'Technicals' armed with a variety of weapons. Chadian forces inflicted a series of sharp defeats on Libyan troops, leading to a decision to withdraw from Chad.

Sino-Vietnamese War 1979–89

■ LANG SON, 1979

During the Sino-Vietnamese War, invading Chinese troops fought defending Vietnamese units for control of the strategic gateway city of Lang Son. Between 27 February and 3 March 1979, coordinated People's Liberation Army armour and infantry methodically cleared the countryside, destroyed the surrounding Vietnamese mountain-top artillery positions, and captured the city. Both sides sustained heavy casualties. On 5 March 1979, Chinese forces demolished the city's southern bridge and withdrew.

Soviet War in Afghanistan 1979–89

■ SOVIET INVASION, 27 DECEMBER 1979–MARCH 1980

Soviet-backed communists, led by Nur Mohammed Taraki, seized power in an April 1978 coup. The new Democratic Republic of Afghanistan's legislative reforms, which defied Afghan cultural traditions, helped to incite rebellion by tribal leaders and Islamist militants, known as *mujahidin*. To help bolster the government, between 1978 and 1979 the Soviet Union deployed a military mission of 5000 advisors. These soldiers trained, equipped and supported the DRA Army's 40,000 troops. Meanwhile, skirmishes between government and rebel factions intensified throughout 1979, further destabilizing the government. Many Afghan officers, who had been trained by the Soviets, defected to the rebel warlords and the *mujahidin*, as the DRA Army became increasingly demoralized and unreliable. Taraki made several blunders, most notably at Herat in March 1979. There, rioters attacked government forces along with Soviet advisors and their families. The DRA's 17th Division mutinied and joined the rebels. Eventually, loyal troops crushed the uprising, supported by Soviet Il-28 Beagle bombers, but 5000 Afghans and 100 Russians had been killed. Taraki appealed for more Soviet troops, but Leonid Brezhnev's government refused.

As the rebellion teetered on the brink of all-out civil war, the DRA began to unravel politically. Hafizullah Amin, a rival in Taraki's cabinet, led a coup and assassinated the president. In the autumn of 1979, Soviet Defence Minister Marshal Dmitri

Ustinov became convinced that the situation required direct action. Against the advice of his general staff, Ustinov authorized the temporary commitment of between 75,000 and 80,000 Soviet troops.

Unable to rely on erstwhile allies in the Afghan Government, Russian military advisors already in-country helped set the stage for the invasion. They undermined the DRA's combat readiness by sabotaging radio sets and requesting maintenance inspections of Afghan vehicles and inventories of Afghan weapons and ammunition. The effect was to disable bureaucratically and disarm some of the DRA's mechanized units. The Red Army attacked across the border on 27 December. Within one week, more than 50,000 Russian troops had arrived. CGen Yuri Tukharinov's Fortieth Army included four divisions, five separate brigades, three separate regiments and air support.

The invasion's first waves came aboard Antonov transport planes, which landed troops at Kabul and Bagram. Motorized rifle divisions followed through Kuska and Termez. The Soviets' first objectives were to seize the capital, the major highways to Herat and Kandahar and the Salang Pass connecting southern Afghanistan with the Hindu Kush. On 28 December, Russian special forces units (*Spetznaz*) stormed Kabul's Darulaman Palace. They captured government offices, assassinated Amin, and installed Babrak Karmal as the new president. The speed of the invasion, coupled with the DRA's poor military readiness, had ensured the Soviets' early success.

By the beginning of March, the Russians and their Afghan allies launched their first offensive, into the rebel-held Kunar valley. Opposing the invaders was a confederation of warlord militias and as many as 40 groups of *mujahidin* fighters (comprising 100,000–200,000 men in total). The Soviet invasion had helped to weld disparate factions into a broad-based bloc of resistance to the foreigners and the puppet regime. By

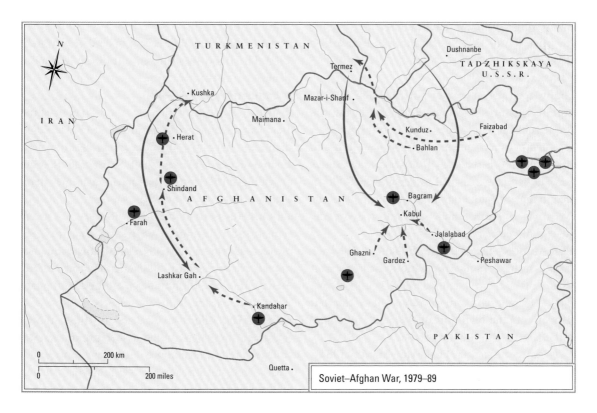

Soviet–Afghan War, 1979–89

1982, the Soviet military presence rose to more than 100,000 men. The Russians also brought substantial air support to their troops and those of their allies in-country, totalling almost 400 fixed-wing planes and more than 200 helicopters, such as the Mi-24 Hind gunship.

Despite their military superiority, however, Russian and Afghan Government troops were doomed to a bitter nine-year war of attrition that ground on through 1989 and cost the lives of more than 14,400 Soviet soldiers and more than 1.3 million Afghans.

Iran–Iraq War 1980–88

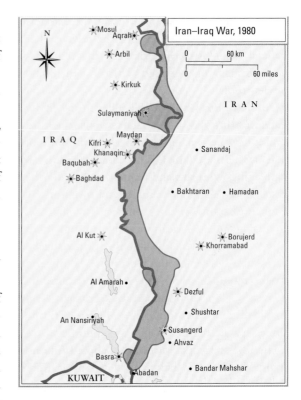

■ IRAQI INVASION OF IRAN, 22 SEPTEMBER 1980

September 1980 saw Iraq launch an invasion of Iran. The Iraqi leader, Saddam Hussein, wished to see Iraq become the dominant state in the Persian Gulf, and sought to exploit the chaos in Iran following the revolution in that country. Although the invasion enjoyed the benefit of surprise and saw some early Iraqi gains, increasingly fierce resistance meant that the invasion had stalled by December 1980.

■ BASRA, 1980–88

The strategically important port of Basra was the target of a number of Iranian attacks during the Iran–Iraq War. The largest and most significant occurred between January and February 1987, in one of the bloodiest battles of a particularly vicious war. The Iranians managed to get within 16km of the city, but an Iraqi counter-attack on 28 January 1987 turned the tide, and the battle was over by the end of February.

■ OPERATIONS *DAWN 5 & 6*, FEBRUARY 1984

Part of a larger Iranian operation (*Badr*) to gain control of the Basra–Baghdad highway in February 1984, Operations *Dawn 5* and *6* made limited gains around the Iraqi port of Basra before stalling in the face of stout Iraqi resistance.

■ OPERATION *KHAIBAR*, FEBRUARY–MARCH 1984

In the aftermath of Operation *Dawn 5*, the Iranians launched a new front at the Lakes of the Hawizah

Marshes between 14 February and 19 March 1984. The Iraqis were driven out of the Majnoon Islands as a result.

■ TANKER WAR, 1984–88

A phase of the war which saw the warring parties attacking oil tankers (of all nations) in a bid to deny their opponents the finances from oil, using fast air strikes. The USA and the USSR responded by providing protection to oil tankers in the Persian Gulf.

■ IRAQI AIR OFFENSIVE, 1985–88

Iranian successes during Operation *Badr* in 1985 prompted Saddam Hussein to launch major air and missile attacks against Iranian cities, particularly Tehran. To offset the advantage enjoyed by Iranian fighter aircraft, the Iraqis also made use of SCUD missiles. The offensive escalated in 1986, when the Iraqis began bombing passenger trains and civilian aircraft, reaching a further peak in 1987 with attacks on 65 Iranian cities, in which many civilians were killed and wounded.

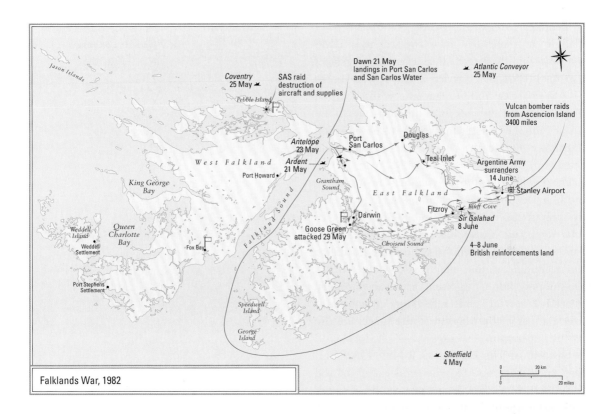

Falklands War, 1982

◼ KARBALA, 12–14 MAY 1986

An operation during the Iran–Iraq War between 12 and 14 May 1986, which saw the Iranians recapture Mehran from the Iraqis, who had seized it earlier in the month in response to the Iranian capture of al-Faw.

◼ KIRKUK REGION, AL-ANFAL CAMPAIGN, 1987–88

A campaign launched in Kurdish areas in northern Iraq, particularly around Kirkuk, by Saddam Hussein. The main operations occurred in 1987–88. Around 4500 Kurdish villages were destroyed, with possibly as many as 2.25 million people killed.

Falklands War 1982

◼ ARGENTINE INVASION OF THE FALKLANDS, 2 APRIL 1982

The Argentine junta under Gen Leopoldo Galtieri planned to seize the Falkland Islands (*Las Islas Malvinas*) from Britain no later than the end of

1983, in a bid to end the long-standing dispute over sovereignty between the two countries. Prompted by fears of an increase in British military strength in the area, the plan was brought forward. On 2 April 1982, Argentina invaded the islands and seized South Georgia.

◼ SOUTH GEORGIA, 25 APRIL 1982

The first notable British action of the Falklands conflict, South Georgia was recaptured on 25 April by Royal Marines and Special Air Service troops after helicopter landings. The Argentine garrison surrendered without resistance.

◼ OPERATION *BLACK BUCK*, MAY–JUNE 1982

Operation *Black Buck* was a series of raids by Royal Air Force Vulcan bombers in support of British operations in the Falklands, beginning on 1 May 1982. The raids were the longest-range bombing missions in history at the time.

◼ FALKLANDS AIR WAR, MAY–JUNE 1982

The nature of the Falklands campaign created serious problems for both the British and the

Argentines. Most of the British combat airpower had to be generated from two carriers, HMS *Invincible* and the larger HMS *Hermes*, using Fleet Air Arm (FAA) Sea Harriers and Royal Air Force (RAF) Harrier VSTOL aircraft, while for the Argentines, the distance from the mainland to the islands and the lack of a proper air-to-air refuelling capability meant that Argentine aircraft could spend little time over the Falklands.

The Sea Harriers proved vital to British success, both protecting the fleet and offering defence to the troops on the ground, while the RAF Harriers made a notable contribution to several land battles. The Argentine pilots were noted for their courageous and effective low-level attacks on shipping. Often forgotten, British air transport, maritime patrol and refuelling aircraft also made a major contribution to the success of the British operation.

■ SINKING OF THE *BELGRANO*, 2 MAY 1982

In one of the more controversial events of the Falklands War, the Argentine cruiser *General Belgrano* was sunk by the British submarine HMS *Conqueror* on 2 May 1982. The controversy arose from the fact that the *Belgrano* was outside the British Exclusion Zone when attacked, but of more significance was the fact that this loss led to the Argentine Navy withdrawing to home ports, from which they did not re-emerge.

■ BRITISH NAVAL LOSSES IN THE FALKLANDS CAMPAIGN, MAY–JUNE 1982

In the course of the fight for the Falklands, the British sustained a number of shipping losses, all as the result of air attack. The destroyer HMS *Sheffield* had to be abandoned after being struck by a missile on 4 May 1982. HMS *Ardent* was sunk on 21 May, followed by HMS *Antelope* on the 24th. *Antelope* had survived a bombing raid, but was destroyed after an unexploded bomb detonated during attempts to defuse it. The next day (25 May) saw HMS *Coventry* sunk by bombing, and the container ship *Atlantic Conveyer* lost after another Exocet attack. The landing ships *Sir Galahad* and *Sir Tristram* were both badly damaged in the air

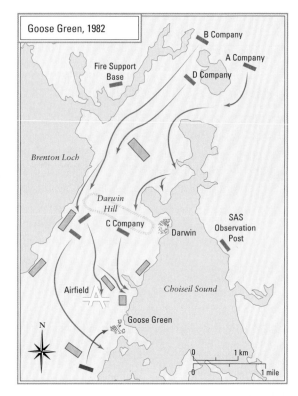

attacks on Bluff Cove, the former later being towed out to sea and sunk. In addition to these losses, a number of other ships were damaged by bomb and missile attacks. The losses could have been much more severe, but for the fact that many Argentine bombs, released at low level, had insufficient time to arm and therefore did not explode.

■ LOSS OF HMS *SHEFFIELD*, 4 MAY 1982

The British Type 42 destroyer *Sheffield* was struck by an Exocet anti-shipping missile launched by Argentine Super Etendard aircraft on 4 May 1982. The ship was badly damaged by fire and abandoned.

■ SAN CARLOS LANDINGS, 21 MAY 1982

On 21 May 1982, the British launched Operation *Sutton*, the invasion to retake the Falkland Islands. Amphibious landings occurred at San Carlos, enabling the British to establish a beachhead and then a lodgement with little opposition. San Carlos Water became the scene of repeated air attacks by the Argentines in a bid to sink British shipping over the next few days, but although losses were sustained by the British, the invasion force was not to be dislodged.

■ GOOSE GREEN, 27–28 MAY 1982

On 27–28 May 1982, 2nd Battalion, the Parachute Regiment attacked Argentine positions at Darwin and Goose Green. Fighting was particularly heavy, and the commanding officer of 2 Para was killed leading a charge on enemy positions. Determined fighting by British paratroopers, aided by an air strike on an Argentine gun position on the second afternoon, helped turn the battle and the Argentines surrendered. British forces were now able to break out from San Carlos.

■ MOUNT KENT, 30 MAY 1982

Elements of the British 22 Special Air Service (SAS) Regiment were inserted onto Mount Kent as a precursor to the arrival of a company of 42 Commando, Royal Marines, by helicopter later that night. The mountain was a critical position from which British forces could attack other Argentine-held mountain ranges outside Port Stanley.

■ BLUFF COVE, 8 JUNE 1982

The arrival of 5th Infantry Brigade off the Falklands on 1 June 1982 enabled the British to plan for a two-pronged advance on the capital of Port Stanley. The Welsh Guards were to support the attack on the southern flank, and were ferried from Port San Carlos to Bluff Cove by the landing ships *Sir Galahad* and *Sir Tristram*. The ships were attacked by Argentine aircraft on 8 June. Fifty-six British troops were killed.

■ MOUNT HARRIET, 11–12 JUNE 1982

One of three engagements between British and Argentine forces on this night, in which 42 Commando, Royal Marines, seized Mount Harriet from defending Argentine troops, giving the British an important key position overlooking Port Stanley.

■ MOUNT LONGDON, 11–12 JUNE 1982

A major battle between British and Argentine forces on the night of 11–12 June 1982. The 3rd Battalion, the Parachute Regiment was tasked with seizing Mount Longdon, one of the key hills

outside Port Stanley. The battle saw particularly heavy fighting and was distinguished by dogged Argentine defence before the paratroopers ultimately prevailed in the early morning of 12 June.

■ WIRELESS RIDGE, 13–14 JUNE 1982

A battle between 2nd Battalion, the Parachute Regiment and Argentine forces, which gave the British control of one of the major hills within 8km of Port Stanley.

■ TUMBLEDOWN, 13–14 JUNE 1982

A key battle between British and Argentine forces on the night of 13–14 June 1982, which saw the Scots Guard dislodge enemy forces from one of the highest points overlooking Port Stanley. By 09:00 on 12 June, the high ground to the east of the mountain had also been seized, and Argentine soldiers could be seen streaming back into Port Stanley.

■ PORT STANLEY, 14 JUNE 1982

Port Stanley, the capital of the Falklands, was the ultimate objective of the British counter-invasion of the Falklands, but there was considerable concern that the British forces would have to conduct street-to-street fighting, with the risk of heavy civilian casualties. This fear was not realized, as in the aftermath of the fighting on Mount Tumbledown, it became clear that the Argentine defensive position was compromised. The Argentine commander, Gen Menendez, therefore surrendered on 14 June 1982.

Invasion of Grenada 1983

■ OPERATION *URGENT FURY*, 25 OCTOBER–3 NOVEMBER 1983

In 1983, political instability in the Commonwealth nation of Grenada saw the overthrow and murder of the government of Maurice Bishop by a faction of his revolutionary New Jewel movement. The governor-general, Sir Paul Scoon, was placed under house arrest. The Organization of Eastern Caribbean States appealed to the United States for assistance, which President Ronald Reagan, concerned by the links between the coup plotters and Cuba, was more than willing to provide. Operation *Urgent Fury* began on 25 October 1983, with several thousand American troops landing at key points on the island, most notably in the form of a parachute assault on Port Salines airfield. Over the course of the next few days, there was notably hard fighting, until on 3 November all US objectives had been taken, and the operation was declared over.

Sri Lankan Civil War 1983–2009

■ COLOMBO, 23–29 JULY 1983
On the Jaffna peninsula, militants with the separatist Liberation Tigers of Tamil Eelam (LTTE) ambushed a Sri Lankan Army patrol called '44-Bravo', killing 13 men with assault-rifle fire and hand grenades. In the capital, Colombo, some members of the majority Sinhalese population were outraged. They attacked Tamils and their

Sri Lanka, 1983–2009

Area claimed by Tamils

property in the city, sparking clashes with the police. The violence, which resulted in many deaths, helped to foment the coming civil war.

■ OPERATION *LIBERATION*, 26 MAY–JUNE 1987
Eight thousand Sri Lankan Army soldiers launched a campaign to re-conquer territory on Jaffna, an LTTE haven. At the Thondamanaru Bridge, Sri Lankan engineers endured many casualties to open the mined route to Vadamarachchi. With helicopter gunship support, government troops advanced, capturing Nelliady, Udupiddy and Valvettithurai by 28 May. Indian intervention led Sri Lankan President Junius Richard Jayewardene to order a ceasefire in June. LTTE commander Velupillai Prabhakaran escaped. Each side suffered more than 600 killed.

■ ELEPHANT'S PASS, 10 JULY–9 AUGUST 1991
Five thousand LTTE fighters attacked a Sri Lankan Army base at Elephant Pass. There, the rebels used roadblocks and anti-aircraft guns to trap 800 soldiers of the Sinha Regiment, which took many casualties before driving off the Tamil attack.

■ POONERYN, 11–12 NOVEMBER 1993
At the eighteenth-century Portuguese fortress of Pooneryn and at the nearby Nagathevanthurai naval base, LTTE fighters surprised the government garrison. The Tigers killed more than 400 soldiers and captured many weapons and vehicles, as well as several naval combatant craft.

■ MULLAITIVU I, 18–25 JULY 1996
Operation *Unceasing Waves* involved more than 4000 Tamil rebels attacking the headquarters of the Sri Lankan 215th Brigade. LTTE fighters overran the base on 19 July. More than 1200 government soldiers and 300 Tamils died in the fighting.

■ KILINOCHCHI I, 26 JULY–3 OCTOBER 1996
The Sri Lankan 53rd Division launched Operation *Sath Jaya*, an effort to oust rebels from Elephant Pass and Kilinochchi, seize the A9 highway and open a supply route to Jaffna. As many as 500 government troops and more than 120 LTTE fighters died.

■ KILINOCHCHI II, 27–29 SEPTEMBER 1998
As part of the LTTE's Operation *Unceasing Waves II,* rebels waged a successful battle to recapture

Kilinochchi, near the Sri Lankan Army base at Elephant Pass. More than 400 government troops and more than 500 Tamils died in fierce hand-to-hand combat.

■ OPERATION *UNCEASING WAVES III*, 22–23 APRIL 2000

In the second major battle at Elephant Pass, LTTE fighters successfully besieged a large Sri Lankan Army base. Rebel artillery battered the base ahead of an infantry assault. 'Black Tiger' suicide bombers stormed the government perimeter. The army fled north. LTTE fighters captured several artillery pieces, heavy machine guns, small arms and ammunition as well as many government armoured vehicles. More than 1000 soldiers and 3500 rebels died in the fighting.

■ TRINCOMALEE, AUGUST 2006

In Sri Lanka's Eastern Province, the LTTE cut the water supply to agricultural fields, prompting a renewed military campaign by the Sri Lankan Army. Government troops attacked LTTE artillery positions north and south of the port, in scenes of heavy fighting.

■ JAFFNA PENINSULA, 11 AUG–29 OCT 2006

In an effort to cut government supply lines, LTTE fighters made a futile attempt to capture the Sri Lankan naval base at Jaffna. In October, a government counter-offensive stalled just as it penetrated rebel-held territory. The six-year old stalemate continued.

■ SAMPUR, 28 AUGUST–4 SEPTEMBER 2006

In August 2006 the Sri Lankan government attacked LTTE artillery positions that had been threatening the major naval base at Trincomalee. After a month of fighting, government troops captured the town. It was the first major reversal for the LTTE since 2002.

■ DAKSHINA NAVAL BASE, 18 OCTOBER 2006

At the tourist resort Galle, south of Colombo, LTTE fighters disguised as fishermen infiltrated a government naval base. Two suicide bomb boats rammed the decommissioned submarine chaser SLNS *Parakramabahu*, destroying it at the pier. In the fracas that followed, the rebels sank three

Sri Lankan Navy gunboats and destroyed an oil tank ashore with a rocket-propelled grenade. Government naval vessels returned fire, sinking all the attackers. One government sailor and a civilian were killed and as many as 24 others injured.

■ KOKKADICHOLAI, 28 MARCH 2007

Having launched a final operation to clear the LTTE rebels from Eastern Province, Sri Lankan Special Operations Forces (SOF) captured the base at Kokkadicholai, clearing the way to seize the A5 highway in April.

■ MALLAVI, 2 SEPTEMBER 2008

The 3rd Brigade of the Sri Lankan 57th Division, advancing north toward Kilinochchi, defeated an LTTE force at this important administrative centre for the rebels. As many as 65 LTTE rebels died in the fighting.

■ VAVUNIYA AIR BASE, 9 SEPTEMBER 2008

Under covering fire from LTTE artillery, 'Black Tiger' suicide squads attacked the government bases at Wanni and Vavuniya. As rebel infiltrators closed in, LTTE light aircraft made a surprise attack on the airfield using improvised bombs.

■ MANKULAM, 16 NOVEMBER 2008

Government Task Force 3 met stiff LTTE resistance south of Muhamalai. Supported by low-altitude bombing from Sri Lankan Air Force jets, the government troops moved west of the A9 highway to flank rebel positions in the town.

■ KILINOCHCHI III, 23 NOVEMBER 2008–2 JANUARY 2009

The Sri Lankan 57th Division, under MGen Jagath Dias (with Task Force 1), breached Tamil defences around the LTTE's de facto capital, attacking from three directions. Both sides suffered casualties in fierce fighting before the city fell.

■ MULLAITIVU II, 25 JANUARY 2009

The 59th Division captured this important rebel naval base and submarine manufacturing facility. In February, another 'Sea Tiger' base at Chalai fell. In May, during a battle at Vellamullivaikkal, government SOF commandos killed LTTE commander Prabhakaran, effectively ending the organized rebellion.

Ugandan Civil War 1987–2009

■ **GARAMBA OFFENSIVE, 14 DECEMBER 2008–15 MARCH 2009**

In Operation *Lightning Thunder*, Uganda, the Democratic Republic of Congo and Southern Sudan troops jointly attacked the Lord's Resistance Army (LRA) at its base in Congo's Garamba National Park. Although the soldiers were unable to lure the LRA into a pitched battle, the campaign forced Joseph Kony's fighters to flee into more remote regions. The LRA retaliated, launching guerilla attacks in which they killed 1000 people in Congo and the Sudan.

Somali Civil War 1991–

MOGADISHU I, 3–4 OCTOBER 1993

In the autumn of 1993, with an international peacekeeping force of US, Pakistani and Malaysian troops in the city, Mogadishu was the scene of

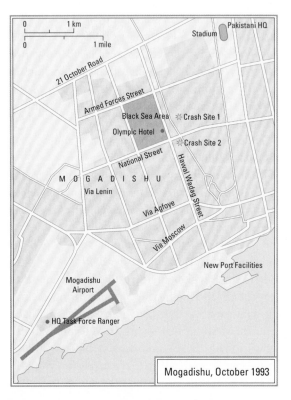

Mogadishu, October 1993

increasing violence between warring Somali factions. In September, militia carried out several attacks on US and UN checkpoints and patrols. On 25 September, militia shot down a US H-60 Black Hawk helicopter, killing three soldiers. On 3 October, a battle began between Mohammed Farah Aidid's militia and the Americans' 'Task Force Ranger', a mounted patrol supported by helicopters. In the opening minutes of the battle, militants shot down a Special Operations Forces (SOF) MH-60. The ensuing rescue operation embroiled US and UN troops in an intense firefight that resulted in 18 Americans and one Malaysian killed, and more than 100 US and UN troops wounded. The Somalis endured more than 1000 casualties, including several hundred killed.

■ **MOGADISHU II, 7 MAY–11 JULY 2006**

Militia of the Islamic Courts Union (ICU), under Sheikh Sharif Ahmed, confronted the fighters of local warlords in May 2006. By early June, the ICU controlled more than 80 percent of the city. Somali Prime Minister Ali Mohammed Gedi requested international military aid.

■ **BAIDOA, 20–26 DECEMBER 2006**

At the Somali government's transitional capital, 3000 troops, backed by a 5000-man Ethiopian expeditionary force, attacked the ICU in Somalia's Bay Region. The offensive forced the Islamists to retreat toward the coast.

■ **BANDIRADLEY, 23–25 DECEMBER 2006**

Several hundred Somali fighters, backed by 500 Ethiopian troops, armour, artillery and helicopter gunships, opened a second front against the ICU at Somalia's semi-autonomous Puntland State, along the Ethiopian border. The invasion forced the ICU militiamen to flee south.

■ **BELEDWEYNE, 24–25 DECEMBER 2006**

Having captured the town of Beledweyne in August 2006 amid in-fighting among local clans, the ICU ousted the regional governor. An Ethiopian armoured column attacked, flanking the ICU's militia and driving them south to Jowhar.

■ **JOWHAR, 27 DECEMBER 2006**

The Ethiopian and Somali transitional government

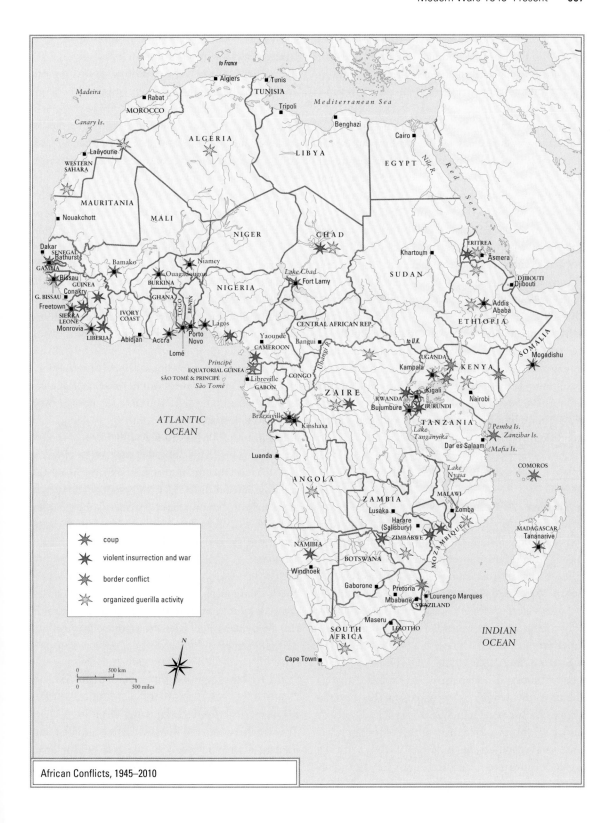

Madeira

to France
Algiers   Tunis
TUNISIA
Rabat
MOROCCO   Tripoli
Mediterranean Sea
Benghazi
Cairo
Canary Is.
Laâyoune
ALGERIA   LIBYA
WESTERN
SAHARA   EGYPT

Nile R.

Red Sea

MAURITANIA   MALI   NIGER   CHAD
SUDAN   ERITREA
Khartoum   Asmera
Nouakchott
DJIBOUTI
Djibouti

Dakar   SENEGAL
Bathurst   Bamako   Niamey   Lake Chad   Fort Lamy
GAMBIA   Bissau   Ouagadougou   NIGERIA
GUINEA   BURKINA
G. BISSAU   Conakry   GHANA   TOGO   BENIN
Freetown   IVORY   Lagos   CENTRAL AFRICAN REP.
SIERRA   COAST   Accra   Porto   Yaounde   Bangui
LEONE   Novo   CAMEROON
Monrovia   Abidjan   Lomé
LIBERIA   *Principé*   *to U.K.*   UGANDA
EQUATORIAL GUINEA   Kampala   KENYA
SÃO TOMÉ & PRINCIPE   Libreville   CONGO
São Tomé   GABON   ZAIRE   Kigali   Nairobi
RWANDA
Brazzaville   Bujumbura   BURUNDI
Kinshasa   TANZANIA
Luanda   *Lake*
Tanganyika   *Pemba Is.*
Zanzibar Is.
Dar es Salaam   *Mafia Is.*

Addis
Ababa
ETHIOPIA   SOMALIA
Mogadishu

ATLANTIC
OCEAN

Lake
Nyasa   COMOROS
ANGOLA   ZAMBIA   MALAWI
Lusaka   Zomba
Harare   MADAGASCAR
(Salisbury)   Tananarive
ZIMBABWE
NAMIBIA   MOZAMBIQUE
BOTSWANA
Windhoek
Gaborone   Pretoria
Mbabane   Lourenço Marques
SWAZILAND
Maseru   LESOTHO
SOUTH
AFRICA   INDIAN
OCEAN
Cape Town

✳	coup
✳	violent insurrection and war
✳	border conflict
✳	organized guerilla activity

N

0   500 km
0   500 miles

African Conflicts, 1945–2010

advance cornered ICU militia 90km north of Mogadishu. Again, Ethiopian armour and air support proved decisive, driving the ICU fighters out of the town they had seized the previous June.

■ JILIB, 31 DECEMBER 2006–1 JANUARY 2007

Fleeing toward the Kenyan border, 3000 ICU militants made a stand at Jilib. Ethiopian MiG-23 Flogger attack jets bombarded ICU positions, followed by artillery fire ahead of the Ethiopian and government assault troops.

■ RAS KAMBONI, 5–12 JANUARY 2007

Ethiopian and Somali Government troops attacked the ICU's last stronghold on the Kenyan border. Ethiopian airpower helped to dig out the entrenched Islamists. US AC-130H/U gunships based at Djibouti participated in some destructive airstrikes.

■ MOGADISHU III, 7 MAY–1 OCTOBER 2009

More than 2500 al-Shabaab and Hizbul Islam rebels attacked the Somali coalition government (including former ICU fighters) in Mogadishu, killing 126 soldiers and capturing most of the city, although the government retained some neighbourhoods.

Nagorno-Karabakh 1988–94

■ KHOJALY, 26 FEBRUARY 1992

In response to artillery attacks from Armenian forces, which forced the population of Khojaly into a troglodyte existence, Armenian separatist troops, back by mechanized units of the Russian 366th Motorized Rifle Regiment, seized Khojaly, a large Azeri town in Nagorno-Karabakh. In addition to many Azeri soldiers, civilians also were killed in the attack.

■ SHUSHA, 8–9 MAY 1992

One thousand Armenian separatist troops stormed the town's Azeri garrison. In a well-known tank engagement, an Armenian T-72 was knocked out, but Armenian troops overwhelmed the Azeri defences, including a GRAD rocket artillery battery, to seize Azerbaijan's last mountain stronghold in the region.

■ OPERATION GORANBOY, 12 JUNE 1992–MARCH 1993

More than 80,000 Azeri troops, with armour and attack-helicopter support, launched a major offensive to crush the Armenian separatist movement. The operation began with an attack at Askeran, after which the Azeris had gained ground at Agbulak, Arachadzor, Dahraz, Nakhichevanik, Pirdzhamal and Mardakert by 4 July. The Armenian separatists retreated to Stepanakert, along with 30,000 refugees. Armenian separatist troops, with Russian artillery support, stopped the Azeri advance and regained much of the lost territory by spring 1993.

■ MARDAKERT AND MARTUNI, 12 JUNE–2 OCTOBER 1992

Azeri troops, with former Soviet armour, artillery and air support, attacked along a 20km front, capturing Shahumian and portions of Askeran by August. Armenian separatists stopped the advance at Mardakert where, from well-entrenched fighting positions, their anti-tank weapons proved extremely decisive.

■ KELBAJAR, 27 MARCH–3 APRIL 1993

Armenian separatists attacked the Azeri cities of Kelbajar and Fizuli in the first expansion of the fighting beyond the borders of Nagorno-Karabakh. Armenians' armour and artillery bombarded Kelbajar on 29 March, with troops breaking through the city's defences by the beginning of April.

■ AGDAM, 4 JULY 1993

During a season of offensives in the summer of 1993, Armenian separatist artillery bombarded Azeri Raion Agdam. By the end of the month, the Armenians had taken the town, driving out 120,000 refugees.

US Invasion of Panama 1989–90

■ OPERATION JUST CAUSE, 1989–90

Tension between the United States and Panama increased after revelations that the Panamanian dictator, Gen Manuel Noriega, was involved in drug smuggling. In February 1988, he was indicted on drugs charges in the United States. Between 1988 and 1989, Noriega defeated a coup he blamed on the Americans, and overturned the results of elections. In October 1989, a second coup failed. On 15 December 1989, Noriega unwisely declared a state of war with the USA, followed by several provocations. The most serious of these provocations was the killing of a US Marine officer on 16 December, an incident that prompted the US Government into action.

On 20 December, the American President George Bush ordered an invasion, Operation *Just Cause,* to protect American citizens and to capture Noriega. American forces quickly took control of Panama, and Noriega fled to the papal mission in Panama City. After a standoff with American troops, he surrendered on 3 January 1990, effectively bringing Operation *Just Cause* to a conclusion.

First Afghan Civil War 1989-92

■ Jalalabad, 1989
In March of 1989, immediately following the Soviet withdrawal from Afghanistan, Islamist *mujahidin* allies fought the armed forces of the Democratic Republic of Afghanistan (DRA) government led by Mohammed Najibullah Ahmadzai. The attack on Jalalabad resulted in a three-month siege of that city. The *mujahidin* forces struck at the non-secular government with hopes of a decisive battle that would replace the last vestiges of Soviet control in Afghanistan.

■ Kabul, 1992
In 1992, the Najibullah regime collapsed in Afghanistan as a result of the defection of the official army to the *mujahidin*. In April, *mujahidin* forces under Abdul Massoud entered Kabul to defend it against rival *mujahidin* general Gulbuddin Hekmatyar. From April 1992 until the rise of the Taliban in 1995, rocket and mortar attacks between factions resulted in the deaths of thousands of civilians and the exodus of over 500,000 people from Kabul.

First Liberian Civil War 1989–96

■ Gbarnga, May 1990
In the second year of Liberia's civil war, the government troops fell back to this city on Liberia's central plain. Prince Johnson's Independent National Patriotic Front of Liberia (INPFL) fighters crushed government forces. In July, Charles Taylor's National Patriotic Front of Liberia (NPFL) set up a new government in Gbarnga.

■ Monrovia, July 1990
As rebel fighters advanced across Liberia, the Armed Forces of Liberia (AFL) collapsed into an undisciplined rabble. On 30 July 1990, government troops murdered 600 civilians at St Peter's Lutheran Church.

■ Lofa and Bomi Counties, September 1991
Fighters of the United Liberation Movement of Liberia for Democracy (ULIMO), yet another rebel faction, which had experience fighting in Sierra Leone, attacked NPFL positions in Liberia's diamond mining districts.

First Gulf War 1990–91

■ Gulf War–Air Campaign, 16 January–28 February 1991
In the wake of Iraq's August 1990 invasion of Kuwait, an American-led multinational Coalition deployed to Saudi Arabia. To force an Iraqi withdrawal, the Coalition initiated an aerial campaign on the night of 16–17 January 1991, which lasted for 43 days until the ceasefire on 28 February. The Coalition ground campaign lasted for only 100 hours of this 43-day period.

The Coalition air forces deployed 2330 aircraft, whereas the Iraqis fielded just 820, mostly inferior Soviet-supplied equipment. The overall Coalition air war delivered 88,000 tons of munitions in over 100,000 sorties. The campaign also comprised four overlapping phases: a strategic air campaign, a battle to win air superiority over Kuwait, attacks on the Iraqi ground forces and, from 24 February, attacks supporting the unfolding ground offensive.

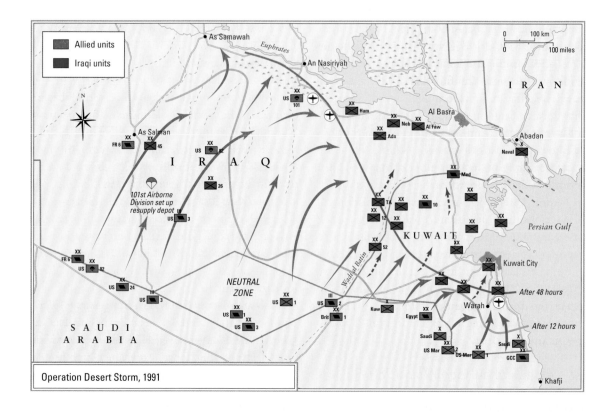

Operation Desert Storm, 1991

In the war's first hours, based on the innovative *Instant Thunder* plan, American F-117A Nighthawk Stealth aircraft flew undetected by Iraqi radars to target strategic enemy command facilities in Baghdad. Following this, Coalition aircraft attacked the infrastructures associated with the enemy's sophisticated 'Kari' air defence system to gain control of the skies, so that aerial operations could be mounted without fear of casualties being caused by enemy aircraft attacks or SAM responses. In phase three, Coalition aircraft attacked Iraqi ground forces to inflict casualties and lower their morale, as well as smash their logistical and command capabilities. Finally, once the ground war commenced, Coalition air forces attacked enemy frontline forces, interdicted Iraqi lines of communication and performed reconnaissance missions.

This sophisticated Coalition air war was hugely effective. It degraded overall Iraqi command and control capability by 90 per cent, smashed their ability to move, destroyed literally hundreds of vehicles and inflicted 40 per cent casualties on the enemy's ground forces, making a significant contribution to the Coalition victory.

■ OPERATION *GRANBY*, AUGUST 1990–APRIL 1991

Granby was the codename given to the deployment to the Persian Gulf of British forces in 1990–91, in response to the Iraqi invasion of Kuwait. *Granby* saw the deployment of the British 1st Armoured Division, a number of Royal Navy ships and a sizable component from the Royal Air Force. A total of 53,462 personnel deployed over the course of the operation, which made the British contribution the second largest after the Americans.

■ OPERATION *DAGUET*, AUGUST 1990–MAY 1991

Following the invasion of Kuwait by Iraq, France contributed air, land and naval forces to the American-led coalition under the codename of Operation *Daguet*. The French contribution was the second largest of European nations, with some 18,000 personnel deployed.

■ KHAFJI, 29 JANUARY–1 FEBRUARY 1991

Even though Coalition air forces had initiated their aerial campaign against Iraqi forces from mid-January 1991, no significant ground operations materialized until 29 January. On this date, 25,000 Iraqi troops from three mobile divisions mounted a surprise attack from south-eastern Kuwait along the coast to the Saudi Arabian town of Al-Khafji. Coalition ground and air forces inflicted heavy casualties as they forced back this incursion. The Coalition suffered 97 casualties, the Iraqis 700.

■ AL BUSAYYAH, 26 FEBRUARY 1991

Fought between American and Iraqi armoured forces, this brief battle saw the Americans take the town with little opposition. The American units involved then moved on to participate in the battle of Medina Ridge the following day, widely regarded as the largest US tank battle in history.

■ PHASE LINE BULLET, 26 FEBRUARY 1991

The battle of Phase Line Bullet was fought on 26 February 1991 by the US 1st and 3rd Armoured Divisions against the Iraqi Tawakalna Republican Guard Division, leading to the latter formation's destruction.

■ WADI AL-BATIN, 16 FEBRUARY 1991

This battle was a successful diversionary operation to convince Iraqi forces that the main weight of the coalition attack to liberate Kuwait would drive through the wadi, tying down and immobilizingIraqi troops.

■ 73RD EASTING, 26 FEBRUARY 1991

The battle of 73rd Easting on 26 February 1991, saw the American 2nd Armored Cavalry Regiment destroy more than 250 Iraqi armoured vehicles of the Iraqi 18th Mechanized and 37th Armoured Brigades of the Tawakalna Division.

■ MEDINA RIDGE, 27 FEBRUARY 1991

On 27 February 1991, the US 1st Armoured Division engaged the 2nd Brigade of the Medina Luminous Division, Iraqi Republican Guard, on the Medina Ridge just outside the city of Basra. The battle lays claim to being the largest tank battle

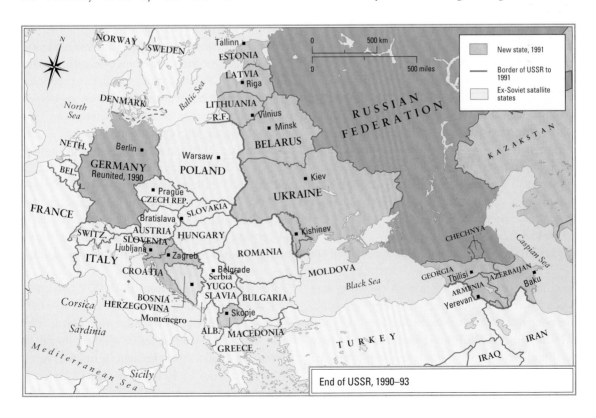

End of USSR, 1990–93

in the US Army's history and saw the effective integration of tanks, attack helicopters and fixed-wing aircraft as the Republican Guard formation was destroyed.

The Iraqis lost over 180 tanks and at least another 125 armoured vehicles during the course of the two-hour battle, including a number of attacks by AH-64 Apache helicopters and A-10 'tankbuster' aircraft. American casualties were remarkably light: only four M1A1 Abrams tanks were sufficiently badly damaged by return fire to be rendered immobile, and there were no American fatalities. The Iraqis, by contrast, lost over 330 dead.

■ NORFOLK, 27 FEBRUARY 1991

This was the final battle of the 1991 Gulf War before a ceasefire came into effect. Taking its name from the codename for the geographical area in which the fighting occurred, the battle saw elements of the US 1st Infantry and 2nd Armored Divisions engage the remnants of the Tawakalna Division of the Iraqi Republican Guard, and ended with the final destruction of that formation.

Break-up of Yugoslavia 1991–99

Slovenia

■ BRNIK, 27 JUNE–4 JULY 1991

With Slovenia's 25 June declaration of independence, a Yugoslavian Peoples' Army (JNA) anti-aircraft battery moved in to capture Brnik airport. Slovenian troops attempted to block its advance, but the JNA column established a base there, which they held until 4 July.

■ ORMOZ, 27 JUNE 1991

Slovenian troops stopped a JNA tank column from the 32nd Mechanized Brigade, under Col Popov, as it attempted to cross the Drava river. Yugoslav tanks, without adequate infantry support, could not penetrate a Slovenian barricade.

■ NOVA GORICA, 28 JUNE–1 JULY 1991

At the Rozna Dolina border crossing on the Italian frontier, Slovenian troops, under Maj Lisjak, destroyed two JNA T-55 tanks and captured three

others. The Slovenians also killed three JNA soldiers, including the company commander, and captured 98. On 29 June, the Slovenians attached the captured tanks to a territorial defence company, boosting its combat power to nine tanks. By 1 July, Slovenian troops had captured all JNA forces at Nova Gorica, as well as the arms depots at Pecovnik, Bukovzlak and Zaloska Gorica.

■ HRVATINI/ANKARAN, 29 JUNE 1991

JNA Special Operations Forces (SOF) attempted a landing near Ankaran, a fishing village on the Adriatic coast near Koper. The Slovenians drove the JNA troops back. After the war, the area became the headquarters of the fledgling Slovenian Navy.

■ KRAKOVSKI FOREST, 1–2 JULY 1991

The 580th Mixed Artillery Brigade of the JNA 306th Light Air Defence Artillery Regiment retreated into the Krakovski Forest, on the Croatian frontier. The Slovenians surrounded and destroyed this brigade after a stubborn fight.

Croatia

■ DALMATIA, JULY–NOVEMBER 1991

Serb nationalists protested Croatian independence by blockading parts of the Dalmatian coast. JNA troops entered the conflict to protect the establishment of an autonomous region of Serbian Krajina. The mechanized troops of Col Ratko Mladic's JNA XIV Corps attacked Croat separatists in Dalmatia, with the heaviest fighting from 15 to 22 September at Sibenik. Croat soldiers put up stiff resistance, repelling powerful thrusts by Serb armoured units and blockading the Yugoslav Navy.

■ VUKOVAR, 24 AUGUST–18 NOVEMBER 1991

In support of Serb nationalists, the JNA deployed to Vukovar 35,000–40,000 armoured troops with air support, under LGen Zivota Panic. The Croatians had 400 soldiers and 300 policemen, with 1000 civilian volunteers. Although outgunned, the Croats put up a stern fight. The Serbs resorted to a crushing artillery barrage before moving in to drive out the defenders. Croat forces destroyed 300 JNA armoured vehicles and inflicted

15,000 casualties, losing more than 1600 of their own men.

■ Operation *Otkos 10*, 31 October–4 November 1991

In western Slavonia, more than 2400 Croat soldiers fought 1750 Serb partisans and JNA troops in the 'Serbian Autonomous Oblast of Western Slavonia'. Croatia captured 270km of territory, breaking the Serb plan to bolster the 'Republic of Serbian Krajina.'

■ Operation *Tigar*, June–July 1992

At Dubrovnik, the JNA left a token force of the Trebinje Corps, following a general redeployment to Bosnia and Herzegovina. The Croatian 1st, 2nd and 4th Guard Brigades launched an offensive to drive the weakened Yugoslav units out.

■ Operation *Maslenica*, 22 Jan–1 Feb 1993

Ten thousand troops of the Croatian Army launched a successful offensive to recapture territory and roll back a Serb and JNA salient that had effectively cut off the Dalmatian coast from the rest of Croatia.

■ Peruca Dam, 28 January 1993

After Operation *Maslenica*, Serb and JNA troops controlled the Peruca hydroelectric dam, which they tried to blow with 30 tons of explosive. Maj Mark Gray, British Royal Marines, part of United Nations Protection Force (UNPROFOR), helped prevent disaster by lowering the water level in Peruca Lake ahead of the Serbs' action.

■ Operation *Medak Pocket*, 9–17 Sep 1993

Twenty-five hundred Croatians from the 9th Guards and 111th Brigades, as well as MUP (Polish) police, attacked Serbs soldiers and civilians in the area of Medak village. UNPROFOR sent Canadian troops, including 2nd Battalion Princess Patricia's Canadian Light Infantry, supported by French armour, into the area as a buffer. The Croats attacked the Canadian troops, beginning a two-week exchange of fire that led to 27 Croatian casualties and four Canadian wounded.

■ Operation *Flash*, 1–3 May 1995

More than 7000 Croatian soldiers attacked Serbian units, killing more than 280 and capturing approximately 1500 Serbian soldiers. The advance drove tens of thousands of ethnic Serbs across the Sava river, with the Croatians gaining 500km of territory.

■ Operation *Storm*, 4 August 1995

In the largest European land battle since WWII, 150,000 Croatian troops defeated a Serb nationalist army to capture thousands of square kilometres of territory. The Croat victory erased the Republic of Serbian Krajina, displacing 200,000 Serbs.

Bosnia and Herzegovina

■ Sarajevo, 5 April 1992–29 February 1996

In March 1992, Bosnia-Herzegovina's ethnic Bosniaks and Croats voted overwhelmingly to secede from Yugoslavia. In response, Bosnian Serbs, backed by units of the Yugoslavian Peoples' Army (JNA), embarked on a violent campaign to carve out an independent Serbian state: Republika Srpska. From 1991 to 1994, many Bosnian Croats, formerly allied to the Bosniaks, began their own campaign to create a separate enclave: Herceg-Bosnia.

Sarajevo became a microcosm of the three-way conflict that followed. In the capital, on 5 April, snipers shot dead two people at a pro-independence rally. The next day, JNA armour seized the city's airport, a railway station and a military training centre. In May, 16 people died when an artillery shell exploded at a Sarajevo bakery. The Bosniaks struck back, attacking a Serbian military barracks. By the end of May, Bosnian Serbs and JNA soldiers had encircled the city and its suburbs. They dug in for a long siege, emplacing tanks and artillery, but they lacked sufficient infantry to take it by force.

During the summer of 1992, snipers began a reign of terror, firing from the surrounding hills at civilians in the city's streets. The Army of the Republic of Bosnia and Herzegovina, under Mustafa Hajrulahovic Talijan, had approximately 40,000 soldiers defending. Thirty thousand soldiers of the Bosnian Serb Sarajevo-Romanija Corps, under Stanislav Galic, were on the offensive. As the war ground down into a bitter contest of attrition, United Nations flights into Sarajevo Airport became the only source of supply for the beleaguered population. In 1993, besieged Sarajevans completed a tunnel from the airport through which humanitarian aid, as well as embargoed weapons, could enter the city. In 1992, the UN had imposed economic sanctions on all parties to the conflict. Additionally, the UN deployed more than 30,000 peacekeeping troops, from 40 nations, under UNPROFOR command, although UN-brokered ceasefires frequently broke down. The major effect of sanctions was to force the JNA to withdraw support from the Bosnian Serbs. Former JNA units joined the Army of Republika Srpska, under Gen Ratko Mladic.

By February 1994, Bosnian Croats and Bosniaks renewed their alliance against Republika Srpska, amid a continuous artillery barrage that killed hundreds and destroyed much of the city's infrastructure, battered by the explosions of more than 300 shells each day. On 5 February 1994, Serbs escalated the violence, lobbing a 120mm mortar shell into the crowded Markale Market, killing 68 civilians and injuring 144 others. A second attack by Serbs on 28 August 1995 killed 37 and wounded a further 90.

NATO air forces intervened from 30 August to 20 September 1995. US, British, French and German warplanes flew some 3500 combat sorties to attack more than 300 Serb targets with precision-guided munitions (PGMs). From February 1992 to July 1994, four internationally brokered peace plans that would have buttressed district governance, or divided Bosnia along ethnic lines, were presented and rejected by both sides. Finally, on 14 December 1995, the warring parties signed the US-brokered peace agreement called the 'Dayton Accord', ending the most serious fighting. In the agreement, Republika Srpska gained 49 per cent of the surrounding hill country, not including the city itself.

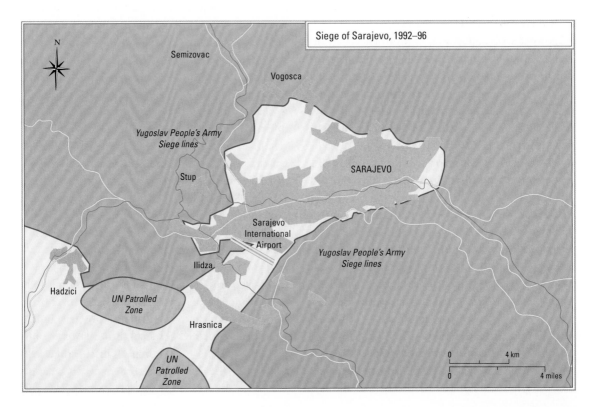

During the four-year siege, Bosnia had lost more than 6000 soldiers and Republika Srpska more than 2000. All told, more than 200,000 people had been killed, with almost three million displaced. In 2006, the International Criminal Tribunal for the Former Yugoslavia, upheld Galic's conviction and life sentence for war crimes.

■ OPERATION *VRBAS 92*, JUNE–OCTOBER 1992

Preceded by a heavy artillery barrage, 16,000 troops of the 30th Krajina Division, under Ratko Mladic, drove 14,000 Bosniak and Croat soldiers from the formerly multi-ethnic town of Jajce on 27 October. Serb troops included the 1st Anti-Armour Artillery Division, 1st, 11th and 17th Infantry Brigades and the 1st Battalion of the Light Infantry Brigade. The Serb victory temporarily ended the war between Republika Srpska and Bosnian Croats, although the conflict with Muslim Bosniaks continued.

■ OPERATION *KORIDOR*, JUNE–JULY 1992

Twenty-eight thousand Republika Srpska Army troops attacked Bosniak and Croat brigades at Bosanska Posavina, in the Sava river valley. Milosovic's objective was to link the two parts of Republika Srpska. Mladic's forces defeated 30,000 Croats, killing 1200 while losing 293 of their own.

■ GORNJI VAKUF/USKOPLJE, JANUARY–APRIL 1993

The 305th and 317th Mountain Brigades of the Bosnian Army's III Corps attacked the Croat 'Ante Starcevic' Brigade at Gornji Vakuf to sever the supply route between territories claimed by the so-called 'Croatian Republic of Herzeg-Bosnia'. The battle divided the ethnically mixed town of 25,000 Bosniaks and Croats. On 14 April, the Bosnian Army launched a major offensive against Croat positions in the Lasva valley, including Uskoplje. Fighting continued in the area through December 1993.

■ MOSTAR, MAY 1993–MARCH 94

After forcing the JNA out in June 1992, Croat and Bosniak forces contested Mostar. More than 10 million rounds of ammunition wrecked much of the central boulevard. A truce left Croats in control of the western part of the old Turkish city, while the Bosniak XIV Corps held the east. Many landmarks of significance to the Serb, Croat and Bosniak communities had been destroyed, including the picturesque Stari Most Bridge, which a Croat tank blasted to destruction on 9 November 1993.

■ OPERATION *BOELLEBANK*, 29 APRIL 1994

At Saraci during Operation *Boellebank*, Bosnian Serb anti-tank missile teams ambushed a Danish UNPROFOR armoured squadron. The Danes' seven Leopard 1A5 main battle tanks returned fire, inflicting as many as 150 casualties in what the Danish press called 'Operation Bully Bashing'.

■ OPERATION *TIGER 94*, 2 JUNE–21 AUG 1994

In the western part of Bosnia, the Bosnian Army's V Corps attacked and routed Serb separatists, under Fikret Abdic. Gen Hamdo Abdic, V Corps commander, lured the Serb leader into a trap. The Bosnian victory destroyed the Serb enclave's military power, although Abdic was able to recapture some of its territory in 1994. In 1995, the territory was overrun by Croatian troops during Operation *Storm*.

■ OPERATIONS *KRIVAJA 95* AND *STUPCANICA 95*, 6–25 JULY 1995

Republika Srpska's Drina Corps defeated the Bosnian 28th Division and entered Srebrenica on 11 July. Dutch UNPROFOR troops, numbering 450, controversially withdrew ahead of the Serb advance, leaving the civilian population unguarded. On 11 July, Dutch NATO warplanes made a limited attack on Republika Srpska tanks. Serb soldiers and mercenaries rounded up and confined the Muslim inhabitant of Srebrenica, eventually carrying out the mass murder of more than 8000 Bosniak men and boys, the killing beginning on 13 July. Elsewhere in the area, the fighting continued. On 25 July, Serb troops defeated the Bosnian 285th Brigade and captured the Bosniak enclave Zepa, continuing a vicious campaign of ethnic cleansing.

The International Criminal Tribunal for the

Former Yugoslavia in The Hague has made numerous indictments of those involved in the Srebrenica massacre, including Mladic and former Republika Srpska leader Radovan Karadzic.

■ **OPERATION *DELIBERATE FORCE*, 30 AUGUST–20 SEPTEMBER 1995**

In 1992–93, the United Nations authorized NATO's 5th Tactical Air Force to defend a no-fly zone over Bosnia. As Serb fighters intensified their war against Bosnian Muslims on the ground, NATO expanded its aerial intervention mission to include close air support for UN peacekeepers, as well as large-scale air strikes with precision-guided munitions against the recalcitrant Serbs. NATO warplanes flew 3535 combat sorties, releasing more than 1100 weapons, ultimately forcing Ratko Mladic to lift the siege of Sarajevo. During *Deliberate Force* in 1995, some 400 aircraft conducted intensive operations against the Army of the Republika Srpska.

Kosovo

■ **OPERATION *ALLIED FORCE*, 24 MARCH 1999**

After Yugoslavian President Slobodan Milosevic ordered 40,000 of his army and police troops to crack down on the breakaway enclave of ethnic Albanians in Kosovo, NATO warplanes once again went into action over the Balkans. The air campaign occurred in three phases, including the destruction of Serbian integrated air defences, strikes against Serbian military targets from the Kosovo border to the 44th Parallel, and strikes against targets north of the 44th Parallel, including Belgrade.

South Ossetia War 1991–92

■ **TSKHINVALI, FEBRUARY 1991–24 JUNE 1992**

Georgian and Ossetian militias clashed over control of Tskhinvali, capital of South Ossetia. Georgian armour successfully blockaded the city, but its assaults were indecisive. The siege left 1000 people dead on both sides and displaced 23,000 Georgians and 100,000 Ossetians.

Sierra Leone Civil War 1991–2002

■ **EASTERN KAILAHUN, 23 MARCH 1991**

The Liberia-based Revolutionary United Front (RUF) invaded Sierra Leone's diamond-rich eastern district. RUF forces pushed toward the interior, sparking an 11-year conflict that killed tens of thousands and displaced over 2.5 million people.

■ **OPERATION *BARRAS*, 2000**

Operation *Barras* was the codename for a combined operation by elements of the 22nd Special Air Service Regiment, the Special Boat Service and the Parachute Regiment 1st Battalion during the British intervention in the civil war in Sierra Leone. The operation was launched against a group of fighters known as the West Side Boys, who had taken hostage soldiers from the Royal Irish Regiment, plus their Sierra Leonean liaison officer, on 25 August 2000. When the West Side Boys broke off discussions, it was thought that the hostages' lives were in danger. On the morning of 10 September 2000, the West Side Boys' camp at Rokel Creek was attacked. In the course of the assault all the hostages were recovered. The rebel leader, Foday Kallay, was captured and at least 25 members of the West Side Boys were killed. British casualties were one fatality and a dozen wounded.

Yemen Civil War 1994

■ **AMRAN, 27 APRIL 1994**

Although billeted together, the South Yemeni 3rd Armoured and North Yemeni 1st Armoured Brigades attacked each other in late April 1994. Two hundred tanks clashed for three days. As many as 400 were killed and the Southern Brigade's tanks were all but annihilated.

First Chechen War 1994–96

■ **GROZNY, 31 DEC 1994–8 FEB 1995**

Chechnya had declared its independence from Russia on 6 September 1991. By 1994, factions were fighting for control of Grozny, a capital city consisting of 490,000 ethnic Chechens and Russians. Russian President Boris Yeltsin authorized his security services to enter Chechnya and restore order, favouring the establishment of a Russian-backed government. The Russian Army and MVD internal security service provided 24,000 men (comprising 34 battalions), supported by 80 tanks and 90 attack helicopters.

The Russian force surrounded Grozny from three sides, attempting to blockade the city's 4500–10,000 Chechen separatist fighters. However, poor training for urban combat would prove costly for the invaders. Chechen rebels, though comparatively lightly equipped and with even less training, made better use of their urban battlespace, effectively luring Russian armoured columns into several inescapable ambushes. The Chechen fighters organized themselves into 25-man 'kill teams', with machine gunners, RPG-7 rocket-propelled grenade launchers and supporting riflemen. On 31 December, several 'kill teams' ambushed the Russian 81st Motorized Rifle Regiment in the northern part of Grozny. The fighters attacked from the upper storeys of structures along Pervomayskaya Street. They delivered anti-tank rocket fire onto the regiment from above, where its armoured fighting vehicles were most vulnerable. The 131st Brigade was similarly caught out at Grozny's railway station, where Chechen fighters radioed 'Welcome to Hell!' before destroying several armoured vehicles with close-range RPG fire. The Russians developed tactics to counter Chechen ambuscades, using artillery fire to destroy buildings along their route of advance, thereby eliminating hiding places. Between 4 and 17 January, the Russians renewed the momentum of their offensive, capturing the presidential palace and the northern half of the city. By 8 February, the Russians had driven the Chechen rebels south of the Sunzha river. Much of Grozny lay in ruins.

■ SOUTHERN MOUNTAINS, FEBRUARY–JUNE 1995

South of Grozny, the hill country rises gradually to the heights of the Caucasus Mountains, the Chechen traditional homeland. The Russian offensive continued into the mountains, seizing

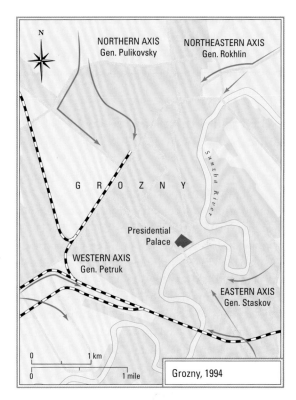

Grozny, 1994

Novye Promysly, Aldy and Chernoreche by the end of February. By June, the Russians had conquered much of the countryside. Perhaps 5000 Russian soldiers and as many as 30,000 Chechens had died. Chechen warlord Shamil Basayev took 1500 Russian hostages at the Budyonnovsk hospital, sparking a siege in which 120 civilians died.

■ BAMUT, 14–19 APRIL 1995

At Bamut village, a former Soviet strategic missile site south-west of Grozny, 1000 Chechen rebels repulsed a Russian attack. Russian artillery bombarded the city with Grad rockets ahead of a successful mechanized advance on 18 April. On 19 April, Chechen artillery, situated in the hills overlooking Bamut, drove the invaders out and the battle descended into a bitter stalemate.

Cenepa War 1995

■ PERUVIAN OFFENSIVE, 28 JAN–28 FEB 1995

In a border dispute, Peruvian infantry, supported by

Russian-built Mi-8 and Mi-17 attack helicopters, failed to dislodge Ecuadorian troops from their outpost at Tiwintza. The Peruvians called in more powerful aircraft, but Ecuadorian fighters drove off the attack planes.

Eritrean–Ethiopian War 1998–2000

■ **BADME, 6 MAY 1998–27 FEBRUARY 1999**
Two Eritrean armoured brigades rolled into Badme, claiming the 400km triangular territory along the Ethiopian border. Local Tigrayan militia resisted, sparking another war between the neighbouring nations. In February 1999, an Ethiopian counter-attack penetrated 10km into Eritrea.

■ **VELESSA, 16 MAY 1999–18 JUNE 2000**
Ethiopian troops launched a two-day assault on Velessa south of Asmara, the Eritrean capital. The Eritreans halted Gen Tsadkan Gebre-Tensae's advance, destroying many tanks and killing hundreds of enemy soldiers.

Operation *Desert Fox*

■ *DESERT FOX*, **16–19 DECEMBER 1998**
In December 1998 American and British warplanes carried out a series of coordinated strikes designed to destroy Iraq's weapons research and development capabilities. The allies worked through a list of a hundred targets that included integrated air defence systems, military command-and-control and other resources. The operation involved as many as 600 combat sorties flown by more than 300 aircraft, including US Air Force B-52 and B-1 Lancer bombers. The US Navy also launched 325 Tomahawk cruise missiles.

Second Liberian Civil War 1999–2003

■ **MONROVIA, 18 JULY–14 AUGUST 2003**
Siege of the Liberian capital between 18 July and 14 August 2003, during the Second Liberian Civil War. Monrovia was surrounded by rebel troops from Liberians United for Reconciliation and Democracy (LURD), aiming to force the overthrow of President Charles Taylor. Several attempts to capture the city failed and several hundred civilians were killed by LURD shelling. The siege ended with Taylor's resignation and the arrival of a West African peacekeeping force.

Second Chechen War 1999–2000

■ **INVASION OF DAGESTAN, 7 AUGUST–28 SEPTEMBER 1999**
Chechen warlord Shamil Basayev with 1500–2000 Muslim fighters, invaded Dagestan, ostensibly to support a separatist movement. Basayev quickly captured Ansalta, Rakhata and Shadroda before declaring Dagestani independence. The local population resisted. The Russian MVD's North Caucasus Military District, under Gen Viktor Kazantsev, intervened. From 4 to 16 September, Basayev carried out a systematic bombing campaign against Russian apartment blocks, killing more than 290 civilians. Russia saw the violent incursion as justification for a second war against Chechnya.

■ **RUSSIAN AIR CAMPAIGN, 26 AUG–SEP 1999**
Following the invasion of Dagestan by Chechen militants in July 1999, the Russians launched a fully fledged and punishing air campaign against Chechnya from 26 August, with the intention of destroying the militant groups involved. The attacks moved on to the Chechen capital Grozny from 23 September, with a number of key targets such as the airport, bridges, communications centres and the oil refinery being struck and severely damaged or destroyed. The air campaign served as a precursor for a major Russian land offensive, bringing more bloodshed and violence to Chechnya and its people.

■ **SAMASHKI, 23–27 OCTOBER 1999**
Ahead of an infantry assault, Russian rocket artillery smashed this village of approximately 12,000 people at the western edge of Chechnya. According to Human Rights Watch, the attacks killed and injured several civilians.

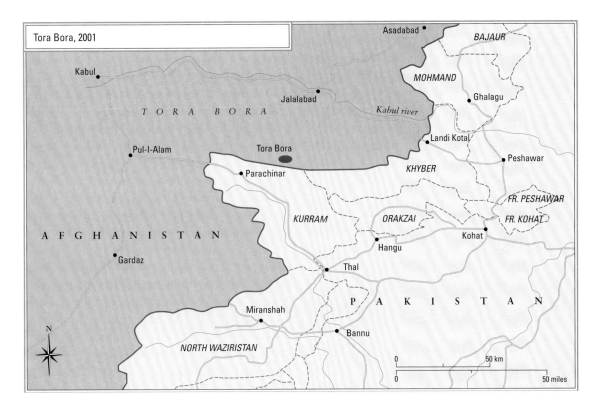

Tora Bora, 2001

■ GROZNY, 25 DEC 1999–6 FEB 2000

The Russian invasion force comprised 80,000 soldiers from the Ministry of Defence and another 30,000 from the MVD, as well as a loyal Chechen brigade under Beslan Gantamirov. Four thousand Chechen fighters were entrenched at Grozny. Having learned painful lessons from their costly invasion and expulsion in 1995–96, the Russian strategy was first to level the city with massive artillery and air strikes ahead of an infantry assault. The Russian forces fired SCUD-B ballistic missiles with devastating thermo-baric warheads and TOS-1 incendiary rockets in massive 'fire strikes' aimed at destroying Chechen fighting positions and shattering morale. On 13 December, Russian soldiers seized Grozny's eastern suburbs.

From 23 December until the end of January, the Russians slowly battled their way across the now-destroyed city. On 1 February, the Chechen rebels began to withdraw. Basayev lost a foot while crossing a minefield to escape.

■ ALKHAN-YURT, DECEMBER 1999

South of Grozny, Russian airborne troops under LGen Vladimir Shamanov pillaged the town of Alkhan-Yurt, committing 17 confirmed murders of civilians. Human rights groups claimed that the Russians carried out such abuses throughout their campaigns in Chechnya.

Afghanistan 2001–

■ MAZAR-E SHARIF, 19 OCTOBER–10 NOVEMBER 2001

At the outset of Operation *Enduring Freedom*, US Army Special Operations Forces (SOF) arrived in northern Afghanistan to join Afghan rebels in overthrowing the Taliban. At Mazar-e Sharif, Boeing CH-47 Chinooks of the 160th Special Operations Aviation Regiment (SOAR) airlifted a 12-man SOF unit to a landing zone south of the city. The Americans joined forces with warlord Abdur Dostum's Northern Alliance, calling air

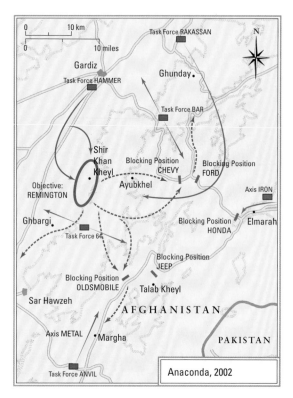

Anaconda, 2002

strikes against Taliban command posts, armoured vehicles and troops. Dostum moved into Mazar-e Sharif on 10 November.

■ KUNDUZ, 11–23 NOVEMBER 2001
Northern Alliance fighters, with US SOF support, defeated 13,000 Taliban and al-Qaeda fighters at Kunduz. American aerial bombardment destroyed Taliban vehicles, leaving the insurgents with no choice but surrender on 24 November. The victors claimed 2000 enemy fighters killed and more than 3500 captured.

■ QALA-I-JANGI, 25 NOVEMBER–1 DECEMBER 2001
At the old fortress of Qala-i-Jangi in Mazar-e Sharif, the Northern Alliance imprisoned 300–500 Taliban and al-Qaeda fighters captured during the siege, as well as those taken at the battles of Taloquon and Kunduz. Northern Alliance soldiers failed to search the prisoners, some of whom had smuggled weapons into the prison. A riot broke out as Central Intelligence Agency (CIA) agents

interrogated al-Qaeda militants. Prisoners killed one of the CIA agents and overran the Qala-i-Jangi fort's armoury, seizing more weapons and fighting back.

US and British SOF teams, supported by air strikes, assisted Afghan forces quelling the bloody, week-long uprising. At one point, Northern Alliance troops brought the 100mm rifle of a Russian-built T-55 tank to bear against the captured armoury. Only 86 prisoners survived the battle. The Northern Alliance lost 73 Afghan soldiers. An American infantry company from the 10th Mountain Division deployed from Uzbekistan to help re-secure the prison.

■ KANDAHAR, 22 NOVEMBER–7 DECEMBER 2001
Harried by Eastern Alliance fighters and local Afghan militia, the Taliban withdrew from Kandahar. The US Marine Corps' 15th Marine Expeditionary Unit and NATO Special Forces entered the city as Hamid Karzai was named President of Afghanistan.

■ TORA BORA, DECEMBER 2001
South of Jalalabad, Taliban and al-Qaeda fighters had fortified their positions in the Tora Bora Mountains. US SOF and local Afghan rebels, under warlord Hazrat Ali, launched an offensive to dislodge their enemies. Coalition forces moved cautiously into the broken, high-altitude terrain, using horses and donkeys to bear their heavy equipment.

From ridgeline observation posts, SOF units supported the North Alliance advance by calling in air strikes. Night attacks by US AC-130 Spectre gunships poured fire into the Taliban positions. Nevertheless, Ali's forces had difficulty taking and holding ground against determined counter-attacks. By day, the Afghans would advance under American air cover, only to fall back to more defensible positions as darkness fell. Arab al-Qaeda fighters resisted to the death, resulting in what one SOF soldier reported as a 'very hard gunfight'. By mid-December, heavy air strikes on the mountain cave complexes had broken organized Taliban and al-Qaeda resistance.

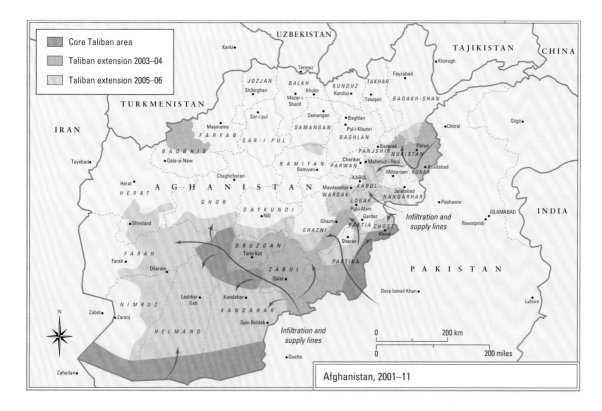

Afghanistan, 2001–11

Legend:
- Core Taliban area
- Taliban extension 2003–04
- Taliban extension 2005–06

■ **OPERATION ANACONDA, 2–19 MARCH 2002**

Operation *Anaconda* was a coordinated attack on Taliban and al-Qaeda positions in the Shahi Kowt valley. It involved US and Coalition SOF, airborne soldiers and light infantry and 1000 Afghan troops. They faced as many as 1000 Taliban and al-Qaeda fighters. Despite the allies enjoying numerical superiority and powerful close air support assets, much of the combat involved bitter hand-to-hand fighting on the valley's steep slopes.

On the night of 3/4 March, US SOF and Rangers became embroiled with al-Qaeda fighters on Takur Ghar Mountain. During an assault landing, militants shot down one helicopter, killing three Rangers and an aircrewman. The remaining Rangers and SOF fought their way up to join their comrades. An al-Qaeda counter-attack failed to dislodge them. By the end of the operation, 15 coalition troops had died along with hundreds of their enemies. Many Taliban and al-Qaeda fighters escaped to Pakistan.

■ **OPERATION MONGOOSE, 27 JANUARY– 3 FEBRUARY 2003**

More than 300 Coalition troops, including elements of the US 82nd Airborne Division, attacked Taliban and al-Qaeda fortifications in the Adi Ghar Mountains, 23km north of Spin Boldak. Operation *Mongoose* followed a battle between soldiers of the International Security Assistance Force (ISAF) and approximately 80 Taliban and al-Qaeda fighters. By the end of the operation, Coalition and Afghan troops cleared 75 caves using explosives as well as precision air strikes to destroy cave complexes that had been used as fighting positions and weapons caches.

■ **OPERATION MOUNTAIN THRUST, 15 JUNE– 31 JULY 2006**

More than 11,000 NATO and Afghan troops attacked Taliban fighters in Uruzgan and Helmand Provinces. US, British, Canadian and Afghan troops sought to establish a permanent NATO presence (via ISAF) in southern Afghanistan, historically a Taliban stronghold. Coalition forces killed more than 1000 Taliban and captured 400, while suffering 155 killed, 106 wounded and 43 of their own captured during the campaign.

■ **PANJWAII, JULY–AUGUST 2006**

In Operation *Zahar*, 2nd Battalion, Princess Patricia's Canadian Light Infantry, with Afghan National Army support, tangled with Taliban guerillas over a mud wall.

■ **OPERATION *MOUNTAIN FURY*, 16 SEPTEMBER 2006–15 JANUARY 2007**

NATO sent 3000 ISAF troops and 4000 Afghan National Army (ANA) troops into the central and eastern Afghan provinces of Ghazni, Khost, Logar Paktika and Paktya to root out Taliban safe havens. The US 10th Mountain Division suffered 150 casualties during October and November. In December, British Royal Marines attacked the Taliban near Garmsir. NATO troops inflicted more than 1000 Taliban casualties. The operation built upon the Canadian-led Operation *Medusa* in Kandahar Province (2–17 September 2006).

■ **OPERATION *FALCON SUMMIT*, 15 DECEMBER 2006–6 JANUARY 2007**

ISAF and ANA troops attacked Taliban positions at Panjwaii and Zhare in Kandahar Province. The force comprised 2000 Canadian troops, including Quebec's Royal 22nd Regiment, supported by Leopard C2 tanks and Light Armoured Vehicles (LAVs). On 19 December, covered by a heavy artillery barrage, the Canadians and Afghans began clearing villages. At Howz-e Madad, approximately 900 Taliban fighters made a futile stand. Canadian, British and American soldiers established a cordon and drove them out.

■ **OPERATION *VOLCANO*, FEBRUARY 2007**

At the Kajaki hydroelectric dam in northern Helmand Province, Royal Marines from 42 Commando, with Royal Engineers, attacked Taliban positions using grenades, mortar bombs and rockets. The British cleared 25 compounds, driving Taliban units away from the area around the dam.

■ **CHORA, 15–19 JUNE 2007**

Taliban guerillas captured three Afghan police

outposts. ISAF Dutch troops counter-attacked with artillery and air support. They killed 71 Taliban before recapturing the posts on 19 June. ISAF and Afghan units lost 20 men, including 16 Afghan police.

■ **WANAT, 13 JULY 2008**

At Wanat village, in Afghanistan's Waygal valley, the US 503rd Parachute Infantry Regiment, with 24 ANA troops, defended against a four-hour Taliban attack on their outpost. Nine Americans died in the fighting.

■ **OPERATION *EAGLE'S SUMMIT*, 27 AUGUST– 5 SEPTEMBER 2008**

In Helmand Province, NATO ground and air forces provided security for a convoy delivering a new turbine to repair the Kajaki Dam's hydroelectric plant. The operation required 4000 troops (including 2000 British and 1000 ANA soldiers), as well as aircraft, to defend against Taliban attack as the convoy of 100 vehicles travelled more than 160km through enemy territory. British soldiers

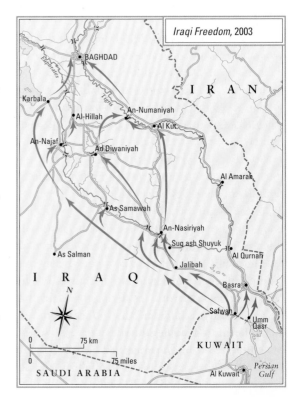

from the Royal Irish Regiment supporting Afghan troops helped clear a way through, killing 100 Taliban without losing any of their own.

■ **OPERATION** *KHANJAR*, **2 JUL–20 AUG 2009**

In July 2009, the US 2nd Marine Expeditionary Brigade (MEB) sent 4000 Marines and more than 600 ANA troops to clear Taliban forces from Nawa and Garmsir districts in central Helmand Province. As the Coalition and ANA forces moved through the Helmand river valley to several hostile villages south of Lashkar Gah, they encountered improvised explosive devices (IEDs) and skirmished with small units of fighters. US air strikes helped break Taliban resistance, although the Taliban finished the battle still in control of parts of Helmand.

■ **OPERATION** *MOSHTARAK*, **13 FEBRUARY– 7 DECEMBER 2010**

More than 15,000 ISAF and Afghan troops successfully ousted the Taliban from Marjah, a major opium-growing district in Helmand Province. Coalition and Afghan SOF helped establish landing sites for Chinooks carrying members of 1st Royal Welsh Battle Group near Showal. Subsequently, US Marines and ANA soldiers landed at Marjah, where they seized a large Taliban weapons cache. Over the next few months, bitter fighting ensued, with daily gun battles interrupting the Coalition's plan to restore Afghan government authority and security to the district.

Iraq 2003–

■ **AIR CAMPAIGN, 19 MARCH–1 MAY 2003**

Aerospace power in Operation *Iraqi Freedom* built on the technologies, tactics and lessons learned in the decade since the Gulf War of 1990–91. In 1991 satellites and unmanned aerial vehicles provided target intelligence and navigation support. Airborne command-and-control correlated data and prioritized targets. Forward air controllers on the ground matched weapons loads to targets. Strike planes laser-designated targets and linked targeting information to real time battlespace data. Advanced sensors assessed damage and helped commanders

redirect attacks. By the end of April, Coalition air forces had deployed 1801 aircraft and flown more than 41,000 combat sorties.

■ **AL-FAW PENINSULA, 20–24 MARCH 2003**

British 3 Commando Brigade Royal Marines led a Coalition force to capture Iraq's al-Faw peninsula at the conjunction of the Tigris and Euphrates rivers. Key objectives of the campaign included seizing Basra, the deepwater port Umm Qasr, and the offshore gas and oil platforms (GOPLATs) Khor al-Amaya and Mina al-Bakr. The 3500-man multinational force included the US 15th Marine Expeditionary Unit (MEU), US Navy SEAL Teams and Polish GROM Special Operations Forces (SOF).

■ **KIRKUK, 20 MARCH–10 APRIL 2003**

Joint Special Operations Task Force North (known as Task Force 'Viking') supported a Kurdish advance south across the Green Line to capture the oil-rich city of Kirkuk. After a 22-day siege, 2000 Kurdish fighters entered the city, supported by US Special Forces and the 173rd Airborne Division.

■ **UMM QASR, 21–25 MARCH 2003**

During the first night of the initial major clash of Operation *Telic* (Britain's reference for the 2003 Iraq War), US and Polish SOF seized the two GOPLATs, Khor al-Amaya and Mina al-Bakr. Ashore, SOF and British 3 Commando Brigade Royal Marines clashed with Iraqi troops, including Fedayeen Saddam internal security forces and Republican Guard units, to secure the port's oil and gas pumping stations.

Meanwhile, air support from RAF GR4 Tornadoes and GR7 Harriers helped destroy Iraqi armoured vehicles, fortified fighting positions and surface-to-air missile (SAM) sites ahead of the invasion. The US 15th MEU, with a platoon of four M1A1 Abrams tanks, helped drive out Iraqi defenders after five days of fighting. With the port secure, Coalition naval minesweepers helped clear the harbours for the imminent arrival of humanitarian aid shipments. As many as 40 Iraqi soldiers died in the fighting. The coalition lost 14 of its own men.

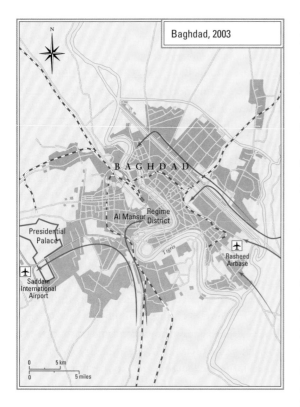

BAGHDAD

Al Mansur Regime District

Presidential Palace

Rasheed Airbase

Saddam International Airport

Tigris

N

0   5 km
0   5 miles

■ BASRA, 21 MARCH–6 APRIL 2003

With the al-Faw peninsula taken, the British 7th Armoured Brigade moved to secure bridges over the Shatt al-Basrah waterway west of Iraq's second largest city. At Abu al-Khasib, 10km southeast of Basra, British 3 Commando Royal Marines battled Iraqi paramilitary units between 30 March and 3 April. Similar actions at Az Zubayr, southwest of Basra, tightened the noose. On 6 April, British troops entered the city as the last of Basra's government resistance fled.

■ AN-NASIRIYAH, 23 MARCH–2 APRIL 2003

The US 2nd Marine Expeditionary Brigade (MEB), comprising 7000 Marines, less its Marine air group and combat service support battalion, formed the core of Task Force 'Tarawa'. This force crossed from Kuwait into Iraq on 21 March with the objective of securing an-Nasiriyah and its two bridges – the Coalition forces' route north to Baghdad led across those bridges.

Prior to the Marines' arrival, the Iraqis ambushed the US Army's 507th Maintenance Company, killing several soldiers and taking six captives. As 'Tarawa' moved through the area on 23 March, they, too, came under attack. Along the Saddam Canal, Iraq's 11th Infantry Division ambushed the Marines, firing RPGs and 100mm T-55 tank shells, destroying eight tracked amphibious assault vehicles and killing 18 Americans. Marine air strikes, including close support by AH-1W Super Cobra helicopters, destroyed 10 Iraqi tanks and blunted the force of their attack.

The Marines came to know the area around the Euphrates river and Saddam Canal bridges as 'ambush alley,' a free-fire zone sheltering Ba'athist Fedayeen Saddam fighters. They struck an American convoy, wounding 60 Marines and destroying 15 of their vehicles. As bitter fighting continued, described by one Marine officer as 'a knife fighting in a phone booth', confusion over the location of friend and foe led to some tragic accidents for the Americans. In one instance, two Marine units fired upon one another during a night patrol, resulting in 31 wounded. In another attack, on 23 March, one Marine was killed and more than a dozen others wounded when a US Air Force A-10 Thunderbolt II mistakenly turned its GAU-8 30mm cannon on their light armoured vehicles (LAVs). In the battles to secure an-Nasiriyah's two bridges, 22 Marines and more than 350 Iraqis were killed.

■ AN-NAJAF, 23–25 MARCH 2003

The US Army's 101st Airborne Division, with a brigade of the 82nd Airborne Division, supported by armoured troops from the US 3rd Infantry and 1st Armored Divisions, moved to an-Najaf. Along the route, Fedayeen Saddam paramilitary fighters lay in ambush, fighting tenaciously despite massive US firepower. During a strong sandstorm, the Americans moved north on Highway 28 and east across the Euphrates at Kifal to complete their encirclement of an-Najaf.

■ GREEN LINE, 26 MARCH 2003–FEBRUARY 2004

Task Force 'Viking' held a line demarcating Kurdish-controlled northern Iraq against 13

Ba'athist divisions. Viking's soldiers and Marines helped to occupy a significant portion of Saddam Hussein's combat power as other American and British units advanced on Baghdad.

■ **BAGHDAD, 3–12 APRIL 2003**

The US Army's 3rd Infantry Division – 18,000 soldiers under MGen Buford Blount – and the 1st Marine Division – 18,000 Marines under MGen James N Mattis – led the attack on the Iraqi capital. The two divisions' M1 Abrams tanks, supported by American and British airpower dropping precision-guided munitions, cut through the defenders, which included 36,000 soldiers of the Iraqi Republican Guard. On 4 April, the 3rd Infantry Division seized the airport while the 1st Marines drove east, completing the city's envelopment. The army sent two armoured columns into Baghdad on so-called 'thunder runs', drawing out the defenders with a provocative attack.

By 7 April, 3rd Infantry Division's tanks had penetrated the city centre, destroying 20 Iraqi armoured fighting vehicles and a host of other materiel. With Baghdad under Coalition control, the commanders counted the cost of the campaign thus far: 42 soldiers killed, 133 wounded; 41 Marines killed, 151 wounded; 19 British troops killed, 36 wounded.

■ **FALLUJAH, 7 NOVEMBER–23 DECEMBER 2004**

Provoked in part by the 31 March murders of four Blackwater Security contractors and a general uprising in April, 2200 US Marines, with US Army and Iraqi Coalition troops in Al Anbar Province, launched Operation *Vigilant Resolve*. The plan marked a failed first attempt, between 5 April and 1 May, to wrest control of Fallujah from an emboldened insurgency, which had approximately 2000 fighters in the city.

The battle proved militarily inconclusive, if deadly: perhaps 600 civilians died in the crossfire along with 200 insurgents and 36 US troops. Coalition forces had gained control of only about 25 per

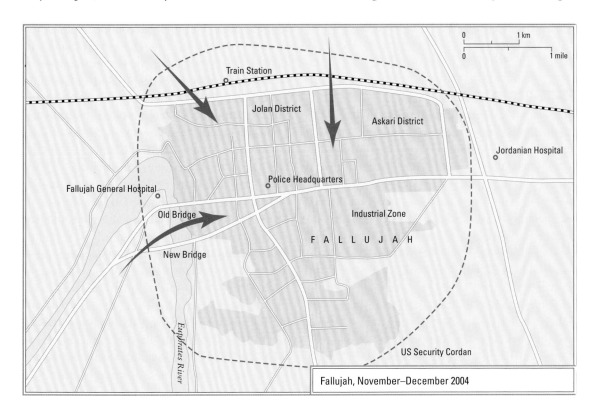

Fallujah, November–December 2004

cent of the city. In the autumn, Abu Musab al-Zarqawi's terrorists had re-established themselves in Fallujah, digging into more than 300 prepared fighting positions. The Coalition launched a new campaign called *al Fajr*, literally, Operation *Dawn*. This involved 25,000 troops in six Marine and two Army battalions and two Iraqi Army battalions. Coalition aircraft and artillery provided direct and indirect fire support. Anticipating a violent clash, all but 400 civilians evacuated the city. The joint task force operation bogged down on the night of 8 November as Army units outran the Marines, who were unaccustomed to heavy breach assault operations. Insurgents took advantage of the halt by shelling one of the Marines' trapped bulldozers, inflicting casualties and destroying equipment. Difficult house-to-house fighting followed, with Coalition troops clearing structures in risky searches for insurgents' ambuscades and weapons caches. The Coalition endured 54 US dead and 425 wounded, eight Iraqi soldiers dead and 43 wounded. The soldiers and Marines killed as many as 2000 insurgents.

Northwest Pakistan 2004–

■ WANA, 16–23 MARCH 2004
At Wana, a task force of approximately 9000–15,000 Pakistani soldiers attacked a stronghold of 400 Taliban and al-Qaeda fighters, sparking the ongoing war. Prompted by US intelligence that an al-Qaeda leader was at the site, Pakistani troops moved into the mountains. The heaviest fighting occurred during the night of 18 March, as both sides struggled to control and hold high ground. The Pakistanis lost 49 soldiers, while the militants lost 55.

■ LAL MASJID SIEGE, JULY 2007
A week-long confrontation between Pakistani security forces and militant Islamists in July 2007. Following an attack by the militants, the Lal Masjid mosque complex was besieged and eventually stormed by Pakistani Special Forces.

■ SWAT VALLEY, OCTOBER–DECEMBER 2007
During autumn 2007, Taliban fighters operating in north-west Pakistan took control of the Swat valley, prompting a large-scale operation by the Pakistan Army to remove them. Fighting began on 25 October with a Taliban suicide bombing against Pakistani troops and, over the course of the next few days, vicious fighting occurred. Although Pakistani forces killed over 100 militants, the Taliban were able to take over several towns and villages, leaving them in control of the Swat district by the end of the first week of November. This was met with a strong Pakistani riposte, during which most of the Taliban's gains were reversed. Two leading Taliban commanders were killed during the fighting and, by the end of November, the Taliban had suffered extremely heavy losses and withdrew from most of Swat valley. Follow-up operations by the Pakistanis to clear pockets of resistance continued until 6 December.

■ MIR ALI, 7–10 OCTOBER 2007
The battle of Mir Ali was a fierce engagement between Pakistani and Taliban forces during which Pakistani troops, with considerable air support, responded to Taliban attacks using improvised explosive devices (IEDs) and several raids on military convoys. Fighting saw heavy applications of Pakistani helicopter gunships and some bombing raids by the Pakistani Air Force. The battle ended with a (short-lived) ceasefire between the Pakistani Army and local tribal groups.

■ BAJAUR, 7 AUGUST 2008–28 FEBRUARY 2009
This major battle between Pakistani and Taliban forces saw Pakistani Frontier Forces drive the Taliban from the strategically important city of Bajaur, destroying the Taliban and Islamist militant presence in the region.

■ OPERATION *BLACK THUNDERSTORM*, 26 APRIL–14 JUNE 2009
Black Thunderstorm was part of the conflict in north-west Pakistan between the government and Taliban forces. It took place between 26 April and 14 June 2009, with the aim of regaining the districts of Lower Dir, Swat, Shangla and Buner from the Taliban. The Pakistani Government counter-offensive was launched following a

Taliban attack on security forces, and had cleared the Lower Dir area of all but a few pockets of resistance within 48 hours. The Pakistani forces then moved against Buner and Daggar, inflicting heavy casualties on the enemy in the process. The third phase of the operation began on 5 May, and by the time it ended on 14 June, the Pakistani armed forces had gained a decisive victory, regaining all the territory taken by the Taliban and inflicting serious losses among the enemy's leadership in the process.

■ **OPERATION** *RAH-E-NIJAT*, **JUNE–DECEMBER 2009**
Rah-e-Nijat was a major Pakistani operation against the Taliban and associated Islamist elements in South Waziristan, conducted between 19 June and 12 December 2009. The operation sought to defeat the Tehrik-i-Taliban Pakistan rebels led by Baitullah Mehsud from South Waziristan. There was fierce fighting before the Pakistani forces drove Mehsud's forces out.

Lebanon War 2006

■ **ISRAELI CAMPAIGN, 12 JULY–14 AUGUST 2006**
Following Hezbollah's rocket attacks and deadly cross-border infiltration, the Israel Defence Forces (IDF) retaliated. Tel Aviv's warplanes struck Hezbollah's long-range rocket launchers and observation posts. A land invasion followed, supported by artillery and naval gunfire, advancing several kilometres inside Lebanon along its border with Israel. The 34 days of fighting involved as many as 10,000 Israeli soldiers and several thousand Hezbollah paramilitary troops. Israel endured 119 combat deaths while Hezbollah lost between 650 and 750 fighters.

■ **HEZBOLLAH CAMPAIGN, 12 JUL–14 AUG 2006**
Hezbollah made the opening move in this campaign of July 2006, launching rocket attacks and infiltrating across the border into Israel. Hezbollah fighters captured two Israeli soldiers. Despite their reputation as guerillas, Hezbollah soldiers engaged the Israelis in a number of conventional, pitched battles.

Internal Lebanese Conflict 2007

■ **TRIPOLI AND NAHR AL-BARED, 20 MAY–7 SEPTEMBER 2007**
At the Nahr al-Bared refugee camp, home to 30,000 Palestinians, the Lebanese Internal Security Force battled Fatah al-Islam militants for three months. Terrorists had killed 27 Lebanese soldiers prior to the conflict. The siege resulted in the deaths of 168 soldiers and 226 militants.

South Ossetia 2008

■ **TSKHINVALI, 8–11 AUGUST 2008**
The city of Tskhinvali was shelled, then occupied by Georgian Government forces on 8 August 2008, as part of the Georgian attempt to regain control of the republic of South Ossetia. The advance was halted by South Ossetian militia and Russian troops who were based in Tskhinvali as part of a peacekeeping force in South Ossetia. More Russian troops arrived in South Ossetia later that day and heavy fighting ensued. By the evening of 8 August, Georgian forces had withdrawn from the city centre, before launching a counter-attack that regained much of the lost ground. However, on 10 August the Russians had arrived in sufficient numbers to clear the Georgian forces completely from Tskhinvali, subsequently driving Georgian troops from all of South Ossetia by 11 August.

■ **KODORI VALLEY, 9–12 AUGUST 2008**
Russian and Abkhaz warplanes attacked Georgian-controlled villages in the Upper Kodori valley, ahead of an invasion by Abkhaz troops under separatist leader Sergei Bagapsh. Russian and Abkhaz units also deployed to Gali and the Inguri river regions, bombing Zugdidi on 10 August. In the Kodori Valley, the Russian military drove out Georgian police units, effectively severing the enclave from Tbilisi's control.

■ **GORI, 13–22 AUGUST 2008**
The city of Gori, near South Ossetia, served as a staging area for the Georgian Army's operations against rebels and Russian units at the battle of

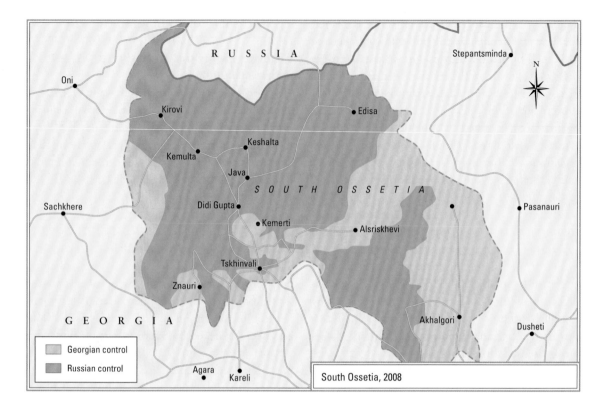

South Ossetia, 2008

Georgian control

Russian control

Tskhinvali (8–11 August). Russian warplanes attacked Gori, bombing civilian and military targets from 9 to 12 August. The airstrikes killed 60 people and led to the evacuation of 56,000 civilians. Georgian military units followed soon after, falling back on Tbilisi as Russian troops moved in to occupy Gori.

Arab Spring 2010–

■ TUNISIA, 17 DEC 2010–14 JAN 2011

Several weeks of clashes between the public and security forces led to the Tunisian President, Zine El Abidine Ben Ali, fleeing the country for Saudi Arabia.

■ EGYPT, 25 JANUARY–11 FEBRUARY 2011

Anti-government protests across Egypt led to the Egyptian Army being deployed. The strength and scale of protests, however, resulted in violent street clashes and the step-down of President Hosni Mubarak on 11 February.

■ LIBYA, 15 FEBRUARY–20 OCTOBER 2011

An uprising against the Gaddafi regime on 15 February 2011 brought heavy fighting between rebels and the Libyan armed forces. Within three days the rebels took control of Benghazi, and from 19 March NATO warplanes begin operations against the Libyan Army, in support of the uprising. After a period of stalemate, the rebels captured Tripoli on 21 August, and the fighting then centred on Gaddafi's stronghold of Sirte. The city fell, and Gaddafi was killed, on 20 October.

■ SYRIA, 18 MARCH 2011–

An uprising against the regime of President Bashar al-Assad brought a bloody response from Syrian armed forces. Heavy fighting in cities such as Daraa, Homs, Baniyas and Latakia led to tens of thousands of deaths, mostly amongst the civilian population, who were victims of some well-publicized massacres. At the time of writing in June 2013, Syria remained in a state of civil war.

RANK ABBREVIATIONS

The following abbreviations have been used for ranks throughout the book:

Army:

Pvt – *Private*
Cpl – *Corporal*
Sgt – *Sergeant*
2nd Lt – *Second Lieutenant*
Lt – *Lieutenant*
Capt – *Captain*
Maj – *Major*
Col – *Colonel*
LCol – *Lieutenant Colonel*
Brig – *Brigadier*
BGen – *Brigadier General*
MGen – *Major General*
LGen – *Lieutenant General*
CGen – *Colonel General*
Gen – *General*
FM – *Field Marshal*

Naval:

Ens – *Ensign*
LCdr – *Lieutenant Commander*
Cdr – *Commander*
RAdm – *Rear Admiral*
VAdm – *Vice Admiral*
Adm – *Admiral*

GENERAL INDEX

Page numbers in *italics* refer to illustrations

Argentau, Austrian Gen 49
Argentina
   Argentine-Brazil (Cisplatine) War 585
   Argentine Civil War 625
   Central American Wars (1830–1905) 627
   Falklands War 901–3
   Gran Colombia Peru War 585
   Park Revolution 764
   Revolution 627
   South American Wars (1815–30) 577–9, 583
   South American Wars (1830–1905) 625, 626
Argos 43, 46, 58, 67, 72
Argus, USS (brig 16 1804) 564
Argyll, Archibald, Marquis and 8th Earl of 395, 396
Argyll, Archibald Campbell, 5th Earl of 317, 318
Argyll, John, 2nd Duke of 410–11
Arista, General Mariano 646–7
Aritomo, Field Marshal Yamagata 728
Aritomo, General Yamagata 729
Arius, River 89
Arizona 605–7
Ark Royal, HMS 837
Arma di Colgnia (Venetian galleasse 1657) 298
Arma di Midelborgo (Venetian galleasse 1657) 298
Armenia
   Ancient Wars 33, 131, 134, 136, 153, 154, 159, 160
   Crimean War 654
   Medieval Wars 183, 205, 207
   Nagorno Karabakh 908
Armfeldt, Lt Gen Carl Gustaf 418
Arminius, Germanic chieftain 131–3
Armistead, Brigadier General Lewis 683
Arnold, Col Benedict 451, 452, 455, 458–9, 472, 473
arquebusiers 316
   Arabian 321
   Japanese 326, 329, 330, 335, 353, 354, 355
   Korean 356
   Moroccan 363
   Ottoman 321
   Portuguese 321
   Russian 348
   Spanish 315–16, 339
Arran, Earl of 317, 323
Arromanches 879
Arteaga, General Luis 627
Arthur, King 161
artillery
   Austrian 769
   British 450, 776, 778, 831
   Burgundian 264, 287
   Chinese 49, 199, 200
   Crusader 252
   English 267, 274
   Ferrarese 305, 306
   French 272, 283, 306, 307, 315, 498, 516, 523–4, 541, 558, 774
   French Republican 500
   German 769, 774
   Hanoverian 411, 441
   howitzers 527, 553
   Hungarian 254
   Hussite 252, 253
   Japanese 333
   Korean naval types 353, 355

Lithuanian 307
Moldavian 256
Mongol 237, 239
mortars 369, 405, 480, 541
Mughal 304
North Vietnamese 886
Ottoman 212, 254, 256
Prussian 442
Roman 85, 135
Russian 348, 529, 783, 785
Scottish 307
siege 405, 428, 483, 484, 490, 537, 539, 541, 543, 566, 573
Soviet 816
Spanish train 465, 467
Swedish 405, 418, 568
Swedish 3-pdr regimental guns 378
Syrian 870
Teutonic 244
see also cannon
Asahina Yasumoto 327
Asai Hisamasa 326
Asai Nagamasa 326, 328, 329
Asakura Yoshikage 329
Asano Yukinaga 356
Ashanti 727
Ashby, Colonel Turner 670
Ashe, Gen John 464
Ashikaga Haruuji 320
Ashikaga Yoshiaki, Shogun 319, 329
Ashraf, Shah of Iran 414
Ashworth, Lt Gen 537
Aske, Robert 322
Aslan Bey 588
Aspendos, Lycia 63
Assiniboine 609, 618
Assyria 37, *39,* 40, 41, *42,* 43–5, 171
Astley, Sir Jacob 395
Ataga Khan 303
Atahualpa, Inca (King of Peru) 311
Athens 58, 59, 60, 61, 63, 64
   and Macedon 89
   Social War 73–4
   and Sparta 64, 66–73, 89
Atkinson, General Henry 599
Atlantic Conveyor, SS 902
Atlantic convoys 835, 837–8
atomic bombs 859, 861, 864
Attalus, King of Pergamon 85, 86
Attica, Greece 61, 70
Attila the Hun 149–51
Auchmuty, Brig-Gen Sir Samuel 506
Auffenberg, Austrian Gen 514
Augereau, Marshal, Duc de Castiglione 495, 496, 520, 535
Augusta, HMS (3rd rate 64 1763) 459
Augustus, Emperor 132, 133
Augustus II, King of Poland and Saxony 415, 416
Aurangzeb, Mughal Emperor 304, 399
Aurelian, Emperor 144–5
Austen, Admiral Charles 597
Austin, Stephen 632
Australia
   6th Division 856
   7th Division 848, 849

INDEX OF BATTLES & SIEGES

Page numbers in *italics* refer to illustrations